Sixth Edition

Consumer Behavior

Wayne D. Hoyer
University of Texas at Austin

Deborah J. MacInnis
University of Southern California

Rik Pieters
Tilburg University

SOUTH-WESTERN
CENGAGE Learning·

Australia · Brazil · Japan · Korea · Mexico · Singapore · Spain · United Kingdom · United States

Consumer Behavior, Sixth Edition,
International Edition
Wayne D. Hoyer, Deborah J. MacInnis, and
Rik Pieters

Senior Vice President, LRS/Acquisitions &
Solutions Planning: Jack W. Calhoun

Editorial Director, Business & Economics:
Erin Joyner

Executive Editor: Michael Roche

Developmental Editor: Sarah Blasco

Editorial Assistant: Megan Fischer

Marketing Manager: Gretchen Swann

Media Editor: John Rich

Manufacturing Planner: Ron Montgomery

Senior Marketing Communications Manager:
Jim Overly

Art and Cover Direction,
Production Management, and
Composition: PreMediaGlobal

Photo Researcher: © Terri Miller/ E-Visual
Communications, Inc.

Cover Image: © Africa Studio/Shutterstock

Rights Acquisitions Specialist: Deanna Ettinger
(image), Audrey Pettengill (text)

Exam*View*® is a registered trademark of eInstruction Corp. Windows is a
registered trademark of the Microsoft Corporation used herein under
license. Macintosh and Power Macintosh are registered trademarks of
Apple Computer, Inc. used herein under license.

© 2008 Cengage Learning. All Rights Reserved.

Cengage Learning WebTutor™ is a trademark of Cengage Learning.

Library of Congress Control Number: 2012941536

International Edition:

ISBN-13: 978-1-133-27449-0

ISBN-10: 1-133-27449-8

Cengage Learning International Offices

Asia
www.cengageasia.com
tel: (65) 6410 1200

India
www.cengage.co.in
tel: (91) 11 4364 1111

Australia/New Zealand
www.cengage.com.au
tel: (61) 3 9685 4111

Latin America
www.cengage.com.mx
tel: (52) 55 1500 6000

Brazil
www.cengage.com.br
tel: (55) 11 3665 9900

UK/Europe/Middle East/Africa
www.cengage.co.uk
tel: (44) 0 1264 332 424

Represented in Canada by Nelson Education, Ltd.
www.nelson.com
tel: (416) 752 9100 / (800) 668 0671

Cengage Learning is a leading provider of customized learning solutions
with office locations around the globe, including Singapore, the
United Kingdom, Australia, Mexico, Brazil, and Japan. Locate your
local office at: **www.cengage.com/global**

For product information: **www.cengage.com/international**
Visit your local office: **www.cengage.com/global**
Visit our corporate website: **www.cengage.com**

Printed in the United States of America
2 3 4 5 6 7 16 15 14 13

To my wonderful family, Shirley, David, Stephanie, and Lindsey and to my parents Louis and Doris for their tremendous support and love. To all of you, I dedicate this book.

WAYNE D. HOYER
Austin, Texas
August 2012

To my loving family and devoted friends. You are my life-spring of energy and my center of gravity.

DEBORAH J. MACINNIS
Los Angeles, California
August 2012

To Trees who loves me and Thomas who knew everything.

RIK PIETERS
Tilburg, Netherlands
August 2012

About the Authors

Wayne D. Hoyer

Wayne D. Hoyer is the James L. Bayless/William S. Farish Fund Chair for Free Enterprise in the McCombs School of Business at the University of Texas at Austin. He received his Ph.D. in Consumer Psychology from Purdue University in 1980. He also holds an honorary doctorate from the University of Bern in Switzerland. His major area of study is Consumer Psychology and his research interests include consumer information processing and decision making, customer relationship management and new product development, and advertising information processing (including miscomprehension, humor, and brand personality). Wayne has published over 100 articles in various publications including the *Journal of Consumer Research, Journal of Marketing, Journal of Marketing Research, Journal of Advertising Research*, and *Journal of Retailing*. A 1998 article in the *Journal of Marketing Research* (with Susan Broniarczyk and Leigh McAlister) won the O'Dell Award in 2003 for the article that had the most impact in the marketing field over that five-year period. In addition to Consumer Behavior, he has co-authored two books on the topic of advertising miscomprehension. He is a current area editor for the *Journal of Marketing*, a former associate editor for the *Journal of Consumer Research* and serves on eight editorial review boards including the *Journal of Marketing Research, Journal of Consumer Research*, and *Journal of Consumer Psychology*. His major areas of teaching include consumer behavior, customer strategy, and marketing communications. He has also taught internationally at the University of Mannheim, the University of Muenster, and the Otto Beisheim School of Management (all in Germany), the University of Bern in Switzerland, the University of Cambridge (UK), and Thammasat University in Thailand. He has also been the Montezemolo Visiting Research Fellow in the Judge School of Business and is a Visiting Fellow of Sidney Sussex College at the University of Cambridge (UK).

Deborah J. MacInnis

Debbie MacInnis (Ph.D., University of Pittsburgh 1986) is the Charles L. and Ramona I. Hilliard Professor of Business Administration and Professor of Marketing at the University of Southern California in Los Angeles, CA. She has previously held positions as Chairperson of the Marketing Department and Vice Dean for Research. Debbie has published papers in the *Journal of Consumer Research, Journal of Marketing Research, Journal of Marketing, Journal of Personality and Social Psychology, Psychology and Marketing*, and others in the areas of marketing communications, information processing, imagery, emotions, and branding. She is an Associate Editor for the *Journal of Consumer Research* and the *Journal of Consumer Psychology*. She has also served as a member of the editorial review boards of the *Journal of Consumer Research, Journal of Marketing Research, Journal of Marketing*, and *Journal of the Academy of Marketing Sciences* and has won outstanding reviewer awards from these journals. She has also served on the editorial review boards of other journals in marketing and business. Debbie has served as Conference Co-Chair, Treasurer, and President of the Association for Consumer Research. She has also served as Vice President of Conferences and Research for the Academic Council of the American Marketing Association. She has received major awards for her research, including the Alpha Kappa Psi and Maynard awards, given to the best practice- and theory-based articles, respectively, published in the *Journal of Marketing*. Debbie's research has also been named as a finalist for the Practice Prize Competition for contributions to marketing, and the Converse Award for significant long-term contributions to marketing. She has been named recipient of the Marshall Teaching Innovation Award, the Dean's Award for

Community, and the Dean's Award for Research from the Marshall School of Business. Her classes have won national awards through the SAA National Advertising Competition. Debbie's major areas of teaching include consumer behavior and integrated marketing communications. Debbie lives in Los Angeles with her husband and two children.

Rik Pieters

Rik Pieters is Professor of Marketing at the Tilburg School of Economics and Management (TISEM) of Tilburg University, the Netherlands. He received his Ph.D. in social psychology from the University of Leiden in 1989. Rik believes in interdisciplinary work, and that imagination, persistence and openness to surprise are a person's biggest assets. He has published over 90 articles in marketing, psychology, economics, and statistics. His work has appeared in *Journal of Consumer Psychology, Journal of Consumer Research, Journal of Marketing, Journal of Marketing Research, Marketing Science, Management Science,* and *International Journal of Research in Marketing.* He has published in the *Journal of Personality and Social Psychology, Organizational Behavior and Human Decision Processes, European Journal of Social Psychology, Emotion, Psychological Science,* and *Journal of Economic Literature.* Currently, Rik is an Associate Editor of the *Journal of Marketing Research.* His research concerns attention and memory processes in marketing communication, and the role of emotions in consumer decision making. He has served as Co-Chair of the Association for Consumer Research annual conference, and has co-organized special conferences on visual marketing, social communication, and service marketing and management. He has taught internationally at Pennsylvania State University; University of Innsbruck, Austria; Koc University, Turkey; and the University of Auckland, New Zealand. He has won best teaching awards at the school and university levels. He has been Strategy Director for National and International clients at the Prad/FCB advertising agency, Amsterdam office. He bakes bread, rides bikes, and drinks hoppy, fermented barley beverages, all except the first in moderation. In his spare time, he works.

Brief Contents

Part 1 An Introduction to Consumer Behavior 1

Chapter 1 Understanding Consumer Behavior 2
Appendix Developing Information About
Consumer Behavior 28

Part 2 The Psychological Core 43

Chapter 2 Motivation, Ability, and Opportunity 44
Chapter 3 From Exposure to Comprehension 72
Chapter 4 Memory and Knowledge 99
Chapter 5 Attitudes Based on High Effort 127
Chapter 6 Attitudes Based on Low Effort 157

Part 3 The Process of Making Decisions 183

Chapter 7 Problem Recognition and Information Search 184
Chapter 8 Judgment and Decision Making Based on High Effort 213
Chapter 9 Judgment and Decision Making Based on Low Effort 241
Chapter 10 Post-Decision Processes 267

Part 4 The Consumer's Culture 297

Chapter 11 Social Influences on Consumer Behavior 298
Chapter 12 Consumer Diversity 329
Chapter 13 Household and Social Class Influences 355
Chapter 14 Psychographics: Values, Personality, and Lifestyles 382

Part 5 Consumer Behavior Outcomes and Issues 413

Chapter 15 Innovations: Adoption, Resistance, and Diffusion 414
Chapter 16 Symbolic Consumer Behavior 442
Chapter 17 Marketing, Ethics, and Social Responsibility in Today's
Consumer Society 472

Contents

Preface xiii

Part 1 An Introduction to Consumer Behavior 1

Chapter 1 Understanding Consumer Behavior 2

INTRODUCTION: Panera Bread: More than Bread 2

Defining Consumer Behavior 3
Consumer Behavior Involves Goods, Services, Activities, Experiences, People, and Ideas 3
Consumer Behavior Involves More than Buying 4
Consumer Behavior Is a Dynamic Process 5
Consumer Behavior Can Involve Many People 5
Consumer Behavior Involves Many Decisions 5
Consumer Behavior Involves Emotions and Coping 9

What Affects Consumer Behavior? 10
The Psychological Core: Internal Consumer Processes 11
The Process of Making Decisions 12
The Consumer's Culture: External Processes 12
Consumer Behavior Outcomes and Issues 13

Who Benefits from the Study of Consumer Behavior? 14
Marketing Managers 14
Ethicists and Advocacy Groups 14
Public Policy Makers and Regulators 15

Academics 15
Consumers and Society 15

Marketing Implications of Consumer Behavior 15
Developing and Implementing Customer-Oriented Strategy 16
Selecting the Target Market 16
Developing Products 16
Positioning 17
Making Promotion and Marketing Communications Decisions 18
Making Pricing Decisions 19
Making Distribution Decisions 20

Summary 22

CONSUMER BEHAVIOR CASE: How Unilever's Brands Connect with Consumers 22

Endnotes 23

Appendix Developing Information About Consumer Behavior 28

Consumer Behavior Research Methods 28

Surveys 29
Focus Groups 30
Interviews 30
Storytelling 31
Photography and Pictures 31
Diaries 31
Experiments 32
Field Experiments 33
Conjoint Analysis 33
Observations and Ethnographic Research 33
Purchase Panels 34
Database Marketing 34
Netnography 34
Psychophysiological Reactions and Neuroscience 35

Types of Consumer Researchers 36
In-House Marketing Research Departments 36
External Marketing Research Firms 37
Advertising Agencies and Media Planning Firms 37
Syndicated Data Services 38
Retailers 38
Research Foundations and Trade Groups 38
Government 39
Consumer Organizations 39
Academics and Academic Research Centers 39

Ethical Issues in Consumer Research 39
The Positive Aspects of Consumer Research 40
The Negative Aspects of Consumer Research 40

Summary 41

Endnotes 41

Part 2 The Psychological Core 43

Chapter 2 Motivation, Ability, and Opportunity 44

INTRODUCTION: Movie Tavern Markets Food and a Flick 44

Consumer Motivation and Its Effects 45
High-Effort Behavior 45
High-Effort Information Processing and Decision Making 45
Felt Involvement 47

What Affects Motivation? 48
Personal Relevance 48
Values 49
Needs 49

Goals 53
Goals and Emotions 55
Self-Control and Goal Conflict 55
Perceived Risk 58
Inconsistency with Attitudes 60
Consumer Ability: Resources to Act 60
Financial Resources 60
Cognitive Resources 61
Emotional Resources 61
Physical Resources 61
Social and Cultural Resources 62
Education and Age 62

Consumer Opportunity 62
Time 63
Distraction 63
Complexity, Amount, Repetition, and Control of
    Information 63
Summary 65
CONSUMER BEHAVIOR CASE: USAA: Million of Customers,
    One Bank Branch 65
Endnotes 66

Chapter 3   From Exposure to Comprehension   72
INTRODUCTION: Wax or Real? Welcome to Madame Tussauds 72

Exposure and Consumer Behavior 73
Factors Influencing Exposure 73
Selective Exposure 73
Attention and Consumer Behavior 76
Characteristics of Attention 76
Focal and Nonfocal Attention 77
Customer Segments Defined by Attention 80
Habituation 80
Perception and Consumer Behavior 80
Perceiving Through Vision 81
Perceiving Through Hearing 81
Perceiving Through Taste 82
Perceiving Through Smell 82

Perceiving Through Touch 82
When Do We Perceive Stimuli? 84
How Do Consumers Perceive a Stimulus? 86
Comprehension and Consumer Behavior 87
Source Identification 87
Message Comprehension 88
Consumer Inferences 90
Summary 92
CONSUMER BEHAVIOR CASE: How Under Armour
    Gets Noticed 93
Endnotes 94

Chapter 4   Memory and Knowledge   99
INTRODUCTION: The Unforgettable Apple 99

What Is Memory? 100
Sensory Memory 100
Working Memory 102
Long-Term Memory 102
Explicit Memory, Implicit Memory, and Processing Fluency 103
How Memory Is Enhanced 104
Knowledge Content, Structure, and Flexibility 105
Knowledge Content: Schemas and Scripts 106
Knowledge Structure: Categories 111
Knowledge Flexibility 114
Why Consumers Differ in Knowledge
    Content and Structure 115

Memory and Retrieval 116
Retrieval Failures 116
Retrieval Errors 117
Enhancing Retrieval 117
Characteristics of the Stimulus 118
Summary 120
CONSUMER BEHAVIOR CASE: Nostalgia Marketing Brings
    Memories Back 120
Endnotes 121

Chapter 5   Attitudes Based on High Effort   127
INTRODUCTION: Prestige Watches Have Timeless Appeal 127

What Are Attitudes? 128
The Importance of Attitudes 128
The Characteristics of Attitudes 128
Forming and Changing Attitudes 129
The Cognitive Foundations of Attitudes 131
Direct or Imagined Experience 131
Reasoning by Analogy or Category 131
Values-Driven Attitudes 132
Social Identity-Based Attitude Generation 132
Analytical Processes of Attitude Formation 132
How Cognitively Based Attitudes Are Influenced 135
Communication Source 136

The Message 138
The Affective (Emotional) Foundations of Attitudes 141
How Affectively Based Attitudes Are Influenced 143
The Source 143
The Message 144
Attitude Toward the Ad 146
When Do Attitudes Predict Behavior? 146
Summary 148
CONSUMER BEHAVIOR CASE: Volkswagen's Drive to Become the
    World's Top Automaker 149
Endnotes 150

Chapter 6   Attitudes Based on Low Effort   157

INTRODUCTION: Snacks Go Social and Mobile   157

High-Effort Versus Low-Effort Routes to Persuasion   158

Unconscious Influences on Attitudes When Consumer Effort Is Low   160
Thin-Slice Judgments   160
Body Feedback   160

Cognitive Bases of Attitudes When Consumer Effort Is Low   161

How Cognitive Attitudes Are Influenced   162
Communication Source   162
The Message   162
Message Context and Repetition   164

Affective Bases of Attitudes When Consumer Effort Is Low   164

The Mere Exposure Effect   164
Classical and Evaluative Conditioning   165
Attitude Toward the Ad   167
Mood   168

How Affective Attitudes Are Influenced   169
Communication Source   169
The Message   171

Summary   175

CONSUMER BEHAVIOR CASE: The Old Spice Man Spices Up Brand Marketing   176

Endnotes   177

Part 3   The Process of Making Decisions   183

Chapter 7   Problem Recognition and Information Search   184

INTRODUCTION: Quick Response Codes for Quick Information   184

Problem Recognition   185
The Ideal State: Where We Want to Be   185
The Actual State: Where We Are Now   187

Internal Search: Searching for Information from Memory   188
How Much Do We Engage in Internal Search?   188
What Kind of Information Is Retrieved from Internal Search?   189
Is Internal Search Always Accurate?   193

External Search: Searching for Information from the Environment   194

Where Can We Search for Information?   195
How Much Do We Engage in External Search?   198
What Kind of Information Is Acquired in External Search?   203
Is External Search Always Accurate?   204
How Do We Engage in External Search?   204

Summary   206

CONSUMER BEHAVIOR CASE: Searching for a Search Engine   207

Endnotes   208

Chapter 8   Judgment and Decision Making Based on High Effort   213

INTRODUCTION: Cars Load Up on Gizmos and Gadgets   213

High-Effort Judgment Processes   214
Judgments of Likelihood and Goodness/Badness   214
Mental and Emotional Accounting   216
Biases in Judgment Processes   216

High-Effort Decisions and High-Effort Decision-Making Processes   218
Deciding Which Brands to Consider   219
Deciding Which Criteria Are Important to the Choice   220

Deciding What Brand to Choose: Thought-Based Decisions   222
Decisions Based on Brands   223
Decisions Based on Product Attributes   224
Decisions Based on Gains and Losses   225

Deciding What Brand to Choose: High-Effort Feeling-Based Decisions   226
Appraisals and Feelings   227

Affective Forecasts and Choices   227
Imagery   228

Additional High-Effort Decisions   229
Decision Delay   229
Decision Making When Alternatives Cannot Be Compared   229

What Affects High-Effort Decisions?   230
Consumer Characteristics   230
Characteristics of the Decision   231
Group Context   233

Summary   234

CONSUMER BEHAVIOR CASE: Harley-Davidson Wheels into India   235

Endnotes   236

Chapter 9   Judgment and Decision Making Based on Low Effort   241

INTRODUCTION: Need Dorm Stuff? Hop on the Bullseye Bus!   241

Low-Effort Judgment Processes   242
The Representativeness Heuristic   242
The Availability Heuristic   242

Low-Effort Decision-Making Processes   245
Unconscious Low-Effort Decision Making   245
Conscious Low-Effort Decision Making   245
Using Simplifying Strategies When Consumer
    Effort Is Low   246

Learning Choice Tactics   247
Reinforcement   247
Punishment   247
Repeat Purchase   248
Choice Tactics Depend on the Product   248

Low-Effort Thought-Based Decision Making   249
Performance as a Simplifying Strategy   249

Habit as a Simplifying Strategy   249
Brand Loyalty as a Simplifying Strategy   251
Price as a Simplifying Strategy   253
Normative Influences as a Simplifying Strategy   256

Low-Effort Feeling-Based Decision Making   256
Feelings as a Simplifying Strategy   256
Brand Familiarity   257
Decision Making Based on Variety-Seeking Needs   258
Buying on Impulse   259

Summary   260

CONSUMER BEHAVIOR CASE: Bargain-a-Day Deal Appeal   261

Endnotes   262

Chapter 10   Post-Decision Processes   267

INTRODUCTION: Companies Go Social for Improved Customer Service   267

Post-Decision Dissonance and Regret   268
Dissonance   268
Regret   268

Learning from Consumer Experience   270
A Model of Learning from Consumer Experience   271
What Affects Learning?   272

**How Do Consumers Make Satisfaction or
    Dissatisfaction Judgments?   273**
Satisfaction/Dissatisfaction Based on Thoughts   275
Satisfaction/Dissatisfaction Based on Feelings   279

Responses to Dissatisfaction   281
Complaints   281

Responding to Service Recovery   282
Responding by Negative Word of Mouth   283

Is Customer Satisfaction Enough?   283

Disposition   285
Disposing of Meaningful Objects   286
Recycling   287

Summary   289

CONSUMER BEHAVIOR CASE: What to Do with Old
    Cell Phones?   290

Endnotes   291

Part 4   The Consumer's Culture   297

Chapter 11   Social Influences on Consumer Behavior   298

INTRODUCTION: Buzz Sends Angry Birds Soaring   298

Sources of Influence   299
Marketing and Nonmarketing Sources   299
How Do These General Sources Differ?   301
Opinion Leaders   303

Reference Groups as Sources of Influence   305
Types of Reference Groups   305
Characteristics of Reference Groups   306
Reference Groups Affect Consumer Socialization   309

Normative Influence   310
How Normative Influence Can Affect Consumer
    Behavior   311

What Affects Normative Influence Strength   312

Informational Influence   316
Factors Affecting Informational Influence Strength   316
Descriptive Dimensions of Information   318
The Pervasive and Persuasive Influence of Word of
    Mouth   318

Summary   322

CONSUMER BEHAVIOR CASE: Big Buying on Black Friday
    and Cyber Monday   322

Endnotes   323

Chapter 12   Consumer Diversity   329

INTRODUCTION: Serving Shrimp Burgers in Beijing and Potato Tacos in Bangalore   329

How Age Affects Consumer Behavior   330
Age Trends in the United States   330
Teens and Millennials   330
Generation X   334

Boomers   335
Seniors   336

**How Gender and Sexual Orientation
    Affect Consumer Behavior   337**

Sex Roles   337
Differences in Acquisition and Consumption Behaviors   338
Gender and Sexual Orientation   339

How Regional Influences Affect Consumer Behavior   340
Regions Within the United States   340
Regions Across the World   341

How Ethnic Influences Affect Consumer Behavior   342
Ethnic Groups Within the United States   343

Ethnic Groups Around the World   347

The Influence of Religion   347

Summary   348

CONSUMER BEHAVIOR CASE: Marketing to Teens
   Worldwide via Music   349

Endnotes   350

Chapter 13   Household and Social Class Influences   355

INTRODUCTION: Marketing to "$2 a Day" Consumers   355

How the Household Influences Consumer Behavior   356
Types of Households   356
Households and Family Life Cycle   358
Changing Trends in Household Structure   358

Roles That Household Members Play   361
The Roles of Spouses   362
The Role of Children   363

Social Class   364
Types of Social Class Systems   364
Social Class Influences   365
How Social Class Is Determined   366

How Social Class Changes over Time   367
Upward Mobility   368
Downward Mobility   368
Social Class Fragmentation   368

How Does Social Class Affect Consumption?   369
Conspicuous Consumption and Voluntary Simplicity   369
Status Symbols and Judging Others   370
Compensatory Consumption   370
The Meaning of Money   371

The Consumption Patterns of Specific Social Classes   372
The Upper Class   372
The Middle Class   373
The Working Class   373
The Homeless   373

Summary   376

CONSUMER BEHAVIOR CASE: IKEA's Household
   Appeal   376

Endnotes   377

Chapter 14   Psychographics: Values, Personality, and Lifestyles   382

INTRODUCTION: The Dazzle of Customizing via Zazzle   382

Values   383
How Values Can Be Described   385
The Values That Characterize Western Cultures   386
Why Values Change   391
Influences on Values   391
How Values Can Be Measured   393

Personality   396
Research Approaches to Personality   396
Determining Whether Personality Characteristics
   Affect Consumer Behavior   398

Lifestyles   401
Lifestyle and Behavior Patterns   401

Voluntary Simplicity   402

**Psychographics: Combining Values,
   Personality, and Lifestyles   404**
VALS™   404
Other Applied Psychographic Research   404

Summary   406

CONSUMER BEHAVIOR CASE: Earache Treatment, Aisle 3:
   The Rise of Retail Walk-In Clinics   406

Endnotes   407

Part 5 Consumer Behavior Outcomes and Issues   413

Chapter 15   Innovations: Adoption, Resistance, and Diffusion   414

INTRODUCTION: Will Consumers Pay with Their Phones?   414

Innovations   415
Defining an Innovation   415
Innovations Characterized by Degree of Novelty   417
Innovations Characterized by Benefits Offered   418
Innovations Characterized by Breadth   418
Innovations and Cocreation   418

Resistance Versus Adoption   419
Whether Consumers Adopt an Innovation   419

How Consumers Adopt an Innovation   420
When Consumers Adopt Innovations   422

Diffusion   425
How Offerings Diffuse Through a Market   425
Factors Affecting the Shape of the Diffusion Curve   426
How Diffusion Relates to the Product Life Cycle   427

Influences on Adoption, Resistance, and Diffusion   427
Characteristics of the Innovation   427

Uncertainty   429
Consumer Learning Requirements   430
Social Relevance   433
Legitimacy and Adaptability   433
Characteristics of the Social System   435

The Consequences of Innovations   436
Summary   436
CONSUMER BEHAVIOR CASE: It Is Brewing: Single-Serve Coffeemakers Are Hot   437
Endnotes   438

Chapter 16   Symbolic Consumer Behavior   442

INTRODUCTION: Spin It Again: The Vinyl LP Is Back   442

Sources and Functions of Symbolic Meaning   443
Meaning Derived from Culture   443
Meaning Derived from the Consumer   445
The Emblematic Function   446
The Role Acquisition Function   448
The Connectedness Function   451
The Expressiveness Function   452
Multiple Functions   452
Symbols and Self-Concept   453

Special Possessions and Brands   455
Special Brands   455
Types of Special Possessions   455
The Characteristics That Describe Special Possessions   456
Why Some Products Are Special   457

Consumer Characteristics Affect What Is Special   457
Rituals Used with Special Possessions   458
Disposing of Special Possessions   459

Sacred Meaning   459

The Transfer of Symbolic Meaning Through Gift Giving   461
The Timing of Gifts   461
Three Stages of Gift Giving   461

Summary   465

CONSUMER BEHAVIOR CASE: Bicycles: More than Pedal Power   466

Endnotes   467

Chapter 17   Marketing, Ethics, and Social Responsibility in Today's Consumer Society   472

INTRODUCTION: Pepsi Refresh Pours on the Community Grants   472

In Search of Balance   473
Self-interest Versus the Interests of Others   473
Immediate Versus Long-Term Interests   475
"Dark Side" Versus "Bright Side" Outcomes   475

Marketing Ethics, Consumer Ethics, and Deviant Consumer Behavior   476
Acquisition Controversies   477
Consumption Controversies   483
Disposition Controversies   487

Social Responsibility Issues in Marketing   488
Environmentally Conscious Behavior   488

Charitable Behavior   490
Community Involvement   490

How Can Consumers Resist Marketing Practices?   491

Summary   491

CONSUMER BEHAVIOR CASE: Marketing Baby Carrots Like Junk Food   492

Endnotes   493

Glossary G-1

Name/Author Index I-1

Company/Product Index I-20

Subject Index I-25

Preface

At just about every moment of our lives, we engage in some form of consumer behavior. When we watch an ad on TV, send a text message to friends about a movie we just saw, brush our teeth, go to a ball game or to a beach party, visit a website on the Internet, download a new CD, or even throw away an old pair of shoes, we are behaving as a consumer. Being a consumer reaches into every part of our lives. Of course, we are much more than just consumers. We are students, team mates, family members, employees, citizens, voters, neighbors, basketball fans, ice-cream lovers, bloggers, inventors, and more. This book is dedicated to our role as consumers.

Given its omnipresence, the study of consumer behavior has critical implications for areas such as marketing, public policy, and ethics. It also helps us learn about ourselves—why we buy certain things, why we use them in a certain way, and how we get rid of them.

In this book we explore the fascinating world of consumer behavior, looking at a number of interesting and exciting topics. Some of these are quickly identified with our typical image of consumer behavior. Others may be surprising. We hope you will see why we became stimulated and drawn to this topic from the very moment we had our first consumer behavior course as students. We hope you will also appreciate why we choose to make this field our life's work, and why we are dedicated to this textbook.

WHY THE NEW EDITION OF THIS BOOK?

There are a number of consumer behavior books on the market. An important question concerns what this book has to offer and what distinguishes it from other texts. As active researchers in the field of consumer behavior, our overriding goal was to continue providing a treatment of the field that is up to date and cutting edge. There has been an explosion of research on a variety of consumer behavior topics over the last 20 years. Our primary aim was to provide a useful summary of this material for students of marketing. However, in drawing on cutting-edge research, we wanted to be careful not to become too "academic." Instead, our objective is to present cutting-edge topics in a manner that is accessible and easy for students to understand.

Specific changes and improvements to the sixth edition of this book include:

▶ Shorter length and more streamlined prose, making the content easier for students to process

▶ Coverage of the latest research from the academic field of consumer behavior

▶ New end-of-chapter cases, giving students the opportunity to discuss real-world consumer issues and to apply and use the concepts discussed in each chapter

▶ New coverage of research and behavioral concepts related to such topics as emotions, social media, unconscious consumer behavior, privacy, and obesity

▶ Numerous new advertisements offering concrete illustrations of consumer behavior concepts in action

▶ Numerous new examples highlighting how all kinds of organizations use insights into consumer behavior to improve their marketing effectiveness

▶ New database analysis exercises offering students an opportunity to make marketing decisions based on consumer demographics and behavior styles

▶ Improved synergistic supplemental materials

TEXTBOOK FEATURES

As award-winning teachers, we have tried to translate our instructional abilities and experience into the writing of this text. The following features have been a natural outgrowth of these experiences.

Conceptual Model

First, we believe that students can learn best when they see the big picture—when they understand what concepts mean, how these concepts are used in business practice, and how these relate to one another. In our opinion, consumer behavior is too often presented as a set of discrete topics with little or no relationship to one another. We have therefore developed an overall conceptual model that helps students grasp the big picture and see how the chapters and topics are themselves interrelated. Each chapter is linked to other chapters by a specific model that fits within the larger model. Further, the overall model guides the organization of the book. This organizing scheme makes the chapters far more *integrative* than most other books.

Practical Orientation, with an Emphasis on Globalization and Social Media

Second, we believe that insights into consumer behavior are interesting in and of themselves, but also that they should be relevant to managerial practice. The ultimate goal of consumer behavior theory and research is to improve the decision making ability of managers in profit and nonprofit organizations who aim to cater to consumers' needs. Rather than merely translating general psychological or sociological principles and theories to a consumer context, this book is dedicated to understanding consumer behavior in order to improve managerial practice. Given our notion that students enjoy seeing how the concepts in consumer behavior can apply to business practice, a second objective of the book was to provide a very practical orientation. We include a wealth of contemporary real-world examples to illustrate key topics. We also try to broaden students' horizons by providing a number of international examples. Given the importance of online consumer behavior, the new edition also fully treats the advent and implications of the new social media. It provides numerous examples of consumer behavior in an Internet and social media context.

Current and Cutting-Edge Coverage

Third, we provide coverage of the field of consumer behavior that is as current and up to date as possible (including many of the recent research advances). This includes several *novel chapters* that often do not appear in other textbooks: "Symbolic Consumer Behavior," "Low Effort Attitude Change," "Low Effort Decision Making," and "Ethics, Social Responsibility, and the Dark Side of Consumer Behavior and Marketing." These topics are at the cutting edge of consumer behavior research and are likely to be of considerable interest to students.

Balanced Treatment of Micro and Macro Topics

Fourth, our book tries to provide a balanced perspective on the field of consumer behavior. Specifically we give treatment to both psychological (micro) consumer behavior topics (e.g., attitudes, decision making) and sociological (macro) consumer behavior topics (e.g., subculture, gender, social class influences). Also, although we typically teach consumer behavior by starting with the more micro topics and then moving up to more macro topics, we realize that some instructors prefer the reverse sequence.

Broad Conceptualization of the Subject

Fifth, we present a broad conceptualization of the topic of consumer behavior. While many books focus on what products or services consumers *buy,* consumer behavior scholars have recognized that the topic of consumer behavior is much broader. Specifically, rather than studying buying per se, we recognize that consumer behavior includes a *set* of decisions (what, whether, when, where, why, how, how often, how much, how long) about *acquisition* (including, but not limited to buying), *usage,* and *disposition* decisions. Focusing on more than what products or services consumers buy provides a rich set of theoretical and practical implications for our both understanding of consumer behavior and the practice of marketing.

Finally, we consider the relevance of consumer behavior to *many constituents,* not just marketers. Chapter 1 indicates that CB is important to marketers, public policy makers, ethicists and consumer advocacy groups, and consumers themselves (including students' own lives). Some chapters focus exclusively on the implications of consumer behavior for public policy makers, ethicists, and consumer advocacy groups. Other chapters consider these issues as well, though in less detail.

CONTENT AND ORGANIZATION OF THE BOOK

One can currently identify two main approaches to the study of consumer behavior: a "micro" orientation, which focuses on the individual psychological processes that consumers use to make acquisition, consumption, and disposition decisions, and a "macro" orientation, which focuses on group behaviors and the symbolic nature of consumer behavior. This latter orientation draws heavily from such fields as sociology, culture theory, and anthropology. Both orientations are represented in this book. The current book and overall model have been structured around a "micro to macro" organization based on the way we teach this course and the feedback that we have received from reviewers.

Chapter 1 in Part 1, "An Introduction to Consumer Behavior," presents an introduction to consumer behavior and provides students with an understanding of the breadth of the field, and its importance to marketers, advocacy groups, public policy makers, and consumers themselves. It also presents the overall model that guides the organization of the text. An Appendix, which follows Chapter 1, introduces methods by which consumer research is conducted.

Part 2, "The Psychological Core," focuses on the inner psychological processes that affect consumer behavior. We see that consumers' acquisition, usage, and disposition behaviors and decisions are greatly affected by the amount of effort they put into engaging in behaviors and making decisions. Chapter 2 describes three critical factors that affect effort: the (1) *motivation* or desire, (2) *ability* (knowledge and information), and (3) *opportunity* to engage in behaviors and make decisions. In Chapter 3, we then examine how information in consumers' environments (ads, prices, product features, word-of-mouth communications, etc.) is internally processed by consumers— how they come in contact with these stimuli (*exposure*), notice them (*attention*), and *perceive* them (perception—and how we attempt to understand or *comprehend* them on a deeper level). Chapter 4 continues by discussing how we compare new stimuli to our knowledge of existing stimuli, in a process called *categorization*. Also, because consumers often must remember the information they have previously stored in order to make decisions, this chapter examines the important topic of consumer *memory*. In Chapters 5 and 6, we see how *attitudes* are formed and changed depending on whether the amount of effort consumers devote to forming an attitude is *high* or *low* and whether attitudes are cognitively or affectively based.

Whereas Part 2 examines some of the internal factors that influence consumers' decisions, a critical domain of consumer behavior involves understanding how consumers make acquisition, consumption, and disposition decisions. Thus, in Part 3, "The Process of Making Decisions," we examine the sequential steps of the consumer decision-making process. In Chapter 7, we examine the initial steps of this process—*problem recognition* and *information search*. Similar to the attitude change processes described earlier, we next examine the consumer decision-making process, both when *effort is high* (Chapter 8) and when it is *low* (Chapter 9). Further, in both chapters we examine these important processes from both a cognitive and an affective perspective. Finally, the process does not end after a decision has been made. In Chapter 10, we see how consumers determine whether they are *satisfied* or *dissatisfied* with their decisions and how they *learn* from choosing and consuming products and services.

Part 4, "The Consumer's Culture," reflects a "macro" view of consumer behavior that examines how various aspects of *culture* affect consumer behavior. First, Chapter 11 considers how, when, and why the specific *reference groups* (friends, work group, clubs) to which we belong can influence acquisition, usage, and disposition decisions and behaviors. Then, we see how *consumer diversity* (in terms of age, gender, sexual orientation, region, ethnicity, and religion) can affect consumer behavior in Chapter 12. Chapter 13 then examines how *social class* and *households* characteristics influence acquisition, usage, and disposition behaviors. Finally, Chapter 14 examines how external influences affect our *personality, lifestyle,* and *values,* as well as consumer behavior.

Finally, Part 5, "Consumer Behavior Outcomes and Issues," examines the effects of the numerous influences and decision processes discussed in the previous three parts. Chapter 15 builds on the topics of internal decision making and group behavior by examining how consumers adopt new offerings, and how their *adoption* decisions affect the spread or *diffusion* of an offering through a market. Because products and services often reflect deep-felt and significant meanings (e.g., our favorite song or restaurant), Chapter 16 focuses on the exciting topic of *symbolic consumer behavior*. Finally, Chapter 17 examines *marketing, ethics,* and *social responsibility,* and focuses on marketing and consumer ethics, as well as marketing practices that have been the focus of social commentary in recent years.

PEDAGOGICAL ADVANTAGES

Based on our extensive teaching experience, we have incorporated a number of features that should help students learn about consumer behavior.

Chapter Opening Cases

Each chapter begins with a case scenario about an actual company or situation that illustrates key concepts discussed in the chapter and their importance to marketers. This will help students grasp the "big picture" and understand the relevance of the topics from the start of the chapter.

Chapter Opening Model

Each chapter also begins with a conceptual model that shows the organization of the chapter, the topics discussed, and how they relate both to one another and to other chapters. Each model reflects an expanded picture of one or more of the elements presented in the overall conceptual model for the book (described in Chapter 1).

Marketing Implication Sections

Numerous *Marketing Implications sections* are interspersed throughout each chapter. These sections illustrate how various consumer behavior concepts can be applied to the practice of marketing, including such basic marketing functions as market segmentation, target market selection, positioning, market research, promotion, price, product, and place decisions. An abundance of marketing examples (from both the United States and abroad) provide concrete applications and implementations of the concepts to marketing practice.

Marginal Glossary

Every chapter contains a set of key terms that are both highlighted in the text and defined in margin notes. These terms and their definitions should help students identify and remember the central concepts described in the chapter.

Rich Use of Full-Color Exhibits

Each chapter contains a number of illustrated examples, including photos, advertisements, charts, and graphs. These illustrations help to make important topics personally relevant and engaging, help students remember the material, and make the book more accessible and aesthetically pleasing, thereby increasing students' motivation to learn. All diagrams and charts employ full color, which serves to both highlight key points and add to the aesthetic appeal of the text. Each model, graph, ad, and photo also has an accompanying caption that provides a simple description and explanation of how the exhibit relates to the topic it is designed to illustrate.

End-of-Chapter Summaries

The end of each chapter provides students with a simple and concise summary of topics. These summaries are a good review tool to use with the conceptual model to help students to get the big picture.

End-of-Chapter Questions

Each chapter includes a set of review and discussion questions designed to help students recall and more deeply understand the concepts in the chapter.

End-of-Chapter Cases

Each chapter ends with a short case that describes an issue pertinent to the topics discussed in the text. By applying chapter content to real-world cases, students have a chance to make the concepts we discuss more concrete. Many of the cases involve brands that students are familiar with, heightening engagement with the material.

COMPLETE TEACHING PACKAGE

A variety of ancillary materials have been designed to help the instructor in the classroom. All of these supplements have been carefully coordinated to support the text and provide an integrated and synergistic set of materials for the instructor. Dr. Angeline G. Close of the University of Texas at Austin authors the revised and modern instructor's supplements. She brings a modern approach, and includes experiential aspects of consumer behavior to the supplements. Her objective in this project is twofold:

▶   Enhance the student learning experience via more interactive and visually engaging supplements.

▶   Help instructors, especially newer instructors, by giving modern supplements that are synergistic to each other. That is, the text, the Instructor's Manual, Test Bank, PowerPoint presentations, and quizzes reinforce the same learning objectives and content.

How to Access the Supplements

Consumer Behavior's, 6th Edition, Instructor's Manual, Test Bank, and PowerPoint® supplements are available on the Instructor's Resource CD. These supplements, as well as some additional content, such as online quizzes, are also available on the Instructor's Companion Site.

Instructor's Manual

The Instructors' Manual is updated to be synergistic with all other supplements. Included for each chapter are a chapter summary, learning objectives, chapter outline, review/discussion answers, end-of-chapter case solutions, end-of-chapter exercise solutions, Internet exercise solutions, discussion questions, and experiential learning exercises to enhance student learning.

Test Bank

A new Test Bank is available for *Consumer Behavior's*, 6th Edition, also updated to be synergistic with the text and other supplements. Each Test Bank question has a new system of potential choices. One, there is a clearly defined correct choice. There are two or three other choices that are clearly incorrect for a precise reason (as indicated by the readings). Then, there is a choice that is clearly wrong or not relevant at all. The number of "all of the above" and "none of the above" choices has been reduced. The new Test Bank has a text page reference and AACSB requirement tags (e.g., ethics).

Test Bank, ExamView® Format

This electronic software for the Test Bank allows instructors to generate and change tests easily on the computer. The program will print an answer key appropriate to each version for the test you have devised, and it allows you to customize the printed appearance of the test.

PowerPoint® Presentation Package

A package of professionally developed PowerPoint® slides is available for use by adopters of this textbook. These lecture PowerPoint® slides outline the text content, including key figures and tables. *Consumer Behavior's*, 6th Edition, will have more user friendly, experiential presentations to enhance student learning and break up the monotony of text-based lectures. Also, participation probes are now included, to entice student feedback and interaction with the course and instructor.

Videos

A completely new video package, available online or DVD, has been provided to supplement and enliven class lectures and discussion. Videos contain real-world scenarios that illustrate certain concepts in a given chapter. The clips are intended to be interesting, to ground the concepts in real life for students, and to provide an impetus for stimulating student input and involvement. A Video Guide is also available to help instructors integrate the videos with various text chapters.

WebTutor™ (for WebCT® and Blackboard®)

Online learning is growing at a rapid pace. Whether you are looking to offer courses at a distance or in a Web-enhanced classroom, South-Western, a part of Cengage Learning, offers you a solution with WebTutor. WebTutor provides instructors with text-specific content that interacts with the two leading systems of higher education course management: WebCT and Blackboard.

WebTutor is a turnkey solution for instructors who want to begin using technology like Blackboard or WebCT but do not have Web-ready content available or do not want to be burdened with developing their own content. WebTutor uses the Internet to turn everyone in your class into a front-row student. WebTutor offers interactive study guide features including quizzes, concept reviews, discussion forums, video clips, and more. Instructor tools are also provided to facilitate communication between students and faculty.

Student Companion Site

The free student companion site provides a number of additional resources to help students study and test their learning.

ACKNOWLEDGMENTS

Special recognition is extended to Marian Wood, whose assistance was crucial to the completion of this project. Her tireless work on this project is greatly appreciated. We have also been extremely fortunate to work with a wonderful team of dedicated professionals from Cengage Learning. We are very grateful to Sarah Blasco, Fred Burns, Joanne Dauksewicz, Colleen Farmer, and Julie Low whose enormous energy and enthusiasm spurred our progress on this sixth edition. We also appreciate the efforts of Angeline Close of the University of Texas at Austin for her work on the Instructor's Manual, Test Bank, and PowerPoint slides. The quality of this book and its ancillary package has been helped immensely by the insightful and rich comments of a set of researchers and instructors who served as reviewers. Their thoughtful and helpful comments had real impact in shaping the final product. In particular, we wish to thank:

Larry Anderson
Long Island University

Mike Ballif
University of Utah

Sharon Beatty
University of Alabama

Sandy Becker
Rutgers Business School

Russell Belk
University of Utah

Joseph Bonnice
Manhattan College

Timothy Brotherton
Ferris State University

Carol Bruneau
University of Montana

Margaret L. Burk
Muskingum College

Carol Calder
Loyola Marymount University

Paul Chao
University of Northern Iowa

Dennis Clayson
University of Northern Iowa

Joel Cohen
University of Florida

Sally Dibb
University of Warwick

Richard W. Easley
Baylor University

Richard Elliott
Lancaster University

Abdi Eshghi
Bentley College

Frank W. Fisher
Stonehill College

Ronald Fullerton
Providence College

Philip Garton
Leicester Business School

Peter L. Gillett
University of Central Florida

Debbora Heflin
Cal Poly, Pomona

Elizabeth Hirschman
Rutgers University

Raj G. Javalgi
Cleveland State University

Harold Kassarjian
UCLA

Patricia Kennedy
University of Nebraska, Lincoln

Robert E. Kleine
Arizona State University

Stephen K. Koernig
DePaul University

Scott Koslow
University of Waikato

Robert Lawson
William Patterson University

Phillip Lewis
Rowan College of New Jersey

Kenneth R. Lord
SUNY, Buffalo

Peggy Sue Loroz
Gonzaga University

Bart Macchiette
Plymouth State College

Michael Mallin
Kent State University

Lawrence Marks
Kent State University

David Marshall
University of Edinburgh

Ingrid M. Martin
California State University, Long Beach

Anil Mathur
Hofstra University

A. Peter McGraw
University of Colorado, Boulder

Matt Meuter
California State University, Chico

Martin Meyers
University of Wisconsin, Stevens Point

Vince Mitchell
UMIST

Lois Mohr
Georgia State University

Risto Moisio
California State University, Long Beach

Rebecca Walker Naylor
University of South Carolina

James R. Ogden
Kutztown University

Thomas O'Guinn
University of Illinois

Marco Protano
New York University

Judith Powell
Virginia Union University

Michael Reilly
Montana State University

Anja K. Reimer
University of Miami

Gregory M. Rose
The University of Mississippi

Mary Mercurio Scheip
Eckerd College

Marilyn Scrizzi
New Hampshire Technical College

John Shaw
Providence College

C. David Shepherd
University of Tennessee, Chattanooga

Robert E. Smith
Indiana University

Eric Richard Spangenberg
Washington State University

Bruce Stern
Portland State University

Barbara Stewart
University of Houston

Jane Boyd Thomas
Winthrop University

Phil Titus
Bowling Green State University

Carolyn Tripp
Western Illinois University

Rajiv Vaidyanathan
University of Minnesota, Duluth

Stuart Van Auken
California State University, Chico

Kathleen D. Vohs
University of Minnesota

Janet Wagner
University of Maryland

John Weiss
Colorado State University

Tommy E. Whittler
University of Kentucky

Carolyn Yoon
University of Michigan

An Introduction to Consumer Behavior

PART 1

1 Understanding Consumer Behavior   2

Appendix: Developing Information about Consumer Behavior   28

IN PART ONE, you will learn that consumer behavior involves much more than purchasing products. In addition, you will find out that marketers continuously study consumer behavior for clues to who buys, uses, and disposes of what goods and services, as well as clues to when, where, why, and how they make decisions.

Chapter 1 defines consumer behavior and examines its importance to marketers, advocacy groups, public policy makers, and consumers. The chapter also presents the overall model that guides the organization of this book. As this model indicates, consumer behavior covers four basic domains: (1) the psychological core, (2) the process of making decisions, (3) the consumer's culture, and (4) consumer behavior outcomes and issues. In addition, you will read about the implications of consumer behavior for marketing activities.

The Appendix focuses on consumer behavior research and its special implications for marketers. You will learn about various research methods, types of data, and ethical issues related to consumer research. With this background, you will be able to understand how consumer research helps marketers develop more effective strategies and tactics for reaching and satisfying customers.

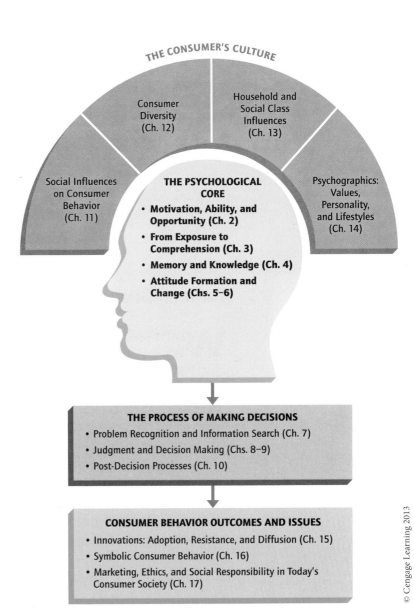

THE CONSUMER'S CULTURE

Consumer Diversity (Ch. 12)

Household and Social Class Influences (Ch. 13)

Social Influences on Consumer Behavior (Ch. 11)

THE PSYCHOLOGICAL CORE
- **Motivation, Ability, and Opportunity (Ch. 2)**
- **From Exposure to Comprehension (Ch. 3)**
- **Memory and Knowledge (Ch. 4)**
- **Attitude Formation and Change (Chs. 5–6)**

Psychographics: Values, Personality, and Lifestyles (Ch. 14)

THE PROCESS OF MAKING DECISIONS
- Problem Recognition and Information Search (Ch. 7)
- Judgment and Decision Making (Chs. 8–9)
- Post-Decision Processes (Ch. 10)

CONSUMER BEHAVIOR OUTCOMES AND ISSUES
- Innovations: Adoption, Resistance, and Diffusion (Ch. 15)
- Symbolic Consumer Behavior (Ch. 16)
- Marketing, Ethics, and Social Responsibility in Today's Consumer Society (Ch. 17)

CHAPTER 1

UNDERSTANDING CONSUMER BEHAVIOR

After studying this chapter, you will be able to

1. Define consumer behavior and explain the components that make up the definition.

2. Identify the four domains of consumer behavior shown in Exhibit 1.6 that affect acquisition, usage, and disposition decisions.

3. Discuss the benefits of studying consumer behavior.

4. Explain how companies apply consumer behavior concepts when making marketing decisions.

© ZUMA Wire Service/Alamy

INTRODUCTION

Panera Bread: More than Bread

When Ron Shaich, the founder of Panera Bread, looks at fast-food burger restaurants, he sees "self-service gasoline stations for the human body." In contrast, Panera Bread is designed to "bring real food to people in environments that engage them." The Missouri-based chain of more than 1,500 bakery-cafés emphasizes the wholesome quality of its artisanal breads, salads, sandwiches, and soups. The friendly atmosphere and comfortable surroundings invite customers to linger, use the free Wi-Fi, and enjoy the aroma of fresh-baked bread.

The 10 million customers who belong to the restaurant's loyalty program make more than 40 percent of all Panera purchases. "We are able to track individually what people do," Shaich explains, which means "we're actually able to market to you in a way that's unique to you." As a result, Panera can surprise loyal customers by offering an occasional reward that each will like, such as a free pastry for those who tend to buy breakfast or coffee. As a company with a conscience, Panera donates cash and unsold bakery items to feed the hungry. It also operates a handful of nonprofit Panera Cares restaurants, where customers pay what they wish, to provide meals to those in need and serve the community at large. These restaurants post no prices, only a suggested donation for each item. Are people responding? Yes: 60 percent of customers donate the suggested amount, 20 percent donate more, and 20 percent donate less.[1]

Panera Bread and other businesses know that their success depends on understanding consumer behavior and trends so that they can create goods and services that consumers will want, like, use, and recommend to others. Panera is concerned not only with the foods its customers prefer but also with its social responsibility to local communities, which affects customers' reactions toward the company. Charities, schools, government agencies, and other organizations are also interested in how consumers behave and how marketing can influence consumers' thoughts, feelings, and actions.

This chapter provides a general overview of (1) what consumer behavior is, (2) what factors affect it, (3) who benefits from studying it, and (4) how marketers apply consumer behavior concepts. Because you are a consumer, you probably have some thoughts about these issues. However, you may be surprised at how broad the domain of consumer behavior is, how many factors help explain it, and how important the field is to marketers, ethicists and consumer advocates, public policy makers and regulators, and consumers like yourself. You will also get a glimpse of the marketing implications of consumer behavior, previewing how we will connect consumer behavior concepts with practical applications throughout this book.

DEFINING CONSUMER BEHAVIOR

Consumer behavior The totality of consumers' decisions with respect to the acquisition, consumption, and disposition of goods, services, time, and ideas by human decision-making units (over time).

If you were asked to define **consumer behavior**, you might say it refers to the study of how a person buys products. However, consumer behavior really involves quite a bit more, as this more complete definition indicates:

Consumer behavior reflects the totality of consumers' decisions with respect to the acquisition, consumption, and disposition of goods, services, activities, experiences, people, and ideas by (human) decision-making units [over time].[2]

This definition has some very important elements, summarized in Exhibit 1.1. The following sections present a closer look at each element.

Consumer Behavior Involves Goods, Services, Activities, Experiences, People, and Ideas

Consumer behavior means more than just the way that a person buys tangible products such as bath soap and automobiles. It also includes consumers' use of services, activities, experiences, and ideas such as going to the dentist, attending a concert, taking a trip, and donating to UNICEF.[3] In addition, consumers make decisions about people, such as voting for politicians, reading books by certain authors, seeing movies or TV shows starring certain actors, and attending concerts featuring favorite bands.

Another example of consumer behavior involves choices about the consumption of time, a scarce resource. Will you check to see what's happening on Facebook, search for a YouTube video, watch a sports event live, or record a program and watch it later, for instance?[4] How we use time reflects who we are, what our lifestyles are like, and how we are both the same and different from others.[5] Because consumer behavior includes the consumption of so many things, we use the simple term **offering** to encompass these entities.

Offering A product, service, activity, experience, or idea offered by a marketing organization to consumers.

Consumer Behavior reflects:

the totality of decisions	about the consumption	of an offering	by decision-making units	over time
Whether What Why How When Where How much/ How often/ How long	Acquisition Usage Disposition	Products Services Activities Experiences People Ideas	Information gatherer Influencer Decider Purchaser User	Hours Days Weeks Months Years

Marketing Strategies and Tactics

Consumer Behavior Involves More than Buying

How consumers buy is extremely important to marketers. However, marketers are also intensely interested in consumer behavior related to using and disposing of an offering:

Acquisition The process by which a consumer comes to own an offering.

▶ *Acquiring.* Buying represents one type of **acquisition** behavior. As shown later in this chapter, acquisition includes other ways of obtaining goods and services, such as renting, leasing, trading, and sharing. It also involves decisions about time as well as money.[6] For example, when consumers experience a loss (i.e., make a purchase that does not work out well), they will perceive the time period until the next purchase as being shorter (because they want to remove negative feeling).[7] Consumers sometimes find themselves interrupted during a consumption experience; studies show interruption actually makes a pleasant experience seem more enjoyable when resumed.[8] Deadlines can also affect acquisition behavior: Consumers tend to procrastinate in redeeming coupons and gift cards with far-future deadlines, but move more quickly when deadlines are closer. Why? Because they do not want to regret having missed out and they expect to have more time to enjoy and indulge themselves with the acquisition in the future.[9]

Usage The process by which a consumer uses an offering.

▶ *Using.* After consumers acquire an offering, they use it, which is why **usage** is at the very core of consumer behavior.[10] Whether and why we use certain products can symbolize something about who we are, what we value, and what we believe. The products we use on Christmas (e.g., making desserts from scratch or buying them in a bakery) may symbolize the event's significance and how we feel about our guests. The music we enjoy (Lady Gaga or Paul McCartney) and the jewelry we wear (earrings or engagement rings) can also symbolize who we are and how we feel. Moreover, marketers must be sensitive to when consumers are likely to use a product,[11] whether they find it effective,[12] whether they control their consumption of it,[13] and how they react after using it—do they spread positive or negative word-of-mouth reviews about a new film, for instance?[14]

Disposition The process by which a consumer discards an offering.

▶ *Disposing.* **Disposition**, how consumers get rid of an offering they have previously acquired, can have important implications for marketers.[15] Consumers can give away their used possessions, sell them on eBay, or lend them to others. "Vintage" clothing stores now sell older clothes (disposed of by the original owners) that buyers find stylish. Eco-minded consumers often seek out biodegradable products made from recycled materials or choose goods that do not pollute

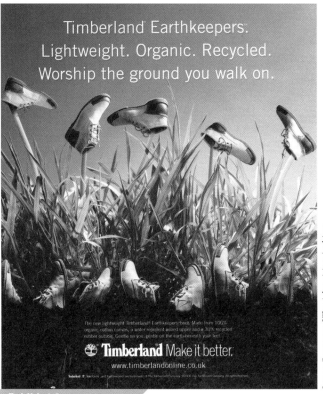

Image Courtesy of The Advertising Archives

Exhibit 1.2

Disposition
Consumers dispose of old products they acquired in a number of ways, oftentimes through recycling or vintage shops.

when disposed of (see Exhibit 1.2). Municipalities are also interested in how to motivate earth-friendly disposition.[16] Marketers see profit opportunities in addressing disposition concerns. Terra-Cycle, for example, markets tote bags, pencil cases, and other products made from used packaging and recycled materials. In North and South America, Europe, and the Baltic, it partners with firms such as PepsiCo to collect mountains of discarded packaging and turn them into usable products for sale.[17]

Consumer Behavior Is a Dynamic Process

The sequence of acquisition, consumption, and disposition can occur over time in a dynamic order—hours, days, weeks, months, or years, as shown in Exhibit 1.1. To illustrate, assume that a family has acquired and is using a new car. Usage provides the family with information—whether the car drives well and is reliable—that affects when, whether, how, and why members will dispose of the car by selling, trading, or junking it. Because the family always needs transportation, disposition is likely to affect when, whether, how, and why its members acquire another car in the future.

Entire markets are designed around linking one consumer's disposition decision to other consumers' acquisition decisions. When consumers buy used cars, they are buying cars that others have disposed of. From eBay's online auctions to Goodwill Industries' secondhand clothing stores, from consignment shops to used books sold online, many businesses exist to link one consumer's disposition behavior with another's acquisition behavior.

Broader changes in consumer behavior occur over time, as well. Fifty years ago, consumers had far fewer brand choices and were exposed to fewer marketing messages. In contrast, today's consumers are more connected, easily able to research offerings online, access communications and promotions in multiple media, and check what others think of brands with a quick search or social media post. Consumers can also collaborate with marketers or with each other to create new products.[18] For example, thousands of consumers participate when Mountain Dew requests ideas for new soft-drink flavors, product logos, and new ads.[19] Then, consumers become cocreators of products.

Consumer Behavior Can Involve Many People

Consumer behavior does not necessarily reflect the action of a single individual. A group of friends, a few coworkers, or an entire family may plan a birthday party or decide where to have lunch, exchanging ideas in person, on the phone, via social media, or by e-mail or text message. Moreover, the individuals engaging in consumer behavior can take on one or more roles. In the case of a car purchase, for example, one or more family members might take on the role of information gatherer by researching different models. Others might assume the role of influencer and try to affect the outcome of a decision. One or more members may take on the role of purchaser by actually paying for the car, and some or all may be users. Finally, several family members may be involved in the disposal of the car.

Consumer Behavior Involves Many Decisions

Consumer behavior involves understanding whether, why, when, where, how, how much, how often, and for how long consumers will buy, use, or dispose of an offering (look back at see Exhibit 1.1).

Whether to Acquire/Use/Dispose of an Offering
Consumers must decide whether to acquire, use, or dispose of an offering. They may need to decide whether to spend or save their money when they earn extra cash.[20] How much they decide to spend may be influenced by their perceptions of how much they recall spending in the past.[21]

Exhibit 1.3

U.S. Consumer Spending, by Age
Consumers in different age groups have different needs and spend different amounts on necessities and nonnecessities.

Age of Consumer (in years)	Annual Average Spending per Household (in $)	Annual Average Spending on Housing, Food, and Transportation	Annual Average Spending on Entertainment and Education
Under 25	28,119	19,248	3,143
25–34	46,494	31,098	3,312
35–44	57,301	36,829	4,252
45–54	58,708	35,858	5,231
55–64	52,463	31,617	3,909
65 and older	37,562	23,506	2,224

Source: Adapted from "Age of Reference Person: Average Annual Expenditures and Characteristics," *Consumer Expenditure Survey,* October 2010, U.S. Department of Labor, U.S. Bureau of Labor Statistics, Table 3, www.bls.gov.

They may need to decide whether to order a pizza, clean out a closet, or download a movie. Some consumers collect items, for example, a situation that has created a huge market for buying, selling, transporting, storing, and insuring collectible items.[22] Decisions about whether to acquire, use, or dispose of an offering are often related to personal goals, safety concerns, or a desire to reduce economic, social, or psychological risk.

What Offering to Acquire/Use/Dispose Of

Consumers make decisions every day about what to buy; in fact, each U.S. household spends an average of $138 per day on goods and services.[23] In some cases, we make choices among product or service *categories* such as buying food versus downloading new music. In other cases, we choose between *brands* such as whether to buy a Kindle or a NOOK e-book reader. Our choices multiply daily as marketers introduce new products, sizes, and packages. Exhibit 1.3 shows some of the spending patterns of U.S. consumers in particular age groups.

Why Acquire/Use/Dispose of an Offering

Consumption can occur for a number of reasons. Among the most important reasons, as you will see later, are the ways in which an offering meets someone's needs, values, or goals. Some consumers acquire tattoos as a form of self-expression, to fit into a group, or to express their feelings about someone or something. In New York City, the Social Tattoo Project provides free tattoos of Twitter hashtags to highlight social causes (#poverty for example).[24] Taking the self-expression of tattoos into the automotive arena, Ford has offered dozens of vinyl wrap "tattoos" for buyers to use in personalizing their Ford Focus cars.[25]

Sometimes our reasons for using an offering are filled with conflict, which leads to some difficult consumption decisions. Teenagers may smoke, even though they know it is harmful, because they think smoking will help them gain acceptance. Some consumers may be unable to stop acquiring, using, or disposing of products. They may be physically addicted to products such as cigarettes, or they may have a compulsion to eat, gamble, or buy.

Why an Offering Is Not Acquired/Used/Disposed Of

Marketers also try to understand why consumers do *not* acquire, use, or dispose of an offering. For example, consumers may delay buying a tablet computer because they believe that the product will soon be outdated or that some firms will leave this market, leaving them without after-sale support or service. At times, consumers who want to acquire or consume an offering are unable to do so because what they want is unavailable. Ethics and social responsibility can also play a role. Some consumers may want to avoid products made in factories with questionable labor practices or avoid movies downloaded, copied, and shared without permission.[26]

How to Acquire/Use/Dispose of an Offering

Marketers gain a lot of insight by understanding how consumers acquire, consume, and dispose of an offering.

Exhibit 1.4

Eight Ways to Acquire an Offering

There are many ways that consumers can acquire an offering.

Acquisition Method	Description
Buying	Buying is a common acquisition method used for many offerings.
Trading	Consumers might receive a good or service as part of a trade.
Renting or leasing	Instead of buying, consumers rent or lease cars, furniture, vacation homes, and more.
Bartering	Consumers (and businesses) can exchange goods or services without having money change hands.
Gifting	Each society has many gift-giving occasions as well as informal or formal rules dictating how gifts are to be given, what is an appropriate gift, and how to respond to a gift.
Finding	Consumers sometimes find goods that others have lost (hats left on a bus) or thrown away.
Stealing	Because various offerings can be acquired through theft, marketers have developed products to deter this acquisition method, such as alarms to deter car theft.
Sharing	Another method of acquisition is by sharing or borrowing. Some types of "sharing" are illegal and border on theft, as when consumers copy and share movies.

Ways of Acquiring an Offering

How do consumers decide whether to acquire an offering in a store or mall, online, or at an auction?[27] How do they decide whether to pay with cash, a check, a debit card, a credit card, an electronic system such as PayPal, or a "mobile wallet" payment app on their smartphones?[28] These examples relate to consumers' buying decisions, but Exhibit 1.4 shows that consumers can acquire an offering in other ways. *Sharing* is a form of acquisition, such as sharing possessions within a family or sharing videos via YouTube.[29]

Ways of Using an Offering

In addition to understanding how consumers acquire an offering, marketers want to know how consumers use an offering.[30] For obvious reasons, marketers want to ensure that their offering is used correctly. Improper usage of offerings like cough medicine or alcohol can create health and safety problems.[31] Because consumers may ignore label warnings and directions on potentially dangerous products, marketers who want to make warnings more effective have to understand how consumers process label information.

Ways of Disposing of an Offering

Sometimes nothing but the packaging remains of an offering (such as food) after it has been consumed. This leaves only a decision about whether to recycle or not, and how. Consumers who want to dispose of a tangible product have several options:[32]

▶ *Find a new use for it.* Using an old toothbrush to clean rust from tools or making shorts out of an old pair of jeans shows how consumers can continue using an item instead of disposing of it.

▶ *Get rid of it temporarily.* Renting or lending an item is one way of getting rid of it temporarily.

▶ *Get rid of it permanently.* Throwing away an item, sending it a recycling center, trading it, giving it away, or selling it are all ways to get rid of it permanently. However, some consumers refuse to throw away things that they regard as special, even if the items no longer serve a functional purpose.

When to Acquire/Use/Dispose of an Offering

The timing of consumer behavior can depend on many factors, including our perceptions of and attitudes toward time itself. Consumers may think in terms of whether it is "time for me" or "time for others" and whether acquiring or using an offering is planned or spontaneous.[33] In cold weather, our tendency to rent movies, call for a tow truck, or shop for clothes is greatly enhanced. At the same time, we are less likely to eat ice cream, shop for a car, or look for a new home during cold weather. Time of day influences many consumption decisions, which is why Panera Bread is starting to add drive-throughs to accommodate breakfast customers in a hurry.[34]

Our need for variety can affect when we acquire, use, or dispose of an offering. We may decide not to eat a sandwich for lunch today if we have already had it every other day this week. Transitions such as graduation, birth, retirement, and death also affect when we acquire, use, and dispose of offerings. For instance, we buy wedding rings when we get married. When we consume can be affected by traditions influenced by our families, our culture, and the area in which we live.

Decisions about when to acquire or use an offering are also affected by knowing when others might or might not be buying or using it. Thus, we might choose to go to the gym when we know that others will *not* be doing so. In addition, we may wait to buy until we know something will be on sale; even if we have to line up to buy something popular, we are likely to continue waiting if we see many people joining the line behind us.[35] Also, waiting to consume a pleasurable product such as candy increases our enjoyment of its consumption, even though we may be frustrated by having to wait.[36]

Another decision is when to acquire a new, improved version of a product we already own. This can be a difficult decision when the current model still works well or has sentimental value. However, marketers may be able to affect whether and when consumers buy upgrades by providing economic incentives for replacing older products.[37]

Where to Acquire/Use/Dispose of an Offering

Transitions such as graduation, birth, retirement, and death also affect when we acquire, use, and dispose of offerings. Consumers have more choices of where to acquire, use, and dispose of an offering than they have ever had before, including making purchases in stores, by mail, by phone, and over the Internet. The Internet has changed where we acquire, use, and dispose of goods. Many consumers buy online via computer or mobile phone because they like the convenience or the price or to acquire unique products.[38] And as the success of craigslist shows, the Internet can help people dispose of goods that are then acquired by others.

In addition to acquisition decisions, consumers also make decisions about where to consume various products. For example, the need for privacy motivates consumers to stay home when using products that determine whether they are ovulating or pregnant. On the other hand, wireless connections allow consumers in public places to make phone calls, post messages to social media sites, play computer games, and download photos or music from anywhere in the world. Consumers can also make charitable donations via text messages.[39]

Finally, consumers make decisions regarding where to dispose of goods. Should they toss an old magazine in the trash or the recycling bin? Should they store an old photo album in the attic or give it to a relative? Older consumers, in particular, may worry about what will happen to their special possessions after their death and about how to divide heirlooms without creating family conflict. These consumers hope that mementos will serve as a legacy for their heirs.[40] A growing number of consumers are recycling unwanted goods through recycling agencies or nonprofit groups or giving them directly to other consumers through websites like The Freecycle Network (www.freecycle.org) (see Exhibit 1.5).

How Much, How Often, and How Long to Acquire/Use/Dispose of an Offering

Consumers must make decisions about how much of a good or service they need; how often they need it; and how much time they will spend in acquisition, usage, and disposition.[41] Usage decisions can vary widely from person to person and from culture to culture. For example, consumers in Switzerland eat twice as much chocolate as consumers in Russia.[42]

Exhibit 1.5

Where to Dispose
Consumers have a number of options of places to dispose of goods, such as this recycling website.

Sales of a product can be increased when the consumer (1) uses larger amounts of the product, (2) uses the product more frequently, or (3) uses it for longer periods of time. Bonus packages may motivate consumers to buy more of a product, but does this stockpiling lead to higher consumption? In the case of food products, consumers are more likely to increase consumption when the stockpiled item requires no preparation.[43] Usage may also increase when consumers sign up for flat-fee pricing covering unlimited consumption of telephone services or other offerings. However, because many consumers who choose flat-fee programs overestimate their likely consumption, they often pay more than if they had chosen per-usage pricing.[44]

Some consumers experience problems because they engage in more acquisition, usage, or disposition than they should. For example, they may have a compulsion to overbuy, overeat, smoke, or gamble too much. Researchers are also investigating what affects consumers' abilities to control consumption temptations and what happens when self-control falters, an issue for anybody who has tried to diet or make other changes to consumption habits.[45]

Consumer Behavior Involves Emotions and Coping

Consumer researchers have studied the powerful role that emotions play in consumer behavior.[46] Positive and negative emotions as well as specific emotions like hope,[47] fear,[48] regret,[49] guilt,[50] embarrassment,[51] and general moods[52] can affect how consumers think, the choices they make, how they feel after making a decision, what they remember, and how much they enjoy an experience. Emotions like love sometimes describe how we feel about certain brands or possessions.[53] Consumers often use products to regulate their feelings—as when a scoop of ice cream seems like a good antidote to a bad quiz score.[54] Researchers have also studied how service employees' emotions can affect consumers' emotions outside of their awareness.[55] And low-level emotions can be very important in low-effort situations (e.g., the low-level feelings we get from viewing a humorous ad).

Because issues related to consumer behavior can involve stress, consumers often need to cope in some way.[56] Researchers have studied how consumers cope with difficult choices and an overwhelming array of goods from which to choose;[57] how consumers use goods and services to cope with stressful events[58] like having cancer; and how they cope with losing possessions due to divorce, natural disasters, moving to a residential-care facility, and other incidents.[59] They have even studied the coping behavior of certain market segments, such as low-literacy consumers, who often find it challenging to understand the marketplace without being able to read.[60]

WHAT AFFECTS CONSUMER BEHAVIOR?

The many factors that affect acquisition, usage, and disposition decisions can be classified into four broad domains, as shown in the model in Exhibit 1.6: (1) the psychological core, (2) the process of making decisions, (3) the consumer's culture, and (4) consumer behavior outcomes. Although the four domains are presented in separate sections of this book, each domain is related to all the others. For example, to make decisions that affect outcomes like buying new products, consumers must first engage in processes described in the psychological core. They need to be motivated, able, and have the opportunity to be exposed to, perceive, and attend to information. They need to think about and comprehend this information, develop attitudes about it, and form memories they can retrieve during the decision process.

The cultural environment also affects what motivates consumers, how they process information, and the kinds of decisions they make. Age, gender, social class, ethnicity, families, friends, and other factors affect consumer values and lifestyles and, in turn, influence the decisions that consumers make and how and why they make them. In the following overview, we illustrate the interrelationships among the domains with an example of a vacation decision.

Exhibit 1.6

A Model of Consumer Behavior

Consumer behavior encompasses four domains: (1) the consumer's culture, (2) the psychological core, (3) the process of making decisions, and (4) consumer behavior outcomes and issues. As the exhibit shows, Chapters 2–17 of this book relate to the four parts of this overall model.

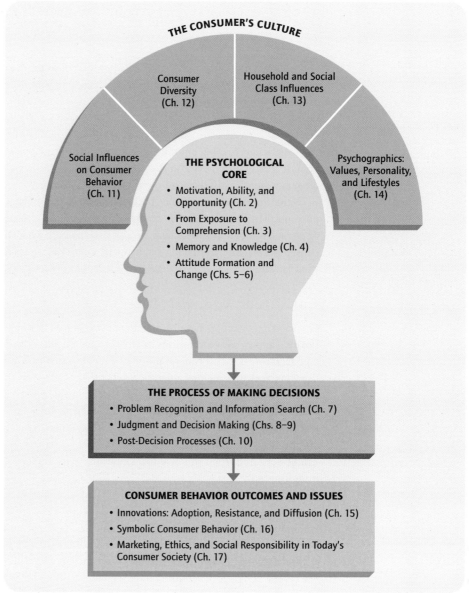

© Cengage Learning 2013

The Psychological Core: Internal Consumer Processes

Before consumers can make decisions, they must have some source of knowledge or information upon which to base their decisions. This source—the psychological core—covers motivation, ability, and opportunity; exposure, attention, perception, and comprehension; memory and knowledge; and attitudes about an offering.

Motivation, Ability, and Opportunity

Consider the case of a consumer named Jason who is deciding on a ski vacation. In Jason's mind, the vacation decision is risky because it will consume a lot of money and time, and he does not want to make a bad choice. Therefore, Jason is motivated to learn as much as he can about various vacation options, think about them, and imagine what they will be like. He has put other activities aside to give himself the opportunity to learn and think about this vacation. Because Jason already knows how to ski, he has the ability to determine what types of ski vacations he would find enjoyable. Whether he focuses on concrete things (how much the trip will cost) or abstract things (how much fun he will have) depends on how soon he plans to travel and how well the place he plans to visit fits with his self-concept.[61]

Exposure, Attention, Perception, and Comprehension

Because Jason is motivated to decide where to go on vacation and has both the ability and opportunity to do so, he will make sure he is exposed to and attends to any information relevant to his decision. He might look at travel ads and websites, read travel-related articles, check Twitter for special deals, and talk with friends and travel agents. Jason will probably not attend to *all* vacation information; however, he is likely to be exposed to information he will never consciously perceive or pay attention to. He must identify what he has perceived—is it an ad or something else?—and then determine what country or mountain resort is involved, all as part of the comprehension process. He might infer that Kitzbühel, Austria, is a reasonably priced vacation destination because a website shows information consistent with this interpretation, for example.

Memory and Knowledge

Whether Jason can store what he learns about ski resorts in his memory—and whether he can recall that information later—depends, in part, on his motivation, ability, and opportunity. As he learns something new about ski resorts, he will organize that knowledge according to categories such as "places to stay on a ski vacation." Jason will also associate each new piece of information with other concepts he knows, such as "expensive" or "eco-friendly." Note that Jason may *store* information in memory, but his choices will be based only on the information that can be *retrieved* from memory—a key point for marketers seeking to create strong brand images and develop memorable communications (see Exhibit 1.7).

Forming and Changing Attitudes

Jason is likely to form attitudes toward the vacations he has categorized and comprehended. He may have a favorable attitude toward Kitzbühel because a website describes it as affordable, educational, and fun. However, his attitudes might change as he encounters new information. Attitudes do not always predict behavior. For example, although many of us have a positive attitude toward working out, our attitude and our good intentions do not always culminate in a trip to the gym. For this reason, attitudes and choices are considered as separate topics.

It's not just a "don't miss."

It's a "never forget."

2 PARK ADVENTURE PASSPORT

When you include Busch Gardens® in your travel plans, it's not just about a Florida holiday. It's about a family discovery. Because there's something for every family member to experience and remember throughout the park - from a real-life safari to world-class thrill rides. All just an hour from Orlando.

Add the amazing encounters and electrifying rides of SeaWorld® Orlando with an Adventure Passport, a special two-park ticket which includes unlimited free coach rides from Orlando to Busch Gardens. If you don't get to see everything in two days, come back as often as you wish during the rest of your holiday®. This ticket is not available at the parks' front gates, so be sure to buy yours before leaving home.

Busch GARDENS. TAMPA BAY, FL

For holidays and tickets to Busch Gardens, call Virgin Holidays at 0871 222 0304 or visit virginholidays.com/buschgardens

Image Courtesy of The Advertising Archives

The Process of Making Decisions

As shown in Exhibit 1.6, the processes that are part of the psychological core are intimately tied to the process of making decisions. This domain involves four stages: problem recognition, information search, decision making, and postpurchase evaluation.

Problem Recognition and the Search for Information

Problem recognition occurs when we realize that we have an unfulfilled need. Jason realized that he needed a vacation, for example. His subsequent search for information gave him insight into where he might go, how much the vacation might cost, and when he might travel. He also examined his financial situation. Elements of the psychological core are invoked in problem recognition and search because once Jason realizes that he needs a vacation and begins his information search, he is exposed to information, attends to and perceives it, categorizes and comprehends it, and forms attitudes and memories.

Making Judgments and Decisions

Jason's decision is characterized as a *high-effort decision*, meaning that he is willing to invest a lot of time and to exert mental and emotional energy in making it. He identifies several criteria that will be important in making his choices: the trip should be fun and exciting, safe, educational, and affordable. Not all decisions involve a lot of effort. Jason also faces low-effort decisions such as what brand of toothpaste to take on the trip.

Again, the psychological core is invoked in making decisions. With a high-effort decision, Jason will be motivated to be exposed to lots of information, think about it deeply, analyze it critically, and form attitudes about it. He may have lasting memories about this information because he has thought about it so much. Consumers are not always aware of what they are thinking and how they are making their choices, so Jason might not be able to explain what affected his choices (background music in a travel agency might even be an influence).[62] Yet the emotions he thinks he will experience from different options (excitement, relaxation) may well influence his ultimate choice.[63] With a low-effort decision, such as what brand of toothpaste to buy, he would probably engage in less information search and process information less deeply, resulting in less enduring attitudes and memories.

Making Postdecision Evaluations

This step allows the consumer to judge, after the fact, whether the decision made was the correct one and whether to purchase that offering again. When he returns from his vacation, Jason will probably evaluate the outcome of his decisions. If his expectations were met and if the vacation was everything he thought it would be, he will feel satisfied. If the vacation exceeded his expectations, he will be delighted. If it fell short of them, he will be dissatisfied. Once again, aspects of the psychological core are invoked in making postdecision evaluations. Jason may expose himself to information that validates his experiences, he may update his attitudes, and he may selectively remember aspects of his trip that were extremely positive or negative.

The Consumer's Culture: External Processes

Why did Jason decide to go on a skiing trip in the first place? In large part, our consumption decisions and how we process information are affected by our culture. **Culture** refers to the typical or expected behaviors, norms, and ideas that characterize a group of people. It can be a powerful influence on all aspects of human behavior. Jason had certain feelings, perceptions, and attitudes because of the unique combination of groups to which he belongs and the influence they have on his values, personality, and lifestyle.

Reference Groups and Other Social Influences

When Jason sees groups of others he perceives as similar to himself, he regards them as **reference groups**, people whose values he shares and whose opinions he respects. He might also want to emulate the behavior of people whom he admires and to listen to the advice they offer through *word of mouth* (in person, on Facebook, on Twitter, etc.). Athletes, musicians, or movie stars sometimes serve as reference groups, influencing how we evaluate information and the choices we make

Culture The typical or expected behaviors, norms, and ideas that characterize a group of people.

Reference group A group of people consumers compare themselves with for information regarding behavior, attitudes, or values.

(see Exhibit 1.8). Reference groups can also make us feel as if we should behave in a certain way. Jason may feel some pressure to go to Kitzbühel because his friends think that doing so is cool.

Diversity Influences

Jason is a member of many regional, ethnic, and religious groups that directly or indirectly affect the decisions he makes. For example, although his decision to ski at a place far from home is fairly typical for a North American man launched on his career, a consumer from a developing nation or a single woman from a different culture may not have made the same choice. Also, his age, gender, and educational background may all affect his impressions of what constitutes a good vacation, accounting for his interest in a European ski trip. Consider the vacation choices shown in Exhibit 1.9, and try to imagine the background factors that predispose consumers to choose these as vacation options.

Household and Social Class Influences

Because Jason is a member of the upper middle class and lives with his parents, these household and social class influences may affect his decision to go to a luxurious European ski resort with friends rather than join his family at a rustic ski area near home.

Values, Personality, and Lifestyles

The choices Jason makes are based, in part, on his beliefs, his personality, and his activities, interests, and opinions. Thus, he may be attracted to a European ski trip because he wants a vacation that he thinks will be exciting and out of the ordinary. He also anticipates that this vacation will test his ability to manage on his own and give himself a sense of accomplishment.

Consumer Behavior Outcomes and Issues

As Exhibit 1.6 shows, the psychological core, decision-making processes, and the consumer's culture affect consumer behavior outcomes such as the symbolic use of products and the diffusion of ideas, products, or services through a market. They also influence and are influenced by issues of ethics and social responsibility.

© AP Images/PRNewsFoto/BodybyMilk.com

Exhibit 1.8

Influence of Reference Groups

Reference groups are people whose values we share and whose opinions we value, as evidenced in the Got Milk? campaigns.

Exhibit 1.9

Vacation Choices

The word "vacation" means different things to different people. Can you see how factors like social class, ethnic status, lifestyle, economic conditions, group affiliations, and gender affect the kinds of vacations that appeal to us? These examples show that some marketers are successful because they understand what their customers value.

On vacation, would you like to . . .

Learn how to walk on the moon?   Space Camp is the place for you! You'll experience the weightlessness of space flight, launch a rocket, and take a simulated trip to Mars or the Moon. The price for would-be astronauts (adults and children alike) is $699–$899 per week.

Volunteer to restore parklands?   Through the Sierra Club, you can travel to wildlife refuges and parks around the United States when you help preserve wilderness areas and keep up hiking trails. Along with a reasonable price tag—a six-day stay in the Grand Canyon to replant native vegetation costs $525, not including transportation—you'll get an insider's view of the local area plus the satisfaction of helping the planet.

See where penguins play?   On a National Geographic cruise, you'll start from the tip of South America and sail through Drake Passage. Then you'll travel by kayak along Antarctica's edge, home to penguins, whales, and other marine life. If your itinerary includes the Falkland Islands and South Georgia, you'll pay up to $38,000 (airfare is extra).

Sources: Based on information on www.spacecamp.com; www.sierraclub.org; and www.expeditions.com.

Symbols External signs that consumers use to express their identity.

Consumer Behaviors Can Symbolize Who We Are

The groups we belong to and our sense of self can affect the **symbols** or external signs we use, consciously or unconsciously, to express our actual or desired identity. For example, while skiing, Jason may wear a North Face parka and Bollé goggles to communicate his status as an experienced skier. He might also take home objects, such as postcards and T-shirts, that symbolize his vacation.

Consumer Behaviors Can Diffuse Through a Market

After Jason makes his vacation decision, he may tell others about his prospective trip, which, in turn, could influence their vacation decisions. In this way, the idea of going to Kitzbühel on vacation may diffuse, or spread, to others. Had Jason resisted going to Kitzbühel (perhaps because he thought it was too expensive or too far away), he might have communicated information that would make others less likely to vacation there. Thus, the diffusion of information can have both negative and positive effects for marketers.

Consumer Behavior, Ethics, and Social Responsibility

Sometimes consumers face potentially conflicting priorities: They try to balance an immediate outcome against a long-term outcome, or try to balance their own interests against the interests of others. For instance, a consumer who steals may acquire something right away, but the long-term outcome is personally risky and also problematic to society. Similarly, marketing decisions may involve conflicting priorities and sometimes lead to ethical questions, such as whether marketing efforts promote obesity, whether advertising affects self-image, and whether marketing invades consumers' privacy.

On the other hand, both consumers and marketers can and do use marketing for constructive purposes, balancing short- and long-term horizons plus the interests of themselves and others. These efforts by marketers and consumers may be relatively narrow—focusing on satisfying the needs of a particular consumer segment—or much broader, such as protecting the environment or improving the community. In the example of Jason choosing a ski vacation, he might decide to stay at an eco-friendly resort that conserves water and uses energy from clean sources. Or he may decide to buy his gear secondhand on eBay or from a retailer that is transparent about its environmental impact.[64]

WHO BENEFITS FROM THE STUDY OF CONSUMER BEHAVIOR?

Why do people study consumer behavior? The reasons are as varied as the four different groups who use consumer research: marketing managers, ethicists and advocates, public policy makers and regulators, and consumers.

Marketing Managers

Marketing The activity, set of institutions, and processes for creating, communicating, delivering, and exchanging offerings with value for individuals, groups, and society.

The study of consumer behavior provides critical information to marketing managers for developing marketing strategies and tactics. The American Marketing Association's definition of **marketing** shows why marketing managers need to learn about consumer behavior:

> *Marketing is the activity, set of institutions, and processes for creating, communicating, delivering, and exchanging offerings that have value for customers, clients, partners, and society at large.*

As this definition makes clear, marketers need consumer behavior insights to understand what consumers and clients value; only then can they develop, communicate, and deliver appropriate goods and services. See the Appendix for more about marketing research.

Ethicists and Advocacy Groups

Marketers' actions sometimes raise important ethical questions. Concerned consumers sometimes form advocacy groups to create public awareness of inappropriate practices. They also influence other consumers as well as the targeted companies through strategies such as media statements and boycotts. For example, U.S. advocacy groups such as the Consumer Federation of America and Consumer Watchdog worry about companies tracking what consumers do online. They and other groups support a "do not track" mechanism that would allow consumers to opt out of online tracking systems; the Federal Trade Commission wants more transparent disclosure of what is being collected and how it will be used.[65] We explore various ethical issues throughout this book and go into more detail in Chapter 17.

Public Policy Makers and Regulators

Understanding consumer behavior is crucial for legislators, regulators, and government agencies in developing policies and rules to protect consumers from unfair, unsafe, or inappropriate marketing practices. In turn, marketers' decisions are affected by these public policy actions. Consider the regulatory limits on tobacco marketing that are designed to discourage underage consumers from smoking and to inform consumers of smoking's health hazards. The United States, Canada, and many other nations already ban cigarette advertising on television and radio. Canada also requires large graphic warning labels on each pack.[66]

Understanding how consumers comprehend and categorize information is important for recognizing and guarding against misleading advertising. For instance, researchers want to know what impressions an ad creates and whether these impressions are true. They also want to know how marketing influences consumers' decisions to comply with product usage instructions, such as using medical treatments as prescribed.[67] And consumer behavior research helps government officials understand and try to improve consumer welfare.[68]

Academics

Understanding consumer behavior is important in the academic world for two reasons. First, academics disseminate knowledge about consumer behavior when they teach courses on the subject. Second, academics generate knowledge about consumer behavior when they conduct research focusing on how consumers act, think, and feel when acquiring, using, and disposing of offerings. In turn, such academic research is useful to marketing managers, advocacy groups, policy makers, regulators, and others who need to understand consumer behavior.

Consumers and Society

Understanding consumer behavior enables marketers and other organizations to provide tools for more informed decision-making. For example, research indicates that we better understand the differences among brands when we can view a chart, matrix, or grid comparing brands and their attributes.[69] Thus, matrices such as those presented in the *Consumer Reports* magazine or on its website are likely to help many consumers make better decisions.

Product, service, and communications developments to protect certain consumer segments have also grown out of understanding how consumers behave. Many people want to protect children against inappropriate advertising or guard themselves against invasion of privacy. Some companies have changed their marketing voluntarily, whereas others have waited until legislators, regulators, or advocacy groups forced them to make changes. Finally, a better understanding of consumer behavior can pave the way for programs that benefit society. As discussed in Chapter 17, research on disposition behavior has the potential to aid recycling programs and other environmental activities, just as research on charitable donations can help nonprofit groups design communications to attract contributors.

MARKETING IMPLICATIONS OF CONSUMER BEHAVIOR

As you learn about consumer behavior, you may wonder how marketers use different consumer behavior insights. Starting with Chapter 2, you will find numerous sections titled "Marketing Implications" that illustrate how marketers apply consumer behavior concepts in the real world. In general, consumer research helps marketers to develop product-specific plans, as well as broader strategies for market segmentation, targeting, and positioning, and to make decisions about the components of the marketing mix.

Developing and Implementing Customer-Oriented Strategy

Marketing is designed to *provide value to customers*. Thus, marketers must conduct research to understand the various groups of consumers within the marketplace so that they can develop a strategy and specific offerings that will provide such value. Once they develop and implement a suitable strategy, marketers need research to determine how well it is working and whether it is delivering the expected results (such as increasing market share or improving profits).

How Is the Market Segmented?

What one consumer values in a product may not be the same as what another consumer values. Consider the market for orange juice, which can be offered from concentrate, fresh squeezed, with other juices, and in other combinations. For example, Minute Maid, owned by Coca-Cola, stopped offering fresh-squeezed and switched to concentrate more than 25 years ago. Recently, however, it added three varieties of "Pure Squeezed" orange juice to its product line. A Minute Maid executive explains that although many consumers enjoy the current product line, "there's a segment of consumers who have an affinity for the not-from concentrate [juice]."[70] Clearly, research helps marketers understand the different groups that make up a market and whether they can make an offering to appeal to one or more of these groups.

How Profitable Is Each Segment?

Consumer research can help marketers identify consumers who have needs that are not being met and can reveal the size and profitability of each segment. For example, Daimler has identified a potentially profitable segment of affluent auto buyers interested in upscale compact cars. It is introducing a series of Mercedes-Benz compact cars specifically for this segment, fully equipped with accessories like USB ports for consumers' digital devices, all part of its effort to regain the lead in the premium auto market by 2020.[71]

What Are the Characteristics of Consumers in Each Segment?

After determining how the market is segmented and whether it is potentially profitable, marketers need to learn about the characteristics of consumers in each segment, such as their age, education, and lifestyle. This information helps marketers project whether the segment is likely to grow or to shrink over time, a factor that affects future marketing decisions. For example, sales of fitness goods and services are expected to rise as aging baby boomers strive to stay fit.

Are Customers Satisfied with Existing Offerings?

Marketers often do considerable research to learn whether consumers are currently satisfied with the company's offerings and marketing. For example, Harley-Davidson executives regularly ride with members of the Harley Owners Group to find out firsthand what satisfies motorcycle buyers and what else they are looking for. They also invite customers to submit their own videos online illustrating individual Harley-Davidson experiences, and ask social media users to comment on proposed ad campaigns. This research all helps the company come up with new product ideas and new ways to promote bikes to current and potential customers.[72]

Selecting the Target Market

Understanding consumer behavior helps marketers determine which consumer groups are appropriate targets for marketing tactics and how heavy users of a product differ from light users.[73] Marketers also need to identify who is likely to be involved in acquisition, usage, and disposition decisions. U.S. home builders like Toll Brothers, for example, are interested in the trend of multigenerational families living in one home. They know that some, if not all, of the family members will want some say in the home purchase, and therefore the homes must have features that will appeal to all the relatives involved in the decision.[74]

Developing Products

Developing goods and services that satisfy consumers' wants and needs is a critical marketing activity. Marketers apply consumer research when making a number of decisions about products and branding.

What Ideas Do Consumers Have for New Products?

First, marketers need to design an offering that matches what consumers in the target market want. As noted earlier, sometimes customers collaborate with marketers or with each other on the development of innovative new offerings. The jewelry firm Swarovski is one of many companies that have used online competitions to tap the creativity of their customers in designing new products.[75] The entire inventory of Chicago-based online T-shirt company Threadless comes from designs submitted by consumers. After a round of voting by consumers (online or via social media), Threadless puts the highest-scoring items into production—with a ready segment of buyers who have a taste for such individualistic designs.[76]

What Attributes Can Be Added to or Changed in an Existing Offering?

Marketers often use research to determine when and how to modify or tailor a product to meet the needs of new or existing groups of consumers. For example, the U.S. Postal Service (USPS) knows that many engaged couples still send printed wedding invitations through the mail instead of communicating with friends and relatives electronically. To supplement its regularly updated series of stamps, the USPS designed a stamp specifically for wedding invitations—which generated $375 million in sales within a few years. Now the USPS is adding new wedding-stamp designs and inviting consumers to personalize their own wedding stamps, an increasingly popular option.[77]

How Should the Offering Be Branded?

Consumer research plays a vital role in decisions about choosing a brand and differentiating it from competing brands and from other brands in the company's product portfolio.[78] For example, the Japanese automaker Nissan once marketed cars under the Datsun brand, but eliminated that brand in favor of its corporate name, Nissan, in 1981. Later, the company introduced Infiniti to brand its luxury autos and distinguish them from its other cars. Now, as Nissan eyes sales opportunities in emerging markets, it is bringing back the Datsun brand for small, low-priced cars to be sold in Russia, India, and Indonesia. This strategy allows Nissan to maintain a separate brand image and positioning for each of these product lines.[79]

What Should the Package and Logo Look Like?

Many marketers use consumer research to test alternative packaging and logos. Research shows, for instance, that consumers are likely to think that food (including cookies) is good for them if it comes in green packaging.[80] This information is valuable in the design of packages for products with a "healthy" positioning. Research is also vital in decisions about changing packaging and logos.

Positioning

Another strategic choice is deciding how an offering should be positioned in consumers' minds. The desired image should reflect what the product is and how it differs from the competition. For example, the Window of the World theme park in Shenzhen, China, is positioned as a fun place for Chinese consumers who want to see the world's most famous sights without leaving the country. The park features 130 replicas of well-known landmarks such as the pyramids, the White House, and the Eiffel Tower. This positioning is in contrast to another Chinese theme park Disneyland Hong Kong, which offers rides and other traditional amusement park attractions.[81]

How Are Competitive Offerings Positioned?

Marketers sometimes conduct research to see how consumers view other brands in comparison with their own and then plot the results on a graph called a *perceptual map*. Brands in the same quadrant of the map are perceived as offering similar benefits to consumers. The closer companies are to one another on the map, the more similar they are perceived to be, and hence, the more likely they are to be competitors. Marketers can use perceptual maps to determine how their offerings can be positioned as distinct and different from competing offerings, based on appeals that are sustainable over time.[82]

How Should Our Offerings Be Positioned?

Companies use consumer research to understand what image a new offering should have in the eyes of consumers and what messages will effectively support this image.[83] The positioning should suggest that the product is superior in one or more attributes valued by the target market.[84] For example, Procter & Gamble's research found that many consumers weren't satisfied with traditional dry-cleaning establishments, in part because of inconsistent quality and also due to environmental concerns about cleaning chemicals. Seeing this as an opportunity, P&G positioned its Tide Dry Cleaners chain as clean, green, and friendly—using earth-friendly cleaning products, the power of the Tide brand, and attentive customer service.[85]

Should Our Offerings Be Repositioned?

Consumer research can help marketers reposition existing products (i.e., change their image). Consider how the Versus sports cable channel was repositioned. Originally introduced as Outdoor Life Network in 1995, the U.S. cable channel was repositioned as Versus in 2006 to reflect its broader sports coverage. Even with an audience of 70 million households, Versus fell short of rival ESPN's audience of 100 million households. Knowing that consumers are far more familiar with the NBC brand and coverage, thanks to the network's broadcasting of the Olympics and other high-profile events, Comcast repositioned Versus as NBC Sports Network, broadcasting round-the-clock sporting events and related content.[86]

Making Promotion and Marketing Communications Decisions

Research can help companies make decisions about promotional/marketing communications tools, including advertising, sales promotions (premiums, contests, sweepstakes, free samples, coupons, and rebates), personal selling, and public relations. One area receiving attention is the use of techniques to measure consumers' physiological and neurological responses to marketing communications.[87] The rise of social media adds another twist to promotion and communications decisions.[88] Word of mouth—which spreads quickly through social media—that is not marketer-controlled, although it may be marketer-initiated, seems more credible to consumers than messages directly controlled by marketers.[89]

What Are Our Advertising Objectives?

Consumer research can be very useful in determining advertising objectives. It may reveal, for example, that few people have heard of a new brand, suggesting that the advertising objective should be to enhance brand-name awareness. If research indicates that consumers have heard of the brand but don't know anything about it, the advertising objective should be to enhance brand knowledge. If consumers know the brand name but don't know the characteristics of the brand that make it desirable, the advertising should aim to enhance brand knowledge and encourage positive attitudes about it. And if consumers know neither the brand name nor the product's benefits, the advertising should educate the target market about both.

What Should Our Advertising Look Like?

Research can help marketers determine what words and visuals—and what balance of text and images—would be most effective for ad and brand recognition and recall.[90] A brand name is better remembered when placed in an ad that has interesting, unusual, and relevant visuals. If the visuals are interesting but unrelated to the product, consumers may remember the visuals but forget the product's name. Moreover, marketers can research how different groups respond to different wording. For example, saying a product is a good "value for the money" does not work in Spain. Instead, marketers use the phrase "price for product."[91]

Online advertising is also being researched. One finding, for instance, is that customizing e-mail messages for targeted customers is an effective way to boost visits to the brand's website.[92] Another study showed that both emotion and physiological arousal are factors in whether an online ad goes viral. Specifically, an ad is more likely to be spread virally when the content evokes a positive emotional response (such as awe) or a negative emotional response (such as anger).[93]

Where Should Advertising Be Placed?

When marketers select specific media vehicles in which to advertise, they find demographic, lifestyle, and media usage data very useful. As noted earlier, research shows that more people split their time among many different media and that many people use recording technology to avoid commercials. Knowing this, marketers are choosing media with better targeting or more consumer exposure in mind. For example, Ford has used video ads on Facebook's log-out page to promote its sporty Mustang car, taking advantage of the ability to target by location, gender, and age.[94] A growing number of firms are using sponsorship of cause-related events (such as the Avon Walk for Breast Cancer) that attract the interest of consumers in the targeted segments.[95]

When Should We Advertise?

Research may reveal seasonal variations in purchases due to weather-related needs, variations in the amount of discretionary money consumers have (which changes, for instance, before and after Christmas), holiday buying patterns, and the like. In the weeks leading up to Easter, for instance, the chocolate company Cadbury airs TV commercials, places print ads, sponsors special events, and posts Facebook promotions for its chocolate eggs. In Australia, it recently targeted 18- to 30-year-old chocolate lovers with extensive Facebook advertising for new chocolate egg products just before Easter, when this segment is most likely to buy.[96]

Has Our Advertising Been Effective?

Finally, advertisers can research an ad's effectiveness at various points in the advertising development process. Sometimes marketers or ad agencies conduct advertising *copy testing* or *pretesting*, testing an ad's effectiveness before it appears in public. If the objective is creating brand awareness and the tested ad does not enhance awareness, the company may replace it with a new ad. Effectiveness research can also take place after the ads have been placed in the media, such as conducting tracking studies to see whether ads have achieved particular objectives over time.

What About Sales Promotion Objectives and Tactics?

When developing sales promotions, marketers can use research to identify sales promotion objectives and tactics. For example, when Snack Factory wanted to attract new customers to its Pretzel Crisps snacks and increase sales, the firm posted a $1 coupon on Facebook for two weeks. This promotion added 7,000 new Facebook fans and, more importantly, the rate of redemption of the coupons was 87 percent. Without fanfare, Snack Factory switched to a buy one, get one free coupon on Facebook. The new offer went viral, gaining Pretzel Crisps 15,000 new fans in two weeks—plus an impressive 95 percent coupon redemption rate. Now the brand has more than 200,000 "likes" and regularly conducts contests, coupons, and other sales promotions on the social media site.[97] Research can also prevent such pitfalls as offering coupons to certain consumers who won't redeem them for fear of looking stingy.[98]

Have Our Sales Promotions Been Effective?

Consumer research can answer this question. Marketers might compare sales before, during, and after a promotion to determine changes in sales. Research can also indicate whether a free sample has been more effective than a price promotion, whether a free gift enhances value perceptions and purchase intentions, and how consumers react after a sales promotion has been discontinued.[99]

How Can Salespeople Best Serve Customers?

Finally, research can help managers make decisions about salespeople. By tracking store patronage at different times of the day or on different days of the week, retailers can determine the appropriate number of store personnel needed to best serve customers at those times. Research also offers insights into and selecting salespeople and evaluating how well they serve customers. For example, similarity between the consumer and a salesperson or service provider can influence whether customers comply with these marketing representatives.[100] Other studies indicate that how a salesperson presents a product will affect consumers' attitudes toward the salesperson and what consumers learn about the product.[101]

Making Pricing Decisions

The price of a product or service can have a critical influence on consumers' acquisition, usage, and disposition decisions. It is therefore very important for marketers to understand how consumers react to price and to use this information in pricing decisions.

What Price Should Be Charged?

Why do prices often end in 99? Consumer research has shown that people perceive $9.99 or $99.99 to be cheaper than $10.00 or $100.00. Perhaps this is one reason why so many prices end in the number 9.[102] Although economic theory suggests that a decrease in price will increase the likelihood of purchase, too low a price can make consumers suspect the product's quality.[103] In general, consumers respond better to a discount presented as a percentage off the regular price (e.g., 25 percent subtracted from the price) than to a discount presented as a specific amount of money subtracted from the regular price (originally $25, now only $15).[104]

Also, when making a purchase, consumers consider how much they must pay in relation to the price of other relevant brands or to the price they previously paid for that product, so marketers must be aware of these reference prices.[105] When buying multiple units of a service for one bundled price (such as a multiday ski pass), consumers may not feel a great loss if they use only some of the units because they have difficulty assigning value to each unit. In addition, when consumers buy multiple products for one bundled price (such as a case of wine), they are likely to increase their consumption because unit costs seem low.[106]

According to research, how much consumers will pay can even be affected by the price of unrelated products they happen to see first. Thus, the price you would be willing to pay for a T-shirt may vary, depending on whether the prices you noticed for shoes in the store next door were high or low.[107]

Finally, studies indicate that consumers have differing perceptions of what a product is worth, depending on whether they are buying or selling it. Sellers should therefore avoid this *endowment effect*; that is, they should not set a higher price than buyers are willing to pay.[108]

How Sensitive Are Consumers to Price and Price Changes?

Research also suggests that consumers have different views of the importance of price. Some consumers are very price sensitive, meaning that a small change in price will have a large effect on consumers' willingness to purchase the product. Other consumers are price insensitive and thus likely to buy an offering regardless of its price. Marketers can use research to determine which consumers are likely to be price sensitive and when. For fashion or prestige goods, a high price symbolizes status. Thus, status-seeking consumers may be less sensitive to a product's price and pay more than $50 for a T-shirt with a prestigious label.

When Should Certain Price Tactics Be Used?

Research also reveals when consumers are likely to be most responsive to various pricing tactics. For example, consumers have traditionally been very responsive to price cuts on bed linens during January. These "white sales" are effective because consumers have come to anticipate them at that time of the year. Similarly, approximately five million U.S. consumers buy new TVs specifically to watch the Super Bowl every year. Knowing this trend, online and store retailers mount price promotions in the weeks leading up to the Super Bowl, aiming to get their share of these TV purchases.[109]

Making Distribution Decisions

Another important marketing decision involves how products are distributed and sold to consumers in retail stores. Here, too, marketers can use consumer research.

Where and When Are Target Consumers Likely to Shop?

Marketers who understand the value consumers place on time and convenience have developed distribution channels that allow consumers to acquire or use offerings whenever and wherever it is most convenient for them. For example, 24-hour grocery stores, health clubs, catalog ordering, and online ordering systems give consumers flexibility in the timing of their acquisition, usage, and disposition decisions. The U.K. supermarket chain Tesco operates a grocery chain called Home Plus in South Korea. Knowing that many commuters have little time to shop, it set up virtual stores inside busy train stations (see Exhibit 1.10). These "stores" are actually large posters showing grocery shelves stocked with frequently purchased items, each featuring a QR (quick

Targeting Where Consumers Shop
Marketers need to understand how and when consumers best shop. For instance, busy consumers can grocery shop using their smartphones on these boards in subway stations, which is very convenient for them.

© Imaginechina via AP Images

response) code. While they wait for the next train, commuters use their smartphones to scan the QR code of items they want to buy, complete the transaction, and schedule delivery for when they know they will be home.[110]

What Do Customers Want to See in Stores?

Retailers want to carry the assortment of merchandise best suited to consumers who shop in their stores. Walmart now invites consumers to watch videos submitted by companies that have developed new products. Because consumers vote for the items they would like to see in their local Walmart store, the retailer gains insight into its customers' preferences and can expand its merchandise assortment accordingly.[111]

How Should Stores Be Designed?

Supermarkets are generally designed with similar or complementary items stocked near one another because research shows that consumers think about items in terms of categories based on products' similar characteristics or use. Thus, stores stock peanut butter near jelly because the products are often used together. Consumer research can also help marketers develop other aspects of their retail environments. Studies show that bright colors and up-tempo music make consumers move quickly through a store; subdued colors and quiet music have the opposite effect.[112]

Store design also depends on whether consumers are shopping for fun or seeking to quickly accomplish a particular task like buying a certain item.[113] During the back-to-school shopping season, for instance, Target stores display dorm-room products together for consumer convenience.[114] Knowing that some consumers simply like to shop, retailers are increasingly creating more exciting and aesthetically pleasing store environments.[115] For example, in Shanghai, the distinctive glass exterior, spiral staircase, and gleaming white logo of the Apple store has made such an impression on shoppers that some competitors have opened look-alike stores elsewhere in China.[116]

Stores and retail websites can be designed to convey a very specific image and for friendly functionality on devices used by targeted consumer groups. After the Apple iPad became popular, many retail sites redesigned their Web pages to look better on a tablet computer screen and to be sure features worked properly on all touch-screen devices, including mobile phones. The apparel retailer Abercrombie & Fitch even added an online playlist so customers who shop via the Internet can click to hear the same songs that play in its stores.[117]

SUMMARY

Consumer behavior involves understanding the set of decisions (what, whether, why, when, how, where, how much, and how often) that an individual or group of consumers makes over time about the acquisition, use, or disposition of goods, services, ideas, or other offerings. The psychological core exerts considerable influence on consumer behavior. A consumer's motivation, ability, and opportunity affect his or her decisions and influence what a person is exposed to, what he or she pays attention to, and what he or she perceives and comprehends. These factors also affect how consumers categorize and interpret information, how they form and retrieve memories, and how they form and change attitudes. Each aspect of the psychological core has a bearing on the consumer decision-making process, which involves (1) problem recognition, (2) information search, (3) judgments and decision making, and (4) evaluating satisfaction with the decision.

Consumer behavior is affected by the consumer's culture and by the typical or expected behaviors, norms, and ideas of a particular group. Consumers belong to a number of groups, share their cultural values and beliefs, and use their symbols to communicate group membership. Household and social class influences are involved in consumer behavior, as are each individual's values, personality, and lifestyles. Consumer behavior can be symbolic and express an individual's identity. It is also indicative of how quickly an offering spreads throughout a market. Further, ethics and social responsibility play a role in consumer behavior.

Marketers study consumer behavior to gain insights that will lead to more effective marketing strategies and tactics. Ethicists and advocacy groups are keenly interested in consumer behavior, as are public policy makers and regulators who want to protect consumers from unsafe or inappropriate offerings. Consumers and society can both benefit as marketers learn to make products more user-friendly and to show concern for the environment. Finally, studying consumer behavior helps marketers understand how to segment markets and how to decide which to target, how to position an offering, and which marketing-mix tactics will be most effective.

Questions for Review and Discussion

1. How is consumer behavior defined?
2. What is an offering?
3. What are some of the factors in the psychological core that affect consumer decisions and behavior?
4. What are aspects of the consumer's culture influence decisions and behavior?
5. How is *marketing* defined?
6. How can public policy decision makers, advocacy groups, and marketing managers use consumer research?
7. What kinds of marketing questions can companies use consumer behavior research to answer?
8. How can you benefit from studying consumer behavior?

CONSUMER BEHAVIOR CASE

How Unilever's Brands Connect with Consumers

From soap to soup, Unilever markets a wide range of personal care products, foods, and household cleaners under popular brands like Dove, Bertolli, Lipton, Lux, Axe, Sunsilk, Surf, and Omo. Two billion consumers buy its products every day, adding up to annual revenue of $62 billion. The Anglo-Dutch company constantly conducts research to learn more about what consumers want and need, identifying even seemingly small changes that can make a big difference in the daily lives of people worldwide.

One of the company's most memorable marketing initiatives has been Dove's "Campaign for Real Beauty." Based on extensive consumer research into women's attitudes and emotions, the campaign uses ads, YouTube videos, special events, and other communications to counter beauty stereotypes and make the point that real beauty is more than skin deep. By linking its soap brand to messages reinforcing positive self-esteem for women of all ages, races, sizes, and shapes, Dove has won the admiration and loyalty of consumers in many countries.

Unilever's Ragú food brand has been courting parents with Facebook and YouTube communications that encourage ongoing conversations with marketers and

Investigation," *Journal of Consumer Psychology* 13, no. 1, 2003, pp. 177–183.

39. Emily Glazer, "Donate Safely Through Text," *Wall Street Journal*, March 3, 2012, www.wsj.com.

40. Linda L. Price, Eric J. Arnould, and Carolyn Folkman Curasi, "Older Consumers' Disposition of Special Possessions," *Journal of Consumer Research*, September 2000, pp. 179–201.

41. Morris B. Holbrook and Meryl P. Gardner, "How Motivation Moderates the Effects of Emotion on the Duration of Consumption," *Journal of Business Research*, July 1998, pp. 241–252.

42. "Nestle: Recession Stunts Russian Confectionery Market Growth," *Confectionery News*, August 16, 2011, www.confectionerynews.com.

43. Pierre Chandon and Brian Wansink, "When Are Stockpiled Products Consumed Faster?" *Journal of Marketing Research*, August 2002, pp. 321–335.

44. Joseph C. Nunes, "A Cognitive Model of People's Usage Estimations," *Journal of Marketing Research* 38, November 2000, pp. 397–409.

45. Kathleen D. Vohs and Ronald J. Faber, "Spent Resources: Self-Regulatory Resource Availability Affects Impulse Buying," *Journal of Consumer Research* 33, no. 4, 2007, pp. 537–548; Suresh Ramanathan and Geeta Menon, "Time-Varying Effects of Chronic Hedonic Goals on Impulsive Behavior," *Journal of Marketing Research*, November 2006, pp. 628–641; Fritz Strack, Lioba Werth, and Roland Deutsch, "Reflective and Impulsive Determinants of Consumer Behavior," *Journal of Consumer Psychology* 16, no. 3, 2006, pp. 205–216; Xueming Luo, "How Does Shopping with Others Influence Impulsive Purchasing?" *Journal of Consumer Psychology* 15, no. 4, 2005, pp. 288–294; Rosellina Ferraro, Baba Shiv, and James R. Bettman, "Let Us Eat and Drink, for Tomorrow We Shall Die: Effects of Mortality Salience and Self-Esteem on Self-Regulation in Consumer Choice," *Journal of Consumer Research* 32, no. 1, 2005, pp. 65–75; and Anirban Mukhopadhyay and Gita Venkataramani Johar, "Where There Is a Will, Is There a Way? Effects of Lay Theories of Self-Control on Setting and Keeping Resolutions," *Journal of Consumer Research* 31, no. 4, 2005, pp. 779–786.

46. Allison R. Johnson and David W. Stewart, "A Re-Appraisal of the Role of Emotion in Consumer Behavior: Traditional and Contemporary Approaches," in ed. Naresh Malhotra, *Review of Marketing Research*, vol. 1, 2004, pp. 1–33; and R. P. Bagozzi, M. Gopinath, and P. U. Nyer, "The Role of Emotions in Marketing," *Journal of the Academy of Marketing Science* 27, no. 2, 1999, pp. 184–206.

47. Deborah J. MacInnis and Gustavo deMello, "The Concept of Hope and its Relevance to Product Evaluation and Choice," *Journal of Marketing*, January 2005, pp. 1–14; and Gustavo DeMello, Deborah J. MacInnis, and David W. Stewart, "Threats to Hope: Effects on Reasoning About Product Information," *Journal of Consumer Research* 34, no. 2, 2007, pp. 153–161.

48. Kirsten Passyn and Mita Sujan, "Self-Accountability Emotions and Fear Appeals: Motivating Behavior," *Journal of Consumer Research* 32, March 2006, pp. 583–589; and O. Shehryar and D. Hunt, "A Terror Management Perspective on the Persuasiveness of Fear Appeals," *Journal of Consumer Psychology* 15, no. 4, 2005, pp. 275–287.

49. Eric A. Greenleaf, "Reserves, Regret, and Rejoicing in Open English Auctions," *Journal of Consumer Research* 31, no. 2, 2004, pp. 264–273; Marcel Zeelenberg and Rik Pieters, "A Theory of Regret Regulation 1.0," *Journal of Consumer Psychology* 17, no. 1,

2007, pp. 3–18; Ran Kivetz and Anat Keinan, "Repenting Hyperopia: An Analysis of Self-Control Regrets," *Journal of Consumer Research* 33, no. 2, 2006, pp. 273–282; and Lisa J. Abendroth and Kristin Diehl, "Now or Never: Effects of Limited Purchase Opportunities on Patterns of Regret over Time," *Journal of Consumer Research* 33, no. 3, 2006, pp. 342–351.

50. Darren W. Dahl, Heather Honea, and Rajesh V. Manchanda, "The Three Rs of Interpersonal Consumer Guilt: Relationship, Reciprocity, Reparation," *Journal of Consumer Psychology* 15, no. 4, 2005, pp. 307–315; and Brian Wansink and Pierre Chandon, "Can 'Low-Fat' Nutrition Labels Lead to Obesity?" *Journal of Marketing Research*, November 2006, pp. 605–617.

51. Darren Dahl, Rajesh V. Manchanda, and Jennifer J. Argo, "Embarrassment in Consumer Purchase: The Roles of Social Presence and Purchase Familiarity," *Journal of Consumer Research*, December 2001, pp. 473–483.

52. Georgios A. Bakamitsos, "A Cue Alone or a Probe to Think: The Dual Role of Affect in Product Evaluations," *Journal of Consumer Research*, December 2006, pp. 403–412; Eduardo Andrade, "Behavioral Consequences of Affect: Combining Evaluative and Regulatory Mechanisms," *Journal of Consumer Research*, December 2005, pp. 355–362; and Harper A. Roehm and Michelle L. Roehm, "Revisiting the Effect of Positive Mood on Variety Seeking," *Journal of Consumer Research*, September 2005, pp. 330–336.

53. Aaron C. Ahuvia, "Beyond the Extended Self: Loved Objects and Consumers' Identity Narratives," *Journal of Consumer Research* 32, June 2005, pp. 171–184.

54. Joel B. Cohen and Eduardo B. Andrade, "Affective Intuition and Task-Contingent Affect Regulation," *Journal of Consumer Research* 31, no. 2, 2004, pp. 358–367; and Nitika G. Barg, Brian Wansink, and J. Jeffrey Inman, "The Influence of Incidental Affect on Consumers' Food Intake," *Journal of Marketing*, January 2007, pp. 194–206.

55. Thorsten Hennig-Thurau, Markus Groth, and Michael Paul, "Are All Smiles Created Equal? How Emotional Contagion and Emotional Labor Affect Service Relationships," *Journal of Marketing*, July 2006, pp. 58–73.

56. Adam Duhachek and Dawn Iacobucci, "Consumer Personality and Coping: Testing Rival Theories of Process," *Journal of Consumer Psychology* 15, no. 1, 2005, pp. 52–63; and Adam Duhachek, "Coping: A Multidimensional, Hierarchical Framework of Responses to Stressful Consumption Episodes," *Journal of Consumer Research* 32, no. 1, 2005, pp. 41–53.

57. Sheena Leek and Suchart Chanasawatkit, "Consumer Confusion in the Thai Mobile Phone Market," *Journal of Consumer Behavior* 5, no. 6, 2006, pp. 518–532.

58. Teresa M. Pavia and Marlys J. Mason, "The Reflexive Relationship Between Consumer Behavior and Adaptive Coping," *Journal of Consumer Research* 31, no. 2, 2004, pp. 441–454.

59. Linda L. Price, Eric Arnould, and Carolyn Folkman Curasi, "Older Consumers' Dispositions of Special Possessions," *Journal of Consumer Research*, September 2000, pp. 179–201.

60. Natalie Ross Adkins and Julie L. Ozanne, "The Low Literate Consumer," *Journal of Consumer Research* 32, no. 1, 2005, pp. 93–105.

61. John G. Lynch and G. Zauberman, "Construing Consumer Decision Making," *Journal of Consumer Psychology* 17, no. 2, 2007, pp. 107–112.

62. John A. Bargh, "Losing Consciousness: Automatic Influences on Consumer Judgment, Behavior, and Motivation," *Journal of Consumer Research*, September 2002, pp. 280–285; Stewart Shapiro, "When an Ad's Influence Is Beyond Our Conscious Con-

trol," *Journal of Consumer Research*, June 1999, pp. 16–36; and Ap Dijksterhuis, Pamela K. Smith, Rick B. Van Baaren, and Daniel H. J. Wigboldus, "The Unconscious Consumer: Effects of Environment on Consumer Behavior," *Journal of Consumer Psychology* 15, no. 3, 2005, pp. 193–202.

63. Deborah J. MacInnis, Vanessa M. Patrick, and C. Whan Park, "Not as Happy as I Thought I'd Be? Affective Misforecasting and Product Evaluations," *Journal of Consumer Research*, March 2007, pp. 479–490; and Deborah J. MacInnis, Vanessa M. Patrick, and C. Whan Park, "Looking Through the Crystal Ball: Affective Forecasting and Misforecasting in Consumer Behavior," *Review of Marketing Research* 2, 2006, pp. 43–80.

64. See, for example, Linn Viktoria Rampl, Tim Eberhardt, Reinhard Schutte, and Peter Kenning, "Consumer Trust in Food Retailers: Conceptual Framework and Empirical Evidence," *International Journal of Retail & Distribution Management* 40, no. 4, 2012, pp. 254–272.

65. Morgan Little, "FTC Pushes for 'Do Not Track,' Draws Comparison to 'Big Brother,'" *Los Angeles Times*, March 27, 2012, www .latimes.com; Grant Gross, "Privacy Groups Support New Do-not-track Bill," *PC Magazine*, May 9, 2011, www.pcmag.com; and Byron Acohido, "Web Tracking Has Become a Privacy Time Bomb," *USA Today*, August 4, 2011, www.usatoday.com.

66. Chantal Mack, "New Tobacco Warnings Become Mandatory," *Post Media News*, March 21, 2012, www.canada.com; and Melissa Healy, "Cigarette Packages in Medical Journals: New Look for a New Age," *Los Angeles Times*, August 4, 2011, www.latimes.com.

67. Douglas Bowman, Carrie M. Heilman, and P. B. Seetharaman, "Determinants of Product-Use Compliance Behavior," *Journal of Marketing Research*, August 2004, pp. 324–338.

68. Dipankar Chakravarti, "Voices Unheard: The Psychology of Consumption in Poverty and Development," *Journal of Consumer Psychology* 16, no. 4, 2006, pp. 363–376.

69. James R. Bettman, *An Information Processing Theory of Consumer Choice* (Reading, Mass.: Addison-Wesley, 1979).

70. Jeremiah McWilliams, "Coca-Cola to Sell Not-from-concentrate Minute Maid Orange Juice," *Atlanta Journal-Constitution*, August 19, 2011, www.ajc.com/business.

71. Christiaan Hetzner and Marton Dunai, "Daimler to Launch 4-Door Compact Coupe in 2013," *Reuters*, March 29, 2012, www .reuters.com; and Marty Padgett, "Mercedes-Benz 'CLC' Coming to New York Auto Show," *Washington Post*, March 6, 2012, www .washingtonpost.com.

72. David Booth, "The New Harley-Davidson Wants You," *Edmonton Journal (Canada)*, March 20, 2012, www.edmontonjournal.com; and Dale Buss, "Can Harley Ride the New Wave?" *Brandweek*, October 25, 2004, p. 203.

73. Robert D. Jewell and H. Rao Unnava, "Exploring Differences in Attitudes Between Light and Heavy Brand Users," *Journal of Consumer Psychology* 14, no. 1–2, 2004, pp. 75–80.

74. John Gittelsohn, "Homebuilders Target In-Laws, Dogs as Extended Families Grow," *Businessweek*, November 17, 2011, www .businessweek.com.

75. Johann Füller, Katja Hutter, and Rita Faullant, "Why Co-Creation Experience Matters? Creative Experience and Its Impact on the Quantity and Quality of Creative Contributions," *R&D Management*, June 2011, pp. 259–273.

76. John Jantsch, "How Threadless Nailed the Crowdsource Model," *Social Media Today*, April 7, 2011, www.socialmediatoday.com.

77. Vincent M. Mallozzi, "The Honor of Your Postage Is Requested," *New York Times*, February 19, 2012, p. ST-17.

78. Judith Lynne Zaichkowsky, "Strategies for Distinctive Brands," *Brand Management* 17, no. 8, 2010, pp. 548–560.

79. Jerry Hirsch, "Nissan to Bring Back Datsun Car Brand in Selected Markets," *Los Angeles Times*, March 20, 2012, www.latimes.com.

80. Robert McNatt, "Hey, It's Green—It Must Be Healthy," *Business-Week*, July 13, 1998, p. 6.

81. Daniel Roberts, "By the Numbers: Tourism, Wow!" *Fortune*, July 4, 2011, pp. 10–11; and Huang Lan and Huan Cao, "Around the World in a Day," *China Daily*, August 3, 2011, www.chinadaily .com.cn.

82. Cheng-Wen Lee and Chi-Shun Liao, "The Effects of Consumer Preferences and Perceptions of Chinese Tea Beverages on Brand Positioning Strategies," *British Food Journal* 111, no. 1, 2009, pp. 80–96.

83. See Claudiu V. Dimofte and Richard F. Yalch, "Consumer Response to Polysemous Brand Slogans," *Journal of Consumer Research* 33, no. 4, 2007, pp. 515–522.

84. See Alexander Chernev, "Jack of All Trades or Master of One? Product Differentiation and Compensatory Reasoning in Consumer Choice," *Journal of Consumer Research* 33, no. 4, 2007, pp. 430–444.

85. Rich Laden, "Local Businessman Joins P&G, Panda Express in Dry Cleaning Venture," *Gazette (Colorado Springs, CO)*, March 5, 2012, www.gazette.com; Ray A. Smith, "The New Dirt on Dry Cleaners," *Wall Street Journal*, July 28, 2011, www.wsj.com; and Andrew Martin, "Smelling an Opportunity," *New York Times*, December 8, 2010, www.nytimes.com.

86. Sofia M. Fernandez, "NBC Sports Network Official Launch Replaces Versus on Monday," *Hollywood Reporter*, January 2, 2012, www.hollywoodreporter.com; and Michael McCarthy, "Versus Set to Become the NBC Sports Network," *USA Today*, August 1, 2011, www.usatoday.com.

87. See, for instance, Thales Teixeira, Michel Wedel, and Rik Pieters, "Emotion-Induced Engagement in Internet Video Ads," *Journal of Marketing Research*, forthcoming; and Adam W. Craig, Yuliya Komarova Loureiro, Stacy Wood, and Jennifer M.C. Vendemia, "Suspicious Minds: Exploring Neural Processes During Exposure to Deceptive Advertising," *Journal of Marketing Research*, forthcoming (posted online December 22, 2011).

88. Hyoungkoo Khang, Eyun-Jung Ki, and Lan Ye, "Social Media Research in Advertising, Communication, Marketing, and Public Relations, 1997–2010," *Journalism & Mass Communication Quarterly*, published online March 14, 2012, http://jmq.sagepub .com.

89. W. Glynn Mangold and David J. Faulds, "Social Media: The New Hybrid Element of the Promotion Mix," *Business Horizons* 52, 2009, pp. 357–365.

90. Anocha Aribarg, Rik Pieters, and Michel Wedel, "Raising the Bar: Bias-Adjustment of Advertising Recognition Tests," *Journal of Marketing Research*, June 2010, pp. 387–400.

91. Charlotte Clarke, "Language Classes," *Marketing Week*, July 24, 1997, pp. 35–39.

92. Asim Ansari and Carl Mela, "E-Customization," *Journal of Marketing Research*, May 2003, pp. 131–145.

93. Jonah Berger and Katherine L. Milkman, "What Makes Online Content Viral?" *Journal of Marketing Research*, forthcoming, posted online November 22, 2011.

94. Cotton Delo, "Facebook Sets High Asking Price for Log-Out Ads," *Advertising Age*, March 23, 2012, www.adage.com; and "Facebook Eyes Big Ad Opportunity from Log-Out Ads," *Forbes*, March 28, 2012, www.forbes.com.

95. Carolyn J. Simmons and Karen L. Becker-Olsen, "Achieving Marketing Objectives Through Social Sponsorships," *Journal of Marketing*, October 2006, pp. 154–169.

96. Clare Kermond, "Cadbury Hatches Plan for Three Easter Products," *Canberra Times (Australia)*, March 30, 2012, www.canberratimes.com.au.

97. "Case Study: Snack Brand Doubles Facebook 'Likes' Through Social Coupon," *emarketer.com*, August 16, 2011, www.emarketer.com.

98. Laurence Ashworth, Peter R. Darke, and Mark Schaller, "No One Wants to Look Cheap: Trade-offs Between Social Disincentives and the Economic and Psychological Incentives to Redeem Coupons," *Journal of Consumer Psychology* 15, no. 4, 2005, pp. 295–306.

99. Sucharita Chandran and Vicki G. Morwitz, "The Price of 'Free'-dom: Consumer Sensitivity to Promotions with Negative Contextual Influences," *Journal of Consumer Research* 33, no. 3, 2006, pp. 384–392; Priya Raghubir, "Free Gift with Purchase: Promoting or Discounting the Brand?" *Journal of Consumer Psychology* 14, no. 1–2, 2004, pp. 181–186; and Luc Wathieu, A. V. Muthukrishnan, and Bart J. Bronnenberg, "The Asymmetric Effect of Discount Retraction on Subsequent Choice," *Journal of Consumer Research* 31, no. 3, 2004, pp. 652–657.

100. Stephanie Dellande, Mary C. Gilly, and John L. Graham, "Gaining Compliance and Losing Weight: The Role of the Service Provider in Health Care Services," *Journal of Marketing* 68, July 2004, pp. 78–91; and Sean Dwyer, Orlando Richard, and C. David Shepherd, "An Exploratory Study of Gender and Age Matching in the Salesperson–Prospective Customer Dyad," *Journal of Personal Selling and Sales Management*, Fall 1998, pp. 55–69.

101. Thomas E. DeCarlo, "The Effects of Sales Message and Suspicion of Ulterior Motives on Salesperson Evaluation," *Journal of Consumer Psychology* 15, no. 3, 2005, pp. 238–249.

102. Thomas Manoj and Vicki Morwitz, "Penny Wise and Pound Foolish: The Left-Digit Effect in Price Cognition," *Journal of Consumer Research* 32, no. 1, 2005, pp. 54–64; and Robert M. Schindler and Patrick N. Kirby, "Patterns of Rightmost Digits Used in Advertising Prices: Implications for Nine-Ending Effects," *Journal of Consumer Research*, September 1997, pp. 192–201.

103. Jacob Jacoby, Jerry Olson, and Rafael Haddock, "Price, Brand Name, and Product Composition Characteristics as Determinants of Perceived Quality," *Journal of Applied Psychology*, December 1971, pp. 470–479; and Kent B. Monroe, "The Influence of Price Differences and Brand Familiarity on Brand Preferences," *Journal of Consumer Research*, June 1976, pp. 42–49.

104. Devon DelVecchio, H. Shanker Krishnan, and Daniel C. Smith, "Cents or Percent? The Effects of Promotion Framing on Price Expectations and Choice," *Journal of Marketing*, July 2007, pp. 158–170. For more on pricing effects associated with regular and discount prices, see Keith S. Coulter and Robin A. Coulter, "Distortion of Price Discount Perceptions: The Right Digit Effect," *Journal of Consumer Research*, August 2007, pp. 162–173.

105. Daniel J. Howard and Roger A. Kerin, "Broadening the Scope of Reference Price Advertising Research: A Field Study of Consumer Shopping Involvement," *Journal of Marketing*, October 2006, pp. 185–204; Tridib Mazumdar, S. P. Raj, and Indrajit Sinha, "Reference Price Research: Review and Propositions," *Journal of Marketing*, October 2005, pp. 84–102; Ziv Carmon and Dan Ariely, "Focusing on the Forgone: How Value Can Appear So Different to Buyers and Sellers," *Journal of Consumer Research* 27, December 2000, pp. 360–370; and Tridib Mazumdar and Purushottam Papatla, "An Investigation of Reference Price Segments," *Journal of Marketing Research* 37, May 2000, pp. 246–258.

106. Dilip Soman and John T. Gourville, "Transaction Decoupling: How Price Bundling Affects the Decision to Consume," *Journal of Marketing Research* 38, February 2001, pp. 30–44.

107. Joseph C. Nunes and Peter Boatwright, "Incidental Prices and Their Effect on Willingness to Pay," *Journal of Consumer Research*, November 2004, pp. 457–466.

108. Dhananjay Nayakankuppam and Himanshu Mishra, "The Endowment Effect: Rose-Tinted and Dark-Tinted Glasses," *Journal of Consumer Research* 32, no. 3, 2005, pp. 390–395.

109. Andrea Chang, "TV Prices Plunge Ahead of Super Bowl," *Los Angeles Times*, February 3, 2012, www.latimes.com.

110. Olivia Solon, "Tesco Brings the Supermarket to Time-poor Commuters in South Korea," *Wired*, June 30, 2011, www.wired.co.uk.

111. Dale Buss, "Walmart Crowdsources New Product Ideas," *BrandChannel*, January 23, 2012, www.brandchannel.com.

112. Ronald E. Milliman, "The Influence of Background Music on the Behavior of Restaurant Patrons," *Journal of Consumer Research*, September 1986, pp. 286–289; Richard Yalch and Eric Spannenberg, "Effects of Store Music on Shopping Behavior," *Journal of Services Marketing*, Winter 1990, pp. 31–39; and Joseph A. Bellizi, Ayn E. Crowley, and Ronald W. Hasty, "The Effects of Color in Store Design," *Journal of Retailing*, Spring 1983, pp. 21–45.

113. Velitchka D. Kaltcheva and Barton A. Weitz, "When Should a Retailer Create an Exciting Store Environment?" *Journal of Marketing*, January 2006, pp. 107–118.

114. Sarah Nassauer, "A Season (or 13) for Shopping," *Wall Street Journal*, August 17, 2011, www.wsj.com.

115. Risto Moisio and Eric J. Arnould, "Framework in Marketing: Drama Structure, Drama Interaction, and Drama Content in Shopping Experiences," *Journal of Consumer Behavior* 4, no. 4, 2005, pp. 246–256; and Robert V. Kozinets, John F. Sherry, Diana Storm, Adam Duhachek, Krittinee Nuttavuthisit, and Benét DeBerry-Spence, "Ludic Agency and Retail Spectacle," *Journal of Consumer Research* 31, no. 3, 2004, pp. 658–672.

116. "U.S. Patent for Apple Store in Shanghai," *Shanghai Daily*, March 23, 2012, www.china.org.cn.

117. Kevin Woodward, "February Survey: Web Site Design And Usability," *Internet Retailer*, February 1, 2012, www.internetretailer.com; and Zak Stambor, "A Consistent Feel," *Internet Retailer*, November 30, 2011, www.internetretailer.com.

118. "Unilever Ramps Up Hispanic Marketing," *Media Post*, April 2, 2012, www.mediapost.com; Anna Maria Virzi, "How Unilever Connects with Hispanics on Facebook," *ClickZ*, February 28, 2012, www.clickz.com; Louise Lucas, "Changing Lives," *Financial Times*, March 20, 2012, www.ft.com; Louise Jack, "Unilever CEO Paul Polman on the Packaged Goods Giant's Creative Shift," *Fast Company*, January 12, 2012, www.fastcocreate.com; Ann-Christine Diaz, "Behind the work: Ragu and BFG9000's Tips for Finicky Eaters," *Advertising Age*, March 20, 2012, www.adage.com; and Ekaterina Walter, "Marketing to Women," *Fast Company*, March 19, 2012, www.fastcompany.com.

DEVELOPING INFORMATION ABOUT CONSUMER BEHAVIOR

Consumer behavior research helps marketers determine what customers need, how they behave, what they think, and how they feel. Based on research, marketers make decisions about how to profitably satisfy consumer needs. This appendix explains the tools used to collect information about consumers, describes the organizations involved in research, and introduces ethical issues in research.

CONSUMER BEHAVIOR RESEARCH METHODS

Primary data Data originating from a researcher and collected to provide information relevant to a specific research project.

Secondary data Data collected for some other purpose that is subsequently used in a research project.

Researchers collect and analyze two types of data for marketing purposes: primary and secondary. Data collected for its own purpose is called **primary data**. When marketers gather data using surveys, focus groups, experiments, and the like to support their own marketing decisions, they are collecting primary data. Data collected by an entity for one purpose and subsequently used by another entity for a different purpose is called **secondary data**. For example, after the government collects census data for tax purposes, marketers can use the results as secondary data to estimate the size of markets in their own industry.

A number of tools are available in the consumer researcher's "tool kit" for gathering primary data, some based on what consumers say and some on what they do (see Exhibit A.1). Researchers may collect data from relatively few people or compile data from huge samples of consumers. Each of these tools can provide unique insights that, when combined, reveal very different perspectives on the complex world of consumer behavior. This is research with a purpose: to guide companies in making more informed decisions and achieving marketing results.

Surveys

Survey A method of collecting information from a sample of consumers, predominantly by asking questions.

One of the most familiar research tools is the **survey**, a method of collecting information from a sample of consumers, usually by asking questions, to draw quantitative conclusions about a target population. Some questions may be open-ended, with the consumer filling in the blanks; other questions may ask consumers to use a rating scale or check marks. Surveys can be conducted in person, through the mail, over the phone, or by using the Web. The online retailer Lands' End uses questionnaires posted on the SurveyMonkey site to obtain consumer input on all kinds of issues, from quality perceptions to buying priorities.[1]

Although companies often undertake specialized surveys to better understand a specific customer segment, some organizations carry out broad-based surveys that are made available to marketers. The U.S. Bureau of the Census is a widely used source of demographic information. Its Census of Population and Housing, conducted every ten years, asks U.S. consumers a series of questions regarding their age, marital status, gender, household size, education, and home ownership. This data base, available online (www.census.gov), helps marketers learn about population shifts that might affect their offerings or their industry.

Survey data can also help marketers understand media usage and product purchasing patterns. For example, the Pew Research Center surveys consumers in different age groups about their Internet usage. After one recent survey, the organization reported: "On any given day, 53% of all the young adults ages 18–29 go online for no particular reason except to have fun or to pass the time."

Tools for Primary Research Investigating Consumer Behavior

There are many different types of tools available to research and get information on consumer behavior.

Tool	Description
Survey	A written instrument that asks consumers to respond to a predetermined set of research questions.
Focus group	A form of interview involving 8 to12 people who, led by a moderator, discuss a product or other marketing stimulus.
Interview	One-on-one discussion in which an interviewer asks a consumer questions related to consumption behavior and decisions.
Storytelling	Consumers are asked to tell stories about acquisition, usage, or disposition experiences.
Photography and pictures	Showing photographs or pictures to consumers (or asking consumers to take photos or draw pictures) as a way to elicit comments about marketing stimuli.
Diaries	Asking consumers to maintain a written or online diary about product purchasing, media usage, and related behavior.
Experiments	Conducting experiments under laboratory conditions to determine whether and how specific marketing phenomena affect consumer behavior.
Field experiments	Conducting experiments such as market tests in the real world, to determine actual consumer reaction to marketing stimuli.
Conjoint analysis	A research technique designed to determine the relative importance and appeal of different levels of an offering's attributes.
Observations and ethnographic research	Observing consumers at home or in stores to understand behavior and gain insights that will lead to more effective marketing decisions.
Purchase panels	Tracking what consumers buy on different occasions or in different places.
Database marketing	Combining all research data about consumers and their purchases into a database that can be analyzed to identify behavior patterns as insights for developing marketing programs.
Netnography	Tracking and analyzing online comments and consumer activities to understand consumers' thoughts, feelings, and actions relative to marketing stimuli.
Psychophysiological reactions and neuroscience	Examining physiological reactions (e.g., eye movements) and applying neuroscience techniques (e.g., measuring brain activity) to understand consumer behavior.

By contrast, Pew reported that fewer than half of seniors were using the Internet as a fun diversion.[2] Researchers are even studying how to encourage survey response. In one study, more consumers completed a survey they received in the mail when the package was topped by a Post-it note asking them to participate.[3]

Surveys can also be used to collect sensitive information from consumers, by ensuring that their responses to the questions are completely anonymous. In a regular survey, consumers might underreport negative behaviors (e.g., shoplifting, tax evasion, binge drinking, smoking) or overreport positive behaviors (e.g., giving to charity, reading books, studying, eating vegetables). Recent developments in market research techniques allow deep insights into the sensitive behaviors of consumers, while still safeguarding their anonymity.[4]

One technique to collect valid information about such sensitive topics is by having consumers use a randomization device (e.g., flipping a coin) while answering the questions. The randomization device determines whether consumers should truthfully respond to a question or provide an answer given by the device. For example, researchers might give consumers a coin and ask them to flip it before responding "yes" or "no" to the question "Have you ever shoplifted?" If the coin shows "tails," consumers are to answer truthfully. If it shows "heads," they are to flip again. Then, if the coin shows "tails," they answer "yes"; if it shows "heads," they answer "no." Researchers can determine which percentage of all answers is due to the randomization device, and which percentage is true.

> **Focus group** A form of interview involving 8 to 12 people; a moderator leads the group and asks participants to discuss a product, concept, or other marketing stimulus.

Focus Groups

Unlike a survey, which may collect input from hundreds of people responding individually to the same questionnaire, a **focus group** brings together small groups of consumers to discuss an issue or an offering. Led by a trained moderator, participants express their opinions about a given product or topic, which can be particularly useful in identifying and testing new product ideas. Focus groups provide qualitative insights into consumer attitudes as opposed to the quantitative (numerical) data resulting from surveys. When Nebraska was readying a new marketing plan to boost state tourism, researchers held focus groups to learn about consumers' perceptions of and attitudes toward the state's varied attractions. Officials put together a tourism plan after determining that some tourists are attracted by Nebraska's "open spaces," while others prefer Omaha's faster pace.[5]

A related technique is the computer-based focus group, in which consumers go to a computer lab where their individual comments are displayed anonymously on a large screen for viewing by the group. This method can help researchers gather information on sensitive topics, as can focus groups conducted by telephone or online rather than in person. However, the anonymity prevents researchers from collecting other relevant data, such as nonverbal reactions conveyed by facial expressions and body language that would be available in a traditional focus group.

Some companies convene customer advisory boards, small groups of customers that meet with marketing and service executives once or twice a year (face to face, online, or by phone) to discuss offerings, competitive products, future needs, acquisition and usage problems, and related issues. Board meetings serve not just as research but also as a tool for strengthening customer relations.[6] To illustrate, Premier Bank of Tallahassee, Florida, asks its two customer boards for feedback on branch services, new product ideas, and community involvement.[7]

> **Exhibit A.2**
>
> **Interviews**
> One-on-one interviews with consumers can provide useful feedback to companies or market researchers, especially on sensitive subjects.

© Michael Newman/PhotoEdit

Interviews

Like focus groups, interviews involve direct contact with consumers (see Exhibit A.2). Interviews are often more appropriate than focus groups when the topic is sensitive, embarrassing, confidential, or emotionally charged. They provide more in-depth data than surveys when the researcher wants to "pick consumers' brains."

In some interviews, researchers ask customers about the process they use to make a purchase decision. One research company assigns professional interviewers to tape-record consumers' thoughts while they shop for groceries. This research helps marketers understand how factors in the shopping environment affect purchasing. Interviews can also uncover broader attitudes that affect behavior across product categories. When the Underwriters Laboratories interviewed hundreds of consumers in the United States, Germany, China, and India, it found a belief that high-tech firms were bringing new products to market more quickly than needed. The interviews revealed concerns about the fast pace of new technology and about new products being introduced because companies wanted new products to sell, not necessarily because the products were innovative.[8]

Traditional interviews require a trained interviewer who attempts to establish rapport with consumers. Interviewers also note nonverbal behaviors like fidgeting, voice pitch changes, and folded arms and legs as clues to whether the respondent is open to the discussion or whether certain questions are particularly sensitive. Researchers often record interviews for later transcription so they can examine the results using qualitative or quantitative analysis. Sometimes researchers videotape nonverbal responses that cannot be captured in the transcription process and analyze the interviews later to identify patterns or themes.

Storytelling

Storytelling A research method by which consumers are asked to tell stories about product acquisition, usage, or disposition experiences. These stories help marketers gain insights into consumer needs and identify the product attributes that meet these needs.

Another tool for conducting consumer research is **storytelling**, in which consumers tell researchers stories about their experiences with a product. At Patagonia, which markets outdoor clothing and accessories, researchers collect consumer stories about backpacking and other outdoor experiences for use in developing the company's catalogs and online product descriptions. Storytelling not only provides information relevant to the marketing of the product but also shows that Patagonia is in touch with its customers and values what they say.[9]

Although storytelling involves the real stories of real consumers, sometimes marketers ask consumers to tell or write stories about hypothetical situations that the marketer has depicted in a picture or scenario.[10] The idea is that a consumer's needs, feelings, and perceptions are revealed by the way he or she interprets what is depicted in the picture or scenario. For example, researchers may show a picture of a woman at the entrance to a Zara store with a thought bubble above her head and ask consumers to write what they imagine the woman is thinking. Such stories can reveal what consumers think of a particular store, purchase situation, and so on.

Photography and Pictures

Some researchers use a technique in which they show pictures of experiences that consumers have had in order to help consumers remember and report experiences more completely.[11] Researchers may also ask consumers to draw or collect pictures that represent their thoughts and feelings about the topic at hand. Still another practice is to ask consumers to photograph their belongings or assemble a collage of pictures that reflects their lifestyles. Researchers then ask about the pictures and the meaning behind them or have the consumer write an essay, which can help integrate the images and thoughts suggested by the pictures.[12]

Diaries

Asking consumers to keep diaries can provide important insights into their behavior, including product purchasing and media usage. Diaries often reveal how friends and family affect consumers' decisions about clothes, music, fast foods, videos, concerts, and so on. When Unilever was planning a new deodorant, it asked a group of women to keep an "armpit diary" noting how often they shaved, what their underarms looked like, and how frequently they used deodorant. Finding that the women were concerned about the condition of their underarm skin, Unilever created a moisturizing deodorant product and promoted its skin-care benefits.[13]

The research firm NPD Group asks more than three million consumers worldwide to maintain online diaries tracking their purchases in dozens of product categories. Companies buy NPD's diary data to learn whether consumers are brand loyal or brand switching and whether they are heavy or light product users. By linking the data with demographic data, marketers can learn even more about these consumers. Marketers targeting U.S. consumers can also examine yearly data from the government's Consumer Expenditure Diary Survey. As part of this research, selected consumers record all their household purchases of goods and services in certain categories, such as foods, beverages, and nonprescription medical items, during a two-week period. The results provide insights into how purchasing differs by age, home owners versus renters, and other consumer characteristics.

Experiments

Consumer researchers can conduct experiments to determine whether certain marketing phenomena affect consumer behavior (see Exhibit A.3). For example, they might design an experiment to learn whether consumers' attitudes toward a brand are affected by the brand name as opposed to factors such as product features, package, color, logo, room temperature, or the consumer's mood. With experiments, researchers randomly assign consumers to receive different "treatments" and then observe the effects of these treatments. To illustrate, consumers might be assigned to groups that are shown different brand names. The researchers collect data about participants' attitudes toward the name and compare attitudes across groups. In a taste-test experiment, they might randomly assign consumers to groups and then ask each group to taste a different product. Comparing evaluations of the product across the groups will show which product is preferred.

Independent variable The "treatment" or the entity that researchers vary in a research project.

An important aspect of such experiments is that the groups are designed to be identical in all respects except the treatment, called the **independent variable**. Thus, in a taste-test experiment, only the taste of the food or beverage is varied. Everything else is the same across

Experiments

Laboratory testing and field experiments with consumers, such as taste testing, with is one way to research new products and marketing trends.

© Tom Williams/Roll Call/Getty Images

groups—consumers eat or drink the same amount of the product, at the same temperature, from the same kind of container, in the same room, in the presence of the same experimenter, and so on. After consumers taste and rate the product, researchers can compare the groups' responses to see which taste is preferred. Because the groups are identical in all other respects, researchers know that any differences between the two groups are caused by the treatment (the food's taste).

Field Experiments

Market test A study in which the effectiveness of one or more elements of the marketing mix is examined by evaluating sales of the product in an actual market, e.g., a specific city.

Although experiments are often conducted in controlled laboratory situations, marketers can plan and implement experiments in the real world, known as "field experiments." One type of field experiment, a **market test**, reveals whether an offering is likely to sell in a given market and which marketing-mix elements most effectively enhance sales. Suppose marketers want to determine how much advertising support to give to a new product. They could select two test markets of a similar size and demographic composition and spend a different amount of money on advertising in each market. By observing product sales in the two markets over a set period, the marketers would be able to tell which level of advertising expenditure resulted in higher sales.

Before Dr Pepper Snapple introduced its Dr Pepper Ten soft drink throughout the United States—targeting men who drink diet beverages—it tested the product's 10-calorie formula and the supporting marketing mix in six cities. In addition to gauging consumer response to the taste and name, the company wanted to determine how men and women would react to its male-oriented packaging and advertising. As a result of this market test, Dr Pepper Snapple learned that men responded positively—and that women were intrigued enough to try Dr Pepper Ten at least once.[14]

Conjoint Analysis

Conjoint analysis A research technique to determine the relative importance and appeal of different levels of an offering's attributes.

Many marketers use the sophisticated research technique of **conjoint analysis** to determine the relative importance and appeal of different levels of an offering's attributes. To start, researchers identify the attributes of the offering, such as package size, specific product features, and price points. Next, they determine the levels to be tested for each attribute (e.g., large or small size). Then they ask consumers to react to a series of product concepts that combine these attributes in different ways.

For example, researchers might ask how likely consumers are to buy a large container of liquid Tide laundry detergent that has added stain removal power and costs $4.75; they might also ask how likely consumers are to buy a small container of Tide that lacks added stain removal power and costs $2.50. By analyzing the responses to different combinations, the researchers can see how important each attribute (e.g., size, price) is and the level of a given attribute that customers prefer. Academic researchers have used this methodology to understand, among other things, how much weight consumers give to environmental factors versus price and other attributes when they buy wooden furniture.[15]

Observations and Ethnographic Research

At times, researchers observe consumers to gain insight into potentially effective product, promotion, price, and distribution decisions. The maker of Huggies disposable diapers, Kimberly-Clark, uses observational research to see how consumers react to new packaging and new shelf positions as they "shop" in virtual store environments customized to look like specific chain stores. The results not only help Kimberly-Clark's marketers make product and promotion decisions, but they also help Walmart, Target, and other retailers make decisions about buying and displaying Kimberly-Clark products.[16]

Ethnographic research In-depth qualitative research using observations and interviews (often over-repeated occasions) of consumers in real-world surroundings. Often used to study the meaning that consumers ascribe to a product or consumption phenomenon.

Some companies conduct **ethnographic research**, in which researchers interview and observe (and perhaps videotape) how consumers behave in real-world surroundings. (Ethnographic research can also be applied to Internet activities, as discussed later in this appendix.) Speck, a store located in the high-tech center of California's Silicon Valley, is not in business to make sales of iPhones and other electronic gadgets. Instead, it serves as a retail location for observing and interviewing shoppers as they browse the showcases, handle new products, ask questions, test product functions, and offer comments about the merchandise. "It's a marketing laboratory," explains Speck's CEO. "Sales are nice, but our goal is to be able to talk to people."[17]

Purchase Panels

Sometimes marketers try to understand consumer behavior by tracking what consumers buy on different purchase occasions. This kind of research simply records whether a behavior occurred. Such behavioral data may be collected from special panel members, from a representative sample of the general population, or from the marketer's target market. Every time panel members go shopping, the cash register records their purchases. By merging purchase data with demographic data, marketers can tell who is purchasing a product, whether those consumers are also buying competitors' products, and whether a coupon or other sales promotion was involved. Marketers can also use these data to determine whether, for example, the shelf space allocated to a product, or added advertising in the test area, affected panel members' purchases.

A growing number of firms, including Del Monte Foods, Procter & Gamble, and Coca-Cola, also conduct research through a proprietary online purchase panel. For instance, Del Monte's research firm set up a password-protected "I Love My Dog" website and invited 400 dog owners to participate in answering questions about dog food products. Feedback from participants helped Del Monte select flavors for its Snausages Breakfast Bites dog treats.[18]

Database Marketing

Data mining Searching for patterns in a company database that offer clues to customer needs, preferences, and behaviors.

Marketers can dig deeper into consumer behavior if they combine different forms of consumer research into a common database. This database might contain information about targeted consumers' demographics and lifestyles combined with data about their purchases in various product categories over time, their media habits, and their usage of coupons and other promotional devices. Using **data mining**, the company then searches for patterns in the database that offer clues to customer needs, preferences, and behaviors.[19]

Walmart is at the cutting edge of the data-mining movement. It follows every piece of merchandise from warehouse to store shelf by using radio frequency identification tags. Every item sold at the checkout is recorded, along with the item's price, the time of sale, and the store location. These data are reported to Walmart hourly and daily by product, by category, by store, by supplier, and so on. The retailer analyzes what else goes into the shopping cart, store by store and region by region, for clues to pricing products in different categories. Walmart also pays attention to what its 11 million Facebook fans say and do online. Data mining helps the company identify promising new store locations and profile each store's shoppers so it can stock the right assortment of goods in appropriate quantities. Walmart can even use data mining to be sure that extra quantities of storm-related merchandise gets to individual stores in advance of hurricanes or other extreme weather situations, based on what customers in those stores have bought before and after storms in previous years.[20]

Netnography

Netnography Observing and analyzing the online behavior and comments of consumers.

Researchers can use a variety of methods for **netnography**, ethnographic research techniques adapted for the observation and analysis of consumers' online behavior and comments.[21] Many marketers and digital advertising firms use tracking software or other methods to observe which websites consumers visit, which pages they look at, how long they visit each site, and related data. By analyzing consumer browsing patterns, researchers can determine how to make websites more user-friendly and how to better target online advertising as well as how to make other decisions about online marketing activities. One study looked at consumers' use of websites to buy automobiles and found that the best predictor of purchase was not the use of sophisticated decision-making aids or the number of repeat visits but rather how long consumers browsed and navigated through the site.[22] Google analyzes the search words entered by each consumer, so it can position relevant advertising adjacent to search the results. To give consumers more information about its ad targeting and allow them to opt out of all ads or ads from particular advertisers, Google has also begun posting "Why these ads?" links near ad messages.[23]

However, privacy advocates are concerned that tracking software—especially when used without the consumer's knowledge or consent—is intrusive. Even though most marketing websites post privacy policies to explain what details they collect and how they use the data, these policies are rarely on the home page and are not always easy to understand. To protect personal privacy, the European Union now requires companies to obtain consumers' consent before using tracking "cookies" to follow anyone's online activities.[24] Canada requires marketers to disclose how they are tracking consumers online, what information is collected, and how it will be used. "Some people like receiving ads targeted to their specific interests," explains Canada's privacy commissioner. "Others are extremely uncomfortable with the notion of their online activities being tracked. People's choices must be respected."[25]

Increasingly, consumers are posting comments on social media pages, brand forums, and websites, talking about their brand likes and dislikes, discussing good and bad experiences with offerings, and reacting to what both marketers and other consumers say online. However, researchers are still learning to interpret the intentions, attitudes, and emotions inherent in messages on Twitter, Facebook, blogs, and other sites. Tools such as automated content analysis and sophisticated data-mining tools are useful in extracting insights with the goal of fine-tuning marketing elements.[26]

Procter & Gamble, the company behind Tide, Bounty, and many other big brands, looks carefully at the level of social media buzz stimulated by each TV program that carries its TV ads. The TV networks are also very interested in such information. CBS, for example, looks at both the number of messages and the sentiment behind the messages (are the messages positive or negative?).[27] Charming Shoppes, a retailer of plus-size women's clothing, digs deeply into comments in e-mails, online product reviews, and Web-based brand communities to understand what satisfies its customers and what they would like improved.[28]

Psychophysiological Reactions and Neuroscience

Most marketing research involves either collecting verbal responses from consumers (e.g., answers to questions and self-reports about media and purchase behaviors) or observing consumer behavior (e.g., under laboratory conditions, in real life, or online). In contrast, the psychophysiological reactions of consumers to marketing actions (e.g., eye and muscle movements) are often automatic and rapid, unable to be verbalized by consumers. The range of potential *psychophysiological reactions* that can be measured is virtually limitless, including pupil dilation, eye movements, skin conductance, facial muscle movements, electrical activity of the brain (using electroencephalogram), and heart rate. Psychophysiological reactions to marketing are an important source of information that cannot easily be collected in any other way.

Neuroscience is the scientific study of the nervous system, which includes the brain, the spinal cord, and the retina. Developments in neuroscience have led to the introduction of new methodologies to collect data on fundamental brain processes involved in consumer behavior. (Note that in marketing, the term *neuro* is often applied in a more general sense to all research techniques that involve some kind of psychophysiological measurement, such as eye tracking.)

Today, consumer researchers are gaining deeper insights by measuring physiological reactions and applying neuroscience to understand how consumers respond to various marketing stimuli.[29] By recording moment-to-moment eye movements and interpreting emotions from facial expressions, for example, researchers can determine which ad messages or websites attract and retain attention. Marketers can then apply this learning to increase the "stopping power" of ad messages and websites. In another study, researchers were able to suggest, based on these physiological measurements, how marketers could engage consumers so they will not click away from online video ads.[30]

Neuroscientists are seeking to understand consumer behavior by watching which parts of the brain become activated when consumers make a decision, view an ad, or select an investment.[31] For instance, Frito-Lay learned through neuroscience research that consumers like the orange cheesy residue left on their fingers when they eat Cheetos snacks. Based on this insight, Frito-Lay has played up the messy-fingers angle in its ads and on its Facebook page.[32] Although neuroscience research raises concerns about manipulation, one advertising executive notes: "Observing brain activity and setting up models for behavior is not the same as forcing a brain into making a consumption decision."[33]

TYPES OF CONSUMER RESEARCHERS

Exhibit A.4

Who Conducts Consumer Research?
A number of different organizations conduct research on consumers, although they differ in their objectives. Some do research for application, some for consumer protection, and some for obtaining general knowledge about consumers.

Many entities use market research to study consumer behavior for different reasons, as shown in Exhibit A.4. Organizations such as consumer goods and service companies, ad agencies, and marketing research firms conduct research to make decisions about marketing a specific product or service. Government organizations collect consumer information so as to set laws designed to protect consumers. Academics conduct research to protect consumers or simply to understand why and how consumers behave as they do.

In-House Marketing Research Departments

The benefits of conducting "in-house" research (conducted by the company for the company) are that the information collected can be kept within the company and that opportunities for information to leak to competitors are minimized. However, internal departments are sometimes viewed

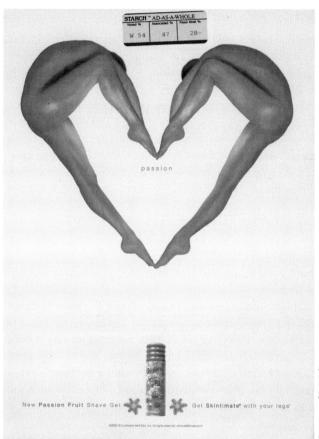

STARCH™ AD-AS-A-WHOLE
Noted %	Associated %	Read Most %
W 54	47	28-

passion

New Passion Fruit Shave Gel Get Skintimate® with your legs™

Exhibit A.5

Working with an External Marketing Research Firm
Companies like Starch collect data on what, if anything, consumers remember from an ad. The numbers noted on the stickers placed at the top of the ad indicate the percentage of respondents sampled who remembered having seen or read various parts of the ad.

as less objective than outside research firms since they may have a vested interest in the research results. For example, employees may be motivated to show that the company is making good decisions, a situation that may unwittingly bias the nature of their research or the outcomes they report. Consequently, some companies use outside research companies to gather their consumer research.

External Marketing Research Firms

External research firms often help design a specific research project before it begins. They develop measuring instruments to measure consumer responses, collect data from consumers, analyze the data, and develop reports for their clients (see Exhibit A.5). Research firms specializing in neuroscience have helped PayPal, ESPN, Intel, Frito-Lay, and others fine-tune their marketing messages and plan new offerings.[34]

Some marketing research firms are "full service" organizations that perform a variety of marketing research services; others specialize in a particular type of research. The GfK Group, for instance, conducts media research, brand awareness research, and other consumer behavior research. In its Starch Advertising Research studies, dozens of readers of a specific magazine go through a recent issue with a trained interviewer. The interviewer asks whether consumers have seen each ad in the issue and whether they saw the picture in each ad, read the headline, read the body copy, and saw the ad slogan. The company compiles reports about the percentage of respondents who saw each part of each ad and sells the results to advertisers who want to determine whether their ads were seen and read more than other ads in the same issue or product category.

Advertising Agencies and Media Planning Firms

Full-service advertising agencies and media planning firms conduct research to better understand what advertising messages and media will appeal to their clients' target markets. For example, the international home-furnishings chain IKEA recently asked MEC Global and Ogilvy & Mather to develop a campaign to increase the amount its customers spend during each transaction. When agency researchers studied the buying and consumption behavior of 35-year-old IKEA customers, both in stores and in their homes, they found that these shoppers associated the retailer with accessory merchandise, rather than major furniture pieces and sets. The researchers also discovered that IKEA shoppers were looking for creative ideas they could adapt to personalize their living spaces. On the basis of this research, the agencies developed a multimedia campaign that focused on how the store offers choices for furnishing entire rooms with personal flair. In addition to TV, the campaign included print ads, online promotions, and a brand community where consumers could upload photos of rooms they furnished and decorated with IKEA products, as inspiration for other consumers. The results: IKEA's overall sales increased more than 7 percent—and sales of living room sets rose 9 percent.[35]

Some advertising agencies have departments to test advertising concepts as part of the service they provide to clients. Agencies may also conduct advertising pretesting, using drawings of ads or finished ads, to make sure that an ad is fulfilling its objectives *before* it is placed in the media. In addition, agencies often conduct tracking studies to monitor advertising effectiveness over time. Tracking studies can determine whether the percentage of target market consumers who are aware of a brand has changed as a function of the amount, duration, and timing of its advertising.

Syndicated Data Services

Syndicated data services are companies that collect and then sell the information they collect, usually to firms that market products and services to consumers. For example, the Yankelovich Monitor study collects data on consumer lifestyles and social trends using 90-minute interviews at the homes of approximately 2,500 adults. Its annual reports describing current and projected lifestyle trends help advertising agencies and company marketers develop content for promotional messages, choose media, identify new product ideas, plan positioning strategy, and make other marketing decisions.

Nielsen is a syndicated data service that tracks the TV viewing habits of thousands of participating U.S. households. Using digital set-top equipment, it records which TV shows each household member is viewing and when. In addition, during "sweeps weeks," it asks two million U.S. consumers to keep a diary indicating the shows they watch. Based on these data, Nielsen assigns a rating that indicates the number and percentage of all households watching a particular TV program, and a specific commercial, along with demographic analyses of the audience. This is how advertisers know how many viewers tune in to watch the Super Bowl, for instance.

By combining demographic and TV viewing behavior—including viewing on personal computers and cell phones, not just on home TV sets—Nielsen can describe the audience for individual shows. Networks, cable stations, and independent channels use this information to determine whether TV shows should be renewed and how much they can charge for advertising time on a particular show. In general, advertisers will pay more to advertise on very popular shows (those with higher Nielsen ratings). Advertisers who buy Nielsen data can assess which TV shows they should advertise in, basing their decisions on how well the audience's demographic characteristics match the sponsor's target market. Nielsen also conducts research into consumers' use of the Internet, video games, mobile devices, and other media that carry ad messages.

Retailers

Large retail chains often conduct consumer research. By using electronic scanners to track sales of a brand or product category, they can determine which are their best and worst-selling items and see how consumers respond to coupons, discounts, and other promotions. Because salespeople often interact directly with customers, retailers sometimes use research to measure customer satisfaction and determine how they can improve service quality. Often retailers use research to uncover new needs and understand brand perceptions. Raymond, a clothing chain based in India, recently conducted research to learn more about consumers' preferences and brand attitudes within the United Arab Emirates and Saudi Arabia. Having learned that Gulf-region consumers accept its brand and feel an emotional connection with it, Raymond is proceeding with stores designed specifically for these markets.[36]

Research Foundations and Trade Groups

Research foundation A nonprofit organization that sponsors research on topics relevant to the foundation's goals.

Many research foundations and trade groups collect consumer research. A **research foundation** is a nonprofit organization that sponsors research on topics relevant to the foundation's goals. As an example, the nonprofit Advertising Research Foundation seeks to improve the practice of advertising, marketing, and media research. It sponsors conferences and webinars, and publishes reports related to research in these areas. The Marketing Science Institute is another nonprofit organization that sponsors academic research to uncover information useful to marketers.

Trade group A professional organization made up of marketers in the same industry.

Specialized trade groups may also collect consumer research to better understand the needs of consumers in their own industries. A **trade group** is an organization formed by people who work in the same industry, such as the Recording Industry Association of America, a group whose members are involved in the recorded music industry through recording, distribution, or retailing activities. This organization has sponsored a host of research projects, including studies to understand how American music tastes have changed over the years.

Recall Notice

Recall of the Wooden Pull Toy Wagon with Blocks
under the brand names "First Learning" and "My Kidz"
bearing the UPC numbers 834162002158 and 834162002165
Lead Hazard
Sold between August 2005 and August 2007

UPC: 834162002165   UPC: 834162002158

UPC: 834162002165   UPC: 834162002158

UPC: 834162002165   UPC: 834162002158

The paints decorating this item may contain lead levels in excess of federal standards.
Lead is toxic if ingested by young children and can cause adverse health effects.

**Consumers should immediately take the
recalled item away from children and
return it to KB Toys for a merchandise credit.**

For additional information, visit: www.recall.kbtinfo.com
or contact KB Toys, Monday through Friday between 9am and 5pm EST,
toll-free at (888) 843-9520.

To be posted through January 2008
In cooperation with the U.S. Consumer Product Safety Commission

© AFP/Getty Images/Newscom

Exhibit A.6

Consumer Protection
Government agencies, such as the Consumer Product Safety Commission, are designed for consumer protection, and can issue recall notices such as this one for items unfit for consumer consumption.

Government

Although government agencies do not use research to help market an offering, businesses frequently use government research for marketing purposes, as when they examine census data to estimate the size of various demographic markets. U.S. government studies by agencies such as the Consumer Products Safety Commission, the Department of Transportation, and the Food and Drug Administration are specifically designed for consumer protection (see Exhibit A.6). As an example, the Federal Trade Commission (FTC) conducts research on potentially deceptive, misleading, or fraudulent advertising. One issue the FTC continues to study, for example, is how consumers perceive goods and services advertised using phrases that suggest environmentally friendly properties. After conducting research, the FTC recently issued guidelines for how marketers are permitted to use specific phrases (e.g., "renewable materials") to avoid misleading consumers about "green" claims.[37] Research can also help resolve court cases involving marketing issues such as whether consumers are confusing a new product's trademark with an established product's trademark, a situation that could hurt the established brand.[38]

Consumer Organizations

Independent consumer organizations also conduct research, generally for the purpose of protecting or informing consumers. Consumers Union is an independent, nonprofit testing and information organization designed to serve consumers. The organization publishes the well-known *Consumer Reports* magazine. Many of the products described in *Consumer Reports* are tested in Consumers Union's independent product-testing lab, and the results are posted on the organization's website (www.consumersunion.org).

Academics and Academic Research Centers

Although academic research involving consumers can be used for marketing and may have implications for public policy, studies often are designed simply to enhance our general understanding of consumer behavior. Much of the research reported in this book describes state-of-the-art academic studies. Some academic research centers focus on a specific aspect of consumer behavior. For example, to learn more about media consumption, researchers from Ball State University's Center for Media Design observed 101 consumers from the time they woke up until the time they went to sleep. They found that consumers actually spend more time with TV, radio, newspapers, and online media than is reflected in conventional media research.[39] Another example is the Restaurant of the Future, on the campus of Wageningen University in the Netherlands, where researchers experiment with lighting, plates, food arrangement, seasonings and ingredients, and other details to see their effects on what and how much students and faculty eat.[40]

ETHICAL ISSUES IN CONSUMER RESEARCH

Although marketers rely heavily on consumer research in the development of successful goods and services, the conduct of this research raises important ethical issues. As the following sections show, consumer research has both positive and negative aspects. See Chapter 17 and about public policy for more discussion of ethical issues.

The Positive Aspects of Consumer Research

Both consumers and marketers can benefit from consumer research. Consumers generally have better acquisition, usage, and disposition experiences. Meanwhile, marketers can learn to build stronger customer relationships by paying attention to consumer research. As a consequence, fewer new products may fail, and more products of interest to consumers will be brought to market, making for a more efficient and effective marketplace.

Better Consumer Experiences

Because consumer research helps marketers become more customer focused, consumers can have better designed products, better customer service, clearer usage instructions, more information that helps them make good decisions, and more satisfying acquisition and postpurchase experiences. Consumer research (by government and consumer organizations) also plays a role in protecting consumers from unscrupulous marketers.

Potential for Building Customer Relationships

Research can help marketers identify ways of establishing and enhancing relationships with customers through a better understanding of their needs, attitudes, and behavior. Interestingly, U.S. consumers have a more favorable view of marketing today than they did in the 1980s and 1990s, particularly in regard to retailing and distribution.[41] Being aware of these kinds of broad trends in consumer sentiment is a good foundation from which to approach relationship building.

The Negative Aspects of Consumer Research

Consumer research is a very complex process with a number of potentially negative aspects. These include the difficulty of conducting research in foreign countries, the high costs of conducting research, concerns about invasion of privacy, and the use of deceptive practices.

Studying Consumer Behavior in Different Countries

Marketers who want to research consumer behavior in other countries face special challenges. For instance, focus groups are not appropriate in all countries or situations. U.S. marketers often put husbands and wives together in a focus group to explore attitudes toward products like furniture. However, this approach won't work in countries like Saudi Arabia, where women are unlikely to speak freely and are highly unlikely to disagree with their husbands in such settings. Focus groups must also be conducted differently in Japan, where cultural pressures dictate against a person's disagreeing with the views of a group.

Although telephone interviewing is common in the United States, it is far less prevalent in developing nations. Marketers must also consider a country's literacy rate when planning survey research. At a minimum, researchers should word questions carefully and check to ensure that the meaning is being accurately conveyed by first translating questions into the other language and then translating them back into the original language.

Companies may not be able to directly compare secondary data gathered in another country with data gathered in the United States, in part because of different collection procedures or timing. Countries may also use different categorization schemes for describing demographics like social class and education level. Moreover, different or fewer syndicated data sources may be available in other countries, a situation that limits the research available to marketers. Finally, conducting research to examine consumers' online behavior and analyze online comments may be more challenging because of legal, cultural, and language differences from country to country.

Potentially Higher Marketing Costs

Some consumers worry that the process of researching consumer behavior leads to higher marketing costs, which in turn translate into higher product prices. Some marketers, however, argue that they can market to their customers more efficiently if they know more about them. For example, product development, advertising, sales promotion costs, and distribution costs will be lower if marketers know exactly what consumers want and how to reach them.

Invasion of Consumer Privacy

A potentially more serious and widespread concern is that in the process of conducting and use of research—especially database marketing—marketers may invade consumers' privacy. Consumers worry that marketers know too much about them and that personal data, financial data, and behavioral data may be sold to other companies or used inappropriately without their knowledge or consent. For example, after two U.S. shopping centers followed shoppers' cell phone signals to track consumers' movements (anonymously) from store to store, legislators objected on privacy grounds. The research company made plans to offer a convenient opt-out feature for consumers who do not wish to be tracked in that way. Such systems are already in limited use in Europe and Australia.[42] However, privacy requirements vary from country to country. In some areas, researchers must obtain consumers' permission before collecting and storing personal data.

Deceptive Research Practices

Finally, unscrupulous researchers may engage in deceptive practices. One such practice is lying about the sponsor of the research (e.g., saying it is being conducted by a nonprofit organization when it is really being conducted by a for-profit company). Another deceptive practice is promising that respondents' answers will remain anonymous when in fact the company adds identifying information to the data in order to be able to market to these consumers later on. Unscrupulous researchers may also promise to compensate respondents but fail to deliver on this promise.[43] Such deceptive practices are not allowed under the strict codes of conduct developed by professional organizations such as ESOMAR (European Society for Opinion and Market Research) and the Marketing Research Association.

SUMMARY

Consumer research is a valuable tool that helps marketers design better marketing programs, aids in the development of laws and public policy decisions regarding product safety, and promotes our general understanding of how consumers behave and why. Researchers use a variety of techniques, including collecting data on what consumers say and what they do. These tools may involve data collection from relatively few individuals or from many individuals and may study consumers at a single point in time or track their behavior across time.

Some companies have internal marketing research departments to collect data; others use external research firms to conduct studies. Advertising agencies and syndicated data services are two types of outside agencies that conduct consumer research. Large retail chains often use electronic scanners to track sales of a brand or product category. Research foundations, trade groups, the government, consumer organizations, academics, and academic research centers also collect consumer information. Research supports a consumer-oriented view of marketing and can help companies improve consumption experiences and strengthen customer relationships. However, critics say research may invade consumers' privacy and lead to higher marketing costs; in addition, unscrupulous marketers can misuse consumer information.

ENDNOTES

1. Miguel Helft, "SurveyMonkey Says!" *Fortune*, September 26, 2011, p. 68.
2. "What Are You Doing on the Web? Most Under 30 Are Wasting Time," *Los Angeles Times*, December 2, 2011, www.latimes.com.
3. Randy Garner, "Post-It Note Persuasion: A Sticky Influence," *Journal of Consumer Psychology* 15, no. 2, 2005, pp. 230–237.
4. Martijn G. de Jong, Rik Pieters, and Jean-Paul Fox, "Reducing Social Desirability Bias Through Item Randomized Response: An Application to Measure Underreported Desires," *Journal of Marketing Research*, February 2010, pp. 14–27.
5. Scott Koperski, "Tourism Focus Group Held," *Beatrice Daily Sun (Nebraska)*, December 17, 2011, www.beatricedailysun.com.
6. "Getting Close to the Customer," *Knowledge@Wharton*, May 5, 2004, http://knowledge.wharton.upenn.edu.
7. Melanie Scarborough, "Customers as Advisers," *Community Banker*, January 2008, p. 20.

8. Steve Lohr, "Are We Suffering Global Gadget Fatigue?" *New York Times*, December 12, 2011, www.nytimes.com.

9. Ronald B. Lieber and Joyce E. Davis, "Storytelling: A New Way to Get Close to Your Customer," *Fortune*, February 3, 1997, pp. 102–108.

10. Sandra Yin, "Marketing Tools: The Power of Images," *American Demographics*, November 2001, pp. 32–33.

11. Deborah D. Heisley and Sidney J. Levy, "Autodriving: A Photoelicitation Technique," *Journal of Consumer Research*, December 1991, pp. 257–272.

12. Robin A. Coulter, Gerald Zaltman, and Keith S. Coulter, "Interpreting Consumer Perceptions of Advertising," *Journal of Advertising* 30, Winter 2001, pp. 1–21; and Morris B. Holbrook, "Collective Stereographic Photo Essays," *International Journal of Research in Marketing*, July 1998, pp. 201–221.

13. Christine Bittar, "Up in Arms," *Brandweek*, June 18, 2001, pp. 17–18.

14. Steven R. Thompson, "Dr Pepper to Test More 10-Calorie Drinks in Columbus," *Dallas Business Journal*, December 20, 2011, www.bizjournals.com; and Mae Anderson, "Dr Pepper Ten 'Not for Women,'" *USA Today*, October 10, 2011, www.usatoday.com.

15. Roy C. Anderson and Eric N. Hansen, "The Impact of Environmental Certification on Preferences for Wood Furniture: A Conjoint Analysis Approach," *Forest Products Journal*, March 2004, pp. 42–50.

16. Ellen Byron, "A Virtual View of the Store Aisle," *Wall Street Journal*, October 3, 2007, p. B1.

17. Daniel Terdiman, "In Silicon Valley, a Retail Store as Product Laboratory," *CNet News*, August 18, 2011, http://news.cnet.com.

18. Emily Steel, "The New Focus Groups: Online Networks," *Wall Street Journal*, January 14, 2008, p. B6.

19. Jennifer Lach, "Data Mining Digs In," *American Demographics*, July 1999, pp. 38–45.

20. Geoff Colvin, "Walmart's Makeover," *Fortune*, December 26, 2011, pp. 50–55; Steve Lohr, "Reaping Results: Data-Mining Goes Mainstream," *New York Times*, May 20, 2007, p. BU-3; Constance L. Hays, "What They Know About You," *New York Times*, November 14, 2004, sec. 3, pp. 1, 9; and Jon Hamilton, "Big-Box Stores' Hurricane Prep Starts Early," *NPR*, August 26, 2011, www.npr.org.

21. Robert V. Kozinets, "The Field Behind the Screen: Using Netnography for Marketing Research in Online Communities," *Journal of Marketing Research*, February 2002, pp. 61–72; and Jonathan Reynolds and Jiyao Xun, "Applying Netnography to Market Research: The Case of the Online Forum," *Journal of Targeting, Measurement, and Analysis for Marketing*, March 2010, p. 17.

22. Caterina Sismeiro and Randolph E. Bucklin, "Modeling Purchase Behavior at an E-Commerce Web Site: A Task-Completion Approach," *Journal of Marketing Research*, August 2004, pp. 306–323.

23. Tom Loftus, "Google Aims to Answer the 'Why?' Behind Ad Targeting," *Wall Street Journal*, November 1, 2011, www.wsj.com.

24. "Cookie Law Deferred for One Year," *BBC News*, May 25, 2011, www.bbc.co.uk.

25. Etan Vlessing, "Canada's Privacy Czar Tells Advertisers to Curb Online Tracking," *Hollywood Reporter*, December 6, 2011, www.hollywoodreporter.com.

26. "Can Twitter Predict the Future?" *Economist*, June 4, 2011, p. 12.

27. David Talbot, "A Social-Media Decoder," *Technology Review*, November–December 2011, p. 44ff.

28. Elisabeth Horwitt, "Listening to the Voice of the Customer," *ComputerWorld*, October 10, 2011, p. 28.

29. See Hilke Plassmann, Carolyn Yoon, Fred M. Feinberg, and Baba Shiv, "Consumer Neuroscience," in *International Encyclopedia of Marketing, Volume 3—Consumer Behavior*, volume editors Richard P. Bagozzi and Ayalla A. Ruvio, editors in chief Jagdish N. Sheth and Naresh K. Malhotra (Wiley Publishing, 2011).

30. Thales Texeira, Michel Wedel, and Rik Pieters, "Emotion-Induced Engagement in Internet Video Ads," *Journal of Marketing Research*, April 2012, pp. 144–159.

31. Carolyn Yoon, Angela H. Gutchess, Fred Feinberg, and Thad A. Polk, "A Functional Magnetic Resonance Imaging Study of Neural Dissociations Between Brand and Person Judgments," *Journal of Consumer Research* 33, no. 1, 2006, pp. 31–40; and Colin F. Camerer, George F. Loewenstein, and Drazen Prelec, "Neuroeconomics: How Neuroscience Can Inform Economics," *Journal of Economic Literature*, March 2005, pp. 9–64.

32. Adam L. Penenberg, "NeuroFocus Uses Neuromarketing to Hack Your Brain," *Fast Company*, August 8, 2011, www.fastcompany.com.

33. Amber Haq, "This Is Your Brain on Advertising," *BusinessWeek Online*, October 8, 2007, www.businessweek.com.

34. Adam L. Penenberg, "NeuroFocus Uses Neuromarketing to Hack Your Brain."

35. Emma Hutchings, "IKEA Campaign Highlights the Craftsman to Transform 'Consumer Perceptions,'" *PSFK*, December 15, 2011, www.psfk.com.

36. Manoj Nair, "Raymond Tailors Retail Strategy to Expand in Gulf Markets," *Gulf News*, December 22, 2011, www.gulfnews.com.

37. Lee van der Voo, "New FTC Rules Take Swipe at Greenwashing," *Sustainable Business Oregon*, October 8, 2010, www.sustainablebusinessoregon.com.

38. Chris Pullig, Carolyn J. Simmons, and Richard G. Netemeyer, "Brand Dilution: When Do New Brands Hurt Existing Brands?" *Journal of Marketing*, April 2006, pp. 52–66.

39. Joe Mandese, "Observers Rock Research," *Television Week*, March 1, 2004, p. 35.

40. Frank Browning, "The Restaurant of the Future: A Living Lab," *NPR*, May 17, 2009, www.npr.org; and Marlise Simons, "In the Netherlands, Eat, Drink, and Be Monitored," *New York Times*, November 26, 2007, p. A4.

41. John F. Gaski and Michael J. Etzel, "National Aggregate Consumer Sentiment Toward Marketing: A Thirty-Year Retrospective and Analysis," *Journal of Consumer Research* 31, no. 4, 2005, pp. 859–867.

42. Annalyn Censky, "Malls Stop Tracking Shoppers' Cell Phones," *CNN Money*, November 28, 2011, www.cnn.com.

43. Kenneth C. Schneider and Cynthia K. Holm, "Deceptive Practices in Marketing Research: The Consumer's Viewpoint," *California Management Review*, Spring 1982, pp. 89–97.

The Psychological Core

PART 2

2 Motivation, Ability, and Opportunity   44

3 From Exposure to Comprehension   72

4 Memory and Knowledge   99

5 Attitudes Based on High Effort   127

6 Attitudes Based on Low Effort   157

CONSUMER BEHAVIOR IS greatly affected by the amount of effort that consumers put into their consumption behaviors and decisions. Chapter 2 describes three critical factors that affect effort: the (1) motivation, (2) ability, and (3) opportunity consumers have to engage in behaviors and make decisions. Chapter 3 discusses how consumers come into contact with marketing stimuli (exposure), notice them (attention), and perceive them.

Chapter 4 continues the topic by discussing how consumers put information into memory, compare information with their existing knowledge, and retrieve it from memory. Chapter 5 describes what happens when consumers exert a great deal of effort in forming and changing attitudes. Finally, Chapter 6 discusses how attitudes can be influenced when consumer effort is low.

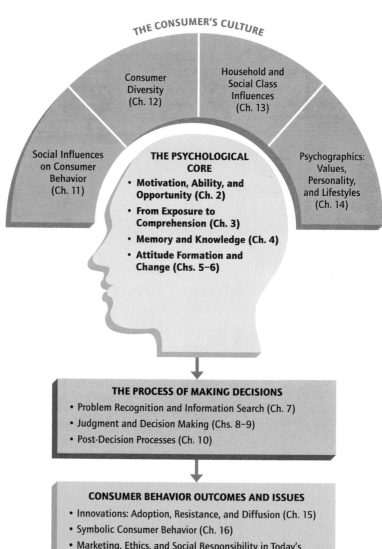

THE CONSUMER'S CULTURE

Consumer Diversity (Ch. 12)

Household and Social Class Influences (Ch. 13)

Social Influences on Consumer Behavior (Ch. 11)

THE PSYCHOLOGICAL CORE
- Motivation, Ability, and Opportunity (Ch. 2)
- From Exposure to Comprehension (Ch. 3)
- Memory and Knowledge (Ch. 4)
- Attitude Formation and Change (Chs. 5–6)

Psychographics: Values, Personality, and Lifestyles (Ch. 14)

THE PROCESS OF MAKING DECISIONS
- Problem Recognition and Information Search (Ch. 7)
- Judgment and Decision Making (Chs. 8–9)
- Post-Decision Processes (Ch. 10)

CONSUMER BEHAVIOR OUTCOMES AND ISSUES
- Innovations: Adoption, Resistance, and Diffusion (Ch. 15)
- Symbolic Consumer Behavior (Ch. 16)
- Marketing, Ethics, and Social Responsibility in Today's Consumer Society (Ch. 17)

CHAPTER 2

MOTIVATION, ABILITY, AND OPPORTUNITY

After studying this chapter, you will be able to

1. Discuss the four types of influences that affect the consumer's motivation to process information, make a decision, or take an action.

2. Explain how financial, cognitive, emotional, physical, social, and cultural resources, plus age and education,

can affect the individual's ability to engage in consumer behaviors.

3. Identify the three main types of influences on the consumer's opportunity to process information and acquire, consume, or dispose of products.

© Andre Jenny/Alamy

INTRODUCTION

Movie Tavern Markets Food and a Flick

Dinner and a movie? Yes—together! Movie Tavern is part of the nationwide trend toward pairing dinner *with* a movie. With so many consumers watching movies at home on cable TV or streamed from the Internet, it can be a challenge to fill cinema seats night after night, day after day. To draw time-pressured audiences into its theaters, Movie Tavern offers two complementary leisure-time activities that delight the senses and provide a unique, affordable experience. Headquartered in Texas, Movie Tavern has 16 U.S. multiscreen locations where consumers can see the latest film hits (in 3D too) and enjoy a casual meal delivered to their easy-chair seats. Grown-ups can sip margaritas and eat full-course dinners or just have dessert, while children snack on mini-corn dogs and a milk shake.

Movie Tavern faces growing competition from big industry players like AMC Entertainments, which operates its own "Fork & Screen" program, and Regal, which offers the "Cinebarre" dine-in program at selected theaters. Movie Tavern's CEO says one appeal is that "dinner and a movie is a two-and-a-half hour experience, rather than a four-hour experience." Breakfast screenings of family-friendly movies are available on weekend mornings, and some Movie Taverns also air operas and other special events in HD. The popcorn is always fresh and hot, no matter what time of day.[1]

Movie Tavern understands that consumer motivation, ability, and opportunity exert a powerful influence on a consumer's acquisition, usage, and disposition decisions. The movie-and-meal combination is consistent with achieving goals such as saving time and money and with meeting needs for food as well as for socializing. The movie-and-meal deal allows consumers to attain two goals at the same time (eat and watch). Making it fast and easy for consumers to find out about Movie Tavern's latest movies and menu items (from ads, the company's website, on-site signage, and other sources) increases the ability and opportunity for purchasing and consumption.

Whether motivated consumers actually achieve a goal depends on whether they have the *ability* and the *opportunity* to achieve it. Ability depends on five categories of resources plus age and education. Opportunity is determined by time, distractions, and the complexity, amount, repetition, and control of information to which consumers are exposed.

CONSUMER MOTIVATION AND ITS EFFECTS

Motivation An inner state of arousal that provides energy needed to achieve a goal.

Motivation comes from the Latin word "movere," which means "to move." Motivation is what moves people. It is defined as "an inner state of arousal," with the aroused energy directed to achieving a goal.[2] The motivated consumer is energized, ready, and willing to engage in a goal-relevant activity. For example, if you learn that a much-anticipated electronic game will be released next Tuesday, you may be motivated to be ready to buy and download early that morning. Consumers can be motivated to engage in behaviors, make decisions, or process information, and this motivation can be seen in the context of acquiring, using, or disposing of an offering. Let's look first at the effects of motivation, as shown in Exhibit 2.1.

High-Effort Behavior

One outcome of motivation is behavior that takes considerable effort. For example, if you are motivated to buy a good car, you will research vehicles online, look at ads, visit dealerships, and so on. Likewise, if you are motivated to lose weight, you will buy low-fat foods, eat smaller portions, and exercise. Motivation not only drives behaviors consistent with a goal but also creates a willingness to expend time and energy engaging in these behaviors. Thus, someone motivated to buy a smartphone may earn extra money for it, drive through a storm to reach the store, and then wait in line to buy it. Note, however, that consumers try to match anticipated and actual effort. If they believe their anticipated effort will be too much—if it is too much trouble to wait on line, for instance—they will simplify the decision (by ordering online or waiting until the next day). Conversely, if consumers think an important decision will be too simple, they will complicate it with extra effort.[3]

High-Effort Information Processing and Decision Making

Motivation also affects how we process information and make decisions.[4] When consumers are highly motivated to achieve a goal, they are more likely to pay careful attention to it, think about it, attempt to understand or comprehend goal-relevant information, evaluate that information critically, and try to remember it for later use. This takes a lot of effort. For example, if you are motivated to buy a new piano keyboard, you might scour websites looking for a sale. If someone mentions an online retailer that has keyboard sales from time to time, you might subscribe to that retailer's promotional e-mails.

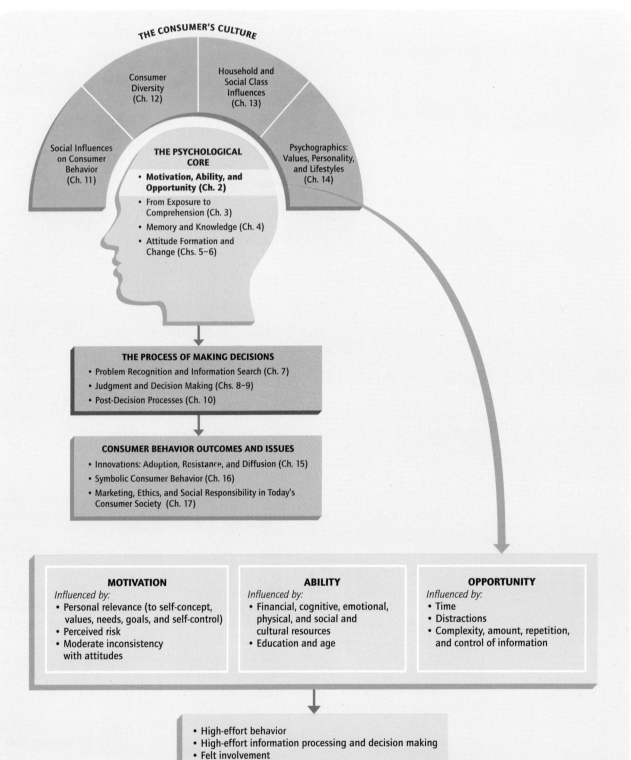

THE CONSUMER'S CULTURE

Consumer Diversity (Ch. 12)

Household and Social Class Influences (Ch. 13)

Social Influences on Consumer Behavior (Ch. 11)

THE PSYCHOLOGICAL CORE
- **Motivation, Ability, and Opportunity (Ch. 2)**
- From Exposure to Comprehension (Ch. 3)
- Memory and Knowledge (Ch. 4)
- Attitude Formation and Change (Chs. 5–6)

Psychographics: Values, Personality, and Lifestyles (Ch. 14)

THE PROCESS OF MAKING DECISIONS
- Problem Recognition and Information Search (Ch. 7)
- Judgment and Decision Making (Chs. 8–9)
- Post-Decision Processes (Ch. 10)

CONSUMER BEHAVIOR OUTCOMES AND ISSUES
- Innovations: Adoption, Resistance, and Diffusion (Ch. 15)
- Symbolic Consumer Behavior (Ch. 16)
- Marketing, Ethics, and Social Responsibility in Today's Consumer Society (Ch. 17)

MOTIVATION
Influenced by:
- Personal relevance (to self-concept, values, needs, goals, and self-control)
- Perceived risk
- Moderate inconsistency with attitudes

ABILITY
Influenced by:
- Financial, cognitive, emotional, physical, and social and cultural resources
- Education and age

OPPORTUNITY
Influenced by:
- Time
- Distractions
- Complexity, amount, repetition, and control of information

- High-effort behavior
- High-effort information processing and decision making
- Felt involvement

© Cengage Learning 2013

Exhibit 2.1

Chapter Overview: Motivation, Ability, and Opportunity

Motivation, ability, and opportunity (MAO) to engage in various consumer behaviors are affected by many factors. Outcomes of high MAO include (1) goal-relevant behavior, (2) high-effort information processing and decision making, and (3) felt involvement.

However, when consumers have low motivation, they devote little effort to processing information and making decisions. For example, your motivation to purchase the best paper clips on the market is likely to be low. You would devote little attention to learning about the characteristics of paperclips, and you would not stop to think about what it would be like to use various types of paperclips (colored or uncolored, aluminum or steel, small or large). You may use decision-making shortcuts, such as deciding to buy the cheapest brand or the same brand you bought the last time.[5] This is, in fact, how consumers tend to buy common grocery products.

Most research on consumer behavior has focused on consumers' motivation to process information *accurately*, as just described. Recent research has focused on a different type of motivation involved in information processing that is called **motivated reasoning**. When consumers engage in motivated reasoning, they process information in a biased way so that they can obtain the particular conclusion they want to reach.[6]

For example, if your goal is to lose weight, and you see an ad for a diet product, you might process the ad in a biased way to convince yourself that the product will work for you. If we want to believe that we are not vulnerable to the ill effects of smoking, we may be more likely to smoke if we are aware of smoking cessation products that are touted as "remedies." Because remedies exist to help stop smoking, we can use motivated reasoning to convince ourselves that smoking is not so bad after all.[7]

As another example, because we want to think about good things that can happen to us rather than bad things, we may underestimate the likelihood of facing problems such as becoming ill—and fail to take preventive steps to avoid doing so.[8] We may be particularly prone to motivated reasoning when our self-esteem is at stake or when we desperately hope to achieve a particular goal (like weight loss) or avoid a negative outcome (like becoming ill).[9] Motivated reasoning is a developing field, and most of the discussion that follows focuses on the motivation to process information accurately.

Felt Involvement

A final outcome of motivation is that it evokes a psychological state in consumers called *involvement*. Researchers use the term **felt involvement** to refer to the psychological experience of the motivated consumer.[10]

Types of Involvement

Felt involvement can be (1) enduring, (2) situational, (3) cognitive, or (4) affective.[11]

Enduring involvement exists when we show interest in an offering or activity over a long period of time.[12] Car enthusiasts are intrinsically interested in cars and exhibit enduring involvement in them. Enthusiasts engage in activities that reveal this interest (e.g., going to car shows, visiting car websites, and going to dealerships). In most instances, consumers experience **situational (temporary) involvement** with an offering or activity. For example, consumers who exhibit no enduring involvement with cars may be involved in the car-buying process when they are in the market for a new car. After they buy the car, their involvement with new cars declines dramatically.

Researchers also distinguish between cognitive and affective involvement.[13] **Cognitive involvement** means that the consumer is interested in thinking about and processing information related to his or her goal. The goal therefore includes learning about the offering. A figure-skating fan who is interested in learning all about ice-dance champions Meryl Davis and Charlie White and the technicalities of their performances would be exhibiting cognitive involvement. **Affective involvement** means that the consumer is willing to expend emotional energy in or has heightened feelings about an offering or activity. The consumer who listens to music to experience intense emotions or to relive a particular event in life is exhibiting strong affective involvement.

Objects of Involvement

As many of this chapter's examples indicate, consumers may exhibit cognitive and/or affective involvement in objects. These objects can include *a product or retail category* such as cars or cosmetic stores or can involve *experiences* such as white-water rafting.[14] You might be involved with clothing because you enjoy shopping for such products and see them as important for your self-expression.[15]

Motivated reasoning
Processing information in a way that allows consumers to reach the conclusion that they want to reach.

Felt involvement
Self-reported arousal or interest in an offering, activity, or decision.

Enduring involvement
Long-term interest in an offering, activity, or decision.

Situational (temporary) involvement Temporary interest in an offering, activity, or decision, often caused by situational circumstances.

Cognitive involvement
Interest in thinking about and learning information pertinent to an offering, activity, or decisions.

Affective involvement
Interest in expending emotional energy and evoking deep feelings about an offering, activity, or decision.

Consumers can also exhibit cognitive and/or affective *involvement with a brand* by being emotionally attached to it, as one might be with a particular musical band or one's iPod. When one is emotionally attached to and involved with a brand, one views the brand as an extension of oneself and feels a great deal of passion toward the brand.[16] Consumers can also be *involved with ads* that are interesting or relevant to them.[17] In Japan, ads that emphasize interpersonal relationships, social circumstances, and nonverbal expressions generate more involvement than ads with clearly articulated and spoken messages.[18] Consumers may also be *involved with a medium* (like TV, newspapers, or the Internet) or with a particular article or show in which an ad is placed. The Super Bowl's huge global audience demonstrates how involved consumers are with this televised event. A person may get so involved in interacting with a particular company's website that he or she may view it as "play."[19]

Response involvement Interest in certain decisions and behaviors.

Consumers involved in certain decisions and behaviors are experiencing **response involvement**.[20] For example, consumers may be highly involved in the process of deciding between brands. Because consumers can be involved with many different entities, it is important to specify the *object of involvement* when using the term *involvement*. For instance, consumers who are involved with brands because they are attached to them are unlikely to be involved in deciding which brand to buy since they already think their brand is the best. Similarly, consumers can be very involved in an ad because it is funny or interesting, yet they may not be involved in the advertised brand because they are loyal to another brand.

We are motivated to behave, process information, or engage in effortful *decision making* about things that we feel are personally relevant. And we will experience considerable involvement when buying, using, or disposing of them. Think about all the behaviors that you engaged in when deciding where to go to college—obtaining applications and information packets, searching the Web, visiting campuses, weighing the information about each school, and choosing the school you will attend. You probably found the task of making this decision personally involving and were interested, enthusiastic, and perhaps overwhelmed during the process. Finally, we are also motivated to think deeply about issues pertinent to a given decision when we believe we will have to justify or explain our decisions.[21]

WHAT AFFECTS MOTIVATION?

Because motivation can affect outcomes of interest to marketers (like goal-relevant behaviors such as purchasing, effortful information processing, and felt involvement), it is important for marketers to understand what affects motivation. If marketers know what the drivers of consumer motivation are, they may be able to predict consumers' motivation to think about, be involved with, and/or process information about their brand or ad and then develop marketing tactics to influence this motivation. As shown in Exhibit 2.1, motivation is affected when consumers regard something as (1) personally relevant; (2) consistent with their values, needs, goals, emotions, and self-control processes; (3) risky; and/or (4) moderately inconsistent with their prior attitudes.

Personal Relevance

Personal relevance Something that has a direct bearing on the self and has potentially significant consequences or implications for our lives.

Something will be motivating to the extent it has **personal relevance**—that is, the extent to which it has a direct bearing on and significant implications for your life.[22] For example, if you learn that your laptop computer's battery is being recalled because it can overheat and cause a fire, you will probably find this issue to be personally relevant. Careers, romantic relationships, a car, an apartment or house, clothes, and hobbies are likely to be personally relevant because their consequences are significant for you. This relevance fuels your motivation to process information, make decisions, and take actions.

Consistency with Self-Concept

Self-concept Our mental view of who we are.

Any kind of offering (a good, a service, a person, a place) may be personally relevant to the extent that it bears on your **self-concept**, or your view of yourself and the way you think others view you. Self-concept helps us define who we are, and it frequently motivates our behavior.[23] Note that different parts of a self-concept can be salient at different times.[24] When we buy clothing, we are often making a statement about some aspect of who we are—such as a professional, a student, or a sports fan. Identifying with a brand and making an emotional connection with it strengthens brand loyalty and makes those consumers less price sensitive toward that brand.[25] Harley-Davidson customers, for instance, see the brand as relevant to their self-concept and are therefore loyal. In a similar way, reality TV shows can be relevant when viewers identify with the lives of the people on the show.[26]

Values

Values Abstract, enduring beliefs about what is right/wrong, important, or good/bad.

Consumers are more motivated to attend to and process information when they find it relevant to their **values**—abstract beliefs that guide what people regard as important or good. Thus, if you see intellectual development as very important, you are likely to be motivated to engage in behaviors that are consistent with this value, such as pursuing a college degree. Other values may include family security, protecting the environment, and feeling fit (see Exhibit 2.2). (You'll read more about values in Chapter 14.)

Needs

Need An internal state of tension caused by disequilibrium from an ideal/desired physical or psychological state.

Consumers also find things personally relevant when they have a bearing on activated needs. A **need** is an internal state of tension caused by disequilibrium from an ideal or desired state. For example, at certain times of the day, your stomach begins to feel uncomfortable. You realize it is time to get something to eat, and you are motivated to direct your behavior toward certain outcomes (such as opening the refrigerator). Eating satisfies your need and removes the tension—in this case, hunger. Once you are motivated to satisfy a particular need, objects unrelated to that need seem less attractive. Thus, if you are motivated to fix your hair because you're having a bad hair day, a product such as styling gel will seem more attractive and important than, say, popcorn.[27] Needs can also lead us away from a product or service: You might stay away from the dentist because you want to avoid pain.

What needs do consumers experience? Psychologist Abraham Maslow's theory groups needs into the five categories shown in Exhibit 2.3: (1) physiological (the need for food, water, and sleep); (2) safety (the need for shelter, protection, and security); (3) social (the need for affection, friendship, and to belong); (4) egoistic (the need for prestige, success, accomplishment, and self-esteem); and (5) self-actualization (the need for self-fulfillment and enriching experiences).[28] Within this hierarchy, lower-level needs generally must be satisfied before higher-level needs become activated. Before we can worry about prestige, we must meet lower-level needs for food, water, and so on.

Although Maslow's hierarchy brings useful organization to the complex issue of needs, it is of course too simplistic. First, needs are not always ordered exactly as in this hierarchy. Some consumers might place a higher priority on buying lottery tickets than on buying necessities such as food. Also, consumers may be able to appreciate art and engage in cultural activities even when they feel insecure or socially excluded. Thus, lower-order needs need to be fulfilled before higher-order needs become important to consumers. Moreover, the hierarchy ignores the intensity of needs and the resulting effect on motivation. Finally, the ordering of needs may

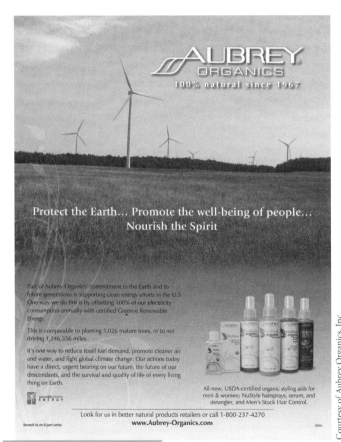

Courtesy of Aubrey Organics, Inc.

Exhibit 2.2

Values

Consumers are more motivated by ads if they appeal to their values, such as organic products that advertise protecting the environment.

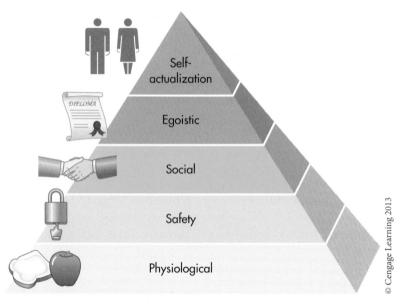

© Cengage Learning 2013

Exhibit 2.3

Maslow's Hierarchy of Needs

Maslow suggested that needs can be categorized into a basic hierarchy. People fulfill lower-order needs (e.g., physiological needs for food, water, sleep) before they fulfill higher-order needs.

© Cengage Learning 2013

Exhibit 2.4

Categorizing Needs

Needs can be categorized according to whether they are (1) social or nonsocial and (2) functional, symbolic, or hedonic in nature. This categorization method helps marketers think about consumers' needs.

Functional need Need that motivates the search for offerings that solve consumption-related problems.

not be consistent across cultures. In some societies, for instance, social needs and belonging may be higher in the hierarchy than egoistic needs. Still, it is a useful idea that individuals and cultures share certain basic needs, that these are somehow hierarchically organized, and that these needs influence consumer motivation and specific decisions.

Types of Needs

Another way to categorize needs is as (1) social and nonsocial needs or as (2) functional, symbolic, and hedonic needs[29] (see Exhibit 2.4).

▶ *Social needs* are externally directed and relate to other individuals. Fulfilling these needs thus requires the presence or actions of other people. For example, the need for status drives our desire to have others hold us in high regard; the need for support drives us to have others relieve us of our burdens; the need for models reflects a wish to have others show us how to behave. We may be motivated to buy products like Hallmark cards or use social media such as Facebook because they help us achieve a need for affiliation. In fact, consumers may even spend on illegal products such as drugs to satisfy a higher-level need like becoming part of a group.[30] Other products may be valued because they are consistent with our need for status or our need to be unique. We also have antisocial needs—needs for space and psychological distance from other people. Plane seats that are too close together violate our need for space and motivate us to escape the confining environment.

▶ *Nonsocial needs* are those for which achievement is not based on other people. Our needs for sleep, novelty, control, uniqueness, and understanding, which involve only ourselves, can affect the usage of certain goods and services (see Exhibit 2.5). We might purchase the same brand repeatedly to maintain consistency in our world—or we might buy something different to fulfill a need for variety.

▶ *Functional needs* may be social or nonsocial. **Functional needs** motivate the search for products that solve consumption-related problems. For example, you might consider buying a product like a car with side air bags because it appeals to your safety needs (a functional, nonsocial need). For mothers with young children, hiring a nanny would solve the need for support (a functional, social need).

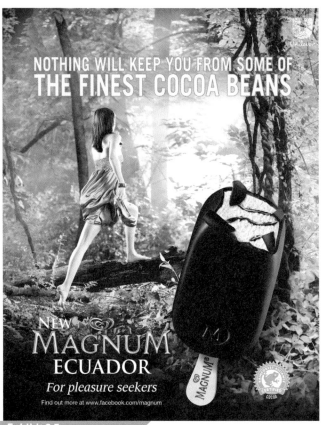

NOTHING WILL KEEP YOU FROM SOME OF
THE FINEST COCOA BEANS

NEW
MAGNUM.
ECUADOR
For pleasure seekers
Find out more at www.facebook.com/magnum

Image Courtesy of The Advertising Archives

Exhibit 2.5

Needs
Consumers respond to ads that resonate with their specific needs, such as non-social needs, like this ad for ice cream that targets pleasure and uniqueness.

Symbolic need Need that relates to how we perceive ourselves, how we are perceived by others, how we relate to others, and the esteem in which we are held by others.

Hedonic need Need that relates to sensory pleasure.

▶ *Symbolic needs* affect how we perceive ourselves and how others perceive us. Achievement, independence, and self-control are **symbolic needs** because they are connected with our sense of self. Similarly, our need for uniqueness is symbolic because it drives consumption decisions about how we express our identity.[31] The need to avoid rejection and the need for achievement, status, affiliation, and belonging are symbolic because they reflect our social position or role. For example, some consumers wear stylish Christian Louboutin shoes to express their social standing.[32]

▶ *Hedonic needs* include needs for sensory stimulation, cognitive stimulation, and novelty (nonsocial hedonic needs) and needs for reinforcement, sex, and play (social hedonic needs). These **hedonic needs** reflect our inherent desires for sensory pleasure. In fact, consumers exposed to sexual marketing cues tend to buy sense-rewarding products, like snacks, more quickly than when such cues are not present.[33] If the desire to satisfy hedonic needs is intense enough, it can inspire fantasizing about specific goods, simultaneously pleasurable and discomforting.[34] Consumers in India may go to luxury shopping areas like Mumbai's Palladium Mall for the eye-catching ambiance.[35]

▶ *Needs for cognition and stimulation* also affect motivation and behavior. Consumers want to understand the world themselves and see some structure in it. Consumers with a high need for cognition[36] (a need for understanding and mental stimulation) enjoy being involved in mentally taxing activities like reading and deeply processing information when making decisions. People with a low need for cognition may prefer activities that require less thought, such as watching TV, and are less likely to actively process information during decision making. In addition, consumers often need other kinds of stimulation. Those with a high optimum stimulation level enjoy a lot of sensory stimulation and tend to be involved in shopping and seeking brand information.[37] They also show heightened involvement in ads. Consumers with thrill-seeking tendencies enjoy activities like skydiving or white-water rafting. In contrast, consumers who feel overstimulated want to get away from people, noise, and demands—a desire revealed in the popularity of vacations at nature retreats or monasteries.

Characteristics of Needs
All of the preceding needs share several characteristics:

▶ *Needs are dynamic.* Needs are never fully satisfied; satisfaction is only temporary. Clearly, eating once will not satisfy our hunger forever. Also, as soon as one need is satisfied, new needs emerge. After we have eaten a meal, we might feel the need to be with others (the need for affiliation). Thus, needs are dynamic because daily life is a constant process of need fulfillment.

▶ *Needs exist in a hierarchy.* Although several needs may be activated at any one time, some assume more importance than others. You may experience a need to eat during an exam, but your need for achievement may assume a higher priority—so you stay to finish the test. Despite this hierarchy, many needs may be activated simultaneously and influence your acquisition, usage, and disposition behaviors. Thus, your decision to plan your next holiday with friends over dinner may be driven by a combination of needs for stimulation, companionship, and food.

> ▶ *Needs can be internally or externally aroused.* Although many needs are internally activated, some needs can be externally cued. Smelling pizza cooking in the apartment next door may, for example, affect your perceived need for food.

> ▶ *Needs can conflict.* There are various types of need conflicts.

Approach-avoidance conflict An inner struggle about acquiring or consuming an offering that fulfills one need but fails to fulfill another.

> ▶ An **approach-avoidance conflict** occurs when the consumer wants both to engage in the behavior and to avoid it. Teenagers may experience an approach-avoidance conflict in deciding whether to smoke cigarettes. Although they may believe that others will think they are cool for smoking (consistent with the need to belong and affiliate), they also know that smoking is bad for them (incompatible with the need for safety).

Approach-approach conflict An inner struggle about which offering to acquire when each can satisfy an important but different need.

> ▶ An **approach-approach conflict** occurs when the consumer must choose between two or more equally desirable options that fulfill different needs. A consumer who is invited to a career-night function (consistent with achievement needs) might experience an approach-approach conflict if he is invited to see a basketball game with friends (consistent with affiliation and stimulation needs) on the same evening. This person will experience conflict if he views both options as equally desirable.

Avoidance-avoidance conflict An inner struggle about which offering to acquire when neither can satisfy an important but different need.

> ▶ An **avoidance-avoidance conflict** occurs when the consumer must choose between two equally undesirable options, such as going home alone right after a late meeting (not satisfying a need for safety) or waiting another hour until a friend can drive her home (not satisfying a need for convenience). Conflict occurs when neither option is desirable.

Identifying Needs

Because needs influence motivation and its effects, marketers are keenly interested in identifying and measuring them. However, consumers are often unaware of their needs and have trouble communicating them to researchers. Inferring needs from consumers' behaviors is also difficult because a given need might not be linked to a specific behavior. In other words, the same need (for example, affiliation) can be exhibited in various and diverse behaviors (visiting friends, going to the gym), and the same behavior (going to the gym) can reflect various needs (affiliation, achievement). Consider the activity of shopping. One study found that when women shop in drugstores, they are seeking information about items that provide peace of mind (satisfying needs for safety and well-being). When they shop in club stores like Costco, they are seeking adventure and entertainment (satisfying the need for stimulation).[38]

Inferring needs in a cross-cultural context is particularly difficult. For example, some research indicates that U.S. consumers use toothpaste primarily for its cavity-reducing capabilities (a functional need). In contrast, consumers in England and some French-speaking areas of Canada use toothpaste primarily to freshen breath (a hedonic need). French women drink mineral water so they will look better (a symbolic need), whereas German consumers drink it for its health powers (a functional need).[39]

Given these difficulties, marketers sometimes use indirect research techniques to uncover consumers' needs.[40] One technique is to ask consumers to interpret a set of relatively ambiguous stimuli such as cartoons, word associations, incomplete sentences, and incomplete stories. Using Exhibit 2.6, one consumer might reveal needs for esteem by interpreting the man in the cartoon as thinking, "My friends will think I'm really cool for riding in this car!" Another might reveal needs for affiliation by filling in the cartoon with "I could take all my friends for rides with me."

When one study asked cigarette smokers why they smoked, most said they enjoyed it and believed that smoking in moderation was fine. However, when they were given incomplete sentences like "People who never smoke are ___," research participants filled in the blanks with words like *happier* and *wiser*. And when given sentences like "Teenagers who smoke are ___," respondents answered with words like *crazy* and *foolish*. These smokers were clearly more concerned about smoking than their explicit answers indicated.[41]

SURVEY

A. Cartoon drawing:
What do you think the people in this cartoon are thinking?

B. Sentence completion:
Fill in the blanks with the first word that comes to your mind:

1. The perfect gift_____.

2. The gifts I still treasure_____.

3. If I give a gift to myself_____.

C. Tell a story:
Tell a story about the gift being unwrapped in this picture.

Exhibit 2.6

Uncovering Consumers' Needs

Marketers sometimes uncover consumers' needs using ambiguous stimuli like cartoon drawings, sentence completion tasks, and tell-a-story tasks. The idea is that consumers will project their needs, wishes, and fantasies onto these ambiguous stimuli.

Goal Outcome that we would like to achieve.

Exhibit 2.7

Consumer Goals

Consumers are more likely to be involved in ads when brands are touted as relevant to consumers' goals (e.g., losing weight).

MORE LOVE, LESS HANDLE.

BEN & JERRY'S Original U.S. Recipe **Cherry Garcia** LOW FAT FROZEN YOGURT
with Cherries & Dark Chocolatey Cho...

BEN & JERRY'S Original U.S. Recipe **Chocolate Fudge Brownie** LOW FAT FROZEN YOGURT
with Chocolate Brownie Pieces

NEW! Ben & Jerry's Frozen Yogurt - only 3% fat

Image Courtesy of The Advertising Archives

Goals

Goals are also an important influence on personal relevance and motivation.[42] A **goal** is a particular end state or outcome that a person would like to achieve. Goals are more specific and concrete than needs. For instance, you might have the goals to lose weight before the summer season starts, to save a particular amount of money to buy new furniture, or to study every day for an upcoming exam (see Exhibit 2.7).

Goal Setting and Pursuit

Consumers set goals that they try to pursue over time. Goal setting comprises what to pursue (such as losing weight or saving money) and at what level (such as losing four pounds or saving $500).[43] As shown in Exhibit 2.8, activities during goal pursuit follow a certain sequence. After setting a goal (losing four pounds in one month), consumers are motivated to form a goal intention, plan to take action (seek out low-fat foods, join a gym), implement and control the action (through diet and exercise), and evaluate success or failure in attaining the goal (check weight each week). Consumers use what they learn by achieving or not achieving the goal as feedback for future goal setting and pursuit. Consumer behavior is a continuous cycle of setting goals, pursuing them, determining success and failure of goal pursuit, and adapting the goals.

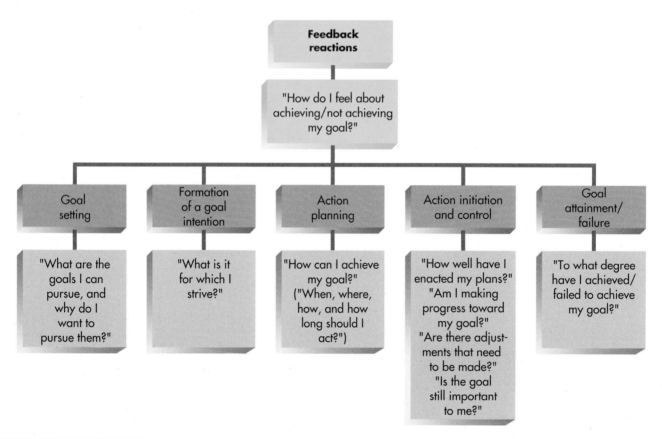

Exhibit 2.8

Goal Setting and Pursuit in Consumer Behavior

The process of setting and pursuing goals is circular: How a person feels about achieving or not achieving a goal affects what new goals that person sets and why. This process affects the individual's motivation to initiate or continue behaviors relevant to the goal that has been set.

Source: Richard P. Bagozzi and Utpal Dholakia, "Goal Setting and Goal Striving in Consumer Behavior," *Journal of Marketing*, vol. 63, 1999, p. 20. Reprinted with permission of American Marketing Association.

Goals and Effort

Consumers vary in how much effort they exert to achieve a goal. You might want to lose weight but might not put much effort into doing so. Furthermore, if you perceive that you have failed in achieving a goal (such as saving a certain amount of money), you will be less motivated and, subsequently, may perform even more poorly in relation to that goal.[44] The more easily consumers can visualize their goals, the more motivated and committed they are to putting in efforts toward those goals.[45] Some research also shows that the amount of effort people exert to achieve a goal depends not only on how important the goal is to them but also on how well they are doing in achieving other, potentially unrelated, goals. For example, if you are making progress toward a goal of getting good grades, you may also choose to pursue a different goal, such as starting a new exercise routine.[46]

The amount of effort put into achieving a goal also depends on whether consumers have feedback demonstrating their progress toward the goal. You will tend to stick with an exercise routine, for instance, if you notice improvements in your strength and endurance.[47] If you succeed in achieving a recurring goal (such as earning a free travel ticket with frequent-flyer points), you will increase your effort to reach the same goal in the future—but only if the goal remains challenging.[48] Yet when you are optimistic about your future pursuit of a goal, you will be more motivated to do something when you see your action as a *commitment* to the goal, not as *making progress* toward the goal.[49] Importantly, people often strive to attain multiple goals, such as trying to lose weight, save money, achieve at work, and be a good friend, parent, and spouse. When they are close to attaining one of their goals, people tend to reduce effort on pursuing that goal ("coasting to the finish") and redirect it to other goals. Thus, losing the first three pounds of weight may go faster than losing the last pound, not just because it is harder, but because the consumer's confidence in losing the final pound has been diminished and therefore attention has been shifted to the goal of saving money.

Types of Goals

Although goals (i.e., weight loss) are more concrete than needs (i.e., safety), they can vary in being more *concrete* or *abstract*. Some goals are concrete. They are specific to a given behavior or action and determined by the situation at hand. If you are tired, one of your goals for the evening might be to go to bed early. If you are often late for class, one of your goals might be to arrive on time. Other goals are more abstract and endure over a long period, such as being a good student or looking beautiful.[50]

Goals also differ in whether they are *promotion-focused* or *prevention-focused*. With promotion-focused goals, consumers are motivated to act in ways to achieve positive outcomes; that is, they focus on hopes, wants, and accomplishments. With prevention-focused goals, consumers are motivated to act in ways that avoid negative outcomes; they focus on responsibilities, safety, and guarding against risks. However, only consumers who believe that the world is changeable—that their actions make a difference—will be influenced by messages that are framed by a promotion or prevention focus.[51]

To illustrate, if you were going to buy a new car, would you focus on how much fun you would have driving it (promotion-focused goal) or on how much you would have to pay for insurance (prevention-focused goal)? Alternatively, if you were trying to diet, would you be more likely to focus on how good you would feel if you avoided that slice of cake or how bad you would feel if you ate it?[52] One last important point: Sometimes consumers make a decision simply because they want to experience the choice, rather than because they are pursuing a goal (prevention or promotion). They may plan, for instance, a vacation, search information about it, and make a destination choice to explore and express their preferences.[53]

Goals and Emotions

The extent to which we are successful or unsuccessful in attaining our goals determines how we feel: We feel good when we make sufficient progress towards goal attainment or have attained our goals (saved enough to buy a new bike) and feel bad when we make insufficient progress toward goal attainment or have failed to attain our goals (stop smoking). According to **appraisal theory**, our emotions are determined by how we think about or "appraise" a situation or outcome. As Exhibit 2.9 shows, appraisal theory proposes that we feel positive emotions like pleasure and pride when an outcome is consistent with our goals. Appraisal theory also posits that other appraisal dimensions affect how we feel—dimensions like normative/moral compatibility (is the outcome relevant to what is expected of us or what we should do?), certainty (is the outcome certain to occur or not?), and agency (was I the cause of the outcome, did someone else or the environment cause it, or did it happen by chance?).

To illustrate Exhibit 2.9, consumers might feel proud when a good outcome happens, when we are the cause of that outcome, and when the outcome is consistent with what we should have done. In contrast, we might feel sad when an outcome is inconsistent with our goals and we see it as being caused by the situation or by bad luck.[54] Research also shows that consumers driven by envy will pay more for a product because others who are socially admired have it (benign envy) or pay more for a product because others who are socially admired do not have it (malicious envy).[55]

In some instances, actions and outcomes will result in specific emotions rather than generally feeling good or bad. If a product doesn't work, consumers might feel guilty, angry, sad, or frustrated, depending on who is seen as being responsible for the product not working. Because emotions play a powerful role in attitudes, choices, and satisfaction, later chapters will return to the role of appraisals in consumers' emotions.[56]

Self-Control and Goal Conflict

Consumers use **self-control** to regulate their feelings, thoughts, and behavior in line with their long-term goals.[57] Self-control conflicts arise when we face decisions about actions related to goals that are in conflict. The mental effort involved in making such a decision may result in **ego depletion**,

Appraisal theory A theory of emotion that proposes that emotions are based on an individual's assessment of a situation or an outcome and its relevance to his or her goals.

Self-control Process consumers use to regulate feelings, thoughts, and behavior in line with long-term goals.

Ego depletion Outcome of decision-making effort that results in mental resources being exhausted.

Caused by...	**Good for Me** (consistent with my goals)		**Bad for Me** (inconsistent with my goals)		
	Certain	Uncertain	Certain	Uncertain	
Self	Pride	Hope Excitement	Guilt Shame	Fear Anxiety	Relevant to what I should do or should have done
	Happiness	Hope Excitement	Distress	Fear Anxiety	Irrelevant to what I should do or should have done
Other	Admiration Love	Hope Excitement	Contempt Disgust Envy	Fear Anxiety	Relevant to what I should do or should have done
	Gratitude Love	Hope Excitement	Anger Enraged Resentful	Fear Anxiety	Irrelevant to what I should do or should have done
Environment	Satisfied Relieved Delighted	Hope Excitement Interest Challenge	Disappointed Threatened Frustrated Regret	Fear Anxiety	Relevant to what I should do or should have done
	Pleased Delighted Relieved	Hope Excitement	Miserable Bored	Fear Anxiety	Irrelevant to what I should do or should have done
Not Sure	Glad Delighted	Hope Excitement	Pity	Fear Anxiety	Relevant to what I should do or should have done
	Happiness Joy	Hope Excitement	Sadness Miserable	Fear Anxiety	Irrelevant to what I should do or should have done

Exhibit 2.9

Appraisal Theory

Consumer emotions are formed based on how they appraise a situation or outcome, including from other sources and how it pertains to their goals.

Source: Adapted from Based on Allison Johnson and David Stewart, "A Re-Appraisal of the Role of Emotion in Consumer Behavior: Traditional and Contemporary Approaches," *Review of Marketing Research*, vol. 1 (New York: M.E. Sharpe, 2005), pp. 3–34.

which means the consumer's ability to control his or her behavior is impaired. In other words, such challenges deplete a consumer's mental energy, which in turn reduces decision quality.

Suppose one of your goals is to eat healthy and another is to enjoy tasty, not-so-healthy treats. Confronted with the choice of candy or yogurt, you may choose the yogurt in pursuit of your healthy goal. A little later, when choosing between potato chips and brown rice, your self-control might crumble and the chips would win because of ego depletion. Time plays a role in your self-control: If you repeatedly face the same choice (candy or yogurt), and you first choose yogurt, this initial decision reinforces your self-control and you are more likely to choose yogurt later.[58] Thus, on one hand, you can train to gain self-control. On the other hand, you may indulge today because you optimistically believe you will not indulge in the future when faced with similar choices.[59] Conflicts like these present a challenge to mental processing: When evaluating the nutritional value of a meal that combines opposites such as healthy foods and indulgent treats, consumers tend to underestimate the overall calorie content.[60]

Consumers seeking to exert self-control are caught in a psychological conflict between *desire*, which is a short-term, hedonic force (we want that candy NOW, even if we feel regret later) and *willpower*, which is a long-term, more utilitarian force (we think and act to stop ourselves from having that candy now, to have a long-term healthy lifestyle).[61] Interestingly, research shows a mind-body connection in self-control. If you imagine that your willpower withstands your immediate desires, you may "firm your muscles." In fact, physically firming one's muscles will carry through in firming willpower to resist tempting actions (eating candy now), as long as consumers perceive the long-term benefits.[62]

Goals and self-control are related in other ways. Consumers frequently have *goals to regulate how they feel*. If you feel depressed, you might have a goal of trying to make yourself feel better, perhaps by eating an ice cream cone or going to the movies. These goals describe why consumers who are feeling sad may think that "retail therapy" will cheer them up.[63] Consumers also regulate their feelings by thinking about how to arrange consumption activities for maximal pleasure. For example, when on vacation, you may plan what you want to do and in what order, so you can maximize the overall pleasure.[64]

In addition, consumers have *goals to regulate what they do*, hoping to achieve important goals.[65] Consumers who actively pursue a self-control goal may lapse when the offering they want (candy, for instance) is far away, in distance or in time, because they focus more on the pleasure (good taste) and less on the cost (gaining weight). If they cannot access product information from external sources (such as a nutrition label) and instead rely on memory, consumers are also more likely to lose self-control and consume because they focus on the pleasure.[66] People regulate their spending, as well. They tend not to spend when they perceive the purchase as one large amount ($20) rather than as many smaller amounts (10 purchases of $2). In fact, when consciously exerting self-control over their spending, consumers prefer to receive money in large-denomination bills rather than smaller bills.[67]

Finally, note that although self-control can help consumers progress toward long-term goals, exerting it can be associated with negative feelings such as anger or regret.[68] Thus, firming one's muscles may help willpower, and exerting willpower may firm one's muscles and carry over into feeling angry. These connections between the mind (feeling angry, exerting willpower) and body (firming one's muscles) are an example of the **embodiment** of the mind.

Embodiment Connection between mind and body that influences consumer self-control and behavior.

Marketing Implications

An understanding of consumers' self-concept, needs, goals, and self-control processes is important in many areas of marketing strategy and tactics. For example, marketers frequently use needs, goals, or values to segment and target specific markets. Targeting the growing segment of vegetarian consumers, Earthbound Farm offers organically grown fruits and vegetables, as well as premade salads mixed with beans and whole grains for convenience and added nutrition.[69] In particular, marketers should keep consumer self-concept, needs, goals, and self-control in mind when planning for communications, product development and positioning, and influencing specific behaviors.

Enhance Motivation to Process Communications

Marketers can enhance consumers' motivation to process and act on promotional material by making the information as personally relevant as possible and appealing to consumers' self-concepts, values, needs, or goals. Similarly, salespeople can explore consumers' underlying reasons for making a purchase and tailor sales pitches to those reasons. In advertising, messages can use a narrative structure to stimulate narrative processing, helping consumers connect the advertised brand with their self-concept.[70] Consumers tend to think more about messages that match their self-concept.[71] Thus, if you see yourself as being extroverted, you are likely to be stimulated to process an ad if it portrays a brand appropriate for extroverted people.

Consumers who value advancement or achievement will find an ad more personally relevant if it appeals to those values. For instance, charity: water, a nonprofit organization dedicated to bringing safe drinking water to developing nations, appeals to achievement by showing how contributors can make a difference. The charity has nearly 200,000 Facebook "likes" and more than 1.3 million Twitter followers. The founder explains: "There are solutions, and we can show people those solutions. It's a story full of hope and redemption."[72]

Product Development and Positioning

Marketers can develop goods or services with features and benefits to help consumers achieve their self-control goals. For instance, Weight Watchers and other weight-loss organizations offer tips and tools for avoiding unhealthy eating (self-control goal) as well as feedback on progress toward reaching the goal. Bundled offerings, in particular, may allow consumers to achieve more than one goal or satisfy more than one need in a single consumption episode.[73] For example, the SUBWAY chain's FRESH FIT line of sandwiches is designed to help consumers achieve weight-loss goals while also helping to satisfy hedonic needs and cravings for variety.[74] Sometimes marketers try to appeal to consumers' unrecognized needs or goals. Betsy Kaufman did this with Eggies, a plastic mold for cooking hard-boiled eggs. She came up with the idea in her kitchen and brought it to Edison Nation, which now markets Eggies as a product for consumers who want easy, perfect hard-boiled eggs every time.[75]

In general, a new good or service is likely to be better suited to consumers' needs—and more valued—when consumers are actively involved in its development.[76] This *co-creation* process is increasingly important for customer relationship building. Still, marketers launching a new product might want to target consumers with promotion-focused goals. Why? Buying a new product may bring many new benefits, but there are also potential costs (money and uncertainty) in making the change. Prevention-focused consumers tend to preserve the status quo by staying with the option they know, making them less receptive to new products.[77] Companies can also improve offerings to help consumers make decisions involving conflicting goals or needs. The frozen yogurt chain TCBY now offers self-serve counters where customers dish out their own desserts, choose toppings, and pay by the ounce. "If calories are an issue or budget is an issue, [customers are] in control," explains an executive.[78]

Encouraging Specific Behaviors

Marketers can also use the mind-body connection to influence behavior in support of purchase decisions. For example, a real estate agent who wants to emphasize the spacious, open floorplan of a home could use physical movements such as turning his or her head all the way from left to right and gesturing across the space with his or her arms, encouraging prospective buyers to do the same. Similarly, a furniture salesperson can have consumers sit on a sofa in the store and imagine relaxing on it at home. Such physical actions can help move consumers closer toward purchase decisions. —————————————

Perceived risk The extent to which the consumer is uncertain about the consequences of an action, for example, buying, using, or disposing of an offering.

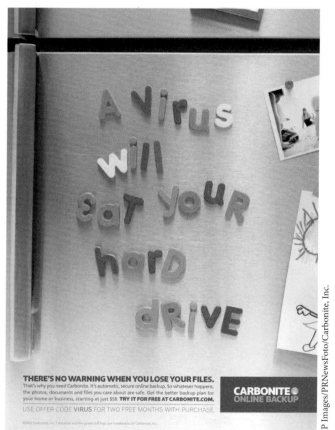

Perceived Risk

Exhibit 2.1 shows that another factor of consumers' motivation to process information about a product or brand is **perceived risk**, the extent to which the consumer is uncertain about the personal consequences of buying, using, or disposing of an offering.[79] If negative outcomes are likely or positive outcomes are unlikely, perceived risk is high. Consumers are more likely to pay attention to and carefully process marketing communications when perceived risk is high (see Exhibit 2.10). As perceived risk increases, consumers tend to collect more information and evaluate it carefully.

Perceived risk can be associated with any product or service, but it tends to be higher (1) when little information is available about the offering; (2) when the offering is new; (3) when the offering has a high price; (4) when the offering is technologically complex; (5) when brands differ fairly substantially in quality and might cause the consumer to make an inferior choice; (6) when the consumer has little confidence or experience in evaluating the offering; or (7) when the opinions of others are important, and the consumer is likely to be judged on the basis of the acquisition, usage, or disposition decision.[80]

Perceptions of risk vary across cultural groups. In particular, high levels of risk tend to be associated with many more products in less-developed countries, perhaps because the products in these countries are generally of poorer quality.[81] Also, perceived risk is typically higher when travelers purchase goods in a foreign country.[82]

In addition, risk perceptions vary within a culture.[83] For example, men in Western cultures take more risks in stock market investments than women take, and younger consumers take more risks than older ones take.

Types of Perceived Risk

It is useful to distinguish six types of risk that consumers can perceive:[84]

Performance risk The possibility that the offering will perform less than expected.

Financial risk The extent to which buying, using, or disposing of an offering is perceived to have the potential to create financial harm.

Physical (or safety) risk The extent to which buying, using, or disposing of an offering is perceived to have the potential to create physical harm or harm one's safety.

Social risk The extent to which buying, using, or disposing of an offering is perceived to have the potential to do harm to one's social standing.

Psychological risk The extent to which buying, using, or disposing of an offering is perceived to have the potential to harm one's sense of self and thus create negative emotions.

Time risk The extent to which buying, using, or disposing of the offering is perceived to have the potential to lead to loss of time.

▶ **Performance risk** reflects uncertainty about whether the product or service will perform as expected. Northland Volkswagen in Calgary, Canada, reassures used car buyers by offering "Certified Pure" VW vehicles that have been thoroughly conditioned and are sold with a two-year limited warranty plus two years' of roadside assistance service.[85]

▶ **Financial risk** is higher if an offering is expensive, such as the cost of buying a home. When consumers perceive high product-category risk due to high price levels, research suggests that their buying decisions can be improved if they research offerings using websites such as epinions.com.[86]

▶ **Physical (or safety) risk** refers to the potential harm a product or service might pose to one's safety. Many consumer decisions are driven by a motivation to avoid physical risk. For example, consumers often shy away from buying perishable groceries that have passed the stated expiration date because they are afraid of getting sick from eating spoiled food.[87]

▶ **Social risk** is the potential harm to one's social standing that may arise from buying, using, or disposing of an offering. According to research, antismoking ad messages that conveyed the severe social disapproval risk of smoking cigarettes were more effective in influencing teens' intentions not to smoke than ad messages stressing the health consequences of smoking, such as disease.[88]

▶ **Psychological risk** reflects consumers' concern about the extent to which a product or service fits with the way they perceive themselves. To illustrate, if you see yourself as an environmentalist, buying disposable diapers may be psychologically risky.

▶ **Time risk** reflects uncertainties about the length of time that must be invested in buying, using, or disposing of the product or service. Time risk may be high if the offering involves considerable time commitment, if learning to use it is a lengthy process, or if it entails a long commitment period (such as a subscription to cable television services that requires a two-year contract).

Risk and Involvement

As noted earlier, products can be described as either high- or low-involvement products. Some researchers have classified high- versus low-involvement products in terms of the amount of risk they pose to consumers. Consumers are likely to be more involved in purchasing products such as homes and computers than in purchasing picture frames or coffee because the former generate higher levels of performance, financial, safety, social, psychological, or time risk and can therefore have more extreme personal consequences.

High risk is generally uncomfortable for consumers. As a result, they are usually motivated to engage in any number of behaviors and information-processing activities to reduce or resolve risk. To reduce the uncertainty component of risk, consumers can collect additional information by conducting online research, reading news articles, engaging in comparative shopping, talking to friends or sales specialists, or consulting an expert. Consumers also reduce uncertainty by being brand loyal (buying the same brand that they did the last time), ensuring that the product should be at least as satisfactory as their last purchase.

In addition, consumers attempt to reduce the consequence component of perceived risk through various strategies. Some consumers may employ a simple decision rule that results in a safer choice. For example, someone might buy the most expensive offering or choose a heavily advertised brand in the belief that this brand is of higher quality than other brands. When decision risk is high, consumers may be willing to consider less conventional alternatives, particularly when they do not trust traditional products or practices. For example, consumers who believe that conventional medical treatments are too technological or dehumanizing may be open to other healing alternatives.[89]

> **Marketing Implications**

When perceived risk is high, marketers can either reduce uncertainty or reduce the perceived consequences of failure. DARN TOUGH VERMOUNT, which markets highly durable athletic socks priced at $20 per pair, reduces both financial and performance risk by offering a lifetime guarantee: If a sock ever wears out, the buyer gets a new pair free.[90] When risk is low, consumers are less motivated to think about the brand or product and its potential consequences. Marketers sometimes need to enhance risk perceptions to make their messages more compelling. For instance, the Scottish government's alcohol moderation campaign, which ran online, in print, and on radio, highlighted negative effects of excessive drinking with the slogan "Every time you have a drink, it adds up to more than you think."[91]

Interestingly, consumers do not always see a particular action as risky, even when it is. For example, many people fail to realize the risks of unprotected sex, a situation that explains why condom sales are not higher. Despite the health benefits of using sunscreen, some consumers don't appreciate the risk they take when they suffer sunburn. This is why New Zealand, which leads the world in melanoma skin cancer mortality rates, has created a Sun Protection Alert graphic for media use in reminding consumers to use sunscreen and avoid the sun during specific hours.[92] Marketers can also enhance consumers' understanding of how behavior can create risky negative outcomes. When consumers think about the role their own behavior plays in acquiring AIDS, they are more likely to follow the advice in ads about reducing that risk.[93] _____

Inconsistency with Attitudes

A final factor affecting motivation, shown in Exhibit 2.1, is the extent to which new information is consistent with previously acquired knowledge or attitudes. We tend to be motivated to process messages that are moderately inconsistent with our knowledge or attitudes because such messages are perceived as moderately threatening or uncomfortable. Therefore, we try to eliminate or at least understand this inconsistency.[94] For example, if a consumer sees a car ad that mentions slightly negative information about the brand she currently owns—such as the brand's getting lower gas mileage than a competitor—she will want to process the information to understand and perhaps resolve the uncomfortable feeling.

On the other hand, consumers are less motivated to process information that is highly inconsistent with their prior attitudes. Thus, for instance, someone who is loyal to the Hertz brand would not be motivated to process information from a comparative ad suggesting that Hertz is bad or that other brands are better. The consumer would simply reject the other brands as nonviable options.

CONSUMER ABILITY: RESOURCES TO ACT

Ability The extent to which consumers have the resources needed to make an outcome happen.

Motivation may not result in action unless a consumer has the ability to process information, make decisions, or engage in behaviors. **Ability** is defined as the extent to which consumers have the necessary resources to make the outcome happen.[95] If our ability to process information is high, we may engage in active decision making. As shown in Exhibit 2.1, (1) financial resources, (2) cognitive resources, (3) emotional resources, (4) physical resources, and (5) social and cultural resources can affect consumers' abilities to process information about brands and make decisions about and engage in buying, usage, and disposition. In turn, these five resources can be affected by other factors, including education and age.

Financial Resources

In some situations, consumers can use money instead of other resources to enhance their ability to make decisions and take actions. For example, many consumers hire financial planners for investment guidance and pay tour guides to show them around a particular area. Obviously, the lack of money constrains consumers who might otherwise have the motivation to engage in a behavior that involves acquisition. Although motivated consumers who lack money can still process information and make buying decisions, they are definitely constrained in their immediate ability to buy from marketers. See Chapter 13 for an in-depth discussion of the meaning of money.

Cognitive Resources

Consumers vary greatly in their knowledge about and experience of an offering.[96] They can gain knowledge from product or service experiences such as ad exposures, interactions with salespeople, information from friends or the media, previous decision making or product usage, or memory. A number of studies have compared the information-processing activities of consumers who have a lot of product knowledge or expertise with those of consumers who do not.[97] Knowledgeable consumers, or "experts," are better able to think deeply about information than are equally motivated but less knowledgeable consumers, or "novices." These differences in prior knowledge clearly affect how consumers make decisions. For example, consumers trying to lease a car rarely understand the concept of capitalized costs (the figure used to determine lease payments) or the need to negotiate lower costs to lower their payments. The inability to understand these costs may result in a less than optimal decision.[98]

According to research, novices and experts process information in different ways.[99] Experts can process information stated in terms of attributes (what the product has—such as a 500-gigabyte hard drive), whereas novices process information better when it's stated in terms of benefits (what the product can do—such as store a lot of data). Novices may be able to process information when marketers provide a helpful analogy (e.g., can hold a library's worth of data).[100] In particular, an analogy is persuasive when consumers can transfer their knowledge of one product's attributes to an unfamiliar product and can allocate the resources needed to process this mapping.[101]

Also, consumers may have difficulty evaluating a service provider when they lack product knowledge or experience (or simply because the service outcome is not easy to evaluate, such as whether the doctor provided the best possible advice). In such situations, consumers may judge service providers using *heuristics*, simple cues or rules of thumb such as whether the medical staff was friendly or whether the examination room was clean and in good order.[102] Finally, consumers can differ in *cognitive style*, or their preferences for ways information should be presented. Some consumers are adept at processing information visually (checking a map for directions), whereas others prefer to process information verbally (listening to a GPS unit give verbal directions).

Emotional Resources

Consumers' ability to experience empathy and sympathy can affect their processing of information and their decisions about brand choices, consumption, disposition, spending, and so on. Emotional resources also affect the actions consumers take to participate in charitable events or donate to causes. For example, many marketers offer pink-themed products during October, which is Breast Cancer Awareness Month, and donate part of the purchase price to the fight against breast cancer (see Exhibit 2.11). According to research, 84 percent of all U.S. consumers buy pink-themed products during October because they want to help battle the disease.[103]

Physical Resources

Physical capabilities—"body power"—can affect how, when, where, and whether consumers make decisions and take actions. As discussed earlier in this chapter, the mind-body connection can play a role in consumers' self-control, for example. Physical resources also influence consumers' ability to use certain goods or services. Even when consumers do not accurately assess their

Exhibit 2.11

Emotional Resources
Some ads appeal to a consumers' emotions, such as advertising a product that donates to breast cancer awareness.

© AP Images/PRNewsFoto/National Breast Cancer Foundation

physical resources, these resources will affect their decisions. For instance, consumers who feel they are physically capable may decide to take a strenuous hike or buy challenging exercise equipment.

Social and Cultural Resources

Who consumers know (their social relationships) and the cultural knowledge and experiences they have can affect their acquisition, consumption, and disposition behavior. For example, studies show that college freshmen with solid social and cultural resources are more likely to continue into their second year of school, rather than dropping out.[104] The extent of a consumer's social resources also plays a role in whether marketing activities conducted on Facebook or in other social media will generate strong word of mouth support and referrals to potential buyers or brand fans.

Education and Age

Education and age have also been related to the ability to process information and make decisions. Specifically, better-educated consumers will have more cognitive resources to use in processing complex information and making decisions. Age also accounts for differences in physical resources and processing ability. Older children seem to be more sensitive to the fact that the benefits of searching for information sometimes outweigh the costs, whereas younger children don't seem to have this same ability.[105] Old age has been associated with a decline in certain cognitive skills and thus reduced ability to process information. In one study, older consumers took more time to process nutrition information and made decisions that were less accurate than those of younger consumers.[106]

Marketing Implications

Factors affecting ability suggest several implications for marketers. First, marketers should be sure that targeted consumers have sufficient prior knowledge to process marketing communications. If not, the company may need to develop educational messages as a first step. Marketers also need to be sensitive to the potentially different processing styles, education levels, and ages of each segment. For example, highly motivated but visually oriented parents may be unable to assemble furniture if the written instructions are too complex and thus incompatible with their processing style. IKEA's furniture assembly instructions are appropriate for a broad audience because they have only illustrations and numbers. IKEA even has a website, the Share Space, where customers can post photos after they've assembled their purchases—reassuring others that they can do this, too.[107]

Knowing that a lack of money constrains purchase behaviors, marketers can facilitate first-time and repeat buying by providing monetary aid. Car manufacturers have enhanced consumers' purchasing ability—and boosted sales—by offering low- or no-down-payment programs, low financing rates, and rebates. Marketers can also provide education and information (through advertising, websites, mobile marketing, social media, point-of-purchase displays, and other communications) that help consumers better process information, make more informed decisions, and engage in consumption behaviors.

CONSUMER OPPORTUNITY

The final factor affecting whether motivation results in action is consumers' opportunity to engage in a behavior. For example, a consumer may be highly motivated to work out and have sufficient money to join a health club (ability); however, he may be so busy that he has little opportunity to actually go. Thus, even when motivation and ability are high, someone may not take action or make decisions because of three key influences: (1) lack of time, (2) distraction, and (3) the complexity, amount, repetition, and control of information.

Time

Time can affect the consumer's opportunity to process information, make decisions, and perform certain behaviors. Some studies show that time-pressured consumers are more likely to buy things for themselves during the Christmas season because this is one of the few opportunities they have to shop.[108] Time affects leisure-time consumption behavior as well. Knowing that would-be gardeners have little time (or patience) to plant, weed, and water, companies are successfully marketing seed-embedded mats, low-maintenance plants, and fast-maturing trees.[109]

Consumers under time pressure to make a decision will engage in limited information processing. For example, a consumer who has to buy 30 items during a 15-minute grocery shopping trip will not have time to process a lot of information about each item. Time-pressured consumers not only process less information but also put more weight on negative information and are quicker to reject brands because of negative features.[110] When motivation to process information is low, consumers feeling moderate time pressure will tend to process information systematically. However, if time pressure is quite high or quite low, consumers are unlikely to process details systematically.[111] The more time consumers have to think about consumption problems, the more creative they tend to be at coming up with novel solutions.[112] In an advertising context, consumers have limited opportunity to process information when a message is presented in a short period; when they cannot control the pace of message presentation, as is the case with TV and radio ads; or when they fast-forward through commercials.[113]

Distraction

Distraction refers to any aspect of a situation that diverts consumers' attention. For example, an important exam can divert a consumer's attention from a yoga class she really wants to take. If someone talks while a consumer is viewing an ad or making a decision, that distraction can inhibit the consumer's ability to process the information. Certain background factors in an ad, such as music or attractive models, can also distract consumers from an advertised message.[114] Consumers may be distracted from TV commercials if the program during which the commercials appear is very involving.[115] Distraction seems to influence the effect of consumers' thoughts on their choices, not the effect of their emotions on choices.[116]

Complexity, Amount, Repetition, and Control of Information

The complexity of the information to which consumers are exposed can affect their opportunity to process it. Consumers find technical or quantitative information more difficult to handle than nontechnical and qualitative data, a situation that inhibits processing.[117] Many technological and pharmaceutical products entail complex information. In addition, research shows that messages containing pictures without words tend to be ambiguous and therefore hard to process.[118] Marketers can, however, use visualization tools to communicate complex information and facilitate processing.[119]

Information may also be complex if the individual must sift through a huge volume of it. That's why Lowe's, the home improvement retailer, offers consumers the opportunity to educate themselves about repair projects quickly and conveniently by viewing how-to videos or downloading articles in Spanish or English.[120] However, when consumers' resources are limited or depleted from processing information (the experience of ego depletion), they will tend to shift from deliberative reasoning and rational consideration of data to more effortless intuitive reasoning in making decisions.[121]

Moreover, although consumers' ability to process information is limited by time, distraction, and the quality and complexity of the information, one factor—repetition—actually enhances it.[122] If consumers are repeatedly exposed to information, they can more easily process it because they have more chances to think about, scrutinize, and remember the information. Advertisers who use television and radio, in particular, must therefore plan to get their messages to the target audience more than once to enhance the opportunity for processing. However, research suggests that when a brand is unfamiliar, consumers may react negatively to repeated advertising, thereby reducing communication effectiveness. In contrast, consumers show more patience for repetition of ads attributed to known, familiar brands.[123]

Consumers remember and learn more when they can control the flow of information by determining what information is presented, for how long, and in what order. With print ads, for example, consumers have a lot of control over which messages they pay attention to, how long they spend processing each message, and the order in which they process the messages. They have more opportunity to select what is appropriate for their own needs and goals, process the information, and apply it to consumption decisions. The same is true for informative company or product review websites. In contrast, consumers exposed to radio or TV commercials have no such control, so they have less opportunity to process and apply the information.[124] As consumers become proficient in controlling the information flow, they can put more effort into processing the content rather than focusing on the control task.[125]

Marketing Implications

Often marketers can do little to enhance consumers' opportunities to process information, make careful decisions, or engage in purchase, usage, or disposition behaviors. For example, advertisers cannot make living rooms less distracting during TV commercials or give consumers more time for shopping. However, companies can play some role in enhancing opportunity.

▶ *Repeating marketing communications* (up to a point) increases the likelihood that consumers will notice and eventually process them. Marketers can also increase the likelihood of processing by presenting messages at a time of day when consumers are least likely to be distracted and pressed for time. Messages should be stated slowly and in simple terms so consumers can understand them. Often companies such as Pepsi will get a message across by restating it in different media (TV commercials, radio ads, billboards, Facebook posts, tweets, and so on.) One caution: Although repetition increases the opportunity to process information, it can also reduce consumers' motivation to process it!

▶ *Reducing time pressure* can lessen distractions for consumers. For example, stores may extend their hours and offer online buying so consumers can shop when they are least distracted and least time pressured. Amazon.com, among other online retailers, allows consumers to "save" items in their shopping carts for later evaluation and purchase.

▶ *Reducing the time needed to buy, use, and learn about a product or service* allows consumers more opportunities to process information and act on their decisions. In stores, clear signs and directories help consumers locate goods more quickly and increase the likelihood that they will actually buy the goods.

▶ *Offering information when and where consumers choose to access it* will open more opportunities for processing and acting on information. Increasingly, companies are using mobile marketing to allow consumers to access product information and place orders via smartphone from anywhere at any time. The U.K. department store Debenhams, for example, has a mobile website optimized for viewing on small phone screens, as well as an iPhone shopping app. Consumers can also receive text messages about special offers, which they can read right away or hold for later viewing. The Sanibel Recreation Center in Florida has posted a QR (quick response) code on the front door to let consumers access details such as hours of operation and day-by-day events.[126]

SUMMARY

Motivation reflects an inner state of arousal that directs the consumer to engage in goal-relevant behaviors, effortful information processing, and detailed decision making. Motivated consumers often experience affective or cognitive involvement. In some cases, this involvement may be enduring; in other cases, it may be situational, lasting only until the goal has been achieved. Consumers experience greater motivation when they regard a goal or object as personally relevant—meaning that it relates to their self-concepts, values, needs, goals, and self-control; when it entails considerable risk; or when it is moderately inconsistent with their prior attitudes.

Even when motivation is high, consumers may not achieve their goals if their ability or opportunity to do so is low. Similarly, if consumers lack the financial, cognitive, emotional, physical, or social and cultural resources, they may not have the ability to make a decision. Age and education also affect ability. In addition, consumers may not achieve the goal if they are attending to information that is incompatible with their processing styles. Highly motivated consumers may also fail to achieve goals if lack of time, distractions, complex or large amounts of information, or lack of control over information flow limit the opportunity to make decisions.

Questions for Review and Discussion

1. How is motivation defined, and how does it affect felt involvement?

2. What are some objects of involvement for consumers?

3. What determines the ranking of needs in Maslow's hierarchy?

4. What types of goals do consumers have?

5. According to appraisal theory, what do emotions have to do with goals?

6. What is self-control and how does it relate to conflicting goals?

7. What are six types of perceived risk, and how does perceived risk affect personal relevance?

8. What five types of resources affect ability to process information and make decisions?

9. Identify some of the elements that contribute to consumer opportunity for processing information and making decisions.

CONSUMER BEHAVIOR CASE

USAA: Million of Customers, One Bank Branch

USAA (United States Automobile Association) maintains only one bank branch to serve more than 8 million consumers worldwide, yet it boasts a 98 percent customer retention rate and often ranks way ahead of competitors in surveys of customer service and satisfaction. Hundreds of banks, brokerage firms, and other financial services firms offer checking and savings accounts, insurance, mortgage loans, and credit cards; some of these have extensive branch systems and ATM networks. So why do consumers choose USAA—and why do they remain customers, year after year?

USAA specializes in serving military personnel and their families, including those on active duty and those who have left the military due to retirement or honorable separation. Although some of its products are available to the general public, the firm's marketing efforts are primarily geared toward consumers in uniform and their spouses and children. Many of these consumers have much in common with nonmilitary consumers: They marry, start a family, buy cars or trucks, look forward to buying a home, save for their children's college education, and as retirement approaches, worry about financial security. However, consumers in this segment also face difficult challenges unique to the military life, such as being deployed many miles from home, frequent or unexpected transfers, lengthy separations from family members, and eventual transition to civilian life.

In marketing to this segment, USAA focuses on these consumers' particular needs, goals, values, and self-concepts. All members of a military family may not be on the same continent for weeks or months at a time, but each adult in the household will still need access to the family's accounts, insurance, and so on. In response, USAA offers a variety of ways to manage money matters at any hour from any location via phone or Internet. It was an early adopter of apps for cell phone banking, including an app for scanning and depositing checks without an in-person branch visit. Customers receive daily text messages with updated balance details, whether they're at home or on overseas assignment. The website is full of details that are available 24/7, and e-mail assistance is just a few clicks away.

For more personalized attention, customers can make a call and speak with one of USAA's 12,000 representatives, who will discuss their needs, inquire about their goals, and then offer advice on choosing the right product. In the past, customers had to determine who to call at USAA when they wanted information—should they contact the banking department or the financial advisory department about retirement accounts? Now USAA makes it easier to get information by phone or online according to life event (getting married or divorced, planning for retirement) or product (home insurance, car loans). And instead of pushing for an immediate purchase, USAA's phone reps are trained to make suggestions that will best serve the customer in the long run. "The answer may be to not buy that product, if that is the right thing to do for the [customer] in that situation," says a top USAA official.

Online at the USAA site, customers can get information at their own pace, including watching video seminars, reading experts' blog entries, and posting questions or comments on customer-only forums. While researching complex issues such as retirement options, any customer can arrange an individual consultation with USAA's financial advisors via videoconference. USAA's professionals do more than answer questions and educate customers about their choices: They also communicate respect for their customers. As one customer observes: "It's not every day I get addressed 'sergeant' by a customer service agent."[127]

CASE QUESTIONS

1. How does USAA enhance consumer motivation by making itself and its offerings personally relevant to customers?
2. What is USAA doing to facilitate consumers' ability and opportunity to process information about its services and make informed financial decisions?
3. What types of needs (functional, symbolic, hedonic, social, nonsocial) are USAA's customers likely to experience? How does USAA respond to these needs?
4. Does USAA do anything to reduce perceived risk? Explain your answer.

ENDNOTES

1. Carrie Rickey, "'Potter,' Panini, and Pino," *Philadelphia Inquirer*, July 24, 2011, www.philly.com/inquirer; Pamela McClintock, "The Evolving Upscale Movie Experience," *Hollywood Reporter*, April 1, 2011, p. 52; Michelle Keras, "Dinner and a Movie," *Montgomery News (PA)*, July 14, 2011, www.montgomerynews.com; and Karen Robinson-Jacobs, "'Eat-'n'-Watch' Movie Race Focuses on Dallas-Fort Worth Area," *Dallas Morning News*, June 23, 2010, www.dallasnews.com.

2. C. Whan Park and Banwari Mittal, "A Theory of Involvement in Consumer Behavior: Problems and Issues," in ed. J. N. Sheth, *Research in Consumer Behavior* (Greenwich, Conn.: JAI Press, 1979), pp. 201–231; and Deborah J. MacInnis, Christine Moorman, and Bernard J. Jaworski, "Enhancing and Measuring Consumers' Motivation, Opportunity, and Ability to Process Brand Information from Ads," *Journal of Marketing*, October 1991, pp. 32–53.

3. Rom Y. Schrift, Oded Netzer, and Ran Kivetz, "Complicating Choice," *Journal of Marketing Research*, April 2011, pp. 308–326.

4. Deborah J. MacInnis and Bernard J. Jaworski, "Information Processing from Advertisements: Toward an Integrative Framework," *Journal of Marketing*, 53, October 1989, pp. 1–23; Scott B. MacKenzie and Richard A. Spreng, "How Does Motivation Moderate the Impact of Central and Peripheral Processing on Brand Attitudes and Intentions?" *Journal of Consumer Research*, March 1992, pp. 519–529; Richard E. Petty and John T. Cacioppo, *Communication and Persuasion* (New York: Springer-Verlag, 1986); Anthony Greenwald and Clark Leavitt, "Audience Involvement in Advertising: Four Levels," *Journal of Consumer Research* 11, June 1984, pp. 581–592; Ronald C. Goodstein, "Category-Based Applications and Extensions in Advertising: Motivating More Extensive Ad Processing," *Journal of Consumer Research*, June 1993, pp. 87–99; and Ellen Garbarino and Julie A. Edell, "Cognitive Effort, Affect, and Choice," *Journal of Consumer Research*, September 1997, pp. 147–158.

5. Wayne D. Hoyer, "An Examination of Consumer Decision Making for a Common Repeat Purchase Product," *Journal of Consumer Research*, December 1984, pp. 822–829.

6. Kurt A. Carlson, Margaret G. Meloy, and J. Edward Russo, "Leader-Driven Primacy: Using Attribute Order to Affect Consumer Choice," *Journal of Consumer Research* 32, no. 4, 2006, pp. 513–518; Nidhi Agrawal and Durairaj Maheswaran, "Motivated Reasoning in Outcome-Bias Effects," *Journal of Consumer Research* 31, no. 4, 2005, pp. 798–805; Getta Menon, Lauren G. Block, and Suresh Ramanathan, "We're at as Much Risk as We're Led to Believe: The Effect of Message Cues on Judgments of Health Risk," *Journal of Consumer Research*, March 2002, pp. 533–549; Shailendra Jain and Durairai Maheswaran, "Motivated Reasoning: A Depth-of-Processing Perspective," *Journal of Consumer Research* 26, no. 4, 2000, pp. 358–371; and Ziva Kunda, "The Case for Motivated Reasoning," *Psychological Bulletin*, 1990, pp. 480–498.

7. Lisa E. Bolton, Joel B. Cohen, and Paul N. Bloom, "Does Marketing Products as Remedies Create 'Get Out of Jail Free Cards'?" *Journal of Consumer Research* 33, no. 1, 2006, pp. 71–81.

8. Ying-Ching Lin, Chien-Huang Lin, and Priya Raghubir, "Avoiding Anxiety, Being in Denial, or Simply Stroking Self-Esteem: Why Self-Positivity?" *Journal of Consumer Psychology* 13, no. 4, 2003, pp. 464–477.

9. Gustavo de Mello, Deborah J. MacInnis, and David W. Stewart, "Threats to Hope: Effects on Reasoning About Product Information," *Journal of Consumer Research*, August 2007, pp. 153–161; and Deborah J. MacInnis and Gustavo de Mello, "The Concept of Hope and Its Relevance to Product Evaluation and Choice," *Journal of Marketing*, January 2005, pp. 1–14.

10. Richard L. Celsi and Jerry C. Olson, "The Role of Involvement in Attention and Comprehension Processes," *Journal of Consumer Research*, September 1988, pp. 210–224.

11. Marsha L. Richins, Peter H. Bloch, and Edward F. McQuarrie, "How Enduring and Situational Involvement Combine to Create Involvement Responses," *Journal of Consumer Psychology*, September 1992, pp. 143–154; Peter H. Bloch and Marsha L. Richins, "A Theoretical Model for the Study of Product Importance Perceptions," *Journal of Marketing*, Summer 1983, pp. 69–81; Celsi and Olson, "The Role of Involvement in Attention and Comprehension Processes"; Andrew A. Mitchell, "The Dimensions of Advertising Involvement," in ed. Kent Monroe, *Advances in Consumer Research* 8 (Ann Arbor, Mich.: Association for Consumer Research, 1981), pp. 25–30; and Marsha L. Richins and Peter H. Bloch, "After the New Wears Off: The Temporal Context of Product Involvement," *Journal of Consumer Research*, September 1986, pp. 280–285.

12. Michael J. Houston and Michael L. Rothschild, "Conceptual and Methodological Perspectives on Involvement," in ed. S. Jain, *Research Frontiers in Marketing: Dialogues and Directions* (Chicago: American Marketing Association, 1978), pp. 184–187; Richins and Bloch, "After the New Wears Off: The Temporal Context of Product Involvement"; and Gilles Laurent and Jean-Noel Kapferer, "Measuring Consumer Involvement Profiles," *Journal of Marketing Research*, February 1985, pp. 41–53.

13. C. Whan Park and S. Mark Young, "Consumer Response to Television Commercials: The Impact of Involvement and Background Music on Brand Attitude Formation," *Journal of Marketing Research*, February 1986, pp. 11–24.

14. Judith Lynne Zaichkowsky, "Measuring the Involvement Construct," *Journal of Consumer Research*, December 1985, pp. 341–352; and Laurent and Kapferer, "Measuring Consumer Involvement Profiles."

15. Nina Michaelidou and Sally Dibb, "Product Involvement: An Application in Clothing," *Journal of Consumer Behaviour* 5, no. 5, 2006, pp. 442–453.

16. Jennifer Aaker, Susan Fournier, and S. Adam Brasel, "When Good Brands Do Bad," *Journal of Consumer Research*, June 2004, pp. 1–16; and Matthew Thomson, Deborah J. MacInnis, and C. W. Park, "The Ties that Bind: Measuring the Strength of Consumers' Emotional Attachments to Brands," *Journal of Consumer Psychology* 15, no. 1, 2005, pp. 77–91.

17. J. Craig Andrews, Syed H. Akhter, Srinivas Durvasula, and Darrel D. Muehling, "The Effect of Advertising Distinctiveness and Message Content Involvement on Cognitive and Affective Responses to Advertising," *Journal of Current Issues and Research in Advertising*, Spring 1992, pp. 45–58; Laura M. Bucholz and Robert E. Smith, "The Role of Consumer Involvement in Determining Cognitive Response to Broadcast Advertising," *Journal of Advertising*, March 1991, pp. 4–17; Darrel D. Muehling, Russell N. Laczniak, and Jeffrey J. Stoltman, "The Moderating Effects of Ad Message Involvement: A Reassessment," *Journal of Advertising*, June 1991, pp. 29–38; and Scott B. MacKenzie and Richard J. Lutz, "An Empirical Examination of the Structural Antecedents of Attitude Toward the Ad in an Advertising Pretesting Context," *Journal of Marketing*, April 1989, pp. 48–65.

18. Barbara Mueller, "Standardization vs. Specialization: An Examination of Westernization in Japanese Advertising," *Journal of Advertising Research*, January–February 1992, pp. 15–24.

19. Ann E. Schlosser, "Computers as Situational Cues: Implications for Consumers Product Cognitions and Attitudes," *Journal of Consumer Psychology* 13, no. 1 and 2, 2003, pp. 103–112; and Charla Mathwick and Edward Rigdon, "Play, Flow, and the Online Search Experience," *Journal of Consumer Research* 31, no. 2, 2004, pp. 324–332.

20. Houston and Rothschild, "Conceptual and Methodological Perspectives in Involvement"; Peter H. Bloch, Daniel Sherrell, and Nancy Ridgway, "Consumer Search: An Extended Framework," *Journal of Consumer Research*, June 1986, pp. 119–126; Peter H. Bloch, Nancy M. Ridgway, and Scott A. Dawson, "The Shopping Mall as Consumer Habitat," *Journal of Retailing*, Spring 1994, pp. 23–42; Richard L. Celsi, Randall L. Rose, and Thomas W. Leigh, "An Exploration of High-Risk Leisure Consumption Through Skydiving," *Journal of Consumer Research*, June 1993, pp. 1–23; Eric J. Arnould and Linda L. Price, "River Magic: Extraordinary Experience and the Extended Service Encounter," *Journal of Consumer Research*, June 1993, pp. 24–45; Morris B. Holbrook and Elizabeth C. Hirschman, "The Experiential Aspects of Consumption," *Journal of Consumer Research*, September 1982, pp. 132–140; Elizabeth C. Hirschman and Morris B. Holbrook, "Experience Seeking," *Journal of Marketing*, Summer 1982, pp. 92–101; and Morris B. Holbrook, Robert W. Chestnut, Terence A. Oliva, and Eric A. Greenleaf, "Play as a Consumption Experience," *Journal of Consumer Research*, September 1984, pp. 728–739.

21. Yinlong Zhang and Vikas Mittal, "Decision Difficulty: Effects of Procedural and Outcome Accountability," *Journal of Consumer Research* 32, no. 3, 2005, pp. 465–472.

22. Celsi and Olson, "The Role of Involvement in Attention and Comprehension Processes"; Greenwald and Leavitt, "Audience Involvement in Advertising"; Laurent and Kapferer, "Measuring Consumer Involvement Profiles"; Zaichkowsky, "Measuring the

Involvement Construct"; Michael L. Rothschild, "Perspectives on Involvement: Current Problems and Future Directions," in ed. Tom Kinnear, *Advances in Consumer Research* 11 (Ann Arbor, Mich.: Association for Consumer Research, 1984), pp. 216–217; Andrew A. Mitchell, "Involvement: A Potentially Important Mediator of Consumer Behavior," in ed. William L. Wilkie, *Advances in Consumer Research*, vol. 6 (Ann Arbor, Mich.: Association for Consumer Research, 1979), pp. 191–196; and Petty and Cacioppo, *Communication and Persuasion.*

23. Banwari Mittal, "I, Me, and Mine: How Products Become Consumers' Extended Selves," *Journal of Consumer Behaviour* 5, no. 6, 2006, pp. 550–562. For more background, see M. Joseph Sirgy, "Self-Concept in Consumer Behavior: A Critical Review," *Journal of Consumer Research*, December 1982, pp. 287–300.

24. Americus Reed II, "Activating the Self-Importance of Consumer Selves," *Journal of Consumer Research* 31, no. 2, 2004, pp. 286–295.

25. Christian Homburg, Jan Wieseke, and Wayne D. Hoyer, "Social Identity and the Service-Profit Chain," *Journal of Marketing*, March 2009, pp. 38–54; and David Sprott, Sandor Czellar, and Eric Spangenberg, "The Importance of a General Measure of Brand Engagement and Validation of a Scale," *Journal of Marketing Research*, February 2009, pp. 92–104.

26. Randall L. Rose and Stacy L. Wood, "Paradox and the Consumption of Authenticity Through Reality Television," *Journal of Consumer Research* 32, no. 2, 2005, pp. 284–296.

27. C. Miguel Brendl, Arthur B. Markman, and Claude Messner, "The Devaluation Effect: Activating a Need Devalues Unrelated Objects," *Journal of Consumer Research*, March 2003, pp. 463–473.

28. Abraham H. Maslow, *Motivation and Personality*, 2nd ed. (New York: Harper & Row, 1970).

29. C. Whan Park, Bernard J. Jaworski, and Deborah J. MacInnis, "Strategic Brand Concept–Image Management," *Journal of Marketing*, October 1986, pp. 135–145.

30. Nicole L. Mead, Roy F. Baumeister, Tyler F. Stillman, Catherine D. Rawn, and Kathleen D. Vohs, "Social Exclusion Causes People to Spend and Consume Strategically in the Service of Affiliation," *Journal of Consumer Research*, February 2011, pp. 902–919.

31. Judy Harris and Michael Lynn, "The Manifestations and Measurement of the Desire to Be a Unique Consumer," *Proceedings of the 1994 AMA Winter Educators' Conference*, Chicago; Kelly Tepper, "Need for Uniqueness: An Individual Difference Factor Affecting Nonconformity in Consumer Responses," *Proceedings of the 1994 AMA Winter Educators' Conference*, Chicago; and Kelly Tepper Tian, William O. Bearden, and Gary L. Hunter, "Consumers' Need For Uniqueness: Scale Development and Validation," *Journal of Consumer Research* 28, June 2001, pp. 50–66.

32. "Lay Off My Red-Soled Shoes," *Economist*, August 20, 2011, www.economist.com/node/21526357.

33. Bram Van den Bergh, "Bikinis Instigate Generalized Impatience in Intertemporal Choice," *Journal of Consumer Research*, June 2008, pp. 85-97.

34. Russell W. Belk, Güliz Ger, and Soren Askegaard, "The Fire of Desire: A Multisited Inquiry into Consumer Passion," *Journal of Consumer Research*, December 2003, pp. 326–351.

35. Payal Khandelwal, "A Luxe Life," *Financial Express (India)*, August 23, 2011, www.financialexpress.com/news.

36. John T. Cacioppo and Richard E. Petty, "The Need for Cognition," *Journal of Personality and Social Psychology*, February 1982, pp. 116–131; Douglas M. Stayman and Frank R. Kardes, "Spontaneous Inference Processes in Advertising: Effects of Need for Cognition and Self-Monitoring on Inference Generation and Utilization," *Journal of Consumer Psychology* 1, no. 2, 1992, pp. 125–142; and John T. Cacioppo, Richard Petty, and Katherine Morris, "Effects of Need for Cognition on Message Evaluation, Recall, and Persuasion," *Journal of Personality and Social Psychology*, October 1993, pp. 805–818.

37. P. S. Raju, "Optimum Stimulation Level," *Journal of Consumer Research*, December 1980, pp. 272–282; and Jan-Benedict E. M. Steenkamp and Hans Baumgartner, "The Role of Optimum Stimulation Level in Exploratory Consumer Behavior," *Journal of Consumer Research*, December 1992, pp. 434–448.

38. Stuart Elliott, "Study Tries to Help Retailers Understand What Drives the Shopping Habits of Women," *New York Times*, January 17, 2001, p. C6.

39. Robert Roth, *International Marketing Communications* (Chicago: Crain Books, 1982), p. 5.

40. H. Murray, *Thematic Apperception Test Manual* (Cambridge, Mass.: Harvard University Press, 1943); Harold Kassarjian, "Projective Methods," in ed. Robert Ferber, *Handbook of Marketing Research* (New York: McGraw-Hill, 1974), pp. 85–100; Ernest Dichter, *Packaging the Sixth Sense: A Guide to Identifying Consumer Motivation* (Boston: Cahners Books, 1975); Dennis Rook, "Researching Consumer Fantasy," in ed. Elizabeth C. Hirschman, *Research in Consumer Behavior*, vol. 3 (Greenwich, Conn.: JAI Press, 1990), pp. 247–270; David Mick, M. De Moss, and Ronald Faber, "A Projective Study of Motivations and Meanings of Self-Gifts," *Journal of Retailing*, Summer 1992, pp. 122–144; and Mary Ann McGrath, John F. Sherry, and Sidney J. Levy, "Giving Voice to the Gift: The Use of Projective Techniques to Recover Lost Meanings," *Journal of Consumer Psychology* 2, no. 2, 1993, pp. 171–191.

41. Harold H. Kassarjian and Joel B. Cohen, "Cognitive Dissonance and Consumer Behavior," *California Management Review*, Fall 1965, pp. 55–65; see also Kenneth E. Runyon and David W. Stewart, *Consumer Behavior*, 3rd ed. (Columbus, Ohio: Merrill, 1987).

42. Sharon Shavitt, Suzanne Swan, Tina M. Lowrey, and Michaela Wanke, "The Interaction of Endorser Attractiveness and Involvement in Persuasion Depends on the Goal That Guides Message Processing," *Journal of Consumer Psychology* 3, no. 2, 1994, pp. 137–162; Robert Lawson, "Consumer Decision Making Within a Goal-Driven Framework," *Psychology and Marketing*, August 1997, pp. 427–449; and Ingrid W. Martin and David W. Stewart, "The Differential Impact of Goal Congruency on Attitudes, Intentions, and the Transfer of Brand Equity," *Journal of Marketing Research*, November 2001, pp. 471–484.

43. Richard P. Bagozzi and Utpal Dholakia, "Goal Setting and Goal Striving in Consumer Behavior," *Journal of Marketing* 63, 1999, pp. 19–32.

44. Dilip Soman and Amar Cheema, "When Goals Are Counterproductive," *Journal of Consumer Research*, June 2004, pp. 52–62.

45. Amar Cheema and Rajesh Bagchi, "The Effect of Goal Visualization on Goal Pursuit," *Journal of Marketing*, March 2011, pp. 109–123.

46. Ayelet Fishbach and Ravi Dhar, "Goals as Excuses or Guides: The Liberating Effect of Perceived Goal Progress on Choice," *Journal of Consumer Research* 32, no. 3, 2005, pp. 370–377.

47. Joseph C. Nunes and Xavier Drèze, "The Endowed Progress Effect: How Artificial Advancement Increases Effort," *Journal of Consumer Research* 32, no. 4, 2006, pp. 504–512.

48. Xavier Drèze and Joseph C. Nunes, "Recurring Goals and Learning," *Journal of Marketing Research*, April 2011, pp. 268–281.

49. Ying Zhang, Ayelet Fishback, and Ravi Dhar, "When Thinking Beats Doing: The Role of Optimistic Expectations in Goal-Based Choice," *Journal of Consumer Research*, February 2008.

50. Richard P. Bagozzi and Utpal Dholakia, "Goal Setting and Goal Striving in Consumer Behavior," *Journal of Marketing* 63, 1999, pp. 19–32.

51. Shailendra Pratap Jain, Pragya Mathur, and Durairaj Maheswaran, "The Influence of Consumers' Lay Theories on Approach/Avoidance Motivation," *Journal of Marketing Research,* February 2009, pp. 56–65.

52. Rui (Juliet) Zhu and Joan Meyers-Levy, "Exploring the Cognitive Mechanism that Underlies Regulatory Focus Effects," *Journal of Consumer Research* 34, no. 1, 2007, pp. 89–98; Jing Wang and Angela Y. Lee, "The Role of Regulatory Focus in Preference Construction," *Journal of Marketing Research*, February 2006, pp. 28–38; Utpal M. Dholakia, Mahesh Gopinath, Richard P. Bagozzi, and Rajan Nataraajan, "The Role of Regulatory Focus in the Experience and Self-Control of Desire for Temptations," *Journal of Consumer Psychology* 16, no. 2, 2006, pp. 163–175; and Jens Förster, E. Tory Higgins, and Lorraine Chen Idson, "Approach and Avoidance Strength During Goal Attainment," *Journal of Personality and Social Psychology*, November 1998, pp. 1115–1131.

53. Jinhee Choi and Ayelet Fishbach, "Choice as an End Versus a Means," *Journal of Marketing Research*, June 2011, pp. 544–554.

54. Allison R. Johnson and David W. Stewart, "A Reappraisal of the Role of Emotion in Consumer Behavior," in ed. Naresh K. Malhotra, *Review of Marketing Research*, (London: M.E. Sharpe, 2005), pp. 3–34.

55. Niels van de Ven, Marcel Zeelenberg, and Rik Pieters, "The Envy Premium in Product Evaluation," *Journal of Consumer Research*, April 2011, pp. 984–998.

56. Seunghee Han, Jennifer S. Lerner, and Dacher Keltner, "Feelings and Consumer Decision Making: The Appraisal-Tendency Framework," *Journal of Consumer Psychology* 17, no. 3, 2007, pp. 158–168.

57. Kathleen D. Vohs and Roy F. Baumeister, "Understanding Self-Regulation: An Introduction," in ed. Roy F. Baumeister and Kathleen D. Vohs, eds. *Handbook of Self-Regulation: Research, Theory, and Applications* (New York: Guilford Press, 2004), pp. 1–9.

58. Siegried Dewitte, Sabrina Bruyneel, and Kelly Geyskens, "Self-Regulating Enhances Self-Regulation in Subsequent Consumer Decisions Involving Similar Response Conflicts," *Journal of Consumer Research*, October 2009, pp. 394–405.

59. Uzma Khan and Ravi Dhar, "Where There Is a Way, Is There a Will?" *Journal of Experimental Psychology*, 136, 2007, pp. 277–288.

60. Alexander Chernev and David Gal, "Categorization Effects in Value Judgments," *Journal of Marketing Research*, August 2010, pp. 738–747.

61. For more about strategies for reducing desire and increasing willpower, see Stephen J. Hoch and George F. Loewenstein, "Time-Inconsistent Preferences and Consumer Self-Control," *Journal of Consumer Research,* March 1991, pp. 492–507.

62. Iris W. Hung and Aparna A. Labroo, "From Firm Muscles to Firm Willpower: Understanding the Role of Embodied Cognition in Self-Regulation," *Journal of Consumer Research,* April 2011, pp. 1046-1064.

63. Eduardo B. Andrade, "Behavioral Consequences of Affect: Combining Evaluative and Regulatory Mechanisms," *Journal of Consumer Research* 32, no. 2, 2005, pp. 355–362.

64. Nathan Novemsky and Ravi Dhar, "Goal Fulfillment and Goal Targets in Sequential Choice," *Journal of Consumer Research* 32, no. 3, 2005, pp. 396–404.

65. Anirban Mukhopadhyay and Gita Venkataramani Johar, "Where There Is a Will, Is There a Way? Effects of Lay Theories of Self-Control on Setting and Keeping Resolutions," *Journal of Consumer Research* 31, no. 4, 2005, pp. 779–786.

66. Remi Trudel and Kyle B. Murray, "Why Didn't I Think of That?" *Journal of Marketing Research*, August 2011, pp. 701–712.

67. Priya Raghubir and Joydeep Srivastava, "The Denomination Effect," *Journal of Consumer Research*, December 2009, pp. 701–713.

68. David Gal and Wendy Liu, "Grapes of Wrath: The Angry Effects of Self-Control," *Journal of Consumer Research*, October 2011, pp. 445ff.

69. Andy Nelson, "Earthbound Farm Launches Salad Line," *The Packer*, July 28, 2011, www.thepacker.com.

70. Jennifer Edson Escalas, "Narrative Processing: Building Consumer Connections to Brands," *Journal of Consumer Psychology* 14, no. 1/2, 2004, pp. 168–180.

71. Nidhi Agrawal and Durairaj Maheswaran, "The Effects of Self-Construal and Commitment on Persuasion," *Journal of Consumer Research* 31, no. 4, 2005, pp. 841–849; and S. Christian Wheeler, Richard E. Petty, and George Y. Bizer, "Self-Schema Matching and Attitude Change: Situational and Dispositional Determinants of Message Elaboration," *Journal of Consumer Research* 31, no. 4, 2005, pp. 787–797.

72. Gina Pace, "Creating Marketing Campaigns That Matter," *Inc.*, May 16, 2011, www.inc.com.

73. Ravi Dhar and Itamar Simonson, "Making Complementary Choices in Consumption Episodes," *Journal of Marketing Research* 36, February 1999, pp. 29–44.

74. Karlene Lukovitz, "Subway Takes on Grease in Product Launch Spots," *MediaPost*, August 17, 2011, www.mediapost.com; and "Subway Launches Program to Help Consumers Keep Diet Resolutions," *Nation's Restaurant News*, January 2, 2006, p. 18.

75. Amy Wallace, "You Bring an Idea, and They'll Do the Rest," *New York Times*, June 12, 2011, p. BU3.

76. Wayne D. Hoyer, Rajesh Chandy, Matilda Dorotic, Manfred Krafft, and Siddharth S. Singh, "Consumer Cocreation in New Product Development," *Journal of Service Research* 13 (3), 2010, pp. 283–296.

77. Alexander Chernev, "Goal Orientation and Consumer Preference for the Status Quo," *Journal of Consumer Research* 31, no. 3, 2004, pp. 557–565.

78. Jaime Levy Pessin, "Yogurt Chains Give Power to the People," *Wall Street Journal*, August 22, 2011, www.wsj.com.

79. Raymond A. Bauer, "Consumer Behavior as Risk Taking," in ed. Robert S. Hancock, *Dynamic Marketing for a Changing World* (Chicago: American Marketing Association, 1960), pp. 389–398; Grahame R. Dowling, "Perceived Risk: The Concept and Its Measurement," *Psychology and Marketing*, Fall 1986, pp. 193–210; and Lawrence X. Tarpey and J. Paul Peter, "A Comparative Analysis of Three Consumer Decision Strategies," *Journal of Consumer Research*, June 1975, pp. 29–37.

80. James R. Bettman, "Perceived Risk and Its Components," *Journal of Marketing Research*, May 1973, pp. 184–190.

81. Dana L. Alden, Douglas M. Stayman, and Wayne D. Hoyer, "The Evaluation Strategies of American and Thai Consumers," *Psychology and Marketing*, March–April 1994, pp. 145–161; and Ugur Yavas, Bronislaw J. Verhage, and Robert T. Green, "Global Consumer Segmentation Versus Local Market Orientation," *Management International Review*, July 1992, pp. 265–272.

82. Vincent W. Mitchell and Michael Greatorex, "Consumer Purchasing in Foreign Countries," *International Journal of Advertising* 9, no. 4, 1990, pp. 295–307.

83. Anonymous, "Marketing Briefs," *Marketing News*, March 1995, p. 11.

84. Jacob Jacoby and Leon Kaplan, "The Components of Perceived Risk," in ed. M. Venkatesan, *Advances in Consumer Research*, vol. 3 (Chicago: Association for Consumer Research, 1972), pp. 382–383; and Tarpey and Peter, "A Comparative Analysis of Three Consumer Decision Strategies."

85. "Pre-Owned and Proud of It at Northland VW," *Calgary Heralod*, August 17, 2011, www.calgaryherald.com.

86. Vanitha Swaminathan, "The Impact of Recommendation Agents on Consumer Evaluation and Choice," *Journal of Consumer Psychology* 13, no. 1&2, 2003, pp. 93–102.

87. Michael Tsiros and Carrie M. Heilman, "The Effect of Expiration Dates and Perceived Risk on Purchasing Behavior in Grocery Store Perishable Categories," *Journal of Marketing*, April 2005, pp. 114–129.

88. Cornelia Pechmann, Guangzhi Zhao, Marvin E. Goldberg, and Ellen Thomas Reibling, "What to Convey in Antismoking Advertisements for Adolescents," *Journal of Marketing*, April 2003, pp. 1–18.

89. Craig J. Thompson, "Consumer Risk Perceptions in a Community of Reflexive Doubt," *Journal of Consumer Research* 32, no. 2, 2005, pp. 235–248.

90. Jessica Shambora, "David vs. Goliath: Darn Tough Vermont vs. Timberland," *Fortune*, February 28, 2011, p. 26.

91. "Scottish Government Reveals Results of Social Marketing Campaigns," *The Drum*, August 18, 2011, www.thedrum.co.uk; and "Scots Gov Launches Alcohol Awareness Social Media Campaign," *The Drum*, January 13, 2011, www.thedrum.co.uk.

92. Kate Mead, "Here Comes the Sun," *Sunday Star Times (New Zealand)*, November 6, 2011, www.stuff.co.nz.

93. Priya Raghubir and Geeta Menon, "AIDS and Me, Never the Twain Shall Meet: The Effects of Information Accessibility on Judgments of Risk and Advertising Effectiveness," *Journal of Consumer Research*, June 1998, pp. 52–63.

94. Shailendra Pratap Jain and Durairaj Maheswaran, "Motivated Reasoning: A Depth-of-Processing Perspective," *Journal of Consumer Research* 26, March 2000, pp. 358–371; and Joan Meyers-Levy and Alice Tybout, "Schema-Congruity as a Basis for Product Evaluation," *Journal of Consumer Research*, June 1989, pp. 39–54.

95. Deborah J. MacInnis and Bernard J. Jaworski, "Information Processing from Advertisements: Toward an Integrative Framework," *Journal of Marketing*, 53, October 1989, pp. 1–23.

96. Joseph W. Alba and J. Wesley Hutchinson, "Dimensions of Consumer Expertise," *Journal of Consumer Research*, March 1987, pp. 411–454. For an excellent overview of measures of consumer knowledge or expertise, see Andrew A. Mitchell and Peter A. Dacin, "The Assessment of Alternative Measures of Consumer Expertise," *Journal of Consumer Research*, December 1996, pp. 219–239.

97. Eric J. Johnson and J. Edward Russo, "Product Familiarity and Learning New Information," *Journal of Consumer Research*, June 1984, pp. 542–550; Merrie Brucks, "The Effects of Product Class Knowledge on Information Search Behavior," *Journal of Consumer Research*, June 1985, pp. 1–16; and Alba and Hutchinson, "Dimensions of Consumer Expertise," *Journal of Consumer Research*, March 1987, pp. 411–454.

98. Oscar Suris, "New Data Help Car Lessees Shop Smarter," *Wall Street Journal*, July 11, 1995, pp. 1, B12.

99. Durairaj Maheswaran and Brian Sternthal, "The Effects of Knowledge, Motivation, and Type of Message on Ad Processing and Product Judgments," *Journal of Consumer Research*, June 1990, pp. 66–73.

100. Jennifer Gregan-Paxton and Deborah Roedder John, "Consumer Learning by Analogy," *Journal of Consumer Research*, December 1997, pp. 266–284.

101. Michelle L. Roehm and Brian Sternthal, "The Moderating Effect of Knowledge and Resources on the Persuasive Impact of Analogies," *Journal of Consumer Research*, September 2001, pp. 257.

102. Michael K. Hui, Xiande Zhao, Xiucheng Fan, and Kevin Au, "When Does the Service Process Matter? A Test of Two Competing Theories," *Journal of Consumer Research* 31, no. 2, 2004, pp. 465–475.

103. Liz Szabo, "Pink Ribbon Marketing Brings Mixed Emotions, Poll Finds," *USA Today*, October 7, 2011, www.usatoday.com.

104. Ryan Wells, "Social and Cultural Capital, Race and Ethnicity, and College Student Retention," *Journal of College Student Retention* 10, no. 2, 2008–9, pp. 103–128.

105. Jennifer Gregan-Paxton and Deborah Roedder John, "Are Young Children Adaptive Decision Makers? A Study of Age Differences in Information Search Behavior," *Journal of Consumer Research*, March 1995, pp. 567–580.

106. Catherine A. Cole and Gary J. Gaeth, "Cognitive and Age-Related Differences in the Ability to Use Nutrition Information in a Complex Environment," *Journal of Marketing Research*, May 1990, pp. 175–184.

107. Lisa Boone, "IKEA Launches Share Space for Customers' Project Photos," *Los Angeles Times*, August 18, 2011, www.latimes.com

108. Cynthia Crossen, "'Merry Christmas to Moi' Shoppers Say," *Wall Street Journal*, December 11, 1997, pp. B1, B14.

109. June Fletcher and Sarah Collins, "The Lazy Gardener," *Wall Street Journal*, June 6, 2001, pp. W1, W16.

110. Peter Wright, "The Time Harassed Consumer: Time Pressures, Distraction, and the Use of Evidence," *Journal of Applied Psychology*, October 1974, pp. 555–561.

111. Rajneesh Suri and Kent B. Monroe, "The Effects of Time Constraints on Consumers' Judgments of Prices and Products," *Journal of Consumer Research*, June 2003, pp. 92–104.

112. C. Page Moreau and Darren W. Dahl, "Designing the Solution: The Impact of Constraints on Consumers' Creativity," *Journal of Consumer Research* 32, no. 1, 2005, pp. 13–22.

113. Danny L. Moore, Douglas Hausknecht, and Kanchana Thamodaran, "Time Compression, Response Opportunity, and Persuasion," *Journal of Consumer Research*, June 1986, pp. 85–99; Priscilla LaBarbera and James Mac-Laughlin, "Time Compressed Speech in Radio Advertising," *Journal of Marketing*, January 1979, pp. 30–36; Shelly Chaiken and Alice Eagly, "Communication Modality as a Determinant of Message Persuasiveness and Message Comprehensibility," *Journal of Personality and Social Psychology*, March 1976, pp. 605–614; Herbert Krugman, "The Impact of Television Advertising," *Public Opinion Quarterly*, Fall 1965, pp. 349–356; and Patricia A. Stout and Benedicta Burda, "Zipped Commercials: Are They Effective?" *Journal of Advertising*, Fall 1989, pp. 23–32.

114. Park and Young, "Consumer Response to Television Commercials"; Deborah J. MacInnis and C. Whan Park, "The Differential Role of Characteristics of Music on High- and Low-Involvement Consumers' Processing of Ads," *Journal of Consumer Research*, September 1991, pp. 161–173; and Shelly Chaiken and Alice Eagly, "Communication Modality as a Determinant of Persuasion: The Role of Communicator Salience," *Journal of Personality and Social Psychology*, August 1983, pp. 605–614.

115. Kenneth Lord and Robert Burnkrant, "Attention Versus Distraction: The Interactive Effect of Program Involvement and Attentional Devices on Commercial Processing," *Journal of Advertising*, March 1993, pp. 47–61; Kenneth R. Lord and Robert E. Burnkrant, "Television Program Effects on Commercial Processing," in ed. Michael J. Houston, *Advances in Consumer Research*, vol. 15 (Provo, Utah: Association for Consumer Research, 1988), pp. 213–218; and Gary Soldow and Victor Principe, "Response to Commercials as a Function of Program Context," *Journal of Advertising Research*, February–March 1981, pp. 59–65.

116. Baba Shiv and Stephen M. Nowlis, "The Effect of Distractions While Tasting a Food Sample: The Interplay of Informational and Affective Components in Subsequent Choice," *Journal of Consumer Research*, December 2004, pp. 599–608.

117. Richard Yalch and Rebecca Elmore-Yalch, "The Effect of Numbers on the Route to Persuasion," *Journal of Consumer Research*, June 1984, pp. 522–527.

118. Noel Capon and Roger Davis, "Basic Cognitive Ability Measures as Predictors of Consumer Information Processing Strategies," *Journal of Consumer Research*, June 1984, pp. 551–564.

119. Nicole H. Lurie and Charlotte H. Mason, "Visual Representation: Implications for Decision Making," *Journal of Marketing*, January 2007, pp. 160–177.

120. Adam Blair, "Lowe's Mounts Multi-Channel Battle Plan," *Retail Information Systems News*, August 23, 2011, http://risnews.edgl.com.

121. Anastasiya Pocheptsova, On Amir, Ravi Dhar, and Roy F. Baumeister, "Deciding without Resources," *Journal of Marketing Research*, June 2009, pp. 344–355.

122. Rajeev Batra and Michael L. Ray, "Situational Effects of Advertising Repetitions: The Moderating Influence of Motivation, Ability, and Opportunity to Respond," *Journal of Consumer Research*, March 1986, pp. 432–435; Carl Obermiller, "Varieties of Mere Exposure: The Effects of Processing Style and Repetition on Affective Response," *Journal of Consumer Research*, June 1985, pp. 17–30; Arno Rethans, John L. Swazy, and Lawrence J. Marks, "The Effects of Television Commercial Repetition, Receiver Knowledge, and Commercial Length: A Test of the Two-Factor Model," *Journal of Marketing Research*, February 1986, pp. 50–61; Sharmistha Law and Scott A. Hawkins, "Advertising Repetition and Consumer Beliefs: The Role of Source Memory," in ed. William Wells, *Measuring Advertising Effectiveness* (Mahwah, N.J.: Lawrence Erlbaum Associates, 1997), pp. 67–75; and Giles D'Sousa and Ram C. Rao, "Can Repeating an Advertisement More Frequently Than the Competition Affect Brand Preference in a Mature Market?" *Journal of Marketing* 59, no. 2, 1995, pp. 32–43.

123. Margaret C. Campbell and Kevin Lane Keller, "Brand Familiarity and Advertising Repetition Effects," *Journal of Consumer Research*, September 2003, pp. 292–304.

124. Dan Ariely, "Controlling the Information Flow: Effects on Consumers' Decision Making and Preferences," *Journal of Consumer Research* 27, September 2000, pp. 233–248.

125. Ibid.

126. "Sanibel Attractions Using QR Codes," *WZVN-TV*, August 19, 2011, www.abc-7.com.

127. Jeremy Quittner, "USAA Tech Overhaul Makes Remote Banking Less Remote," *America Banker*, July 12, 2011, p. 1; "Customer Experience: The Frontline," *Marketing Week*, June 2, 2011, p. 25; Robert L. Mitchell, "Big Business Takes a (Small) Bite of the Apple," *ComputerWorld*, August 22, 2011, p. 12; and Jena McGregor, "USAA's Battle Plan," *Bloomberg Businessweek*, February 18, 2010, www.businessweek.com.

FROM EXPOSURE TO COMPREHENSION

After studying this chapter, you will be able to

1. Discuss why marketers are concerned about consumers' exposure to marketing stimuli and what tactics they use to enhance exposure.

2. Explain the characteristics of attention and how marketers can try to attract and sustain consumers' attention to products and marketing messages.

3. Describe the major senses that are part of perception and outline why marketers are concerned about consumers' sensory perceptions.

4. Discuss the process of comprehension, and outline how marketing-mix elements can affect consumer inferences about products and brands.

© Don Arnold/WireImage/Getty Images

INTRODUCTION

Wax or Real? Welcome to Madame Tussauds

When Madame Tussauds unveils a new figure like Justin Bieber or Helen Mirren, photos and videos of the "twins" make headlines around the world, prompting consumers to try to see which one is wax and which one is real. The company, owned by Merlin Entertainments Group of Poole, England, has been creating lifelike, life-size wax figures of famous people for more than 250 years. These days, visitors to the 13 Madame Tussauds museums find themselves face to face with wax versions of global superstars like Lady Gaga, film stars like Jet Li, athletes like Usain Bolt, singers like Roel van Velzen, and cartoon characters like Astro Boy.

Using a combination of headline-grabbing publicity events, media advertising, Facebook photos, YouTube videos, and other marketing activities, Madame Tussauds seeks to get its figures and brand in front of potential visitors on four continents. Every time consumers see real celebrities standing next to identical wax figures and take the next step to guess which one is real and which one is wax, they see for themselves how real Madame Tussauds' figures really are—a case of "seeing is believing."[1]

If consumers are to register any message after being exposed to a photo or video of a product like a wax figure, an ad, or some other marketing element, they must pay attention to it, use their senses to determine its properties, and make sense of it (see Exhibit 3.1). Madame Tussauds counts on people paying closer attention to two seemingly identical celebrities, using their sense of vision to pick out details that might distinguish the real from the wax, and finally coming to understand which is which. A variety of factors affect this four-step process of exposure, attention, perception, and comprehension, which also plays a role in and is influenced by knowledge stored in memory, as described in Chapter 4.

EXPOSURE AND CONSUMER BEHAVIOR

Exposure The process by which the consumer comes in physical contact with a stimulus.

Marketing stimuli Information about offerings communicated either by the marketer (such as ads) or by nonmarketing sources (such as word of mouth).

Before an ad, a tweet, a product sample, or a store display can affect consumers, they must be exposed to it. **Exposure** means coming into physical contact with a stimulus. **Marketing stimuli** contain information about products or brands and other offerings communicated by either the marketer (via ads, Facebook messages, salespeople, brand symbols, packages, prices, and so on) or by nonmarketing sources (e.g., news media, word of mouth, and consumer reviews of a product).

Consumers can be exposed to marketing stimuli at any stage of the decision-making process. To some extent, they can select what they will be exposed to and avoid other stimuli, as you know from your own experience. Because exposure is critical to influencing consumers' thoughts and feelings, marketers want consumers to be exposed to stimuli that portray their offerings in a favorable light or at a time when consumers may be interested in such products.

Factors Influencing Exposure

The *position of an ad within a medium* can affect exposure. Consumers' exposure to magazine ads is greatest when they appear on inside cover (next to the table of contents) or on the back cover because the ads are in view whenever the magazine is placed face down. Also, consumers are most likely to be exposed to ads placed next to articles or within TV programs that interest them.[2] Exposure to commercials is greatest when they air at the beginning or end of a commercial break within a program, because consumers are still involved in the program or are waiting for the program to resume. Some advertisers sponsor commercial-free TV programs in which the company gets product placement within the show or airs a single ad before or after the show.

Moreover, *product distribution* and *shelf placement* affect consumers' exposure to brands and packages. The more stores carrying the product or brand, the greater the likelihood that consumers will encounter it. Likewise, the product's location or the amount of shelf space allocated to it can increase exposure to a product. Products displayed at the end of an aisle or placed from waist to eye level get more exposure than those in other positions. Sales of some products increase because of their higher exposure in displays at checkout counters in supermarkets, automotive stores, and restaurants.[3]

Selective Exposure

While marketers can work very hard to affect consumers' exposure to certain products and brands, ultimately consumers are the ones who control their exposure to marketing stimuli. In other words, consumers can and do actively seek out certain stimuli and avoid or resist others. One reason consumers want to avoid ads is that they are exposed to so many that they cannot possibly process them all. Consumers avoid ads for product categories they do not use (indicating that the ads are

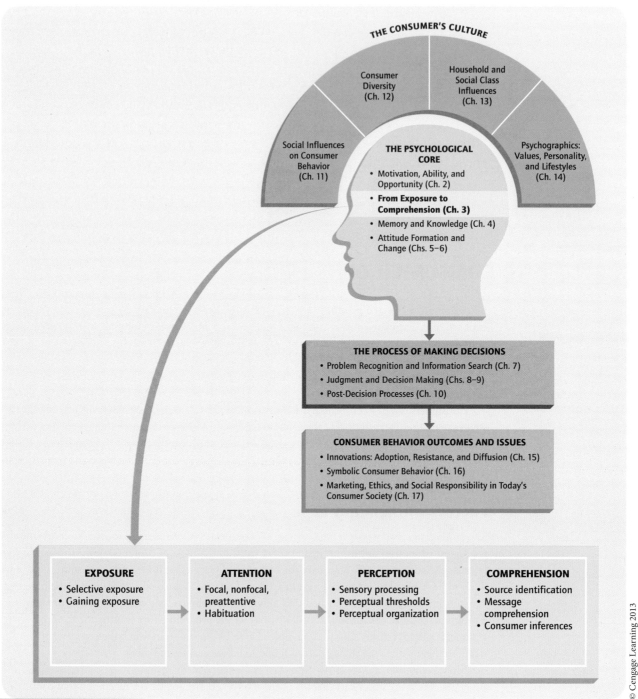

THE CONSUMER'S CULTURE

Consumer Diversity (Ch. 12)

Household and Social Class Influences (Ch. 13)

Social Influences on Consumer Behavior (Ch. 11)

Psychographics: Values, Personality, and Lifestyles (Ch. 14)

THE PSYCHOLOGICAL CORE
- Motivation, Ability, and Opportunity (Ch. 2)
- **From Exposure to Comprehension (Ch. 3)**
- Memory and Knowledge (Ch. 4)
- Attitude Formation and Change (Chs. 5–6)

THE PROCESS OF MAKING DECISIONS
- Problem Recognition and Information Search (Ch. 7)
- Judgment and Decision Making (Chs. 8–9)
- Post-Decision Processes (Ch. 10)

CONSUMER BEHAVIOR OUTCOMES AND ISSUES
- Innovations: Adoption, Resistance, and Diffusion (Ch. 15)
- Symbolic Consumer Behavior (Ch. 16)
- Marketing, Ethics, and Social Responsibility in Today's Consumer Society (Ch. 17)

EXPOSURE	**ATTENTION**	**PERCEPTION**	**COMPREHENSION**
• Selective exposure • Gaining exposure	• Focal, nonfocal, preattentive • Habituation	• Sensory processing • Perceptual thresholds • Perceptual organization	• Source identification • Message comprehension • Consumer inferences

© Cengage Learning 2013

Exhibit 3.1

Chapter Overview: From Exposure to Comprehension

Before you can pay attention to a marketing stimulus, you must be exposed to it. When you allocate mental resources to a stimulus, you can perceive it and, finally, comprehend what it is, in the context of what you already know.

irrelevant to them); they also tend to avoid ads they have seen before because they know what these ads will say. When consumers avoid stimuli they find distracting—such as online ads located near content they want to focus on—they are likely to form negative attitudes toward those brands.[4]

Consumers' avoidance of marketing stimuli is a major problem for marketers.[5] One survey reveals that 54 percent of U.S. consumers and 68 percent of German consumers avoid ads.[6] During a TV ad, consumers can leave the room, do something else, or avoid it entirely by zipping and zapping

Exhibit 3.2

Selective Exposure
Consumers can selectively control what marketing stimuli they view.

Zipping Fast-forwarding through commercials on a program recorded earlier.

Zapping Use of a remote control to switch channels during commercial breaks.

(see Exhibit 3.2). With **zipping**, consumers record TV shows with a DVR (digital video recorder) and fast-forward through the commercials when viewing the shows later. Consumers zip through up to 75 percent of the ads in recorded shows—yet they can still identify the brand or product category in many of the ads.[7] Even if zipping occurs, an ad with extensive brand information in the center of the screen can have a positive influence on brand attitude.[8] Also, despite zipping, prior exposure to an ad improves consumers' recall of the message but increases consumers' tendency to avoid previously seen ads.[9]

With **zapping**, consumers avoid ads by switching to other channels during commercial breaks. Approximately 20 percent of consumers zap at any one time; more than two-thirds of households with cable TV zap regularly. Men zap more than women do. People are more likely to zap commercials at the half-hour or hour mark than during the program itself.[10]

Thanks to technology, consumers use zipping and zapping to gain control over what they are exposed to, when, where, and for how long. Consumers are increasingly taking charge of where and when they are exposed to certain stimuli, by watching entertainment online, for example, or by downloading programs to view via cell phone or computer, now or later. Millions of consumers also use software to block ads that would otherwise open, move, or flash when they view a Web page.[11] At times, consumers may resist other brand-related stimuli, not just advertising. For example, studies show that consumers tend to resist negative word of mouth about brands they are likely to choose and, conversely, resist positive word of mouth about brands they are unlikely to choose.[12]

Marketing Implications

Marketers start the process of gaining exposure by selecting media, such as Internet sites, television, radio, and product placements, and developing communications for targeted consumers. For example, to connect with younger consumers—often the most style-conscious and interested in self-expression—adidas coordinates multiple brand and product messages in multiple media. Many of the ads attract attention because they star celebrities such as singer Katy Perry and basketball player Derrick Rose. The firm is testing digital store displays that use facial recognition to identify the gender and age of shoppers and then present appropriate products. Finally, adidas's flagship NEO stores feature eye-catching and colorful displays and head-to-toe outfits geared to the fashion tastes of teenagers in India, China, Russia, and Europe.[13]

Marketers are trying other ways of gaining exposure for marketing stimuli, including advertising on airport jetways, sports stadium turnstiles, and supermarket floors. For example, Chrysler sponsors mobile billboards and NASCAR cars during automotive events such as the annual Woodward Dream Cruise in suburban Detroit.[14] Mobile marketing is a fast-growing field as marketers experiment with coupons, apps, offers, contests, and other content viewed on consumers' cell phones.[15] Marketers such as Woolworths in Australia and Tesco in South Korea are testing virtual grocery shelves, projected on the walls of transit stations, to increase exposure and encourage purchasing via cell phone.[16] These are all ways that marketers increase the "reach" of messages about their products and brands.

Marketers want to get their messages or products noticed without alienating consumers, a real challenge when consumers feel bombarded by marketing stimuli. Therefore, some marketers are reaching out through media not yet saturated with messages. For example, some companies participate in "transaction-based marketing" by arranging to have a website link embedded in consumers' online bank statements. Consumers can choose to click and see the offer or ignore the link, giving them control over such communications.[17] Targeted e-mail marketing allows firms to communicate regularly with consumers, offering product updates, promotional deals, and other content. Although Internet users resent uninvited messages from companies, many will agree to receive e-mail if they see a benefit and can control the timing.[18]

Television networks are trying to hold viewers using such techniques as switching ads to mid-program or airing 30- or 60-second mini-movies in the middle of a block of commercial. BBC America, for example, recently aired an AT&T-sponsored 60-second animated scene featuring well-known characters during a commercial break in a *Doctor Who* episode. The network aired a "stay tuned for the break" notice as a "DVR buster," according to a BBC America executive.[19] And for commercials that will air during high-profile TV programs such as the Super Bowl, advertisers are encouraging exposure by offering online previews, mobile marketing extras, and social media promotions that build buzz.[20]

ATTENTION AND CONSUMER BEHAVIOR

Attention How much mental activity a consumer devotes to a stimulus.

While exposure reflects whether consumers encounter a stimulus, **attention** reflects how much mental activity they devote to it. A certain amount of attention is necessary for information to be perceived—for it to activate people's senses. After consumers perceive information, they may pay more attention to it and continue with the higher-order processing activities discussed in the next few chapters. Thus, attention enables consumers to learn more efficiently from their exposure to marketing stimuli and make more informed decisions.

Characteristics of Attention

Attention has three key characteristics, as shown in Exhibit 3.3: (1) it is limited; (2) it is selective; and (3) it is capable of being divided.

Attention Is Limited

Attention is limited. Consumers cannot possibly attend to all stimuli in the environment, even if they would want to see everything. However, consumers can attend to multiple stimuli (such as products on store shelves) only if processing them is relatively automatic, well practiced, and effortless.[21] When trying to learn a new skill, for instance, like playing an instrument or ordering books online, we need to pay close attention to each specific activity. With practice, we integrate sequences of activities and our attention is freed up for other things.

Attention Is Selective

Because attention is limited, consumers need to select what to pay attention to and simultaneously what *not* to pay attention to. Being surrounded by a potentially overwhelming number of stimuli,

Exhibit 3.3

Three Characteristics of Attention

Characteristic	Example
Attention is limited: Consumers may miss some stimuli, especially when in unfamiliar surroundings.	While watching TV with friends, a consumer may reduce the volume to pay more attention to what friends are saying.
Attention is selective: Consumers decide what to focus on at any one time, choosing not to focus on or mentally process other stimuli.	Shoppers cannot focus on every display or product in a store, so they must decide which they will pay attention to.
Attention can be divided: Consumers can allocate some attention to one task and some to a different task.	While paying attention to their driving, consumers can also notice ads on billboards posted along a highway.

we pay less attention to things we have seen many times before.[22] Attention can also be affected by goals: If we look at a package with the goal of learning how to use the product, we may be more likely to read the directions than to read about its ingredients.[23]

Attention Can Be Divided

We can divide our attentional resources, allocating some attention to one task and some to another. At the same time, we can become distracted when one stimulus draws attention from another; if we are distracted from an ad, we devote less attention to it.[24]

Focal and Nonfocal Attention

These three characteristics of attention raise questions about what happens when we focus on a stimulus (*focal attention*) while simultaneously being exposed to other stimuli (*nonfocal attention*). For example, can we process any information from a roadside billboard in our peripheral vision if we are focusing on the traffic on the road ahead of us? This example is about the information processing that can take place during nonfocal attention.

Preattentive processing
The nonconscious processing of stimuli in peripheral vision.

▶ *Preattentive processing.* To the extent that we can process information from our peripheral vision even if we are not aware of doing so, we are engaged in **preattentive processing**. With preattentive processing, most of our attentional resources are devoted to one thing, leaving limited resources for something else. We devote just enough attention to an object in our peripheral vision to process *something* about it, but we are usually not aware that we are absorbing and processing that information.

▶ *Hemispheric lateralization.* Some studies have found that our ability to process preattentively depends on (1) whether the stimulus in peripheral vision is a picture or a word and (2) whether it is placed to the right side or the left side of the focal item. These factors are influential because of how the two halves of the brain—the two hemispheres—process information. The right hemisphere is best at processing music, grasping visual and spatial information, forming inferences, and drawing conclusions. The left hemisphere is best at processing units that can be combined, performing tasks such as counting, processing unfamiliar words, and forming sentences.[25] When we focus on stimuli centrally, information is processed by both hemispheres.

▶ *Preattentive processing, brand name liking, and choice.* Do preattentively processed stimuli affect feelings about or choices of brands? Research suggests that consumers will like a brand name more if they have processed it preattentively than if they have not been exposed to it.[26] Preattentive processing makes a brand name familiar, and we like familiar things.[27] Preattentive processing of an ad can also affect consumers' consideration of a product, even when they do not remember seeing the ad.[28] Emotions can also play a factor in preattentive processing. If TV commercials can engage consumers emotionally, they can build strong brands even at low attention levels.[29] Research also indicates that emotionally charged headlines in print ads can be processed preattentively, resulting in higher ad and brand awareness.[30]

Marketing Implications

Although consumers can process general information (such as logos and brand names) preattentively, specific information (such as about ingredients and directions for use) will have more impact when consumers devote full attention to it. Unfortunately, a marketing stimulus competes with many other stimuli for attention, and consumers may have limited motivation and opportunity to attend to marketing stimuli. Consequently, marketers often take steps to attract consumers' attention by making the stimulus (1) personally relevant, (2) pleasant, (3) surprising, and/or (4) easy to process. They can use various research methods to gauge consumers' attention to ads, packages, and products, as shown in Exhibit 3.4.

1. *Make stimuli personally relevant.* Stimuli are personally relevant when they appeal to our needs, values, emotions, or goals.[31] If you are hungry, for example, you are more likely to pay attention to food ads and packages. Products such as candy bars may make use of this by appealing to the need for energy to keep going, or the need for "a break" between tasks. A second way is to show sources similar to the target audience, such as "typical consumers" in an ad.[32] A third way to increase personal relevance is by using dramas, mini-stories that depict the experiences of actors or consumers through a narrative in one or more ads. A fourth way to draw consumers into the ad is to ask rhetorical questions, such as "Would you like to win a million dollars?"[33] These questions appeal to the consumer by including the word *you* and by asking the consumer (if only for effect) to consider answering the question.

2. *Make stimuli pleasant.* Because people tend to approach things that are inherently pleasant, marketers can increase consumers' attention to marketing stimuli by:

   ▶ *Using attractive models.* Ads containing attractive models have a higher probability of being noticed because the models arouse positive feelings or basic sexual attraction.[34] Clearly, individual and cultural differences influence opinions about what is attractive. Some people enjoy seeing naked models in ads, while others find these images offensive. Ultrathin models represent a Western standard of beauty; elsewhere in the world, such models could be perceived as undernourished and unattractive.

   ▶ *Using music.* Familiar songs and popular entertainers can attract us in pleasant ways.[35] Chevrolet has run commercials featuring the cast of the TV show *Glee* singing a jingle from the company's past, "See the USA in Your Chevrolet." The promotions manager explains that the firm is "trying to have the *Glee* fan become the Chevrolet fan."[36]

   ▶ *Using humor.* Humor can be an effective attention-getting device.[37] For example, a commercial for Berlitz language schools shows a London double-decker bus landing, flying-saucer style, in Middle Eastern cities as locals flee. The tag line is: "Don't be an alien in a foreign country."[38] Although roughly one in five TV ads contains humor, some are more successful at evoking laughter (and retaining viewers' attention) than others.[39]

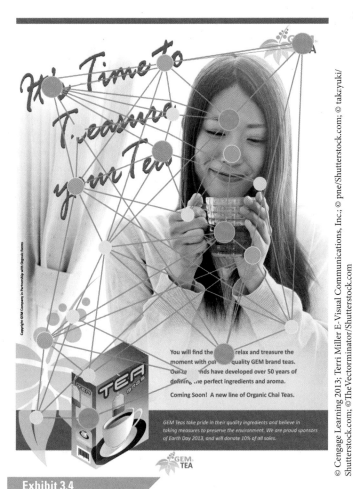

You will find the [ ] relax and treasure the moment with our [ ] quality GEM brand teas. Our [ ] nds have developed over 50 years of defining the perfect ingredients and aroma.

Coming Soon! A new line of Organic Chai Teas.

GEM Teas take pride in their quality ingredients and believe in taking measures to preserve the environment. We are proud sponsors of Earth Day 2013, and will donate 10% of all sales.

GEM TEA

Copyright GEM Company in Partnership with Organic Farms

© Cengage Learning 2013; Terri Miller E-Visual Communications, Inc.; © pne/Shutterstock.com; © takeyuki/Shutterstock.com; © TheVectorminator/Shutterstock.com

Exhibit 3.4

Studying Eye Movements to Gauge and Improve Attention

Image Courtesy of The Advertising Archives

Capturing Attention
Consumers are more likely to pay attention to ads with unexpected elements.

3. *Make stimuli surprising.* Consumers are likely to process a stimulus when it is surprising by:

▶ *Using novelty.* We are more likely to notice any marketing stimulus (an ad, package, or brand name) that is new or unique, because it stands out relative to other stimuli. When QR (quick response) codes were new and novel, ads and labels with the boxy codes attracted attention. Although novel stimuli attract attention, we do not always like them better. For example, we may dislike food with a taste unlike that of foods we usually eat. Thus, the factors that make a stimulus novel may not be the same factors that make it likable.

▶ *Using unexpectedness* (see Exhibit 3.5). Unexpected stimuli may not necessarily be new to us, but their placement or content differs from what we are used to, arousing curiosity and causing us to analyze them further to make sense of them.[40] In fact, unexpectedness can affect the extent to which consumers perceive an ad as humorous.[41] For example, slapstick comedy has nothing to do with buying car tires, so consumers are apt to notice when Bridgestone uses such humor in TV commercials.[42]

▶ *Using a puzzle.* Visual rhymes, antitheses, metaphors, and puns are puzzles that attract attention in ads, because they require resolution. To understand puns and metaphors, a shared cultural background is needed, which makes it hard to use them in multinational campaigns—American consumers may not readily understand ads developed in other countries.[43] Although ads that use a puzzle may capture and hold attention, it is important that consumers can solve it to prevent boomerang effects.

4. *Make stimuli easy to process.* Marketers can enhance attention by boosting consumers' ability to process the stimuli. Four characteristics make a stimulus easy to process:

Prominence The intensity of stimuli that causes them to stand out relative to the environment.

▶ *Prominent stimuli.* Prominent stimuli stand out relative to the environment because of their intensity. The size or length of the stimulus can affect its **prominence**. For example, consumers are more likely to notice larger or longer ads than smaller or shorter ones.[44] Increasing the amount of space devoted to text within an ad increases the viewers' attention to the entire message; making ads less cluttered focuses attention on the brand, price, and promotion aspects of the message.[45] Movement also increases prominence, which is why attention tends to be enhanced when a commercial uses dynamic, fast-paced action.[46] Movement attracts attention even in the visual periphery, which is why Web ads often make use of it. Also, when choosing among competing products, consumers tend to buy products in packages that appear to be taller than others. Even the ratio of the dimensions of rectangular products or packages can subtly affect consumer preferences.[47]

Concreteness The extent to which a stimulus is capable of being imagined.

▶ *Concrete stimuli.* Stimuli are easier to process if they are concrete rather than abstract.[48] **Concreteness** is defined as the extent to which we can imagine a stimulus. Notice how easily you can develop images of the concrete words in Exhibit 3.6 compared with your response to the abstract words. Concreteness applies to brand names as well, which is why a dishwashing liquid such as Sunlight may attract more attention than a competing brand named Joy.

▶ *Amount of competing stimuli.* A stimulus is easier to process when few things surround it to compete for your attention.[49] You are more likely to notice a billboard when driving down a deserted rural highway than when in a congested, sign-filled city, just as you are more likely to notice a brand name in a visually simple ad than in one that is visually cluttered. Companies seek moments and locations where competition for attention with their stimuli is limited.

Exhibit 3.6

Concreteness and Abstractness
We may pay more attention to things that are concrete and capable of generating images than we do to things that are abstract and difficult to represent visually.

Concrete Words	Abstract Words
Apple	Aptitude
Bowl	Betrayal
Cat	Chance
Cottage	Criterion
Diamond	Democracy
Engine	Essence
Flower	Fantasy
Garden	Glory
Hammer	Hatred
Infant	Ignorance
Lemon	Loyalty
Meadow	Mercy
Mountain	Necessity
Ocean	Obedience

Source: Allan Paivio et al., *Journal of Experimental Psychology,* Monograph Supplement, January 1968, pp. 1–25. Copyright © 1968 by the American Psychological Association. Adapted with permission.

Habituation The process by which a stimulus loses its attention-getting abilities by virtue of its familiarity.

> ▶ *Contrast with competing stimuli.* Contrast captures attention. Color newspaper ads stand out because they are surrounded by black and white, just as black-and-white TV ads stand out during TV shows broadcast in color. For contrast, some winemakers put images of unusual animals on their labels to help bottles stand out on the shelf.[50] In a study on retail advertising, it was found that attention was highest when an ad differed from the other ads, and when these other ads were very similar to each other.[51]

Therefore, attention to a stimulus is high when its signal-to-noise ratio is high. Prominent and concrete stimuli have a high "signal," whereas the "noise" is low when there are few competing stimuli and the stimulus contrasts with those competitors (i.e., because competing ads all look the same). ───────────────

Customer Segments Defined by Attention

If we do pay attention to things that are relevant, pleasant, surprising, and easy to process, can we identify consumer segments that are more affected by relevance, pleasantness, surprise, and ease of processing? The answer appears to be yes. Researchers have identified a group of consumers who paid minimal attention to an ad because the elements were not relevant to them. A second group focused on visually pleasant elements of the ad, such as the picture. The last group spent the longest time looking at the ad and devoted equal time to the picture, package, headline, and body text, perhaps because they viewed the product as personally relevant and its purchase as potentially risky. Hence, the consumers needed sustained attention to properly evaluate the ad's information.[52]

Habituation

When a stimulus becomes familiar, it can lose its attention-getting ability, a result called **habituation**. For example, think about the last time you purchased something new for your bedroom (such as a picture). For the first few days, you probably noticed the object every time you entered the room. Over time, however, you probably noticed the item less and less, as you became habituated to it.

In the same way, consumers become habituated to ads, packages, and other marketing stimuli. To counter this, marketers can alter the stimulus periodically. For example, many companies develop multiple ads that communicate the same basic message but in different ways and different media. Habituation also explains why marketers sometimes change packaging to attract consumers' attention anew. Campbell Soup Company is starting to package soups in pouches, an unusual type of packaging for this category, in part to attract attention.[53]

PERCEPTION AND CONSUMER BEHAVIOR

Perception The process of determining the properties of stimuli using vision, hearing, taste, smell, and touch.

After we have been exposed to a stimulus and have devoted at least some attention to it, we are in a position to perceive it. **Perception** is the process of determining the properties of stimuli using one or more of our five senses: vision, hearing, taste, smell, and touch. For instance, consumers judge how much soft drink a can will contain based on its width and height, how much food a plate contains based on the size of the plate, which car will drive fastest based on the color (red or green) and the engine's sound (low pitched or high pitched), which fabric softener will make clothes softest based on its smell and color, and so on. Consumers constantly and mostly automatically determine such properties of marketing stimuli using their senses and knowledge of the world. Some of these perceptions are about physical properties such as the size, color, pitch, loudness, smell, and softness of stimuli, while others are meanings associated with these properties.

Perceiving Through Vision

What arouses our visual perception?

▶ *Size and shape.* Consumers perceive that packages in eye-catching shapes contain more of a product.[54] When product or package size is changed, consumers are less sensitive when the change involves only one dimension (height or length or width) than when the change involves all three dimensions. Thus, consumers may "supersize" their order when a product is enlarged along only one dimension, but "downsize" when the product is enlarged along all dimensions, a change more easily perceived.[55]

▶ *Lettering.* The size and style of the lettering on a product or in an ad can attract attention and support brand recognition and image.[56] The distinctive Coca-Cola script, for instance, is not only eye-catching but also is instantly identified with the soft-drink brand.

▶ *Image location on package.* Where product images are located on a package can influence consumers' perceptions and preferences. Images located near the package top, on the left side, or at top-left add to the perception of a product as "lighter." On packages of products where "lighter" is perceived positively—such as healthy snacks—the images should be placed in these "lighter" locations.[57]

▶ *Color.* Color is a crucial factor in visual perception. A color can be described according to hue, saturation, and lightness. *Hue* is the pigment contained in the color. Colors can be classified into two broad categories of hues: warm colors such as red, orange, and yellow and cool colors such as green, blue, and violet. *Saturation* (also called *chroma*) refers to the richness of the color, leading to distinctions such as pale pink or deep, rich pink. *Lightness* refers to the depth of tone in the color. A saturated pink could have a lot of lightness (a fluorescent pink) or a lot of darkness (a mauve).

▶ *Effects of color on physiological responses and moods.* Color can influence our physiological responses and moods: Warm colors generally encourage activity and excitement, whereas cool colors are more soothing and relaxing. Thus, cool colors are more appropriate in places such as spas or doctors' offices, where it is desirable for consumers to feel calm or to spend time making decisions. Warm colors are more appropriate in environments such as health clubs and fast-food restaurants, where high levels of activity are desirable.

▶ *Color and liking.* Colors can have a great effect on consumers' liking of a product. Dirt Devil vacuum cleaners and Sunbeam Toasters, for example, now come in fashion colors like teal blue, targeting college students and graduates who are setting up households for the first time.[58] Steel, another popular choice, feels "industrial," which fits certain lifestyles.

Perceiving Through Hearing

Sound represents another form of sensory input. Perception of sounds depends on its intensity.[59] Consumers are more likely to notice loud music or voices and stark noises. When the announcer in a radio or TV ad speaks more quickly, the faster pace disrupts consumers' processing of the information; a low-pitched voice speaking syllables at a faster-than-normal rate induces more positive ad and brand attitudes.[60] When a company uses one person to speak the voice-over lines during many of its ads or plays the same jingle in many commercials, consumers associate those sounds with the product or brand. McDonald's, NBC, Harley-Davidson, and other firms consciously seek to define a certain *sonic identity*—using certain music or sounds to identify a brand.[61]

Further, consumers infer product attributes and form evaluations using information gleaned from hearing a brand's sounds, syllables, and words—a process known as *sound symbolism*.[62] For instance, the name of Nissan's LEAF electric car reminds consumers of the product's environmental benefits. In addition, because electric cars are very quiet, Nissan created a pleasant, turbine-like hum as a distinctive, non–gasoline-engine noise to signal LEAF's smooth acceleration and deceleration.[63]

Perceiving Through Taste

Food and beverage marketers must stress taste perceptions in their marketing stimuli. For example, the major challenge for marketers of low-calorie and low-fat products is to provide healthier foods that still taste good and that are perceived as such. Yet what tastes good to one person may not taste good to another, and consumers from different cultural backgrounds may have different taste preferences. Interestingly, tasting or sampling a product is the in-store marketing tactic that most influences consumer purchasing, even though stand-alone, in-store displays—perceived through vision—are the marketing tactic that shoppers notice the most.[64] "If you see a four-pack of Oogavé sodas on the grocery shelf alongside all the other soda options, you may not put it in your shopping cart," explains the head of the small Colorado-based company that makes these all-natural drinks. "But once you've tried it, you'll go looking for it."[65]

Perceiving Through Smell

If you were blindfolded, you (like most consumers) would probably have a hard time identifying many supermarket items based on smell.[66] However, consumers also differ in their ability to label odors. Compared with younger consumers, the elderly have a harder time identifying smells,[67] and men in general are worse at the task than are women.[68] Marketers are concerned with the effects of smell on consumer responses, product trial, liking, and buying.

▶ *Effects of smells on physiological responses and moods.* Smell produces both physiological and emotional responses. Some studies show that people can feel tense or relaxed depending on whether or not a scent is present and what it is.[69] This theory has been key to the development of aromatherapy. Some of our most basic emotions are also linked to smell. For example, children hate having their security blankets washed, in part because washing removes comforting smells. In addition, the smell of the ocean, freshly baked cookies, or apple pie can revive emotional or childhood memories.[70]

▶ *Smells and product trial.* Smell (often in combination with other sensory perceptions) can entice consumers to try or buy a food product. Research suggests that scents in the air can be effective stimuli when related to the product being sold—yet the fit between scent and product is crucial. Thus, a flowery aroma would be more appropriate for a lingerie store than for a coffee bar.[71] Some "scratch-and-sniff" ads for perfumes and after-shave lotions are doused with the product to increase sensory processing. However, this technique can backfire if consumers are offended by or have allergic reactions to scents.

▶ *Smell and liking.* Retailers, in particular, recognize that smells can attract consumers. For example, The NetCost supermarket in New York City adds grapefruit aromas in its produce department to attract shoppers. Since NetCost began doing this, fruit and vegetable sales have increased 7 percent.[72] Similarly, grocery retailers often locate in-store bakeries up front so that the aroma of fresh bread can be smelled at the main entrance.

▶ *Smell and buying.* Providing a pleasant-smelling environment can have a positive effect on shopping behavior by encouraging more attention to relevant stimuli that consumers encounter, and encouraging consumers to linger longer.[73] M&M World, for example, in London pumps chocolate aromas throughout the store to put consumers in the mood for buying its products.[74]

Perceiving Through Touch

Although individual preferences vary, touch (both what we touch with our fingers and the way things feel as they come in contact with our skin) is an important aspect of many offerings.[75] Consumers like some products because of their feel. Some consumers buy skin creams and baby products for their soothing effect on the skin. In fact, consumers who have a high need for touch tend to like products that provide this opportunity.[76] When considering products with material properties, such as clothing or carpeting, consumers prefer goods they can touch in stores more than products they only see and read about online or in catalogs.[77]

Merely touching a product (or imagining the action of touching it) can increase a consumer's perceived ownership of the item. Also, consumers who are briefly touched by a salesperson are more likely to have positive feelings and more likely to evaluate both the store and the salesperson positively. In addition, customers who are touched by the salesperson are more likely to comply with the salesperson's requests.[78] However, reaction to touch in sales situation differs from culture to culture. Consumers in Latin America are more comfortable with touching and embracing than U.S. consumers. In Asia, touching between relative strangers is seen as inappropriate.[79] Another interesting finding is that consumers have higher evaluations of a product that has been touched by an attractive member of the opposite sex, such as a good-looking salesperson or model.[80] This finding shows the symbolic nature of consumer behavior, which Chapter 16 treats in further detail.

Marketing Implications

Sensory marketing is the process of systematically managing consumers' perception and experiences of marketing stimuli.[81] Many companies seek to enhance consumer perception of marketing stimuli by appealing to the five senses (see Exhibit 3.7)

Vision

Because colors can strongly influence attention to and liking of a product, marketers often rely on the advice of "color forecasters" when deciding which colors to use in products and on packages. Why? Because color can make consumers believe they are buying products that are very current or spark nostalgia for earlier times. Color is also important in perceptions of service marketers and their staff. For example, MGM Grand hotel in Las Vegas projects a contemporary image by updating the color and style of employees' uniforms when it redecorates restaurants and other hotel facilities.[82]

Hearing

Fast music, like that played at aerobics classes, tends to energize; in contrast, slow music can be soothing. The type of music being played in a retail outlet can affect shopping behavior.[83] A fast tempo creates a more rapid traffic flow, whereas a slow tempo can increase sales as much as 38 percent because it encourages leisurely shopping (although consumers are unaware of this influence).[84] A fast tempo is more desirable in some restaurants because consumers will eat faster, facilitating greater turnover and higher sales.[85] For example, radio ads for the In-N-Out hamburger chain use a slightly retro, fast-paced jingle to reflect both old-fashioned quality and speedy service.[86] Likable and familiar music can induce good moods, whereas discordant sounds can induce bad moods. This effect is important to note because, as you will see in later chapters, bad moods may affect how people feel about products and consumption experiences.[87]

Taste

Marketers often try to monitor consumers' tastes through taste tests. Many food and beverage products are thoroughly taste tested before they are introduced. Ads or food packages sometimes ask consumers to compare the product's taste with that of competing products. However, consumers are not always good at discerning taste, so marketers should consider adding descriptive words or pictures to marketing communications about foods, restaurants, and the like.[88] To engage consumers, some marketers mention taste in an unexpected way. For instance, the slogan of Buckley's

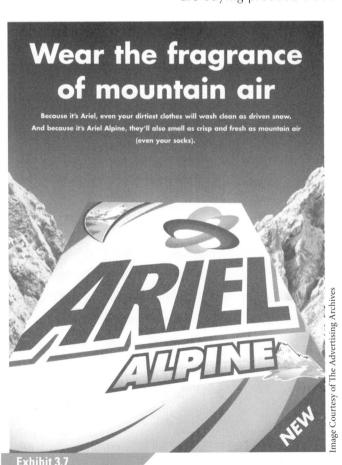

Image Courtesy of The Advertising Archives

Exhibit 3.7

Perception Through Senses
Some products are valued because of the smells they evoke.

Cough Mixture is "It Tastes Awful. And It Works." The company has built on this slogan to launch viral campaigns that keep brand awareness high during cold and cough season.[89]

Smell

Obviously, we like some products—for example, perfumes and scented candles—for the smells they produce. However, we may like other products, such as mouthwashes and deodorants, because they mask aromas. Procter & Gamble's Febreze, for example, started as an odor eliminator. After company research showed how strongly consumers are influenced by scents, marketers introduced aromas into Febreze and added these aromas to many P&G products for the home and laundry. Due to multimedia marketing that reinforces positive perceptions of these Febreze scents, P&G sells more than $1 billion worth of Febreze products yearly.[90]

However, smell does not always work to the marketers' advantage: Some consumers may dislike a product scent or find it irritating. In addition, some consumers value particular products because they have no smell, such as unscented deodorants, carpet cleaners, and laundry detergents. Finally, consumers' preferences for smells differ across cultures. Only one smell (cola) is universally regarded as pleasant, a finding that is good news for companies like Coca-Cola and Pepsi that are expanding globally.[91]

Touch

Knowing that consumers prefer to try products before they buy them, many retailers and manufacturers offer trial sizes, samples, and opportunities to handle products. The Bass Pro Shops sporting goods stores, for example, offer hands-on demonstrations of products for sale. Companies often set up tables or exhibits in transportation hubs and busy shopping districts so consumers can get a feel for products in person. When South Korea's Dongsuh Foods opened a two-week "pop-up" café in a trendy urban area to promote instant coffee, it hired a popular actor to serve coffee to consumers on opening day.[92] Getting consumers to taste the coffee was clearly the main goal, but having an attractive actor touch the product may have also influenced perceptions in a positive way. ⎯⎯⎯⎯⎯⎯⎯⎯

When Do We Perceive Stimuli?

Our senses are exposed to numerous inputs at any given time. To perceive each one would be overwhelming and extremely difficult. Fortunately, our sensory processing is simplified by the fact that many stimuli do not enter our conscious awareness. For us to perceive something, it must be sufficiently intense. The intensity of a smell can be measured by the concentration of the stimulus in a substance or in the air. Stimulus intensity of sounds can be measured in decibels and frequencies, and stimulus intensity of colors can be measured by properties like lightness, saturation, and hue. In the area of touch, stimulus intensity can be measured in terms of pounds or ounces of pressure. In terms of taste, the bitterness of beers is measured in IBUs (International Bitterness Units).

Absolute Thresholds

Absolute threshold The minimal level of stimulus intensity needed to detect a stimulus.

The **absolute threshold** is the minimum level of stimulus intensity needed for a stimulus to be perceived. In other words, the absolute threshold is the amount of intensity needed for a person to detect a difference between something and nothing. Suppose you are driving on the highway and a billboard is in the distance. The absolute threshold is that point at which you can first see the billboard. Before that point, the billboard is below the absolute threshold and not sufficiently intense to be seen.

Differential Thresholds

Differential threshold/ just noticeable difference (j.n.d.) The intensity difference needed between two stimuli before they are perceived to be different.

Whereas the absolute threshold deals with whether or not a stimulus can be perceived, the **differential threshold** refers to the intensity difference needed between two stimuli before people can perceive that the stimuli are *different*. Thus, the differential threshold is a relative concept; it is often called the **just noticeable difference (j.n.d.)**. For example, when you get your eyes checked, the eye doctor often shows you a row of letters through different sets of lenses. If you can detect a difference between the two lenses, the new lens is different enough to have crossed the differential threshold.

Weber's law The stronger the initial stimulus, the greater the additional intensity needed for the second stimulus to be perceived as different.

Weber's law, outlined by psychophysiologist Ernst Weber, states that the stronger the initial stimulus, the greater the additional intensity needed for the second stimulus to be perceived as different. This relationship is shown in the following formula:

$$\frac{\Delta s}{S} = K$$

where S is the initial stimulus value, Δs is the smallest change (Δ) in a stimulus capable of being detected, and K is a constant of proportionality.

Imagine that a marketer finds, through testing, that 1 ounce would need to be added to a 10-ounce package before consumers notice that the two packages contain different amounts. The marketer has a 50-ounce box and wants to know how much to add before consumers detect a difference. According to Weber's law, $K = 1/10$ or 0.10. To determine how much would need to be added, would solve for Ds as follows:

$$\frac{\Delta s}{50} = 0.10$$

The answer is 0.10 of the package weight, or 5 ounces.

Marketing Implications

Thresholds have a number of implications in marketing situations.

Absolute Threshold

Obviously, consumers will only consciously perceive a marketing stimulus when it is sufficiently high in intensity to be above the absolute threshold. Thus, if images or words in a commercial are too small or the sound level is too low, the stimulus will not be consciously perceived.

Differential Threshold

Sometimes marketers *do not* want consumers to notice a difference between two stimuli. In some cases, marketers might not want consumers to notice that they have decreased a product's size or increased its price, a situation that raises ethical concerns. Yet more companies are shrinking packages and contents rather than raising prices. For example, when *Consumer Reports* asked Häagen-Dazs why it reduced the amount of ice cream in its containers by two fluid ounces, the company explained: "Due to the cost of ingredients and facilities costs, it was either change the size of the container or raise the price."[93]

In other instances, marketers *do* want consumers to perceive a difference between two stimuli. For example, McDonald's once increased the size of its regular hamburger patty by 25 percent but left the price the same, hoping that consumers would notice the change.[94] Note that differential thresholds vary from sense to sense. For example, since our sense of smell is not well developed, we may fail to differentiate the smell of two versions of the same object.

Subliminal Perception

"Limen" is the Latin word for threshold, and "sub" means below. Subliminal stimuli are presented below the threshold level of conscious awareness. If such stimuli still have an effect, this is evidence of **subliminal perception**. Subliminal perception is different from preattentive processing. In the case of preattentive processing, our attention is directed at something other than the stimulus—for instance, at a magazine article instead of an ad in our peripheral vision. With subliminal perception, our attention is directed squarely at the stimulus that is being presented subliminally. Also, with preattentive processing, the stimulus is fully present—if you shift your attention and look directly at the ad or billboard, you can easily see it. In contrast, subliminal stimuli are presented so quickly or are so degraded that the very act of consciously perceiving is not possible, even if you try hard.

Subliminal perception The activation of sensory receptors by stimuli presented below the perceptual threshold.

Subliminal perception has been the subject of controversy since a widely known but fraudulent study claimed that consumers at a movie theater bought more popcorn and Coca-Cola after being subliminally exposed to extremely brief on-screen messages that read "Eat popcorn" and "Drink Coke."[95] This study that was never published and perhaps never conducted still led to much public debate because it appeared to show that advertising could manipulate consumers against their will.[96] What is the evidence? It is important to distinguish between "weak" and "strong" effects of subliminal advertising.

A "strong" effect would be when subliminal advertising could influence people against their will. There is very little evidence for this theory though. Recent studies show that subliminal perception can enhance persuasion only when the subliminal stimulus fits with the consumer's current goals or motivations.[97] In other words, consumers who are hungry and ready to eat will be more motivated to act on a subliminal message about popcorn than if they have just had a meal. Here, both a subliminal stimulus and a motivated consumer make the difference for behavioral effects to occur.

A "weak" effect would be when subliminal advertising could influence people in ways that are consistent with their current goals or motivations. Unlike the strong effect, there is now much evidence for the weak effect. If consumers are subliminally exposed to a word (e.g., razor), they will recognize that word faster than they recognize words to which they have not been exposed subliminally.[98] This research shows that subliminal stimuli can activate various meanings in consumers. In one study, when consumers were exposed subliminally to either the IBM or the Apple brand logo, those exposed to the Apple logo exhibited more creativity when completing a subsequent task. Apple is known for its creativity, and consumers subliminally primed by its logo responded creatively in an automatic way when motivated, without being conscious of any influence.[99] Of course, such subliminal stimuli do not immediately make a Steve Jobs out of most people, but they may temporarily activate forms of divergent thinking that most people have access to and appreciate. Stimuli that are perceived subliminally may also affect consumers' feelings. Consumers were found to have stronger responses to ads with sexual subliminal implants than to those without them.[100]

Overall, research suggests that the effects of subliminal perception are limited, and difficult to obtain outside of controlled laboratory situations.[101] Still, researchers continue to investigate when and how subliminal advertising works to understand fundamental perception processes, also using neuroscience methods.[102] Exposing consumers to the message at or *above* the threshold level of awareness should generally have just as much, if not more, impact than subliminal stimuli, making the use of subliminal stimuli unnecessary.[103] Moreover, subliminal advertising is banned in the United States, the United Kingdom, Australia, and the Netherlands, among other countries.[104]

How Do Consumers Perceive a Stimulus?

Consumers tend not to perceive a single stimulus in isolation; rather, they organize and integrate it in the context of the other things around it. Also, many stimuli are really a complex combination of numerous simple stimuli that consumers must organize into a unified whole using **perceptual organization**. This process represents a somewhat higher, more meaningful level of processing than simply having stimuli register on our sensory receptors (see Exhibit 3.8). Four basic principles related to perceptual organization are figure and ground, closure, grouping, and bias for the whole.

The principle of **figure and ground** suggests that people interpret stimuli in contrast to a background (see Exhibit 3.9). The figure is well defined and in the forefront—the focal point of attention—whereas the ground is indefinite and in the background. Advertisers should plan for important brand information to be the figure, and not let the background detract from the figure.

Perceptual organization The process by which stimuli are organized into meaningful units.

Figure and ground The principle that people interpret stimuli in the context of a background.

CHOCOLATE, CARAMEL AND NUTS. DEVOUR THEM.

bluebunny.com   So good, it speaks for itself.

BLUE BUNNY
Champ!

Wells Enterprises, with permission.

Exhibit 3.8

Perceptional Organization
Consumers organize multiple simple stimuli into one unified whole, making an ad like this successful.

© Maurice Savage/Alamy

Exhibit 3.9

Figure and Ground

Sometimes marketers play with reversals of figure and ground to attract and retain attention in creative ways, as in this Baskin-Robbins logo. Initially, you may see a large B and R, the "figure," and the rest of the logo is "ground." Then you may discover that number 31 shown in pink, which refers to the original number of ice-cream flavors that Baskin-Robbins is famous for. When you focus on the pink number 31, you cannot see the letters BR. The switching between 31 and BR illustrates figure-ground reversals to convey the brand message.

Closure refers to the fact that individuals have a need to organize perceptions so that they form a meaningful whole. Even if a stimulus is incomplete, our need for closure will lead us to see it as complete. The key to using the need for closure is to provide consumers with an incomplete stimulus. For example, putting a well-known television ad on the radio can get consumers thinking about the message. The radio version of the ad is an incomplete stimulus, and the need for closure leads consumers to picture the visual parts of the ad. In a television campaign for a coffee brand in Europe, the first stage was a voice-over repeatedly saying ". . . and then there is coffee, brand X coffee, good coffee." In the second stage of the campaign, the voice-over only said: "and then . . . ." so that consumers could complete the sentence themselves. Because of consumers' strong need for closure, such appeals may have positive effects on brand attitude.[105]

Grouping refers to the fact that we often group stimuli to form a unified picture or impression, making it easier to process them. We view similar or nearby objects as belonging together. Marketers can influence the image or perception of an offering by grouping it with other products. In a store, consumers may perceive a table setting as elegant when the napkins, napkin holders, silverware, dishes, and serving bowls are cleverly grouped.

Bias for the whole means that consumers perceive more value in the whole of something than in two or more parts that are equivalent to the whole. Thus, you are more likely to make a $20 purchase if you have two $5 bills and a $10. In contrast, if you have a single $20 bill, your bias for the whole makes you less willing to spend it.[106]

COMPREHENSION AND CONSUMER BEHAVIOR

Closure The principle that individuals have a need to organize perceptions so that they form a meaningful whole.

Grouping The tendency to group stimuli to form a unified picture or impression.

Bias for the whole The tendency to perceive more value in a whole than in the combined parts that make up a whole.

Comprehension The process of extracting higher-order meaning from what we have perceived in the context of what we already know.

Source identification The process of determining what the perceived stimulus actually is.

So far, we have been exposed to a marketing stimulus, focused our attention on it, and used our senses to perceive it. Now, we have to identify what it is and understand the message it conveys. These are the two critical elements in **comprehension**, which is the process of extracting higher-order meaning from what we have perceived in the context of what we already know. Sometimes it is immediately clear that a stimulus to which we are exposed is an ad for a car brand, but the message the car brand wants to convey may be less clear. In that case, the *message comprehension* is challenged. But increasingly, it may be hard to identify whether the stimulus that we are exposed to is an ad or something else, which represents a challenge of *source identification*.

Source Identification

Source identification is the process of determining what the stimulus that we have detected actually is. Chapter 4 explains in more detail how we use categorization processes to quickly accomplish this identification. Imagine opening a magazine and quickly looking at a page. Source identification is the rapid, perhaps automatic process of determining what the page contains. Is it an ad, or something else? If it is an ad, what brand or product is being advertised? Research shows that consumers are very good at identifying the products and brands in ads—when the ads are typical for the category. In fact, after only 100 milliseconds (just a brief, single glance) consumers already know that something is an ad rather than editorial information (such as an article). And if the ad is typical, they know which product category and even which brand is being advertised. Ads that are atypical for the product category require more than a single glance to communicate what they are for, which is why marketers try to retain consumers' attention long enough to allow for source identification.[107]

Because of techniques such as *product placement* (arranging for a product to be shown in a movie, TV show, or digital game), it is not always easy to know whether something is really a marketing message. Blurring of the lines occurs in other media, as well. Is that magazine article actually an *advertorial* (advertising that takes the form of editorial content) or a story unconnected with a sponsor? Is that TV program an *infomercial* (a long-form commercial sponsored by a marketer) or a news story about a product or brand? Commercial stimuli try to look noncommercial because that may increase their credibility—although that compromises source identification by consumers. The U.S. Federal Trade Commission (FTC) requires that advertorials and infomercials be clearly labeled as such, but these disclosures generally attract less attention than the rest of the message.

Message Comprehension

Once we have identified the source as a marketing message and determined what product or brand is involved, we can start to comprehend its message—make sense out of it—on a number of levels. In particular, marketers are concerned with (1) objective and subjective comprehension of messages; (2) the possibility of miscomprehension; (3) the effect of motivation, attitude, and opportunity on comprehension; and (4) the effect of culture.

Objective and Subjective Comprehension

Objective comprehension The extent to which consumers accurately understand the message a sender intended to communicate.

Subjective comprehension What the consumer understands from the message, regardless of whether this understanding is accurate.

Objective comprehension refers to whether the meaning that consumers take from a message is consistent with what the message actually stated. **Subjective comprehension** is the different or additional meaning consumers attach to the message, whether or not these meanings were intended.[108] Whereas *objective comprehension* reflects whether we accurately understand what a sender intended to communicate, *subjective comprehension* reflects what we understand, accurate or not. Marketing mix elements such as price and advertising have a powerful influence on what we think a message is saying. You may infer that a dental gum is as powerful at whitening teeth as whitening toothpastes because the package art has white sparkles, the model in the ad has very white teeth, and the package displays phrases like "whitening agent." Yet the product may not be an effective whitening agent, and the words on the package may not actually say that it is, as you will see later in this chapter.

Miscomprehension

Miscomprehension occurs when consumers inaccurately construe the meaning contained in a message. Several studies have found a surprisingly high level of miscomprehension of TV and magazine ads. The estimated rate of objective comprehension was only about 70 percent for TV ads and 65 percent for print ads. Moreover, the rates of miscomprehension for directly asserted information and implied information were fairly equal, as were miscomprehension rates for programming, editorial material, and advertising.[109]

In addition to miscomprehending advertising messages, consumers sometimes miscomprehend product descriptions and usage instructions. The insurance company Aflac (American Family Life Assurance Company) changed its advertising messages after research showed that consumers misunderstood some of its offerings (see Exhibit 3.10). The famous duck that quacks the company's name is still in Aflac ads, having helped boost brand recognition to more than 90 percent. However, the ads now focus on the benefits of the company's insurance, with messages like "When I'm hurt and miss work, Aflac gives me cash to help pay bills that my health insurance doesn't pay."[110]

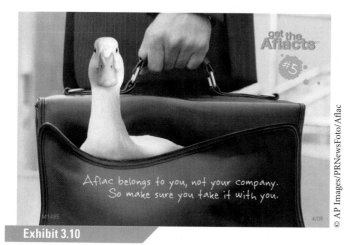

Aflac belongs to you, not your company. So make sure you take it with you.

© AP Images/PRNewsFoto/Aflac

Exhibit 3.10

Avoiding Miscomprehension

Aflac's ad combines a brand cue (the duck) with a clear message of their services to avoid miscomprehension.

Effect of MAO

Consumers may not comprehend a marketing message when they have low motivation and limited opportunity to process it, when the message is complex or shown for only a few seconds, or when the message is viewed only once or twice.[111] Experts are better able to comprehend information about a highly innovative product when prompted by marketing messages that help them make the connections and tap existing knowledge in more than one category.[112] Regarding ability, one study found that although consumers want to see nutritional information on packaging (implying high motivation to process it), most do not comprehend it once they have read it.[113] Still, comprehension may improve with expertise and ability, which is the reason that adults often better comprehend the finer points of a message than young children do.[114]

Effect of the Culture

Consumers in low-context cultures such as those in North America and northern Europe generally separate the words and meanings of a communication from the context in which the message appears. In these cultures, consumers place more emphasis on what is said than on the surrounding visuals. But in high-context cultures (such as many in Asia), much of a message's meaning is implied indirectly and communicated nonverbally rather than stated explicitly through words. The message sender's characteristics, such as social class, values, and age, also play an important role in message interpretation.[115] Language differences further raise the possibility of miscomprehension, as does the meaning that consumers in different cultures attach to words.[116] For example, in the United Kingdom, a *billion* is "a million million," whereas in the United States, a billion means "a thousand million."

Marketing Implications

Marketers may enhance consumer comprehension and awareness with a variety of tactics.

Marketers can improve objective comprehension in several ways.[117] When consumers accurately identify the advertised product and brand, much is already gained because people can access their prior knowledge. Keeping the message simple helps too. Another is to repeat the message—stating it multiple times within the same communication and repeating it on multiple occasions. Presenting information in different forms, such as both visually and verbally in a TV commercial, can also help consumers form an accurate mental picture.[118] In fact, consumers who have had more exposure to a brand's marketing messages will be better able to process brand information and have more positive attitudes toward it.[119] Ease in perceiving and processing information is known as **perceptual fluency**. The earlier in life that consumers encounter a brand, and the more regularly they encounter it, the more quickly they will be able to recognize it. As a result, perceptual fluency is high for established brands that have been known for years, compared with new brands just entering the market.[120]

Subjective comprehension involves some interaction between what is in a message and what consumers already know. As a result, a marketer can strongly influence what consumers subjectively perceive by designing a message to be consistent with their prior knowledge. When consumers know little about a new product, marketers may be able to convey information effectively by drawing an analogy between the product and something with similar benefits. For example, a marketer may try to communicate the idea that a particular brand of boots is waterproof, soft, and lightweight by using the analogy of a duck.[121]

Product placements are on the rise as marketers seek to counter advertising avoidance and associate their brands with popular media. *American Idol*, for example, is among the leaders in TV product placements, such as when its judges sip from Coca-Cola-labeled cups.[122] Knowing that Chinese audiences responded positively to earlier *Transformers* movies, Lenovo and other Chinese marketers arranged for product placement in *Transformers 3* to showcase their brands in a blockbuster Hollywood movie.[123] Marketers pay some celebrities with large numbers of Twitter followers, such as Snoop Dogg, for tweeting about brands and offerings.[124] (As required by the FTC, sponsored tweets must be labeled as such, using hashtags such as #spon or #ad.) Such product placements blur the boundaries between commercial and noncommercial stimuli and

Perceptual fluency
The ease with which information is processed.

may make it harder for consumers to identify the goals and messages of the programs and their contents.

At times, marketers may (knowingly or unknowingly) create inferences that do not accurately characterize an offering, which results in miscomprehension.[125] For instance, Taiwan's Fair Trade Commission recently fined Colgate for a comparative TV commercial in which the competing toothpaste brand wasn't sufficiently disguised. The ad was intended to convey Colgate's superiority in reducing teeth sensitivity. However, the commission said consumers could be misled into thinking that the competing brand was an inferior toothpaste, even though it also contained ingredients proven to reduce sensitivity.[126] _____

Consumer Inferences

Specific elements of the marketing mix can affect the correct or incorrect inferences consumers make about an offering during comprehension. *Inferences* are the conclusions that consumers draw or interpretations that they form based on the message. Such inferences may lead to conclusions such as (1) if brand A contains attribute 1 then it will also contain attribute 2 (congruent) or (2) if brand A contains attribute 1 then it will not contain attribute 2 (incongruent). Here, we look at the effect of brand names and symbols, product features and packaging, price, and retail atmospherics and display.

Brand Names and Symbols

Subjective comprehension of a marketing communication can be based on the inferences consumers make from a brand symbol. For example, the Pillsbury Doughboy has slimmed down over the years because the company's marketers were afraid that consumers would infer that he was fat from eating Pillsbury products.

Brand names themselves can create subjective comprehension and inferences. For example, alphanumeric brand names like BMW's X6 tend to be associated with technological sophistication. When presented with brand names such as X-500 and X-700, consumers tend to prefer names with higher numerical values, inferring that the product will have advanced attributes.[127] In addition, consumers tend to make inferences when they evaluate a brand extension by carrying over certain features linked to the parent brand.[128]

Descriptive names can also create inferences. Brand names such as Speedo for bathing suits may create inferences about the particular brand's benefits.[129] Some brand names lead to inappropriate or outdated inferences about the product, especially after new features are added. When Verizon Wireless, for example, expanded its video-on-demand offerings for cell phone users, it signaled the update by changing the name from V Cast to Verizon Video.[130]

Product Features and Packaging

Consumers may subjectively comprehend aspects of an offering based on inferences they make from the product and the way that it is packaged. For example, consumers may infer that a product with a low repair record also has a long warranty.[131] As another example, a consumer who encounters a large, multipack item may use prior knowledge about the correlation between price and package size to infer that the large-sized brand is also a good buy.[132]

Consumers make taste inferences based on nutritional information presented about food products, inferences that affect their buying and consumption decisions. Some research shows that consumers who are given nutritional information about a product are more likely to see it as healthier than when they are not given nutritional information. However, they will also infer that the healthier product will not taste as good as an unhealthier product.[133] Moreover, consumers infer that products with unusual flavors or color names are better than products that use common flavors or color names.[134]

When consumers are searching for information about whether a product will deliver a particular benefit, exposure to irrelevant attributes leads to inferences that the product will not necessarily perform as desired.[135] In highly competitive categories, where differences among products seem minimal, consumers may infer that although the dominant brand is good on observable attributes it has a disadvantage on some unobservable attribute.[136]

Knowledge about a product's country of origin can affect the way consumers think about it.[137] Just as we stereotype people based on where they were born, we stereotype products based on where they were made. Consumers in developing countries, for instance, often infer higher quality for brands perceived as foreign.[138] Conversely, consumers in some nations believe their country's products are superior to those made elsewhere. Japanese consumers, for example, tend to infer that made-in-Japan products are higher quality than made-in-America products. Therefore, Samsonite markets its pricier luggage in Japan by stressing that the products are designed and made in Japan.[139] Consumers are more likely to make inferences about a brand based on its country of origin when they are unmotivated to process brand information or when their processing goal guides attention toward origin information.[140] If consumers dislike a country's political or social policies, they may respond negatively to its products.[141]

Package characteristics can also stimulate inferences. Although consumers may make inferences about one brand if its packaging looks much like that of the market leader, they do not necessarily react negatively to the copycat brand.[142] As bargain-hunting consumers increasingly seek out cost-effective store brands, more retailers are redesigning their packaging to point up the differences between store and national brands. Walgreens, for example, has renamed and repackaged its store-brand merchandise to stand out and look more distinctive next to national brands.[143]

Price

Consumers sometimes (but not always) make inferences about an offering's quality based on its price.[144] They may know from prior experience that price and quality tend to be correlated in a particular product category, and then infer that a high-priced product is also high in quality.[145] Consumers often make this inference when they believe that brands differ in quality, when they perceive that choosing a low-quality product can be risky, and when they have no information about the brand's quality before they buy it.[146] When consumers use price as a shortcut to infer quality, they may overestimate the relationship between price and quality.[147]

Retail Atmospherics, Displays, and Distribution

Comprehension can be influenced by retailers' marketing tactics. The inferences you make when walking into a warehouse-type store like Costco are likely to be different from the inferences you make entering a more upscale, service-oriented store like Nordstrom. Atmospherics are a major tool used to develop, elaborate, and change store images. The Duane Reade drug store in New York City's financial district is nothing like the typical drug store, urban or suburban. Housed in a former bank building with marble walls and vaulted ceilings, this store has a two-story lobby and a holographic "greeter" who talks up special features such as the stock ticker, manicure center, and sushi stations.[148]

The context of a product display is also important. In particular, it may lead consumers to rely more on external cues—meaning that a brand's positioning could be undermined by a store's inappropriate retail display decisions.[149] Exhibit 3.11 shows that lighting and signs are the two atmospheric elements that consumers say exert the most influence on their in-store behavior.

Moreover, consumers may draw inferences from the way an offering is distributed. For example, food trucks have not traditionally been associated with innovative, top-quality meals or snacks. These days, however, consumers expect novel tastes when they approach one of the many gourmet food trucks crisscrossing streets from Portland, Oregon, to Portland, Maine. Many food trucks announce their routes via Twitter or mobile apps, adding an "insider" association to the experience of being in the right place at the right time.[150]

Exhibit 3.11

Which Atmospheric Elements Exert the Most Influence?
Certain atmospheric elements are perceived by consumers to influence their shopping and buying behavior.

Source: From "Measuring Shopper Response," *Chain Store Age,* January 2004, pp. 3B+. Reprinted with permission of Lebhar-Friedman, Inc.

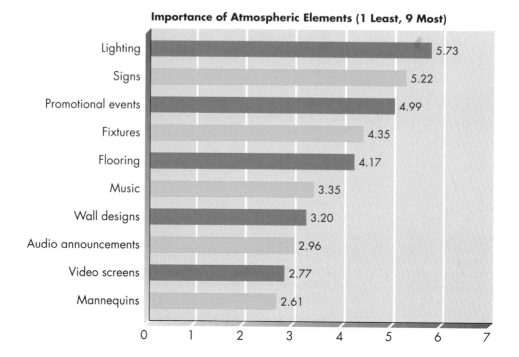

Importance of Atmospheric Elements (1 Least, 9 Most)

Element	Value
Lighting	5.73
Signs	5.22
Promotional events	4.99
Fixtures	4.35
Flooring	4.17
Music	3.35
Wall designs	3.20
Audio announcements	2.96
Video screens	2.77
Mannequins	2.61

SUMMARY

For a marketing stimulus to have an impact, consumers must be exposed to it, allocate some attention to it, and perceive it. Consumers need a basic level of attention to perceive a stimulus before they can use additional mental resources to process the stimulus at higher levels. Exposure occurs when the consumer is presented with a marketing stimulus. Attention occurs when the consumer allocates processing capacity to the stimulus. Attention is limited, selective, and divided, and may be focal or nonfocal. Consumers perceive a stimulus by using one or more of their five senses.

Perceptual thresholds determine the point at which stimuli are perceived. Consumers can sometimes perceive things outside of their conscious level of awareness, a phenomenon called subliminal perception. Perceptual organization occurs when consumers organize a set of stimuli into a coherent whole, affected by the principles of figure and ground, closure, grouping, and bias for the whole. Comprehension is the process of extracting higher-order meaning from what consumers have perceived in the context of what they know. This starts with source identification ("what is it actually?") and continues with message comprehension ("what about it?"), including objective comprehension (accurately understanding what is stated) and subjective comprehension (what consumers understand from the message). Finally, consumers may make correct or incorrect inferences from various elements of the marketing mix during the comprehension process.

Questions for Review and Discussion

1. How do zipping and zapping affect consumers' exposure to marketing stimuli such as products and ads?

2. What is attention, and what are its three key characteristics?

3. In what ways do prominence and habituation affect consumer attention?

4. What is perception, and what methods do we use to perceive stimuli?

5. Differentiate between the absolute threshold and the differential threshold, and explain how these concepts relate to Weber's law.

6. Identify four principles of perceptual organization and describe why marketers need to know about them.

7. Discuss how source identification and message comprehension affect consumers' comprehension of a stimulus.

8. What are some ways that companies can use marketing-mix elements such as brand names and symbols to affect consumer inferences?

CONSUMER BEHAVIOR CASE

How Under Armour Gets Noticed

The Nike swoosh may be one of the most recognized logos in the world of sports, but the Under Armour logo (an interlocking U and A) is increasingly in the spotlight as the company gets noticed on and off the field. Founded in 1996 by Kevin Plank, once a member of the University of Maryland's football team, Under Armour designs apparel and gear to help athletes feel and do their best in hot or cold weather, in sports arenas or on the track. How can a latecomer to a fast-growing industry dominated by global giants such as Nike get noticed?

A little-known brand name was only one of Under Armour's early challenges. Another was that many of its first products (such as undershirts that wick away moisture) were not actually visible to onlookers. In contrast, the logos of competing brands were visible and often prominent on athletic shoes, shirts, and caps. So the company initially positioned itself as "a brand for the next generation of athletes." Whereas Nike was sponsoring well-known, established athletes, Under Armour's sponsorships went to up-and-comers known for their dedication and athleticism. Its first endorsement deal was with a Dallas Cowboys football player who had been at University of Maryland with Under Armour's founder. More recently, the company's performance apparel has been spotted on endorsers such as Heather Mitts (soccer), Cam Newtown (football), and Derrick Williams (basketball).

As its sponsored athletes do well, and their teams win games and even championships, Under Armour's brand gains attention and visibility. Although not every rising star becomes a sports legend, the brand still gets exposure as these athletes receive media coverage, become established in their sports, and appear in Under Armour ads. Now that the company rings up more than $1 billion in yearly revenue from the sale of clothing, footwear, and accessories for men, women, and children, it can also afford some high-profile deals, such as being endorsed by Tom Brady of the New England Patriots.

The Under Armour website features the brand mission—"Make all athletes better"—and puts its "Universal guarantee of performance" in a conspicuous position, offering a full refund if customers are ever dissatisfied with a product for any reason. The diversity of models and athletes on the Under Armour site and in its ads, often shown participating in a sport, invites a broad range of consumers to identify with the brand.

The close ties between Under Armour and the University of Maryland have led to additional opportunities for brand and product exposure. To grab attention and sell more team merchandise, college and professional football teams are switching to more fashionable uniforms and gear, with flashier colors and styles. As part of this trend, Under Armour has designed 32 different items for football players at the University of Maryland to wear. Fans, competing teams, and the media can't help but notice the eye-catching combinations of shirts, pants, and helmets worn by team members on different days—with Under Armour's now-familiar logo on each item.

What's ahead for Under Armour? The company is expanding into Europe and beyond, relying on distribution and marketing communications to reach more consumers, both casual and serious athletes. It is using social media such as YouTube, Twitter, and Facebook to engage consumers, showcase its sports endorsers, and increase brand and product visibility. Just as important, new products are in the pipeline, along with new technology that enhances Under Armour's differentiation.[151]

CASE QUESTIONS

1. What is Under Armour doing to make its brand personally relevant, surprising, and easy to process?
2. What role do objective and subjective comprehension play in Under Armour's ability to market its products by sponsoring up-and-coming athletes?
3. Why would Under Armour want to be sure that consumers can clearly see different models as well as its mission and guarantee on the brand's website?

ENDNOTES

1. Sarah Danckert, "Merlin Set to Weave Magic with Theme-Park Portfolio," *The Australian*, February 23, 2012, p. 30; Hugo Martin, "A Heated Wax Museum War Takes Shape in Hollywood," *Los Angeles Times*, December 21, 2011, www.latimes.com; and "Waxing on with Celebrities at Madame Tussauds Tokyo," *Yomiuri Shimbun*, December 16, 2011, www.yomiuri.co.jp/dy.

2. Adam Finn, "Print Ad Recognition Readership Scores: An Information Processing Perspective," *Journal of Marketing Research*, May 1988, pp. 168–177.

3. John Battle, "Cashing in at the Register," *Aftermarket Business*, September 1, 1994, pp. 12–13.

4. Brittany R.L. Duff and Ronald J. Faber, "Missing the Mark: Advertising Avoidance and Distractor Devaluation," *Journal of Advertising*, Summer 2011, pp. 51–62.

5. Paul Surgi Speck and Michael T. Elliott, "Predictors of Advertising Avoidance in Print and Broadcast Media," *Journal of Advertising*, Fall 1997, pp. 61–76.

6. Amy L. Webb, "More Consumers Are Ignoring Ads, Survey Shows," *Wall Street Journal Europe*, June 18, 2001, p. 29.

7. Erik du Plessis, "Digital Video Recorders and Inadvertent Advertising Exposure," *Journal of Advertising Research*, June 2009, pp. 236ff; and Steve McClellan, "It's Inescapable: DVRs Here to Stay," *Television Week*, November 29, 2004, p. 17.

8. S. Adam Brasel and James Gips, "Breaking through Fast-Forwarding: Brand Information and Visual Attention," *Journal of Marketing*, November 2008, pp. 31–48.

9. Steven Bellman, Anika Schweda, and Duane Varan, "The Residual Impact of Avoided Television Advertising," *Journal of Advertising*, Spring 2010, pp. 67–81.

10. Dean M. Krugman, Glen T. Cameron, and Candace McKearney White, "Visual Attention to Programming and Commercials," *Journal of Advertising*, Spring 1995, pp. 1–12; and S. Siddarth and Amitava Chattopadhyay, "To Zap or Not to Zap: A Study of the Determinants of Channel Switching During Commercials," *Marketing Science* 17, no. 2, 1998, pp. 124–138.

11. Noam Cohen, "An Ad Blocker Opens the Gate, Ever So Slightly," *New York Times*, January 1, 2012, www.nytimes.com; and Steven M. Edwards, Hairong Li, and Joo-Hyun Lee, "Forced Exposure and Psychological Reactance," *Journal of Advertising*, Fall 2002, pp. 83–95.

12. Robert East, Kathy Hammond, and Wendy Lomax, "Measuring the Impact of Positive and Negatove Word of Mouth on Brand Purchase Probability," *International Journal of Research in Marketing* 25, 2008, pp. 215–224.

13. Julie Cruz, "Adidas Targets Teenage Girls for $1.3 Billion in Sales," *Bloomberg News*, February 13, 2012, www.bloomberg.com; Shan Li and David Sarno, "Advertisers Scan Faces to Tailor Pitches," *Los Angeles Times*, August 21, 2011, www.latimes.com; Gabriel Beltrone, "Ad of the Day: Adidas," August 9, 2011, www.adweek.com; and Kiran Aditham, "Sid Lee Goes 'All In' for Adidas' Biggest Marketing Campaign Ever," *Mediabistro*, March 16, 2011, www.mediabistro.com.

14. Mary M. Chapman, "Big Three Increase Their Financial Footprint on Woodward Dream Cruise," *New York Times*, August 19, 2011, www.nytimes.com.

15. Yardeena Arar, "Mobile Advertising: The Next Generation," *PC World*, August 15, 2011, www.pcworld.com.

16. Chris Griffith, "Woolworths Unveils Virtual Supermarket in Sydney," *The Australian*, February 20, 2012, www.theaustralian.com.

17. "Ads, Coupons Popping up in Bank Statements," *WSB-TV*, August 23, 2011, www.wsbtv.com.

18. For more about consumer control of e-mail advertising, see Ray Kent and Hege Brandal, "Improving Email Response in a Permission Marketing Context," *International Journal of Market Research*, Winter 2003, pp. 489–504.

19. Andrew Hampp, "AT&T to Help Tell the Story of 'Doctor Who,'" *Advertising Age*, August 26, 2011, www.adage.com; and Bill Carter, "NBC Is Hoping Short Movies Keep Viewers from Zapping," *New York Times*, August 4, 2003, p. C1.

20. Carolyn Said, "A Whole New Ballgame for Super Bowl Ads," *San Francisco Chronicle*, January 31, 2012, www.sfgate.com.

21. L. Hasher and R. T. Zacks, "Automatic and Effortful Processes in Memory," *Journal of Experimental Psychology: General*, September 1979, pp. 356–388; W. Schneider and R. M. Shiffrin, "Controlled and Automatic Human Information Processing," *Psychological Review*, January 1977, pp. 1–66; and R. M. Shiffrin and W. Schneider, "Controlled and Automatic Human Information Processing," *Psychological Review*, March 1977, pp. 127–190.

22. Rik Pieters, Edward Rosbergen, and Michel Wedel, "Visual Attention to Repeated Print Advertising: A Test of Scanpath Theory," *Journal of Marketing Research* 36, November 1999, pp. 424–438.

23. Rik Pieters and Michel Wedel, "Goal Control of Attention to Advertising: The Yarbus Implication," *Journal of Consumer Research*, August 2007, pp. 224–233.

24. Scott B. MacKenzie, "The Role of Attention in Mediating the Effect of Advertising on Attribute Importance," *Journal of Consumer Research*, September 1986, pp. 174–195; and Richard E. Petty and Timothy C. Brock, "Thought Disruption and Persuasion," in eds. Richard E. Petty, Thomas Ostrom, and Timothy C. Brock, *Cognitive Responses in Persuasion* (Hillsdale, N.J.: Lawrence Erlbaum, 1981), pp. 55–79.

25. Chris Janiszewski, "Preconscious Processing Effects," *Journal of Consumer Research*, September 1988, pp. 199–209; and Joan Meyers-Levy, "Priming Effects on Product Judgments," *Journal of Consumer Research*, June 1989, pp. 76–87.

26. Chris Janiszewski, "Preattentive Mere Exposure Effects," *Journal of Consumer Research*, December 1993, pp. 376–392; Janiszewski, "Preconscious Processing Effects"; and Chris Janiszewski, "The Influence of Print Advertisement Organization on Affect Toward a Brand Name," *Journal of Consumer Research* 17, June 1990, pp. 53–65.

27. Janiszewski, "Preattentive Mere Exposure Effects"; Stewart Shapiro and Deborah J. MacInnis, "Mapping the Relationship Between Preattentive Processing and Attitudes," in eds. John Sherry and Brian Sternthal, *Advances in Consumer Research*, vol. 19 (Provo, Utah: Association for Consumer Research, 1992), pp. 505–513.

28. Stewart Shapiro, "When an Ad's Influence Is Beyond Our Conscious Control," *Journal of Consumer Research* 26, June 1999, pp. 16–36; and Stewart Shapiro, Deborah J. MacInnis, and Susan E. Heckler, "The Effects of Incidental Ad Exposure on the Formation of Consideration Sets," *Journal of Consumer Research*, June 1997, pp. 94–104.

29. Robert Heath, "Emotional Engagement: How Television Builds Big Brands at Low Attention," *Journal of Advertising Research*, March 2009, pp. 62–73.

30. Jesper H. Nielsen, Stewart A. Shapiro, and Charlotte H. Mason, "Emotionality and Semantic Onsets: Exploring Orienting Attention Responses in Advertising," *Journal of Marketing Research*, December 2010, pp. 1138–1150.

31. Richard L. Celsi and Jerry C. Olson, "The Role of Involvement in Attention and Comprehension Processes," *Journal of Consumer Research*, September 1988, pp. 210–224.

32. Arch Woodside and J. William Davenport Jr., "The Effect of Salesman Similarity and Expertise on Consumer Purchasing Behavior," *Journal of Marketing Research*, May 1974, pp. 198–202.

33. Robert E. Burnkrant and Daniel J. Howard, "Effects of the Use of Introductory Rhetorical Questions Versus Statements on Information Processing," *Journal of Personality and Social Psychology*, December 1984, pp. 1218–1230.

34. Grant McCracken, "Who Is the Celebrity Endorser? Cultural Foundations of the Endorsement Process," *Journal of Consumer Research*, December 1989, pp. 310–321; and Jeffrey Burroughs and Richard A. Feinberg, "Using Response Latency to Assess Spokesperson Effectiveness," *Journal of Consumer Research*, September 1987, pp. 295–299.

35. Deborah J. MacInnis and C. Whan Park, "The Differential Role of Characteristics of Music on High- and Low-Involvement Consumers' Processing of Ads," *Journal of Consumer Research*, September 1991, pp. 161–173; David W. Stewart and David H. Furse, *Effective Television Advertising: A Study of 1000 Commercials* (Lexington, Mass.: Lexington Books, 1986); James J. Kellaris and Robert J. Kent, "An Exploratory Investigation of Responses Elicited by Music Varying in Tempo, Tonality, and Texture," *Journal of Consumer Psychology*, March 1993, pp. 381–402; and James J. Kellaris, Anthony Cox, and Dena Cox, "The Effects of Background Music on Ad Processing Contingency Explanation," *Journal of Consumer Research*, October 1993, pp. 114–126.

36. "Glee the USA in Your Chevrolet and Win," *AutoTrader*, May 26, 2011, www.autotrader.com.

37. Brian Sternthal and Samuel Craig, "Humor in Advertising," *Journal of Marketing*, October 1973, pp. 12–18; and Thomas Madden and Marc G. Weinberger, "The Effect of Humor on Attention in Magazine Advertising," *Journal of Advertising*, September 1982, pp. 8–14.

38. Iain Akerman, "Berlitz—Don't Be an Alien," *Campaign Middle East*, February 28, 2011, www.campaignme.com.

39. Josephine L. C. M. Woltman Elpers, Ashesh Mukherjee, and Wayne D. Hoyer, "Humor in Television Advertising: A Moment-to-Moment Analysis," *Journal of Consumer Research*, December 2004, pp. 592–598.

40. Satya Menon and Dilip Soman, "Managing the Power of Curiosity for Effective Web Strategies," *Journal of Advertising*, Fall 2002, pp. 1–14; Yih Hwai Lee, "Manipulating Ad Message Involvement Through Information Expectancy," *Journal of Advertising* 29, no. 2, Summer 2000, pp. 29–42; and Joan Meyers-Levy and Alice Tybout, "Schema Congruity as a Basis for Product Evaluation," *Journal of Consumer Research*, June 1989, pp. 39–54. Characteristics of music can also cause surprise; see James Kellaris and Ronald Rice (1993), "The Influence of Tempo, Loudness and Gender of Listener on Responses to Music," *Psychology and Marketing* 10, no. 1, pp. 15–29.

41. Dana L. Alden, Ashesh Mukherjee, and Wayne D. Hoyer, "The Effects of Incongruity, Surprise and Positive Moderators on Perceived Humor in Television Advertising," *Journal of Advertising* 29, no. 2, Summer 2000, pp. 1–15; and Elpers, Mukherjee, and Hoyer, "Humor in Television Advertising: A Moment-to-Moment Analysis."

42. Mae Anderson, "Super Bowl Ads: Slapstick, Cameos Strike a Funny Note," *The Statesman (Austin, Tex.)*, February 6, 2011, www.statesman.com.

43. Edward F. McQuarrie and David Glen Mick, "Visual Rhetoric in Advertising," *Journal of Consumer Research* 26, June 1999, pp. 37–54.

44. Rik Pieters and Michel Wedel, "Attention Capture and Transfer in Advertising: Brand, Pictorial, and Text-size Effects," *Journal of Marketing*, April 2004, pp. 36–50.

45. Ibid.

46. S. Shyam Sundar and Sriram Kalyanaraman, "Arousal, Memory, and Impression-Formation Effects of Animation Speed in Web Advertising," *Journal of Advertising*, Spring 2004, pp. 7–17; Werner Krober-Riel, "Activation Research," *Journal of Consumer Research*, March 1979, pp. 240–250; and Morris B. Holbrook and Donald R. Lehmann, "Form vs. Content in Predicting Starch Scores," *Journal of Advertising Research*, August 1980, pp. 53–62.

47. Priya Raghubir and Eric A. Greenleaf, "Ratios in Proportion: What Should the Shape of the Package Be?" *Journal of Marketing*, April 2006, pp. 95–107; Priya Raghubir and Aradhna Krishna, "Vital Dimensions in Volume Perception: Can the Eye Fool the Stomach?" *Journal of Marketing Research* 36, August 1999, pp. 313–326; and Aradhna Krishna, "Interaction of Senses: The Effect of Vision Versus Touch on the Elongation Bias," *Journal of Consumer Research* 32, no. 4, 2006, pp. 557–566.

48. Mackenzie, "The Role of Attention in Mediating the Effect of Advertising on Attribute Importance."

49. Chris Janiszewski, "The Influence of Display Characteristics on Visual Exploratory Search Behavior," *Journal of Consumer Research*, December 1998, pp. 290–301.

50. Walter Nicholls, "The U.S. Is Turned On to Wine," *Washington Post*, January 2, 2008, www.washingtonpost.com.

51. Rik Pieters, Michael Wedel, and Jie Zhang, "Optimal Feature Advertising Design under Competitive Clutter," *Management Science*, November 2007, pp. 1815–1828.

52. Edward Rosbergen, Rik Pieters, and Michel Wedel, "Visual Attention to Advertising: A Segment-Level Analysis," *Journal of Consumer Research*, December 1997, pp. 305–314.

53. Paul Ziobro, "Campbell Thinks Outside the Can for New Soup Packaging," *Wall Street Journal*, February 22, 2012, www.wsj.com.

54. Valerie Folkes and Shashi Matta, "The Effect of Package Shape on Consumers' Judgments of Product Volume," *Journal of Consumer Research*, September 2004, pp. 390–401.

55. Pierre Chandon and Nailya Ordabayeva, "Supersize in One Dimension, Downsize in Three Dimensions: Effects of Spatial Dimensionality on Size Perceptions and Preferences," *Journal of Marketing Research*, December 2009, pp. 739–753.

56. John R. Doyle, Paul A. Bottomley, "Dressed for the Occasion: Font-Product Congruity in the Perception of Logotype," *Journal of Consumer Psychology* 16, no. 2, 2006, pp. 112–123.

57. Xiaoyan Deng and Barbara E. Kahn, "Is Your Product on the Right Side? The 'Location Effect' on Perceived Product Heaviness and Package Evaluation," *Journal of Marketing Research*, December 2009, pp. 725–738.

58. Sarah Nassauer, "A Season (or 13) for Shopping," *Wall Street Journal*, August 17, 2011, www.wsj.com; and Greg Morago, "Shapely Stuff Makes Waves," *Hartford Courant*, March 23, 2007, p. H1

59. Peter H. Lindsay and Donald A. Norman, *Human Information Processing: An Introduction to Psychology*, 2nd ed. (New York: Academic Press, 1977).

60. Amitava Chattopadhyay, Darren W. Dahl, Robin J. B. Ritchie, and Kimary N. Shahin, "Hearing Voices: The Impact of Announcer Speech Characteristics on Consumer Response to Broadcast Advertising," *Journal of Consumer Psychology* 13, no. 3, 2003, pp. 198–204.

61. Hannah Booth, "Sound Minds: Brands These Days Need to Sound Good as Well as Look Good," *Design Week*, April 15, 2004, p. 163.

62. Eric Yorkston and Geeta Menon, "A Sound Idea: Phonetic Effects of Brand Names on Consumer Judgments," *Journal of Consumer Research*, June 2004, pp. 43–51.

63. Chris Dearden, "Electric Vehicles Find Their Voice," *New Zealand Herald*, August 27, 2011, www.nzherald.co.nz.

64. Kate Fitzgerald, "In-Store Media Ring Cash Register," *Advertising Age*, February 9, 2004, p. 43.

65. Kathryn Tuggle, "More Businesses Turning to Free Samples to Drum up Business," *Fox Business*, August 15, 2011, http://small-business.foxbusiness.com.

66. Trygg Engen, *The Perception of Odors* (New York: Academic Press, 1982); and Trygg Engen, "Remembering Odors and Their Names," *American Scientist*, September–October 1987, pp. 497–503.

67. T. Schemper, S. Voss, and W. S. Cain, "Odor Identification in Young and Elderly Persons," *Journal of Gerontology*, December 1981, pp. 446–452; and J. C. Stevens and W. S. Cain, "Smelling via the Mouth: Effect of Aging," *Perception and Psychophysics*, September 1986, pp. 142–146.

68. W. S. Cain, "Odor Identification by Males and Females: Prediction vs. Performance," *Chemical Senses*, February 1982, pp. 129–142.

69. M. S. Kirk-Smith, C. Van Toller, and G. H. Dodd, "Unconscious Odor Conditioning in Human Subjects," *Biological Psychology* 17, 1983, pp. 221–231.

70. Pamela Weentraug, "Sentimental Journeys: Smells Have the Power to Arouse Our Deepest Memories, Our Most Primitive Drives," *Omni*, August 1986, p. 815; Howard Erlichman and Jack N. Halpern, "Affect and Memory," *Journal of Personality and Social Psychology*, May 1988, pp. 769–779; and Frank R. Schab, "Odors and the Remembrance of Things Past," *Journal of Experimental Psychology: Learning, Memory and Cognition*, July 1990, pp. 648–655.

71. Anick Bosmans, "Scents and Sensibility: When Do (In)Congruent Ambient Scents Influence Product Evaluations?" *Journal of Marketing*, July 2006, pp. 32–43.

72. Josh Sanburn, "NYC Grocery Store Pipes in Artificial Food Smells," *Time*, July 20, 2011, www.moneyland.time.com.

73. Maureen Morrin and S. Ratneshwar, "Does It Make Sense to Use Scents to Enhance Brand Memory?" *Journal of Marketing Research*, February 2003, pp. 10–25.

74. "The Smell of Commerce," *The Independent* (London), August 16, 2011, www.independent.co.uk.

75. Joann Peck and Terry L. Childers, "Individual Differences in Haptic Information Processing," *Journal of Consumer Research*, December 2003, pp. 430–442.

76. Joann Peck and Jennifer Wiggins, "It Just Feels Good: Customers' Affective Response to Touch and Its Influence on Persuasion," *Journal of Marketing*, October 2006, pp. 57–69.

77. Deborah Brown McCabe and Stephen M. Nowlis, "The Effect of Examining Actual Products or Product Descriptions on Consumer Preference," *Journal of Consumer Psychology* 13, no. 4, 2003, pp. 431–439.

78. Jacob Hornik, "Tactile Stimulation and Consumer Response," *Journal of Consumer Research*, December 1992, pp. 449–458.

79. Sak Onkvisit and John J. Shaw, *International Marketing: Analysis and Strategy* (Columbus, Ohio: Merrill, 1989).

80. Jennifer J. Argo, Darren W. Dahl, and Andrea C. Morales, "Positive Consumer Contagion: Responses to Attractive Others in a Retail Context," *Journal of Marketing Research*, December 2008, pp. 690–701.

81. Aradhna Krishna, Editor, *Sensory Marketing: Research on the Sensuality of Products* (New York: Routledge, 2010).

82. Sonya Padgett, "Designer Creates Uniforms MGM Workers Want to Wear," *Las Vegas Review-Journal*, August 28, 2011, www.lvrj.com.

83. Ronald E. Milliman, "Using Background Music to Affect the Behavior of Supermarket Shoppers," *Journal of Marketing*, Summer 1982, pp. 86–91.

84. Colleen Bazdarich, "In a Buying Mood? Maybe It's the Muzak," *Business 2.0*, March 2002, p. 100.

85. Ronald E. Milliman, "The Influence of Background Music on the Behavior of Restaurant Patrons," *Journal of Consumer Research*, September 1986, pp. 286–289; and Richard Yalch and Eric Spannenberg, "Effects of Store Music on Shopping Behavior," *Journal of Services Marketing*, Winter 1990, pp. 31–39.

86. Barry Shlachter, "Fort Worth's Newest Burger Joint Draws In-N-Out Crowd," *Fort Worth Star-Telegram*, August 11, 2011, www.star-telegram.com.

87. Gerald J. Gorn, "The Effects of Music in Advertising on Choice Behavior," *Journal of Marketing*, Winter 1982, pp. 94–101; C. Whan Park and S. Mark Young, "Consumer Response to Television Commercials," *Journal of Marketing Research*, February 1986, pp. 11–24; and MacInnis and Park, "The Differential Role of Characteristics of Music on High- and Low-Involvement Consumers' Processing of Ads."

88. JoAndrea Hoegg and Joseph W. Alba, "Taste Perception: More (and Less) than Meets the Tongue," *Journal of Consumer Research*, March 2007, pp. 490–498.

89. Bruce Watson, "Turning Foul Flavors into Sweet Success," *Daily Finance*, September 11, 2010, www.dailyfinance.com; and Jeanne Whalen, "Foul Taste Is Part of the Cure," *Wall Street Journal*, November 5, 2007, p. B4.

90. Charles Duhigg, "How Companies Learn Your Secrets," *New York Times*, February 16, 2012, www.nytimes.com; and Karl Greenburg, "P&G: Febreze Makes Scents That Make Happiness," *Media Post*, July 10, 2011, www.mediapost.com.

91. Maxine Wilkie, "Scent of a Market," *American Demographics*, August 1995, pp. 40–49.

92. "Pop-Up Stores Are the New Marketing Trend," *Chosunilbo*, February 16, 2012, http://english.chosun.com.

93. "Downsized! More and More Products Lose Weight," *Consumer Reports*, February 2011, pp. 18–19.

94. Richard Gibson, "Bigger Burger by McDonald's: A Two Ouncer," *Wall Street Journal*, April 18, 1996, p. B1.

95. Stuart Rogers, "How a Publicity Blitz Created the Myth of Subliminal Advertising," *Public Relations Quarterly*, Winter 1992, pp. 12–18.

96. Martha Rogers and Christine A. Seiler, "The Answer Is No," *Journal of Advertising Research*, March–April 1994, pp. 36–46; W. B. Key, *Subliminal Seduction* (Englewood Cliffs, N.J.: Prentice-Hall, 1973); Matthew Fitzgerald, *Media Sex-ploitation* (Englewood Cliffs, N.J.: Prentice-Hall, 1976); W. B. Key, *The Clamplate Orgy* (Englewood Cliffs, N.J.: Prentice-Hall, 1980); Martha Rogers and Kirk H. Smith, "Public Perceptions of Subliminal Advertising," *Journal of Advertising Research*, March–April 1993, pp. 10–19; and Michael Lev, "No Hidden Meaning Here: Survey Sees Subliminal Ads," *New York Times*, June 16, 1991, pp. 22, S12.

97. Erin J. Strahan, Steven J. Spencer, and Mark P. Zanna, "Subliminal Priming and Persuasion: Striking While the Iron Is Hot," *Journal of Experimental Social Psychology*, 2002, pp. 556–568;

Johan C. Karremans, Wolfgang Stroebe, and Jasper Claus, "Beyond Vicary's Fantasies: The Impact of Subliminal Priming and Brand Choice," *Journal of Experimental Social Psychology*, 2006, pp. 792–798.

98. A. J. Marcel, "Conscious and Unconscious Perception," *Cognitive Psychology*, June 1983, pp. 197–237; and A. J. Marcel, "Conscious and Unconscious Perception," *Cognitive Psychology*, September 1983, pp. 238–300.

99. Grainne M. Fitzsimons, Tanya L. Chartrand, and Gavan J. Fitzsimons, "Automatic Effects of Brand Exposure on Motivated Behavior: How Apple Makes You 'Think Different,'" *Journal of Consumer Research*, June 2008, pp. 21–35.

100. Ronald C. Goodstein and Ajay Kalra, "Incidental Exposure and Affective Reactions to Advertising," Working paper No. 239, School of Management, University of California at Los Angeles, January 1994.

101. Sharon Beatty and Del I. Hawkins, "Subliminal Stimulation: Some New Data and Interpretation," *Journal of Advertising*, June 1989, pp. 4–9; Myron Gable, Henry T. Wilkens, Lynn Harris, and Richard Feinberg, "An Evaluation of Subliminally Embedded Sexual Stimuli and Graphics," *Journal of Advertising*, March 1987, pp. 26–32; Dennis L. Rosen and Surendra N. Singh, "An Investigation of Subliminal Embed Effect on Multiple Measures of Advertising Effectiveness," *Psychology and Marketing*, March–April 1992, pp. 157–173; J. Steven Kelly, "Subliminal Embeds in Print Advertising," *Journal of Advertising*, September 1979, pp. 20–24; Anthony R. Pratkanis and Anthony G. Greenwald, "Recent Perspectives on Unconscious Processing," *Psychology and Marketing*, Winter 1988, pp. 337–353; and Joel Saegert, "Why Marketing Should Quit Giving Subliminal Advertising the Benefit of the Doubt," *Psychology and Marketing*, March–April 1987, pp. 157–173.

102. David Penn, "Looking for the Emotional Unconscious in Advertising," *International Journal of Market Research* 48, no. 5, 2006, pp. 515–524.

103. Timothy E. Moore, "Subliminal Advertising: What You See Is What You Get," *Journal of Marketing*, Spring 1982, pp. 38–47.

104. Cahal Milmo, "Power of the Hidden Message Revealed," *Independent (UK)*, September 28, 2009, www.independent.co.uk.

105. Donna M. Webster and Arie W. Kruglanski, "Cognitive and Social Consequences of the Need for Cognitive Closure," *European Review of Social Psychology* 18, 1997, pp. 133–173.

106. Himanshu Mishra, Arul Mishra, and Dhananjay Nayakankuppam, "Money: A Bias for the Whole," *Journal of Consumer Research* 32, no. 4, 2006, pp. 541–549.

107. Rik Pieters and Michel Wedel, "Ad Gist: Ad Communication in a Single Eye Fixation," *Marketing Science*, January–February 2012, pp. 59–73.

108. David G. Mick, "Levels of Subjective Comprehension in Advertising Processing and Their Relations to Ad Perceptions, Attitudes, and Memory," *Journal of Consumer Research*, March 1992, pp. 411–424.

109. Jacob Jacoby, Wayne D. Hoyer, and David A. Sheluga, *Miscomprehension of Televised Communication* (New York: American Association of Advertising Agencies, 1980); and Jacob Jacoby and Wayne D. Hoyer, *The Comprehension and Miscomprehension of Print Communications: An Investigation of Mass Media Magazines* (New York: Advertising Education Foundation, 1987); see also Jacob Jacoby and Wayne D. Hoyer, "The Miscomprehension of Mass-Media Advertising Claims: A Re-Analysis of Benchmark Data," *Journal of Advertising Research*, June–July 1990, pp. 9–17; Jacob Jacoby and Wayne D. Hoyer, "The Comprehension–Miscomprehension of Print Communication," *Journal of Consumer Research*, March 1989, pp. 434–444; and Fliece R. Gates, "Further Comments on the Miscomprehension of Televised Advertisements," *Journal of Advertising*, Winter 1986, pp. 4–10.

110. Rupal Parekh, "Insurer Chooses Successor for Fired Gilbert Gottfried," *Advertising Age*, April 26, 2011, www.adage.com; and Suzanne Vranica, "Aflac Partly Muzzles Iconic Duck," *Wall Street Journal*, December 2, 2004, p. B8.

111. Gary J. Gaeth and Timothy B. Heath, "The Cognitive Processing of Misleading Advertising in Young and Old Adults," *Journal of Consumer Research*, June 1987, pp. 43–54; Deborah Roedder and John and Catherine A. Cole, "Age Differences in Information Processing," *Journal of Consumer Research*, December 1986, pp. 297–315; and Catherine A. Cole and Michael J. Houston, "Encoding and Media Effects on Consumer Learning Deficiencies in the Elderly," *Journal of Marketing Research*, February 1987, pp. 55–63.

112. Richard L. Celsi and Jerry C. Olson, "The Role of Involvement in Attention and Comprehension Processes," *Journal of Consumer Research*, September 1988, pp. 210–224.

113. Jacob Jacoby, Robert W. Chestnut, and William Silberman, "Consumer Use and Comprehension of Nutrition Information," *Journal of Consumer Research*, September 1977, pp. 119–127.

114. C. Page Moreau, Donald R. Lehmann, and Arthur B. Markman, "Entrenched Knowledge Structures and Consumer Response to New Products," *Journal of Marketing Research*, February 2001, pp. 14–29.

115. Edward T. Hall, *Beyond Culture* (Garden City, N.Y.: Anchor Press/Doubleday, 1976); and Onkvisit and Shaw, *International Marketing: Analysis and Strategy*.

116. Onkvisit and Shaw, *International Marketing: Analysis and Strategy*.

117. Wayne D. Hoyer, Rajendra K. Srivastava, and Jacob Jacoby, "Examining Sources of Advertising Miscomprehension," *Journal of Advertising*, June 1984, pp. 17–26; Julie A. Edell and Richard Staelin, "The Information Processing of Pictures in Print Advertisements," *Journal of Consumer Research*, June 1983, pp. 45–61; and Ann Beattie and Andrew A. Mitchell, "The Relationship Between Advertising Recall and Persuasion," in eds. Linda F. Alwitt and Andrew A. Mitchell, *Psychological Processes and Advertising Effects* (Hillsdale, N.J.: Lawrence Erlbaum, 1985), pp. 129–156.

118. David Luna, "Integrating Ad Information," *Journal of Consumer Psychology* 15, no. 1, pp. 38–51.

119. Angela Y. Lee and Aparna A. Labroo, "The Effect of Conceptual and Perceptual Fluency on Brand Evaluation," *Journal of Marketing Research*, May 2004, pp. 151–165.

120. Andrew W. Ellis, Selina J. Holmes, and Richard L. Wright, "Age of Acquisition and the Rrecognition of Brand Names," *Journal of Consumer Psychology* 20, 2010, pp. 43–52.

121. Jennifer Gregan-Paxton and Deborah Roedder John, "Consumer Learning by Analogy: A Model of Internal Knowledge Transfer," *Journal of Consumer Research*, December 1997, pp. 266–284.

122. "Product Placement: Is TV Selling Out?" *Seattle Post-Intelligencer*, January 31, 2012, www.seattlepi.com.

123. Abe Sauer, "Hollywood's New China Deal a Goldmine for Product Placement," *Brand Channel*, February 21, 2012, www.brandchannel.com.

124. Lauren Dugan, "Celebs Are Paid $2,500–$8,000 Per Sponsored Tweet," *Media Bistro*, January 31, 2012, www.mediabistro.com.

125. Richard D. Johnson and Irwin P. Levin, "More Than Meets the Eye: The Effect of Missing Information on Purchase Evaluations," *Journal of Consumer Research*, September 1985, pp. 169–177; Frank Kardes, "Spontaneous Inference Processes in Advertising," *Journal of Consumer Research*, September 1988, pp. 225–233; and Joseph W. Alba and J. Wesley Hutchinson, "Dimensions of Consumer Expertise," *Journal of Consumer Research*, March 1987, pp. 411–454.

126. "Colgate Receives Fine of NT $400,000 in Biased Advertising Case: FTC," *China Post*, August 6, 2011, www.chinapost.com.tw; and "Taiwan Fair Trade Commission Decisions," August 2011, www.ftc.gov.

127. Kunter Gunasti and William T. Ross Jr., "How and When Alphanumeric Brand Names Affect Consumers," *Journal of Marketing Research*, December 2010, pp. 1177–1192.

128. Michaela Wänke, Herbert Bless, and Norbert Schwarz, "Context Effects in Product Line Extensions," *Journal of Consumer Psychology* 7, no. 4, 1998, pp. 299–322.

129. Teresa Pavia and Janeen Arnold Costa, "The Winning Number: Consumer Perceptions of Alpha-Numeric Brand Names," *Journal of Marketing*, July 1993, pp. 85–99; France Leclerc, Bernd H. Schmitt, and Laurette Dube, "Foreign Branding and Its Effects on Product Perceptions and Attitudes," *Journal of Marketing Research*, May 1994, pp. 263–270; and Mary Sullivan, "How Brand Names Affect the Demand for Twin Automobiles," *Journal of Marketing Research*, May 1998, pp. 154–165.

130. "Verizon Recasts V Cast Mobile Video," *Consumer Reports Online*, August 24, 2011, www.consumerreports.org.

131. Susan M. Broniarczyk and Joseph W. Alba, "The Role of Consumers' Intuitions in Inference Making," *Journal of Consumer Research*, December 1994, pp. 393–407.

132. Gary T. Ford and Ruth Ann Smith, "Inferential Beliefs in Consumer Evaluations," *Journal of Consumer Research*, December 1987, pp. 363–371.

133. Rajagopal Raghunathan, Rebecca Walker Naylor, and Wayne D. Hoyer, "The Unhealthy = Tasty Intuition and Its Effects on Taste Interferences, Enjoyment, and Choice of Food Products," *Journal of Marketing*, October 2006, pp. 170–184.

134. Elizabeth G. Miller and Barbara E. Kahn, "Shades of Meaning: The Effect of Color and Flavor Names on Consumer Choice," *Journal of Consumer Research* 32, no. 1, 2005, pp. 86–92.

135. Tom Meyvis and Chris Janiszewski, "Consumers' Beliefs About Product Benefits," *Journal of Consumer Research*, March 2002, pp. 618–635.

136. Alexander Chernev and Gregory S. Carpenter, "The Role of Market Efficiency Intuitions in Consumer Choice," *Journal of Marketing Research*, August 2001, pp. 349–361.

137. Peeter W. J. Verlegh, Jan-Benedict E. M. Steenkamp, and Matthew T. G. Meulenberg, "Country-of-origin Effects in Consumer Processing of Advertising Claims," *International Journal of Research in Marketing*, June 2005, pp. 127–139; Sung-Tai Hong and Robert S. Wyer Jr., "Determinants of Product Evaluation," *Journal of Consumer Research*, December 1990, pp. 277–288; Durairaj Maheswaran, "Country of Origin as a Stereotype," *Journal of Consumer Research*, September 1994, pp. 354–365; Sung-Tai Hong and Robert S. Wyer Jr., "Effects of Country of Origin and Product-Attribute Information on Product Evaluation," *Journal of Consumer Research*, September 1989, pp. 175–187; Johny K. Johansson, Susan P. Douglas, and Ikujiro Nonaka, "Assessing the Impact of Country of Origin on Product Evaluations," *Journal of Marketing Research*, November 1985, pp. 388–396; and Wai-Kwan Li and Robert S. Wyer Jr., "The Role of Country of Origin

in Product Evaluations," *Journal of Consumer Psychology* 2, 1994, pp. 187–212.

138. Rajeev Batra, Venkatram Ramaswamy, Dana L. Alden, Jan-Benedict E. M. Steenkamp, and S. Ramachander, "Effects of Brand Local and Non-local Origin on Consumer Attitudes in Developing Countries," *Journal of Consumer Psychology* 9, no. 2, 2000, pp. 83–95.

139. Enid Tsui, "Samsonite Makes Its Case for Japan," *Financial Times*, August 30, 2011, www.ft.com; and Zeynep Gürhan-Canli and Durairaj Maheswaran, "Cultural Variations in Country of Origin Effects," *Journal of Marketing Research*, August 2000, pp. 309–317.

140. Zeynep Gürhan-Canli and Durairaj Maheswaran, "Determinants of Country-of-Origin Evaluations," *Journal of Consumer Research*, June 2000, pp. 96–108.

141. Sung-Tai Hong and Dong Kyoon Kang, "Country-of-Origin Influences on Product Evaluations," *Journal of Consumer Psychology* 16, no. 3, 2006, pp. 232–239.

142. Luk Warlop and Joseph W. Alba, "Sincere Flattery: Trade-Dress Imitation and Consumer Choice," *Journal of Consumer Psychology*, 2004, pp. 21–27.

143. Sandra M. Jones, "Nice! Touch Comes to Walgreens Shelves as Store Brands Get Makeover," *Chicago Tribune*, August 18, 2011, www.chicagotribune.com.

144. Frank R. Kardes, Maria L. Cronley, James J. Kellaris, and Steven S. Posavac, "The Role of Selective Information Processing in Price–Quality Inference," *Journal of Consumer Research*, September 2004, pp. 368–374.

145. Donald Lichtenstein and Scott Burton, "The Relationship Between Perceived and Objective Price-Quality," *Journal of Marketing Research*, November 1989, pp. 429–443; Etian Gerstner, "Do Higher Prices Signal Higher Quality?" *Journal of Marketing Research*, May 1985, pp. 209–215; Susan M. Petroshius and Kent B. Monroe, "Effect of Product-Line Pricing Characteristics on Product Evaluations," *Journal of Consumer Research*, March 1987, pp. 511–519; Akshay R. Rao and Kent B. Monroe, "The Moderating Effect of Prior Knowledge on Cue Utilization in Product Evaluations," *Journal of Consumer Research*, September 1988, pp. 253–264; and Cornelia Pechmann and S. Ratneshwar, "Consumer Covariation Judgments: Theory or Data Driven?" *Journal of Consumer Research*, December 1992, pp. 373–386.

146. Thomas T. Nagle and Reed K. Holden, *The Strategy and Tactics of Pricing*, 2nd ed. (Englewood Cliffs, N.J.: Prentice-Hall, 1995), pp. 84–85.

147. Maria L. Cronley, Steven S. Posavac, Tracy Meyer, Frank R. Kardes, and James J. Kellaris, "Selective Hypothesis Testing Perspective on Price–Quality Inference and Inference-Based Choice," *Journal of Consumer Psychology* 15, no. 2, 2005, pp. 159–169.

148. Anne Kadet, "Yes, It's Still a Drugstore," *Wall Street Journal*, August 20, 2011, www.wsj.com.

149. Lauranne Buchanan, Carolyn J. Simmons, and Barbara A. Bickart, "Brand Equity Dilution," *Journal of Marketing Research*, August 1999, pp. 345–355.

150. Daniel P. Smith, "America's Top 20 Food Trucks," *QSR Magazine*, February 2011, www.qsrmagazine.com; and Kim Severson, "Should Cities Drive Food Trucks Off the Streets?" *New York Times*, July 17, 2011, p. SR-3.

151. Chris Sorenson, "An Underdog with Attitude," *Maclean's*, September 12, 2011, p. 46; Rosemary Feitelberg, "Under Armour's Unofficial All-Star Team," *WWD*, December 1, 2011, p. 12c; Andrea K. Walker, "Under Armour's Rookie Strategy for Endorsement Deals," *Baltimore Sun*, July 25, 2011, www.baltimoresun.com; and "Football or Fashion Show?" *New York Times*, October 24, 2011, p. 4.

CHAPTER 4

MEMORY AND KNOWLEDGE

After studying this chapter, you will be able to

1. Distinguish among sensory, working, long-term, implicit, and explicit memory, and explain why marketers must be aware of these different types of memory.

2. Describe how schemas and scripts affect consumers' knowledge content.

3. Explain how and why the content and structure of knowledge, including associative networks, categories, and prototypicality, are relevant to marketers.

4. Discuss what memory retrieval is, how it works, and how marketers try to affect it.

© JEFF PACHOUD/AFP/Getty Images

INTRODUCTION

The Unforgettable Apple

Computers were expensive, serious products when Apple chose its brand name and adopted a rainbow-striped, stylized apple logo for its personal computers. Competing against big-business behemoths like IBM, upstart Apple wanted to differentiate itself through a warm, approachable brand personality reflecting its computers' distinctive design and user-friendly functionality.

Through the years, the Apple logo and its products' names evolved as the company introduced one innovation after another: the iPod, iPhone, Apple TV, iPad, and more. Apple's version of the click-wheel iPod redefined digital music players; its touch-screen iPads were pioneer products in the tablet computer category. When the first iPad was introduced in 2010, Apple sold three million within 80 days; when the third-generation iPad was introduced in 2012, Apple sold three million in the first *weekend*. Although Apple's rainbow-striped apple logo was replaced by stylish apple logos in white, black, or metallic grey long ago, the brand's associations with cutting-edge technology and customer-friendly features have not changed.[1] So what is Apple, actually? Does it offer the same products as Samsung, Dell, or IBM do? What do we remember about Apple, and what do we know of it? What is its brand personality?

As you saw in Chapter 3, once we are exposed to a stimulus (like the Apple brand or logo) and attend to it, we use our senses to perceive and comprehend it (the Apple brand stands for well-designed, playful electronics, not fruit nor stuffy machines). Sensory input is the starting point for memory and knowledge. We can store inputs such as a brand name, a logo (like the Apple), or an advertising image in memory for some period of time, ranging from moments to years, to be retrieved for later use. Memory may be explicit or implicit, depending on whether we are aware of trying to retrieve information. The content of our knowledge and the way we structure knowledge in memory (i.e., what we know about Apple) affects our ability to relate new information to what we already know and our ability to retrieve memory. Finally, retrieval can be enhanced in a variety of ways, improving our ability to call on knowledge in memory during any part of the decision-making process (see Exhibit 4.1). For example, seeing the Apple logo helps us remember the brand.

WHAT IS MEMORY?

Consumer memory The persistence of learning over time, via the storage and retrieval of information, either consciously or unconsciously.

Retrieval The process of remembering or accessing what was previously stored in memory.

Consumer memory is the persistence of learning over time, via the storage and retrieval of information, which can occur consciously or unconsciously. **Retrieval** is the process of remembering or accessing what was previously stored in memory. We constantly store and remember information that we learn about things, experiences, and evaluations. Specifically, we might remember what brands, products, and companies we have used in the past (things); what we paid; the features of these products or services; how, where, when, and why we bought and used them, and on what occasions (experiences)[2]; and whether or not we liked them (evaluations). The information we store and retrieve is learned from various sources—marketing communications, the media, word of mouth, and personal experience. We may retain it in memory for an instant, for a few minutes, or a long time depending on the type of memory employed: sensory memory, working memory, or long-term memory.

Sensory Memory

Sensory memory Input from the five senses stored temporarily in memory.

Sensory memory is the ability to temporarily store input from all our five senses. Information is stored automatically and retained only briefly in sensory memory, generally from a quarter of a second to several seconds.[3] *Echoic memory* is sensory memory of things we hear, while *iconic memory* is sensory memory of things we see. For instance, you may have found that when someone asks you a question, and you are not really listening, you can say, "What did you say?" and actually "play back" what the person said. Iconic memory is at work when you drive by a sign and see it quickly and then only later realize what the sign was advertising. *Olfactory memory* is at play, for example, when the smell of freshly baked bread still lingers in your mind right after having left a bakery. If the information in sensory memory is relevant, consumers are motivated to process it further and keep it active. This occurs in working memory.

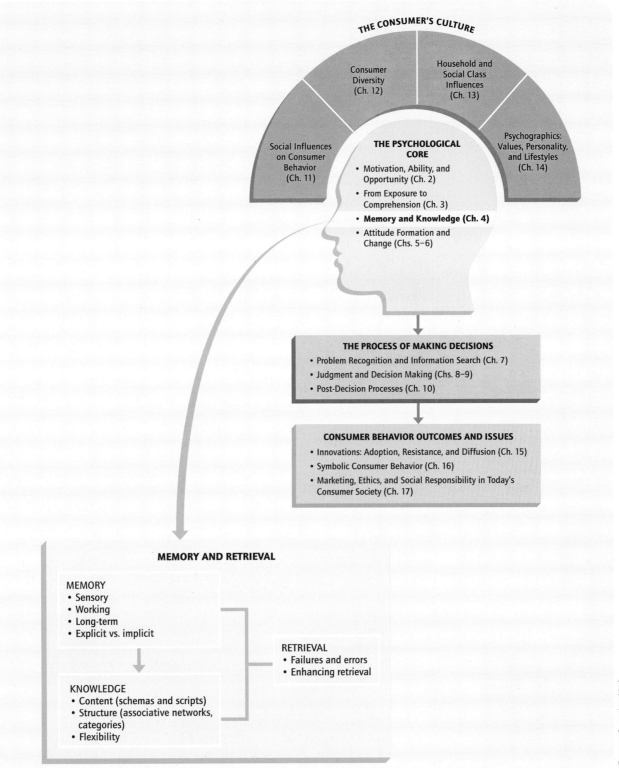

THE CONSUMER'S CULTURE

Consumer Diversity (Ch. 12)

Household and Social Class Influences (Ch. 13)

Social Influences on Consumer Behavior (Ch. 11)

Psychographics: Values, Personality, and Lifestyles (Ch. 14)

THE PSYCHOLOGICAL CORE
- Motivation, Ability, and Opportunity (Ch. 2)
- From Exposure to Comprehension (Ch. 3)
- **Memory and Knowledge (Ch. 4)**
- Attitude Formation and Change (Chs. 5–6)

THE PROCESS OF MAKING DECISIONS
- Problem Recognition and Information Search (Ch. 7)
- Judgment and Decision Making (Chs. 8–9)
- Post-Decision Processes (Ch. 10)

CONSUMER BEHAVIOR OUTCOMES AND ISSUES
- Innovations: Adoption, Resistance, and Diffusion (Ch. 15)
- Symbolic Consumer Behavior (Ch. 16)
- Marketing, Ethics, and Social Responsibility in Today's Consumer Society (Ch. 17)

MEMORY AND RETRIEVAL

MEMORY
- Sensory
- Working
- Long-term
- Explicit vs. implicit

KNOWLEDGE
- Content (schemas and scripts)
- Structure (associative networks, categories)
- Flexibility

RETRIEVAL
- Failures and errors
- Enhancing retrieval

© Cengage Learning 2013

Exhibit 4.1

Chapter Overview: Memory and Knowledge

Marketers need to understand how consumers store and retrieve information about things, experiences, and evaluations. Information may remain in memory temporarily, be moved to working memory for further processing, and finally be stored in our long-term memory. Knowledge content, structure, and flexibility affect our ability to relate new information to what we already know. Marketers can try to enhance retrieval to overcome failures and errors and increase the likelihood that information will be retrieved from memory.

Working Memory

Working memory (WM) is the portion of memory where we "encode" or interpret incoming information and keep it available for further processing. As you read this book, you are using your working memory to comprehend what you read. Working memory is where most of our conscious information processing takes place. It is both limited in capacity and short-lived in time. Also, it requires attention to retain information.[4]

Information processing in working memory can take one of several forms. When we think about an object—say, an apple—we might use *discursive processing* and represent it with the word *apple*. Alternatively, we could represent it visually as a picture of an *apple* or in terms of its smell, its feel, what it sounds like when we bite into it, or what it tastes like. Representing the visual, auditory, tactile, gustatory, and/or olfactory properties of an apple uses *imagery processing*.[5] Unlike discursive processing, an object in imagery processing bears a close resemblance to the thing being represented.[6] Therefore, if you were asked to imagine an apple and a car, imagery processing would ensure that you preserve their relative sizes.

Information represented either as words or images can be elaborated, or thought about more deeply.[7] When motivation, ability, and opportunity (MAO) is low, working memory might consist of a simple reproduction of an object—for example, the word *skier* or a visual image of a skier. When MAO is high, however, consumers can use elaborated imagery processing to engage in daydreams, fantasies, visual problem-solving, or elaborated discursive processing to think about upcoming events or work out solutions to current problems.

Marketing Implications

Working memory, particularly imagery processing, has several key implications for marketers:

1. *Imagery can improve the amount of information that can be processed.* Adding more information to ads, websites, or packages, like lists of attributes, can create information overload and hamper discursive processing. By stimulating imagery, more information can be processed and retained. To illustrate, www.brides.com offers a virtual dressing room where brides can upload their photos and digitally try on gowns, a tactic that might help consumers better imagine how they would look in particular styles.[8]

2. *Imagery can stimulate future choice.* When we make choices, we often imagine what consuming the product or service will be like. For example, our choice of a vacation may be greatly influenced by what we imagine it will be like. We value some of the products we buy (e.g., novels or music) because of the imagery they provide.[9] Consumers who immerse themselves in thoughts of using a product or having an experience similar to one simulated in an ad will tend to have positive attitudes toward the ad and the product.[10] Stimulating consumers to imagine how they would use a product can improve product attitudes even more when the context in which the imagery processing occurs is similar to the situation in which products are normally used.[11]

3. *Realistic imagery can improve consumer satisfaction.* We may create an elaborate image or fantasy of what the product or consumption experience will be like (how great we will look in a new car or how relaxing a vacation will be). If reality does not confirm our imagery, however, we may feel dissatisfied. Realizing this possibility, some marketers help consumers establish realistic imagery. For example, paint brands such as Behr and Benjamin Moore offer apps that let consumers browse colors on their cell phone screens and "paint" virtual rooms to envision the effect before they buy paint.[12]

Long-Term Memory

Long-term memory (LTM) is that part of memory where information is permanently stored for later use. The two major types of long-term memory are episodic and semantic memory.

Episodic (autobiographical) memory Knowledge we have about ourselves and our personal, past experiences.

Episodic (or **autobiographical**) **memory** represents knowledge about ourselves and what has happened to us in our past, including emotions and sensations tied to past experiences.[13] These memories tend to be primarily sensory, involving visual images, sounds, smells, tastes, and tactile sensations. For example, we may have episodic memories that relate to product acquisition, such as a specific shopping trip to find a birthday present for a good friend[14] or consumption such as eating at a particular restaurant. Because we each have a unique set of experiences, episodic memory tends to be very personal and idiosyncratic.

Episodic memory can influence how products and services are evaluated. For example, if you once ate at a particular restaurant and found a hair in your food, the memory of this experience might prevent you from eating there again. This is a form of *operant conditioning*, where one vivid event produces strong lasting memory (see Chapter 10 for more about this concept). Positive experiences would have the opposite effect. Also, you may remember how much you paid for something the last time you made that purchase,[15] and this memory can affect your future choices. For instance, you may decide not to buy something if you think you overpaid last time or will overpay this time.

Consumers' expectations about choices do not always match their episodic memories of similar experiences. Consumers who consider indulging in a purchase expect to have more negative than positive feelings when there is no good justification for the indulgence. Yet in one study, consumers reported episodic memories of having enjoyed a recent indulgence, whether or not they "earned" it.[16]

Semantic memory General knowledge about an entity, detached from specific episodes.

Much of what we have stored in memory consists of facts and general knowledge unrelated to specific episodes in our life's history. This is called **semantic memory**. For example, we have memory for the concept called "cola." We know that colas are liquid, come in cans and bottles, are fizzy and brown in color, and are sweet. This knowledge holds for colas in general. It is not tied to any specific consumption experience that we had.

Marketing Implications

Various techniques can leverage the power of episodic memory for marketing.

1. *Promote empathy and identification.* Episodic memories can play a role in creating identification with characters or situations in ads. For example, if an ad for Hefty bags can make consumers think about incidents in which their own garbage bags split open, consumers may be better able to relate to the ad showing inferior bags splitting apart while Hefty bags remain strong.

2. *Cue and preserve episodic memories.* Consumers value some brands or products and have a positive attitude toward some ads because they promote episodic memories by creating feelings of nostalgia—a fondness for the past.[17] Many consumers preserve personal memories of graduations, the birth of a child, and so on, creating opportunities for marketers of goods and services that help consumers document these occasions. Thanks to consumer interest in making scrapbooks to preserve memories, Provo Craft, maker of the Cricut paper cutter, has increased sales beyond $400 million annually.[18]

3. *Reinterpret past consumption experiences.* Advertising can affect episodic memories, such as how a consumer remembers past experiences with the advertised product.[19] One study had consumers sample good- and bad-tasting orange juices and then watch ads that described the products' good taste. Those exposed to the ads remembered the bad-tasting juice as being better tasting than it actually was.[20]

Explicit memory When consumers are consciously aware that they remember something.

Implicit memory Memory without any conscious attempt at remembering something.

Explicit Memory, Implicit Memory, and Processing Fluency

Memory may be explicit or implicit. **Explicit memory** is when consumers are consciously aware that they remember something. For instance, consumers may remember that they visited a particular website, and what they ordered from the site. **Implicit memory** is when consumers are not consciously aware that they remember something. Implicit memory makes it easier to process information that we have encountered before. This ease-of-processing or *processing fluency* leads to feelings of familiarity. So consumers may not remember that they actually visited a particular website before, but may instead experience a sense of familiarity with it. Much of our memory is implicit, and this is efficient. It would overburden our information-processing ability to constantly and consciously remember everything we encountered and did before.

Suppose you are driving down the highway at high speed and pass a billboard bearing the word *Caterpillar* (a brand of tractors). Later you are asked whether you remember seeing a billboard and, if so, what was on it. You have no explicit memory of the billboard and its message. But if you are asked to say the first word you can think of that begins with *cat-*, you might answer "caterpillar." Why? Because when you are asked for a word that begins with *cat-*, your implicit memory brings the brand to mind.

Exposure to brands via advertising and other marketing stimuli enhances perceptual fluency, making it easier for consumers to recognize a brand and leading to more favorable brand attitudes.[21] Positive attitudes also tend to result with higher conceptual fluency, the ease with which an ad or other stimulus comes to mind and its meaning can be processed. Thus, processing fluency is a key element in implicit memory and in learning new behaviors. (Learning is described in more detail in Chapter 10.)

How Memory Is Enhanced

Because we must attend to something before we can remember it, many of the factors that affect attention (described in Chapter 3) also affect memory and, ultimately, recognition and recall. Explicit memory expresses itself in two forms. **Recognition** occurs when we remember having seen, heard, smelled, touched, or tasted something before after being reexposed to it. Brand and ad recognition ("Have you seen this particular ad for Bertolli Olive Oil before?") are common examples. **Recall** occurs when we remember having seen, heard, smelled, touched, or tasted something before *without* being reexposed to it in the present. Brand recall could be tapped with the question: "Which ads do you remember seeing yesterday?"

Several techniques help to improve working memory and increase the likelihood that information will be transferred to long-term memory, namely chunking, rehearsal, recirculation, and elaboration. A *chunk* is a group of items that are processed as a unit. For example, phone numbers are typically grouped into three chunks: the area code, the exchange, and four numbers. Whereas chunking reduces the likelihood that information will be lost from working memory, rehearsal improves the transfer of information to long-term memory. *Rehearsal* means that we actively and consciously interact with the material that we are trying to remember, perhaps by silently repeating or actively thinking about the information and its meaning. In marketing contexts, rehearsal is likely to occur only when consumers are motivated to process and remember information.

Information can also be transferred to long-term memory by *recirculation*. Just as water is recirculated when it goes through the same pipe again and again, information is recirculated through your working memory when you encounter it repeatedly. Unlike rehearsal, with recirculation we make no active attempt to remember the information. Brand recall is greater when information is repeated at different times rather than when it is presented over and over at one time.[22]

Finally, through **elaboration**, we transfer information into long-term memory by processing it at deeper levels of meaning.[23] We can try to remember through rote memorization or rehearsal; however, this type of processing is not always effective over a long period. If you have ever rote memorized material for an exam, you probably noticed that you forgot most of what you had learned within a few days. More enduring memory is established when we try to relate information to prior knowledge and past experiences. If you see an ad for a new product, for instance, you might elaborate on it by thinking about how you would use the product, and therefore keep the brand and the ad in your memory.

Recognition The process of identifying whether we have previously encountered a stimulus when reexposed to it.

Recall The ability to retrieve information from memory without being reexposed to it.

Elaboration Transferring information into long-term memory by processing it at deeper levels.

Marketing Implications

Marketers can apply chunking, rehearsal, recirculation, and elaboration to help consumers remember their brands, communications, or offerings.

Chunking

Marketers can increase the likelihood that consumers will hold information in short-term memory and transfer it to long-term memory by providing larger bits of information that chunk together smaller bits. For example, acronyms reduce several pieces of information to one chunk. Brand names like KFC and H&M are examples of chunking in a marketing context. Similarly, marketers can facilitate consumers' memory for telephone numbers by using words rather than individual numbers (800-LUNGUSA). Also, ads might draw conclusions that summarize or chunk disparate pieces of information into a single attribute or benefit.

Rehearsal

When motivation is low, marketers may use tactics such as jingles, sounds, and slogans to instigate rehearsal. For example, Under Armour, which makes athletic footwear, created ads in which a pounding, rhythmic beat echoed the sound of athletes' feet hitting the ground as they raced, spiked a basketball, or caught a football. Connecting the sound with athletic achievement supported by Under Armour shoes, a professional athlete asks the audience, "Do you hear footsteps? Or are they hearing yours?"[24] Sometimes these techniques work too well, as you may know from going through the day singing a commercial's jingle over and over.

Recirculation

Recirculation is an important principle for marketing because it explains why repetition of marketing communications affects memory, particularly in low-involvement situations.[25] Marketers can strengthen the effect of recirculation by creating different ads that repeat the same basic message and repeating the brand name frequently. Studies show that spaced exposures of alternating messages in involving media such as TV commercials and less involving media such as billboards can be highly effective.[26] However, when one brand repeatedly advertises product claims that are similar to claims promoted repeatedly by a close competitor, this may confuse consumers, rather than enhance their memory.[27]

Elaboration

Several strategies mentioned in previous chapters can enhance the likelihood that consumers will elaborate on information. Unexpected or novel stimuli can attract attention and induce elaboration.[28] For example, GEICO's choice of a gecko as a character for its insurance ads is intended to make consumers think about the connection. Elaboration may also explain why moderate levels of humor in an ad enhance both encoding and retrieval of the product's claims, whereas strong humor inhibits elaboration of the claims.[29] Further, the ability to elaborate may vary across individuals. Older people may have less ability to elaborate on information from marketing messages, perhaps because their working memory is more limited. Children may elaborate less because they have less knowledge, which makes it more difficult for them to think extensively about an ad message.[30]

KNOWLEDGE CONTENT, STRUCTURE, AND FLEXIBILITY

Knowledge content reflects the information we have already learned and stored in memory about brands, companies, stores, people, how to shop, and so on. *Knowledge structure* describes how we organize knowledge (both episodic and semantic) in memory. When we say we "know" something, it has to do with what we have encountered (knowledge content) and the way in which that knowledge is organized in memory (knowledge structure). Both content and structure are flexible, as discussed later in this chapter.

Knowledge Content: Schemas and Scripts

Knowledge content is not stored in memory as a bunch of random facts. Instead, content takes the form of schemas or scripts. As the next sections explain, schemas are a form of semantic knowledge: knowledge about "*what*" objects and people are, and what they mean to a consumer. Scripts are a form of procedural knowledge: knowledge about "*how*" to do things with the objects and people and are related to episodic memory.

Schemas and Associative Networks

Schema The set of associations linked to a concept.

A **schema** is the group of associations or *associative network* linked to an object or person (more in general to a "concept").[31] A schema for the concept *banana* has many associations—it has 100 calories, is yellow, and bruises easily, and the peel can be slippery if stepped on. We have schemas for *people* (mothers, Lady Gaga, working-class people), *salespeople* (cosmetics salesperson, car salesperson), *ads* (Taco Bell ads, GEICO ads), *companies* (Apple, Costco) *places* (LEGOLAND, the Taj Mahal), and so on. The banana example is an illustration of a *product category schema*. We also have schemas for brands, which can be influenced by marketing actions (see Exhibit 4.2). We even have a *self-schema*, and sometimes consider whether a brand's schema fits with it.[32] Schemas thus contain subjective knowledge about "what" something is. Of course, our subjective knowledge of products, brands, and ourselves may be inconsistent with objective facts.

Exhibit 4.3 represents one consumer's scheme or associative network for the category "vacations," specifically for a St. Moritz ski vacation. The associations are learned based on personal experiences and other information, such as from mass media, word-of-mouth, or advertising. Some associations in the network represent episodic memories and others represent semantic memory.

Notice that in Exhibit 4.3, the links in the associative network vary in strength. Strong links (depicted by the thick lines) are firmly established in memory because they have been rehearsed, recirculated, chunked, and elaborated extensively. Others (depicted by the dashed lines) are weakly established in memory, because they are encountered infrequently, are rarely accessed, or have not been thoroughly processed.

Exhibit 4.2

Marketers Use Ads, Packages, and Product Attributes to Enhance Consumers' Knowledge About an Offering

Marketers often want consumers to know more about their products (eg., that Olay now has a new body wash product). Ads, packages, and product attributes are useful ways of getting this knowledge across.

Exhibit 4.3

An Associative Network for Vacations

An associative network is a set of concepts connected by links. When one concept is activated, others may become activated via the links. Concepts connected by strong links are more likely to activate each other than are those connected by weak links.

Spreading of activation The process by which retrieving a concept or association spreads to the retrieval of a related concept or association.

Priming The increased sensitivity to certain concepts and associations due to prior experience based on implicit memory.

Because associations in the network are linked, activating one part of the associative network leads to a **spreading of activation** to other parts of the network. Using the example in Exhibit 4.3, when the "St. Moritz" concept is activated in the consumer's associative network, the strong link between "St. Moritz" and "expensive" will make the consumer think about "expensive." Because the link connecting "St. Moritz" and "expensive" is very strong, the activation will spread to adjacent concepts in the associative network, particularly along strong links. This spreading of activation will likely lead the consumer to remember the town of St. Moritz and may also activate "Switzerland" and "long lines." Activation from "Switzerland" may, in turn, spread to the concept "chocolate."

Of course, concepts like "Switzerland," "chocolate," and "expensive" are linked to many associative networks, not just to one. The consumer may think about chocolate when prompted to think about St. Moritz, but chocolate may be strongly linked to other associative networks that can be cued through spreading of activation. Spreading of activation explains why we sometimes have seemingly random thoughts as the activation spreads from one associative network to another. If the consumer's motivation and opportunity to process information are high, the number of activated links can also be quite high.[33]

Spreading of activation may take place consciously. Then, a consumer who sees the purple Milka chocolate bar might think about Alpine cows and the rich milk they give for the Milka chocolate. Spreading of activation may also take place outside of conscious awareness. This concept is called **priming**: the increased sensitivity to certain concepts and associations due to prior experience based on implicit memory. It occurs when a concept is activated by a stimulus (such as when the "Milka" brand activates the concept "Switzerland") and this activation influences consumers' associations, positively or negatively, outside of awareness.

The associations in schemas can be described along several dimensions.[34] First, associations vary in what they are about—their content. One schema for banana might include associations that reflect its (1) attributes (yellow, long, 100 calories), (2) benefits (nutritious, low in fat), (3) values (being a healthy person, a sweet tooth), (4) consumption occasions (as a snack, dessert),

(5) consumption locations (at home, school), (6) brands (Turbana, Chiquita), and so on. Consumers often use associations with brands and attributes to predict what a product's benefits will be.[35] Also, the associations in schemas vary in terms of how abstract or concrete they are. Locations to eat a banana are more concrete, whereas the values expressed by eating a banana are more abstract.

Most importantly, the associations in schemas vary in three dimensions that are crucial to building and maintaining strong brands:

1. *Favorability.* Associations can vary in favorability. Associating a banana with 100 calories might result in a favorable evaluation.
2. *Uniqueness.* Associations vary in their uniqueness: the extent to which they are also related to other concepts. "Fast service" is not unique to McDonald's, but the Big Mac is.
3. *Salience.* Associations vary in their salience, or how easily they come to mind. For example, a consumer might always think of the Golden Arches when hearing the McDonald's name. Less salient associations may be remembered only in certain contexts. Thus, the association that McDonald's offers breakfast burritos may be less salient than other associations, and a consumer may think about it only if someone starts talking about fast-food breakfast items.[36] Brands aim to be linked to favorable, unique, salient associations.

Specific Schemas: Brand Image and Personality

Brand image Specific type of schema that captures what a brand stands for and how favorably it is viewed.

A **brand image** is a specific type of schema that captures what a brand stands for and how favorably consumers view it. For example, our brand image of McDonald's may be favorable, and it may include such associations as a family-friendly place and fast food. An image does not represent *all* the associations linked to a schema—only those that are most salient and that make the brand different from others in the category. Thus, although we may know that McDonald's also serves low-fat foods, this knowledge need not be used to form our brand image. We also have images for other marketing entities like stores, companies, places, and countries.[37]

Brand personality The set of associations included in a schema that reflect a brand's personification.

Schemas can include specific associations that reflect the **brand's personality**—that is, the way that the consumer would describe the brand if it were a person.[38] One study found that many brands could be described according to such dimensions as sincerity, competence, ruggedness, etc., as shown in Exhibit 4.4. As you might expect, a celebrity endorser's personality can reinforce associations with the endorsed brand's personality.[39] Perceptions of masculinity and femininity are important to brand personality, as well, and have important implications for choice of endorser, among other marketing decisions.[40]

Because brand personalities have cultural meaning and reflect cultural values, a global brand may be perceived slightly differently in different cultures.[41] Brand personalities can also be updated based on consumers' exposure to new information.[42] In addition, consumers who are encouraged to have an anthropomorphic image of a product such as a car—seeing it as if it was alive, not an inanimate object—are less willing to replace it.[43]

Another key element that marketers must consider is the fit between the consumer's actual personality and the brand's personality. A consumer will react to a good fit with the feeling that the brand's personality is "like who I really am." Also, research suggests that using a brand with a certain personality can help shape a consumer's personality.[44] Brand personality has an even stronger influence on the consumer's emotional attachment to a brand when involvement, self-esteem, and public self-consciousness are high. The trend toward cocreation—consumers collaborating with companies to shape brand personality—can go a long way toward enhancing the fit with actual personality.[45]

Scripts

Script A special type of schema that represents knowledge of a sequence of actions involved in performing an activity.

A **script** represents our knowledge of a sequence of actions involved in performing an activity.[46] For example, you may have a script for how to arrange roses bought from the store: You open the cellophane wrapping, get scissors, fill a vase with water, run the roses under water, cut them, and arrange them in the vase. This script helps you complete the task quickly and easily. But when you do something for the first time, such as assembling a piece of furniture, not having a script may prolong the task. Some brands and stimuli may activate scripts in consumers' minds, such as when an ad for IKEA makes you think about how to walk through the store and finish the trip with a visit to the restaurant.

Source: Reprinted with permission from *Journal of Marketing Research*, published by the American Marketing Association, Jennifer L. Aaker, August 1997, vol. 34, pp. 347–356.

Exhibit 4.4

A Brand Personality Framework

One researcher found that many brands can be described according to one or more of the five personality types depicted here. Which dimensions best characterize Pepsi's brand personality? Which describe the personalities of Dell? Volkswagen? Google? Smucker's?

Marketing Implications

Knowledge content is important to marketers. Brands with favorable, unique, and salient associations that are meaningful to consumers have high *brand equity* and are valuable to the company.[47] Such strong brands can command a higher price and have a more loyal following of consumers. Therefore, marketers need to identify and understand the various favorable, unique, and salient associations that consumers link to a particular brand.[48] Moreover, consumers as young as middle-school age start to associate brand images with their self-images.[49] Understanding the associations that consumers see as part of themselves or want to see as part of themselves helps marketers to create, maintain, change, and protect brand images and personalities.

Creating Brand Images and Personalities

When an offering is new, the marketer has to create a schema, image, and/or personality to help consumers understand what it is, what it can do for them, and how it differs from competing offerings. Creating schemas and images for a company is also important so that consumers understand the types of products it offers. For example, GEICO, the insurance firm with the gecko brand character, wants consumers to know it offers motorcycle insurance as well as car insurance. That association is why it is a lead sponsor of the annual Sturgis motorcycle rally in South Dakota.[50]

Creating Brand Extensions

Brand extension Using the brand name of a product with a well-developed image on a product in a different category.

Marketers create a **brand extension** when they use the brand name of a product with a well-developed image (like Dove soap) on a product in a different category (e.g., Dove Deodorant, which belongs to the antiperspirant category, see Exhibit 4.5). Brand extensions have two general effects.

First, a transfer of associations takes place from the original brand schema (Dove Soap) to the new branded product (Dove Deodorant).[51] If consumers like the original brand, these feelings will improve their evaluations of the brand extension.[52] Consumers tend to like brand extensions more when the product fits in some way with the parent brand and when they really like the parent brand.[53] The fit between brand extension and parent brand or family may be based on similar attributes or benefits, usage goals, or targets.[54] Evaluations of brand extensions can be affected by a consumer's mood and involvement in processing brand information.[55] Moreover, consumers exposed to brand extensions can more quickly categorize the parent brand correctly. Given the speed at which consumers are exposed to marketing

Image Courtesy of The Advertising Archives

Exhibit 4.5

Brand Extensions

Certain products can market their success with one product by expanding their brand to other products, like Dove did with their soap and new deodorant.

stimuli when shopping, this faster categorization can be an advantage for marketers.[56]

Second, a transfer of meaning from the new branded product (Dove Deodorant) to the original brand schema (Dove Soap) may take place. One concern is that brand extensions may make the brand schema less coherent and may dilute the brand's image.[57] For example, if the Jeep name appears on too many different products—wheelbarrows, clothing—consumers may be confused about what this automotive brand really stands for. On the other hand, sometimes consumers accept a brand extension more readily when the brand is already linked to quite different products because some of the attributes or benefits in one category make the brand extension seem like a good product.[58]

There are cross-cultural differences in brand extension effects. One study found that brand dilution would be more pronounced in Eastern cultures, compared with the effect in Western cultures, if an unsuccessful brand extension is similar to an existing product and consumer motivation is high. This occurs because of differences in processing conflicting information about the brand and the products to which it is linked (i.e., Eastern cultures are more able to deal with conflicting information).[59] Further, the "stretch-ability" of a brand depends on consumers' ability to process relationships and accept the perceived fit between the parent brand and other products on which it appears, which can vary from culture to culture.[60]

Maintaining Brand Images and Personalities

Once created, marketers must maintain and develop the brand images and personalities. Over time, consistent advertising can help to accomplish this.[61] To develop the brand images and personalities, a company may offer multiple brand extensions (the way Dove did with antiperspirant), link the product to an appropriate sponsorship (the way GEICO did with the motorcycle rally), or highlight additional features and benefits.[62]

Changing Brand Images and Personalities

If a brand or product image becomes stale, outdated, or linked to negative associations, marketers need to add new and positive associations. For example, when Burger King wanted to change its image to quality, fresh fast food, it stopped using the King brand character, added guacamole-topped burgers, wraps, and oatmeal, and advertised its fresh, healthy ingredients.[63]

Protecting Brand Images and Personalities

Brand images and personalities may be threatened during crises that involve potential harm, such as reports of contaminated products or health problems that are linked to specific products. The way that a company responds to a crisis affects its brand image, but research indicates that consumers' prior expectations also play a critical role. Companies whose customers held a strong, positive image of the brand prior to the crisis suffered less image damage than did companies whose customers had lower expectations. Therefore, firms with weaker brand images should act aggressively to support their brands after a crisis.[64]

Interestingly, firms with a "sincere" brand personality may have difficulty reestablishing strong customer relations after a crisis because fundamental perceptions of the brand have deteriorated. In contrast, firms with an "exciting" brand personality may have an easier time reinvigorating customer relationships after a crisis because consumers are less surprised by nonroutine experiences with such brands.[65]

Knowledge Structure: Categories

Taxonomic category
How consumers classify a group of objects in memory in an orderly, often hierarchical way, based on their similarity to one another.

Consumers have various associations with each of the objects and people surrounding them. They also have the natural tendency to group these objects and people together in categories that share certain characteristics, called **taxonomic categories**.[66] A taxonomic category is a specifically defined division within an orderly classification of objects with similar objects in the same category. For example, our schemas for Coke, Pepsi, Diet Coke, and other brands can be clustered in a category called soft drink; we might also use subcategories to cluster specific brands and separate them from others. Thus, we might have one subcategory for diet soft drinks and a different subcategory for nondiet *soft drinks*. In turn, soft drinks may be part of a larger beverage category that also includes coffees, teas, juices, and bottled waters, as shown in Exhibit 4.6.

Once we have categorized an object, we know what it is, what it is like, and what it is similar to. Still, consumers do not always categorize offerings correctly. For example, the Timberland brand helps consumers put its Earthkeepers boots in the category of "eco-friendly products" through its slogan, "Tough boot, gentle footprint" and a Green Index label showing how green the boots really are.[67] When consumers encounter a product or service provider that does not seem to fit the category, they may elaborate more on the information about that provider. And when they categorize the provider as a member of the category, they may infer that the provider has features or attributes typical of the category.[68]

On the other hand, marketers may sometimes want consumers to mentally recategorize a product. For example, General Motors faced this situation when it launched an electric-gas hybrid model of Cadillac, a car traditionally known for luxury. The Cadillac ELR uses engine technology similar to that of the all-electric Chevrolet Volt. GM may be able to build on high awareness of the Volt's gas-saving technology as it encourages consumers to properly categorize the Cadillac ELR.[69]

Graded Structure and Prototypicality

Things within the same taxonomic category share similar features, which are different from the features of objects in other categories. A category member such as Diet Coke shares many associations with members of its own category of diet colas but shares few associations with members of other categories. In Exhibit 4.6, Diet Coke has associations a–d, and Diet Pepsi has many but not

Exhibit 4.6

Taxonomic Category Structure

Objects can be organized in ordered, hierarchically structured categories, with similar objects in the same category. For example, herbal and nonherbal teas are subordinate to the basic-level category of teas. Teas, coffees, and soft drinks are members of the superordinate category beverages. The letters under each brand signify attributes linked with each brand. Brands with the same letters have the same attributes. For example, three brands share a common attribute "a" (e.g., caffeine) while only Diet Coke and Diet Pepsi share attribute "b" (e.g., low calorie).

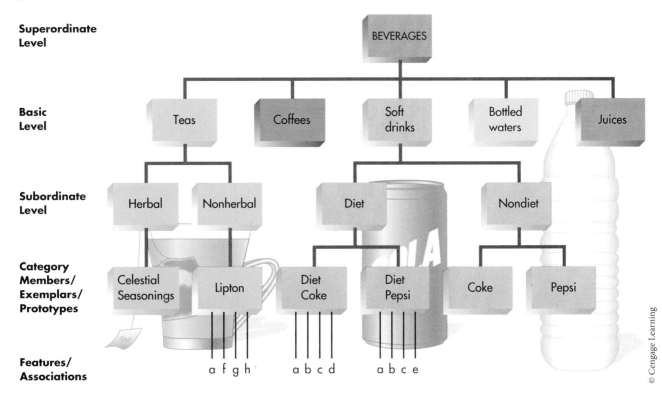

© Cengage Learning

all of the same associations (a–c and e). In this category, you might view Diet Coke as a better example of a soft drink than a lesser-known diet drink. The fact that category members vary in how well they are perceived to represent a category illustrates the principle of *graded structure*.[70]

Within a category, some category members represent the category better than others. The **prototype** is the category member perceived to be the best example of the category, like Disney being the prototypical theme park, and apple pie being the prototypical pie. **Prototypicality** is the extent to which category members are considered to be representative of the category. A diamond ring may be a more prototypical engagement gift than a tattoo or a nose piercing. To many consumers, the iPad may be the prototypical tablet computer. Exhibit 4.7 identifies brands generally regarded as prototypes in their product categories.

Several factors affect whether a consumer regards something as a category prototype.[71] The first is shared associations: A prototype shares the most associations with other members of its own category and shares the fewest with members from different categories. The second is the frequency with which an object is encountered as a category member. Third, the first or "pioneer" brand in a category—such as Amazon for online books and music—may also be a prototype because it sets a standard against which later brands are compared.[72]

Hierarchical Structure

Another way in which taxonomic categories are structured is hierarchically, which affects the number of associations. As Exhibit 4.6 indicates, taxonomic categories can be hierarchically organized into basic, subordinate, and superordinate levels. The broadest level of categorization is the *superordinate level*, where objects share a few associations but also have many different ones. Finer discriminations among these objects are made at the *basic level*. Beverages might be more finely represented by categories such as teas, coffees, and soft drinks. The finest level of differentiation exists at the *subordinate level*. For example, soft drinks might be subdivided into categories of diet and nondiet soft drinks. As you can see, consumers use more associations to describe objects in a progression from the superordinate to the basic to the subordinate levels.

The hierarchical structure of information stored in memory is also influenced by environmental cues. People who ignore environmental cues tend to integrate information and form general brand beliefs, whereas those who pay attention to environmental cues store information in a more context-specific way and do not form general beliefs about product categories.[73]

Prototype The best example of a cognitive (mental) category.

Prototypicality When an object is representative of its category.

© Cengage Learning 2013

Exhibit 4.7

Prototypical Brands

Brands viewed as the best examples of a product category are called *prototypical brands*. Prototypical brands tend to have many features in common with other brands in the category, are encountered frequently, and may have been the first entrant in the product category.

Product Category	Prototypical Brands
Bologna	Oscar Mayer
Car rental service	Hertz
Cold cereal	Kellogg's
Eco-friendly car	Toyota Prius
Greeting cards	Hallmark
Hamburgers	McDonald's
Hook-and-loop fastener	Velcro
Ketchup	Heinz
Laundry detergent	Tide
Motorcycle	Harley-Davidson
Online retailer	Amazon.com
Smart phone	iPhone
Social media	Facebook
Soup	Campbell's
Tablet computer	iPad
Theme park	Disney

Correlated Associations

When an associative network contains attributes that are linked in the consumer's mind, these attributes are *correlated*. With automobiles, consumers may expect the size of a car to be negatively correlated with fuel efficiency, or the price to be positively correlated with quality or luxury. Although the attributes may be correlated in consumers' minds, they may or may not actually be correlated. Knowledge about correlated attributes or benefits can significantly affect consumers' inferences about a new brand and the kinds of communications marketers need to create to overcome potentially false inferences. Contrary to the correlations in some consumers' minds, for example, healthy food options can be tasty, and tasty options can be healthy.

When consumers are developing a schema or when they are confronted with ambiguous information, they can mistakenly believe that if a product in a particular category has a type of attribute, other products in that category have similar attributes.[74] To understand these illusory correlations, consider this example: Just as some smokers mistakenly thought that "clean" smokeless cigarettes were safer than regular cigarettes, they may also mistakenly believe that low-toxin and natural cigarettes are safer.[75] Clearly understanding such illusory and real associations between attributes is crucial for marketers and policy makers.

Marketing Implications

Prototypes are the main point of comparison used by consumers to categorize a new brand. Therefore, a brand can develop its identity by being positioned as being either similar to or different from the prototype. Because the prototype best defines the category and is well liked, a new brand positioned as being similar to it may appeal to that same (large) segment of consumers. Thus, consumers may well have a positive response to products that look similar to the prototype, including copycat competitors.[76]

Positioning away from the prototype can be an effective way to differentiate a brand. For instance, the small size of the Mercedes-Benz Smart ED electric car (see Exhibit 4.8) clearly differentiates it from the full-size green-car prototype, the Toyota Prius.[77] This tactic can also work with pricing, because consumers judge whether a product's price is high or low by comparing it with the prices of several category members, not just with the price of the prototype.[78]

Exhibit 4.8

Differentiating from the Prototype

Since products are often compared to prototypes, new brands and products can differentiate themselves by positioning themselves away from the prototype, such as the new Mercedes-Benz Smart ED electric car whose small size differentiates it from the green-car prototype, the Toyota Prius.

Applying the concept of correlated associations, when two brands with similar brand concepts become cosponsors of an event such as a soccer championship, a positive image transfer can occur.[79] Understanding consumers' hierarchical category structure also helps marketers identify their competitors and influence perceptions of category attributes and prototypical products.[80] For instance, basic, subordinate, and superordinate category levels have implications for retail store design and merchandising. In grocery stores, objects in taxonomically similar categories are usually shelved together, as are items in the same basic- and subordinate-level categories. Thus, most grocery stores have a dairy (superordinate level) section with shelves for milk, yogurt, cheese, and so on (basic level). Thus, soy milks are typically sold in the supermarket's refrigerated milk section to help consumers find them among category members. ───────────────────────────────

Knowledge Flexibility

The content and structure of a consumer's associative networks and categorizations are flexible and adaptable to the requirements of the tasks that he or she faces. This flexibility depends, in part, on the consumer's specific goals and the time to implement these goals.

Goal-Derived Categories

Goal-derived category Things viewed as belonging in the same category because they serve the same goals.

Taxonomic categories are fairly stable and based on the similarity between objects in terms of attributes ("all drinks that are carbonated"). Consumers may also organize their knowledge in **goal-derived categories**. A goal-derived category contains things that consumers view as similar because they serve the same goal, even though they may belong to different taxonomic categories.[81] "Lighter, water, beef jerky, and a tent" may belong to the goal-directed category "things to take on a camping trip," while "cookies, classical music, tea, and flowers," might be part of the category "gifts to take to your grand-dad."

Because consumers have different goals over time, they also have goal-derived categories that change flexibly. Thus, Diet Coke might be part of the taxonomic categories of diet colas, soft drinks, and beverages and also a member of goal-derived categories such as "things to have for lunch" and "things to take on a picnic." And, like taxonomic categories, goal-derived categories exhibit graded structure.

Construal Level

The associations that become activated in consumers' associative networks depend on the time to implementing the goals. That is, when consumers are far away from implementing a goal, more abstract knowledge about the desirability of attaining the goal becomes salient (the "why"). This is useful because it helps people to move toward the goal and block out competing goals. However, when people are close to implementing a goal, more concrete knowledge about the feasibility of attaining the goal becomes salient (the "how").[82] This helps people to prepare for the required activity and perform well.

To illustrate, when your wedding day is months away, more abstract associations such as the "union of souls" and "the joy of sharing thoughts and values" are salient in the associative network "my marriage." Yet, as the designated day draws near, more concrete associations about "who to invite" and "which dishes to have on the buffet" become salient. That is, the activated knowledge varies from very abstract to very concrete levels, and the time to act is an important determinant of this.[83]

Construal level theory Theory describing the different levels of abstractness in the associations that a consumer has about concepts (people, products, brands, and activities) and how the consumer's psychological distance from these concepts influences his or her behavior.

Construal level theory describes the different levels of abstractness in the associations that a consumer has about concepts (people, products, brands, and activities) and how the consumer's psychological distance from these concepts influences his or her behavior.[84] Attributes of products and brands may have concrete or abstract associations, depending on the time to act, which is an aspect of psychological distance. For instance, the price of a product may be an indicator of quality when the purchase is far in the future; yet price may also be an indicator of the "pain" of paying when a consumer is in the store, and ready to buy (or not).[85]

Marketing Implications

Positioning an offering as relevant to a goal can be an important marketing objective. To illustrate, in Japan, Nestlé's Kit Kat brand translates into something like "If I try, I will win." Thus, Kit Kat candy bars are positioned as "lucky things to eat before school exams."[86]

Supermarkets also apply the idea of goal-derived category structures. Many stores display baby bottles, diapers, and baby food in the same aisle despite these products' taxonomic differences. But these products are part of a goal-derived category—"things you need to take care of a baby." Parents can therefore easily find the items they need in one handy location. Retailers use a hybrid of taxonomic (all frozen products) and goal-derived categories (baby products, impulse products) to manage their assortments across the available store space.

When consumers are made aware of the specific set of brands they will have to choose from in the future, they might focus on the concrete associations that they actually will focus on when having to make the final choice. That might help them make accurate decisions.[87] Other factors such as mood may also influence the abstractness of the associations that become salient: Consumers in a positive mood tend to think more abstractly, while those in a negative mood tend to think more concretely.[88] _____

Why Consumers Differ in Knowledge Content and Structure

Goals and their timing influence the content and structure of knowledge *within* the minds of consumers. The consumer's culture and level of expertise influence the structure and content of knowledge *between* consumers. That is, the associations that consumers link to a concept may vary considerably across cultures.[89] In Europe, the Philips brand is associated with consumer electronics while in U.S. markets Philips is closely associated with light bulbs, which it also makes.[90] Cultural groups also vary in how they organize taxonomic and goal-derived categories. In the United States, the category "breakfast products" includes cereal and eggs for many consumers, whereas in Japan it may include fish and rice.

Culture can affect how associations are correlated, as well. For example, price and store size may be negatively correlated in U.S. consumers' knowledge because big stores like Costco and Walmart tend to price products lower than small stores do. In contrast, price and store size may be positively correlated in India and Sri Lanka because large stores in those countries tend to price products higher to cover higher costs.

Prior experience plays a role in the content and structure of consumers' knowledge and the flexibility of using their knowledge. Therefore, consumers vary in their ability to process information based on how much prior experience they have. For instance, experts are consumers with a lot of prior experience and their knowledge and flexibility is well developed.

Experts differ from novices in several ways.[91] First, expert consumers have a richer associative network with more associations, and more concrete and abstract associations linked to a concept than novices have. Second, they have more graded and refined taxonomic structure of categories. Third, they exhibit more flexibility in activating suitable associations (concrete or abstract) and categories (superordinate and subordinate) than novices. As a consequence, experts learn better which brands might be appropriate for different usage situations, organize such information by specific product subcategories, and are less motivated than novices to learn about a new product.[92]

Experts can also make finer distinctions among brands. For example, car experts would have many subordinate categories for cars, such as vintage cars and roadsters. Yet consumers are sometimes overconfident in their knowledge and think that they know more than they actually do.[93] Experts furthermore tend to evaluate a brand more favorably when product information is presented in such a way that they feel they are progressing toward their goal of making a decision.

They also react favorably when the information presentation involves abstract associations, because these are motivating and the consumers already have access to the concrete associations themselves.[94]

MEMORY AND RETRIEVAL

Marketers not only want consumers to store information in memory, properly categorized, and with favorable, unique associations—they want consumers to retrieve this information from memory when making decisions. You have already seen how information becomes salient within the minds of consumers over time, and between consumers due to culture and expertise. Marketers also want to understand and influence more specifically how consumers retrieve this information from memory and remember the information.

Marketing communication aims to increase the memorability (recall and recognition) of a brand name and logo, the brand's attributes, benefits, and perhaps personality.[95] Of course, memorable ads are not necessarily the most effective for the brand (see Exhibit 4.9). In one study, consumers who watched the commercials during the Super Bowl incorrectly attributed the advertising slogan of one telecommunications firm to as many as 13 other companies.[96] More importantly, the likelihood that a particular brand is chosen depends on whether it is remembered when consumers make a choice, independent of the attitude that consumers have toward brands.[97] Clearly, marketers want to avoid retrieval failures and retrieval errors for their brand when consumers make a choice.

Retrieval Failures

Three elements in particular contribute to retrieval failures: decay, interference, and serial-position effects.

Decay

Decay The weakening of memory strength over time.

Decay occurs when memory strength deteriorates over time, for instance, because it has not been used. Thus, we tend to forget entire events or small details from childhood because they happened so long ago. Decay is reduced by repetition of the information, such as by advertising, and by recirculation, such as when repeatedly retrieving it from memory.

Interference

Interference When the strength of a memory deteriorates over time because of competing memories.

Interference occurs when the strength of a memory deteriorates over time because of the presence of other memories that compete with it.[98] Similarity between products, brands, and ads increase the likelihood of memory interference. Suppose you watch an ad that focuses on car brand

© AP Images/PRNewsFoto/Kia Motors America

A's safety, followed by a similar ad that focuses on car brand B's speed. You may then remember that some brand excels in safety but forget which brand it is.[99] Competitive advertising affects interference. When an established brand promotes a new attribute, consumers' knowledge of the brand's old attributes can interfere with retrieval of information about the new one. Yet when competitive advertising is present, consumers are able to suppress older attribute information and effectively retrieve the new attribute information, an accomplishment that works to the brand's advantage.[100]

Interference also affects marketing across cultures. For instance, a study of how interference affects bilingual consumers concluded that second-language messages are not retrieved as well as first-language messages. To reduce interference, marketers could use visual and textual cues that reinforce each other. This tactic helps consumers to process second-language messages, thereby improving retrieval.[101]

Moreover, interference can result when one concept is activated so frequently that we cannot activate a different one. Suppose you are trying to recall the 10 items that you have on your grocery list. Chances are good that you can recall several items very easily and a few more with some difficulty, but the last ones are probably impossible to remember. In trying to remember the missing items, you keep remembering the items you have already recalled, and these recollections interfere with your ability to activate the missing ones.[102]

Serial-Position Effects: Primacy and Recency

Primacy and recency effect The tendency to show greater memory for information that comes first or last in a sequence.

Decay and interference can be used to explain **primacy and recency effects**—that is, the fact that the things we encountered first or last in a sequence are often those most easily remembered. As an example of primacy effects, consumers are likely to remember the first ad during a commercial break because there is no other ad information to interfere with it. That information may also be less likely to decay if they rehearse it. Sampling two desirable products (such as two new songs), consumers tend to prefer the second sample, because of recency effects.[103] Considering primacy and recency effects, many advertisers believe that the best placement for an ad is either first or last in a commercial sequence or in a magazine. Research supports the importance of being first, but the evidence in support of being last is not as strong.[104]

Retrieval Errors

Memory is not always accurate or complete and may be subject to selection, confusion, and distortion. Memory is selective when you only remember the good things that happened on your last vacation but not the bad things that happened. Memory can be confused, as when you remember your friend telling you a great story about a new movie, when it was really your neighbor who told you. This example is a form of *source confusion* because you accurately remember the story about the movie but confuse who the source of the story was.

Finally, memory can be distorted, as when you remember experiences or events that actually did not happen. Perhaps you remember that a waitress who treated you badly at a restaurant clunked your coffee down loudly on the table, and asked for a larger tip. While this "memory" is consistent with the "bad waitress" experience, it might not have actually happened.[105] And virtual interaction with a product leads to more false memories because it generates vivid images that consumers later come to believe were real occurrences.[106]

Enhancing Retrieval

Given the importance of retrieval, marketers need to understand how they can enhance the likelihood that consumers will remember something about specific brands. In addition to memory-enhancing factors mentioned earlier in this chapter, retrieval is affected by: (1) the characteristics of the stimulus itself, (2) what the stimulus is linked to, (3) the way the stimulus is processed, and (4) the consumer's characteristics.

Characteristics of the Stimulus

Key characteristics of the stimulus that affect retrieval are salience, prototypicality, redundant cues, and the medium.

▶ *Salience.* Salient objects tend to attract attention and induce greater elaboration, thereby creating stronger memories.[107] Research has shown that consumers remember longer commercials better than shorter ones and bigger print ads better than smaller ones.[108]

▶ *Prototypicality.* We are better able to recognize and recall prototypical or pioneer brands because these have been frequently rehearsed and recirculated and are linked to many other concepts in memory. The fact that we tend to remember these brands may explain why they have been so successful over time and why so many companies fight to establish themselves as category leaders.[109]

▶ *Redundant cues.* Memory is enhanced when the information items to be learned seem to go together naturally. Marketers can enhance consumers' memory for brands by advertising two complementary products together (such as Jif peanut butter with Smucker's jelly) and explaining why they go together.[110] Event sponsorship enhances memory when the brand is prototypical and the event relates to the brand's core meaning. Even if no clear link exists between the event and the sponsor, sponsor recall can be improved if the company explains why the sponsorship makes sense.[111]

▶ *The medium in which the stimulus is processed.* Researchers are exploring whether certain media are more effective than others at enhancing consumer memory. Compared to magazines, television may be more effective because it combines visual and auditory information. Some studies suggest that consumers tend not to look at or remember Internet ads, whereas other studies suggest online ads can be as or even more effective than traditional media in generating brand memory.[112]

What the Stimulus Is Linked To

Retrieval cue A stimulus that facilitates the activation of memory.

Retrieval can also be affected by what the stimulus is linked to in memory. A **retrieval cue** is some stimulus that facilitates the activation of memory.[113] For example, if you want to remember to go to a sale at Macy's, you might leave a note on your desk that says, "Macy's." The note serves as a retrieval cue when you see it some time later and remember the sale.

Retrieval cues can be generated internally or externally. Internally, a thought can cue another thought, as in "Today is November 8. Oh no, it's my sister's birthday!" An external stimulus such as a vending machine, a viral ad video, or an in-store display could also serve as a retrieval cue. Pictures or videos of ourselves engaging in an activity can serve as powerful retrieval cues, too.[114] Effective retrieval cues may differ from culture to culture. One study found sounds to be more effective retrieval cues for English-language ads, whereas visuals were more for Chinese-language ads.[115]

Brand name is a vitally important retrieval cue.[116] Yet the impact of a brand name as a retrieval cue is not the same for recognition as it is for recall.[117] If marketers want consumers to *recognize* the brand on the store shelf, it is important to have high-frequency words or names to which consumers have been heavily exposed—for example, Axe or Old Spice. If the goal is to have consumers *recall* the brand and its associations, choose brand names that (1) evoke rich imagery (Old El Paso), (2) are novel or unexpected (Kindle), or (3) suggest the offering and its benefits (Mr. Clean).

Unfamiliar brands have a retrieval advantage when the name of the brand fits well with the product function, whereas familiar brands have a retrieval advantage when the name features unusual spelling.[118] Images closely related to the brand name also serve as retrieval cues.[119] Revealing the brand name early in an ad message strengthens the memory association between the brand and the consumer's evaluation of the message content, an effect that influences retrieval.[120] Finally, logos, packages, and brand logos and typefaces can also act as retrieval cues.[121] The picture of the girl with the umbrella is likely to cue consumers to remember the Morton seasoning products depicted in Exhibit 4.10.

Exhibit 4.10

The Package as Retrieval Cue

Packages sometimes contain information that helps consumers remember what they saw in an ad. The girl with the umbrella (who shows that Morton salt still pours even when it rains) is used as a retrieval cue on all Morton seasoning products.

How a Stimulus Is Processed in Working Memory

Another factor affecting retrieval is the way information is processed in working memory. One consistent finding is that messages processed through imagery tend to be better remembered than those processed discursively. Imagery apparently creates a greater number of associations in memory, which, in turn, enhance retrieval.[122] This is because mental images are processed as pictures *and* as words. This *dual coding* provides extra associative links in memory, enhancing the likelihood that the item will be retrieved, whereas information encoded verbally is processed just one way and has only one retrieval path. Dual coding is one reason that marketers often use the audio portion of well-known TV ads as radio commercials. When consumers hear the familiar verbal message, they may provide their own imagery of the visual part.

Consumer Characteristics Affecting Retrieval

Consumers' mood and expertise can affect retrieval.[123] First, being in a positive mood can enhance our recall of stimuli in general. Second, we are more likely to recall information that is consistent with our mood. In other words, if we are in a positive mood, we are more likely to recall positive information. Several explanations account for these mood effects. One is that feelings consumers associate with a concept are linked to the concept in memory. Thus, your memory of DisneyWorld may be associated with the feeling of having fun. If you are in a mood for fun, the "fun" concept may be activated, and this activation may spread to the concept of "DisneyWorld."[124] People also appear to process information in more detail when mood is intense than when it is not. More detailed processing leads to greater elaboration and higher levels of recall.[125] Furthermore, mood influences both elaboration and rehearsal. Thus, consumers in a positive mood are more likely to readily learn brand names and engage in brand rehearsal.[126]

Compared with novices, experts have more complex category structures in memory with a greater number of higher- and lower-level categories and more detail within each category. Therefore, experts' associative networks are more interconnected than the networks of novices. The complex linkages and the spreading of the activation concept explain why experts can recall more brands, brand attributes, and benefits than novices.[127] On the other hand, when experts comparing product descriptions infer information that is not actually described, they may base their judgments at least in part on these false memories because of their highly developed category structures and schema.[128]

SUMMARY

Consumer memory is the persistence of learning over time, via the storage and retrieval of information, which can occur consciously or unconsciously. Retrieval is remembering or accessing what is stored in memory. Sensory memory (iconic and echoic) involves a very brief analysis of sensory inputs. Working memory is where we interpret incoming information, involving discursive and imagery processing. Long-term memory represents the permanent memory store, covering both episodic and semantic memory. Explicit memory involves active efforts to remember what's in memory; implicit memory involves remembering without conscious awareness. Chunking, rehearsal, recirculation, and elaboration are useful for influencing working memory.

Knowledge content is represented by a set of associations about an object or an activity linked in schemas and scripts. Knowledge in long-term memory is organized according to associative networks, with concepts connected by associations or links. By the spreading of activation in associative networks, some information becomes more salient than others. Objects in memory are stored according to taxonomic categories; within the same taxonomic category, objects share similar features, which differ from the features of objects in other categories. A prototype is perceived as the best example of its category. Taxonomic categories are structured hierarchically, organized into superordinate, basic, and subordinate levels. Knowledge content and structure are flexible. Objects may become part of the same category because they contribute to the same goal, and more or less abstract associations may become activated depending on the time until consumers make the choice or take the action.

People forget because of retrieval failures (due to decay, interference, and primacy and recency effects), or they may retrieve information that is not accurate. Factors that facilitate retrieval include the characteristics of the stimulus, what it is linked to, the way it is processed, and the characteristics of consumers.

Questions for Review and Discussion

1. How are sensory, working, and long-term memory linked?
2. What techniques can enhance the storage of information in long-term memory?
3. What is a schema and how can the associations in a schema be described?
4. Why are some links in a semantic or associative network weak, whereas others are strong?
5. What are taxonomic categories and how do consumers use them to structure knowledge in memory?
6. What is a category prototype, and what affects prototypicality?
7. What does it mean to say that consumers organize knowledge according to goal-derived categories?
8. How do high- (abstract) and low-level (concrete) associations differ, and what does this mean for knowledge structure?
9. Which three elements affect retrieval failures?
10. How can consumers' ability to retrieve information in memory be enhanced?

CONSUMER BEHAVIOR CASE

Nostalgia Marketing Brings Memories Back

Many different marketers, from cat-food manufacturers to insurance firms, are evoking positive memories of the past to capture the imagination of consumers through nostalgia marketing. Whether they're bringing back old jingles, slogans, images, logos, characters, or brands, marketers want to jolt consumers' memories. Feeling pressured by today's fast-paced, high-tech world, many consumers are receptive to familiar ads and products they associate with their younger days and bygone times they remember fondly.

Meow Mix cat food, owned by Del Monte Foods, recently resumed the use of its decades-old advertising jingle, after a 16-year hiatus. The jingle is a series of "meows" set to a simple tune that plays as viewers watch cats "mouth" the words during the commercials. "The Meow Mix Jingle brings back a sense of nostalgia and is a classic advertising spot that many people can even recite by memory," explained the brand's marketing director. The jingle is so memorable that 50 percent of consumers surveyed *before* the new ads aired said they had heard the jingle during the previous 18 months, even though it had not been used for more than a decade.

Comic-strip characters from the 1960s are helping MetLife appeal to consumers who smile when they see Charlie Brown, Snoopy, and other Peanuts characters in the insurance company's ads and social media posts. Before debuting a new commercial during the Super Bowl, MetLife used its Facebook to post "comments" by Peanuts characters. After the game, MetLife posted additional character scenes online to keep the buzz going. Why use nostalgia for Snoopy to market life insurance? "It definitely takes people back, and we wanted to start a dialogue," says a company executive.

Volkswagen, Audi, and other car companies frequently play on nostalgia for old rock songs to reach target audiences. One Volkswagen commercial recently featured a 1960s James Brown hit, while an Audi ad featured a 1980s song by Echo and the Bunnymen. H&M has marketed its men's clothing with hit songs from the past such as the Animals' *Please Don't Let Me Be Misunderstood*. Nostalgia for childhood snacks has helped Cadbury market its Wispa chocolate bar and Nestlé market its Kit Kat bars.

The long-running TV program *Mad Men*, which focused on characters rising in the advertising industry of the 1950s and 1960s, provided numerous opportunities for advertisers to evoke nostalgia for the period. Unilever created retro-look commercials to air in Europe during the program's fourth season. During the U.K. premiere of *Mad Men's* fifth season, Sky Atlantic ran well-known British TV commercials from the 1960s for Fairy Liquid, Tetley Tea, and other brands, heightening viewer anticipation for a nostalgic look back at ads they hadn't seen for many years.

When the U.S. magazine *Newsweek* put *Mad Men* on its cover, it suggested that advertisers submit ads with a 1965 look. That issue included a Spam ad with flower-power colors and fonts; a Dunkin' Donuts ad with 1960s images of the donut shop; a Hush Puppies shoe ad based on the company's actual 1960s ads; a new Mercedes-Benz sports car advertised in 1960s style; and a reprint of a 1960s Johnnie Walker Red liquor ad. Media coverage of the issue and its special ads increased sales and boosted traffic to websites where the ads were posted, adding a 21st-century angle to the 20th-century nostalgic appeal.[129]

CASE QUESTIONS

1. Using the concepts in this chapter, explain why Meow Mix would return to its old advertising jingle 16 years after the company stopped using it.
2. What role do episodic and semantic memory play in the use of nostalgia marketing?
3. How is MetLife's use of Peanuts comic-strip characters in its ads likely to affect consumers' schemas? Would you have these characters posting on Facebook as part of the campaign? Why or why not?

ENDNOTES

1 Chandra Steele, "History of the iPad," *PC Magazine*, March 12, 2012, www.pcmag.com; Abe Sauer, "Steve Jobs and the Evolution of the Apple Logo: 'Don't Make It Cute,'" *Brand Channel*, October 9, 2011, www.brandchannel.com; and Dean Crutchfield, "Why the Apple Won't Crumble," *Forbes*, March 13, 2012, www.forbes.com.

2. Loraine Lau-Gesk, "Understanding Consumer Evaluations of Mixed Affective Experiences," *Journal of Consumer Research* 32, no. 1, 2005, pp. 23–28.

3. R. N. Haber, "The Impending Demise of the Icon: A Critique of the Concept of Iconic Storage in Visual Information Processing," *The Behavioral and Brain Sciences*, March 1983, pp. 1–54.

4. Nader T. Tavassoli and Jin K. Han, "Scripted Thought: Processing Korean Hancha and Hangul in a Multimedia Context," *Journal of Consumer Research*, December 2001, pp. 482–493.

5. Deborah J. MacInnis and Linda L. Price, "The Role of Imagery in Information Processing: Review and Extensions," *Journal of Consumer Research*, March 1987, pp. 473–491.

6. Allan Paivio, "Perceptual Comparisons Through the Mind's Eye," *Memory and Cognition*, November 1975, pp. 635–647; Stephen M. Kosslyn, "The Medium and the Message in Mental Imagery," *Psychological Review*, January 1981, pp. 46–66; and MacInnis and Price, "The Role of Imagery in Information Processing."

7. Morris B. Holbrook and Elizabeth C. Hirschman, "The Experiential Aspects of Consumption," *Journal of Consumer Research*, September 1982, pp. 132–140; and Alan Richardson, "Imagery: Definitions and Types," in ed. Aness Sheikh, *Imagery: Current Theory, Research, and Application* (New York: Wiley, 1983), pp. 3–42.

8. "Visitors Can Try on Dresses in Virtual Dressing Room on Brides.com," *Long Island Press*, August 28, 2011, www.longislandpress.com.

9. Martin S. Lindauer, "Imagery and the Arts," in ed. Aness Sheikh, *Imagery: Current Theory, Research, and Application* (New York: Wiley, 1983), pp. 468–506.

10. Jennifer Edson Escalas, "Imagine Yourself in the Product," *Journal of Advertising*, Summer 2004, pp. 37–48.

11. Iris W. Hung and Robert S. Wyer Jr., "Shaping Consumer Imaginations: The Role of Self-Focused Attention in Product Evaluations," *Journal of Marketing Research*, April 2011, pp. 381–392.

12. Dennis Hockman, "Home Design Right at Hand," *Baltimore Sun*, August 25, 2011, www.baltimoresun.com.

13. Hans Baumgartner, Mita Sujan, and James R. Bettman, "Autobiographical Memories, Affect, and Consumer Information Processing," *Journal of Consumer Psychology* 1, no. 1, 1992, pp. 53–82.

14. See Kathryn A. Braun-LaTour, Michael S. LaTour, and George M. Zinkham, "Using Childhood Memories to Gain Insight into Brand Meaning," *Journal of Marketing*, April 2007, pp. 45–60.

15. Marc Vanhuele, Gilles Laurent, and Xavier Drèze, "Consumers' Immediate Memory for Prices," *Journal of Consumer Research* 33, no. 2, 2006, pp. 163–172.

16. Jing Xu and Norbert Schwarz, "Do We Really Need a Reason to Indulge?" *Journal of Marketing Research*, February 2009, pp. 25–36.

17. Darrel D. Muehling and Vincent J. Pascal, "An Empirical Investigation of the Differential Effects of Personal, Historical, and Non-Nostalgic Advertising on Consumer Responses," *Journal of Advertising*, Summer 2011, pp. 107–122; Darrel D. Muehling and David E. Sprott, "The Power of Reflection: An Empirical Examination of Nostalgia Advertising Effects," *Journal of Advertising*, Fall 2004, pp. 25–36; Morris B. Holbrook, "Nostalgia and Consumer Preferences," *Journal of Consumer Research*, September 1993, pp. 245–256; and Morris B. Holbrook and Robert M. Schindler, "Echoes of the Dear Departed Past," in eds. Rebecca H. Holman and Michael R. Solomon, *Advances in Consumer Research*, vol. 18 (Provo, Utah: Association for Consumer Research, 1991), pp. 330–333.

18. Jack Neff, "Scrapbooking Gets Reinvented to Suit New Digital Reality," *Advertising Age*, July 25, 2011, p. 8.

19. Kathryn A. Braun-LaTour, Michael S. LaTour, Jacqueline E. Pickrell, and Elizabeth F. Loftus, "How and When Advertising Can Influence Memory for Consumer Experience," *Journal of Advertising*, Winter 2004, pp. 7–25.

20. Kathryn A. Braun, "Postexperience Advertising Effects on Consumer Memory," *Journal of Consumer Research*, March 1999, pp. 319–334.

21. Angela Y. Lee and Aparna A. Labroo, "The Effect of Conceptual and Perceptual Fluency on Brand Evaluation," *Journal of Marketing Research*, May 2004, pp. 151–165.

22. Noel Hayden, "The Spacing Effect: Enhancing Memory for Repeated Marketing Stimuli," *Journal of Consumer Psychology* 16, no. 3, 2006, pp. 306–320.

23. F. I. M. Craik and R. S. Lockhart, "Levels of Processing," *Verbal Learning and Verbal Behavior*, December 1972, pp. 671–684.

24. Elizabeth Olson, "Under Armour Applies Its Muscle to Shoes," *New York Times*, August 8, 2011, www.nytimes.com.

25. Alan G. Sawyer, "The Effects of Repetition," in eds. G. David Hughes and Michael L. Ray, *Buyer/Consumer Information Processing* (Chapel Hill, N.C.: University of North Carolina Press, 1974), pp. 190–219; George E. Belch, "The Effects of Television Commercial Repetition on Cognitive Response and Message Acceptance," *Journal of Consumer Research*, June 1982, pp. 56–66; H. Rao Unnava and Robert E. Burnkrant, "Effects of Repeating Varied Ad Executions on Brand Name Memory," *Journal of Marketing Research*, November 1991, pp. 406–416; and Murphy S. Sewall and Dan Sarel, "Characteristics of Radio Commercials and Their Recall Effectiveness," *Journal of Marketing*, January 1986, pp. 52–60.

26. Chris Janiszewski, Hayden Noel, and Alan G. Sawyer, "Re-Inquiries: A Meta-Analysis of the Spacing Effect in Verbal Learning," *Journal of Consumer Research*, June 2003, pp. 138–149; see also Sara L. Appleton, Robert A. Bjork, and Thomas D. Wickens, "Examining the Spacing Effect in Advertising," *Journal of Consumer Research* 32, no. 2, 2005, pp. 266–276.

27. Sharmistha Law, "Can Repeating a Brand Claim Lead to Memory Confusion?" *Journal of Marketing Research*, August 2002, pp. 366–378.

28. Susan E. Heckler and Terry L. Childers, "The Role of Expectancy and Relevancy in Memory for Verbal and Visual Information," *Journal of Consumer Research*, March 1992, pp. 475–492.

29. H. Shanker Krishnan, "A Process Analysis of the Effects of Humorous Advertising Executions on Brand Claims Memory," *Journal of Consumer Psychology*, 2003, pp. 230–245.

30. Catherine A. Cole and Michael J. Houston, "Encoding and Media Effects on Consumer Learning Deficiencies in the Elderly," *Journal of Marketing Research*, February 1987, pp. 55–64; and Deborah Roedder John and John C. Whitney Jr., "The Development of Consumer Knowledge in Children," *Journal of Consumer Research*, March 1986, pp. 406–418.

31. Lawrence W. Barsalou, *Cognitive Psychology: An Overview for Cognitive Scientists* (Hillsdale, N.J.: Lawrence Erlbaum, 1992); James R. Bettman, "Memory Factors in Consumer Choice," *Journal of Marketing*, Spring 1979, pp. 37–53; and Merrie Brucks and Andrew A. Mitchell, "Knowledge Structures, Production Systems and Decision Strategies," in ed. Kent B. Monroe, *Advances in Consumer Research*, vol. 8 (Ann Arbor, Mich.: Association for Consumer Research, 1982), pp. 750–757.

32. Vanitha Swaminathan, Karen L. Page, and Zeynep Gurhan-Canli, "'My' Brand or 'Our' Brand: The Effects of Brand Relationship Dimensions and Self-Construal on Brand Evaluations," *Journal of Consumer Research*, August 2007, pp. 248–259.

33. Joseph W. Alba and J. Wesley Hutchinson, "Dimensions of Consumer Expertise," *Journal of Consumer Research*, March 1987, pp. 411–454.

34. Deborah J. MacInnis, Kent Nakamoto, and Gayathri Mani, "Cognitive Associations and Product Category Comparisons," in eds. John F. Sherry and Brian Sternthal, *Advances in Consumer Research*, vol. 19 (Provo, Utah: Association for Consumer Research, 1992), pp. 260–267; and Kevin L. Keller, "Conceptualizing, Measuring, and Managing Customer-Based Brand Equity," *Journal of Marketing*, January 1993, pp. 1–22.

35. Stijn M. J. Van Osselaer and Chris Janiszewski, "Two Ways of Learning Brand Associations," *Journal of Consumer Research*, September 2001, pp. 202–223.

36. Beth Kowitt, "Why McDonald's Wins in Any Economy," *Fortune*, September 5, 2011, pp. 70–78.

37. Zeynep Gurhan-Canli and Rajeev Batra, "When Corporate Image Affects Product Evaluations: The Moderating Role of Perceived Risk," *Journal of Marketing Research*, May 2004, pp. 197–205.

38. Joseph T. Plummer, "How Personality Makes a Difference," *Journal of Advertising Research*, December 1984–January 1985, pp. 27–31; William D. Wells, Frank J. Andriuli, Fedele J. Goi, and Stuart Seader, "An Adjective Check List for the Study of 'Product Personality,'" *Journal of Applied Psychology*, October 1957, pp. 317–319; and Jennifer L. Aaker, "Dimensions of Brand Personality," *Journal of Marketing Research*, August 1997, pp. 347–356.

39. Rajeev Batra and Pamela Miles Homer, "The Situational Impact of Brand Image Beliefs," *Journal of Consumer Psychology* 14, no. 3, 2004, pp. 318–330.

40. Bianca Grohmann, "Gender Dimensions of Brand Personality," *Journal of Marketing Research*, February 2009, pp. 105–111.

41. Yongjun Sung and Spencer F. Tinkham, "Brand Personality Structures in the United States and Korea," *Journal of Consumer Psychology* 15, no. 4, 2005, pp. 334–350.

42. Gita V. Johar, Jaideep Sengupta, and Jennifer L. Aaker, "Two Roads to Updating Brand Personality Impressions: Trait Versus Evaluative Inferencing," *Journal of Marketing Research*, November 2005, pp. 458–469.

43. Jesse Chandler and Norbert Schwarz, "Use Does Not Wear Ragged the Fabric of Friendship: Thinking of Objects as Alive Makes People Less Willing to Replace Them," *Journal of Consumer Psychology*, 2010, pp. 138–145.

44. Ji Kyung Park and Deborah Roedder John, "Got to Get You into My Life: Do Brand Personalities Rub Off on Consumers?" *Journal of Consumer Research*, December 2010, pp. 655–669.

45. Lucia Malar, Harley Krohmer, Wayne D. Hoyer, and Bettina Nyffenegger, "Emotional Brand Attachment and Brand Personality: The Relative Importance of the Actual and the Ideal Self," *Journal of Marketing*, July 2011, pp. 35–52.

46. Thomas W. Leigh and Arno J. Rethans, "Experiences in Script Elicitation Within Consumer Decision-Making Contexts," in eds. Richard P. Bagozzi and Alice M. Tybout, *Advances in Consumer Research*, vol. 10 (Ann Arbor, Mich.: Association for Consumer Research, 1983), pp. 667–672; Roger C. Shank and Robert P. Abelson, *Scripts, Plans, Goals, and Understanding* (Hillsdale, N.J.: Lawrence Erlbaum, 1977); Ruth Ann Smith and Michael J. Houston, "A Psychometric Assessment of Measures of Scripts in Consumer Memory," *Journal of Consumer Research*, September 1985, pp. 214–224; R. A. Lakshmi-Ratan and Easwar Iyer, "Similarity Analysis of Cognitive Scripts," *Journal of the Academy of Marketing Science*, Summer 1988, pp. 36–43; and C. Whan Park, Easwar Iyer, and Daniel C. Smith, "The Effects of Situational Factors on In-Store Grocery Shopping Behavior," *Journal of Consumer Research*, March 1989, pp. 422–432.

47. See Girish N. Punj and Clayton L. Hillyer, "A Cognitive Model of Customer-Based Brand Equity for Frequently Purchased Products," *Journal of Consumer Psychology* 14, no. 1 & 2, 2004, pp. 124–131; Kevin Lane Keller, *Building, Measuring, and Managing Brand Equity*, 2nd ed. (Upper Saddle River, N.J.: Prentice-Hall, 2003), p. 60; and Roland T. Rust, Valarie Z. Zeithaml, and Katherine N. Lemon, *Driving Customer Equity* (New York: Free Press, 2000), pp. 80–87.

48. Deborah Roedder John, Barbara Loken, Kyeongheui Kim, and Alokparna Basu Monga, "Brand Concept Maps," *Journal of Marketing Research*, November 2006, pp. 549–563.

49. Lan Nguyen Chaplin and Deborah Roedder John, "The Development of Self-Brand Connections in Children and Adolescents," *Journal of Consumer Research* 32, no. 1, 2005, pp. 119–129.

50. Bryan Harley, "Rats Hole Custom Bike Show Sturgis 2011," *Motorcycle USA*, August 12, 2011, www.motorcycle-usa.com; and Steve Miller, "Signs Point to Smaller Rally Crowd," *Rapid City Journal (S.D.)*, August 15, 2011.

51. Tom Meyvis and Chris Janiszewski, "When Are Broader Brands Stronger Brands?" *Journal of Consumer Research* 31, no. 2, 2004, pp. 346–357; Sheri Bridges, Kevin Lane Keller, and Sanjay Sood, "Communication Strategies for Brand Extensions," *Journal of Advertising* 29, no. 4, Winter 2000, pp. 1–11; Elyette Roux and Frederic Lorange, "Brand Extension Research," in eds. Fred von Raiij and Gary Bamoussy, *European Advances in Consumer Research*, vol. 1 (Provo, Utah: Association for Consumer Research, 1993), pp. 492–500; C. Whan Park, Bernard J. Jaworski, and Deborah J. MacInnis, "Strategic Brand Concept–Image Management," *Journal of Marketing*, October 1986, pp. 135–145; David A. Aaker and Kevin L. Keller, "Consumer Evaluations of Brand Extensions," *Journal of Marketing*,

January 1990, pp. 27–41; Bernard Simonin and Julie A. Ruth, "Is a Company Known by the Company It Keeps?" *Journal of Marketing Research*, February 1998, pp. 30–42; C. Whan Park, Sung Youl Jun, and Allan D. Shocker, "Composite Branding Alliances," *Journal of Marketing Research*, November 1996, pp. 453–466; MacInnis, Nakamoto, and Mani, "Cognitive Associations and Product Category Comparisons"; David M. Bousch et al., "Affect Generalization to Similar and Dissimilar Brand Extensions," *Psychology and Marketing*, 1987, pp. 225–237; and Susan M. Baroniarczyk and Joseph W. Alba, "The Importance of the Brand in Brand Extension," *Journal of Marketing Research*, May 1994, pp. 214–228.

52. Catherine W. M. Yeung and Robert S. Wyer Jr., "Does Loving a Brand Mean Loving Its Products? The Role of Brand-Elicited Affect in Brand Extension Evaluations," *Journal of Marketing Research*, November 2005, pp. 495–506.

53. Huifang Mao and H. Shanker Krishnan, "Effects of Prototype and Exemplar Fit on Brand Extension Evaluations: A Two-Process Contingency Model," *Journal of Consumer Research* 33, no. 1, 2006, pp. 41–49; Franziska Volkner and Henrik Sattler, "Drivers of Brand Extension Success," *Journal of Marketing*, April 2006, pp. 18–34; David Bousch, Shannon Shipp, Barbara Loken, Esra Genturk, Susan Crocket, Ellen Kennedy, Bettie Minshall, Dennis Misurell, Linda Rochford, and John Strobel, "Affect Generalization to Similar and Dissimilar Brand Extensions," *Psychology and Marketing* 4, no. 3, 1987, pp. 225–237; and Rainer Greifender, Herbert Bless, and Thorston Kurschmann, "Extending the Brand Image on New Products," *Journal of Consumer Behavior* 6, no. 1, 2007, pp. 19–31.

54. Ingrid Martin and David Stewart, "The Differential Impact of Goal Congruence on Attitudes, Intentions, and the Transfer of Brand Equity," *Journal of Marketing Research*, November 2001, pp. 471–484; and Alokparna Basu Monga and Deborah Roedder John, "Cultural Differences in Brand Extension Evaluation," *Journal of Consumer Research* 33, no. 4, 2007, pp. 529–536. See also Shailendra Pratap Jain, Kalpesh Kaushik Desai, and Huifang Mao, "The Influence of Chronic and Situational Self-Construal on Categorization," *Journal of Consumer Research* 34, no. 1, 2007, pp. 66–76; and Sandra Milberg, C. W. Park, and Robert Lawson, "Evaluation of Brand Extensions," *Journal of Consumer Research* 18, no. 2, 1991, pp. 185–193.

55. Michael J. Barone, "The Interactive Effects of Mood and Involvement on Brand Extension Evaluations," *Journal of Consumer Psychology* 15, no. 3, 2005, pp. 263–270.

56. Maureen Morrin, "The Impact of Brand Extensions on Parent Brand Memory Structures and Retrieval Processes," *Journal of Marketing Research*, November 1999, pp. 517–525.

57. Deborah Roedder John, Barbara Loken, and Christopher Joiner, "The Negative Impact of Extensions," *Journal of Marketing* 62, January 1998, pp. 19–32.

58. Meyvis and Janiszewski, "When Are Broader Brands Stronger Brands?"

59. Sharon Ng, "Cultural Orientation and Brand Dilution: Impact of Motivation Level and Extension Typicality," *Journal of Marketing Research*, February 2010, pp. 186–198.

60. Rohini Ahluwalia, "How Far Can a Brand Stretch? Understanding the Role of Self-Construal," *Journal of Marketing Research*, June 2008, pp. 337–350.

61. Kathryn A. LaTour and Michael S. LaTour, "Assessing the Long-term Impact of a Consistent Advertising Campaign on Consumer Memory," *Journal of Advertising*, Summer 2004, pp. 49–61.

62. See Kevin P. Gwinner and John Eaton, "Building Brand Image Through Event Sponsorship," *Journal of Advertising* 28, no. 4, Winter 1999, pp. 47–57.

63. Candice Choi, "Burger King Launches New Menu to Boost Sagging Sales," *Chicago Sun-Times*, April 2, 2012, www.suntimes.com; Dale Buss, "Burger King, Quaker Hope Oatmeal Sticks," *Brand Channel*, August 29, 2011, www.brandchannel.com; and Bruce Horovitz, "Burger King Freshens Fast-food Image, Kicks King to the Curb," *USA Today*, August 19, 2011, www.usatoday.com.

64. Niraj Dawar and Madan M. Pillutla, "Impact of Product-Harm Crises on Brand Equity," *Journal of Marketing Research*, May 2000, pp. 215–226.

65. Jennifer Aaker, Susan Fournier, and S. Adam Brasel, "When Good Brands Do Bad," *Journal of Consumer Research*, June 2004, pp. 1–16.

66. Eleanor Rosch, "Principles of Categorization," in eds. E. Rosch and B. Lloyd, *Cognition and Categorization* (Hillsdale, N.J.: Lawrence Erlbaum, 1978), pp. 119–160.

67. Jacquelyn A. Ottman, "Earth to Eco-Labels," *Media Post*, August 17, 2011, www.mediapost.com.

68. Shashi Matta and Valerie S. Folkes, "Inferences About the Brand from Counterstereotypical Service Providers," *Journal of Consumer Research* 32, no. 2, 2005, pp. 196–206.

69. Greg Migliore, "GM Transplants Chevrolet Volt Technology into the Cadillac ELR Hybrid," *Auto Week*, August 17, 2011, www.autoweek.com.

70. Rosch, "Principles of Categorization"; Barsalou, *Cognitive Psychology*; and Madhubalan Viswanathan and Terry L. Childers, "Understanding How Product Attributes Influence Product Categorization: Development and Validation of Fuzzy Set-Based Measures of Gradedness in Product Categories," *Journal of Marketing Research*, February 1999, pp. 75–94.

71. Lawrence Barsalou, "Ideals, Central Tendency, and Frequency of Instantiation as Determinants of Graded Structure in Categories," *Journal of Experimental Psychology: Learning, Memory and Cognition*, October 1985, pp. 629–649; Barbara Loken and James Ward, "Alternative Approaches to Understanding the Determinants of Typicality," *Journal of Consumer Research*, September 1990, pp. 111–126; James Ward and Barbara Loken, "The Quintessential Snack Food: Measurement of Product Prototypes," in ed. Richard J. Lutz, *Advances in Consumer Research*, vol. 13 (Provo, Utah: Association for Consumer Research, 1986), pp. 126–131; and Gregory S. Carpenter and Kent Nakamoto, "Consumer Preference Formation and Pioneering Advantage," *Journal of Marketing Research*, August 1989, pp. 285–298.

72. Hyeong Min Kim, "Evaluations of Moderately Typical Products: The Role of Within- Versus Cross-Manufacturer Comparisons," *Journal of Consumer Psychology* 16, no. 1, 2006, pp. 70–78.

73. Sharon Ng and Michael J. Houston, "Field Dependency and Brand Cognitive Structures," *Journal of Marketing Research*, April 2009, pp. 279–292.

74. See Amos Tversky and Daniel Kahneman, "Extensional Versus Intuitive Reasoning: The Conjunction Fallacy," *Psychological Review*, October 1983, pp. 293–315.

75. Bob Garfield, "Softly Lit or Blunt, 'Less Toxic' Cigarette Ads Hint at Health," *Advertising Age*, November 12, 2001, p. 58; and Suein Hwang, "Smokers May Mistake 'Clean' Cigarette for Safe," *Wall Street Journal*, September 30, 1995, pp. B1, B2.

76. Luk Warlop and Joseph W. Alba, "Sincere Flattery: Trade-Dress Imitation and Consumer Choice," *Journal of Consumer Psychology* 14, no. 1/2, 2004, pp. 21–27.

77. John Schwartz, "Seems Like a No-Brainer," *New York Times*, August 26, 2011, www.nytimes.com.

78. Ronald W. Niedrich, Subhash Sharma, and Douglas H. Wedell, "Reference Price and Price Perceptions," *Journal of Consumer Research*, December 2001, pp. 339–354.

79. Francois A. Carrillat, Eric G. Harris, and Barbara A. Lafferty, "Fortuitous Brand Image Transfer," *Journal of Advertising*, Summer 2010, pp. 109–123.

80. Barbara Loken, Christopher Joiner, and Joann Peck, "Category Attitude Measures: Exemplars as Inputs," *Journal of Consumer Psychology*, no. 2, 2002, pp. 149–161.

81. Barsalou, *Cognitive Psychology*.

82. Yaacov Trope, Nira Liberman, and Cheryl Wakslak, "Construal Levels and Psychological Distance: Effects on Representation, Prediction, Evaluation, and Behavior," *Journal of Consumer Psychology* 17, no. 2, 2007, pp. 83–95.

83. Klaus Fiedler, "Construal Level Theory as an Integrative Framework for Behavioral Decision-Making Research and Consumer Psychology," *Journal of Consumer Psychology* 17, no. 2, 2007, pp. 101–106.

84. Yaacov Trope and Nira Liberman, "Temporal Construal," *Psychological Review*, 110, no. 3, 2003, pp. 403–421.

85. Dengfeng Yan and Jaideep Sengupta, "Effects of Construal Level on the Price-Quality Relationship," *Journal of Consumer Research*, August 2011, pp. 376–389.

86. Michael Fitzpatrick, "Japan: Kit Kat Sales Boosted by Lucky Translation," *Just-Food.com*, February 3, 2005, www.just-food.com.

87. Frank R. Kardes, Maria L. Cronley, and John Kim, "Construal-Level Effects on Preference Stability, Preference–Behavior Correspondence, and the Suppression of Competing Brands," *Journal of Consumer Psychology* 16, no. 2, 2006, pp. 135–144.

88. Aparna A. Labroo and Vanessa M. Patrick, "Psychological Distancing: Why Happiness Helps You See the Big Picture," *Journal of Consumer Research*, February 2009, pp. 800–809.

89. Eleanor Rosch, "Human Categorization," in ed. N. Warren, *Studies in Cross-Cultural Psychology* (New York: Academic Press, 1977), pp. 1–49; A. D. Pick, "Cognition: Psychological Perspectives," in eds. H. C. Triandis and W. Lonner, *Handbook of Cross-Cultural Psychology* (Boston: Allyn & Bacon, 1980), pp. 117–153; and Bernd Schmitt and Shi Zhang, "Language Structure and Categorization: A Study of Classifiers in Consumer Cognition, Judgment and Choice," *Journal of Consumer Research*, September 1998, pp. 108–122.

90. Beth Snyder Bulik, "Philips: We're Not Just Light Bulbs," *Advertising Age*, June 25, 2007, www.adage.com.

91. Alba and Hutchinson, "Dimensions of Consumer Expertise"; Deborah Roedder John and John Whitney Jr., "The Development of Consumer Knowledge in Children," *Journal of Consumer Research*, March 1986, pp. 406–417; Merrie Brucks, "The Effects of Product Class Knowledge on Information Search Behavior," *Journal of Consumer Research*, June 1985, pp. 1–16; and Deborah Roedder John and Mita Sujan, "Age Differences in Product Categorization," *Journal of Consumer Research*, March 1990, pp. 452–460; see also Andrew A. Mitchell and Peter A. Dacin, "The Assessment of Alternative Measures of Consumer Expertise," *Journal of Consumer Research*, December 1996, pp. 219–239; and C. Whan Park, David L. Mothersbaugh, and Lawrence Feick, "Consumer Knowledge Assessment," *Journal of Consumer Research*, June 1994, pp. 71–82.

92. Elizabeth Cowley and Andrew A. Mitchell, "The Moderating Effect of Product Knowledge on the Learning and Organization of

Product Information," *Journal of Consumer Research*, December 2003, pp. 443–454; and Stacy L. Wood and John G. Lynch Jr., "Prior Knowledge and Complacency in New Product Learning," *Journal of Consumer Research*, December 2002, pp. 416–426.

93. Joseph W. Alba and J. Wesley Hutchinson, "Knowledge Calibration," *Journal of Consumer Research*, September 2000, pp. 123–156.

94. Jiewen Hong and Brian Sternthal, "The Effects of Consumer Prior Knowledge and Processing Strategies on Judgments," *Journal of Marketing Research*, April 2010, pp. 301–311.

95. Larry Percy and John R. Rossiter, "A Model of Brand Awareness and Brand Attitude in Advertising Strategies," *Psychology and Marketing*, July–August 1992, pp. 263–274.

96. Bonnie Tsui, "Bowl Poll: Ads Don't Mean Sales," *Advertising Age*, February 5, 2001, p. 33.

97. Angela Y. Lee, "Effects of Implicit Memory on Memory-Based Versus Stimulus-Based Brand Choice," *Journal of Marketing Research*, November 2002, pp. 440–454.

98. Rik G. M. Pieters and Tammo H. A. Bijmolt, "Consumer Memory for Television Advertising: A Field Study of Duration, Serial Position and Competition Effects," *Journal of Consumer Research*, March 1997, pp. 362–372; Raymond Burke and Thomas K. Srull, "Competitive Interference and Consumer Memory for Advertisements," *Journal of Consumer Research*, June 1988, pp. 55–68; Kevin Keller, "Memory and Evaluation Effects in Competitive Advertising Environments," *Journal of Consumer Research*, March 1991, pp. 463–476; Tom J. Brown and Michael L. Rothschild, "Reassessing the Impact of Television Advertising Clutter," *Journal of Consumer Research*, June 1993, pp. 138–147; Robert J. Kent and Chris T. Allen, "Competitive Interference Effects in Consumer Memory for Advertising," *Journal of Marketing*, July 1994, pp. 97–105; and H. Rao Unnava and Deepak Sirdeshmukh, "Reducing Competitive Ad Interference," *Journal of Marketing Research*, August 1994, pp. 403–411.

99. Anand Kumar and Shanker Krishnan, "Memory Interference in Advertising: A Replication and Extension," *Journal of Consumer Research*, March 2004, pp. 602–661; and Anand Kumar, "Interference Effects of Contextual Cues in Advertisements on Memory for Ad Content," *Journal of Consumer Psychology* 9, no. 3, 2000, pp. 155–166.

100. Robert D. Jewell and H. Rao Unnava, "When Competitive Interference Can Be Beneficial," *Journal of Consumer Research*, September 2003, pp. 283–291.

101. David Luna and Laura A. Peracchio, "Moderators of Language Effects in Advertising to Bilinguals," *Journal of Consumer Research*, September 2001, pp. 28–43.

102. Joseph W. Alba and Amitava Chattopadhyay, "Effects of Context and Part-Category Cues on Recall of Competing Brands," *Journal of Marketing Research*, August 1985, pp. 340–349; Joseph W. Alba and Amitava Chattopadhyay, "Salience Effects in Brand Recall," *Journal of Marketing Research*, November 1986, pp. 363–369; and Manoj Hastak and Anusre Mitra, "Facilitating and Inhibiting Effects of Brand Cues on Recall, Consideration Set, and Choice," *Journal of Business Research*, October 1996, pp. 121–126.

103. Dipayan Biswas, Dhruv Grewal, and Anne Roggeveen, "How the Order of Sampled Experiential Products Affects Choice," *Journal of Marketing Research*, June 2010, pp. 508–519.

104. Rik Pieters and Tammo H. A. Bijmolt, "Consumer Memory for Television Advertising: A Field Study of Duration, Serial Position, and Competition Effects," *Journal of Consumer Research*, March 1997, pp. 362–372; and Burke and Srull, "Competitive Interference and Consumer Memory for Advertising."

105. Elizabeth F. Loftus, "When a Lie Becomes Memory's Truth: Memory and Distortion after Exposure to Misinformation," *Current Directions in Psychological Science*, August 1992, pp. 121–123.

106. Ann E. Schlosser, "Learning Through Virtual Product Experiences," *Journal of Consumer Research* 33, no. 3, 2006, pp. 377–383.

107. Joseph W. Alba, J. Wesley Hutchinson, and John G. Lynch Jr., "Memory and Decision Making," in eds. Thomas S. Robertson and Harold Kassarjian, *Handbook of Consumer Behavior* (Englewood Cliffs, N.J.: Prentice-Hall, 1991), pp. 1–49.

108. Rik G. M. Pieters and Tammo H. A. Bijmolt, "Consumer Memory for Television Advertising: A Field Study of Duration, Serial Position, and Competition Effects," *Journal of Consumer Research*, March 1997, pp. 362–372; David W. Stewart and David H. Furse, *Effective Television Advertising: A Study of 1000 Commercials* (Cambridge, Mass.: Marketing Science Institute, 1986); and Pamela Homer, "Ad Size as an Indicator of Perceived Advertising Costs and Effort: The Effects on Memory and Perceptions," *Journal of Advertising*, Winter 1995, pp. 1–12.

109. Frank R. Kardes and Gurumurthy Kalyanaram, "Order of Entry Effects on Consumer Memory and Judgment," *Journal of Marketing Research*, August 1992, pp. 343–357; Frank Kardes, Murali Chandrashekaran, and Ronald Dornoff, "Brand Retrieval, Consideration Set Composition, Consumer Choice, and the Pioneering Advantage," *Journal of Consumer Research*, June 1993, pp. 62–75; and Frank H. Alpert and Michael A. Kamins, "An Empirical Investigation of Consumer Memory, Attitude, and Perceptions Toward Pioneer and Follower Brands," *Journal of Marketing*, October 1995, pp. 34–44.

110. Sridar Samu, H. Shankar Krishnan, and Robert E. Smith, "Using Advertising Alliances for New Product Introduction," *Journal of Marketing*, January 1999, pp. 57–74.

111. T. Bettina Cornwell, Michael S. Humphreys, Angela M. Maguire, Clinton S. Weeks, and Cassandra L. Tellegen, "Sponsorship-Linked Marketing: The Role of Articulation in Memory," *Journal of Consumer Research* 33, no. 3, 2006, pp. 312–321.

112. Rex Briggs and Nigel Hollis, "Advertising on the Web," *Journal of Advertising Research*, March–April 1997, pp. 33–45.

113. Michael Pham and Gita Venkataramani Johar, "Contingent Processes of Source Identification," *Journal of Consumer Research*, December 1997, pp. 249–265.

114. Deborah D. Heisley and Sidney J. Levy, "Autodriving: A Photoelicitation Technique," *Journal of Consumer Research*, December 1991, pp. 257–272.

115. Nader T. Tavassoli and Yih Hwai Lee, "The Differential Interaction of Auditory and Visual Advertising Elements with Chinese and English," *Journal of Marketing Research*, November 2003, pp. 468–480.

116. Charles D. Lindsey and H. Shanker Krishnan, "Retrieval Disruption in Collaborative Groups due to Brand Cues," *Journal of Consumer Research* 33, no. 4, 2007, pp. 470–478.

117. Joan Meyers-Levy, "The Influence of a Brand Name's Association Set Size and Word Frequency on Brand Memory," *Journal of Consumer Research*, September 1989, pp. 197–207; and Alba and Hutchinson, "Dimensions of Consumer Expertise."

118. Tina M. Lowrey, L. J. Shrum, and Tony M. Dubitsky, "The Relation Between Brand-Name Linguistic Characteristics and Brand-Name Memory," *Journal of Advertising*, Fall 2003, pp. 7–17.

119. Jaideep Sengupta and Gerald J. Gorn, "Absence Makes the Mind Grow Sharper: Effects of Element Omission on Subsequent Recall," *Journal of Marketing Research*, May 2002, pp. 186–201.

120. William E. Baker, Heather Honea, and Cristel Antonia Russell, "Do Not Wait to Reveal the Brand Name," *Journal of Advertising*, Fall 2004, pp. 77–85.

121. Judith Lynne Zaichkowsky, "Strategies for Distinctive Brands," *Brand Management* 17, no. 8, 2010, pp. 548–560; and Terry L. Childers and Jeffrey Jass, "All Dressed Up with Something to Say: Effects of Typeface Semantic Associations on Brand Perceptions and Consumer Memory," *Journal of Consumer Psychology*, 2002, pp. 93–106.

122. Cole and Houston, "Encoding and Media Effects on Consumer Learning Deficiencies in the Elderly"; and Sharmistha Law, Scott A. Hawkins, and Fergus I. M. Craik, "Repetition-Induced Belief in the Elderly: Rehabilitating Age-Related Memory Deficits," *Journal of Consumer Research*, September 1998, pp. 91–107.

123. Alice M. Isen, "Some Ways in Which Affect Influences Cognitive Processes: Implications for Advertising and Consumer Behavior," in eds. Alice M. Tybout and P. Cafferata, *Advertising and Consumer Psychology* (Lexington, Mass.: Lexington Books, 1989), pp. 91–117; see also Patricia A. Knowles, Stephen J. Grove, and W. Jeffrey Burroughs, "An Experimental Examination of Mood Effects on Retrieval and Evaluation of Advertisement and Brand Information," *Journal of the Academy of Marketing Science*, Spring 1993, pp. 135–143; Gordon H. Bower, "Mood and Memory," *American Psychologist*, February 1981, pp. 129–148; Gordon H. Bower, Stephen Gilligan, and Kenneth Montiero, "Selectivity of Learning Caused by Affective States," *Journal of Experimental Psychology: General*, December 1981, pp. 451–473; and Alice M. Isen, Thomas Shalker, Margaret Clark, and Lynn Karp, "Affect, Accessibility of Material in Memory, and Behavior," *Journal of Personality and Social Psychology*, 1978, pp. 1–12.

124. Alice M. Isen, "Toward Understanding the Role of Affect in Cognition," in eds. Robert S. Wyer and Thomas K. Srull, *Handbook of Social Cognition* (Hillsdale, N.J.: Lawrence Erlbaum, 1984), pp. 179–236.

125. Alice M. Isen, "Some Ways in Which Affect Influences Cognitive Processes: Implications for Advertising and Consumer Behavior," in eds. Patricia Cafferata and Alice M. Tybout, *Cognitive and Affective Responses to Advertising* (Lexington, Mass.: Lexington Books, 1989), pp. 91–118.

126. Angela Y. Lee and Brian Sternthal, "The Effects of Positive Mood on Memory," *Journal of Consumer Research* 26, September 1999, pp. 115–127.

127. Alba and Hutchinson, "Dimensions of Consumer Expertise."

128. Ravi Mehta, Joandrea Hoegg, and Amitav Chakravarti, "Knowing Too Much: Expertise-Induced False Recall Effects in Product Comparison," *Journal of Consumer Research*, October 2011, pp. 535–554.

129. Tanya Irwin, "Infectious Meow Mix Jingle Returns," *Media Post*, March 13, 2012, www.mediapost.com; Joanne Ostrow, "Pop Culture Nostalgia Rules in Super Bowl Ads," *Denver Post*, February 6, 2012, www.denverpost.com; Matthew Sturdevant, "MetLife's Cartoon Ads are the Latest in Nostalgia Marketing," *Hartford Courant*, February 7, 2012, www.courant.com; Florence Waters, "Mad Men Gets Sixties' Commercial Breaks," *Telegraph (UK)*, March 27, 2012, www.telegraph.co.uk; and Laura Slattery, "Everybody's Looking for a Piece of This Mad World," *Irish Times*, March 22, 2012, www.irishtimes.com.

ATTITUDES BASED ON HIGH EFFORT

After studying this chapter, you will be able to

1. Discuss how marketers can apply various cognitive models to understand and influence consumers' attitudes based on high-effort thought processes.

2. Describe some of the methods for using the communication source and the message to favorably influence consumers' attitudes.

3. Explain how and why a company might try to change consumers' attitudes by influencing their feelings.

Nautilus Chronograph

PATEK PHILIPPE
GENEVE

Image Courtesy of The Advertising Archives

INTRODUCTION

Prestige Watches Have Timeless Appeal

Luxury, tradition, and achievement—Rolex, Panerai, Patek Philippe, Tag Heuer, and others use such themes in marketing high-end watches to affluent consumers around the world. Switzerland's Rolex, known for its status-symbol watches, promotes its sponsorship of the Royal Ocean Racing Club and other yacht groups to reinforce a long-standing connection with this upper-class sport. To attract and engage well-to-do buyers, Rolex also advertises in luxury lifestyle magazines, provides product details via mobile marketing, and arranges endorsements from successful sports figures such as golfer Phil Mickelson.

Panerai, based in Italy, sponsors regattas to associate its handcrafted, precision watches with traditional yacht craftsmanship. Patek Philippe reinforces its positioning as a fine Swiss timepiece brand with advertising and through carefully chosen retail locations, including an elegant boutique in the heart of Zurich's luxury shopping district, where the world's top watchmakers have stores. Tag Heuer, part of France's LVMH Group, has signed Bollywood star Shah Rukh Khan to endorse its watch brand in print ads and personal appearances. Tag Heuer's lead designer explains that buyers connect with these high-end watches on a strong, emotional level: "It's a purchase of passion."[1]

The marketing activities of luxury watchmakers illustrate several important points that stem directly from concepts covered in the preceding chapter. Consumers probably have certain beliefs about brands such as Rolex that are based on the mental associations they have linked to them (Rolex watches are expensive; Rolex watches are status symbols). These beliefs can affect consumers' attitudes (whether they like a certain brand or a particular style) and their behavior (whether they will travel to a store that carries Rolex watches). Finally, attitudes can be based on the offering's functional features (precise time-keeping ability) or the emotional aspects (feeling proud to own a prestige brand). How marketers help consumers form positive brand attitudes based on new beliefs and associations, and to influence buying decisions, are central issues addressed in this chapter.

WHAT ARE ATTITUDES?

Attitude A relatively global and enduring evaluation of an object, issue, person, or action.

An **attitude** is an overall evaluation that expresses how much we like or dislike an object, issue, person, or action.[2] Attitudes are learned, and they tend to persist over time. Our attitudes also reflect our overall evaluation of something based on the set of associations linked to it. This is the reason why we have attitudes toward brands, product categories, ads, people, stores, websites, activities, and so forth.

The Importance of Attitudes

Cognitive function How attitudes influence our thoughts.

Affective function How attitudes influence our feelings.

Connative function How attitudes influence our behavior.

Attitudes are important because they (1) guide our thoughts (the **cognitive function**), (2) influence our feelings (the **affective function**), and (3) affect our behavior (the **connative function**). We decide which ads to read, whom to talk to, where to shop, and where to eat, based on our attitudes. Likewise, attitudes influence our behavior in acquiring, consuming, and disposing of an offering. Thus, marketers need to change attitudes in order to influence consumer decision making and change consumer behavior.

The Characteristics of Attitudes

Favorability The degree to which we like or dislike something.

Attitude accessibility How easily an attitude can be remembered.

Attitude confidence How strongly we hold an attitude.

Attitude persistence How long our attitude lasts.

Attitude resistance How difficult it is to change an attitude.

Ambivalence When our evaluations regarding a brand are mixed (both positive and negative).

Attitudes can be described in terms of five main characteristics: favorability, attitude accessibility, attitude confidence, persistence, and resistance. **Favorability** refers to how much we like or dislike an attitude object. **Attitude accessibility** refers to how easily and readily an attitude can be retrieved from memory.[3] If you went to a movie last night, you can probably remember fairly easily what your attitude toward it was, just as you can easily remember your attitude toward an important object, event, or activity (such as your first car).

Attitudes can also be described in terms of their strength, or **attitude confidence**. In some cases we hold our attitudes very strongly and with a great deal of confidence, whereas in other cases we feel much less certain about them. Attitudes may also vary in their **persistence**, or endurance. The attitudes we hold with confidence may last for an extremely long time, whereas others may be very brief. In addition, attitudes can be described in terms of their **resistance** to subsequent change.[4] Consumers may change attitudes easily when they are not loyal to a particular brand or know little about a product. However, attitude change is more difficult when consumers are brand loyal or consider themselves experts in the product category.

Finally, attitudes may be described in terms of **ambivalence**, as when we have strong positive evaluations of one aspect of a brand and strong negative evaluations of other aspects of the brand. Interestingly, someone else's opinion will tend to influence us more when our attitudes are ambivalent, even when we do not see that person as being particularly knowledgeable about the product or category. So if you are shopping, and you can find both good and bad reasons to buy the product, you may be more influenced to buy it if encouraged by a friend.[5]

Forming and Changing Attitudes

Marketers can better create or influence consumers' attitudes toward new offerings and novel behaviors when they understand how attitudes are formed. This understanding also helps marketers plan strategies for changing consumer attitudes about existing offerings and established behaviors. Exhibit 5.1 summarizes general approaches to attitude formation and change processes that are discussed in this and the next chapter.

The Foundation of Attitudes

As Exhibit 5.1 shows, one approach to attitude formation suggests that attitudes are based on *cognitions* (thoughts) or beliefs.[6] This means that attitudes can be based on thoughts we have about information received from an external source (such as advertising, salespeople, Facebook, or a friend) or on information we recall from memory. One study shows that ad messages with information about product function—what a product's features can do, for example—can provoke thinking about the product and stimulate positive product attitudes.[7]

A second approach suggests that attitudes are based on *emotions*. Sometimes we have a favorable attitude toward an offering simply because it feels good or seems right. Likewise, we can acquire attitudes by observing and vicariously experiencing the emotions of others who use an offering. For example, if you see that people riding skateboards are having fun, you may believe that if you rode one, you would, too. In fact, research suggests that both the hedonic aspect (related to the experience of product use) and the utilitarian aspect (related to the product's function) affect attitudes toward product categories and individual brands.[8]

The Role of Effort in Attitude Formation and Change

How much extensive thinking or *elaboration* consumers put forth affects their attitude formation and change processes as well. As discussed in Chapter 2, consumers sometimes have high motivation, ability, and opportunity (MAO) to process information and make decisions. When MAO is high, consumers are more likely to devote a lot of effort toward and become quite involved in forming or changing attitudes and making decisions. Some researchers have used the term

Attitudes are based on:

	Cognitions (thoughts)	Affect (feelings/emotions)
High Effort Central-Route Processing (Chapter 5)	• Direct or imagined experience • Reasoning by analogy or category • Values-driven attitudes • Social identity-based attitude generation • Analytical attitude construction	• Emotional processing • Affective response • Attitude toward the ad
Low Effort Peripheral-Route Processing (Chapter 6)	• Simple beliefs • Unconscious influences • The environment	• The mere exposure effect • Classical and evaluative conditioning • Attitude toward the ad • Mood

Consumers' elaboration (consideration) of a message (based on their motivation, ability, and opportunity [MAO])

© Cengage Learning 2013

Exhibit 5.1

General Approaches to Attitude Formation and Change

Consumers can form attitudes in four basic ways, depending on whether elaboration is high or low and whether the processing is cognitive or affective. This chapter examines the ways in which attitudes can be formed and changed when consumer effort is high.

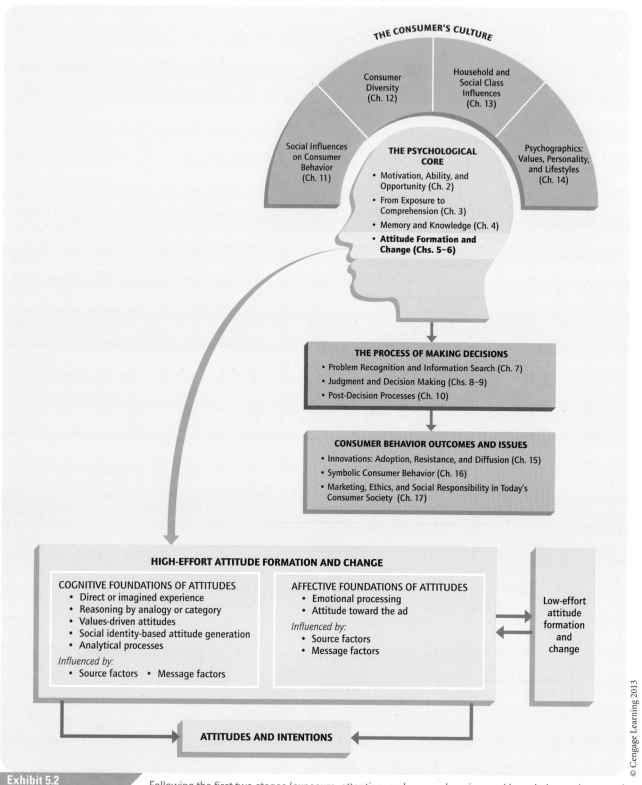

Exhibit 5.2

Chapter Overview: Attitude Formation and Change, High Consumer Effort

Following the first two stages (exposure, attention, and comprehension; and knowledge and memory), consumers can either form or change their attitudes. This chapter explains how consumers form high-effort attitudes based on both cognition and affect. It also shows how marketers can influence attitudes through source factors and message factors.

Central-route process-ing The attitude formation and change process when effort is high.

central-route processing to describe the process of attitude formation and change when thinking about a message requires some effort.[9] Processing is central because consumers' attitudes are based on a careful and effortful analysis of the true merits or central issues contained within the message. As a result of this extensive and laborious processing, consumers form strong, accessible, and confidently held attitudes that are persistent and resistant to change.

When MAO is low, however, consumers' attitudes are based on a more tangential or superficial analysis of the message, not on an effortful analysis of its true merits. Because these attitudes tend to be based on peripheral or superficial cues contained within the message, the term **peripheral-route processing** has been used to describe attitude formation and change that involves limited effort (or low elaboration) on the part of the consumer.

Peripheral-route pro-cessing The attitude formation and change process when effort is low.

This chapter focuses on several ways in which consumers form and change attitudes when effort (i.e., MAO) is high. The next chapter focuses on how consumers form and change attitudes when effort is low. Because attitudes tend to be more accessible, persistent, resistant to change, and held with confidence when consumers' MAO to process information is high, much of the chapter focuses on what affects the favorability of consumers' attitudes.

As shown in Exhibit 5.2, when consumers are likely to devote a lot of effort to processing information, marketers can influence consumer attitudes either (1) *cognitively*—influencing the thoughts or beliefs they have about the offering or (2) *affectively*—influencing the emotional experiences consumers associate with the offering. Furthermore, marketers can try to influence consumers' attitudes through characteristics of the source used in a persuasive communication, the type of message used, or some combination of both. After attitudes are formed, they may play a powerful role in influencing consumers' intentions and actual behavior.

THE COGNITIVE FOUNDATIONS OF ATTITUDES

Researchers have proposed various theories to explain how thoughts are related to attitudes when consumers devote a lot of effort to processing information and making decisions. This section focuses on five cognitive models: (1) direct or imagined experience; (2) reasoning by analogy or category; (3) values-driven attitudes; (4) social identity-based attitude generation; and (5) analytical processes of attitude construction, including expectancy-value models such as the theory of reasoned action (TORA) and the theory of planned behavior.

Direct or Imagined Experience

Elaborating on actual experience with a product or service (or even imagining what that experience could be like) can help consumers form positive or negative attitudes. You are likely to form an attitude after test-driving a new car or watching a movie preview, for instance, or even simply by imagining what it would be like to drive that car or watch that movie. JC Penney's "Pennies from Heaven" fundraising campaign to benefit after-school programs asks consumers to "imagine what a penny can do" and reminds them that a lot of small change can make a big difference.[10] One more point: You will have a more favorable attitude toward a product like a new car if you use imagery to elaborate on the positive aspects of buying and using it.[11]

Reasoning by Analogy or Category

Consumers also form attitudes by considering how similar a product is to other products or to a particular product category. For instance, if you have never sipped a chilled bottle of Starbucks Frappuccino, but you think it might be similar to the hot Starbucks coffees that you like, your reasoning would lead you to form a positive attitude toward the Frappuccino. As another example, if a tiny keyring-mounted flash drive is advertised as having the portability and convenience of a Swiss Army knife, you might form a positive attitude toward it because the analogy involves a product you like (the knife).[12]

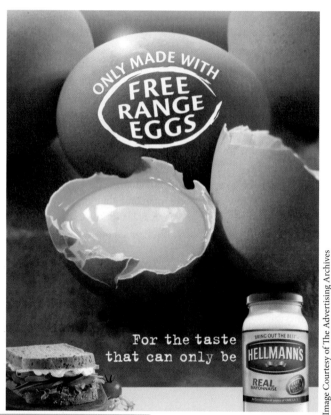

Exhibit 5.3

Value-Driven Ads
Consumers are more responsive to ads that reflect their individual values.

Cognitive response
Thought we have in response to a communication.

Counterargument (CA)
Thought that disagrees with the message.

Support argument (SA)
Thought that agrees with the message.

Source derogation (SD)
Thought that discounts or attacks the source of the message.

Values-Driven Attitudes

Another way that attitudes are generated or shaped is based on individual values.[13] Suppose that environmental protection is one of your most strongly held values. When you think about buying new sneakers, you might have a more positive attitude about a brand that uses recycled materials than you would about a brand that uses nonrecyclable materials. Thus, your values shape your attitude toward those brands (see Exhibit 5.3). This is also true for consumers who value authenticity and therefore form a positive attitude toward a brand or offering they perceive to be genuine, real, and true.[14] An example that illustrates this value-driven attitude is Barilla highlighting the authenticity of its Italian food products by having its Bologna-trained executive chef demonstrate for consumers the actual cooking techniques used in Italy.[15]

Social Identity-Based Attitude Generation

The way that consumers view their own social identities can play a role in forming their attitudes toward products or brands. If you consider yourself a very serious sports fan, for instance, that may be a defining aspect of your identity. In turn, you will tend to form positive attitudes toward a brand or product (such as the brand of sports apparel endorsed by your favorite athlete) that enables you to express this social identity.[16] Thus, for example, consumers who see themselves as dedicated snowboarding fans may form positive feelings toward the Northstar Ski Resort in Lake Tahoe, where X Games star Shaun White has designed a half-pipe.[17]

Analytical Processes of Attitude Formation

Consumers sometimes use a more analytical process of attitude formation in which, after being exposed to marketing stimuli or other information, they form attitudes based on their cognitive responses. **Cognitive responses** are the thoughts a person has when he or she is exposed to a communication, which may take the form of recognitions, evaluations, associations, images, or ideas.[18] Suppose a man sees an ad for the impotency drug Cialis. In response, he might think, "I really need a product like this," "This product will never work," or "The guy in the ad was paid to praise this product." These spontaneously generated thoughts will, according to cognitive response models, influence his attitude toward Cialis.[19] Positive thoughts can have a favorable impact on attitudes, whereas negative thoughts can have a negative effect.

Cognitive Responses to Communications

According to the cognitive response model, consumers exert a lot of effort in responding to the message—enough effort to generate counterarguments, support arguments, and source derogations.

▶ **Counterarguments (CAs)** are thoughts that express disagreement with the message. In the earlier example of a man seeing an ad for Cialis, such thoughts might be "This product will never work" or "This product will not cure my problem."

▶ **Support arguments (SAs)** are thoughts that express agreement with the message. The man may think "This sounds great" or "I really need a product like this."

▶ **Source derogations (SDs)** are thoughts that discount or attack the message source. Seeing the Cialis ad, the man might think "The guy is lying" or "The guy in the ad was paid to say this."

Counterarguments and source derogations, in particular, result in a less favorable initial attitude or resistance to attitude change. Thoughts like "It will never work" or "The guy was paid to say this" are likely to lead to a negative attitude toward Cialis. However, consumers do not blindly accept and follow suggestions made in persuasive messages; rather, they may use their knowledge about marketers' goals or tactics to effectively cope with or resist these messages.[20] In fact, consumers do think about how marketers try to influence consumer behavior—and, in turn, these thoughts allow consumers to formulate counterarguments or support arguments in response to marketing activities.[21] Moreover, the presence of support arguments ("This sounds great") results in positive attitudes toward the offering.

Research shows that when consumers resist persuasion and become aware of their own resistance, this awareness reinforces their initial attitudes. In high-elaboration situations, consumers confronted with a persuasive message that conflicts with their own attitudes will generate counterarguments that strengthen their initial attitudes—but only when the message is from an expert source.[22]

Marketing Implications

Although marketers want consumers to be exposed to and to comprehend their marketing messages, they also want consumers' responses to be positive rather than negative. Consumers who generate counterarguments and source derogations will have weak or even negative attitudes toward an offering. To combat this reaction, marketers should test consumers' cognitive responses to communications before running the ads. By asking consumers to think aloud while they view the ad or to record their thoughts right after seeing it, marketers can classify the responses, identify problems, and strengthen the message.

Consumers tend to generate more counterarguments and fewer support arguments when the message content differs from what they already believe. Thus, a message supporting handgun control will generate a lot of counterarguments among National Rifle Association members. This **belief discrepancy** creates more counterarguments because consumers want to maintain their existing belief structures and do so by arguing against the message.[23] Consumers also generate more counterarguments and fewer support arguments when the message is weak. For example, saying that Gillette disposable razors come in many colors is not a strong and compelling reason to buy one. In such a situation, consumers may derogate the source (Gillette) or generate counterarguments ("Who cares about color?").[24]

Consumers come up with more support arguments and fewer counterarguments when they are involved with the TV program in which a commercial appears. The program distracts consumers from counterarguing, enhancing the message's persuasive impact.[25] Another way to decrease counterarguments is through the *disrupt-then-reframe technique*. Disrupting consumers' cognitive processing of the communication in an odd but subtle way ("400 pennies a day vs. $4 a day") clears the way for more effective persuasion when the message is reframed (with a statement such as "this is an incredible bargain").[26] Finally, consumers react more favorably to communications when they are in a good mood: They often want to preserve this mood, so they resist counterarguing.[27]

Expectancy-Value Models

Expectancy-value models are analytical processes that explain how consumers form and change attitudes based on (1) the beliefs or knowledge they have about an object or action and (2) their evaluation of these particular beliefs.[28] According to this model, you might like a Volkswagen because you believe it is reliable, moderately priced, and environmentally friendly—and you think it is good for a car to have these traits.

The expectancy-value model known as the **theory of reasoned action (TORA)** provides an expanded picture of how, when, and why attitudes predict consumer behavior, particularly in the United States.[29] As shown in Exhibit 5.4, the model proposes that **behavior (B)** is a function of a person's **behavioral intention (BI)**, which in turn is determined by (1) the person's **attitude toward the act (A_{act})** and (2) the **subjective norms (SN)** that operate in the situation. Consistent with most expectancy-value models, A_{act} is determined by the consumer's *beliefs* (b_i) about the consequences of engaging in the behavior and the consumer's *evaluation* (e_i) of these consequences. SNs are determined by the consumer's *normative beliefs* (NB_j)—or what the consumer thinks someone else wants him or her to do—and the consumer's *motivation to comply* (MC_j) with this person.

Belief discrepancy When a message is different from what consumers believe.

Expectancy-value model A widely used model that explains how attitudes form and change.

Theory of reasoned action (TORA) A model that provides an explanation of how, when, and why attitudes predict behavior.

Behavior (B) What we do.

Behavioral intention (BI) What we intend to do.

Attitude toward the act (A_{act}) How we feel about doing something.

Subjective norm (SN) How others feel about our doing something.

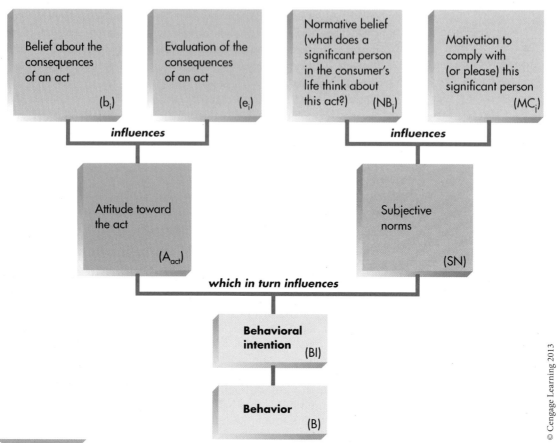

© Cengage Learning 2013

Exhibit 5.4

The Theory of Reasoned Action

TORA is an expectancy-value model that proposes how beliefs influence attitudes and norms, which in turn affect behavior.

Normative influence
How other people influence our behavior through social pressure.

Note that the TORA model takes into account how other people in the social environment influence consumer behavior. In some situations, **normative influences** from others can play a powerful role in how people behave. Hotels use normative influences to encourage eco-friendly behavior when they place signs in guest rooms saying "the majority of guests reuse their towels," in the hope that guests will not request freshly laundered towels every day.[30] Also, trying to predict BIs from attitudes, as in the TORA model, is much easier than trying to predict actual behaviors because many situational factors could cause a consumer not to engage in an intended behavior.[31] For example, you may *intend* to buy a Volkswagen, but you may not because you are short of money.

The TORA model assumes that attitudes are accessible since they can only guide behavior if consumers can retrieve them. Attitude confidence and less ambivalence will also increase the relationship between attitudes and behavior.[32] In addition, an extension of TORA, the **theory of planned behavior**, seeks to predict behaviors over which consumers have incomplete control by examining their perceived behavioral control.[33] For instance, older consumers who see an ad promoting the health benefits of taking blood pressure medication will be more likely to obtain and take the product if they form a positive attitude toward making this change, form intentions to change, and perceive that they have some control over this consumption behavior.

Theory of planned behavior An extension of the TORA model that predicts behaviors over which consumers perceive they have control.

Marketing Implications

Marketers need to understand not only what attitudes consumers have but also why consumers have these attitudes and how these attitudes can be changed. The TORA model is useful for analyzing the reasons why consumers may like or dislike an offering, whether they intend to engage in or resist a behavior, and who else might be influential and therefore should also be targeted.

Such models also provide useful guidance on how marketers can change attitudes, intentions, and (marketers hope) behavior through these major strategies:

1. *Change beliefs*. One possible strategy would be to change the strength of the beliefs that consumers associate with the consequences of acquiring an offering. Marketers could try to (1) strengthen beliefs that the offering has positive, important consequences or (2) lessen the belief that it has negative consequences. Although marketers commonly use this strategy when consumers are more likely to consider the message, inducing such change is not easy when consumers have strong prior beliefs. When South Korea's Hyundai first entered global markets such as the United States and South Africa, its cars were perceived as low-price, low-quality products. In recent years, Hyundai has sought to change those beliefs by advertising the good quality, high-tech features, and updated styling of its Genesis and Elantra models.[34]

2. *Change evaluations*. Another way to change attitudes is to change consumers' evaluations of the consequences. Consumers' attitudes become more positive when their beliefs are more positive or less negative. For instance, makers of biodiesel-blended heating oil are targeting home-owners with messages that explain the environmental benefits of "bioheat" compared with traditional fuel oil.[35] Interestingly, research shows that a campaign promoting a product category winds up changing the relative importance of the attributes that consumers use to evaluate brands in that category.[36]

3. *Add a new belief*. A third strategy is to add a new belief altogether that would make the consumer's attitude more positive. This strategy is particularly effective when a brand has existing features that are considered inferior, quality perceived to be lower, or a higher price than that of its competitors.[37] After the 2010 oil spill that damaged the Gulf Coast, Florida wanted vacationers to know that most beaches remained clean and beautiful. So the tourism commission asked local residents to post photos of their favorite beaches to floridalive.com, a special site with web-cam feeds as well as photos to reinforce the idea that many beaches were undamaged.[38] Note that adding novel attributes to a low-complexity product is likely to encourage positive beliefs and a more positive attitude toward that product.[39]

4. *Encourage attitude formation based on imagined experience*. Marketers can communicate information through ads featuring vivid language, detailed pictures, instructions, or virtual-reality demonstrations to encourage consumers to imagine the experience. Doing this may produce positive brand attitudes as long as consumers are good at imagining things and as long as they focus on positive aspects rather than potentially negative aspects.[40] For example, the U.K.-based online retailer Banana Flame offers a virtual dressing room experience: When consumers stand in front of their computer's webcam, they can see, on the screen, how a particular garment is likely to look on them.[41]

5. *Target normative beliefs*. Another strategy is to develop communications that specifically target strong normative beliefs as a way of influencing behavior. For example, Outagamie County, Wisconsin, is fighting heavy drinking among teens with billboards citing surveys showing that "70 percent of area high school students say it is *not okay* to binge drink."[42] On the other hand, condom ads have been unsuccessful in increasing sales because they have *not* stressed normative beliefs (what others will think of you if you do not use them).[43] The importance of normative beliefs does, however, vary across cultures. In countries that stress group values over those of the individual (such as Japan, among other Asian nations), appeals to normative beliefs take on greater significance.[44]

HOW COGNITIVELY BASED ATTITUDES ARE INFLUENCED

As Exhibit 5.2 indicates, both the communication source and the message influence how favorable a consumer's attitude will be. Here we explore how marketing communications can affect consumers' cognitively based attitudes when the processing effort is extensive.

Communication Source

Among consumers who process information extensively, those with attitudes based on cognitions are likely to be influenced by believable information. This means that marketing messages must be credible to generate support arguments, restrict counterarguments and source derogations, and increase belief strength. Several factors, including source credibility and company reputation, enhance the credibility of a message.

Source Credibility

Credibility Extent to which the source is trustworthy, expert, or has status.

In many marketing messages, information is presented by a spokesperson, usually a celebrity, an actor, a company representative, or a real consumer. In a sales situation, the salesperson is a spokesperson for the company and the offering. Both the **credibility** of these sources and the credibility of the company influence consumers' attitudes.[45] According to research, consumers tend to evaluate product information more thoughtfully when source credibility is low than when source credibility is high.[46]

Sources are credible when they have one or more of three characteristics: trustworthiness, expertise, and status. First, someone perceived as trustworthy is more likely to be believed than someone who is not. Pfizer, for instance, has featured user testimonials in ads for smoking-cessation medicine because consumers "liked the authenticity—to really connect their experiences with what they have heard from others," explains a marketing executive.[47] Consumers tend to see other consumers' opinions as less biased than official sources, which is why many check product reviews posted on bizrate.com, yelp.com, and other review sites. Research shows that high-quality online reviews (and a high number of reviews) have a positive effect on the purchasing intentions of online shoppers.[48]

Second, we are more likely to accept a message from someone perceived as knowledgeable or as *an expert* about the topic than from someone who has no experience with it. A salesperson who demonstrates extensive product knowledge will be more credible than an uninformed one. Consumers do, in fact, make buying decisions based on recommendations from expert sources such as *Consumer Reports*—and consumers will quickly change their buying patterns when the magazine retracts its findings.[49] Third, someone with a high position or social status can also be perceived as credible; this is why many firms feature their CEOs or founders in their ads or on their websites. Tom Dickinson is a credible source not only because he founded Blendtec, which makes blenders for home and restaurant use, but also because of his "Will It Blend?" viral videos showing how his products can blend almost anything, from iPhones to lumber.[50]

Research shows that credible sources have considerable impact on the acceptance of the message when consumers' prior attitudes are negative, when the message deviates greatly from their prior beliefs, when the message is complex or difficult to understand, and when there is a good "match" between product and endorser.[51] Moreover, source credibility can influence consumer attitudes by influencing the confidence consumers have in their thoughts about the message.[52]

Yet, credible sources will have less impact when consumers hold their existing attitude with confidence (so that even a credible source will not convince them otherwise) and when they have a high degree of ability to generate their own conclusions from the message (they have a lot of product-relevant knowledge, particularly if it is based on direct experience).[53] Also, consumers are less likely to believe that a source is credible when the source (e.g., a celebrity) endorses multiple products.[54] Finally, trust is an important element of credibility for spokescharacters such as the GEICO Gecko. Specifically, trust in a spokescharacter results in favorable brand attitudes if the consumer has had little experience with that brand.[55]

Marketing Implications

David Beckham's soccer achievements make him a credible, trusted endorser for adidas sports shoes and apparel.[56] Expert sources can also be popular, another factor that can contribute to an effective ad. Interestingly, one survey indicated that women endorsers are often seen as more popular and credible than male endorsers.[57] However, the company or product risks losing some credibility if a celebrity endorser gets into trouble or quits. For instance, AT&T, Gatorade, and other marketers cancelled their endorsement contracts with golfer Tiger Woods after his personal problems made headlines worldwide.[58]

Ordinary people may also be perceived as credible endorsers. Companies such as Pizza Hut and Cathay Pacific Airways have featured employees in their ad campaigns and online marketing because the employees add realism and help make an emotional connection with consumers.[59] Also note that a low-credibility source *can* be effective in some circumstances. In particular, if a low-credibility source argues against his or her own self-interest, positive attitude change can result.[60] Political ads, for example, may feature a member of the opposing party who endorses a rival candidate. In addition, the impact of a low-credibility source can actually increase over time (assuming the message is powerful). This **sleeper effect** occurs because the consumer's memory of the source can decay more rapidly than his or her memory of the message.[61] Thus, consumers may remember the message but not the source. _____

Sleeper effect Consumers forget the source of a message more quickly than they forget the message.

Company Reputation

When marketing communications do not feature an actual person, consumers judge credibility by the reputation of the company delivering the message.[62] People are more likely to believe—and change their attitudes based on—messages from companies with a reputation for producing quality products, dealing fairly with consumers, or being trustworthy. Online, a company can enhance its reputation and engender positive reactions by sponsoring content on relevant websites; banner ads highly targeted to a site's audience can also elicit positive attitudes toward the company.[63] More specifically, a brand's perceived trustworthiness exerts more influence on consumers' consideration and behavior than its expertise.[64]

Marketing Implications

Knowing that reputation influences consumer perceptions and credibility, companies generally work hard to develop a positive image through corporate advertising. Toyota, 3M, Siemens, and other companies have become known for their environmental records and earth-friendly products, which is why they top the list of the world's greenest brands (see Exhibit 5.5).[65] Many firms use advertising, social media, and public relations to communicate their involvement in charitable activities and environmental initiatives. The clothing retailer H&M, based in Sweden, showcases its support of UNICEF's All for Children Project in ads, a Facebook page, and Flickr photo-sharing.[66] _____

Exhibit 5.5

Top 10 Global Green Brands
A company's reputation for eco-friendly operations can influence perceptions of its credibility and consumer attitudes toward its brands.

These are the world's most environmentally friendly brands, as ranked by INTERBRAND:
1. Toyota (based in Japan)
2. 3M (based in the United States)
3. Siemens (based in Germany)
4. Johnson & Johnson (based in the United States)
5. Hewlett-Packard (based in the United States)
6. Volkswagen (based in Germany)
7. Honda (based in Japan)
8. Dell (based in the United States)
9. Cisco (based in the United States)
10. Panasonic (based in Japan)

Source: Adapted from INTERBAND, www.interbrand.com/en/best-global-brands/Best-Global-Green-Brands/2011-Report/BestGlobalGreenBrandsTable-2011.aspx.

Strong argument A presentation that features the best or central merits of an offering in a convincing manner.

The Message

Just as consumers evaluate whether or not the source is credible when their processing effort is high, they also evaluate whether or not the message is credible. Three factors affect the credibility of a message: the quality of its argument, whether it is a one- or two-sided message, and whether it is a comparative message.

Argument Quality

One of the most critical factors affecting whether a message is credible concerns whether it uses strong arguments.[67] **Strong arguments** present the best features or central merits of an offering in a convincing manner. Messages can also present supporting research or endorsements, such as the *Good Housekeeping* Seal, which is awarded only to products that pass the company's lab testing (see Exhibit 5.6).[68] Strong arguments are likely to be more persuasive if consumers are exposed to such messages after thinking about what they could have done differently to avoid a purchasing experience that led to an undesirable outcome.[69] In addition, strong arguments have a greater effect on behavioral intentions when consumers focus on the process of using the product rather than on the outcome of using it, especially for low-to moderate-involvement products.[70] Combining a strong argument with an implicit conclusion in an ad message engenders more favorable brand attitudes and buying intensions among consumers with a high need for cognition.[71] Moreover, consumers are more persuaded by a message containing a strong argument when they devote sufficient cognitive resources to processing the information.[72]

Infomercials—commercial messages that can last 30 to 60 minutes—allow companies enough time to fully explain complicated, technologically advanced, or innovative goods and services. In recent years, some marketers have turned to shorter infomercials—often only two minutes long—to sell products that require more demonstration or explanation than can be squeezed into a 30- or 60-second TV commercial. Infomercials generally include the address of a website or Facebook page where consumers can see more details and place orders.[73]

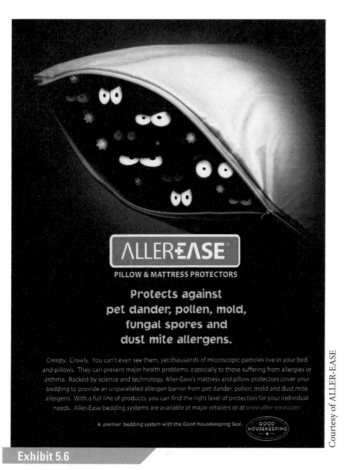

Courtesy of ALLER-EASE

ALLER·EASE
PILLOW & MATTRESS PROTECTORS

Protects against pet dander, pollen, mold, fungal spores and dust mite allergens.

Creepy. Crawly. You can't even see them, yet thousands of microscopic particles live in your bed and pillows. They can present major health problems, especially to those suffering from allergies or asthma. Backed by science and technology, Aller-Ease's mattress and pillow protectors cover your bedding to provide an unparalleled allergen barrier from pet dander, pollen, mold and dust mite allergens. With a full line of products, you can find the right level of protection for your individual needs. Aller-Ease bedding systems are available at major retailers or at www.aller-ease.com

A *premier* bedding system with the Good Housekeeping Seal.

Exhibit 5.6

Argument Quality

An example of a strong argument message is one based on research and backed by the Good Housekeeping Seal of approval.

Marketing Implications

If messages are weak, consumers are unlikely to think that they offer credible reasons for buying. Saying that a person should buy a particular brand of mattress because it comes in decorator fabrics is not very convincing. Nevertheless, messages do not always have to focus on substantive features of a product or service. Less important features can actually play a key role in influencing consumers' attitudes when brands are similar and many competitors emphasize the same important attributes.[74] Also, a message should match the amount of effort consumers want to use to process it. A message that is too simple or too complicated is unlikely to be persuasive.[75] ————

One- Versus Two-Sided Messages

One-sided message A marketing message that presents only positive information.

Two-sided message A marketing message that presents both positive and negative information.

Most marketing messages present only positive information. These are called **one-sided messages**. In some instances, however, a **two-sided message**, containing both positive and negative information about an offering, can be effective. For example, Buckley's Cough Mixture is marketed using blunt two-sided ad messages such as "It tastes awful. And it works" and "Disgustingly effective."[76] Like strong arguments, two-sided messages may affect consumers' attitudes by making the message more credible (i.e., they increase belief strength) and reducing counterarguments. When consumers see negative information in an ad, they tend to infer that the company is honest, a belief that adds to source credibility.[77] By providing reasons for consumers to be interested in the offering despite these problems, the ad encourages consumers to add a new belief. Note that the persuasive effect of two-sided messages depends, in part, on how much negative information is presented and on the interplay of negative and positive attributes.[78]

Marketing Implications

Two-sided messages seem to be particularly effective (1) when consumers are initially opposed to the offering (they already have negative beliefs) or (2) when they will be exposed to strong countermessages from competitors.[79] However, consumers who are exposed to many competing ads during a short period are likely to have difficulty recalling a particular brand's message, which in turn will hurt sales.[80] Two-sided messages are also well received by more intelligent consumers, who prefer neutral, unbiased messages. However, the use of two-sided advertising is not always in the marketer's best interest. In general, the positive effects of two-sided messages on brand attitudes occur only if the negative message is about an attribute that is not extremely important.

Comparative Messages

Comparative message
A message that makes direct comparisons with competitors.

Comparative messages show how much better the offering is than a competitor's. Two types of comparative messages have been identified.[81] The most common type is the *indirect comparative message*, in which the offering is compared with those of unnamed competitors (such as "other leading brands" or "Brand X"). This strategy can improve consumers' perceptions of a moderate-share brand relative to other moderate-share brands (but not to the market leader).[82] Marketers must remember, however, that the effectiveness of comparative advertising differs from culture to culture.[83] In Korea, a culture that values harmony, comparative advertising seems overly confrontational and is rarely used, whereas this technique is frequently used in the United States.

With *direct comparative advertising*, advertisers explicitly name and attack a competitor or set of competitors on the basis of an attribute or benefit (see Exhibit 5.7). This approach is usually used when the offering has a feature that is purportedly better than that of a competitor's. Salespeople frequently use this technique to convince consumers of the advantages of their offering over the competition. Comparative advertising is also used in political campaigns, where it generates more counterarguments and fewer source derogations than negative political advertising does. This result may be due to the different styles of information processing that the two types of messages encourage.[84] However, consumers exposed to negative political messages find them less useful for decision making and have more negative attitudes toward political campaigns than do consumers exposed to positive political advertising.[85]

In general, direct comparative messages are effective in generating attention and brand awareness and in positively increasing message processing, attitudes, intentions, and behavior.[86] They do not, however, have high credibility, as noted earlier. These messages are particularly effective for new brands or low-market-share brands attempting to take sales away from more popular brands.[87] Advertising for the new or low-share brand can enhance consumers' attitudes by highlighting how the brand is different from or better than other brands, giving consumers a credible reason for purchasing it. In fact, comparative advertising that stresses differentiation can spur consumers to note the dissimilarities of competing brands.[88] Messages comparing two brands perceived as dissimilar will elicit more elaboration, especially among consumers with a low need for cognition, precisely because the brands are different.[89]

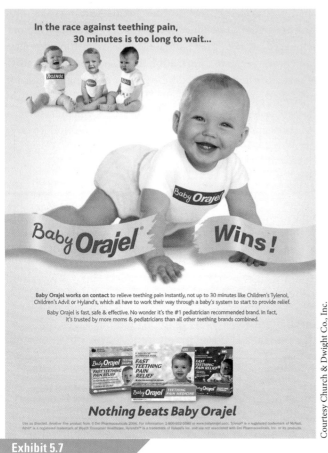

In the race against teething pain,
30 minutes is too long to wait...

Baby Orajel Wins!

Baby Orajel works on contact to relieve teething pain instantly, not up to 30 minutes like Children's Tylenol,
Children's Advil or Hyland's, which all have to work their way through a baby's system to start to provide relief.

Baby Orajel is fast, safe & effective. No wonder it's the #1 pediatrician recommended brand. In fact,
it's trusted by more moms & pediatricians than all other teething brands combined.

Nothing beats Baby Orajel

Courtesy Church & Dwight Co., Inc.

Exhibit 5.7

Comparative Messages

Ads may compare their products with competitors in direct comparative messaging.

Comparative messages are especially effective when they contain other elements that make them believable—such as a credible source or objective and verifiable claims (a strong argument)[90]—and when the featured attribute or benefit is important within the product category.[91] Still, a message that indirectly indicates a brand's superiority on featured attributes when compared with all competitors is more effective at positioning that brand within the overall market than a noncomparative or direct comparison ad is.[92] Also, consumers who originally receive information in a noncomparative ad and are then exposed to a comparative ad will revise their evaluations more than they will when subsequently exposed to another noncomparative ad.[93] Comparative ads that refer to competitors in a negative way are perceived as less believable and more biased; they cause consumers to develop more counterarguments and fewer support arguments than do comparative ads without negative competitive references.[94]

Marketers should also consider consumers' goals when preparing comparative ads. Promotion-focused consumers, whose goal is to maximize their gains and positive outcomes, will be more responsive to claims that Brand X is superior to Brand Y; prevention-focused consumers, who want to minimize their loss and risk, will be more skeptical of superiority claims and more responsive to claims that Brand X is similar or equivalent to Brand Y.[95] Note that positively framed comparative messages (Brand X performs better than Brand Y) are more effective for promotion-focused consumers (refer to Chapter 2), whereas negatively framed messages (Brand Y has more problems than Brand X) are more effective for prevention-focused consumers.[96] Positively framed comparative messages encourage more cognitive processing and prompt consumers to consider other brand information—sparking their buying intentions if the additional information supports the positive argument.[97]

Marketing Implications

When MAO is high, consumers exert more effort in processing direct comparative messages and are less likely to confuse the advertised brand with its competition.[98] Further, when consumers use analytical processing, a comparative ad will be more persuasive than a noncomparative ad; when consumers use imagery processing, a noncomparative ad will be more persuasive.[99] For instance, the SUBWAY sandwich chain has used comparative messages urging consumers to buy their lower-fat, lower-calorie sandwiches, which help consumers make a choice between fast-food categories based on attributes such as nutrition.[100] Bear in mind, however, that comparative messages are not useful in changing a consumer's negative first impression of a brand or company.[101]

All information contained in a comparative message must be factual and verifiable; otherwise, competitors may consider taking legal action. Although comparative ads are widely used in the United States and Latin America, they are illegal in some countries and closely regulated in the European Union.[102] Some consumers dislike comparative advertising. Japanese consumers, for example, respond better to a softer sell than they do to comparative ads.[103] Aggressive use of direct comparative ads can draw complaints from consumers as well as from competitors, and stimulate regulatory scrutiny.[104] Also, messages that compare a company's new, improved product to the same company's original product will be effective only when the improved functions are seen as atypical for that product. Otherwise, consumers are likely to discount the novelty of the new functionality.[105]

THE AFFECTIVE (EMOTIONAL) FOUNDATIONS OF ATTITUDES

Most of the early consumer research on attitudes when MAO and processing effort are high has focused on the cognitive models of attitude formation. Now, however, researchers are recognizing that consumers might exert a lot of mental energy in processing a message on an emotional basis. Emotional reactions, independent of cognitive structure, may serve as a powerful way of creating attitudes that are favorable, enduring, and resistant to change.[106] This section examines when and how attitudes can be changed through consumers' feelings when MAO and processing effort are high.

When affective involvement with an object or decision is high, consumers can experience fairly strong emotional reactions to or engagement with a stimulus. *Engagement* refers to the extent to which consumers are emotionally connected to a product or ad.[107] A high level of engagement means strong feelings that can, in turn, influence attitudes. In this case, the consumer's *feelings* act as a source of information, and consumers will rely on these feelings to evaluate the stimulus.[108]

Feelings are more likely to influence attitude change when they fit with or are viewed as relevant to the offering.[109] For example, someone who is in love might have a more positive attitude toward an expensive perfume than someone who is not experiencing this emotion would. Consumers tend to like a brand or product when there is a close match between their *emotional receptivity* (predisposition for a certain level of emotion) and the emotional intensity expressed in an ad or by a salesperson.[110] Feelings can also be a factor when consumers see others experiencing strong emotion while using an offering or when situational factors hamper the consumer's effort to develop a cognitive attitude.[111] Thus, consumers under severe time pressure could simply recall a previous emotional experience rather than develop a cognitive attitude.

In marketing situations, certain factors can activate experiences or episodes from memory that may be associated with strong emotions.[112] For example, you might experience positive emotions such as joy and excitement if you suddenly see an ad for the car you just bought. If you are a dog lover, you might experience affective involvement toward a message featuring a cute dog (see Exhibit 5.8). It is small wonder that dogs have, in fact, been included in print advertising for decades.[113]

Attitudes can also be formed through an emotional route to persuasion called *regulatory fit*. Recall that Chapter 2 identified two types of goals consumers might have—promotion- and prevention-focused. Consumers with promotion-focused goals are motivated to act in ways to achieve positive outcomes, focusing on hopes, wants, and accomplishments. In contrast, consumers with prevention-focused goals are motivated to avoid negative outcomes, focusing on responsibilities, safety, and guarding against risks.

Research suggests that a consumer's attitude toward a product depends on the fit between the consumer's goal and the strategies available to achieve that goal. For example, a promotion-focused consumer who sees an ad showing how great it feels to drive a certain car (promotion goal) will be more persuaded than if the ad emphasized safety features. The ad emphasizing safety would, in fact, be more persuasive for consumers with prevention-focused goals. Why? People just feel right when there is a fit between their regulatory goals and the strategies available to help them achieve their goals. This feeling makes them more certain about their attitude evaluation and more likely to regard their attitude or choice as valuable.[114]

When consumers are emotionally involved in a message, they tend to process it on a general level rather than analytically.[115] This process involves the generation of images or feelings, called

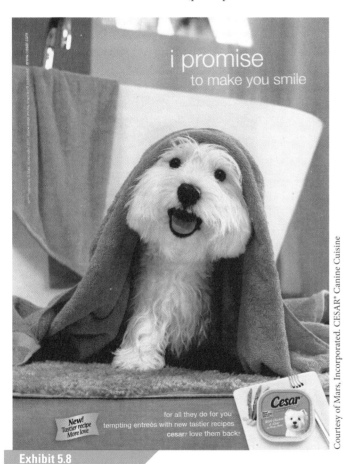

Courtesy of Mars, Incorporated. CESAR® Canine Cuisine

i promise
to make you smile

New!
Tastier recipe
More love

for all they do for you
tempting entrees with new tastier recipes
cesar: love them back?

Cesar

Exhibit 5.8

Man's Best Friend in Advertising

Pet owners feel strong emotions towards dogs, so an ad featuring a cute dog can be used to stimulate affective involvement.

Affective response
When consumers generate feelings and images in response to a message.

affective responses (or ARs),[116] rather than cognitive responses. In fact, affective responses are generally more influential than cognitive responses in shaping consumers' attitudes toward trying a product.[117] Affective responses are particularly important when the ad builds toward a "peak emotional experience."[118] Consumers can either recall an emotional experience from memory or vicariously place themselves in the situation and experience the emotions associated with it.[119] These feelings will then influence their attitudes, especially if the consumers' emotional receptivity matches the ad's emotional intensity.[120] Consumers focused on goals involving their hopes and aspirations tend to rely on their affective responses to an ad, whereas consumers focused on their responsibilities and obligations tend to rely more on message content.[121]

Emotional appeal A message designed to elicit an emotional response.

Cross-cultural differences can also influence the effectiveness of **emotional appeals**. One study found that messages evoking ego-focused responses (such as pride or happiness) led to more favorable attitudes in group-oriented cultures, whereas empathetic messages led to more positive attitudes in individualistic cultures.[122] The reason for this apparent reversal is that the appeal's novelty or uniqueness increases the motivation to process and consider the message.

Negative emotions sometimes have a positive effect on attitude change. In one study, the exposure to a public service announcement about child abuse initially created negative emotions (sadness, anger, fear) but then led to a feeling of empathy, and this response led to a decision to help.[123] In addition, consumers can actively try to avoid making decisions associated with strong negative emotions by making choices to minimize these emotions.[124]

Note that cognition can still influence whether experienced feelings will affect consumer attitudes. For feelings to have a direct impact on their attitudes, consumers must cognitively link them to the offering.[125] To illustrate, if you saw a bank ad showing a tender scene of a father holding his baby, you might experience an immediate emotional response (warmth and joy). However, this feeling will affect your attitude toward the bank only if you consciously make a connection between the feeling and the bank ("This bank makes me feel good" or "I like this bank because it cares about people"). Also, an advertising message that relies on emotional appeal will be more effective in helping heavy users of the product access the brand name than in helping light users access the brand name.[126]

Marketing Implications

Marketers can try to influence emotions as a way of affecting consumer attitudes. In particular, marketers can try to ensure that the emotions experienced in a particular situation will be positive. Car salespeople, for example, may try to do everything possible to please customers so they will develop positive attitudes toward the dealer and the car. The importance of creating positive emotions also explains why airlines, financial institutions, and other service providers place a high value on being friendly. For example, L.L.Bean has earned a reputation for customer-oriented service, thanks to its flexible merchandise return policy and its responsive, courteous call-center representatives.[127]

Another way to influence consumers' attitudes and emotions is by focusing attention on the emotional experience of product usage.[128] For instance, Subaru recently ran a commercial in which an anxious father stands next to his Subaru while his five-year-old daughter sits in the driver's seat. The father nervously gives her last-minute safety instructions about driving by herself for the first time. Finally, as he hands over the keys, the audience sees that the driver is now a teenager ready for a solo drive. By portraying an emotional situation that many parents can identify with, Subaru called attention to its vehicles' safety features and specific benefits that buyers will appreciate.[129]

Marketing communications can potentially trigger strong emotions in consumers, although the ability to trigger these emotions is typically quite limited—ads are better at creating low-level moods than they are at creating intense emotions. Think about how commercials that show people enjoying sips of ice-cold Coca-Cola seek to put viewers in a good mood. Nevertheless, in situations in which affective involvement in the product or service is often high, marketers may be able to generate the images and feelings necessary to change attitudes. This outcome most often occurs in categories in which a strong pleasure-seeking or symbolic motivation is present—when feelings or symbolic meanings are critical. To illustrate, T-Mobile has used emotional appeals in its advertising, emphasizing the person-to-person connections that its phone services make possible.[130]

HOW AFFECTIVELY BASED ATTITUDES ARE INFLUENCED

Attractiveness A source characteristic that evokes favorable attitudes if a source is physically attractive, likable, familiar, or similar to ourselves.

Match-up hypothesis Idea that the source must be appropriate for the product/service.

When MAO and effort are high and attitudes are affectively (emotionally) based, several strategies shown in Exhibit 5.1 can be employed to change attitudes. As with cognitively based attitudes, marketers can use characteristics of the source and the message to change consumers' attitudes by affecting their emotions.

The Source

Perceived **attractiveness** is an important source characteristic affecting high-effort, emotionally based attitudes. Research on source attractiveness suggests that when consumers' MAO and effort are high, attractive sources tend to evoke favorable attitudes if the sources are appropriate for the offering category (e.g., a luxury automobile, fashion, cosmetics, and beauty treatments).[131] This effect has been called the **match-up hypothesis** (the source should match the offering). The relevant attractive source probably enhances attitudes, either by making the ad informative and likable or by affecting consumers' beliefs that the product must be good. A source that is attractive but not relevant can distract the consumer from the message's ideas.[132]

Research suggests that the match-up hypothesis may be even more powerful for expert sources than for attractive sources, which may explain why tennis star Li Na's endorsement of Nike tennis clothing has been particularly effective in China.[133] In addition, she has been signed as an attractive source to communicate the benefits of upscale products such as Rolex watches and Mercedes-Benz cars to a worldwide audience.[134]

The relationship between attractiveness and attitude change applies to selling encounters as well. Consumers perceive physically attractive salespeople as having more favorable selling skills and are more likely to yield to their requests.[135] Customers also tend to be attracted to and to buy from salespeople whom they perceive as similar to themselves.[136]

Nespresso. What else?

Available from Nespresso Boutiques, department stores & kitchenware specialists
Discover more at www.nespresso-whatelse.com

NESPRESSO.
Coffee, body and soul

Image Courtesy of The Advertising Archives

Exhibit 5.9

The Importance of Attractiveness

Ads often use attractive models to stimulate positive feelings towards the ad and the product.

Marketing Implications

Although attractiveness is most often thought of in terms of physical features, sources can also be attractive if they are perceived as similar, likable, or familiar (in terms of physical appearance or opinions).[137] One example is Nespresso's deal with actor George Clooney to appear in ads and on in-store posters promoting coffee machines in Europe, Japan, and Russia (see Exhibit 5.9). Clooney was chosen not just because of his likability but also because "he's a worldwide citizen . . . and a humanist," says Nespresso's CEO.[138]

The Message

Just as marketers can use characteristics of the source to understand and influence affective processing, they can also use characteristics of the message to influence consumers. In particular, emotional appeals and fear appeals are two important message characteristics.

Emotional Appeals and Emotional Contagion

Marketers sometimes attempt to influence consumers' attitudes by using appeals that elicit emotions such as love, desire, joy, hope, excitement, daring, fear, anger, shame, or rejection. Disgust can be a powerful emotion that, even when stimulated unintentionally through humor or another aspect of a message, can engender negative attitudes and purchase intentions.[139] Moreover, because consumers try to minimize emotions like shame and guilt, an appeal based on these emotions may not be effective.[140] Emotional appeals based on conflicting emotions (such as happiness and sadness) can result in less favorable attitudes among consumers who are less accepting of such contradictions.[141]

Emotional contagion A message designed to induce consumers to vicariously experience a depicted emotion.

In general, positive emotions are intended to attract consumers to the offering, whereas the negatives are intended to create anxiety about what might happen if consumers do not use the offering. Messages or salespeople can also use flattery to elicit positive attitudes.[142] And when consumers identify with and feel a strong emotional connection with a brand or company, they pay more attention to it and are more loyal, as well.[143] Not surprisingly, sales personnel who understand how to interpret and appropriately influence a consumer's emotional state will be more effective in influencing attitudes and buying decisions, as well as reinforcing customer loyalty.[144]

However, emotional appeals may limit the amount of product-related information consumers can process.[145] This can occur because consumers may be thinking more about feeling good than about the product's features, a situation that inhibits cognition about the product and its benefits. Thus, emotional appeals are more likely to be effective when the emotional arousal relates to product consumption or usage, an occurrence that is common when hedonic or symbolic motivations are important. Research suggests that emotional appeals more effectively influence consumer behavior when the type of product being advertised has been on the market for some time. In contrast, ads featuring expert sources and strong arguments are more effective for products in younger markets.[146]

Exhibit 5.10

Emotional Contagion

Marketers sometimes attempt to influence consumers' attitudes by using appeals that elicit emotions such as love, desire, joy, hope, and excitement. When consumers feel these emotions in response to an ad, emotional contagion has occurred.

Image Courtesy of The Advertising Archives

Messages that apply the principle of **emotional contagion** depict people expressing an emotion, with the goal of inducing consumers to vicariously experience that emotion (see Exhibit 5.10). As an example, a U.K. McDonald's commercial shows smiling children enjoying Happy Meals while *Glad All Over*, an upbeat 1960s song, plays in the background. Consumers who "catch" that happy feeling from the children's smiles are likely to transfer it to McDonald's and Happy Meals.[147] When consumers are drawn into a message through warm, positive feelings, they become more interested and their attitudes become more positive toward the ad, especially if the message is affectively intense.[148] Still, consumers who see sad-faced victims in a charity's ads will also feel sad and will be more inclined to donate to the cause.[149]

Finally, when consumers become immersed in a message's emotionally charged story, they focus less on the costs and more on the positive outcomes of consumption. In the context of an ad featuring lottery winners, for example, consumers who feel lucky would be drawn into the narrative and focus on the good fortune of winning rather than on the low probability of actually hitting the jackpot.[150]

Marketing Implications

Typically, marketers attempt to arouse emotions by using techniques such as music, emotional scenes or facial expressions, visuals, sex, and attractive sources. For example, a recent Ad Council campaign focused on the emotions surrounding the adoption of a dog or cat from a local pet shelter, with visuals and voiceovers featuring happy pet owners and contented pets. The multimedia campaign, with the tag line "A person is the best thing to happen to a shelter pet. Be that person—Adopt, " helped increase adoptions over a two-year period.[151] However, arousing emotions can be a challenge unless the message has personal relevance for the consumer. ————————————————————————

Fear Appeals

Fear appeal A message that stresses negative consequences.

Fear appeals attempt to elicit fear or anxiety by stressing the negative consequences of either engaging or not engaging in a particular behavior. By arousing this fear, marketers hope consumers will be motivated to think about the message and behave in the desired manner.[152] But is fear an effective appeal? Early studies found that fear appeals were ineffective because consumers' perceptual defense helped them block out and ignore the message (due to its threatening nature).[153] This research provides one explanation of why the surgeon general's warning on cigarette packages and ads has been largely ineffective. However, more recent research indicates that fear appeals can work under certain conditions.[154] For example, fear appeals that evoke guilt, regret, or challenge can motivate behavior because they play to feelings of self-accountability that are experienced when the consumer does or does not do something, such as applying sun screen to avoid cancer.[155]

Terror management theory (TMT) A theory which deals with how we cope with the threat of death by defending our world view of values and beliefs.

Terror management theory (TMT) provides additional insight into the use of fear appeals. According to this theory, we develop a worldview of values and beliefs to cope with the terror of knowing that we will die someday, despite our innate impulse toward self-preservation. To avoid being paralyzed by anxiety, we may respond to messages that highlight the threat of death by more strongly defending our worldview. A high-fear appeal using a threat of fatal consequences may be ineffective, therefore, because consumers elaborate so much on the threat that they cannot process the message's suggested change in behavior. So the nature of the fear appeal—specifically, whether it makes mortality more salient—can influence consumers' emotions, their elaboration, and their attitudes.[156]

Marketing Implications

When can fear appeals be effective? First, the appeal must suggest an immediate action that will reduce the consumer's fear. Consider how Carbonite markets its online backup services. "We found that the only thing that sells our product is fear," says the company's CEO, David Friend. "The fact that you might wake up tomorrow and your hard drive is dead and all your photos are gone." Carbonite's messages on radio, Facebook, and Twitter stress that consumers can prevent data loss by signing up to try its backup services.[157]

Second, the level of fear must be generally moderate for the appeal to be effective.[158] If the fear induced is too intense, the consumer's perceptual defense will take over and the message will not have an impact. Third, at higher levels of involvement, lower levels of fear can be generated because the consumer has a higher motivation to process the information.[159] Factors such as personality, product usage, and socioeconomic status also have an impact on the effectiveness of fear appeals.[160] Finally, the source providing the information must be credible; otherwise, the consumer can easily discount the message by generating counterarguments and source derogations. ————————————————————————

ATTITUDE TOWARD THE AD

Attitude toward the ad (A_{ad}) Whether the consumer likes or dislikes an ad.

Although most attitude research has focused on consumers' attitude toward the brand, some evidence suggests that the overall **attitude toward the ad (A_{ad})** in which the brand is advertised will influence consumers' brand attitudes and behavior.[161] In other words, if we see an advertisement and like it, our liking for the ad may rub off on the brand and thereby make our brand attitude more positive. Most A_{ad} research has been done in the context of low-effort processing. However, researchers are finding that A_{ad} can also have an impact when consumers devote considerable effort to processing the message.

Three major factors have been found to lead to a positive A_{ad} in the context of high effort.[162] First, more *informative* ads tend to be better liked and to generate positive responses.[163] These reactions to the ad will, in turn, have a positive influence on brand attitudes, a factor called the **utilitarian (or functional) dimension**. For example, consumers often like promotions on the Internet because these are seen as more informative than promotions in other media. On the other hand, consumers may have negative attitudes toward ads that are not informative. A good example is the rising negativity toward political ads that are viewed as "mudslinging" and that provide little useful information about the candidates.[164]

Utilitarian (or functional) dimension When an ad provides information.

Hedonic dimension When an ad creates positive or negative feelings.

Second, consumers can like an ad if it creates positive feelings or emotions (the **hedonic dimension**).[165] We tend to like ads that either make us feel good or elicit positive experiences from our memory. This positive attitude can transfer to the brand and make our beliefs about the brand (b_i) more positive as well.[166] Finally, consumers can like an ad because it is interesting—that is, it arouses curiosity and attracts attention. When consumers exert a lot of effort and thoughtfully elaborate on a message, it can be viewed as interesting and generate a positive A_{ad}.

Marketing Implications

Marketers use a variety of techniques to enhance the hedonic dimension of ad messages, especially online, and to engage consumers to generate a positive A_{ad}. For example, Audi recently launched an advertising series consisting of eight two-minute episodes called "Untitled Jersey City Project." Along with online extras such as clues and character insights, these ads were created to engage consumers who like the mystery and excitement of a fast-paced dramatic storyline. Throughout the episodes, the AUDI A6 could be seen weaving in and out of traffic through Jersey City streets.[167]

WHEN DO ATTITUDES PREDICT BEHAVIOR?

Marketers are interested not only in how attitudes are formed and can be changed but also in knowing whether, when, and why attitudes will predict behavior. The TORA model comes closest to providing this information by predicting which factors affect consumers' BIs. However, as previously noted, what we intend to do does not always predict what we actually will do. Therefore, marketers also need to consider which factors affect the attitude-behavior relationship. These are some of the factors that affect whether a consumer's attitudes will influence his or her behavior:

▶ *Level of involvement/elaboration.* Attitudes are more likely to predict behavior when cognitive involvement is high and consumers elaborate or think extensively about the information that gives rise to their attitudes.[168] Attitudes also tend to be strong and enduring and therefore more predictive of a consumer's behavior when affective involvement is high. Thus, attitudes toward emotionally charged issues such as owning a handgun or getting an abortion tend to be strongly held and related to behavior. What if consumers are faced with inconsistencies about a brand and learn, for example, that it rates higher against competitors on one attribute but lower on another attribute? Here, the attitude-behavior relationship is weakened if consumers do not attempt to resolve the inconsistency through elaboration.[169]

▶ *Knowledge and experience.* Attitudes are more likely to be strongly held and predictive of behavior when the consumer is knowledgeable about or experienced with the object of the attitude.[170] When making a computer-buying decision, for example, an expert is more likely to form an attitude that is based on more detailed and integrated information than is a novice. This attitude would then be more strongly held and more strongly related to behavior.

▶ *Analysis of reasons.* Research shows that asking consumers to analyze their reasons for brand preference increases the link between attitude and behavior in situations in which behavior is measured soon after attitudes are measured. Marketers should take this finding into account when planning consumer research to support a new product introduction.[171]

▶ *Accessibility of attitudes.* Attitudes are more strongly related to behavior when they are accessible or "top of mind."[172] Conversely, if an attitude cannot be easily remembered, it will have little effect on behavior. Direct experience (product usage) generally increases attitude accessibility for attributes that must be experienced (e.g., tasted, touched), whereas advertising can produce accessible attitudes for search attributes (e.g., price, ingredients), especially when the level of repetition is high.[173] Also, consumers asked about their purchase intentions toward a product in a particular category are more likely to choose brands toward which they have positive and accessible attitudes; research itself can make attitudes more accessible for brands in that category, thereby changing behavior.[174]

▶ *Attitude confidence.* As noted earlier, sometimes we are more certain about our evaluations than we are at other times. Therefore, another factor affecting the attitude-behavior relationship is attitude confidence. Confidence tends to be stronger when the attitude is based either on a greater amount of information or on more trustworthy information. And when we are confident, our attitudes are more likely to predict our behaviors.[175] Not surprisingly, strongly held attitudes have more influence on consumers' consideration and choice of brand alternatives than weakly held attitudes.[176] When consumers feel that they have depleted their mental resources (ego depletion) in thoroughly processing the message, they will be more confident of their attitudes, which, in turn, means that their attitudes will exert more influence over buying decisions.[177]

▶ *Specificity of attitudes.* Attitudes tend to be good predictors of behavior when we are very specific about the behavior that they are trying to predict.[178] Thus, if we wanted to predict whether people will take skydiving lessons, measuring their attitudes toward skydiving in general would be less likely to predict behavior than would measuring their attitudes specifically toward skydiving lessons.

▶ *Attitude-behavior relationship over time.* When consumers are exposed to an advertising message but do not actually try the product, their attitude confidence declines over time. Marketers should therefore plan their advertising schedules to reactivate consumer attitudes and attitude confidence through message repetition. On the other hand, trial-based brand attitudes are likely to decline over time even though advertising-based attitudes do not. As a result, marketers should use communications to reinforce the effects of the trial experience and thereby reactivate the attitude.[179]

▶ *Emotional attachment.* Emotional attachment to a brand is a stronger predictor of actual purchase behavior than brand attitudes.[180] The more emotionally attached consumers are to a brand—the more they feel bonded or connected to it—the more likely they will be to purchase it repeatedly over time. In fact, such consumers are more willing to pay a price premium for the brand to which they are committed and remain loyal even if it is involved in a product crisis such as a recall.[181] To increase the emotional attachment, marketers should develop and project a brand personality that fits well with the consumer's actual self-image.[182] Note that consumers who are emotionally attached to a brand will be aroused by negative information about that brand, motivating them to generate more counterarguments against the negative information.[183]

▶   *Situational factors.* Intervening situational factors can prevent a behavior from being performed and can thus weaken the attitude-behavior relationship.[184] For instance, you might have a very positive attitude toward Porsche, but you might not buy one because you cannot afford to. In another situation, if you had gone to buy the car, your attitude might not have resulted in a purchase if the dealership had none available. In other circumstances, the usage situation may alter the attitude. For example, your attitudes toward different wines might depend on whether you are buying wine for yourself or for a friend.

▶   *Normative factors.* According to the TORA model, normative factors are likely to affect the attitude-behavior relationship. For example, you may like going to the ballet, but you may not go because you think your friends will make fun of you for doing so. Although your attitude is positive and should lead to the behavior of attending the ballet, you are more motivated to comply with normative beliefs.

▶   *Personality variables.* Finally, certain personality types are more likely to exhibit stronger attitude-behavior relationships than are others. Individuals who like to devote a lot of thought to actions will evidence stronger attitude-behavior relationships because their attitudes will be based on high elaboration thinking.[185] Also, people who are guided more by their own internal dispositions (called *low self-monitors*) are more likely to exhibit similar behavior patterns across situations and therefore more consistent attitude-behavior relationships.[186] People who are guided by the views and behaviors of others (called *high self-monitors*), on the other hand, try to change their behavior to adapt to every unique situation. Thus, a high self-monitor's choice of beer might depend on the situation; a low self-monitor would choose the same beer regardless of the circumstances.

SUMMARY

When consumers' MAO to engage in a behavior or to process a message is high, consumers tend to devote considerable effort to forming their attitudes and to message processing. An attitude is a relatively global and enduring evaluation about an offering, issue, activity, person, or event. Attitudes can be described in terms of their favorability, accessibility, confidence, persistence, and resistance. Consumers' thoughts and feelings in response to this situation can affect their attitudes, through either a cognitive or an affective route to persuasion.

Five types of cognitive models show how thoughts relate to attitudes in high-consumer-effort situations: (1) direct or imagined experience, (2) reasoning by analogy or category, (3) values-driven attitudes, (4) social identity-based attitude generation, and (5) analytical processes of attitude construction, including expectancy-value models such as the TORA and the theory of planned behavior. Under the cognitive response model, consumers exert a lot of effort in responding to the message—enough effort to generate counterarguments, support arguments, and source derogations. Under elaborative processing,

messages can be effective if they have a credible source or a strong argument, present positive and negative information (under certain circumstances), or involve direct comparisons (if the brand is not the market leader).

Consumers can experience emotions when they are affectively involved with a communication or when the message involves an emotional appeal. In either case the consumer processes the communication, and the positive or negative feelings that result can determine attitudes. When attitudes are affectively based, sources that are likable or attractive can have a positive impact on affective attitude change. Emotional appeals can affect communication processing if they are relevant to the offering. Fear appeals, a type of emotion-eliciting message, are explained, in part, by terror-management theory. A consumer's attitude toward the ad (A_{ad}) can play a role in the attitude change process if the ad is informative or associated with positive feelings. The A_{ad} can then rub off on brand beliefs and attitudes.

Finally, attitudes will better predict a consumer's behavior when (1) involvement is high, (2) knowledge is high,

(3) reasons are analyzed, (4) attitudes are accessible, (5) attitudes are held with confidence, (6) attitudes are specific, (7) the attitude-behavior relationship does not decline over time, (8) emotional attachment is high, (9) no situational factors are present, (10) normative factors are not in operation, and (11) we are dealing with certain personality types.

Questions for Review and Discussion

1. What are attitudes, and what three functions do they serve?

2. How do expectancy-value models seek to explain attitude formation?

3. What role does credibility play in affecting consumer attitudes based on cognitions?

4. What are the advantages and disadvantages of offering a two-sided message about a product?

5. Contrast emotional and fear appeals. Why is each effective? Which do you consider most compelling for products in which you are interested?

6. What three factors may lead to a positive attitude toward the ad (A_{ad}) when consumers devote a lot of effort to processing a message? How can marketers apply these factors when designing advertising messages?

CONSUMER BEHAVIOR CASE

Volkswagen's Drive to Become the World's Top Automaker

Volkswagen Group, Europe's largest automaker, is accelerating toward its goal of passing Toyota to become the world's largest automaker by 2018. Based in Wolfsburg, Germany, Volkswagen has introduced many distinctively styled vehicles over the years, including the Beetle, which was recently redesigned and relaunched in North America amid a flurry of multimedia marketing communications.

The latest Beetle model lacks the bud vase that graced the dashboard of the previous model, a small but noticeable change that may steer consumers away from the idea that the Beetle is a "chick car." Another pointed hint about the target market: Ads with the headline "It's a boy" over an image of the redesigned Beetle. A third clue is a new emphasis on sleek styling and powerful performance, as evidenced by the campaign's tagline: "That's the power of German engineering."

Overall, however, Volkswagen wants to give consumers a good feeling about its cars. One TV commercial showed a 30-ish man driving around town in the new black Beetle. As he sits at red lights or inches ahead in traffic, he gets friendly hand-slaps from a pedestrian, a truck driver, a police officer on horseback, a construction worker, and a group of cyclists, all to the toe-tapping tune of "The Clapping Song." Why the focus on friendly reactions? Eric Wilson, Volkswagen of America's marketing communications manager, observes that the Beetle is "the world's most iconic car, and when people see it, they smile, they connect with the driver, and the driver connects with them."

When the redesigned Beetle was introduced in Canada, Volkswagen invited consumers to download a free app that activates special on-screen digital animation when the phone is pointed at billboards and transit poster ads around Toronto, Montreal, and Vancouver. Brought to life on the smartphone screen, the Beetle seems to roar from one billboard to another and race through tunnels on the transit ads. The company used messages on YouTube and in other social media to build awareness and engage consumers in the animated ads. Here, Volkswagen wanted to emphasize the Beetle's more aggressive personality and performance, to distinguish it from the cute Beetles of the past.

To introduce its new Passat model, Volkswagen posted an online preview of a clever 60-second commercial that gained millions of YouTube views and thousands of Twitter comments days before its network television Super Bowl debut. In "The Force," a youngster in a Darth Vader costume prowls the house trying in vain to use the force to do something to his dog, his sister's doll, a sandwich, and other things. When his father's new Passat coasts to a stop in the driveway, the child rushes past dad and tries to use the force on the car. After a moment, the car roars to life, and its headlights illuminate a surprised and delighted Darth. Then the audience gets a glimpse of dad, out of sight in the kitchen, smiling as he holds up his keychain and presses the Passat's remote starter.

This feel-good commercial had already gone viral before the Super Bowl kickoff, capturing upwards of 10 million YouTube views. As the game progressed, social media sites buzzed with positive reactions to "The Force." The commercial, among the most popular and critically acclaimed of all the Super Bowl ads, continued to draw online views and reinforce the Passat's family-friendly image for many months.

Volkswagen's sales are up, but it still faces a number of challenges in its drive to the top, including competition from other global automakers, economic uncertainty in numerous markets, and relatively tepid demand for new cars as many consumers keep the brakes on personal spending. But when consumers are thinking about a new car, Volkswagen wants them to have positive thoughts and feelings about its cars.[187]

CASE QUESTIONS

1. What is Volkswagen doing to change consumers' beliefs and evaluations of its cars or encourage them to add new beliefs about its cars? Explain your answer.
2. What message characteristics are particularly important to Volkswagen's ability to try to influence consumers' affective attitudes toward its cars?
3. How is Volkswagen applying the principle of emotional contagion in its marketing communications?
4. Describe how Volkswagen employs the utilitarian dimension, the hedonic dimension, and the arousal of curiosity to influence consumers' attitudes toward its ads. Which do you think is most important in this product category, and why?

ENDNOTES

1. Sylvia Pennington, "Lure of Luxury," *Sydney Morning Herald (Australia)*, September 9, 2011, www.smh.com; Anusha Subramanian, "SRK's Superhero Power," *Business Today (India)*, September 27, 2011, http://businesstoday.intoday.in; Richard Donkin, "Watchmakers: Time and Tide United as Brands Battle for an Edge," *Financial Times*, September 20, 2011, www.ft.com; "Swiss Street Key to Global Branding for Watchmakers," *Reuters*, October 6, 2011, www.reuters.com; and Rimma Kats, "Rolex Taps Mobile to Make Print Ad More Interactive," *Mobile Marketer*, April 23, 2010, www.mobilemarketer.com.

2. Richard E. Petty, H. Rao Unnava, and Alan J. Strathman, "Theories of Attitude Change," in eds. Thomas S. Robertson and Harold H. Kassarjian, *Handbook of Consumer Behavior* (Englewood Cliffs, N.J.: Prentice-Hall, 1991), pp. 241–280.

3. Ida E. Berger and Andrew A. Mitchell, "The Effect of Advertising on Attitude Accessibility, Attitude Confidence, and the Attitude–Behavior Relationship," *Journal of Consumer Research*, December 1989, pp. 269–279; and Joel B. Cohen and Americus Reed II, "A Multiple Pathway Anchoring and Adjustment (MPAA) Model of Attitude Generation and Recruitment," *Journal of Consumer Research* 33, no. 1, 2006, pp. 1–15.

4. Rohini Ahluwalia, "Examination of Psychological Processes Underlying Resistance to Persuasion," *Journal of Consumer Research*, September 2000, pp. 217–232.

5. Joseph R. Priester and Richard E. Petty, "The Gradual Threshold Model of Ambivalence," *Journal of Personality and Social Psychology* 71, 1996, pp. 431–449; Joseph R. Priester, Richard E. Petty, and Kiwan Park, "Whence Univalent Ambivalence?" *Journal of Consumer Research* 34, no. 1, 2007, pp. 11–21; and Martin R. Zemborain and Gita Venkataramani Johar, "Attitudinal Ambivalence and Openness to Persuasion," *Journal of Consumer Research* 33, no. 4, 2007, pp. 506–514.

6. Martin Fishbein and Icek Ajzen, *Belief, Attitude, Intention, and Behavior: An Introduction to Theory and Research* (Reading, Mass.: Addison-Wesley, 1975).

7. Lizbieta Lepkowska-White, Thomas G. Brashear, and Marc G. Weinberger, "A Test of Ad Appeal Effectiveness in Poland and the United States," *Journal of Advertising*, Fall 2003, pp. 57–67.

8. Kevin E. Voss, Eric R. Spangenburg, and Bianca Grohmann, "Measuring the Hedonic and Utilitarian Dimensions of Consumer Attitude," *Journal of Marketing Research*, August 2003, pp. 310–320.

9. Petty, Unnava, and Strathman, "Theories of Attitude Change"; and Richard Petty and John T. Cacioppo, *Communication and Persuasion* (New York: Springer, 1986).

10. "JCPenney Supports Youth Programs One Penny at a Time," *Retailing Today*, July 22, 2011, www.retailingtoday.com.

11. Cohen and Reed, "A Multiple Pathway Anchoring and Adjustment (MPAA) Model of Attitude Generation and Recruitment;" F. P. Bone and S. P. Ellen, "The Generation and Consequences of Communication-Evoked Imagery," *Journal of Consumer Research*, June 1992, pp. 93–104; Punam Anand Keller and Ann L. McGill, "Differences in the Relative Influence of Product Attributes under Alternative Processing Conditions: Attribute Importance Versus Attribute Ease of Imagability," *Journal of Consumer Psychology* 3, no. 1, 1994, pp. 29–49; and Pham, Michel Tuan, Joel B. Cohen, John W. Pracejus, and G. David Hughes, "Affect Monitoring and the Primacy of Feelings in Judgment," *Journal of Consumer Research* 28, September 2001, pp. 167–188.

12. Anton Olsen, "Review: Victorinox Swiss Army Slim Flash Drive," *Wired*, August 18, 2011, www.wired.com; and Jennifer Gregan-Paxton and Deborah Roedder John, "Consumer Learning by Analogy: A Model of Internal Knowledge Transfer," *Journal of Consumer Research* 24, December 1997, pp. 266–284.

13. Cohen and Reed, "A Multiple Pathway Anchoring and Adjustment (MPAA) Model of Attitude Generation and Recruitment."

14. Michael B. Beverland and Francis J. Farrelly, "The Quest for Authenticity in Consumption: Consumers' Purposive Choice of Authentic Cues to Shape Experienced Outcomes," *Journal of Consumer Research*, February 2010, pp. 838–856.

15. Abby Scalf, "Barilla Chef Shares His Recipe," *Daily Herald (Arlington Heights, Ill.)*, October 11, 2011, www.dailyherald.com.

16. Americus Reed II, "Activating the Self-Importance of Consumer Selves," *Journal of Consumer Research* 31, September 2004, pp. 286–295; and Sharon Shavitt and Michelle R. Nelson, "The Social-Identity Function in Person Perception," in eds. Gregory Maio and James M. Olson, *Why We Evaluate: Functions of Attitudes* (Mahwah, N.J.: Lawrence Erlbaum, 2000), pp. 37–57.

17. Jason Blevins, "Vail Resorts Lands Endorsement Deal with Shaun White," *Denver Post*, August 17, 2011, www.denverpost.com.

18. Peter L. Wright, "Message-Evoked Thoughts: Persuasion Research Using Thought Verbalizations," *Journal of Consumer Research*, September 1980, pp. 151–175.

19. Jerry C. Olson, Daniel R. Toy, and Philip A. Dover, "Do Cognitive Responses Mediate the Effects of Advertising Content on Cognitive Structure?" *Journal of Consumer Research*, December 1982, pp. 245–262.

20. Marian Friestad and Peter Wright, "The Persuasion Knowledge Model: How People Cope with Persuasion Attempts," *Journal of Consumer Research*, June 1994, pp. 1–31.

21. Peter Wright, "Marketplace Metacognition and Social Intelligence," *Journal of Consumer Research*, March 2002, pp. 677–682.

22. Zakary L. Tormala and Richard E. Petty, "Source Credibility and Attitude Certainty: A Metacognitive Analysis of Resistance to Persuasion," *Journal of Consumer Psychology* 14, no. 4, 2004, pp. 427–442.

23. Daniel R. Toy, "Monitoring Communication Effects," *Journal of Consumer Research*, June 1982, pp. 66–76.

24. Petty, Unnava, and Strathman, "Theories of Attitude Change."

25. Punam Anand and Brian Sternthal, "The Effects of Program Involvement and Ease of Message Counterarguing on Advertising Persuasiveness," *Journal of Consumer Psychology* 1, no. 3, 1992, pp. 225–238; and Kenneth R. Lord and Robert E. Burnkrant, "Attention Versus Distraction: The Interactive Effect of Program Involvement and Attentional Devices on Commercial Processing," *Journal of Advertising*, March 1993, pp. 47–60.

26. Bob M. Fennis, Enny H. H. J. Das, and Ad Th. H. Pruyn, "'If You Can't Dazzle Them with Brilliance, Baffle Them with Nonsense': Extending the Impact of the Disrupt-Then-Reframe Technique of Social Influence," *Journal of Consumer Psychology* 14, no. 3, 2004, pp. 280–290; and B. P. Davis and E. S. Knowles, "A Disrupt-Then-Reframe Technique of Social Influence," *Journal of Personality and Social Psychology* 76, 1999, pp. 192–199.

27. Deborah J. MacInnis and Whan C. Park, "The Differential Role of Characteristics of Music on High- and Low-Involvement Consumers' Processing of Ads," *Journal of Consumer Research*, September 1991, pp. 161–173; and Rajeev Batra and Douglas M. Stayman, "The Role of Mood in Advertising Effectiveness," *Journal of Consumer Research*, September 1990, pp. 203–214.

28. William L. Wilkie and Edgar A. Pessemier, "Issues in Marketing's Use of Multi-Attribute Models," *Journal of Marketing Research*, November 1973, pp. 428–441.

29. Richard P. Bagozzi, Nancy Wong, Shuzo Abe, and Massimo Bergami, "Cultural and Situational Contingencies and the Theory of Reasoned Action," *Journal of Consumer Psychology* 9, no. 2, 2000, pp. 97–106.

30. Noah J. Goldstein, Robert B. Cialdini, and Vladas Griskevicius, "A Room with a Viewpoint: Using Social Norms to Motivate Environmental Conservation in Hotels," *Journal of Consumer Research*, October 2008, pp. 472–482.

31. Icek Ajzen and Martin Fishbein, "Prediction of Goal-Directed Behavior: Attitudes, Intentions, and Perceived Behavioral Control," *Journal of Experimental Social Psychology*, September 1980, pp. 453–474; and Blair H. Sheppard, Jon Hartwick, and Paul R. Warshaw, "The Theory of Reasoned Action," *Journal of Consumer Research*, December 1988, pp. 325–342.

32. Cohen and Reed, "A Multiple Pathway Anchoring and Adjustment (MPAA) Model of Attitude Generation and Recruitment."

33. Arti Sahni Notani, "Moderators of Perceived Behavioral Control's Predictiveness in the Theory of Planned Behavior," *Journal of Consumer Psychology* 7, no. 3, 1998, pp. 247–271.

34. Ryan Beene, "Hyundai Future Products: New Entries Seek Upscale Niches," *Auto Week*, August 22, 2011, www.autoweek.com; and Irma Venter, "Hyundai SA Now Seeks Edge in Product, Not Price, as It Unveils New Elantra," *Engineering News*, August 30, 2011, www.engineeringnews.co.za.

35. Erin Voegele, "Building Out for Bioheat," *Biodiesel Magazine*, September 8, 2011, www.biodieselmagazine.com.

36. Amitav Chakravarti and Chris Janiszewski, "The Influence of Generic Advertising on Brand Preferences," *Journal of Consumer Research*, March 2004, pp. 487–502.

37. Stephen M. Nowlis and Itamar Simonson, "The Effect of New Product Features on Brand Choice," *Journal of Marketing Research*, February 1996, pp. 36–46.

38. Jennifer Rooney, "How Florida Bounced Back from the Oil Spill," *Advertising Age*, January 3, 2011, www.adage.com.

39. Ashesh Mukherjee and Wayne D. Hoyer, "The Effect of Novel Attributes on Product Evaluation," *Journal of Consumer Research*, December 2001, pp. 462–472.

40. Petia K. Petrova and Robert B. Cialdini, "Fluency of Consumption Imagery and the Backfire Effects of Imagery Appeals," *Journal of Consumer Research* 32, no. 3, 2005, pp. 442–452; Punam Anand Keller and Ann L. McGill, "Differences in the Relative Influence of Product Attributes Under Alternative Processing Conditions," *Journal of Consumer Psychology* 3, no. 1, 1994, pp. 29–49; and Michel Tuan Pham, "Representativeness, Relevance, and the Use of Feelings in Decision Making," *Journal of Consumer Research* 25, September 1998, pp. 144–159.

41. David Murphy, "Zugara Brings Webcam-Augmented Clothes Shopping to Life," *PC Magazine*, August 7, 2011, www.pcmag.com.

42. Lindsay Veremis, "Anti-drinking Billboards Hit Outagamie County," *WLUK-TV*, August 17, 2011, www.fox11online.com.

43. Laura Bird, "Condom Campaign Fails to Increase Sales," *Wall Street Journal*, June 23, 1994, p. B7

44. Barbara Mueller, "Reflections of Culture: An Analysis of Japanese and American Advertising Appeals," *Journal of Advertising Research*, June–July 1987, pp. 51–59.

45. Yong-Soon Kang and Paul M. Herr, "Beauty and the Beholder: Toward an Integrative Model of Communication Source Effects," *Journal of Consumer Research* 33, no. 1, 2006, pp. 123–130; and Ronald E. Goldsmith, Barbara A. Lafferty, and Stephen J. Newell, "The Impact of Corporate Credibility and Celebrity Credibility on Consumer Reaction to Advertisements and Brands," *Journal of Advertising* 29, no. 3, Fall 2000, pp. 43–54; also see Brian Sternthal, Ruby R. Dholakia, and Clark Leavitt, "The Persuasive

Effect of Source Credibility," *Public Opinion Quarterly*, Fall 1978, pp. 285–314.

46. Joseph R. Priester, "The Influence of Spokesperson Trustworthiness on Message Elaboration, Attitude Strength, and Advertising Effectiveness," *Journal of Consumer Psychology* 13, no. 4, 2003, pp. 408–421.

47. Jonathan D. Rockoff, "Trusting Other Patients' Drug Advice," *Wall Street Journal*, February 25, 2010, www.wsj.com.

48. Der-Juinn Horng, Sheng-Hsien Lee, and Chin-Lung Lin, "The Effects of Online Reviews on Purchasing Intention," *Social Behavior and Personality: An International Journal*, February 2011, p. 71.

49. Uri Simonsohn, "Lessons from an 'Oops' at *Consumer Reports*," *Journal of Marketing Research*, February 2011, pp. 1–12.

50. Spencer Healey, "Blendtec Guy Blends at UVU," *UVU Review (Utah)*, October 17, 2011, www.uvureview.com.

51. Amna Kirmani and Baba Shiv, "Effects of Source Congruity on Brand Attitudes and Beliefs," *Journal of Consumer Psychology* 7, no. 1, 1998, pp. 25–48.

52. Pablo Briñol, Richard E. Petty, and Zakary L. Tormala, "Self-Validation of Cognitive Responses to Advertisements," *Journal of Consumer Research*, March 2004, pp. 559–573.

53. Chenghuan Wu and David R. Schaffer, "Susceptibility to Persuasive Appeals as a Function of Source Credibility and Prior Experience with the Attitude Object," *Journal of Personality and Social Psychology*, April 1987, pp. 677–688.

54. Carolyn Tripp, Thomas D. Jensen, and Les Carlson, "The Effects of Multiple Endorsements by Celebrities on Consumers' Attitudes and Intentions," *Journal of Consumer Research*, March 1994, pp. 535–547.

55. Judith A. Garretson and Ronald W. Niedrich, "Spokes-Characters: Creating Character Trust and Positive Brand Attitudes," *Journal of Advertising* 33, no. 2, Summer 2004, pp. 25–36.

56. "The Question Is—Who Isn't Wearing Adidas Originals?" *Manchester Evening News*, August 18, 2011, www.menmedia.co.uk/manchestereveningnews.

57. Kevin Goldman, "Women Endorsers More Credible than Men, a Survey Suggests," *Wall Street Journal*, October 22, 1995, p. B1.

58. Bloomberg. "Tiger Woods Dropped by Tag Heuer," *Advertising Age*, August 8, 2011, www.adage.com; and Cathy Yingling, "Beware the Lure of Celebrity Endorsers," *Advertising Age*, September 24, 2007, p. 19.

59. Joan Voight, "Selling Confidence," *Adweek Southwest*, August 20, 2001, p. 9; and Ken Bruno, "Marketers Turn Employees into Ad Stars," *Forbes*, September 23, 2010, www.forbes.com.

60. Sternthal, Dholakia, and Leavitt, "The Persuasive Effect of Source Credibility."

61. Darlene B. Hannah and Brian Sternthal, "Detecting and Explaining the Sleeper Effect," *Journal of Consumer Research*, September 1984, pp. 632–642.

62. Marvin E. Goldberg and Jon Hartwick, "The Effects of Advertiser Reputation and Extremity of Advertising Claim on Advertising Effectiveness," *Journal of Consumer Research*, September 1990, pp. 172–179.

63. Karen L. Becker-Olsen, "And Now, a Word from Our Sponsor," *Journal of Advertising*, Summer 2003, pp. 17–32.

64. Tülin Erdem and Joffre Swait, "Brand Credibility, Brand Consideration, and Choice," *Journal of Consumer Research*, June 2004, pp. 191–198.

65. Candace Lombardi, "Toyota, 3M, Siemens Top Green Brands in Survey," *CNet News*, July 27, 2011, http://news.cnet.com.

66. Kelly O'Reilly, "H&M to Launch Children's Collection for UNICEF," *NBC New York*, June 15, 2011, www.nbcnewyork.com.

67. Petty, Unnava, and Strathman, "Theories of Attitude Change"; and Charles S. Areni and Richard J. Lutz, "The Role of Argument Quality in the Elaboration Likelihood Model," in ed. Michael J. Houston, *Advances in Consumer Research*, vol. 15 (Provo, Utah: Association for Consumer Research, 1987), pp. 197–203.

68. "Marketers, Get Ready: Good Housekeeping Makes More Product Tests Public," *Advertising Age*, September 13, 2011, www.adage.com.

69. Parthasarathy Krishnamurthy and Anuradha Sivararman, "Counterfactual Thinking and Advertising Responses," *Journal of Consumer Research*, March 2002, pp. 650–658.

70. Jennifer Edson Escalas and Mary Frances Luce, "Process Versus Outcome Thought Focus and Advertising," *Journal of Consumer Psychology*, 2003, pp. 246–254; and Jennifer Edson Escalas and Mary Frances Luce, "Understanding the Effects of Process-Focused Versus Outcome-Focused Thought in Response to Advertising," *Journal of Consumer Research*, September 2004, pp. 274–285.

71. Brett A. S. Martin, Bodo Lang, and Stephanie Wong, "Conclusion Explicitness in Advertising," *Journal of Advertising*, Winter 2003–2004, pp. 57–65.

72. Keith S. Coulter and Girish N. Punj, "The Effects of Cognitive Resource Requirements, Availability, and Argument Quality on Brand Attitudes," *Journal of Advertising* 33, no. 4, Winter 2004, pp. 53–64.

73. Bridget McCrea, "A Winning Combination," *Response*, March 2011, pp. 36+.

74. Timothy B. Heath, Michael S. McCarthy, and David L. Mothersbaugh, "Spokesperson Fame and Vividness Effects in the Context of Issue-Relevant Thinking," *Journal of Consumer Research*, March 1994, pp. 520–534.

75. Laura A. Peracchio, "Evaluating Persuasion-Enhancing Techniques from a Resource Matching Perspective," *Journal of Consumer Research*, September 1997, pp. 178–191.

76. Patrick Di Justo, "Minty, Piney, Sticky … I Guess I Feel Better," *Wired*, November 2009, p. 39; and Jeanne Whalen, "Foul Taste Is Part of the Cure," *Wall Street Journal*, November 5, 2007, p. B4.

77. See Gerd Bohner, Sabine Einwiller, Hans-Peter Erb, and Frank Siebler, "When Small Means Comfortable: Relations Between Product Attributes in Two-Sided Advertising," *Journal of Consumer Psychology*, 13(4), 2003, pp. 454–463.

78. Martin Eisend, "Two-Sided Advertising: A Meta-Analysis," *International Journal of Research in Marketing* 23, no. 2, June 2006, pp. 187–198.

79. Michael A. Kamins and Henry Assael, "Two-Sided Versus One-Sided Appeals: A Cognitive Perspective on Argumentation, Source Derogation, and the Effect of Disconfirming Trial on Belief Change," *Journal of Marketing Research*, February 1984, pp. 29–39.

80. See Peter J. Danaher, Andre Bonfrer, and Sanjay Dhar, "The Effect of Competitive Advertising Interference on Sales for Packaged Goods," *Journal of Marketing Research*, April 2008, pp. 211–225.

81. Cornelia Pechmann and David W. Stewart, "The Effects of Comparative Advertising on Attention, Memory, and Purchase Intentions," *Journal of Consumer Research*, September 1990, pp. 180–191.

82. Pechmann and Stewart, "The Effects of Comparative Advertising on Attention, Memory, and Purchase Intentions"; and

Rita Snyder, "Comparative Advertising and Brand Evaluation: Toward Developing a Categorization Approach," *Journal of Consumer Psychology* 1, no. 1, 1992, pp. 15–30.

83. Yung Kyun Choi and Gordon E. Miracle, "The Effectiveness of Comparative Advertising in Korea and the United States," *Journal of Advertising* 33, no. 4, Winter 2004, pp. 75–87.

84. Patrick Meirick, "Cognitive Responses to Negative and Comparative Political Advertising," *Journal of Advertising*, Spring 2002, pp. 49–62.

85. Bruce E. Pinkleton, Nam-Hyun Um, and Erica Weintraub Austin, "An Exploration of the Effects of Negative Political Advertising on Political Decision Making," *Journal of Advertising*, Spring 2002, pp. 13–25.

86. Dhruv Grewal, Sukumar Kavanoor, Edward F. Fern, Carolyn Costley, and James Barnes, "Comparative Versus Noncomparative Advertising," *Journal of Marketing*, October 1997, pp. 1–15.

87. Pechmann and Stewart, "The Effects of Comparative Advertising on Attention, Memory, and Purchase Intentions."

88. Kenneth C. Manning, Paul W. Miniard, Michael J. Barone, and Randall L. Rose, "Understanding the Mental Representations Created by Comparative Advertising," *Journal of Advertising* 3, no. 2, Summer 2001, pp. 27–39.

89. Joseph R. Priester, John Godek, D. J. Nayankuppum, and Kiwan Park, "Brand Congruity and Comparative Advertising," *Journal of Consumer Psychology* 14, no. 1–2, 2004, pp. 115–123.

90. Jerry B. Gotlieb and Dan Sarel, "Comparative Advertising Effectiveness," *Journal of Advertising* 20, no. 1, 1991, pp. 38–45; and Koprowski, "Theories of Negativity."

91. Cornelia Pechmann and S. Ratneshwar, "The Use of Comparative Advertising for Brand Positioning: Association Versus Differentiation," *Journal of Consumer Research*, September 1991, pp. 145–160.

92. Paul W. Miniard, Michael J. Barone, Randall L. Rose, and Kenneth C. Manning, "A Further Assessment of Indirect Comparative Advertising Claims of Superiority Over All Competitors," *Journal of Advertising* 35, no. 4, Winter 2006, pp. 53–64.

93. A. V. Muthukrishnan and S. Ramaswami, "Contextual Effects on the Revision of Evaluative Judgments: An Extension of the Omission-Detection Framework," *Journal of Consumer Research*, June 1999, pp. 70–84.

94. Shailendra Pratap Jain and Steven S. Posavac, "Valenced Comparisons," *Journal of Marketing Research* 41, no. 1, February 2004, pp. 46–58.

95. Shailendra Pratap Jain, Nidhi Agrawal, and Durairaj Maheswaran, "When More May Be Less: The Effects of Regulatory Focus on Responses to Different Comparative Frames," *Journal of Consumer Research* 33, no. 1, 2006, pp. 91–98.

96. Shailendra Pratap Jain, Charles Lindsey, Nidhi Agrawal, and Durairaj Maheswaran, "For Better or For Worse? Valenced Comparative Frames and Regulatory Focus," *Journal of Consumer Research* 34, no. 1, 2007, pp. 57–65.

97. Anne L. Roggeveen, Dhruv Grewal, and Jerry Gotlieb, "Does the Frame of a Comparative Ad Moderate the Effectiveness of Extrinsic Information Cues?" *Journal of Consumer Research* 33, no. 1, 2006, pp. 115–122.

98. Pechmann and Stewart, "The Effects of Comparative Advertising on Attention, Memory, and Purchase Intentions."

99. Debora Viana Thompson and Rebecca W. Hamilton, "The Effects of Information Processing Mode on Consumers' Responses to Comparative Advertising," *Journal of Consumer Research* 32, no. 4, 2006, pp. 530–540.

100. Karlene Lukovitz, "Subway Takes on Grease in Product Launch Spots," *Mediapost*, August 17, 2011, www.mediapost.com; and Kate Macarthur, "Why Big Brands Are Getting into the Ring," *Advertising Age*, May 21, 2007, p. 6.

101. A. V. Muthukrishnan and Amitava Chattopadhyay, "Just Give Me Another Chance: The Strategies for Brand Recovery from a Bad First Impression," *Journal of Marketing Research*, May 2007, pp. 334–345.

102. Dennis Amschewitz, Sarah Bailey, Paola Gelato, and Janna van Olst, "This Article Is Better Than Yours," *Managing Intellectual Property*, April 2011, n.p.; and John Tylee, "New 'Honesty' Laws Could Render Many Campaigns Illegal," *Campaign*, March 17, 2000, p. 16.

103. Barbara Mueller, "Reflections of Culture: An Analysis of Japanese and American Advertising Appeals," *Journal of Advertising Research*, June–July 1987, pp. 51–59.

104. "Number of Complaints Is Soaring, Reports ASA," *Grocer*, May 14, 2011, p. 5.

105. Paschalina (Lilia) Ziamou and S. Ratneshwar, "Innovations in Product Functionality: When and Why Are Explicit Comparisons Effective?" *Journal of Marketing*, April 2003, pp. 49–61.

106. H. Onur Bodur, David Brinberg, and Eloïse Coupey, "Belief, Affect, and Attitude: Alternative Models of the Determinants of Attitude," *Journal of Consumer Psychology* 9, no. 1, 2000, pp. 17–28.

107. Stephen D. Rappaport, "Lessons from Online Practice: New Advertising Models," *Journal of Advertising Research*, June 2007, pp. 135–141.

108. Michel Tuan Pham, "Representativeness, Relevance, and the Use of Feelings in Decision Making," *Journal of Consumer Research*, September 1998, pp. 144–159.

109. MacInnis and Park, "The Differential Role of Characteristics of Music on High- and Low-Involvement Consumers' Processing of Ads."

110. Yih Hwai Lee and Elison Ai Ching Lim, "When Good Cheer Goes Unrequited: How Emotional Receptivity Affects Evaluation of Express Emotion," *Journal of Marketing Research*, December 2010, pp. 1151–1161.

111. Deborah J. MacInnis and Douglas M. Stayman, "Focal and Emotional Integration: Constructs, Measures and Preliminary Evidence," *Journal of Advertising*, December 1993, pp. 51–66; and Chris T. Allen, Karen A. Machleit, and Susan Schultz Kleine, "A Comparison of Attitudes and Emotions as Predictors of Behavior at Diverse Levels of Behavioral Experience," *Journal of Consumer Research*, March 1992, pp. 493–504.

112. Deborah J. MacInnis and Bernard J. Jaworski, "Two Routes to Persuasion in Advertising," *Review of Marketing* 10, 1990, pp. 1–25.

113. See Nancy Spears and Richard Germain, "1900–2000 in Review: The Shifting Role and Face of Animals in Print Advertisements in the Twentieth Century," *Journal of Advertising*, Fall 2007, pp. 19–33.

114. Tamar Avnet and E. Tory Higgins, "How Regulatory Fit Affects Value in Consumer Choices and Opinions," *Journal of Marketing Research*, February 2006, pp. 1–10; Tamar Avnet and E. Tory Higgins, "Response to Comments on 'How Regulatory Fit Affects Value in Consumer Choices and Opinions,'" *Journal of Marketing Research*, February 2006, pp. 24–27; Jennifer L. Aaker and Angela Y. Lee, "Understanding Regulatory Fit," *Journal of Marketing Research*, February 2006, pp. 15–19; Aparna A. Labroo and Angela Y. Lee, "Between Two Brands: A Goal Fluency Account of Brand Evaluation," *Journal of Marketing Research*, August 2006, pp. 374–385; and Junsang Yeo and Jongwon Park, "Effects of Parent-Extension Similarity and Self-Regulatory Focus on

Evaluations of Brand Extensions," *Journal of Consumer Psychology* 16, no. 3, 2006, pp. 272–282.

115. Whan C. Park and Mark S. Young, "Consumer Response to Television Commercials: The Impact of Involvement and Background Music on Brand Attitude Formation," *Journal of Marketing Research*, February 1986, pp. 11–24.

116. Rajeev Batra and Michael L. Ray, "Affective Responses Mediating Acceptance of Advertising," *Journal of Consumer Research*, September 1986, pp. 234–249.

117. Jooyoung Kim and Jon D. Morris, "The Power of Affective Response and Cognitive Structure in Product-Trial Attitude Formation," *Journal of Advertising* 36, no. 1, Spring 2007, pp. 95–106.

118. Hans Baumgartner, Mita Sujan, and Dan Padgett, "Patterns of Affective Reactions to Advertisements: The Integration of Moment-to-Moment Responses into Overall Judgments," *Journal of Marketing Research*, May 1997, pp. 219–232.

119. Deborah J. MacInnis and Bernard J. Jaworski, "Information Processing from Advertisements: Toward an Integrative Framework," *Journal of Marketing*, October 1989, pp. 1–23.

120. Lee and Lim, "When Good Cheer Goes Unrequited."

121. Michel Tuan Pham and Tamar Avnet, "Ideals and Oughts and the Reliance on Affect Versus Substance in Persuasion," *Journal of Consumer Research*, March 2004, pp. 503–518.

122. Jennifer L. Aaker and Patti Williams, "Empathy Versus Pride: The Influence of Emotional Appeals Across Cultures," *Journal of Consumer Research*, December 1998, pp. 241–261.

123. Richard P. Bagozzi and David J. Moore, "Public Service Announcements: Emotions and Empathy Guide Prosocial Behavior," *Journal of Marketing*, January 1994, pp. 56–57.

124. May Frances Luce, "Choosing to Avoid: Coping with Negatively Emotion-Laden Consumer Decisions," *Journal of Consumer Research*, March 1998, pp. 409–433.

125. Joel B. Cohen and Charles S. Areni, "Affect and Consumer Behavior," in eds. Thomas S. Robertson and Harold H. Kassarjian, *Handbook of Consumer Behavior* (Englewood Cliffs, N.J.: Prentice-Hall, 1991), pp. 188–240.

126. Robert D. Jewell and H. Rao Unnava, "Exploring Differences in Attitudes Between Light and Heavy Brand Users," *Journal of Consumer Psychology* 14, no. 1/2, 2004, pp. 75–80.

127. Jena McGregor, "Customer Service Champs 2010: L.L. Bean," *Bloomberg Businessweek*, February 18, 2010, www.businessweek.com.

128. See Miranda R. Goode, Darren W. Dahl, and C. Page Moreau, "The Effect of Experiential Analogies on Consumer Perceptions and Attitudes," *Journal of Marketing Research*, April 2010, pp. 274–286.

129. Sean Gregory, "The Top 10 Everything of 2010," *Time*, December 9, 2010, www.time.com; and Amy Tokic, "New Subaru Ad Promotes Brand's Safety," *Auto Guide*, August 8, 2010, www.autoguide.com.

130. "T-Mobile Captures Emotions," *Marketing Week*, January 13, 2011, p. 4.

131. Petty, Unnava, and Strathman, "Theories of Attitude Change."

132. Harry C. Triandis, *Attitudes and Attitude Change* (New York: Wiley, 1971).

133. Brian D. Till and Michael Busler, "The Match-Up Hypothesis: Physical Attractiveness, Expertise, and the Role of Fit on Brand Attitude, Purchase Intent, and Brand Beliefs," *Journal of Advertising* 29, no. 3, Fall 2000, pp. 1–13.

134. Mike Bastin, "Celebrity Endorsements Can Backfire," *China Daily*, August 26, 2011, http://europe.chinadaily.com.cn.

135. Peter H. Reingen and Jerome B. Kernan, "Social Perception and Interpersonal Influence: Some Consequences of the Physical Attractiveness Stereotype in a Personal Selling Situation," *Journal of Consumer Psychology* 2, no. 1, 1993, pp. 25–38.

136. Scott Ward and Frederick E. Webster Jr., "Organizational Buying Behavior," in eds. Thomas S. Robertson and Harold H. Kassarjian, *Handbook of Consumer Behavior* (Englewood Cliffs, N.J.: Prentice-Hall, 1991), pp. 419–458.

137. Herbert Simon, Nancy Berkowitz, and John Moyer, "Similarity, Credibility, and Attitude Change," *Psychological Bulletin*, January 1970, pp. 1–16.

138. Louise Lucas, "Beauty and the Brands," *Financial Times*, August 29, 2011, www.ft.com.

139. Terence A. Shimp and Elnora W. Stuart, "The Role of Disgust as an Emotional Mediator of Advertising Effects," *Journal of Advertising*, Spring 2004, pp. 43–53.

140. Nidhi Agrawal and Adam Duhachek, "Emotional Compatibility and the Effectiveness of Antidrinking Messages," *Journal of Marketing Research*, April 2010, pp. 263–273.

141. Patti Williams and Jennifer L. Aaker, "Can Mixed Emotions Peacefully Coexist?" *Journal of Consumer Research*, March 2002, pp. 636–649.

142. Elaine Chan and Jaideep Sengupta, "Insincere Flattery Actually Works," *Journal of Marketing Research*, February 2010, pp. 122–133.

143. See Christian Homburg, Jan Wieseke, and Wayne D. Hoyer, "Social Identity and the Service-Profit Chain," *Journal of Marketing*, March 2010, pp. 38–54; and David Sprott, Sandor Czellar, and Eric Spangenberg, "The Importance of a General Measure of Brand Engagement on Market Behavior," *Journal of Marketing Research*, February 2009, pp. 92–104.

144. Blair Kidwell, David M. Hardesty, Brian R. Murtha, and Shibin Sheng, "Emotional Intelligence in Marketing Exchanges," *Journal of Marketing*, January 2011, pp. 78–95.

145. Batra and Stayman, "The Role of Mood in Advertising Effectiveness."

146. Rajesh K. Chandy, Gerard J. Tellis, Deborah J. MacInnis, and Pattana Thaivanich, "'What to Say When' Advertising Appeals in Evolving Markets," *Journal of Marketing Research*, November 2001, pp. 399–414.

147. "McDonald's—Happy Box," *Campaign*, July 29, 2011, p. 7.

148. Jennifer Edson Escalas, Marian Chapman Moore, and Julie Edell Britton, "Fishing for Feelings? Hooking Viewers Helps!" *Journal of Consumer Psychology* 14, no. 1 and 2, 2004, pp. 105–114.

149. Deborah A. Small and Nicole M. Verrochi, "The Face of Need: Facial Emotion Expression on Charity Advertisements," *Journal of Marketing Research*, December 2009, pp. 777–787.

150. Brent McFerran, Darren W. Dahl, Gerald J. Gorn, and Heather Honea, "Motivational Determinants of Transportation into Marketing Narratives," *Journal of Consumer Psychology* 20, 2010, pp. 306–316.

151. "Shelter Pet Adoption," Ad Council, www.adcouncil.org.

152. John F. Tanner, James B. Hunt, and David R. Eppright, "The Protection Motivation Model: A Normative Model of Fear Appeals," *Journal of Marketing*, July 1991, pp. 36–45.

153. Michael L. Ray and William L. Wilkie, "Fear: The Potential of an Appeal Neglected by Marketing," *Journal of Marketing*, January 1970, pp. 54–62.

154. Ibid.

155. Kirsten Passyn and Mita Sujan, "Self-Accountability Emotions and Fear Appeals: Motivating Behavior," *Journal of Consumer Research* 32, no. 4, 2006, pp. 583–589.

156. Omar Shehryar and David M. Hunt, "A Terror Management Perspective on the Persuasiveness of Fear Appeals," *Journal of Consumer Psychology* 15, no. 4, 2005, pp. 275–287.

157. Scott Kirsner, "The Carbonite File," *Boston Globe*, May 12, 2011, www.boston.com; and Scott Kirsner, "Dueling Data Backup Firms Are Rare Bright Spot," *Boston Globe*, January 25, 2009, www.boston.com.

158. Herbert J. Rotfeld, "Fear Appeals and Persuasion: Assumptions and Errors in Advertising Research," in eds. James H. Leigh and Claude R. Martin, *Current Issues and Research in Advertising* (Ann Arbor, Mich.: Graduate School of Business Administration, University of Michigan, 1990), pp. 155–175.

159. John J. Wheatley, "Marketing and the Use of Fear- or Anxiety-Arousing Appeals," *Journal of Marketing*, April 1971, pp. 62–64; and Peter L. Wright, "Concrete Action Plans in TV Messages to Increase Reading of Drug Warnings," *Journal of Consumer Research*, December 1979, pp. 256–269.

160. John J. Burette and Richard L. Oliver, "Fear Appeal Effects in the Field: A Segmentation Approach," *Journal of Marketing Research*, May 1979, pp. 181–190.

161. MacInnis and Jaworski, "Two Routes to Persuasion in Advertising."

162. Thomas J. Olney, Morris B. Holbrook, and Rajeev Batra, "Consumer Responses to Advertising: The Effects of Ad Content, Emotions, and Attitude Toward the Ad on Viewing Time," *Journal of Consumer Research*, March 1991, pp. 440–453.

163. Paul W. Miniard, Sunil Bhatla, and Randall L. Rose, "On the Formation and Relationship of Ad and Brand Attitudes," *Journal of Marketing Research*, August 1990, pp. 290–303.

164. Sally Goll Beatty, "Executive Fears Effects of Political Ads," *Wall Street Journal*, April 29, 1996, p. B6.

165. Julie A. Edell and Richard E. Staelin, "The Information Processing of Pictures in Print Advertisements," *Journal of Consumer Research*, June 1983, pp. 45–60.

166. Scott B. MacKenzie, Richard J. Lutz, and George E. Belch, "The Role of Attitude Toward the Ad as a Mediator of Advertising Effectiveness," *Journal of Marketing Research*, May 1986, pp. 130–143; and Pamela M. Homer, "The Mediating Role of Attitude Toward the Ad: Some Additional Evidence," *Journal of Marketing Research*, February 1990, pp. 78–86.

167. Dan Minahan, "Game of Thrones Director Wraps Audi Drama Series," *Shoot Online*, October 21, 2011, www.shootonline.com.

168. Richard E. Petty, John T. Cacioppo, and David W. Schumann, "Central and Peripheral Routes to Advertising Persuasion," *Journal of Consumer Research*, September 1983, pp. 134–148.

169. Jaideep Sengupta and Gita Venkataramani Johar, "Effects of Inconsistent Attribute Information on the Predictive Value of Product Attitudes," *Journal of Consumer Research*, June 2002, pp. 39–56.

170. Robert E. Smith and William R. Swinyard, "Attitude-Behavior Consistency: The Impact of Product Trial Versus Advertising," *Journal of Marketing Research* 20, no. 3, August 1983, pp. 257–267; and Russell H. Fazio and Mark P. Zanna, "Direct Experience and Attitude–Behavior Consistency," in ed. Leonard Berkowitz, *Advances in Experimental Social Psychology* (New York: Academic Press, 1981), pp. 162–202.

171. Jaideep Sengupta and Gavan J. Fitzsimons, "The Effects of Analyzing Reasons for Brand Preferences: Disruption or Reinforcement?" *Journal of Marketing Research* 37, August 2000, pp. 318–330.

172. Russell H. Fazio, Martha C. Powell, and Carol J. Williams, "The Role of Attitude Accessibility in the Attitude-to-Behavior Process," *Journal of Consumer Research*, December 1989, pp. 280–288; and Berger and Mitchell, "The Effect of Advertising on Attitude Accessibility, Attitude Confidence, and the Attitude–Behavior Relationship."

173. Smith and Swinyard, "Attitude–Behavior Consistency"; and Alice A. Wright and John G. Lynch, "Communication Effects of Advertising vs. Direct Experience When Both Search and Experience Attributes Are Present," *Journal of Consumer Research*, March 1995, pp. 708–718.

174. Vicki G. Morwitz and Gavan J. Fitzsimons, "The Mere-Measurement Effect: Why Does Measuring Intention Change Actual Behavior?" *Journal of Consumer Psychology* 14, no. 1/2, 2004, pp. 64–74; and Pierre Chandon, Vicki G. Morwitz, and Werner J. Reinartz, "Do Intentions Really Predict Behavior? Self-Generated Validity Effects in Survey Research," *Journal of Marketing* 69, no. 2, April 2005, pp. 1–14.

175. Berger, "The Nature of Attitude Accessibility and Attitude Confidence."

176. Joseph R. Priester, Dhananhjay Nayakankuppam, Monique A. Fleming, and John Godek, "The A2SC2 Model: The Influence of Attitudes and Attitude Strength on Consideration and Choice," *Journal of Consumer Research*, March 2004, pp. 574–587.

177. Echo Wen Wan, Derek D. Rucker, Zakary L. Tormala, and Joshua J. Clarkson, "The Effect of Regulatory Depletion on Attitude Certainty," *Journal of Marketing Research*, June 2010, pp. 531–541.

178. Fishbein and Ajzen, *Belief, Attitude, Intention, and Behavior*.

179. Shanker H. Krishnan and Robert E. Smith, "The Relative Endurance of Attitudes, Confidence, and Attitude–Behavior Consistency," *Journal of Consumer Psychology* 7, no. 3, 1998, pp. 273–298.

180. Whan C. Park, Deborah J. MacInnis, Joseph Priester, Andreas B. Eisingerich, and Dawn Iacobucci, "Brand Attachment and Brand Attitude Strength: Conceptual and Empirical Differentiation of Two Critical Brand Equity Drivers," *Journal of Marketing*, November 2010, pp. 1–17.

181. Matt Thomson, Deborah J. MacInnis, and Whan C. Park, "The Ties that Bind: Measuring the Strength of Consumers' Emotional Attachments to Brands," *Journal of Consumer Psychology* 15, no. 1, 2005, pp. 77–91; Whan C. Park and Deborah J. MacInnis, "What's In and What's Out: Questions on the Boundaries of the Attitude Construct," *Journal of Consumer Research* 33, no. 1, 2006, pp. 16–18; Whan C. Park, Deborah J. MacInnis, and Joseph Priester, "Brand Attachment as a Strategic Brand Exemplar," forthcoming in ed. Bernd H. Schmitt, *Handbook of Brand and Experience Management* (Elgar Publishing, 2009); Rohini Ahluwalia, Robert Burnkrant, and H. Rao Unnava, "Consumer Response to Negative Publicity," *Journal of Marketing Research* 37, no. 2 (May 2000), pp. 203–214; Michael D. Johnson, Andreas Herrmann, and Frank Huber, "The Evolution of Loyalty Intentions," *Journal of Marketing* 70, April 2006, 122–132; and Matthew Thomson, "Human Brands: Investigating Antecedents to Consumers' Strong Attachments to Celebrities," *Journal of Marketing* 70, no. 3, July 2006, pp. 104–119.

182. Lucia Malar, Harley Krohmer, Wayne D. Hoyer, and Bettina Nyffenegger, "Emotional Brand Attachment and Brand Personality: The Relative Importance of the Actual and the Ideal Self," *Journal of Marketing*, July 2011, pp. 35–52.

183. Sekar Raju and H. Rao Unnava, "The Role of Arousal in Commitment," *Journal of Consumer Research* 33, no. 2, 2006, pp. 173–178.

184. Krishnan and Smith, "The Relative Endurance of Attitudes, Confidence, and Attitude–Behavior Consistency."

185. John T. Cacioppo, Richard E. Petty, Chuan Fang Kao, and Regina Rodriguez, "Central and Peripheral Routes to Persuasion," *Journal of Personality and Social Psychology* 51, 1986, pp. 1032–1043.

186. Mark Snyder and William B. Swan Jr., "When Actions Reflect Attitudes: The Politics of Impression Management," *Journal of Personality and Social Psychology* 34, 1976, pp. 1034–1042.

187. Stuart Elliott, "Clap Clap, Here Comes the Beetle," *New York Times*, September 8, 2011, www.nytimes.com; Matt Semansky, "Volkswagen Canada Augments Reality in OOH Campaign," *Marketing Magazine (Canada)*, October 26, 2011, www.marketingmag.ca; Todd Wasserman, "VW's 'The Force' Super Bowl Ad Goes Viral," *Mashable*, February 3, 2011, www.mashable.com; Gabriel Beltrone, "Ad of the Day: Volkswagen," *Adweek*, September 27, 2011, www.adweek.com; Bob Garfield, "VW Finds Viral Force with Cute Ad, But So What?" *Advertising Age*, February 7, 2011, www.adage.com; Robert Klara, "Volkswagen Beetle Nipped in Bud," *Adweek*, April 22, 2011, www.adweek.com; and Chris Bryant, "Volkswagen Sales Surge Across Its Brands," *Financial Times*, October 27, 2011, www.ft.com.

CHAPTER 6

ATTITUDES BASED ON LOW EFFORT

After studying this chapter, you will be able to

1. Outline some issues marketers face in trying to change consumers' attitudes when processing effort is low.

2. Explain the role of unconscious influences on attitudes and behavior in low-effort situations.

3. Discuss how consumers form beliefs based on low-processing effort and explain how marketers can influence those beliefs.

4. Describe how consumers form attitudes through affective reactions when cognitive effort is low.

5. Highlight how marketers can use the communication source, message, and context to influence consumers' feelings and attitudes when processing effort is low.

© MARCUS BRANDT/EPA/Newscom

INTRODUCTION

Snacks Go Social and Mobile

Snacks aren't just waiting for you at the grocery store—they want to be your friend, tweet to you, and leap onto your phone screen. Nutella, the Italian hazelnut-chocolate spread now available worldwide, is one of the top snack foods on Facebook. It has attracted more than 11.5 million "likes" plus 100,000 comments on consumers' personal pages through a combination of contests and promotions that invite interaction. Brand owner Ferrero invites Facebook visitors to click to any one of 13 country sites, from the Netherlands to Australia to Russia, for recipes, fun facts, and nutrition data. Cadbury's seasonal Crème Eggs (spring themes for Easter, Screme Eggs for Halloween) are also social and mobile, with 2 million "likes" and numerous videos and games on Facebook. Crème Eggs offers a cell phone app for brand promotions that can be tailored by location and rotate messages during the day, encouraging repeat contacts.

Texas-based Frito-Lay uses social media to engage fans of its snack brands (including Doritos, Lay's, Tostitos, and Sun Chips) via Facebook, YouTube, Twitter, and QR (quick response) codes. To emphasize its "farm-fresh" ingredients, Frito-Lay arranged for its brands to be featured in the popular FarmVille game on Facebook. More than 2 million consumers "like" Frito-Lay's Facebook page, which includes an ever-changing array of messages, photos, fan comments, and links to YouTube videos demonstrating snack recipes and new products in the works. Consumers can use their cell phones to scan the QR codes on Frito-Lay packages and receive coupons and additional information.[1]

The different approaches used by snack brands illustrate how marketers can influence attitudes even when consumers devote little effort to processing a message. Because consumers tend not to actively process message arguments or become emotionally involved in messages about snacks, marketers must use other techniques to create positive evaluations of their brands, increase situational involvement, raise awareness of need situations, and stimulate purchasing and consumption. Snack marketers like Cadbury and Frito-Lay see new opportunities to connect with consumers and communicate messages through social media and mobile marketing. This chapter discusses how marketers apply these and other techniques such as sex, humor, attractive sources, and emotion to influence attitudes even when consumers make little effort to process the message.

HIGH-EFFORT VERSUS LOW-EFFORT ROUTES TO PERSUASION

When consumers are either unwilling or unable to exert a lot of effort or devote emotional resources to processing the central idea behind a marketing communication, we characterize it as a *low-effort situation*. In such a situation, consumers are unlikely to think about what the product means to them, relate empathetically to the characters in the ad, or generate arguments against or in support of the brand message. When processing effort is low, consumers are passive recipients of the message and usually do not form strong beliefs or accessible, persistent, resistant, or confident attitudes. In fact, attitudes formed under low-effort processing may not even be stored in memory, allowing consumers to form attitudes anew each time they are exposed to a message.[2] Marketers must therefore use a strategy that takes into account these effects of lower-level processing.

One approach is to create communications that use a different route. Instead of focusing on the key message arguments, the message will be more effective if it takes the **peripheral route to persuasion**.[3] Processing is called *peripheral* when consumers' attitudes are based not on a detailed consideration of the message or their ability to relate to the brand empathetically but on other easily processed aspects of the message, such as the source or visuals, called **peripheral cues**. In particular, consumer attitudes can persist over time if peripheral cues such as visuals are related to the offering.[4]

Just as there are both cognitive and affective routes to persuasion when processing effort is high, so too can consumers form low-effort attitudes in both a cognitive and an affective manner. Marketers can try to design their ads to enhance the likelihood that consumers' thoughts (the cognitive base), feelings (the affective base), or both will be favorable. Exhibit 6.1 provides a framework for thinking about the peripheral bases of consumer behavior, including unconscious influences on attitude formation and change.

Marketers need to understand how consumers form attitudes with low effort because, in most cases, consumers will have limited motivation, ability, and/or opportunity (MAO) to process marketing communications. Think about the countless marketing messages you receive every day. How many actually attract your attention and stimulate you to think about the ad and the way that you feel about the offering? When the television is on, do you channel surf during commercials or tune them out because they feature products you do not care about? These behaviors pose challenges for marketers.

Peripheral route to persuasion Aspects other than key message arguments that are used to influence attitudes.

Peripheral cues Easily processed aspects of a message, such as music, an attractive source, picture, or humor.

Exhibit 6.1

Chapter Overview: Attitude
Formation and Change:
Low Consumer Effort

Attitudes can be formed unconsciously as well as cognitively and affectively in low-effort situations, although not in the same way as they are in high-effort situations. Low-effort cognition involves simple beliefs, and affect involves mere exposure, classical and evaluative conditioning, attitude toward the ad, and mood. Marketers can also influence consumer attitudes cognitively and affectively using source, message, and context factors.

UNCONSCIOUS INFLUENCES ON ATTITUDES WHEN CONSUMER EFFORT IS LOW

Recent research indicates that much processing in low-effort situations occurs below conscious awareness. This means that consumers form attitudes on both cognitive and affective bases without being aware of how or why they have done so. For example, a consumer browsing in a store may unconsciously be affected by various aspects of the shopping environment.[5] As another example, when people must stand in line to acquire something (make a purchase, get on a flight), they will perceive the product or experience as more valuable—and have a more positive attitude toward it—as they make progress toward the front of the line.[6] In particular, two unconscious influences being researched are thin-slice judgments based on brief observations and cues from body feedback.

Thin-Slice Judgments

Thin-slice judgments
Evaluations made after very brief observations.

Thin-slice judgments are assessments consumers make after brief observations despite receiving minimal information input. Studies show that consumers can form surprisingly accurate impressions through thin-slice judgments, even though they are not doing so on a conscious level.[7] For example, a consumer may unconsciously form an assessment about a salesperson after a moment of observation or interaction. (This same effect may occur when students judge a professor's class performance after brief observation.) Such an assessment can influence the consumer's decision to buy and satisfaction with the sale. Also, when consumers glance at a product and unconsciously perceive it to have a friendly human face—such as an upturned car grille that seems to be a smile—they are likely to have a positive attitude toward that product.[8] At the same time, an overabundance of information, knowledge, or analysis can impair this kind of intuitive assessment.[9]

Body Feedback

Even though consumers may not consciously monitor their own physical reactions, body feedback can influence attitudes and behavior in some circumstances, which is why researchers are studying mind-body connections in more detail. For instance, consumers who were induced to nod had more positive evaluations of favorable brands; when induced to shake their heads, consumers had more negative evaluations. Similarly, pushing up on a table led to more positive evaluations; pushing down led to more negative evaluations. However, consumers must know the meaning of the body feedback they experience in order to explain their behavior. If they do not recognize that nodding signals agreement, this feedback cue will have no effect on their attitude or behavior.[10] Also, as discussed in Chapter 2, the mind-body connection can affect consumer behavior. As one example, physically firming muscles may help consumers exert self-control in choices such as picking a healthy snack rather than an unhealthy one.[11]

Marketing Implications

Marketers can try to enhance thin-slice judgments and induce positive body feedback, even though consumers will not be consciously aware of these influences. For example, a consumer may unconsciously form an assessment about a salesperson after a moment or two of conversation. Applying body feedback theory, many marketers make product packaging intriguing or attractive enough to cause consumers to pick up a product. In one test, high school students began buying baby carrots after the vegetables were repackaged like popular chip snacks and displayed in bright orange vending machines.[12]

Also, marketers should aim to have consumers read ad copy from top to bottom (and then from bottom to top) to simulate nodding "yes." Such body movements could tip the scale in favor of a purchase if the consumer has a positive perception of the product. Applying unconscious influences in marketing can be tricky, however, because of their complex interactions with conscious influences.[13] For example, after a redesign of the Mazda3 sports car turned the grille into a wide grin, reviewers complained that the car seemed less "aggressive."[14] _____

COGNITIVE BASES OF ATTITUDES WHEN CONSUMER EFFORT IS LOW

Simple inferences Beliefs based on peripheral cues.

Heuristics Simple rules of thumb that are used to make judgments.

Frequency heuristic Belief based simply on the number of supporting arguments or amount of repetition.

Truth effect When consumers believe a statement simply because it has been repeated a number of times.

Chapter 5 explains how consumers' beliefs form an important cognitive basis for their attitudes. When processing effort is low, attitudes may be based on a few simple and not very strong beliefs because consumers have not processed the message deeply. Interestingly, because these beliefs are not very strong, marketers may actually be *more* successful in changing them than when consumers' processing effort is high.

The attitudes of low-effort consumers may be less resistant to attack than those of high-effort consumers because the low-effort people may "let their guard down" and not resist the message or develop counterarguments. So a company that wants to change consumers' false beliefs about a product will be more successful if it uses a direct refutation to rebut a direct product claim.[15] Also, ads that focus consumers on the process of using the advertised product make consumers more likely to think about a plan to buy the product—and open the way to persuasion by strong message claims.[16]

When processing effort is low, consumers may acquire simple beliefs by forming **simple inferences** based on simple associations. For example, consumers may infer that a brand of champagne is elegant because it is shown with other elegant things, such as a richly decorated room or a woman in an evening dress. If an ad is perceived to be similar to the prototypical ad for a product or service category, consumers may believe that the offering is just like the prototypical brand and may develop similar attitudes toward both.[17] Inferred beliefs may also come from consumers' superficial analysis of the product's brand name, country of origin, price, or color.

In addition, consumers can form simple beliefs based on attributions or explanations for an endorsement.[18] If consumers attribute an endorsement to a desire to earn a lot of money, they will not find the message believable. The ad is apt to be credible if consumers perceive that the endorser truly cares about the offering. When Maria Sharapova appears in Nike ads for the tennis clothing she's designed, she's believable because she has an insider's understanding of the sport and is known for her sense of style on and off the court (see Exhibit 6.2).[19]

Finally, consumers can aid judgments by forming **heuristics**, or simple rules of thumb, that are easy to invoke and require little thought.[20] For example, consumers could use the heuristic "If it is a well-known brand, it must be good" to infer that brands with more frequent ads are also higher in quality.[21] A special type of heuristic is the **frequency heuristic**, with which consumers form a belief based on the number of supporting arguments.[22] They may think, "It must be good because there are ten reasons why I should like it." Research also indicates that consumers are likely to have stronger beliefs about a product when they hear the same message repeatedly, which is known as the **truth effect**.[23] Rather than thinking about and evaluating the information, consumers use familiarity with the message to judge its accuracy ("This 'rings a bell,' so it must be true").

© AP Images/PRNewsFoto/NIKE, Inc.

Exhibit 6.2

Endorsement
Maria Sharapova shows off her custom Nike apparel she's designed.

HOW COGNITIVE ATTITUDES ARE INFLUENCED

Marketers need to consider multiple factors when trying to influence cognitive attitudes. The strength and importance of consumers' beliefs is one factor. Another factor is the likelihood that consumers will form favorable beliefs based on the inferences, attributions, and heuristics they use in processing the message. In designing communications that overcome these hurdles, marketers must consider three major characteristics of a communication: (1) the communication source, (2) the message, and (3) the context in which the message is delivered and the use of repetition.

Communication Source

Characteristics of the source play an important role in influencing consumers' beliefs when their processing effort is low. Credible sources can serve as peripheral cues for making a simplified judgment, such as "Statements from experts can be trusted" or "Products endorsed by an expert must be good."[24] Note that source expertise is used here as a simple cue in judging the credibility of the message, and unlike the case in high-effort situations, little cognitive effort is required to process the message. Marketers may also increase the chances that consumers will believe the endorsement of a product by using an endorser who does not advertise many other products.

The Message

The message itself can influence attitudes in a number of ways when consumers' processing effort is low.

Category- and Schema-Consistent Information

Many elements of a communication affect the inferences that consumers make about a message. For example, consumers may infer that a brand has certain characteristics based on its name ("Healthy Choice soups must be good for me"). They may make inferences about quality based on price, as discussed in Chapter 4, or about attributes based on color, such as when blue suggests coolness. Thus, in designing ads for low-effort consumers, marketers pay close attention to the immediate associations consumers have about easily processed visual and verbal information. These associations are likely to be consistent with category and schema information stored in the consumer's memory.

Many Message Arguments

The frequency heuristic can also affect consumers' beliefs about the message. As a simplifying rule, consumers do not actually process all the information but form a belief based on the number of supporting arguments. For example, when Kraft introduced its MiO concentrated fruit flavors for water, its Facebook promotions and TV commercials featured three arguments to encourage belief formation: MiO flavors make water tastier, MiO-flavored water is more fun to drink, and MiO flavors can be combined for variety.[25] Note that low-effort attitudes can be affected by how easily consumers remember the message arguments. Simply being able to recall some of the arguments can enhance a consumer's preference for the advertised brand.[26]

Simple Messages

In low-processing situations, a simple message is more likely to be effective because consumers will not have to process a lot of information. Marketers often want to convey basic information about why a particular brand is superior, especially when a point of differentiation distinguishes it from the competition. Thus, rather than overloading low-processing consumers with details, marketers should use a simple message with one or two key points. When Glad advertises its ForceFlex garbage bags, the words and pictures focus on one simple point: The bags stretch when stuffed, but they do not break (see Exhibit 6.3). When marketing food products on the basis of convenience, marketers should focus attention on one important functional benefit through a literal, direct assertion, such as "ready in just 15 minutes."[27]

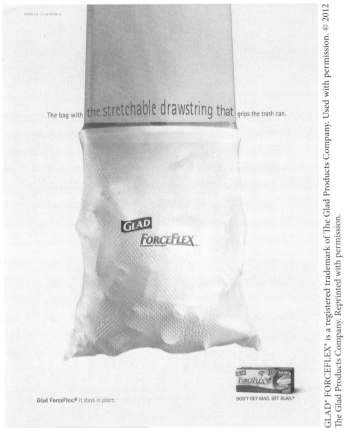

The bag with **the stretchable drawstring that** grips the trash can.

GLAD
FORCEFLEX

Glad ForceFlex.® It stays in place.   DON'T GET MAD, GET GLAD.®

GLAD® FORCEFLEX® is a registered trademark of The Glad Products Company. Used with permission. © 2012 The Glad Products Company. Reprinted with permission.

Exhibit 6.3

Simple Message
When effort is low, consumers will not process a lot of information, so advertisers need to provide simple messages, like in this ad.

Self-referencing Relating a message to one's own experience or self-image.

Mystery ad An ad in which the brand is not identified until the end of the message.

Involving Messages

Marketers will sometimes want to *increase* consumers' situational involvement with the message to ensure that the information is received. One common strategy is to increase the extent to which consumers engage in **self-referencing**, or relating the message to their own experience or self-image.[28] A self-referencing strategy can be effective in developing positive attitudes and intentions, especially if it is used at moderate levels and consumers' involvement is not too low.[29] Some marketers use nostalgia in messages to encourage self-referencing and influence positive attitudes.[30]

Remembering and using the consumer's name in a personal selling context also increases purchase behavior.[31] Consumers will have more favorable attitudes toward a brand that is highly descriptive on a personality dimension that they consider important or self-descriptive.[32] New Balance, which makes high-performance sneakers, prefers not to showcase celebrity endorsers but instead to emphasize consumers' passion for doing their best at sports they love, a dimension with which many consumers identify.[33] A mainstream ad with dominant culture cues may stimulate self-referencing among members of a subculture as well as among members of the dominant culture and lead to favorable ad attitudes. If the ad has subcultural cues rather than dominant culture cues, however, it will induce self-referencing and positive ad attitudes only among subculture members.[34]

Marketing Implications

Marketers can increase self-referencing by (1) directly instructing consumers to self-reference ("Think of the last time you had a good meal ... "), (2) using the word *you* in the ad, (3) asking rhetorical questions ("Wouldn't you like your clothes to look this clean?"),[35] or (4) showing visuals of situations to which consumers can easily relate. Kodak, for example, uses Facebook messages and coupons to encourage self-referencing by suggesting that consumers print their old Facebook images and share special memories with family and friends.[36] However, when a rhetorical question in an ad attracts special attention, consumers wonder why the question is there, shifting their processing effort to the message style instead of the message content.[37]

The **mystery ad** (sometimes called the "wait and bait" ad), which does not identify the brand until the end, if at all, is another way to arouse consumers' curiosity and involvement. Some movies use mystery ads to build audience interest in advance of their release dates. In particular, the mystery ad is effective in generating category-based processing and storing brand associations in memory.[38]

Marketers can also employ other techniques to increase situational involvement and processing effort. Online marketers can use avatars to induce more arousal and involve consumers in the website experience.[39] Scratch-and-sniff print ads often increase processing effort because many consumers cannot resist trying something new. Also, inviting consumers to experience simulated product usage online increases involvement and advertising effectiveness more than an online ad message alone would.[40] The Lego site, for example, features interactive games where players create virtual animals and cities using virtual Lego blocks, demonstrating the product's functionality and fun.[41]

Message Context and Repetition

Although source and message factors can influence consumers' attitudes, the context in which the message is delivered can affect the strength of consumers' beliefs and the prominence (or salience) of those beliefs for the consumers. In particular, a company can use message *repetition* to help consumers acquire basic knowledge of important product features or benefits, enhancing the strength and salience of their beliefs. Consumers do not try to process this information actively; rather, the constant repetition increases recall through effortless or **incidental learning**. For example, you may have a prominent belief about milk's health benefits because you have been repeatedly exposed to the long-running "Got Milk?" milk mustache ad campaign.

Incidental learning
Learning that occurs from repetition rather than from conscious processing.

Repetition may enhance brand awareness, make a brand name more familiar,[42] make it easier to recognize in the store, increase the likelihood that consumers will remember it and be better able to process it when making a purchasing decision,[43] and increase consumers' confidence in the brand.[44] Also, as you have seen, repetition can make claims more believable (the truth effect)—an effect that gets even stronger when ads are spaced out over time.[45] TV commercials that air within the context of similar programming (i.e., humorous ads aired during comedy shows) are more likable and better understood by consumers expending low-processing effort.[46] Similarly, ads that fit into the context of the magazines where they appear elicit more positive feelings and are better remembered than ads not in tune with magazine context.[47]

AFFECTIVE BASES OF ATTITUDES WHEN CONSUMER EFFORT IS LOW

The establishment of low-level beliefs based on peripheral cues is not the only way that consumers can form attitudes about brands with little effort. Attitudes can also be based on consumers' affective or emotional reactions to these easily processed peripheral cues. These low-effort affective processes may be due to (1) the mere exposure effect, (2) classical and evaluative conditioning, (3) attitude toward the ad (A_{ad}), and (4) consumer mood.

The Mere Exposure Effect

Mere exposure effect
When familiarity leads to a consumer's liking an object.

According to the **mere exposure effect**, we tend to prefer familiar objects to unfamiliar ones.[48] Therefore, our attitudes toward an offering such as a new style of clothing should change as we become more and more familiar with it, regardless of whether we perform any deep cognitive analysis of it. The mere exposure effect may explain why many of the top 30 brands in the 1930s are still in the top 30 today. It also explains why the music industry likes to have recordings featured on the radio or in TV music videos. Through repeated exposure, consumers become familiar with the music and come to like it.

Because most demonstrations of the mere exposure effect have occurred in tightly controlled laboratory studies, some experts question whether it generalizes to the real world.[49] It is also possible that repeated exposure reduces uncertainty about the stimulus or increases consumers' opportunity to process it[50] and that these factors (rather than mere familiarity) are what affect consumers' attitudes. However, research shows that mere exposure can help an unknown brand compete against other unknown brands if product performance characteristics are equivalent and consumers invest little processing effort at the time of brand choice.[51] Also, when consumers can easily process the information from a stimulus to which they have been exposed in the past, they mistakenly believe that the ease in processing is due to liking, truth, or acceptability.[52]

Marketing Implications

If the mere exposure effect is valid, marketers may be able to enhance consumers' liking of a new product or service by repeatedly exposing consumers to the offering or messages about it. Research suggests that when consumers' MAO is low, marketers need creative tactics for increasing consumers' exposure to products and messages, perhaps by using the right medium, the right placement within the medium, optimal shelf placement, and sampling.

Consistent with the mere exposure effect, some smaller companies are embarking on ad campaigns to create brand-name familiarity and liking, which are especially important for new brands. For instance, CM Photographics, a small wedding photography business, has been building its brand and generating thousands of dollars worth of orders by advertising on Facebook.[53]

Some companies pay to have their logos displayed at sporting events, knowing that there will be repeated exposures as race cars go around the track or players move around the field. However, repeated exposures will build familiarity and liking only up to a point.[54] After this, consumers typically experience **wearout**, which means they become bored with the stimulus, and brand attitudes can actually become negative.[55] In fact, once a persuasive ad has effectively reached the targeted consumer segment, wearout causes a loss of persuasiveness.[56] Interestingly, although consumers are irritated by repeated direct mail requests for contributions to charities, their attitude and behavior toward the charities is not negatively affected, perhaps because charities are viewed differently than businesses.[57]

Research shows that when consumers are familiar with a brand, wearout may occur later.[58] Also, the use of rational arguments to promote a well-known brand in a mature product category tends to be less effective than the use of affectively based tactics because consumers have been exposed to the product information many times before.[59] Still, in low-effort processing situations, brand evaluations do not suffer when consumers are repeatedly exposed to messages about product features.[60]

Marketers can overcome wearout by creating different executions for the same message or variants on the same offering; this is the reason why many advertisers develop a series of ads rather than a single execution.[61] The goal is to get the same message across in many different ways, as Ireland's official tourism agency is doing by creating a three-year multimedia campaign featuring numerous iconic sights such as the Ring of Kerry.[62] The mere exposure effect may not be the only reason that repetition affects brand attitudes. When repetition allows consumers greater opportunity to process information about specific aspects of the brand and the ways that it relates to other brands in the category, brand attitudes improve.[63] _____

Classical and Evaluative Conditioning

One way of influencing attitudes based on low effort is **classical conditioning**, producing a response to a stimulus by repeatedly pairing it with another stimulus that automatically produces this response. Classical conditioning became well known from a study in the 1900s by the Russian scientist Ivan Pavlov. Normally, hungry dogs will salivate automatically just at the sight of food. Pavlov discovered that he could condition hungry dogs to salivate at the sound of a bell. How did he do that?

According to Pavlov, the food was an *unconditioned stimulus (UCS)*, and the salivation response to the food was an *unconditioned response (UCR)* (see the top half of Exhibit 6.4). A stimulus is unconditioned when it automatically elicits an involuntary response. In this situation, the dogs automatically salivated when they saw meat powder. In contrast, a *conditioned stimulus (CS)* is something that does not automatically elicit an involuntary response by itself. Until Pavlov rang the bell at the same time that the food was presented, the bell alone could not make the dogs salivate. By repeatedly pairing the CS (the bell) with the UCS (the meat powder), the involuntary UCR (salivation) was created. The dogs associated the food and the bell so closely that eventually just the ringing bell made them salivate. Because the response could now be evoked in the presence of the CS, the response was said to be a *conditioned response (CR)*. (This is the same phenomenon that makes cats come running when they hear the can opener.)

Evaluative conditioning is a special case of classical conditioning that produces an affective response by repeatedly pairing a neutral *CS* (such as a brand) and an emotionally charged *UCS* (such as a well-liked celebrity).[64] This process is shown in the bottom half of Exhibit 6.4. Here, the goal is not to encourage a physiological behavior (salivating, as in Pavlov's classical conditioning) but to encourage a psychological one (positive feeling toward or preference for the CS).

Certain unconditioned stimuli (such as a happy scene or a catchy jingle) automatically elicit an UCR such as joy. By repeatedly pairing one of these unconditioned stimuli with a CS such as a brand name, marketers may be able to evoke the same emotional response (now the CR) to the

Wearout Becoming bored with a stimulus.

Classical conditioning Producing a response to a stimulus by repeatedly pairing it with another stimulus that automatically produces this response.

Evaluative conditioning A special case of classical conditioning, producing an affective response by repeatedly pairing a neutral conditioned stimulus with an emotionally-charged unconditioned stimulus.

© Cengage Learning 2013

Exhibit 6.4

Classical and Evaluative Conditioning

In classical conditioning (top), an unconditioned stimulus, or UCS (e.g., food), will automatically produce an unconditioned physiological response, or UCR (e.g., salivation). By repeatedly pairing the UCS with a conditioned stimulus, or CS (e.g., a bell), the CS can be conditioned to produce the same response, a conditioned response, or CR (e.g., salivation). In evaluative conditioning (bottom), a special case of classical conditioning, the UCS may be a pleasant scene and the CS a soft drink. Here, repeatedly pairing the UCS and the CS results in a CR of positive affect, rather than a physiological response. Can you think of any other situations in which this process occurs?

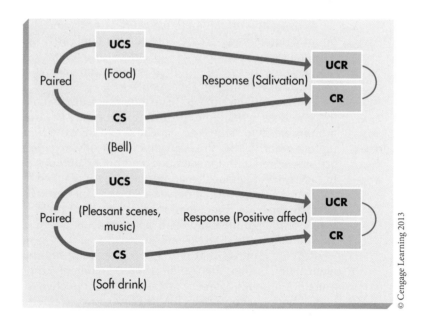

CS—that is, the brand name itself. Similarly, consumers might be conditioned to have a *negative* emotional response to an offering such as cigarettes if ads or package labels repeatedly show the product with stimuli that elicit a negative emotional response (such as pictures of badly stained teeth or diseased lungs). This is why some countries require graphic warning labels on cigarette packages, and research shows that these warnings have been effective in encouraging smokers to quit in Brazil, Thailand, and several other nations.[65]

Marketing Implications

In one of the first consumer studies to demonstrate classical/evaluative conditioning, subjects viewed a slide of a blue or beige pen matched with a one-minute segment of either pleasant or unpleasant music. Subjects who heard pleasant music selected the pen they viewed with that music 79 percent of the time, whereas only 30 percent of those who heard the unpleasant music selected the pen they had viewed.[66] Although these findings could be interpreted in different ways (subjects may have done what they thought the experimenter wanted them to do, or the music may have put the consumers in a better mood),[67] more recent, tightly controlled studies have found support for classical and evaluative conditioning. For example, by using unconditioned stimuli such as *Star Wars* music and pleasing pictures, experimenters have affected consumers' attitudes toward such conditioned stimuli as geometric figures, colas, and toothpaste.[68] Research also shows that attitudes created by classical conditioning can be fairly enduring over time.[69] Brand attitudes influenced by evaluative conditioning are fairly enduring as well, especially when different affective unconditioned stimuli are paired with the CS (the brand).[70] Finally, when consumers have limited or depleted attentional resources, they may not make the connection between the CS and the UCS, which in turn can impair the evaluative conditioning response.[71]

Overall, research suggests that conditioning is most likely to occur under the following circumstances:

▶ The conditioned stimuli–unconditioned stimuli link is relatively novel or unknown. This is the reason why marketers often use unique visuals, such as pictures of beautiful scenery, exciting situations, or pleasing objects, as unconditioned stimuli to create positive feelings.

▶ The CS precedes the unconditioned stimulus (*forward conditioning*). Conditioning is weaker when the UCS is presented first (*backward conditioning*) or at the same time as the conditioned stimulus (*concurrent conditioning*).

▶ The CS is paired consistently with the UCS.

▶ The consumer is aware of the link between the conditioned and unconditioned stimuli.

▶ A logical fit exists between the conditioned and unconditioned stimuli, such as between Derrick Williams of the Minnesota Timberwolves basketball team and the brand he endorses, Under Armour's basketball apparel.[72]

Interestingly, the first condition can cause problems for marketers because unconditioned stimuli are often well-known celebrities, music, or visuals for which consumers possess many associations. This finding might suggest that using highly visible celebrities is not as effective a strategy for creating a classical conditioning effect. Other research indicates that the problem can be overcome by using highly familiar stimuli such as popular personalities because they elicit very strong feelings. Some marketers do not shy away from endorsers associated with multiple brands. Bollywood actress Kareena Kapoor endorses more than a dozen brands in India, yet Unilever's Lakme cosmetics brand recently signed her as its spokesperson because of Kapoor's popularity.[73]

Another area of investigation is how choices are affected when consumers are exposed to a stimulus (such as a product message) that activates attitudes without conscious thought. One study found that consumers are likely to rely on their unconscious, conditioned attitudes in situations where they have not explicitly evaluated product attribute information—even when they have both motivation and opportunity to retrieve product information from memory.[74] Even now, researchers are investigating these issues in more detail to understand the mechanisms that trigger response and their short- and long-term effects. ────────────────

Attitude Toward the Ad

Another concept that has been useful in understanding the affective bases of attitudes in low-effort situations is the consumer's attitude toward the ad (A_{ad}). Sometimes consumers like an ad so much that they transfer their positive feelings from the ad to the brand.[75] Thus, you may decide that you really like Frito-Lay snacks because the company's ads or YouTube videos are humorous.

One study found that consumers' beliefs or knowledge about the brand did not fully account for brand attitudes and that A_{ad} provided a significant additional explanation—brands with liked ads were evaluated more favorably.[76] Furthermore, research in India, Greece, Denmark, New Zealand, and the United States revealed that the A_{ad} principle was globally applicable.[77] An Advertising Research Foundation project suggests that consumers' attitudes toward ads may be the best indicator of advertising effectiveness.[78]

The **dual-mediation hypothesis** is a somewhat more complex explanation of the relationship between consumers' liking of an ad and brand attitude (see Exhibit 6.5).[79] According to

Dual-mediation hypothesis Explains how attitudes toward the ad influence brand attitudes.

Exhibit 6.5

The Dual-Mediation Hypothesis

This hypothesis explains how attitudes toward the ad (A_{ad}) can influence attitudes toward the brand (A_b) and intentions (I_b). When you read an ad, you can have responses (C_{ad}) that are both cognitive (this ad has information about a brand) and affective (positive feelings from finding the ad). These responses may cause you to like the ad (A_{ad}), a reaction that can then either (1) make you more accepting of brand beliefs (C_b), leading to a more positive brand attitude (A_b); or (2) give you positive feelings that transfer over to the brand (I like the ad, so I like the brand). Both processes lead to an increase in intention to purchase.

this hypothesis, consumers can have a favorable attitude toward an ad either because they find it believable or because they feel good about it. Thus, the dual-mediation hypothesis proposes that A_{ad} can affect attitudes toward the brand (A_b) either through believability or liking. These responses, in turn, may positively affect consumers' intentions to purchase (I_b).

Marketing Implications

Based on attitude-toward-the-ad theory, marketers may be able to make consumers' A_b more positive by providing ads that please consumers. Thus, by using techniques such as humor, music, pleasant pictures, and sex (all of which will be discussed in more detail shortly), marketers can encourage positive attitudes toward the ad. Kellogg's, for instance, has aired emotion-evoking commercials online and on TV for Frosted Flakes, showing fathers and sons playing sports and then sitting down for a bowl of cereal together, with the tagline: "Share what you love with who you love."[80]

In addition, the effect of ad attitudes on A_b may depend on whether consumers already have a strong attitude toward the brand. When brands are well known and attitudes about them have been formed, consumers may not like the brand more just because they like the ad. However, when brands are new or not well known, consumers' liking of the ad can play a more significant role in their liking of the brand.[81] Studies also suggest that the effect of A_{ad} on attitude toward the brand dissipates over time.[82] As memory of the ad fades, liking of the ad and the brand becomes weaker.

Mood

Affective attitudes can also be influenced by the consumer's mood. Here, a stimulus creates a positive or a negative mood; in turn, this mood can affect the consumer's reactions to any other stimulus they happen to evaluate. Thus, we are more likely to say that we like something if we are in a good mood or say that we dislike something if we are in a bad mood. Mood can therefore bias attitudes in a *mood-congruent direction*. Note that mood is different from classical conditioning because mood (1) does not require a repeated association between two stimuli; and (2) can affect consumers' evaluations of any object, not just the stimulus.

According to one study, consumers in a good mood who have a tentative preference for a certain brand tend to ignore negative information about that brand as well as information about a competitor.[83] Another study found that although consumers tend to like a brand extension less when the product is not very similar to the parent product, consumers in a good mood are more likely to like a brand extension that is moderately similar to the parent product than consumers who are not in a good mood.[84] A good mood can act as a resource by increasing elaboration and helping consumers think creatively and see relationships among brands. Specific emotions, not just a general good or bad mood, can also influence attitudes when MAO is low, as long as the emotions are consistent with the consumer's goals.[85] Moreover, consumers in a good mood tend to give more weight to positive information when evaluating a product, whereas consumers in a bad mood give more weight to negative information.[86]

Consumers may like a brand better when they are put in a good mood by its ads or the programs in which the ads appear. Research has focused on the kinds of emotions or moods that ads invoke and the variety of ways these factors might affect consumers' A_b.[87] One study identified three major categories of affective responses: (1) *SEVA* (surgency, elation, vigor, and activation), which is present when the communication puts the consumer in an upbeat or happy mood; (2) *deactivation feelings*, which include soothing, relaxing, quiet, or pleasant responses; and (3) *social affection*, which are feelings of warmth, tenderness, and caring.[88] Another study found that ad-induced feelings of warmth and humor could have a direct and positive impact on A_b.[89] Thus, when ads for Huggies disposable diapers picture tender moments between babies and parents, they may also generate positive feelings for the brand.

> **Marketing Implications**

On the assumption that mood affects consumer behavior, retailers can use physical sur-roundings and the behavior of store employees to put consumers in a good mood. Warm colors such as red and orange tend to be more stimulating and exciting, whereas cool colors such as blue, green, and violet tend to be more soothing.[90] Warm colors are more likely to draw customers to an outlet but can also create tension, whereas cool colors are more relaxing but do not attract customers.[91] Therefore, when the goal is to stimulate quick purchases or activity, warm colors are more appropriate, a situation that explains why Target and Costco stores use a red-based color scheme. Warm colors are also appropriate for health clubs, sports stadiums, and fast-food restaurants, where a high level of activity and energy is desirable. Cool colors are more appropriate when the goal is to have consumers feel calm or spend time deliberating. For instance, Apple's modernistic stores are decorated in white, black, tan, and grey to provide a clean, uncluttered environment for showcasing high-tech products to shoppers.[92]

Researchers examining how lighting influences mood have found that brighter in-store lighting tends to increase the extent to which shoppers examine and handle merchandise.[93] Brighter lighting does not, however, increase the amount of time con-sumers spend shopping or the number of purchases they make. A salesperson's mood can influence consumers as well. Consumers in a bad mood are likely to feel worse and downgrade their judgments of the product being sold when they interact with salespeople who seem to be unhappy (unless the decision is so important that they are motivated to shake off their bad mood).[94]

HOW AFFECTIVE ATTITUDES ARE INFLUENCED

When consumers apply little processing effort and form attitudes based on feelings, the same three factors that influence cognitive reasoning also influence affective attitudes: the communication source, the message, and the context. Again, these factors are based on low-effort processes such as mere exposure, classical conditioning, A_{ad}, and mood.

Communication Source

Under conditions of low effort, two factors play a major role in determining whether or not the communication source evokes favorable affective reactions: its physical attractiveness and its likability. These two factors help to explain why marketers like to feature celebrities in ads.

Attractive Sources

Many ads feature attractive models, spokespersons, or celebrities, reflecting the long-held belief that beauty sells—especially in the beauty business. Research studies in a number of nations gener-ally support this notion. One study in Romania found that attractive models in beauty ads stimu-lated positive ad and product evaluations, but mixed self-judgments. Yet, after a two-week trial of a product advertised by attractive models, these consumers experienced positive self-judgments.[95] When consumers' motivation to process an advertised message is low, attractive sources enhance the favorability of consumers' A_b regardless of whether the message arguments are strong or weak.[96] Consumers also rate ads with attractive models as more appealing, eye-catching, and inter-esting than ads with unattractive models. These ratings may affect consumers' attitudes toward the products these models sponsor.[97]

Moreover, attractiveness can have beneficial effects on advertiser believability and actual pur-chase.[98] These effects can occur for both male and female models (consumers are more strongly attracted to models of the opposite sex) and have been found to operate for direct-mail responses, point-of-purchase displays, and personal-selling interactions.[99] Race may be an important factor

Exhibit 6.6

Influence of Communication Source

Companies use popular movie stars or celebrities like Angelina Jolie to generate positive feelings toward the ad and the product.

A single journey can change the course of a life.
Cambodia, May 2011.

Follow Angelina Jolie on louisvuittonjourneys.com

LOUIS VUITTON

Image Courtesy of The Advertising Archives

as well.[100] One study showed that African American consumers who identified strongly with African American culture responded more favorably to ads with African American models. Attractive sources make a difference in personal selling too. In one study, consumers had more positive attitudes and stronger buying intentions when attractive salespeople tried to persuade than when unattractive salespeople were involved.[101]

Note that in the context of high affective involvement, attractive sources directly influence brand-based attitudes because the sources are directly relevant to the product being considered (perfume, fashion, lingerie, etc.) and are thus a central part of the message. In the context of low-effort processing, attractive sources serve as a peripheral cue used to increase situational involvement and to generate a positive A_{ad}.

Likable Sources

The likability of the source can influence affective attitudes.[102] For instance, the Paris-based luxury goods company Louis Vuitton has found Angelina Jolie to be a likable and attractive endorser in international ads for its upscale luggage (see Exhibit 6.6).[103] Consumers also have more favorable attitudes toward brands that use likable celebrity voice-overs.[104] Likable sources may serve as unconditioned stimuli, create a positive mood that affects consumers' evaluations of the ad or brand, and make consumers feel more positive about the endorsed product. Online ads in which consumers assume an avatar to interact virtually with the product can lead to more positive A_b and purchase intentions because consumers feel positive about the endorser (themselves).[105] Sometimes, the source can be physically unattractive but have features or a personality that consumers like. We tend to like people of average looks because they are more similar to ourselves and we can relate to them. In addition, disabled people are effective, likable models in ads for the U.K. department store Debenhams because marketers want to represent diversity and because consumers admire courageous individuals.[106]

Celebrity Sources

Physical attractiveness and likability explain why celebrities and well-known cartoon characters are among the most widely used sources. In this case, the presence of celebrities essentially increases the likelihood that consumers will like the ad (A_{ad}). In particular, celebrity sources can be effective when they are related to the offering (the match-up hypothesis).[107] Teenage consumers find athletes to be especially influential endorsers: The sports stars stimulate discussion about the brand and encourage brand loyalty.[108]

Spokescharacters of long tenure sometimes need makeovers to remain attractive to contemporary eyes. That's why Planters, a Kraft Foods brand, gave its Mr. Peanut character a retro look for nostalgic appeal and hired actor Robert Downey, Jr., as the character's first voice.[109] Spokescharacters may engender trust even if they are not directly relevant to the advertised product; trust, in turn, influences A_b.[110] Spokescharacters may be most effective in ads for hedonic services such as restaurants.[111]

Nonprofit organizations also use celebrities to attract attention and influence attitudes. Tennis champion Novak Djokovic and other celebrity endorsers for UNICEF "are of huge value," says the nonprofit's head of celebrity relations. "When a celebrity talks, people listen; there is no better messenger."[112] Using a celebrity endorser entails some risk because the spokesperson might become ill, break the law, or have another problem that could put the brand in a negative light. Yet research shows that a company can actually enhance its reputation by associating with an endorser who is perceived by consumers as having little blame for a problem (such as falling ill).[113]

The Message

Just as the source can influence consumers' feelings and moods, so too can characteristics associated with the message. These message characteristics include pleasant pictures, music, humor, sex, emotional content, and context.

Pleasant Pictures

Marketers frequently use pleasant pictures to influence consumers' message processing. Visual stimuli can serve as a CS, affect consumers' mood, or make an ad likable by making it interesting. Research has generally supported the view that pleasant pictures can affect ad and A_b when they are processed peripherally, beyond the effect they have on consumers' beliefs about the product.[114] A picture of a sunset, for instance, can influence the choice of a soft drink.[115] As another example, because consumers associate visual art with luxury, the luxury image carries over to ads and packages featuring art.[116] Many advertisers use high-powered special effects rivaling those seen in movies for their TV and online ads. In fact, video ads are now the fastest-growing category of online advertising.[117]

Music

Music is frequently used as a communications tool by many domestic and international companies, including South Korea's Kia Motors, which has used LMFAO's *Rock Party Anthem* to advertise its Soul model in America.[118] Further, the use of music is progressing beyond the traditional use of the "jingle." Sometimes, the music ads become popular and drive album sales, as was the case with U2, whose album *How to Dismantle an Atomic Bomb* became a huge hit after the song "Vertigo" was featured in an iPod TV commercial.[119]

The popularity of music as a marketing device should not be surprising given that music has been shown to stimulate a variety of positive effects.[120] First, music can be an effective CS for a classical conditioning strategy. NBC and other brands use musical "tags" to serve as retrieval cues and add to the brand identity. Second, music can put the consumer in a positive mood and lead to the development of positive attitudes. Third, music can be effective in generating positive feelings such as happiness, serenity, excitement, and sentimentality. Fourth, background music in ads can stimulate emotional memories of experiences or situations.[121] If a song in an ad reminds you of your high school days or of an old romance, the emotions associated with these memories may transfer to an ad, a brand, a store, or other attitude object. Several studies have found that music can have a positive effect on purchase intentions.[122]

Exhibit 6.7 shows several musical characteristics and the emotional responses they may elicit. Whether or not music evokes a positive affective response depends on the music's structure. The style of music used and the product meanings it conveys can vary considerably across different cultures.[123] Marketers must therefore be careful to match their music to the desired affective responses.

Exhibit 6.7

Musical Characteristics for Producing Various Emotional Expressions

Research has pinpointed the specific effect that various aspects of music can have on feelings. As shown here, the mode, tempo, pitch, rhythm, harmony, and volume of music can influence whether individuals feel serious, sad, sentimental, serene, humorous, happy, excited, majestic, or frightened.

Musical Element	Emotional Expression								
	Serious	**Sad**	**Sentimental**	**Serene**	**Humorous**	**Happy**	**Exciting**	**Majestic**	**Frightening**
MODE	Major	Minor	Minor	Major	Major	Major	Major	Major	Minor
TEMPO	Slow	Slow	Slow	Slow	Fast	Fast	Fast	Medium	Slow
PITCH	Low	Low	Medium	Medium	High	High	Medium	Medium	Low
RHYTHM	Firm	Firm	Flowing	Flowing	Flowing	Flowing	Uneven	Firm	Uneven
HARMONY	Consonant	Dissonant	Consonant	Consonant	Consonant	Consonant	Dissonant	Dissonant	Dissonant
VOLUME	Medium	Soft	Soft	Soft	Medium	Medium	Loud	Loud	Varied

Source: Gordon C. Bruner, "Music, Mood, and Marketing," *Journal of Marketing,* October 1990, p. 100. Reprinted by permission.

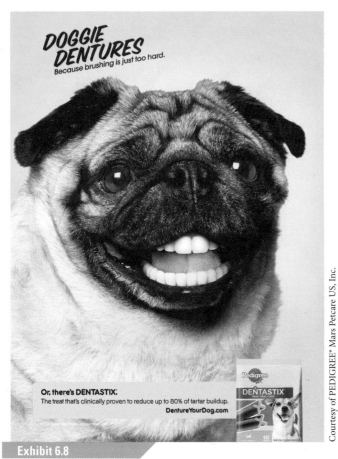

DOGGIE DENTURES
Because brushing is just too hard.

Or, there's DENTASTIX.
The treat that's clinically proven to reduce up to 80% of tartar buildup.
DentureYourDog.com

Pedigree
DENTASTIX
ORAL CARE

Courtesy of PEDIGREE® Mars Petcare US, Inc.

Exhibit 6.8

Humor in Advertising

Humor is a widely used technique in advertising.

Humor

An ad can use humor in many different ways, including puns, understatements, jokes, ludicrous situations, satire, and irony. Humor is common in TV advertising: 24 to 42 percent of all commercials contain some form of humor.[124] Although not as widespread in other media as in TV, use of humor is nevertheless extensive, particularly in radio.[125] The popularity of humor as a message device is not surprising because it works, increasing consumers' liking of the ad and the brand (see Exhibit 6.8).[126]

Humor appears to be more appropriate for low-involvement offerings in which generating positive feelings about the ad is critical.[127] Unless humor is tied or related to the offering, however, consumers will only pay attention to the humor and ignore the brand.[128] In fact, consumers will have higher recall of an ad when the humor is strong and relates to the message.[129] Consumers who feel the need to seek out amusement and wittiness will develop more favorable attitudes toward humorous ads—and may have less favorable attitudes toward ads with lower levels of humorous content.[130]

How consumers react during a TV ad affects their evaluations of the message as well. Consumers in one study rated TV ads as more humorous when the ad created surprise followed by a humorous response.[131] TV and online ads depicting comedic violence stimulate greater involvement with the message and greater likability. Although these ads do not affect A_b, they do generate buzz and have high pass-along rates, which is why many Super Bowl ads that feature this type of humor go "viral" and gain widespread Internet exposure.[132]

Marketing Implications

Humor tends to work best on TV and radio because these media allow for greater expressiveness than do other media.[133] For example, the Boston Bruins hockey team airs funny commercials instead of the more serious sports-themed ads that most teams favor, in order to give the brand a distinct personality.[134] However, humor is more effective with certain audiences than with others. In particular, younger, more educated males tend to respond most positively—apparently because aggressive and sexual types of humor appear more frequently than other types of humor, and men enjoy this type of humor more than women do.[135] Also, humor appears to be more effective for consumers who have either a lower need for cognition or a positive attitude toward the advertised brand.[136]

Finally, humor can be used effectively throughout the world. One study examined humorous ads from Germany, South Korea, Thailand, and the United States and found that most humorous ads in all four countries contained the same basic structure—contrasts between expected/possible and unexpected/impossible events.[137] However, ads in Korea and Thailand tended to emphasize humor related to group behavior and unequal status relationships, whereas ads in the other two countries focused the humor on individuals with equal status. In all four countries, humor was more likely to be used for marketing pleasure-oriented products. In addition, not all countries appear to employ humor more often for low-involvement products than for high-involvement ones. German and Thai ads, for example, used humor equally for both types of products, and U.K. firms tend to use humorous ads more than U.S. firms do.[138] Humor is most common in U.S. ads for foods and beverages. In China, however, humor is most prevalent in consumer electronics ads, while in France, humor is most prevalent in ads for services (see Exhibit 6.9).[139] Finally, research finds that the effect of humor varies from culture to culture, depending on the way humor is employed in the ad and the cultural orientation of the consumer.[140]

Exhibit 6.9

Humor in U.S., Chinese, and French Advertising: Top Five Product Categories

Country	Product Categories
United States	1. Food and beverages
	2. Automobiles
	3. Services
	4. Medicine
	5. Beauty and personal care
China	1. Consumer electronics
	2. Automobiles
	3. Services
	4. Household appliances
	5. Beauty and personal care
France	1. Services
	2. Food and beverages
	3. Automobiles
	4. Household appliances
	5. Consumer electronics

Source: Adapted from Michel Laroche, Marcelo Vinhal Nepomuceno, Liang Huang, and Marie-Odile Richard, "What's So Funny?" *Journal of Advertising Research* 51, no. 2 (2011): Table 4, p. 409.

Sex

Sex as a communication technique appears in two major forms: sexual suggestiveness and nudity. Sexual suggestiveness involves situations that either portray or imply sexual themes or romance. Another use of sex is through nudity or partial nudity, a technique often used by brands in the fragrance industry.[141] Research shows that consumers prefer mildly provocative ads and that such ads can even be effective in promoting social causes that have some connection to sex (match-up hypothesis).[142] Men tend to have a generally positive attitude toward an ad with sexual cues. Women, however, tend to dislike such ads but soften their attitudes when relationship commitment is involved.[143] Further, men who are exposed to sexual cues in ads exhibit more impulsive behavior and are more likely to buy or consume right away rather than waiting.[144]

Although the percentage of ads with sexual overtones has not changed over the years, the type of sex appeal depicted has. From 1964 to 1984, the use of sex in the United States became more overt and blatant.[145] As the country became more conservative in the late 1980s, ads became more playful and subtler—suggestive rather than blunt.[146] In recent years, public response and regulatory scrutiny have prompted some advertisers to tone down their use of sexual references and imagery in traditional advertising.[147] At the same time, some advertisers (like Go Daddy, the Internet hosting service) have a strategy of airing a slightly risqué TV commercial as a teaser, to attract viewers for a sexier ad posted directly on the brand website. "We start with an edgy TV ad and have a much edgier Internet-only version," explains Go Daddy's CEO. "The formula works for us. It gets people to our website."[148]

Marketing Implications

Research on sexual themes in messages suggests that they can be effective in several ways. Sexual messages attract the consumer's attention[149] and can evoke emotional responses such as arousal, excitement, or even lust, which in turn can affect consumers' moods and their attitudes toward the ad and the brand.[150] Funny ads featuring sexy women drawn to men wearing Axe brand body spray have been quite effective for Unilever.[151]

For some consumers, however, sexual messages can create negative feelings such as embarrassment, disgust, or uneasiness, any of which would have a negative effect. In particular, women are more likely to react negatively to ads with sexy female models.[152] Men are much more likely than women to buy a product featured in an ad with sexual content. Yet, 61 percent of the respondents in one study said they would be less likely to buy products advertised with sexual imagery. In this research, 53 percent of the respondents preferred love imagery over sex imagery in advertising.[153]

One survey indicated that 84 percent of females and 72 percent of males believe that TV ads place too much emphasis on sex. In another survey, 49 percent said they have been embarrassed in front of friends or family by sexy TV ads, and 47 percent indicated they would not buy a product if they found an ad offensive.[154] The lesson for marketers is that sexual themes should be used carefully and not be demeaning, sexist, or offensive.

Whether consumers will have a positive or negative reaction to a sexual ad often depends on whether the sexual content is appropriate for the product/service. One study found that using a seductive model to sell body oil was very appealing, but having a nude model endorse a ratchet set was not.[155] Thus, sexual themes would be relevant for products such as perfume, cologne, suntan lotion, and lingerie but inappropriate for tools, computers, and household cleaners.

Finally, consumer reaction to sexual messages varies from culture to culture. In some societies, such as in Europe, sexual attitudes are fairly open, and the use of sex in advertising is more widespread than it is in other countries. German and Thai TV commercials typically show more nudity than U.S. and Chinese commercials, for example.[156] In areas where attitudes are more conservative (such as Muslim and some Asian countries), the use of sex is much more restricted. Showing intimacy and kissing, as many U.S. ads do, would be inappropriate and even offensive in these cultures. Consumers in different countries reacted differently to a public service ad for breast cancer awareness in which men admired an attractive woman wearing a sun-dress while an announcer stated, "If only women paid as much attention to their breasts as men do." Japanese consumers appreciated the humor, but French consumers disliked the sexual overtones and light treatment of a serious problem.[157]

Emotional Content

Marketers can plan communications to accommodate or enhance consumers' existing MAO and processing effort in the presence of cognitive attitudes. The same holds true for affective attitudes, which is where emotionally involving messages come into play. Note that emotional appeals can be concrete (linked to a specific experience or emotion, such as the joy of winning a race) or abstract (less specific, such as feeling hopeful). Concrete emotional appeals are more effective in stimulating short-term behavioral intentions, whereas abstract emotional appeals are more effective in stimulating long-term intentions.[158]

Transformational advertising Ads that try to increase emotional involvement with the product or service.

One special type of emotional message is called **transformational advertising**.[159] The goal of a transformational ad is to associate the experience of using the product with a unique set of psychological characteristics. These ads try to increase emotional involvement by making the use of the product or service a warmer, more exciting, more pleasing, and richer experience as opposed to the approach taken by informational ads, which only present factual information. Coca-Cola, for example, uses transformational advertising to convey that "Coke is a part of the pleasure of everyday life, the pleasure of aliveness, relaxation, and being connected," says the company's chief marketing officer. Diet Coke is also taking this approach with ads targeting consumers in their 20s. "We've learned the brand needs to have wit, self-deprecation, and optimism," explains a Coke marketing executive.[160]

Dramas Ads with characters, a plot, and a story.

Dramas can also increase emotional involvement in a message. A drama message has characters, a plot, and a story about the use of the product or service.[161] The aim is to involve consumers emotionally and influence positive attitudes through both sympathy and empathy.[162] Bertolli did this for its frozen Italian entrées by using TV commercials and an online-only advertising miniseries about three celebrities who travel to Italy to learn the secrets of authentic Italian cooking from contemporary culinary experts. Although the point of frozen food is convenience, Bertolli is differentiating its products on the basis of quality, not just speed of preparation.[163]

Message Context

The program or editorial context in which an ad appears can affect consumers' evaluation of the message. First, ads embedded in a happy TV program may be evaluated more positively than those in sad programs, especially if the ads are emotional.[164] Similarly, how well we like the program can affect our feelings about the ad and the brand.[165] One explanation of this reaction is that the programs influence us to process information in a manner consistent with our mood. Or, according to the excitation transfer hypothesis, we may mistakenly attribute to the ad our feelings about the TV program.[166]

One note of caution: A TV program can become too arousing and can therefore distract viewers from the ads. In an interesting study that compared consumers' reactions to ads broadcast during the Super Bowl, ad responses in the winning city were inhibited in contrast to those in the losing and neutral cities.[167] Another study shows that placing ads in violent programs can inhibit processing and ad recall.[168]

SUMMARY

Marketers can use a variety of techniques to change consumers' attitudes when motivation, ability, and opportunity (MAO) are low and consumers use little effort to process information, make decisions, or engage in behavior. Often consumers form attitudes unconsciously, without being aware of how or why they have done so. Two unconscious influences in low-effort situations are thin-slice judgments and body feedback. When attitudes of low MAO consumers are based on cognitive processing, the message should affect their beliefs, which may be formed by simple inferences, attributions, or heuristics. Marketers can also affect the salience, strength, or favorability of consumers' beliefs on which attitudes are based. Source credibility, information consistent with the offering category, the number of message arguments, simple arguments, and repetition can all influence beliefs.

According to the mere exposure effect, when effort (MAO) is low, consumers' attitudes toward an offering become more favorable as consumers become more familiar with it. Classical conditioning predicts that consumers' attitudes toward an offering (the conditioned stimulus) are enhanced when it is repeatedly paired with a stimulus (the unconditioned stimulus) that evokes a positive response (the unconditioned response). Evaluative conditioning, a special case of classical conditioning, produces an emotional response (positive or negative) by repeatedly pairing a conditioned stimulus and an emotionally charged unconditioned stimulus. Attitude toward the ad is also a factor: If consumers like an ad, these positive feelings may be transferred to the brand. Consumers' moods and their tendency to evaluate an offering in accordance with their moods can also affect their attitudes.

Finally, marketers can use marketing communications to induce favorable attitudes based on affective processes when consumers' motivation, ability, opportunity, and effort are low. Characteristics of the source (attractiveness, likability), the message (attractive pictures, pleasant music, humor, sex, emotionally involving messages), and the context (repetition, program or editorial context) can all influence affective attitudes.

Questions for Review and Discussion

1. How can unconscious influences affect consumer attitudes and behavior in low-effort situations?

2. What role do source, message, context, and repetition play in influencing consumers' cognitive attitudes in low-effort situations?

3. What is the mere exposure effect, and why is it important to consumers' affective reactions?

4. How do classical conditioning and evaluative conditioning apply to consumers' attitudes when processing effort is low?

5. Explain the dual-mediation hypothesis. What are the implications for affecting consumers' brand attitudes?

6. In low-effort situations, what characteristics of the message influence consumers' affective response?

7. What are the advantages and disadvantages of featuring celebrities in advertising messages?

The Old Spice Man Spices Up Brand Marketing

When Isaiah Mustafa appeared in a 2010 Super Bowl commercial with a towel wrapped around his waist and a bottle of Old Spice body wash in one hand, he kicked off a long-running viral marketing campaign that has rejuvenated the brand's sales. Mustafa, a former NFL wide receiver, smiled into the camera and addressed women viewers, saying he was "the man your man could smell like" if they used Old Spice. The combination of his wryly funny lines, winning delivery, and buff physique made the commercial an instant YouTube hit. Suddenly, Old Spice, a pre–World War II brand that zoomed to prominence in the 1960s and 1970s, was an overnight social media sensation, with Facebook fans, Twitter comments, and consumer-generated spoof videos stirring up conversation around the world. The Old Spice Man campaign, created by ad agency Wieden & Kennedy for brand owner Procter & Gamble, had successfully added a relevancy and an affective appeal that was attracting and entertaining a younger audience than the brand's traditional customer base—and boosting sales significantly.

As soon as the first Isaiah Mustafa ad went viral, the agency followed up with a second commercial in the same humorous vein, again featuring the bare-chested Old Spice Man. Again, public response was so enthusiastic that the campaign geared up for a new and unprecedented socialmedia blitz. This time, Old Spice invited users of Twitter, Reddit, and Digg—including celebrities and athletes such as Ellen DeGeneres, Demi Moore, and Apolo Ohno—to submit questions for the Old Spice Man to answer. As hundreds of questions poured in, consumers voted for the ones they wanted to see answered. Next, in a marathon three-day studio session, the agency scripted and Mustafa starred in 186 brief YouTube videos responding to individual questioners in typical wry style. When Kevin Rose of Digg.com tweeted that he wasn't feeling well, the Old Spice Man answered with a "get well" video that Rose immediately mentioned to his more than 1 million Twitter followers.

The concentrated barrage of targeted, personalized tweets and entertaining videos stirred up enormous positive word of mouth among consumers. Just as important, Old Spice was the subject of many stories on TV and radio, in the blogosphere, in newspapers and magazines, and seemingly everywhere on the Internet where news commentators posted articles, podcasts, or videos. All the media coverage (which the brand did not pay for) fueled even more consumer interest in Old Spice. Within days of the Old Spice Man's answer videos appearing online, the brand's Facebook page collected more than 600,000 "likes" and the online videos were viewed more than 7 million times.

Procter & Gamble supported the social media campaign with discount coupons and other promotional efforts that reinforced brand awareness and offered an incentive to buy and try Old Spice products right away. Old Spice sales quickly skyrocketed, and the brand captured the market leader position, despite competition from Unilever's Axe, Beiersdorf's Nivea, and Henkel's Right Guard brands.

A year later, Procter & Gamble launched a new chapter in the Old Spice Man story. This time, Fabio—the model and star of many romance novel covers—appeared in online videos challenging Isaiah Mustafa for the title of Old Spice Man. This tongue-in-cheek mano a mano competition consisted of 39 back-and-forth videos that drew millions of viewers and tens of thousands of social media comments. Consumers clicked to vote for the Old Spice Man they preferred, and after several days of hectic and humorous exchanges, Mustafa and Fabio appeared in one final video announcing that Mustafa had retained his title. The big winner was, of course, Old Spice, which gained even more brand awareness and enjoyed higher sales. Now Procter & Gamble is taking the Old Spice Man campaign on the road to universities and cities where consumers can try branded products and have their photos taken in poses reminiscent of the original Old Spice Man commercial.[169]

CASE QUESTIONS

1. How is Old Spice using evaluative conditioning to influence consumers' affective attitudes? Identify the conditioned stimulus, unconditioned stimulus, unconditioned response, and conditioned response in this situation.

2. What role does the dual-mediation hypothesis play in the Old Spice Man's marketing success?

3. What aspects of the communication source are involved in influencing affective attitudes toward Old Spice?

4. Do you think consumers will maintain a positive attitude toward Old Spice if the Old Spice Man campaign suspends messages for more than one or two months? Explain your answer.

ENDNOTES

1. Jed Singer, "Facebook: Top 20 Snack Brands," *Social Media Week*, June 8–9, 2011, http://socialmediaweek.org; Brian Quinton, "Frito-Lay Thanks Fans for Record 'Likes' After NYC Live Event," *Promo Magazine*, May 4, 2011, http://promomagazine.com; Jennifer Horn, "Cadbury Skips the QR Code," *Media in Canada*, August 23, 2011, http://mediaincanada.com; and Stuart Elliott, "Marketer Puts Its 'Chips' on Time Square," *New York Times*, April 10, 2011, www.times.com.

2. Norbert Schwarz, "Attitude Research: Between Ockham's Razor and the Fundamental Attribution Error," *Journal of Consumer Research* 33, no. 1, 2006, pp. 19–21.

3. Richard E. Petty and John T. Cacioppo, *Attitudes and Persuasion: Classic and Contemporary Approaches* (Dubuque, IA: William C. Brown, 1981); and Richard E. Petty, John T. Cacioppo, and David Schumann, "Central and Peripheral Routes to Advertising Effectiveness: The Moderating Role of Involvement," *Journal of Consumer Research*, September 1983, pp. 135–146.

4. Jaideep Sengupta, Ronald C. Goodstein, and David S. Boninger, "All Cues Are Not Created Equal: Obtaining Attitude Persistence under Low Involvement Conditions," *Journal of Consumer Research*, March 1997, pp. 315–361.

5. Ap Dijksterhuis, Pamela K. Smith, Rick B. Van Baaren, and Daniel H. J. Wigboldus, "The Unconscious Consumer: Effects of Environment on Consumer Behavior," *Journal of Consumer Psychology* 15, no. 3, 2005, pp. 193–202.

6. Minjung Koo and Ayelet Fishbach, "A Silver Lining of Standing in Line," *Journal of Marketing Research*, August 2010, pp. 713–724.

7. Nalini Ambady, Mary Ann Krabbenhoft, and Daniel Hogan, "The 30-Sec Sale: Using Thin-Slice Judgments to Evaluate Sales Effectiveness," *Journal of Consumer Psychology* 16, no. 1, 2006, pp. 4–13.

8. Jan R. Landwehr, Ann L. McGill, and Andreas Herrmann, "It's Got the Look: The Effect of Friendly and Aggressive 'Facial' Expressions on Product Liking and Sales," *Journal of Marketing*, May 2011, pp. 132–146.

9. Frank R. Kardes, "When Should Consumers and Managers Trust Their Intuition?" *Journal of Consumer Psychology* 16, no. 1, 2006, pp. 20–24.

10. Jens Förster, "How Body Feedback Influences Consumers' Evaluation of Products," *Journal of Consumer Psychology* 14, no. 4, 2004, pp. 416–426. See also Ronald S. Friedman and Jens Förster, "The Effects of Approach and Avoidance Motor Actions on the Elements of Creative Insight," *Journal of Personality and Social Psychology* 79, no. 4, 2000, pp. 477–492.

11. Iris W. Hung and Aparna A. Labroo, "From Firm Muscles to Firm Willpower," *Journal of Consumer Research*, April 2011, pp. 1046–1064.

12. Bruce Horovitz, "Baby Carrots Take on Junk Food with Hip Marketing Campaign," *USA Today*, September 3, 2010, www.usatoday.com.

13. Itamar Simonson, "In Defense of Consciousness: The Role of Conscious and Unconscious Inputs in Consumer Choice," *Journal of Consumer Psychology* 15, no. 3, 2005, pp. 211–217.

14. "Mazda3 Review: What the Auto Press Says," *U.S. News and World Report*, October 19, 2011, http://usnews.rankingsandreviews.com.

15. Gita V. Johar and Anne L. Roggeveen, "Changing False Beliefs from Repeated Advertising: The Role of Claim-Refutation Alignment," *Journal of Consumer Psychology* 17, no. 2, 2007, pp. 118–127.

16. Jennifer Edson Escalas and Mary Frances Luce, "Understanding the Effects of Process-Focused versus Outcome-Focused Thought in Response to Advertising," *Journal of Consumer Research* 13, no. 2, 2004, pp. 274–285.

17. Ronald C. Goodstein, "Category-Based Applications and Extensions in Advertising: Motivating More Extensive Ad Processing," *Journal of Consumer Research*, June 1993, pp. 87–99.

18. Valerie S. Folkes, "Recent Attribution Research in Consumer Behavior: A Review and New Directions," *Journal of Consumer Research*, March 1988, pp. 548–656.

19. Rosemary Feitelberg, "Maria Sharapova: Golden Girl," *WWD*, August 29, 2011, www.wwd.com; and Jean Folger, "Winning Celebrities and the Companies They Endorse," *San Francisco Chronicle*, August 22, 2011, www.sfgate.com.

20. Shelly Chaiken, "Heuristic versus Systematic Information Processing and the Use of Source versus Message Cues in Persuasion," *Journal of Personality and Social Psychology* 39, 1980, pp. 752–766. See also "The Heuristic Model of Persuasion," in eds. Mark P. Zanna, J. M. Olson, and C. P. Herman, *Social Influence: The Ontario Symposium*, vol. 5 (Hillsdale, N.J.: Lawrence Erlbaum, 1987), pp. 3–49.

21. Amna Kirmani, "Advertising Repetition as a Signal of Quality: If It's Advertised So Much, Something Must Be Wrong," *Journal of Advertising*, Fall 1997, pp. 77–86.

22. Joseph W. Alba and Howard Marmorstein, "The Effects of Frequency Knowledge on Consumer Decision Making," *Journal of Consumer Research*, June 1987, pp. 14–25.

23. Scott A. Hawkins and Stephen J. Hoch, "Low-Involvement Learning: Memory without Evaluation," *Journal of Consumer Research*, September 1992, pp. 212–225; and Lynn Hasher, David Goldstein, and Thomas Toppino, "Frequency and the Conference of Referential Validity," *Journal of Verbal Learning and Verbal Behavior*, February 1977, pp. 107–112.

24. S. Ratneshwar and Shelly Chaiken, "Comprehension's Role in Persuasion: The Case of Its Moderating Effect on the Persuasive Impact of Source Cues," *Journal of Consumer Research*, June 1991, pp. 52–62.

25. Barry Silverstein, "Kraft Whets Appetites for Flavored Water with Facebook Freebies, Sassy Gay Friend," *BrandChannel*, February 22, 2011, www.brandchannel.com.

26. Alice M. Tybout, Brian Sternthal, Prashant Malaviya, Georgios A. Bakamitsos, and Se-Bum Park, "Information Accessibility as a Moderator of Judgments: The Role of Content versus Retrieval Ease," *Journal of Consumer Research* 32, no. 1, 2005, pp. 76–85.

27. Nancy Spears, "On the Use of Time Expressions in Promoting Product Benefits," *Journal of Advertising*, Summer 2003, pp. 33–44.

28. Jennifer Edson Escalas, "Self-Referencing and Persuasion: Narrative Transportation versus Analytical Elaboration," *Journal of Consumer Research* 33, no. 4, 2007, pp. 421–429.

29. Patricia M. West, Joel Huber, and Kyeong Sam Min, "Altering Experienced Utility: The Impact of Story Writing and Self-Referencing on Preferences," *Journal of Consumer Research* 31, no. 3, 2004, pp. 623–630; Robert E. Burnkrant and H. Rao Unnava, "Effects of Self-Referencing on Persuasion," *Journal of Consumer Research*, June 1995, pp. 17–26; Sharon Shavitt and Timothy C. Brock, "Self-Relevant Responses in Commercial Persuasion," in eds. Jerry C. Olson and Keith Sentis, *Advertising and Consumer Psychology* (New York: Praeger, 1986), pp. 149–171; Kathleen Debevec and Jean B. Romeo, "Self-Referent Processing in Perceptions of Verbal and Visual Commercial Information," *Journal of Consumer Psychology* 1, no. 1, 1992, pp. 83–102; and Joan Myers-Levy and Laura A. Peracchio, "Moderators of the Impact of Self-Reference on Persuasion," *Journal of Consumer Research*, March 1996, pp. 408–423.

30. Darrel D. Muehling and Vincent J. Pascal, "An Empirical Investigation of the Differential Effects of Personal, Historical, and Non-Nostalgic Advertising on Consumer Responses," *Journal of Advertising*, Summer 2011, pp. 107–122.

31. Daniel J. Howard, Charles Gengler, and Ambuj Jain, "What's in a Name? A Complimentary Means of Persuasion," *Journal of Consumer Research*, September 1995, pp. 200–211.

32. Jennifer L. Aaker, "The Malleable Self: The Role of Self-Expression in Persuasion," *Journal of Marketing Research* 36, February 1999, pp. 45–57.

33. "New Balance Launches Ad Campaign," *Boston Globe*, March 1, 2011, www.boston.com; and Jenn Abelson, "Sneaker Company Taps Chief," *Boston Globe*, April 18, 2007, p. F1.

34. Anne M. Brumbaugh, "Source and Nonsource Cues in Advertising and Their Effects on the Activation of Cultural and Subcultural Knowledge on the Route to Persuasion," *Journal of Consumer Research*, September 2002, pp. 258–269.

35. Robert E. Burnkrant and Daniel J. Howard, "Effects of the Use of Introductory Rhetorical Questions versus Statements on Information Processing," *Journal of Personality and Social Psychology*, December 1984, pp. 1218–1230; and James M. Munch, Gregory W. Boller, and John L. Swazy, "The Effects of Argument Structure and Affective Tagging on Product Attitude Formation," *Journal of Consumer Research*, September 1993, pp. 294–302.

36. Krystal Peak, "Kodak Offers Free Printing of Facebook Pictures," *VatorNews*, October 13, 2011, http://vator.tv/n/202b.

37. Rohini Ahluwalia and Robert E. Burnkrant, "Answering Questions about Questions: A Persuasion Knowledge Perspective for Understanding the Effects of Rhetorical Questions," *Journal of Consumer Research*, June 2004, pp. 26–42.

38. Russell H. Fazio, Paul M. Herr, and Martha C. Powell, "On the Development and Strength of Category-Brand Associations in Memory: The Case of Mystery Ads," *Journal of Consumer Psychology* 1, no. 1, 1992, pp. 1–14.

39. Liz C. Wang, Julie Baker, Judy A. Wagner, and Kirk Wakefield, "Can a Retail Website Be Social?" *Journal of Marketing*, July 2007, pp. 143–157.

40. David A. Griffin and Qimei Chen, "The Influence of Virtual Direct Experience (VDE) on On-Line Ad Message Effectiveness," *Journal of Advertising*, Spring 2004, pp. 55–68.

41. Hiawatha Bray, "'Advergames' Spark Concerns of Kids Being Targeted," *Boston Globe*, July 30, 2004, www.bostonglobe.com.

42. Joseph W. Alba, J. Wesley Hutchinson, and John G. Lynch, "Memory and Decision Making," in eds. Thomas S. Robertson and Harold H. Kassarjian, *Handbook of Consumer Behavior* (Englewood Cliffs, N.J.: Prentice-Hall, 1991).

43. Chris Janiszewski and Tom Meyvis, "Effects of Brand Logo Complexity, Repetition, and Spacing on Processing Fluency and Judgment," *Journal of Consumer Research*, June 2001, pp. 18–32; and H. Rao Unnava and Robert E. Burnkrant, "Effects of Repeating Varied Ad Executions on Brand Name Memory," *Journal of Marketing Research*, November 1991, pp. 406–416.

44. Ida E. Berger and Andrew A. Mitchell, "The Effect of Attitude Accessibility, Attitude Confidence, and the Attitude–Behavior Relationship," *Journal of Consumer Research*, December 1989, pp. 269–279.

45. Prashant Malaviya and Brian Sternthal, "The Persuasive Impact of Message Spacing," *Journal of Consumer Psychology* 6, no. 3, 1997, pp. 233–256.

46. Patrick De Pelsmacker, Maggie Geuens, and Pascal Anckaert, "Media Context and Advertising Effectiveness: The Role of Context Appreciation and Context/Ad Similarity," *Journal of Advertising*, September 2002, pp. 49–61.

47. Marjolein Moorman, Peter C. Neijens, and Edith G. Smit, "The Effects of Magazine-Induced Psychological Responses and Thematic Congruence on Memory and Attitude toward the Life in a Real-Life Setting," *Journal of Advertising*, Winter 2002, pp. 27–40.

48. See, for instance, Xiang Fang, Surendra Singh, and Rohini Ahluwalia, "An Examination of Different Explanations for the Mere Exposure Effect," *Journal of Consumer Research* 34, no. 1, 2007, pp. 99–103.

49. Carl Obermiller, "Varieties of Mere Exposure: The Effects of Processing Style and Repetition in Affective Response," *Journal of Consumer Research*, June 1985, pp. 17–30.

50. Arno Rethans, John L. Swazy, and Lawrence J. Marks, "The Effects of Television Commercial Repetition, Receiver Knowledge, and Commercial Length," *Journal of Marketing Research*, February 1986, pp. 50–61.

51. William E. Baker, "When Can Affective Conditioning and Mere Exposure Directly Influence Brand Choice?" *Journal of Advertising* 28, no. 4, Winter 1999, pp. 31–46.

52. Chris Janiszewski and Tom Meyvis, "Effects of Brand Logo Complexity, Repetition, and Spacing on Processing Fluency and Judgment," *Journal of Consumer Research* 28, June 2001, pp. 18–32.

53. Zak Stambor, "Facebook Looks to Lure Small Business Advertisers," *Internet Retailer*, September 26, 2011, www.internetretailer.com.

54. Herbert Krugman, "Why Three Exposures May Be Enough," *Journal of Advertising Research*, December 1972, pp. 11–14.

55. George E. Belch, "The Effects of Television Commercial Repetition on Cognitive Response and Message Acceptance," *Journal of Consumer Research*, June 1982, pp. 56–65.

56. Margaret Henderson Blair, "An Empirical Investigation of Advertising Wearin and Wearout," *Journal of Advertising Research* 40, November 2000, p. 95.

57. Merel van Diepen, Bas Donkers, and Philip Hans Franses, "Does Irritation Induced by Charitable Mailings Reduce Donations?" *International Journal of Research in Marketing* 26, 2009, pp. 180–188.

58. Margaret C. Campbell and Kevin Lane Keller, "Brand Familiarity and Advertising Repetition Effects," *Journal of Consumer Research*, September 2003, pp. 292–304.

59. Deborah J. MacInnis, Ambar G. Rao, and Allen M. Weiss, "Assessing When Increased Media Weight of Real-World Advertisements Helps Sales," *Journal of Marketing Research*, November 2002, pp. 391–407.

60. Christie L. Nordhielm, "The Influence of Level of Processing on Advertising Repetition Effects," *Journal of Consumer Research*, December 2002, pp. 371–373.

61. Marian Burke and Julie A. Edell, "Ad Reactions over Time," *Journal of Consumer Research*, June 1986, pp. 114–118; and Curtis P. Haugtvedt, David W. Schumann, Wendy L. Schneier, and Wendy L. Warren, "Advertising Repetition and Variation Strategies," *Journal of Consumer Research*, June 1994, pp. 176–189.

62. Ishbel Macleod, "Tourism Ireland Begin Filming for Three-Year Global Advertising Campaign," *The Drum (UK)*, October 21, 2011, http://thedrum.co.uk.

63. Prashant Malaviya, "The Moderating Influence of Advertising Context on Ad Repetition Effects: The Role of Amount and Type of Elaboration," *Journal of Consumer Research* 34, no. 1, 2007, pp. 32–40.

64. Steven Sweldens, Stijn M. J. van Osselaer, and Chris Janiszewski, "Evaluative Conditioning Procedures and the Resilience of Conditioned Brand Attitudes," *Journal of Consumer Research*, October 2010, pp. 473-489.

65. "Graphic Warnings on Cigarette Packets Do Help Smokers to Kick the Habit," *Daily Mail Reporter (UK)*, May 27, 2011, www.dailymail.co.uk.

66. Gerald J. Gorn, "The Effects of Music in Advertising on Choice Behavior: A Classical Conditioning Approach," *Journal of Marketing*, Winter 1982, pp. 94–101.

67. Calvin Bierley, Frances K. McSweeny, and Renee Vannieuwkerk, "Classical Conditioning of Preferences for Stimuli," *Journal of Consumer Research*, December 1985, pp. 316–323; James J. Kellaris and Anthony D. Cox, "The Effects of Background Music in Advertising," *Journal of Consumer Research*, June 1989, pp. 113–118; and Chris T. Allen and Thomas J. Madden, "A Closer Look at Classical Conditioning," *Journal of Consumer Research*, December 1985, pp. 301–315.

68. Bierley, McSweeny, and Vannieuwkerk, "Classical Conditioning of Preferences for Stimuli"; Elnora W. Stuart, Terence A. Shimp, and Randall W. Engle, "Classical Conditioning of Consumer Attitudes," *Journal of Consumer Research*, December 1987, pp. 334–349; Terence A. Shimp, Elnora W. Stuart, and Randall W. Engle, "A Program of Classical Conditioning Experiments Testing Variations in the Conditioned Stimulus and Context," *Journal of Consumer Research*, June 1991, pp. 1–12; and Chris T. Allen and Chris A. Janiszewski, "Assessing the Role of Contingency Awareness in Attitudinal Conditioning with Implications for Advertising Research," *Journal of Marketing Research*, February 1989, pp. 30–43.

69. Randi Priluck Grossman and Brian D. Till, "The Persistence of Classically Conditioned Brand Attitudes," *Journal of Advertising*, Spring 1998.

70. Sweldens, van Osselaer, and Janiszewski, "Evaluative Conditioning Procedures and the Resilience of Conditioned Brand Attitudes."

71. Gordy Pleyers, Olivier Corneille, Vincent Yzerbyt, and Olivier Luminet, "Evaluative Conditioning May Incur Attentional Costs," *American Psychological Association* 35, no. 2, 2009, pp. 279–285.

72. Michael McCarthy, "Under Armour's Derrick Williams Takes Aim at Nike," *USA Today*, July 22, 2011, www.usatoday.com; and Terence A. Shimp, "Neo-Pavlovian Conditioning and Its Implications for Consumer Theory and Research," in eds. Thomas S. Robertson and Harold H. Kassarjian, *Handbook of Consumer Behavior* (Englewood Cliffs, N.J.: Prentice-Hall, 1991), pp. 162–187.

73. Andrew Buncombe, "Bollywood Goldrush: India's Stars Get Ahead in Advertising," *Independent*, August 8, 2011, www.independent.co.uk.

74. Melanie A. Dempsey and Andrew A. Mitchell, "The Influence of Implicit Attitudes on Choice When Consumers Are Confronted with Conflicting Attribute Information," *Journal of Consumer Research*, December 2010, pp. 614–625.

75. Aparna A. Labroo and Suresh Ramanathan, "The Influence of Experience and Sequence of Conflicting Emotions on Ad Attitudes," *Journal of Consumer Research* 33, no. 4, 2007, pp. 523–528; Steven P. Brown and Douglas M. Stayman, "Antecedents and Consequences of Attitude toward the Ad: A Meta-analysis," *Journal of Consumer Research*, June 1993, pp. 34–51; Andrew A. Mitchell and Jerry C. Olson, "Are Product Attribute Beliefs the Only Mediator of Advertising Effects on Brand Attitudes?" *Journal of Marketing Research*, August 1981, pp. 318–322; Terence A. Shimp, "Attitude toward the Ad as a Mediator of Consumer Brand Choice," *Journal of Advertising* 10, no. 2, 1981, pp. 9–15; and Christian M. Derbaix, "The Impact of Affective Reactions on Attitudes toward the Advertisement and the Brand: A Step toward Ecological Validity," *Journal of Marketing Research*, November 1995, pp. 470–479.

76. Mitchell and Olson, "Are Product Attribute Beliefs the Only Mediator of Advertising Effects on Brand Attitudes?"

77. Srinivas Durvasula, J. Craig Andrews, Steven Lysonski, and Richard G. Netemeyer, "Assessing the Cross-National Applicability of Consumer Behavior Models: A Model of Attitude toward Advertising in General," *Journal of Consumer Research*, March 1993, pp. 626–636.

78. Russell I. Haley and Allan L. Baldinger, "The ARF Copy Research Validity Project," *Journal of Advertising Research*, April–May 1991, pp. 11–32.

79. Elizabeth S. Moore and Richard J. Lutz, "Children, Advertising, and Product Experiences: A Multimethod Inquiry," *Journal of Consumer Research* 27, June 2000, pp. 31–48; Scott B. MacKenzie, Richard J. Lutz, and George E. Belch, "The Role of Attitude toward the Ad as a Mediator of Advertising Effectiveness: A Test of Competing Explanations," *Journal of Marketing Research*, May 1986, pp. 130–143; Pamela M. Homer, "The Mediating Role of Attitude toward the Ad: Some Additional Evidence," *Journal of Marketing Research*, February 1990, pp. 78–86; and Brown and Stayman, "Antecedents and Consequences of Attitude toward the Ad."

80. E. J. Schultz, "A Tiger at 60," *Advertising Age*, August 29, 2011, www.adage.com.

81. Brown and Stayman, "Antecedents and Consequences of Attitude toward the Ad."

82. Marian Chapman Burke and Julie A. Edell, "Ad Reactions over Time: Capturing Changes in the Real World," *Journal of Consumer Research*, June 1986, pp. 114–118; and Amitava Chattopadhyay and Prakash Nedungadi, "Does Attitude toward the Ad Endure?" *Journal of Consumer Research*, June 1992, pp. 26–33.

83. Margaret G. Meloy, "Mood Driven Distortion of Product Information," *Journal of Consumer Research* 27, December 2000, pp. 345–359.

84. Michael J. Barone, Paul W. Miniard, and Jean B. Romeo, "The Influence of Positive Mood on Brand Extension Evaluations," *Journal of Consumer Research* 26, March 2000, pp. 386–400.

85. Anick Bosmans and Hans Baumgartner, "Goal-Relevant Emotional Information," *Journal of Consumer Research* 32, no. 3, 2005, pp. 424–434.

86. Rashmi Adaval, "Sometimes It Just Feels Right: The Differential Weighting of Affect-Consistent and Affect-Inconsistent Product Information," *Journal of Consumer Research* 28, June 2001, pp. 1–17.

87. Julie A. Edell and Marian Chapman Burke, "The Power of Feelings in Understanding Advertising Effects," *Journal of Consumer Research*, December 1987, pp. 421–433; Douglas M. Stayman and David A. Aaker, "Are All Effects of Ad-Induced Feelings Mediated by A$_{ad}$?" *Journal of Consumer Research*, December 1988, pp. 368–373; and Morris B. Holbrook and Rajeev Batra, "Assessing the Role of Emotions as Mediators of Consumer Responses to Advertising," *Journal of Consumer Research*, December 1987, pp. 404–420.

88. Rajeev Batra and Michael L. Ray, "Affective Responses Mediating Acceptance of Advertising," *Journal of Consumer Research*, September 1986, pp. 234–249.

89. David A. Aaker, Douglas M. Stayman, and Michael R. Hagerty, "Warmth in Advertising: Measurement, Impact, and Sequence Effects," *Journal of Consumer Research*, March 1986, pp. 365–381.

90. Ayn E. Crowley, "The Two-Dimension Impact of Color on Shopping," *Marketing Letters* 4, no. 1, 1993, pp. 59–69.

91. Joseph A. Bellizzi, Ayn E. Crowley, and Ronald W. Hasty, "The Effects of Color in Store Design," *Journal of Retailing*, Spring 1983, pp. 21–45.

92. Nick Bilton, "Bits Pics: Inside Apple's New Grand Central Store," *New York Times*, August 17, 2011, www.nytimes.com.

93. Charles S. Areni and David Kim, "The Influence of In-Store Lighting on Consumers' Examination of Merchandise in a Wine Store," *International Journal of Research in Marketing*, March 1994, pp. 117–125.

94. Nancy M. Puccinelli, "Putting Your Best Face Forward: The Impact of Customer Mood on Salesperson Evaluation," *Journal of Consumer Psychology* 16, no. 2, 2006, pp. 156–162.

95. Camelia C. Micu, Robin A. Coulter, and Linda L. Price, "How Product Trials Alters the Effects of Model Attractiveness," *Journal of Advertising*, September 2009, pp. 69–81.

96. Curt Haugtvedt, Richard E. Petty, John T. Cacioppo, and T. Steidley, "Personality and Ad Effectiveness: Exploring the Utility of Need for Cognition," in ed. Michael J. Houston, *Advances in Consumer Research*, vol. 15 (Provo, Utah: Association for Consumer Research, 1988), pp. 209–212.

97. Susan M. Petroshius and Kenneth E. Crocker, "An Empirical Analysis of Spokesperson Characteristics on Advertisement and Product Evaluations," *Journal of the Academy of Marketing Science*, Summer 1989, pp. 217–225; and Lynn R. Kahle and Pamela M. Homer, "Physical Attractiveness of the Celebrity Endorser," *Journal of Consumer Research*, March 1985, pp. 954–961.

98. Michael A. Kamins, "An Investigation into the 'Match-Up' Hypothesis in Celebrity Advertising," *Journal of Advertising* 19, no. 1, 1990, pp. 4–13: and Marjorie J. Caballero and Paul J. Solomon, "Effects of Model Attractiveness on Sales Response," *Journal of Advertising* 13, no. 1, 1984, pp. 17–23.

99. Lynn R. Kahle and Pamela M. Homer, "Physical Attractiveness of the Celebrity Endorser," *Journal of Consumer Research*, March 1985, pp. 954–961; Kathleen Debevec and Jerome B. Kernan, "More Evidence on the Effects of a Presenter's Physical Attractiveness," in ed. Thomas C. Kinnear, *Advances in Consumer Research*, vol. 11 (Provo, Utah: Association for Consumer Research, 1984), pp. 127–132; Marjorie J. Caballero and William M. Pride, "Selected Effects of Salesperson Sex and Attractiveness in Direct Mail Advertising," *Journal of Marketing*, January 1984, pp. 94–100; Shelly Chaiken, "Communicator Physical Attractiveness and Persuasion," *Journal of Personality and Social Psychology*, August 1979, pp. 1387–1397; and Peter H. Reingen and Jerome B. Kernan, "Social Perception and Interpersonal Influence," *Journal of Consumer Psychology* 2, no. 1, 1993, pp. 25–38.

100. Tommy E. Whittler and Joan Scattone Spira, "Model's Race: A Peripheral Cue in Advertising Messages?" *Journal of Consumer Psychology* 12, no. 4, 2002, pp. 291–301.

101. M. Reinhard, M. Messner, and S. Ludwig Sporer, "Explicit Persuasive Intent and Its Impact on Success at Persuasion—the Determining Roles of Attractiveness and Likeableness," *Journal of Consumer Psychology* 16, no. 3, 2006, pp. 249–259.

102. Yong-Soon Kang and Paul M. Herr, "Beauty and the Beholder: Toward an Integrative Model of Communication Source Effects," *Journal of Consumer Research* 33, no. 1, 2006, pp. 123–130; Richard E. Petty, H. Rao Unnava, and Alan J. Strathman, "Theories of Attitude Change," in eds. Thomas S. Robertson and Harold H. Kassarjian, *Handbook of Consumer Behavior* (Englewood Cliffs, N.J.: Prentice-Hall, 1991), pp. 241–280; and Kahle and Homer, "Physical Attractiveness of the Celebrity Endorser."

103. Tim Nudd, "Angelina Jolie Hardly Seems Natural in First Louis Vuitton Ad," *Adweek*, June 13, 2011, www.adweek.com.

104. Mark R. Forehand and Andrew Perkins, "Implicit Assimilation and Explicit Contrast: A Set/Reset Model of Response to Celebrity Voice-Overs," *Journal of Consumer Research* 32, no. 3, 2005, pp. 435–441.

105. Sun Joo Ahn and Jeremy N. Bailenson, "Self-Endorsing versus Other-Endorsing in Virtual Environments," *Journal of Advertising*, Summer 2011, pp. 93–106.

106. Tamara Abraham, "Wheelchair-User Becomes First Disabled Model to Star in Major High Street Campaign," *Daily Mail (UK)*, February 26, 2010, www.dailymail.co.uk.

107. Sengupta, Goodstein, and Boninger, "All Cues Are Not Created Equal."

108. Alan J. Bush, Craig A. Martin, and Victoria D. Bush, "Sports Celebrity Influence on the Behavioral Intentions of Generation Y," *Journal of Advertising Research*, March 2004, pp. 108–118.

109. Stuart Elliott, "Mr. Peanut's New Look? Old School," *New York Times*, November 7, 2010, www.nytimes.com.

110. Judith A. Garretson and Ronald W. Niedrich, "Spokes-Characters," *Journal of Advertising*, Summer 2004, pp. 25–36.

111. Marla Royne Stafford, Thomas F. Stafford, and Ellen Day, "A Contingency Approach: The Effects of Spokesperson Type and Service Type on Service Advertising Perceptions," *Journal of Advertising*, Summer 2002, pp. 17–34.

112. James Waterson, "Novak Djokovic Appointed UNICEF Serbia Ambassador," *Tennis Now*, August 29, 2011, www.tennisnow.com; and Peter Ford and Gloria Goodale, "Why Stars and Charities Need Each Other," *Christian Science Monitor*, January 13, 2005, p. 1.

113. Therese A. Louie and Carl Obermiller, "Consumer Response to a Firm's Endorser (Dis)Association Decisions," *Journal of Advertising*, Winter 2002, pp. 41–52.

114. Mitchell and Olson, "Are Product Attributes Beliefs the Only Mediator of Advertising Effects on Brand Attitudes?"; Andrew A. Mitchell, "The Effect of Verbal and Visual Components of Advertisements on Brand Attitudes and Attitude toward the Advertisement," *Journal of Consumer Research*, March 1986, pp. 12–24; and Paul W. Miniard, Sunil Bhatla, Kenneth R. Lord, Peter R. Dickson, and H. Rao Unnava, "Picture-Based Persuasion Processes and the Moderating Role of Involvement," *Journal of Consumer Research*, June 1991, pp. 92–107.

115. Paul W. Miniard, Deepak Sirdeshmukh, and Daniel E. Innis, "Peripheral Persuasion and Brand Choice," *Journal of Consumer Research*, September 1992, pp. 226–239.

116. Henrik Hagtvedt and Vanessa M. Patrick, "Art Infusion: The Influence of Visual Art on the Perception and Evaluation of Consumer Products," *Journal of Marketing Research*, June 2008, pp. 379–389.

117. Robert Hof, "What Double-Dip? Online Ads Keep Clicking—for Now," *Forbes*, September 28, 2011, www.forbes.com.

118. Chris Woodyard, "Kia Brings Back the Hamsters in TV Ad This Sunday," *USA Today*, August 26, 2011, www.usatoday.com.

119. "Mark Sandman, An Instant Classic," *Wall Street Journal*, December 28, 2004, p. D8.

120. Gordon C. Bruner, "Music, Mood, and Marketing," *Journal of Marketing*, October 1990, pp. 94–104; Gerald J. Gorn, "The Effects of Music in Advertising on Choice Behavior," *Journal of Marketing*, Winter 1982, pp. 94–101; Judy I. Alpert and Mark I. Alpert, "Background Music as an Influence in Consumer Mood and Advertising Responses," in ed. Thomas K. Srull, *Advances in Consumer Research*, vol. 16 (Provo, Utah: Association for Consumer Research, 1989), pp. 485–491; Meryl Paula Gardner, "Mood States and Consumer Behavior: A Critical Review," *Journal of Consumer Research*, December 1985, pp. 281–300; and C. Whan Park and S. Mark Young, "Consumer Response to Television Commercials," *Journal of Marketing Research*, February 1986, pp. 11–24.

121. Juliet Rui and Joan Meyers-Levy, "Distinguishing between the Meanings of Music," *Journal of Marketing Research*, August 2005, pp. 333–345.

122. Mark Alpert and Judy Alpert, "Background Music as an Influence in Consumer Mood and Advertising Responses," *Advances in Consumer Research* 16, Fall 1989, pp. 485–491; and Stout and Leckenby, "Let the Music Play."

123. Noel M. Murray and Sandra B. Murray, "Music and Lyrics in Commercials: A Cross-Cultural Comparison between Commercials Run in the Dominican Republic and the United States," *Journal of Advertising*, Summer 1996, pp. 51–64.

124. Marc G. Weinberger and Harlan E. Spotts, "Humor in U.S. vs. U.K. TV Advertising," *Journal of Advertising* 18, no. 2, 1989, pp. 39–44; and Paul Surgi Speck, "The Humorous Message Taxonomy," in eds. James H. Leigh and Claude R. Martin, *Current Research and Issues in Advertising* (Ann Arbor, Mich.: University of Michigan, 1991), pp. 1–44.

125. Thomas J. Madden and Marc G. Weinberger, "Humor in Advertising: A Practitioner View," *Journal of Advertising Research*, August–September 1984, pp. 23–29; Stewart and Furse, "Effective Television Advertising," *Marketing News*, October 24, 1986, Vol. 20 Issue 22, 1/9p; Thomas J. Madden and Marc C. Weinberger, "The Effects of Humor on Attention in Magazine Advertising," *Journal of Advertising* 1, no. 3, 1982, pp. 8–14; and Marc C. Weinberger and Leland Campbell, "The Use and Impact of Humor in Radio Advertising," *Journal of Advertising Research*, December–January 1991, pp. 44–52.

126. Martin Eisend, "A Meta-analysis of Humor in Advertising," *Journal of the Academy of Marketing Science* 37, 2009, pp. 191–203; George E. Belch and Michael A. Belch, "An Investigation of the Effects of Repetition on Cognitive and Affective Reactions to Humorous and Serious Television Commercials," in ed. Thomas C. Kinnear, *Advances in Consumer Research*, vol. 11 (Provo, Utah: Association for Consumer Research, 1984), pp. 4–10; Calvin P. Duncan and James E. Nelson, "Effects of Humor in a Radio Advertising Experiment," *Journal of Advertising* 14, no. 2, 1985, pp. 33–40, 64; Betsy D. Gelb and Charles M. Pickett, "Attitude-toward-the-Ad: Links to Humor and to Advertising Effectiveness," *Journal of Advertising* 12, no. 2, 1983, pp. 34–42; and Betsy D. Gelb and George M. Zinkhan, "The Effect of Repetition on Humor in a Radio Advertising Study," *Journal of Advertising* 15, no. 2, 1986, pp. 15–20, 34.

127. Harlan E. Spotts, Marc. G. Weinberger, and Amy L. Parsons, "Assessing the Use and Impact of Humor on Advertising Effectiveness: A Contingency Approach," *Journal of Advertising*, Fall 1997, pp. 17–32.

128. Brian Sternthal and Samuel Craig, "Humor in Advertising," *Journal of Marketing* 37, no. 4, 1973, pp. 12–18; Calvin P. Duncan, "Humor in Advertising: A Behavioral Perspective," *Journal of the Academy of Marketing Science* 7, no. 4, 1979, pp. 285–306; and Weinberger and Campbell, "The Use and Impact of Humor in Radio Advertising."

129. Thomas W. Cline and James J. Kellaris, "The Influence of Humor Strength and Humor–Message Relatedness on Ad Memorability," *Journal of Advertising*, Spring 2007, pp. 55–67.

130. Thomas W. Cline, Moses B. Altsech, and James J. Kellaris, "When Does Humor Enhance or Inhibit Ad Responses?" *Journal of Advertising*, Fall 2003, pp. 31–45.

131. Josephine L. C. M., Woltman Elpers, Ashesh Mukherjee, and Wayne D. Hoyer, "Humor in Television Advertising: A Moment-to-Moment Analysis," *Journal of Consumer Research*, December 2004, pp. 592–598.

132. Mark R. Brown, Roop K. Bhadury, and Nigel K. Li Pope, "The Impact of Comedic Violence on Viral Advertising Effectiveness," *Journal of Advertising*, Spring 2010, pp. 49–65.

133. Madden and Weinberger, "Humor in Advertising"; Weinberger and Campbell, "The Use and Impact of Humor in Radio Advertising"; and Weinberger and Spotts, "Humor in U.S. vs. U.K. TV Advertising."

134. Thomas Grillo and Donna Goodison, "Arnold Scores Boston Bruins Ads," *Boston Herald*, August 20, 2011, www.bostonherald.com.

135. Madden and Weinberger, "Humor in Advertising"; and Thomas W. Whipple and Alice E. Courtney, "How Men and Women Judge Humor," in eds. James H. Leigh and Claude R. Martin, *Current Research and Issues in Advertising* (Ann Arbor, Mich.: University of Michigan, 1981), pp. 43–56.

136. Yong Zhang, "Responses to Humorous Advertising: The Moderating Effect of Need for Cognition," *Journal of Advertising*, Spring 1996; and Amitava Chattopadhyay and Kunal Basu, "Prior Brand Evaluation as a Moderator of the Effects of Humor in Advertising," *Journal of Marketing Research*, November 1989, pp. 466–476.

137. Dana L. Alden, Wayne D. Hoyer, and Chol Lee, "Identifying Global and Culture-Specific Dimensions of Humor in Advertising: A Multi-National Analysis," *Journal of Marketing*, April 1993, pp. 64–75; and Dana L. Alden, Wayne D. Hoyer, Chol Lee, and Guntalee Wechasara, "The Use of Humor in Asian and Western Advertising: A Four-Country Comparison," *Journal of Asia-Pacific Business* 1, no. 2, 1995, pp. 3–23.

138. Weinberger and Spotts, "Humor in U.S. vs. U.K. TV Advertising."

139. Michel Laroche, Marcelo Vinhal Nepomuceno, Liang Huang, and Marie-Odile Richard, "What's So Funny?" *Journal of Advertising Research* 51, no. 2, 2011, pp. 404–416.

140. Yih Hwai Lee and Elison Ai Ching Lim, "What's Funny and What's Not," *Journal of Advertising*, Summer 2008, pp. 71–84.

141. Sean Poulter, "Beyonce Turns Up the Heat a Little Too Much," *Daily Mail (UK)*, November 17, 2010, www.dailymail.co.uk.

142. Nigel K. Li Pope, Kevin E. Voges, and Mark R. Brown, "The Effect of Provocation in the Form of Mild Erotica on Attitude to the Ad and Corporate Image," *Journal of Advertising*, Spring 2004, pp. 69–82.

143. Darren W. Dahl, Jaideep Sengupta, and Kathleen D. Vohs, "Sex in Advertising: Gender Differences and the Role of Relationship Commitment," *Journal of Consumer Research*, August 2009, pp. 215–231; and Jaideep Sengupta and Darren W. Dahl, "Gender-Related Reactions to Gratuitous Sex Appeals in Advertising," *Journal of Consumer Psychology* 18, 2008, pp. 62–78.

144. Bram Van den Bergh, Siegried Dewitte, and Luk Warlop, "Bikinis Instigate Generalized Impatience in Intertemporal Choice," *Journal of Consumer Research*, June 2008, pp. 85–97.

145. Lawrence Soley and Gary Kurzbard, "Sex in Advertising: A Comparison of 1964 and 1984 Magazine Advertisements," *Journal of Advertising* 15, no. 3, 1986, pp. 46–54.

146. Cyndee Miller, "We've Been 'Cosbyized,' " *Marketing News*, April 16, 1990, pp. 1–2; and Joshua Levine, "Marketing: Fantasy, Not Flesh," *Forbes*, January 22, 1990, pp. 118–120.

147. Vranica, "Anheuser-Busch Kicks Edgy Super Bowl Ad to Curb."

148. Susanna Kim, "Go Daddy Hopes Super Bowl Ads Are Risque Again," *ABC News*, February 4, 2011, www.abcnews.go.com.

149. Robert S. Baron, "Sexual Content and Advertising Effectiveness: Comments on Belch et al. (1981) and Caccavale et al. (1981)," in ed. Andrew A. Mitchell, *Advances in Consumer Research*, vol. 9 (Ann Arbor, Mich.: Association for Consumer Research, 1982), pp. 428–430.

150. Michael S. LaTour, Robert E. Pitts, and David C. Snook-Luther, "Female Nudity, Arousal, and Ad Response: An Experimental Investigation," *Journal of Advertising* 19, no. 4, 1990, pp. 51–62.

151. Evan I. Schwartz, "When Advertising Becomes the Show," *MIT Technology Review*, October 22, 2010, www.technologyreview.com; and Laura Petrecca, "Axe Ads Turn Up the Promise of Sex Appeal," *USA Today*, April 17, 2007, p. 3B.

152. Marilyn Y. Jones, Andrea J. S. Stanaland, and Betsy D. Gelb, "Beefcake and Cheesecake: Insights for Advertisers," *Journal of Advertising*, Summer 1998, pp. 33–52.

153. John Fetto, "Where's the Lovin'?" *American Demographics*, February 28, 2001.

154. Miller, "We've Been 'Cosbyized'"; and "Poll on Ads: Too Sexy," *Wall Street Journal*, March 8, 1993, p. B5.

155. Robert A. Peterson and Roger A. Kerin, "The Female Role in Advertisements," *Journal of Marketing*, October 1977, pp. 59–63.

156. Michelle R. Nelson and Hye-Jin Paek, "Nudity of Female and Male Models in Primetime TV Advertising Across Seven Countries," *International Journal of Advertising* 27, no. 5, 2008, pp. 715–744.

157. Sak Onkvisit and John J. Shaw, "A View of Marketing and Advertising Practices in Asia and Its Meaning for Marketing Managers," *Journal of Consumer Marketing*, Spring 1985, pp. 5–17; and Sarah Ellison, "Sex-Themed Ads Often Don't Travel Well," *Wall Street Journal*, March 31, 2000, p. B7.

158. Cenk Bulbul and Geeta Menon, "The Power of Emotional Appeals in Advertising," *Journal of Advertising Research*, June 2010, pp. 169–180.

159. M. Friestad and Esther Thorson, "Emotion-Eliciting Advertising: Effect on Long-Term Memory and Judgment," in ed. R. J. Lutz, *Advances in Consumer Research*, vol. 13 (Provo, Utah: Association for Consumer Research, 1986), pp. 111–116.

160. Natalie Zmuda, "Diet Coke Pours on Marketing Activity," *Advertising Age*, September 1, 2011, www.adage.com; Theresa Howard, "Coke Adds Spark to Ad Campaign," *USA Today*, April 3, 2006, p. 3B; and Christina Cheddar Berk, "Coke to Debut 'Real' Ad on 'Idol,'" *Wall Street Journal*, January 17, 2005, p. B3.

161. Barbara B. Stern, "Classical and Vignette Television Advertising Dramas: Structural Models, Formal Analysis, and Consumer Effects," *Journal of Consumer Research*, March 1994, pp. 601–615; William D. Wells, "Lectures and Dramas," in eds. Pat Cafferata and Alice M. Tybout, *Cognitive and Affective Responses to Advertising* (Lexington, Mass.: D. C. Heath, 1988); and John Deighton, Daniel Romer, and Josh McQueen, "Using Dramas to Persuade," *Journal of Consumer Research*, December 1989, pp. 335–343.

162. Jennifer Edson Escalas and Barbara B. Stern, "Sympathy and Empathy: Emotional Responses to Advertising Dramas," *Journal of Consumer Research*, March 2003, pp. 566–578.

163. Elaine Wong, "Why Bertolli Is Using Webisodes to Promote Frozen Dinners," *Adweek*, March 4, 2010, www.adweek.com.

164. Marvin E. Goldberg and Gerald J. Gorn, "Happy and Sad TV Programs: How They Affect Reactions to Commercials," *Journal of Consumer Research*, December 1987, pp. 387–403; and John P. Murray Jr. and Peter A. Dacin, "Cognitive Moderators of Negative-Emotion Effects," *Journal of Consumer Research*, March 1996, pp. 439–447.

165. John P. Murray, John L. Lastovicka, and Surendra Singh, "Feeling and Liking Responses to Television Programs," *Journal of Consumer Research*, March 1992, pp. 441–451.

166. S. N. Singh and Gilbert A. Churchill, "Arousal and Advertising Effectiveness," *Journal of Advertising* 16, no. 1, 1987, pp. 4–10.

167. Mark A. Pavelchak, John H. Antil, and James M. Munch, "The Super Bowl: An Investigation into the Relationship among Program Context, Emotional Experience, and Ad Recall," *Journal of Consumer Research*, December 1988, pp. 360–367.

168. Sally Beatty, "Madison Avenue Should Rethink Television Violence, Study Finds," *Wall Street Journal*, December 1, 1998, p. B8.

169. Hollie Shaw, "Old Spice Guy Beats Fabio in 'Mano a Mano' Contest," *Advertising Age*, July 28, 2011, www.adage.com; Craig Reiss, "Businesses Can Learn from the Old Spice Man Viral Marketing Campaign," *Entrepreneur*, July 18, 2010, www.entrepreneur.com; Gary Vaynerchuk, "Old Spice Man Marketing, Redux," *Fast Company*, March 10, 2011, www.fastcompany.com; Jack Neff, "Old Spice Is Killing It on YouTube Again, But Sales Are Down Double-Digits," *Advertising Age*, August 4, 2011, www.adage.com; and Sebastian Joseph, "Old Spice Man Tour to Visit a City Near You," *Marketing Week (UK)*, October 7, 2011, www.marketingweek.co.uk.

The Process of Making Decisions

PART THREE examines the sequential steps in the consumer decision-making process. Chapter 7 explores the initial steps of this process—problem recognition and information search. Consumers must first realize they have a problem before they can begin the process of making a decision about solving it. They must then collect information to help make this decision.

As with attitude change, decision making is affected by the amount of effort consumers expend. Chapter 8 examines the decision-making process when consumer effort is high and explores how marketers can influence this extensive decision process. Chapter 9 focuses on decision making when consumer effort is low and discusses how marketers can influence this kind of decision process. Chapter 10 looks at how consumers determine whether they are satisfied or dissatisfied with their decisions and how they learn from choosing and consuming products and services.

THE CONSUMER'S CULTURE

Consumer Diversity (Ch. 12)

Household and Social Class Influences (Ch. 13)

Social Influences on Consumer Behavior (Ch. 11)

THE PSYCHOLOGICAL CORE
- Motivation, Ability, and Opportunity (Ch. 2)
- From Exposure to Comprehension (Ch. 3)
- Memory and Knowledge (Ch. 4)
- Attitude Formation and Change (Chs. 5–6)

Psychographics: Values, Personality, and Lifestyles (Ch. 14)

THE PROCESS OF MAKING DECISIONS
- Problem Recognition and Information Search (Ch. 7)
- Judgment and Decision Making (Chs. 8–9)
- Post-Decision Processes (Ch. 10)

CONSUMER BEHAVIOR OUTCOMES AND ISSUES
- Innovations: Adoption, Resistance, and Diffusion (Ch. 15)
- Symbolic Consumer Behavior (Ch. 16)
- Marketing, Ethics, and Social Responsibility in Today's Consumer Society (Ch. 17)

© Cengage Learning 2013

CHAPTER 7

PROBLEM RECOGNITION AND INFORMATION SEARCH

After studying this chapter, you will be able to

1. Describe how consumers recognize a consumption problem and show why marketers must understand this part of the decision-making process.

2. Discuss what happens when consumers conduct an internal search to solve a consumption problem and identify some of the ways in which marketers can affect internal searches.

3. Explain why and how consumers conduct an external search to solve a consumption problem.

4. Identify opportunities and the challenges that marketers face in trying to influence external searches.

© iStockphoto.com/roccomontoya

INTRODUCTION

Quick Response Codes for Quick Information

Those block-shaped, black-and-white QR (quick response) codes are popping up all over the marketing landscape—on products, in store displays, in ads, on billboards, almost anywhere a consumer may show up with smartphone in hand. Consumers simply download a QR app, point the phone at the code, and see whatever information the marketer has linked to it—photos, videos, music, written descriptions, contest clues, coupons, and anything else that can be displayed on or downloaded to a phone.

Suppose your car is being repaired and you rent a Mazda6 from Enterprise Rent-A-Car. You like the way it drives, and you realize that it might be a good idea to replace your old car. You try to recall what you know about car brands and features, but your information is limited. So you use your phone to scan the QR code stuck to the side window of your rented Mazda and you read about that car's options and performance. On your way home, you pass an AUDI billboard and park across the street to aim your phone at its enlarged QR code. This gives you details about the A7 model and dealer locations where you can take a test-drive. Later that evening, you drive past a nearby Ford dealership and you stop to use the QR codes to check each model's fuel efficiency rating. At home, you check car magazine ads (many with QR codes for further information) and look up reviews online as you consider which car you might like to buy.[1]

This example shows how marketing stimuli can be helpful in the early stages of the consumer decision-making process. Driving a rental while your car is being repaired helps you recognize a problem, as shown in Exhibit 7.1. Thinking about car brands and features represents internal search. Using QR codes to get details on various models, looking at car ads, browsing at dealerships, and going online to read reviews are all part of external information search. Whether problem recognition, internal information search, and external information search proceed sequentially, simultaneously, or in a different order, these three stages are useful in explaining the basic processes that characterize consumer decision making.

PROBLEM RECOGNITION

Problem recognition
The perceived difference between an actual and an ideal state.

Ideal state The way we want things to be.

Actual state The way things actually are.

The consumer decision process generally begins when the consumer identifies a consumption problem that needs to be solved ("I need a new car" or "I would like some new clothes"). **Problem recognition** is the perceived difference between an ideal and an actual state. This is a critical stage in the decision process because it motivates the consumer to action (see Exhibit 7.2).

The **ideal state** is the way that consumers would like a situation to be (having an excellent camera or wearing attractive clothing). The **actual state** is the real situation as consumers perceive it now. Problem recognition occurs if consumers become aware of a discrepancy between the actual state and the ideal state ("My car needs frequent repairs" or "My clothing is out of date"). The greater the discrepancy between the actual and the ideal states, and the higher the level of motivation, ability, and opportunity (MAO), the more likely consumers are to act. If consumers do not perceive a problem, their motivation to act will be low.

Problem recognition relates to consumption and disposition as well as to acquisition. Consumers can recognize problems such as needing to decide what to make for dinner, which item of clothing to wear, or whether to replace an old appliance. Because problem recognition stimulates many types of consumer decision making, it is important to understand what contributes to differences between the ideal and the actual states.

The Ideal State: Where We Want to Be

Where do we get our notion of the ideal state? Sometimes we rely on simple expectations, usually based on past experience, about everyday consumption and disposition situations and how products or services fulfill our needs. For example, we consider how we might look in certain clothes, how clean our house should be, how much fun it would be to vacation in a particular location, which old products we should keep, and so on. The ideal state also can be a function of our future goals or aspirations. For example, many consumers might want to drive a car that will provide them with social status (a Lexus, Mercedes, or Porsche) or to join a club that will bring them admiration or acceptance by others.

Both expectations and aspirations are often stimulated by our own personal motivations—what we want to be based on our self-image—and by aspects of our own culture. Some societies are more materialistic than others, and therefore the desire for many goods and services may be greater in those cultures. Likewise, social class can exert an influence: Many consumers want to be accepted by members of their class or to raise their social standing, leading them to aspire to a higher ideal state.

THE CONSUMER'S CULTURE

Consumer Diversity (Ch. 12)

Household and Social Class Influences (Ch. 13)

Social Influences on Consumer Behavior (Ch. 11)

THE PSYCHOLOGICAL CORE
- Motivation, Ability, and Opportunity (Ch. 2)
- From Exposure to Comprehension (Ch. 3)
- Memory and Knowledge (Ch. 4)
- Attitude Formation and Change (Chs. 5–6)

Psychographics: Values, Personality, and Lifestyles (Ch. 14)

THE PROCESS OF MAKING DECISIONS
- **Problem Recognition and Information Search (Ch. 7)**
- Judgment and Decision Making (Chs. 8–9)
- Post-Decision Processes (Ch. 10)

CONSUMER BEHAVIOR OUTCOMES AND ISSUES
- Innovations: Adoption, Resistance, and Diffusion (Ch. 15)
- Symbolic Consumer Behavior (Ch. 16)
- Marketing, Ethics, and Social Responsibility in Today's Consumer Society (Ch. 17)

PROBLEM RECOGNITION AND INFORMATION SEARCH

PROBLEM RECOGNITION (IDEAL VERSUS ACTUAL STATE)

INTERNAL INFORMATION SEARCH
- Extent
- Type of information retrieved
- Search biases

EXTERNAL INFORMATION SEARCH
- Where search occurs
- Extent
- Type of information acquired
- How information is searched

© Cengage Learning 2013

Exhibit 7.1

Chapter Overview: Problem Recognition and Information Search

The first step in the consumer decision-making process involves problem recognition (the consumer recognizes a problem that needs to be solved). Next, the consumer searches for information to solve the problem either internally from memory or externally from outside sources (such as experts, magazines, or ads). How much consumers search, what they search for, and the process they go through while searching are all discussed in this chapter.

Exhibit 7.2

An Ideal State
Consumers may respond to upscale ads, like this one for Jimmy Choo, because that is their ideal state.

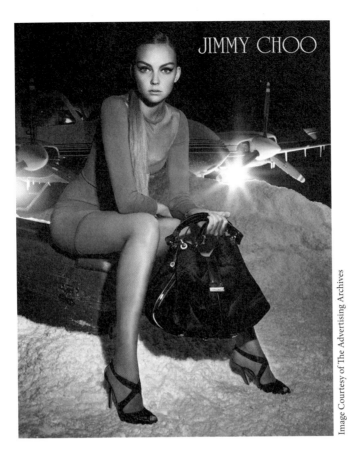

Image Courtesy of The Advertising Archives

Reference groups also play a critical role because we strive to be accepted by others and because reference groups serve as a guide to our behavior.

Finally, major changes in personal circumstances, such as getting a promotion or becoming a parent, can instigate new ideal states. When you graduate and start a new job, you are likely to develop new ideal states related to where you live, what you wear, what you drive, and so forth. Newly affluent consumers in South Korea, for example, are increasingly interested in buying world-famous status-symbol brands that signify wealth, such as Hermès purses.[2]

The Actual State: Where We Are Now

Like our perception of the ideal state, our perception of the actual state can be influenced by a variety of factors. Often these are simple physical factors, such as running out of a product, having a product malfunction (the cell phone breaks) or become obsolete (the digital music player has insufficient storage), or unexpectedly needing a service (a cavity requires dental work). Needs also play a critical role. If you are hungry or thirsty or if friends make fun of your clothes, your actual state would not be acceptable. Finally, external stimuli can suddenly change your perceptions of the actual state. If someone tells you that Mother's Day is next Sunday, for example, you might suddenly realize that you have not bought a card or present yet.

Marketing Implications

Marketing can help put consumers in a state of problem recognition and motivate them to start the decision process, leading them to acquire, consume, or dispose of a product or service. In general, marketers use two major techniques to try to stimulate problem recognition. First, they can attempt to create a new ideal state. Thirty years ago, few people gave much thought to the performance or style of their athletic shoes. Today we are bombarded with marketing messages featuring athletic shoes that will make us run faster, jump higher, and look more fashionable—a new ideal state.

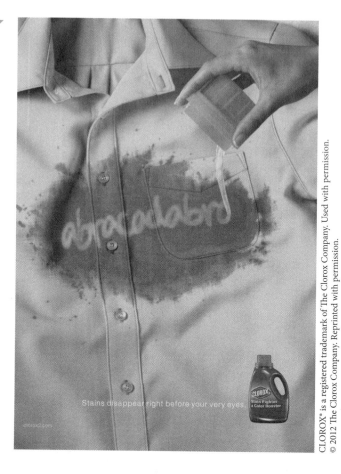

Exhibit 7.3

Targeting the Ideal State
Marketers can target the ideal state by showing consumers how the product is the solution to their problems.

Second, marketers can try to encourage our dissatisfaction with the actual state, as Saks Fifth Avenue did by fostering shoppers' dissatisfaction with ordinary shopping bags. When Saks created boldly stylish, eco-friendly, reusable bags to hold purchases, it encouraged consumers to view free bags as personal statements about fashion and environmental consciousness. Now many upscale retailers worldwide offer elegant shopping bags. This trend has led some status-conscious South Korean consumers to buy luxury-brand shopping bags from other consumers.[3]

Whether they create a new ideal state or stimulate dissatisfaction with the actual state, marketers are more likely to have their offering chosen if they position it as the solution to the consumer's problem (see Exhibit 7.3). For example, the name of Procter & Gamble's Mr. Clean Magic Eraser sponges and mops suggest that they help consumers quickly and easily "erase" dirt for a cleaner home.

INTERNAL SEARCH: SEARCHING FOR INFORMATION FROM MEMORY

Internal search The process of recalling stored information from memory.

After problem recognition has been stimulated, the consumer will usually begin the decision process to solve the problem. Typically, the next step is **internal search**. As discussed in Chapter 4, almost all decision making involves some form of memory processing. Consumers have stored in memory a variety of information, feelings, and past experiences that can be recalled when making a decision.

Because consumers have limited capacity or ability to process information—and because memory traces can decay over time—consumers are likely to recall only a small subset of stored information when they engage in internal search. Researchers are investigating (1) the extent of the search, (2) the nature of the search, and (3) the process by which consumers recall information, feelings, and experiences and enter them into the decision process.

How Much Do We Engage in Internal Search?

The degree of internal search can vary widely from the simple recall of only a brand name to more extensive searches through memory for relevant information, feelings, and experiences. On a general level, researchers know that the effort consumers devote to internal search depends on their MAO to process information. Thus, consumers will attempt to recall more information when felt involvement, perceived risk, or the need for cognition is high. In addition, consumers can engage in active internal search only if the information is stored in memory. Consumers with a greater degree of knowledge and experience therefore have a greater ability to search internally. Finally, consumers can recall information from memory only if they have the opportunity to do so. Time pressure or distractions will limit internal search.

What Kind of Information Is Retrieved from Internal Search?

Much of the research on the role of internal search in consumer judgment and decision making has focused on what is recalled. Specifically, researchers have examined the recall of four major types of information: (1) brands, (2) attributes, (3) evaluations, and (4) experiences.[4]

Recall of Brands

Consideration (or evoked set) The subset of top-of-mind brands evaluated when making a choice.

The set of brands that consumers recall from memory whenever problem recognition has been stimulated is an important aspect of internal search that greatly affects decision making. Rather than remembering all available brands in any given situation, consumers tend to recall a subset of two to eight brands known as a **consideration** or **evoked set**.[5] For example, someone buying toothpaste might consider Colgate and Crest rather than all possible brands. With product proliferation, however, the number of offerings has increased dramatically. Colgate-Palmolive alone offers more than a dozen toothpaste brands (including Colgate Total and Ultrabrite), a situation that increases competition for inclusion in the consideration set.[6]

In general, the consideration set consists of brands that are "top of mind," or easy to remember, when a consumer is making a decision. For instance, some U.S. consumers fly rather than take the train—even when taking the train is faster and cheaper—simply because they do not consider the possibility of train travel. Conversely, in India, airlines are using marketing to encourage consumers to consider flying rather than taking the train or bus when they travel long distances. The effort has been successful: The number of air travelers is increasing by nearly 20 percent every year.[7]

A small consideration set is usually necessary because consumers' ability to recall brand information decreases as the size of the set increases. However, even if they do not recall the entire set from memory, stored information aids the recognition process. For example, stored information can help consumers identify brands on the shelf. This is one reason why L'Oréal is stepping up advertising in India, where it distributes shampoo and other personal-care products through 600,000 stores, in competition with Unilever and Procter & Gamble.[8] By increasing brand recognition and stored information, L'Oréal hopes to strengthen their brand in the consumers' consideration set.

Studies indicate that consideration sets vary in terms of their size, stability, variety, and *preference dispersion* (the equality of preferences toward brands or products in the set). On more familiar occasions and in more familiar locations, such as when buying snacks at the local movie theater, consumers have consideration sets that are less stable, are larger in size, and have slightly more variety. In such situations, consumers tend to have stronger preferences for one or two items in the consideration set. This phenomenon suggests that a company should enhance its product's linkage with an occasion or situation familiar to consumers—such as eating on the run—to increase the chance that the product will be retrieved from memory as part of the consideration set.[9]

According to research, brands that are recalled are more likely to be chosen.[10] However, a brand's simply being recalled does not guarantee that it will be in a consumer's consideration set because consumers can recall a number of brands and then reject undesirable alternatives. Also, consumers' choices can be altered by the simple manipulation of which brands they recall, even though this manipulation may not change their product preferences. Thus, if consumers cannot recall brands from memory to form a consideration set, the set will tend to be determined by external factors such as the availability of products on the shelf or the suggestions of salespeople.[11]

Researchers have looked at the following factors that increase the possibility of consumers' recalling a particular brand during internal search and including that brand in their consideration set:

▶ *Prototypicality.* When consumers engage in internal search, they more easily recall brands that are closest to the prototype or that most resemble other category members, making these more likely to be included in the consideration set than brands that are not typical of the category.[12] For example, Apple's iPad created the category of tablet computer, which it still dominates. This brand is more likely than other brands to be in the consideration set when problem recognition for the product exists (see Exhibit 7.4).

▶ *Brand familiarity.* Well-known brands are more easily recalled during internal search than unfamiliar brands because the memory links associated with these brands tend to be stronger. As a result, companies need to repeat marketing communications continually to keep brand awareness high and associations strong. In Asian cultures, ads with high-meaning pictures and words (e.g., Superman fences with a picture of Superman) are very effective in increasing brand-name recall.[13] Even in low-MAO situations in which little processing occurs, incidental ad exposure can increase the likelihood of a brand's inclusion in the consideration set.[14] This explains why global brands such as McDonald's have high familiarity worldwide and are likely to be in many consumers' consideration sets. Brand familiarity helps consumers recognize which of the many brands in the store should be attended to and reduces misidentification of brands.[15]

▶ *Goals and usage situations.* As discussed in Chapter 5, consumers have goal-derived and usage-specific categories in memory, such as drinks to bring to the beach, and the activation of these categories will determine which brands they recall during internal search.[16] Therefore, marketers can attempt to associate products with certain goals and usage situations. For example, an ad for Kellogg's Frosted Flakes cereal features ESPN anchor Rece Davis, targeting fathers with the tagline "share what you love with who you love." Here, the usage situation is breakfast-time and the goal is to strengthen father-child connections. A Kellogg marketer explains: "Dad loves to share the things that he is passionate about with his kid, and Frosted Flakes and sports are two of those things."[17]

▶ *Brand preference.* Brands toward which the consumer has positive attitudes tend to be recalled more easily and tend to be included in the consideration set more often than brands that evoke negative attitudes.[18] This tendency highlights the importance of developing positive brand attitudes. In Nigeria, Star beer encourages positive attitudes by appealing to strong patriotic feelings with a campaign built on the slogan "I am Nigeria…and Star is my beer."[19]

▶ *Retrieval cues.* By strongly associating the brand with a retrieval cue, marketers can increase the chance that the brand will be included in the consumer's consideration set. Think of the Target red-and-white bull's-eye. The retailer is emphasizing this cue as it expands into Canada, where many consumers may already be familiar with the bull's-eye because they've bought from Target's U.S. stores (see Exhibit 7.5).[20] Packaging can also be an important retrieval cue for food products. Therefore, Coca-Cola's iconic glass bottle is still featured in some promotions, even though the bottles are now made with recycled and recyclable plastic.[21]

Recall of Attributes

For a variety of reasons, we access only a small portion of the information stored in memory during internal search. Often we cannot remember specific facts about a product or service because our memory of details decreases over time. Thus, the attribute information we recall tends to be in summary or simplified form rather than in its original detail. For example, we would be more likely to remember that a car gets good gas mileage or that filling the tank is not expensive than to remember the actual miles per gallon the car gets or the exact price of the gas.

Image Courtesy of The Advertising Archives

Exhibit 7.4

Prototypicality

When you think of a "tablet," Apple's iPad probably comes to mind first, as it is the prototype of the tablet category.

Exhibit 7.5

Retrieval Cues

Brands can create strong retrieval cues, increasing the likelihood of being included in consumers' consideration set. Target stores have done this with their bull's-eye logo, which helps them be known around the world.

Nevertheless, consumers can often recall *some* details when they engage in internal search, and the recalled attribute information can strongly influence their brand choices.[22] As a result, researchers have been very interested in determining which factors influence the recall of attribute information in the information search and decision-making processes. These are some of the major variables they have identified:

▶ *Accessibility or availability.* Information that is more accessible or available—having the strongest associative links—is the most likely to be recalled and entered into the decision process.[23] Information that is perceived as being easy to recall is also more likely to be accessible.[24] Simply reminding consumers of the ease of information retrieval can affect their judgments in some situations.[25] Marketers can make information more accessible by repeatedly drawing attention to it in communications or by making the information more relevant.[26]

Diagnostic information That which helps us discriminate among objects.

▶ *Diagnosticity.* **Diagnostic information** helps us distinguish objects from one another. If all brands of computers are the same price, then price is not diagnostic, or useful, when consumers are making a decision. On the other hand, if prices vary, consumers can distinguish among them, so the information is diagnostic.[27] If information is both accessible and diagnostic, it has a very strong influence in the decision-making process.[28] However, if accessible information is not diagnostic, it is less likely to be recalled.

Research shows that negative information tends to be more diagnostic than positive or neutral information because the former is more distinctive.[29] Because most brands are associated with positive attributes, negative information makes it easier for consumers to categorize the brand as different from other brands. Unfortunately, consumers tend to give negative information greater weight in decisions, increasing the chances that alternatives with negative qualities will be rejected. Therefore, marketers should avoid associating their offerings with negative information, plan two-sided messages that counter negative information, or divert attention from the negative feature.

In addition, marketers can identify which attributes tend to be most diagnostic for a particular category and seek a competitive advantage on one or more of these attributes. This is what Chevrolet did with its recharge-anywhere electric car Volt, which is drawing attention from environmentally conscious consumers. The Volt name suggests the all-electric attribute that sets the car apart from its competitors.[30]

Salient attribute Attribute that is "top of mind" or more important.

▶ *Salience.* Research has clearly shown that consumers can recall very **salient** (prominent) **attributes** even when their opportunity to process is low.[31] The Apple iPad's distinctive look and foldable Smart Cover are salient attributes for consumers interested in tablet computers, for example.

In addition, price is a highly salient attribute for many consumers. Note that consumers do not always have a strong belief about the salience of an attribute.[32] Thus, a marketer of stereo systems can improve consumers' recall of its products' sound quality by providing information that makes this attribute more salient, an action that in turn facilitates brand choice.[33] By repeatedly calling attention to an attribute in marketing messages, marketers can increase a product's salience and its impact on the decision.[34] For example, companies such as Hershey's are mentioning in their marketing that recent research suggests health benefits from eating dark chocolate.

However, an attribute can be highly salient but not necessarily diagnostic. If you are buying a watch, for example, the attribute "tells time" would be highly salient but not very diagnostic. For information to be recalled and entered into the decision, it must have **attribute determinance**, which means the information is both salient and diagnostic.[35] When Dunkin' Donuts introduced a new breakfast sandwich, the marketing emphasized not only eat-on-the-go convenience but also the use of egg whites, a salient attribute for health-conscious consumers.[36]

> *Vividness.* Vivid information is presented as concrete words, pictures, or instructions to imagine (e.g., imagine yourself on a tropical beach) or through word-of-mouth communication. For example, a photo of a hand holding the paperback-sized Kindle e-book reader is vivid information. Vivid information is easier to recall than less dramatic information, but it only tends to influence judgment and decision making when consumers have not formed a strong prior evaluation, especially one that is negative.[37] Also, vividness affects attitudes only when the effort required to process the information matches the amount of effort the consumer is willing to put forth.[38] Otherwise, vivid and nonvivid information affect consumer attitudes in about the same way.

> *Goals.* The consumer's goals will determine which attribute is recalled from memory. If one of your goals in taking a vacation is to economize, you are likely to recall price when considering possible vacation destinations. Marketers can identify important goals that guide the choice process for consumers and can then position their offerings in the context of these goals, such as offering economy vacation packages.

Recall of Evaluations

Because our memory for specific details decays rapidly over time, we find overall evaluations or attitudes (i.e., our likes and dislikes) easier to remember than specific attribute information. In addition, our evaluations tend to form strong associative links with the brand. This tendency is the reason that it is important for a marketer to encourage positive attitudes toward its brand or offering, whether it is a product, service, person, or place. A growing number of marketers are doing this via social media. The owners of Forty Putney Road Bed and Breakfast in Brattleboro, Vermont, reinforce positive attitudes by offering travel tips via Twitter. "A few really good followers, that have a bunch of their own followers, will spread your message better than having a large number of unengaged followers yourself," says one of the innkeepers.[39]

Evaluations are also more likely to be recalled by consumers who are actively evaluating the brand when they are exposed to relevant information. For example, if you are ready to buy a new computer and suddenly see an ad for a particular brand, you will probably determine whether you like the brand when you see the ad. This activity is called **online processing**.[40] Afterward, you will more likely recall this evaluation rather than the specific information that led to it. Many times, however, consumers do not have a brand-processing goal when they see or hear an ad. In such cases they do not form an evaluation and are therefore better able to recall specific attribute information, assuming that their involvement was high and the information was processed.[41] Moreover, consumers are more likely to use online processing in evaluating family brands when the brands within that family have low variability and share many attributes.[42]

Recall of Experiences

Internal search can involve the recall of experiences from autobiographical memory in the form of specific images and the effect associated with them.[43] Like information in semantic memory, experiences that are more vivid, salient, or frequent are the most likely to be recalled. For example, if you have an experience with a product or service that is either unusually positive or unusually negative, you are likely to recall these vivid experiences later. Furthermore, if you repeatedly have a

Attribute determinance Attribute that is both salient and diagnostic.

Online processing When a consumer is actively evaluating a brand as he/she views an ad for it.

positive experience with a product or service, it will be easier to recall. To illustrate, minor league baseball is known for wacky promotions that make the in-stadium experience more exciting and memorable. During their season, the South Bend Silver Hawks team in Indiana holds a memorable "Half-Way to Halloween" costume contests for all ages.[44] Research suggests that although advertising may affect how accurately consumers can recall their product experiences, their recall of the product's evaluations is not necessarily affected.[45]

Marketing Implications

Obviously marketers want consumers to recall positive experiences related to certain products or services. Marketers often deliberately associate their products or services with common positive experiences or images to increase their recall from consumers' memory. For example, the Macy's department store chain generates considerable goodwill through its Thanksgiving Day Parade and its Independence Day fireworks displays in New York City, both of which draw millions of television and Internet viewers every year (see Exhibit 7.6).

Marketers should also monitor reviews posted online and in social media for negative recall experiences. It is important for marketers to respond to comments about negative experiences with speedy, satisfactory responses that are more salient. For instance, after Dell was stung by a lot of negative customer comments a few years ago, the company set up a central "listening post" to scour the Web and social media for conversations about its brand and products. There are companies that can be hired to do this now, such as reputation.com. The company also created several Twitter accounts specifically for handling customers' complaints. Now, a Dell executive says, "we've seen a significant decline in negative commentary about our products and services, proof that the ability to listen and respond instantly is a smart investment in any company's future and a way to continually improve both business and customer relations."[46]

Is Internal Search Always Accurate?

In addition to being influenced by factors that affect what we recall, we all have processing biases that alter the nature of internal search. These search biases can sometimes lead to the recall of information that results in a less-than-optimal judgment or decision. Three biases have important implications for marketing: confirmation bias, inhibition, and mood.

Exhibit 7.6

Recall of Experiences
Marketers can associate their products with positive events, like the Macy's Thanksgiving Day Parade, to promote positive customer recall.

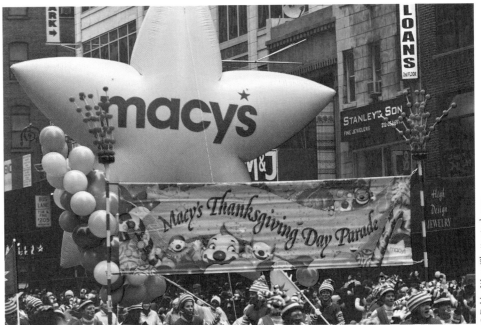

Confirmation Bias

Confirmation bias Tendency to recall information that reinforces or confirms our over all beliefs rather than contradicting them, thereby making our judgment or decision more positive than it should be.

Confirmation bias refers to our tendency to recall information that reinforces or confirms our overall beliefs rather than contradicting them, thereby making our judgment or decision more positive than it should be. This phenomenon is related to the concept of *selective perception*—we see what we want to see—and occurs because we strive to maintain consistency in our views. When we engage in internal search, we are more likely to recall information about brands we like or have previously chosen than information about brands we dislike or have rejected. Furthermore, when the confirmation bias is operating, we are more likely to recall positive rather than negative information about favored brands. This response can be a problem because, as mentioned earlier, negative information tends to be more diagnostic. Nevertheless, we sometimes recall contradictory evidence. In fact, we may recall moderately contradictory information because we had consciously thought about it when we first tried to understand it.[47] In most instances, however, consumers tend to recall information that reinforces their overall beliefs.

Inhibition

Inhibition The recall of one attribute inhibiting the recall of another.

Another internal search bias is associated with limitations in consumers' processing capacity[48] In this case, all the variables that influence the recall of certain attributes—such as accessibility, vividness, and salience—can actually lead to the **inhibition** of recall for other diagnostic attributes.[49] In buying a house, for example, a consumer might recall information such as the selling price, number of bathrooms, and square footage but may not recall other important attributes such as the size of the lot. Inhibition can also lead to a biased judgment or decision because consumers may remember but still ignore important and useful information.

Mood

Recall from Chapter 6 that consumers engaged in internal search are most likely to recall information, feelings, and experiences that match their mood.[50] With this knowledge in mind, advertisers are aware that marketing communications that put consumers in a good mood through the use of humor or attractive visuals can enhance the recall of positive attribute information.

Marketing Implications

From a marketing perspective, confirmation bias presents a real problem when consumers search internally for only positive information about the competition. One way marketers attack this problem is to draw attention to negative aspects of competitive brands through comparative advertising. For example, Apple has done this with ads comparing its easy-to-use computer operating systems with those made by Microsoft for PCs.[51] By presenting comparative information in a convincing and credible way, marketers may be able to overcome confirmation bias.

Inhibition is an important aspect of internal search for two reasons. First, consumers may not always consider key aspects of a brand when making a decision because they recall other, more accessible attributes instead. If these nonrecalled attributes reflect features that differentiate the brand from others (i.e., if the attributes are diagnostic), the company may want to highlight them in marketing communications. Marketers can sometimes offset the effect of their brand's disadvantages and/or their competitors' advantages by drawing attention to more vivid or accessible attributes. ⎯⎯⎯⎯⎯⎯

EXTERNAL SEARCH: SEARCHING FOR INFORMATION FROM THE ENVIRONMENT

External search The process of collecting information from outside sources, for example, magazines, dealers, ads.

Sometimes a consumer's decision can be based entirely on information recalled from memory. At other times, information may be missing or some uncertainty may surround the recalled information. Then consumers engage in an **external search** of outside sources, such as dealers, trusted friends or relatives, published sources (magazines, pamphlets, or books), advertisements, the

Internet, or the product package. Consumers use external search to collect additional information about which brands are available as well as about the attributes and benefits associated with brands in the consideration set.

Prepurchase search A search for information that aids a specific acquisition decision.

Two types of external search are prepurchase search and ongoing search. **Prepurchase search** occurs in response to the activation of problem recognition. As an example, consumers seeking to buy a new car or truck can get information by visiting dealers, searching edmunds.com and other websites, checking quality rankings, searching social media sites for tips and opinions, talking to friends, and reading *Consumer Reports*. Online prepurchase search is so commonplace that Honda recently launched a series of Web-only car videos supported by TV ads. The rationale, according to a Honda marketer: "The web portion is really the important part, because when you're wanting to reach online people who are shopping for cars, that's where they are."[52]

Ongoing search A search that occurs regularly, regardless of whether the consumer is making a choice.

Ongoing search occurs on a regular and continual basis, even when problem recognition has not been activated.[53] A consumer might consistently read automotive magazines, visit automotive websites, and go to car shows because he or she has a high degree of enduring involvement in cars. Exhibit 7.7 contrasts these two types of searches.

Researchers have examined five key aspects of the external search process: (1) the source of information, (2) the extent of external search, (3) the content of the external search, (4) search typologies, and (5) the process or order of the search.

Where Can We Search for Information?

For either prepurchase or ongoing search, consumers can acquire information from a number of external sources:[54]

▶   *Retailer search.* Visits or calls to stores or dealers, including the examination of package information or pamphlets about brands; in particular, consumers believe they save time by going to stores that are clustered together.[55]

▶   *Media and social media search.* Information from advertising, online ads, manufacturer-sponsored websites and forums, and other types of marketer-produced communications, as well as from Facebook, Twitter, blogs, and other social media sources.

▶   *Interpersonal search.* Advice from friends, relatives, neighbors, coworkers, and/or other consumers, whether sought in person, by phone, online, text message, or in another way. Sites

Exhibit 7.7

Types of Information Searches

Consumers can engage in two major types of external search. Prepurchase search occurs in response to problem recognition; the goal is to make better purchase decisions. Ongoing search results from enduring involvement and occurs on a continual basis (independent of problem recognition). In the latter, consumers search for information because they find searching enjoyable (they like to browse).

	Prepurchase Search	**Ongoing Search**
Determinants	• Involvement in the purchase • Market environment • Situational factors	• Involvement with the product • Market environment • Situational factors
Motives	To make better purchase decisions	• Build a bank of information for future use • Experience fun and pleasure

Outcomes	• Increased product and market knowledge
	• Better purchase decisions
	• Increased satisfaction with the purchase outcome
		• Increased product and market knowledge leading to
		  – future buying efficiencies
		  – personal influence
		• Increased impulse buying
		• Increased satisfaction from search, and other outcomes

Sources: Michael Totty, "So Much Information ..." *Wall Street Journal*, December 9, 2002, p. R4; and Subodh Bhat, Michael Bevans, and Sanjit Sengupta, "Measuring Users' Web Activity to Evaluate and Enhance Advertising Effectiveness," *Journal of Advertising*, Fall 2002, pp. 97–106.

such as yelp.com and tripadvisor.com offer consumer-generated reviews of restaurants, stores, and other goods and services, for instance.

▶ *Independent search.* Contact with independent sources of information, such as books, non-brand-sponsored websites like shopping.com, government pamphlets, or magazines.

▶ *Experiential search.* Using product samples or product/service trials (such as a test-drive) or experiencing the product online.

Traditionally, retailer and media searches, followed by experiential search, have been the most frequently used forms of search. These increase when a consumer's involvement is higher and knowledge is lower.[56] This finding is significant for marketers because such sources are under their most direct control. Other research indicates that consumers browse two or more sources of information (such as the Internet and catalogs) before making a buying decision.[57] Therefore, marketers and retailers should ensure that their brand information is consistent across the various sources.

Consumers increase their use of interpersonal sources as their brand knowledge decreases. Apparently, when consumers' knowledge is limited, they are motivated to seek out the opinions of others. Furthermore, when consumers believe that their purchase and consumption of certain items (usually hedonic or symbolic products and services such as fashion, music, and furniture) will be judged by others, they tend to seek out interpersonal sources.[58]

Experiential search is also critical for hedonic products and services. Given the importance of sensory stimulation, consumers want to get a "feel" for the offering, so they often try on clothing or listen to a new song before they buy. When Burberry was getting ready to launch a new Burberry Body fragrance in U.K. markets, it created a Facebook app where consumers could request a free sample. Burberry not only drew thousands of "likes" with this sampling offer, it also invited and received feedback on the new product.[59]

Cultural characteristics play a role in external search as well. According to research, consumers who are members of subcultural groups and not culturally assimilated—fully integrated into the surrounding culture—tend to conduct a wider search of external sources. And members of subcultural groups who identify with the surrounding culture are more likely to search for information among media advertisements. Thus, marketers should create informative advertising messages when targeting these consumer segments.[60] Although independent search tends to increase as available time increases, time spent on this type of search is generally quite minimal.

Internet Sources

Without leaving their keyboards or smartphones, consumers can use the Internet to search through mounds of data online, locate any details needed to make purchase decisions, and buy. In fact, consumers can use the Internet to get information from all five of the sources just mentioned. Sometimes consumers search for specific information; at other times they simply browse.[61] Consumers tend to use the same Internet search sources over and over, although the emergence of new online sites can disrupt this inertia.[62] One study suggests that women and older consumers visit websites longer than others do.[63] Speed, user control, and two-way communication capability are key elements of website interactivity for conducting online searches.[64] Interestingly, consumers may perceive that a site downloads quickly when its color has a relaxing effect.[65]

In general, consumers who have a pleasant experience with a company's website will have more positive attitudes toward the site and its brands.[66] Consumers report higher satisfaction and stronger buying intentions when searching and shopping on sites that use an avatar—an animated "person"—to deliver information.[67] For example, IKEA's Anna is an animated customer service representative that answers online shoppers' questions about the store, its products, and its services. These virtual shopping agents are particularly effective for introducing newcomers to a website's offerings and guiding them through the search and service process.[68] Internet ads can also encourage current customers to search and buy again. Research shows that the number of exposures to Internet ads, number of websites visited, and number of pages viewed all have a positive effect on repeat purchasing.[69]

In addition to conducting keyword searches on sites such as Google, consumers can use social media (such as Facebook and Twitter, as well as blogs) to research brands and products. Many download and use mobile phone-based shopping apps such as RedLaser to compare prices.[70] Some use shopping agents such as Shopping.com to organize their search results according to price, retail source, and other attributes. However, consumers do not always accurately assess whether a shopping agent's recommendations are appropriate and effective in a particular buying situation. Thus, consumers may make poor buying decisions by using an inferior shopping agent and by choosing offers they should have avoided.[71] Also, when consumers using a shopping agent receive recommendations about unfamiliar products, they check additional recommendations for familiar products as a context in which to evaluate the unfamiliar products.[72] Over time, analyzing consumers' buying patterns can improve shopping agents' recommendations.[73] Still, consumers who make numerous visits to a website may not buy even when the site offers tools to help them make better decisions.[74]

Information Overload

Consumers today have access to so much information that they can actually become overloaded. Depending on the way in which the information is structured, an overload can lead to a decline in decision quality.[75] Some search sites therefore apply more efficient search techniques that prioritize results by identifying the most popular or frequently accessed sites.[76] An ordered list with the "best" result presented first may actually encourage consumers to keep exploring less-than-optimal options, resulting in less-than-optimal buying decisions. On the other hand, consumers whose searches uncover increasingly better options may have more positive brand evaluations and be motivated to search for superior choices.[77]

Despite the potential for overload, does decision quality suffer when consumers desire more choice options? Some research indicates that choice overload can occur in situations where the problem is complex and the consumer has difficulty dealing with complexity.[78] However, other research suggests that increasing the number of options does not generally reduce choice quality. Nevertheless, marketers should always be sensitive to the amount of information presented in order to ensure that overload does not occur.

Simulations

Advances in technology and graphics have dramatically improved the online experience. Website developers can now simulate the retail experience as well as product trials by creating sites that incorporate special and interactive effects including audio, video, zoom, panoramic views, streaming media, and three-dimensional product representations that can be manipulated. Creating a virtual product experience has a positive effect on consumer product knowledge and brand attitude, thereby reducing perceived risk and increasing purchase intention.[79] A growing number of colleges and universities, including Oregon Institute of Technology and Syracuse University, are offering virtual campus tours that can be viewed online, on mobile apps, or on Facebook.[80]

The Online Community

Often people with a common interest or condition related to a product or service go online to share ideas by using websites, discussion forums, text chat, and other tools.[81] Research indicates that the most common interactions focus on product recommendations and how-to-use-it advice.[82] Often this information can be very influential in the consumer's decision process because it is not controlled by marketers and is therefore seen as more credible.

In fact, one study shows that 80 percent of consumers changed their mind about buying a good or service after reading a negative review online. On the other hand, positive reviews influenced the buying decisions of 87 percent of consumers surveyed.[83] Moreover, consumers place a higher value on the input of reviewers who respond quickly to inquiries and provide a good deal of information.[84] In addition, reviews written by people whose tastes seem to be similar to the consumer's are more persuasive than reviews written by people with dissimilar tastes.[85] For instance, the electronics retailer Newegg is part of a trend toward identifying which reviewers have actually purchased the product from the site and inviting manufacturers to respond to customer comment. These enhancements help consumers understand the context of product reviews and make more informed decisions.

An increasing number of retailers and manufacturers are tracking consumers' online information search and purchase patterns to provide additional assistance and recommendations. For example, consumers who rent or stream movies from Netflix are encouraged to rate them so that the site can recommend other movies based on what each consumer liked and didn't like. This is Netflix's way of adding movies to the consideration set and providing more information for consumer decision making.

Marketing Implications

Consumers are buying online more frequently, making bigger purchases, and choosing a wider variety of products than they did in the early days of the Internet. Still, online marketers tend to be less successful when shoppers cannot judge the quality of a product such as a sofa (as the defunct furniture retailer Living.com found out) or when consumers perceive that the delivery cost is high relative to the cost of individual items such as groceries (as the defunct online grocer Webvan.com found out).[86] Facilitating extended searches for even inexpensive items like books can boost sales significantly, as Amazon.com learned with its "LOOK INSIDE!" feature, which lets consumers read pages from individual books.[87] When shopping for homes and other major purchases, many consumers use the Internet or mobile apps to search for information and then complete the purchase in person, although a small number will buy without any personal experience of the offering.

Many consumers see product choice as riskier when they lack access to experiential information until after they have completed an online purchase.[88] Sometimes consumers search but then abandon their online shopping carts because of frustration over the time and effort needed to check out; some do not buy because they get no information about shipping fees and taxes until they reach the final screen, or they balk at the fees at the last minute.[89] In some cases, consumers fill their shopping carts for entertainment purposes rather than with a specific purchase in mind; in other cases, they fill their carts as part of the search and return to buy later.[90] Among consumers who abandon carts several times over the course of a month, 48 percent will buy if the marketer makes another approach—and this group will spend more, too, suggesting that filling and leaving an online cart is simply part of the buying decision process for these consumers.[91] Vintage Tub & Bath, an online retailer of bathroom fixtures, uses a series of e-mails to engage consumers who had abandoned carts, encouraging them to return and click to buy—with considerable success.[92]

To learn which online tactics are most effective for their site and products, marketers track consumers' search and purchase behaviors using appropriate measurements. Vintage Tub & Bath tracks how many would-be buyers abandon their carts before they complete the purchase, how many open the retailer's e-mails, how many click on an offer in the e-mail, and how many e-mails are received before a consumer actually buys. Note that marketers need specific strategies for individual markets because activities that are effective with U.S. consumers will not be effective everywhere. So, for instance, the Web-based book retailer Flipkart offers the usual credit card and debit card options to its customers in India. In addition, it allows buyers to pay cash for their books when delivered or set up a monthly payment plan for their purchases—options not commonly available to U.S. buyers of books online.[93]

How Much Do We Engage in External Search?

Much of the research on external search has concentrated on examining how much information consumers acquire prior to making a judgment or decision. One of the key findings is that the degree of search activity is usually quite limited, even for purchases that are typically considered important.[94]

With more consumers shopping online, search activity is increasing because online sources are very convenient. Yet consumers' Internet search patterns can differ depending on type of product. Specifically, when researching *experience goods* (products that cannot easily be evaluated until after purchase and use), consumers tend to dig into the details and spend some time on each web page. Consumer-contributed product reviews and multimedia sources such as video demonstrations are particularly helpful during such searches because they enable consumers to better understand these products before the purchase. On the other hand, when researching *search goods* (products that can be evaluated before purchase and use), consumers tend to cast the net wider, searching more sites but spending less time on each web page.[95]

Nevertheless, information search can vary widely from a simple hunt for one or two pieces of information to a very extensive search relying on many sources. In an attempt to explain this variance, researchers have identified a number of causal factors that relate to our motivation, ability, and opportunity to process information.

Motivation to Process Information

As the motivation to process information increases, external search will generally be more extensive. Six factors increase our motivation to conduct an external search: (1) involvement and perceived risk, (2) the perceived costs of and benefits resulting from the search, (3) the nature of the consideration set, (4) relative brand uncertainty, (5) attitudes toward the search, and (6) the level of discrepancy of new information.

▶ *Involvement and perceived risk.* To understand how involvement relates to external search, recall the distinction from Chapter 2 between situational involvement—a response to a particular situation—and enduring involvement—an ongoing response. Higher situational involvement will generally lead to a greater prepurchase search,[96] whereas enduring involvement relates to an ongoing search regardless of whether problem recognition exists.[97] Thus, consumers with high enduring involvement with cars are more likely to read automotive magazines, visit car shows and car-related websites, and seek out other information about cars on a regular basis.

Because perceived risk is a major determinant of involvement, it should not be surprising that when consumers face riskier decisions, they engage in more external search activity. One of the key components of perceived risk is uncertainty regarding the consequences of behavior, and consumers use external search as a way to reduce this uncertainty.[98] Consumers are more likely to search when they are uncertain about which brand to choose than when they are uncertain about a brand's specific attribute. Consumers also search more when they are evaluating services rather than products because services are intangible and hence perceived as more uncertain.[99] Finally, consumers will have higher motivation to search if the consequences are more serious, such as those entailing high financial or social risk. This situation explains why consumers often search more extensively for information about higher-priced products or services.

▶ *Perceived costs and benefits.* External search activity is also greater when its perceived benefits are high relative to its costs.[100] In these situations, consumers who search will benefit by reducing their uncertainty and increasing the likelihood of their making a better decision, obtaining a better value, and enjoying the shopping process. The costs associated with external search are time, effort, inconvenience, and money (including traveling to stores and dealers). All these factors place psychological or physical strain on the consumer. In general, consumers tend to continue searching until they perceive that the costs outweigh the benefits. The desire to reduce searching costs explains why many supermarkets now offer a variety of nontraditional items like electronics and furniture, becoming places "where people do all their gift shopping."[101] As noted earlier, consumers who uncover increasingly better options will be motivated to keep searching for superior options.[102] Even so, consumers tend to minimize their initial search investment, delay further searches after making a choice, and underestimate the future costs (both search and usage) of switching to another offering.[103]

▶ *Consideration set.* If the consideration set contains a number of attractive alternatives, consumers will be motivated to engage in external search to decide which alternative to select. On the other hand, a consideration set that contains only one or two brands reduces the need to search for information.

▶ *Relative brand uncertainty.* When consumers are uncertain about which brand is the best, they are more motivated to engage in external search.[104] They also engage in more external search to learn about features when brands vary along unique dimensions, even though continued search may reduce their satisfaction with the eventual decision.[105]

▶ *Attitudes toward search.* Some consumers like to search for information and do so extensively.[106] These consumers generally have positive beliefs about the value and benefits of their search. In particular, extensive search activity appears to be strongly related to the belief that "when important purchases are made quickly, they are regretted."[107] Other consumers simply hate searching and do little of it.

Researchers have identified two groups of Internet searchers.[108] Experienced searchers are the most enthusiastic and heaviest users of the Internet, whereas moderate and light users see it as a source of information only, not a source of entertainment or fun. To appeal to the latter group, some companies have created interesting and engaging games to stimulate consumers to search.[109]

▶ *Discrepancy of information.* Whenever consumers encounter something new in their environment, they will try to categorize it by using their stored knowledge. If it does not fit into an existing category, consumers will try to resolve this incongruity by engaging in information search, especially when incongruity is at a moderate level and the consumer has limited knowledge about the product category.[110] Consumers are likely to reject highly incongruous information.[111] Marketers can capitalize on this tendency by introducing moderate discrepancies between their brand and other brands. For example, Diet Pepsi recently debuted a tall, skinny can distinctly different from the usual soft-drink can, prompting consumers to dig a little deeper in resolving this discrepancy (see Exhibit 7.8).[112]

The same general process applies to the search for information about new products. If a new product is moderately discrepant or incongruent with existing categories of products, the consumer will be motivated to resolve this discrepancy.[113] In particular, consumers explore the most salient attributes in greater depth rather than search for a lot of additional attributes. From a marketing perspective, this behavior suggests that positioning new products as moderately different from existing brands may induce consumers to search for more information that might, in turn, affect their decision-making process.

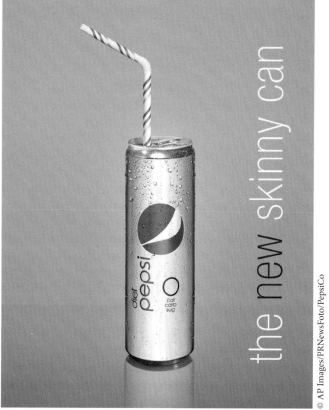

the new skinny can

© AP Images/PRNewsFoto/PepsiCo

Ability to Process Information

External search is also strongly influenced by the consumer's ability to process information. Researchers have studied the ways that three variables affect the extent of external information search: (1) consumer knowledge, (2) cognitive abilities, and (3) demographic factors.

▶ *Consumer knowledge.* Common sense suggests that expert consumers search less because they already have more complex knowledge stored in memory. However, research results on this subject have been mixed.[114] Part of the problem stems from the way that *knowledge* is defined. Some studies have measured *subjective knowledge*, the consumer's perception about what he or she knows relative to what others know. *Objective knowledge* refers to the actual information stored in memory that can be measured with a formal knowledge test. Researchers have linked objective knowledge to information search, although both types of knowledge are somewhat related. One study found that subjective knowledge influences the locations where consumers search for information as well as the quality of their choices.[115]

Specifically, several studies have found an inverted-U relationship between knowledge and search.[116] Consumers with moderate levels of knowledge search the most. They tend to have a higher level of motivation and at least some basic knowledge, which helps them to interpret new information. Experts, on the other hand, search less because they have more knowledge stored in memory, and they also know how to target their search to the most relevant or diagnostic information, ignoring that which is irrelevant—except when the search involves new products. Because experts have more developed memory structures, they have an advantage when learning novel information and can acquire more information about new products.

▶ *Cognitive abilities.* Consumers with higher basic cognitive abilities, such as a high IQ and the ability to integrate complex information, not only are more likely to acquire more information than consumers with little or no knowledge but also are able to process this information in more complex ways.[117]

▶ *Demographics.* As researchers continue to investigate whether certain types of consumers search more than others, they have discovered a few consistent patterns. For instance, consumers with higher educations tend to search more than less educated consumers do. This situation results because consumers with more education have at least moderate levels of knowledge and better access to information sources than the less educated do.[118]

Opportunity to Process Information

Consumers who have the motivation and ability to search for information must still have the opportunity to process that information before an extensive search can take place. Situational factors that might affect the search process include (1) the amount of information, (2) the information format, (3) the time available, and (4) the number of items being chosen.

▶ *Amount of information available.* In any decision situation, the amount of information available to consumers can vary greatly, depending on the number of brands on the market, the attribute information available about each brand, the number of retail outlets or dealers, and the number of other sources of information, such as magazines or knowledgeable friends. In general, consumers do more searching as the amount of available information increases, suggesting that the Internet and social media can generate greater external search, not to mention cell phone access to price comparisons. If information is restricted or not available, however, consumers have a hard time engaging in extensive external search.

▶ *Information format.* The format in which information is presented can also strongly influence the search process. Sometimes information is available from diverse sources or locations, but consumers must expend considerable effort to collect it (contacting different companies or stores, for instance). In contrast, presenting information in a manner that reduces consumer effort can enhance information search and usage, particularly when the consumer is in the decision mode.[119] As an example, U.S. regulations require foods to carry a concise, easy-to-read nutrition label (see Exhibit 7.9), thereby improving opportunity to process.[120] A related study found that consumers increase their use of nutritional information when the rewards of good nutrition are made more explicit.[121] In addition, consumers will engage in more leisurely exploratory searches if the information surrounding an object is visually simple and uncluttered.[122] The order in which options are presented can also influence attitude and preference.[123] If consumers hear a familiar song and then listen to a newer version of that song by another musical group, for example, they tend to prefer the familiar version because they encountered it first.

Nutrition Facts

Serving Size 3/4 Cup (27g)

Amount Per Serving	Cereal	With 1/2 Cup Skim Milk
Calories	90	130
Calories from Fat	10	10
	Daily Value (%)	
Total Fat 1g*	**2**	**2**
Saturated Fat 0 g	**0**	**0**
Trans Fat 0 g	**0**	**0**
Cholesterol 0 mg	**0**	**0**
Sodium 190 mg	**8**	**11**
Potassium 85 mg	**2**	**8**
Total Carbohydrate 23 g	**8**	**10**
Dietary Fiber 5 g	**20**	**20**
Sugars 5 g		
Protein 2 g		
Vitamin A	0	4
Vitamin C	10	15
Calcium	0	15
Iron	2	2

Exhibit 7.9

Information Format

Public policy makers have tried to make nutrition labels easier for consumers to understand and use by improving the format of this information. How easy do you think it is to understand the nutrition information in this exhibit?

Source: From Peter H. Bloch, Daniel L. Sherrell and Nancy M. Ridgeway, "Consumer Search: An Extended Framework," *Journal of Consumer Research*, June 1986, p. 120. Reprinted with permission of University of Chicago Press.

▶ *Time availability.* Consumers who face no time restrictions have more opportunity to search. If consumers are under time pressure, however, they will severely restrict their search activity.[124] Further, consumers will spend less time getting information from different sources as time pressure increases.[125] Time pressure is one of the main reasons that consumers search and shop on the Internet. One study found that when consumers revisit a website for search reasons, they spend less total time on the site because they look at fewer pages, not because they spend less time looking at each page.[126]

▶ *Number of items being chosen.* When consumers are making a decision about multiple items, research suggests that they will conduct a more extensive search with less variability in search patterns than if the decision involves the purchase or use of only one item.[127]

Marketing Implications

The extent to which consumers search for external information has important implications for marketing strategy. If many consumers tend to search extensively for a particular product or service, marketers can facilitate this process by making information readily available and easily accessible at the lowest cost and with the least consumer effort. To do this, marketers should consider redesigning their product packaging, websites, ads, and other promotional materials to add information that will alter consumers' attitudes and change their buying behavior. A growing number are including QR (quick response) codes in various marketing elements so that consumers can get more information via cell phone, as you saw in this chapter's opening example. Exhibit 7.10 shows how marketers can use QR codes to stimulate information search and processing.

Exhibit 7.10

Marketing with QR Codes

Do:

- *Have a purpose.* What is the purpose of the QR code? For example, do you want consumers to scan the code so they can watch an instructional video or to download a discount coupon?

- *Explain what will happen.* Let consumers know why they should scan the code. For example, an ad might state: "Scan this code for an exclusive discount."

- *Plan for the small screen.* Whatever content you offer, be sure it looks good shrunk to the size of a phone screen. The words must be readable and graphics must be clear on the small screen.

- *Monitor and evaluate QR code usage.* Beyond monitoring the number of consumers who scan the code daily and weekly, track how much time they spend with the information (do they watch the entire 60-second video?). Also determine how many are repeat visitors and how many click to the brand's Facebook page or website.

Don't:

- *Let design overpower the code.* Consumers should be able to see and scan the QR code wherever it's placed (on a product label or tag, in a magazine ad, etc.)

- *Post once and forget it.* Change the content from time to time to encourage repeat visits and provide additional information if and when consumers search again.

- *Link to content not valued by the audience.* Reward customers for taking the time to scan the code by offering interesting, beneficial content such as exclusive discounts, contests, or interviews with brand spokespeople.

- *Miss the chance to extend the relationship.* Invite consumers who scan the code to subscribe to an e-newsletter or "like" the brand on Facebook for special offers, product specifications, and more details.

Sources: Based on information in Karen M. Kroll, "Decoding ROI in Marketing's QR Codes," *COMPUTERWORLD*, November 14, 2011, www.computerworld.com; Tim Donnelly, "How to Use QR Codes to Market Your Business," *Inc.*, December 16, 2010, www.inc.com; Matthias Galica, "5 Big Mistakes to Avoid in Your QR Code Marketing Campaign," *Mashable*, August 2, 2011, www.mashable.com; and Hamilton Chan, "5 Steps for a Successful QR Code Marketing Campaign," *Mashable*, November 11, 2011, www.mashable.com.

Companies should also provide information about salient and diagnostic attributes, particularly if the brand has a differential advantage. Otherwise, if consumers cannot get the information they need, they may eliminate the brand from their consideration set. Novices, in particular, tend to be influenced by visual cues such as pictures and colors that focus their attention on selected attributes, a factor that affects their external search and, ultimately, their brand choices.[128]

Moreover, marketers can segment the market for a product or service according to search activity. One study identified six clusters of searchers in the purchase of a car.[129] Another found that consumers who search online for cars are younger and better educated and conduct more searches than those who do not use the Internet—and that they would have searched more extensively if they could not have used the Internet.[130] In high-tech markets, older consumers tend to search information channels that provide fairly uncomplicated information, whereas better educated consumers tend to search all information channels.[131]

Determining which search activities are commonly used for a particular product helps marketers plan to meet the information needs of their targeted consumers. Low-search consumers, for example, will focus on getting a good deal, whereas high searchers will need a lot of attention and information to offset their low levels of confidence and prior satisfaction. Marketers can be very selective in providing low searchers with information, emphasizing only those attributes that are most salient and diagnostic.

Marketers can attempt to stimulate external search by providing information in a highly accessible manner. Macys, for example, is testing free Wi-Fi service in its department stores to encourage consumers to use mobile apps for searching and shopping. The retailer is also setting up a cosmetics kiosk where consumers can research beauty products in selected stores.[132] Such opportunities for additional search may lead low searchers to information that will change their attitudes and affect their buying decisions. Marketers can also provide consumers with incentives to search. _____

What Kind of Information Is Acquired in External Search?

Researchers are interested in the types of information that consumers acquire during an external search because this information can potentially play a crucial role in influencing the consumers' judgments and decision making. When searching external sources, consumers usually acquire information about brand name, price, and other attributes.

Brand Name Information

Brand name is the most frequently accessed type of information because it is a central node around which other information can be organized in memory.[133] Thus, when we know the brand name, we can immediately activate other relevant nodes. For example, we can draw on prior knowledge and associations if we know the brand name is Whirlpool.

Price Information

Price is often the focus of consumer search because it tends to be diagnostic and can be used to make inferences about other attributes such as quality and value.[134] One study found that when price and quality are not directly correlated for a product category, consumers who use quality-screening agents to search for purchase options online are actually more sensitive to price differences.[135] Yet the search for price is less important than we might expect (due to the low overall extent of search), and it does not become more important when price variations increase and costs are higher.[136] In line with construal level theory (see Chapter 4), consumers will rely more on price as a quality cue when the decision is psychologically distant—when it relates to someone else, for instance.[137]

Even when consumers search on the basis of price, prior brand preference plays a role in how other information is processed.[138] Specifically, consumers who switch to a lower-price product during their search still retain some preference for the brand they preferred before search, which tends to bias their information processing in favor of that preferred brand. Consumers who search for price across multiple stores and over a period of time do, in fact, save more than those who search only one way.[139] Also, if marketers announce a product's price before it is launched, consumers who encounter that information in early searches will integrate it as a quality-related element later, when the product is available.[140] Finally, the importance of price depends on the culture. For example, compared to other countries, consumers in Japan have not traditionally been fond of discounters. However, this has changed as many now search for bargains in low-price stores such as Costco and UNIQLO.[141]

Information About Other Attributes

After brand and price, attribute information for which consumers will search depends on which attributes are salient and diagnostic in the offering category (see Exhibit 7.11). Consumers are more likely to access information that is relevant to their goals. For example, if a major goal in choosing a snack is to eat healthy, a consumer would probably collect information about each snack's ingredients, how much fat it contains, and how many calories. Note that size labels on food packages affect perceptions because consumers tend to rely on simple heuristics (like number of portions) rather than closely examining the details (such as number of ounces).[142] Also, when consumers switch goals from one purchase occasion to the next, as when looking for an economy car instead of one that is fast, the search they perform for the second task is more efficient because they can transfer the knowledge from the first task.[143]

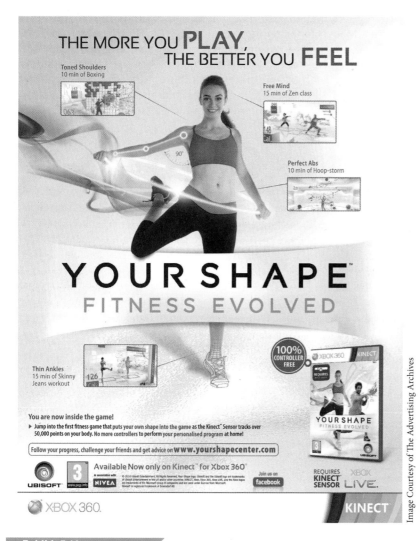

Exhibit 7.11

Attributes

Consumers respond to ads that show attributes that are both salient and diagnostic.

Is External Search Always Accurate?

Consumers can be just as biased in their search for external information as they are during internal search. In particular, consumers tend to search for external information that confirms rather than contradicts their overall beliefs. In one study, consumers with a strong price-quality belief tended to search more for higher priced brands.[144] Unfortunately, confirmation bias can lead consumers to avoid important information, resulting in a less-than-optimal decision outcome. Thus, if a lower priced, high-quality brand were available, consumers might never acquire information about it and therefore never select it for purchase.

How Do We Engage in External Search?

External search follows a series of sequential steps that can provide further insight into the consumer's decision. These steps include orientation, or getting an overview of the product display; evaluation, or comparing options on key attributes; and verification, or confirming the choice.[145] Researchers have examined the order of information acquisition during evaluation, in particular, because they assume that information acquired earlier in the decision process plays a more significant role than information acquired later.[146] Once a brand emerges as the leader early in the search process, subsequent information acquisition and evaluation are distorted in favor of that brand.[147]

Search Stages

Consumers access different sources and use different decision criteria at different stages of the search process. In the early stages, mass media and marketer-related sources tend to be more influential, whereas interpersonal sources are more critical when the actual decision is made.[148] Early in a search, consumers are more likely to access information that is especially salient, diagnostic, and goal related. However, if they can recall salient, diagnostic information from memory, they will have little need to search for it externally. Therefore, consumers will search first for information on attributes that provoke greater uncertainty or are less favorable.[149]

Early in a search, consumers will use simpler criteria to screen out options and then apply more detailed decision rules later in the search process. How highly a brand ranks early in the search may have little influence on the likelihood that the consumer will select it later in the process.[150] Because consumers tend to search first for brands with a higher perceived attractiveness, it is important for marketers to encourage positive brand attitudes. Consumers who are new to a product or service category will start by searching for information about low-risk, well-known brands; then search lesser known brands; and then consolidate the information leading to a preference for brands that provide the greatest utility.[151]

Searching by Brand or Attribute

Two major types of processes are (1) *searching by brand*, in which consumers acquire all the needed information on one brand before moving on to the next, and (2) *searching by attribute*, in which consumers compare brands in terms of one attribute at a time, such as by price.[152] Consumers generally prefer to process by attribute because doing so is easier.

Consumers are very sensitive to the manner in which information is stored in memory and the format in which it is presented in the store.[153] If information is organized by brand, as is the case in most stores where all the information is on packages, consumers will process information by brand. Experts, in particular, tend to process by brand because they have more brand-based knowledge. The fact that consumers are accustomed to processing by brand may bias processing, however, even when information is organized by attribute.[154] In addition, different search strategies affect consumers' decision processes differently.[155] Consumers who process by brand remain high in uncertainty until the very end of the search process, whereas those who search by attribute gradually reduce their uncertainty.

Nevertheless, consumers with less knowledge will take advantage of opportunities to process by attribute, such as by viewing information in a matrix in *Consumer Reports* or in another format that simplifies searching. One study found that presenting lists of nutritional information in the grocery store is popular with consumers. The *Consumer Reports* rating charts, which provide information about the top brands and best buys in various product categories in a simple format, are popular sources of information. As noted earlier, search engines and shopping agents also make it easier for consumers to process by attribute, especially by price.

Marketing Implications

Marketers have to make the specific information that consumers seek easily and readily available by emphasizing it in communications, whether printed, online, broadcast, accessed through mobile app, or presented through the sales force. It is important to remember that consumers are less likely to choose a brand that performs poorly on attributes that are accessed frequently. Therefore, marketers should be sure that their offerings perform well on attributes that are heavily accessed, including price.

When marketers promise to match the lowest price that consumers can find, such policies spark more extensive searching when search costs are low (as consumers look for the lowest price) but less extensive searching when search costs are high (and consumers perceive that the policy signals low prices).[156] Sainsbury's, a major U.K. grocery chain, recently introduced Brand Match, a price-matching policy, to reassure consumers that it has low prices, after rivals such as Tesco and Morrisons began aggressive marketing campaigns focused on price cuts. "Brand Match is giving [consumers] a guarantee that they can do their shopping at Sainsbury's and not miss out on deals on their favorite brands," explains the CEO.[157] Finally, companies can pay search sites such as Google to make brand information available in a prominently positioned sponsored link when consumers perform certain keyword searches. _____

SUMMARY

This chapter examined the three initial stages of the consumer judgment and decision-making process. Problem recognition, the first stage, is the perceived difference between an ideal state and the actual state. When there is a discrepancy between these two states, the consumer may be motivated to resolve it by engaging in decision making.

Internal search is the recall of information, experiences, and feelings from memory. The extent of internal search generally increases as motivation, ability, and opportunity increase. Aspects of an offer that are more salient, diagnostic, vivid, and related to goals are the most likely to be recalled. Several biases apply to internal search: confirmation bias (the tendency to remember information that reinforces our overall beliefs); inhibition (the recall of some information inhibits the recall of other attributes; and mood (the tendency to recall mood-congruent information).

When consumers need more information or are uncertain about recalled information, they engage in external search, acquiring information from outside sources through prepurchase search (in response to problem recognition) or ongoing search (which continues regardless of problem recognition). During external search, consumers can acquire information from retailers, media and social media, other people, and independent sources and by experiencing the product. Retailer and media searches account for the most search activity, but interpersonal sources increase in importance as consumer knowledge decreases and normative factors increase.

Consumers will conduct a more extensive search when they have a higher motivation and opportunity to process information.

Situational factors affect the consumer's opportunity to process the information. Brand name and price are the most accessed attributes in an external search. Consumers also tend to exhibit a confirmation bias in their external search. More salient and diagnostic information tends to be accessed earlier. Finally, consumers tend to process either by brand or by attribute. Attribute search is easier and preferred, but often the information is not organized to facilitate such processing.

Questions for Review and Discussion

1. How does a discrepancy between the ideal state and the actual state affect consumer behavior?

2. What factors affect the inclusion of brands in the consideration set, and why would a company want its brand in the consideration set?

3. How does confirmation bias operate in internal and external searches for information?

4. What five broad groups of sources can consumers consult during external search?

5. How do involvement, perceived risk, perceived costs and benefits, and the consideration set affect a consumer's motivation to conduct an external search?

6. When would a consumer be more likely to conduct an external search by brand rather than by attribute? Which search process would a marketer prefer consumers to use—and why?

CONSUMER BEHAVIOR CASE

Searching for a Search Engine

There's a big marketing battle brewing among the search engines of the world. Google is so widely used that many consumers talk of "Googling" a product or service when they mean they're going to do some Internet research. But as dominant as Google may be in some countries—it handles two out of every three online searches in the United States, for instance—it does face competition, both locally and globally. Still, because of Google's firmly entrenched position, other search engines have to start by stirring consumers to recognize a problem with their current search engine.

The most aggressive of Google's search competitors is bing, introduced by parent company Microsoft in 2009. Within months, bing had arranged to become the official search engine of Yahoo!, one of the web's original search sites. Thanks to this deal, bing improved its share and now holds about 15 percent of the U.S. search market, pulling nearly even with the market share of Yahoo! worldwide, however, bing holds only a tiny share of the search market, whereas Google still controls more than 80 percent of the global search market.

To increase brand awareness, to put itself in the consideration set, and bring consumers to its search site, bing runs ads on TV and in movie theaters to promote itself as a "decision engine." The messages, delivered with a dash of humor, suggest that consumers can avoid information overload and find just what they need by searching on bing, whether they're looking for how-to videos, holiday gift ideas, airline flights, or movie showtimes.

For its part, Google is pouring on the warm feelings in its ads to engage consumers emotionally and retain their loyalty. Ads portray Google as the place to search for long-lost friends, for example, among other search stories with affective appeal. In essence, Google is reminding consumers: "Remember how it felt when you did those successful searches through our site? Use Google when you're searching for something you care about, whether it's videos, images, news, maps, or more."

Google also wants to be sure that mobile users continue to choose its search site when using their phones to locate information about goods and services. Currently, Google is responsible for more than 90 percent of U.S. mobile searches. However, that may change as many search sites gear up in earnest for this fast-growing segment.

Other search engines have captured considerable market share outside the United States by optimizing their searches and the look of their sites and results to meet local needs and preferences. Baidu, for example, is the market leader in Chinese-language searches, and Yandex is the leader in Russian-language searches.

In addition, various niche search sites want consumers to choose them for specialized searches. VideoSurf, now owned by Microsoft, enables consumers to search for specific content among 50 million online video clips. It is being marketed in connection with Microsoft's Xbox system as a way for consumers to locate sports or music videos to stream to their TVs. Mocavo, used to search for names of ancestors, is marketed through mentions on genealogy blogs and websites. Wolfram Alpha calls itself a "computational knowledge engine" that can help users search for data about mathematics, statistics, engineering, units and measures, and more. Infomine searches academic resource collections available online. findsounds.com enables consumers to locate and listen to sound effects posted on the web. spezify.com emphasizes colorful and intuitive visual display rather than a simple text listing of results. No matter what kind of search consumers want to conduct online, there's a site to help them locate exactly what they want.[158]

CASE QUESTIONS

1. Why is achieving a significant level of brand familiarity especially important for Google's competitors?
2. What are the search sites doing to increase consumers' motivation, ability, and opportunity to process external information?
3. Are consumers likely to search by brand or search by attribute when comparing search sites? Which process is likely to favor the specialized search sites?
4. Given the role of prototypicality in recall of search engine brands, what do you think niche search sites should do to get into the consideration set?

ENDNOTES

1. Kelsey Volkmann, "Enterprise Adds QR Codes to Cars," *St. Louis Business Journal*, November 8, 2011, www.bizjournals.com; Giselle Tsirulnik, "Audi A7 Times Square Billboard Engages Pedestrians via Mobile," *Mobile Marketer*, April 19, 2011, www.mobilemarketer.com; Dale Buss, "Nissan's QR Marketing Enables 'After Hours' Shopping," *Brand Channel*, August 8, 2011, www.brandchannel.com; and Candace Lombardi, "New Car Labels Offer QR Codes but No Grades," *CNet*, May 25, 2011, www.cnet.com.

2. "Hermes Can't Keep Up with Demand for Birkin Bag," *Chosun Ilbo*, September 2, 2011, http://english.chosun.com.

3. "One Example of How Much Koreans Love Luxury," *Wall Street Journal*, August 17, 2011, www.wsj.com; and Michael Barbaro, "Never Mind What's in Them, Bags Are the Fashion," *New York Times*, December 16, 2007, www.nytimes.com.

4. Joseph W. Alba, J. Wesley Hutchinson, and John G. Lynch, "Memory and Decision Making," in eds. Thomas C. Roberton and Harold H. Kassarjian, *Handbook of Consumer Behavior* (Englewood Cliffs, N.J.: Prentice-Hall, 1991).

5. John R. Hauser and Birger Wernerfelt, "An Evaluation Cost Model of Consideration Sets," *Journal of Consumer Research*, March 1990, pp. 393–408.

6. Jack Neff, "Colgate Keeps Triclosan in Its $1B Total Brand," *Advertising Age*, January 24, 2011, p. 5.

7. Karthikeyan Sundaram and Mehul Srivastava, "Billionaires Struggle to Turn Booming Travel in India into Airline Profits," *Bloomberg Businessweek*, November 14, 2011, www.businessweek.com; Heather Timmons, "For India's Airlines, Passengers Are Plentiful but Profits Are Scarce," *New York Times*, May 8, 2007, p. C8; and Susan Carey, "Even When It's Quicker to Travel by Train, Many Fly," *Wall Street Journal*, August 29, 1997, pp. B1, B5.

8. Shailaja Sharma, "L'Oreal Says Sticking Real Close to Consumers Is the Key to the India Game," *Daily News & Analysis*, September 9, 2011, n. p.

9. Kalpesh Kaushik Desai and Wayne D. Hoyer, "Descriptive Characteristics of Memory-Based Consideration Sets: Influence of Usage Occasion Frequency and Usage Location Familiarity," *Journal of Consumer Research* 27, December 2000, pp. 309–323.

10. Prakash Nedungadi and J. Wesley Hutchinson, "The Prototypicality of Brands: Relationships with Brand Awareness, Preference, and Usage," in eds. Elizabeth C. Hirschman and Morris B. Holbrook, *Advances in Consumer Research*, vol. 12 (Provo, Utah: Association for Consumer Research, 1985), pp. 498–503; and Prakash Nedungadi, "Recall and Consumer Consideration Sets: Influencing Choice Without Altering Brand Evaluations," *Journal of Consumer Research*, December 1990, pp. 263–276.

11. Alba, Hutchinson, and Lynch, "Memory and Decision Making."

12. Nedungadi and Hutchinson, "The Prototypicality of Brands"; and James Ward and Barbara Loken, "The Quintessential Snack Food: Measurement of Product Prototypes," in ed. Richard J. Lutz, *Advances in Consumer Research*, vol. 13 (Provo, Utah: Association for Consumer Research, 1986), pp. 126–131.

13. Siew Meng Leong, Swee Hoon Ang, and Lai Leng Tham, "Increasing Brand Name Recall in Print Advertising Among Asian Consumers," *Journal of Advertising*, Summer 1996, pp. 65–82.

14. Stewart Shapiro, Deborah J. MacInnis, and Susan E. Heckler, "The Effects of Incidental Ad Exposure on the Formation of

15. Alba, Hutchinson, and Lynch, "Memory and Decision Making."

16. S. Ratneshwar and Allan D. Shocker, "Substitution in Use and the Role of Usage Context in Product Category Structures," *Journal of Marketing Research*, August 1991, pp. 281–295.

17. E.J. Schultz, "A Tiger at 60," *Advertising Age*, August 29, 2011, www.adage.com.

18. Nedungadi and Hutchinson, "The Prototypicality of Brands"; and Ward and Loken, "The Quintessential Snack Food."

19. "Nigeria's Mad Men," *Economist*, April 30, 2011, p. 72.

20. John Springer, "Target Looks to Wallet Share, Canada for Growth," *Supermarket News*, August 29, 2011, http://supermarketnews.com.

21. Lara O'Reilly, "Coca-Cola Replaces Packaging with More Eco-Friendly Bottles," *Marketing Week*, September 12, 2011, www.marketingweek.co.uk.

22. Gabriel Biehal and Dipankar Chakravarti, "Consumers' Use of Memory and External Information in Choice: Macro and Micro Perspectives," *Journal of Consumer Research*, March 1986, pp. 382–405.

23. Gabriel Biehal and Dipankar Chakravarti, "Information Accessibility as a Moderator of Consumer Choice," *Journal of Consumer Research*, June 1983, pp. 1–14.

24. Michaela Waenke, Gerd Bohner, and Andreas Jurkowitsch, "There Are Many Reasons to Drive a BMW?" *Journal of Consumer Research*, September 1997, pp. 170–177.

25. Shai Danziger, Simone Moran, and Vered Rafaely, "The Influence of Ease of Retrieval on Judgment as a Function of Attention to Subjective Experience," *Journal of Consumer Psychology* 16, no. 2, 2006, pp. 191–195.

26. Meryl Paula Gardner, "Advertising Effects on Attributes Recalled and Criteria Used for Brand Evaluations," *Journal of Consumer Research*, December 1983, pp. 310–318; Scott B. MacKenzie, "The Role of Attention in Mediating the Effect of Advertising on Attribute Importance," *Journal of Consumer Research*, September 1986, pp. 174–195; and Priya Raghubir and Geeta Menon, "AIDS and Me, Never the Twain Shall Meet," *Journal of Consumer Research*, June 1998, pp. 52–63.

27. Fellman and Lynch, "Self-Generated Validity and Other Effects of Measurement"; and John G. Lynch, Howard Marmorstein, and Michael F. Weigold, "Choices from Sets Including Remembered Brands," *Journal of Consumer Research*, September 1988, pp. 169–184.

28. Carolyn L. Costley and Merrie Brucks, "Selective Recall and Information Use in Consumer Preferences," *Journal of Consumer Research*, March 1992, pp. 464–474; and Geeta Menon, Priya Raghubit, and Norbert Schwarz, "Behavioral Frequency Judgments," *Journal of Consumer Research*, September 1995, pp. 212–228.

29. Paul M. Herr, Frank R. Kardes, and John Kim, "Effects of Word-of-Mouth and Product-Attribute Information on Persuasion," *Journal of Consumer Research*, March 1991, pp. 454–462.

30. Bryan Roth, "Volts Give Car-Sharing a New Charge," *Duke Today*, August 31, 2011, http://today.duke.edu.

31. Walter Kintsch and Tuen A. Van Dyk, "Toward a Model of Text Comprehension and Production," *Psychological Review*, September 1978, pp. 363–394; and S. Ratneshwar, David G. Mick, and Gail Reitinger, "Selective Attention in Consumer Information Processing," in eds. Marvin E. Goldberg, Gerald Gorn, and Richard W. Pollay, *Advances in Consumer Research*,

Consideration Sets," *Journal of Consumer Research*, June 1997, pp. 94–104.

vol. 17 (Provo, Utah: Association for Consumer Research, 1990), pp. 547–553.

32. Jacob Jacoby, Tracy Troutman, Alfred Kuss, and David Mazursky, "Experience and Expertise in Complex Decision Making," in ed. Richard J. Lutz, *Advances in Consumer Research*, vol. 13 (Provo, Utah: Association for Consumer Research, 1986), pp. 469–475.

33. Stewart Shapiro and Mark T. Spence, "Factors Affecting Encoding, Retrieval, and Alignment of Sensory Attributes in a Memory-Based Brand Choice Task," *Journal of Consumer Research*, March 2002, pp. 603–617.

34. Gardner, "Advertising Effects on Attributes Recalled and Criteria Used for Brand Evaluations"; and Mackenzie, "The Role of Attention in Mediating the Effect of Advertising on Attribute Importance."

35. Mark I. Alpert, "Identification of Determinant Attributes," *Journal of Marketing Research*, May 1971, pp. 184–191.

36. M.R.F. Buckley, "Coffee, Doughnut Giant Has Recipe for Success," *WCVB-TV*, August 14, 2011, www.thebostonchannel.com.

37. Jolita Kiselius and Brian Sternthal, "Examining the Vividness Controversy," *Journal of Consumer Research*, March 1986, pp. 418–431; and Herr, Kardes, and Kim, "Effects of Word-of-Mouth and Product-Attribute Information on Persuasion."

38. Punam Anand Keller and Lauren G. Block, "Vividness Effects," *Journal of Consumer Research*, December 1997, pp. 295–304.

39. Lynn Monty, "Word of Mouth? In #BTV, It's the Word of Tweet," *Burlington Free Press (Vermont)*, September 8, 2011, www.burlingtonfreepress.com.

40. Reid Hastie and Bernadette Park, "The Relationship Between Memory and Judgment Depends on Whether the Judgment Task Is Memory-Based or On-Line," *Psychological Review*, June 1986, pp. 258–268; and Barbara Loken and Ronald Hoverstad, "Relationships Between Information Recall and Subsequent Attitudes," *Journal of Consumer Research*, September 1985, pp. 155–168.

41. Biehal and Chakravarti, "Consumers' Use of Memory and External Information in Choice: Macro and Micro Perspectives"; and Jong-Won Park and Manoj Hastak, "Memory-Based Product Judgments," *Journal of Consumer Research*, December 1994, pp. 534–547.

42. Zeynep Gürhan-Canli, "The Effect of Expected Variability of Product Quality and Attribute Uniqueness on Family Brand Evaluations," *Journal of Consumer Research*, June 2003, pp. 105–114.

43. Hans Baumgartner, Mita Sujan, and James R. Bettman, "Autobiographical Memories, Affect, and Consumer Information Processing," *Journal of Consumer Psychology* 1, no. 1, 1992, pp. 53–82.

44. Geoff Morrow, "The Best and Wackiest Minor League Baseball Promotions," *Patriot-News (Mechanicsburg, PA)*, June 6, 2010, www.pennlive.com.

45. Elizabeth Cowley and Eunika Janus, "Not Necessarily Better, but Certainly Different: A Limit to the Advertising Misinformation Effect on Memory," *Journal of Consumer Research*, June 2004, pp. 229–235.

46. Jason Duty, "Customer Support in the Virtual Era," *Forbes.com*, September 12, 2011, www.forbes.com.

47. Michael J. Houston, Terry L. Childers, and Susan E. Heckler, "Picture–Word Consistency and the Elaborative Processing of Advertisements," *Journal of Marketing Research*, November 1987, pp. 359–369.

48. Joseph W. Alba and Amitava Chattopadhyay, "Salience Effects in Brand Recall," *Journal of Marketing Research*, November 1986,

pp. 363–369; and Kiselius and Sternthal, "Examining the Vividness Controversy."

49. Alba and Chattopadhyay, "Salience Effects in Brand Recall"; and Kiselius and Sternthal, Examining the Vividness Controversy."

50. Gordon H. Bower, "Mood and Memory," *American Psychologist*, February 1981, pp. 129–148; Gordon H. Bower, Stephen Gilligan, and Kenneth Montiero, "Selectivity of Learning Caused by Affective States," *Journal of Experimental Psychology: General*, December 1981, pp. 451–473; and Alice M. Isen, Thomas Shalker, Margaret Clark, and Lynn Karp, "Affect, Accessibility of Material in Memory, and Behavior," *Journal of Personality and Social Psychology*, January 1978, pp. 1–12.

51. Matthew Creamer, "Microsoft Plans Blitz to Fend Off Apple," *Advertising Age*, December 3, 2007, www.adage.com.

52. Joni Grey, "Honda Offers 'Good Reasons' to Buy Its Cars in Multimedia Push," *Advertising Age*, September 13, 2011, www.adage.com.

53. Peter H. Bloch, Daniel L. Sherrell, and Nancy M. Ridgway, "Consumer Search: An Extended Framework," *Journal of Consumer Research*, June 1986, pp. 119–126.

54. Sharon E. Beatty and Scott M. Smith, "External Search Effort," *Journal of Consumer Research*, June 1987, pp. 83–95.

55. Charles M. Brooks, Patrick J. Kaufmann, and Donald P. Lichtenstein, "Travel Configuration on Consumer Trip-Chained Store Choice," *Journal of Consumer Research* 31, no. 2, 2004, pp. 241–248.

56. Beatty and Smith, "External Search Effort."

57. See Judi Strebel, Tulim Erdem, and Joffre Swait, "Consumer Search in High Technology Markets," *Journal of Consumer Psychology* 14, no. 1–2, 2004, pp. 96–104.

58. David F. Midgley, "Patterns of Interpersonal Information Seeking for the Purchase of a Symbolic Product," *Journal of Marketing Research*, February 1983, pp. 74–83.

59. Sarah Shearman, "Burberry Rolls Out Facebook Sampling Drive," *Marketing*, August 19, 2011, www.marketingmagazine.co.uk.

60. Denver D'Rozario and Susan P. Douglas, "Effect of Assimilation on Prepurchase External Information-Search Tendencies," *Journal of Consumer Psychology* 8, no. 2, 1999, pp. 187–209.

61. Niranjan J. Raman, "A Qualitative Investigation of Web-Browsing Behavior," in eds. Merrie Brucks and Deborah J. MacInnis, *Advances in Consumer Research*, vol. 24 (Provo, Utah: Association for Consumer Research, 1997), pp. 511–516.

62. Wendy W. Moe and Sha Yang, "Inertia Disruption: The Impact of a New Competitive Entrant on Online Consumer Search," *Journal of Marketing*, January 2009, pp. 109–121.

63. Peter J. Danaher, Guy W. Mullarkey, and Skander Essegaier, "Factors Affecting Web Site Visit Duration: A Cross-Domain Analysis," *Journal of Marketing Research*, May 2006, pp. 182–194.

64. Sally J. McMillan and Jang-Sun Hwang, "Measures of Perceived Interactivity: An Exploration of the Role of Direction of Communication, User Control, and Time in Shaping Perceptions of Interactivity," *Journal of Advertising*, Fall 2002, pp. 29–42; and Yuping Liu and L. J. Shrum, "What Is Interactivity and Is It Always Such a Good Thing," *Journal of Advertising*, Winter 2002, pp. 53–64.

65. Gerald J. Gorn, Amitava Chattopadhyay, Jaideep Sengupta, and Shashank Tripathi, "Waiting for the Web: How Screen Color Affects Time Perception," *Journal of Marketing Research*, May 2004, pp. 215–225.

66. Charla Mathwick and Edward Rigdon, "Play, Flow, and the On-line Search Experience," *Journal of Consumer Research*, September 2004, pp. 324–332.

67. Martin Holzwarth, Chris Janiszewski, and Marcus M. Neumann, "The Influence of Avatars on Online Consumer Shopping Behavior," *Journal of Marketing*, June 2006, pp. 19–36.

68. Clemens F. Kohler, Andrew J. Rohn, Ko de Ruyter, and Martiin Wetzels, "Return on Interactivity: The Impact of Online Agents on Newcomer Adjustment," *Journal of Marketing*, March 2011, pp. 93–108.

69. Puneet Manchanda, Jean-Pierre Dubé, Khim Yong Goh, and Pradeep K. Chintagunta, "The Effect of Banner Advertising on Internet Purchasing," *Journal of Marketing Research*, February 2006, pp. 98–108.

70. "Back-to-School Spending Tests Your Wallet and Your Patience," *Reuters*, September 6, 2011, www.reuters.com.

71. Andrew D. Gershoff, Susan M. Broniarczyk, and Patricia M. West, "Recommendation or Evaluation? Task Sensitivity in Information Source Selection," *Journal of Consumer Research*, December 2001, pp. 418–438.

72. Alan D. J. Cooke, Harish Sujan, Mita Sujan, and Barton A. Weitz, "Marketing the Unfamiliar: The Role of Context and Item-Specific Information in Electronic Agent Recommendations," *Journal of Marketing Research*, November 2002, pp. 488–497.

73. Dan Ariely, John G. Lynch Jr., and Manuel Aparicio IV, "Learning by Collaborative and Individual-Based Recommendation Agents," *Journal of Consumer Psychology* 14, no. 1–2, 2004, pp. 81–95.

74. Caterina Sismeiro and Randolph E. Bucklin, "Modeling Purchase Behavior at an E-Commerce Web Site," *Journal of Marketing Research*, August 2004, pp. 306–323.

75. Nicholas H. Lurie, "Decision Making in Information-Rich Environments: The Role of Information Structure," *Journal of Consumer Research*, March 2004, pp. 473–486.

76. Ross Kerber, "Direct Hit Uses Popularity to Narrow Internet Searches," *Wall Street Journal*, July 2, 1998, p. B4.

77. Kristen Diel, "When Two Rights Make a Wrong: Searching Too Much in Ordered Environments," *Journal of Marketing Research*, August 2005, pp. 313–322; and Kristen Diel and Gal Zauberman, "Searching Ordered Sets," *Journal of Consumer Research* 31, no. 4, 2005, pp. 824–832.

78. Benjamin Scheibehenne, Rainer Greifeneder, and Peter M. Todd, "Can There Ever Be Too Many Options? A Meta-Analytical Review of Choice Overload," *Journal of Consumer Research*, October 2010, pp. 409–425.

79. Hairong Li, Terry Daugherty, and Frank Biocca, "Impact of 3-D Advertising on Product Knowledge, Brand Attitude, and Purchase Intention: The Mediating Role of Presence," *Journal of Advertising*, Fall 2002, pp. 43–57.

80. Bridget Carey, "Virtual Tours May Help Draw Students," *Register-Guard (Eugene, OR)*, September 4, 2011, www.registerguard.com.

81. Eileen Fischer, Julia Bristor, and Brenda Gainer, "Creating or Escaping Community? An Exploratory Study of Internet Consumers' Behaviors," in eds. Kim P. Corfman and John G. Lynch, *Advances in Consumer Research*, vol. 23 (Provo, Utah: Association for Consumer Research, 1996), pp. 178–182; and John Buskin, "Tales from the Front," *Wall Street Journal*, December 7, 1998, p. R6.

82. Neil A. Granitz and James C. Ward, "Virtual Community: A Sociocognitive Analysis," in eds. Kim P. Corfman and John G.

Lynch, *Advances in Consumer Research*, vol. 23 (Provo, Utah: Association for Consumer Research, 1996), pp. 161–166.

83. Sarah Mahoney, "Study: Negative Reviews Grow More Powerful," *MediaPost*, August 31, 2011, www.mediapost.com.

84. Allen M. Weiss, Nicholas H. Lurie, and Deborah J. MacInnis, "Listening to Strangers: Whose Responses Are Valuable, How Valuable Are They, and Why?" *Journal of Marketing Research*, August 2008, pp. 425–436.

85. Rebecca Walker Naylor, Cait Poynor Lamberton, and David A. Norton, "Seeing Ourselves in Others: Reviewer Ambiguity, Egocentric Anchoring, and Persuasion," *Journal of Marketing Research*, June 2011, pp. 617–631.

86. Holly Vanscoy, "Life after Living.com," *Smart Business*, February 2001, pp. 68–10; and Clare Saliba, "With Webvan Gone, Where Will Online Shoppers Turn?" *E-Commerce Times*, July 10, 2001, www.ecommercetimes.com.

87. John C. Ryan, "Dipping into Books Online," *Christian Science Monitor*, November 13, 2003, p. 12.

88. Stacy L. Wood, "Remote Purchase Environments: The Influence of Return Policy Leniency on Two-Stage Decision Process," *Journal of Marketing Research* 38, May 2001, pp. 157–169.

89. Dave Fazekas, "How to Solve the Free Shipping Challenge," *Multichannel Merchant*, November 14, 2011, www.multichannelmerchant.com.

90. Monika Kukar-Kinney and Angeline G. Close, "The Determinants of Consumers' Online Shopping Cart Abandonment," *Journal of the Academy of Marketing Science* 38, 2010, 240–250.

91. Charles Nicholls, "Can Shopping Cart Abandonment Predict Online Buying Behavior?" *ClickZ*, September 13, 2011, www.clickz.com.

92. Zak Stambor, "Vintage Tub & Bath Finds Abandonment E-mails Help Its Message Sink In," *Internet Retailer*, March 23, 2011, www.internetretailer.com.

93. Nivedita Mookerji & Dilasha Seth, "Casting the Net Wider," *Business Standard (India)*, September 12, 2011, www.business-standard.com/india.

94. Jacob Jacoby, Robert W. Chestnut, Karl Weigl, and William A. Fisher, "Prepurchase Information Acquisition," in ed. Beverlee B. Anderson, *Advances in Consumer Research*, vol. 3 (Cincinnati, Ohio: Association for Consumer Research, 1976), pp. 306–314; and Jacob Jacoby, Robert W. Chestnut, and William Silberman, "Consumer Use and Comprehension of Nutrition Information," *Journal of Consumer Research*, September 1977, pp. 119–128.

95. Peng Huang, Nicholas H. Lurie, and Sabyasachi Mitra, "Searching for Expreience on the Web: An Empirical Examination of Consumer Behavior for Search and Experience Goods," *Journal of Marketing*, March 2009, pp. 55–69.

96. John O. Claxton, Joseph N. Fry, and Bernard Portis, "A Taxonomy of Prepurchase Information Gathering Patterns," *Journal of Consumer Research*, December 1974, pp. 35–42.

97. Bloch, Sherrell, and Ridgway, "Consumer Search: An Extended Framework."

98. R. A. Bauer, "Consumer Behavior as Risk Taking," in ed. Robert S. Hancock, *Dynamic Marketing for a Changing World* (Chicago: American Marketing Association, 1960), pp. 389–398; and Rohit Deshpande and Wayne D. Hoyer, "Consumer Decision Making: Strategies, Cognitive Effort, and Perceived Risk," in *1983 Educators' Conference Proceedings* (Chicago: American Marketing Association, 1983), pp. 88–91.

99. Keith B. Murray, "A Test of Services Marketing Theory," *Journal of Marketing*, January 1991, pp. 10–25; and Joel E. Urbany, Peter R. Dickson, and William L. Wilkie, "Buyer Uncertainty and Information Search," *Journal of Consumer Research*, September 1989, pp. 208–215.

100. David J. Furse, Girish N. Punj, and David W. Stewart, "A Typology of Individual Search Strategies Among Purchasers of New Automobiles," *Journal of Consumer Research*, March 1984, pp. 417–431; Narasimhan Srinivasan and Brian T. Ratchford, "An Empirical Test of a Model of External Search for Automobiles," *Journal of Consumer Research*, September 1991, pp. 233–242; and Jacob Jacoby, James J. Jaccard, Imran Currim, Alfred Kuss, Asim Ansari, and Tracy Troutman, "Tracing the Impact of Item-by-Item Information Accessing on Uncertainty Reduction," *Journal of Consumer Research*, September 1994, pp. 291–303.

101. Calmetta Y. Coleman, "Selling Jewelry, Dolls, and TVs Next to Corn Flakes," *Wall Street Journal*, November 19, 1997, pp. B1, B8.

102. Diehl and Zauberman, "Searching Ordered Sets."

103. Gal Zauberman, "The Intertemporal Dynamics of Consumer Lock-In," *Journal of Consumer Research*, December 2003, pp. 405–419.

104. Sridhar Moorthy, Brian T. Ratchford, and Debabrata Talukdar, "Consumer Information Search Revisited," *Journal of Consumer Research*, March 1997, pp. 263–277.

105. Jill G. Griffin and Susan M. Broniarczyk, "The Slippery Slope: The Impact of Feature Alignability on Search and Satisfaction," *Journal of Marketing Research*, April 2010, pp. 323–334.

106. Calvin P. Duncan and Richard W. Olshavsky, "External Search: The Role of Consumer Beliefs," *Journal of Marketing Research*, February 1982, pp. 32–43; and Girish N. Punj and Richard Staelin, "A Model of Information Search Behavior for New Automobiles," *Journal of Consumer Research*, September 1983, pp. 181–196.

107. Duncan and Olshavsky, "External Search: The Role of Consumer Beliefs."

108. Kathy Hammond, Gil McWilliam, and Andrea Narholz Diaz, "Fun and Work on the Web: Differences in Attitudes between Novices and Experienced Users," in eds. Joseph W. Alba and J. Wesley Hutchinson, *Advances in Consumer Research*, vol. 25 (Provo, Utah: Association for Consumer Research, 1998), pp. 372–378.

109. Joan E. Rigdon, "Advertisers Give Surfers Games to Play," *Wall Street Journal*, October 28, 1996, pp. B1, B6.

110. Laura A. Peracchio and Alice M. Tybout, "The Moderating Role of Prior Knowledge in Schema-Based Product Evaluation," *Journal of Consumer Research*, December 1996, pp. 177–192.

111. Joan Meyers-Levy and Alice Tybout, "Schema-Congruity as Basis for Product Evaluation," *Journal of Consumer Research*, June 1989, pp. 39–54.

112. Natalie Zmuda, "Skinny Pepsi Can Launch Is Heavy with Controversy," *Advertising Age*, February 21, 2011, www.adage.com.

113. Julie L. Ozanne, Merrie Brucks, and Dhruv Grewal, "A Study of Information Search Behavior during Categorization of New Products," *Journal of Consumer Research*, March 1992, pp. 452–463.

114. Punj and Staelin, "A Model of Consumer Information Search Behavior for New Automobiles"; and Kiel and Layton, "Dimensions of Consumer Information Seeking."

115. Christine Moorman, Kristin Diehl, David Brinberg, and Blair Kidwell, "Subjective Knowledge, Search Locations, and Consumer Choice," *Journal of Consumer Research*, December 2004, pp. 673–680.

116. Merrie Brucks, "The Effects of Product Class Knowledge on Information Search Behavior," *Journal of Consumer Research*, June 1985, pp. 1–16; James R. Bettman and C. Whan Park, "Effects of Prior Knowledge and Experience and Phase of the Choice Process on Consumer Decision Processes: A Protocol Analysis," *Journal of Consumer Research*, December 1980, pp. 234–248; Eric J. Johnson and J. Edward Russo, "Product Familiarity and Learning New Information," *Journal of Consumer Research*, June 1984, pp. 542–550; P. S. Raju, Subhas C. Lonial, and W. Glyn Mangold, "Differential Effects of Subjective Knowledge, Objective Knowledge, and Usage Experience on Decision Making," *Journal of Consumer Psychology* 4, no. 2, 1995, pp. 153–180; and Joseph W. Alba and J. Wesley Hutchinson, "Dimensions of Consumer Expertise," *Journal of Consumer Research*, March 1987, pp. 411–454.

117. Noel Capon and Roger Davis, "Basic Cognitive Ability Measures as Predictors of Consumer Information Processing Strategies," *Journal of Consumer Research*, June 1984, pp. 551–563.

118. For a summary of a number of studies, see Joseph W. Newman, "Consumer External Search: Amount and Determinants," in eds. Arch Woodside, Jagdish Sheth, and Peter Bennett, *Consumer and Industrial Buying Behavior* (New York: North-Holland, 1977), pp. 79–94; and Charles M. Schaninger and Donald Sciglimpaglia, "The Influences of Cognitive Personality Traits and Demographics on Consumer Information Acquisition," *Journal of Consumer Research*, September 1981, pp. 208–216.

119. Scott Painton and James W. Gentry, "Another Look at the Impact of Information Presentation Format," *Journal of Consumer Research*, September 1985, pp. 240–244.

120. J. Edward Russo, Richard Staelin, Catherine A. Nolan, Gary J. Russell, and Barbara L. Metcalf, "Nutrition Information in the Supermarket," *Journal of Consumer Research*, June 1986, pp. 48–70.

121. Christine Moorman, "The Effects of Stimulus and Consumer Utilization of Nutrition Information," *Journal of Consumer Research*, December 1990, pp. 362–374.

122. Chris Janiszewski, "The Influence of Display Characteristics on Visual Exploratory Search Behavior," *Journal of Consumer Research*, December 1998, pp. 290–301.

123. Mario Pandelaere, Kobe Millet, and Bram Van den Bergh, "Madonna or Don McLean? The Effect of Order of Exposure on Relative Liking," *Journal of Consumer Psychology* 20, 2010, 442–451.

124. William L. Moore and Donald L. Lehman, "Validity of Information Display Boards," *Journal of Marketing Research*, November 1980, pp. 296–307; and C. Whan Park, Easwar S. Iyer, and Daniel C. Smith, "The Effects of Situational Factors on In-Store Grocery Shopping Behavior," *Journal of Consumer Research*, March 1989, pp. 422–433.

125. John R. Hauser, Glen L. Urban, and Bruce D. Weinberg, "How Consumers Allocate Their Time When Searching for Information," *Journal of Marketing Research*, November 1993, pp. 452–466.

126. Randolph E. Bucklin and Catarina Sismeiro, "A Model of Web Site Browsing Behavior Estimated on Click-Stream Data," *Journal of Marketing Research*, August 2003, pp. 249–267.

127. Alhassan G. Abdul-Muhmin, "Contingent Decision Behavior," *Journal of Consumer Psychology* 8, no. 1, 1999, pp. 91–111.

128. Naomi Mandel and Eric J. Johnson, "When Web Pages Influence Choice: Effects of Visual Primes on Experts and Novices," *Journal of Consumer Research*, September 2002, pp. 235–245.

129. Furse, Punj, and Stewart, "A Typology of Individual Search Strategies among Purchasers of New Automobiles."

130. Brian T. Ratchford, Myung-Soo Lee, and Debabrata Talukdar, "The Impact of the Internet on Information Search for Automobiles," *Journal of Marketing Research*, May 2003, pp. 193–209.

131. Judi Strebel, Tülin Erdem, and Joffre Swait, "Consumer Search in High Technology Markets: Exploring the Use of Traditional Information Channels," *Journal of Consumer Psychology*, 2004, pp. 96–104.

132. Nanette Byrnes, "More Clicks at the Bricks," *Business Week*, December 17, 2007, pp. 50–52; and Katherine Field Boccaccio, "Macy's Launches Tech Pilots at Namesake and Bloomingdale's Stores," *Chain Store Age*, September 13, 2011, www.chainstoreage.com.

133. Jacob Jacoby, Robert W. Chestnut, and William A. Fisher, "A Behavioral Process Approach to Information Acquisition in Nondurable Purchasing," *Journal of Marketing Research*, November 1978, pp. 532–544.

134. Kent B. Monroe, "The Influence of Price Differences and Brand Familiarity on Brand Preferences," *Journal of Consumer Research*, June 1976, pp. 42–49.

135. Kristin Diehl, Laura J. Kornish, and John G. Lynch Jr., "Smart Agents: When Lower Search Costs for Quality Information Increase Price Sensitivity," *Journal of Consumer Research*, June 2003, pp. 56–71.

136. Dhruv Grewal and Howard Marmorstein, "Market Price Variation, Perceived Price Variation, and Consumers' Price Search Decision for Durable Goods," *Journal of Consumer Research*, December 1994, pp. 453–460.

137. Dengfeng Yan and Jaideep Sengupta, "Effects of Construal Level on the Price-Quality Relationship," *Journal of Consumer Research*, August 2011, pp. 376–389.

138. Kurt A. Carlson, Margaret G. Meloy, and Daniel Lieb, "Benefits Leader Reversion: How a Once-Preferred Product Recaptures Its Standing," *Journal of Marketing Research*, December 2009, pp. 788–797.

139. Dinesh K. Gauri, K. Sudhir, and Debabrata Talukdar, "The Temporal and Spatial Dimensions of Price Search: Insights from Matching Household Survey and Purchase Data," *Journal of Marketing Research*, April 2008, pp. 226–240.

140. Torsten Bornemann and Christian Homburg, "Psychological Distance and the Dual Role of Price," *Journal of Consumer Research*, October 2011, pp. 490–504.

141. Michiyo Nakamoto, "Tesco's Exit Adds to Japan's Tough Reputation," *Financial Times*, September 1, 2011, www.ft.com; and "Japan's Fast Retailing Rebuilds Units by Tapping Uniqlo Strength," *AsiaPulse News*, December 27, 2007, n.p.

142. Nilufer Z. Aydinoglu and Aradhna Krishna, "Guiltless Gluttony: The Asymmetric Effect of Size Labels on Size Perceptions and Consumption," *Journal of Consumer Research*, April 2011, pp. 1095–1112.

143. Cynthia Huffman, "Goal Change, Information Acquisition, and Transfer," *Journal of Consumer Psychology* 5, no. 1, 1996, pp. 1–26.

144. Deborah Roedder John, Carol A. Scott, and James R. Bettman, "Sampling Data for Covariation Assessment," *Journal of Consumer Research*, March 1986, pp. 406–417.

145. J. Edward Russo and France Leclerc, "An Eye-Fixation Analysis of Choice for Consumer Nondurables," *Journal of Consumer Research*, September 1994, pp. 274–290.

146. Jacoby et al., "Prepurchase Information Acquisition."

147. J. Edward Russo, Margaret G. Meloy, and Husted Medvec, "Predecisional Distortion of Product Information," *Journal of Marketing Research*, November 1998, pp. 438–452.

148. Carol A. Berning and Jacob Jacoby, "Patterns of Information Acquisition in New Product Purchases," *Journal of Consumer Research*, September 1974, pp. 18–22.

149. Itamar Simonson, Joel Huber, and John Payne, "The Relationship between Prior Brand Knowledge and Information Acquisition Order," *Journal of Consumer Research*, March 1988, pp. 566–578.

150. Wendy W. Moe, "An Empirical Two-Stage Choice Model with Varying Decision Rules Applied to Internet Clickstream Data," *Journal of Marketing Research*, November 2006, pp. 680–692; and Amitav Chakravarti, Chris Janiszewski, and Gulden Ulkumen, "The Neglect of Prescreening Information," *Journal of Marketing Research*, November 2006, pp. 642–653.

151. Carrie M. Heilman, Douglas Bowman, and Gordon P. Wright, "The Evolution of Brand Preference and Choice Behaviors of Consumers New to a Market," *Journal of Marketing Research* 37, May 2000, pp. 139–155.

152. Jacoby et al., "Prepurchase Information Acquisition"; and James R. Bettman, *An Information Processing Theory of Consumer Choice* (Reading, Mass.: Addison-Wesley, 1979).

153. Eric J. Johnson and J. Edward Russo, "Product Familiarity and Learning New Information," *Journal of Consumer Research*, June 1984, pp. 542–550; and James R. Bettman and P. Kakkar, "Effects of Information Presentation Format on Consumer Information Acquisition Strategies," *Journal of Consumer Research*, March 1977, pp. 233–240.

154. Raj Sethuraman, Catherine Cole, and Dipak Jain, "Analyzing the Effect of Information Format and Task on Cutoff Search Strategies," *Journal of Consumer Psychology* 3, 1994, pp. 103–136.

155. Jacoby et al., "Tracing the Impact of Item-by-Item Information Accessing on Uncertainty Reduction."

156. Joydeep Srivastava and Nicholas Lurie, "A Consumer Perspective on Price-Matching Refund Policies," *Journal of Consumer Research*, September 2001, pp. 296–307.

157. Ruki Sayid, "Sainsbury's Takes Price War to Rivals," *Daily Mirror (UK)*, November 10, 2011, www.mirror.co.uk.

158. Jamie Yap, "Google's Search Lead Entrenched But Not Unbeatable," *ZDNet Asia*, November 21, 2011, www.zdnetasia.com; Lee Kaelin, "Microsoft Purchases Video Search Engine Firm VideoSurf," *Tech Spot*, November 23, 2011, www.techspot.com; Michael Boland, "Google's Battle for the Mobile Web," *Search Engine Watch*, November 25, 2011, www.searchenginewatch.com; Michael Liedtke, "Bing Hitches Holiday Hopes to Rudolph the Reindeer," *Associated Press*, November 23, 2011, www.businessweek.com; and Clint Boulton, "Google Search Stays 65% Course, Bing Closes on Yahoo," *eWeek*, November 13, 2011, www.eweek.com.

CHAPTER 8

JUDGMENT AND DECISION MAKING BASED ON HIGH EFFORT

After studying this chapter, you will be able to

1. Distinguish between judgment and decision making, and indicate why both processes are important to marketers.

2. Explain how cognitive decision-making models differ from affective decision-making models and why marketers are interested in both types of models.

3. Identify the types of decisions faced by consumers in high-effort situations and discuss how marketers can try to influence these decisions.

4. Outline the ways that consumer characteristics, decision characteristics, and other people can influence high-effort decisions.

© Jason Alden/Bloomberg via Getty Images

INTRODUCTION

Cars Load Up on Gizmos and Gadgets

What *can't* cutting-edge cars do? Ford's SYNC onboard system will read incoming text messages and Twitter updates aloud. Its MyFord Touch allows drivers to touch a screen or use voice commands to crank up the heat, start the defroster, make phone calls, and more. Toyota's Entune dashboard system lets drivers view updated weather maps, stream music from the Web, and even buy movie tickets with a click.

The trend toward loading cars and trucks with high-tech safety and communications features has been accelerating ever since General Motors introduced its innovative hands-free OnStar system in 1996, allowing drivers to speak with a live representative when they need emergency help. These days, OnStar offers a range of voice-activated services, from monitoring engine performance to posting Facebook messages with a verbal command. The world's automakers are adding increasingly sophisticated safety gadgetry with every model year. For instance, the Volkswagen Sharan will be equipped with sensors so it can shift into reverse and park itself at a signal from the driver's phone, without colliding with the curb, cars, or people. Nissan is readying sensors to alert drivers when other cars are moving into their lane or when they accidentally step on the wrong pedal. The list goes on and on as every automaker gets into the race to add new technology now.

Gizmos and gadgets are the latest marketing battleground for automotive manufacturers who must understand the types of judgments that car buyers make (such as that electronics can make a car safer) and the criteria that most influence buying decisions (the ability to stay connected on the go, the security of being able to drive and park safely). In addition, marketers must understand the emotions and feelings that influence consumer decisions (e.g., that a car makes you feel good). This chapter examines high-effort judgments and decisions (see Exhibit 8.1), the kind of judgments and decisions that consumers make when their motivation, ability, and opportunity to process information relevant to the decision are high. By carefully analyzing the factors that enter into judgment and decision making, marketers can acquire valuable insights that help them develop and market offerings to consumers.[1]

HIGH-EFFORT JUDGMENT PROCESSES

Judgment Evaluation of an object or estimate of likelihood of an outcome or event.

Decision making Making a selection among options or courses of action.

Think about the last time you went to a restaurant. While reviewing the menu, you probably considered some items and thought about how good they would be before making your final choice. You were making **judgments**—evaluations or estimates regarding the likelihood of events. Judgment is a critical input into the decision process, but it is not the same as **decision making**, which involves making a selection among options or activities.

In a consumer context, *judgments* are evaluations or estimates regarding the likelihood that products and services possess certain features or will perform in a certain manner.[2] Judgments do not require a decision. Thus, if you see an ad for a new Italian restaurant, you can form a judgment as to whether you will like it, how different it will be from other Italian restaurants, or how expensive it will be. These judgments can serve as important inputs into your decision about whether to eat at the restaurant, but they do not require that you decide whether to go there or not.

Judgment and decision making can also involve different processes.[3] For example, one study found that consumers searched attributes in a different order when they were making judgments than when they were making decisions.[4] Another found that whether consumers' familiarity with a product helped or hurt the amount of information they could recall about it depended on whether they were making judgments or making decisions about the brands.[5] Given the importance of judgment in consumers' information processing, marketers need to understand judgments about (1) likelihood, (2) goodness or badness, and (3) mental and emotional accounting.

Judgments of Likelihood and Goodness/Badness

Estimation of likelihood Judging how likely it is that something will occur.

One kind of judgment is an **estimation of likelihood**, the determination of the probability that something will occur. Estimations of likelihood appear in many consumer contexts. For example, when we buy a good or service, we can attempt to estimate the likelihood that it will break down, the likelihood that others will like it, and the likelihood that it will satisfy our needs. When we view an ad, we can assess the likelihood that it is truthful.

Judgment of goodness/badness Evaluating the desirability of something.

Judgments of goodness/badness reflect our evaluation of the desirability of the offering's features. For example, if you are planning a trip, you might judge whether the fact that Europe is cold this time of year or the fact that European travel can be expensive is good or bad. Chapter 5 discussed judgments of goodness and badness in the section on high-effort attitudes. The research presented there suggested that a consumer combines judgments about product attributes or actions associated with a product to form an evaluation of or attitude toward the product or service. Judgments of goodness and badness not only are affected by the attributes of a product; they are also

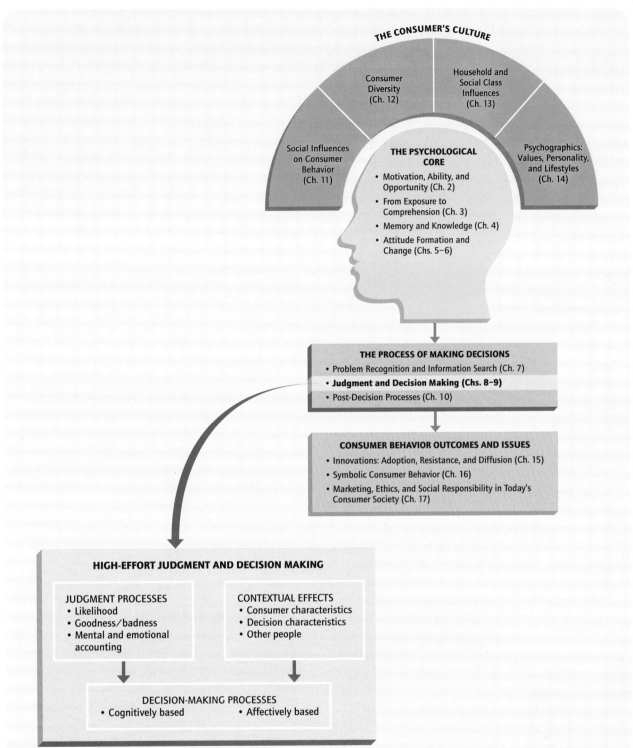

THE CONSUMER'S CULTURE

Consumer Diversity (Ch. 12)

Household and Social Class Influences (Ch. 13)

Social Influences on Consumer Behavior (Ch. 11)

THE PSYCHOLOGICAL CORE
- Motivation, Ability, and Opportunity (Ch. 2)
- From Exposure to Comprehension (Ch. 3)
- Memory and Knowledge (Ch. 4)
- Attitude Formation and Change (Chs. 5–6)

Psychographics: Values, Personality, and Lifestyles (Ch. 14)

THE PROCESS OF MAKING DECISIONS
- Problem Recognition and Information Search (Ch. 7)
- Judgment and Decision Making (Chs. 8–9)
- Post-Decision Processes (Ch. 10)

CONSUMER BEHAVIOR OUTCOMES AND ISSUES
- Innovations: Adoption, Resistance, and Diffusion (Ch. 15)
- Symbolic Consumer Behavior (Ch. 16)
- Marketing, Ethics, and Social Responsibility in Today's Consumer Society (Ch. 17)

HIGH-EFFORT JUDGMENT AND DECISION MAKING

JUDGMENT PROCESSES
- Likelihood
- Goodness/badness
- Mental and emotional accounting

CONTEXTUAL EFFECTS
- Consumer characteristics
- Decision characteristics
- Other people

DECISION-MAKING PROCESSES
- Cognitively based
- Affectively based

© Cengage Learning 2013

Exhibit 8.1

Chapter Overview: Judgment and Decision Making Based on High Consumer Effort

After problem recognition and search, consumers can engage in some form of judgment or decision making, which can vary in terms of processing effort (from high to low). This chapter looks at high-effort judgment and decision processes. Judgments serve as inputs into decision making, which can be cognitively or affectively based. Contextual effects also influence this process.

affected by how we feel. Specifically, consumers tend to form judgments of goodness or badness more quickly and consistently based, in part, on the intensity and direction of their affective responses.[6]

When making judgments about likelihood and goodness/badness, consumers often employ an **anchoring and adjustment process**.[7] They first anchor the judgment based on some initial value and then adjust or "update" the evaluation as they consider additional information. The initial value can be information or an affective response readily available from memory; it can also be attribute information from the external environment that is encountered first.[8] Consumer values and normative influences can also be strong determinants of the initial value.

To illustrate, Walt Disney is strongly associated with the United States and, thanks to theme parks, animated movies, and memorable cartoon characters, has a strong brand image worldwide. So when Disney opened a series of English-language schools in China, it used the "Disney" name as a positive initial anchor and encouraged consumers to see the schools—where cartoon characters are incorporated into lessons—as an update to that anchor. And, despite high tuition, Disney's schools are thriving in China.[9] Additional information from experience may adjust this initial value upward or downward, but the judgment is more likely to be positive, based on the Disney image. If the prior evaluation of Disney had been negative, the anchor would probably have resulted in a negative judgment. Thus, the same anchor can lead to two different judgments, depending on how the anchor is perceived.

Imagery, or visualization, also plays a major role in judgments of likelihood and goodness and badness. Consumers can try to construct an image of an event, such as how they will look and feel behind the wheel of a new car, to estimate its likelihood or judge its goodness or badness. Visualizing an event can actually make it seem more likely to occur because consumers may form a positive bias when they imagine themselves using the product.[10] Imagery may also lead consumers to overestimate how satisfied they will be with a product or service.[11] Imagery may also cause consumers to focus on vivid attributes and weigh those attributes more heavily when forming judgments.[12]

Mental and Emotional Accounting

As consumers, we use **mental accounting** to categorize spending and saving decisions into "accounts" we mentally designate for specific consumption transactions, goals, or situations. For example, we might have a "vacation" account (to pay for a trip), an "emergency" account (money held in reserve for unexpected expenses), and a "credit card" account (for credit purchases), each associated with a budget range or a dollar amount. The way we mentally account for our money influences judgments about what, when, where, why, how, and how much we should spend or save, borrow, make payments, and behave as a consumer over time. For instance, one study found that consumers were more willing to use a mobile payment service to make everyday purchases if it was linked to a credit card rather than a savings or checking account because of these consumers' mental accounting categories.[13]

The related concept of **emotional accounting** suggests that the intensity of the positive or negative feelings associated with each "account" is another important influence on buying behavior.[14] Money received under negative circumstances (from a seriously ill relative, for instance) is more likely to be spent on a utilitarian purchase (such as tuition) than on a hedonic purchase (a trip) because the utilitarian purchase helps counter the negative feelings. Clearly, mental and emotional accounting will vary from consumer to consumer, so marketers must research and understand the attitudes and feelings of their target markets.

Biases in Judgment Processes

Judgments are not always objective. Biases and other factors may compromise the quality of the consumer's decision[15] and affect consumer judgment in a variety of ways:

▶ *Confirmation bias.* If consumers are susceptible to a confirmation bias (see previous chapter) they will focus more on judgments that confirm what they already believe and will hold those judgments with more confidence. They may ignore information that runs counter to their judgments. Of course, overweighting confirming information and underweighting contrary information in forming judgments can reduce consumers' tendencies to search for more information because they believe they know almost everything about the product.[16] Therefore, the confirmation bias can set consumers up for making less-than-optimal choices.

Anchoring and adjustment process Starting with an initial evaluation and adjusting it with additional information.

Imagery Imagining an event in order to make a judgment.

Mental accounting Categorizing spending and saving decisions into "accounts" mentally designated for specific consumption transactions, goals, or situations.

Emotional accounting The intensity of positive or negative feelings associated with each mental "account" for saving or spending.

▶ *Self-positivity bias.* Consumers can make judgments about the extent to which they or others are vulnerable to having bad things happen to them (e.g., contracting AIDS, getting into an automobile accident). Interestingly, research finds that consumers have a self-positivity bias when making these judgments about the likelihood that bad outcomes will happen. That is, they tend to believe that bad things are more likely to happen to other people than to themselves. As such, they might not process messages that suggest that they themselves might be vulnerable to risks.[17] This is bad news for some marketers (e.g., health-care marketers, insurance marketers) who want to remind consumers that bad things can indeed happen to them.

▶ *Negativity bias.* With a negativity bias, consumers give negative information more weight than positive information when they are forming judgments. Consumers seem to weigh negative information more heavily in their judgments when they are forming opinions about something that is very important to them and for which they wish to have as accurate a judgment as possible (e.g., which college to attend). But consumers do not engage in a negativity bias when they are already committed to a brand. For example, if you love the school you are now attending, you are unlikely to think much about (or may even discount) any negative information you hear about it.[18]

▶ *Mood and bias.* Mood can bias consumer judgments in several ways.[19] First, your mood can serve as the initial anchor for a judgment. If you are in a good mood when browsing a menu, you will probably respond positively to new items you might try. Second, moods bias consumers' judgments by reducing their search for and attention to negative information. The reason for this phenomenon is that consumers want to preserve their good mood, and encountering negative information may not serve that goal. Third, mood can bias judgments by making consumers overconfident about the judgments they are reaching.[20]

▶ *Prior brand evaluations.* When consumers judge a brand to be good based on their past exposure to it, they may subsequently fail to learn (and view as important) information about the brand's attributes that affect its actual quality.[21] In effect, the favorable brand name "blocks" learning about quality-revealing product attributes that should affect consumers' judgments.

▶ *Prior experience.* Customers learn from their previous experiences, which can be helpful but may also bias judgments during future decisions. Imagine you are customizing a product (such as a laptop computer) to your own specifications. Based on your experience with decisions made early in the process, you will find subsequent decisions to be easier or more difficult. If later decisions are easier than earlier decisions, you will be more likely to upgrade to expensive features.[22]

▶ *Difficulty of mental calculations.* When comparing various prices or discounts, the ease or difficulty of calculating the difference will affect consumers' judgment of the size of these differences. When consumers have little difficulty mentally calculating the difference between two or more prices or discounts, they may think the numerical differences are larger than in reality, which will bias their judgment of the choices.[23]

Marketing Implications

Marketers can do several things to make sure that their brand serves as a positive anchor in anchoring adjustment decisions. First, they can focus consumers' attention on those attributes that place the brand as the best in its class. For example, by focusing attention on easy use and chic design, Apple has made its iPad the anchor for tablet computers. Marketers can also try to affect the set of other products that consumers use in their adjustment.[24] The Swedish firm Bike by Me encourages buyers to think of fashion when they think of its stylish bicycles, because every piece (frame, rims, tires, etc.) can be customized by color.[25]

When consumers are exposed to a brand extension, the existing brand name and its positive associations often serve as the anchor for judgments of the new product. A product's country of origin can also serve as an anchor and influence subsequent judgments.[26] For example, although the Kenny Rogers Roasters, a chain of American-style rotisserie-chicken restaurants, is down to a single U.S. outlet, it is quite popular in

Asia, where the local franchiser operates 140 restaurants and rings up more than $100 million in annual revenue.[27]

Marketers can also affect judgments of goodness and badness in several ways. First, making consumers feel good (e.g., by manipulating their moods or *priming* consumers with positive feelings before giving them information) will lead them to evaluate the offering more positively.[28] Second, marketers can affect judgments of goodness and badness by asking consumers to imagine the attributes or benefits of a product or service. A particular kind of pizza will be judged as better than other kinds when consumers imagine how delicious it tastes. It will be judged as worse when consumers imagine the grease it might have floating on the top of it.

Finally, marketers can affect consumers' perceptions of how probable things are (i.e., likelihood estimates). Research shows that consumers primed to consider their family ties are more likely to take a financial risk because they realize that their family can help cushion a monetary loss. However, consumers are less likely to take a social risk when thinking about family ties because of the way that a negative outcome might affect their family.[29] Marketers can also try to reduce consumers' self-positivity judgments. A study on consumers' self-positive bias regarding the likelihood that they could contract AIDS was reduced when consumers were shown that people very similar to them have also gotten AIDS and when they were made to think about actions that they engage in that could result in getting AIDS.[30] Enumerating many (versus few) risk behaviors that can make a person vulnerable to a bad outcome (e.g., contracting AIDS) can also reduce his or her self-positivity bias.[31]

HIGH-EFFORT DECISIONS AND HIGH-EFFORT DECISION-MAKING PROCESSES

Acquisition, usage, and disposition all involve some sort of consumer decision—even if the decision is not to select any of the alternatives, which may happen when a great deal of uncertainty exists.[32] In some cases, the consumer first makes a decision about whether or not to buy and then focuses on the selection decision.[33] The selection decision can, in turn, involve other decisions such as decisions about (a) what offerings to consider, (b) what factors are important to the choice, (c) what choice to actually make, (d) whether to make a decision now or to delay a decision, and (e) how to make choices when alternatives cannot be compared. We consider each of these kinds of decisions in this chapter (see Exhibit 8.2). When consumers' motivation, ability, and opportunity (MAO) to process information relevant to a decision are high, consumers put a lot of effort into making these decisions.

Deciding which brands to consider	Deciding what is important to the choice	Deciding what offerings to choose	Deciding whether to make a decision now	Deciding when alternatives cannot be compared

• Consideration set	• Goals
	• Time
	• Framing
		• Thought-based decisions
		  ◆ Brands
		  ◆ Product attributes
		  ◆ Gains and losses
		• Feeling-based decisions
		  ◆ Appraisals and feelings
		  ◆ Affective forecasts
			• Decision delay	

Exhibit 8.2

Types of Decisions That Consumers Face in High-Effort Situations

In high-effort situations, consumers are often confronted with a variety of different types of decisions to make. This exhibit outlines the major ones.

© Cengage Learning 2013

Deciding Which Brands to Consider

Inept set Options that are unacceptable when making a decision.

Inert set Options toward which consumers are indifferent.

Consumers today face more options than ever before.[34] With so many available options, they often find themselves first deciding whether brands fall into an **inept set** (those that are unacceptable), an **inert set** (those they treat with indifference), and a consideration set (those they want to choose among).[35]

The consideration set is very important to marketers because it affects what brands consumers are choosing among and hence whom the marketer is competing against. Decisions tend to be easier when the consideration set contains brands that can be easily compared.[36] Still, just because a brand is in a consideration set does not mean that it will get much of the consumers' attention.[37] But if it does get a lot of attention, consumers are more likely to select it and to be willing to pay more for it than for the other alternatives.[38] If they focus on one brand at a time, they tend to judge that brand more positively than they would the average of the best brands within that category.[39]

A consumer's evaluation of a brand in the consideration set depends on the other brands to which it is compared. If one brand is clearly more attractive or dominant than the others, making a choice does not require much effort. Changing the alternatives in the consideration set can, however, have a major impact on the consumer's decision, even without a change in preferences.[40] For example, a good brand can look even better when an inferior brand is added to the consideration set. This **attraction effect** occurs because the inferior brands increase the attractiveness of the dominant brand, making the decision easier.[41]

Attraction effect When the addition of an inferior brand to a consideration set increases the attractiveness of the dominant brand.

Marketing Implications

The most important implication is that it is critical for a company to get its brand into the consumer's consideration set; otherwise, there is little chance that the brand will be chosen. Repetition of the brand name and messages in marketing communications are needed to ensure that the brand name is "top of mind." Another way to try to gain an advantage is by promoting comparisons of the brand with inferior rather than with equal or superior competitors. Doing this maximizes the attraction effect and results in a more positive evaluation of the brand. Also, marketers can increase sales of a high-margin item simply by offering a higher-priced option.[42] Thus, Amazon.com might increase the sales of its lowest-priced Kindle e-book reader by offering higher-priced models with much more functionality (see Exhibit 8.3). Even if the higher-priced models aren't best-sellers, they would make the lower-priced model look like a good deal.

Exhibit 8.3

Attraction Effect
Sometimes a higher-priced option can make a lower-priced option look like a better deal, as is the case with the Kindle products.

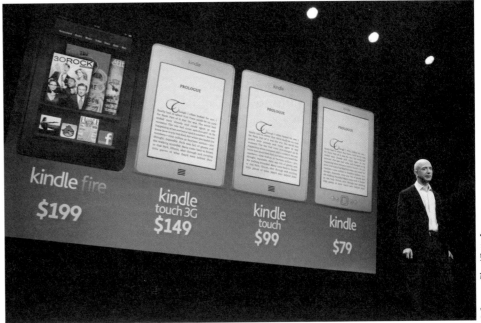

© Spencer Platt/Getty Images

Deciding Which Criteria Are Important to the Choice

Before consumers can choose a specific offering from among a set of brands in a consideration set, they need to determine which criteria are relevant to the decision and how important each criterion is to their decision. The relevance and importance of various decision criteria, in turn, depend on consumers' goals, the timing of their decision, and how the decision is framed or represented.

Goals

Goals clearly affect the criteria that will drive a consumer's choice. For example, one goal might be to buy an economical car you can afford; another might be to buy a car that will impress your friends. Consumers whose goal is to influence others will use different criteria when choosing among brands than those used by consumers who do not have this goal.[43]

When the goal is to make a decision, consumers may evaluate products with unique, positive attributes and shared negative attributes as more favorable than products with unique, negative attributes that share positive attributes.[44] If the goal is flexibility in choice, the consumer will seek out a large assortment of choices; if the goal is to simplify the choice, the consumer will seek out a small assortment.[45]

In addition, consumers' goals may change during the decision process. For example, before you go to a store, you may be less certain about what you want to buy—but once you are in the store, your goals may become more certain and concrete.[46] Whether the consumers' goals are prevention- or promotion-focused will also affect their decisions. Promotion-focused consumers, whose goal is to maximize gains and positive outcomes, will put more emphasis on whether they think they have the skills and capacity to use the product to achieve the goal they seek and put less emphasis on the effectiveness of the product itself. Prevention-focused consumers, who are more risk-averse, emphasize the product's efficacy rather than their own skills and capacities to use it.[47]

Time

The timing of a decision also affects which criteria drive our choices. As you learned in Chapter 4, *construal level theory* relates to how we think about (or construe) an offering. Whether we use high- (abstract) or low-level (concrete) construals depends on whether we are making a decision about what to buy/do right now or about something we might buy/do in the future.[48] If the decision is about something we will buy or do immediately (e.g., what restaurant to go to right now), our choices tend to be based on *low-level construals*—specific, concrete elements such as how close it is to home, how much dinner will cost there, and who is coming along. The opposite is true for decisions we anticipate making later: our criteria tend to be more general and abstract (e.g., which restaurant will create the best dining experience). When the decision outcome will be realized far in the future, consumers may consider the hedonic aspects of a decision (how good it will make me feel) to be more important than the more rational aspects of the decision (can I really afford it?).[49]

Framing

Decision framing The initial reference point or anchor in the decision process.

The way in which the task is defined or represented, **decision framing**, can affect how important a criterion is to our choice. Because the frame serves as the initial anchor in the decision process, all subsequent information is considered in light of that frame.

Early research on framing studied people's willingness to take risks in a gamble. Results showed that people are more willing to take risks when a choice is framed as avoiding a loss rather than as acquiring a gain.[50] Other research has found that messages framed in terms of loss are more persuasive when consumers are in a good mood, whereas messages framed in terms of gain are more persuasive when consumers are in a bad mood.[51] Framing gains and losses also applies to buying and selling: When the outcomes are equally positive, buyers feel better about not losing money while sellers feel better about achieving gains. But when the outcomes are equally negative, buyers feel worse about losses while sellers feel worse about not gaining anything.[52]

Decisions can also be framed in terms of how the problem is structured in the external environment, such as whether beef is presented as 75 percent lean or as 25 percent fat.[53] Framing the time period can affect decisions as well. Consumers perceive health hazards as being more immediate and concrete if they are framed as occurring every day but regard them as less immediate and more abstract if they are framed as occurring every year.[54] In another study, industrial buyers who used low price as an initial reference point were less willing to take risks than buyers with a medium- or high-price point.[55] Likewise, consumers react more positively when marketers frame the cost of a product as a series of small payments (pennies a day) instead of as a large one-time expense.[56] Moreover, a product framed in the context of higher-priced options will be judged as being less expensive than one framed in the context of lower-priced options.[57]

Whether a decision is framed positively (How good is this product?) or negatively (How bad is this product?) influences the evaluation differently.[58] Consumers are more likely to choose a brand with negatively framed claims about a competitor when elaboration is low, but higher elaboration may lead them to conclude that the tactics being used are unfair.[59]

Priming certain attributes, such as reliability and creativity, can significantly alter consumers' judgments of both comparable alternatives like different brands of cameras and noncomparable alternatives like computers and cameras.[60] This priming causes consumers to focus their processing on specific attributes rather than on abstract criteria. Priming hedonic or symbolic attributes—such as associations—with political concerns (e.g., reduce toxic waste) rather than with functional ones (e.g., no more hassles) can produce a higher willingness to pay for items or social programs.[61] Consumers primed to respond to a question about liking a product (i.e., one framed positively) answered more quickly than when they were primed to respond to a question about disliking a product (one framed negatively).[62]

LEGO® Games. Play a new way.

ONE OF 10 NEW GAMES NOW AVAILABLE IN THE BOARD GAMES AISLE!

Create and customize with NEW LEGO Games, a whole new way of spending fun, quality time with the family! LEGO Games are designed to be a new game every time they are played, encouraging children of all ages to build the game differently or change the dice to keep game play fresh and exciting.

Build game nights to new heights.

For more information visit: games.LEGO.com

Follow us at: Facebook.com/LEGOGames

LEGO and the LEGO logo are trademarks of the LEGO Group. © 2010 The LEGO Group.

LEGO and the LEGO logo are trademarks of the LEGO Group of Companies. © 2012 The LEGO Group. Photo used here by special permission.

Exhibit 8.4

Usage-Context
Sometimes ads try to stimulate purchase by relating to consumer's values (such as playing together as a family) and targeting consumers who already know the product (i.e., LEGO® toys).

Marketing Implications

Goals, decision timing, and framing have important implications for positioning and market segmentation. First, marketers can position an offering as being consistent with consumers' goal-related or usage categories. That way, marketers can influence the way that consumers frame the decision, and consumers will be more likely to consider the brand and important related information. For example, the Chevy Volt is marketed as an eco-friendly, compact car for consumers who want to protect the environment and spend less on gas. Second, marketers can identify and market to large segments of consumers who have similar goal-related or usage-context categories. Thus, for example, the LEGO Group created board games—complete with boards to be built from LEGO bricks—for the segment of families that play games together (see Exhibit 8.4).[63]

Another marketing strategy is to frame or reframe the decision. For example, a marketer might emphasize emotional benefits rather than functional benefits of a product. The Melt, a new chain of grilled-cheese restaurants, focuses on its sandwiches, tomato soup, and chocolate chip cookies as nostalgic food that "just makes people happy."[64] Sales promotions generally are more successful when framed as gains rather than as a reduced loss—consumers prefer getting something free rather than getting a discount. And consumer decisions can be framed by the location of products in the store, a strategy that influences comparisons. For example, placing wine next to gourmet foods may frame the consumer's decision more broadly as planning to have a nice, romantic meal rather than simply as buying a bottle of wine.

DECIDING WHAT BRAND TO CHOOSE: THOUGHT-BASED DECISIONS

Researchers have proposed various decision-making models, each of which may accurately describe how consumers make these high-effort decisions. Being opportunistic and adaptive, consumers do not follow a uniform process every time they make a decision.[65] Instead, they choose a model or use bits and pieces of various models, depending on the situation, and they may employ one or more decision rules, sometimes just because they want a change.[66] Furthermore, the choices consumers make may be related to other choices. For example, making one decision (buying a computer) can lead to yet another decision (buying a printer).[67]

Cognitive decision-making models describe how consumers systematically use information about attributes to reach a decision. Researchers also recognize that consumers may make decisions on the basis of feelings or emotions, using **affective decision-making models**.[68] Therefore, marketers need to know how consumers make choices when the decision is either cognitive or more emotional in nature.

Decision-making styles can vary across cultures.[69] Some North Americans, for example, tend to be analytical, rely on factual information, and search for solutions to problems. In contrast, in Asian cultures, and particularly in Japan, logic is sometimes less important than the *kimochi*—the feeling. Similarly, many Saudi Arabians are more intuitive in their decision making and avoid persuasion based on empirical reasoning. Russians may place more emphasis on values than on facts, and Germans tend to be theoretical and deductive. In North American and European cultures, decisions are usually made by individuals who control their own fate. In Asian cultures, the group is of primary importance, and actions are regarded as arising at random or from other events rather than as being controlled by individuals.

Cognitive models describe the processes by which consumers combine information about attributes to reach a decision in a rational, systematic manner. Two types of cognitive models are (1) compensatory versus noncompensatory and (2) brand versus attribute (see Exhibit 8.5).

With a **compensatory model**, consumers evaluate how good each of the attributes of the brands in their consideration set is (i.e., they make judgments about goodness and badness) and weight them in terms of how important the attributes are to their decisions. The brand that has the best overall score (attribute goodness times importance summed across all of the brand's attributes) is the one consumers choose. This is a kind of mental cost-benefit analysis in which a negative evaluation of one attribute can be compensated for (hence the name *compensatory*) by the positive features on others. To illustrate, for some U.S. consumers, a negative feature of Chinese products is that they are not made in America. However, this evaluation can be overcome if the products rate highly on other criteria deemed important, such as price.

With a **noncompensatory model**, consumers use negative information to evaluate brands and immediately eliminate from the consideration set those that are inadequate on any one or more important attributes.[70] These models are called *noncompensatory* because a negative rating on a key attribute eliminates the brand, as is the case when some U.S. consumers reject a product because it is foreign-made. Noncompensatory models require less cognitive effort than compensatory models do because consumers set up **cutoff levels** for each attribute and reject any brand with attribute rankings below the cutoff. Thus, if brands in consumers' consideration set are similar in attractiveness, they must put more effort into making a decision and will probably use a compensatory model.[71]

Cognitive decision-making model The process by which consumers combine items of information about attributes to reach a decision.

Affective decision-making model The process by which consumers base their decision on feelings and emotions.

Compensatory model A mental cost-benefit analysis model in which negative features can be compensated for by positive ones.

Noncompensatory model A simple decision model in which negative information leads to rejection of the option.

Cutoff level For each attribute, the point at which a brand is rejected with a noncompensatory model.

	Compensatory	Noncompensatory
Processing by Brand	Multiattribute models	Conjunctive model Disjunctive model
Processing by Attribute	Additive difference model	Lexicographic model Elimination-by-aspects model

© Cengage Learning 2013

Exhibit 8.5

Types of Cognitive Choice Models

Cognitive decision-making models can be classified along two major dimensions: (a) whether processing occurs one brand at a time or one attribute at a time, and (b) whether they are compensatory (bad attributes can be compensated for by good ones) or noncompensatory (a bad attribute eliminates the brand).

Marketing Implications

Given that different models can lead to different choices, marketers may sometimes want to change the process by which consumers make a decision. For example, if most consumers are using a compensatory strategy, switching them to a noncompensatory strategy may be advantageous, particularly if competitors' products have a major weakness. By convincing consumers not to accept a lower level of an important attribute—that is, not to compensate for the attribute—marketers might prompt some consumers to reject competitors' products from consideration. For example, sales of the ITALIKA motorbike have soared in Mexico because the product is not only affordable, it can be conveniently financed and serviced through the 1,100 Elektra stores where it is sold. Those attributes are important to consumers—and competing bikes don't have the same convenient financing and servicing arrangements.[72]

When consumers reject a brand using a noncompensatory strategy, marketers can try to switch them to using a compensatory strategy by arguing that other attributes compensate for a negative. To illustrate, advertising for high-priced, premium brands often stresses the reasons why its offerings are worth the extra money so that consumers do not reject them on price alone.

Decisions Based on Brands

In making a decision, consumers may evaluate *one brand at a time*. Thus, a consumer making a laptop purchase might collect information about an Apple model and make a judgment about it before moving on to the next brand. This type of **brand processing** occurs frequently because the environment—advertising, dealerships, and so on—is often organized by brands.

Brand processing Evaluating one brand at a time.

Much research has focused on brand-based compensatory models, also called **multiattribute expectancy-value models**.[73] One multiattribute model, the theory of reasoned action (TORA), was discussed in Chapter 5. Note that when considering multiple attributes, consumers tend to give more weight to those that are compatible with their goals.[74] Multiattribute models can be emotionally taxing as well as cognitively taxing when consumers need to make tradeoffs among attributes.[75] For instance, consumers facing emotionally difficult tradeoffs between price and quality may cope by choosing the offering with the best quality.[76] Some consumers may simply avoid making tradeoffs between conflicting attributes.[77]

Multiattribute expectancy-value model A type of brand-based compensatory model.

Using a **conjunctive model**, consumers set up *minimum* cutoffs for *each* attribute that represent the absolute lowest value they are willing to accept.[78] For example, consumers might want to pay less than $10 per hour to rent a car and therefore reject an alternative with a higher hourly cost. Thus, the car-sharing program WeCar charges Duke University students $9 per hour to rent a Chevy Volt.[79] Because the cutoffs represent the bare minimum belief strength levels, the psychology of a conjunctive model is to rule out unsuitable alternatives (i.e., get rid of the "bad ones") as soon as possible, something that consumers do by weighing negative information.

Conjunctive model A noncompensatory model that sets minimum cutoffs to reject "bad" options.

The **disjunctive model** is similar to the conjunctive model, with two important exceptions. First, the consumer sets up *acceptable* levels for the cutoffs—levels that are more desirable (i.e., find the "good ones"). So even though $10 per hour may be the highest payment a consumer will accept for a car rental, $7 or $8 per hour may be more acceptable, especially if the rental will cover several hours. Second, the consumer bases evaluations on several of the *most important* attributes rather than on all of them, putting the weight on positive information. Using the descriptions provided above, see if you can decide which brand you would choose from among the set of brands in Exhibit 8.6, using first the multiattribute decision-making model, then the conjunctive, and finally the disjunctive model. Note that consumers may use several of these decision-making models. When the consideration set is large, they might use the conjunctive or disjunctive model to eliminate undesirable brands and then make their final choice among the brands that remain, using the multiattribute model.[80]

Disjunctive model A noncompensatory model that sets acceptable cutoffs to find options that are "good."

Exhibit 8.6

Which Apartment Would You Choose?

Imagine that you visited five apartments (A, B, C, D, and E) and were trying to decide which to rent. You have determined what attributes you get (cost is the most important attribute followed by size and then location). After visiting each apartment, you rate how good each apartment is on each attribute. Which apartment would you rent if you used the following decision rules? Note that different decision rules can lead to different choices.

Evaluations of brands as good or bad based on information retrieved from memory or generated through external search (5 = very good on this attribute; 1 = not at all good on this attribute).

Importance weight of this attribute based on needs, values, goals (higher score means more important: weights add up to 100).

Evaluative Criteria	A	B	C	D	E	Importance
Cost	5	3	4	4	2	35
Size	3	4	5	4	3	25
Location	5	5	5	2	5	20
View	1	3	1	4	1	15
Has a pool	3	3	4	3	5	5

Apartment Chosen Based on the:
1. Compensatory Model (sum of Eval x Imp) _____
2. Conjunctive Model (set minimum cutoff of 2) _____
3. Disjunctive Model (set acceptable cutoff of 3) _____
4. Lexicographic Model (compare on EC in order of Imp) _____
5. Elimination by Aspects Model (set acceptable cutoff of 3) _____

Answers: 1 = C; 2 = B or D; 3 = B; 4 = A; 5 = B

© Cengage Learning 2013

Marketing Implications

Brand-based compensatory models help marketers understand which alternatives consumers may choose or reject and the beliefs that consumers have about the outcomes or attributes associated with a product. If consumers do not strongly believe that positive outcomes or attributes are associated with a decision, marketers should stress these outcomes or attributes through marketing to strengthen consumers' beliefs. For example, Megabus markets its intercity bus services on the basis of low price. It emphasizes its modern vehicles with Wi-Fi and power outlets at every seat, rather than the duration of trips (longer compared with train and air travel) and the inflexibility of trips (compared with private cars).[81]

Marketers can address shortcomings by altering the product and communicating its improvements to consumers. However, when companies make changes to remove competitive disadvantages, they may draw consumers away from competitive offerings, but they may also be reducing differentiation. Therefore, marketers should consider the long-term effects of improvements.[82] Decision models can also help marketers better plan communications. Research shows that consumers with little commitment to a brand will put more weight on negative information because they perceive it as more diagnostic.[83] This is why Radisson, which had aging U.S. hotel properties and struggled with perceptions of undistinguished service, introduced its upscale Radisson Blu from Europe to revitalize its U.S. brand image.[84]

Decisions Based on Product Attributes

Attribute processing
Comparing brands, one attribute at a time.

The previous discussion described how consumers make choices when they first process information one brand at a time. Here, we discuss **attribute processing**, which occurs when consumers compare across brands *one attribute at a time*, such as comparing each brand on price. Although most consumers prefer attribute processing because it is easier than brand processing, they cannot always find information available in a manner that facilitates it. This situation accounts for the increasing popularity of shopping agents. One study found that the inclusion of an attribute in a shopping agent's recommendations list gives that attribute more prominence.[85]

Additive difference model Compensatory model in which brands are compared by attribute, two brands at a time.

Lexicographic model A noncompensatory model that compares brands by attributes, one at a time in order of importance.

Elimination-by-aspects model Similar to the lexicographic model but adds the notion of acceptable cutoffs.

According to the **additive difference model**, brands are compared by attribute, *two brands at a time.*[86] Consumers evaluate differences between the two brands on each attribute and then combine them into an overall preference. This process allows tradeoffs between attributes—that is, a positive difference on one attribute can offset a negative difference on another.

With the **lexicographic model**, consumers order attributes in terms of importance and compare the options one attribute at a time, starting with the most important. If one option dominates, the consumer selects it. In the case of a tie, the consumer proceeds to the second most important attribute and continues in this way until only one option remains. A tie can occur if the difference between two options on any attribute is below the just noticeable difference: one brand priced at $2.77 and one priced at $2.79 would likely be regarded as being tied on price.

The **elimination-by-aspects model** is similar to the lexicographic model but incorporates the notion of an *acceptable cutoff.*[87] This model is not as strict as the lexicographic model, and more attributes are likely to be considered. Consumers first order attributes in terms of importance and then compare options on the most important attribute. Those options below the cutoff are eliminated, and the consumer continues the process until only one option remains. Again using the information shown in Exhibit 8.6, think about which brand you would select if you were to use the various decision models described in this exhibit.

Marketing Implications

The additive difference model helps marketers determine which attributes or outcomes exhibit the greatest differences among brands and use this knowledge to improve and properly position their brand. On one hand, if a brand performs below a major competitor on a certain attribute, the company needs to enhance consumers' beliefs about that product's superiority. On the other hand, if a brand performs significantly better than competitors on a key attribute, marketers should enhance consumer beliefs by positioning the offering around this advantage. Kyochon Chicken, a Korean restaurant chain specializing in fried chicken, for example, has expanded outside Asia by emphasizing its unique crispy, cooked-to-order chicken dishes. Its first U.S. outlet opened in 2007, and the chain continues to open restaurants on both coasts. "Americans have long been accustomed to the flavor of KFC chicken," explains a Kyochon executive. "For them, the soy sauce-coated chicken wing was brand new and attractive."[88]

If many consumers are employing a lexicographic model, and a brand is weak on the most important attribute, the company needs to improve this feature in order to have its brand selected. Also, marketers can try to change the order of importance of attributes so that a major brand advantage is the most critical attribute.

Identifying consumers' cutoff levels can be very useful for marketers. If an offering is beyond any of the cutoffs that many consumers set, it will be rejected frequently. This result means marketers must change consumers' beliefs about these attributes. For example, consumers concerned that an electric car won't take them far enough on a single charge may be reassured by the growing number of recharging stations being installed across the country. Whole Foods Market has noticed great interest in the recharging stations at its stores in Connecticut, Colorado, and Texas.[89] Marketers can also influence brand choice by affecting how attributes are framed (i.e., whether they are framed negatively or positively). Consumers may not like or choose a brand that is framed as having 25 percent fat and may like a brand framed as being 75 percent lean better. While both brands have the same amount of fat, one is framed in terms of a positive (lean); the other in terms of a negative (fat).[90]

Decisions Based on Gains and Losses

The previous discussion describes the different types of models that consumers can use to make decisions. However, research shows that the decisions consumers make also depend on whether the consumer is motivated to seek gains or to avoid losses. According to *prospect theory*, losses loom larger than gains for consumers even when the two outcomes are of the same magnitude.[91]

Endowment effect
When ownership increases the value of an item.

For example, when asked to set a price for an item to be exchanged, sellers typically ask for a much higher price (because they are experiencing a loss of the item) than buyers are willing to pay (gaining the item). This has been called the **endowment effect** because ownership increases the value (and loss) associated with an item.

Similarly, consumers have a much stronger reaction to price increases than to price decreases and may be more reluctant to upgrade to higher-priced durable items. Thus, consumers may avoid making decisions to a greater degree when a decision involves losses relative to gains. This effect has been demonstrated across a variety of products/services including wine, lottery tickets, basketball tickets, and pizza toppings.

In addition, the consumer's promotion- and prevention-focused goals will impact this process. For instance, prevention-focused consumers tend to preserve the status quo instead of making a decision that will result in a change because they want to avoid losses. In contrast, promotion-focused consumers are more willing to try new things if they think that changing from the status quo will help them achieve their goals of growth and development.[92]

Marketing Implications

Prospect theory has a number of important marketing implications. First, consumers will be more risk averse and unwilling to buy the product when the decision involves losses. Thus, marketers must make an effort to reduce risks and potential losses. This situation is one of the key reasons that manufacturers and retailers make offers such as the "full money-back guarantee" or "no money down for 12 months with no interest" as well as provide warranty programs. Procter & Gamble's Swiffer house-cleaning products come with a 30-day money-back guarantee, for example, advertised with the tagline: "You have nothing to lose but the dirt."[93]

Second, consumers will react more negatively to price increases or higher-priced items than they will react positively to price decreases. Thus, marketers need to carefully consider the amount of the price increase (i.e., the greater the increase, the stronger the negative reaction). Further, this suggests that if possible, marketers should try to frame these increases as gains rather than losses (i.e., the increased benefit the consumer might get from the higher-priced item). When Nissan increased the base price of its Leaf electric car, it also added many new features as standard, including heated seats and a fast-charge connection, emphasizing that these enhancements were the most requested by consumers (and worth the extra price).[94] ⎯⎯⎯⎯

DECIDING WHAT BRAND TO CHOOSE: HIGH-EFFORT FEELING-BASED DECISIONS

Just as consumers can make high-effort thought-based decisions, so too can they make high-effort feeling-based decisions. With affective decision making, consumers make a decision because the choice feels right rather than because they have made a detailed, systematic evaluation of offerings. Or they may decide that the chosen option feels like a perfect fit, regardless of their prior cognitive processing.[95] Consumers who make decisions based on feelings tend to be more satisfied afterward than those who make decisions based on product attributes.[96] Moreover, emotions can also help thought-based decision making since emotions can help consumers gather their thoughts and make judgments more quickly.[97]

As explained in Chapter 6, brands can be associated with positive emotions such as love, joy, pride, and elation as well as with negative emotions such as guilt, hate, fear, anxiety, anger, sadness, shame, and greed. These emotions can be recalled to play a central role in the decision process, particularly when consumers perceive them as relevant to the offering.[98] This affective processing is frequently experience-based.[99] In other words, consumers select an option based on their recall of past experiences and the associated feelings. When consumers choose among brands in memory, they must work harder to process information, so their feelings carry considerable weight. In contrast, when they choose among brands based on information in ads or other external stimuli, they can focus more on the offering's attributes and less on their feelings.[100]

WEAR IT AND BLOOM
A rose is not just a rose. Stack our floral inspired RING UPON RING series with the beautifully hand-carved rose in black onyx, set in sterling silver.

be inspired at pandora.net

PANDORA
UNFORGETTABLE MOMENTS

Image Courtesy of The Advertising Archives

Exhibit 8.7

Affective Decision Making

Consumers sometimes make purchase decisions based on how they feel, as opposed to product attributes. Ads for Pandora jewelry, seen here, feature good feelings and memories.

Consumer feelings are particularly critical for offerings with hedonic, symbolic, or aesthetic aspects.[101] Feelings also influence decisions about what we will consume and for how long.[102] We tend to buy offerings that make us feel good more often and for longer periods than we buy offerings that do not have these effects. Note that consumers sometimes buy a product, such as jewelry, simply to make themselves feel better (see Exhibit 8.7). In other situations, they may make a choice because of a negative feeling, buying a product out of guilt or shame.

Appraisals and Feelings

As discussed in Chapter 2, *appraisal theory* examines how our emotions are determined by the way that we think about or "appraise" the situation, a field being explored by many researchers.[103] This theory also explains how and why certain emotions (including those carried over from previous decisions) can affect future judgments and choices. People who are fearful tend to see more risk in new situations than do people who are angry, for example.

In situations involving disposition of objects, people who are disgusted tend to view this activity as an opportunity to get rid of their current possessions while people who are sad tend to view it as an opportunity to change their circumstances.[104] Even the emotional reaction to a desired product being out of stock can affect a consumer's feelings about and appraisals of subsequent purchases in the same environment.[105]

Consumers also consider how they will feel if a hedonic experience is interrupted. Although consumers prefer that a positive experience (such as watching a movie) be uninterrupted, they actually enjoy it more with an interruption, because the pleasure is intensified after the break. Similarly, their appraisal of a negative experience may cause them to want an interruption, yet research shows that interrupting such experiences actually increases irritation.[106] Finally, consumers appraise their feelings of envy when considering a purchase. If their appraisal is benign envy, they will put a premium on purchases to keep up with higher-status consumers; if their appraisal is malicious envy, they will put a premium on purchases that set them apart from higher-status consumers.[107]

Affective Forecasts and Choices

Affective forecasting
A prediction of how you will feel in the future.

Consumers' predictions of what they will feel in the future—**affective forecasting**—can influence the choices they make today. For instance, someone may buy a dishwasher after forecasting the relief she will feel at having an appliance to handle this time-consuming chore. You may decide to go to Mexico instead of Colorado over spring break because you think the Mexico trip will make you feel more relaxed. As shown in Exhibit 8.8, we can forecast (1) how we think we will feel as a

Exhibit 8.8

Affective Forecasting

Affective forecasting occurs when consumers try to predict how they will feel in a future consumption situation. Specifically, they try to predict what feelings they will have, how strongly these feelings will be, and how long the feelings will last.

What Will I Feel?	How Much Will I Feel It?	How Long Will I Feel This Way?
• Valence (good or bad) • Nature of feeling (specific emotion such as happiness, regret, guilt, shame)	• Intensity	• Duration

© Cengage Learning 2013

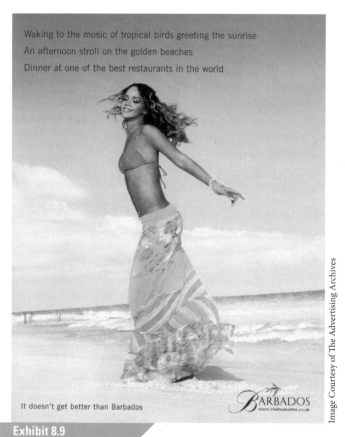

Waking to the music of tropical birds greeting the sunrise

An afternoon stroll on the golden beaches

Dinner at one of the best restaurants in the world

It doesn't get better than Barbados

BARBADOS
www.visitbarbados.co.uk

Image Courtesy of The Advertising Archives

Exhibit 8.9

Stimulating Imagery Through Advertising

Ads sometimes try to induce consumers to imagine themselves in certain situations. When they do, consumers may experience the feelings and emotions that are associated with this situation.

result of a decision, (2) how intensely we will have this feeling, and (3) how long this feeling will last. Any one of these forecasts can affect our decision about whether to go to Mexico. Affective forecasting is not always accurate, however, and we can be wrong about any or all of the above-noted forecasts.[108] Consequently, after our vacation, instead of feeling relaxed, we may feel stressed; instead of feeling extremely relaxed, we may feel only mildly relaxed; or instead of feeling relaxed for a week, our postvacation feelings of relaxation may only last until we reach home (and see the pile of work we now have to do).

While anticipating postdecision levels of happiness (or relaxation, as illustrated in the example above) can impact the choices consumers make, so too can anticipated regret about making a wrong decision impact the choices consumers make. For instance, if they are participating in an auction and anticipate feeling deep regret should another bidder win, consumers will place a higher bid on an item than they would otherwise have placed.[109] Similarly, consumers who anticipate regret at later finding out that today's sale price was better than a future sale price are more likely to buy the item on sale now.[110]

Imagery

Imagery plays a key role in emotional decision making.[111] Consumers can attempt to imagine themselves consuming the product or service and can use any emotions they experience as input for the decision. In choosing a vacation, you can imagine the excitement you might experience by being in each destination (see Exhibit 8.9). If these images are pleasant (or negative), they will exert a positive (or negative) influence on your decision process. Imagery can also ignite consumer desire for and fantasizing about certain products.[112] Inviting consumers to interact with a product through an online demonstration can evoke vivid mental images of product use and increase purchase intentions.[113]

Adding information actually makes imagery processing easier because more information makes it easier for consumers to form an accurate image (whereas it may lead to *information overload* under cognitive processing). For instance, consumers who see an ad asking them to imagine how good they would feel using the advertised product are likely to react positively and like the product more.[114] Moreover, imagery encourages brand-based processing because images are organized by brand rather than by attribute. Also, companies that design new products by encouraging customers to imagine or create a new image rather than recall one from memory can produce more original product designs.[115]

Marketing Implications

Marketers can employ a variety of advertising, sales, and promotional techniques to add to the emotional experience and imagery surrounding an offering. Good service or pleasant ambiance in a hotel, restaurant, or store, for example, can produce consumers' positive feelings and experiences that may influence their future choices. This is why the Ritz-Carlton hotel chain spends so much time and money training its 35,000 employees to deliver exemplary service and make every guest feel pampered. The hotel's advertising focuses on the emotional experience, "measuring a stay in the number of memories, so you get your memory's worth, not just your money's worth," explains the ad agency. Thanks to Ritz-Carlton's reputation for quality service, it can also market service training programs to other businesses and facilities, like the Erlanger Health System in Chattanooga, Tennessee.[116]

ADDITIONAL HIGH-EFFORT DECISIONS

In addition to deciding which brands to include in a consideration set, deciding what is important to the choice, and deciding what offerings to choose, consumers in high-effort situations face two more key decisions. First, should they delay the decision or make it right now? And second, how can they make a decision when the alternatives cannot be compared?

Decision Delay

If consumers perceive the decision to be too risky or if it entails an unpleasant task, they may delay making a decision.[117] They may also delay if they have too many attractive choices that are difficult to compare.[118] Another reason for delaying a decision is if consumers feel uncertain about how to get product information. Delaying a decision can affect a consumer's evaluation of brands that have features in common, regardless of whether those features are positive or negative. Specifically, the delay seems to make the shared features easier to recall and therefore has a greater impact on consumers' evaluations of the brands being considered.[119]

Marketing Implications

Should marketers encourage consumers to decide on a purchase right away? Many sales promotion techniques, including coupons and discounts, are available only to consumers who act quickly. On the other hand, if consumers delay making their decisions, marketers may have more time to offer additional information to bolster the chances that their brand will be chosen. Nissan used this strategy to good advantage when it hyped its Leaf electric car many months in advance of the U.S. launch, using traditional media and public relations as well as Facebook, Twitter, and other social media. By the time the car was available in dealerships—in limited quantities—the company had a waiting list of 20,000 consumers eager to buy.[120]

Decision Making When Alternatives Cannot Be Compared

Consumers sometimes need to choose from a set of options that cannot be directly compared on the same attributes. For instance, you might be trying to select entertainment for next weekend and may have the choice of going to the movies, eating at a nice restaurant, renting a video, or attending a party. Each alternative has different attributes, making comparisons among them difficult.

In making these **noncomparable decisions**, consumers adopt either an alternative-based strategy or an attribute-based strategy.[121] Using the **alternative-based strategy** (also called *top-down processing*), they develop an overall evaluation of each option—perhaps using a compensatory or affective strategy—and base their decision on it. For example, if you were deciding on weekend entertainment, you could evaluate each option's pros and cons independently and then choose the one you liked the best.

Using the **attribute-based strategy**, consumers make comparisons easier for themselves by forming abstract representations that will allow them to compare the options. In this strategy (also called *bottom-up processing*), the choice is constructed or built up. To make a more direct comparison of options for an entertainment decision, for example, you could construct abstract attributes for them such as "fun" or "likelihood of impressing a date." Because using abstractions simplifies the decision-making process, consumers tend to use them even when the options are easy to compare.[122]

Note that both strategies can be employed in different circumstances. When the alternatives are less comparable, consumers tend to use an alternative-based strategy because it is harder for them to create attribute abstractions.[123] Alternative-based strategies also suit consumers who have well-defined goals because they can easily recall the various options and their results. For example, if your goal is to find enjoyable things to do with a date, you could immediately recall a set of options like going to a movie or eating out, along with your overall evaluation of each option. You would then pick the option with the strongest evaluation. On the other hand, when consumers lack well-defined goals, they tend to use attribute-based processing.

Noncomparable decision The process of making a decision about products or services from different categories.

Alternative-based strategy Making a non-comparable choice based on an overall evaluation.

Attribute-based strategy Making a non-comparable choice by making abstract representations of comparable attributes.

Remember that price is often the one attribute on which alternatives can be compared directly. Consumers typically use price to screen alternatives for the consideration set rather than as the main basis of comparison among noncomparable alternatives. Thus, when selecting from among entertainment alternatives, you might use cost to generate a set of options that are reasonably affordable, then use an alternative- or attribute-based strategy to make the final decision.

Marketing Implications

Because of the way that consumers approach noncomparable decisions, marketers should look at each product's or brand's competition in broad terms as well as understand how the product or brand stacks up to specific competitors. For example, when consumers are deciding where to go on vacation, their alternatives may reflect competition between different types of destinations (such as cities or beaches), activities (such as going to museums or going surfing), and so on. Therefore, marketers might identify the abstract attributes that consumers use to make these noncomparable evaluations. For instance, stressing an attribute like "fun" could make it easier for consumers to compare products. Also, communications about destinations like Scotland could feature multiple attributes (golf courses, fishing areas, historic landmarks) and suggest how visiting the destination will fit the "fun" attribute.[124] Pricing is also an important marketing tactic for getting a brand into the consideration set when consumers cannot directly compare the attributes of various alternatives. Thus, tourism marketers often use pricing promotions to attract consumers' attention and encourage them to make further comparisons based on their goals or on individual attributes. _____

WHAT AFFECTS HIGH-EFFORT DECISIONS?

As you have seen, consumers can use many different strategies when making decisions. However, the best strategy to use for making a specific decision depends on the consumer and the nature of the decision.[125] This final section looks at how characteristics of (a) consumers, (b) the situation they are in, and (c) the group that they are a part of can affect their decisions.

Consumer Characteristics

Characteristics associated with consumers—such as their expertise, mood, extremeness aversion, time pressure, and metacognitive experiences—can affect the decisions they make.

Expertise

Consumers are more likely to understand their preferences and decisions when they have detailed consumption vocabularies—meaning that they can articulate exactly why they like or dislike the brands that they do. For example, a consumer who is an expert in wine may know that he or she likes wines that are buttery, dry, and smooth, whereas a novice might not know how to articulate these preferences.[126] Consumers who have this "consumption vocabulary" can use more attributes and information when making a decision. Expert consumers have more brand-based prior experience and knowledge and, as a result, tend to use brand-based decision strategies.[127] These consumers know how to identify relevant information and ignore irrelevant attributes in their decision making. When consumers consider complex information, they may simplify the processing task by focusing more on brand effects and less on attributes, especially if they face more than one complex choice task.[128]

Mood

Consumers who are in a reasonably good mood are more willing to process information and take more time in making a decision than those who are not in a good mood.[129] When in a good mood, consumers pay closer attention to the set of brands being considered and think about a higher number of attributes connected with each brand, a process that can result in more extreme (positive or negative) evaluations.[130] Another study showed that consumers in a high-arousal mood—feeling excited or very sad, for instance—tend to process information less thoroughly. Recall is also affected: Consumers in a bad mood are more likely to accurately recall what a marketing message said, a factor that may affect what attributes they consider when making their choices.[131]

Mood can also influence how positively consumers judge products and their attributes.[132] One study found that when consumers' moods were subconsciously influenced by music, consumers in a good mood rated a set of audio speakers more positively than did consumers in a bad mood.[133] Interestingly, consumers may deliberately manipulate their moods to help themselves improve their decision performance.[134] Finally, consumers in a good mood are more willing to try new products because they perceive lower probabilities of incurring losses.[135]

Time Pressure

As time pressure increases, consumers initially try to process information relevant to their choices faster.[136] If doing this does not work, they base their decision on fewer attributes and place heavier weight on negative information, eliminating bad alternatives by using a noncompensatory decision strategy. Time pressure, one of the major reasons that consumers fail to make intended purchases, can reduce shopping time and the number of impulsive purchases.[137] Time pressure also affects consumers' decisions to delay their choices.[138] Moreover, whether a consumer is present- or future-oriented can lead to different motivations and choices for different products.[139] *Present-oriented consumers* want to improve their current well-being and prefer products that help them to do so, such as relaxing vacations and entertaining books. *Future-oriented consumers* want to develop themselves and select life-enriching vacations and books.

Extremeness Aversion

Consumers tend to exhibit **extremeness aversion**, meaning that options for a particular attribute that are perceived as extreme will seem less attractive than those perceived as intermediate. This tendency is the reason that people often find moderately priced options more attractive than options that are either very expensive or very inexpensive.

When consumers see the attributes of one alternative as being equally dispersed (rather than very close together or very far apart), they will view this alternative as the compromise option even when it is not at the overall midpoint among options.[140] According to the **compromise effect**, a brand will gain share when it is seen as the intermediate or compromise choice rather than as an extreme choice.[141] Also, consumers prefer a brand with attributes that score equally well on certain criteria more than a brand that has unequal scores across attributes, a phenomenon known as **attribute balancing**.[142]

Metacognitive Experiences

One final set of consumer characteristics that affects the decision-making process is that of **metacognitive experiences**. These are factors based on our decision-processing experience, such as how easy it is to recall information in memory and to form thoughts as well as how easy it is to process new information.[143] Metacognitive experiences affect decisions beyond formal knowledge by influencing retrieval ease, inferences, and biases. Thus, it is not just the content of the information that influences the decision; rather, *how* this information is processed is also critical.

According to one study, the pleasant experience of being able to process a brand name easily can lead to a consumer's favorable attitudes toward that brand. Yet in some cases in which consumers can process information about the brand more easily—such as seeing the mention of product benefits in an ad message—they may develop less favorable attitudes toward the brand because they may attribute that ease of processing to the persuasiveness of the information rather than to the attractiveness of the brand itself. Other studies have found that individuals are more likely to regard a statement as true when it is printed in an easy-to-read color or if the words rhyme.[144] In short, metacognitive experiences affect choices in concert with stimuli and consumer characteristics such as mood.[145]

Characteristics of the Decision

In addition to consumer characteristics, decision characteristics can affect how consumers make their choices. Two decision characteristics of particular note are the availability of information on which to base a decision and the presence of trivial attributes.

Extremeness aversion Options that are extreme on some attributes are less attractive than those with a moderate level of those attributes.

Compromise effect When a brand gains share because it is an intermediate rather than an extreme option.

Attribute balancing Picking a brand because it scores equally well on certain attributes rather than faring unequally on these attributes.

Metacognitive experiences How the information is processed beyond the content of the decision.

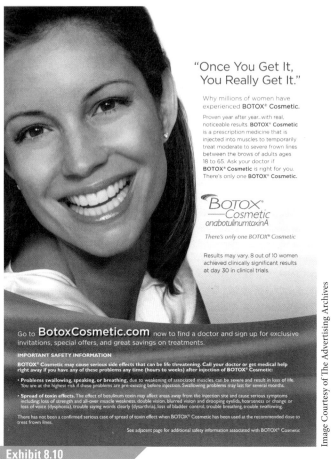

"Once You Get It, You Really Get It."

Why millions of women have experienced BOTOX® Cosmetic.

Proven year after year...with real, noticeable results. BOTOX® Cosmetic is a prescription medicine that is injected into muscles to temporarily treat moderate to severe frown lines between the brows of adults ages 18 to 65. Ask your doctor if BOTOX® Cosmetic is right for you. There's only one BOTOX® Cosmetic.

BOTOX® Cosmetic
onabotulinumtoxinA

There's only one BOTOX® Cosmetic

Results may vary. 8 out of 10 women achieved clinically significant results at day 30 in clinical trials.

Go to BotoxCosmetic.com now to find a doctor and sign up for exclusive invitations, special offers, and great savings on treatments.

IMPORTANT SAFETY INFORMATION

BOTOX® Cosmetic may cause serious side effects that can be life threatening. Call your doctor or get medical help right away if you have any of these problems any time (hours to weeks) after injection of BOTOX® Cosmetic:

• **Problems swallowing, speaking, or breathing,** due to weakening of associated muscles, can be severe and result in loss of life. You are at the highest risk if these problems are pre-existing before injection. Swallowing problems may last for several months.

• **Spread of toxin effects.** The effect of botulinum toxin may affect areas away from the injection site and cause serious symptoms including: loss of strength and all-over muscle weakness, double vision, blurred vision and drooping eyelids, hoarseness or change of loss of voice (dysphonia), trouble saying words clearly (dysarthria), loss of bladder control, trouble breathing, trouble swallowing.

There has not been a confirmed serious case of spread of toxin effect when BOTOX® Cosmetic has been used at the recommended dose to treat frown lines.

See adjacent page for additional safety information associated with BOTOX® Cosmetic

Image Courtesy of The Advertising Archives

Exhibit 8.10

Information Availability

Providing relevant information is important in consumer purchasing, but the marketer must be aware not to provide too much information or the consumer will experience information overload and most likely will not process all this information.

Information Availability

The amount, quality, and format of the information can affect the decision-making strategy that consumers use. When a consumer has more information, the decision becomes more complex, and the consumer must use a more detailed decision-making strategy, such as the multiattribute choice strategy. Having more information will lead to making a better choice only up to a point, however; after that, the consumer will experience information overload.[146] For example, pharmaceutical firms are legally required to provide detailed prescription information and to disclose side effects of medications in their ads, yet the amount of such information can be overwhelming.

If the information provided is useful and relevant to our decision criteria, decision making is less taxing, and we can make better decisions.[147] Essentially, we can narrow the consideration set relatively quickly because we can focus on those attributes that are most important to our decision. Hence, it is better for marketers to focus on providing relevant information, not just more information (see Exhibit 8.10). If the information provided is not useful or if some information is missing, we will need to infer how the product might rate on that attribute, perhaps by using other attributes of the brand in question to make that inference.[148]

If the available information is ambiguous, consumers are more likely to stay with their current brand than to risk purchasing a new competitive brand—even a superior one.[149] Consumers also can compare numerical attribute information faster and more easily than they can compare verbal information.[150] For example, to help parents select video games, a group of manufacturers developed a rating system to indicate the amount of sex and violence in their games. Finally, decisions are sometimes affected by information about attributes to which consumers have been exposed in a previous choice.[151]

Information Format

The format of the information—the way that it is organized or presented in the external environment—can also influence the decision strategy that consumers use. If information is organized by brand, consumers will likely employ a brand-based decision-making strategy such as a compensatory, conjunctive, or disjunctive model. If information is organized by attribute or in a matrix, consumers can use an attribute-processing strategy. For example, one study found that organizing yogurt by flavor instead of by brand encouraged more comparison shopping on the basis of attribute processing.[152]

Sometimes consumers will even restructure information into a more useful format, especially in a matrix. Consumers are less likely to choose the cheapest brand of consumer electronics product when the offerings are organized by model (similar offerings by different companies grouped together) rather than by brand.[153] Thus, companies with high-priced brands would want the display to be organized by model, whereas companies offering low-priced brands would prefer a brand-based display.

The presence of a narrative format for presenting information about brands can also impact consumers' choices. When researchers presented consumers with a narrative message about vacations, the consumers used holistic processing to sequence and evaluate the information. The narrative structure is similar to the way in which consumers acquire information in daily life, so processing was easier. In processing the narrative, consumers did not consider individual features, a situation that meant negative information had less impact.[154] Also note that consumers who tend to elaborate on the potential benefits and potential risks of the outcome before making a decision are less susceptible to information format biases.[155]

Trivial Attributes

Consumers sometimes finalize decisions by looking at trivial attributes. For example, if three brands in the consideration set are perceived as equivalent with the exception that one contains a trivial attribute, the consumer is likely to choose the brand with the trivial attribute (arguing that its presence may be useful). If, however, two of the three brands in the consideration set have a particular trivial attribute, the consumer is likely to choose the one without that attribute (arguing that the attribute is unnecessary). In both cases, the trivial attribute was used to complete and justify the decision.[156]

Group Context

Finally, consumers' decisions can be affected by the presence of a group, such as when a group of people is dining out and each member is deciding what to order. As each group member makes a decision in turn, he or she attempts to balance two sets of goals: (1) goals that are attained by the individual's action alone (*individual alone*) and (2) goals that are achieved depending on the actions of both the individual and the group (*individual group*).[157] Because consumers may have to choose a different alternative to achieve each set of goals, they cannot always achieve both sets of goals simultaneously in group settings.

In a group, consumers face three types of individual-group goals, as shown in Exhibit 8.11:

▶ *Self-presentation.* Consumers seek to convey a certain image through the decisions they make in a group context. When consumers want to use unique choices as positive self-presentation cues or to express their individuality, the result will be variety seeking at the group level. Yet consumers are often more concerned about social norms and therefore make similar choices to blend in, resulting in uniformity at the group level.

▶ *Minimizing regret.* Consumers who are risk averse and want to minimize regret will tend to make choices that are similar to those made by the rest of the group, leading to uniformity at the group level. Making this choice allows group members to avoid any disappointment they might feel if someone else's choice seemed better than their own.

▶ *Information gathering.* Consumers can learn more about the different choices each has made through interaction with other group members. Whether members actually share choices or simply share their reactions, the result is variety in the totality of choices within the group when consumers see information gathering as a priority. However, when group members are more concerned with self-presentation or loss aversion than with information gathering, they will make similar choices, resulting in group uniformity.

Exhibit 8.11

Goal Classes That Affect Consumer Decision Making

Consumers are not always able to achieve both individual-alone and individual-group goals when making decisions in the context of a group. Trying to achieve individual-group goals can result in either group variety or group uniformity, while trying to achieve individual-alone goals allows the consumer to satisfy his or her own taste through the decision.

Source: From Dan Ariely and Jonathan Levav, "Sequential Choice in Group Settings: Taking the Road Less Traveled and Less Enjoyed," *Journal of Consumer Research*, December 2000, p. 281. Reprinted with permission of The University of Chicago Press.

Note: In cases where informational social influence is present during the decision process, an outcome of group uniformity or variety seeking can result.

When making a decision in a group context, we try to balance these three individual-group goals with our individual-alone goals. In most group situations, the result is group uniformity, even though individual members may ultimately feel less satisfied by the outcome.

Marketing Implications

Marketers can develop some interesting strategies by understanding how consumer characteristics affect high-effort decisions. One technique is to sell a new, improved model alongside the old model at the same price, a tactic that makes the new one look better. In addition, marketers need to think about the information in their ads and on their packaging because irrelevant information can sometimes influence consumers' decisions—even in the presence of more relevant information.[158]

Providing the right amount of information at the right time is a challenge marketers face all over the world. One study found that consumers in Romania and Turkey have experienced great confusion in judging quality and making choices because "there are so many alternatives now."[159] Marketers should therefore present a few key points, not a flood of information. However, providing too little information can also hamper decision making, resulting in poorer quality decisions and a lower level of satisfaction. A lack of both products and information has been a major problem in some former communist countries.[160]

Finally, marketers can use communications to make individual-group goals a higher priority in group situations, leading to more uniformity of choice in favor of the advertised brand. Beer marketers, for instance, often show group members enjoying only the advertised brand, an image that reinforces strong social norms and encourages consumers to order that brand when they drink in a social setting. _____

SUMMARY

Judgments involve forming evaluations or estimates—not always objective—of the likelihood of the occurrence of events, whereas decisions entail choosing from among options or courses of action. Consumers make judgments about likelihood, about goodness or badness, and using mental accounting.

Once they recognize a problem, consumers may address it by using cognitive decision-making models (deciding in a rational, systematic manner) or affective decision-making models (deciding on the basis of their feelings or emotions). Consumers face a number of other decisions in high-effort situations: which brands to consider (developing the consideration set), what is important to the choice (how it is affected by goals, decision timing, and decision framing), what offerings to choose, whether to make a decision now, and what to do when alternatives cannot be compared.

In thought-based decisions about offerings, consumers may use compensatory or noncompensatory models, process by brand or by attribute, and consider gains versus losses. Feeling-based decisions about offerings may rely on appraisals and feelings, affective forecasts and choices, and imagery. Finally, three types of contextual factors that can influence the decision

process are (1) consumer characteristics, (2) decision characteristics, and (3) the presence of a group.

Questions for Review and Discussion

1. How does consumer judgment differ from consumer decision making?

2. What is the anchoring and adjustment process, and how does it affect consumer judgment?

3. How do consumers use compensatory and noncompensatory decision-making models?

4. Explain how consumers use their goals, decision timing, and framing to decide which criteria are important for a particular choice.

5. Why do marketers need to know that attribute processing is easier for consumers than brand processing?

6. How do appraisals and feelings as well as affective forecasting influence consumer decision making?

7. What three contextual elements affect consumer decision making?

CONSUMER BEHAVIOR CASE

Harley-Davidson Wheels into India

Can Milwaukee-based Harley-Davidson roar into India—the world's second-largest market for motorcycles, after China—and attract buyers despite strong competition from local and global bike brands? With more than a century of tradition behind its iconic American brand, Harley-Davidson isn't starting from scratch in India. It enjoys high brand recognition worldwide and began planning for a presence in India in 2005. Two years later, a U.S.-India trade deal paved the way for foreign-made, heavy-weight bikes like Harley-Davidson to be imported and sold throughout the country. Once Harley-Davidson had the green light to go into high gear, it began recruiting dealers in five metropolitan areas.

Marketers for Harley-Davidson see India's economy growing rapidly. Its expanding middle class has both considerable buying power and an appetite for world-class, brand-name products. Most of these consumers have seen Harley-Davidson bikes in Hollywood movies, and some have met Harley-Davidson owners or tested Harley-Davidson bikes at cycling events. Harley-Davidson's research shows that affluent motorcycle enthusiasts tend to own more than one bike (one for weekday commuting and another for weekend trips, for instance). "These are people who have worked hard, earn well, and can now allow themselves the chance to explore their passions," explains the managing director.

Still, Harley-Davidson must compete against long-established bike brands such as Royal Enfield, which has its own loyal customer base. Consumers in India can compare Royal Enfield's four-stroke engines—responsible for the "thumper" sound associated with the brand—with Harley-Davidson's more powerful V-twin engines, which produce that brand's signature thundering sound. Looking at price, they will find Royal Enfield's bikes carry a lower price tag than Harley-Davidson's, in part because of import duties. Consumers concerned about the availability of repair services will also compare Harley-Davidson's handful of dealerships with Royal Enfield's countrywide dealership network.

Harley-Davidson's unique image of independence and individuality is a clear point of differentiation. The company also has other competitive advantages. One is that it offers a full range of motorcycles and accessories, with customization options that bike buyers particularly value. The company is developing special customization kits so buyers in India can mix and match Harley-Davidson engines and parts to create one-of-a-kind motorcycles, as they do in other markets.

A second competitive advantage is that only Harley-Davidson buyers can join the Harley Owners Group (HOG), a global group whose one million-plus members are invited to events such as bike training "boot camp," weekend rides, and film festivals exclusively for Harley-Davidson owners. HOG members also get to attend the company's owners-only rock concerts featuring top Indian bands. "We want to give bike lovers the full ownership experience in India," Harley-Davidson's managing director says about local HOG activities.

A third advantage is that Harley-Davidson dealerships permit buyers to test-drive every bike in the product line, which not every competitor allows. Test-drives help buyers try out the various features, experience firsthand the difference between individual models, and form an impression of how it would feel to ride a Harley-Davidson bike.

Harley-Davidson is starting out strong in India. Before the first bike was delivered, the company had hundreds of preorders. As in most of the world, the majority of buyers are men. Unlike most Harley-Davidson markets, however, here the fastest growth in sales is to men in their 30s and 40s. Women are also being targeted, according to the director of marketing in India: "While we strongly believe Harley-Davidson is more of a state of mind and it transcends gender and age, we see a tremendous potential with Indian women riders." In fact, Harley-Davidson is already the most popular brand among U.S. women bike buyers, a trend that could spread to India in the coming years.[161]

CASE QUESTIONS

1. How is Harley-Davidson using marketing to influence emotional aspects of the motorcycle buying process?
2. What role are consumer characteristics likely to play in a consumer's decision to buy a Harley-Davidson in India?
3. In terms of the anchoring and adjustment process, what challenges and opportunities does Harley-Davidson face in marketing to Indian consumers?

4. Using the consumer behavior concepts in this chapter, explain the marketing thinking behind allowing buyers to test-drive any of the Harley-Davidson bikes. Do you agree with this marketing decision? Why or why not?

5. How might consumers use thought-based decision models when considering a motorcycle purchase in India? What are the implications for Harley-Davidson?

ENDNOTES

1. "Ford to Upgrade MyFord Touch in 250,000 Vehicles," *Washington Post*, November 6, 2011, www.washingtonpost.com; "Connected Cars: A New Risk," *Consumer Reports*, October 2011, pp. 47–51; "Autoficial Intelligence," *Economist*, September 17, 2011, pp. 67–68; and "Nissan Adds Drivetrain and Safety Features for Mass-market Models," *CNet*, October 19, 2011, www.cnet.com.

2. Michael D. Johnson and Christopher P. Puto, "A Review of Consumer Judgment and Choice," in ed. Michael J. Houston, *Review of Marketing* (Chicago: American Marketing Association, 1987), pp. 236–292.

3. Eloise Coupey, Julie R. Irwin, and John W. Payne, "Product Category Familiarity and Preference Construction," *Journal of Consumer Research*, March 1998, pp. 459–468.

4. Itamar Simonson, Joel Huber, and John Payne, "The Relationship between Prior Brand Knowledge and Information Acquisition Order," *Journal of Consumer Research*, March 1988, pp. 566–578.

5. Eric J. Johnson and J. Edward Russo, "Product Familiarity and Learning New Information," *Journal of Consumer Research*, June 1984, pp. 528–541.

6. Michel Tuan Pham, Joel B. Cohen, John W. Pracejus, and G. David Hughes, "Affect Monitoring and the Primacy of Feelings in Judgment," *Journal of Consumer Research*, September 2001, pp. 167–188.

7. Gita Venkataramani Johar, Kamel Jedidi, and Jacob Jacoby, "A Varying-Parameter Averaging Model of Online Brand Evaluations," *Journal of Consumer Research*, September 1997, pp. 232–247; and Daniel Kahneman and Amos Tversky, "On the Psychology of Prediction," *Psychology Review*, July 1973, pp. 251–275.

8. Joan Meyers-Levy and Alice M. Tybout, "Context Effects at Encoding and Judgment in Consumption Settings: The Role of Cognitive Resources," *Journal of Consumer Research*, June 1997, pp. 1–14.

9. "Middle Kingdom Meets Magic Kingdom," *Economist*, August 28, 2010, p. 52.

10. John Carroll, "The Effect of Imagining an Event on Expectations for the Event," *Journal of Experimental Social Psychology*, January 1978, pp. 88–96

11. Deborah J. MacInnis and Linda L. Price, "The Role of Imagery in Information Processing: Review and Extensions," *Journal of Consumer Research*, March 1987, pp. 473–491.

12. Baba Shiv and Joel Huber, "The Impact of Anticipating Satisfaction on Consumer Choice," *Journal of Consumer Research* 27, September 2000, pp. 202–216.

13. Irene C. L. Ng and Nick K.T. Yip, "Theoretical Foundations in the Pricing of Intermediating Services: The Case of Payments Via Mobile Phones," *Journal of Revenue and Pricing Management* 9, no. 3, 2010, pp. 217–227.

14. Jonathan Levav and A. Peter McGraw, "Emotional Accounting: How Feelings about Money Influence Consumer Choice," *Journal of Marketing Research*, February 2009, pp. 66–80.

15. Arul Mishra and Dhananjay Nayakankuppam, "Consistency and Validity Issues in Consumer Judgments," *Journal of Consumer Research* 33, no. 3, 2006, pp. 291–303.

16. Calvin P. Duncan and Richard W. Olshavsky, "External Search: The Role of Consumer Beliefs," *Journal of Marketing Research*, February 1982, pp. 32–43.

17. Geeta Menon, Lauren G. Block, and Suresh Ramanathan, "We're at as Much Risk as We Are Led to Believe," *Journal of Consumer Research*, March 2002, pp. 533–549.

18. Rohini Ahluwalia, "Re-Inquiries: How Prevalent Is the Negativity Effect in Consumer Environments?" *Journal of Consumer Research*, September 2002, pp. 270–279; and Rohini Ahluwalia, H. Rao Unnava, and Robert E. Burnkrant, "The Moderating Effect of Commitment on the Spillover Effect of Marketing Communications," *Journal of Marketing Research*, November 2001, pp. 458–470.

19. Meryl Paula Gardner, "Mood States and Consumer Behavior: A Critical Review," *Journal of Consumer Research*, December 1985, pp. 281–300.

20. Margaret G. Meloy, J. Edward Russo, and Elizabeth Gelfand, "Monetary Incentives and Mood," *Journal of Marketing Research*, May 2006, pp. 267–275.

21. Stijn M. J. Van Osselaer and Joseph W. Alba, "Consumer Learning and Brand Equity," *Journal of Consumer Research* 27, June 2000, pp. 1–16.

22. Keith Wilcox and Sangyoung Song, "Discrepant Fluency in Self-Customization," *Journal of Marketing Research*, August 2011, pp. 729–740.

23. Manoj Thomas and Vicki G. Morwitz, "The Ease-of-Computation Effect," *Journal of Marketing Research*, February 2009, pp. 81–91.

24. Paul M. Herr, "Priming Price: Prior Knowledge and Context Effects," *Journal of Consumer Research*, June 1989, pp. 67–75.

25. Benoit Faucon, "The Rise of the Designer Bike," *Wall Street Journal*, April 1, 2011, www.wsj.com; and "Consumers Are Finding New Ways to Flaunt Their Status," *Economist*, December 4, 2010, p. 86.

26. Sung-Tai Hong and Robert S. Wyer Jr., "Effects of Country-of-Origin and Product-Attribute Information," *Journal of Consumer Research*, September 1989, pp. 175–187.

27. Maureen Morrison, "Now-Rare U.S. Brands Thriving Overseas," *Advertising Age*, September 5, 2011, www.adage.com.

28. James R. Bettman and Mita Sujan, "Effects of Framing on Evaluation of Comparable and Noncomparable Alternatives by Expert and Novice Consumers," *Journal of Consumer Research*, September 1987, pp. 141–151.

29. Naomi Mandel, "Shifting Selves and Decision Making: The Effects of Self-Construal Priming on Consumer Risk-Taking," *Journal of Consumer Research*, June 2003, pp. 30–40.

30. Priya Raghubir and Geeta Menon, "AIDS and Me, Never the Twain Shall Meet," *Journal of Consumer Research*, June 1998, pp. 52–63.

31. Menon, Block, and Ramanathan, "We're as at Much Risk as We Are Led to Believe."

32. Ravi Dhar and Itamar Simonson, "The Effect of Forced Choice on Choice," *Journal of Marketing Research*, May 2004, pp. 146–160; and Ravi Dhar, "Consumer Preference for a No-Choice Option," *Journal of Consumer Research*, September 1997, pp. 215–231.

33. Ravi Dhar and Stephen M. Nowlis, "To Buy or Not to Buy," *Journal of Marketing Research*, November 2004, pp. 423–432.

34. "The Rise of the Superbrands," *Economist*, February 5, 2005, pp. 63–65.

35. F. May and R. Homans, "Evoked Set Size and the Level of Information Processing in Product Comprehension and Choice Criteria," in ed. William D. Perrault, *Advances in Consumer Research*, vol. 4 (Chicago: Association for Consumer Research, 1977), pp. 172–175.

36. Amitav Chakravarti and Chris Janiszewski, "The Influence of Macro-Level Motives on Consideration Set Composition in Novel Purchase Situations," *Journal of Consumer Research*, September 2003, pp. 244–258.

37. Frank R. Kardes, David M. Sanbonmatsu, Maria L. Cronley, and David C. Houghton, "Consideration Set Overvaluation," *Journal of Consumer Psychology*, 2002, pp. 353–361.

38. Steven S. Posavac, David M. Sanbonmatsu, and Edward A. Ho, "The Effects of Selective Consideration of Alternatives on Consumer Choice and Attitude–Decision Consistency," *Journal of Consumer Psychology*, 2002, pp. 203–213.

39. Steven S. Posavac, David M. Sanbonmatsu, Frank R. Kardes, and Gavan J. Fitzsimons, "The Brand Positivity Effect: When Evaluation Confers Preference," *Journal of Consumer Research*, December 2004, pp. 643–651.

40. Ryan Hamilton, Jiewen Hong, and Alexander Chernev, "Perceptual Focus Effects in Choice," *Journal of Consumer Research*, August 2007, pp. 187–199; and Itamar Simonson and Amos Tversky, "Choice in Context: Tradeoff Contrast and Extremeness Aversion," *Journal of Marketing Research*, August 1992, pp. 281–295.

41. Jongwon Park and JungKeun Kim, "The Effects of Decoys on Preference Shifts," *Journal of Consumer Psychology* 15, no. 2, 2005, pp. 94–107; Joel Huber, John W. Payne, and Christopher Puto, "Adding Asymmetrically Dominated Alternatives," *Journal of Consumer Research*, June 1982, pp. 90–98; Srinivasan Ratneshwar, Allan D. Shocker, and David W. Stewart, "Toward Understanding the Attraction Effect," *Journal of Consumer Research*, March 1987, pp. 520–533; Sanjay Mishra, U. N. Umesh, and Donald E. Stem, "Antecedents of the Attraction Effect," *Journal of Marketing Research*, August 1993, pp. 331–349; Yigang Pan, Sue O'Curry, and Robert Pitts, "The Attraction Effect and Political Choice in Two Elections," *Journal of Consumer Psychology* 4, no. 1, 1995, pp. 85–101; Sankar Sen, "Knowledge, Information Mode, and the Attraction Effect," *Journal of Consumer Research*, June 1998, pp. 64–77; Timothy B. Heath and Subimal Chatterjee, "Asymmetric Decoy Effects on Lower-Quality Versus Higher-Quality Brands," *Journal of Consumer Research*, December 1995, pp. 268–284; and Elizabeth Cowley and John R. Rossiter, "Range Model of Judgments," *Journal of Consumer Psychology* 15, no. 3, 2005, pp. 250–262.

42. Simonson, "Get Closer to Your Consumers by Understanding How They Make Choices."

43. Rebecca W. Hamilton, "Why Do People Suggest What They Do Not Want? Using Context Effects to Influence Others' Choices," *Journal of Consumer Research*, March 2003, pp. 492–506.

44. Jim Wang and Robert S. Wyer Jr., "Comparative Judgment Processes: The Effects of Task Objectives and Time Delay on Product Evaluations," *Journal of Consumer Psychology*, 2002, pp. 327–340.

45. Alexander Chernev, "Decision Focus and Consumer Choice among Assortments," *Journal of Consumer Research* 33, no. 1, 2006, pp. 50–59.

46. Leonard Lee and Dan Ariely, "Shopping Goals, Goal Concreteness, and Conditional Promotions," *Journal of Consumer Research* 33, no. 1, 2006, pp. 60–70.

47. Punam A. Keller, "Regulatory Focus and Efficacy of Health Messages," *Journal of Consumer Research* 33, no. 1, 2006, pp. 109–114.

48. John G. Lynch and G. Zauberman, "Construing Consumer Decision Making," *Journal of Consumer Psychology* 17, no. 2, 2007, pp. 107–112.

49. Ran Kivetz and Itamar Simonson, "Self-Control for the Righteous: Toward a Theory of Precommitment to Indulgence," *Journal of Consumer Research*, September 2002, pp. 199–217.

50. Daniel Kahneman and Amos Tversky, "Prospect Theory," *Econometrica*, March 1979, pp. 263–291.

51. Punan Anand Keller, Isaac M. Lipkus, and Barbara K. Rimer, "Affect, Framing, and Persuasion," *Journal of Marketing Research*, February 2003, pp. 54–64.

52. Ashwani Monga and Rui Zhu, "Buyers versus Sellers: How They Differ in Their Responses to Framed Outcomes," *Journal of Consumer Psychology* 15, no. 4, 2005, pp. 325–333.

53. I. P. Levin, "Associative Effects of Information Framing on Human Judgments," Paper presented at the annual meeting of the Midwestern Psychological Association, May 1987, in Chicago, Ill.

54. Sucharita Chandran and Geeta Menon, "When a Day Means More Than a Year: Effects of Temporal Framing on Judgments of Health Risk," *Journal of Consumer Research*, September 2004, pp. 375–389.

55. Christopher P. Puto, W. E. Patton, and Ronald H. King, "Risk Handling Strategies in Industrial Vendor Selection Decisions," *Journal of Marketing*, January 1987, pp. 89–98.

56. John T. Gourville, "Pennies-a-Day: The Effect of Temporal Reframing on Transaction Evaluation," *Journal of Consumer Research*, March 1998, pp. 395–408.

57. Rashmi Adaval and Kent B. Monroe, "Automatic Construct and Use of Contextual Information for Product and Price Evaluations," *Journal of Consumer Research*, March 2002, pp. 572–588.

58. Yaacov Schul and Yoav Ganzach, "The Effects of Accessibility of Standards and Decision Framing on Product Evaluations," *Journal of Consumer Psychology* 4, no. 1, 1995, pp. 61–83.

59. Baba Shiv, Julie A. Edell, and John W. Payne, "Factors Affecting the Impact of Negatively and Positively Framed Ad Messages," *Journal of Consumer Research*, December 1997, pp. 285–294.

60. James R. Bettman and Mita Sujan, "Effects of Framing on Evaluation of Comparable and Noncomparable Alternatives by Expert and Novice Consumers," *Journal of Consumer Research* 14, no. 2, 1987, pp. 141–154.

61. Donald P. Green and Irene V. Blair, "Framing and Price Elasticity of Private and Public Goods," *Journal of Consumer Psychology* 4, no. 1, 1995, pp. 1–32.

62. Paul M. Herr and Christine M. Page, "Asymmetric Association of Liking and Disliking Judgments: So What's Not to Like?" *Journal of Consumer Research*, March 2004, pp. 588–601.

63. "LEGO Bricks and Flicks," *Economist*, May 7, 2011, p. 70.

64. Josh Ozersky, "Cheesed Off: A Childhood Staple Becomes a Fad," *Time*, September 5, 2011, www.time.com.

65. Itamar Simonson, "Get Closer to Your Consumers by Understanding How They Make Choices," *California Management Review*, Summer 1993, pp. 68–84; John W. Payne, James R. Bettman, and Eric J. Johnson, "The Adaptive Decision-Maker," in ed. Robin M. Hogarth, *Insights in Decision Making: A Tribute to Hillel Einhorn* (Chicago: University of Chicago Press, 1990).

66. Aimee Drolet, "Inherent Rule Variability in Consumer Choice: Changing Rules for Change's Sake," *Journal of Consumer Research*, December 2002, pp. 293–305. James R. Bettman, Mary Frances Luce, and John W. Payne, "Constructive Consumer Choice Processes," *Journal of Consumer Research*, December 1998, pp. 187–217; James R. Bettman, Mary Frances Luce, and John W. Payne, "Constructive Consumer Choice Processes," *Journal of Consumer Research*, December 1998, pp. 187–217; Denis A. Lussier and Richard W. Olshavsky, "Task Complexity and Contingent Processing in Brand Choice," *Journal of Consumer Research*, September 1979, pp. 154–165; and Eric J. Johnson and Robert J. Meyer, "Compensatory Choice Models of Noncompensatory Processes," *Journal of Consumer Research*, June 1984, pp. 542–551.

67. Sanjay Sood, Yuval Rottenstreich, and Lyle Brenner, "On Decisions That Lead to Decisions: Direct and Derived Evaluations of Preference," *Journal of Consumer Research*, June 2004, pp. 17–18.

68. Seymour Epstein, "Integration of the Cognitive and the Psychodynamic Unconscious," *American Psychologist*, August 1994, pp. 709–724.

69. Mariele K. De Mooij and Warren Keegan, *Worldwide Advertising* (London: Prentice-Hall International, 1991).

70. Peter Wright, "Consumer Choice Strategies: Simplifying vs. Optimizing," *Journal of Marketing Research*, February 1975, pp. 60–67; and Noreen Klein and Stewart W. Bither, "An Investigation of Utility-Directed Cutoff Selection," *Journal of Consumer Research*, September 1987, pp. 240–256.

71. Simonson, "Get Closer to Your Consumers by Understanding How They Make Choices."

72. "Buzzing into Brazil," *Economist*, August 20, 2011, p. 61.

73. For a review of multiattribute models, see William L. Wilkie and Edgar A. Pessemier, "Issues in Marketing's Use of Multiattribute Models," *Journal of Marketing Research*, November 1983, pp. 428–441; and Blair H. Sheppard, Jon Hartwick, and Paul R. Warshaw, "The Theory of Reasoned Action," *Journal of Consumer Research*, December 1988, pp. 325–342.

74. Alexander Chernev, "Goal-Attribute Compatibility in Consumer Choice," *Journal of Consumer Psychology*, 2004, pp. 141–150.

75. Mary Frances Luce, "Choosing to Avoid: Coping with Negatively Emotion-Laden Consumer Decisions," *Journal of Consumer Research*, March 1998, pp. 409–433; and Ellen C. Garbarino and Julie A. Edell, "Cognitive Effort, Affect, and Choice," *Journal of Consumer Research*, September 1997, pp. 147–158.

76. Mary Frances Luce, John W. Payne, and James R. Bettman, "Emotional Trade-off Difficulty and Choice," *Journal of Marketing Research* 36, May 1999, pp. 143–159.

77. Aimee Drolet and Mary Frances Luce, "The Rationalizing Effects of Cognitive Load on Emotion-Based Tradeoff Avoidance," *Journal of Consumer Research*, June 2004, pp. 63–77; see also Tiffany Barnett White, "Consumer Trust and Advice Acceptance: The Moderating Roles of Benevolence, Expertise, and Negative Emotions," *Journal of Consumer Psychology* 15, no. 2, 2005, pp. 141–148.

78. David Grether and Louis Wilde, "An Analysis of Conjunctive Choice," *Journal of Consumer Research*, March 1984, pp. 373–385.

79. Bryan Roth, "Volts Give Car-Sharing a New Charge," *Duke Today*, August 31, 2011, http://today.duke.edu.

80. Lussier and Olshavsky, "Task Complexity and Contingent Processing in Brand Choice"; and Johnson and Meyer, "Compensatory Choice Models of Noncompensatory Processes."

81. Ben Austen, "The Mega Bus," *Bloomberg Businessweek*, April 11, 2011, pp. 63–67.

82. Timothy B. Heath, Gangseog Ryu, Subimal Chatterjee, Michael S. McCarthy, David L. Mothersbaugh, Sandra Milberg, and Gary J. Gaeth, "Asymmetric Competition in Choice and the Leveraging of Competitive Disadvantages," *Journal of Consumer Research* 27, December 2000, pp. 291–308.

83. Rohini Ahluwalia, Robert E. Burnkrant, and H. Rao Unnava, "Consumer Response to Negative Publicity: The Moderating Role of Commitment," *Journal of Marketing Research* 37, May 2000, pp. 203–214.

84. Josh Noel, "Radisson Betting on Blu," *Chicago Tribune*, August 26, 2011, www.chicagotribune.com; and Paris Wolfe, "Radisson's Brand Transformation Progresses," *Lodging Hospitality*, August 25, 2011, http://lhonline.com.

85. Gerald Häubl and Kyle B. Murray, "Preference Construction and Persistence in Digital Marketplaces: The Role of Electronic Recommendation Agents," *Journal of Consumer Psychology*, 2003, pp. 75–91.

86. Amos Tversky, "Intransitivity of Preferences," *Psychological Review*, January 1969, pp. 31–48.

87. Amos Tversky, "Elimination by Aspects: A Theory of Choice," *Psychological Review*, July 1972, pp. 281–299.

88. "Korean Restaurant Chains Seek Success Abroad," *Korea Herald*, September 9, 2011, www.koreaherald.com.

89. Jeff DeLong, "Retail Outlets Adding Electric Car Charging Stations," *USA Today*, January 18, 2011, www.usatoday.com.

90. Irwin Levin, "Associative Effects of Information Framing," *Bulletin of the Psychonomic Society*, March 1987, pp. 85–86.

91. Nathan Novemsky and Daniel Kahneman, "The Boundaries of Loss Aversion," *Journal of Marketing Research*, May 2005, pp. 119–128; Colin Camerer, "Three Cheers—Psychological, Theoretical, Empirical—for Loss Aversion," *Journal of Marketing Research*, May 2005, pp. 129–133; and Dan Ariely, Joel Huber, and Klaus Wertenbroch, "When Do Losses Loom Larger Than Gains?" *Journal of Marketing Research*, May 2005, pp. 134–138.

92. Alexander Chernev, "Goal Orientation and Consumer Preference for the Status Quo," *Journal of Consumer Research* 31, no. 3, 2004, pp. 557–565.

93. Swiffer website, www.swiffer.com/coupons-and-promotions/money-back-guarantee.

94. Matt Burns, "Nissan Adds New Features to the Leaf for 2012 Including a Higher Price," *TechCrunch*, July 19, 2011, www.techcrunch.com.

95. Douglas E. Allen, "Toward a Theory of Consumer Choice as Sociohistorically Shaped Practical Experience," *Journal of Consumer Research*, March 2002, pp. 515–532.

96. Peter R. Darke, Amitava Chattopadhyay, and Laurence Ashworth, "The Importance and Functional Significance of Affective Cues in Consumer Choice," *Journal of Consumer Research* 33, no. 3, 2006, pp. 322–328; and Stephen J. Hoch and George F. Lowenstein, "Time-Inconsistent Preferences and Consumer Self-Control," *Journal of Consumer Research*, March 1991, pp. 492–507.

97. Michel Tuan Pham, "The Logic of Feeling," *Journal of Consumer Psychology* 14, no. 4, 2004, pp. 360–369.

98. Michel Tuan Pham, "Representativeness, Relevance, and the Use of Feelings in Decision Making," *Journal of Consumer Research*, September 1998, pp. 144–159.

99. Epstein, "Integration of the Cognitive and the Psychodynamic Unconscious."

100. Yuval Rottenstreich, Sanjay Sood, and Lyle Brenner, "Feeling and Thinking in Memory-Based Versus Stimulus-Based Choices," *Journal of Consumer Research* 33, no. 4, 2007, pp. 461–469.

101. Pham, "Representativeness, Relevance, and the Use of Feelings in Decision Making"; Morris B. Holbrook and Elizabeth C. Hirschman, "The Experiential Aspects of Consumption," *Journal of Consumer Research*, September 1982, pp. 132–140; and Erica Mina Okada, "Justification Effects on Consumer Choice of Hedonic and Utilitarian Goods," *Journal of Marketing Research*, February 2005, pp. 43–53.

102. Stacy L. Wood and James R. Bettman, "Predicting Happiness: How Normative Feeling Rules Influence (and Even Reverse) Durability Bias," *Journal of Consumer Psychology* 17, no. 3, 2007, pp. 188–201; and Morris B. Holbrook and Meryl P. Gardner, "An Approach to Investigating the Emotional Determinants of Consumption Durations: Why Do People Consume What They Consume for as Long as They Consume It?" *Journal of Consumer Psychology* 2, no. 2, 1993, pp. 123–142.

103. See Jennifer S. Lerner, Seunghee Han, and Dacher Keltner, "Feelings and Consumer Decision Making: Extending the Appraisal-Tendency Framework," *Journal of Consumer Psychology* 17, no. 3, 2007, pp. 184–187; J. Frank Yates, "Emotional Appraisal Tendencies and Carryover: How, Why, and … Therefore?" *Journal of Consumer Psychology* 17, no. 3, 2007, pp. 179–183; and Baba Shiv, "Emotions, Decisions, and the Brain," *Journal of Consumer Psychology* 17, no. 3, pp. 174–178.

104. Seunghee Han, Jennifer S. Lerner, and Dacher Keltner, "Feelings and Consumer Decision Making: The Appraisal-Tendency Framework," *Journal of Consumer Psychology* 17, no. 3, 2007, pp. 158–168.

105. Ibid.

106. Leif D. Nelson and Tom Meyvis, "Interrupted Consumption: Disrupting Adaptation to Hedonic Experiences," *Journal of marketing Research*, December 2008, pp. 654–664.

107. Niels van de Ven, Marcel Zeelenberg, and Rik Pieters, "The Envy Premium in Product Evaluation," *Journal of Consumer Research*, April 2011, pp. 984–998.

108. Deborah J. MacInnis, Vanessa M. Patrick, and C. Whan Park, "Not as Happy as I Thought I'd Be? Affective Misforecasting and Product Evaluations," *Journal of Consumer Research*, March 2007, pp. 479–490; and Deborah J. MacInnis, Vanessa M. Patrick, and C. Whan Park, "Looking Through the Crystal Ball: Affective Forecasting and Misforecasting in Consumer Behavior," *Review of Marketing Research* 2, 2006, pp. 43–80.

109. Eric A. Greenleaf, "Reserves, Regret, and Rejoicing in Open English Auctions," *Journal of Consumer Research* 31, no. 2, 2004, pp. 264–273.

110. I. Simonson, "The Influence of Anticipating Regret and Responsibility on Purchase Decisions," *Journal of Consumer Research* 19, 1992, pp. 105–118.

111. Ann L. McGill and Punam Anand Keller, "Differences in the Relative Influence of Product Attributes under Alternative Processing Conditions," *Journal of Consumer Psychology* 3, no. 1, 1994, pp. 29–50; and MacInnis and Price, "The Role of Imagery in Information Processing: Review and Extensions."

112. Russell W. Belk, Güliz Ger, and Søren Askegaard, "The Fire of Desire: A Multisited Inquiry into Consumer Passion," *Journal of Consumer Research*, December 2003, pp. 326–351.

113. Ann E. Schlosser, "Experiencing Products in the Virtual World: The Role of Goal and Imagery in Influencing Attitudes versus Purchase Intentions," *Journal of Consumer Research*, September 2003, pp. 184–198.

114. Jennifer Edson Escalas, "Imagine Yourself in the Product," *Journal of Advertising*, Summer 2004, pp. 37–48.

115. Darren W. Dahl, Amitava Chattopadhyay and Gerald J. Gorn, "The Use of Visual Mental Imagery in New Product Design," *Journal of Marketing Research* 36, February 1999, pp. 18–28.

116. Stuart Elliott, "Luxury Hotels Market the Memories They Can Make," *New York Times*, September 13, 2011, www.nytimes.com; Carmine Gallo, "Employee Motivation the Ritz-Carlton Way," *BusinessWeek*, February 29, 2008, www.businessweek.com; and Molly Gamble, "Luxury Hotel Chain Ritz-Carlton to Help Tennessee Hospital Achieve Service Excellence," *Becker's Hospital Review*, August 26, 2011, www.beckershospitalreview.com.

117. Eric A. Greenleaf and Donald R. Lehmann, "Reasons for Substantial Delay in Consumer Decision Making," *Journal of Consumer Research*, September 1995, pp. 186–199.

118. See Benjamin Scheibehenne, Rainer Greifeneder, and Peter M. Todd, "Can There Ever Be Too Many Options? A Meta-Analytic Review of Choice Overload," *Journal of Consumer Research*, October 2010, pp. 409–425.

119. Thomas A. Brunner and Michaela Wänke, "The Reduced and Enhanced Impact of Shared Features on Individual Brand Evaluations," *Journal of Consumer Psychology* 16, no. 2, 2006, pp. 101–111.

120. "Nissan's Leaf Sales Spike in April," *Nashville Business Journal*, May 3, 2011, www.bizjournals.com.

121. Michael D. Johnson, "Consumer Choice Strategies for Comparing Noncomparable Alternatives," *Journal of Consumer Research*, December 1984, pp. 741–753; and Michael D. Johnson, "Comparability and Hierarchical Processing in Multialternative Choice," *Journal of Consumer Research*, December 1988, pp. 303–314.

122. Kim P. Corfman, "Comparability and Comparison Levels Used in Choices Among Consumer Products," *Journal of Marketing Research*, August 1991, pp. 368–374.

123. C. Whan Park and Daniel Smith, "Product-Level Choice: A Top-Down or Bottom-Up Process?" *Journal of Consumer Research*, December 1989, pp. 289–299

124. "Visit Scotland Targets Golfers with Latest Tourism Campaign," *New Media Age*, January 31, 2008, n.p.

125. Girish N. Punj and David W. Stewart, "An Interaction Framework of Consumer Decision Making," *Journal of Consumer Research*, September 1983, pp. 181–196.

126. Patricia M. West, Christina L. Brown, and Stephen J. Hoch, "Consumption Vocabulary and Preference Formation," *Journal of Consumer Research*, September 1996, pp. 120–135.

127. Johnson and Russo, "Product Familiarity and Learning New Information"; and James R. Bettman and C. Whan Park, "Effects of Prior Knowledge and Experience and Phase of the Choice Process on Consumer Decision Processes, A Protocol Analysis," *Journal of Consumer Research*, December 1980, pp. 234–248.

128. Joffre Swait and Wiktor Adamowicz, "The Influence of Task Complexity on Consumer Choice," *Journal of Consumer Research*, June 2001, pp. 135–148.

129. Elaine Sherman and Ruth Belk Smith, "Mood States of Shoppers and Store Image: Promising Interactions and Possible Behavioral Effects," in eds. Paul Anderson and Melanie Wallendorf, *Advances in Consumer Research*, vol. 14 (Provo, Utah: Association for Consumer Research, 1987), pp. 251–254.

130. Rashmi Adaval, "How Good Gets Better and Bad Gets Worse: Understanding the Impact of Affect on Evaluations of Known Brands," *Journal of Consumer Research*, December 2003, pp. 352–367.

131. Stewart Shapiro, Deborah J. MacInnis, and C. Whan Park, "Understanding Program-Induced Mood Effects: Decoupling Arousal from Valence," *Journal of Advertising*, Winter 2002, pp. 15–26.

132. Catherine W. M. Yeung and Robert S. Wyer Jr., "Affect, Appraisal, and Consumer Judgment," *Journal of Consumer Research*, September 2004, pp. 412–424.

133. Gerald J. Gorn, Marvin E. Goldberg, and Kunal Basu, "Mood, Awareness, and Product Evaluation," *Journal of Consumer Psychology* 2, no. 3, 1993, pp. 237–256.

134. Joel B. Cohen and Eduardo B. Andrade, "Affective Intuition and Task-Contingent Affect Regulation," *Journal of Consumer Research*, September 2004, pp. 358–367.

135. Alexander Fedorikhin and Catherine A. Cole, "Mood Effects on Attitudes, Perceived Risk, and Choice: Moderators and Mediators," *Journal of Consumer Psychology* 14, no. 1/2, 2004, pp. 2–12.

136. Payne, Bettman, and Johnson, "The Adaptive Decision-Maker."

137. C. Whan Park, Easwar S. Iyer, and Daniel C. Smith, "The Effects of Situational Factors on In-Store Grocery Shopping Behavior: The Role of Store Environment and Time Available for Shopping," *Journal of Consumer Research*, March 1989, pp. 422–433.

138. Ravi Dhar and Stephen M. Nowlis, "The Effect of Time Pressure on Consumer Choice Deferral," *Journal of Consumer Research* 25, March 1999, pp. 369–384.

139. Michelle M. Bergadaa, "The Role of Time in the Action of the Consumer," *Journal of Consumer Research*, December 1990, pp. 289–302.

140. Alexander Chernev, "Extremeness Aversion and Attribute-Balance Effects in Choice," *Journal of Consumer Research*, September 2004, pp. 249–263.

141. Ran Kivetz, Oded Netzer, and V. Srinivasan, "Alternative Models for Capturing the Compromise Effect," *Journal of Marketing Research*, August 2004, pp. 237–257; and Ravi Dhar, Anil Menon, and Bryan Maach, "Toward Extending the Compromise Effect to Complex Buying Contexts," *Journal of Marketing Research*, August 2004, pp. 258–261.

142. Alexander Chernev, "Context Effects without a Context: Attribute Balance as a Reason for Choice," *Journal of Consumer Research* 32, no. 2, 2005, pp. 213–223.

143. Norbert Schwarz, "Metacognitive Experiences in Consumer Judgment and Decision Making," *Journal of Consumer Psychology* 14, no. 4, 2004, pp. 332–348.

144. Rolf Reber and Norbert Schwarz, "Effects on Perceptual Fluency on Judgments of Truth," *Consciousness and Cognition*, 8, 1999, 338–342; and Matthew S. McGlone and Jessica Tofighbakhsh, "Birds of a Feather Flock Conjointly(?): Rhyme as Reason in Aphorisms," *Psychological Science* 11, no. 1, 2000, 424–428.

145. See Joel Huber, "A Comment on Metacognitive Experiences and Consumer Choices," *Journal of Consumer Psychology* 14, no. 4, 2004, pp. 356–359; and Norbert Schwarz, "Metacognitive Experiences: Response to Commentaries," *Journal of Consumer Psychology* 14, no. 4, 2004, pp. 370–373.

146. Jacob Jacoby, "Perspectives on Information Overload," *Journal of Consumer Research*, March 1984, pp. 569–573; and Kevin Lane Keller and Richard Staelin, "Effects of Quality and Quantity of Information on Decision Effectiveness," *Journal of Consumer Research*, September 1987, pp. 200–213.

147. Keller and Staelin, "Effects of Quality and Quantity of Information on Decision Effectiveness."

148. Ran Kivetz and Itamar Simonson, "The Effects of Incomplete Information on Consumer Choice," *Journal of Marketing Research* 37, November 2000, pp. 427–448.

149. A. V. Muthukrishnan, "Decision Ambiguity and Incumbent Brand Advantage," *Journal of Consumer Research*, June 1995, pp. 98–109.

150. Madhubalan Viswanathan and Sunder Narayanan, "Comparative Judgments of Numerical and Verbal Attribute Labels," *Journal of Consumer Psychology* 3, no. 1, 1994, pp. 79–100.

151. Joseph R. Priester, Utpal M. Dholakia, and Monique A. Fleming, "When and Why the Background Contrast Effect Emerges," *Journal of Consumer Research* 31, no. 3, 2004, pp. 491–501; Joel Huber, John W. Payne, and Christopher Puto, "Adding Asymmetrically Dominated Alternatives: Violations of Regularity and the Similarity Hypothesis," *Journal of Consumer Research*, June 1982, pp. 90–98; and Ravi Dhar and Itamar Simonson, "Making Complementary Choices in Consumption Episodes," *Journal of Marketing Research*, February 1999, pp. 29–44.

152. Itamar Simonson and Russell S. Winer, "The Influence of Purchase Quantity and Display Format on Consumer Preference for Variety," *Journal of Consumer Research*, June 1992, pp. 133–138.

153. Itamar Simonson, Stephen Nowlis, and Katherine Lemon, "The Effect of Local Consideration Sets on Global Choice between Lower Price and Higher Quality," *Marketing Science*, Fall 1993.

154. Rashmi Adaval and Robert S. Wyer Jr., "The Role of Narratives in Consumer Information Processing," *Journal of Consumer Psychology* 7, no. 3, 1998, pp. 207–245.

155. Gergana Y. Nenkov, J. Jeffrey Inman, John Hulland, and Maureen Morrin, "The Impact of Outcome Elaboration on Susceptibility to Contextual and Presentation Biases," *Journal of Marketing Research*, December 2009, pp. 764–776.

156. Christina L. Brown and Gregory S. Carpenter, "Why Is the Trivial Important? A Reasons-Based Account for the Effects of Trivial Attributes on Choice," *Journal of Consumer Research*, March 2000, pp. 372–385.

157. Dan Ariely and Jonathan Levav, "Sequential Choice in Group Settings," *Journal of Consumer Research* 27, December 2000, pp. 279–290.

158. Stijn M. J. van Osselaer, Joseph W. Alba, and Puneet Manchanda, "Irrelevant Information and Mediated Intertemporal Choice," *Journal of Consumer Psychology* 14, no. 3, 2004, pp. 257–270.

159. Guliz Ger, "Problems of Marketization in Romania and Turkey," in eds. Clifford Schultz, Russell Belk, and Guliz Ger, *Consumption in Marketizing Economies* (Greenwich, Conn.: JAI Press, 1995).

160. Sabrina Tavernise, "In Russia, Capitalism of a Certain Size," *New York Times*, July 29, 2001, sec. 3, p. 6; and Guliz Ger, Russell Belk, and Dana-Nicoleta Lascu, "The Development of Consumer Desire in Marketing and Developing Economies," in eds. Leigh McAlister and Michael L. Rothschild, *Advances in Consumer Research*, vol. 20 (Provo, Utah: Association for Consumer Research, 1993), pp. 102–107.

161. "Harley, the Century-old Iconic Brand," *Economic Times (India)*, November 6, 2011, www.economictimes.indiatimes.com; "Harley Davidson Enjoys Romance with Indian Women," *Economic Times (India)*, July 19, 2011, www.economictimes.indiatimes.com; Arathi Gunnupuri, "Harley Davidson India Opens for 'Mumbikers,'" *CNN Go*, September 22, 2010, www.cnngo.com; Sara Sidner, "Harley-Davidson to Build Bikes in India," *CNN*, November 4, 2010, www.cnn.com; Penny MacRae, "Harley-Davidson 'Hogs' Ride into India," *AsiaOne*, July 18, 2010, www.asiaone.com; and Rudraneil Sengupta, "Anoop Prakash, Man Behind the Machine," *livemint.com*, September 2, 2011, www.livemint.com.

CHAPTER 9

JUDGMENT AND DECISION MAKING BASED ON LOW EFFORT

After studying this chapter, you will be able to

1. Identify the types of heuristics that consumers can use to make simple judgments.

2. Explain why marketers need to understand both unconscious and conscious decision-making processes in low-effort situations.

3. Show how the hierarchy of effects and operant conditioning explain consumers' low-effort decision making.

4. Discuss how consumers make thought-based low-effort decisions using performance-related tactics, habit, brand loyalty, price-related tactics, and normative influences.

5. Describe how consumers make affect-based low-effort decisions using feelings as a simplifying strategy, brand familiarity, variety seeking, and impulse purchasing.

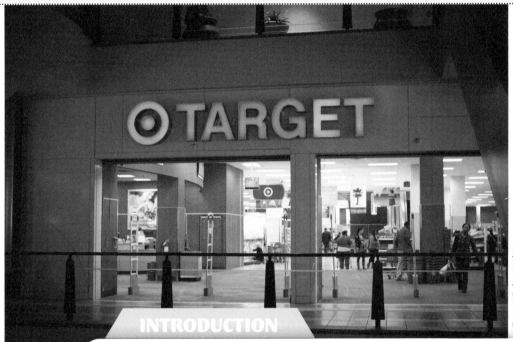

© Frances Roberts/Alamy

INTRODUCTION

Need Dorm Stuff? Hop on the Bullseye Bus!

Since 2007, tens of thousands of college students have taken Target up on its offer to give them a free ride to the nearest Target store for an exclusive after-hours shopping trip to stock up on dorm-room items and personal-care products such as toothpaste. Most of the dorm residents at the University of Utah have hopped on the bus to enjoy free snacks, a dance party, in-store contests, and lots of company as they wheel their carts down Target's aisles at midnight. At the University of Central Florida, thousands of students flock to the local Target every fall, while local cheerleaders shout cheers and the store's mascot dances along.

This annual back-to-school shopping event, which has spread to more than 65 colleges and universities, is not for freshmen only: at University of North Carolina, returning students like to hop on the Target bus and enjoy the late-night event alongside incoming students. For their part, school administrators see the event as a safe, alcohol-free environment where students can mix and mingle while they shop for what they need and want. Target offers an online checklist that students can customize in advance and then send to their cell phones or print out for

241

shopping convenience. To build excitement before students even hop on the bus, Target posts promotions on its Facebook page and offers mobile coupons that can be redeemed in the store. And when the party's over, students simply haul their shopping bags back on the bus for a quick ride back to the dorm.[1]

Target's back-to-school shopping events illustrate several factors discussed in this chapter. When consumers have low motivation, ability, and opportunity (MAO) to process information (as when purchasing everyday products like shampoo), their judgment and decision processes are different and involve less effort than when MAO is high (as when buying luxury goods). Consumers may simplify their decisions by repeatedly buying a brand they like or from a store they like. Or they may be guided by their feelings toward a familiar brand or store (such as Target). Also, the marketer can try to increase the excitement (or situational involvement) by offering free merchandise and coupons on its website, through social media, or in the store.

This chapter examines the nature of low-effort judgment and decision making, as shown in Exhibit 9.1. The focus here is on the cognitive and affective shortcuts or heuristics that consumers use to make judgments and decisions, as well as on how consumers make unconscious and conscious decisions in low-effort situations.

LOW-EFFORT JUDGMENT PROCESSES

Chapter 8 showed that when effort is high, consumers' judgments—such as estimations of likelihood, judgments of goodness/badness, and mental accounting—can be cognitively complex. In contrast, when MAO is low, individuals are motivated to simplify the cognitive process by using heuristics, or rules of thumb, to reduce the effort involved in making judgments.[2] Two major types of heuristics are representativeness and availability.

The Representativeness Heuristic

Representativeness heuristic Making a judgment by simply comparing a stimulus with the category prototype or exemplar.

One way that consumers can make simple estimations or judgments is to make comparisons with the category prototype or exemplar. This categorization process is called the **representativeness heuristic**.[3] For example, if you want to estimate the likelihood that a new laundry detergent is of high quality, you might compare it with your prototype for detergents, such as Tide. If you see that the new brand is similar to the prototype, you will assume that it is also of high quality. This is the reasoning behind packaging many store brands so that they look similar to leading brands in product categories. The retailers hope that the outward similarity will suggest to consumers that the store products possess the same good qualities.

Like any shortcut, the representativeness heuristic can also lead to biased judgments. For instance, consumers who see Hallmark as the prototype of a greeting card may assume that it offers only paper-based products. To overcome these biased judgments, Hallmark has added a variety of tech-enhanced products, including e-cards and storybooks with voice-capture technology so children can hear a family member read the book out loud.[4]

The Availability Heuristic

Availability heuristic Basing judgments on events that are easier to recall.

Judgments can also be influenced by the ease with which instances of an event can be brought to mind, a shortcut called the **availability heuristic**.[5] Consumers are more likely to recall more accessible or more vivid events, a tendency that influences their judgments—even though they may be unaware of this effect.[6] To illustrate, suppose that years ago you purchased a DVD player that needed constant repair. Today you may still recall your anger and disappointment when

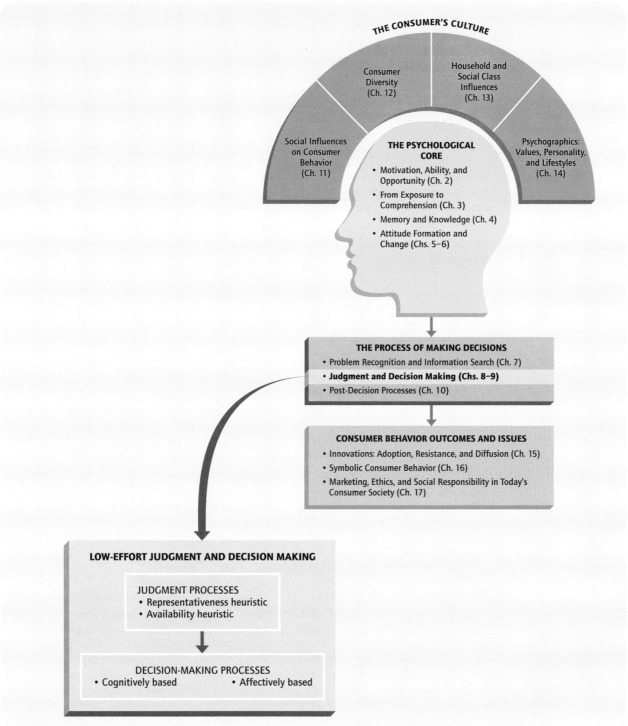

THE CONSUMER'S CULTURE

Consumer Diversity (Ch. 12)

Household and Social Class Influences (Ch. 13)

Social Influences on Consumer Behavior (Ch. 11)

THE PSYCHOLOGICAL CORE
- Motivation, Ability, and Opportunity (Ch. 2)
- From Exposure to Comprehension (Ch. 3)
- Memory and Knowledge (Ch. 4)
- Attitude Formation and Change (Chs. 5–6)

Psychographics: Values, Personality, and Lifestyles (Ch. 14)

THE PROCESS OF MAKING DECISIONS
- Problem Recognition and Information Search (Ch. 7)
- Judgment and Decision Making (Chs. 8–9)
- Post-Decision Processes (Ch. 10)

CONSUMER BEHAVIOR OUTCOMES AND ISSUES
- Innovations: Adoption, Resistance, and Diffusion (Ch. 15)
- Symbolic Consumer Behavior (Ch. 16)
- Marketing, Ethics, and Social Responsibility in Today's Consumer Society (Ch. 17)

LOW-EFFORT JUDGMENT AND DECISION MAKING

JUDGMENT PROCESSES
- Representativeness heuristic
- Availability heuristic

DECISION-MAKING PROCESSES
- Cognitively based
- Affectively based

© Cengage Learning 2013

Exhibit 9.1

Chapter Overview: Judgment and Decision Making: Low Consumer Effort

In low-effort processing situations, consumers tend to use heuristics or ways of simplifying the judgment or decision. Both cognitively based heuristics (performance-based tactics, habit, price-related tactics, brand loyalty, and normative influences) and affectively based heuristics (affect-related tactics, variety seeking, and impulse) are used to make decisions.

you see this brand. Your experiences greatly color your estimations of the quality of this brand, even though the brand might actually have few breakdowns today. Word-of-mouth communication is another example of accessible information that leads to use of the availability heuristic. If a friend says she had problems with a certain brand of DVD player, this information is likely to affect your estimates of the brand's quality, even though her experience might have been an isolated event.

Base-rate information
How often an event really occurs on average.

These judgments are biased because we tend to ignore **base-rate information**—how often the event really occurs—in favor of information that is more vivid or accessible. One study demonstrated this effect in the context of estimating the probability that refrigerators would break down.[7] One group was given a set of case histories told by consumers, and another was given actual statistics about the incidence of appliance breakdown. People who read the case histories provided breakdown estimates that were 30 percent higher than those of the statistics group. Another study found that consumers can use both base-rate and case information, but their judgment depends on how the information is structured.[8] As case history information becomes more specific, consumers rely less on base rates. Another reason that we do not use more base-rate information is that it is often not available.

Law of small numbers
The expectation that information obtained from a small number of people represents the larger population.

A related bias is the **law of small numbers**, whereby people expect information obtained from a small sample to be typical of the larger population.[9] If friends say that a new song by a particular group is really good or that the food at a particular restaurant is terrible, we believe that information, even if most people do not feel that way. In fact, reliance on small numbers is another reason that word-of-mouth communication can be so powerful. We tend to have confidence that the opinions of friends or relatives are more reflective of the majority than they may actually be.

Marketing Implications

Both the representativeness and availability heuristics are important to marketers.

The Representativeness Heuristic

This heuristic suggests that companies position offerings close to a prototype that has positive associations in consumers' minds. However, when the shortcut leads to a judgment that is negatively biased, marketers must take steps to overcome it. For example, some consumers view merchandise made in China as the prototype for cheaply made products. Chinese companies such as Haier (home appliances) and Lenovo (computers) are working to overcome this bias by designing cutting-edge products and opening local manufacturing facilities in the United States and other countries where they market.[10]

The Availability Heuristic

Marketers can attempt either to capitalize on or to overcome the availability bias. To capitalize, they can provide consumers with positive and vivid product-related experiences through the use of marketing communications, or they can ask consumers to imagine such situations. Both strategies will increase consumers' estimates that these events will occur. Or marketers can attempt to stimulate positive word-of-mouth communication. For instance, *Entertainment Weekly* magazine invites consumers to participate in live online chats with its editors and post to Twitter or Facebook while watching popular TV shows. The idea is to get consumers talking about *Entertainment Weekly* and the TV shows.[11]

Marketers can attempt to overcome the availability bias by providing consumers with base-rate information about the general population. If this information is vivid and specific (such as "chosen 2 to 1 over its competitors"), it can help consumers make a less biased judgment. The Internet is an excellent vehicle for providing base-rate information. To illustrate, consumers interested in buying books at Amazon.com can see a summary rating, read consumer-submitted reviews, and click to preview the book. The availability bias is also a common problem in the context of sweepstakes and lotteries. Although the likelihood of their winning is exceedingly small, consumers often overestimate the odds because they are exposed to highly vivid and available images of winners in the media. Regulators have attempted to overcome this bias by requiring marketers to clearly post the odds of winning.

LOW-EFFORT DECISION-MAKING PROCESSES

Most low-effort judgment and decision situations are not very important in consumers' lives relative to other decisions in their lives. Clearly, career and family decisions are far more important than deciding which toothpaste or peanut butter to buy. Thus, the consumer usually does not want to devote a lot of time and effort to these relatively mundane decisions.[12] So how do consumers make decisions in these low-elaboration situations? Researchers suggest that such decisions are sometimes made unconsciously and sometimes consciously, but with little effort.

Unconscious Low-Effort Decision Making

In some low-effort situations, consumers may make a decision without being consciously aware of how or why they are doing so. As much as 50 percent of all shopping decisions are made spontaneously and unconsciously while consumers are in the store.[13] Such unconscious choices may be strongly affected by environmental stimuli such as the fragrance of a perfume in a department store.[14] With "all of the other senses, you think before you respond, but with scent, your brain responds before you think," observes one expert.[15] Other environmental stimuli that might trigger choices and behavior without the consumer's being consciously aware of the effect are novel shapes, color, brand logos, certain places or social situations, and the presence of other people.[16]

Several influences mentioned in Chapter 6 play a role in unconscious, low-effort decision making. For example, evaluative conditioning can influence attitudes and unconscious brand choices.[17] In addition, consumers may form accurate yet unconscious impressions through thin-slice judgments.[18] Consumers may have a positive attitude toward a product they unconsciously perceive as having a friendly human face—such as a car that seems to smile.[19] Body feedback can also play a role. In one study, consumers who were induced to nod had more positive evaluations of positively valenced brands (and more negative evaluations when induced to shake their heads).[20] Another factor affecting unconscious evaluations of products is how the floor feels to a shopper. The comfortable feeling of standing on carpeting prompts shoppers to evaluate nearby products as less comforting than products that are not close at hand.[21]

Some researchers argue that certain choices represent goal-related behavior (e.g., buying fast food), even though consumers are pursuing the goal almost automatically, without conscious thought.[22] Others point out that although many consumer behaviors operate on a conscious level, unconscious choices and behaviors are also important, even if poorly understood and unpredictable.[23] More research is needed to explain how and why consumers use unconscious decision making.

Marketing Implications

Because environmental stimuli strongly influence unconscious choices, many hotels, stores, and restaurants scent the air with aromas that serve as unconscious reminders of certain products, brands, or situations. Upscale hotels often create signature scents for their lobbies. The scent in the Ritz-Carlton hotel in South Beach, Florida, has hints of mango and peach, while a citrus-and-clove fragrance wafts through the lobby of the Kimpton's EPIC in Miami.[24] Marketers can also use music, color, displays, and other sensory cues.

Conscious Low-Effort Decision Making

Traditional hierarchy of effects Sequential steps used in decision making involving thinking, then feeling, then behavior.

In the previous chapter, you saw that consumers have certain beliefs about each alternative that are combined to form an attitude that leads to a conscious behavior or a choice. The consumer engages in *thinking*, which leads to *feelings*, which result in behaving, a progression known as the hierarchy of effects. However, studies show that this **traditional hierarchy of effects** does not apply to all decision-making situations.[25]

Low-effort hierarchy of effects Sequence of thinking-behaving-feeling.

Instead, researchers have proposed a **hierarchy of effects for low-effort situations** that follows a *thinking-behaving-feeling* sequence.[26] The consumer enters the decision process with a set of low-level beliefs based on brand familiarity and knowledge obtained from repeated exposures to advertising, in-store exposure, or prior usage. In the absence of any attitude, these beliefs serve as the foundation for the decision or behavior. After making the decision and while using the product, the consumer evaluates the brand and may or may not form an attitude, depending on how strongly the brand is liked or satisfies needs.

Some researchers have challenged the belief-behavior link in the low-involvement hierarchy, saying that consumers sometimes base a decision solely on how they feel rather than on what they think.[27] For example, you might select a new candy or download a TV program based on positive feelings rather than on beliefs or knowledge. Here, the sequence would be feeling, behaving, and thinking. This type of decision making, which clearly does occur, suggests that consumers can process in both a cognitive and an affective manner—a factor in many low-elaboration situations.

Using Simplifying Strategies When Consumer Effort Is Low

Low-effort purchases represent the most frequent type of decisions that consumers make in everyday life. One in-store study of laundry detergent purchases found that the median amount of time taken to make a choice was only 8.5 seconds.[28] A study of coffee and tissues found very low levels of decision activity, particularly among consumers who purchased the product frequently and had a strong brand preference.[29] Some research has examined consumer decision processes across a number of product categories and has even questioned whether there is any decision process at all.[30] Other research suggests that if you have low motivation and ability, you may simply delegate a buying decision by asking someone else to make the decision. Of course, the outcome will depend on how well the other person knows you.[31]

Under low motivation and low processing opportunity, how a marketing message is framed will influence how consumers react. A negatively framed marketing message is more effective than a positively framed message low MAO, for instance.[32] Research also shows that consumers with a low need for cognition are more susceptible to the influence of a negatively framed message.[33] And when a decision is framed in terms of subtracting unwanted options from a fully loaded product, consumers will choose more options with a higher total option price than they will if the decision is framed in terms of adding wanted items to a base model.[34]

A decision process probably does occur in low-effort situations, but it is simpler, involves less effort, and is qualitatively different from processes that occur when MAO is high. Two other factors influence the low-MAO decision process. First, the goal is not necessarily to find the best possible brand, called *optimizing*, as is the case with high-elaboration decisions. To optimize here would require more effort than consumers are typically willing to expend. Instead, consumers are more willing to **satisfice**, to find a brand that is good enough to simply satisfy their needs. The effort required to find the best brand may simply not be worth it.[35]

Satisfice Finding a brand that satisfies a need even though the brand may not be the best brand.

Second, most low-elaboration decisions are made frequently and repeatedly. In these decisions, consumers may rely on previous information and judgments of satisfaction or dissatisfaction from past consumption. Think of all the times that you have purchased toothpaste, breakfast cereal, and shampoo. You have acquired information by using these products and by seeing ads, checking websites, talking to friends, and so forth. Instead of searching for information every time you are in the store, you can simply remember previous decisions and use that information to make your next choice.

Choice tactics Simple rules of thumb used to make low-effort decisions.

In these common, repeat-purchase situations, consumers can develop decision heuristics called **choice tactics** for quick, effortless decision making.[36] Rather than comparing various brands in detail, consumers apply these rules to simplify the decision process. The study of laundry detergents mentioned earlier supports this view.[37] When consumers were asked how they made their choices, several major categories of tactics emerged, including *price tactics* (it's the cheapest or it's on sale), *affect tactics* (I like it), *performance tactics* (it cleans clothes better), and *normative tactics* (my mother bought it). Other studies have identified *habit tactics* (I buy the same brand I bought last time), *brand-loyalty tactics* (I buy the same brand for which I have a strong preference), and *variety-seeking tactics* (I need to try something different). Research has found similar patterns in Singapore, Germany, Thailand, and the United States.[38]

Consumers can develop a choice tactic for each repeat-purchase, low-elaboration decision in the product or service category. If the consumer's decision is observed only once, it will appear very limited. Because all prior purchases serve as input to the current decision, it is important to look at a whole series of choices and consumption situations to fully understand consumer decision making. Thus, low-effort decision making is very dynamic in nature.

LEARNING CHOICE TACTICS

Operant conditioning
The view that behavior is a function of reinforcements and punishments received in the past.

To understand low-elaboration decision making, marketers need to know how consumers learn to apply choice tactics. Certain concepts from the behaviorist tradition in psychology are relevant to understanding the way that consumers learn. **Operant conditioning** views behavior as a function of previous actions and of the reinforcements or punishments obtained from these actions.[39] For example, while you were growing up, your parents may have given you a reward for making good grades or an allowance for mowing the lawn. You learned that these were good behaviors, and you were more likely to do these things again because you had been rewarded for them.

Reinforcement

Reinforcement usually comes from a feeling of satisfaction that occurs when we as consumers perceive that our needs have been adequately met. This reinforcement increases the probability that we will purchase the same brand again. For example, if you buy Crest toothpaste and are impressed by the results after using it, your purchase will be reinforced, and you will be more likely to buy this brand again. In one study, past experience with a brand was by far the most critical factor in brand choice—more important than quality, price, and familiarity.[40] Other research has shown that the information that consumers receive from product trials tends to be more powerful and influential than that received from advertising.[41] The thoughts and emotions experienced during a trial can have a particularly powerful influence on evaluations.[42] Reinforcement in the form of frequent-buyer rewards can also be effective. One study found that consumers actually accelerated their purchasing as they got closer to earning a reward.[43]

Note that consumers often perceive few differences among brands of many products and services.[44] Thus, they are unlikely to develop a strong positive brand attitude when no brand is seen as clearly better than another. As long as the consumer is not dissatisfied, the choice tactic he or she used will be reinforced. Suppose you buy the cheapest brand of paper towels. If this brand at least minimally satisfies your needs, you are likely to buy the cheapest brand again—and it may be a different brand next time. Thus, reinforcement can occur for either the brand or the choice tactic.

Punishment

Alternatively, consumers can have a bad experience with a product or service, form a negative evaluation of it, and never purchase it again. In operant conditioning terms, this experience is called *punishment*. If you did something bad when you were growing up, your parents may have punished you to make sure that you would not behave that way again. In a consumer context, punishment occurs when a brand does not meet our needs and we are dissatisfied, so we learn not to buy that brand again. Punishment may also lead consumers to reevaluate the choice tactic and use a different tactic for the next purchase. If you buy the cheapest brand of trash bags, and the bags burst when you take out the trash, you could either employ a new tactic (buy the most expensive or the most familiar brand) or upgrade your tactic (buy the cheapest *national* brand).

Repeat Purchase

Consumers learn when the same act is repeatedly reinforced or punished over time, a process summarized in Exhibit 9.2. This process occurs whenever we buy a common, repeat-purchase product. Thus, we learn and gradually acquire a set of choice tactics that will result in making a satisfactory choice in each decision situation. Decision-making models have traditionally ignored the key role of consumption in the decision process, focusing more attention on the processing that occurs immediately prior to the decision. But clearly what takes place while the product is being consumed has important implications for future acquisition, usage, and disposition decisions. In other words, whether the consumer forms a positive or negative evaluation of the brand or tactic can be an important input into future decisions.

Choice Tactics Depend on the Product

The choice tactics we use often depend on the product category that we are considering.[45] For example, we might be brand loyal to Heinz ketchup but always buy the cheapest trash bags. The tactic we learn for a product category depends on which brands are available and our experiences with them. The amount of advertising, price variations, and the number and similarity of brands also influence the type of tactic that we employ.[46] Interestingly, the study from Singapore mentioned earlier found a greater similarity in the tactics that consumers use for the same product in different cultures (the United States and Singapore) than in tactics that they use for different products in the same culture.[47] In general, our experiences help us learn what works for each product, and we use these tactics to minimize our decision-making effort for future purchases.

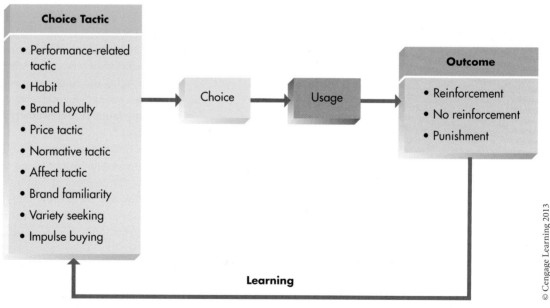

© Cengage Learning 2013

Exhibit 9.2

The Learning Process

This diagram shows how the outcome of a decision can help consumers learn which choice tactic to apply in a given situation. After consumers apply one of the seven basic types of tactics to make a choice, they take the brand home and use it. During consumption, they can evaluate the brand, an action that results in one of three basic outcomes: reinforcement (satisfaction leading to positive attitude and repurchase), no reinforcement (leading to tactic reinforcement, but no attitude toward the brand), or punishment (leading to a negative attitude, no repurchase, and tactic reevaluation).

LOW-EFFORT THOUGHT-BASED DECISION MAKING

Each tactic consumers learn for making low-elaboration decisions can have important implications for marketers. As in high-elaboration decisions, these strategies can be divided into two broad categories: thought-based and feeling-based decision making. This section examines cognitive-based decision making, which includes performance-related tactics, habit, brand loyalty, price-related tactics, and normative influences.

Performance as a Simplifying Strategy

Performance-related tactics Tactics based on benefits, features, or evaluations of the brand.

When the outcome of the consumption process is positive reinforcement, consumers are likely to use **performance-related tactics** to make their choices. These tactics can represent an overall evaluation (works the best) or focus on a specific attribute or benefit (gets teeth whiter, tastes better, or has quicker service). Satisfaction is the key: Satisfied consumers are likely to develop a positive evaluation of the brand or service and repurchase it based on its features.

Marketing Implications

A principal objective of marketing strategy should be to increase the likelihood of satisfaction through offering quality. Only then can a brand consistently achieve repeat purchases and loyal users. Kohl's, for example, offers basic clothing products as well as higher-quality private-label fashion lines by Jennifer Lopez and Marc Anthony. Customers appreciate the product quality and the quality of services such as the department store's no-hassle returns. In turn, customers' preference for Kohl's has boosted its sales and profits.[48]

Advertising can play a central role in influencing performance evaluations by increasing the consumer's expectation of positive reinforcement and satisfaction and lessening the negative effects of an unfavorable consumption experience.[49] Because we see what we want to see and form our expectations accordingly, marketers should select product features or benefits that are important to consumers, help to differentiate the brand from competitors, and convince consumers that they will be satisfied if they buy the product. Earthbound Organic, which markets organically grown vegetables and fruits, makes a good impression by stacking romaine lettuce leaves in one direction within the bag, which research shows consumers prefer. Within salad kits, it packages grain and bean add-ins separately from greens to preserve quality and texture.[50]

Sales promotions such as free samples, price deals, or coupons are often used to induce consumers to try an offering. Marketers hope that if consumers find the product satisfactory, they will continue to buy it after the promotions end. However, these strategies only work if product performance satisfies and reinforces the consumer. They will not overcome dissatisfaction due to poor product quality or other factors. Another caution is that consumers may perceive a price promotion as a signal of lower quality when they are not category experts, when the promotion is not typical of the industry, and when the brand's past behavior is inconsistent. Domino's, for instance, has been working to change quality perceptions after years of emphasizing price via coupons and other promotions. "Over time you're going to see the overall quality of Domino's getting elevated from where it used to be," says the CEO. "Consumers really need to see and taste these pizzas to believe them." Therefore, when launching Artisan Pizzas, Domino's ads focused on the freshness and quality of the ingredients as well as the gourmet flavor combinations.[51]

Habit as a Simplifying Strategy

Habit Doing the same thing time after time.

Humans are creatures of **habit**. Once we find a convenient way of doing things, we tend to repeat it without really thinking: following the same routine every morning, driving the same route to work or school, shopping at the same stores. We do these things because they make life simpler and more manageable.

Sometimes consumers' acquisition, usage, and disposition decisions are based on habit, too. Habit is one of the simplest, most effortless types of consumer decision making, characterized by (1) little or no information seeking and (2) little or no evaluation of alternatives. However, habit does not require a strong preference for an offering; rather, it simply involves repetitive behavior and regular purchase.[52] Decision making based on habit also reduces risk.[53] Consumers know the brand will satisfy their needs because they have bought it a number of times in the past. Research supports the effect of habit on low-priced, frequently purchased products. Yet the longer consumers wait to make their next purchase in a product category, the less likely they are to buy the brand that they habitually purchase.[54]

Marketing Implications

Habit-based decision making has several important implications for marketers who want to develop repeat-purchase behavior and to sell their offerings to habitual purchasers of both that brand and competing products.

Developing Repeat-Purchase Behavior

Getting consumers to acquire or use an offering repeatedly is important because repeat purchases lead to profitability. Marketers can use an operant conditioning technique called **shaping** that leads consumers through a series of steps to a desired response: purchase.[55] Companies often use sales promotions to shape repeat purchasing. First, they might offer a free sample to generate brand trial, along with a high-value coupon to induce. The next step might be to provide a series of lower-value coupons to promote subsequent repurchase, hoping that when the incentives end, consumers will continue to buy the product by habit.

Shaping Leading consumers through a series of steps to create a desired response.

Marketing to Habitual Purchasers of Other Brands

Another major marketing goal is to break consumers' habits and induce them to switch to the company's brand. Because the habitual consumer does not have a strong brand preference, this goal is easier to achieve than it is for brand-loyal consumers. To induce brand switching, marketers use *sales promotion* techniques, such as demonstrations (online or in person), pricing deals, coupons, free samples, and premiums intended to capture consumers' attention and get them to try the new brand (see Exhibit 9.3). Sales of Bobbi Brown cosmetics at Macy's, for instance, skyrocketed after the brand put up an in-store quick response (QR) code that consumers scanned with their smartphones to view an online makeup video by founder Bobbi Brown.[56] Once the old habit is broken, consumers may continue to purchase the new brand either because they like it or because they have developed a new habit.

Marketers can also break habits by introducing *a new and unique benefit* that satisfies consumers' needs better than existing brands. This differential advantage then needs to be heavily promoted to get the word out to consumers. For example, after the entertainment rental company Netflix set separate fees for DVD-by-mail rentals and instant streaming rentals, its 25 million subscribers became a target for rival Blockbuster and its parent, DISH Network. DISH Network began promoting a $10 monthly "all you can view" Blockbuster movie pass with unique benefits: DVDs rented by mail can be

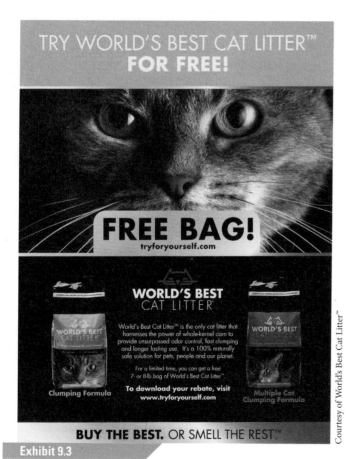

Courtesy of World's Best Cat Litter™

Exhibit 9.3

Sales Promotions
Companies often try to get consumers to switch brands by touting their products as superior and utilizing sales promotions for free trials or discounted prices.

exchanged at any Blockbuster store for another movie, and thousands of movies can be streamed to TVs or computers instantly without extra cost. The unique benefits and attractive price helped DISH sign up new subscribers and gave disgruntled Netflix customers an alternative.[57]

Finally, *distribution policies* are very important for habitual purchasing. In general, the greater the amount of shelf space a brand has in the store, the more likely the brand is to get consumers' attention. A product's location may be enough to capture the habitual consumer's attention and plant the idea in his or her mind to buy something else. An end-of-aisle display may increase a brand's sales by 100 to 400 percent.[58] In one study, eye-catching displays increased sales of frozen dinners by 245 percent, laundry detergent by 207 percent, and salty snacks by 172 percent.[59]

Marketing to Habitual Purchasers of One's Own Brand

Marketers do not want repeat-purchase customers to break their buying habits. Because habitual consumers are susceptible to competitors' deals, marketers need to offer comparable deals to build resistance to switching. This situation explains why a fare cut by any one airline is usually matched immediately by all of its major competitors.

Distribution and inventory control are also used to prevent habitual consumers from switching to another brand. Without a strong preference, consumers are more likely to break the habit and buy another brand if their usual brand is out of stock rather than to go to another store. In one study, 63 percent of consumers said they would be willing to buy another brand of groceries if their preferred brand were not available.[60] Widespread distribution can ensure that the consumer is not forced to buy something else, one reason why Deep River Snacks, a fast-growing marketer of all-natural chips, has arranged for wider supermarket distribution.[61]

Finally, advertising can induce resistance to switching. By occasionally reminding the consumer of a reason for buying the brand and keeping the brand name "top of mind," marketers may be able to keep consumers from switching. ━━━━━━━━━━━━━━

Brand Loyalty as a Simplifying Strategy

Brand loyalty Buying the same brand repeatedly because of a strong preference for it.

Brand loyalty occurs when consumers make a conscious evaluation that a brand or service satisfies their needs to a greater extent than others do and decide to buy the same brand repeatedly for that reason.[62] Essentially, brand loyalty results from *very* positive reinforcement of a performance-related choice tactic. Brand loyalty can also develop when a consumer becomes skillful in using a particular offering, such as a specific brand of money-management software. Faced with the learning curve needed to switch to a different brand of software, the consumer tends to remain brand loyal because of *cognitive lock-in*.[63]

Note that the level of commitment to the brand distinguishes brand loyalty from habit. The higher the degree of brand loyalty, the stronger this evaluation becomes over time. For instance, if you buy Heinz ketchup and decide that it is thicker and tastes better than other brands, you will purchase it again. If this evaluation is reinforced repeatedly, you will develop strong brand loyalty. Consumers can also be **multibrand loyal**, committed to two or more brands that they purchase repeatedly.[64] For example, if you prefer and purchase only Coke and Sprite, you exhibit multibrand loyalty for soft drinks.

Multibrand loyalty Buying two or more brands repeatedly because of a strong preference for them.

Brand loyalty results in low-effort decision making because the consumer does not need to process information when making a decision and simply buys the same brand each time. However, because of their strong commitment to the brand or service, brand-loyal consumers have a relatively high level of involvement with the *brand* regardless of whether their involvement with the product or service category is high or low. Thus, even though ketchup might typically be thought of as a low-involvement product, the brand-loyal consumer can exhibit a high level of involvement toward the brand, for example, Heinz. Brand loyalty also affects choice of retail outlet: Loyalty to a bricks-and-mortar retail brand can lead to higher intentions to shop at that brand's online outlet.[65]

Marketing Implications

Brand-loyal consumers form a solid base on which companies can build brand profitability. By identifying the characteristics of these consumers, marketers might discover ways to strengthen brand loyalty. Unfortunately, doing this is difficult because marketers cannot obtain a general profile of the brand-loyal consumer that applies to all product categories.[66] In fact, brand loyalty depends on the product category; the consumer who is loyal for ketchup may not be loyal for peanut butter. This situation means that marketers must assess brand loyalty for each specific category.

Identifying Brand-Loyal Customers

One way that marketers can identify brand-loyal consumers is to focus on consumer purchase patterns. Consumers who exhibit a particular sequence of purchases (three to four consecutive purchases of the same brand) or proportion of purchases (seven or eight out of 10 purchases for the same brand) are considered brand loyal.[67] The problem is that because brand loyalty involves both repeat purchases *and* a commitment to the brand, purchase-only measures do not accurately distinguish between habitual and brand-loyal consumers. To truly identify the brand-loyal consumer, marketers must assess both repeat-purchase behavior and brand preference. In one study, a measure that looked only at repeat-purchase behavior identified more than 70 percent of the consumer sample as brand loyal. Adding brand preference as a qualifier reduced the percentage to less than 50 percent.[68]

With the availability of scanner data and online buying information, marketers now have a wealth of information about consumer purchase patterns that they can analyze to understand how coupons or pricing changes affect buying. Nevertheless, firms that want to study brand loyalty should be measuring both purchase patterns and preference.

Developing Brand Loyalty

Companies seek to develop brand loyalty because they know these customers have a strong brand commitment and are more resistant to competitive efforts and switching than other consumers are. However, the widespread use of pricing deals in the United States has gradually eroded consumer loyalty toward many brands, leading more consumers to buy on the basis of price. Therefore, marketers are now striving to develop consumer loyalty through nonprice promotions or through less drastic price promotions. For example, in the United Kingdom, Energizer batteries and Wilkinson Sword razor blades have cut back on price promotions, preferring to differentiate their brands through other techniques, such as making a contribution to designated charities for each product purchase.[69]

Developing Brand Loyalty Through Product Quality

One obvious and critical way to develop brand loyalty is to satisfy the consumer with a high-quality product (see Exhibit 9.4). Consumers may also become brand loyal to high-quality brands that are perceived to be priced fairly, a result that explains why some companies have lowered prices on major brands.[70]

Developing Brand Loyalty Through Sales Promotions

Many companies cultivate brand loyalty through sales promotions such as discount coupons to brand loyalists and giveaways. Lone Star Steakhouse, for instance, has offered

THAT
UNIQUE
KELLOGG'S QUALITY

If it doesn't say Kellogg's on the box, then it won't be Kellogg's in the box. As it's been since 1906, when W. K. Kellogg started making cereal from only the finest ingredients.

Kellogg's
Bringing our best to you.

CORN FLAKES

Image Courtesy of The Advertising Archives

Exhibit 9.4

Using Quality to Encourage Brand Loyalty
Having high-quality products is a key way to develop brand loyalty.

coupons and other special offers to consumers who enroll in its E-Club program through Facebook.[71]

Frequent-buyer programs build loyalty by encouraging consumers to buy a product or service repeatedly so that they can earn points toward free trips or other rewards. Marketers must take care, however, in planning loyalty rewards and program requirements. The reward should have some brand connection if it is to increase accessibility of favorable brand associations. However, if the reward is too valuable, it will draw more attention than the brand itself.[72] Also, consumers perceive more value in a loyalty program when they think that they have an advantage in earning points.[73] Moreover, consumers who must do more to earn loyalty points will tend to choose luxury rewards (especially when they feel guilty about luxury consumption).[74] Another important point to note is that customers who do not spend enough to maintain their frequent-buyer status will become less loyal if the program "demotes" them to a lower level.[75]

Marketing to Brand-Loyal Consumers of Other Brands

Marketers want to induce brand-loyal users of competitive brands to switch to their brands. However, because these consumers are strongly committed to other brands, getting them to switch is extremely difficult. As a result, it is usually better to avoid these consumers and to try to market toward nonloyal or habitual consumers, except when a brand has a strong point of superiority or differentiation when compared with the competition. In this case, the superior attribute might be enough to persuade brand-loyal consumers to switch. For example, Coca-Cola's high-tech Freestyle vending machine allows consumers to custom-mix their own soft drinks in moments, with nearly 200 different flavor combinations. There's even a Freestyle app. Given the novelty and the ability to mix to taste, the Freestyle has become a point of differentiation for Coca-Cola in its rivalry with PepsiCo.[76]

Price as a Simplifying Strategy

Price-related tactics
Simplifying decision heuristics that are based on price.

Consumers are most likely to use **price-related tactics** such as buying the cheapest brand, buying the brand on sale, or using a coupon when they perceive few differences among brands and when they have low involvement with the brands in the consideration set. One study found that 9 out of 10 shoppers entered the store with some strategy for saving money.[77] Although price is a critical factor in many decisions, consumers generally do not remember price information, even for a brand they have just selected.[78] This reaction occurs because price information is always available in the store, so consumers have little motivation to remember it. Note that consumers who worry about losing money are more concerned about price, whereas those who are sensitive to gains look at brand features as well as price.[79]

Marketing Implications

Sometimes marketers mistakenly assume that consumers always look for the lowest possible price. Although this assumption is true in some instances, a more accurate statement is that consumers have a **zone of acceptance** regarding what constitutes an appropriate range of prices for a particular category.[80] As long as the brand falls within this price range, consumers will consider it but reject brands falling either above or below the range. For example, all the major fast-food chains have created value menus to appeal to price-conscious consumers, with a variety of items priced at about $1 each (see Exhibit 9.5). At the same time, Wendy's has successfully sold more expensive items such as its main-dish salads by promoting the new flavors and the fresh, healthy ingredients.[81]

Zone of acceptance The acceptable range of prices for any purchase decision.

Consumers may reject low-priced products because they infer that something is wrong with the products. Buyers would be suspicious of a pair of expensive designer jeans on sale for $9.99. As noted earlier, consumers sometimes use price as a heuristic to judge quality (higher price means higher quality). Retailers must also consider that consumers view store design (layout and ambiance) as a pricing cue and expect higher

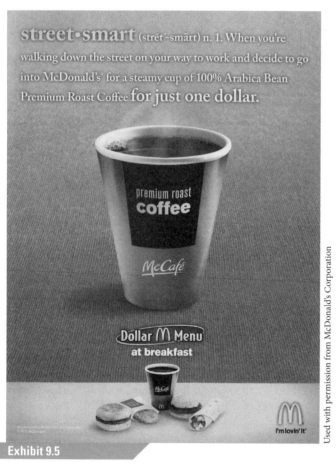

street·smart (strēt′-smärt) n. 1. When you're walking down the street on your way to work and decide to go into McDonald's for a steamy cup of 100% Arabica Bean Premium Roast Coffee **for just one dollar.**

Dollar M Menu **at breakfast**

i'm lovin' it

Used with permission from McDonald's Corporation

Exhibit 9.5

Price as a Simplifying Strategy
Sometimes companies stress low price and good value in their ads.

prices at stores that look upscale.[82] Finally, when stores that have high selling costs advertise low prices, the revenue generated may not justify the increased cost of servicing the customers who respond.[83] _____

Price Perceptions

Consumer perceptions play an important role in the use of price-related tactics. Remember that for consumers to perceive two prices as different, the variation must be at or above the just noticeable difference. Thus, consumers might not care if one brand of toothpaste is priced at $1.95 and another at $1.99. Consumers also compare a product's price with an internal reference price for such products that is based on past prices paid, competing product prices, and other factors, including incidental products in some cases.[84] Typically, consumers use a range of prices rather than a single price point when they think of products.[85]

In addition, perceptual processes play a role in the consumer's reaction to different price points. Research has consistently indicated that consumers perceive odd prices (those ending with an odd number) as significantly lower than even prices (those ending with an even number); a DVD priced at $15.99 will be perceived as less expensive than one priced at $16.00.[86] Consumers who see a much higher-priced item in a catalog that also has moderately priced products will form a higher reference point for the moderately priced items.[87]

Consumers tend to be more responsive to price decreases than they are to price increases.[88] Lowering the price of an offering will increase sales to a greater degree than increasing price by the same amount will decrease sales. Moreover, when a company heavily discounts a product on an infrequent basis, consumers will perceive the average price as lower than if the product goes on sale often but with less of a price reduction.[89] One study found that when companies establish a purchase or time limit, consumers perceive the deal as more valuable, but only when motivation to process is low.[90]

How companies describe the deal can also make a difference. One study found that comparing the sale price to the "regular price" worked better in the store, whereas comparison to competitors' prices was more effective at home.[91] Also, paying for products in a foreign currency (as when traveling) affects price perceptions and spending behavior: When the foreign currency is valued as a multiple of the home-country currency (such as 7 Swedish krona = $1), consumers tend to spend more than when the foreign currency is valued as a fraction (such as 0.7 euros = $1).[92] Consumers tend to perceive a price increase as less fair if they learn about it from a personal source (such as a sales rep) rather than from nonpersonal sources such as a store sign.[93]

The Deal-Prone Consumer

Deal-prone consumer
A consumer who is more likely to be influenced by price.

Marketers are interested in identifying **deal-prone consumers** because this segment is suitable for more directly targeted price-related strategies, but research findings on this issue have been mixed. One study found that deal-prone consumers are more likely to be lower-income, older, and less educated than non-deal-prone consumers; other studies have found that higher-income consumers have better access to price information and are therefore more able to act on it.[94] Part of the problem is that consumers react differently to different types of deals: Some will be more responsive to coupons, whereas others will be more responsive to price cuts and to rebates.[95]

Marketing Implications

Marketers can use a variety of pricing techniques, including coupons, price-offs, rebates, and two-for-ones, as long as the savings are at or above the just noticeable difference and within the zone of acceptance.

Deals and Deal Sites

The importance of deals is evidenced by the deep price cuts supermarkets have made, spurred by stiff competition from Walmart, Costco, and other discounters. Many brands have lowered their prices in response to competition from store brands, which are promoted as being equal in quality to national brands but priced lower. Although many shoppers like shopping online because they can search for price deals, some companies prefer not to attract consumers who use price-comparison sites or apps. Now some retailers are offering their own apps to encourage shoppers to check prices and buy while in the store or from the company's website.[96] Also, many consumers check daily deal sites such as Living-Social and Google Offers for special price offers (see the case at the end of this chapter for more about this trend).[97]

The Importance of Value

Many consumers are looking for good value—that is, a high-quality brand at a good price. SUBWAY's $5 foot-long sandwich menu has helped the chain compete with other fast-food companies even during a bad economy, for example.[98] Value does not always mean lower price: Consumers will pay more if they believe the offering provides an important benefit that consumers are convinced is worth the extra cost. Heinz, the ketchup company, for example, has done this with its "Dip & Squeeze" packets. Developed to replace the usual single-serve ketchup packets in fast-food restaurants, the new packet is easy to open and less messy for dipping French fries or squirting ketchup onto food. Target, Kroger, and other retailers now sell 10 packets for $1.99, a price premium over buying Heinz ketchup in the traditional bottle.[99]

Special Pricing

If marketers use pricing deals too often, consumers will perceive the special price as the regular price and will not buy unless the brand is on sale—resulting in lost profits. This result has happened in the past to several food chains. Too many deals can also damage brand loyalty as consumers become too deal oriented and switch brands more often. Thus, deals tend to work best when used intermittently and selectively. Lower brand loyalty has become a major concern in numerous product categories in the United States and is the reason that many firms want to move toward brand-building strategies such as advertising and sampling.[100]

The use of pricing deals also varies with the country. Coupons are common in the United States: More than 300 billion are offered by manufacturers and retailers every year, although only a small fraction are actually redeemed. Digital coupons—obtained by visiting coupon websites, branded websites, social media sites, daily-deal coupon sites, or via mobile marketing—account for about 10 percent of all coupons redeemed in the United States.[101] Digital coupons are expanding in other countries, as well; for instance, in India, more than 10 percent of consumers with Internet access have used digital coupon sites.[102]

Price Consciousness Is Not Static

Consumers tend to be more price conscious in difficult economic times than in times of prosperity. In many countries, stores that sell merchandise at one low, fixed price—one dollar, one pound sterling, or 100 yen—generally did well during the recent recession, fueled by higher consumer demand for low-priced everyday items. Daiso Japan, which operates thousands of 100-yen stores, has been expanding into other countries, including Australia, targeting bargain hunters interested in deep-discount goods.[103] But it's not just low-income consumers who seek deals during tough times: The fastest-growing segment of Dollar General's U.S. customer base is consumers from households with an annual income over $70,000.[104] Some of these consumers return to their former buying patterns once the economy improves, and some continue their new frugality.

Normative Influences as a Simplifying Strategy

Normative choice tactics Low-elaboration decision making that is based on others' opinions.

Sometimes other individuals can influence consumers' low-elaboration decision making. For instance, a college freshman may buy the brand of laundry detergent that his mother uses at home; a sophomore might buy clothing that her friends like. Our use of such **normative choice tactics** can result from (1) *direct influence*, in which others try to manipulate us; (2) *vicarious observation*, in which we observe others to guide our behavior; and (3) *indirect influence*, in which we are concerned about the opinions of others. Normative tactics are particularly common among inexperienced consumers who have little knowledge. Online communication can increase the importance of normative influence in decision making because consumers can contact each other so easily. If normative tactics are particularly evident in a product or service category, companies can emphasize these motivations in advertising. Marketers can also attempt to stimulate word-of-mouth communication, as described in Chapter 11.

LOW-EFFORT FEELING-BASED DECISION MAKING

The final category of low-effort strategies covers decisions that are based more on feelings than on cognitive processing. These types of strategies include affective tactics, brand familiarity, variety seeking, and impulse purchasing.

Feelings as a Simplifying Strategy

Affect Low-level feelings.

At times, consumers will select a brand or service because they like it, even though they may not know why. This behavior relies on very basic, low-level feelings, or **affect**. Affect differs from cognitive strategies such as performance-related attitudes in that it does not necessarily result from a conscious recognition of need satisfaction and is usually weaker than an attitude. Simply being in the presence of someone you like who is smiling happily can make you smile and feel happy—and, in turn, can have a positive influence on your evaluation of a product.[105]

Affect is most likely to be part of the decision process when the offering is hedonic (rather than functional) and when other factors, such as performance evaluations, price, habit, and normative influences, are not in operation. If you buy Hellmann's mayonnaise because it best satisfies your needs or if you usually buy only the cheapest brand of paper towels, affect is less likely to influence your decision. However, when these factors do not operate in low-effort situations, affect can play a central role. Interestingly, research shows that trying to suppress feelings ties up cognitive resources and undermines consumers' ability to judge product performance—leading them to rely more on feelings when making the choice.[106]

Affect-related tactics Tactics based on feelings.

Affect referral A simple type of affective tactic whereby we simply remember our feelings for the product or service.

Affect-related tactics use a form of category-based processing.[107] In other words, we associate brands with global affective evaluations we recall from memory when making a choice, a process called **affect referral** or the "How do I feel about it?" heuristic.[108] For instance, when we hear the name *Starbucks*, we might associate it with general feelings of happiness, and we might decide to get coffee there based on these feelings rather than on a detailed evaluation of Starbucks. In one study, consumers choosing between a healthy dessert and a less healthy chocolate cake chose the dessert associated with the most positive affect (the cake) when they had little opportunity to think about the choice. When they had more time to think, they chose the healthier dessert, a reaction that suggests that affect referral is more of a factor under low processing effort.[109] Another study found that positive feelings toward promotions can also transfer not only to the promoted product but to unrelated products as well.[110]

Whenever a consumer encounters a new brand, he or she can also compare it with other brands in the same category. To the extent that the new brand is similar to previously encountered brands, the affect associated with that category can be transferred to the new instance and influence choice.[111] On the other hand, if the new brand is perceived as being dissimilar, the consumer is more likely to switch to piecemeal processing, evaluating attributes in the manner described in

SOME COMBINATIONS
WERE JUST MEANT TO BE.

Campbell's Goldfish
Tomato SOUP

Tomato soup with Goldfish® crackers. Made for each other, to make your kids smile.
It's amazing what soup can do.

Courtesy of Campbell Soup Company

Exhibit 9.6

Co-Branding
Sometimes companies engage in co-branding by advertising two different brands together.

Brand familiarity
Easy recognition of a well-known brand.

Co-branding An arrangement by which the two brands form a partnership to benefit from the power of both.

the previous chapter.[112] For example, when Unilever introduced new damaged-hair shampoos under its Dove brand, the director of Unilever Hair Brands explained, "Intrinsic to Dove is to be about 'real beauty,' and each category has a different take on what that means. In the hair category, 'real beauty' is about having not damaged, not overly dry hair, having healthy hair." As a result of extending this brand to shampoos, consumers may be able to evaluate the new Dove products on their own merits.[113]

Brand Familiarity

Affect can also be generated from **brand familiarity** (through the mere exposure effect). In one study, beer drinkers with well-established brand preferences could not distinguish their preferred brand from others in a blind taste test.[114] However, when the beers were identified, consumers rated the taste of their preferred brand significantly higher than that of the others. Another study found that "buying the most familiar brand" was a dominant choice tactic for inexperienced purchasers of peanut butter. Even when the quality of the most familiar brand was manipulated to be lower than that of unfamiliar brands, consumers still greatly preferred the familiar brand.[115] Another study found that brand name was a more important heuristic cue in low-elaboration situations than in high-elaboration ones.[116]

These findings were replicated in a study in Singapore, suggesting that the impact of brand familiarity may be a cross-cultural phenomenon.[117] Coca-Cola is a household name due, in part, to its consistent, highly visible marketing. Yet aggressively promoted local brands can outsell Coca-Cola and other global brands in certain areas. Local brand IRN-BRU, for instance, outsells Coca-Cola in Scotland.[118]

Many companies now engage in **co-branding**, an arrangement by which two brands form a partnership to benefit from the combined power and familiarity of the two.[119] The ice-cream chain Cold Stone Creamery has successfully co-branded its sundaes with Oreo cookies, Jelly Belly jelly beans, and other well-known brands.[120] And Southern Comfort is seeking higher sales by co-branding with TABASCO sauce in a new flavored liquor, Southern Comfort Fiery Pepper.[121] See another example in Exhibit 9.6.

Marketing Implications

Given that feelings can play an important role in the decision process, marketers can attempt to create and maintain brand familiarity, build category-based associations, and generate affect through advertising that creates positive attitudes toward the ad. By creating positive affect toward their brand, marketers can increase the probability that, all other things being equal, their brand will be selected.

Affect plays a key role in determining aesthetic responses to marketing stimuli, especially when visual properties are the only basis for judgment. In Yellow Pages advertising, for example, consumers are more likely to consider firms with color ads and more likely to call those with product-enhancing color.[122] One study showed that two key aspects of a product's design generate more positive affective responses to the product.[123] These are **unity**, which means that the visual parts of the design connect in a meaningful way, and *prototypicality*, which means that the object is representative of its category.

Unity When all the visual parts of a design fit together.

Brands that have positive cross-cultural affect can be marketed internationally. The U.S. image has benefited many firms that market in China; for instance, KFC—the first U.S. fast-food firm to enter the country—now dominates the fast-food category, despite the presence of McDonald's and other U.S.-based chains.[124] Similarly, positive affect for Italian cooking has helped Barilla capture 25 percent of the pasta market in the United States.[125] In particular, hedonic offerings—those that involve style or taste—rely heavily on affective associations.

Decision Making Based on Variety-Seeking Needs

Variety seeking Trying something different.

Optimal stimulation level (OSL) The level of arousal that is most comfortable for an individual.

Sensation seeker A consumer who actively looks for variety.

Vicarious exploration Seeking information simply for stimulation.

Another common consumer-choice tactic in low-effort situations is to try something different, a phenomenon called **variety seeking**. A consumer might regularly buy Starbucks coffee but one day have an urge to try Dunkin' Donuts coffee—then return to Starbucks for later coffee purchases. Consumers seek variety for two major reasons: *satiation* and *boredom*.[126] If you had the same food for dinner every night or watched only one movie over and over, satiation would occur, driving you to do something different. Consumer decisions that occur repeatedly can become monotonous. This result explains why some consumers switch for the sake of change, even though they would have derived more immediate enjoyment from repeating their usual choice.[127] Another reason consumers seek variety in public situations is because they anticipate that others will evaluate their decision more positively.[128] Consumers may engage in variety seeking because they perceive the costs of switching to a new product to be lower than do consumers who are not variety seekers.[129]

However, variety seeking is not expressed in every product category. It is most likely to occur when involvement is low, there are few differences among brands, and the product is more hedonic than functional.[130] It also tends to occur when consumers become satiated with a particular sensory attribute of a product, such as its smell, taste, touch, and visual appearance.[131] Marketers can therefore reduce consumers' boredom simply by providing more variety in a product category (see Exhibit 9.7).[132] In fact, demonstrating to consumers that they have a variety of categories from which to choose—*the mere categorization effect*—can increase feelings of satisfaction with conscious decisions in low-effort situations.[133] Also note that when consumers have more variety from which to choose, they tend to select choices they can easily justify.[134]

Consumers are motivated to relieve their boredom because their level of arousal falls below the **optimal stimulation level (OSL)**—an internal ideal level of stimulation.[135] Repetitive purchasing causes the internal level of stimulation to fall below the OSL, and buying something different is a way of restoring it. In addition, certain consumers need more stimulation and are less tolerant of boredom than others are. These **sensation seekers** are more likely to engage in variety seeking and to be among the first to try new and trendy products; therefore, these consumers are a good market for new offerings.[136]

Note that purchasing something different is only one way to seek stimulation. Consumers can also express their variety drive by engaging in vicarious exploration.[137] **Vicarious exploration** occurs when consumers collect information about a product, either by reading or talking with others or by putting themselves in stimulating shopping environments. For example, many people like to go to stores simply to look around or browse—not to buy, just to increase their stimulation.

Image Courtesy of The Advertising Archives

Exhibit 9.7

Courting Variety Seekers
Sometimes consumers need variety in their choices, so advertisers can promote multiple choices in their ads.

> ## Marketing Implications

Marketers should recognize consumers' need for variety and accommodate these needs appropriately, as Frito-Lay does by introducing new flavors and PepsiCo does by introducing new cans on a regular basis. Marketers can attempt to induce brand switching among variety seekers by encouraging consumers to "put a little spice into life" and try something different. The Flying Bison Brewing Company, in Buffalo, New York, offers a 12-pack of assorted flavors of its unique beers, such as the seasonally brewed Octoberfest.[138] However, consumers may not like *too* much variety. Note that simply altering the way that the product assortment is presented (e.g., how items are arranged on the store shelves) can increase consumers' perceptions of variety and trigger higher consumption, a finding that is particularly relevant for food retailers.[139]

Buying on Impulse

Impulse purchase An unexpected purchase based on a strong feeling.

Another common decision process that has a strong affective component is the **impulse purchase**, which occurs when consumers suddenly decide to purchase something they had not planned on buying. Impulse purchases are characterized by (1) an intense or overwhelming feeling of having to buy the product immediately, (2) a disregard for potentially negative purchase consequences, (3) feelings of euphoria and excitement, and (4) a conflict between control and indulgence.[140] In Asian countries, where interdependence and emotional control are emphasized and power distance belief is high (meaning people accept disparities in power or prestige), consumers engage in less impulse purchasing than do consumers in Western countries, where personal independence and hedonistic pleasures are emphasized.[141] Impulse purchasing and consumption, especially when related to unfulfilled pleasure-seeking needs, are often triggered by the consumer's exposure to an external stimulus, such as an in-store display, a Web ad, or a TV ad with a phone number.[142]

Some research suggests that impulse purchases are prompted by a failure of consumers' self-control.[143] Applying self-control is taxing, a factor that explains why consumers who exert self-control in one area—such as not eating sweets while dieting—may be less able to maintain self-control in another area and will therefore buy something on impulse.[144] Making a series of decisions can deplete consumers' self-control even further.[145] Yet consumers may be unable to control impulse purchasing even when they engage in a great deal of conscious processing.[146] Among the methods that consumers can use to effectively limit impulse buys are making shopping lists, visiting fewer aisles or departments, making shorter and more frequent shopping trips, and paying with cash.[147]

Recent research indicates that consumers may, through the use of mental accounting, plan to buy "on impulse" based on an amount they mentally allocate for unspecified in-store purchasing.[148] Researchers estimate that anywhere from 27 to 62 percent of consumer purchases can be considered impulse buys.[149] However, it is important to distinguish between impulse buying and partially planned purchases, or those for which the consumer has an intention to buy the product category but uses the store display to decide which brand to select. When this distinction is made, the proportion of impulse purchases is usually lower.[150]

The tendency to engage in impulse purchasing varies; some consumers can be considered highly impulsive buyers, whereas others are not.[151] The tendency to buy on impulse is probably related to other traits such as general acquisitiveness and materialism, sensation seeking, and a liking for recreational shopping.[152] If the costs of impulsiveness are made salient or if normative pressure such as the presence of others with negative opinions is high, consumers will engage in less impulse purchasing.[153] The presence of peers increases the urge to make impulse purchases, while the presence of family members has the opposite effect.[154] Interestingly, some research suggests that physiological factors, such as eating foods that enhance levels of neurotransmitters, can contribute to impulse buying.[155]

Marketing Implications

Marketers can influence impulse purchases in a number of ways. Many stores organize their merchandise to maximize impulse purchases. As discussed earlier in this chapter, eye-level and eye-catching displays, including end-of-aisle displays and blinking lights, can increase sales dramatically—mostly of impulse items.[156] Package design can also increase impulse purchases—the reason that Kleenex tissues introduced boxes designed like ice-cream cones for summer displays and boxes designed like cake slices for winter displays.[157] Consumers' preshopping goals ("stocking up on basics" or "taking advantage of a special deal") have been shown to affect unplanned buying. Also, although outside-the-store marketing alone does not directly influence impulse buying, the combination of outside-the-store and in-store marketing can encourage consumers to make unplanned purchases.[158]

Impulse purchasing tends to decline in difficult economic times. In China, for example, where constant inflation is causing steady price increases, research shows consumers are doing more planning for purchases and cutting back on impulse buys.[159] On the other hand, some U.S. consumers are, even during recession, indulging themselves with affordable luxuries such as visiting BLO, Drybar, or other salons that only wash, dry, and style hair.[160]

SUMMARY

This chapter examines the nature of consumer judgment and decision making when motivation, ability, and opportunity—and consequently elaboration—are low. In these situations, consumers often make judgments using simplified heuristics or decision rules. When using the representativeness heuristic, consumers base their judgments on comparisons to a category prototype. When using the availability heuristic, they base their judgments on accessibility of information.

Sometimes low-effort decisions are made unconsciously, sometimes consciously. Unconscious decisions may be strongly affected by environmental cues. Conscious low-effort decision making can follow a hierarchy of effects in which thinking leads to behaving and results in feeling; in contrast, the hierarchy of effects for high-effort decision making is typically thinking-feeling-behaving. For simplicity, consumers making low-effort decisions may satisfice rather than optimize. They may also devise choice tactics over repeat purchase occasions through a process similar to operant conditioning. Cognitively based choice tactics include performance, habit, brand loyalty, price, and normative influences; affective-based choice tactics include affect referral, brand familiarity, variety seeking, and impulse buying.

Questions for Review and Discussion

1. How do base-rate information and the law of small numbers bias judgments made on the basis of the availability heuristic?

2. How is the high-effort hierarchy of effects similar to and different from the low-effort hierarchy?

3. How do unconscious factors influence consumer behavior?

4. What operant conditioning concepts apply to consumer learning?

5. Why is quality an important ingredient in cognitive-based decision making?

6. What is brand loyalty, and what role does it play in low-effort decision making?

7. How do price and value perceptions affect low-effort decision making?

8. When is affect likely to be more of a factor in low-effort decision making?

9. If habit is a simplifying strategy, why do consumers sometimes seek variety?

CONSUMER BEHAVIOR CASE

Bargain-a-Day Deal Appeal

Every day a big new deal—that's the appeal of bargain-a-day websites like Living Social, Google Offers, and kgbdeals. Although the details vary from site to site, the idea is the same: Consumers click to buy a coupon good for a deeply discounted deal on a national or local product or service. One day, the featured deal might be a specialty pizza for 50 percent off the regular price; the next day, it might be a custom photo book for 75 percent off the regular price—or even 90 percent off. Offers are typically valid for only a day or two. The list of marketers offering deals goes on and on: bakeries and boutiques, spas and stores, clothing companies and cafes have used deal sites to attract new customers who might otherwise not give them a try.

LivingSocial, which often posts deals on "social experiences" such as restaurants and travel destinations, is steadily expanding within the United States, Canada, and the United Kingdom. Another deal site, kgbdeals, is increasingly popular in the United States and Europe.

Google Offers—one of the newer sites—aggregates deals from a number of different sites eager to ride the wave of Google's worldwide brand recognition. With its digital marketing expertise, Google Offers is especially focused on matching consumers with appropriate offers in their local area. "We believe that people want more deals that are personal to them," an executive explains. For a better match, Google invites consumers to take a "personalization quiz," indicating which categories of deals (shopping, food and drink, kids and family, and so on) interest them.

When deal sites were in their infancy, the eye-popping introductory offers got consumers buzzing and drew crowds of bargain hunters. Consumers tried a new service provider or product, evaluated the results, and then figured out whether to buy from that marketer a second time. If the initial experience was positive, consumers might be willing to buy at full price. But even if they weren't completely satisfied, consumers would have been able to sample the offer without spending very much.

Soon companies large and small jumped on the deal-a-day bandwagon to bring in newcomers, hoping that these customers would be so happy that they would ultimately become loyal purchasers. Marketers also looked forward to selling deal-seekers additional goods or services and encouraging them to upgrade to more expensive offerings. Often the first deal was a money-loser for the marketer, an opportunity to establish a relationship with hordes of new customers that might, in time, lead to profits and word-of-mouth referrals.

These days, some industry experts worry that "deal fatigue" is setting in as consumers sign up for multiple deal sites and receive offer after offer in their e-mailboxes or via mobile apps. Marketers are also concerned that deal-a-day regulars will become so accustomed to deep discounts that they won't buy unless they believe the price is as low as it can possibly go. Meanwhile, marketers have no guarantee that they'll wind up with as many repeat buyers as they expected, and many disappointed firms are avoiding deal sites. How will deal-a-day sites fare in the future?[161]

CASE QUESTIONS

1. Once a consumer has used a deal-a-day site, how are learning choice tactics likely to affect their subsequent decisions?
2. In what way might deal sites affect the zone of acceptance for a product or category? What are the implications for marketers?
3. Is it reasonable for a marketer to expect that a consumer who is loyal to a different brand would switch to its brand after trying a deeply discounted offer on a deal site? Explain your answer.
4. What role do you think variety seeking plays in a consumer's decision to use deal-a-day sites?

ENDNOTES

1. Natasha Singer, "On Campus, It's One Big Commercial," *New York Times*, September 10, 2011, www.nytimes.com; Jennifer Pritchard, "Annual After-Hours Event Is Right on Target," *Central Florida Future*, August 21, 2011, www.centralfloridafuture.com; Laura Schmitz, "Target Opens Exclusively to U Students," *Daily Utah Chronicle*, August 22, 2011, www.dailyutahchronicle.com; and Allison Enright, "Target's Back-to-school Promotion Merges Online and Offline Shopping," *Internet Retailer*, August 4, 2011, www.internetretailer.com.

2. Rohit Deshpande, Wayne D. Hoyer, and Scott Jeffries, "Low Involvement Decision Processes: The Importance of Choice Tactics," in eds. R. F. Bush and S. D. Hunt, *Marketing Theory: Philosophy of Science Perspectives* (Chicago: American Marketing Association, 1982), pp. 155–158; Alan Newell and Herbert A. Simon, *Human Problem Solving* (Englewood Cliffs, N.J.: Prentice-Hall, 1972); and Daniel Kahneman and Amos Tversky, "On the Psychology of Prediction," *Psychological Review*, July 1973, pp. 237–251.

3. Daniel Kahneman and Amos Tversky, "Subjective Probability: A Judgment of Representativeness," *Cognitive Psychology*, July 1972, pp. 430–454.

4. "Digital Tells New Tale in Greeting Card Aisle," *MMR*, May 16, 2011, p. 34.

5. Valerie S. Folkes, "The Availability Heuristic and Perceived Risk," *Journal of Consumer Research*, June 1988, pp. 13–23; and Johnson and Puto, "A Review of Consumer Judgment and Choice," in ed. Michael J. Houston, *Review of Marketing* (Chicago: American Marketing Association, 1987), pp. 236–292.

6. Geeta Menon and Priya Raghubir, "Ease-of-Retrieval as an Automatic Input in Judgments: A Mere-Accessibility Framework?" *Journal of Consumer Research*, September 2003, pp. 230–243.

7. Peter R. Dickson, "The Impact of Enriching Case and Statistical Information on Consumer Judgments," *Journal of Consumer Research*, March 1982, pp. 398–408.

8. Chezy Ofir and John G. Lynch Jr., "Context Effects on Judgment under Uncertainty," *Journal of Consumer Research*, September 1984, pp. 668–679.

9. Amos Tversky and Daniel Kahneman, "Belief in the Law of Small Numbers," *Psychological Bulletin*, August 1971, pp. 105–110; and Amos Tversky and Daniel Kahneman, "Judgment Under Uncertainty: Heuristics and Biases," *Science*, September 1974, pp. 1124–1131.

10. Marc Worth, "Chinese Brands: When Will They Succeed?" *Forbes*, September 22, 2011, www.forbes.com.

11. Nat Ives, "Entertainment Weekly Adds Co-Viewing Platform for TV Shows from 'Glee' to Football," *Advertising Age*, September 16, 2011, www.adage.com.

12. Wayne D. Hoyer, "An Examination of Consumer Decision Making for a Common Repeat Purchase Product," *Journal of Consumer Research*, December 1984, pp. 822–829.

13. Martin Lindstrom, *Buyology: Truth and Lies About Why We Buy* (New York: Doubleday, 2008).

14. Ap Dijksterhuis, Pamela K. Smith, Rick B. van Baaren, and Daniel H. J. Wigboldus, "The Unconscious Consumer: Effects of Environment on Consumer Behavior," *Journal of Consumer Psychology* 15, no. 3, 2005, pp. 193–202.

15. James Vlahos, "Scent and Sensibility," *Key (New York Times Real Estate Magazine)*, Fall 2007, pp. 68–73.

16. Michal Maimaran and S. Christian Wheeler, "Circles, Squares, and Choice: The Effect of Shape Arrays on Uniqueness and Variety Seeking," *Journal of Marketing Research*, December 2008, pp. 731–740; and Tanya L. Chartrand, "The Role of Conscious Awareness in Consumer Behavior," *Journal of Consumer Psychology* 15, no. 3, 2005, pp. 203–210.

17. Melanie A. Dempsey and Andrew A. Mitchell, "The Influence of Implicit Attitudes on Choice When Consumers Are Confronted with Conflicting Attribute Information," *Journal of Consumer Research*, December 2010, pp. 614–625.

18. Nalini Ambady, Mary Ann Krabbenhoft, and Daniel Hogan, "The 30-Sec Sale: Using Thin-Slice Judgments to Evaluate Sales Effectiveness," *Journal of Consumer Psychology* 16, no. 1, 2006, pp. 4–13.

19. Jan R. Landwehr, Ann L. McGill, and Andreas Herrmann, "It's Got the Look: The Effect of Friendly and Aggressive 'Facial' Expressions on Product Liking and Sales," *Journal of Marketing*, May 2011, pp. 132–146.

20. Jens Förster, "How Body Feedback Influences Consumers' Evaluation of Products," *Journal of Consumer Psychology* 14, no. 4, 2004, pp. 416–426. See also Ronald S. Friedman and Jens Förster, "The Effects of Approach and Avoidance Motor Actions on the Elements of Creative Insight," *Journal of Personality and Social Psychology* 79, no. 4, 2000, pp. 477–492.

21. Joan Meyers-Levy, Rui Zhu, and Lan Jiang, "Context Effects from Bodily Sensations: Examining Bodily Sensations Induced by Flooring and the Moderating Role of Product Viewing Distance," *Journal of Consumer Research*, June 2010.

22. Chris Janiszewski and Stijn M. J. van Osselaer, "Behavior Activation Is Not Enough," *Journal of Consumer Psychology* 15, no. 3, 2005, pp. 218–224.

23. Ap Dijksterhuis and Pamela K. Smith, "What Do We Do Unconsciously? And How?" *Journal of Consumer Psychology* 15, no. 3, 2005, pp. 225–229.

24. Hannah Sampson, "South Florida Hotels Discover Scents Make Sense," *Miami Herald*, June 6, 2011, www.miamiherald.com.

25. Herbert E. Krugman, "The Impact of Television Advertising: Learning Without Involvement," *Public Opinion Quarterly*, Fall 1965, pp. 349–356.

26. Michael L. Ray, *Marketing Communications and the Hierarchy of Effects* (Cambridge, Mass.: Marketing Science Institute, 1973).

27. Robert B. Zajonc, "Feeling and Thinking: Preferences Need No Inferences," *American Psychologist*, February 1980, pp. 151–175; and Robert B. Zajonc and Hazel B. Markus, "Affective and Cognitive Factors in Preferences," *Journal of Consumer Research*, September 1982, pp. 122–131.

28. Hoyer, "An Examination of Consumer Decision Making for a Common Repeat Purchase Product."

29. Cathy J. Cobb and Wayne D. Hoyer, "Direct Observation of Search Behavior in the Purchase of Two Nondurable Products," *Psychology and Marketing*, Fall 1983, pp. 161–179.

30. Richard W. Olshavsky and Donald H. Granbois, "Consumer Decision Making: Fact or Fiction?" *Journal of Consumer Research*, September 1979, pp. 93–100.

31. Andrew D. Gershoff and Gita Venkataramani Johar, "Do You Know Me? Consumer Calibration of Friends' Knowledge," *Journal of Consumer Research* 32, no. 4, 2006, pp. 496–503.

32. Baba Shiv, Julie A. Edell Britton, and John W. Payne, "Re-Inquiries: Does Elaboration Increase or Decrease the Effectiveness of Negatively Versus Positively Framed Messages?" *Journal of Consumer Research*, June 2004, pp. 199–208.

33. Yong Zhang and Richard Buda, "Moderating Effects of Need for Cognition on Responses to Positively versus Negatively Framed Advertising Messages," *Journal of Advertising*, Summer 1999, pp. 1–15.

34. C. Whan Park, Sung Youl Jun, and Deborah J. MacInnis, "Choosing What I Want Versus Rejecting What I Do Not Want: An Application of Decision Framing to Product Option Choice Decisions," *Journal of Marketing Research*, May 2000, pp. 187–202.

35. William E. Baker and Richard J. Lutz, "An Empirical Test of an Updated Relevance–Accessibility Model of Advertising Effectiveness," *Journal of Advertising* 29, no. 1, Spring 2000, pp. 1–13.

36. Deshpande, Hoyer, and Jeffries, "Low Involvement Decision Processes: The Importance of Choice Tactics."

37. Hoyer, "An Examination of Consumer Decision Making for a Common Repeat Purchase Product."

38. Siew Meng Leong, "Consumer Decision Making for Common, Repeat-Purchase Products: A Dual Replication," *Journal of Consumer Psychology* 2, no. 2, 1993, pp. 193–208; and Dana L. Alden, Wayne D. Hoyer, and Guntalee Wechasara, "Choice Strategies and Involvement, A Cross-Cultural Analysis," in ed. Thomas K. Srull, *Advances in Consumer Research*, vol. 16 (Provo, Utah: Association for Consumer Research, 1989), pp. 119–126.

39. Walter A. Nord and J. Paul Peter, "A Behavior Modification Perspective on Marketing," *Journal of Marketing*, Spring 1980, pp. 36–47; and Michael Rothschild and William C. Gaidis, "Behavioral Learning Theory: Its Relevance to Marketing and Promotions," *Journal of Marketing*, Spring 1981, pp. 70–78.

40. Holly Heline, "Brand Loyalty Isn't Dead—But You're Not Off the Hook," *Brandweek*, June 7, 1994, p. 14.

41. Robert E. Smith and William R. Swinyard, "Information Response Models: An Integrated Approach," *Journal of Marketing*, Winter 1982, pp. 81–93; and Robert E. Smith and William R. Swinyard, "Attitude–Behavior Consistency: The Impact of Product Trial vs. Advertising," *Journal of Marketing Research*, August 1983, pp. 257–267.

42. Deanna S. Kempf and Robert E. Smith, "Consumer Processing of Product Trial and the Influence of Prior Advertising: A Structural Modeling Approach," *Journal of Marketing Research*, August 1998, pp. 325–338.

43. Ran Kivetz, Oleg Urminsky, and Yuhuang Zheng, "The Goal-Gradient Hypothesis Resurrected: Purchase Acceleration, Illusionary Goal Progress, and Customer Retention," *Journal of Marketing Research*, February 2006, pp. 39–58.

44. Michael L. Rothschild and Michael J. Houston, "The Consumer Involvement Matrix: Some Preliminary Findings," in eds. Barnett A. Greenberg and Danny N. Bellenger, *Proceedings of the American Marketing Association Educators' Conference*, Series no. 41, 1977, pp. 95–98.

45. Wayne D. Hoyer, "Variations in Choice Strategies Across Decision Contexts: An Examination of Contingent Factors," in ed. Richard J. Lutz, *Advances in Consumer Research*, vol. 13 (Provo, Utah: Association for Consumer Research, 1986), pp. 32–36.

46. Wayne D. Hoyer and Cathy J. Cobb-Walgren, "Consumer Decision Making Across Product Categories: The Influence of Task Environment," *Psychology and Marketing*, Spring 1988, pp. 45–69.

47. Leong, "Consumer Decision Making for Common, Repeat-Purchase Products: A Dual Replication."

48. "Kohl's 3rd-quarter Profit Rises," *Wall Street Journal*, November 10, 2011, www.wsj.com.

49. Robert E. Smith, "Integrating Information from Advertising and Trial: Processes and Effects on Consumer Response to Product Information," *Journal of Marketing Research*, May 1993, pp. 204–219.

50. Sarah Nassauer, "Marketers Hope Guest Veggies Will Get Americans to Eat More Greens," *Wall Street Journal*, July 27, 2011, www.wsj.com.

51. Rae Ann Fera, "Should 'Domino's' and 'Artisan' Be Used in the Same Pizza Ad?" *Fast Company*, September 26, 2011, www.fastcompany.com; and Priya Raghubir and Kim Corfman, "When Do Price Promotions Affect Pretrial Brand Evaluations?" *Journal of Marketing Research* 36, May 1999, pp. 211–222.

52. Adwait Khare and J. Jeffrey Inman, "Habitual Behavior in American Eating Patterns: The Role of Meal Occasions," *Journal of Consumer Research* 32, no. 4, 2006, pp. 567–575; and Jacob Jacoby and David B. Kyner, "Brand Loyalty vs. Repeat Purchasing Behavior," *Journal of Marketing Research*, February 1973, pp. 1–9.

53. Ted Roselius, "Consumer Rankings of Risk Reduction Methods," *Journal of Marketing*, January 1971, pp. 56–61.

54. P. B. Seetharaman, Andrew Ainslie, and Pradeep K. Chintagunta, "Investigating Household State Dependence Effects Across Categories," *Journal of Marketing Research* 36, November 1999, pp. 488–500.

55. Rothschild and Gaidis, "Behavioral Learning Theory."

56. Stephanie Rosenbloom, "Want More Information? Just Scan Me," *New York Times*, September 21, 2011, www.nytimes.com.

57. Erik Gruenwedel, "The New Adventures of Old Blockbuster," *Home Media Magazine*, September 26, 2011, www.homemediamagazine.com; and Ben Fritz, "Dish Network Taking on Netflix," *Los Angeles Times*, September 23, 2011, www.latimes.com.

58. Gary F. McKinnon, J. Patrick Kelly, and E. Doyle Robinson, "Sales Effects of Point-of-Purchase In-Store Signing," *Journal of Retailing*, Summer 1981, pp. 49–63.

59. Kathleen Deveny, "Displays Pay Off for Grocery Marketers," *Wall Street Journal*, October 15, 1992, pp. B1, B5.

60. "Brand Loyalty in the Food Industry," *The Food Institute Report*, November 5, 2001, p. 3.

61. Elaine Pofeldt, "David vs. Goliath," *Fortune*, September 26, 2011, p. 57.

62. George S. Day, "A Two-Dimensional Concept of Brand Loyalty," *Journal of Advertising Research*, August–September 1969, pp. 29–36; Jacoby and Kyner, "Brand Loyalty vs. Repeat Purchasing Behavior"; and Jacob Jacoby and Robert W. Chestnut, *Brand Loyalty: Measurement and Management* (New York: Wiley, 1978).

63. Kyle B. Murray and Gerald Häubl, "Explaining Cognitive Lock-In: The Role of Skill-Based Habits of Use in Consumer Choice," *Journal of Consumer Research* 34, no. 1, 2007, pp. 77–88.

64. Jacob Jacoby, "A Model of Multi-Brand Loyalty," *Journal of Advertising Research*, June–July 1971, p. 26.

65. Her-Sen Doong, Gordon R. Foxall, and Hui-Chih Wang, "An Investigation of Consumers' Webstore Shopping," *International Journal of Information Management*, June 2011, pp. 210–216.

66. Ronald E. Frank, William F. Massy, and Thomas L. Lodahl, "Purchasing Behavior and Personal Attributes," *Journal of Advertising Research*, December 1969–January 1970, pp. 15–24.

67. R. M. Cunningham, "Brand Loyalty—What, Where, How Much," *Harvard Business Review*, January–February 1956, pp. 116–128; and "Customer Loyalty to Store and Brand," *Harvard Business Review*, November–December 1961, pp. 127–137.

68. Day, "A Two-Dimensional Concept of Brand Loyalty."

69. Rosie Baker, "Price Promotions Are Here to Stay," *Marketing Week*, September 15, 2011, www.marketingweek.co.uk.

70. Heline, "Brand Loyalty Isn't Dead—But You're Not Off the Hook."

71. Jack Neff, "How Brands Should Think about Facebook: A Loyalty Program," *Ad Age*, September 1, 2011, www.adage.com.

72. Michelle L. Roehm, Ellen Bolman Pullins, and Harper A. Roehm Jr., "Designing Loyalty-Building Programs for Packaged Goods Brands," *Journal of Marketing Research*, May 2002, pp. 202–213.

73. Ran Kivetz and Itamar Simonson, "The Idiosyncratic Fit Heuristic: Effort Advantage as a Determinant of Consumer Response to Loyalty Programs," *Journal of Marketing Research*, November 2003, pp. 454–467.

74. Ran Kivetz and Itamar Simonson, "Earning the Right to Indulge: Effort as a Determinant of Customer Preferences toward Frequency Program Rewards," *Journal of Marketing Research*, May 2002, pp. 155–170.

75. Tillmann Wagner, Thorsten Hennig-Thurau, and Thomas Rudolph, "Does Customer Demotion Jeopardize Loyalty?" *Journal of Marketing*, May 2009, pp. 69–85.

76. Don Worthington, "Moe's Drinks Go High-Tech at Manchester Restaurant," *The Herald (Rock Hill, S.C.)*, September 26, 2011, www.heraldonline.com.

77. Laurie Petersen, "The Strategic Shopper," *Adweek's Marketing Week*, March 30, 1992, pp. 18–20.

78. Peter D. Dickson and Alan G. Sawyer, "Methods to Research Shoppers' Knowledge of Supermarket Prices," in ed. Richard J. Lutz, *Advances in Consumer Research*, vol. 12 (Provo, Utah: Association for Consumer Research, 1986), pp. 584–587.

79. Tulin Erdem, Glenn Mayhew, and Baohung Sun, "Understanding Reference-Price Shoppers: A Within- and Cross-Category Analysis," *Journal of Marketing Research*, November 2001, pp. 445–457.

80. Chris Janiszewski and Donald R. Lichtenstein, "A Range Theory Account of Price Perception," *Journal of Consumer Research* 25, March 1999, pp. 353–368; and Kent B. Monroe and Susan M. Petroshius, "Buyers' Perception of Price: An Update of the Evidence," in eds. Harold H. Kassarjian and Thomas S. Robertson, *Perspectives in Consumer Behavior*, 3rd ed. (Dallas, Tex.: Scott-Foresman, 1981), pp. 43–55.

81. Maureen Morrison, "The Value-Meal Index, or Why $1 Hamburgers Are Still Hot," *Advertising Age*, June 27, 2011, p. 13.

82. Julie Baker, A. Parasuraman, Dhruv Grewal, and Glenn B. Voss, "The Influence of Multiple Store Environment Cues on Perceived Merchandise Value and Patronage Intentions," *Journal of Marketing*, April 2002, pp. 120–141.

83. Jiwoong Shin, "The Role of Selling Costs in Signaling Price Image," *Journal of Marketing Research*, August 2005, pp. 302–312.

84. Lisa E. Bolton, Luk Warlop, and Joseph W. Alba, "Consumer Perceptions of Price (Un)Fairness," *Journal of Consumer Research*, March 2003, pp. 474–491; and Joseph C. Nunes and Peter Boatwright, "Incidental Prices and Their Effect on Willingness to Pay," *Journal of Marketing Research*, November 2004, pp. 457–466.

85. Tuo Wang, R. Venkatesh, and Rabikar Chatterjee, "Reservation Price as a Range: An Incentive-Compatible Measurement Approach," *Journal of Marketing Research*, May 2007, pp. 200–213.

86. Mark Stiving and Russell S. Winer, "An Empirical Analysis of Price Endings with Scanner Data," *Journal of Consumer Research*, June 1997, pp. 57–76; and Zarrel V. Lambert, "Perceived Prices as Related to Odd and Even Price Endings," *Journal of Retailing*, Fall 1975, pp. 13–22.

87. Aradhna Krishna, Mary Wagner, Carolyn Yoon, and Rashmi Adaval, "Effects of Extreme-Priced Products on Consumer Reservation Prices," *Journal of Consumer Psychology* 16, no. 2, 2006, pp. 176–190.

88. Kent B. Monroe, "The Influence of Price Differences and Brand Familiarity on Brand Preferences," *Journal of Consumer Research*, June 1976, pp. 42–49.

89. Joseph W. Alba, Carl F. Mela, Terence A. Shimp, and Joel E. Urbany, "The Effect of Discount Frequency and Depth on Consumer Price Judgments," *Journal of Consumer Research*, September 1999, pp. 99–114.

90. J. Jeffrey Inman, Anil C. Peter, and Priya Raghubir, "Framing the Deal: The Role of Restrictions in Accentuating Deal Value," *Journal of Consumer Research*, June 1997, pp. 68–79.

91. Dhruv Grewal, Howard Marmorstein, and Arun Sharma, "Communicating Price Information Through Semantic Cues," *Journal of Consumer Research*, September 1996, pp. 148–155.

92. Priya Raghubir and Joydeep Srivastava, "Effect of Face Value on Product Valuation in Foreign Currencies," *Journal of Consumer Research*, December 2002, pp. 335–347.

93. Margaret C. Campbell, "'Says Who?!' How the Source of Price Information and Affect Influence Perceived Price (Un)Fairness," *Journal of Marketing Research*, May 2007, pp. 261–271.

94. *Supermarket Shoppers in a Period of Economic Uncertainty* (New York: Yankelovich, Skelly, & White, 1982), p. 53; and Robert Blattberg, Thomas Buesing, Peter Peacock, and Subrata K. Sen, "Who Is the Deal-Prone Consumer?" in ed. H. Keith Hunt, *Advances in Consumer Research*, vol. 5 (Ann Arbor, Mich.: Association for Consumer Research, 1978), pp. 57–62.

95. Donald R. Lichtenstein, Richard G. Netemeyer, and Scot Burton, "Assessing the Domain Specificity of Deal Proneness: A Field Study," *Journal of Consumer Research*, December 1995, pp. 314–326.

96. Mark Hachman, "Retailers Discover Useful In-Store Apps Keep Shoppers from Escaping," *PC Magazine*, September 27, 2011, www.pcmag.com.

97. John Pietz, "Daily Deal Duel," *Crain's Chicago Business*, November 9, 2011, www.chicagobusiness.com.

98. "Fast-Food Chains Bringing Back Cheap Eats with Special Deals," *Chicago Sun-Times*, September 27, 2011, www.suntimes.com.

99. "Heinz Ketchup Package Redesign Squirts into Stores," *Bloomberg Businessweek*, September 19, 2011, www.businessweek.com.

100. Kathleen Deveny, "How Country's Biggest Brands Are Faring at the Supermarket," *Wall Street Journal*, March 24, 1994, p. B1.

101. David Pitt, "Now That Have Gone Digital, It's Hip to Be Frugal, Executive Says," *Boston Globe*, September 8, 2011, www.boston.com.

102. "Trend for Coupon Sites Growing in India," *The Independent (U.K.)*, July 31, 2011, www.indendent.co.uk.

103. "100 Yen Stores—That's $2.80—Come to Australia," *CNN Go*, September 15, 2011, www.cnngo.com.

104. Sean Gregory, "The Buck Shops Here," *Time*, January 2, 2011, pp. 55–56.

105. Daniel J. Howard and Charles Gengler, "Emotional Contagion Effects on Product Attitudes," *Journal of Consumer Research*, September 2001, pp. 189–201.

106. Cheng Qui, Yih Hwai Lee, and Catherine W. M. Yeung, "Suppressing Feelings: A Double-edged Sword to Consumer Judgment and Choice," *Journal of Consumer Psychology* 19, 2009, pp. 427–439.

107. Susan T. Fiske, "Schema Triggered Affect: Applications to Social Perception," in eds. Margaret S. Clark and Susan T. Fiske, *Affect and Cognition: The 17th Annual Carnegie Symposium on Cognition* (Hillsdale, N.J.: Lawrence Erlbaum, 1982), pp. 55–77; and Mita Sujan, James R. Bettman, and Harish Sujan, "Effects of Consumer Expectations on Information Processing and Selling Encounters," *Journal of Marketing Research*, November 1986, pp. 346–353.

108. Peter L. Wright, "An Adaptive Consumer's View of Attitudes and Choice Mechanisms as Viewed by an Equally Adaptive Advertiser," in ed. William D. Wells, *Attitude Research at Bay* (Chicago: American Marketing Association, 1976), pp. 113–131.

109. Baba Shiv and Alexander Fedorikhin, "Heart and Mind in Conflict: The Interplay of Affect and Cognition in Consumer Decision Making," *Journal of Consumer Research* 26, December 1999, pp. 278–292.

110. Rebecca Walker Naylor, Rajagopal Raghunathan, and Suresh Ramanathan, "Promotions Spontaneously Induce a Positive Evaluative Response," *Journal of Consumer Psychology* 16, no. 3, 2006, pp. 295–305.

111. Susan T. Fiske and Mark A. Pavelchak, "Category-Based Versus Piecemeal-Based Affective Responses: Developments in Schema-Triggered Affect," in eds. R. M. Sorrentino and E. T. Higgins, *The Handbook of Motivation and Cognition: Foundations of Social Behavior* (New York: Guilford, 1986), pp. 167–203; and David M. Boush and Barbara Loken, "A Process-Tracing Study of Brand Extension Evaluation," *Journal of Marketing Research*, February 1991, pp. 16–28.

112. Fiske, "Schema Triggered Affect: Applications to Social Perception"; and Mita Sujan, "Consumer Knowledge: Effects on Evaluation Strategies Mediating Consumer Judgments," *Journal of Consumer Research*, June 1985, pp. 31–46.

113. "Dove Campaign Stars Rashida Jones, Focuses on Common Complaints: Bad Hair Days," *Washington Post*, September 19, 2011, www.washingtonpost.com.

114. Ralph I. Allison and Kenneth P. Uhl, "Influence of Beer Brand Identification on Taste Perception," *Journal of Marketing Research*, August 1964, pp. 36–39.

115. Wayne D. Hoyer and Stephen P. Brown, "Effects of Brand Awareness on Choice for a Common, Repeat-Purchase Product," *Journal of Consumer Research*, September 1990, pp. 141–148.

116. Leong, "Consumer Decision Making for Common, Repeat-Purchase Products: A Dual Replication."

117. M. Carole Macklin, "Preschoolers' Learning of Brand Names from Visual Cues," *Journal of Consumer Research*, December 1996, pp. 251–261.

118. Peter Woodifield, "A.G. Barr First-Half Net Income Rises 12% on Sales, Taxes," *Bloomberg News*, September 27, 2011, www.bloomberg.com.

119. Eric Yang, "Co-brand or Be Damned," *Brandweek*, November 21, 1994, pp. 21–24.

120. Dan Beem, "The Case for Co-Branding," *Forbes*, March 16, 2010, www.forbes.com.

121. Bruce Schreiner, "Southern Comfort Mixing with Tabasco," *Bloomberg Businessweek*, September 9, 2011, www.businessweek.com.

122. Karen V. Fernandez and Dennis L. Rosen, "The Effectiveness of Information and Color in Yellow Pages Advertising," *Journal of Advertising* 29, no. 2, Summer 2000, pp. 61–73.

123. Robert W. Veryzer and J. Wesley Hutchinson, "The Influence of Unity and Prototypicality on Aesthetic Responses to New Product Designs," *Journal of Consumer Research*, March 1998, pp. 374–394.

124. Mark Brandau, "China: A Look at Strategies from McDonald's, Yum! Brands," *Nation's Restaurant News*, September 9, 2011, www.nrn.com; and "McDonald's China Strategy," *Los Angeles Times*, September 17, 2007, p. C4.

125. "Big Portions: Barilla," *Economist*, June 23, 2007, p. 75.

126. M. Venkatesan, "Cognitive Consistency and Novelty Seeking," in eds. Scott Ward and Thomas S. Robertson, *Consumer Behavior: Theoretical Sources* (Englewood Cliffs, N.J.: Prentice-Hall, 1973), pp. 354–384; and Leigh McAlister, "A Dynamic Attribute Satiation Model of Variety Seeking Behavior," *Journal of Consumer Research*, September 1982, pp. 141–150.

127. Rebecca K. Ratner, Barbara E. Kahn, and Daniel Kahneman, "Choosing Less-Preferred Experiences for the Sake of Variety," *Journal of Consumer Research* 26, June 1999, pp. 1–15.

128. Rebecca K. Ratner and Barbara E. Kahn, "The Impact of Private versus Public Consumption on Variety-Seeking Behavior," *Journal of Consumer Research*, September 2002, pp. 246–257.

129. Rosario Vázquez-Carrasco and Gordon R. Foxall, "Positive versus Negative Switching Barriers: The Influence of Service Consumers' Need for Variety," *Journal of Consumer Behavior* 5, no. 4, 2006, pp. 367–379.

130. Hans C. M. Van Trijp, Wayne D. Hoyer, and J. Jeffrey Inman, "Why Switch? Product Category-Level Explanations for True Variety Seeking," *Journal of Marketing Research*, August 1996, pp. 281–292; and Wayne D. Hoyer and Nancy M. Ridgway, "Variety Seeking as an Explanation for Exploratory Purchase Behavior: A Theoretical Model," in ed. Thomas C. Kinnear, *Advances in Consumer Research*, vol. 11 (Ann Arbor, Mich.: Association for Consumer Research, 1984), pp. 114–119.

131. J. Jeffrey Inman, "The Role of Sensory-Specific Satiety in Attribute-Level Variety Seeking," *Journal of Consumer Research* 28, June 2001, pp. 105–120.

132. Saatya Menon and Barbara E. Kahn, "The Impact of Context on Variety Seeking in Product Choices," *Journal of Consumer Research*, December 1995, pp. 285–295.

133. Cassie Mogilner, Tamar Rudnick, and Sheena S. Iyengar, "The Mere Categorization Effect," *Journal of Consumer Research*, August 2008, pp. 201–215.

134. Aner Sela, Jonah Berger, and Wendy Liu, "Variety, Vice, and Virtue: How Assortment Size Influences Option Choice," *Journal of Consumer Research*, April 2009, pp. 941–951.

135. Erich A. Joachimsthaler and John L. Lastovicka, "Optimal Stimulation Level–Exploratory Behavior Models," *Journal of Consumer Research*, December 1984, pp. 830–835.

136. Albert Mehrabian and James Russell, *An Approach to Environmental Psychology* (Cambridge, Mass.: MIT Press, 1974).

137. Linda L. Price and Nancy M. Ridgway, "Use Innovativeness, Vicarious Exploration and Purchase Exploration: Three Facets of Consumer Varied Behavior," in ed. Bruce Walker, *American Marketing Association Educators' Conference Proceedings* (Chicago: American Marketing Association, 1982), pp. 56–60.

138. Elizabeth Carey, "Local Brewery Says 'Cheers!'" *Buffalo Business First*, September 15, 2011, www.bizfournals.com/buffalo.

139. Barbara E. Kahn and Brian Wansink, "The Influence of Assortment Structure on Perceived Variety and Consumption Quantities," *Journal of Consumer Research*, March 2004, pp. 519–533.

140. Fritz Strack, Lioba Werth, and Roland Deutsch, "Reflective and Impulsive Determinants of Consumer Behavior," *Journal of Consumer Psychology* 16, no. 2, 2006, pp. 205–216; and Dennis W. Rook,

"The Buying Impulse," *Journal of Consumer Research*, September 1987, pp. 189–199; and Craig J. Thompson, William B. Locander, and Howard R. Pollio, "The Lived Meaning of Free Choice: Existential–Phenomenological Description of Everyday Consumer Experiences of Contemporary Married Women," *Journal of Consumer Research*, December 1990, pp. 346–361.

141. Yinlong Zhang, Karen Page Winterich, and Vikas Mittal, "Power Distance Belief and Impulsive Buying," *Journal of Marketing Research*, October 2010, pp. 945–954; and Jacqueline J. Kacen and Julie Anne Lee, "The Influence of Culture on Consumer Impulsive Buying Behavior," *Journal of Consumer Psychology* 12, no. 2, 2002, pp. 163–176.

142. See Suresh Ramanathan and Geeta Menon, "Time-Varying Effects of Chronic Hedonic Goals on Impulsive Behavior," *Journal of Marketing Research*, November 2006, pp. 628–641.

143. Roy F. Baumeister, "Yielding to Temptation: Self-Control Failure, Impulsive Behavior, and Consumer Behavior," *Journal of Consumer Research*, March 2002, pp. 670–676.

144. Kathleen D. Vons and Ronald J. Faber, "Spent Resources: Self-Regulatory Resource Availability Affects Impulse Buying," *Journal of Consumer Research* 33, no. 4, 2007, pp. 537–548.

145. Kathleen D. Vohs, "Self-Regulatory Resources Power the Reflective System: Evidence from Five Domains," *Journal of Consumer Psychology* 16, no. 3, 2006, pp. 217–223.

146. Deborah J. MacInnis and Vanessa M. Patrick, "Spotlight on Affect: Affect and Affective Forecasting in Impulse Control," *Journal of Consumer Psychology* 16, no. 3, 2006, pp. 224–231.

147. J. Jeffrey Inman, Russell S. Winer, Rosellina Ferraro, "The Interplay Among Category Characteristics, Customer Characteristics, and Customer Activities on In-Store Decision Making," *Journal of Marketing*, September 2009, pp. 19–29.

148. Karen M. Stilley, J. Jeffrey Inman, and Kirk L. Wakefield, "Planning to Make Unplanned Purchases?" *Journal of Consumer Research*, August 2010, pp. 264–278.

149. J. Jeffrey Inman and Russell S. Winer, "Where the Rubber Meets the Road: A Model of In-store Consumer Decision Making," *Marketing Science Institute Report Summary*, December 1998, pp. 98–122; "How We Shop … From Mass to Market," *Brandweek*, January 9, 1995, p. 17; and Danny Bellenger, D. H. Robertson, and Elizabeth C. Hirschman, "Impulse Buying Varies by Product," *Journal of Advertising Research*, December 1978–January 1979, pp. 15–18.

150. Cathy J. Cobb and Wayne D. Hoyer, "Planned vs. Impulse Purchase Behavior," *Journal of Retailing*, Winter 1986, pp. 384–409.

151. Rook, "The Buying Impulse."

152. Russell W. Belk, "Materialism: Trait Aspects of Living in a Material World," *Journal of Consumer Research*, December 1985, pp. 265–280; P. S. Raju, "Optimum Stimulation Level: Its Relationship to Personality, Demographics, and Exploratory Behavior," *Journal of Consumer Research*, December 1980, pp. 272–282; and Danny Bellenger and P. K. Korgaonkar, "Profiling the Recreational Shopper," *Journal of Retailing*, Fall 1980, pp. 77–92.

153. Dennis W. Rook and Robert J. Fisher, "Normative Influences on Impulsive Buying Behavior," *Journal of Consumer Research*, December 1995, pp. 305–313; and Radhika Puri, "Measuring and Modifying Consumer Impulsiveness: A Cost–Benefit Accessibility Framework," *Journal of Consumer Psychology* 5, no. 2, 1996, pp. 87–114.

154. Xueming Luo, "How Does Shopping with Others Influence Impulsive Purchasing?" *Journal of Consumer Psychology* 15, no. 4, 2005, pp. 288–294.

155. Arul Mishra and Himanshu Mishra, "We Are What We Consume: The Influence of Food Consumption on Impulsive Choice," *Journal of Marketing Research*, December 2010, pp. 1129–1137.

156. Inman and Winer, "Where the Rubber Meets the Road: A Model of In-store Consumer Decision Making."

157. Sarah Nassauer, "A Season (or 13) for Shopping," *Wall Street Journal*, August 17, 2011, www.wsj.com.

158. David R. Bell, Daniel Corsten, and George Knox, "From Point of Purchase to Path to Purchase," *Journal of Marketing*, January 2011, pp. 31–45.

159. Shaun Rein, "Rein: Chinese Women Keep Shopping Despite the Gloom," *CNBC*, September 26, 2011, www.cnbc.com.

160. Elizabeth Holmes, "New Chains Court Women Who Want Polished Locks," *Wall Street Journal*, September 28, 2011, www.wsj.com.

161. Michael Oliveira, "Canada Loves Daily Deal Sites, Even More than U.S.: Survey," *Globe and Mail (Canada)*, March 21, 2012, www.theglobeandmail.com; Zak Stambor, "Google Aims for Daily Deal Dominance," *Internet Retailer*, November 8, 2011, www.internetretailer.com; Sara Yin, "Will Groupon Addicts Force Deeper Black Friday Discounts?" *PC Magazine*, November 1, 2011, www.pcmag.com; Rolfe Winkler, "Googe Offers New Threat to Groupon," *Wall Street Journal*, October 31, 2011, www.wsj.com; Dave Lee, "Have Daily Deal Sites Like Groupon Had Their Day?" *BBC News*, November 3, 2011, www.bbc.co.uk/news; and Sheila Shayon, "kgbdeals: The 'Special Agents' of Daily Deals," *Brand Channel*, July 19, 2011, www.brandchannel.com.

POST-DECISION PROCESSES

After studying this chapter, you will be able to

1. Distinguish between the dissonance and the regret that consumers may experience after acquisition, consumption, or disposition.

2. Explain how consumers can learn from experience and why marketers need to understand this postdecision process.

3. Discuss how consumers judge satisfaction or dissatisfaction with their decisions about acquisition, consumption, or disposition.

4. Describe how consumers may dispose of something, why this process is more complex for meaningful objects, and what influences consumer recycling behavior.

INTRODUCTION

Companies Go Social for Improved Customer Service

When Delta Air Lines passengers are grounded by weather delays, they can tweet for immediate help in booking a new flight. Virgin Atlantic Airways keeps customers worldwide informed about changes in departures or arrivals through a Twitter-based automated flight status system. Whirlpool checks its Facebook page for complaints cheers that customers post about its appliances, and makes it a point to respond. College Hunks Hauling Junk, a rubbish-removal service, monitors comments on social media sites so that it can resolve any complaints quickly. Standard Chartered Bank's customers in India can tweet or text for assistance with account questions.

These are only a few examples of the many marketers using social media to deliver speedier, more personalized customer service; to keep customers informed about delays and other service issues; and to react to complaints in a timely manner. With the extensive reach of social media, one angry comment about bad service or a faulty product can reach hundreds or thousands of people in a very short time. No wonder so many companies are logging onto social media for customer service. "The whole idea is to work to address issues so they don't escalate," explains a Delta Air Lines spokesperson. Resolving complaints via social media does more than eliminate dissatisfaction: It also demonstrates, in a very public way, that the company listens and responds to its customers.[1]

This example illustrates several key topics in this chapter. First, it highlights the importance of customer satisfaction as the foundation of successful businesses. Second, it shows how customer satisfaction depends on good performance, creating positive feelings, and perceptions of equity (a fair exchange). Third, it illustrates how consumers learn about offerings by experiencing them directly, as customers do when flying on Delta Air Lines or tweeting for help from service representatives. Finally, it demonstrates how a business can counter customer dissatisfaction by doing a good job of handling complaints. All of these phenomena occur after the consumer has made a decision. This chapter examines the four post-decision processes shown in Exhibit 10.1: dissonance and regret, consumer learning, satisfaction/dissatisfaction, and disposition—all of which have important implications for marketers.

POST-DECISION DISSONANCE AND REGRET

Consumers are not always confident about their acquisition, consumption, or disposition decisions. They may feel uncertain about whether they made the correct choice or may even regret the decision that they made, as the following sections show.

Dissonance

After you make an acquisition, consumption, or disposition decision, you may sometimes feel uncertain about whether you made the correct choice. You might wonder whether you should have bought a shirt or dress other than the one you did, or whether you should have worn something else to a party, or whether you should have kept an old teddy bear instead of throwing it away. **Post-decision dissonance** is most likely to occur when more than one alternative is attractive and the decision is important.[2]

Post-decision dissonance
A feeling of anxiety over whether the correct decision was made.

Post-decision dissonance can influence consumer behavior because it creates anxiety that the consumer would like to reduce, especially when motivation, ability, and opportunity (MAO) are high. One way of reducing dissonance is to search for additional information from sources such as experts and magazines. This search is very selective and is designed to make the chosen alternative more attractive and the rejected ones less attractive, thereby reducing dissonance.

Regret

Post-decision regret
A feeling that one should have purchased another option.

Post-decision regret occurs when consumers perceive an unfavorable comparison between the performance of the chosen option and the performance of the options not chosen.[3] If you consider three cars before making your purchase decision and then find out that the resale value of the car that you bought is much lower than that of either of the two options, you may regret your purchase and wish that you had chosen one of the other cars. In fact, research indicates that you may feel regret even if you have no information about the unchosen alternatives—especially if you

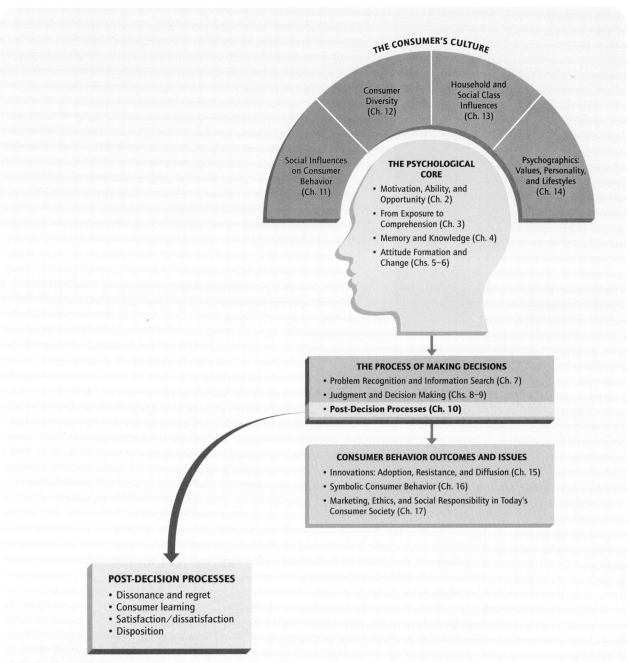

THE CONSUMER'S CULTURE

Consumer Diversity (Ch. 12)

Household and Social Class Influences (Ch. 13)

Social Influences on Consumer Behavior (Ch. 11)

Psychographics: Values, Personality, and Lifestyles (Ch. 14)

THE PSYCHOLOGICAL CORE
- Motivation, Ability, and Opportunity (Ch. 2)
- From Exposure to Comprehension (Ch. 3)
- Memory and Knowledge (Ch. 4)
- Attitude Formation and Change (Chs. 5–6)

THE PROCESS OF MAKING DECISIONS
- Problem Recognition and Information Search (Ch. 7)
- Judgment and Decision Making (Chs. 8–9)
- Post-Decision Processes (Ch. 10)

CONSUMER BEHAVIOR OUTCOMES AND ISSUES
- Innovations: Adoption, Resistance, and Diffusion (Ch. 15)
- Symbolic Consumer Behavior (Ch. 16)
- Marketing, Ethics, and Social Responsibility in Today's Consumer Society (Ch. 17)

POST-DECISION PROCESSES
- Dissonance and regret
- Consumer learning
- Satisfaction/dissatisfaction
- Disposition

© Cengage Learning 2013

Exhibit 10.1

Chapter Overview: Post-Decision Processes

The decision does not end after consumers have made a choice or purchase. Consumers can experience dissonance (anxiety over whether they made the correct decision) or regret after a purchase, learn about the offering by using it, experience satisfaction or dissatisfaction with it, and eventually dispose of it.

cannot reverse your decision, have a negative outcome from your chosen alternative, or have made a change from the status quo (see Exhibit 10.2).

Moreover, although consumers feel short-term regret if they do not buy during a limited-time purchase opportunity, this regret goes away over time.[4] Consumers who avoid guilt by exercising self-control and not splurging on a hedonic choice like an expensive but exciting vacation may later regret this decision and feel that they missed out by not living in the moment.[5]

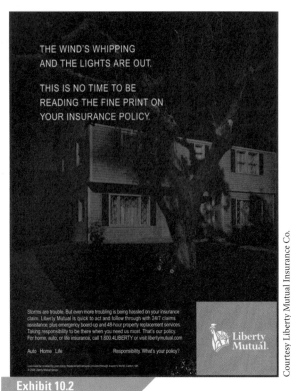

Courtesy Liberty Mutual Insurance Co.

THE WIND'S WHIPPING
AND THE LIGHTS ARE OUT.

THIS IS NO TIME TO BE
READING THE FINE PRINT ON
YOUR INSURANCE POLICY.

Exhibit 10.2

Advertising Based on Feelings of Regret
Sometimes ads try to stimulate feelings of regret in order to purchase their product.

Furthermore, suppose consumers are dissatisfied with a purchase outcome and decide to switch to a different alternative. Will they regret switching? Even if this new alternative turns out to have a negative outcome, consumers will feel less regret because they believe that their decision to switch was justified.[6] Consumers can also regulate postpurchase regret by focusing on what they can learn from this decision to improve future decisions.[7] Finally, breaking a major decision into a series of smaller decisions can reduce the difficulty of making those choices and reduce the tendency to feel regret about the overall decision.[8]

Marketing Implications

By helping consumers reduce post-decision dissonance and regret, marketers can diminish negative feelings related to the offering. For example, Subaru of America gives each vehicle owner a free subscription to its quarterly *Drive* magazine and a free monthly e-newsletter. It also reinforces positive feelings by offering owners a free, personalized "Badge of Ownership" and inviting them to submit photos of themselves with their cars for the Subaru website and Facebook page. These activities help to reduce dissonance or regret and encourage positive attitudes toward the brand. Consumers may also reduce dissonance and regret by reading supporting information in advertisements or online after a purchase.

LEARNING FROM CONSUMER EXPERIENCE*

Earlier chapters explained how consumers acquire knowledge through processes such as information search, exposure to marketing communications, and observation of others. From a practical perspective, we most often think about this type of consumer learning because much of it is under the direct control of the company, which provides information through marketing communications. However, these efforts are often limited because of their low credibility.[9] Consumers assume that these messages are intended to persuade them to buy the offering and are therefore generally skeptical about the marketing claims.

Experiences that occur during acquisition, consumption, or disposition, however, can be equally—if not more—important sources of consumer knowledge for several reasons. First, the consumer tends to be more motivated to learn under these circumstances. Actually experiencing an event is more involving and interesting than being told about it, and the consumer has more control over what happens. Simply investigating the various alternatives is a learning experience. However, if consumers become too attached to the alternatives during the decision process, they may feel uneasy after making a choice because they had to forgo the other alternatives.[10]

Second, information acquired from experience is more vivid and therefore easier to remember than other types of information.[11] However, the information gained from experiential learning is not always accurate and may, in fact, be biased and erroneous.[12] Information about attributes that must be experienced through taste, touch, or smell exerts a stronger influence on consumers' future behavior when it comes from experience or product trial than when it is acquired from ads or word of mouth.[13] An ad can state that a product will taste good, but actually eating it is more likely to generate

---

*Some of this section draws heavily from an article by Stephen J. Hoch and John Deighton, "Managing What Consumers Learn from Experience," *Journal of Marketing*, April 1989, pp. 1–20.

a strong attitude. On the other hand, repeated exposure to ads can approximate the effect of direct experience when it comes to search or informational attributes such as price or ingredients, resulting in consumers holding strong beliefs about those characteristics.[14]

A Model of Learning from Consumer Experience

Hypothesis testing
Testing out expectations through experience.

Hypothesis generation
Forming expectations about the product or service.

Exposure to evidence
Actually experiencing the product or service.

Encoding of evidence
Processing the information one experiences.

Integration of evidence
Combining new information with stored knowledge.

Consumers can learn from experience by engaging in a process of **hypothesis testing**. On the basis of past experience or another source such as word of mouth or advertising, consumers can form a hypothesis or expectation about a product or service, a consumption experience, or a disposition option and then set out to test it. Such hypotheses are important because without them consumers are less likely to gather the evidence that they need to learn. Researchers have proposed that consumers go through four basic stages in testing hypotheses for learning: (1) hypothesis generation, (2) exposure to evidence, (3) encoding of evidence, and (4) integration of evidence and prior beliefs (see Exhibit 10.3). The following example illustrates these four stages.

Suppose a consumer sees an ad for a new Steve Carell movie. He also remembers some of Carell's previous movies, such as Date Night. Based on all this information, he generates a hypothesis (**hypothesis generation**) about the quality of the new movie ("It must be great"). Next, he seeks out **exposure to evidence** to either confirm or disprove this hypothesis by going to see the new movie. While watching it, he can assess whether or not it is in fact great, a step called **encoding the evidence**. After watching the movie, the consumer can **integrate the evidence** with his existing knowledge or beliefs. If he really likes it, confirming the hypothesis, he may have learned that "you can always count on a Steve Carell movie to be great." However, if he does not like it, he may form the new belief that "not all Carell films are great, and I must be careful in the future."

Consumers can form hypotheses in relation to any aspect of consumer behavior: acquisition ("using an app to buy groceries will be fun"), consumption ("listening to the concert will be fun"), or disposition ("getting rid of used textbooks will be easy"). Learning from experience is also important when consumers use a shopping agent or app, or when they react to recommendations from retail sites such as amazon.com. Using feedback from repeated hypothesis tests, the agent or site learns what the consumer likes and can present more appropriate options.[15]

The consumer's hypothesis and experience of brand personality also influence learning. If a firm with a "sincere" brand personality suffers a crisis, it may have difficulty reconnecting with customers because its fundamental perceptions of the brand have deteriorated. However, firms with an "exciting" brand personality may reinvigorate customer relationships more easily after a crisis because consumers are less surprised by nonroutine experiences with such brands.[16]

Exhibit 10.3

A Model of Learning from Experience

Consumers can acquire a lot of information about products and services by actually experiencing them. This entire process is influenced by consumer familiarity, motivation to process, and the ambiguity of the information.

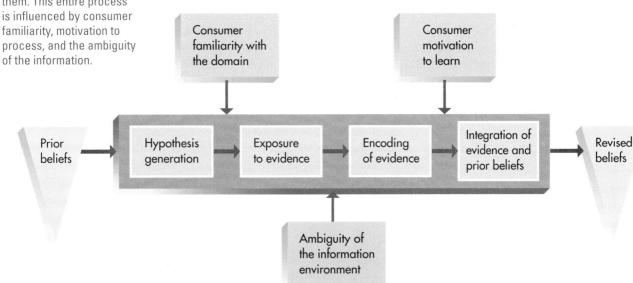

Source: Stephen J. Hoch and John Deighton, "Managing What Consumers Learn from Experience," *Journal of Marketing*, April 1989, pp. 1–20. Reprinted by permission.

What Affects Learning?

Four factors affect learning from experience: (1) motivation, (2) prior familiarity or ability, (3) ambiguity of the information environment or lack of opportunity, and (4) processing biases.

Motivation

When consumers are motivated to process information, they will generate a number of hypotheses and seek out information to confirm or disprove them, actively engaging in the process of learning from experience. Consider what happened when shoppers told qvc.com that they could not judge a certain handbag's size from the product photo. The company quickly posted photos showing women of different heights holding the purse. This information helped consumers learn more about the purse; in fact, those who viewed the photos were more likely to buy the purse than those who did not view the photos.[17] Note that when motivation is low, consumers will generate few or no hypotheses and will be less likely to learn unless the learning process involves the simpler processes of classical or operant conditioning (see Chapters 6 and 9). Still, marketers can facilitate learning when motivation is low, as shown later in this chapter.

Prior Knowledge or Ability

Consumers' prior knowledge or ability affects the extent to which they learn from experience. When knowledge is high, consumers are likely to have well-defined beliefs and expectations and are therefore unlikely to generate new hypotheses. Also, experts are less likely than those with moderate knowledge to search for information.[18] Both of these factors inhibit learning. In contrast, low-knowledge consumers lack skills to develop hypotheses to guide the learning process.[19] Without guiding hypotheses, consumers have difficulty collecting evidence and learning. Thus, moderately knowledgeable consumers are the most likely to generate hypotheses and learn from experience. Interestingly, experts do have an advantage in learning information about new products and services due to their more extensive knowledge base.[20]

Ambiguity of the Information Environment or Lack of Opportunity

Some situations do not provide the opportunity for consumers to learn from experience, which means that consumers may lack sufficient information to confirm or disprove hypotheses.[21] Such **ambiguity of information** occurs because many offerings are similar in quality and consumers can glean little information from the experience. Moreover, making the initial choice in a context of ambiguity affects consumers' certainty about the decision and, if the actual experience is uninformative, can lead to persistent preferences for the chosen option's attributes.[22]

Ambiguous information can strongly affect consumers' ability to learn from experience. On the one hand, when consumers have difficulty determining product quality (for such products as beer and motor oil), they tend to support their hypotheses with information from advertising or word of mouth. Because consumers cannot disprove the information by experiencing the product, they see the product as being consistent with their prior expectations.[23] Thus, for many years consumers believed that Listerine prevented colds because the claim could not be disproved by usage. Obviously, the marketer in such a situation has an unfair advantage, a situation that explains why deception in advertising is an important topic.

On the other hand, when evidence is unambiguous and the product is clearly good or bad, consumers base their perceptions on actual experience and learn a great deal. Unambiguous information tends to be better remembered and to have more impact on future decisions.[24] When evidence is ambiguous, evaluations by both experts and novices are strongly influenced by country-of-origin expectations (e.g., knowing that a product was made in Japan), but when evidence is unambiguous, experts ignore this information and make evaluations based on actual quality.[25]

Processing Biases

The confirmation bias and overconfidence can pose major hurdles to the learning process, particularly when evidence is ambiguous.[26] Specifically, these biases inhibit learning by making consumers avoid both negative and highly diagnostic information. For example, a consumer who believes that all Japanese products are of high quality may ignore contrary evidence and learn nothing new about these products. Also, negative information is important to the learning process because it

Ambiguity of information When there is not enough information to confirm or disprove hypotheses.

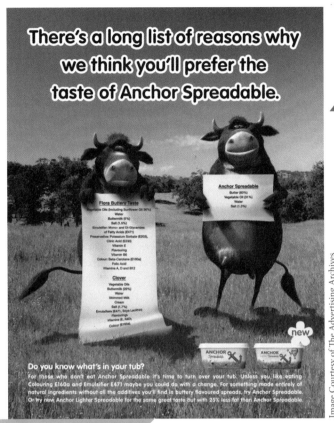

There's a long list of reasons why we think you'll prefer the taste of Anchor Spreadable.

Do you know what's in your tub?
For those who don't eat Anchor Spreadable it's time to turn over your tub. Unless you like eating Colouring E160a and Emulsifier E471 maybe you could do with a change. For something made entirely of natural ingredients without all the additives you'll find in buttery flavoured spreads, try Anchor Spreadable. Or try new Anchor Lighter Spreadable for the same great taste but with 25% less fat than Anchor Spreadable.

Image Courtesy of The Advertising Archives

Exhibit 10.4

Encouraging Learning to Facilitate Switching
Sometimes marketers can encourage learning about their brand in order to get consumers to switch.

Top dog A market leader or brand that has a large market share.
Underdog A lower-share brand.

provides a more balanced picture of the situation and allows consumers to more accurately test hypotheses. Research has also shown that the acquisition of disproving evidence has a strong and rapid impact on consumer learning.[27]

Marketing Implications

Ambiguous information and processing biases often inhibit consumer learning about products and services. These biases have important strategic implications, depending on the offering's market position.[28]

Top-Dog Strategies

A product, service, or business that is the market leader or has a large market share is called a **top dog**. Limitations on learning are advantageous to top dogs because consumers will simply confirm existing beliefs and expectations and be overconfident, particularly when the motivation to learn is low. When motivation to learn is high, the consumer will try to acquire information that could be disproving and lead to a switch. To avoid this, the top dog can state specific claims that justify consumers' evaluation of the brand. Or the top dog can encourage consumers not to acquire new information, which is called *blocking exposure to evidence*. If top-dog evidence is unambiguous, the consumer simply needs reinforcement of messages telling why the brand is satisfying—called *explaining the experience*—and encouragement to try it. Coca-Cola's "Live positively" slogan is a good example.

Underdog Strategies

Underdogs (lower-share brands) want to encourage consumer learning because new information may lead consumers to switch brands. First, when consumers are not motivated, underdogs can instigate learning through comparisons of their brand with the market leader, side-by-side displays, or information provided online (see Exhibit 10.4). The underdog needs a strong and distinct advantage if it is to overcome overconfidence and confirmation biases.

Second, underdogs can create expectations and use promotions to provide the actual experience for consumers. If the evidence is ambiguous, consumers' expectations are not likely to be disconfirmed. For example, the Czech beer brand Budweiser Budvar, which competes with Anheuser-Busch's U.S. Budweiser beer in many global markets, promotes its quality ingredients and traditional brewing methods. The brand recently ran a taste test on its Facebook page to highlight the differences between its beer and the U.S. Bud brand, which has a large international market share.[29]

Finally, facilitating product trial is critical when consumers' motivation to learn is low and the evidence is unambiguous because the evidence will lead to a positive learning experience.

HOW DO CONSUMERS MAKE SATISFACTION OR DISSATISFACTION JUDGMENTS?

Satisfaction The feeling that results when consumers make a positive evaluation or feel happy with their decision.

After consumers have made acquisition, consumption, or disposition decisions, they can evaluate the outcomes of their decisions. If their evaluations are positive—if they believe their needs or goals have been met—they feel **satisfaction**. Thus, you could feel satisfied with the purchase of a new smartphone, a haircut, a buying experience, a salesperson, or a retail outlet.[30] When consumers have a

Dissatisfaction The feeling that results when consumers make a negative evaluation or are unhappy with a decision.

negative evaluation of an outcome, they feel **dissatisfaction**. Dissatisfaction occurs if you did not enjoy a movie, were unhappy with a salesperson, or wished you had not thrown something away. Dissatisfaction can be related to feelings of tolerance, distress, sadness, regret, agitation, and outrage.[31]

Most of the research on satisfaction and dissatisfaction has focused on offerings that consumers can evaluate on *utilitarian dimensions*, or how well the product or service functions (good or bad), as well as on *hedonic dimensions*, or how the product makes someone feel (happy, excited, delighted, sad, regretful, or angry).[32] In fact, all aspects of the product or brand experience—its sensory, affective, behavioral, and cognitive appeals—can influence satisfaction and loyalty.[33] In judging satisfaction, consumers make a conscious comparison between what they thought would happen and the actual performance.[34]

Satisfaction also varies with consumer involvement, consumer characteristics, and time.[35] High-involvement consumers tend to express higher satisfaction immediately after a purchase, probably due to their more extensive evaluation, but their satisfaction declines over time. Lower-involvement consumers exhibit lower satisfaction at first, but their satisfaction increases with greater usage over time. Note that when consumers make their own choices of hedonic products (such as buying a ticket for next week's concert), they are more satisfied when they delay consumption only a short time after making the decision. If choices are made for them by others, however, consumers' satisfaction will decrease the longer that consumption is delayed.[36]

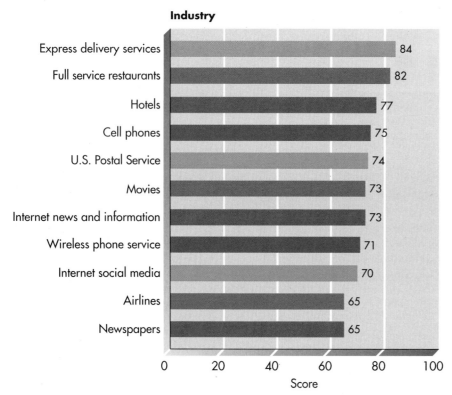

Industry

Note: Higher scores indicate higher satisfaction.

Exhibit 10.5

The American Consumer Satisfaction Index

The ACSI measures customer satisfaction performance across a variety of different industries. Here are a few examples.

Source: Data from ACSI, 2007.

Marketing Implications

Customer satisfaction is critical to business success because satisfied customers are willing to pay higher prices, particularly if they buy the product repeatedly.[37] They are also more likely to remain customers, be brand loyal, and be committed to the product.[38] Also, they will tell others about their experiences, increasing the likelihood that those consumers will then buy the product.[39] Attracting new customers is more expensive than marketing to existing customers, a situation that means retaining satisfied customers is cost-efficient.[40] When the product category is important to the consumer, satisfaction can also lead to more frequent purchasing, especially when it is convenient for the consumer to buy.[41]

When they make purchases, consumers tend to spend more on the brand or with the company that gives them satisfaction in that product category.[42] For example, the founder of Zane's Cycles in Branford, Connecticut, estimates that over a lifetime of purchasing bicycles, parts, and service, the average customer will spend $12,500, which is why his store aims to provide superior customer service to encourage repeat purchasing.[43] In fact, some studies have linked customer satisfaction with company profitability. A key consideration for publicly traded corporations is that improvements in customer satisfaction can pay off in more positive stock recommendations to investors, as well.[44]

Not surprisingly, many companies actively monitor customer satisfaction. The American Customer Satisfaction Index (ACSI) monitors satisfaction with a variety of industries and firms (see Exhibit 10.5). Global marketers should be aware, however, that cultural, socioeconomic, and political factors can influence customer satisfaction levels in individual nations.[45] Marketers should also aim for satisfaction when responding to customers' questions and concerns because (1) these tend to be highly loyal customers and (2) these consumers will influence others through word of mouth after the contact.[46]

Finally, marketers must understand the roots of dissatisfaction because of the potential for negative outcomes such as negative word-of-mouth communication, complaints, and lower sales and profits. For instance, if a department store loses 167 customers a month, it will lose $2.4 million in sales (and $280,000 in profit) in just one year.[47] One study found that it takes 12 positive experiences to overcome a single negative one and that the cost of attracting a new customer is five times the cost of keeping an existing one.[48]

Satisfaction/Dissatisfaction Based on Thoughts

Just as consumers make decisions based on thoughts and feelings, they also judge satisfaction or dissatisfaction based on thoughts and feelings. Thought-based judgments of satisfaction/dissatisfaction can relate to (1) whether consumers' thoughts and expectations about the offering are confirmed or disconfirmed by its actual performance, (2) thoughts about causality and blame, and (3) thoughts about fairness and equity.

Expectations and Performance: The Disconfirmation Paradigm

Disconfirmation The existence of a discrepancy between expectations and performance.

Expectation Belief about how a product/service will perform.

As diagrammed in Exhibit 10.6, **disconfirmation** occurs when there is a discrepancy, positive or negative, between our prior expectations and the product's actual performance (see the red arrows in the exhibit).[49] In this case, **expectations** are desired product/service outcomes and include "pre-consumption beliefs about overall performance, or … the levels or attributes possessed by a product (service)."[50] For example, you might expect a Japanese car to be reliable and fuel efficient, expectations based on advertising, inspection of the product, prior experience with similar offerings, and the experiences of other referent consumers.[51]

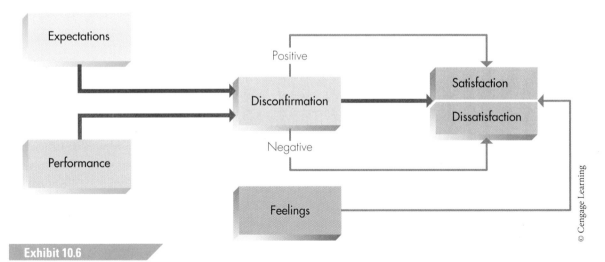

Exhibit 10.6

The Disconfirmation Paradigm

Here the disconfirmation paradigm shows how satisfaction or dissatisfaction can occur. Using an example of a new Steve Carell movie, the consumer enters the situation with expectations ("Steve Carell movies are entertaining"). Once she sees the movie, she can evaluate it (performance). If she finds it more entertaining than she expected, positive disconfirmation has occurred, and she will be satisfied. If the movie is less entertaining than she expected, a negative disconfirmation and dissatisfaction will result. Expectations (the likelihood of seeing the movie as entertaining), performance (whether the movie actually is good), and feelings (positive or negative emotions experienced during viewing) will also affect satisfaction/dissatisfaction (independent of disconfirmation).

Performance The measurement of whether the product/service actually fulfills consumers' needs.

Performance measures whether these expected outcomes have been achieved. Performance can either be *objective*—based on the actual performance, which is fairly constant across consumers—or *subjective*—based on individual feelings, which can vary across consumers. The objective performance of a car describes how well it runs and how economical its gas mileage is, whereas subjective performance might include an assessment of how stylish it is or "how good it makes me feel." Better-than-expected performance leads to a *positive disconfirmation* and to satisfaction. If performance is as good as expected, a *simple confirmation* has occurred, and this condition will also lead to satisfaction. In contrast, if performance is lower than expected, the result is *negative disconfirmation* and dissatisfaction.

Customers' evaluation of services is also susceptible to disconfirmation.[52] Here, customers have expectations related to price and service performance and to intangible characteristics of the facilities and the personnel.[53] Surprisingly, consumers who focus on the service provider's obligations (e.g., to respond to their needs) will be more dissatisfied with service failures if they are on friendly terms with the provider. Yet in the same situation, consumers will be less dissatisfied if they focus on their own obligations within the relationship.[54] One way online retailers such as Amazon can manage expectations and avoid dissatisfaction is by providing plenty of information, such as stating the cutoff date for ordering merchandise to be delivered by Christmas. Note that if consumers participate in a service expecting to achieve a goal such as weight loss, they are more satisfied when they successfully follow the instructions and achieve the goal.[55]

Although the disconfirmation paradigm is similar to the learning process, satisfaction and dissatisfaction are based on a formal evaluation, whereas the learning process may not be. Also, satisfaction need not be transaction-specific and is subject to change—in fact, it can be affected by social influences such as family members and may be closely related to consumers' satisfaction with their own lives.[56]

Consumers who have many choices will feel more satisfied when they decide on an option that turns out well, and they can give themselves credit for making a good decision (but they will be dissatisfied if they choose an option that turns out to be bad because they will blame themselves for making a bad decision).[57] Interestingly, consumers who have many choices may be optimistic about their chosen product's performance at first, but this optimism will fade over time.[58] Another study shows that consumers may experience greater negative disconfirmation and therefore less satisfaction when they choose an option from a large assortment.[59]

When consumers expect to evaluate an offering, they will pay closer attention to negative aspects during consumption and therefore will provide less favorable quality and satisfaction evaluations—unless they have low expectations at the outset.[60] Distrust, another consequence of negative disconfirmation, can carry over even to unrelated products or firms.[61] Also, customers who buy at a discount may perceive that they benefit less from the product's consumption than if they had paid full price.[62] Even when price has no bearing on a product's quality, consumers' beliefs about the price-quality relationship will affect their experience of the product's performance.[63] And in some cultures, superstition-driven expectations (such as preference for a "lucky" number of items in a package) can play a role in product or service evaluation and disconfirmation.[64]

Exhibit 10.6 shows that performance, expectations, and feelings can affect satisfaction, *independent* of disconfirmation (as reflected by the blue arrows).[65] To fully understand why satisfaction or dissatisfaction occurs, we must account for all these dimensions together and separately. The simple fact that a product performs well will have a positive influence on satisfaction, independent of expectations.[66] Likewise, the poor performance of a product or service alone can lead to dissatisfaction.[67] If you buy a new computer, and it does not work well, you could be dissatisfied—even without having had any prior expectations about it. How feelings affect satisfaction and dissatisfaction will be explored later in this chapter.

Marketing Implications

Based on the disconfirmation paradigm, better performance leads to fulfilled expectations and satisfaction. Expectations created by marketers about product performance can also influence satisfaction or dissatisfaction. Raising consumers' expectations of how well the product or service will perform can increase ratings of product performance.[68] Whole Foods Market, the natural foods grocery chain, has cooking coaches on staff to advise

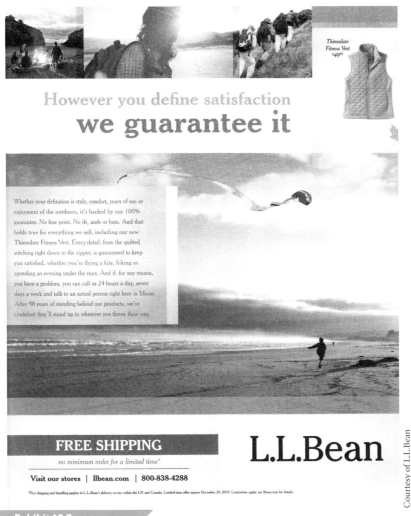

However you define satisfaction
we guarantee it

Thinsulate Fitness Vest $49⁹⁵

Whether your definition is style, comfort, years of use or enjoyment of the outdoors, it's backed by our 100% guarantee. No fine print. No ifs, ands or buts. And that holds true for everything we sell, including our new Thinsulate Fitness Vest. Every detail, from the quilted stitching right down to the zipper, is guaranteed to keep you satisfied, whether you're flying a kite, hiking or spending an evening under the stars. And if, for any reason, you have a problem, you can call us 24 hours a day, seven days a week and talk to an actual person right here in Maine. After 98 years of standing behind our products, we're confident they'll stand up to whatever you throw their way.

FREE SHIPPING
no minimum order for a limited time*

Visit our stores | llbean.com | 800-838-4288

*Free shipping and handling applies to L.L.Bean's delivery service within the US and Canada. Limited-time offer expires December 20, 2010. Limitations apply, see llbean.com for details.

L.L.Bean

Courtesy of L.L.Bean

Exhibit 10.7

Guarantees
Companies can create positive expectations that lead to satisfaction simply by offering a good warranty or guarantee on their products, so customers do not have much to lose.

Attribution theory A theory of how individuals find explanations for events.

shoppers about questions such as how to select dried chili peppers and how to prepare faro. In-store technology provides instant access to additional recipes and cooking tips, helping consumers understand what to expect from the fresh foods they buy at Whole Foods Market.[69] On the other hand, marketers are setting themselves up for a potential negative disconfirmation and dissatisfaction if customer expectations are too high, and companies make promises they cannot keep.

Providing consumers with a good warranty or guarantee can create positive expectations that will lead to satisfaction (see Exhibit 10.7).[70] Zane's Cycles provides a lifetime service guarantee for every bicycle—covering parts and service—as well as a 30-day test ride period, enabling buyers to determine whether they selected the bike that best fits their needs. The guarantee and test-ride period are both promoted on Zane's Facebook page, its website, and in the store.[71]

Causality and Blame: Attribution Theory

Attribution theory explains how individuals think about explanations for or causes of effects or behavior.[72] In a marketing context, when a product or service does not fulfill consumers' needs, they will attempt to find an explanation based on three factors:

▶ *Stability.* Is the cause of the event temporary or permanent?

▶ *Focus.* Is the problem consumer or marketer related?

▶ *Controllability.* Is the event under the customer's or marketer's control?

Customers are more likely to be dissatisfied if the cause is perceived to be permanent, marketer related, and not under the customer's control. Suppose you find a crack in the windshield of your new car. If you perceive that this is only a chance or temporary occurrence, beyond the control of the marketer (maybe a rock hit the window while you were driving), you will probably not be dissatisfied. On the other hand, if you discover that many other consumers have had a similar problem—that is, the cause is more permanent, company related, and under the company's control—you will probably be dissatisfied.

Attribution theory also applies to services. For instance, consumers were dissatisfied with a travel agent if the problem they had experienced was permanent and under the firm's control.[73] In a study of passengers delayed at an airport, attributions were found to explain the desire either to complain or to fly the same airline again. If consumers saw the delay as permanent and under the airline's control, they were more likely to complain and less likely to fly the airline again.[74] Consumers who can choose whether to participate in a service are likely to attribute at least part of any negative outcome to their own involvement, whereas they will attribute a good part of any positive outcome to their own participation.[75] Satisfaction with services also depends on whether the consumer holds the company responsible for the outcome and believes the outcome stems from a stable or unstable cause.[76] Finally, consumers are more satisfied when companies exert extra effort to serve them, even when the offerings are not that great.[77]

Marketing Implications

Attribution theory can provide marketers with guidance in how to deal with potential or existing perceptions of consumer dissatisfaction. If the cause of the dissatisfaction actually is permanent, marketer related, and under the marketer's control, something must be done to correct the problem or provide the consumer with restitution. In the banking industry, many banks are marketing value-added services such as financial advice, electronic bill payment, and mobile banking in an attempt to satisfy customers. First Tennessee Bank, for example, recently introduced an app that lets consumers photograph a check and deposit it via cell phone, along with other digital banking services. "We're allowing [consumers] to check their balance, pay bills and deposit checks, all from the palm of their hand," explains a bank official.[78]

Fairness and Equity: Equity Theory

Equity theory A theory that focuses on the fairness of exchanges between individuals, which helps in understanding consumer satisfaction and dissatisfaction.

Equity theory focuses on the nature of exchanges between individuals and their perceptions of these exchanges. In marketing, it has been applied to examining the exchange between a buyer and a seller or a more general institution.[79] According to equity theory, consumers form perceptions of their own inputs and outputs into a particular exchange and compare these perceptions with their perceptions of the inputs and outputs of the salesperson, dealer, or company. For example, when buying a car, a consumer's inputs might include information search, decision-making effort, psychological anxiety, and money. The output would be a satisfactory car. Seller inputs might include a quality product, selling effort, and a financing plan; seller output might be a fair profit.

Fairness in the exchange The perception that people's inputs are equal to their outputs in an exchange.

For equity to occur, the buyer must perceive **fairness in the exchange**. Thus, the car buyer might perceive a fair exchange if he or she purchased a desirable car at a fair price. Satisfaction is even higher if consumers perceive that they have gotten a bargain.[80] Consumers will be dissatisfied if they perceive inequity in an exchange—for example, if the salesperson did not pay enough attention to the buyer. For equity to occur, the consumer must perceive that the seller is also being dealt with fairly. Nevertheless, fairness perceptions tend to be self-centered, biased more toward buyer outcomes and seller inputs, than to buyer inputs and seller outcomes.[81]

Moreover, research shows that consumers judge the equity of the payment exchanged for service usage by asking themselves, "Am I using this service enough, given what I pay for it?" They will perceive the exchange as more equitable when they have high expectations of service usage levels at first or when the service performance exceeds their normative expectations. When they perceive the price/usage exchange to be more equitable, they will be more satisfied.[82] Also, perceptions of equity can shift over time. For instance, as the end of a car's warranty period approaches, owners become increasingly dissatisfied with attributes they believe can be remedied; in turn, these attributes become more highly related to product quality satisfaction.[83]

Equity theory complements the disconfirmation paradigm in that equity theory specifies another way dissatisfaction can occur. In other words, both types of processes can operate at the same time. However, whereas the disconfirmation paradigm focuses on expectations and performance, equity theory is concerned with more general interpersonal norms governing what is wrong or right and with a consideration of the outcomes for both the seller and the buyer.

Marketing Implications

As long as consumers perceive that their inputs and outputs are equitable in relation to those of the seller, they will be satisfied. This reaction is true in terms of the offering itself as well as in terms of interactions with employees when resolving a complaint. In other words, consumers who perceive that they have been treated fairly in the complaint process will be more satisfied, more likely to buy again, and more likely to spread positive word of mouth.[84] However, if an inequity exists, consumers will be dissatisfied.

Marketers must work toward providing fair exchanges, even though consumers' perceptions of fairness tend to be biased toward themselves. One area in which marketers can directly affect equity perceptions is the salesperson-customer interaction.

Salespeople must make every effort to ensure that their inputs match customer inputs by listening to consumer needs, answering questions, and trying to provide a good deal. At Chow Tai Fook, a Hong Kong-based jewelry chain with 1,500 stores across China, salespeople serve tea to browsing customers and, when asked to bargain on price, offer discounts in a respectful but responsive way.[85] Promotions can also increase perceptions of fairness in an exchange. Offering a lower price or a free gift with purchase can make consumers feel that they are getting more out of the exchange. _____

Satisfaction/Dissatisfaction Based on Feelings

Consumers can also judge satisfaction and dissatisfaction on the basis of feelings, specifically (1) experienced emotions (and coping with these emotions) and (2) mispredictions about emotions.

Experienced Emotions and Coping

Post-decision feeling
Positive or negative emotion experienced while using the products or services.

The positive and negative **post-decision feelings** we experience help to explain satisfaction or dissatisfaction judgments (independent of disconfirmation, as you saw in Exhibit 10.6).[86] If we feel good (or bad) while using a product or service, we are more likely to be satisfied (or dissatisfied), independent of our expectations and evaluations of its performance. Consumers who are happy or content are most likely to be satisfied, followed by those who experience pleasant surprise. In fact, most consumers around the world find enjoyment and satisfaction in their buying experiences. One study found that more than 90 percent of durable goods purchases were associated with positive feelings.[87] In fact, research suggests that actively building strong, positive emotional bonds with customers can enhance both satisfaction and loyalty.[88]

Dissatisfaction is most likely to strike consumers who feel angry or upset, followed by those who experience unpleasant surprise.[89] Feelings expressed by service employees also affect customer satisfaction. When employees appear to be expressing genuinely positive emotions, consumers are more satisfied with the service encounter.[90]

Consumers who are dissatisfied with a purchase, consumption, or disposition decision may need to cope with the feelings of stress that dissatisfaction involves.[91] How they cope depends on whether they feel threatened or challenged by the stress and whether they think that they have the motivation, ability, and opportunity to deal with it. For example, a consumer might cope with a technological product failure by reading the instruction manual (active coping), by calling a friend who knows that technology (instrumental support seeking), or by denying that the failure has occurred (see Exhibit 10.8).

Exhibit 10.8

Coping with Dissatisfaction Due to Consumption Problems

Consumers may cope with dissatisfaction through active coping, expressive support seeking, or avoidance.

Active Coping	**Expressive Support Seeking**	**Avoidance**
ACTION COPING • I concentrate on ways the problem could be solved • I try to make a plan of action RATIONAL THINKING • I analyze the problem before reacting • I try to control my emotions POSITIVE THINKING • I try to look on the bright side of things	EMOTIONAL VENTING • I take time to express my emotions • I delve into my feelings to understand them INSTRUMENTAL SUPPORT • I ask friends with similar experience what they did • I try to get advice from someone about what to do EMOTIONAL SUPPORT • I seek out others for comfort • I rely on others to make me feel better	AVOIDANCE • I avoid thinking about it • I try to take my mind off of it by doing other things DENIAL • I deny that the event has happened • I refuse to believe that the problem has occurred

Source: Adapted from Adam Duhachek, "Coping: A Multidimensional, Hierarchical Framework of Responses to Stressful Consumption Episodes," *Journal of Consumer Research*, 32, June 2005, pp. 41–53.

Consumers' satisfaction evaluations also tend to be tied to specific consumption situations—we may be satisfied (or not) with the offering as we are using it at the current time. Even if we are satisfied now, however, we may not be satisfied the next time we use it.[92] Thus, satisfaction differs from an attitude, which is relatively enduring and less dependent on the specific situation.[93] In addition, research shows that feelings tend to have more influence on satisfaction judgments early on, but this influence decreases over time. Conversely, thoughts have more influence on satisfaction judgments as time goes on.[94] Note that a post-decision evaluation can differ from a pre-decision evaluation in that after using the product, a consumer may judge different attributes and cutoff levels than he or she did before.[95] For example, after trying frozen microwave pizza, you might decide that you like the taste less than you thought you would.

Mispredictions About Emotions

While post-decision feelings can affect satisfaction judgments, so too can the difference between how we thought the product would make us feel and how it actually makes us feel, a phenomenon known as affective forecasting (see Chapter 8). In other words, we tend to be more dissatisfied not only when a product fails to perform as we thought it would but also when a product makes us feel worse than we forecast that it would. This phenomenon may be a fairly common occurrence because people tend to be poor predictors of how decisions, experiences, and outcomes will make them feel.[96] Thus, even when we eagerly anticipate enjoying a new product before the purchase, our satisfaction with its performance can fade as we grow accustomed to the performance over time.[97] Affective forecasting applies to services as well as tangible products. When we predict the outcome of uncertain events (such as who will be voted off a reality TV program), we enjoy those events less than people who make no predictions. Why? Because we are wary of anticipated regret.[98]

Marketing Implications

Marketers should make sure that customers' feelings about trying, buying, and using their offerings are as positive as possible. Some marketers use promotions to increase consumers' positive feelings. For example, Capital One, which markets banking and credit card services, has promoted its brand through integration with popular Facebook games such as *FarmVille*, aiming to enhance positive feelings among the more than 100 million players.[99]

Businesses and nonprofits can build relationships with consumers and contributors by encouraging their involvement and identification with the organization through communications and other activities.[100] Harley-Davidson, for example, works hard to get and keep its customers emotionally involved with the brand. Customers receive invitations to owners-only special events and acquire a sense of community through extensive marketing contacts, both online and offline. Combined with a quality product and top performance, these marketing activities have helped Harley-Davidson win high customer satisfaction and long-term loyalty.

Finally, knowing that dissatisfied consumers may feel stress, companies can aid in the coping process by providing a feedback mechanism and expert advice. For example, the well-trained Genius Bar experts in Apple stores stand ready to listen to customer complaints or inquiries and to offer knowledgeable ideas and solutions (see Exhibit 10.9).[101]

Exhibit 10.9

Decreasing Customer Dissatisfaction

Some companies help elevate consumer's dissatisfaction after purchase by providing mechanisms for feedback or technical support, like the Apple Genius bar.

© Presselect/Alamy

RESPONSES TO DISSATISFACTION

Marketers must understand the nature of consumers' responses to dissatisfaction because a variety of mostly negative consequences can result. Specifically, dissatisfied consumers can decide to (1) take no action, (2) discontinue purchasing the product or service, (3) complain to the company or to a third party and perhaps return the item, or (4) engage in negative word-of-mouth communication.[102] The last two behaviors are of special interest to consumer researchers.

Complaints

Surprisingly, the majority of dissatisfied consumers do not complain.[103] Nevertheless, even a few consumer complaints can indicate marketing-related problems that need attention. When consumers complain, they can voice their dissatisfaction to a manufacturer, the retailer, regulatory agencies, the media, or to peers through websites such as yelp.com and social media sites. Customers can also use apps such as Gripe to broadcast complaints on Facebook and Twitter simultaneously via cell phone.[104] Sometimes consumers seek formal redress through legal means or from governmental agencies. Thus, marketers need to focus on when complaints are likely to occur and which consumers tend to complain.

Complaining is more likely when motivation, ability, and opportunity are high. It is also more likely as the level of dissatisfaction or the severity of the problem increases.[105] In equity theory terms, the unfairness of the exchange is higher, and the consumer is more motivated to act.[106] However, the severity of the dissatisfaction alone does not explain complaining behavior. In particular, consumers are less likely to act if they perceive that complaining will take a lot of time and effort, that their chances of benefiting from doing so are low, or that the offering is insignificant.[107]

The more the blame or attribution for dissatisfaction is placed on someone else, particularly on the company or on society in general, the greater the motivation and likelihood of complaining.[108] Thus, consumers are more likely to complain when they feel removed from the problem—that is, when the perceived cause is permanent, marketer related, and volitional.[109] If dissatisfaction is so strong that complainers want "revenge" against the company, they will even resort to a suboptimal alternative, such as switching to a more costly competing product.[110]

You might expect that consumers who are aggressive and self-confident would be more likely to complain than those who are not[111] or that consumers with more experience or knowledgeability about how to complain might be more likely to do so than their less savvy counterparts. Neither idea has been strongly supported by evidence, although findings suggest experience may influence the likelihood of consumer complaints. Consumers are more likely to complain when they have the time and formal channels of communication to do so.

Research suggests that there are four types of complainers.[112] *Passives* are the least likely to complain. *Voicers* are likely to complain directly to the retailer or service provider. *Irates* are angry consumers who are most likely to engage in negative word of mouth, stop buyingpatronage, and complain to the provider but not to a third party such as the media or government. *Activists* engage heavily in all types of complaining, including to a third party. Activists can now reach thousands of people by posting negative comments on blogs, on websites, or in social media such as Twitter.[113]

Although there is no one best way to handle complaints, customer characteristics can provide insights to guide marketers in developing the most appropriate response.[114] In particular, companies should pay close attention to four customer characteristics when preparing complaint-resolution policies and practices:

▶ *Customer's perceptions of the problem.* How severe does the problem seem to be? Is the company seen as being responsible for the problem? How important is the product to the customer?

▶ *Customer-company relationship.* How often does the customer buy from the company? How long has the customer been buying from the company?

▶ *Customer psychographics.* Does the customer have a propensity to complain? Consumers are more likely to complain when they are experts or are self-confident and aggressive. How much appreciation of quality does the customer exhibit?

▶ *Personal characteristics.* What is the age of the customer? What is the gender of the customer?

In general, consumers are more concerned with the fairness of a company's resolution to a complaint—the redress—than with the fairness of the procedure for handling complaints or the fairness of the interactions with the company's representatives.[115] Companies that respond quickly and offer solutions that complainers view as fair (such as a refund) are more likely to earn positive word of mouth and win repeat business.

Marketing Implications

Although a large percentage of consumers do not complain, it is still in the marketer's best interests to be responsive when any consumers do. Speedy response is important: 57 percent of the consumers in one survey said that how quickly a website responds to e-mail influences their decision to buy from that site in the future.[116] Clearly, consumers will be more satisfied and more likely to buy again if they get a speedy response, especially if it involves getting money back or a fair exchange/refund policy. Airtel, a telecommunications firm in India, recognizes the importance of responding quickly and heading off negative word of mouth—especially among users of social media or websites. "Online, these situations are fraught with risk," says an airtel manager. "Unlike call centers, conversation online is one-to-many and a bad response to one can spread like wildfire."[117]

At the same time, dissatisfied consumers who have been treated fairly can become even more loyal in the future, leading to positive word of mouth. Nissan, for instance, moves very quickly to answer complaints that appear on Facebook and other places online. In the interest of transparency, the automaker never takes down negative comments from its Facebook page, which has 260,000 fans. Nor does it request that customers post compliments after Nissan has fixed the problem. "But when they decide on their own to do that, that's a great message for those 260,000 [Facebook] fans to see," a Nissan marketer observes.[118]

However, if consumers experience more than one problem with a company, their satisfaction and repurchase intent will drop, even if the problems are quickly resolved. In fact, they will rate the second problem as even more severe than the first and are more likely to see a pattern in which the company is to blame.[119] Thus, not only do companies need an efficient and responsive mechanism for handling problems; they also must make changes to avoid similar lapses in the future. For instance, when the Massachusetts-based supermarket chain Big Y studied the slow progress of customers through its self-checkout lanes, it learned that delays were caused by issues such as customer confusion over what to do with coupons. Finding that its customers were more satisfied with full-service checkouts, Big Y removed its self-checkouts.[120]

Positive disconfirmation of warranty and service expectations—a better-than-expected response—can result in satisfaction with the complaint resolution.[121] Also note that sometimes a company may want to encourage complaints because dissatisfied consumers who do not complain are more likely to stop buying.[122] But when companies are too responsive to complaints—that is, too eager to please—customers may be more likely to complain, even when a complaint is not justified, because they perceive a greater likelihood of compensation.[123] Still, by encouraging complaints when they are justified and by actively managing customer problems, the company can retain valued consumers. _____

Responding to Service Recovery

If customers are dissatisfied, marketers need to find ways of making up for this dissatisfaction to win back the customers' business. How consumers will respond to service recovery efforts will depend on their expectations.[124] When consumers expect to maintain a good relationship despite a mishap, the business should sincerely apologize and promise to prevent such mishaps in the future. When consumers expect to respond aggressively and to control the situation, the business should take their complaints seriously, give them choices, and help them feel in control. When consumers expect a rational response based on costs and benefits, the business should offer a discount or some other benefit to restore some level of satisfaction.

Marketing Implications

Research indicates that consumers prefer service recovery efforts that correspond to the type of failure experienced.[125] In the case of inattentive service, for instance, restoring good service and quickly apologizing can reduce dissatisfaction and help restore satisfaction. When dissatisfied consumers perceive that the cause of the service problem is permanent, marketer related, and under the firm's control when in fact it is not, marketers need to correct these misperceptions. Providing consumers with logical explanations for service failure, especially if it was not the company's fault, or providing some form of compensation such as a gift or refund can often reduce consumers' feelings of dissatisfaction.[126] _____

Responding by Negative Word of Mouth

When consumers are unhappy with a product or service, they are often motivated to tell others in order to relieve their frustration and to convince others not to purchase the product or to do business with the company. **Negative word-of-mouth communication** is more likely to occur when the problem is severe, when consumers are unhappy with the company's responsiveness, and when consumers perceive that the company is at fault.[127] Negative word of mouth can be troublesome because it tends to be highly persuasive and very vivid (and therefore easily remembered) and because consumers place great emphasis on it when making decisions.[128] It also may influence other consumers to stop (or never begin) doing business with the company.

Negative word of mouth can go global very quickly as consumers air gripes on blogs, social media sites, and specialized websites such as yelp.com—even in cases where the information may be unfair, nasty, or inappropriate.[129] In one study, 59 percent of the consumers surveyed said they regularly use social media to air complaints about negative experiences with products or businesses. The same study found that 74 percent of participants were influenced in their buying decisions by the comments they found about companies in social media and other online sources.[130] Understanding the power of negative comments in social media, Dell—among a growing number of companies—actively monitors social media, analyzes the comments it finds, and responds quickly when issues arise.[131]

Negative word-of-mouth communication The act of consumers saying negative things about a product or service to other consumers.

Marketing Implications

Marketers need to be responsive to negative word of mouth, make an effort to identify the reason for or source of the difficulty, and take steps to rectify or eliminate the problem with restitution or communications. Consider what happened when JCPenney began promoting a girls' T-shirt bearing the slogan "I'm too pretty to do my homework so my brother has to do it for me." Controversy quickly spread across social media as consumers complained that the shirt was sexist. Within 24 hours, JCPenney withdrew the shirt and issued this public apology: "We agree that the 'Too Pretty' T-shirt does not deliver an appropriate message, and we have immediately discontinued its sale. We would like to apologize to our customers." Because the retailer moved quickly to rectify the situation and made a sincere apology, it showed that its customers' concerns are taken seriously.[132] _____

IS CUSTOMER SATISFACTION ENOUGH?

Although customer satisfaction should be an extremely important goal for any firm, some have questioned whether satisfaction alone is enough to keep customers loyal. As evidence, they point out that 65 to 85 percent of customers who defect to competitors' brands say that they had been either satisfied or very satisfied with the product or service they left.[133] When consumers are not strongly satisfied, they are more prone to defect.[134] Other studies have found a low correlation between satisfaction and repurchase.[135] Thus, customers may need to be "extremely satisfied" or need a stronger reason to stay with a brand or company.[136] Moreover, loyalty depends on whether the product is competitively superior, consumers find its superiority desirable, and the product can be part of a social network that the company is able to maintain.[137]

Customer retention The practice of keeping customers by building long-term relationships.

A key goal for any marketer should therefore be **customer retention**, the practice of working to satisfy customers with the intention of developing long-term relationships with them. A customer-retention strategy attempts to build customer commitment and loyalty by continually paying close attention to all aspects of customer interaction, especially after-sales service. Customer loyalty programs can, over the long term, strengthen relationships with customers and increase purchasing.[138] Specifically, profits can be increased through repeat sales, reduced costs, and referrals.[139] Customer relationship management systems can help companies learn more about their customers, information that, in turn, helps marketers better serve, satisfy, and retain customers.[140]

Marketing Implications

Given the cost of acquiring new customers and the potential profit in repeat purchasing, companies should take steps such as the following to retain their customers:[141]

▶ *Care about customers.* Two-thirds of consumers defect because they believe that the company does not care about them. Thus, demonstrating a little caring can go a long way. For instance, Cole Hardware, a family-owned retail chain in San Francisco, offers a lot of service extras. Seniors who need a lift to the store can call for a ride. The store will lend customers a digital camera to photograph a project for which they need help in selecting tools or materials. Cole offers discounts to students, seniors, and other special groups. And, showing it cares for the planet, the retailer serves as a recycling center for electronics and other items.[142]

▶ *Remember customers between sales.* Companies can contact consumers to make sure that they are not having any problems with the offering or to acknowledge special occasions such as birthdays. Marketers that do most or all of their business online often communicate between transactions through e-mail newsletters and requests for feedback about purchased products and services. Crutchfield, for example, a $250 million catalog and Web retailer of electronics products, does all this and more for its customers. It also alerts customers to its ever-expanding list of online videos that show how to choose, install, and use many of the items sold by the company. And customers are invited to e-mail their comments to owner Bill Crutchfield directly from the home page.[143]

▶ *Build trusting relationships.* Provide consumers with expertise and high-quality offerings that meet their needs, now and into the future. For example, USAA Federal Savings Bank trains its employees to discuss customers' needs more broadly and suggest meaningful long-term alternatives. Even if a particular product is under consideration, employees may recommend that a customer "not buy that product, if that is the right thing to do for the member in that situation," notes a senior USAA manager. This is one reason for USAA's 98 percent customer retention rate.[144]

▶ *Monitor the service-delivery process.* Companies should monitor customer service and make every effort to respond quickly and with care when an offering requires service or repairs. Many service firms use *mystery shoppers*, consumers or researchers who pose as customers to test the quality of service at each location. For instance, Santander Bank regularly uses mystery shoppers to check on customer service in its U.K. branches. Brown Bear Car Wash in Seattle also uses mystery shoppers to monitor service at its 40 locations.[145]

▶ *Provide extra effort.* Companies that put special effort into satisfying customers are more likely to build lasting relationships than companies that do the minimum. Ocado, for example, an online grocery shopping service operating in the United Kingdom, adds extra convenience by allowing customers to choose a one-hour window for their purchases to be delivered. "It would be cheaper for us to offer a two-hour slot, but it's better for the customer that we can offer them one," an Ocado executive explains. Ocado also empowers its drivers to resolve customer complaints on the spot, another plus that helps keep its time-strapped customers loyal despite increasing competition.[146] _____

DISPOSITION

Exhibit 10.10

Disposition Options
Disposition often means throwing things away; however, there are many additional ways of disposing of an offering (e.g., give away, trade, recycle). In addition, disposition can involve one person (personal focus), two or more people (interpersonal focus), or society in general (societal focus).

At the most basic level, *disposition* is the throwing away of meaningless or used-up items without giving the action much thought, yet research shows that disposition is actually a much richer and more detailed process.[147] We tend to think of possessions as physical things, but they can be defined much more broadly as anything that reflects an extension of the self, including one's body and body parts, other persons, pets, places, services, time periods, and events. For example, you could end a relationship, give a friend an idea, donate an organ, abandon an unhealthy lifestyle, use up all your leisure time, or discontinue your cable TV service. Thus, the study of disposition relates to all of these types of possessions.

Many options are available when a consumer decides that a possession is no longer of immediate use, as outlined in Exhibit 10.10.[148] Note that disposition can be *temporary* (loaning or renting the item) or *involuntary* (losing or destroying the item).[149] Here we will focus on permanent, voluntary disposition.

Consumers often have logical and reasonable motives behind their disposition actions.[150] For example, people sell things to earn an economic return and come out ahead. In contrast, they may

A TAXONOMY OF VOLUNTARY DISPOSITION

Methods	Personal Focus	Interpersonal Focus	Societal Focus
Give away: usually to someone who can use it.	Necessarily requires another person as receiver.	Donate body organs; give clothes to the needy; give a baby up for adoption; give an idea to a friend.	Give land to new settlers; give surplus food to the poor; give military advice to an ally.
Trade or exchange it for something else.	Skin grafts; trade sleep time for work time; trade work time for shopping for bargains.	Trade a car; trade stock; barter; exchange ideas with a colleague; switch boyfriends/girlfriends. Swap meets.	Trade tanks for oil; exchange effluent water for a golf course.
Recycle: convert it to something else.	Convert barn beams to paneling; make a quilt of scraps; eat turkey sandwiches after Thanksgiving.	Recycle newspapers; recycle aluminum cans; manufacturers' recycling of defective parts.	Recycle waste water; convert a slum to a model neighborhood; recycle war ruins as national monuments.
Sell: convert it to money.	Necessarily requires another person as buyer; prostitution; sell one's artwork; sell ideas.	Businesses; sell blood; sell ideals to attain political goals.	Sell wheat; sell weapons; sell land.
Use up: consumption is equivalent to disposal.	Eat food; drive car using up the fuel; shoot ammo; spend one's time; burn wood.	Use employee's time and energy; use someone else's money; use the neighbor's gas.	Use natural fuels or electricity; use a nation's productive capacity; use people as soldiers in wars.
Throw away: discard in a socially acceptable manner.	Put things in the trash; flush the toilet; use a garbage disposal; discard an idea.	Neighborhood cleanup; divorce; end a relationship; resign or retire from a job.	Dump garbage in the oceans; bury nuclear waste.
Abandon: discard in a socially unacceptable manner.	Abandon car on the roadside; abandon morals; abandon an unhealthy, unhappy lifestyle.	Abandon one's child or family; abandon a pet on someone's doorstep; abandon another's trust.	Abandon Vietnam; abandon the Shah of Iran; abandon old satellites in space; abandon the poor.
Destroy: physically damage with intent.	Tear up personal mail; commit suicide; burn house down; shred old pictures.	Raze a building; murder; euthanasia; cremation; abort a child; commit arson.	Conduct war; genocide; execute prisoners; carry out a revolution; burn a flag.

Source: Melissa Martin Young and Melanie Wallendorf, "Ashes to Ashes, Dust to Dust: Conceptualizing Consumer Disposition of Possessions," in *Proceedings, Marketing Educators' Conference* (Chicago: American Marketing Association, 1989), pp. 33–39. Reprinted by permission.

choose to donate something without getting a tax deduction, or they may pass an item along out of a desire to help someone as well as a desire not to let the product go to waste. Situational and product-related factors can also affect disposition options.[151] For example, when consumers have limited time or storage space, they may be more likely to dispose of a possession by throwing it away, giving it away, or abandoning it. Consumers disposing of a possession of high value are likely to sell it or to give it to someone special rather than to throw it away. In general, the frequency of different disposition behaviors varies by product category.

Research has examined how consumers dispose of unwanted gifts.[152] They can be laterally recycled (swapped, sold, or passed on to someone else), destroyed, or returned. Destruction is a way of getting revenge against the giver but is usually more of a fantasy than a real action. Retailers need to be aware that returning a gift to a store can be a negative emotional experience for consumers. Disposition can involve more than one individual, as when consumers give old clothes to someone, sell a car, or participate in a neighborhood cleanup, or it can consist of activities of a collective or societal nature, such as recycling waste water.[153]

Disposing of Meaningful Objects

Although disposition often means simply getting rid of unwanted, meaningless, or used-up possessions, the process is more involved for certain significant items. Possessions can sometimes be important reflections of the self that are infused with significant symbolic meaning.[154] They define who we are, and they catalog our personal history.[155] In these situations, disposition involves two processes: physical detachment and emotional detachment.

Physical detachment Physically disposing of an item.

Emotional detachment Emotionally disposing of a possession.

We most often think of disposition in terms of **physical detachment**, the process by which the item is physically transferred to another person or location. However, **emotional detachment** is a more detailed, lengthy, and sometimes painful process. Often, consumers remain emotionally attached to possessions long after they have become physically detached. For example, it may take a person years to come to grips with selling a valued house or car. Giving up a baby or pet for adoption is an example of difficult emotional detachment that sometimes results in grief and mourning. In fact, some pack rats have a difficult time disposing of even minimally valued possessions—as evidenced by overflowing basements, closets, and garages. Even when an item can be traded in for a discount on a new replacement, emotional attachment enhances the value consumers perceive in the old item, complicating the disposition and purchase decision.[156] Research based on mental accounting shows that consumers who trade a product in place more weight on receiving a favorable trade-in value than on paying the lowest price for the new item.[157]

The disposition process can be particularly important during periods of role transition, such as puberty, graduation, and marriage.[158] In these instances, consumers dispose of possessions that are symbols of old roles. Upon getting married, for example, many people dispose of items that signify old relationships, such as pictures, jewelry, and gifts. The disposition of shared possessions is a critical process during divorce. Two types of such disposition have been identified: *disposition to break free*, in which the goal is to free oneself from the former relationship, and *disposition to hold on*, in which the intent is to cling to possessions with the hope that the relationship can be repaired.[159] Consumers also specify how their possessions will be distributed upon their death. This can include giving away valued items to important family members, other individuals, and organizations such as charities and schools as well as distributing monetary wealth through a will.

Marketing Implications

Marketers need to understand disposition for several reasons. First, disposition decisions often influence later acquisition decisions. Thus, someone who must buy a new refrigerator because the old one stopped working may decide that the old one did not last long enough and may eliminate this brand from future consideration. By understanding why consumers dispose of older brands, particularly when a problem has occurred, marketers may be able to improve their offerings for the future.

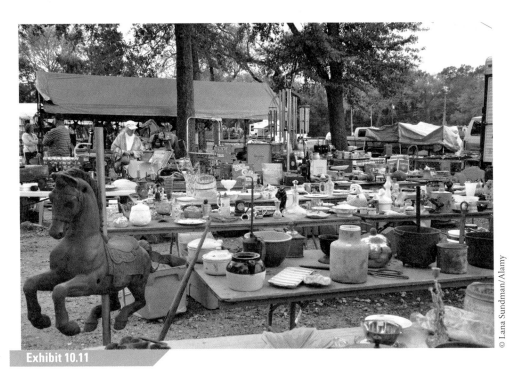

© Lana Sundman/Alamy

Exhibit 10.11

The Disposition Process

Consumers can dispose of unwanted items in a variety of ways, such as through online auctions, yard sales, or flea markets.

Second, marketers have become interested in the way that consumers trade, sell, or give away items for secondhand purchases through used-merchandise retail outlets and websites, flea markets, garage sales, and classified ads in newspapers and online (see Exhibit 10.11). Flea markets are popular, not only because they are a different way of disposing of and acquiring products but also because of the hedonistic experience they provide.[160] Consumers enjoy searching and bargaining for items, the festive atmosphere—almost like a medieval fair—and the social opportunities. This enjoyment is also true of consumers who use sites such as eBay and craigslist to search for and buy goods. In fact, eBay provides apps for cell phones and tablet computers so consumers can search and buy at any time, from anywhere.[161]

Third, product disposition behaviors can sometimes have a major impact on society in general. For example, if product life can be extended by getting consumers to trade or resell items, waste and resource depletion could be reduced. Fourth, by examining broad disposition patterns, marketers can gain important insights. For example, one study examined household garbage to identify group differences in food consumption.[162] Researchers found that the region of the country accounted most strongly for differences in consumption patterns, followed by cultural status. For example, lobster is especially popular in New England—so much so that McDonald's outlets in Maine sell lobster rolls in season. ————————————————————

Recycling

Because of concerns about conserving natural resources, studying disposition behaviors can provide valuable insights for the development of recycling programs (see Exhibit 10.12). In light of this fact, a number of researchers have been interested in examining factors that relate to recycling.[163] For instance, studies show that attitudes toward recycling influence waste recycling and recycling shopping behaviors.[164] More consumers are participating in recycling than ever before, in part because they are more informed about the issues and in part because behaving in an eco-friendly way gives them a good feeling.[165] The most useful variables in understanding consumer recycling are motivation, ability, and opportunity to recycle.

Motivation to Recycle

Consumers are more likely to recycle when they perceive that the benefits outweigh the costs, including money, time, and effort.[166] Immediate benefits or goals include avoiding filling up landfills, reducing waste, reusing materials, and saving the environment. Higher-order goals are to promote health and avoid sickness, achieve life-sustaining ends, and provide for future generations.[167] These benefits are likely to vary across segments. For example, focusing on environmental effects may have little meaning in neighborhoods where violence is a major problem.[168] Also, consumers who perceive that their efforts will have an impact are more motivated to recycle than consumers who do not.[169] Having a clean, convenient place to bring recyclable materials improves consumer motivation as well.

Exhibit 10.12

What Do U.S. Consumers Recycle?
Car batteries are by far the most recycled products in the United States.

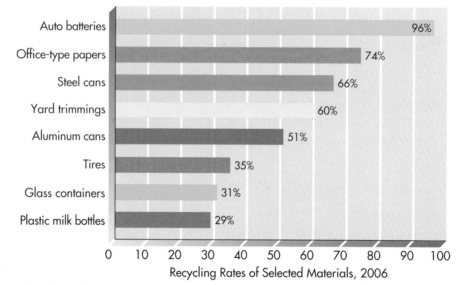

Recycling Rates of Selected Materials, 2006

- Auto batteries: 96%
- Office-type papers: 74%
- Steel cans: 66%
- Yard trimmings: 60%
- Aluminum cans: 51%
- Tires: 35%
- Glass containers: 31%
- Plastic milk bottles: 29%

Source: Data from U.S. Environmental Protection Agency, www.epa.gov.

Ability to Recycle

Consumers who know how to recycle are more likely to do so than those who do not.[170] One study of German consumers found that a lack of knowledge led to incorrect disposal and therefore less recycling.[171] Consumers must also possess general knowledge about the positive environmental effects of recycling and must remember to recycle as part of their daily routine.

Opportunity to Recycle

If separating, storing, and removing recyclable materials is difficult or inconvenient, consumers will usually avoid doing so. A program in Germany that offered color-coded, large plastic containers on wheels for recyclable materials was quite successful. In addition, consumers must break old waste disposal habits and develop new recycling behaviors. Providing easy-to-use containers also helps consumers in this regard (see Exhibit 10.13). Also, consumers who buy products such as soft drinks for consumption on the go have fewer opportunities to recycle the empty bottles and cans.[172]

Exhibit 10.13

Recycling
Providing color-coded recycling containers makes consumers more willing to recycle since it is easy and convenient.

Marketing Implications

Marketers can facilitate recycling by increasing consumers' MAO to recycle. Special incentives such as contests can increase motivation. Communications that focus on the negative consequences of not recycling and that are conveyed in person are especially effective in increasing motivation.[173] The only drawback is that these techniques must be reintroduced periodically because their effects are usually temporary.

Marketers can increase consumers' ability to recycle by teaching them how to recycle through personally relevant and easy-to-remember communications from community leaders, flyers, or public service announcements in traditional and social media. Also, offering tags to place on the refrigerator door can remind consumers to recycle.[174] Offering easily recycled products is another way to increase the opportunity to recycle.

Providing separate containers so that recyclable items can easily be put out and collected along with the trash can increase the opportunity to recycle. Portland, Oregon, for example, is one of a growing number of U.S. cities putting bottle, can, and paper recycling containers in public areas. Retailers often set up recycling centers for bottles and cans purchased at their stores, as well as for unwanted plastic bags. For instance, the U.K. grocery chain Tesco offers frequent-buyer points and cash to encourage recycling of small electronics and TVs at its recycling centers. Colleges and universities are also helping to motivate recycling behavior by providing convenient bins for used batteries and other recyclable items.

Finally, making products and packaging as environmentally friendly as possible—and promoting the benefits of doing so—can help marketers attract consumers who like the convenience of *not* having to recycle. Heinz, PepsiCo, and other companies are using bottles that decompose more quickly than traditional plastic containers, another step toward using packaging that need not be recycled.[175] Trash can also be the raw material of new products. TerraCycle, for example, specializes in creating and marketing purses from used juice pouches, among other products. "Waste does not exist," reads one slogan in the company's offices.[176]

SUMMARY

Consumers sometimes develop post-decision dissonance—a feeling of anxiety or uncertainty regarding a purchasing decision after it has been made. On occasion, they may feel regret when they perceive an unfavorable comparison between the performance of the chosen option and the performance of the unchosen options. These feelings of regret can directly influence the consumer's intention to buy the same product in the future. Consumers can learn from experience through hypothesis testing, in which they try to confirm or disprove expectations by actually engaging in acquisition, consumption, or disposition of a product. This process is influenced by motivation, prior knowledge (familiarity), ambiguity of information, and two types of biases: the confirmation bias and overconfidence.

Satisfaction is both a subjective feeling and an objective evaluation that a decision has fulfilled a need or goal. Dissatisfaction occurs when consumers have negative feelings and believe that their goals or needs have not been fulfilled. Thought-based judgments of satisfaction/dissatisfaction can relate to (1) whether consumers' thoughts and expectations about the offering are confirmed or disconfirmed by its performance (the disconfirmation paradigm), (2) thoughts about causality and blame (attribution theory), and (3) thoughts about fairness and equity (equity theory). Consumers also judge satisfaction and dissatisfaction on the basis of feelings, specifically (1) experienced emotions (and coping with these emotions) and (2) mispredictions about emotions.

Consumers can respond to dissatisfaction by complaining, reacting to service recovery, and engaging in negative word of mouth. Finally, consumers can dispose of products in various ways, actions that have important implications for marketing strategy and for an understanding of consumer behavior. Recycling, one form of disposition, depends on consumers' motivation, ability, and opportunity to act.

Questions for Review and Discussion

1. How does post-decision dissonance differ from post-decision regret, and what effect do these have on consumers?

2. Describe how consumers acquire information about goods and services by learning from their experiences with the commodities.

3. How do expectations and performance contribute to disconfirmation?

4. Define *attribution theory* and *equity theory*, and explain how they relate to dissatisfaction.

5. What is the role of feelings in influencing satisfaction and dissatisfaction?

6. Why is complaining important to marketers, and how should complaints be handled?

7. What influence can experienced emotions and mispredictions about emotions have on consumer satisfaction or dissatisfaction?

8. In what eight ways can consumers dispose of something?

9. Why is it important for marketers to consider both physical and emotional detachment aspects of consumer disposition?

CONSUMER BEHAVIOR CASE

What to Do with Old Cell Phones?

Every year, millions of consumers answer the call to upgrade their cell phones—and that means deciding what to do with the used cell phone being replaced. Some people reuse their cell phones by giving them to another family member or saving them in case the new phone happens to break. Others simply toss their old cell phones into the trash, even though such electronics have materials that shouldn't be in landfills. What else can consumers do with their old phones?

One option is to trade it in. Retailers such as Target, Costco, RadioShack, and Amazon.com have trade-in programs that give consumers store credit for used cell phones in decent shape. Another option is to sell the old phone. Sometimes the sale is to an individual, handled privately or via sites such as ebay.com. More often, consumers prefer the convenience of selling to a business that refurbishes and resells electronic goods (or recycles them responsibly if they have no resale value).

Michigan-based ReCellular is among the market leaders in this industry, with $100 million in annual revenue. Consumers click to the company's website, look up the phone's make and model, indicate the condition of the phone, and see how much ReCellular will pay for it. To complete the transaction, they download a prepaid shipping label and send the phone to ReCellular, which confirms the condition and then mails payment. The company deletes any personal data, makes any needed repairs, replaces worn or missing parts, tests the phones to ensure they're in good working order, and then sells them to consumers in domestic and international markets.

Businesses like ReCellular are thriving as the world emerges from recession and consumers seek to cash in on unused goods. Today's cell phones are more sophisticated than the phones of just a few years ago, which means they're worth more when sold. Even basic models can fetch some money because there is always some level of demand for low-priced, no-frills used phones. ReCellular handles more than five million old phones every year, selling more than half of its refurbished units to U.S. consumers and the remainder to distributors in developing countries.

There are also other disposition possibilities for old phones. A growing number of nonprofit organizations are appealing for used cell phones they can sell to raise money for worthy causes. For example, Hope Phones and several other groups recently banded together to collect 20,000 used cell phones, with the goal of buying prenatal medical equipment to use in Nepal and the Democratic Republic of Congo. "If you can help save a woman and give her a chance to have a healthy baby by simply donating a phone," says a manager at the United Nations Foundation, which is involved in the effort, "that's a powerful opportunity for you to engage and connect with someone else."

As another example, Cell Phones for Soldiers, founded in 2004, asks consumers to donate used cell phones as a fundraiser for buying phone cards for U.S. military members stationed far from home. The 2,000 U.S. AT&T stores are among the many collection points, and AT&T provides free downloadable shipping labels for consumers who can't get to a store to drop off phones in person. Every year, the charity raises enough money to send phone cards with a combined value of more than 10 million minutes of talk time so American men and women in uniform all around the world can call family and friends for free.

In the end, whether reused, resold, recycled, or donated, outdated cell phones have a value and a future somewhere in the world.[177]

CASE QUESTIONS

1. The quote from a U.N. foundation manager talks about donating a cell phone as a "powerful opportunity . . . to engage and connect with someone else." Does this quote refer to motivation, ability, or opportunity to recycle a cell phone by donating it? Explain your answer.

2. How do the concepts of physical and emotional detachment apply to the way consumers decide to dispose of their used cell phones?

3. Why would Amazon.com, which has no physical retailing presence, be as interested in encouraging cell phone trade-ins, same as RadioShack and Target?

4. Once consumers have sold their used phones to a company like ReCellular, how is learning likely to affect their beliefs about this disposition option?

ENDNOTES

1. Sarah E. Needleman, "Many Outlets, One Voice," *Wall Street Journal*, November 14, 2011, www.wsj.com; Randall Stross, "Consumer Complaints Made Easy. Maybe Too Easy," *New York Times*, May 28, 2011, www.nytimes.com; Mary Jane Credeur, "Delta Monitors Twitter to Remedy Customer Complaints," *Bloomberg Businessweek*, August 16, 2010, www.businessweek.com; Lauren Indvik, "Virgin Atlantic Launches Flight Status Bot on Twitter," *Mashable*, November 15, 2011, http://mashable.com; and T. E. Raja Simhan and M. Ramesh, "StanChart to Use Social Media Sites to Improve Customer Service," *The Hindu Business Line*, November 14, 2011, www.thehindubusinessline.com.

2. For a review, see William H. Cummings and M. Venkatesan, "Cognitive Dissonance and Consumer Behavior: A Review of the Evidence," *Journal of Marketing Research*, August 1976, pp. 303–308; also see Dieter Frey and Marita Rosch, "Information Seeking After Decisions: The Roles of Novelty of Information and Decision Reversibility," *Personality and Social Psychology Bulletin*, March 1984, pp. 91–98.

3. Michael Tsiros and Vikas Mittal, "Regret: A Model of Its Antecedents and Consequences in Consumer Decision Making," *Journal of Consumer Research* 26, March 2000, pp. 401–417.

4. Lisa J. Abendroth and Kristin Diehl, "Now or Never: Effects of Limited Purchase Opportunities on Patterns of Regret over Time," *Journal of Consumer Research* 33, no. 3, 2006, pp. 342–351.

5. Ran Kivetz and Anat Keinan, "Repenting Hyperopia: An Analysis of Self-Control Regrets," *Journal of Consumer Research* 33, no. 2, 2006, pp. 273–282.

6. J. Jeffrey Inman and Marcel Zeelenberg, "Regret in Repeat Purchase Versus Switching Decisions," *Journal of Consumer Research*, June 2002, pp. 116–128.

7. Rik Pieters and Marcel Zeelenberg, "A Theory of Regret Regulation 1.0," *Journal of Consumer Psychology* 17, no. 1, 2007, pp. 3–18; J. Jeffrey Inman, "Regret Regulation: Disentangling Self-Reproach from Learning," *Journal of Consumer Psychology* 17, no. 1, 2007, pp. 19–24; and Rik Pieters and Marcel Zeelenberg, "A Theory of Regret Regulation 1.1," *Journal of Consumer Psychology* 17, no. 1, 2007, pp. 29–35.

8. Neal J. Roese, Amy Summerville, and Florian Fessel, "Regret and Behavior: Comment on Zeelenberg and Pieters," *Journal of Consumer Psychology* 17, no. 1, 2007, pp. 25–28.

9. Stephen J. Hoch and John Deighton, "Managing What Consumers Learn from Experience," *Journal of Marketing*, April 1989, pp. 1–20.

10. Ziv Carmon, Klaus Wertenbroch, and Marcel Zeelenberg, "Option Attachment: When Deliberating Makes Choosing Feel Like Losing," *Journal of Consumer Research*, June 2003, pp. 15–29.

11. Allan Pavio, *Imagery and Verbal Processes* (New York: Holt, Rinehart, & Winston, 1981).

12. Eric M. Eisenstein and J. Wesley Hutchinson, "Action-Based Learning: Goals and Attention in the Acquisition of Market Knowledge," *Journal of Marketing Research*, May 2006, pp. 244–258.

13. Robert E. Smith and William R. Swinyard, "Information Response Models," *Journal of Marketing*, Winter 1982, pp. 81–93; and Deanna S. Kempf and Robert E. Smith, "Consumer Processing of Product Trial and the Influence of Prior Advertising," *Journal of Marketing Research*, August 1998, pp. 325–338.

14. Ida E. Berger and Andrew A. Mitchell, "The Effect of Advertising on Attitude Accessibility, Attitude Confidence, and the Attitude-Behavior Relationship," *Journal of Consumer Research*, December 1989, pp. 269–279; and Alice A. Wright and John G. Lynch Jr., "Communication Effects of Advertising vs. Direct Experience When Both Search and Experience Attributes Are Present," *Journal of Consumer Research*, March 1995, pp. 708–718.

15. Patricia M. West, "Predicting Preferences: An Examination of Agent Learning," *Journal of Consumer Research*, June 1996, pp. 68–80.

16. Jennifer Aaker, Susan Fournier, and S. Adam Brasel, "When Good Brands Do Bad," *Journal of Consumer Research*, June 2004, pp. 1–16.

17. Bob Tedeschi, "To Raise Shopper Satisfaction, Web Merchants Turn to Videos," *New York Times*, July 2, 2007, p. C4.

18. Merrie Brucks, "The Effects of Product Class Knowledge on Information Search Behavior," *Journal of Consumer Research*, June 1985, pp. 1–16.

19. Joseph W. Alba and J. Wesley Hutchinson, "Dimensions of Consumer Expertise," *Journal of Consumer Research*, March 1987, pp. 411–454.

20. Eric J. Johnson and J. Edward Russo, "Product Familiarity and Learning New Information," *Journal of Consumer Research*, June 1984, pp. 542–551.

21. Stephen J. Hoch and Young-Won Ha, "Consumer Learning: Advertising and the Ambiguity of Product Experience," *Journal of Consumer Research*, October 1986, pp. 221–233.

22. A. V. Muthukrishnan and Frank R. Kardes, "Persistent Preferences for Product Attributes," *Journal of Consumer Research*, June 2001, pp. 89–104.

23. Paul Herr, Steven J. Sherman, and Russell H. Fazio, "On the Consequences of Priming," *Journal of Experimental Social Psychology*, July 1983, pp. 323–340; and Hoch and Ha, "Consumer Learning: Advertising and the Ambiguity of Product Experience."

24. Reid Hastie, "Causes and Effects of Causal Attributions," *Journal of Personality and Social Psychology*, July 1984, pp. 44–56; and Thomas K. Srull, Meryl Lichtenstein, and Myron Rothbart, "Associative Storage and Retrieval Processes in Person Memory," *Journal of Experimental Psychology: General* 11, no. 6, 1985, pp. 316–435.

25. Durairaj Maheswaran, "Country of Origin as a Stereotype: Effects of Consumer Expertise and Attribute Strength on Product Evaluations," *Journal of Consumer Research*, September 1994, pp. 354–365.

26. John Deighton, "The Interaction of Advertising and Evidence," *Journal of Consumer Research*, December 1984, pp. 763–770; and Hoch and Ha, "Consumer Learning: Advertising and the Ambiguity of Product Experience."

27. Bernard Weiner, "Spontaneous Causal Thinking," *Psychological Bulletin*, January 1985, pp. 74–84.

28. Hoch and Deighton, "Managing What Consumers Learn from Experience."

29. "A Facebook Face-Off for Battle of the Buds," *Grocer*, July 9, 2011, p. 27.

30. Youjae Yi, "A Critical Review of Consumer Satisfaction," *Review of Marketing* (Chicago: American Marketing Association, 1992), pp. 68–123.

31. Richard L. Oliver, "Processing of the Satisfaction Response in Consumption," *Journal of Consumer Satisfaction, Dissatisfaction, and Complaining Behavior* 2, 1989, pp. 1–16; and Haim Mano and Richard L. Oliver, "Assessing the Dimensionality and Structure of the Consumption Experience," *Journal of Consumer Research*, December 1993, pp. 451–466.

32. Mano and Oliver, "Assessing the Dimensionality and Structure of the Consumption Experience."

33. J. Josko Brakus, Bernd H. Schmitt, and Lia Zarantonello, "Brand Experience: What Is It? How Is It Measured? Does It Affect Loyalty?" *Journal of Marketing*, May 2009, pp. 52–68.

34. Michael D. Johnson, Eugene W. Anderson, and Claes Fornell, "Rational and Adaptive Performance Expectations in a Customer Satisfaction Framework," *Journal of Consumer Research*, March 1995, pp. 695–707.

35. Marsha L. Richins and Peter H. Bloch, "Post-purchase Satisfaction: Incorporating the Effects of Involvement and Time," *Journal of Business Research*, September 1991, pp. 145–158; and Vikas Mittal and Wagner A. Kamakura, "Satisfaction, Repurchase Intent, and Repurchase Behavior," *Journal of Marketing Research*, February 2001, pp. 131–142.

36. Elaine Chan and Anirban Mukhopadhyay, "When Choosing Makes a Good Thing Better: Temporal Variations in the Valuation of Hedonic Consumption," *Journal of Marketing Research*, June 2010, pp. 497–507.

37. Christian Homburg, Nicole Koschate, and Wayne D. Hoyer, "Do Satisfied Customers Really Pay More? A Study of the Relationship Between Customer Satisfaction and Willingness to Pay," *Journal of Marketing*, April 2005, pp. 84–96.

38. David M. Szymanski and David H. Henard, "Customer Satisfaction: A Meta-Analysis of the Empirical Evidence," *Journal of the Academy of Marketing Science* 29, no. 1, 2001, pp. 16–35; and Anders Gustafsson, Michael D. Johnson, and Inger Roos, "The Effects of Customer Satisfaction, Relationship Commitment Dimensions, and Triggers on Customer Retention," *Journal of Marketing*, October 2005, pp. 210–218.

39. Todd A. Mooradian and James M. Oliver, "'I Can't Get No Satisfaction': The Impact of Personality and Emotion on Postpurchase Processes," *Psychology and Marketing* 14, no. 4, 1997, pp. 379–393; and Xueming Luo and Christian Homburg, "Neglected Outcomes of Customer Satisfaction," *Journal of Marketing*, April 2007, pp. 133–149.

40. Gustafsson et al., "The Effects of Customer Satisfaction, Relationship Commitment Dimensions, and Triggers on Customer Retention."

41. Kathleen Seiders, Glenn B. Voss, and Dhruv Grewal, "Do Satisfied Customers Buy More? Examining Moderating Influences in a Retailing Context," *Journal of Marketing*, October 2005, pp. 26–43.

42. Bruce Cooil, Timothy L. Keiningham, and Lerzan Aksoy, "A Longitudinal Analysis of Customer Satisfaction and Share of Wallet: Investigating the Moderating Effect of Customer Characteristics," *Journal of Marketing*, January 2007, pp. 67–83.

43. "The True Value of Customer Service," *Costco Connection*, August 2011, p. 11.

44. Xueming Luo, Christian Homburg, and Jan Wieseke, "Customer Satisfaction, Analyst Stock Recommendations, and Firm Value," *Journal of Marketing Research*, December 2010, pp. 1041–1058.

45. Forrest V. Morgeson III, Sunil Mithas, Timothy L. Keiningham, and Lerzan Aksoy, "An Investigation of the Cross-National Determinants of Customer Satisfaction," *Journal of the Academy of Marketing Science*, April 2011, pp. 198–215.

46. Douglas Bowman and Das Narayandas, "Managing Customer-Initiated Contacts with Manufacturers," *Journal of Marketing Research*, August 2001, pp. 281–297.

47. Terry Vavra, "Learning from Your Losses," *Brandweek*, vol. 33 no. 46, December 7, 1992.

48. Charlotte Klopp and John Sterlickhi, "Customer Satisfaction Just Catching on in Europe," *Marketing News*, May 28, 1990.

49. Richard L. Oliver, "A Cognitive Model of the Antecedents and Consequences of Satisfaction Decisions," *Journal of Marketing Research*, November 1980, pp. 460–469; and Yi, "A Critical Review of Consumer Satisfaction," p. 92; see also Douglas M. Stayman, Dana L. Alden, and Karen H. Smith, "Some Effects of Schematic Processing on Consumer Expectations and Disconfirmation Judgments," *Journal of Consumer Research*, September 1992, pp. 240–255.

50. Yi, "A Critical Review of Consumer Satisfaction;" and Stayman, Alden, and Smith, "Some Effects of Schematic Processing on Consumer Expectations and Disconfirmation Judgments."

51. Praveen K. Kopalle and Donald R. Lehman, "The Effects of Advertised and Observed Quality on Expectations About New Product Quality," *Journal of Marketing Research*, August 1995, pp. 280–291; Stephen A. LaTour and Nancy C. Peat, "The Role of Situationally-Produced Expectations, Others' Experiences, and Prior Experiences in Determining Satisfaction," in ed. Jerry C. Olson, *Advances in Consumer Research* (Ann Arbor, Mich.: Association for Consumer Research, 1980), pp. 588–592; and Ernest R. Cadotte, Robert B. Woodruff, and Roger L. Jenkins, "Expectations and Norms in Models of Consumer Satisfaction," *Journal of Marketing Research*, August 1987, pp. 305–314.

52. Ruth N. Bolton and James H. Drew, "A Multistage Model of Customers' Assessments of Service Quality and Value," *Journal of Consumer Research*, March 1991, pp. 375–384; and Michael D. Johnson, Eugene W. Anderson, and Claes Fornell, "Rational and Adaptive Performance Expectations in a Customer Satisfaction Framework," *Journal of Consumer Research*, March 1995, pp. 695–707.

53. Glenn B. Voss, A. Parasuraman, and Dhruv Grewal, "The Roles of Price, Performance, and Expectations in Determining Satisfaction in Service Exchanges," *Journal of Marketing*, October 1998, pp. 46–61; and A. Parasuraman, Valerie A. Zeithaml, and Leonard L. Berry, "SERVQUAL: A Multiple-Item Scale for Measuring Consumer Perceptions of Service Quality," *Journal of Retailing*, Spring 1988, pp. 12–36.

54. Lisa C. Wan, Michael K. Hui, and Robert S. Wyer Jr., "The Role of Relationship Norms in Responses to Service Failures," *Journal of Consumer Research,* August 2011, pp. 260–277.

55. Stephanie Dellande, Mary C. Gilly, and John L. Graham, "Gaining Compliance and Losing Weight," *Journal of Marketing*, July 2004, pp. 78–91.

56. Susan Fournier and David Glen Mick, "Rediscovering Satisfaction," *Journal of Marketing* 63, October 1999, pp. 5–23.

57. Simona Botti and Ann L. McGill, "When Choosing Is Not Deciding: The Effect of Perceived Responsibility on Satisfaction," *Journal of Consumer Research* 33, no. 2, 2006, pp. 211–219.

58. Ashwani Monga and Michael J. Houston, "Fading Optimism in Products: Temporal Changes in Expectations About Performance," *Journal of Marketing Research*, November 2006, pp. 654–663.

59. Kristin Diel and Cait Poynor, "Great Expectations?! Assortment Size, Expectations, and Satisfaction," *Journal of Marketing Research*, April 2010, pp. 312–322.

60. Chezy Ofir and Itamar Simonson, "In Search of Negative Customer Feedback," *Journal of Marketing Research* 38, May 2001, pp. 170–182.

61. Peter Darke, Laurence Ashworth, and Kelley Main, "Great Expectations and Broken Promises," *Journal of the Academy of Marketing Science*, Summer 2010, pp. 347–362.

62. Baba Shiv, Ziv Carmon, and Dan Ariely, "Placebo Effects of Marketing Actions," *Journal of Marketing Research*, November 2005, pp. 383–393.

63. Caglar Irmak, Lauren G. Block, and Gavan J. Fitzsimons, "The Placebo Effect in Marketing," *Journal of Marketing Research*, November 2005, pp. 406–409.

64. Lauren Block and Thomas Kramer, "The Effect of Superstitious Beliefs on Performance Expectations," *Journal of the Academy of Marketing Science* 37, 2009, pp. 161–169.

65. David K. Tse and Peter C. Wilson, "Models of Consumer Satisfaction Formation," *Journal of Marketing Research*, May 1988, pp. 204–212; Richard L. Oliver, "Cognitive, Affective, and Attribute Bases of the Satisfaction Response," *Journal of Consumer Research*, December 1993, pp. 418–430; and Richard L. Oliver and Wayne S. DeSarbo, "Response Determinants in Satisfaction Judgments," *Journal of Consumer Research*, March 1988, pp. 495–507.

66. Gilbert A. Churchill and Carol Supranant, "An Investigation into the Determinants of Customer Satisfaction," *Journal of Marketing Research*, November 1982, pp. 491–504; Richard L. Oliver and William O. Bearden, "The Role of Involvement in Satisfaction Processes," in eds. Richard P. Bagozzi and Alice M. Tybout, *Advances in Consumer Research*, vol. 10 (Ann Arbor, Mich.: Association for Consumer Research, 1983), pp. 250–255; and Paul G. Patterson, "Expectations and Product Performance as Determinants of Satisfaction for a High Involvement Purchase," *Psychology and Marketing*, September–October 1993, pp. 449–465.

67. Robert A. Westbrook and Michael D. Reilly, "Value-Percept Disparity," in eds. Richard P. Bagozzi and Alice M. Tybout, *Advances in Consumer Research*, vol. 10 (Ann Arbor, Mich.: Association for Consumer Research, 1983), pp. 256–261.

68. Richard W. Olshavsky and John A. Miller, "Consumer Expectations, Product Performance, and Perceived Product Quality," *Journal of Marketing Research*, February 1972, pp. 469–499.

69. Bonnie S. Benwick, "Shop Till You Learn Something New at the Market," *Washington Post*, June 7, 2011, www.washingtonpost.com.

70. Diane Halstead, Cornelia Droge, and M. Bixby Cooper, "Product Warranties and Post-purchase Service," *Journal of Services Marketing* 7, no. 1, 1993, pp. 33–40; and Joshua Lyle Wiener, "Are Warranties Accurate Signals of Product Reliability?" *Journal of Consumer Research*, September 1985, pp. 245–250.

71. Gina Pace, "Making Life Easier for His Customers," *Inc.*, May 9, 2011, www.inc.com.

72. Bernard Weiner, "Reflections and Reviews: Attributional Thoughts About Consumer Behavior," *Journal of Consumer Research* 27, December 2000, pp. 382–287; Valerie S. Folkes, "Consumer Reactions to Product Failure," *Journal of Consumer Research*, March 1984, pp. 398–409; Valerie S. Folkes, "Recent Attribution Research in Consumer Behavior," *Journal of Consumer Research*, March 1988, pp. 548–565; and Richard W. Mizerski, Linda L. Golden, and Jerome B. Kernan, "The Attribution Process in Consumer Decision Making," *Journal of Consumer Research*, September 1979, pp. 123–140.

73. Mary Jo Bitner, "Evaluating Service Encounters," *Journal of Marketing*, April 1990, pp. 69–82.

74. Valerie S. Folkes, Susan Koletsky, and John L. Graham, "A Field Study of Causal Inferences and Consumer Reaction," *Journal of Consumer Research*, March 1987, pp. 534–539.

75. Neeli Bendapudi and Robert P. Leone, "Psychological Implications of Customer Participation in Co-Production," *Journal of Marketing*, January 2003, pp. 14–28.

76. Michael Tsiros, Vikas Mittal, and William T. Ross Jr., "The Role of Attributions in Customer Satisfaction," *Journal of Consumer Research*, September 2004, pp. 476–483.

77. Andrea C. Morales, "Giving Firms an E for Effort: Consumer Responses to High-Effort Firms," *Journal of Consumer Research* 31, no. 4, 2005, pp. 806–812.

78. Ellis Smith, "First Tennessee Unveils Mobile Check Deposit," *Chattanooga Times Free Press*, September 29, 2011, www.timesfreepress.com.

79. Richard L. Oliver and John E. Swan, "Equity and Disconfirmation Paradigms as Influences on Merchant and Product Satisfaction," *Journal of Consumer Research*, December 1989, pp. 372–383; and Elaine G. Walster, G. William Walster, and Ellen Berscheid, *Equity: Theory and Research* (Boston: Allyn & Bacon, 1978).

80. Peter R. Darke and Darren W. Dahl, "Fairness and Discounts: The Subjective Value of a Bargain," *Journal of Consumer Psychology* 13, no. 3, 2003, pp. 328–338.

81. Richard L. Oliver and John L. Swan, "Consumer Perceptions of Interpersonal Equity and Satisfaction in Transactions," *Journal of Marketing*, April 1989, pp. 21–35.

82. Ruth N. Bolton and Katherine N. Lemon, "A Dynamic Model of Customers' Usage of Services," *Journal of Marketing Research* 36, May 1999, pp. 171–186.

83. Rebecca J. Slotegraaf and J. Jeffrey Inman, "Longitudinal Shifts in the Drivers of Satisfaction with Product Quality," *Journal of Marketing Research*, August 2004, pp. 269–280.

84. James G. Maxhamm III and Richard G. Netemeyer, "Firms Reap What They Sow: The Effects of Shared Values and Perceived Organizational Justice on Customers' Evaluations of Complaint Handling," *Journal of Marketing*, January 2003, pp. 46–62.

85. Jason Chow and Prudence Ho, "Huge for Its Bling, Unknown in West," *Wall Street Journal*, November 12, 2011, www.wsj.com.

86. Diane M. Phillips and Hans Baumgartner, "The Role of Consumption Emotions in the Satisfaction Response," *Journal of Consumer Psychology* 12, no. 3, 2002, pp. 243–252; Robert A. Westbrook and Richard L. Oliver, "The Dimensionality of Consumption Emotion Patterns and Consumer Satisfaction," *Journal of Consumer Research*, June 1991, pp. 84–91; and Mano and Oliver, "Assessing the Dimensionality and Structure of the Consumption Experience."

87. Robert A Westbrook, "Product/Consumption-Based Affective Responses and Postpurchase Processes," *Journal of Marketing Research* 24, August 1987, pp. 258–270.

88. Chi Kin (Bennett) Yim, David K. Tse, and Kimmy Wa Chan, "Strengthening Customer Loyalty Through Intimacy and Passion," *Journal of Marketing Research*, December 2008, pp. 741–56.

89. Westbrook and Oliver, "The Dimensionality of Consumption Emotion Patterns and Consumer Satisfaction."

90. Thorsten Hennig-Thurau, Markus Groth, and Michael Paul, "Are All Smiles Created Equal?" *Journal of Marketing*, July 2006, pp. 58–73.

91. Adam Duhachek and Dawn Iacobucci, "Consumer Personality and Coping," *Journal of Consumer Psychology* 15, no. 1, 2005, pp. 52–63; and Adam Duhachek, "Coping: A Multidimensional, Hierarchical Framework of Responses to Stressful Consumption Episodes," *Journal of Consumer Research* 32, June 2005, pp. 41–53.

92. Jing Wang, Nathan Novemsky, and Ravi Dhar, "Anticipating Adaptation to Products," *Journal of Consumer Research*, August 2009, pp. 149–159.

93. Richard L. Oliver, "Measurement and Evaluation of Satisfaction Processes in Retail Settings," *Journal of Retailing*, Fall 1981, pp. 25–48.

94. Christian Homburg, Nicole Koschate, and Wayne D. Hoyer, "The Role of Cognition and Affect in the Formation of Customer Satisfaction: A Dynamic Perspective," *Journal of Marketing*, July 2006, pp. 21–31; and Stacy L. Wood and C. Page Moreau, "Loathing? How Emotion Influences the Evaluation and Early Use of Innovations," *Journal of Marketing*, July 2006, pp. 44–57.

95. Sarah Fisher Gardial, D. Scott Clemons, Robert B. Woodruff, David W. Schumann, and Mary Jane Burns, "Comparing Consumers' Recall of Prepurchase and Postpurchase Evaluation Experiences," *Journal of Consumer Research*, March 1994, pp. 548–560.

96. Vanessa M. Patrick, Deborah J. MacInnis, and C. Whan Park, "Not As Happy As I Thought I'd Be? Affective Misforecasting and Product Evaluations," *Journal of Consumer Research* 33, no. 4, 2007, pp. 479–489; Daniel T. Gilbert, Elizabeth C. Pinel, Timothy D. Wilson, Stephen J. Blumberg, and Thalia P. Wheatley, "Immune Neglect: A Source of Durability Bias in Affective Forecasting," *Journal of Personality and Social Psychology* 75, no. 3, 1998, pp. 617–638; and George Loewenstein and David A. Schkade, "Wouldn't It Be Nice? Predicting Future Feelings," in eds. N. Schwartz, D. Kahneman, and E. Diener, *Well-Being: The Foundations of Hedonic Psychology* (New York: Russell Sage Foundation, 1999), pp. 85–105.

97. Wang, Novemsky, and Dhar, "Anticipating Adaptation to Products."

98. Naomi Mandel and Stephen M. Nowlis, "The Effect of Making a Prediction about the Outcome of a Consumption Experience on the Enjoyment of That Experience," *Journal of Consumer Research*, June 2008, pp. 9–20.

99. Todd Wasserman, "Capital One Now in CityVille, FarmVille, & Pioneer Trail," *Mashable*, September 19, 2011, http://mashable.com.

100. C. B. Bhattacharya and Sankar Sen, "Consumer-Company Identification: A Framework for Understanding Consumers' Relationships with Companies," *Journal of Marketing*, April 2003, pp. 76–88; and Dennis B. Arnett, Steve D. German, and Shelby D. Hunt, "The Identify Salience Model of Relationship Marketing Success: The case of nonprofit marketing," *Journal of Marketing*, April 2003, pp. 89–105.

101. Yukari Iwatani Kane and Ian Sherr, "Secrets from Apple's Genius Bar: Full Loyalty, No Negativity," *Wall Street Journal*, June 15, 2011, www.wsj.com.

102. Ralph L. Day, "Modeling Choices Among Alternative Responses to Dissatisfaction," in ed. Thomas C. Kinnear, *Advances in Consumer Research*, vol. 11, (Provo, Utah: Association for Consumer Research, 1984), pp. 496–499; and Marsha L. Richins, "Word-of-Mouth Communication as Negative Information," *Journal of Marketing*, Winter 1983, pp. 68–78.

103. Day, "Modeling Choices Among Alternative Responses to Dissatisfaction"; and Arthur Best and Alan R. Andreasen, "Consumer Response to Unsatisfactory Purchases," *Law and Society*, Spring 1977, pp. 701–742.

104. Stross, "Consumer Complaints Made Easy. Maybe Too Easy."

105. William O. Bearden and Jesse E. Teel, "Selected Determinants of Consumer Satisfaction and Complaint Reports," *Journal of Marketing Research*, February 1983, pp. 21–28.

106. Cathy Goodwin and Ivan Ross, "Consumer Evaluations of Responses to Complaints," *Journal of Services Marketing*, Summer 1990, pp. 53–61.

107. Day, "Modeling Choices Among Alternative Responses to Dissatisfaction"; and Jagdip Singh and Roy D. Howell, "Consumer Complaining Behavior: A Review," in eds. H. Keith Hunt and Ralph L. Day, *Consumer Satisfaction, Dissatisfaction, and Complaining Behavior* (Bloomington, Ind.: Indiana University Press, 1985).

108. S. Krishnan and S. A. Valle, "Dissatisfaction Attributions and Consumer Complaint Behavior," in ed. William L. Wilkie, *Advances in Consumer Research* (Miami, Fla.: Association for Consumer Research, 1979), pp. 445–449.

109. Folkes, "Consumer Reactions to Product Failure."

110. Nada Nasr Bechwati and Maureen Morrin, "Outraged Customers: Getting Even at the Expense of Getting a Good Deal," *Journal of Consumer Psychology* 13, no. 4, 2003, pp. 440–453.

111. Kjell Gronhaug and Gerald R. Zaltman, "Complainers and Noncomplainers Revisted: Another Look at the Data," in ed. Kent B. Monroe, *Advances in Consumer Research* (Ann Arbor, MI: Association for Consumer Research, 1981), pp. 159-165.

112. Jagdip Singh, "A Typology of Consumer Dissatisfaction Response Styles," *Journal of Retailing*, Spring 1990, pp. 57–99.

113. Dan Fost, "On the Internet, Everyone Can Hear Your Complaint," *New York Times*, February 25, 2008, p. C6.

114. Christian Homburg, Andreas Furst, and Nicole Koschate, "On the Importance of Complaint Handling Design: A Multi-level Analysis of the Impact in Specific Complaint Situations," *Journal of the Academy of Marketing Science* 38, 2010, pp. 265–287.

115. Chiara Orsingher, Sara Valentini, and Matteo de Angels, "A Meta-analysis of Satisfaction with Complaint Handling in Services," *Journal of the Academy of Marketing Science* 38, 2010, pp. 169–186.

116. Tiffany Kary, "Online Retailers Fumble on Customer Care," *CNET News.com*, January 3, 2002, http://cnet.com.

117. Ishan Srivastava, "Mobile Complaint? Your Tweet May Help," *Times of India*, September 22, 2011, www.timesofindia.com.

118. Lindsay Chappell, "Nissan: Facebook May Replace Phone Banks," *Automotive News*, July 25, 2011, p. 6.

119. James G. Maxham III and Richard G. Netemeyer, "A Longitudinal Study of Complaining Customers' Evaluations of Multiple Service Failures and Recovery Efforts," *Journal of Marketing*, October 2002, pp. 57–71.

120. Stephanie Reitz, "Some Supermarkets Bag Self-Serve Checkouts," *Seattle Times*, September 26, 2011, www.seattletimes.com.

121. Halstead, Droge, and Cooper, "Product Warranties and Postpurchase Service."

122. Claes Fornell and Nicholas M. Didow, "Economic Constraints on Consumer Complaining Behavior," in ed. Jerry C. Olson, *Advances in Consumer Research*, vol. 7 (Ann Arbor, Mich.: Association for Consumer Research, 1980), pp. 318–323; and Claes Fornell and Birger Wernerfelt, "Defensive Marketing Strategy by Customer Complaint Management," *Journal of Marketing Research*, November 1987, pp. 337–346.

123. Claes Fornell and Robert A. Westbrook, "The Vicious Cycle of Consumer Complaints," *Journal of Marketing*, Summer 1984, pp. 68–78.

124. Torsten Ringberg, Gaby Odekerken-Schröder, and Glenn L. Christensen, "A Cultural Models Approach to Service Recovery," *Journal of Marketing*, July 2007, pp. 194–214.

125. Amy K. Smith, Ruth N. Bolton, and Janet Wagner, "A Model of Customer Satisfaction with Service Encounters Involving Failure and Recovery," *Journal of Marketing Research* 36, August 1999, pp. 356–372.

126. Bitner, "Evaluating Service Encounters."

127. Richins, "Word-of-Mouth Communication as Negative Information."

128. Yi, "A Critical Review of Consumer Satisfaction."

129. James McNair, "Company Backlash Strikes Gripe Sites," *Cincinnati Enquirer*, February 7, 2005, www.usatoday.com.

130. Linda Dobel, "Contact Center Managers Should Already Be Rolling with the Flow of Social Media," *TMC*, October 20, 2011, www.tmcnet.com.

131. Jim Tierney, "Listening Is Social Media Cornerstone at Dell," *Multichannel Merchant*, November 3, 2011, www.multichannelmerchant.com.

132. Tim Donnelly, "How to Issue a Great Apology," *Inc.*, September 14, 2011, www.inc.com.

133. Frederick F. Reichheld, *The Loyalty Effect* (Boston: Harvard Business School Press, 1996).

134. Murali Chandrashekaran, Kristin Rotte, Stephen S. Tax, and Rajdeep Grewal, "Satisfaction Strength and Customer Loyalty," *Journal of Marketing Research*, February 2007, pp. 153–163.

135. Priscilla La Barbera and David W. Mazursky, "A Longitudinal Assessment of Consumer Satisfaction/Dissatisfaction," *Journal of Marketing Research*, November 1983, pp. 393–404; and Ruth Bolton, "A Dynamic Model of the Duration of the Customer's Relationship with a Continuous Service Provider," *Marketing Science* 17, no. 1, 1998, pp. 45–65.

136. Thomas O. Jones and W. Earl Sasser, "Why Customers Defect," *Harvard Business Review*, November–December 1995, pp. 88–99.

137. Richard L. Oliver, "Whence Consumer Loyalty?" *Journal of Marketing* 63, 1999, pp. 33–44.

138. Michael Lewis, "The Influence of Loyalty Programs and Short-Term Promotions on Customer Retention," *Journal of Marketing Research*, August 2004, pp. 281–292.

139. Frederick F. Reichheld and W. Earl Sasser, "Zero Defections," *Harvard Business Review*, September 1990, pp. 105–111; Eugene Anderson, Claes Fornell, and Donald H. Lehman, "Customer Satisfaction, Market Share, and Profitability," *Journal of Marketing*, July 1994, pp. 53–66; and Rajendra K. Srivastava, Tassadduq A. Shervani, and Liam Fahey, "Market-Based Assets and Shareholder Value," *Journal of Marketing* 62, no. 1, 1998, pp. 2–18.

140. Werner Reinartz, Manfred Krafft, and Wayne D. Hoyer, "The Customer Relationship Management Process: Its Measurement and Impact on Performance," *Journal of Marketing Research*, August 2004, pp. 293–305; and Suni Mithas, M. S. Krishnan, and Claes Fornell, "Why Do Customer Relationship Management Applications Affect Customer Satisfaction?" *Journal of Marketing*, October 2005, pp. 201–209.

141. Becky Ebenkamp, "The Complaint Department," *Brandweek*, June 18, 2001, p. 21; and Reichheld, *The Loyalty Effect*.

142. "Cole Hardware—Leading the Way in Eco-friendly Retailing," *Hardware Retailing*, July 2011, p. 60.

143. Kasey Wehrum, "Learning and Relearning to Listen," *Inc.*, March 2011, pp. 64–69.

144. Jeremy Quittner, "USAA Tech Overhaul Makes Remote Banking Less Remote," *American Banker*, July 12, 2011, p. 1.

145. Morag Cuddeford-Jones, "Field Marketing: Mystery Shopping," *Marketing Week*, March 10, 2011, p. 29; and "Clean and Green," *Retail Merchandiser*, January–February 2011, p. 94.

146. Lawrence Hene, "Star Order," *Grocer*, July 16, 2011, p. 20.

147. Melissa Martin Young and Melanie Wallendorf, "Ashes to Ashes, Dust to Dust: Conceptualizing Consumer Disposition of Possessions," in *Proceedings, Marketing Educators' Conference* (Chicago: American Marketing Association, 1989), pp. 33–39.

148. Young and Wallendorf, "Ashes to Ashes, Dust to Dust: Conceptualizing Consumer Disposition of Possessions;" see also Erica Mina Okada, "Trade-Ins, Mental Accounting, and Product Replacement Decisions," *Journal of Consumer Research*, March 2001, pp. 433–446; Jacob Jacoby, Carol K. Berning, and Thomas F. Dietvorst, "What About Disposition?" *Journal of Marketing*, April 1977, pp. 22–28; and Gilbert D. Harrell and Diane M. McConocha, "Personal Factors Related to Consumer Product Disposal," *Journal of Consumer Affairs*, Winter 1992, pp. 397–417.

149. Jacoby, Berning, and Dietvorst, "What About Disposition?"; and Young and Wallendorf, "Ashes to Ashes, Dust to Dust: Conceptualizing Consumer Disposition of Possessions."

150. Harrell and McConocha, "Personal Factors Related to Consumer Product Disposal Tendencies."

151. Jacoby, Berning, and Dietvorst, "What About Disposition?"

152. John B. Sherry, Mary Ann McGrath, and Sidney J. Levy, "The Disposition of the Gift and Many Unhappy Returns," *Journal of Retailing*, Spring 1992, pp. 40–65.

153. Young and Wallendorf, "Ashes to Ashes, Dust to Dust: Conceptualizing Consumer Disposition of Possessions."

154. Russell W. Belk, "Possessions and the Extended Self," *Journal of Consumer Research*, September 1988, pp. 139–168.

155. Young and Wallendorf, "Ashes to Ashes, Dust to Dust: Conceptualizing Consumer Disposition of Possessions."

156. Okada, "Trade-Ins, Mental Accounting, and Product Replacement Decisions."

157. Rui (Juliet) Zhu, Zinlei (Jack) Chen, and Srabana Dasgupta, "Can Trade-ins Hurt You? Exploring the Effect of a Trade-in on Consumers' Willingness to Pay for a New Product," *Journal of Marketing Research*, April 2008, pp. 159–170.

158. Melissa Martin Young, "Disposition of Possessions During Role Transitions," in eds. Rebecca H. Holman and Michael R. Solomon, *Advances in Consumer Research*, vol. 18 (Provo, Utah: Association for Consumer Research, 1991), pp. 33–39.

159. James H. Alexander, "Divorce, the Disposition of the Relationship, and Everything," in eds. Rebecca H. Holman and Michael R. Solomon, *Advances in Consumer Research*, vol. 18 (Provo, Utah: Association for Consumer Research, 1991), pp. 43–48.

160. Ibid; Russell W. Belk, John F. Sherry, and Melanie Wallendorf, "A Naturalistic Inquiry into Buyer and Seller Behavior at a Swap Meet," *Journal of Consumer Research*, March 1988, pp. 449–470.

161. Rachel Metz, "eBay Targets Mobile Users, Hoping to Seem Hip," *USA Today*, September 14, 2011, www.usatoday.com.

162. Michael D. Reilly and Melanie Wallendorf, "A Comparison of Group Differences in Food Consumption Using Household Refuse," *Journal of Consumer Research*, September 1987, pp. 289–294.

163. For a review, see L. J. Shrum, Tina M. Lowrey, and John A. McCarty, "Recycling as a Marketing Problem," *Psychology and Marketing*, July–August 1994, pp. 393–416.

164. Abhijit Biswas, Jane W. Licata, Daryl McKee, Chris Pullig, and Christopher Daughtridge, "The Recycling Cycle," *Journal of Public Policy and Marketing* 19, Spring 2000, pp. 93–105.

165. Aaron Baar, "Survey: Americans Much More Likely to Recycle," *Media Post*, October 5, 2011, www.mediapost.com.

166. Rik G. M. Pieters, "Changing Garbage Disposal Patterns of Consumers," *Journal of Public Policy and Marketing*, Fall 1991, pp. 59–76.

167. Richard P. Bagozzi and Pratibha Dabholkar, "Consumer Recycling Goals and Their Effect on Decisions to Recycle," *Psychology and Marketing*, July–August 1994, pp. 313–340.

168. E. Howenstein, "Marketing Segmentation for Recycling," *Environment and Behavior*, March 1993, pp. 86–102.

169. Shrum, Lowrey, and McCarty, "Recycling as a Marketing Problem."

170. Susan E. Heckler, "The Role of Memory in Understanding and Encouraging Recycling Behavior," *Psychology and Marketing*, July–August 1994, pp. 375–392.

171. Pieters, "Changing Garbage Disposal Patterns of Consumers."

172. Susan Warren, "Recycler's Nightmare: Beer in Plastic," *Wall Street Journal*, November 16, 1999, pp. B1, B4.

173. Kenneth R. Lord, "Motivating Recycling Behavior," *Psychology and Marketing*, July–August 1994, pp. 341–358.

174. Heckler, "The Role of Memory in Understanding and Encouraging Recycling Behavior."

175. Simone Sebastian, "Soft Drink Giants Put New Life into Their Containers," *Houston Chronicle*, September 25, 2011, www.chron.com.

176. Penelope Green, "Making Design Out of Rubbish," *New York Times*, August 10, 2011, www.nytimes.com.

177. Marguerite Reardon, "Don't Get Scammed When Selling Your Old iPhone," *CNET*, November 4, 2011, www.cnet.com; James R. Hagerty, "Entrepreneurs Find Gold in Used Phones," *Wall Street Journal*, February 24, 2011, www.wsj.com; Mariamo Diallo, "Used Mobile Phone Campaign Improves Maternal Health," *Voice of America*, October 19, 2011, www.voanews.com; and "Cell Phones Recycled to Help Soldiers," *Wisconsin Rapids Daily Tribune*, November 4, 2011, www.wisconsinrapidstribune.com.

The Consumer's Culture

PART 4

11 Social Influences on Consumer Behavior   298

12 Consumer Diversity   329

13 Household and Social Class Influences   355

14 Psychographics: Values, Personality, and Lifestyles   382

PART FOUR REFLECTS a "macro" view of consumer behavior, examining how various aspects of the consumer's culture affect each other and, individually and in combination, how they affect the consumer's behavior. As Chapter 11 explains, our behavior and decisions can be influenced by certain individuals, specific groups (such as friends and co-workers), and both traditional and social media. Chapter 12 focuses on diversity, specifically on the roles that age; gender; sexual orientation; and regional, ethnic, and religious influences play in consumer behavior.

Chapter 13 looks at various types of households and families and explores how household members influence acquisition and consumption decisions. It also examines how social class affects consumer decisions and behaviors. The combination of diversity, social class, and household influences can affect our values, personality, and lifestyle—the topics covered in Chapter 14. All of these factors influence consumer behavior and therefore have many implications for marketers.

THE CONSUMER'S CULTURE

Consumer Diversity (Ch. 12)

Household and Social Class Influences (Ch. 13)

Social Influences on Consumer Behavior (Ch. 11)

Psychographics: Values, Personality, and Lifestyles (Ch. 14)

THE PSYCHOLOGICAL CORE
- Motivation, Ability, and Opportunity (Ch. 2)
- From Exposure to Comprehension (Ch. 3)
- Memory and Knowledge (Ch. 4)
- Attitude Formation and Change (Chs. 5–6)

THE PROCESS OF MAKING DECISIONS
- Problem Recognition and Information Search (Ch. 7)
- Judgment and Decision Making (Chs. 8–9)
- Post-Decision Processes (Ch. 10)

CONSUMER BEHAVIOR OUTCOMES AND ISSUES
- Innovations: Adoption, Resistance, and Diffusion (Ch. 15)
- Symbolic Consumer Behavior (Ch. 16)
- Marketing, Ethics, and Social Responsibility in Today's Consumer Society (Ch. 17)

© Cengage Learning 2013

SOCIAL INFLUENCES ON CONSUMER BEHAVIOR

After studying this chapter, you will be able to

1. Explain how social influence can come from marketing or nonmarketing sources and can be mass media or personally delivered.

2. Discuss why marketers must pay particular attention to the influence of opinion leaders, both online and offline, and to the effects of social media.

3. Highlight the types and characteristics of reference groups and show how each can affect consumer behavior.

4. Distinguish between normative and informational influence, and explain how marketers can use their knowledge of these types of influence for more effective marketing.

© Zhao Changchun/ZUMA Press/Newscom

INTRODUCTION

Buzz Sends Angry Birds Soaring

How did you first hear about the mobile game in which players use a slingshot to launch irate birds against bad pigs? Did you download the game, try it, and talk about it with friends? If so, you're part of the reason that Angry Birds captured the world's imagination and was downloaded 600 million times in its first two years. High-profile players, such as U.K. Prime Minister David Cameron, made headlines by admitting they were big fans, which only added to the game's popularity.

Rovio, the Finnish company behind Angry Birds, has relied on buzz built through a combination of online activities, social media activities, consumer word of mouth, and public relations to build excitement about the game and seasonal variations, such as Angry Birds Mooncake Festival. It also partners with other firms to branch out into branded entertainment, T-shirts, books, stuffed toys, candies, and other products. With annual revenue now topping $100 million, Rovio has opened an office in China, its second-largest market, and is making big plans for the future. "Angry Birds can be just like Hello Kitty or Mickey Mouse," says Rovio's chief marketing officer.[1]

The information that individuals or groups provide, as **social influences**, can have a big impact on consumers. When you hear about a game from your friends, that information can be very credible. Social influence is also powerful when

Social influence
Information by and implicit or explicit pressures from individuals, groups, and the mass media that affects how a person behaves.

individuals within groups are in frequent contact and can communicate information in a way that builds buzz. Certain people (such as famous politicians) have influence because their power or expertise makes others want to follow what they believe, do, or say. Groups can influence not only what consumers know but also what they do (such as downloading a game). Therefore, marketers need to understand what kinds of social entities create influence, what kinds of influence they create, and how their influence can affect other consumers. Exhibit 11.1 summarizes the social influences that can affect consumers.

SOURCES OF INFLUENCE

Many people learn about products through advertising, Facebook, e-mail, publicity, samples and coupons, personal experience, other people, and other sources. Building buzz, the way Rovio did for Angry Birds, can be effective because it uses the influence of third parties to amplify initial marketing efforts.[2] But which sources have the most impact, and why? Exhibit 11.2 offers some answers to these questions.

Marketing and Nonmarketing Sources

Influence can come from marketing and nonmarketing sources and can be delivered via the mass media or personally.

Marketing Sources Delivered via Mass Media

Marketing source Influence delivered from a marketing agent, for example, advertising, personal selling.

Marketing sources that deliver influence through the mass media (cell 1 in Exhibit 11.2) include advertising, sales promotions, publicity, special events, and social media posts. Macy's and McDonald's try to influence your purchase behavior by promoting special sales or new products in newspapers, on television, and on Facebook. Marketing messages delivered via cell phones also fall under this category. Macy's includes QR (quick response) codes in some ads and store windows. Consumers simply scan the code with a smartphone to view brief interviews with fashion designers or obtain more product information.[3]

Marketing Sources Delivered Personally

Marketing sources can also deliver information personally (cell 3 in Exhibit 11.2). Salespeople, service representatives, and customer service agents are marketing sources of influence who deliver information personally in retail outlets, at consumers' homes or offices, over the phone, or via e-mail or online chat. In some situations, consumers will respond to a marketing agent, such as a salesperson, by making use of the agent's knowledge and assistance to further their personal goals. When consumers worry about undue persuasion, however, they will adopt techniques to fend off unwanted attention.[4] Some buzz-building tactics, such as when companies pay people to blog or tweet about a brand, blur the line between marketing and nonmarketing sources.

Nonmarketing Sources Delivered via Mass Media

Nonmarketing source Influence delivered from an entity outside a marketing organization, for example, friends, family, the media.

As cell 2 in Exhibit 11.2 shows, sources that are not working for marketing companies (**nonmarketing sources**) can also wield influence via mass media–delivered messages. Consumer behavior may be affected by news items about new products, movies, and restaurants; product contamination; accidents involving products; and incidences of product abuse or misuse. Consumers shopping for a new car may learn about recalls and quality problems from TV coverage, Internet sites, blogs, and other media not controlled by marketers.[5] Some may be influenced by information and opinions obtained through a virtual community.[6] Certain media sources are particularly influential. Many consumers, for instance, choose movies based on film critics' recommendations, make

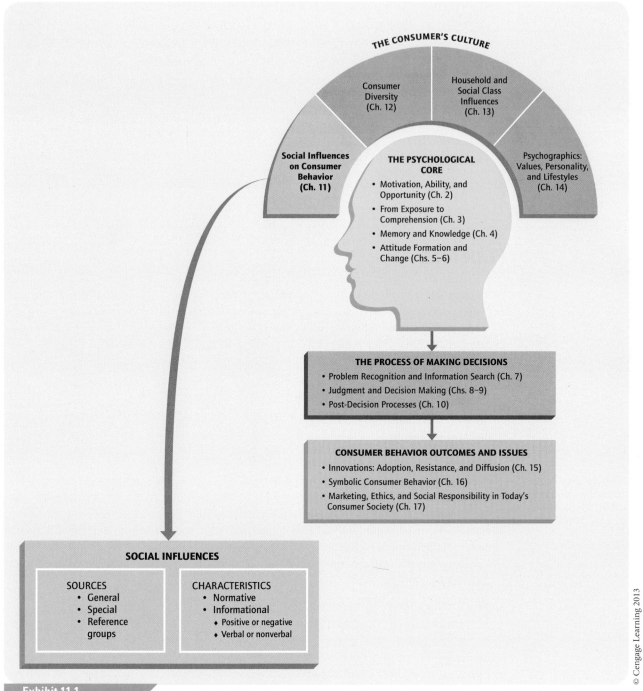

THE CONSUMER'S CULTURE

Consumer Diversity (Ch. 12)

Household and Social Class Influences (Ch. 13)

Social Influences on Consumer Behavior (Ch. 11)

THE PSYCHOLOGICAL CORE
- Motivation, Ability, and Opportunity (Ch. 2)
- From Exposure to Comprehension (Ch. 3)
- Memory and Knowledge (Ch. 4)
- Attitude Formation and Change (Chs. 5–6)

Psychographics: Values, Personality, and Lifestyles (Ch. 14)

THE PROCESS OF MAKING DECISIONS
- Problem Recognition and Information Search (Ch. 7)
- Judgment and Decision Making (Chs. 8–9)
- Post-Decision Processes (Ch. 10)

CONSUMER BEHAVIOR OUTCOMES AND ISSUES
- Innovations: Adoption, Resistance, and Diffusion (Ch. 15)
- Symbolic Consumer Behavior (Ch. 16)
- Marketing, Ethics, and Social Responsibility in Today's Consumer Society (Ch. 17)

SOCIAL INFLUENCES

SOURCES
- General
- Special
- Reference groups

CHARACTERISTICS
- Normative
- Informational
  - Positive or negative
  - Verbal or nonverbal

© Cengage Learning 2013

Exhibit 11.1

Chapter Overview: Social Influences

This chapter describes three sources of influence (general, special, and groups) and the characteristics of influence (normative and informational). Information may be positive or negative, and may be provided verbally or nonverbally.

dining decisions based on restaurant reviews, make buying decisions based on *Consumer Reports* articles, and choose books based on readers' ratings on Amazon.com. Celebrities and other well-known figures may also influence consumers' acquisition, usage, and disposition decisions.

Nonmarketing Sources Delivered Personally

Finally, consumer behavior is influenced by nonmarketing sources who deliver information personally (cell 4 in Exhibit 11.2).[7] Our consumer behavior can be affected by observing how others behave or by **word of mouth**, information about offerings communicated verbally by friends, family, neighbors, casual acquaintances, and even strangers.

Word of mouth Influence delivered verbally from one person to another person or group of people.

Exhibit 11.2

Sources of Influence

Social influence can come from marketing or nonmarketing sources and can be delivered via the mass media or in person. Nonmarketing sources tend to be more credible. Information delivered via the mass media can reach many people but may not allow for a two-way flow of communication.

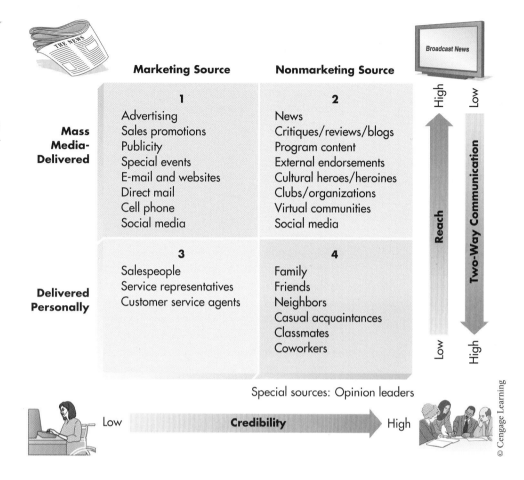

	Marketing Source	**Nonmarketing Source**
Mass Media-Delivered	**1** Advertising Sales promotions Publicity Special events E-mail and websites Direct mail Cell phone Social media	**2** News Critiques/reviews/blogs Program content External endorsements Cultural heroes/heroines Clubs/organizations Virtual communities Social media
Delivered Personally	**3** Salespeople Service representatives Customer service agents	**4** Family Friends Neighbors Casual acquaintances Classmates Coworkers

Reach: High — Low
Two-Way Communication: Low — High

Special sources: Opinion leaders

Credibility: Low → High

Marketing and Nonmarketing Sources Delivered via Social Media

Social media, such as Facebook and YouTube, are increasingly used by both marketing and nonmarketing sources (cells 1 and 2 in Exhibit 11.2). Social media have a mass reach but a more personal feel because consumers choose when, where, and how to access and share content. For example, some Super Bowl ads go viral after being posted on YouTube, multiplying the number of viewers before and after the big game. One of Volkswagen's Super Bowl ads attracted 10 million views during the week before the Super Bowl, continued to attract thousands of viewers during the weeks after the game, and then drew more than one million viewers during the two weeks before the next year's Super Bowl.[8] Consumer-generated ads (nonmarketing sources encouraged or even rewarded by many marketers) can stimulate a range of social media conversations, from positive and negative comments, to debate over content and interest in knowing more about the ad and the brand.[9] Reaction to marketing sources delivered via social media is likely to be positive when the content is entertaining, informative, or is valued in some other way by the consumer audience.[10]

How Do These General Sources Differ?

The influence sources shown in Exhibit 11.2 differ in terms of their reach, capacity for two-way communication, and credibility. In turn, these characteristics affect how much influence each source can have with consumers.

Reach

Mass media sources are important to marketers because they reach large consumer audiences. A 30-second TV commercial during the FIFA World Cup can reach tens of millions of viewers in the United States, Europe, and around the world. The Internet, cell phones, and other technologies are spreading marketing messages, product news, information about the behavior of public figures, and TV programs to an increasingly large audience, thus expanding marketers' reach dramatically.

Capacity for Two-Way Communication

Personally delivered sources of influence are valuable because they allow for a two-way flow of information. For example, a car salesperson may have more influence than a car ad because the salesperson can tailor sales information to fit the buyer's information needs, rebut counter-arguments, reiterate important and/or complex information, and answer the buyer's questions. Personal conversations are often more casual and less purposeful than mass media–delivered information. During a conversation, people are less likely to anticipate what will be said and hence are less likely to take steps to avoid information inconsistent with their own frames of reference. Information from a personal source may also seem more vivid than information from the mass media because the person speaking somehow makes it more real, a factor that may make it more persuasive.[11]

Credibility

While personal and mass media sources differ in their reach and capacity for two-way communication, marketing and nonmarketing sources differ in their credibility. Consumers tend to perceive information delivered through marketing sources as being less credible, more biased, and manipulative. In contrast, nonmarketing sources appear more credible because we do not believe that they have a personal stake in our purchase, consumption, or disposition decisions. We are more likely to believe a *Consumer Reports* article on cars than information from a car salesperson (see Exhibit 11.3). Because nonmarketing sources are credible, they tend to have more influence on consumer decisions than marketing sources do. David Pogue, a *New York Times* technology columnist, is a credible, independent source of information about digital cameras and other consumer electronics.

Specific personal and mass media sources vary in their credibility. We tend to believe information that we hear from people with whom we have close relationships, in part because their similarity to us (and our values and preferences) makes their opinions credible.[12] Certain people are also regarded as more credible than others because they are experts or are generally recognized as having unbiased opinions. For example, research shows that publicity delivered via blogs can generate higher brand attitudes and purchase intensions than publicity delivered via online magazines, simply because of the bloggers' credibility.[13]

Exhibit 11.3

Nonmarketing Sources Enhance Credibility

Nonmarketing sources of influence like *Consumer Reports* can have a powerful impact on consumer' purchase decisions because they are regarded as highly credible.

I CARRY TWO BADGES. THIS ONE'S FOR HOPE.

© Lee/Splash News/Newscom

Exhibit 11.4

Celebrities as Opinion Leaders

Nonmarketing sources can yield powerful influence because they are often seen as more objective and less biased.

> ## Marketing Implications

Marketers can build on these differences in credibility, reach, and two-way communication capability to influence consumer behavior in various ways.

Use Nonmarketing Sources to Enhance Credibility

When possible, marketers should try to have nonmarketing sources feature their offerings (see Exhibit 11.4). Testimonials and word-of-mouth referrals may have considerable impact, particularly if delivered through personal communications.[14] Consumers cannot always determine whether information in the media is from a marketing or nonmarketing source because some magazine and newspaper ads look like editorial content and some articles mention the names of advertisers. Likewise, consumers may have difficulty distinguishing paid testimonials in social media from unpaid mentions. Some Twitter users with large followings may tweet about a brand because they like it or because they're paid to do so. For transparency, the Federal Trade Commission suggests that paid tweets carry a "#spon" or "#ad" tag.[15] Online, marketers can also reach targeted groups by connecting with a virtual community structured around consumers' common interests (such as cooking or sports).[16]

Use Personal Sources to Enhance Two-Way Communication

Marketing efforts may be more effective when personal information sources are used. Hosts of home shopping parties are credible as sales representatives because "people want to buy from people they like and know," says the head of Tastefully Simple, which sells gourmet foods through such parties.[17] Some companies encourage managers and employees to post comments online to a blog or microblogging site (such as Twitter), generating or continuing a dialogue with customers. Best Buy, the electronics retailer, maintains a variety of blogs and Twitter accounts, through which executives and employees engage consumers in social media conversations about new products, tips about technical issues, and answers to customers' questions.[18]

Use a Mix of Sources to Enhance Impact

Because marketing and nonmarketing sources differ in their impact, the effect on consumers may be greatest when marketers use complementary sources of influence. Best Buy benefits from the combination of marketing sources (such as advertising and sales promotions) and nonmarketing sources (such as customer reviews on its website). Some companies stimulate referrals by rewarding customers with discounts or prizes when they refer other people, adding the credibility of a nonmarketing source (current customers) with the inducement of a marketing source (sales promotion).[19] One recent study of bank customers in Germany found that those who were referred by existing customers were significantly more likely to remain loyal and more profitable than average.[20]

Opinion Leaders

Opinion leader An individual who acts as an information broker between the mass media and the opinions and behaviors of an individual or group.

A special source of social influence is the **opinion leader**, someone who acts as an information broker between the mass media and the opinions and behaviors of an individual or group. Opinion leaders have some position, expertise, or firsthand knowledge that makes them particularly important sources of relevant and credible information, usually in a specific domain or product category. Thus, for example, German soccer star Mesut Özil is an opinion leader for sports shoes (which is why Nike pays him for endorsing its products).

Gatekeeper A source that controls the flow of information.

Opinion leaders are regarded as nonmarketing sources of influence, a perception that adds to their credibility. They are not necessarily well-known people; they may be friends and acquaintances or professionals like doctors, dentists, or lawyers who advise patients and clients. Opinion leaders are part of a general category of **gatekeepers**, people who have special influence or power in deciding whether a product or information will be disseminated to a market.

Researchers studying opinion leaders have observed several characteristics.[21] Opinion leaders tend to learn a lot about products, are heavy users of mass media, and tend to buy new products when they are first introduced. Opinion leaders are also self-confident, gregarious, and willing to share product information. They may become opinion leaders because of an intrinsic interest in and enjoyment of certain products—in other words, they have enduring involvement with a product category.[22] Opinion leaders might also like the power of having information and sharing it with others, or they may communicate information because they believe that their actions will help others.[23]

Opinion leaders have influence because they generally have no personal stake in whether their opinions are heeded, so their opinions are perceived as unbiased and credible. They are also regarded as knowledgeable about acquisition, usage, and disposition options because of their product knowledge and experience. These characteristics explain why consumers who enjoy cooking value the comments of celebrity chefs. In fact, after celebrity chefs Jamie Oliver and Delia Smith began promoting the use of shallots in recipes, U.K. sales of shallots rose by 46 percent in one year.[24] However, simply because opinion leaders serve as information brokers does not mean that information only flows from opinion leaders to consumers. Indeed, opinion leaders often get information by seeking it from consumers, manufacturers, and retailers.[25]

Market maven A consumer on whom others rely for information about the marketplace in general.

Whereas opinion leaders are important sources of influence about a particular product or service category, researchers have also identified another special source of influence—a **market maven**, someone who seems to have a lot of information about the marketplace in general.[26] A market maven seems to know all about the best products, the good sales, and the best stores.

Marketing Implications

Marketers use several tactics to influence opinion leaders.

Target Opinion Leaders

Given their potential impact and the fact that they are both seekers and providers of marketplace information, an obvious strategy is to identify and target opinion leaders directly.[27] For example, LEGO, a Danish toymaker, targets adult leaders of LEGO fan groups worldwide, seeking their input and, through them, influencing tens of thousands of fans who meet regularly to swap ideas and show off new LEGO creations.[28]

In Brazil, clothing brands target popular fashion bloggers before placing advertising because bloggers are particularly influential opinion leaders.[29] In another example, toy manufacturers often send free samples to "mommy bloggers," mothers whose blogs attract sizable audiences. The goal is to encourage positive, personal reviews and thereby influence the attitudes and buying behavior of consumers who follow these bloggers. When Spin Master reformulated its Moon Dough molding dough, the company sent samples to hundreds of mommy bloggers. Their positive comments stimulated high interest and resulted in double-digit sales increases within weeks.[30]

Use Opinion Leaders in Marketing Communications

Although opinion leaders' influence may be less effective when delivered through a marketing source, their expertise and association can still support an offering. After the well-known chef Paula Deen announced she had type 2 diabetes, she became a spokesperson for Novo Nordisk's diabetes medication and participated in campaigns to encourage healthier eating and physical activity.[31] As an alternative, marketers may use simulated opinion leaders, such as a dentist's wife endorsing a toothpaste brand, because her affiliation with a dental professional presumably adds credibility.

Refer Consumers to Opinion Leaders

In many cases, marketers ask consumers to contact a knowledgeable opinion leader. Pharmaceutical manufacturers do this by suggesting that consumers consult their doctors (opinion leaders) about how a particular advertised product can help them. Research shows that these opinion leaders can influence the attitudes and behavior of other physicians as well as of consumers.[32] _____

REFERENCE GROUPS AS SOURCES OF INFLUENCE

Social influence is exerted by individuals such as opinion leaders as well as by specific groups of people. A reference group is a set of people with whom individuals compare themselves for guidance in developing their own attitudes, knowledge, and/or behaviors.

Types of Reference Groups

Consumers may relate to three types of reference groups: aspirational, associative, and dissociative. **Aspirational reference groups** are groups we admire and wish to be like but are not currently a member of. For example, a younger brother may want to be like his older brother and other older children. Given the high respect accorded to education in South Korea, teachers often serve as an aspirational reference group for students there. Celebrities and athletes are also admired, which is why tennis champ Li Na has been signed to endorse Nike, Rolex, and other brands marketed in her home country of China.[33]

Associative reference groups are groups to which we actually belong, such as a clique of friends, an extended family, a particular work group, a club, or a school group. The gender, ethnic, geographic, and age groups to which you belong are also associative reference groups with whom you may identify (see Exhibit 11.5). Even consumers who think of themselves as individual-minded react well to products linked to appropriate associative reference groups.[34] However, when consumers misunderstand their relative position in a reference group, they tend to make poor acquisition or consumption decisions.[35] For example, if you believe you are one of the most skillful cyclists or skiers in your class—when in reality, you are just beyond beginner status—you may buy equipment or services unsuited to your capabilities.

Associative reference groups can form around a brand, as is the case with clubs like the HOG (Harley Owners Group), which is made up of Harley-Davidson fans. A **brand community** is a specialized group of consumers with a structured set of relationships involving a particular brand, fellow customers of that brand, and the product in use.[36] A consumer who is a member of a brand community thinks about brand names (e.g., Harley-Davidson), the product category (e.g., motorcycles),

Aspirational reference group A group that we admire and desire to be like.

Associative reference group A group to which we currently belong.

Brand community A specialized group of consumers with a structured set of relationships involving a particular brand, fellow customers of that brand, and the product in use.

Exhibit 11.5

High School Reference Groups

Researchers have found that no matter where you went to high school, the classmates you hung around with were likely to belong to one of five categories: elites, athletes, deviants, academics, and others. What category were you in, and what did students at your school call your group? What "other" groups existed in your school?

- **Elites** are high in peer status and social involvement and are somewhat involved in academics.
- **Athletes** are high in peer status and social involvement but only slightly involved in academics.
- **Deviants** are in the middle on peer status and social involvement and low on academic involvement. They tend to rebel against school.
- **Academics** are high in academic involvement, in the middle on peer status, and relatively low on social involvement.
- **Others** tend to be relatively low in peer status, social involvement, and academic involvement.

Source: Reprinted from Steve Sussman, Pallav Pokhrel, Richard D. Ashmore, and B. Bradford Brown, "Adolescent Peer Group Identification and Characteristics: A Review of the Literature," *Addictive Behaviors*, August 2007, pp. 1620–1627, with permission from Elsevier.

other customers who use the brand (e.g., HOG members), and the marketer that makes and promotes the brand.[37] Members of a brand community not only buy the product repeatedly, but they are extremely committed to it, share their information and enthusiasm with other consumers, and influence other members to remain loyal.[38] Interestingly, such communities may survive even after the brand is discontinued.[39]

Dissociative reference group A group we do not want to emulate.

Dissociative reference groups are groups whose attitudes, values, and behaviors we disapprove of and do not wish to emulate. U.S. citizens, for instance, serve as dissociative reference groups to religious groups in some Arab countries, and neo-Nazis serve as dissociative reference groups for many people in Germany and the United States. Note that the influence of dissociative reference groups can depend, in part, on whether a product is consumed in public or in private.[40]

Marketing Implications

The influence of various reference groups has some important implications for marketers.

Associate Products with Aspirational Reference Groups

Knowing their target consumers' aspirational reference group enables marketers to associate their product with that group and to use spokespeople who represent it. Because celebrities are an aspirational reference group for some, many organizations use celebrities to endorse products or communicate with targeted audiences.[41] For example, Carter Oosterhouse, who hosts home improvement shows on TV channel HGTV, actively participates in Habitat for Humanity home-building projects, using his celebrity status to encourage consumers to donate money or time.[42]

Accurately Represent Associative Reference Groups

Marketers can also identify and appropriately represent target consumers in ads by accurately reflecting the clothing, hairstyles, accessories, and general demeanor of their associative reference groups.[43] To sell products like skateboards and mountain-climbing equipment, for example, many sports marketers develop promotions featuring actual skateboarders and mountain climbers.

Help to Develop Brand Communities

Many brands now create the framework for communities on Facebook or on dedicated websites. These brand communities bring together like-minded consumers, reinforce brand loyalty, encourage positive attitudes toward the brand and its products, and disseminate information about the brand. For example, the Boston Red Sox baseball team maintains a Facebook page with more than three million "likes," plus a website that is home to the Kid Nation and Red Sox Nation brand communities. Before, during, and after baseball season, thousands of Red Sox fans worldwide enjoy interacting within these brand communities.

Avoid Using Dissociative Reference Groups

When appropriate, companies should not use dissociative reference groups in their marketing. Some marketers drop celebrity spokespeople who commit crimes or exhibit other behavior that is offensive to the target market. For example, in an unusual move, retailer Abercrombie & Fitch offered to pay the stars of the controversial TV reality show *Jersey Shore* to *not* wear its clothing. "We understand that the show is for entertainment purposes, but believe this association is contrary to the aspirational nature of our brand, and may be distressing to many of our fans," the retailer stated.[44] _____

Characteristics of Reference Groups

Reference groups can be described according to the degree of contact, formality, similarity among members, group attractiveness, density, degree of identification, and strength of the ties connecting members.

Degree of Contact

Reference groups vary in their degree of contact. We may have direct and extensive contact with some reference groups like our immediate circle of friends or family but may have less contact with others like gangsta rappers. Reference groups with which we have considerable contact tend to exert the greatest influence.[45] A group with which we have face-to-face interaction, such as family, peers, and professors, is a **primary reference group**. In contrast, a **secondary reference group** is one that may influence us even though we have no personal contact with most of its members. We may be members of groups like an Internet chat group or a musical fan club. Although we may interact with some members of the group only through such impersonal communication channels as newsletters, its behavior and values can still influence our behavior.

Formality

Reference groups also vary in formality. Groups like fraternities, athletic teams, clubs, and classes are formally structured, with rules outlining the criteria for group membership and the expected behavior of members. For example, you must satisfy certain requirements—gaining admission, fulfilling class prerequisites—before you can enroll in particular college courses. Once enrolled, you must follow rules for conduct by submitting assignments on time. Other groups are more ad hoc, less organized, and less structured. For example, your immediate group of friends is not formally structured and probably has no official rules. People who attend the same party or vacation on the same cruise also may constitute an informal group.

Homophily: The Similarity Among Group Members

Groups vary in their **homophily**, the similarity among the members. When groups are homophilous, reference-group influence is likely to be strong because similar people tend to see things in the same way, interact frequently, and develop strong social ties.[46] Group members may have more opportunity to exchange information and are more likely to accept information from one another. Because senders and receivers are similar, the information that they share is also likely to be perceived as credible.

Group Attractiveness

The attractiveness of a particular peer group can affect how much consumers conform to the group.[47] When members perceive a group as being very attractive, they have stronger intentions to conform to what the group does—even its illicit consumption behavior. This situation implies that making substance abusers seem less attractive may help U.S. children and teens resist illicit activities.

Density

Dense groups are those in which group members all know one another. For example, an extended family that gets together every Sunday operates as a dense social network. In contrast, the network of faculty at a large university is less dense because its members have fewer opportunities to interact, share information, or influence one another. In South Korea, network density varies by geographic area. A rural village may have high density because its families have known each other for generations whereas many of the 10 million residents of Seoul may not know one another, so network density there is low.

Degree of Identification

Some characteristics of an individual within a group contribute to the ways in which groups vary. One is the degree of identification that a consumer has with a group. Just because people are members of a group does not mean that they use it as a reference group. Even though people may be Hispanic or senior citizens, they need not necessarily regard similar individuals as *part* of their reference group.[48] The influence that a group has on an individual's behavior is affected by the extent to which he or she identifies with it. One study found that consumers who attend sporting events were more likely to buy a sponsor's products when they strongly identified with the team and viewed such purchases as a group norm.[49] Moreover, a marketing stimulus that focuses attention on consumers' identification with a certain group (such as ethnic or religious identity) and is relevant to that identification will more likely elicit a positive response.[50]

Primary reference group Group with whom we have physical face-to-face interaction.

Secondary reference group Group with whom we do not have direct contact.

Homophily The overall similarity among members in the social system.

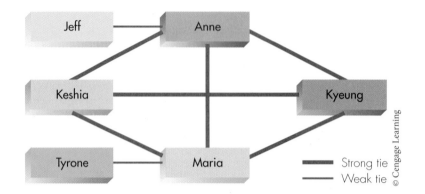

© Cengage Learning

Strong tie

Weak tie

Exhibit 11.6

Tie-Strength and Social Influence

The thick red line shows that Anne has strong ties to three school friends: Maria, Kyeung, and Keshia. The thin red line indicates that Anne is less closely tied to Jeff, someone she knows from her health club. Another thin red line indicates that Maria does not have a close relationship with her distant cousin Tyrone. If you were a marketer, whom would you target in this network? Why?

Tie-strength The extent to which a close, intimate relationship connects people.

Tie-Strength

Another characteristic describing individuals within a group is **tie-strength**.[51] A strong tie means that two people are connected by a close, intimate relationship often characterized by frequent interpersonal contact. A weak tie means that the people have a more distant relationship with limited interpersonal contact. Exhibit 11.6 illustrates these concepts.

Marketing Implications

Marketers pay close attention to the characteristics of reference groups because of their influence on targeting and communication.

Understanding Information Transmission

Homophily, degree of contact, tie-strength, and network density can significantly influence whether, how much, and how quickly information is transmitted within a group. Within dense networks, in which consumers are in frequent contact and are connected by strong ties, information about acquiring, using, and disposing of an offering—or related offerings—is likely to be transmitted quickly. The best way to disseminate information rapidly within a market is to target individuals in dense networks characterized by strong ties and frequent contact. For example, social media users read posted messages and replies of their friends and the brand or products they follow or like—and they spread the word by retweeting, reposting, and adding comments of their own, both positive and negative. General Mills, McDonald's, and other marketers announce new products and promotions on Facebook and Twitter to take advantage of the rapid-fire spread of information.

Formal Reference Groups as Potential Targets

Formal reference groups can provide marketers with clear targets for marketing efforts. For example, the U.K.-based charity Comic Relief targets formal groups like companies, schools, and rugby clubs to encourage fundraising activities in connection with its two major events, Red Nose Day and Sport Relief. Partnering with supporters such as the grocery chain Sainsbury's, the BBC television network, and neighborhood schools, Comic Relief has raised tens of millions of dollars to help children in need.[52]

Homophilous Consumers as Targets

Marketers may use the concept of homophily to market their products. For example, if you log on to amazon.com and find a book you like, the recommendation system points you to more books you might like based on the purchases of consumers who bought the first book. The principle is that you might share the reading tastes of people that the site considers to be similar to you. The same goes for Netflix's movie recommendation system.

Targeting the Network

Sometimes it makes sense for marketers to target the network itself. Verizon Wireless, for example, offers one large pool of monthly cell phone minutes to be shared among family members. Marketers may also encourage referrals by asking consumers to "tell a friend about us." Ticketmaster, for example, has an app that targets users' Facebook networks. Integrated with the Spotify digital music service, the app recommends upcoming entertainment events based on each user's listening history. Users can click on individual concerts to post Facebook messages like "I want to go" or "I just bought tickets," which encourages discussion among friends and purchases of tickets to attend concerts together. "People who are friends on Facebook generally have very similar interests, and Spotify connected with Facebook is a great way to learn what other people are listening to," explains a Ticketmaster executive.[53]

Research shows that within social networks, one-fifth of a user's friends actually influence that user's activity level on the site. As a result, marketers need to study the interactions among social media users when planning to target the network.[54]

Understanding the Strength of Weak Ties

Although weak ties may seem to have little potential for marketers, the opposite is true. Because weak ties often serve as "bridges" connecting groups, they can play a powerful role in propagating information *across* networks.[55] In Exhibit 11.6, for instance, Maria is a bridge between her close friends (Keshia, Kyeung, and Anne) and her distant cousin (Tyrone). Once she gives information to Tyrone, he can communicate it to others with whom he has ties.

In fact, researchers have found that word of mouth spreads more effectively among people with weak ties. Moreover, marketers can use weak ties to identify new networks for marketing efforts. For example, direct-selling organizations like Avon and charitable groups like the American Cancer Society target individual consumers as selling (or fundraising) agents and rely on their interpersonal networks to reach others.[56]

Individuals can tap not only consumers with whom they have strong ties but also those with whom they have weak ties. Girl Scouts, for example, sell cookies to friends and relatives as well as to neighbors, parents' coworkers, and people shopping at grocery stores (see Exhibit 11.7). These are called **embedded markets** because the social relationships among buyers and sellers change the way that the market operates.[57] Thus, your social relationship with a seller may influence the way that you react to his or her selling efforts. You are more likely to buy Girl Scout cookies from a neighbor's daughter than from a girl you have never met, because you want to remain on good terms with your neighbor. Or you can use the Girl Scouts' app to locate the nearest source of Girl Scout cookies in your area.[58]

Embedded market
Market in which the social relationships among buyers and sellers change the way the market operates.

Consumer socialization
The process by which we learn to become consumers.

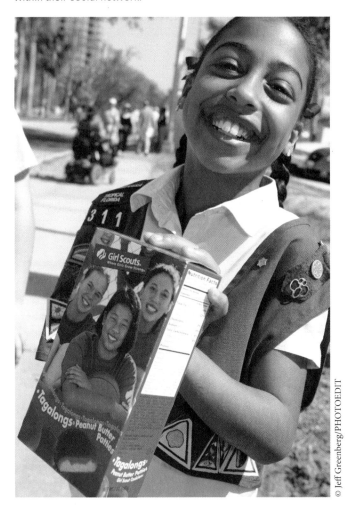

© Jeff Greenberg/PHOTOEDIT

Reference Groups Affect Consumer Socialization

One way that reference groups influence consumer behavior is through socialization, the process by which individuals acquire the skills, knowledge, values, and attitudes that are relevant for functioning in a given domain. **Consumer socialization** is the process by which we learn to become consumers and come to know the value of money; the appropriateness of saving versus spending; and how, when, and where products should be bought and used.[59] Through socialization, consumers learn consumption values as well as gain the knowledge and skills for consumption.[60] Consumer socialization can occur in many ways, as the following sections show.

People as Socializing Agents

Reference groups like family and friends play an important role as socializing agents. Parents may, for example, instill values of thriftiness by directly teaching their children the importance of saving money, letting the children observe them being thrifty, or rewarding children for being thrifty. One study found that direct teaching was most effective for instilling consumer skills in younger children and observational learning was most effective for older children.

Intergenerational influence—information, beliefs, and resources being transmitted from one generation (parents) to the next (children)—affects consumers' acquisition and use of certain product categories and preferred brands.[61] Research shows that children are using brand names as cues for consumer decisions by the time they are 12 years old.[62] Note that parenting styles and socialization patterns vary from culture to culture.[63] In individualistic cultures like Australia and the United States, where many parents are relatively permissive, children develop consumer skills at an earlier age. In contrast, children in a collectivist culture such as India, where parents tend to be stricter, understand advertising practices at a later age.

Moreover, parents affect socialization by influencing what types of products, TV programs, and ads their children are exposed to and how much control they have over buying products that they want.[64] Some observers worry that exposure to these socializing agents encourages children to see the acquisition of material goods as a path to happiness, success, and achievement.[65] Some parents are very concerned about their children's exposure to violent and sexually explicit programming and products and actively regulate what their children watch and what games they play.[66]

The effect of reference groups as socializing agents can change over time. Parents have substantial influence on young children, but their influence wanes as children grow older and interact more with their peers.[67] Similarly, your high school friends probably had a more powerful effect on your values, attitudes, and behaviors when you were younger than they do now. Because we associate with many groups throughout our lives, socialization is a lifelong process.

The Media and the Marketplace as Socializing Agents

TV programs, movies and videos, music, video games, the Internet, and ads can also serve as socializing agents. For example, in ads, boys are sometimes depicted as more knowledgeable, aggressive, active, and instrumental to actions than girls are; these sex role stereotypes can affect children's conceptions of what it is like to be a boy rather than a girl.[68] Consumer products may be used as socializing agents, a situation in which our childhood toys might have influenced who we are and what was expected of us.[69] For instance, parents are likely to give boys sporting equipment, military toys, and vehicles. In contrast, they are more likely to give girls dolls, dollhouses, and domestic toys.[70] Studies show that children of 20 months can already distinguish "boy" toys from "girl" toys. These effects seem to occur at least in part because parents encourage the use of what they consider sex-appropriate toys and discourage cross-sex interests, especially for boys.[71] However, as children mature, they can become more suspicious of media and marketplace socializing agents; teens tend to be particularly skeptical of advertising claims.[72]

Comic Relief, the U.K. charity, is a great example of a company harnessing the socializing power of media for a good cause. By partnering with the BBC television network and inviting involvement through multiple media, Comic Relief uses media to raise money for charity. Millions of people see promotional messages on the BBC leading up to each charity day, and then watch during prime time as entertainers perform and talk about the progress toward the fundraising goal. "There has been a shift to mobile devices and social media already, and we have to be ready for the two-screen fundraising experience," says the charity's head of technology. People who watch the TV show, he adds, "are inspired to do something and, using whatever device is in their hand," they search for more information, or they click or text to donate money.[73]

NORMATIVE INFLUENCE

Thus far you have learned about various sources of influence—general, special, and groups. These sources can exert two types of influence, normative and informational (see Exhibit 11.8). Assume that you are at a dinner interview with a prospective employer who tells you that she is a vegetarian. You may be reluctant to order beef, which you love, because you want to make a good impression.

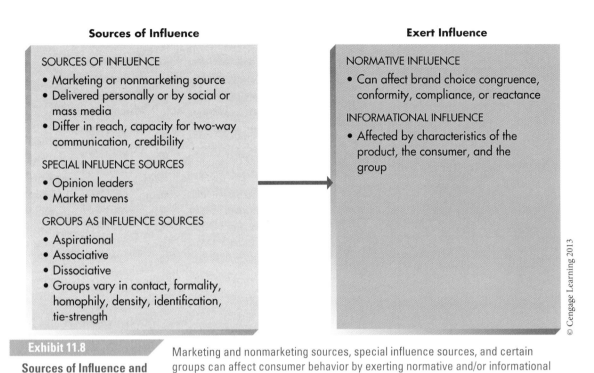

Sources of Influence

Exert Influence

SOURCES OF INFLUENCE

- Marketing or nonmarketing source
- Delivered personally or by social or mass media
- Differ in reach, capacity for two-way communication, credibility

SPECIAL INFLUENCE SOURCES

- Opinion leaders
- Market mavens

GROUPS AS INFLUENCE SOURCES

- Aspirational
- Associative
- Dissociative
- Groups vary in contact, formality, homophily, density, identification, tie-strength

NORMATIVE INFLUENCE

- Can affect brand choice congruence, conformity, compliance, or reactance

INFORMATIONAL INFLUENCE

- Affected by characteristics of the product, the consumer, and the group

© Cengage Learning 2013

Exhibit 11.8

Sources of Influence and Types of Influence

Marketing and nonmarketing sources, special influence sources, and certain groups can affect consumer behavior by exerting normative and/or informational influences.

Norm Collective decision about what constitutes appropriate behavior.

Normative influence is social pressure designed to encourage conformity to the expectations of others.[74] Chapter 5 discusses normative influences in the context of how they affect intentions and consumption decisions. The term normative influence derives from **norms**, society's collective decisions about what behavior should be. For example, we have norms for which brands, stores, and styles are "in" as well as norms that discourage stealing and impulse buying.[75] Morals also exert normative influence about what is right and wrong, and they can strongly influence attitudes—as they do in people's views of cigarette smoking, for example.[76]

Normative influence implies that consumers will be sanctioned, punished, or ridiculed if they do not follow the norms,[77] just as it also implies that they will be rewarded for performing the expected behaviors. To illustrate, a prospective boss may reward you with a job offer or deny you a job, depending on your behavior in the interview. Middle-school girls impose sanctions by treating classmates differently when they do not conform to the dress norm.[78]

How Normative Influence Can Affect Consumer Behavior

Normative influence can have several important effects on consumption behaviors.

Brand-Choice Congruence and Conformity

Brand-choice congruence The purchase of the same brand as members of a group.

Normative influence affects **brand-choice congruence**—the likelihood that consumers will buy what others in their group buy. If you compare the types of clothes, music, hairstyles, and cars that you buy with the selections of your friends, you will probably find that you and your friends make similar choices.[79] The presence of others can influence the enjoyment of shared stimuli (such as going to a movie together) and affect congruence as well.[80] Friends, relatives, and others in your social network may also influence the types of goods and services that you buy as gifts.[81] Simply rehearsing what to say in anticipation of discussing a particular brand purchase with others can change the way that consumers think and feel about the product and its features.[82]

Conformity The tendency to behave in an expected way.

Normative influence can also affect **conformity**, the tendency for an individual to behave as the group behaves. Conformity and brand-choice congruence may be related. For instance, you might conform by buying the same brands as others in your group do,[83] although brand-choice congruence is not the only way for you to conform. You may also conform by performing activities that the group wants you to perform, such as participating in initiation rites or acting in the way that the group acts. For example, your actions at a party might depend on whether you are there with your parents or your friends. In each case, you are conforming to a certain set of expectations regarding appropriate behavior. One study found that the norms established by social and brand relationships can influence consumer behavior as well.[84]

Pressures to conform can be substantial.[85] Research examining group pressure toward underage drinking and drug consumption found that students worried about how others would perceive them if they refused to conform to the group's expected behavior. Other studies have shown that conformity increases as more people in the group conform. However, identity-based thinking ("I am an environmentalist") is very strong and resistant to conformity pressures.[86] Note that conformity varies by culture. Compared with U.S. consumers, for example, Japanese consumers tend to be more group oriented and conform more to group desires.

Compliance versus Reactance

Compliance Doing what the group or social influencer asks.

Compliance, a somewhat different effect of normative influence, means doing what someone explicitly asks you to do. You are complying if, when asked, you fill out a marketing research questionnaire or purchase the products sold at a home party. Parents comply with children by purchasing foods or toys or allowing activities (such as parties) that kids request. In a virtual community, members may *not* comply as readily with the group's desires because the members are anonymous and can withdraw at will.[87]

Reactance Doing the opposite of what the individual or group wants us to do.

When we believe our freedom to choose is being threatened, a boomerang effect occurs and we engage in **reactance**—doing the opposite of what a person or group wants us to do. For example, if a salesperson pressures you too much, you may engage in reactance by refusing to buy whatever he or she is trying to sell, even if you wanted to buy it in the first place.[88] Reactance can occur in brand communities too. When a member feels too much pressure to perform certain rituals or assume certain roles, desire to participate in the community or buy the brand in the future may be lowered.[89]

Social-Relational Theory

According to social-relational theory, consumers conduct their social interactions according to (1) the rights and responsibilities of their relationship with group members, (2) a balance of reciprocal actions with group members, (3) their relative status and authority, and (4) the value placed on different objects and activities. In turn, these relationships and their unspoken rules wield normative influence on consumer behavior.[90] For instance, consumers may regard as taboo transactions in which they are asked to pay for something held to have morally significant value, such as love, friends, family, or even votes in an election. Taboos based on cultural or historical elements may also apply to buying and selling transactions.[91]

What Affects Normative Influence Strength

The strength of normative influence depends on the characteristics of the product, the consumer, and the group to which the consumer belongs.

Product Characteristics

Reference groups can influence two types of decisions: (1) whether we buy a product within a given category and (2) what brand we buy. However, whether reference groups affect product and brand decisions also depends on whether the product is typically consumed in private or in public and whether it is a necessity or a luxury.[92] As Exhibit 11.9 shows, mattresses and hot-water heaters are considered privately consumed necessities, whereas jewelry and inline skates are considered publicly consumed luxuries. This exhibit reflects predictions about when reference groups will affect these decisions.

One prediction is that because we must buy necessity items, reference groups are likely to have little influence on whether we buy such products. However, reference groups might exert some influence on whether we buy a luxury item. For example, your friends will probably not influence whether you buy tissues, a necessity you would buy in any case. But friends might influence whether you get an iPad, in part because luxury products communicate status—something that may be valued by group members. Also, luxury items may communicate your special interests and values

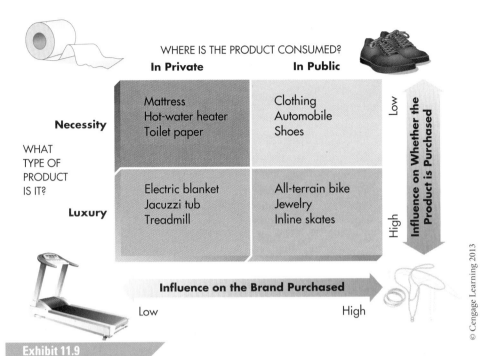

Exhibit 11.9

Reference Group Influences on Publicly and Privately Consumed Products

Reference groups tend to influence consumption of a *product category* only when the product is a luxury (not a necessity). Reference groups tend to influence consumption of a particular *brand* only when the product is consumed in public (not when it is consumed in private). Give some examples of your own to illustrate the matrix.

and thus convey who you are and with whom you associate.

A second prediction is that products consumed in public—such as the cars we drive—give others the opportunity to observe which brand we have purchased (whether it is a Ford F-150 or a Prius). In contrast, few people see which brand of mattress we buy because we consume this product in private. Different brand images communicate different things to people, so reference groups are likely to have considerable influence on the brand we buy when the product is publicly consumed but not when it is privately consumed. Moreover, a publicly consumed product provides opportunities for sanctions, whereas it would be difficult for groups to develop norms and sanctions for violations when the product is consumed privately. Therefore, reference groups influence product category choice for luxuries but not for necessities and they influence brand choice for products consumed in public but not for those consumed in private.[93]

The significance of the product to the group also affects normative influence.[94] Some products designate membership in a certain group. A varsity sports jacket may signify team membership and play a significant role in designating in- and out-group status. The more central a product is to the group, the greater the normative influence the group exerts over its purchase. Finally, whether a product is perceived as embarrassing may also influence acquisition and consumption behavior that occurs in a more public setting.[95]

Consumer Characteristics

The personalities of some consumers make them readily susceptible to influence by others.[96] The trait of competitiveness, for instance, can influence conspicuous consumption behavior.[97] Several researchers have developed the scale of "susceptibility to interpersonal influence," which includes some of the items in Exhibit 11.9. Consumers who are susceptible to interpersonal influence try to enhance their self-image by acquiring products that they think others will approve of. These consumers are also willing to conform to others' expectations about which products and brands to buy.

In addition, a personality characteristic called "attention to social comparison information" (ATSCI) is related to normative influence. Exhibit 11.10 shows several items from an ATSCI scale. People who are high on this personality trait pay close attention to what others do and use this information to guide their own behavior. For example, research shows that people feel lower self-esteem when they are exposed to idealized ad images of financial success or physical attractiveness.[98] When consumers are susceptible to normative influence, they tend to react more positively to communications highlighting product benefits that help them avoid social disapproval.[99]

Tie-strength also affects the degree of normative influence. When ties are strong, individuals presumably want to maintain their relationships with others, so they are therefore motivated to conform to the group's norms and wishes.[100] Normative influence is also affected by a consumer's identification with the group.[101] When a member of a group such as a family or subculture does not identify with that group's attitudes, behaviors, and values, normative reference-group influence will be weak.

Group Characteristics

Finally, the characteristics of the group can impact the degree of normative influence. One characteristic is the extent to which the group can deliver rewards and sanctions, known as the degree of reward power or **coercive power**.[102] To illustrate, your friends probably have more influence over

Coercive power The extent to which the group has the capacity to deliver rewards and sanctions.

© Cengage Learning 2013

Items Indicating Susceptibility to Interpersonal Influence

1. I rarely purchase the latest fashion styles until I am sure my friends approve of them.
2. If other people can see me using a product, I often purchase the brand they expect me to buy.
3. I often identify with other people by purchasing the same products and brands that they purchase.
4. To make sure that I buy the right product or brand, I often observe what others are buying and using.
5. If I have little experience with a product, I often ask my friends about the product.
6. I frequently gather information from friends or family about a product before I buy it.

Items Indicating Attention to Social Comparison Information

1. It is my feeling that if everyone else in a group is behaving in a certain manner, this must be the proper way to behave.
2. I actively avoid wearing clothes that are not in style.
3. At parties, I usually try to behave in a manner that allows me to fit in.
4. When I am uncertain about how to act in a social situation, I look to the behavior of others for cues.
5. I tend to pay attention to what others are wearing.
6. The slightest look of disapproval in the eyes of a person with whom I am interacting is enough to make me change my approach.

Exhibit 11.10

Measuring Susceptibility to Interpersonal Influence and Attention to Social Comparison Information

Individuals differ in whether they are susceptible to influence from others and whether they pay attention to what others do. What conclusions can you draw about yourself based on your answers to these questions? What implications do these questions have for marketers?

Source: Susceptibility to Interpersonal Influence Scale from William O. Bearden, Richard G. Netemeyer and Jesse E. Teel, "Measurement of Consumer Susceptibility to Interpersonal Influence," *Journal of Consumer Research*, March 1989, pp. 472–481. Reprinted with permission of The University of Chicago Press.

your clothing choices than your neighbors do because friends have greater coercive power. That is, they are better able to deliver sanctions if they consider your clothing inappropriate or out of style. In fact, men tend to spend more when they shop with a friend than they would alone, although this does not occur when women shop with a friend. The influence is also different for high self-monitoring, agentic consumers, who tend to spend more when they shop with a friend than when they shop alone.[103]

Group cohesiveness and group similarity also affect the degree of normative influence.[104] Cohesive groups and groups with similar members may communicate and interact on a regular basis. Thus, they have greater opportunity to convey normative influences and deliver rewards and sanctions. Research shows that if a company calls consumers' attention to their cultural identity, their increased awareness of their membership in a particular group can influence their decisions based on group norms.[105] Normative influence tends to be greater when groups are large and when group members are experts.[106] For example, you might be more inclined to buy a bottle of wine recommended by a group of wine experts than one recommended by a casual acquaintance.

Finally, consumers from cultures where collectivism is strong—such as China—are more sensitive to how differences in pricing affect those in their group, compared with consumers from cultures where individualism is strong, such as the United States.[107] This accounts, in part, for why the practice of *tuangou*, the self-organized banding together of consumers to get discounts by shopping as a group, is especially popular in China.[108]

Marketing Implications

Marketers can take a variety of actions based on normative influences and the factors that affect their strength.

Demonstrate Rewards and Sanctions for Product Use/Nonuse

Marketers may be able to create normative influence by using advertising to demonstrate rewards or sanctions that can follow from product use or nonuse. For example, beer or liquor ads often show friends approving of the purchase or consumption of the advertised brand.

Create Norms for Group Behavior

Marketing organizations may create groups with norms to guide consumers' behavior. Members of Weight Watchers who adhere to the norms (by losing weight) are rewarded with group praise. Because influence is greater when consumption is public, another strategy is to make a private behavior public, either in person or online via apps, communities, or websites. Having group discussions about eating behaviors is one way that Weight Watchers makes private information public.

Stimulate Referrals Through Normative Influence

Companies can use normative influence to encourage referrals from current customers. "Bring a friend" promotions are one example. The Swedish retailer IKEA recently used Facebook to promote its "Bring Your Own Friend Day," offering two-for-one specials in its in-store cafeterias plus discounts, gift-card giveaways, decorating seminars, free shopping bags, and more. Its Facebook page suggested sending invitations to friends designated as "my personal shoppers," among other categories. For each Facebook friend invited by an IKEA fan, the company donated $1 to a children's charity, another inducement to spread the word and participate.[109] Although referral programs can pay off in the form of higher sales and profits, marketers need to target and test carefully, because not all customers are equally profitable or loyal.[110]

Create Conformity Pressures

Marketers may also attempt to create conformity. For example, they may actively associate a product with a certain group so that their product becomes a badge of group membership. They may simulate conformity by showing actors in an ad behaving similarly with respect to a product, as some antismoking campaigns do by portraying teens who do not smoke.[111] Conformity may also be enhanced by publicizing others' conformity, a situation that happens at Mary Kay cosmetics parties and at charity fundraisers like telethons.

Use Compliance Techniques

Foot-in-the-door technique A technique designed to induce compliance by getting an individual to agree first to a small favor, then to a larger one, and then to an even larger one.

Door-in-the-face technique A technique designed to induce compliance by first asking an individual to comply with a very large and possibly outrageous request, followed by a smaller and more reasonable request.

Even-a-penny-will-help technique A technique designed to induce compliance by asking individuals to do a very small favor—one that is so small that it almost does not qualify as a favor.

With the **foot-in-the-door technique**, marketers try to enhance compliance by getting a consumer to agree first to a small favor, then to a larger one, and then to an even larger one. For example, a salesperson may first ask a consumer his or her name and then ask what the person thinks of a given product. After complying with these requests, the consumer may be more inclined to comply with the salesperson's ultimate request to purchase the product.[112]

With the **door-in-the-face technique**, the marketer first asks the consumer to comply with a very large and possibly outrageous request, and then presents a smaller and more reasonable request. For example, a salesperson might ask a consumer whether she wants to buy a $500 piece of jewelry. When the consumer says no, the salesperson might then ask if she wants to buy a set of earrings on sale for only $25.[113] Because the consumer perceives that the requester has given something up by moving from a large to a small request, he or she may feel obligated to reciprocate by responding to the smaller request. Moreover, compared to the large initial request, the second seems much more modest.

A third approach is the **even-a-penny-will-help technique**.[114] Here, marketers ask the consumer for a very small favor—so small that it almost does not qualify as a favor. Marketers collecting money for a charity may indicate that even a penny will help those in need. For example, Pennies, a U.K. charity, uses this technique by asking consumers to donate small change electronically when paying by credit card at Domino's Pizza and other participating merchants. If they agree, the purchase is rounded up to the next whole number and the charity receives the few cents' difference.[115] Salespeople making cold calls may even tell prospective clients that even one minute of their time will be valuable. Because people would look foolish denying these tiny requests, they often comply and give an amount appropriate for the situation.

Ask Consumers to Predict Their Behavior

Simply asking consumers to predict their own behavior in taking a certain action often increases the likelihood that they will actually behave in that way.[116] For example, a marketer of products containing recycled parts might ask consumers to predict their behavior in supporting the environment by buying or using products made with reclaimed materials.[117] This request may remind consumers that they have not been doing enough to live up to their own standards in supporting the environment—in turn, leading to purchases that will fulfill the consumers' self-prophecy.

Provide Freedom of Choice

Because reactance usually occurs when people feel that their freedom is being threatened, marketers need to ensure that consumers believe that they have freedom of choice. For example, a salesperson might show a consumer a variety of smartphones, discussing the advantages of each. In this situation, the consumer will feel a greater sense of control over whether to buy at all, and if so, which item to buy. Marketers often offer multiple products within a product line to allow for more choices of features, benefits, and price points, as consumers consider their personal needs and priorities.

Use Expert Service Providers Who Are Similar to Target Customers

Some research shows that consumers are more likely to comply with what a service provider asks (and be more satisfied with the outcome) when the provider and customer have similar attitudes and when the expert clarifies the customer's role.[118] _____

INFORMATIONAL INFLUENCE

Informational influence The extent to which sources influence consumers simply by providing information.

In addition to normative influence, reference groups and other influence sources can exert **informational influence** by offering information to help consumers make decisions.[119] For example, chat groups on Internet travel sites exert informational influence by providing travel tips to prospective travelers. Friends exert informational influence by telling you which movie is playing at the local theater, and the media exert informational influence by reporting that certain foods may be health hazards.

Informational influence can affect how much time and effort consumers devote to information search and decision making. If you can get information easily from a friend, you may be reluctant to conduct an extensive, time-consuming information search when making a decision. Therefore, if you want a new tablet computer, and a trusted friend says that the one he just bought is the best he has ever had, you might simply buy the same one.

Factors Affecting Informational Influence Strength

The extent to which informational influence is strong or weak depends on the characteristics of the product, of the consumer and the influencer, and of the group.

Product Characteristics

Consumers tend to be susceptible to informational influence when considering complex products such as electronic appliances that consumers cannot easily understand how to use.[120] They are also more susceptible to informational influence when they perceive product purchase or usage to be risky.[121] Thus, consumers may be affected by information that they receive about cosmetic surgery, given its formidable financial and safety risks. Consumers may also be more open to informational influence when they themselves cannot tell the difference between brands.[122]

Consumer and Influencer Characteristics

Characteristics of both the consumer and the influencer affect the extent of informational influence. Such influence is likely to be greater when the source or group communicating the information is an expert,[123] especially if the consumer either lacks expertise or has had ambiguous experiences with the product. For example, given their lack of knowledge and confidence about the home-buying process, first-time home buyers may carefully consider the information conveyed by experts such as real estate agents. Personality traits, such as consumers' susceptibility to reference group influence and ATSCI, also influence the extent to which consumers look to others for cues on product characteristics.[124]

Like normative influence, informational influence is affected by tie-strength. Individuals with strong ties tend to interact frequently, a situation that provides greater opportunities for consumers to learn about products and others' reactions to them. Note that informational influence may actually affect the ties between individuals. When people establish social relationships that involve sharing information, for example, they may become friends in the process.[125] Informational influence can also be affected by interactions with strangers online. Specifically, consumers seeking information online will assess how quickly and frequently an information provider—such as an anonymous reviewer—responds to questions and comments.[126]

Finally, culture may affect informational influence. One study found that U.S. consumers were more likely than Korean consumers to be persuaded by information-packed ads. Because the Korean culture often focuses on the group and group compliance, Korean consumers may be more susceptible to normative influence than U.S. consumers are.[127]

Group Characteristics

Group cohesiveness also affects informational influence. Specifically, members of cohesive groups have both greater opportunity and perhaps greater motivation to share information.

Marketing Implications

Marketers can apply informational influence in several ways.

Create Informational Influence by Using Experts

Because source expertise and credibility affect informational influence, marketers can use sources regarded as expert or credible for the product category, as Under Armor does when it uses sports stars such as skier Lindsey Vonn and football player Brandon Jennings in its ads.[128]

Create a Context for Informational Influence

Marketers should try to create a context for informational influence to occur. One way to do this is by hosting or sponsoring special product-related events where people can talk to one another about the company's products. Another way is to host online chats or social media accounts to spark company or brand conversations. Marriott International's website invites public reaction to the CEO's regular blog posts and podcasts, as well as links to interactions with consumers on Twitter, Facebook, and YouTube.[129] In addition, inviting consumers to rate products on the marketers' website provides a forum for online discussion and stimulates word of mouth—especially where ratings vary—which in turn contributes to higher product sales.[130]

Create Informational and Normative Influence

Marketing efforts may be most successful when *both* normative and informational influences are involved. One study found that only 2 percent of consumers donated blood in the absence of any type of influence, but between 4 and 8 percent did so when either informational or normative influence was present. However, when both forms of influence were used, 22 percent of the consumers donated blood.[131] Also, because source similarity enhances both normative and informational influence, advertisers might enhance influence by using sources that are similar to their target audience. Using web-based recommendation systems is another approach to using both normative and informational influence.[132] Finally, marketers can provide clues to product scarcity—such as notifying customers that "due to high demand, only 5 are left in stock." This strategy acts as an informational normative influence and encourages consumers to "join the crowd" and purchase the item, to avoid being left out.[133]

Descriptive Dimensions of Information

In the context of consumer behavior, information can be described by the dimensions of valence and modality.

Valence: Is Information Positive or Negative?

Valence Whether information about something is good (positive valence) or bad (negative valence).

Valence describes whether the information is positive or negative. This distinction is very important because researchers have found that negative and positive information affect consumer behavior in different ways.[134] More than half of dissatisfied consumers engage in negative word of mouth. Moreover, dissatisfied consumers talk to three times more people about their bad experiences than satisfied consumers do about their good experiences.[135] People who like to post online comments about products react more to negative information than do people who read without posting—perhaps because the posters want to make it look like they have high standards.[136]

Researchers hypothesize that people pay more attention to and give more weight to negative information than they do to positive information.[137] Negative information may be diagnostic—that is, it has more significance because it seems to tell us how offerings differ from one another. Most of the information we hear about offerings is positive, so negative information may receive more attention because it is surprising, unusual, and different.[138] Negative information may also prompt consumers to attribute problems to the offering itself, not to the consumer who uses it.[139] Thus, if you learn that a friend got sick after eating at a new restaurant, you may attribute the outcome to bad food rather than to your friend's eating too much.

Modality: Does Information Come from Verbal or Nonverbal Channels?

Another dimension describing influence is the modality through which it is delivered—is it communicated verbally or nonverbally? Although norms about group behavior might be explicitly communicated by verbal description, consumers can also infer norms through observation. For instance, a consumer may learn that a particular brand of can openers is bad either by observing someone struggling with it or by hearing people discuss their experiences with the product.

The Pervasive and Persuasive Influence of Word of Mouth

Marketers are especially interested in word of mouth, both online and offline, which can affect many consumer behaviors. Your neighbor may recommend a hair stylist; you may overhear a stranger say that Nordstrom's semiannual sale is next week.[140] Or you may go to a new movie because your friend posted a positive comment on Facebook. In fact, word of mouth before a movie is released and during its first week in theaters has been shown to strongly influence other consumers' movie-going intentions.[141]

More than 40 percent of U.S. consumers ask family and friends for advice when selecting a doctor, a lawyer, or an auto mechanic, although men and women differ in how often they seek advice and from whom.[142] Importantly, one in five word-of-mouth conversations relates to paid advertising—marketer-sourced content. Moreover, such conversations are more likely to focus on recommendations to buy or try a product, indicating that marketers can have a significant influence on word of mouth through their advertising.[143]

Not only is word of mouth *pervasive*; it is also more *persuasive* than written information is.[144] One study found that word of mouth was the top source affecting food and household product purchases. It was seven times more effective than print media, twice as effective as broadcast media, and four times more effective than salespeople in affecting brand switching.[145] It is also extremely influential in purchases of printed and electronic books. "Even in this digital age, the best sales tool remains word of mouth," says a spokesman for Random House, the largest U.S. book publisher. "Nothing trumps that."[146]

Online Word of Mouth

Online forums, review sites, websites, and e-mail magnify the effect of word of mouth because consumers can notify many people about their good or bad experiences with a few clicks of the mouse. For instance, in any given month, 61 million consumers worldwide read reviews of local businesses that consumers post on yelp.com; tripadvisor.com has 50 million consumer-contributed

Exhibit 11.11

Social Media Word of Mouth
Word-of-mouth is now often real-time due to social media and all its many outlets.

reviews of hotels and other travel businesses. One study of restaurant reviews posted by consumers on yelp.com found that positive ratings translated into revenue increases for independent restaurants, in particular. Why? Positive reviews encouraged consumers to try new, local restaurants, rather than going to nationally advertised chains.[147] Research shows that the most persuasive consumer-generated reviews of a good or service offer evidence to support an overall recommendation ("Buy the Divine chocolate, because it tastes good and is fair trade") and include information about key features ("70% cocoa content").[148]

Customers' purchasing decisions are also influenced by observing what others do online after being exposed to the same online word of mouth. For example, consumers who use amazon.com can read product reviews and then look at the items displayed under the banner "What Other Items Do Customers Buy After Viewing This Item?" This combination is especially influential in the case of products with high word-of-mouth volume.[149]

Social Media Word of Mouth

Social media such as Twitter, YouTube, and Facebook are truly *social*, disseminating word of mouth through public messages and through messages visible only to friends (see Exhibit 11.11). In turn, other consumers may keep the conversation going by reposting or retweeting the original message, echoing it in their own words, rebutting it, recording a video response, or in other ways. These social exchanges can themselves spark word of mouth and get more consumers involved in the conversation and the brand or product. When a product or brand "trends" on Twitter, for example, many users will click to see what others are tweeting about. Similarly, when a YouTube video attracts so many views that it lands on the YouTube home page, that additional exposure is responsible for more views.

Marketers who provide consumers with opportunities to comment via social media during product acquisition or consumption are, in effect, facilitating real-time word of mouth. For example, CBS has instituted Tweet Week and CBS Social Sweep Week to encourage viewers to talk about the network's television programs with each other while programs or previews are being aired. The purpose is to build viewership by building buzz.[150]

Marketing Implications

Viral marketing Rapid spread of brand/product information among a population of people stimulated by brands.

Word of mouth can have a dramatic effect on consumers' product perceptions and an offering's marketplace performance. **Viral marketing**, a rapid spread of brand/product information among a population of people stimulated by brands, contributed in large part to the global success of the Angry Birds games, as mentioned in this chapter's opening case. Marketers want brand or product information to "go viral" because of the opportunity to influence many people in a short period.

Often, small businesses such as hairstylists and preschools cannot afford to advertise in traditional media and rely almost exclusively on word-of-mouth referrals, consumer reviews online, and mentions in social media. Doctors, dentists, and lawyers often rely heavily on word of mouth because they fear that extensive advertising will cheapen their professional image. Moreover, success in some industries (such as entertainment) is ultimately tied to favorable word of mouth. For this reason, companies routinely watch for mentions of their brands online and in social media. Just as important, marketers can actively stimulate discussion by posting information and responding to comments and questions online, often with special emphasis on social media.

Yet word of mouth can have unexpected implications. One study found that consumers with a high need for uniqueness prefer not to provide positive word of mouth for publicly consumed products that they own, although they will provide word of mouth for privately consumed products. Why? Because positive word of mouth often results in higher sales of a product, which would dilute the uniqueness of publicly consumed products, at least in the eyes of these consumers.[151]

Engineering Favorable Word of Mouth

Marketers can try to engineer favorable word of mouth by targeting opinion leaders and using networking opportunities at trade shows, conferences, and public events. Many have social media strategies that include YouTube, Facebook, Twitter, and other popular sites. Film companies routinely post previews on YouTube and on branded sites devoted to each movie, with the goal of building anticipation and prelaunch positive buzz. When consumers are familiar with a brand, positive word of mouth is especially influential, more so than negative word of mouth. On the other hand, consumers resist positive word of mouth about brands they are highly unlikely to purchase (and resist negative word of mouth about brands they are highly likely to purchase).[152] Original products—those that are highly innovative—generate more word of mouth than nonoriginal products. If the product is both original and useful, meaning it meets consumer needs, it is more likely to promote positive word of mouth.[153]

Engineering favorable word of mouth should be an ongoing effort across marketing activities. For instance, an employee group at Gatorade monitors social media mentions, responds to comments, and coordinates social media activities with other marketing efforts. The company integrates its traditional advertising with its social media strategy by, for example, "using the hashtag very purposefully when we're trying to get the conversation going," says a top Gatorade official.[154]

Preventing and Responding to Negative Word of Mouth

Marketers must act to prevent negative word of mouth, whether offline or online, and work to rectify it once it occurs.[155] In the event of a major crisis, a firm must take immediate steps to address the issues, restore confidence, and begin rebuilding its reputation (see Exhibit 11.12).[156]

Rather than ignoring complaints or derogatory comments, firms that empathize with consumers' complaints, address the issues, and respond in a meaningful way will be more successful at reducing negative word of mouth. For example, L.L.Bean closely monitors product reviews posted by customers and responds to negative comments by reexamining the product's improvement potential and, in some cases, withdrawing the product. "There's value in these conversations," explains the chief marketing officer, "but if you're not acting upon them, you're missing it."[157] In fact, one study of negative online comments found that when a firm responds, 33 percent of customers will follow up with a positive comment and 34 percent of customers will take down the original negative comment.[158]

In another example, Bolt Barbers, a barber shop in Los Angeles, has an unusual response to negative Yelp reviews: It publicizes them to attract customers who prefer traditional barber services. "Our 'People Hate Us on Yelp' campaign is a way to help those people find a place that they are going to be comfortable with," says the owner, who notes that "there's no dearth of places you can go to get quaffed, feathered, and texturized. Just don't come to Bolt."[159]

Exhibit 11.12

Restoring a Company's Reputation

Crisis management experts suggest that companies under siege take certain steps (and avoid others) to rebuild their reputation.

DO:	DON'T:
• Listen carefully to understand public perceptions.	• Ignore the crisis.
• Address the issues quickly, consistently, and appropriately.	• Delay your response.
• Be as transparent as possible.	• Evade the issues.
• Make customers your priority.	• Respond with indifference, anger, or impatience.
• Have a contingency plan to win back customers' trust.	• Ignore regular business operations during the crisis.

Handling Rumors and Scandals

Rumors are a special case of negative word of mouth.[160] Scandals can also touch off negative word of mouth, even affecting a company's competitors.[161] Companies should be aware of what consumers are saying about their brands and products, offline, online, and in social media—and be ready to deal with rumors and scandals.

▶ *Do nothing.* Often companies prefer to do nothing because more consumers may actually learn about a rumor from marketers' attempts to correct it. However, this strategy can also backfire. For example, after Nike was accused of condoning low wages and abusive conditions in its Asian factories, its image suffered when it did not respond vigorously to the attacks. The company has since responded in various ways, including putting links to labor standards on its website and severing ties with suppliers that violate those standards. Apple, which produces iPhones and iPads in China, faced similar criticism and now publicizes its annual factory audits, as well as explaining the changes it will make.[162]

▶ *Do something locally.* Some companies react locally, putting the rumor to rest on a case-by-case basis. Procter & Gamble, for example, sent a packet of information about its man-in-the-moon symbol, long rumored to connote devil worship, only to those consumers who called its hotline. In such cases, companies should brief staff members about the rumor and how they should respond to consumers.

▶ *Do something discreetly.* Companies may want to respond discreetly to a rumor. For example, when rumors circulated that oil companies were contriving oil shortages out of greed, the firms ran a public relations campaign highlighting their socially desirable activities. They did not mention the rumor, but the gist of the campaign clearly ran contrary to the rumor's content.

▶ *Do something big.* At times, companies may respond with all the media resources at their disposal. They may use advertising to directly confront and refute the rumor or explain the scandal, create news and conduct media interviews to communicate their perspective, and hire credible outside opinion leaders to help present factual information. For example, when reports surfaced about the all-electric Chevrolet Volt's battery catching fire following government safety tests, parent company General Motors quickly, publicly, and repeatedly pointed to the car's real-world safety record. It offered Volt owners a free GM loaner car to drive while the safety issue was under investigation. Within weeks, GM had redesigned the battery case to reduce the risk of fire and installed it without charge in Volts already on the road. During government hearings, GM's CEO reiterated the company's position that if the battery presented a real fire hazard, "There would be no stalling or working the bureaucratic process. We'd place our customers' sense of safety and peace of mind first, and we would act quickly."[163]

Tracking Word of Mouth

Whether word of mouth is positive (like referrals) or negative (like rumors), companies may want to try to identify the source. Marketers can find out where consumers heard the information and then ask all of those sources where, in turn, they heard the story.[164] Companies such as Dell have special departments devoted to analyzing online and social media comments to see where and when they originated and how they're spreading. With this information, the firms can be prepared to respond accordingly. Marketers can also ask consumers about the specific details that they heard from particular sources, to identify who is distorting information and who is perpetuating the distortions. Then the company can follow up by, for example, thanking or rewarding individuals who communicate positive word of mouth and provide referrals. ⎯⎯⎯⎯⎯

SUMMARY

Consumers are influenced by many sources—marketing and nonmarketing, and those that are delivered through the mass media and those that are delivered personally. Consumers regard nonmarketing sources as more credible than marketing sources. Information delivered personally has less reach but more capacity for two-way communication compared with information from mass media sources. Marketers may want to target opinion leaders, online and offline, who are sources of influence because they are experts in a product category.

Reference groups, people with whom individuals compare themselves, may be associative, aspirational, or dissociative; they can be described according to their degree of contact, formality, homophily, group attractiveness, density, identification, and tie-strength. These influence sources exert normative and informational influence. Normative influence tends to be greater for products that are publicly consumed, considered luxuries, or regarded as a significant aspect of group membership. Normative influence is also strong for individuals who tend to pay attention to social information and when groups are cohesive, members are similar, and the group can deliver rewards and sanctions.

Informational influence operates when individuals affect others by providing information. Consumers are most likely to seek and follow informational influence when products are complex, purchase or use is risky, and brands are distinctive. Social influence varies in valence and modality. Negative information is communicated to more people and given greater weight in decision making than positive information is. Marketers are particularly interested in word of mouth, both positive and negative, online and offline, and in social media.

Questions for Review and Discussion

1. How do sources of influence differ in terms of marketer domination and delivery?

2. How are social media affecting social influence?

3. Why do companies sometimes target opinion leaders for marketing attention?

4. What are the three types of reference groups, and how can these groups be described?

5. How might consumers respond to normative influence?

6. What three techniques can marketers use to encourage consumer compliance?

7. Differentiate between information valence and modality.

8. Why is word of mouth so important for marketers?

CONSUMER BEHAVIOR CASE

Big Buying on Black Friday and Cyber Monday

Black Friday has long been a U.S. shopping tradition. It's named for the day after Thanksgiving (fourth Thursday in November), when retail businesses move from the "red" into the "black"—become profitable—as consumers start buying for Christmas, Hanukkah, or Kwanzaa. Over the years, retailers and product marketers have shaped shoppers' expectations and stimulated word of mouth by offering deep discounts on desirable gift items such as televisions, but in limited quantities. Because consumers have learned that they must arrive early to take advantage of special pricing, many talk about their plans in advance and arrange to shop together, braving lines and crowds to get bargains they'll brag about later.

Media coverage of Black Friday has magnified the focus on bargain hunting and generated even more word-of-mouth excitement in recent years. Not all of the news has been positive: Reports include incidents of violence, long lines at some stores, and complaints from shoppers unable to buy what they wanted. Meanwhile, in the weeks leading up to Black Friday, brand and retail marketers spotlight special pricing and early opening hours in commercials, print ads, radio, and via social media such as Facebook and Twitter.

In 2011, the news that some stores and malls would open at midnight or earlier on the night of Thanksgiving touched off a firestorm of online and offline comments, some in support and some in opposition. When the gigantic Mall of America in Minnesota opened at midnight on Thanksgiving, 15,000 shoppers rushed in, including many Gen Y consumers who told reporters that they preferred late-night shopping to the usual early-morning shopping of Black Friday. By the end of the day, more than 200,000 shoppers had visited the mall, part of the record 86 million U.S. consumers who shopped in stores on that day. Nearly 25 percent of Black Friday shoppers arrived at stores on midnight or earlier, for the few stores that were open. Millions of consumers logged onto retail websites or used their smartphones or tablet computers to shop before or on Black Friday, because many retailers offered special deals in advance.

Cyber Monday, the Monday after Black Friday, is an online shopping "tradition" started by a retail association in 2005. It quickly turned into the busiest online buying day of the year, with consumers clicking to buy from home or at work. Marketers have helped this Internet age tradition along by e-mailing discount offers, posting bargains on sites and Facebook, tweeting about hourly specials, and touting the convenience of buying with a click instead of crowding into stores. Reports in mainstream media, as well as comments on technology blogs and in social media, have also helped to popularize Cyber Monday as an online shopping day.

Individual marketers are hoping to attract customers by advertising their own shopping days during this big buying weekend in November. For example, the telecommunications firm T-Mobile USA recently promoted discounts on smartphones and tablet devices on "Magenta Saturday," named for its brand color.

Mattel has offered deep discounts on toys for "Pink Friday" and "Blue Friday," which coincide with Black Friday. Deal-a-day websites such as livingsocial.com and groupon.com also offer Black Friday specials, targeting bargain seekers who receive offers by e-mail. Watch for even more marketing messages and nonmarketing conversations about these two shopping days as the next holiday buying season approaches.

Extreme shopping days like Black Friday are also common around the globe. For example, on December 27, millions of shoppers in Japan simultaneously shop to prepare for the New Year's festivities.[165]

CASE QUESTIONS

1. What role do you think normative influence and consumer socialization have played in the ongoing popularity of Black Friday and Cyber Monday?

2. What kinds of opinion leaders would you recommend that retailers target to influence consumers' decisions about where and when to shop on Black Friday and Cyber Monday?

3. How is the valence of information about Black Friday and Cyber Monday likely to influence consumers' decisions about where and when to shop on those days?

4. What kind of shopping experiences and emotions do consumers feel when shopping together?

ENDNOTES

1. Sherman So, "Angry Birds Head for China," *Asia Times*, January 18, 2012, www.atimes.com; Gideon Spanier, "It's All to Play for as Mobile and Social Change the Game," *London Evening Standard*, January 18, 2012, www.thisislondon.co.uk; and Oliver Nieburg, "Fazer to Enter Asia with Angry Birds Partnership," *Confectionery News*, January 13, 2012, www.confectionerynews.com.

2. Greg Metz Thomas, "Building the Buzz with the Hive in Mind," *Journal of Consumer Behavior* 4, no. 1, 2004, pp. 64–72.

3. Giselle Tsirulnik, "Macy's Is 2011 Mobile Marketer of the Year," *Mobile Marketer*, December 9, 2011, www.mobilemarketer.com.

4. Amna Kirmani and Margaret C. Campbell, "Goal Seeker and Persuasion Sentry: How Consumer Targets Respond to Interpersonal Marketing Persuasion," *Journal of Consumer Research*, December 2004, pp. 573–582.

5. Robert L. Simison and Joseph B. White, "Reputation for Poor Quality Still Plagues Detroit," *Wall Street Journal*, May 4, 2000, pp. B1, B4.

6. Utpal M. Dholakia, Richard P. Bagozzi, and Lisa Klein Pearo, "A Social Influence Model of Consumer Participation in Network- and Small-Group-Based Virtual Communities," *International Journal of Research in Marketing* 21, 2004, pp. 241–263.

7. See Mehdi Mourali, Michel Larouche, and Frank Pons, "Antecedents of Consumer Relative Preference for Interpersonal Information Sources in Pre-Purchase Search," *Journal of Consumer Behaviour* 4, no. 5, 2005, pp. 307–318.

8. Cotton Delo, "Doritos' Latest Super Bowl Ad Contest Storms Viral Video Chart," *Advertising Age*, January 12, 2012, www.adage.com.

9. Colin Campbell, Leyland F. Pitt, Michael Parent, and Pierre R. Berthon, "Understanding Consumer Conversations Around Ads in a Web 2.0 World," *Journal of Advertising*, Spring 2011, pp. 87–102.

10. David G. Taylor, Jeffrey E. Lewin, and David Strutton, "Friends, Fans, and Followers: Do Ads Work on Social Networks?" *Journal of Advertising Research*, March 2011, pp. 258–275.

11. Frederick Koenig, *Rumor in the Marketplace* (Dover, Mass.: Auburn House, 1985); and Paul M. Herr, Frank R. Kardes, and John Kim, "Effects of Word-of-Mouth and Product-Attribute Information on Persuasion: An Accessibility-Diagnosticity Perspective," *Journal of Consumer Research*, March 1991, pp. 454–462.

12. Dale Duhan, Scott Johnson, James Wilcox, and Gilbert Harrell, "Influences on Consumer Use of Word-of-Mouth

Recommendation Sources," *Journal of the Academy of Marketing Science* 25, Fall 1997, pp. 283–295.

13. Jonas Colliander and Micael Dahlen, "Following the Fashionable Friend: The Power of Social Media," *Journal of Advertising Research*, March 2011, pp. 313–320.

14. Vicki Clift, "Systematically Solicit Testimonial Letters," *Marketing News*, June 6, 1994, p. 7.

15. "Celebrities Paid Thousands for Endorsement Tweets," *CBS News*, November 7, 2011, www.cbsnews.com.

16. See Robert V. Kozinets, "E-Tribalized Marketing?" *European Management Journal*, 1999, pp. 252–264.

17. Susan B. Garland, "So Glad You Could Come. Can I Sell You Anything?" *New York Times*, December 19, 2004, sec. 3, p. 7.

18. Richard S. Levick, "4 Strategic Requirements for Corporate Tweeting," *Fast Company*, January 20, 2012, www.fastcompany.com.

19. Gangseog Ryu and Lawrence Feick, "A Penny for Your Thoughts: Referral Reward Programs and Referral Likelihood," *Journal of Marketing*, January 2007, pp. 84–94.

20. Philipp Schmitt, Bernd Skiera, and Christophe Van den Bulte, "Why Customer Referrals Can Drive Stunning Profits," *Harvard Business Review*, June 2011, www.hbr.org.

21. Jacob Jacoby and Wayne D. Hoyer, "What If Opinion Leaders Didn't Really Know More," in ed. Kent B. Monroe, *Advances in Consumer Research*, vol. 8 (Chicago: Association for Consumer Research, 1980), pp. 299–302; and Robin M. Higie, Lawrence F. Feick, and Linda L. Price, "Types and Amount of Word-of-Mouth Communications about Retailers," *Journal of Retailing*, Fall 1987, pp. 260–277; regarding innovativeness, see Terry L. Childers, "Assessment of the Psychometric Properties of an Opinion Leadership Scale," *Journal of Marketing Research*, May 1986, pp. 184–187.

22. Marsha L. Richins and Teri Root-Shafer, "The Role of Involvement and Opinion Leadership in Consumer Word of Mouth," in ed. Michael J. Houston, *Advances in Consumer Research*, vol. 15 (Provo, Utah: Association for Consumer Research, 1988), pp. 32–36.

23. Audrey Guskey-Federouch and Robert L. Heckman, "The Good Samaritan in the Marketplace," Paper presented at the Society for Consumer Psychology Conference, St. Petersburg, Fla., February 1994.

24. "Why We Love Shallots: Sales Double in a Year Thanks to Jamie and Delia," *Daily Mail (UK)*, January 21, 2011, www.dailymail.co.uk.

25. Lawrence F. Feick, Linda L. Price, and Robin Higie, "People Who Use People," in ed. Richard J. Lutz, *Advances in Consumer Research*, vol. 13 (Provo, Utah: Association for Consumer Research, 1986), pp. 301–305; see also Jagdish N. Sheth, "Word-of-Mouth in Low-Risk Innovations," *Journal of Advertising Research*, June–July 1971, pp. 15–18.

26. Ronald E. Goldsmith, Ronald A. Clark, and Elizabeth Goldsmith, "Extending the Psychological Profile of Market Mavenism," *Journal of Consumer Behavior* 5, no. 5, 2006, pp. 411–419; and Lawrence F. Feick and Linda L. Price, "The Market Maven: A Diffuser of Marketplace Information," *Journal of Marketing*, January 1987, pp. 83–97.

27. See, for example, Dorothy Leonard-Barton, "Experts as Negative Opinion Leaders in the Diffusion of a Technological Innovation," *Journal of Consumer Research*, March 1985, pp. 914–926.

28. Daniel Michaels, "For Some Grown-Ups, Playing with Legos Is a Serious Business," *Wall Street Journal*, November 17, 2011, www.wsj.com.

29. "Eye on Brazil," *WWD*, September 22, 2011, www.com.

30. Mae Anderson, "Mommy Bloggers Can Make or Break Toys," *San Francisco Chronicle*, December 26, 2011, www.sfgate.com.

31. Julia Moskin, "Chef Has Diabetes, and Some Say 'I Told You So,'" *New York Times*, January 17, 2012, www.nytimes.com.

32. Lee Al, "Who Are the Opinion Leaders?" *Journal of Health Communication*, September 2010, pp. 629–655.

33. Malcolm Moore, "Li Poised to Become Richest Woman in Sports," *Telegraph (UK)*, August 2, 2011, www.telegraph.co.uk.

34. Jennifer Edson Escalas and James R. Bettman, "Self-Construal, Reference Groups, and Brand Meaning," *Journal of Consumer Research* 32, no. 3, 2005, pp. 378–389.

35. Andrew D. Gershoff and Katherine A. Burson, "Knowing Where They Stand: The Role of Inferred Distributions of Others in Misestimates of Relative Standing," *Journal of Consumer Research*, October 2011, pp. 407–419.

36. Albert M. Muniz Jr. and Thomas C. O'Guinn, "Brand Community," *Journal of Consumer Research* 27, March 2001, pp. 412–432; and James H. McAlexander, John W. Schouten, and Harold F. Koenig, "Building Brand Community," *Journal of Marketing*, January 2002, pp. 38–54.

37. James H. McAlexander, John W. Schouten, and Harold Koenig, "Building Brand Community," *Journal of Marketing* 66, no. 1, 2002, pp. 38–54.

38. Richard P. Bagozzi and Utpal M. Dholakia, "Antecedents and Purchase Consequences of Customer Participation in Small Group Brand Communities," *International Journal of Research in Marketing* 23, 2006, pp. 45–61.

39. Albert M. Muniz Jr. and Hope Jensen Schau, "Religiosity in the Abandoned Apple Newton Brand Community," *Journal of Consumer Research* 31, no. 4, 2005, pp. 737–747.

40. Katherine White and Darren W. Dahl, "To Be or Not Be? The Influence of Dissociative Reference Groups on Consumer Preferences," *Journal of Consumer Psychology* 16, no. 4, 2006, pp. 404–414.

41. T. L. Stanley, "Heavies of Hip-Hop Lend Phat to Nokia," *Advertising Age*, December 15, 2003, p. 6.

42. Jesse Strauch, "Oosterhouse Helps Build Houses for the Needy," *MSNBC*, January 18, 2012, www.msnbc.msn.com.

43. Basil G. Englis and Michael R. Solomon, "To Be and Not to Be: Lifestyle Imagery, Reference Groups, and the Clustering of America," *Journal of Advertising*, March 1995, pp. 13–28.

44. Elizabeth Holmes, "Abercrombie and Fitch Offers to Pay 'The Situation' to Stop Wearing Its Clothes," *Wall Street Journal*, August 16, 2011, www.wsj.com.

45. A. Benton Cocanougher and Grady D. Bruce, "Socially Distant Referent Groups and Consumer Aspiration," *Journal of Marketing Research*, August 1971, pp. 379–383.

46. Linda L. Price, Lawrence Feick, and Robin Higie, "Preference Heterogeneity and Coorientation as Determinants of Perceived Informational Influence," *Journal of Business Research*, November 1989, pp. 227–242; Jacqueline J. Brown and Peter Reingen, "Social Ties and Word-of-Mouth Referral Behavior," *Journal of Consumer Research*, December 1987, pp. 350–362; Mary C. Gilly, John L. Graham, Mary Wolfinbarger, and Laura Yale, "A Dyadic Study of Interpersonal Information Search," *Journal of the Academy of Marketing Science* 26, no. 2, pp. 83–100; and George Moschis, "Social Comparison and Informal Group Influence," *Journal of Marketing Research*, August 1976, pp. 237–244.

47. Randall L. Rose, William O. Bearden, and Kenneth C. Manning, "Attributions and Conformity in Illicit Consumption: The Mediating Role of Group Attractiveness," *Journal of Public Policy & Marketing* 20, no. 1, Spring 2001, pp. 84–92.

48. Rohit Deshpande, Wayne D. Hoyer, and Naveen Donthu, "The Intensity of Ethnic Affiliation: A Study of the Sociology of Hispanic Consumption," *Journal of Consumer Research*, September 1986, pp. 214–220; and Douglas M. Stayman and Rohit Deshpande, "Situational Ethnicity and Consumer Behavior," *Journal of Consumer Research*, December 1989, pp. 361–371.

49. Robert Madrigal, "The Influence of Social Alliances with Sports Teams on Intentions to Purchase Corporate Sponsors' Products," *Journal of Advertising* 29, no. 4, Winter 2000, pp. 13–24.

50. Americus Reed II, "Activating the Self-Importance of Consumer Selves: Exploring Identity Salience Effects on Judgments," *Journal of Consumer Research*, September 2004, pp. 286–295.

51. Jonathan K. Frenzen and Harry L. Davis, "Purchasing Behavior in Embedded Markets," *Journal of Consumer Research*, June 1990, pp. 1–12; see also Mark S. Granovetter, "The Strength of Weak Ties," *American Journal of Sociology*, May 1973, pp. 1360–1380; Brown and Reingen, "Social Ties and Word-of-Mouth Referral Behavior"; and Jonathan K. Frenzen and Kent Nakamoto, "Structure, Cooperation, and the Flow of Market Information," *Journal of Consumer Research*, December 1993, pp. 360–375.

52. Mark Chillingworth, "A Source of Much Relief for Charity CIO Marcus East," *CIO UK*, December 30, 2011, www.cio.co.uk.

53. Ray Waddell, "Ticketmaster Launches New Facebook App," *Billboard*, January 18, 2012, www.billboard.com.

54. Michael Trusov, Anand V. Bodapati, and Randolph E. Bucklin, "Determining Influential Users in Internet Social Networks," *Journal of Marketing Research*, August 2010, pp. 643–658.

55. Reingen and Kernan, "Analysis of Referral Networks in Marketing"; and Brown and Reingen, "Social Ties and Word-of-Mouth Referral Behavior"; see also Frenzen and Nakamoto, "Structure, Cooperation, and the Flow of Market Information."

56. Nicole Woolsey Biggart, *Charismatic Capitalism* (Chicago: University of Chicago Press, 1989); see also Frenzen and Davis, "Purchasing Behavior in Embedded Markets."

57. Frenzen and Davis, "Purchasing Behavior in Embedded Markets."

58. Kristal Roberts, "Girl Scout Cookie Apps Use GPS Technology to Quench Cookie Cravings," *ABC Action News*, January 17, 2012, www.abcactionnews.com.

59. Scott Ward, "Consumer Socialization," *Journal of Consumer Research*, September 1974, pp. 1–16; George P. Moschis, "The Role of Family Communication in Consumer Socialization of Children and Adolescents," *Journal of Consumer Research*, March 1985, pp. 898–913; George P. Moschis, *Consumer Socialization: A Life Cycle Perspective* (Lexington, Mass.: Lexington Books, 1987); Scott Ward, "Consumer Socialization," in eds. Harold H. Kassarjian and Thomas S. Robertson, *Perspectives in Consumer Behavior* (Glenview, Ill.: Scott-Foresman, 1980), pp. 380–396; and Les Carlson and Sanford Grossbart, "Parental Style and Consumer Socialization of Children," *Journal of Consumer Research*, June 1988, pp. 77–92.

60. Deborah Roedder John, "Consumer Socialization of Children: A Retrospective Look at Twenty-Five Years of Research," *Journal of Consumer Research* 26, December 1999, pp. 183–213.

61. Elizabeth S. Moore, William L. Wilkie, and Richard J. Lutz, "Passing the Torch: Intergenerational Influences as a Source of Brand Equity," *Journal of Marketing*, April 2002, pp. 17–37.

62. Gwen Bachmann Achenreiner and Deborah Roedder John, "The Meaning of Brand Names to Children," *Journal of Consumer Psychology*, 13 (3), 2003, pp. 205–219.

63. Gregory M. Rose, Vassilis Dalakas, and Fredric Kropp, "Consumer Socialization and Parental Style Across Cultures," *Journal of Consumer Psychology* 13 (4), 2003, pp. 366–376.

64. Anirban Mukhopadhyay and Catherine W.M. Yeung, "Building Character: Effects of Lay Theories of Self-Control on the Selection of Products for Children," *Journal of Marketing Research*, April 2010, pp. 240–250.

65. John, "Consumer Socialization of Children: A Retrospective Look at Twenty-Five Years of Research."

66. Ann Walsh, Russell Laczniak, and Les Carlson, "Mothers' Preferences for Regulating Children's Television," *Journal of Advertising*, Fall 1998, pp. 23–36.

67. Moschis, "The Role of Family Communication in Consumer Socialization of Children and Adolescents"; Conway Lackman and John M. Lanasa, "Family Decision Making Theory," *Psychology and Marketing*, March–April 1993, pp. 81–93; and George P. Moschis, *Acquisition of the Consumer Role by Adolescents* (Atlanta, Ga.: Georgia State University, 1978).

68. Beverly A. Browne, "Gender Stereotypes in Advertising on Children's Television in the 1990s," *Journal of Advertising*, Spring 1998, pp. 83–96.

69. See, for example, Greta Fein, David Johnson, Nancy Kosson, Linda Stork, and Lisa Wasserman, "Sex Stereotypes and Preferences in the Toy Choices of 20-Month-Old Boys and Girls," *Developmental Psychology*, July 1975, pp. 527–528; Lenore A. DeLucia, "The Toy Preference Test," *Child Development*, March 1963, pp. 107–117; Judith E. O. Blackmore and Asenath A. LaRue, "Sex-Appropriate Toy Preference and the Ability to Conceptualize Toys as Sex-Role Related," *Developmental Psychology*, May 1979, pp. 339–340; and Nancy Eisenberg-Berg, Rita Boothby, and Tom Matson, "Correlates of Preschool Girls' Feminine and Masculine Toy Preferences," *Developmental Psychology*, May 1979, pp. 354–355.

70. Donna Rouner, "Rock Music Use as a Socializing Function," *Popular Music and Society*, Spring 1990, pp. 97–108; and Thomas L. Eugene, "Clothing and Counterculture: An Empirical Study," *Adolescence*, Spring 1973, pp. 93–112.

71. Fein et al., "Sex Stereotypes and Preferences in the Toy Choices of 20-Month-Old Boys and Girls"; Eisenberg-Berg, Boothby, and Matson, "Correlates of Preschool Girls' Feminine and Masculine Toy Preferences"; and Sheila Fling and Main Manosevitz, "Sex Typing in Nursery School Children's Play," *Developmental Psychology* 7, September 1972, pp. 146–152.

72. Tamara Mangleburg and Terry Bristol, "Socialization and Adolescents' Skepticism Toward Advertising," *Journal of Advertising*, Fall 1998, pp. 11–21.

73. Chillingworth, "A Source of Much Relief for Charity CIO Marcus East."

74. Robert E. Burnkrant and Alain Cousineau, "Informational and Normative Social Influence in Buyer Behavior," *Journal of Consumer Research*, December 1975, pp. 206–215; and Morton Deutsch and Harold B. Gerard, "A Study of Normative and Informational Influence upon Individual Judgment," *Journal of Abnormal and Social Psychology*, November 1955, pp. 629–636.

75. Dennis Rook and Robert Fisher, "Normative Influences on Impulsive Buying Behavior," *Journal of Consumer Research*, December 1995, pp. 305–313.

76. Paul Rozin and Leher Singh, "The Moralization of Cigarette Smoking in the United States," *Journal of Consumer Psychology* 8, no. 3, 1999, pp. 321–337.

77. David B. Wooten, "From Labeling Possessions to Possessing Labels: Ridicule and Socialization Among Adolescents," *Journal of Consumer Research* 33, no. 2, 2006, pp. 188–198.

78. Margaret Talbot, "Girls Just Want to Be Mean," *New York Times Magazine*, February 24, 2002, p. 24.

79. Peter Reingen, Brian Foster, Jacqueline Brown, and Stephen B. Seidman, "Brand Congruence in Interpersonal Relations," *Journal of Consumer Research*, December 1984, pp. 771–783.

80. Rajagopal Raghunathan and Kim Corfman, "Is Happiness Shared Doubled and Sadness Shared Halved? Social Influence on Enjoyment of Hedonic Experiences," *Journal of Marketing Research*, August 2006, pp. 386–394.

81. Tina M. Lowrey, Cele C. Otnes, and Julie A. Ruth, "Social Influences on Dyadic Giving over Time," *Journal of Consumer Research*, March 2004, pp 547–558.

82. Ann E. Schlosser and Sharon Shavitt, "Anticipating Discussion About a Product: Rehearsing What to Say Can Affect Your Judgments," *Journal of Consumer Research*, June 2002, pp. 101–115.

83. James E. Stafford, "Effects of Group Influence on Consumer Brand Preferences," *Journal of Marketing Research*, February 1966, pp. 68–75.

84. Pankaj Aggarwal, "The Effects of Brand Relationship Norms on Consumer Attitudes and Behavior," *Journal of Consumer Research*, June 2004, pp. 87–101.

85. Randall L. Rose, William O. Bearden, and Jesse E. Teel, "An Attributional Analysis of Resistance to Group Pressure Regarding Illicit Drug and Alcohol Consumption," *Journal of Consumer Research*, June 1992, pp. 1–13; Bobby J. Calder and Robert E. Burnkrant, "Interpersonal Influences on Consumer Behavior: An Attribution Theory Approach," *Journal of Consumer Research*, June 1977, pp. 29–38, 71; Solomon E. Asch, "Effects of Group Pressure upon the Modification and Distortion of Judgment," in ed. H. Guetzkow, *Groups, Leadership and Men* (Pittsburgh, Pa.: Carnegie Press, 1951); and Sak Onkvisit and John J. Shaw, *International Marketing: Analysis and Strategy* (Columbus, Ohio: Merrill, 1989); see also Chin Tiong Tan and John U. Farley, "The Impact of Cultural Patterns on Cognition and Intention in Singapore," *Journal of Consumer Research*, March 1987, pp. 540–544.

86. Lisa E. Bolton and Americus Reed II, "Sticky Priors: The Perseverance of Identity Effects on Judgment," *Journal of Marketing Research*, November 2004, pp. 397–410.

87. Utpal M. Dholakia, Richard P. Bagozzi, and Lisa Klein Pearo, "A Social Influence Model of Consumer Participation in Network- and Small-Group-Based Virtual Communities," *International Journal of Research in Marketing* 21, 2004, pp. 241–263.

88. For a general discussion of reactance behavior, see Mona A. Clee and Robert A. Wicklund, "Consumer Behavior and Psychological Reactance," *Journal of Consumer Research*, March 1980, pp. 389–405.

89. Rene Algesheimer, Utpal M. Dholakia, and Andreas Hermann, "The Social Influence of Brand Community," *Journal of Marketing*, July 2005, pp. 19–34.

90. A. Peter McGraw and Philip E. Tetlock, "Taboo Trade-Offs, Relational Framing, and the Acceptability of Exchanges," *Journal of Consumer Psychology* 15, no. 1, 2005, pp. 2–15. See also Gita Venkataramani Johar, "The Price of Friendship: When, Why, and How Relational Norms Guide Social Exchange Behavior," *Journal of Consumer Psychology* 15, no. 1, 2005, pp. 22–27; Barbara E. Kahn, "The Power and Limitations of Social Relational Framing for Understanding Consumer Decision Processes," *Journal of Consumer Psychology* 15, no. 1, 2005, pp. 28–34; and Philip E. Tetlock and A. Peter McGraw, "Theoretically Framing Relational Framing," *Journal of Consumer Psychology* 15, no. 1, 2005, pp. 35–37.

91. Russell W. Belk, "Exchange Taboos from an Interpretive Perspective," *Journal of Consumer Psychology* 15, no. 1, 2005, pp. 16–21.

92. White and Dahl, "To Be or Not Be? The Influence of Dissociative Reference Groups on Consumer Preferences."

93. William O. Bearden and Michael J. Etzel, "Reference Group Influence on Product and Brand Purchase Decisions," *Journal of Consumer Research* 9, no. 2, 1982, pp. 183–194.

94. Robert E. Witt and Grady D. Bruce, "Group Influence and Brand Choice Congruence," *Journal of Marketing Research*, November 1972, pp. 440–443.

95. Jennifer J. Argo, Darren W. Dahl, and Rajesh V. Manchanda, "The Influence of a Mere Social Pressure in a Retail Context," *Journal of Consumer Research* 32, no. 2, 2005, pp. 207–212; and Darren W. Dahl, Rajesh V. Manchanda, and Jennifer J. Argo, "Embarrassment in Consumer Purchase," *Journal of Consumer Research*, December 2001, pp. 473–481.

96. Bobby J. Calder and Robert E. Burnkrant, "Interpersonal Influences on Consumer Behavior," *Journal of Consumer Research*, June 1977, pp. 29–38; William O. Bearden, Richard G. Netemeyer, and Jesse E. Teel, "Measurement of Consumer Susceptibility to Interpersonal Influence," *Journal of Consumer Research*, March 1989, pp. 473–481; and William O. Bearden and Randall L. Rose, "Attention to Social Comparison Information," *Journal of Consumer Research*, March 1990, pp. 461–471.

97. John C. Mowen, "Exploring the Trait of Competitiveness and Its Consumer Behavior Consequences," *Journal of Consumer Psychology*, 2004, pp. 52–63.

98. Charles S. Gulas and Kim McKeage, "Extending Social Comparison," *Journal of Advertising* 29, no. 2, Summer 2000, pp. 17–28.

99. David B. Wooten and Americus Reed II, "Playing It Safe: Susceptibility to Normative Influence and Protective Self-Presentation," *Journal of Consumer Research*, December 2004, pp. 551–556.

100. C. Whan Park and Parker Lessig, "Students and Housewives: Differences in Susceptibility to Reference Group Influence," *Journal of Consumer Research*, September 1977, pp. 102–110.

101. Robert Fisher and Kirk Wakefield, "Factors Leading to Group Identification: A Field Study of Winners and Losers," *Psychology and Marketing*, January 1998, pp. 23–40.

102. John R. French and Bertram Raven, "The Bases of Social Power," in ed. D. Cartwright, *Studies in Social Power* (Ann Arbor, Mich.: Institute for Social Research, 1969), pp. 150–167.

103. Didem Kurt, J. Jeffrey Inman, and Jennifer J. Argo, "The Influence of Friends on Consumer Spending: The Role of Agency-Communion Orientation and Self-Monitoring," *Journal of Marketing Research*, August 2011, pp. 741–754.

104. Reingen et al., "Brand Congruence in Interpersonal Relations"; and Park and Lessig, "Students and Housewives: Differences in Susceptibility to Reference Group Influence."

105. Donnel A. Briley and Robert S. Wyer Jr., "The Effect of Group Membership Salience on the Avoidance of Negative Outcomes," *Journal of Consumer Research*, December 2002, pp. 400–415.

106. Dana-Nicoleta Lascu, William O. Bearden, and Randall L. Rose, "Norm Extremity and Interpersonal Influences on Consumer Conformity," *Journal of Business Research*, March 1995, pp. 200–212.

107. Lisa E. Bolton, Hean Tat Keh, and Joseph W. Alba, "How Do Price Fairness Perceptions Differ Across Culture?" *Journal of Marketing Research*, June 2010, pp. 564–576.

108. Tae-Hyung Kim, Kevin Lam, and Christopher Tsai, "The Groupon Effect in China," *Knowledge@Wharton*, January 3, 2012, http://knowledge.wharton.upenn.edu.

109. Christopher Heine, "IKEA Wants Facebook Fans to Bring Friends to Stores," *ClickZ*, December 20, 2011, www.clickz.com.

110. Philipp Schmitt, Bernd Skiera, and Christophe Van den Bulte, "Referral Programs and Customer Value," *Journal of Marketing*, January 2011, pp. 46–59.

111. Social influence, attitudes toward the ads, and prior trial behavior all affect antismoking beliefs, as discussed in J. Craig Andrews, Richard G. Netemeyer, Scot Burton, D. Paul Moberg, and Ann Christiansen, "Understanding Adolescent Intentions to Smoke," *Journal of Marketing*, July 2004, pp. 110–123.

112. J. L. Freeman and S. Fraser, "Compliance Without Pressure: The Foot-in-the-Door Technique," *Journal of Personality and Social Psychology*, August 1966, pp. 195–202.

113. Robert B. Cialdini, J. E. Vincent, S. K. Lewis, J. Caalan, D. Wheeler, and B. L. Darby, "Reciprocal Concessions Procedure for Inducing Compliance," *Journal of Personality and Social Psychology*, February 1975, pp. 200–215; and John C. Mowen and Robert Cialdini, "On Implementing the Door-in-the-Face Compliance Strategy in a Marketing Context," *Journal of Marketing Research*, May 1980, pp. 253–258; see also Edward Fern, Kent Monroe, and Ramon Avila, "Effectiveness of Multiple Request Strategies," *Journal of Marketing Research*, May 1986, pp. 144–152.

114. Alice Tybout, Brian Sternthal, and Bobby J. Calder, "Information Availability as a Determinant of Multiple Request Effectiveness," *Journal of Marketing Research*, August 1983, pp. 279–290; and John T. Gourville, "Pennies-a-Day: The Effect of Temporal Reframing on Transaction Evaluation," *Journal of Consumer Research*, March 1998, pp. 395–408.

115. Hadley Jones, "Pennies: Electronic Microdonations for Charity at the Point of Sale," *Point of Sale News*, December 29, 2011, http://pointofsale.com.

116. Eric R. Spangenberg and David E. Sprott, "Self-Monitoring and Susceptibility to the Influence of Self-Prophecy," *Journal of Consumer Research* 32, no. 4, 2006, pp. 550–556; and Eric R. Spangenberg and Anthony G. Greenwald, "Social Influence by Requesting Self-Prophecy," *Journal of Consumer Psychology* 8, no. 1, 1999, pp. 61–89.

117. For more about self-prophecy, see Eric R. Spangenberg, David E. Sprott, Bianca Grohmann, and Ronn J. Smith, "Mass-Communicated Prediction Requests," *Journal of Marketing*, July 2003, pp. 47–62.

118. Stephanie Dellande, Mary C. Gilly, and John L. Graham, "Gaining Compliance and Losing Weight," *Journal of Marketing*, July 2004, pp. 78–91.

119. Deutsch and Gerard, "A Study of Normative and Informational Influence upon Individual Judgment"; Park and Lessig, "Students and Housewives: Differences in Susceptibility to Reference Group Influences"; and Dennis L. Rosen and Richard W. Olshavsky, "The Dual Role of Informational Social Influence," *Journal of Business Research*, April 1987, pp. 123–144.

120. Jeffrey D. Ford and Elwood A. Ellis, "A Re-examination of Group Influence on Member Brand Preference," *Journal of Marketing Research* 17, no. 1, 1980, pp. 125–133; and Linda L. Price and Lawrence F. Feick, "The Role of Interpersonal Sources in External Search," in ed. Thomas Kinnear, *Advances in Consumer Research*,

vol. 11 (Ann Arbor, Mich.: Association for Consumer Research, 1984), pp. 250–255.

121. Arch G. Woodside and M. Wayne DeLosier, "Effects of Word-of-Mouth Advertising on Consumer Risk Taking," *Journal of Advertising*, September 1976, pp. 17–26.

122. Henry Assael, *Consumer Behavior and Marketing Action*, 4th ed. (Boston: PWS-Kent, 1992).

123. John R. French and Bertram Raven, "The Bases of Social Power," in ed. D. Cartwright, *Studies in Social Power* (Ann Arbor, Mich.: Institute for Social Research, 1959), pp. 150–167; Dana-Nicoleta Lascu, William Bearden, and Randall Rose, "Norm Extremity and Interpersonal Influences on Consumer Conformity," *Journal of Business Research*, March 1995, pp. 200–212; and David B. Wooten and Americus Reed II, "Informational Influence and the Ambiguity of Product Experience," *Journal of Consumer Psychology* 7, no. 1, 1998, pp. 79–99.

124. Bearden, Netemeyer, and Teel, "Measurement of Consumer Susceptibility to Interpersonal Influence"; and Bearden and Rose, "Attention to Social Comparison Information."

125. Gerald Zaltman and Melanie Wallendorf, *Consumer Behavior: Basic Findings and Management Implications*, 2d ed. (New York: Wiley, 1983); and Reingen et al., "Brand Congruence in Interpersonal Relations."

126. Allen M. Weiss, Nicholas H. Lurie, and Deborah J. MacInnis, "Listening to Strangers: Whose Responses Are Valuable, How Valuable Are They, and Why?" *Journal of Marketing Research*, August 2008, pop. 425–436.

127. Charles R. Taylor, Gordon E. Miracle, and R. Dale Wilson, "The Impact of Information Level on the Effectiveness of U.S. and Korean Television Commercials," *Journal of Advertising*, Spring 1997, pp. 1–18.

128. Andrea K. Walker, "Under Armour's Rookie Strategy for Endorsement Deals," *Baltimore Sun*, July 25, 2011, www.baltimoresun.com.

129. Michael McKean, "Social Media: Don't Just Sign Up. Do It Right!" *Hotel News Now*, August 10, 2011, www.hotelnewsnow.com; and Jane L. Levere, "Wisdom of the Web," January 29, 2008, p. C8. For more about Web-based chatting, see George M. Zinkhan, Hyokjin Kwak, Michelle Morrison, and Cara Okleshen Peters, "Web-Based Chatting," *Journal of Consumer Psychology* 13 (1 and 2), 2003, pp. 17–27.

130. Wendy M. Moe and Michael Trusov, "The Value of Social Dynamics in Online Product Ratings Forums," *Journal of Marketing Research*, June 2011, pp. 444–456.

131. Stephen A. LaTour and Ajay Manrai, "Interactive Impact of Informational and Normative Influence on Donations," *Journal of Marketing Research*, August 1989, pp. 327–335.

132. Asim Ansari, Skander Essegaier, and Rajeev Kohli, "Internet Recommendation Systems," *Journal of Marketing Research* 37, August 2000, pp. 363–375.

133. Erica Van Herpen, Rik Pieters, and Marcel Zeelenberg, "When Demand Accelerates Demand: Trailing the Bandwagon," *Journal of Consumer Psychology* 19, no. 3, 2009, pp. 301–312.

134. Johan Arndt, "Role of Product-Related Conversations in the Diffusion of a New Product," *Journal of Marketing Research*, August 1967, pp. 291–295.

135. Marsha L. Richins, "Negative Word of Mouth by Dissatisfied Consumers," *Journal of Marketing*, January 1983, pp. 68–78.

136. Ann E. Schlosser, "Posting Versus Lurking: Communication in a Multiple Audience Context," *Journal of Consumer Research* 32, no. 2, 2005, pp. 260–265.

137. Herr, Kardes, and Kim, "Effects of Word-of-Mouth and Product-Attribute Information on Persuasion: An Accessibility-Diagnosticity Perspective"; and Richard W. Mizerski, "An Attribution Explanation of the Disproportionate Influence of Unfavorable Information," *Journal of Consumer Research*, December 1982, pp. 301–310.

138. See Suman Basuroy, Subimal Chatterjee, and S. Abraham Ravid, "How Critical Are Critical Reviews?" *Journal of Marketing*, October 2003, pp. 103–117.

139. Daniel Laufer, Kate Gillespie, Brad McBride, and Silvia Gonzalez, "The Role of Severity in Consumer Attributions of Blame," *Journal of International Consumer Marketing* 17, no. 2/3, 2005, pp. 33–50.

140. Brown and Reingen, "Social Ties and Word-of-Mouth Referral Behavior"; Arndt, "Role of Product-Related Conversations in the Diffusion of a New Product"; and Laura Yale and Mary C. Gilly, "Dyadic Perceptions in Personal Source Information Search," *Journal of Business Research*, March 1995, pp. 225–238.

141. Yong Liu, "Word of Mouth for Movies: Its Dynamics and Impact on Box Office Revenue," *Journal of Marketing*, July 2006, pp. 74–89.

142. Chip Walker, "Word of Mouth," *American Demographics*, July 1995, pp. 39–46.

143. Ed Keller and Brad Fay, "The Role of Advertising in Word of Mouth," *Journal of Advertising Research*, June 2009, pp. 154ff.

144. Herr, Kardes, and Kim, "Effects of Word-of-Mouth and Product-Attribute Information on Persuasion: An Accessibility-Diagnosticity Perspective."

145. Elihu Katz and Paul F. Lazarsfeld, *Personal Influence* (Glencoe, Ill.: Free Press, 1955).

146. Allen Pierleoni, "Best-Sellers Lists," *Sacramento Bee*, January 22, 2012, www.sacbee.com.

147. Michael Luca, "Yelp Is Leaving Chains Behind," *Harvard Business Review Blog*, December 7, 2011, http://blogs.hbr.org.

148. Jin Li and Lingjing Zhan, "Online Persuasion: How the Written Word Drives WOM," *Journal of Advertising Research*, March 2011, pp. 239–257.

149. Yubo Chen, Qi Wang, and Jinhong Xie, "Online Social Interactions: A Natural Experiment on Word of Mouth Versus Observational Learning," *Journal of Marketing Research*, April 2011, pp. 238–254.

150. Geoge Schweitzer, "Word-of-mouth Face-off: In-person conversation still dominates," *CNET*, November 3, 2011, www.cnet.com.

151. Amar Cheema and Andrew M. Kaikati, "The Effect of Need for Uniqueness on Word of Mouth," *Journal of Marketing Research*, June 2010, pp. 553–563.

152. Robert East, Kathy Hammond, and Wendy Lomax, "Measuring the Impact of Positive and Negative Word of Mouth on Brand Purchase Probability," *International Journal of Research in Marketing* 25, 2008, pp. 215–224.

153. Sarit Moldovan, Jacob Goldenberg, and Amitava Chattopadhyay, "The Different Roles of Product Originality and Usefulness in Generating Word-of-mouth," *International Journal of Research in Marketing* 28, 2011, pp. 109–119.

154. Natalie Zmuda, "Gatorade's New Selling Point: We're Necessary Performance Gear," *Advertising Age*, January 2, 2012, www.adage.com.

155. A. Coskun and Cheryl J. Frohlich, "Service: The Competitive Edge in Banking," *Journal of Services Marketing*, Winter 1992, pp. 15–23; Jeffrey G. Blodgett, Donald H. Granbois, and Rockney Waters, "The Effects of Perceived Justice on Complainants' Negative Word-of-Mouth Behavior and Repatronage Intentions," *Journal of Retailing*, Winter 1993, pp. 399–429; Karen Maru File, Ben B. Judd, and Russ A. Prince, "Interactive Marketing: The Influence of Participation on Positive Word-of-Mouth Referrals," *Journal of Services Marketing*, Fall 1992, pp. 5–15; and Gary L. Clark, Peter F. Kaminski, and David R. Rink, "Consumer Complaints," *Journal of Services Marketing*, Winter 1992, pp. 41–51.

156. Dallas Lawrence, "6 Tips for Handling Breaking Crises on Twitter," *Mashable*, January 17, 2012, http://mashable.com.

157. Why Terrible Online Reviews Are Actually Good for You," *Advertising Age*, September 15, 2011, www.adage.com.

158. Ekaterina Walter, "How to Respond to Facebook Attacks," *Fast Company*, May 3, 2011, www.fastcompany.com.

159. Stephanie Elam and Julie Brayton, "Does Yelp Help Small Business?" *NBC Los Angeles*, November 15, 2011, www.nbclosangeles.com.

160. Michael Kamins, Valerie Folkes, and Lars Perner, "Consumer Responses to Rumors," *Journal of Consumer Psychology* 6, no. 2, 1997, 165–187.

161. Michelle L. Roehm and Alice M. Tybout, "When Will a Brand Scandal Spill Over, and How Should Competitors Respond?" *Journal of Marketing Research*, August 2006, pp. 366–373.

162. Erica Gies, "Is This Apple's Nike Moment?" *Forbes*, January 20, 2012, www.forbes.com; and Lars Paronen, "Apple Reveals Child Labor at Some Suppliers," *Reuters*, January 13, 2012, www.reuters.com.

163. "GM CEO Says Chevy Volt Fire Problem Handled Properly," *Fox News*, January 25, 2012, www.foxnews.com; and Jake Holmes, "GM Considering Volt Buybacks, Offers Loaner Cars During Fire Investigation," *Motor Trend*, December 2, 2011, www.motortrend.com.

164. Reingen and Kernan, "Analysis of Referral Networks in Marketing."

165. Robert Hof, "Cyter Monday: Marketing Hype No More," *Forbes*, November 28, 2011, www.forbes.com; Wendy Lee, "Bustling Midnight Openings Mean Empty Aisles Come Early Morning," *Star Tribune (Minneapolis)*, November 25, 2011, www.startribune.com; Richard H. Levey and Larry Riggs, "Black Friday Roundup," *Chief Marketer*, November 30, 2011, www.chiefmarketer.com; "Cyber Monday, Green Tuesday . . . Black Friday Isn't the Only Game in Town," *MSNBC*, November 28, 2011, www.msnbc.com; Stuart Elliott, "For Some Marketers, Brand Investment Beats Black Friday," *New York Times*, November 22, 2011, www.nytimes.com; and "Black Friday Weekend Shines as Shoppers Line Up for Deals," *National Retail Federation news release*, November 27, 2011, www.nrf.com/holidays.

CONSUMER DIVERSITY

LEARNING OBJECTIVES

After studying this chapter, you will be able to

1. Explain how the consumer's age affects acquisition, consumption, and disposition behavior, and why marketers need to consider age influences when planning marketing activities.

2. Describe how gender and sexual orientation each affects consumer behavior and how companies can

create more effective marketing by understanding these two influences.

3. Discuss how regional, ethnic, and religious influences can affect consumer behavior and why marketers must consider such influences when targeting specific groups.

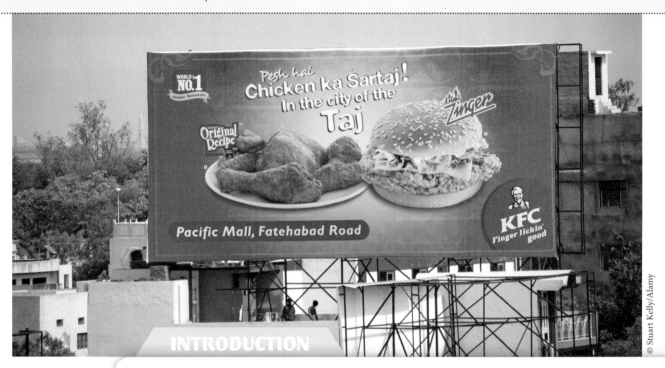

INTRODUCTION

Serving Shrimp Burgers in Beijing and Potato Tacos in Bangalore

When Yum! Brands opens a KFC, Pizza Hut, or Taco Bell restaurant outside the United States, it carefully tailors its offerings to regional and religious preferences. Although KFC is associated with fried chicken dishes in America, its menu in China extends far beyond chicken. There, consumers can order shrimp burgers, egg tarts, fried dough sticks, and other dishes that appeal to local taste buds. KFC also targets particular regions inside China with dishes such as Sichuan spiced tofu chicken. In the Urumqi region of Xinjiang, KFC promotes itself to Muslim Uyghur people as a place to hold parties marking certain religious milestones. And, in line with local customs, home delivery is an option for customers who buy from many of the 3,200 KFC restaurants in China.

In India, KFC initially entered the market with American-style chicken entrees—which quickly proved unpopular. Regrouping, the restaurant chain switched to chicken dishes flavored with local spices and introduced an extensive vegetarian menu for Hindu consumers who eat no meat. Pizza Hut in India offers a wide variety of vegetarian toppings and, for customers of the Jain faith, special toppings without either meat or root vegetables. Finally, Yum! Brands' first Taco Bell restaurant in Bangalore, India, respects religious preferences by serving no beef or pork dishes. Instead, it uses potato in tacos and chicken in burritos, complemented by a menu full of vegetarian dishes prepared with a Taco Bell flavor twist.[1]

Yum! Brands has grown its revenue and profits dramatically in China and India by paying close attention to diversity influences that affect consumer behavior (see Exhibit 12.1). First, the region in which its customers reside—and specific regions within a country, such as the Sichuan area of China—can influence consumer behavior, including the foods and flavors they favor. Second, consumer behavior can vary among subgroups of individuals with unique patterns of religion because of different traditions, customs, and preferences. For instance, many Hindu groups and Jains avoid meat, which is why KFC, Pizza Hut, and Taco Bell serve vegetarian dishes in India. Clearly, to develop and implement effective marketing strategies and tactics, companies must understand how these and other diversity influences (such as age, gender, and sexual orientation) affect consumers.

HOW AGE AFFECTS CONSUMER BEHAVIOR

Marketers often segment consumers by age. The basic logic is that people of the same age are going through similar life experiences and therefore share many common needs, experiences, symbols, and memories, which, in turn, may lead to similar consumption patterns.[2] Regardless of country, age groups are constantly shifting as babies are born, children grow up, adults mature, and people die. This section opens with an overview of U.S. age trends and continues with an examination of four major age groups being targeted by marketers: (1) teens and millennials, also known as Generation Y; (2) Generation X; (3) baby boomers; and (4) seniors.

Age Trends in the United States

The median age of U.S. consumers in 1980 was 30 years. Today, the median age is 37 years, reflecting a huge bulge in the over-40 population. Adults aged 18 and over now make up more than 76 percent of the overall U.S. population (see Exhibit 12.2). Thanks in part to better medical care and healthier lifestyles, people are living longer, which is why the senior market is an attractive target market. Marketers also target age segments of consumers who are entering the workplace and those who are setting up their own households, seeking to build and sustain brand loyalty during these critical periods.

Teens and Millennials

Your own experience may confirm that this segment has considerable influence in household purchases and enjoys a good deal of financial independence. Teens shop more frequently than consumers in other segments, check prices online and via cell phone as well as in stores before they buy, and put a high value on price and convenience.[3] Just as important, U.S. consumers under 18 years of age have hundreds of friends (including social media contacts) whose buying power and brand preferences they may influence.[4] Friends are a major source of information

THE CONSUMER'S CULTURE

Consumer Diversity (Ch. 12)

Household and Social Class Influences (Ch. 13)

Social Influences on Consumer Behavior (Ch. 11)

Psychographics: Values, Personality, and Lifestyles (Ch. 14)

THE PSYCHOLOGICAL CORE
- Motivation, Ability, and Opportunity (Ch. 2)
- From Exposure to Comprehension (Ch. 3)
- Memory and Knowledge (Ch. 4)
- Attitude Formation and Change (Chs. 5–6)

THE PROCESS OF MAKING DECISIONS
- Problem Recognition and Information Search (Ch. 7)
- Judgment and Decision Making (Chs. 8–9)
- Post-Decision Processes (Ch. 10)

CONSUMER BEHAVIOR OUTCOMES AND ISSUES
- Innovations: Adoption, Resistance, and Diffusion (Ch. 15)
- Symbolic Consumer Behavior (Ch. 16)
- Marketing, Ethics, and Social Responsibility in Today's Consumer Society (Ch. 17)

CONSUMER DIVERSITY
- Age influences
- Gender influences
- Sexual orientation
- Regional influences
- Ethnic influences
- Religious influences

© Cengage Learning 2013

Exhibit 12.1

Chapter Overview: Consumer Diversity

This chapter examines how diversity influences such as age, gender, sexual orientation, the region in which one lives, ethnic groups, and religion can affect consumer behavior.

about products, and socializing is one of the major reasons that teens like to shop. Many teens discuss brands in text messages, instant messages, blogs, social networking, and online reviews.[5] Having grown up with recycling, many in this segment consider a product's environmental impact before buying.

A common teen "culture" is spreading around the world, although marketers must take care not to overlook localized culture and its effects on teen consumer behavior.[6] A study of teens in 44 countries reveals common characteristics and attitudes that cross national boundaries in six distinct segments.[7] The "thrills and chills" segment, including teens in the United States, Germany, and other countries, consists of fun-seeking, free-spending consumers from middle- or upper-class backgrounds. Teens in the "resigned" segment, covering Denmark, South Korea, and elsewhere

The U.S. Population by Age
Consumers up to the age of 18 comprise nearly 24 percent of the U.S. population; by comparison, consumers aged 65 and older comprise just under 14 percent of the population.

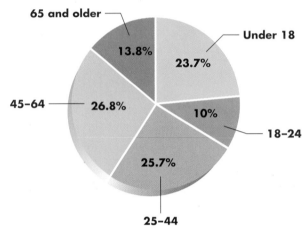

Source: Data from U.S. Census Bureau, 2010 Census.

are alienated from society and have low expectations of the future and of material success. High-aspiration teen "world savers" in Hungary, Venezuela, and other countries are characterized by their altruism. Ambitious teen "quiet achievers" in Thailand, China, and other nations conform to societal norms. "Bootstrappers" in Nigeria, Mexico, the United States, and other countries are family-oriented achievement seekers with hopes for the future. Finally, dutiful and conforming "upholders" in Vietnam, Indonesia, and other nations seek a rewarding family life and uphold traditional values.

Millennial Individuals born between 1980 and 1994; also known as *Generation Y*.

Consumers born during the years 1980 through 1994 are part of the **millennial** generation, also known as **Generation Y**. Millennials are media and tech savvy, having grown up during the Internet era and being accustomed to using various digital gadgets to shop, communicate, listen to music, play games, and so on.[8] According to one study, they seek four benefits from tech devices: immediacy, entertainment, social interaction, and self-expression.[9] This segment is more likely to own laptops or other portable computers, whereas older age groups own desktop personal computers. Also, more than 90 percent of this segment owns a cell phone, which makes millennials an attractive target for upgraded handsets, apps, videos, games, and other mobile-related goods and services.[10]

For economic reasons, many consumers in their 20s and 30s have been delaying their independence or becoming *boomerangers*, meaning they move back in with their parents after college or after being on their own (see Chapter 13 for more about household structure). For example, in California, more than 30 percent of children aged 18 and over now live with their parents, a significant increase over the percentage that lived with their parents in 2000.[11] This trend toward "doubled-up households" isn't confined to the United States: In Australia, for instance, a growing number of adult children aren't leaving home until their mid-20s or later.[12] Boomerangers marry and settle down later and have more discretionary income to spend on entertainment because their parents pay for essentials. Compared with peers who live independently, boomerangers are more likely to buy items like a new car or the latest electronics.

Marketing Implications

U.S. teens are an important target market because they spend money on their own and also influence billions of dollars in family purchases. Around the world, the similarity of teens' tastes, attitudes, and preferences for music, movies, and clothing is partly due to popular entertainment and partly due to the Internet (see Exhibit 12.3). Nonetheless, teens in different regions exhibit some differences, which is why marketers must do their homework before addressing local tastes and behaviors.[13]

Millennial consumers are also a prime target for many marketers because they need to acquire many goods and services during their college years and beyond, as they start their adult lives. In particular, they are often early adopters of new technology,

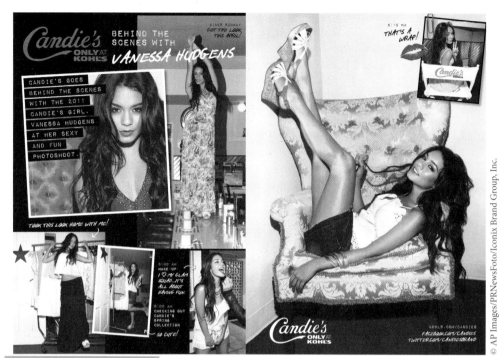

© AP Images/PRNewsFoto/Iconix Brand Group, Inc.

Exhibit 12.3

Targeting to Teens

Advertising to teens, such as the one seen here, is important since teens shop more frequently than other consumers.

intensely interested in brand interactions that take place digitally, and eager to share their brand experiences with others.[14] Moreover, having seen parents and peers struggle during the recent recession, many millennials are debt-averse, which clearly affects how they plan to pay for major purchases.[15]

Brand Loyalty

Research shows that consumers are able to access internal information about brand names learned early in life more quickly and easily than brand names acquired later.[16] Therefore, marketers seek to build early brand awareness and preference among teens and young millennial consumers, working toward having that brand loyalty carry over into adulthood. For example, 50 percent of female teens have developed cosmetic brand loyalties by the age of 15.[17] Mercedes-Benz operates a private online brand community, Generation Benz, for millennial consumers to exchange ideas about cars and respond to Mercedes-Benz's new car concepts. This online community is only one of the ways the company works to develop early brand loyalty by demonstrating its commitment to understanding and meeting the needs of millennials.[18]

Positioning

Some marketers position their products as helpful for dealing with the adolescent pressures of establishing an identity, rebelling, and being accepted by peers. Because teens can be trendsetters, particularly in fashion and music, companies such as Coca-Cola and Pepsi are constantly researching what these consumer like and want. *Teen Vogue*, for example, magazine positions itself as the source for style news and advice with ever-changing print and online content, plus smartphone apps and temporary stores featuring favorite teen fashion brands such as GUESS and bebe.[19] However, teen tastes can change very quickly, and popular products or stores may become overexposed and can quickly lose their cachet.[20]

Advertising Messages

Effective advertising often incorporates symbols, issues, and language to which teens can relate. Because music and sports tend to be the universal languages of teenagers, popular music and sports figures are frequently featured in ads for soft drinks, snacks, and other products. However, messages need to talk *to* teens, not at them. Furthermore, because they have grown up with videos, computers, and texting, today's teens seem to process information faster than older consumers—and they prefer short, snappy phrases to long-winded explanations. Yet using contemporary slang can sometimes be dangerous, because if a phrase is out-of-date when the ad appears, the offering will look "uncool."

Traditional and Social Media

Marketers can target teens and millennials through certain TV networks, TV programs, magazines, radio stations, the Internet, and social media. For example, when the media firm Time Warner launched an antibullying campaign, it began with advertising on the Cartoon Network and then partnered with Facebook to promote an app and a Facebook page for promoting the antibullying message.[21] JCPenney engages teens online and encourages positive word of mouth with social media activities and Web-based tools. During one back-to-school campaign, JCPenney posted online tools to help teens create "haul videos" in which they modeled their latest fashion purchases. The retailer's top marketer notes: "Customers are the new marketers. When it comes to teens, they often want to hear directly from their peers. They are true evangelists."[22]

Other Marketing Activities

Some marketers reach teens through recreation or special events that showcase the brand or product in a lifestyle or sports setting. For example, Red Bull, the energy drink, sponsors musical events and extreme sporting activities such as skateboard demonstrations, to reach its audience of millennials.[23] In addition, marketers of all types are rethinking their distribution strategies to reach teen consumers. The Cleveland Public Library made headlines when it began inviting teens (and others) who hold library cards to legally download music from a special collection for free, as part of a partnership with the Rock and Roll Hall of Fame.[24]

Generation X

Generation X Individuals born between 1965 and 1979.

Individuals born from 1965 to 1979 are often called **Generation X**. In the United States, within this diverse group of 49 million, some are underachievers while some are strong careers and having families. Nonetheless, Gen Xers who believe that they may not be able to match or surpass their parents' level of success may feel a bit disillusioned and less materialistic than other age groups. In fact, compared with consumers who were 30 to 40 years old a decade ago, fewer Gen Xers own their own homes today.[25] In Canada and the United States, many women of this generation are delaying motherhood because of time-sapping work schedules, financial difficulties due to the recession, and shifting societal norms.[26] Yet many Gen Xers are doing well by being at the cutting edge of technology and finding ways to balance their work and personal lives.

Marketing Implications

The Generation X market represents more than $120 billion in spending power. This group takes the time to research a purchase and likes to customize offerings to their personal needs and tastes.[27] Understanding Gen Xers' attitudes and behavior is vital for marketers who seek to reach this group. Campbell Soup, for instance, recognized that Gen Xers prefer the speed of microwave cooking to slower, more traditional stovetop cooking. Based on this insight, the company created microwave heat-and-eat "Soup at Hand" products for quick-serve meals.[28]

Advertising Messages

Born and bred on TV and electronics, Gen Xers tend to be cynical about obvious marketing techniques. They sometimes find objectionable ads that contain exaggerated claims; stereotypes; unpopular products like cigarettes and alcohol; and sexually explicit, political, religious, or social messages. However, Gen Xers do react positively to messages they see as clever or in tune with their values, attitudes, and interests.

Traditional and Social Media

Marketers can reach Gen Xers through media vehicles such as popular or alternative music radio stations and network or cable TV, although this group watches less TV than other groups do.[29] Ads in music-related publications and messages displayed at concerts, sporting events, and popular vacation spots can also be effective. Thus, for example, State Farm, UPS, and Miller, among other companies, sponsor various extreme and college sporting events to attract and retain Gen Xers through such special interests.[30] Increasingly, marketers are using the Internet, mobile marketing, and social media to reach these tech-savvy consumers. AXA Equitable Life Insurance, for example, educates Gen Xers about the value of individual life insurance through an online game called "Pass It On!," which invites players to walk through a virtual New York City streetscape in search of gold. If players buy life insurance for their characters, they gain a shield that protects them as they advance through higher game levels.[31] _____

Boomers

Baby boomers
Individuals born between 1946 and 1964.

The 78 million **baby boomers** born between 1946 and 1964 make up a large and influential U.S. demographic group. Because of their numbers and the fact that many are in their peak earning years, boomers have a lot of buying power (see Exhibit 12.4). Although boomers are a diverse group, they share many common experiences of the 1960s and 1970s, when they grew up. Boomers strongly value individualism and want the freedom to do what they want, when and where they want.[32] Most boomers grew up with TV and as they get older, tend to watch it more. They also spend time browsing the Internet and are increasingly active in social media, although not as active as younger segments. Still, one study shows that boomers spend more on technology than any other segment.[33]

Some researchers have identified subgroups of boomers based on five-year divisions or other definitions, meaning that the oldest and youngest would tend to be the most different—especially since the oldest are now seniors. Research suggests that boomers around the world, like teens around the world, share certain attitudes and values. For example, a majority of U.K. boomers believe that life today is more stressful than it was 50 years ago—a view echoed by most boomers in Mexico, France, and Hong Kong.[34] Despite many differences, boomer parents and their adult children share some common characteristics, such as mothers and daughters often choosing to shop in the same stores.[35] Sometimes boomers are called the "sandwich generation" because so many are simultaneously involved with their children's upbringing and caring for aging parents.

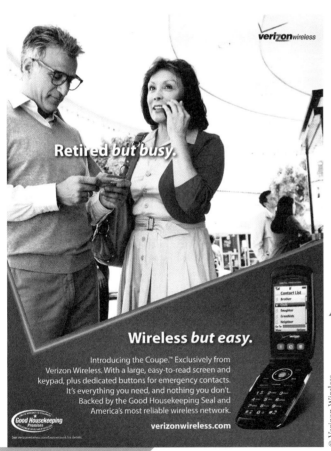

© Verizon Wireless

Exhibit 12.4

Targeting to Boomers

Marketers often try to target and appeal to the lifestyles of baby boomers since they comprise a large segment that has great economic power.

Marketing Implications

Baby boomers have so much buying power that they are the target for many products and services, including cars, housing, travel, entertainment, recreational equipment, and motor homes.[36] For example, many have the time and money to pursue once-in-a-lifetime experiences such as visiting polar regions or playing onstage alongside music icons in the Rock and Roll Fantasy Camp.[37] Harley-Davidson has profited by providing mobile-based apps and social media opportunities for engaging boomer brand enthusiasts and helping them to connect with each other at motorcycling events.[38] Boomers are heavy consumers of financial services as they look toward retirement and juggle expenses such as paying for their children's college educations, helping aging parents, and supporting boomerangers who live at home.

Some firms are developing offerings specifically for the needs of baby boomers. For example, apparel marketers have created jeans in larger sizes and different styles to accommodate the middle-aged physique. The Chico's chain has grown to more than 600 stores by specializing in loose-fitting casual clothing for baby-boom women.[39] The Charming Shoppes clothing chain, which also targets baby-boom women, offers an online recommendation tool to help shoppers find the right apparel for their size and shape.[40] Personal care products, fitness goods and services, cosmetic surgery, and similar offerings are especially attractive to boomers who are sensitive to the idea of aging.[41] General Mills, among other marketers, uses nostalgia to appeal to this segment. Its recent ad campaign for Fiber One brownies featured 1970s comedians Cheech and Chong, for instance.[42]

Seniors

Gray market Individuals over 65 years old.

In the **gray market** of consumers over 65, women outnumber men because women tend to live longer.[43] Because information-processing skills tend to deteriorate with age, seniors are less likely to search for information and more likely to have difficulty remembering information and making more complex decisions.[44] Thus, they tend to engage in simpler, more schematic processing.[45] Furthermore, poor recognition memory makes some seniors susceptible to the "truth effect" (believing that often-repeated statements are true—see Chapter 6).[46] As a result, some may need help or education when making decisions.[47] Nonetheless, younger seniors in particular tend to be healthier and more active than those of previous generations (see Exhibit 12.5). Given recent economic conditions, many are working later in life out of need, to add to their retirement accounts, or to fund special purchases. At the same time, many seniors rekindle their interest in self-expression and affiliation, which they achieve through identity-inspired consumption such as joining hobby groups and paying for lessons.[48]

American Heart Association
Products displaying the heart-check mark meet American Heart Association food criteria for saturated fat and cholesterol for healthy people over age 2.
heartcheckmark.org

WHEN ONE HEART GOES HEART HEALTHY, TWO HEARTS CELEBRATE.

Campbell's

Healthy Request

25 Heart Healthy Soups • Low Cholesterol • 0 Grams Trans Fat • Healthy Level of Sodium

It's amazing what soup can do.

Courtesy of Campbell Soup Company

Exhibit 12.5

Targeting to Seniors

Today's seniors think younger than those of previous generations; and today's advertisements appeal to those values.

Marketing Implications

Seniors represent a critical and growing market for health-related products and services and for retirement communities (particularly in warmer states), as well as for recreational goods and services.[49] In general, seniors tend to be brand-loyal, tend to know more about brands from long-standing experience, may not search extensively when planning high-ticket purchases, and have less motivation and cognitive capacity to deal with new, unfamiliar brands.[50] While some want the latest technology, others care more about basic functionality. For example, Telstra, a global telecommunications firm, runs a "Connected Seniors" program to teach British seniors who are unfamiliar with cell phones how to choose and use one.[51] Many seniors, less mobile than in the past, are heavy Internet and social media users to stay in touch with family members and friends.[52] As with other groups, marketers must carefully research seniors' needs and preferences. In Japan, for instance. Ueshima coffee shops cater to older consumers by having wider aisles, lower tables, and menus with large type.[53]

Advertising and Media

Marketers can target boomers through the use of media geared to this group's interests, including oldies rock 'n' roll programs and websites, activity-specific publications and TV shows, and lifestyle-related events such as home shows. Seniors perceive ads with positive older role models as more credible than those with younger models.[54] However, because of America's youth culture, seniors are less likely to appear in ads—or to be depicted positively—although this situation has been changing over time.[55] Therefore, ads should show seniors as active, contributing members of society, and messages should focus on only a few key attributes. Also, older consumers like and can better recall messages that focus on avoiding negative emotions, possibly because they want to avoid the negative outcomes that are associated with age.[56]

Distribution, Sales, and Promotions

Retailers can design their outlets to provide a more age-friendly shopping environment for baby boomers and seniors, with features such as wider aisles and well-lit aisles and parking lots.[57] Seniors value service, and many develop brand loyalty by taking advantage of discounts offered by retailers such as Kohl's, restaurant chains such as Denny's, and hotels such as Hyatt.[58] However, because older consumers who seek social interaction from telemarketing calls may not recognize fraudulent offers, education and protection are needed to help this segment avoid being victimized by scams.[59] _____

HOW GENDER AND SEXUAL ORIENTATION AFFECT CONSUMER BEHAVIOR

Clearly the two genders, male and female, can differ in traits, attitudes, and activities that affect consumer behavior. The following sections discuss a few key issues that have been the focus of consumer research (complete coverage of the contrasts between men and women is beyond the scope of this book). Remember that these sections describe only general tendencies, which are subject to considerable individual variation.

Sex Roles

Agentic goal Goal that stresses mastery, self-assertiveness, self-efficacy, strength, and no emotion.

Communal goal Goal that stresses affiliation and fostering harmonious relations with others, submissiveness, emotionality, and home orientation.

In most cultures, men and women are expected to behave according to sex-role norms learned very early in childhood. Until recently, males in Western society were expected to be strong, assertive, and emotionless. They were the primary breadwinners and were guided by **agentic goals** that stress mastery, self-assertiveness, and self-efficacy.[60] Women, on the other hand, have been guided more by **communal goals** of forming affiliations and fostering harmonious relations with others and have been expected to be relatively submissive, emotional, and home-oriented.

On a very general level, men tend to be more competitive, independent, externally motivated, and willing to take risks.[61] Expressing "man-of-action" masculinity may take the form of hyper-competitive breadwinner behavior or a rebel approach (including entrepreneurial breadwinner behavior).[62] In contrast, women tend to be cooperative, interdependent, intrinsically motivated, and risk averse. Women's hormonal cycles can also affect product choice, influencing women to prefer appearance-enhancing clothing during fertile days of their monthly cycle.[63] Over time, however, female and male roles have been evolving. In particular, more U.S. women are delaying marriage and childbearing in favor of building a career, as noted earlier. This trend has led to higher standards of living for women and to changes in women's attitudes, particularly an emphasis on independence.

Traditional sex roles are changing in many countries, even those that are very conservative and male dominated. For example, in India, where arranged marriages are still the norm, women's attitudes toward careers, marriage, and the family are undergoing radical changes as more women pursue higher education, build careers, and seek independence.[64] In fact, the earnings of educated women in India, Brazil, Russia, and China are growing faster than those of their male counterparts—and women control two-thirds of the household spending in these nations.[65]

Sex roles and appropriate behavior may vary from one culture to another. Sex roles can, in fact, be influenced by various sources. In a recent Canadian study, 66 percent of teenagers reported experiencing peer pressure to conform to traditional sex roles, and nearly half felt pressure to conform coming from media sources.[66] In the United States, some men feel uncomfortable hugging each other, whereas this behavior is widely accepted in European and Latin societies, often as a greeting.

In general, contemporary ad messages portray stereotyped sex roles less often than in the past. However, stereotyping is still prevalent, mainly in ads that show a man or woman in a particular occupation.[67] And sex roles in ads can provoke differing responses among consumers. For example, women in the Czech Republic react less favorably to ads in which female models are depicted in roles that seem superior to those of male models.[68] Moreover, how sex roles are portrayed in advertising for children can influence consumer attitudes toward the message and the brand. Specifically, children who are open-minded about sex roles and stereotyping will have a more positive attitude toward ads with gender content.[69]

Differences in Acquisition and Consumption Behaviors

Despite sex-role changes, men and women still exhibit a number of differences in their consumption behaviors. Women are more likely to engage in a detailed, thorough examination of a message and to make extended decisions based on product attributes (similar to high motivation, ability, and opportunity [MAO] decision making), whereas men are selective information processors, driven more by overall themes and simplifying heuristics (similar to low-MAO decision making).[70] Men tend to be more sensitive to personally relevant information (consistent with agentic goals), and women pay attention to both personally relevant information and information relevant to others (consistent with communal goals).[71]

Whereas men are more likely to use specific hemispheres of their brain for certain tasks (the right side of the brain for visual and the left side for verbal), women use both hemispheres of their brain for most tasks. Men also appear to be more sensitive to trends in positive emotions experienced during consumption, such as feeling enthusiastic and strong, whereas women display a tendency for negative emotions, such as feeling scared and nervous.[72] In addition, men and women differ in the symbolic meaning that they attach to products and services.[73] Women are more likely to have shared brand stereotypes for fashion goods, whereas men are more consistent in their images of automobiles.

In general, American women see shopping as a pleasurable, stimulating activity and a way of obtaining social interaction, whereas men see shopping merely as a way of acquiring goods and as a chore, especially if they hold traditional sex-role stereotypes. These patterns also hold true in other countries such as Turkey and the Netherlands. Finally, men and women tend to exhibit different eating patterns. In particular, women are more likely to engage in *compensatory eating*—responding to depression or making up for deficiencies such as a lack of social contact by eating.[74]

Marketing Implications

Obviously, many products (such as clothing for men and feminine hygiene products for women) are geared toward gender-specific needs. In addition, certain offerings may be perceived as being more appropriate for one gender than for the other. A tie may be seen as more masculine, whereas a food processor may be seen as more feminine. However, some products are becoming less sex-typed as sex roles evolve. For example, more than 12 percent of Harley-Davidson's motorcycle sales are to women, and the company is attracting more women customers with bikes such as the Switchback, ergonomically suited to women riders.[75] Meanwhile, products that were traditionally perceived as female-oriented are now being positioned as appropriate for men's needs. As an example, Hindustan Unilever advertises Vaseline moisturizers and face cleaners to men in India.[76]

Another important point is that women tend to be more loyal than men to individuals (such as a particular hair stylist), whereas men tend to be more loyal than women to groups (such as a particular company).[77] Gender differences apply to the influence of online product reviews, as well. Women's purchase intentions tend to be more strongly influenced by online reviews than men's purchase intensions.[78]

Targeting a Specific Gender

Marketers often target a particular gender. For example, the home improvement retailer Home Depot is targeting women with coordinated lines of house paints and home décor accessories for easy room makeovers. Lowe's has renovated its U.S. stores with brighter lighting and more informative displays, as well as introducing virtual decorating tools and online wish lists, to attract women do-it-yourselfers. "Women are information gatherers—they want the stores to be inspirational," explains a manager.[79] In India, Titan Industries has become the market leader in wristwatches by targeting women with stylish watches to be worn as elegant jewelry rather than mainly as functional timepieces.[80] Women are often targeted because of their role in household purchases. Procter & Gamble, for instance, targets mothers in particular with ads and social media activities promoting Pampers and other household products.[81]

Studies show that men and women respond differently to emotional advertising.[82] In line with changing sex roles, men in ads are increasingly shown in emotional and caring roles, whereas women are appearing more frequently in important situations and professional positions. A study of magazine ads found a similar trend in Japan as well.[83] Yet traditional roles have not disappeared: In China, where women are increasingly assertive and independent, men are now drawn to marketing that "suggest[s] or reinforce[s] a feeling of control," says an advertising agency manager.[84] Research shows that ads targeting men for a gender-specific product such as perfume (purchased as a gift) are more effective when a male spokesperson is used. In contrast, ads targeting women who buy perfume for themselves are more effective with a female spokesperson.[85]

Traditional and Social Media

Some sex differences still exist in media patterns. Marketers can reach men through certain TV programs, especially sports, and through car and sports magazines such as *Sports Illustrated*. One way that Domino's Pizza reaches men in the 18 to 34 age group is through digital "billboards" inserted into video and online games.[86] To reach female fitness enthusiasts in Malaysia, Nike has sponsored special events with demonstrations of kickboxing and other sports.[87]

Online and social media patterns are important, as well. For example, women tend to use social media more than men and to check social media sites more frequently.[88] This is why some of Nike's social media and online marketing are geared to targeting men and women separately. Nike has a dedicated webpage, NikeWoman, for gender-specific products and a mobile app, Nike Training Club, for helping women achieve the goal of feeling fit.[89]

Gender and Sexual Orientation

Gender Biological state of being male or female.

Sexual orientation A person's preference toward certain behaviors.

Gender refers to a biological state (male or female), whereas **sexual orientation** reflects a person's preference toward certain behaviors. *Masculine* individuals (whether male or female) tend to display male-oriented traits, and *feminine* individuals tend toward female characteristics. In addition, some individuals can be *androgynous*, having both male and female traits. Sexual orientations are important because they can influence consumer preferences and behavior. For example, women who are more masculine tend to prefer ads that depict nontraditional women.[90]

Marketing Implications

An increasing number of marketers are using sexual orientation to target gay and lesbian consumers for a wide range of offerings (see Exhibit 12.6). In part, this strategy is due to a dramatic rise in the number of same-sex U.S. households. Although gay and lesbian consumers tend to dislike and distrust ad messages more than heterosexual consumers do, they are likely to respond to sexual orientation symbols in advertising and to ads that "reflect their lives and culture."[91] They respond to marketing that they perceive as gay friendly (and condemn apparently antigay marketing activities).[92] For instance, the Las Vegas Convention and Visitors Authority promotes a variety of

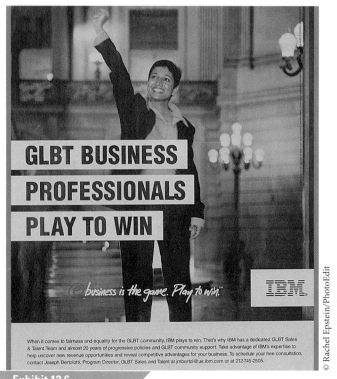

© Rachel Epstein/PhotoEdit

GLBT BUSINESS PROFESSIONALS PLAY TO WIN

business is the game. Play to win.

IBM

When it comes to fairness and equality for the GLBT community, IBM plays to win. That's why IBM has a dedicated GLBT Sales & Talent Team and almost 20 years of progressive policies and GLBT community support. Take advantage of IBM's expertise to help uncover new revenue opportunities and reveal competitive advantages for your business. To schedule your free consultation, contact Joseph Bertolotti, Program Director, GLBT Sales and Talent at jmbertol@us.ibm.com or at 212-745-2505.

Exhibit 12.6

Targeting to Gay and Lesbian Consumers

Companies are increasingly targeting gay and lesbian consumers, such as this bank ad.

gay-themed events to appeal to gay vacationers, and New York City promotes itself as a destination for same-sex weddings.[93]

HOW REGIONAL INFLUENCES AFFECT CONSUMER BEHAVIOR

Because people tend to work and live in the same area, residents in one part of the country can develop patterns of behavior that differ from those in another area. For example, a consumer from New England might enjoy lobster and skiing, whereas someone from Texas may prefer barbecues and rodeos. This section explores how the region in which people live can affect their consumer behavior, both within the United States and in various regions across the world.

Regions Within the United States

The United States is a vast country in which various regions have developed distinctive identities, apart from the overall American culture, based on differing ethnic and cultural histories. For example, California and the Southwest were originally part of Mexico and therefore reflect a Mexican character; the Southwest also has Native American and frontier roots. The eastern seaboard from New England to Georgia reflects the region's roots as the original 13 British colonies. The great expanses of the West and Northwest are reflected in the free-spirited personalities of these regions, and the Deep South from Louisiana to Florida owes some of its character to agriculture as well as to the Confederacy's rebellion during the Civil War. Finally, the Midwest is noted for its farms and agriculture.

These statements represent very broad generalizations. Although each region also has many unique influences and variations that are too numerous to mention, regional differences can affect consumption patterns. Immigration patterns, such as a large number of Mexican-born consumers moving into California and Texas, can add ethnic influences to certain regions as well.[94] For instance, due to a strong Mexican influence, consumers in the Southwest prefer spicy food and dishes such as tortillas and salsa. Interestingly, some Tex-Mex foods, including nachos and chili dogs, were first developed in the United States and then became popular in Mexico.[95]

Clustering The grouping of consumers according to common characteristics using statistical techniques.

Because considerable variation exists in values and lifestyles among consumers within a region, researchers have looked for ways to describe consumers on the basis of more specific characteristics, a technique called *clustering*. **Clustering** is based on the principle that "birds of a feather flock together."[96] This notion suggests that consumers in the same neighborhood tend to buy the same types of cars, homes, appliances, and other products or services.[97] Systems such as Mosaic (from Experian) and PRIZM (from Nielsen Claritas) group areas and neighborhoods into more precise clusters based on consumers' similarities on demographic and consumption characteristics. These systems can define a cluster according to similarity of income, education, age, household type, degree of urbanity, attitudes, and product/service preferences, including the type of car owned and preferred radio format.

For example, PRIZM has identified 66 U.S. consumer segments and grouped them geographically (urban, suburban, second city, and town/rural) as well as by lifestage (according to age and the presence of absence of children at home). Here is a sampling of the individual consumer segments:[98]

▶ *Young Digiterati* are affluent, well-educated, tech-savvy 25- to 44-year-olds in hip urban areas.

▶ *Kids & Cul-de-sac* consumers are upper-middle–income 25- to 44-year-old suburbanites, mostly college grads and home-owners, who live in suburbia with their children.

▶ *Boomtown Singles* are college-educated, lower-middle–income consumers, under the age of 55, living in smaller cities where the singles scene thrives.

▶ *Mobility Blues* are downscale consumers who live in smaller cities, are under the age of 35, and have a high school education.

Marketing Implications

Marketers can develop an offering or communication to appeal to different regions of the United States. For example, Frito-Lay markets "Cajun Herb & Spice" potato chips only in southeastern states, "Chipotle Ranch" chips only in southwestern states, and "Balsamic Sweet Onion" chips only on the west coast. Also, some products are identified with certain regions: Florida orange juice, Hawaiian macadamia nuts, and Texas beef are a few examples. Smaller firms catering to local tastes can develop a loyal following in certain regions. Even though Frito-Lay sells more potato chips across America than all of its smaller competitors combined, Utz potato chips are popular in Pennsylvania and Jays potato chips are popular in Chicago.[99]

Also, marketers can use clustering systems to help find new customers, learn what their customers like, develop new products, buy advertising, locate store sites, and target consumers through media.[100] Retailers use clustering to identify neighborhoods of consumers most likely to purchase certain merchandise. For example, Petco, which sells pet products, uses clustering to pinpoint neighborhoods where home ownership is high because "usually renters don't own animals," a manager says.[101] Clustering systems are also available for other countries and across national borders. Experian's Mosaic Global system clusters consumers into a few common lifestyle categories so that global marketers can target consumers with similar characteristics in different parts of the world. _____

Regions Across the World

Clearly, the area of the world in which a consumer resides can influence consumption patterns. As we have learned, cross-cultural variations exist in just about every aspect of consumer behavior. Some nations are strongly associated with certain products (such as beer in Germany, sports cars in Italy, and sushi in Japan) while the consumption of specific types of products is forbidden in other regions. Drinking alcohol and smoking are not allowed in Muslim countries, and religious restrictions forbid the consumption of pork in Israel and beef in India.

Cultural influences also affect behaviors such as patience. Consumers in Western cultures tend to be less patient and value immediate consumption more than consumers in Eastern cultures do, for instance.[102] In a broader sense, the ways in which cultures differ can affect how consumers think and behave. These differences can be viewed along three main dimensions:

▶ *Individualism versus collectivism.* Consumers from cultures high in individualism (many Western cultures) put more emphasis on themselves as individuals than as part of the group; consumers from cultures high in collectivism (many Eastern cultures) emphasize connections to others rather than their own individuality.[103] Marketers might apply this distinction to the way in which they depict consumers in ads for each culture—as ruggedly individual or as part of a group, for instance.

▶ *Horizontal versus vertical orientation.* Consumers from cultures with a horizontal orientation value equality, whereas consumers from cultures with a vertical orientation put more emphasis on hierarchy.[104] This distinction is especially important to marketers of status-symbol products that will appeal to consumers influenced by vertical orientation.

▶ *Masculine versus feminine.* Consumers from masculine cultures (such as the United States) tend to be more aggressive and focused on individual advancement; in contrast, consumers from feminine cultures (such as Denmark) tend to be more concerned with social relationships.[105] Therefore, advertising with aggressive themes is more likely to strike a chord in masculine cultures than in feminine cultures.

All the consumers in a particular culture may not be affected by cultural influences in the same way, however. The extent of the influence depends on how each consumer processes information and the personal knowledge that he or she relies on when making a judgment.[106]

Marketing Implications

Marketers need to understand global differences in consumer behavior so that they can alter marketing strategy, where necessary, to appeal to specific regions and countries. For example, money-back guarantees give U.S. consumers confidence, but Latin Americans do not believe them because they never expect to get their money back. Also, the strategies of using famous endorsers or being the official product of a sporting event are much more effective in Venezuela and Mexico than in the United States.

Many companies adjust their marketing activities to accommodate global consumer differences.[107] For example, Procter & Gamble developed different versions of a TV ad for Pampers disposable diapers to account for variations in slang and accent in different regions of the German-speaking world. Not heeding important cross-cultural differences can embarrass a company and cause its products to fail. In Germany, Vicks had to change its brand name to *Wicks* because the former term is slang for sexual intercourse.

Marketers should also remember that, as in the United States, consumers in different parts of one country may exhibit different consumer behavior. In Canada, for example, consumers in Quebec have distinctly different food preferences than consumers in British Columbia. Finally, for products available in more than one region, marketers must look at all targeted segments' preferences. General Motors, for example, knows that its Buick vehicles are extremely popular in some parts of China. As a result, the company caters to both U.S. and Chinese consumers' tastes when designing new Buick models.[108]

HOW ETHNIC INFLUENCES AFFECT CONSUMER BEHAVIOR

Ethnic influences are another major factor that affects consumer behavior. It is important to emphasize that the generalizations about ethnic groups discussed in this chapter are only broad group tendencies and may or may not apply to individual consumers. Marketing to any consumer group requires careful research to get beyond stereotypes and to identify specific characteristics and behavioral patterns that can be addressed using appropriate strategies and tactics. Moreover, ethnic influences are only one of the many cultural elements that, in combination, affect how consumers think, feel, and act.

Individuals from many different cultures have come to America over the years. This long history of immigration has created not only a unique national culture but also a number of subcultures or **ethnic groups** within the larger society. Members of these ethnic groups share a common heritage, set of beliefs, religion, and experiences that set them apart from others in society. Larger groups include the Hispanic, African American, Asian, Italian, Irish, Jewish, Muslim, Scandinavian, and Polish subcultures.

Ethnic group Subculture with a similar heritage and values.

These groups are bound together by cultural ties that can, in turn, strongly influence consumer behavior. Moreover, through the process of **acculturation**, members of a subculture must learn to adapt to the host culture. During acculturation, consumers acquire knowledge, skills, and behavior through social interaction, by modeling the behavior of others, and through reinforcement or receipt of rewards for certain behaviors.[109] Acculturation is strongly influenced by family, friends, and institutions such as the media, place of worship, and school and combines with traditional customs to form a unique consumer culture. Meanwhile, members of a larger culture who like to learn about new cultures and think that cultural diversity is important will, at times, adopt a subculture's ethnic-oriented products.[110] Racism can have the opposite effect, prompting racist consumers to avoid products associated with particular ethnic groups.[111]

Acculturation Learning how to adapt to a new culture.

Ethnic Groups Within the United States

The majority of U.S. consumers (sometimes referred to as *Anglos*) can trace their ancestry back to one or more European nations. However, immigration and population trends are leading to greater diversity within the United States, with the three main subcultures—Hispanic American, African American, and Asian American—growing much faster than the general U.S. population.

Multicultural marketing Strategies used to appeal to a variety of cultures at the same time.

However, marketers need not focus on only one of these subcultures. **Multicultural marketing**, the use of strategies that simultaneously appeal to a variety of cultures, is quite popular. This approach requires both long-term commitment and consideration of all targeted groups from the outset, not as an afterthought. McDonald's, for example, estimates that more than 40 percent of its U.S. business comes from subcultural groups, and therefore it actively markets to these groups in multiple media.[112]

Hispanic American Consumers

Hispanic Americans represent one of the largest and most diverse ethnic groups in the United States today, a fast-growing segment in many states.[113] Nearly 39 percent of Hispanic Americans have an income of $50,000 or more, making the segment an attractive one for marketers.[114] Hispanics can also be divided into several groups based on their level of acculturation to the host culture: (1) the *acculturated*, who speak mostly English and have a high level of assimilation; (2) the *bicultural*, who can function in either English or Spanish; and (3) the *traditional*, who speak mostly Spanish.[115] The rate of acculturation can be slow, usually taking four generations, although some Hispanic Americans resist assimilation out of a desire to maintain their ethnic identity.[116]

Intensity of ethnic identification How strongly people identify with their ethnic group.

The consumer's level of acculturation affects consumption patterns, as does the **intensity of ethnic identification**.[117] Consumers who strongly identify with their ethnic group and are less acculturated into the mainstream culture are more likely to exhibit the consumption patterns of the ethnic group. Strong Hispanic identification leads to a higher level of husband-dominant decisions (discussed in greater detail in Chapter 13).[118] Furthermore, strong identifiers are more likely to be influenced by radio ads, billboards, family members, and coworkers and are less likely than weak identifiers to use coupons.[119]

Marketing Implications

Hispanic Americans make up nearly 13 percent of the overall U.S. population and have a combined annual buying power exceeding $1 trillion.[120] Marketers of many goods and services have devised a variety of approaches to reach this growing segment, as the following examples show.

Product Development and Distribution

Marketers are building customer loyalty by developing offerings specifically for Hispanic Americans. For example, an Aspen, Colorado entrepreneur is targeting Hispanic Americans with his U.S.-bottled Oleadas bottled water, labeled in Spanish and English and sold in bottles made from recycled materials.[121] Procter & Gamble has added specially scented household products, such as Brazilian Carnaval Febreze air freshener, to appeal to this segment, and increased the number of products with Spanish-language labeling.[122]

More marketers are tailoring distribution to Hispanic American consumers. Publix, for example, a supermarket chain, operates several Sabor stores designed specifically to cater to Hispanic Americans, with merchandise tailored to the specific tastes and buying habits of local shoppers.[123] Walmart has expanded its distribution for this segment in two ways. First, it increased the shelf space devoted to food products favored by Hispanic American consumers in Texas and other areas. Second, it is testing a Super Mercado store format designed specifically for this segment's shoppers.[124]

Media and Communications

Because Hispanic Americans tend to be concentrated in certain areas and share a common language, many can be targeted in Spanish-language media, including TV,

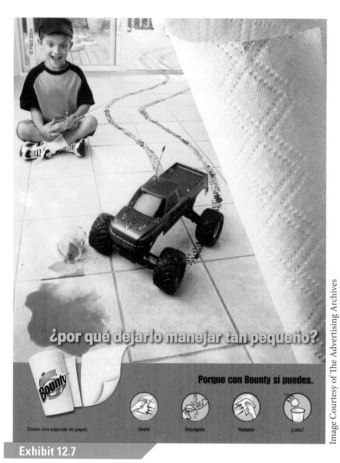

¿por qué dejarlo manejar tan pequeño?

Porque con Bounty sí puedes.

Bounty

Como una esponja de papel.   Usala   Enjuágala   Reúsala   ¡Listo!

Exhibit 12.7

Hispanic American Consumers
Some marketers target to subcultures, such as this one in Spanish.

radio, print, billboards, and websites. In fact, more Hispanic Americans subscribe to digital cable and satellite TV than do Anglos or African Americans.[125] From Univision and Telemundo to *People en Espanol* to Spanish Broadcasting System radio and beyond, marketers have many choices to engage this audience. For example, State Farm Insurance runs Spanish-language commercials on TV as well as on ESPN Deportes, the Spanish language sports station, aiming particularly at consumers under 30 making first-time decisions about auto and home insurance.[126] Hispanic Americans prefer web content that reflects their culture and language. Having Spanish language customer support available for Internet users is especially important for less acculturated Hispanic Americans.[127]

Advertising is particularly important in this segment because many Hispanic Americans prefer prestigious or nationally advertised brands (see Exhibit 12.7). This is why P&G, like many other firms, is spending more to reach the segment and creating English and Spanish language messages that appeal to Hispanic Americans in multiple media. P&G also uses celebrities such as Eva Mendes in its ads for Pantene shampoo to appeal to the segment, and it has Spanish language brand websites for Pampers and other big P&G brands.[128]

Hispanic Americans tend to react positively to ads using ethnic spokespeople, who are perceived as more trustworthy, leading to consumers' having more positive attitudes toward the brand being advertised. This strategy is most effective in environments in which ethnicity is more salient (i.e., the group is in the minority).[129] Ads that draw attention to ethnicity can trigger "ethnic self-awareness" and generate more favorable responses from the targeted group.[130] Marketers who develop ads specifically for Hispanic Americans or other groups should realize that although members of the overall culture also may be exposed to the ads, they are unlikely to react in the same way as the targeted group does because they are less familiar with the cues in the ads.[131] Also, some advertisers try to make ethnic representation in ads proportional to the group's size relative to the general population.[132]

Accommodation theory The more effort one puts forth in trying to communicate with an ethnic group, the more positive the reaction.

Accommodation theory can also apply when marketers develop advertising for Hispanics. This theory predicts that the more effort a source puts into communicating with a group—for example, by using role models and the native language—the greater the response by members of this group and the more positive their feelings. Therefore, advertising in Spanish increases perceptions of the company's sensitivity toward and solidarity with the Hispanic community, creating consumers' positive feelings toward the brand and the firm.[133] Verizon, for example, has developed Spanish language ads and tweets, Facebook pages, and promotions that focus on Hispanic traditions such as the *Quinceañera* party for 15-year-old girls, that target teens, their parents, and their grandparents.[134] Volkswagen shoots some TV commercials twice—once in English, once in Spanish—to reach Hispanic bilinguals and those who have a preference for either Spanish or English.[135]

However, using Spanish messages exclusively can lead to negative ad perceptions. Many ads directed toward Hispanic Americans are delivered in English because these consumers are often bilingual or highly acculturated. An even more effective strategy may involve using both English and Spanish, for example, the method employed by P&G with its bilingual website orgullosa.com and Facebook page featuring beauty and household tips for women.[136] When an ad targeting Hispanic Americans mixes English and Spanish, it is likely to be more persuasive if the text is mainly in Spanish with one word switched to English instead of mainly in English with one Spanish word. Note that consumers may like a code-switching message less if it mixes words incorrectly.[137]

African American Consumers

African Americans represent a large and diverse group—13 percent of the U.S. population—consisting of many subsegments across different levels of income and education, occupations, and regions, from urban to rural areas. One-third of the households have an income of $50,000 or higher, and 20 percent have a college degree or achieved a higher educational level.[138] This segment represents more than $1 trillion in annual buying power.[139]

As with any subculture, African American consumers have some similarities to the general population and also differ in certain ways. For example, African Americans are more likely to believe that people should feel free to live, dress, and look the way that they want to.[140] They also do not necessarily aspire to assimilate with the majority culture.[141] As incomes rise, a strong desire to preserve a cultural identity also develops. A defining element in the consumption patterns of African Americans is the importance of style, self-image, and elegance. Consumption patterns are also related to a strong desire to be recognized and show status. According to research, African Americans often buy premium brands of boys' clothing to make a statement about themselves.[142]

Marketing Implications

African American consumers, like other segments, respond positively to offerings and communications targeted toward them (see Exhibit 12.8). Generally, they are less likely to trust or buy brands that are not advertised.[143] Marketers are addressing this group's specific needs and interests in a number of ways.

Product Development and Distribution

Many marketers focus primarily on products for the unique needs of the African American market. Marketers that make products for the broader U.S. population are also designing products specifically for black consumers, as evidenced by clothing manufacturers that are designing styles deemed more flattering for the physique of African American women. As another example, Hallmark and American Greetings both offer a line of greeting cards created specifically for this segment.[144]

Marketers can also adjust distribution strategies for this segment. For instance, American Airlines operates BlackAtlas, a travel website targeting African Americans, with consumer-generated content and supported by mobile marketing to encourage participation.[145] In some areas where African Americans represent more than 20 percent of the population, JCPenney has developed "Authentic African Boutiques" that offer clothing, handbags, hats, and other accessories imported from Africa. This also taps into the idea that contemporary consumers value authenticity.

Media and Communications

African Americans have more positive attitudes toward ads than do Anglo consumers, according to studies.[146] Research also shows that strong ethnic identifiers among African American consumers act more positively than weak identifiers to ads placed in racially targeted media.[147] Marketers can use multiple media that reach this segment specifically, including TV networks such as

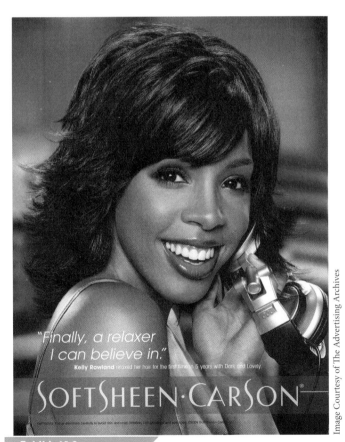

"Finally, a relaxer I can believe in."
Kelly Rowland relaxed her hair for the first time in 5 years with Dark and Lovely.

SOFTSHEEN·CARSON

Image Courtesy of The Advertising Archives

Exhibit 12.8

Targeting to African-American Consumers

Some ads specifically target African-American consumers with specific products or brands.

Black Entertainment Television, targeted websites such as BET.com, magazines such as *Ebony*, and more. Compared with other groups, more African Americans are cable TV subscribers.[148] Moreover, Google's research suggests that African American consumers are more responsive to Web and mobile ads than the overall U.S. population, indicating that digital media are effective for reaching this segment.[149]

Some of the largest U.S. advertisers, including General Motors, Procter & Gamble, and Johnson & Johnson, are investing in ad campaigns specifically for this segment. As noted earlier, subcultures such as African Americans will identify more strongly and have more positive evaluations when the advertising source is of the same ethnic group as the target.[150] Therefore, marketers must take the unique values and expectations of African Americans into account when planning communications, especially since consumers in this segment pay attention to how they are represented in ads.[151]

Marketers must also be aware of the effect that African American models and actors in ads may have on consumers outside the targeted segment. According to Coors's director of ethnic marketing, the company's targeted advertising has boosted the beer's overall sales, not just its sales to African American consumers, "because African American consumers in urban markets have a lot of influence on what's cool with the general market."[152] On the other hand, one study found that some Anglo consumers had less favorable attitudes and were less likely to purchase the product when ads featured African American rather than Anglo actors.[153] This problem is more pronounced when Anglo consumers are prejudiced toward non-Anglos. Yet research suggests that younger Anglo consumers are more accepting of non-Anglo actors, a factor that may reduce the problem over time.[154]

Asian American Consumers

Asian Americans are the third largest and fastest growing major subculture in the United States, making up 5 percent of the population. The Asian American community consists of people from more than 29 countries, from the Indian subcontinent to the Pacific Ocean, each with its own values and customs. The six largest groups include immigrants from China, the Philippines, India, South Korea, Vietnam, and Japan. In light of this tremendous diversity, marketers should research the specific subsegment they wish to target.

Despite individual differences, one common denominator of most Asian cultures is the strong emphasis on the family, tradition, and cooperation.[155] These consumers shop frequently and enjoy shopping with friends. They want brand names and are willing to pay for top quality, even though they react positively to bargains. Asian Americans are more than twice as likely as the average consumer to check prices and products on the Internet before they buy.[156] Consumers in this group also tend to save money, be highly educated, have higher computer literacy, and hold a higher percentage of professional and managerial jobs than the general population does.[157] More tend to be highly assimilated by the second and third generations.

Marketing Implications

Asian Americans are a rapidly growing group with a median income of $65,000, significantly higher than the overall U.S. median income of nearly $50,000. Moreover, 32 percent of Asian American households have an annual income of $100,000 or more, compared with 20 percent of overall U.S. households earning at this income level.[158] Many marketers target this segment, as the following examples show.

Product Development and Distribution

Marketers are increasingly developing more offerings for Asian Americans and tailoring distribution accordingly. To illustrate, EastWest Bank, based in California, has introduced special banking services for this segment and invites its customers to bank in Cantonese, Mandarin, or Vietnamese (Spanish is also an option).[159] Yet caution is needed to avoid missteps: One company mistakenly offered golf balls in a four-pack instead of the usual three-pack, not knowing that the word *four* is considered unlucky because it sounds similar to the word for death in both Japanese and Chinese.

Media and Communications

To reach this diverse group, marketers often use native-language newspapers, magazines, broadcast and cable TV, radio, and, of course, the Internet. Messages delivered to Asian Americans in their native language are often more effective than those delivered in English. Despite the diversity of languages within this subculture, marketers may find the effort worthwhile when many consumers from a single subgroup are concentrated in an area. Subaru, for example, has used a "keeping children safe" theme in U.S. TV commercials produced in Cantonese and Mandarin as well as English.[160] Asian Americans tend to respond to subtle messages that focus on tradition, the family, and cooperation as well as to ads featuring Asian models.[161] _____

Ethnic Groups Around the World

Ethnic subcultures exist in many nations. Although it is beyond the scope of this book to discuss each of the numerous ethnic groups around the world, a few examples illustrate their importance and the challenges and opportunities of reaching specific groups within a particular country.

In Canada, the French-speaking subculture has unique motivations and buying habits.[162] Compared with the rest of the Canadian population, French Canadians use more staples for original or "scratch" cooking; drink more soft drinks, beer, wine, and instant beverages; and consume fewer frozen vegetables, diet drinks, and hard liquor. Canada is home to many other groups, as well, meaning multicultural marketing is important. For instance, to reach the entire country during the nationwide launch of its electric Volt car, Chevrolet Canada relied on marketing messages in English, French, Cantonese, Hindi, Mandarin, Punjabi, and Tamil, delivered on TV and in print, on YouTube, in search-engine ads, and on social media sites.[163]

In Thailand, more than 80 percent of the population is of Thai origin, but several sizable ethnic subcultures still flourish. The largest, 10 percent of the population, has Chinese roots, and this segment has influenced the Thai culture to a significant degree.[164] Chinese consumers in Thailand exert a powerful economic force because they own many businesses; their influence is also felt in art, religion, and food. Other, smaller, ethnic groups in Thailand include people of Laotian, Indian, and Burmese origin.

India has a diverse ethnic population, with more than 80 languages and 120 dialects spoken in the country. Some villagers need travel only 30 miles from home to reach a destination where they are not able to speak the language. As you saw in the opening example, Yum! Brands recognizes how diversity affects consumer behavior in India and other markets, and it fine-tunes its offerings and positioning for each targeted group.

THE INFLUENCE OF RELIGION

A final type of subculture is based on religious beliefs. Religion provides people with a structured set of beliefs and values that serve as a code of conduct or guide to behavior. It also provides ties that bind people together and make one group different from another. According to research, the majority of Americans are either Protestant or Catholic. In comparison, only a small fraction of Americans identify themselves as being Jewish, Mormon, Muslim, Hindu, or a follower of another religion.[165]

Although individual differences certainly come into play, some religious influences or traditions can affect consumer behavior. Born-again Christians, for instance, are less likely to buy on credit, purchase national brands, or attend rock concerts and movies.[166] Religion can also prevent consumption of certain products or services. Mormons are prohibited from using liquor, tobacco, and caffeine, including cola. Orthodox Jews do not eat pork or shellfish, and all meat and poultry to be consumed must be certified as kosher. Muslims cannot eat pork or drink liquor. Catholic consumers may choose to abstain from eating meat on Fridays during the season of Lent.

Religious subcultures are clearly present in many parts of the world. In India, for example, most of the population is Hindu, but large groups of Muslims, Christians, and Sikhs exhibit different patterns of consumption. Because Hindus are predominantly vegetarian, Indian manufacturers of food and cosmetics must use vegetable-based rather than animal-based oils and shortening in their products. The Sikh religion forbids the consumption of beef and tobacco, and the sales of such products are low in areas where many Sikhs live. Finally, the color green has significance for Muslims, a factor that has led to its frequent use on product packages for this group.

Marketing Implications

Marketers can segment the market by focusing on religious affiliation, delivering targeted messages and promotions or using certain media to deliver them. They can target Christian consumers through religious radio and TV stations and programs, which reach millions of U.S. consumers. In addition, marketers can advertise in one of the many publications geared to specific religious affiliations or reach a particular group via specialized websites or social media interaction. Some deep-discount websites target religious groups with carefully tailored offerings. For example, Christian Deals has offered discounts on Christian books, jewelry, and more; jdeal has offered deals on Jewish holiday foods, magazine subscriptions, and other products.[167]

Marketing tactics should demonstrate understanding and respect for the targeted group's beliefs and customs, a strategy that will also generate positive word of mouth. For example, the ITC hotel group now offers Eva floors at its hotels in India exclusively for female travelers. Only women employees serve guests on those floors, providing everything from concierge services to room service. "Many women traveling from Muslim countries may not feel comfortable with male attendants delivering food to their rooms," says an ITC marketing official.[168]

Marketers can also distribute religious products through specialized stores such as King's House in Scottsdale, Arizona, a retail outlet that offers religious artwork, statues, texts, crucifixes, and jewelry. More religious institutions are opening gift shops, snack bars, and even fitness centers, providing distribution opportunities for suitable goods and services.[169] Some marketers use religious symbols and themes in their advertising, which is an effective way to generate a positive reaction from consumers who are religious.[170] However, some marketers avoid products or messages with overt religious meaning, to avoid controversy.

SUMMARY

Six major aspects of consumer diversity have important effects on consumer behavior: age, gender, sexual orientation, regional differences, ethnic differences, and religious differences. Age is a key factor because people of the same age have similar life experiences, needs, symbols, and memories that may lead to similar consumption patterns. Four important age groups are teens and millennials (also known as Generation Y), Generation X, baby boomers, and seniors over 65 years old (the gray market). Gender differences also affect consumer behavior, including the influence of changing sex roles. Men and women differ in terms of their consumer traits, information-processing styles, decision-making styles, and consumption patterns. In addition, more marketers are using sexual orientation to target gay and lesbian consumers for various goods and services.

Consumption patterns may differ in various regions of the United States and the world, leading some marketers to tailor their strategies specifically to these regions. Clustering helps marketers describe consumers in different regions based on similar demographic and consumption characteristics rather

than on geographic location only. The three largest U.S. ethnic groups are African Americans, Hispanic Americans, and Asian Americans. Many marketers are taking a multicultural approach, trying to appeal to several subcultures instead of just one. Finally, religious values and customs can influence consumer behavior and form the basis of some marketing strategies.

Questions for Review and Discussion

1. What type of U.S. consumers are in the Generation X, the millennial generation, and the baby boomer segments?

2. What is the difference between gender and sexual orientation, and why is this distinction important for marketers?

3. What is clustering, and why do marketers use it?

4. What are the three main subcultures within the U.S. population?

5. How do acculturation and intensity of ethnic identification affect consumer behavior?

6. Define the *accommodation theory*, and explain its importance for marketers who target Hispanic Americans.

7. Why would a company adopt multicultural marketing rather than target a single subculture?

8. Why do marketers have to consider regional influences when targeting consumers within the United States or in another country?

9. Identify some of the ways in which religion can influence consumer behavior.

CONSUMER BEHAVIOR CASE

Marketing to Teens Worldwide via Music

Knowing that teenagers in many nations have similar attitudes and tastes, the world's two largest soft drink companies see this group of consumers as an extremely important target market with long-term profit potential. Both Coca-Cola and PepsiCo know that not only do their soft drinks have to taste good, their marketing has to be relevant to capture teens' attention and keep them engaged with the brands as well. Both are using music as part of their strategy for reaching out to teens through their shared interest in new music and bands. Although Coca-Cola and PepsiCo have long been identified with music—Coca-Cola on TV with *American Idol*, PepsiCo with commercials starring legendary performers like Michael Jackson—these new teen campaigns focus on cutting-edge music and involve more interactivity than ever before.

"The number one passion point for teens is music," explains a Coca-Cola senior vice president. During the 2010 World Cup soccer tournament, for example, the company scored a global hit when its TV ads showed the Somali rapper K'naan performing the brand-related "Flag Wavin'" song. The song was released commercially and quickly hit the top of the charts in 18 nations. During another campaign, Coca-Cola invited the popular band Maroon 5 to create a new song based on suggestions and comments submitted by teens via Facebook and Twitter during an intense 24-hour jam session—all streamed live online to a global audience.

For the 2012 Olympics in London, Coca-Cola continued the focus on music with its "Move to the Beat" campaign. A new song written expressly for this campaign, incorporating sports sounds and performed by U.K. singer Katy B, was released before the games began and was featured in TV ads, online ads, mobile marketing, social media posts, and other global marketing activities. "We can't afford not to talk to teens," says a Coca-Cola official. "You can't think, 'Teens already know us,' and skip a couple of years. Every six years there's a new population of teens in the world."

Like Coca-Cola, PepsiCo uses music in marketing to attract teens' attention and to demonstrate its hip factor. In addition to global campaigns featuring music enjoyed by teens in many nations, PepsiCo tailors some marketing events to the musical tastes of teens in specific regions. It has sponsored new-talent festivals in India, for instance, and major rock concerts in Argentina. Knowing that the Grammy Awards are popular among music-loving teens, Pepsi is one of the award program's sponsors. Pepsi's association with the reality TV singing competition, the *X Factor*, is a high-profile way to associate the brand with up-and-coming musical artists who may, with a dash of luck and a lot of talent, blossom into stars who become wildly popular with teen audiences.

PepsiCo is also using social media as a pivotal part of its international marketing to teenagers. During its recent "Summer Time Is Pepsi Time" TV and online campaign, the company pictured parks, beaches, and pools from around the world. Consumers who checked in via foursquare at any three of the sites received special badges and were entered into a sweepstakes for the chance to win prizes. These ads still draw viewers on YouTube, where teens and everybody else can enjoy and share them again and again.[171]

CASE QUESTIONS

1. What long-term results do you think Coca-Cola and PepsiCo hope to achieve by investing heavily in marketing to teens around the world?

2. What are the marketing advantages and disadvantages of associating a soft drink brand such as Coca-Cola or PepsiCo with musical groups that are just beginning their careers? Do you agree with this strategy? Explain.

3. From a consumer behavior perspective, why would these two companies emphasize new music and emerging performers in their ads, rather than well-known songs and groups?

ENDNOTES

1. William Mellor, "McDonald's No Match for KFC in China as Colonel Rules Fast Food," *Bloomberg Businessweek*, January 26, 2011, www.businessweek.com; Carolynne Wheeler, "Yum Brands' Recipe for Fast-Food Success in China? Adapt to Local Tastes," *Globe & Mail (Toronto)*, May 11, 2011, p. B15; Maggie Starvish, "KFC's Explosive Growth in China," *Harvard Business School Working Knowledge*, June 17, 2011, http://hbswk.hbs.edu; "Made for India," *Knowledge@Wharton*, March 12, 2009, http://knowledge.wharton.upenn.edu; and Ron Ruggless, "Taco Bell Opens 1st Unit in India," *Nation's Restaurant News*, April 5, 2010, p. 6.

2. Charles D. Schewe and Geoffrey Meredith, "Segmenting Global Markets by Generational Cohorts: Determining Motivations by Age," *Journal of Consumer Behavior* 4, no. 1, 2004, pp. 51–63.

3. Bryant Ott, "Marketing to Tweeters and Their Facebook Friends," *Gallup Management Journal*, April 11, 2011, n.p.

4. Beth Snyder, "The iGeneration: There's a Market for That," *Advertising Age*, October 17, 2011, www.adage.com.

5. Rick Garlick and Kyle Langley, "Reaching Gen Y on Both Sides of the Cash Register," *Retailing Issues Letter*, Center for Retailing Studies at Texas A&M University, vol. 18, no. 2, 2007, pp. 1–2.

6. Dannie Kjeldgaard and Søren Askegaard, "The Globalization of Youth Culture," *Journal of Consumer Research* 33, no. 2, 2006, pp. 231–247.

7. The Six Value Segments of Global Youth," *Brandweek*, May 22, 2000, pp. 38–44.

8. "Gen Y Embraces Smaller Screens for TV and Online Video Viewing," *E-Marketer*, September 28, 2011, www.emarketer.com; and David Murphy, "Connecting with Online Teenagers," *Marketing*, September 27, 2001, pp. 31–32.

9. Cole J. Engel, Reginald L. Bell, Robert J. Meier, Michael J. Martin, and Joan H. Rumpel, "Young Consumers in the New Marketing Ecosystem: An Analysis of Their Usage of Interactive Technologies," *Academy of Marketing Studies Journal* 15, no. 2, 2011, pp. 23–44.

10. Amanda Mulvihill, "Pew Study: Inside the Tech Generation," *Information Today*, April 2011, p. 10.

11. Hannah Dreier and Paul Burgarino, "Lean Times Force Many Bay Area 'Boomerang Kids' to Return Home as Adults," *Contra Costa Times*, July 19, 2011, www.mercurynews.com.

12. John Masanauskas, "Kids Who Won't Leave Home Put Squeeze on Families," *Herald Sun (Victoria, Australia)*, August 9, 2011, www.heraldsun.com.au.

13. Kerry Capell, "MTV's World," *BusinessWeek*, February 18, 2001, pp. 81–84; and Sally Beatty and Carol Hymowitz, "How MTV Stays Tuned In to Teens," *Wall Street Journal*, March 21, 2000, pp. B1, B4.

14. Lisa Jennings, "Generation App, Study: Millennials Eager to Interact with Brands in Digital Domain," *Nation's Restaurant News*, September 12, 2011, p. 44.

15. Joey Ferguson, "Roughing It: Millennials Are Finding Shelter Amid Financial Fears," *Deseret News (Salt Lake City)*, November 14, 2011, www.deseretnews.com.

16. Andrew W. Ellis, Selina J. Holmes, and Richard L. Wright, "Age of Acquisition and the Recognition of Brand Names: On the Importance of Being Early," *Journal of Consumer Psychology* 20, 2010, pp. 43–52.

17. Paula Dwyer, "The Euroteens (and How to Sell to Them)," *BusinessWeek*, April 11, 1994, p. 84.

18. George Spaulding, "Mercedes Cued into Gen Y and Social Media," *Post and Courier (Charleston, SC)*, November 26, 2011, www.postandcourier.com; and Sheila Shayon, "Mercedes-Benz Woos Gen Y," *BrandChannel*, May 21, 2010, www.brandchannel.com.

19. Erik Sass, "'Teen Vogue' Brings Pop-Up Store to Well-Heeled Masses," *Media Post*, September 8, 2011, www.mediapost.com.

20. Maureen Tkacik, "Fast Times for Retain Chain Behind the 'Euro' Shoe Trend," *Wall Street Journal*, November 21, 2002, p. B1.

21. "Time Warner, Facebook Join Forces to Stop Bullying," *CNN*, July 13, 2011, www.cnn.com; and "Facebook, Time Warner Launch Anti-Bullying App," *Salt Lake Tribune*, September 25, 2011, www.sltrib.com.

22. Emma Jacobs, "Shopping Sprees to Marketing Technique," *Financial Times*, September 29, 2011, www.ft.com.

23. Marshall Heyman, "A Stage for Skaters," *Wall Street Journal*, September 8, 2011, www.wsj.com.

24. John Caniglia, "Libraries Turn the Page to Keep Up with Changing Times," *Plain Dealer (Cleveland, OH)*, September 26, 2011, www.cleveland.com.

25. "Farther Along the Axis," *American Demographics*, May 2004, pp. 21–24.

26. Tralee Pearce, "For Generation X, It's All Work and No Kids, Study Finds," *Globe and Mail (Canada)*, September 21, 2011, www.theglobeandmail.com.

27. Angrisani, "X Marks the Spot."

28. Abram Brown, "Doug Conant Pulled the Brand Out from a Circle of Doom," *Business Insider*, September 15, 2011, www.businessinsider.com.

29. Horst Stipp, "Xers Are Not Created Equal," *Mediaweek*, March 21, 1994, p. 20; and Lisa Marie Petersen, "Previews of Coming Attractions," *Brandweek*, March 1993, pp. 22–23.

30. Brian Grey, "Wild Ride in College Sports Now = Long-Term Good News for Brands," *MediaPost*, September 20, 2011, www.mediapost.com.

31. Matthew Sturdevant, "Marketing Life Insurance Is a Game for AXA Equitable, Online," *Hartford Courant*, November 13, 2011, www.courant.com.

32. Cheryl Russell, "The Power of One," *Brandweek*, October 4, 1993, pp. 27–28, 30, 32.

33. Beth Snyder Bulik, "Boomers—Yes, Boomers—Spend the Most on Tech," *Advertising Age*, October 11, 2010, www.adage.com.

34. Pamela Paul, "Global Generation Gap," *American Demographics*, March 2002, pp. 18–19.

35. Stephen Reily, "How Marketing to Moms Is Like Marketing to Boomers," *MediaPost*, September 29, 2011, www.mediapost.com.

36. Sandra Yin, "More at Home on the Road," *American Demographics*, June 2003, pp. 26–27.

37. Kathy Witt, "Dreams Come True with Bucket-List Adventures," *Modesto Bee (California)*, September 23, 2011, www.modbee.com.

38. Holly Pavlika, "Don't Think Gray, Think Green," *MediaPost*, September 8, 2011, www.mediapost.com.

39. "Specialty Retailer Buys Back Shares, Pays Dividends," *Forbes*, September 14, 2011, www.forbes.com; and John Finotti, "Back in Fashion," *Florida Trend*, January 2002, pp. 16.

40. "Plus-Sized Clothing: Big Business," *Economist*, October 1, 2011, p. 68.

41. Casey Dowd, "Graying Baby Boomers' Quest to Look Younger," *Fox Business*, September 8, 2011, www.foxbusiness.com.

42. Martin Moylan, "Cheech and Chong Get Fired Up Over Fiber," *Minnesota Public Radio*, September 22, 2011, http://minnesota.publicradio.org.

43. Carol M. Morgan, "The Psychographic Landscape of 50-Plus," *Brandweek*, July 19, 1993, pp. 28–32; and Phil Goodman, "Marketing to Age Groups Is All in the Mind Set," *Marketing News*, December 6, 1993, p. 4.

44. Catherine A. Cole and Gary J. Gaeth, "Cognitive and Age-Related Differences in the Ability to Use Nutritional Information in a Complex Environment," *Journal of Marketing Research*, May 1990, pp. 175–184; Catherine A. Cole and Siva K. Balasubramanian, "Age Differences in Consumers' Search for Information," *Journal of Consumer Research*, June 1993, pp. 157–169; and Deborah Roedder John and Catherine A. Cole, "Age Differences in Information Processing," *Journal of Consumer Research*, December 1986, pp. 297–315.

45. Carolyn Yoon, "Age Differences in Consumers' Processing Strategies," *Journal of Consumer Research*, December 1997, pp. 329–342.

46. Sharmistha Law, Scott A. Hawkins, and Fergus I. M. Craik, "Repetition-Induced Belief in the Elderly," *Journal of Consumer Research*, September 1998, pp. 91–107.

47. Catherine A. Cole and Gary J. Gaeth, "Cognitive and Age-Related Differences in the Ability to Use Nutritional Information in a Complex Environment," *Journal of Marketing Research*, May 1990, pp. 175–184; Cole and Balasubramanian, "Age Differences in Consumers' Search for Information"; and John and Cole, "Age Differences in Information Processing."

48. Hope Jensen Schau, Mary C. Gilly, and Mary Wolfinbarger, "Consumer Identity Renaissance: The Resurgence of Identity-Inspired Consumption in Retirement," *Journal of Consumer Research*, August 2009, pp. 255–276.

49. Michael Moss, "Leon Black Bets Big on the Elderly," *Wall Street Journal*, July 24, 1998, pp. B1, B8.

50. Raphaelle Lambert-Pandraud, Gilles Laurent, and Eric Lapersonne, "Repeat Purchasing of New Automobiles by Older Consumers," *Journal of Marketing*, April 2005, pp. 97–113.

51. Simon Rockman, "Are Touch-Screens Good for Seniors?" *Mobile Today (UK)*, October 3, 2011, www.mobiletoday.co.uk.

52. Mary Madden, "Older Adults and Social Media," *Pew Internet and American Life Project*, August 27, 2010, http://pewinternet.org/Reports/2010/Older-Adults-and-Social-Media.aspx.

53. "Turning Silver into Gold," *Economist*, July 30, 2011, p. 60.

54. Ronald E. Milliman and Robert C. Erffmeyer, "Improving Advertising Aimed at Seniors," *Journal of Advertising Research*, December 1989–January 1990, pp. 31–36.

55. Robin T. Peterson, "The Depiction of Senior Citizens in Magazine Advertisements," *Journal of Business Ethics*, September 1992, pp. 701–706; Anthony C. Ursic, Michael L. Ursic, and Virginia L. Ursic, "A Longitudinal Study of the Use of the Elderly in Magazine Advertising," *Journal of Consumer Research*, June 1986, pp. 131–133; and John J. Burnett, "Examining the Media Habits of the Affluent Elderly," *Journal of Advertising Research*, October–November 1991, pp. 33–41.

56. Patti Williams and Aimee Drolet, "Age-Related Differences in Responses to Emotional Advertisements," *Journal of Consumer Research* 32, no. 3, 2005, pp. 343–354.

57. "America's Aging Consumers," *Discount Merchandiser*, September 1993, pp. 16–28; and John and Cole, "Age Differences in Information Processing."

58. Emma Sapong, "Super Saver Seniors," *Buffalo News*, October 3, 2011, www.buffalonews.com.

59. Jinkook Lee and Loren V. Geistfeld, "Elderly Consumers' Receptiveness to Telemarketing Fraud," *Journal of Public Policy & Marketing* 18, no. 2, Fall 1999, pp. 208–217; and John R. Emshwiller, "Having Lost Thousands to Con Artists, Elderly Widow Tells Cautionary Tale," *Wall Street Journal*, August 9, 1996, pp. B1, B5.

60. Joan Meyers-Levy, "The Influence of Sex Roles on Judgment," *Journal of Consumer Research*, March 1988, pp. 522–530.

61. Charles S. Areni and Pamela Kiecker, "Gender Differences in Motivation: Some Implications for Manipulating Task-Related Involvement," in ed. Janeen Arnold Costa, *Gender and Consumer Behavior* (Salt Lake City, Utah: University of Utah Printing Service, 1993), pp. 30–43; and Brenda Giner and Eileen Fischer, "Women and Arts, Men and Sports: Two Phenomena or One?" in ed. Janeen Arnold Costa, *Gender and Consumer Behavior* (Salt Lake City, Utah: University of Utah Printing Service, 1993), p. 149.

62. Douglas B. Holt and Craig J. Thompson, "Man-of-Action Heroes: The Pursuit of Heroic Masculinity in Everyday Consumption," *Journal of Consumer Research*, September 2004, pp. 425–440.

63. Kristina M. Durante, Vladas Griskevicius, Sarah E. Hill, Carin Perilloux, and Norman P. Li, "Ovulation, Female Competition, and Product Choice: Hormonal Influences on Consumer Behavior," *Journal of Consumer Research*, April 2011, pp. 921–934.

64. Chen May Yee, "High-Tech Lift for India's Women," *Wall Street Journal*, November 1, 2000, pp. B1, B4; and Alladi Venkatesh, "Gender Identity in the Indian Context, a Socio-Cultural Construction of the Female Consumer," in ed. Costa, *Gender and Consumer Behavior*, pp. 119–129.

65. Matt Wade, "Business Tigresses Are Burning Bright," *Sydney Morning Herald (Australia)*, September 20, 2011, www.smh.com.au.

66. Tamara Baluja, "Canadian Teens Ambivalent about Gender Equality," *Globe and Mail (Canada)*, September 22, 2011, www.theglobeandmail.com.

67. Martin Eisend, "A Meta-analysis of Gender Roles in Advertising," *Journal of the Academy of Marketing Science*, Fall 2010, pp. 418–440.

68. Timothy M. Smith, Srinath Gopalakrishna, and Paul M. Smith, "Men's and Women's Responses to Sex Role Portrayals in Advertisements," *Journal of Marketing Research*, March 2004, pp. 61–77.

69. Aysen Bakir and Kay M. Palan, "How Are Children's Attitudes Toward Ads and Brands Affected by Gender-Related Content in Advertising?" *Journal of Advertising*, Spring 2010, pp. 35–48.

70. Joan Meyers-Levy and Durairaj Maheswaran, "Exploring Differences in Males' and Females' Processing Strategies," *Journal of Consumer Research*, June 1991, pp. 63–70; William K. Darley and Robert E. Smith, "Gender Differences in Information Processing Strategies," *Journal of Advertising*, Spring 1995, pp. 41–56; and Barbara B. Stern, "Feminist Literary Criticism and the Deconstruction of Ads," *Journal of Consumer Research*, March 1993, pp. 556–566.

71. Meyers-Levy, "The Influence of Sex Roles on Judgment"; and Joan Meyers-Levy, "Priming Effects on Product Judgments," *Journal of Consumer Research*, June 1989, pp. 76–86.

72. Laurette Dube and Michael S. Morgan, "Trend Effects and Gender Differences in Retrospective Judgments of Consumption Emotions," *Journal of Consumer Research*, September 1996, pp. 156–162.

73. Richard Elliot, "Gender and the Psychological Meaning of Fashion Brands," in ed. Janeen Arnold Costa, *Gender and Consumer Behavior* (Salt Lake City, Utah: University of Utah Printing Service, 1993), pp. 99–105.

74. Suzanne C. Grunert, "On Gender Differences in Eating Behavior as Compensatory Consumption," in ed. Janeen Arnold Costa, *Gender and Consumer Behavior*, pp. 74–86.

75. Wevonneda Minis, "Women on a Roll," *Post and Courier (Charleston, S.C.)*, September 25, 2011, www.postandcourier.com; and Clifford Krauss, "Women, Hear Them Roar," *New York Times*, July 25, 2007, pp. C1, C9.

76. Kala Vijayraghavan and Sagar Malviya, Hindustan Unilever's Shift to Personal Products After Soaps and Detergents," *Economic Times (India)*, September 21, 2011, www.economictimes.com.

77. Valentyna Melnyk, Stijn M.J. van Osselaer, and Tammo H.A. Bijmolt, "Are Women more Loyal Customers Than Men? Gender Differences in Loyalty to Firms and Individual Service Providers," *Journal of Marketing*, July 2009, pp. 82–96.

78. Soonyong Bae and Taesik Lee, "Gender Differences in Consumers' Perception of Online Consumer Reviews," *Electronic Commerce Research* 11, no. 2, 2010, pp. 201–214.

79. Stephanie Clifford, "Revamping, Home Depot Woos Women," *New York Times*, January 28, 2011, www.nytimes.com; "Lowe's to Debut New Campaign, Tagline," *Advertising Age*, September 15, 2011, www.adage.com; and Amy Tsao, "Retooling Home Improvement," *BusinessWeek*, February 14, 2005, www.businessweek.com.

80. Scott Anthony, "Three Innovation Lessons from India's Titan Watches," *Bloomberg News*, October 3, 2011, www.bloomberg.com.

81. Rosie Baker, "P&G Readies Olympic Family Campaign," *Marketing Week*, October 5, 2011, www.marketingweek.co.uk.

82. Robert J. Fisher and Laurette Dubé, "Gender Differences in Responses to Emotional Advertising," *Journal of Consumer Research* 31, no. 4, 2005, pp. 850–858.

83. John B. Ford, Patricia Kramer, Earl D. Honeycutt Jr., and Susan L. Casey, "Gender Role Portrayals in Japanese Advertising," *Journal of Advertising*, Spring 1998, pp. 113–124.

84. Geoffrey A. Fowler, "Marketers Take Heed: The Macho Chinese Man Is Back," *Wall Street Journal*, December 18, 2002, p. B1.

85. Thomas W. Whipple and Mary K. McManamon, "Implications of Using Male and Female Voices in Commercials: An Exploratory Study," *Journal of Advertising*, Summer 2002, pp. 79–91.

86. Alex Sood, "The Lost Boys Found: Marketing to Men Through Games," *Fast Company*, March 10, 2011, www.fastcompany.com.

87. "An All-women Fitness Event," *Malaysia Star*, March 20, 2008, http://thestar.com.my.

88. "Social Networking Site Use by Gender, 2005–2011," *Pew Research Center's Internet & American Life Project Studies*, May 2011, www.pewinternet.org.

89. Gillian Shaw, "Getting Off the Couch and Counting Crunches," *Vancouver Sun*, September 27, 2011, www.vancouversun.com.

90. Lynn J. Jaffe and Paul D. Berger, "Impact on Purchase Intent of Sex-Role Identity and Product Positioning," *Psychology and Marketing*, Fall 1988, pp. 259–271.

91. John Fetto, "In Broad Daylight," *American Demographics*, February 2001, pp. 16–20; and Ronald Alsop, "Cracking the Gay Market Code," *Wall Street Journal*, June 29, 1999, p. B1.

92. Steven M. Kates, "The Dynamics of Brand Legitimacy: An Interpretive Study in the Gay Men's Community," *Journal of Consumer Research*, September 2004, pp. 455–464.

93. Dave Berns, "Late to the Party, Las Vegas Businesses Targeting Gay Community," *Vegas Inc.*, July 18, 2011, www.vegasinc.com; and Lisa Fickenscher, "Tourism Industry to Capitalize on Same-Sex Marriage," *Crain's New York Business*, June 27, 2011, www.crainsnewyork.com.

94. Sandra Yin, "Home and Away," *American Demographics*, March 2004, p. 15.

95. Ignacio Vazquez, "Mexicans Are Buying 'Made in USA' Food," *Marketing News*, August 31, 1998, p. 14.

96. Susan Mitchell, "Birds of a Feather," *American Demographics*, February 1995, pp. 40–48.

97. Michael Weiss, "Parallel Universe," *American Demographics*, October 1999, pp. 58–63.

98. Adapted from PRIZM Segment Lookup, *Nielsen MyBestSegments*, www.claritas.com.

99. Chad Terhune, "Snack Giant's Boats Sting Regional Rivals," *Wall Street Journal*, July 29, 2004, pp. B1–B2.

100. Mitchell, "Birds of a Feather."

101. Mike Freeman, "Clusters of Customers," *San Diego Union-Tribune*, December 19, 2004, www.signosandiego.com.

102. Haipeng (Allan) Chen, Sharon Ng, and Akshay R. Rao, "Cultural Differences in Consumer Impatience," *Journal of Marketing Research*, August 2005, pp. 291–301.

103. See Daphna Oyserman, "High Power, Low Power, and Equality," *Journal of Consumer Psychology* 16, no. 4, 2006, pp. 352–356.

104. Sharon Shavitt, Ashok K. Lalwani, Jing Zhang, and Carlos J. Torelli, "The Horizontal/Vertical Dimension in Cross-Cultural Consumer Research," *Journal of Consumer Psychology* 16, no. 4, 2006, pp. 325–342; Joan Meyers-Levy, "Using the Horizontal/Vertical Distinction to Advance Insights into Consumer Psychology," *Journal of Consumer Psychology* 16, no. 4, 2006, pp. 347–351; Jennifer L. Aaker, "Delineating Culture," *Journal of Consumer Psychology* 16, no. 4, 2006, pp. 343–347; and Sharon Shavitt, Ashok K. Lalwani, Jing Zhang, and Carlos J. Torelli, "Reflections on the Meaning and Structure of the Horizontal/Vertical Dimension," *Journal of Consumer Psychology* 16, no. 4, 2006, pp. 357–362.

105. Michelle R. Nelson, Frédéric F. Brunel, Magne Supphellen, and Rajesh V. Manchanda, "Effects of Culture, Gender, and Moral Obligations on Responses to Charity Advertising Across Masculine and Feminine Cultures," *Journal of Consumer Psychology* 16, no. 1, 2006, pp. 45–56.

106. Donnel A. Briley and Jennifer L. Aaker, "When Does Culture Matter? Effects of Personal Knowledge on the Correction of Culture-Based Judgments," *Journal of Marketing Research*, August 2006, pp. 395–408.

107. Steven M. Kates and Charlene Goh, "Brand Morphing," *Journal of Advertising*, Spring 2003, pp. 59–68.

108. "Chinese May Sway Porsche Designs," *Automotive News*, August 22, 2011, p. 26.

109. George P. Moschis, *Consumer Socialization* (Lexington, Mass.: D. C. Heath, 1987); and Lisa Penaloza, "Atravesando Fronteras/Border Crossings," *Journal of Consumer Research*, June 1994, pp. 32–54.

110. Sonya A. Grier, Anne M. Brumbaugh, and Corliss G. Thornton, "Crossover Dreams: Consumer Responses to Ethnic-Oriented Products," *Journal of Marketing*, April 2006, pp. 35–51.

111. Jean-Francois Ouellet, "Consumer Racism and Its Effects on Domestic Cross-Ethnic Product Purchase: An Empirical Test in the United States, Canada, and France," *Journal of Marketing*, January 2007, pp. 113–128.

112. Andrew Hampp, "Major Marketers Tell Radio What They Need," *Advertising Age*, September 15, 2011, www.adage.com.

113. Corey Dade, "Interactive: How Latinos Are Reshaping Communities," *National Public Radio*, October 10, 2011, www.npr.org.

114. "Table 690: Money Income of Households," *Statistical Abstract of the United States 2012*, U.S. Census Bureau, p. 452.

115. Carrie Goerne, "Go the Extra Mile to Catch Up with Hispanics," *Marketing News*, December 24, 1990, p. 13; and Marlene Rossman, *Multicultural Marketing* (New York: American Management Association, 1994).

116. Penaloza, "Atravesando Fronteras/Border Crossings."

117. Humberto Valencia, "Developing an Index to Measure Hispanicness," in eds. Elizabeth C. Hirschman and Morris B. Holbrook, *Advances in Consumer Research*, vol. 12 (Provo, Utah: Association for Consumer Research, 1981), pp. 18–21; and Rohit Deshpande, Wayne D. Hoyer, and Naveen Donthu, "The Intensity of Ethnic Affiliation," *Journal of Consumer Research*, September 1986, pp. 214–220.

118. Cynthia Webster, "Effects of Hispanic Ethnic Identification on Marital Roles in the Purchase Decision Process," *Journal of Consumer Research*, September 1994, pp. 319–331.

119. Cynthia Webster, "The Effects of Hispanic Subcultural Identification on Information Search Behavior," *Journal of Advertising Research*, September–October 1992, pp. 54–62; and Naveen Donthu and Joseph Cherian, "Hispanic Coupon Usage," *Psychology and Marketing*, November–December 1992, pp. 501–510.

120. Ellen Byron, "Hola: P&G Seeks Latino Shoppers," *Wall Street Journal*, September 15, 2011, www.wsj.com.

121. Andre Salvail, "Aspen Company Says Its Bottled Water an Environmentally Sound Alternative," *Aspen Times*, July 21, 2011, www.aspentimes.com.

122. Byron, "Hola: P&G Seeks Latino Shoppers."

123. Bridget Goldschmidt, "Tastes in Translation," *Progressive Grocer*, August 2010, www.progressivegrocer.com.

124. Kevin Cokely, "Grocery Wars Turn to Latino Shoppers," *NBC DFW*, April 11, 2011, www.nbcdfw.com; and Kris Hudson and Ana Campoy, "Hispanics' Hard Times Hit Wal-Mart," *Wall Street Journal*, August 29, 2007, p. A8.

125. Terri C. Albert and Randy D. Jacobs, "Television Attitudes and TV Types of African-Americans, Latinos, and Caucasians," *Journal of Advertising Research*, June 2008, pp. 235–246.

126. Mike Reynolds, "Hispanic TV Summit," *Multichannel News*, September 20, 2011, www.multichannel.com.

127. Nitish Singh, Daniel W. Baack, Arun Pereira, and Donald Baack, "Culturally Customizing Websites for U.S. Hispanic Online Consumers," *Journal of Advertising Research*, June 2008, pp. 224–234.

128. Byron, "Hola: P&G Seeks Latino Shoppers."

129. Rohit Deshpande and Douglas M. Stayman, "A Tale of Two Cities: Distinctiveness Theory and Advertising Effectiveness," *Journal of Marketing Research*, February 1994, pp. 57–64.

130. See Claudia V. Dimofte, Mark R. Forehand, and Rohit Deshpandé, "Ad Schema Incongruity as Elicitor of Ethnic Self-Awareness and Differential Advertising Response," *Journal of Advertising*, Winter 2003–2004, pp. 7–17; and Mark R. Forehand and Rohit Deshpandé, "What We See Makes Us Who We Are: Priming Ethnic Self-Awareness and Advertising Response," *Journal of Marketing Research*, August 2001, pp. 336–348.

131. Anne M. Brumbaugh, "Source and Nonsource Cues in Advertising and Their Effects on the Activation of Cultural and Subcultural Knowledge on the Route to Persuasion," *Journal of Consumer Research*, September 2002, pp. 258–269.

132. Robert E. Wilkes and Humberto Valencia, "Hispanics and Blacks in Television Commercials," *Journal of Advertising*, March 1989, pp. 19–25.

133. Scott Koslow, Prem N. Shamdasani, and Ellen E. Touchstone, "Exploring Language Effects in Ethnic Advertising," *Journal of Consumer Research*, March 1994, pp. 575–585.

134. Chris Daniels, "Consumer Tech Brands Answer Call to Tap Hispanic Audience," *PR Week (US)*, May 2011, p. 18.

135. Laurel Wentz, "With an Ever-Growing Population of 'Fusionistas,' Consistency Is Key," *Advertising Age*, October 17, 2011, p. 28.

136. Laurel Wentz, "Few Marketers Target U.S. Hispanics with Spanish-Language Facebook Fan Pages," *Advertising Age*, September 27, 2011, www.adage.com.

137. David Luna and Laura A. Peracchio, "Advertising to Bilingual Consumers," *Journal of Consumer Research* 31, no. 4, 2005, pp. 760–765; and David Luna, Dawn Lerman, and Laura A. Peracchio, "Structural Constraints in Code-Switched Advertising," *Journal of Consumer Research* 32, no. 3, 2005, pp. 416–423.

138. "Table 229: Educational Attainment by Race and Hispanic Origin, 1970 to 2010," *Statistical Abstract of the United States 2012*, U.S. Census Bureau, p. 151; and "Table 690: Money Income of Households."

139. Irina Slutsky, "'Urban' Trope Misses a Large Swath of Black Consumers," *Advertising Age*, October 11, 2010, p. 15.

140. "Where Blacks, Whites Diverge," *Brandweek*, May 3, 1993, p. 22.

141. Howard Schlossberg, "Many Marketers Still Consider Blacks 'Dark-Skinned Whites,'" *Marketing News*, January 18, 1993, pp. 1, 13.

142. Alan J. Bush, Rachel Smith, and Craig Martin, "The Influence of Consumer Socialization Variables on Attitude Toward Advertising," *Journal of Advertising* 28, no. 3, Fall 1999, pp. 13–24.

143. Corliss L. Green, "Ethnic Evaluations of Advertising," *Journal of Advertising* 28, no. 1, Spring 1999, pp. 49–64; and Pepper Miller and Ronald Miller, "Trends Are Opportunities for Targeting African-Americans," *Marketing News*, January 20, 1992, p. 9.

144. "A Mirror for American Diversity," *MMR*, February 7, 2011, p. 24; and "African-Americans Go Natural," *MMR*, December 17, 2001, p. 43.

145. Giselle Tsirulnik, "American Airlines Mobile Banner Ads Drive BlackAtlas Site Registrations," *Mobile Marketer*, June 18, 2010, www.mobilemarketer.com.

146. Alan J. Bush, Rachel Smith, and Craig Martin, "The Influence of Consumer Socialization Variables on Attitude Toward Advertising," *Journal of Advertising* 28, no. 3, Fall 1999, pp. 13–24.

147. Green, "Ethnic Evaluations of Advertising."

148. Albert and Jacobs, "Television Attitudes and TV Types."

149. Ki Mae Heussner, "Google Study Sees African-Americans More Responsive to Digital Marketing," *Adweek*, September 18, 2011, www.adweek.com.

150. Jennifer L. Aaker, Anne M. Brumbaugh, and Sonya A. Grier, "Nontarget Markets and Viewer Distinctiveness," *Journal of Consumer Psychology* 9, no. 3, 2000, pp. 127–140.

151. Donnel A. Briley, L. J. Shrum, and Robert S. Wyer Jr., "Subjective Impressions of Minority Group Representation in the Media," *Journal of Consumer Psychology* 17, no. 1, 2007, pp. 36–48; and William J. Qualls and David J. Moore, "Stereotyping Effects on Consumers' Evaluation of Advertising," *Psychology and Marketing*, Summer 1990, pp. 135–151.

152. Sonia Alleyne, "The Magic Touch," *Black Enterprise*, June 1, 2004, n.p.

153. Tommy E. Whittler and Joan DiMeo, "Viewers' Reactions to Racial Cues in Advertising Stimuli," *Journal of Advertising Research*, December 1991, pp. 37–46.

154. Tommy E. Whittler, "Viewers' Processing of Source and Message Cues in Advertising Stimuli," *Psychology & Marketing*, July–August 1989, pp. 287–309.

155. Jonathan Burton, "Advertising Targeting Asians," *Far Eastern Economic Review*, January 21, 1993, pp. 40–41.

156. Rebecca Gardyn and John Fetto, "The Way We Shop," *American Demographics*, February 2003, pp. 30–33.

157. "Table 229, Educational Attainment by Race and Hispanic Origin: 1970 to 2010," *Statistical Abstract of the United States 2012*, U.S. Census Bureau, p. 151; and "Asian Americans Lead the Way Online," *Min's New Media Report*, December 31, 2001.

158. "Table 690: Money Income of Households."

159. E. Scott Reckard, "East West Surges into Banking Mainstream," *Los Angeles Times*, February 9, 2011, www.latimes.com.

160. Peter Van Allen, "Subaru Advertising Targets Chinese-Americans, Parents," *Philadelphia Business Journal*, May 20, 2011, www.bizjournals.com/philadelphia.

161. Jonathan Burton, "Advertising Targeting Asians," *Far Eastern Economic Review*, January 21, 1993, pp. 40–41; and Brett A. S. Martin, Christina Kwai-Choi Lee, and Yang Feng, "The Influence of Ad Model Ethnicity and Self-Referencing on Attitudes," *Journal of Advertising*, Winter 2004, pp. 27–37.

162. Onkvisit and Shaw, *International Marketing*; and Charles M. Schaninger, Jacques C. Bourgeois, and W. Christian Buss, "French-English Canadian Subcultural Consumption Differences," *Journal of Marketing*, Spring 1985, pp. 82–92.

163. Simon Houpt and Greg Keenan, "The Biggest Launch in Chevrolet's History," *The Globe and Mail (Canada)*, October 3, 2011, www.theglobeandmail.com

164. Hans Hoefer, *Thailand* (Boston: Houghton Mifflin, 1993).

165. "Major Religious Traditions in the U.S.," *Pew Research Center U.S. Religious Landscape Survey*, 2007, http://religions.pewforum.org/reports.

166. Priscilla L. Barbera, "Consumer Behavior and Born-Again Christianity," in eds. Jagdish N. Sheth and Elizabeth C. Hirschman, *Research in Consumer Behavior* (Greenwich, Conn.: JAI Press, 1988), pp. 193–222.

167. Piet Levy, "Religious Groups Latch on to Groupon Craze," *Houston Chronicle*, September 22, 2011, www.chron.com.

168. Rachel Lee Harris, "Hotels in India Offer Women-Only Floors," *New York Times*, October 16, 2011, p. TR–2.

169. Lisa Miller, "Registers Ring in Sanctuary Stores," *Wall Street Journal*, December 17, 1999, pp. B1, B4; and Elizabeth Bernstein, "Holy Frappuccino!" *Wall Street Journal*, August 3, 2001, pp. W1, W8.

170. Valerie A. Taylor, Diane Halstead, and Paula J. Hayes, "Consumer Responses to Christian Religious Symbols in Advertising," *Journal of Advertising*, Summer 2010, pp. 79–92.

171. Mark Walsh, "Coke's Mildenhall Explains 'Liquid' Marketing," *Media Post*, October 4, 2011, www.mediapost.com; Natalie Zmuda, "Pepsi Beverage Guru Unveils His Plan to Win the World Over," *Advertising Age*, July 11, 2011, www.adage.com; Natalie Zmuda, "Coca-Cola Launches Global Music Effort to Connect with Teens," *Advertising Age*, March 3, 2011, www.adage.com; Natalie Zmuda, "Marketer of the Year: Coca-Cola," *Advertising Age*, November 7, 2011, www.adage.com; Shirley Brady, "Coca-Cola's 2012 Gameplan," *Brand Channel*, September 29, 2011, www.brandchannel.com; and Kenna McHugh, "Pepsi Using Foursquare on Worldwide Social Media Campaign," *Social Times*, July 13, 2011, http://socialtimes.com.

CHAPTER 13

HOUSEHOLD AND SOCIAL CLASS INFLUENCES

After studying this chapter, you will be able to

1. Describe the various types of households and families, and explain how the family life cycle and other forces affect household structure.

2. Discuss the roles that household members play in acquisition and consumption decisions, and how companies can build on these roles to market more effectively.

3. Define the social class hierarchy and identify the major determinants of social class standing.

4. Explain how social class influences consumer behavior and why these influences are considerations when marketers plan strategy and tactics.

5. Outline three key forces that are, over time, changing social class structure in many countries.

© Prashanth Vishwanathan/Bloomberg via Getty Images

INTRODUCTION

Marketing to "$2 a Day" Consumers

Procter & Gamble—known for such blockbuster brands as Puffs, Pampers, and Pantene—aims to serve five billion customers worldwide within the next four years. Reaching that goal means marketing more aggressively to households in developing nations, where income may be as low as $2 a day, but aspirations are high. As these consumers work their way toward the middle class, they're looking for more than basic food and shelter. In home visits and personal interviews, P&G researchers have found that these consumers, like their counterparts in developed nations, want to make a positive impression and they value trusted brands. So P&G is testing products like hair dyes that require little water, an important consideration in rural homes where running water is scarce. And, using its marketing muscle, P&G has built the Pantene hair-care brand into its first $1 billion Asian brand.

In many of the targeted countries, mothers tend to make the buying decisions about household products. Digging deeper, P&G's researchers learned that mothers are especially concerned about the appearance of their family's clothes. With this in mind, P&G created Ariel laundry detergent for effective cleaning without hot water, which many low-income households lack. It also developed a Downy laundry product that gives clothing a long-lasting fragrance, adding a perfume-like aroma that $2-a-day households couldn't otherwise afford. Mothers are such an important target market that P&G has used billboards, print ads, TV commercials, and Facebook posts to proclaim itself the "proud sponsor of Moms" worldwide.[1]

This example illustrates how household influences and social class can affect consumer behavior (see Exhibit 13.1). Mothers in the emerging markets targeted by P&G often exert more influence than other family members in decisions about choosing and using household products (i.e., buying Ariel detergent instead of a competing brand). As a result, P&G reaches out to mothers using a variety of communications and promotions. Social class also affects what and how consumers buy. When lower-status consumers aspire to become middle class, they may buy products to improve their opportunities for advancement or choose a brand preferred by the middle class. As you read this chapter, remember that the generalizations about household and social class are broad group tendencies and may or may not apply to individual consumers.

HOW THE HOUSEHOLD INFLUENCES CONSUMER BEHAVIOR

You know from your own experience how many decisions the members of a household face every day, every week, every month. In fact, some researchers see the household as the most important unit of analysis for consumer behavior because households make many more acquisition, consumption, and disposition decisions than individuals do. Not all households and families are alike, however. This section defines families and households, examines the different types of households, describes the family life cycle, and looks at how families influence decisions and consumption.

Types of Households

Nuclear family Father, mother, and children.

Extended family The nuclear family plus relatives such as grandparents, aunts, uncles, and cousins.

Household A single person living alone or a group of individuals who live together in a common dwelling, regardless of whether they are related.

A *family* is usually defined as a group of individuals living together who are related by marriage, blood, or adoption (see Exhibit 13.2). The most typical unit is the **nuclear family**, consisting of a father, mother, and children. The **extended family** consists of the nuclear family plus relatives such as grandparents, aunts, uncles, and cousins. In the United States, we often think of *family* in terms of the nuclear family, whereas the extended family is the defining unit in many other nations. Yet today, largely due to economic conditions, 21 percent of U.S. adults aged 25 to 34 are living in extended families.[2]

Household is a broader term that includes a single person living alone or a group of individuals who live together in a common dwelling, regardless of whether they are related. Because of later marriages, cohabitation (two people of opposite sex or same sex living together), divorce, dual careers, boomerang children returning to live with their parents, people living longer, and a lower

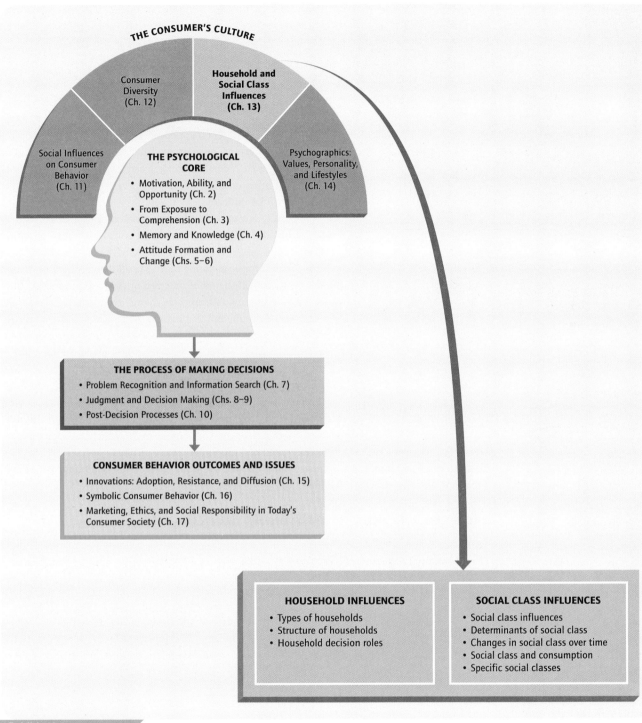

THE CONSUMER'S CULTURE

Consumer
Diversity
(Ch. 12)

**Household and
Social Class
Influences
(Ch. 13)**

Social Influences
on Consumer
Behavior
(Ch. 11)

**THE PSYCHOLOGICAL
CORE**

• Motivation, Ability, and
  Opportunity (Ch. 2)
• From Exposure to
  Comprehension (Ch. 3)
• Memory and Knowledge (Ch. 4)
• Attitude Formation and
  Change (Chs. 5–6)

Psychographics:
Values, Personality,
and Lifestyles
(Ch. 14)

THE PROCESS OF MAKING DECISIONS

• Problem Recognition and Information Search (Ch. 7)
• Judgment and Decision Making (Chs. 8–9)
• Post-Decision Processes (Ch. 10)

CONSUMER BEHAVIOR OUTCOMES AND ISSUES

• Innovations: Adoption, Resistance, and Diffusion (Ch. 15)
• Symbolic Consumer Behavior (Ch. 16)
• Marketing, Ethics, and Social Responsibility in Today's
  Consumer Society (Ch. 17)

HOUSEHOLD INFLUENCES

• Types of households
• Structure of households
• Household decision roles

SOCIAL CLASS INFLUENCES

• Social class influences
• Determinants of social class
• Changes in social class over time
• Social class and consumption
• Specific social classes

© Cengage Learning 2013

Exhibit 13.1

Chapter Overview:
Household and Social
Class Influences

The first section of this chapter examines household influences on consumer
behavior, including the various types of households, trends in household structure,
and the decision roles that household members play in acquiring and using an
offering. Next is a discussion of the determinants of social class (e.g., occupation,
education, income), changes in social class over time, and how social class affects
consumption.

uniqlo undercover   NEW COLLECTION AVAILABLE MARCH 16   www.undercover.uniqlo.com   MADE FOR ALL

Image Courtesy of The Advertising Archives

Exhibit 13.2

Family Life
Families come in all shapes and sizes.

Family life cycle
Different stages of family life, depending on the age of the parents and how many children are living at home.

birth rate, the number of nontraditional households has greatly increased, even as average household size is getting smaller. Exhibit 13.3 shows how U.S. households are changing.

Households and Family Life Cycle

Households can differ in terms of stage in the **family life cycle**. As shown in Exhibit 13.4, families can be characterized in terms of the age of the parents, the number of parents or grandparents present, the age and number of children living at home, and so on.[3] Changes such death or divorce can alter household structure by, for instance, creating single-parent households, as the arrows in Exhibit 13.4 indicate.

Marketers must consider the great variation in needs over the family life cycle and the effect on consumer behavior within households. In general, spending increases as households shift from young singles to young married and then remains high until falling sharply at the older married or older single stages.[4] Still, household buying patterns can change over time: For example, the ongoing decline in U.S. birth rates, coupled with economic recession, has caused sales of disposable diapers to drop in recent years.[5] Marketers should be aware that households in the midst of a life cycle change are more likely to switch brand preferences and be receptive to marketing efforts.[6]

However, these stages do not capture all types of households. Notably missing are same-sex couples (discussed in the next section) and never-married single mothers, two important market segments. Also, pets (cats, dogs, or other animals) are sometimes regarded as special family members and can be an important influence on household spending. In fact, the market for pet-related goods and services exceeds $50 billion.[7]

Changing Trends in Household Structure

Five main factors are altering the basic structure and characteristics of households. These include (1) delayed marriage and cohabitation, (2) dual careers, (3) divorce, (4) smaller families, and (5) same-sex couples.

Delayed Marriage and Cohabitation

In many Western societies, an increasing number of individuals are either delaying or avoiding getting married. Today the median age at which U.S. men first marry is 28; for U.S. women, the median age is 26.[8] This delayed marriage may occur because career is a higher priority, because of

Exhibit 13.3

Changes in Household Types
The composition of U.S. households is changing. In particular, there are more nontraditional families (single mothers and fathers) and nonfamily households (nonrelated people living together and one-person households), even as the percentage of married-couple households drops.

	2000 (Number)	2000 (%)	2010 (Number)	2010* (%)	2000–2010 (Percentage Change)
All Households	104,705,000	100	117,538,000	100	12
Married couples	55,311,000	53	58,410,000	50	6
Single fathers	4,028,000	4	5,580,000	5	39
Single mothers	12,687,000	12	14,843,000	13	17
Nonfamily households	32,680,000	31	38,705,000	33	18

*Numbers may not add to total due to rounding

Source: "Table 59: Households, Families, Subfamilies, and Married Couples, 1980–2010," *U.S. Census Bureau Statistical Abstract of the United States, 2012*, p. 54.

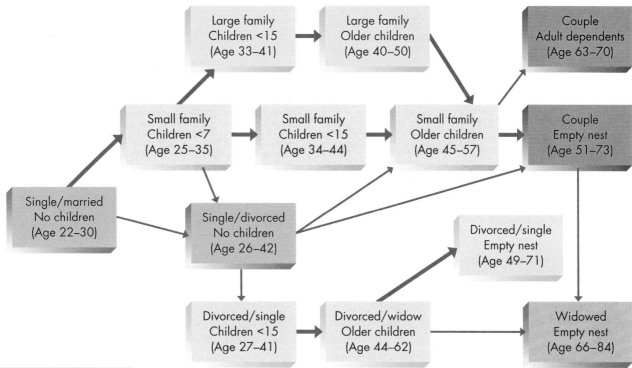

Exhibit 13.4

Household Life Cycles in the United States

This chart depicts how households change as the family life cycle changes. Each box represents a stage in the family life cycle; each line and arrow represents a type of change (marriage, divorce, death, children entering or leaving, aging). Note that this diagram accounts for numerous possibilities (divorce, becoming a single parent, being a childless couple, never marrying). What stage is your family in right now?

Source: Rex Y. Du and Wagner A. Kamakura, "Household Life Cycles and Lifestyles in the United States," *Journal of Marketing Research*, February 2006, Figure 1, p. 126.

cohabitation, or because consumers want to reduce their debt. Marketers look at this trend because single-person households exhibit unique consumption patterns. For example, single men spend more on alcohol, new cars, clothes, and education than married men do. Compared with married women, single women tend to spend more on new cars, shoes, entertainment, and housing (to live in a safe area).[9]

As a result of changing social norms, more consumers are living with members of the opposite sex outside of marriage. Compared with married couples, cohabitating individuals tend to be more self-oriented. Many view possessions as personal rather than joint items in case the relationship does not endure.[10] Nevertheless, many unmarried partners share expenses, and because both are likely to work, they often have higher discretionary income than do married couples of a similar age in which one spouse works.

Dual-Career Families

Dual-career families have several important implications for consumer behavior, starting with higher discretionary spending. These families tend to spend more than other families do on child care, eating out, and services in general. Also, juggling work and family roles, or *role overload*, leaves less time for cooking, housekeeping, and other activities. This is why dual-career families particularly value offerings that save time. No wonder more than half of all fast-food restaurant sales take place in the drive-through lane.[11] In these families, many husbands take on household responsibilities, and a small but growing number of men stay home to care for children.[12] As a result, more ads are geared toward men who, for example, share responsibility for cooking. In Asia, however, such ads may prompt a negative response from both men and women because sex roles are viewed more traditionally, even though more men are handling more housework.

Divorce

More than 4 of every 10 U.S. marriages are likely to end in divorce.[13] Although the trend has recently leveled off, many divorces still occur each year, with important implications for consumer behavior. During this transition, consumers perform critical tasks such as disposing of old possessions, forming a new household, and creating new patterns of consumption.[14] Acquiring goods and services can help consumers form a new identity and relieve stress during and after the divorce. For example, a newly divorced consumer might buy a new car, furniture, or clothing; get a new hairstyle; or go to singles events.

Divorce also influences household structure. If the couple was childless, the newly divorced often adopt the kinds of singles' acquisition and consumption patterns discussed earlier. However, these new singles are typically older and, if they work, have greater discretionary income for housing, transportation, and clothing. Also, divorce creates single-parent families when children are involved, which means that convenience offerings—such as packaged foods—may become a necessity. Compared with married parents, single parents tend to have lower incomes, spend less on most things, and be renters rather than home-owners. Finally, divorced individuals with children form stepfamilies and have unique consumption needs, such as duplicate supplies of clothing and other items that children need when spending time in two households.

Smaller Families

In many countries, the average household size is getting smaller. The average U.S. household size has dropped below three people, even as the number of one-person households has risen.[15] A smaller family means more discretionary income to spend on recreation, vacations, education, and entertainment. Smaller families also can spend more on each child. Childless married couples have more discretionary income than other households and spend more on food, restaurant meals, entertainment, liquor, clothing, and pets.[16]

Same-Sex Couples

According to the U.S. Census, there are more than 645,000 same-sex households in the United States.[17] Despite state-by-state controversies affecting the rights for gay and lesbian couples to marry, the number of same-sex couples is growing, particularly in certain urban areas. Eyeing estimates that New York's same-sex marriage law will attract $400 million in wedding business, New York City has launched a marketing initiative to make the "Big Apple" a gay wedding destination.[18] Around the world, as societal views continue to change, a number of countries now allow same-sex marriage, including Canada, the Netherlands, Belgium, Norway, Iceland, South Africa, and Argentina.[19]

Marketing Implications

Products and services that offer convenience can be marketed specifically to dual-career and divorced households. In two-income families, working wives gain influence over household acquisition and consumption decisions for vacations, cars, and other offerings.[20] Therefore, marketers of costly offerings must appeal to both husband and wife. Nontraditional families are also being targeted: For example, Hallmark offers greeting cards that deal with blended family relationships, without mentioning the word "step."[21] Single men and women are also an attractive target for many marketers. Some stores in the Trader Joe's grocery chain, for example, designate a special "Singles Night" and create romance-themed displays of chocolate and wine for customers who come to mix and mingle as they shop.[22] And marketers can target consumers who are experiencing family life cycle changes such as divorce with offerings that help reduce the stress of these transitions.[23]

Marketers are targeting same-sex couples through sponsorships of gay pride events, ads in targeted magazines such as *Out* and *The Advocate*, specialized websites, billboards in selected neighborhoods, and TV ads depicting same-sex couples.[24] Some marketers that openly target this segment, however, have become targets of conservative groups opposed to homosexuality.[25] Marketers who target same-sex couples also must understand how these consumers make decisions; for instance, purchasing decisions by lesbian couples tend to be made in a more egalitarian manner than decisions in husband- or wife-dominated traditional households are.[26]

ROLES THAT HOUSEHOLD MEMBERS PLAY

Household decision roles Roles that different members play in a household decision.

A key aspect of households is that more than one individual can become involved in acquisition and consumption. This section discusses various elements of household consumer behavior, with particular emphasis on **household decision roles** and how household members influence decision processes. Household members may perform a variety of tasks or roles in acquiring and consuming a product or service:

▶ *Gatekeeper.* Household members who collect and control information important to the decision.

▶ *Influencer.* Household members who try to express their opinions and influence the decision.

▶ *Decider.* The person or persons who actually determine which product or service will be chosen.

▶ *Buyer.* The household member who physically acquires the product or service.

▶ *User.* The household members who consume the product.

Each role can be performed by different household members, by a single individual, a subset of individuals, or the entire household. For example, parents might make the final decision about which movie to download, but the children may play a role, either directly (by stating their preferences) or indirectly (when parents keep their children's preferences in mind). One parent may actually obtain the movie, but the entire family might watch it. Exhibit 13.5 divides household purchases into nine categories, depending on the decision maker and the user.

Instrumental roles Roles that relate to tasks affecting the buying decision.

Expressive roles Roles that involve an indication of family norms.

Household decision roles can be **instrumental**, meaning that they relate to tasks affecting the buying decision, such as when and how much to purchase. Roles can also be **expressive**, which means they indicate family norms, such as choice of color or style.[27] Traditionally, the husband fulfilled the instrumental role and the wife the expressive role, but sex-role changes are altering this pattern.

Conflict can often occur in fulfilling different household roles based on (1) the reasons for buying, (2) who should make the decision, (3) which option to choose, and (4) who gets to use the product or service.[28] Conflict may occur in decisions about "green" consumption, such as using

Exhibit 13.5

Buyers and Users
Household purchase decisions can be made by one, some, or all members of the family. Acquired products and services may be consumed by one, some, or all members. Here is an example of three cells that result from crossing these two factors. Can you think of examples that would fit into the other six cells?

Source: Robert Boutilier, "Pulling the Family's Strings," *American Demographics,* August 1993, pp. 44–48. American Demographics © 1993. Reprinted with permission.

A Purchase Decision Maker

A Consumer		One member	Some members	All members
	One member	1	2 Tennis racket	3
	Some members	4 Sugar Pops	5	6
	All members	7	8	9 Refrigerator

For Example:
1. Mom and Dad go to buy a new tennis racket for Mom. Dad advises Mom on her purchase. Some members are decision makers and one member is a consumer: cell 2.
2. Mom goes to the grocery store to buy Sugar Pops cereal for her children. She'll never eat the stuff. One member is a decision maker and some members are consumers: cell 4.
3. Mom, Dad, and the kids go to the department store to buy a refrigerator. All members are decision makers and all are consumers: cell 9.

organic food and conserving water or energy.[29] In general, households resolve conflicts through problem solving, persuasion, bargaining, and politics, with persuasion and problem solving, the most frequently used methods.[30] Note that resolution is often not systematic and rational, but rather a "muddling-through" process in which the household makes a series of small decisions to arrive at a solution.[31] Moreover, many households avoid rather than confront conflict.

Joint household decisions are more likely when the perceived risk associated with the decision is high, the decision is very important, there is ample time to make a decision, and the household is young. In addition, household members can influence each other in terms of brand preferences and loyalties, information search patterns, media reliance, and price sensitivities.[32]

The Roles of Spouses

Husbands and wives play different roles in making decisions, and the nature of their influence depends on the offering and the couple's relationship. In examining husband-wife influence, a landmark study conducted in Belgium (and replicated in the United States) identified four major decision categories:[33]

Husband-dominant decision Decision made primarily by the male head-of-household.

▶ A **husband-dominant decision** is made primarily by the male head-of-household (e.g., the purchase of lawn mowers and hardware).

Wife-dominant decision Decision made primarily by the female head-of-household.

▶ A **wife-dominant decision** is made primarily by the female head-of-household (e.g., children's clothing, women's clothing, groceries, and toiletries).

Autonomic decision Decision equally likely to be made by the husband or wife, but not by both.

▶ An **autonomic decision** is equally likely to be made by the husband or the wife but not by both (e.g., men's clothing, luggage, toys and games, sporting equipment, and cameras).

Syncratic decision Decision made jointly by the husband and wife.

▶ A **syncratic decision** is made jointly by the husband and wife (e.g., vacations, refrigerators, TVs, living room furniture, financial planning services, and the family car).

As spouses come closer to a final decision, the process tends to move toward syncratic decision making, particularly for more important decisions. These role structures are only generalities, however; the actual influence exerted depends on many factors. First, a spouse who brings more financial resources to the family and has a high involvement level will have more influence on the decision.[34] Second, demographic factors, such as total family income and education, are related to the degree of husband-wife influence.[35] Combined, these factors provide a spouse with a perception of power in the decision-making situation. The higher the degree of perceived power, the more likely the spouse will exert influence.

When the family has a strong traditional sex-role orientation, certain tasks are stereotypically considered either masculine or feminine, and more decisions tend to be husband dominated than they are in less traditional families.[36] For example, Mexican American families tend toward a traditional orientation and husband-dominant decisions. Still, sex-role changes are influencing husband-wife decisions. In Thailand, nearly half of the husbands surveyed said that they decided what foods their households would eat and that they did the family food shopping, traditionally to be considered the wife's role.[37] While men do much of the grocery shopping in many U.S. households, few advertisers target them directly in connection with these decisions.[38] Also in the United States, joint decision making is most common among Anglo families and wife dominance is more prevalent in African American families.

Researchers have found support for the four major patterns of spousal decision roles in a number of countries, although the United States, France, and the Netherlands exhibited a higher level of joint decision making than did Venezuela, where autonomous decisions were more prevalent.[39] Other aspects of spousal decision making have also been studied. For example, through the processes of *bargaining* (which involves a fair exchange) or *concession* (in which a spouse gives in on some points to get what he or she wants in other areas), couples tend to make equitable decisions that result from compromises.[40]

Couples typically follow an informal process for decision making in which they have limited awareness of each other's knowledge and decision strategy.[41] Husbands and wives are generally not good at estimating their spouse's influence and preferences—and in fact, they have less success predicting preferences as relationships progress—but they do learn from previous decisions and make adjustments over time.[42] Further, when the spouses have opposite spending tendencies—one is a spender, one is not—decision making will be marked by conflict, which in turn may have a negative effect on the marriage.[43]

The Role of Children

Children play an important role in household decisions by attempting to influence their parents' acquisition, usage, and disposition behavior. The most common stereotype is that children nag until their parents finally give in. Research finds that the success of such attempts depends on the type of offering, characteristics of the parents, age of the child, and stage of the decision process.[44] Children are more likely to use their influence for child-related products such as cereals, snacks, cars, vacations, and new computer technologies.

Interestingly, children consistently overestimate how much influence they have in most decisions.[45] Children tend to have less influence when parents are more involved in the decision process or are more traditional and conservative. Working and single parents, on the other hand, are more likely to give in because they face more time pressures.[46] Another important finding is that the older the child, the more influence he or she will exert.[47] However, even when the family includes two or more children, parents still exert the most influence over decisions about buying and consuming new offerings.[48] Another point is that parents who believe self-control can be increased over time tend to make buying decisions that will help the child improve self-control.[49]

One study examined the strategies adolescents use in trying to influence parental and family decision making, which include bargaining (making deals), persuasion (trying to influence the decision in their favor), emotional appeals (using emotion to get what they want), and requests (directly asking).[50] Parents, in turn, can use not only the same strategies on their children but also expert (knowledge), legitimate (power), and directive (parental authority) strategies.

The type of household determines the nature of children's influence. Authoritarian households stress obedience, while neglectful households exert little control. Democratic households encourage self-expression, and permissive households remove constraints. Children are more likely to have direct decision control in permissive and neglectful families and are more likely to influence decisions in democratic and permissive ones.[51] Also, children's influence varies at different stages of the decision process. It is greatest early in the decision-making process (problem recognition and information search) and declines significantly in the evaluation and choice phases.[52]

Marketing Implications

Marketers need to recognize that appealing only to deciders or purchasers may be too narrow a strategy, because different household members may play different decision roles. For instance, marketers who exclusively target children for toys ignore the fact that parents are usually influencers, deciders, and purchasers of these products. Therefore, marketers should determine which family members are involved in each acquisition decision and appeal to all important parties.

Companies such as General Mills target mothers who make decisions about products like breakfast cereal using ads as well as product reviews by "mommy bloggers" who have a sizable social media audience.[53] For other decisions, such as family outings, both spouses may play a key role. KidZania play centers—designed for children from 4 to 14 years old—target parents in Mexico, Japan, and the Middle East who want to give their children a taste of different careers. The entrance fee allows children to "play" at various occupations using branded props from sponsors such as Procter & Gamble.[54]

More U.S. children are using the Internet for e-mail, visiting websites, and playing in virtual worlds created especially for youngsters, opening opportunities for established brands and newcomers alike.[55] Children's game sites such as Club Penguin and Moshi Monsters (see Exhibit 13.6) have attracted millions of paid subscribers worldwide because parents see them as a safe place for children to play online.[56] Note that parenting style

Exhibit 13.6

Targeting to Children Consumers
Children's game sites, like Moshi Monsters, combine toys and safe online play areas for kids.

plays an important role in socializing children as consumers and influences how children learn to respond to advertising.[57] Yet marketing to children raises ethical and legal issues; for that reason, websites for children under 13 must comply with the Children's Online Privacy Protection Act and obtain parental permission before collecting information from children.

SOCIAL CLASS

Social class hierarchy
The grouping of members of society according to status, high to low.

Most societies have a **social class hierarchy** that confers higher status to some classes of people than to others. These social classes consist of identifiable groups of individuals whose behaviors and lifestyles differ from those of members of the other classes. Members of a particular social class tend to share similar values and behavior patterns. Note that social classes are loose collections of individuals with similar life experiences, not formal groups with a strong identity.[58]

Many societies view these distinctions as important because they recognize that everyone has a role to play in order for society to function smoothly. However, some roles, such as medical doctor or executive, are more prestigious and more valued than others, such as toll taker or janitor. Nevertheless, the concept of social class is not inherently negative. Even with the inequalities, social class distinctions can help individuals determine what their role in society is or what they would like it to be (their aspirations). Furthermore, all levels of the social class hierarchy make an important contribution to society.

Types of Social Class Systems

Most societies have three major classes: high, middle, and lower. Often, however, finer distinctions are made. The United States, for example, is typically divided into the seven levels presented in Exhibit 13.7, with up to 70 percent of the population concentrated in the middle classes.[59] Although most societies have some kind of hierarchical structure, the size and composition of the classes depend on the relative prosperity of a particular country.[60]

Exhibit 13.7

U.S. Social Classes
Researchers have classified the U.S. social classes in a variety of ways. This exhibit shows a typical classification scheme, with three classes at the top, two in the middle, and two at the lower end of the social classes.

Upper Americans	Upper-upper	The "capital *S* society" world of inherited wealth, aristocratic names
	Lower-upper	Newer social elite, drawn from current professional, corporate leadership
	Upper-middle	The rest of college graduate managers and professionals; lifestyle centers on private clubs, causes, and the arts
Middle Americans	Middle class	Average-pay white-collar workers and their blue-collar friends: live on the "better side of town," try to "do the proper things"
	Working class	Average-pay blue-collar workers; lead "working class lifestyle" whatever the income, school, background, or job
Lower Americans	"A lower group of people but not the lowest"	Working, not on welfare; living standard is just above poverty
	"Real lower-lower"	On welfare, visibly poverty stricken, usually out of work (or have "dirtiest jobs")

Source: From Richard P. Coleman, "The Continuing Significance of Social Class to Marketing," *Journal of Consumer Research*, December 1983, p. 277. Reprinted with permission of The University of Chicago Press.

Compared with the United States, Japan and Scandinavia have an even larger and more predominant middle class with much smaller groups above and below. This distribution means that there is greater equality among people in those two countries than in other societies. The Japanese structure represents a concerted government effort to abolish the social class system and mix together people from all levels of society.[61] Yet the very competitive and selective Japanese educational system still restricts entry to higher-status corporate and government positions. In developing areas such as Latin America and India, the largest concentrations are in the lower classes (see Exhibit 13.8).

In most societies, the upper classes are more similar to each other than they are to other classes within their own countries because the upper classes tend to be more cosmopolitan and international in orientation.[62] The lower classes, on the other hand, are the most likely to be culture bound and the most different from other classes in terms of lifestyles, dress, and eating behaviors. The middle classes are most likely to borrow from other classes as a way to achieve upward social mobility.

Even though members of a particular class may share similar values, they may maintain these values in different ways. In addition, a particular social class may contain different economic substrata. Specifically, families whose income level is 20 to 30 percent more than the median of their class are considered **overprivileged** because they have funds to buy more than basic necessities.[63] **Class average** families have an income level that is average for their social class and can therefore afford the type of symbols expected for their status, such as a house or appropriate clothing. The **underprivileged**, whose incomes are below the median, have trouble meeting class expectations.

Overprivileged Families with an income higher than the average in their social class.

Class average Families with an average income in a particular class.

Underprivileged Families below the average income in their class.

Social Class Influences

Social class structures are important because they strongly affect norms and values and, therefore, behavior. Given that members of a social class interact regularly with each other (both formally and informally), people are more likely to be influenced by individuals in their own social class than by those in other classes. Note that social class influence is not a cultural straitjacket; it merely reflects the fact that people with similar life experiences tend to exhibit similar lifestyles and behaviors.[64]

The norms and behaviors of consumers in one class can also influence consumers in other social classes. A commonly cited theory of class influence is the **trickle-down effect**, whereby lower

Trickle-down effect
Trends that start in the upper classes and then are copied by lower classes.

Exhibit 13.8

Class Structure by Culture
The relative sizes and structures of social classes vary by culture. Japan and Scandinavia, for example, are characterized by a large middle class with few people above or below it. India and Latin America, on the other hand, have a greater proportion of individuals in the lower classes. The United States has a large middle class but also has significant proportions in the upper and lower classes.

Sources: Adapted from Edward W. Cundiff and Marye T. Hilger, *Marketing in the International Environment* (Englewood Cliffs, N.J.: Prentice-Hall, 1988); and Marieke K. de Mooij and Warren Keegan, *Advertising Worldwide* (Englewood Cliffs, N.J.: Prentice-Hall, 1991), p. 96.

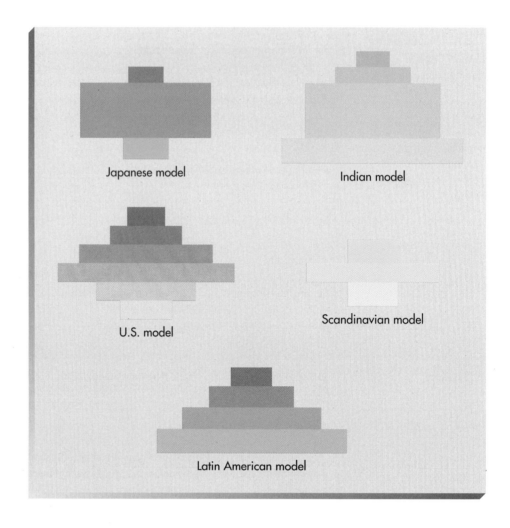

Japanese model

Indian model

U.S. model

Scandinavian model

Latin American model

Status float Trends that start in the lower and middle classes and move upward.

classes, seeking to raise their social standing, copy trends that begin in the upper classes. They also accept upper-class influence if they lack the cultural knowledge to make their own judgments of what is and is not acceptable.[65] For example, the middle class often looks to the upper class for guidance on cultural matters of music, art, and literature. However, the universal validity of the trickle-down theory has been questioned. In some instances, a **status float** can occur, whereby trends (in clothing, music, etc.) start in the lower and middle classes and then spread upward.

How Social Class Is Determined

Examining how social class affects consumer behavior requires a way of classifying consumers into different social classes. Unfortunately, this is a complex task, and the exact determinants of social class have been the subject of considerable debate over the years.

Income Versus Social Class

Income is only weakly related to social class, for several reasons.[66] First, income levels often overlap social classes, particularly at the middle and lower levels. For example, many U.S. blue-collar workers have higher incomes than some white-collar workers, yet they do not have higher social standing. Second, although income increases greatly with age, older workers do not automatically achieve higher social status. Finally, dual-career families may generate a higher than average income but do not necessarily attain higher status. Thus, although income is one factor related to social class, other factors play key roles as well.

Although some researchers argue that income can be a better predictor of consumer behavior than social class, a more common view is that both factors are important in explaining behavior in different situations.[67] Social class is a better predictor of consumption when it reflects lifestyles and values and does not involve high monetary expenditures, such as purchasing clothes or furniture. For example, middle- and lower-class consumers favor different styles of furniture, but middle-class consumers tend to spend more money on home furnishings even when the incomes of both classes of consumers are roughly similar. Income, on the other hand, is more useful in explaining the consumption of costly offerings unrelated to class symbols, such as boats. Both social class and income are needed to explain behaviors that involve status symbols and significant expenditures such as buying a car or, as in Africa, buying an appliance such as a washing machine.[68]

Although income cannot always explain social class, social class can often explain how income is used. As one illustration, upper-class consumers are more likely to invest money, whereas the lower classes are more likely to rely on savings accounts in banks. The key point is that social class aids in the understanding of consumer behavior and that social standing is determined by a variety of factors in addition to income.

Occupation and Education

The greatest determinant of class standing is occupation, particularly in Western cultures. Specifically, some occupations, especially those that require higher levels of education, skill, or training, are viewed as higher in status than others—although perceived status varies from culture to culture. Moreover, individuals with the same occupation tend to share similar income, lifestyles, knowledge, and values.

Education also plays a critical role because it is one of the key determinants of occupation and therefore social class. In fact, educational attainment is considered the most reliable determinant of consumers' income potential and spending patterns.[69] Consider that the median income of a U.S. consumer with a high school education is $21,500, whereas the median income of a college graduate is nearly twice as high, at $42,780.[70] Well-educated consumers not only earn more, they also read and travel more, are healthier, and are often more receptive to new offerings than the rest of the population.[71] Higher education is particularly important for gaining entry into higher-status occupations.

Other Indicators of Social Class

Inherited status Status that derives from parents at birth.

Earned status Status acquired later in life through achievements.

Factors such as area of residence, possessions, family background, and social interactions can also indicate class level. The neighborhood in which we live and the number and types of possessions we have are visible signs that often communicate class standing. In terms of family background, researchers distinguish between **inherited status**, which is adopted from parents at birth, and **earned status**, which is acquired later in life from personal achievements.[72] Inherited status is the initial anchor point from which values are learned and from which upward or downward mobility can occur. As mentioned earlier, members of a social class often interact with each other, so the company we keep also helps us to identify our social standing. Note, however, that the relative importance of these determinants of social class varies from country to country.

Social Class Indexes

Status crystallization When consumers are consistent across indicators of social class income, education, occupation, etc.

All of the preceding factors must be taken into account to determine social class standing, and sociologists have developed a number of indexes to accomplish this task. For this purpose, researchers use indexes such as the *Computerized Status Index* (CSI), which assesses consumers' education, occupation, area of residence, and income. When consumers are consistent across the various dimensions, social class is easy to determine and **status crystallization** occurs. Sometimes, however, individuals are low on some factors but high on others. Thus, a new doctor from an inner-city neighborhood might be inconsistent on factors such as occupation and income. It is also difficult for marketers to neatly categorize such consumers into one social class or another.

HOW SOCIAL CLASS CHANGES OVER TIME

Social class structures are not necessarily static, unchanging systems. Three of the key forces producing an evolution in social class structures in many countries are (1) upward mobility, (2) downward mobility, and (3) social class fragmentation.

Upward Mobility

Upward mobility Raising one's status level.

In many cultures, consumers can raise their status level through **upward mobility**, usually by educational or occupational achievement. In other words, lower- or middle-class individuals can take advantage of educational opportunities, particularly a college education, to gain entry into higher-status occupations. However, the percentage of U.S. college graduates from poverty-level households has remained low for decades, reflecting the challenge of paying for college—especially during tough financial times—and the difficulty of bridging the gap between the lower and middle classes while in college.[73]

Clearly, upward mobility is not guaranteed. The lower classes, particularly some minorities, still face limited economic and cultural resources as well as limited educational opportunities and are statistically less likely than are the upper classes to have access to higher-status occupations.[74] Individuals from higher-status families are twice as likely to maintain their status as members of lower classes are to achieve a higher status. Even after achieving upward mobility, an individual's behavior can still be heavily influenced by his or her former class level because the behaviors associated with the social class in which people grow up are strongly learned.[75] Another important point about upward mobility is that consumers often inaccurately estimate their comparisons with others, which affects their buying decisions.[76]

Note that the degree of upward mobility may vary across cultures. Typically, Western nations offer the most opportunities, although opportunities for upward mobility have actually decreased in the United States, Canada, and Great Britain during some periods.[77] In Arab countries, the upper and middle classes are growing rapidly as a result of oil money and an increase in Western college education.[78] The size of the middle class has been exploding in many developing countries because international trade is making affordable goods more available, dual-career families are earning greater income, and more professionals are needed to support growing economies. As you saw in the opening example, Procter & Gamble sees $2-a-day consumers in developing countries as an important market, in part because many in this segment aspire to be middle class.

Downward Mobility

Downward mobility Losing one's social standing.

Downward mobility, or moving to a lower class, is an increasing trend in some industrialized societies. In the past 25 years, millions of U.S. families have slid downward as jobs were sent overseas or eliminated by technology and companies lowered wages or laid off workers. Although many parents dreamed of providing their children with a better life and higher status, some children may have difficulty reaching their parents' status level, a situation labeled *status panic*.[79] Meanwhile, because of increasing material desires, more upper-middle- and middle-class families are having difficulty maintaining their lifestyles.

Downward mobility creates disappointment and disillusionment. Sometimes acquisition and consumption can help protect personal self-worth. For example, a consumer might buy a new truck or other item to feel good about himself or herself.[80] Alternatively, downward mobility can lead to a loss of possessions, such as a car or home, or to a decrease in consumption if people choose to spend less on items that are less important.

Social Class Fragmentation

Social class fragmentation The disappearance of class distinctions.

Interestingly, the old social class distinctions are beginning to disintegrate—a phenomenon called **social class fragmentation**—due to several factors.[81] First, both upward and downward mobility have blurred class divisions. Second, the increased availability of mass media, especially TV and the Internet is exposing consumers worldwide to the values and norms of diverse classes and cultures, leading some people to adopt elements of other groups' behavior. A third reason is that advances in communication technology have increased interaction across social class lines. These factors have led to the emergence of many social class subsegments with distinct patterns of values and behavior. The United States now has dozens of classes ranging from the suburban elite (super-rich families) to the hardscrabble (poor, single-parent families).[82] Similar trends are occurring in other countries as well. Exhibit 13.9 shows some traditional and emerging classes in Germany.

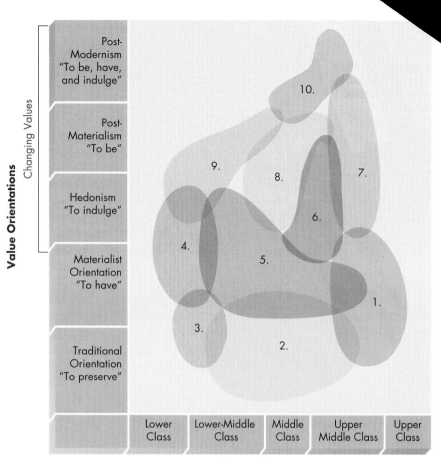

Exhibit 13.9

German Social Classes
This exhibit is a detailed depiction of social class structure in German society. The 10 groups are characterized along two dimensions: social standing (low to upper-middle class) and value orientations (traditional to very modern values).

Source: Based on Mariele De Mooij and Warren Kegan, *Advertising Worldwide* (Englewood Cliffs, N.J.: Prentice Hall, 1991), p. 116.

1. Conservative-Technocratic Milieu: 10%
2. Petty Bourgeois Milieu: 8%
3. Traditional Blue-Collar Milieu: 4%
4. Uprooted Blue-Collar Milieu: 11%
5. Social Climber Milieu: 20%
6. Modern Bourgeois Milieu: 9%
7. Liberal-Intellectual Milieu: 10%
8. Modern No-Collar Milieu: 8%
9. Hedonistic Milieu: 13%
10. Post-Modern Milieu: 7%

HOW DOES SOCIAL CLASS AFFECT CONSUMPTION?

Social class is often viewed as a cause of or motivation for consumer acquisition, consumption, and disposition behaviors. This section examines four major topics: (1) conspicuous consumption and voluntary simplicity, (2) status symbols, (3) compensatory consumption, and (4) the meaning of money.

Conspicuous Consumption and Voluntary Simplicity

Conspicuous consumption The acquisition and display of goods and services to show off one's status.

Conspicuous waste Visibly buying products and services that one never uses.

Voluntary simplicity Limiting acquisition and consumption to live a less material life.

Conspicuous consumption, also related to social class, is an attempt to offset deficiencies or a lack of esteem by devoting attention to consumption.[83] Conspicuously consumed items are important to their owner because of what they tell others.[84] Only if these items are visible will the message be communicated. According to research, both uniqueness and conformity play a role in conspicuous consumption.[85] Even in societies with fewer distinctions between status levels, conspicuous consumption can prompt lower-status consumers to feel socially competitive and increase their consumption to "get ahead of the Joneses."[86] Another explanation, from *terror management theory*, suggests that such materialism helps relieve consumers' anxiety over the inevitability of death.[87]

In addition, consumers can engage in **conspicuous waste**. For example, wealthy individuals may buy houses they never use and pianos that no one plays.[88] On the other hand, some consumers are moving away from conspicuous consumption toward **voluntary simplicity**, consciously limiting their acquisition and consumption for a less material, eco-friendly lifestyle.[89]

Status Symbols and Judging Others

Highly related to conspicuous consumption is the notion that people often judge others on the basis of what they own. In other words, goods or services become **status symbols** to indicate their owners' place in the social hierarchy.[90] Someone who owns an expensive watch or car will likely be viewed as upper class. While some luxury brands send subtle status signals that only members of the upper class will recognize, other brands use highly distinctive logos or other prominent elements to publicly announce status.[91]

Consumers' quest to acquire items that reflect not only their current social class but also their class aspirations can explain some acquisitions and consumption behavior (see Exhibit 13.10). By acquiring items that members of their own social class cannot typically afford, consumers can increase their perception of self-worth. Depictions of the material success of peers can spur the desire for luxurious status symbols as well.[92] Even relatively affordable luxuries—like a posh $20 nail polish or the lowest-priced Mercedes car—"enable less affluent consumers to trade up to higher levels of quality, taste, and aspiration," says a Boston Consulting Group expert. "These are the luxuries that continue to sell even when the economy is shaky, because they often meet very powerful emotional needs."[93]

Interestingly, status symbols can sometimes move in a reverse direction, which is called a **parody display**.[94] For example, middle- and upper-class Brazilians feel hip if they practice capoeira, a blend of dance and martial arts traditionally popular among members of the lower class.[95] In addition, if certain status symbols become widely possessed, they can lose their status connotations and become **fraudulent symbols**. For example, recognizing that luxury brands are often copied to produce low-price knockoffs for the mass market, Coach and others have redesigned their products with subtler logos. The new products are unmistakably upscale but don't "scream 'Coach, Coach, Coach,'" observes a Coach designer.[96]

Compensatory Consumption

Compensatory consumption behavior, also related to social class, is an attempt to offset deficiencies or a lack of esteem by devoting attention to consumption.[97] A consumer who is experiencing frustration or difficulties, particularly in terms of career advancement or status level, may compensate by purchasing status symbols, such as a car or nice clothes, to help restore lost self-esteem. Traditionally, some working-class consumers would exhibit compensatory consumption by mortgaging their future to buy a house and other status symbols. More recently, however, many middle- and upper-middle-class U.S. consumers, disappointed at stalled careers and lower prosperity levels than their parents,

Parody display Status symbols that start in the lower-social classes and move upward.

Fraudulent symbol Symbol that becomes so widely adopted that it loses its status.

Compensatory consumption The consumer behavior of buying products or services to offset frustrations or difficulties in life.

Exhibit 13.10

Conspicuous Consumption and Status Symbols

Sometimes consumers buy items because they signal a message of status or eliteness to others, like expensive eyeglasses or cars.

have exhibited compensatory consumption behavior. Knowing this tendency, some companies have created offerings that are somewhat more affordable than their existing luxury brands.

The Meaning of Money

An important concept related to social class is money. At the most basic level, economists define *money* as a medium of exchange or standard of payment. Under this view, money fulfills a very functional or utilitarian purpose, enabling people to acquire items needed for everyday living. Often, however, money comes to symbolize security, power, love, and freedom.

Consumers learn the meaning of money early in childhood. Parents easily discover that they can control their children by meting out rewards and punishments based on money and by buying or not buying things.[98] Children learn that if they behave, get good grades, or do their chores, their parents will buy things for them. This early learning later translates into adult life when money is viewed as a means of acquiring things that will bring not only happiness and fulfillment but also a sense of status and prestige. In some societies, this belief can lead to an almost insatiable desire and quest for making money, which is enhanced by media coverage of those who have "made it" and by the belief that "it could happen to anyone, including me." This belief is one reason that state lotteries are popular among certain classes.

Marketers must understand money and what it stands for in order to understand consumption patterns. Money allows consumers to acquire status objects as indicators of social class standing or as a way to rise to a higher level through acquisition. However, the increase in credit and debit card usage shows that money need not involve physical cash. Even in nations like Kenya, where cash is the dominant payment method, more consumers are qualifying for credit cards so that they can buy now and pay later.[99]

Money as Both Good and Evil

Money can be perceived as the just reward for hard work and can lead to the acquisition of needed items, a higher quality of life, and the ability to help others and society in general. On the downside, the quest for money can lead to obsession, greed, dishonesty, and potentially harmful practices such as gambling, prostitution, and drug dealing (see Chapter 17). The quest for money can also lead to negative emotions such as anxiety, depression, anger, and helplessness.[100] Moreover, individuals who do not share their wealth with others may be seen as selfish and greedy. Interestingly, consumers with yearly household incomes under $25,000 donate about 4 percent of their income to charities, whereas consumers with household incomes of $100,000 or more contribute less than 3 percent of their income to charities.[101]

Money and Happiness

The popular belief (especially in Western countries) that money can buy happiness is rarely true. After some people acquire tremendous wealth, money can become meaningless and no longer highly desired. Furthermore, wealthy people can often afford to hire others to handle many of the activities that they formerly enjoyed, such as gardening and do-it-yourself projects. And, of course, money simply cannot buy love, health, true friendship, and children, among other things. In fact, as time becomes scarcer than money, consumers are consciously spending time in ways that will make them happy, such as being with friends and family—experiences that cannot be purchased.[102] Still, research suggests that consumers can get more happiness for their money in a number of ways, including buying experiences rather than material possessions, buying multiple small pleasures rather than a few large pleasures, using money to benefit other people, and delaying consumption to prolong the pleasure of anticipation.[103]

One study on money, acquisition, and happiness indicates that acquiring money is distinct from acquiring an offering, because consumers tend to focus on external information—the face value— when acquiring money, rather than the consumption experience it can buy.[104] Another study shows that the positive emotions that consumers feel when they buy an experience (such as a day at a theme park) tend to last longer than the good feelings they have from acquiring and owning a material possession. However, any negative feeling from a bad purchase is forgotten more quickly than a negative feeling from a bad experience.[105]

Also, some consumers will spend money to acquire what they want now, whereas others will engage in self-denial to save. One study found that spenders tend to be healthier and happier than self-deniers, who tend to be unhappy about finances, personal growth, friends, and jobs.[106] Other research suggests that spending less would benefit consumers by lowering debt and increasing the appreciation of positive acquisition experiences.[107]

Marketing Implications

Tapping into the desire for visible signs of upward mobility can be effective in marketing certain offerings. For example, targeting upper-class consumers who want to wear signs of wealth, Bulgari offers a $59,000 pair of designer sunglasses studded with diamonds and sapphires.[108] And among upper-middle-class consumers, the home elevator—priced at $25,000 and up—is becoming a popular status symbol.[109] Downward mobility is also prompting marketers of everyday products, such as Heinz and Coca-Cola, to market products in smaller-size packages that can be sold at lower, more affordable prices.[110] Hallmark now offers "sorry you lost your job" cards, indicating a niche segment large enough for such products.[111]

The use of credit and debit cards is rising in many nations, presenting both opportunities and challenges. However, excess use of credit is also contributing to higher consumer bankruptcy rates, a situation that raises ethical and public policy issues. Increasingly, consumers in the United States, China, and elsewhere are using their cell phones to pay for purchases, instead of cash or credit cards.[112] Another developing trend is the use of noncash payment systems (such as Facebook Credits) to buy online.[113]

THE CONSUMPTION PATTERNS OF SPECIFIC SOCIAL CLASSES

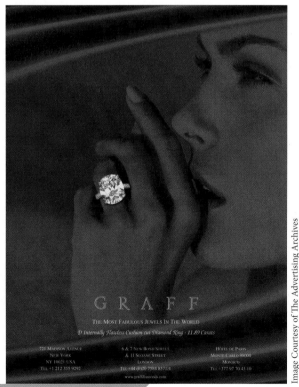

Exhibit 13.11

Targeting to Upper-Class Consumers
Some ads target upper-class consumers with luxury or limited access items.

Image Courtesy of The Advertising Archives

Earlier sections examined how social class influences acquisition and consumption in general. This section extends the discussion by examining, in broad generalities, the consumption patterns of specific social classes. Although class distinctions are becoming blurred, for the sake of simplicity, this discussion will focus on (1) the upper class, (2) the middle class, (3) the working class, and (4) the homeless. Remember that these are broad tendencies and individual behavior may differ; marketers must delve deeper to identify subsegments of consumers with specific and unique consumption patterns.

The Upper Class

The *upper class* of most societies is a varied group of individuals who include the aristocracy, the "old money" of inherited wealth, the new social elite (or nouveaux riches), and the upper-middle class (professionals). In the United States, upper class "old money" consumers tend to save and invest money more than members of other classes. Although many of these consumers are price-conscious, they are more likely than other consumers to carefully research their purchases using product characteristics, not price, as an indicator of quality.[114]

The upper class is small but diverse, and its members share a number of common values and lifestyles that relate to consumption behavior. These consumers tend to view themselves as intellectual, political, and socially conscious, leading to an increase in behaviors such as attending the theater, investing in art and antiques, traveling, and giving time and money to charities and civic issues.[115] Self-expression is also important, resulting in the purchase of high-quality, prestige brands in good taste (see Exhibit 13.11). Even during the recent recession, luxury brands continued to sell well in the United States, China, India, Brazil, and other countries because of upper-class spending.[116]

More than eight million U.S. households are now among the millionaire ranks, and more than 1.1 million have $5 million or more in assets.[117] Contrary to the traditional image of millionaires, one-third of all U.S. households with assets topping $1 million are headed by consumers aged 39 and younger.[118] The average U.S. millionaire is 54 years old, is married with three children, and has an average household net worth of $9.2 million.[119] From a global perspective, more than half of world's millionaires are concentrated in the United States, Japan, and Germany.[120]

The Middle Class

The U.S. *middle class* consists primarily of white-collar workers, many of whom have attended college (although some have not earned a degree). The values and consumption patterns of middle-class consumers vary, yet many look to the upper class for guidance on certain behaviors such as proper dining etiquette, clothing (especially important for those with aspirations of upward mobility), and leisure activities such as golf and tennis. This tendency extends to theater attendance, vacations, and adult education classes for self-improvement. Yet during the past decade, financial difficulties have caused many middle-class families to lose purchasing power and experience lower living standards in a downward mobility trend that may not be reversed until the economy is much stronger.[121]

In Mexico, the middle class has many similarities with the traditional spending patterns of the U.S. middle class: spending much of its disposable income on cars, clothing, vacations, and household goods. However, lower-middle-class households in Mexico have a lower average income (around $14,400) than that of their American counterparts.[122] The middle class is expanding in many developing nations, particularly in India, Brazil, China, and South Korea. In Africa, the middle class is growing rapidly enough to attract the attention of multinational corporations such as Ford, Yum! Brands, and Walmart, looking to tap this segment's increased disposable income.[123]

The Working Class

The *working class* is mainly represented by blue-collar workers. The stereotype of a hard-hatted, middle-aged man is changing as the working class becomes younger, more ethnically diverse, more female, somewhat more educated, and more alienated from employers. Working-class consumers depend heavily on family members for economic and social support in many areas, including job opportunities and advice—particularly for key purchases and help during difficult times.[124] As a result, they tend to have more of a local orientation socially, psychologically, and geographically than other classes. For example, working-class men exhibit strong preferences for local athletic teams, news segments, and vacations.

Consumers in the working class are more likely to spend than to save; however, when they do save, many choose savings accounts over investments and seek financial stability.[125] In addition, working-class consumers are more likely to judge product quality on the basis of price (higher price means higher quality), to shop in discount stores, and to have less product information when purchasing.[126] And they may exhibit distinctly different product preferences than those of consumers in other social classes. For instance, only 15 percent of U.S. adults with an income below $25,000 say they drink wine, compared with 52 percent of adults in the top-income bracket and 28 percent in middle-income brackets.[127]

The Homeless

At the low end of the status hierarchy are *homeless* consumers who lack shelter and live on the streets or in makeshift structures, cars, or vacant houses.[128] The homeless represent a sizable segment of society in some countries. Official U.S. estimates indicate that about 750,000 people are homeless on any given night, although other estimates of this population range above seven million, with the numbers growing during the recent recession.[129] This group includes unemployed or underemployed consumers, drug and alcohol abusers, mentally ill people, members of female-headed households, and people who have experienced financial setbacks such as losing their homes.

An overriding characteristic of the homeless is the struggle for survival. With little or no income, homeless consumers have difficulty acquiring daily necessities such as food, housing, and medical care.[130] They are not helpless but rather are a "resourceful, determined, and capable group that proactively deals with its lack of resources in the consumer environment."[131] A particularly important survival activity for homeless consumers is *scavenging*, finding used or partially used goods that others have discarded. Many vary their scavenging patterns to avoid detection as they move between areas to find the needed items, making this a mobile or nomadic society. Despite their poverty, most homeless consumers have some valued possessions, and they get the maximum use out of items, discarding something only if they have absolutely no further use for it.

Marketing Implications

Social class can serve as an effective way of segmenting the market, thereby influencing product or service development, messages, media selection, and channel selection.

Product or Service Development

Social class motives and values can determine which offerings consumers desire. For example, to satisfy their need for prestige and luxury, many upper-class consumers prefer high-end automobiles, imported wines, fancy restaurants, exotic or deluxe vacations, and couture clothing. Working class consumers want good quality at a fair price, and many offerings—family-rate motels, buffet restaurants, basic versions of branded items—are designed to fulfill this desire. Buying power can be an issue, which is why in Mexico, the Elektra retail chain caters to working-class customers by making credit available for purchases of appliances and cars.[132]

Sometimes marketers develop different product lines for different classes. For example, Procter & Gamble targets higher-class customers with $50 antiaging Olay face creams and lower-class customers with basic $6 Olay skin moisturizers.[133] Many marketers target a particular class, get to know the needs of those consumers in depth, and create offerings specifically for them. For example, Italy-based fashion house Loro Piana targets upper-class customers worldwide by creating fine cashmere and wool clothing that does not flaunt the brand and is not mass marketed, enhancing its aura of exclusivity.[134] Also, marketers can create products that appeal to consumers' aspirations for upward mobility. For example, designer Jason Wu is now reaching beyond couture customers into the middle class with a line of moderately priced clothing sold only in Target stores.[135]

Messages

Advertisers targeting a particular social class within the larger population can be effective by tapping into the group's distinctiveness; when targeting the upper classes, for instance, the advertiser might suggest the group's status as a small, elite group.[136] Other messages for the upper classes might focus on themes of "a just reward for hard work," "you've made it," or "pamper yourself because you deserve it." Certain offerings can be advertised as coveted status symbols; thus, Jaguar, for instance, advertises its XJ8 as a car that wealthy consumers lust after because it combines "beauty and brains." Messages for the working class might take on a more localized orientation, focusing on home and friends as well as favored activities such as hunting and watching sports events. In addition, messages can use typical members of a social class as role models.

Media Exposure

The classes differ in their exposure to certain media. Advertisers try to reach the upper classes through targeted magazines such as the *Robb Report*, special events such as collectible cars shows, sponsorships on public TV and radio, and cultural events. Many marketers think "three screens" when they want to reach middle- and upper-class

Exhibit 13.12

Working-Class Appeal
Stores such as Walmart or the Dollar Tree appeal to working-class consumers with everyday low prices.

consumers: television, personal computer, and cell phone. Tablet computers/e-book readers are a fourth screen for some advertisers, especially since consumers frequently use these electronics while watching TV, for example.[137] Lower-class consumers tend to be heavy watchers of TV and less likely than other classes to read magazines and newspapers. Middle-class consumers, particularly those with only some college education, are unique because they tend to be heavy TV watchers as well as magazine readers.

Channel Selection

Marketers targeting upper-class consumers can make goods available through channels that sell exclusive merchandise with personalized service.[138] For example, Nokia sells its Vertu luxury cell phones through upscale boutiques on prestigious shopping streets such as Rodeo Drive in Beverly Hills.[139] Conspicuous consumption can play a role when consumers want to acquire items in the "correct" store, especially if they can be seen doing so.[140] Dollar stores such as Dollar Tree attract working-class consumers with value pricing of everyday goods. Walmart attracts consumers from lower and middle classes, although the retailer lost some of its most price-conscious shoppers to dollar stores during the recent recession (see Exhibit 13.12).[141]

Note of Caution

Marketers have had difficulty in using social class as a segmentation variable for several reasons. As noted earlier, social class is difficult to assess because a variety of factors such as occupation and income can have opposite effects on class. Also, variations within a class make social class a better predictor of broad behavior patterns, such as conspicuous product-level choice, than of specific behaviors such as brand choice. Finally, because of social class fragmentation, traditional class distinctions may be becoming too broad to be truly useful. Therefore, marketers are using technology to segment markets and to target consumers more precisely through database marketing, the Internet, direct mail, and other tools. ⎯⎯⎯⎯⎯⎯⎯

SUMMARY

Households, which include families and unrelated people living together as well as singles, exert considerable influence on acquisition and consumption patterns. The proportion of nontraditional households has increased because of factors such as (1) later marriages and cohabitation, (2) dual-career families, (3) divorce, (4) smaller families, and (5) same-sex couples. Members can play different roles in the decision process (gatekeeper, influencer, decider, buyer, and user). Also, husbands and wives vary in their influence on the decision process, depending on whether the situation is husband dominant, wife dominant, autonomic, or syncratic. The nature of children's influence on acquisition, usage, and disposition decisions partly depends on whether the household is authoritarian, neglectful, democratic, or permissive. In general, the older the child, the greater the influence.

Individuals in a society can be grouped into status levels (upper, middle, and lower), making up a social class hierarchy. Class distinctions are significant because members of a particular class tend to share common life experiences and therefore also share values and consumer behavior patterns (despite variations within groups). Individuals are most likely to be influenced by members of their own class because they regularly interact with them. Still, influence can cross class lines through the *trickle-down effect* (when lower classes copy upper-class values and behavior) or *status float* (when trends start in the lower classes and spread upward).

A variety of factors determine social class, the most critical of which are occupation and education. Three major trends producing an evolution in social class structure are upward mobility, downward mobility, and social class fragmentation. Social class influences consumer behavior in four major ways: through (1) conspicuous consumption (acquiring and displaying offerings to show class standing) or voluntary simplicity (consciously choosing a less material lifestyle); (2) status symbols (offerings that demonstrate social standing); (3) compensatory consumption (buying as a way to offset some deficiency); and (4) the meaning of money.

Questions for Review and Discussion

1. Define the terms nuclear family, extended family, and household.

2. What five key factors have altered the basic structure and characteristics of households?

3. What five roles might a household member perform in acquiring and consuming something?

4. What is the social class hierarchy?

5. What are the determinants of social class?

6. Why is social class fragmentation taking place?

7. Why would a consumer engage in conspicuous consumption, conspicuous waste, or voluntary simplicity?

8. How does parody display differ from status symbols?

9. Under what circumstances does compensatory consumption occur?

10. Why might a company develop different offerings for consumers in different social classes?

CONSUMER BEHAVIOR CASE

IKEA's Household Appeal

No matter where you live, no matter what kind of household you live in—married with children, same-sex couple, single, single parent, or just roommates—IKEA wants to be "your partner in better living." The Swedish retailer rings up $33 billion in sales through 284 stores in 26 countries, offering stylishly designed furniture and quality housewares at affordable prices. In fact, IKEA continues to lower prices year by year on popular items so it can both attract new customers and stimulate repeat business, even among consumers whose household incomes are stalled or falling. Offering a range of good-better-best products widens the store's appeal to consumers setting up new households, families getting ready for new babies, families where children regularly travel from one parent's household to another, and households that are buying on a limited budget. Also, consumers who might have bought IKEA's top-of-the-line items before the recession now have more choices if they're trading down to less-expensive products.

Shopping at IKEA is deliberately family-friendly. Many of its stores feature a play area where youngsters can be dropped off while parents browse the store for adult or children's furniture and make purchases without their children. The stores also are equipped with restaurants that serve Swedish-style foods for breakfast, lunch, and dinner, and have high chairs for the youngest shoppers. When the IKEA store in Wednesbury, England, added a children's play area and expanded the restaurant, it saw an immediate sales increase and found that the length of the average customer visit had doubled, to about four hours.

Yet not every family member looks forward to an IKEA shopping trip. For Father's Day weekend in Australia, the IKEA store in Sydney set up a temporary Manland, a room where men could watch sports programming and play video games while their wives or girlfriends shopped. "Manland is the perfect solution for both the blokes who find shopping a chore and the ladies who are forced to drag their partners around," said IKEA's PR manager in Australia.

Although targeting singles and couples with advertising that appeals to their needs and wants is nothing new, IKEA was among the pioneers of mainstream advertisers to target gay couples. Its TV commercial showing two men shopping for furniture together caused a stir in part because the men were depicted as a committed couple. A recent—and controversial—billboard for IKEA in Italy features two men holding hands (and a shopping bag) under the headline: "We are open to all families." The ad goes on to say: "With us, you will feel at home. What we want to do is make life easier for everyone, every family, every couple, whoever they are."

IKEA's word-of-mouth reputation for quality and value gives the company an advantage in expanding to new markets. Before the first IKEA store opened in Bangkok, Thailand, the marketing manager acknowledged the presence of competition but also noted that many locals "have traveled abroad or learned from friends about IKEA furniture." In advance of this store opening, IKEA distributed one million copies of a special 16-page catalog featuring items chosen specifically for the Thai market. IKEA's full 370-page catalog is available to consumers worldwide for ideas as well as for shopping. IKEA prints more than 200 million copies each year and makes the catalog available online and via an app.

U.K. consumers who use Facebook were recently invited to create a 3D IKEA bedroom on YouTube and click on items from the company's catalog to furnish it as they wish. IKEA adds the finishing touch by hanging photos from each user's Facebook wall in the bedroom. "We want to be the experts in truly understanding peoples' needs, wants, and dreams to help them live a happier life at home," explains an executive. Of course, any merchandise chosen for the virtual bedroom can be easily ordered for delivery in the real world.[142]

CASE QUESTIONS

1. The Manland experiment lasted only one weekend in one store. What are the marketing advantages and disadvantages of expanding it to other stores? Do you think IKEA should do more with this idea? Why or why not?

2. Would you classify IKEA's products as suitable for conspicuous consumption, voluntary simplicity, and/or compensatory consumption? Explain your answer.

3. IKEA's ads targeting gay couples have drawn criticism as well as acclaim. What effect do you think such controversy has on the retailer's image and appeal?

4. Why would IKEA continue to print millions of catalogs every year, while other retailers are eliminating printed catalogs in favor of online and in-store shopping?

ENDNOTES

1. Molly Prior and Andrea Nagel, "P&G's McDonald Out to Cover Globe," *WWD*, August 12, 2011, p. 1; Dan Sewell, "P&G Readies New Detergent Global Launch," *Boston Globe*, June 14, 2011, www.boston.com; Jennifer Reingold, "Can P&G Make Money in Places Where People Earn $2 a Day?" *Fortune*, January 17, 2011, pp. 58-63; "Procter & Gamble Looks Beyond U.S. Borders," *USA Today*, March 19, 2010, www.usatoday.com; Dan Sewell, "P&G Rushing $3M Water Purifier Aid to East Africa," *Associated Press*, September 21, 2011, www.google.com/hostednews; and "Procter &

Gamble and Innovation in Asia," *Harvard Business Review*, February 3, 2011, www.hbr.org.

2. Rakesh Kochhar and D'Vera Cohn, "Fighting Poverty in a Bad Economy, "Americans Move in with Relatives," *Pew Research Center's Social and Demographic Trends*, October 3, 2011, www.pewsocialtrends.org.

3. Rex Y. Du and Wagner A. Kamakura, "Household Life Cycles and Lifestyles in the United States," *Journal of Marketing Research*, February 2006, pp. 121–132; Mary C. Gilly and Ben M. Enis, "Recycling the Family Life Cycle," in ed. Andrew A. Mitchell,

Advances in Consumer Research, vol. 9 (Ann Arbor, Mich.: Association for Consumer Research, 1982), pp. 271–276; and William D. Danko and Charles M. Schaninger, "An Empirical Evaluation of the Gilly-Enis Updated Household Life Cycle Model," *Journal of Business Research*, August 1990, pp. 39–57.

4. Robert E. Wilkes, "Household Life-Cycle Stages, Transitions, and Product Expenditures," *Journal of Consumer Research*, June 1995, pp. 27–42.

5. Hannah Karp, "How Tough Are Times? Parents Cut Back Diapers," *Wall Street Journal*, October 4, 2011, www.wsj.com.

6. Alan R. Andreasen, "Life Status Changes and Changes in Consumer Preferences and Satisfaction," *Journal of Consumer Research*, December 1984, pp. 784–794.

7. Jason Wachter, "Spending on Pets Rises During Recession," *USA Today*, October 10, 2011, www.usatoday.com.

8. "U.S. Census Bureau Reports Men and Women Wait Longer to Marry," *U.S. Census Bureau*, November 10, 2010, www.census.gov.

9. Patricia Braus, "Sex and the Single Spender," *American Demographics*, November 1993, pp. 28–34.

10 Clark D. Olson, "Materialism in the Home: The Impact of Artifacts on Dyadic Communication," in eds. Elizabeth C. Hirschman and Morris B. Holbrook, *Advances in Consumer Research*, vol. 12 (Provo, Utah: Association for Consumer Research, 1985), pp. 388–393.

11. Karl Taro Greenfeld, "Fast and Furious," *Businessweek*, May 9, 2011, pp. 64–69.

12. See John Fetto, "Does Father Really Know Best?" *American Demographics*, June 2002, pp. 10–11; Pamela Paul, "Meet the Parents," *American Demographics*, January 2002, pp. 42–43; and Linda Thompson and Alexis Walker, "Gender in Families: Women and Men in Marriage, Work, and Parenthood," *Journal of Marriage and the Family*, November 1989, pp. 845–871.

13. Joan Raymond, "The Ex-Files," *American Demographics*, February 2001, pp. 60–64.

14. James H. Alexander, John W. Shouten, and Scott D. Roberts, "Consumer Behavior and Divorce," in eds. Janeen Costa and Russell W. Belk, *Research in Consumer Behavior*, vol. 6 (Greenwich, Conn.: JAI Press, 1993), pp. 153–184.

15. "U.S. Census Bureau Reports Men and Women Wait Longer to Marry," *U.S. Census Bureau*, November 10, 2010, www.census.gov.

16. Pamela Paul, "Childless by Choice," *American Demographics*, November 2001, pp. 45–50.

17. "Census Bureau Releases Estimates of Same-Sex Married Couples," U.S. Census Bureau, September 27, 2011, www.census.gov.

18. Liz Szabo, "Gay Marriage Law Set to Boost New York Tourism," *USA Today*, June 27, 2011, www.usatoday.com.

19. Dan Fastenburg, "International Gay Marriage," *Time*, July 22, 2010, www.time.com.

20. Suraj Commuri and James W. Gentry, "Resource Allocation in Households with Women as Chief Wage Earner," *Journal of Consumer Research* 32, no. 2, 2005, pp. 185–195.

21. Carol Morello, "Blended Families More Common," *Washington Post*, January 23, 2011, www.washingtonpost.com.

22. Jen Christensen, "Grocery Store Provides Dinner (and Maybe a Date)," *Atlanta Journal Constitution*, March 13, 2008, www.ajc.com.

23. Anil Mathur, George P. Moschis, and Euehun Lee, "A Longitudinal Study of the Effects of Life Status Changes on Changes in Consumer Preferences," *Journal of the Academy of Marekting Science*, 2008, vol. 36, pp. 234–246.

24. Sandra Yin, "Coming Out in Print," *American Demographics*, February 2003, pp. 18- 21; and Ronald Alsop, "Corporate Sponsorships at Gay Pride Parades Alienate Some Activists," *Wall Street Journal*, June 22, 2001, p. B1.

25. Andy Bagnall, "Does This Ad Make Me Look Gay?" *Advertising Age*, June 8, 2011, www.adage.com; and Ronald Alsop, "As Same-Sex Households Grow More Mainstream, Businesses Take Note," *Wall Street Journal*, August 8, 2001, pp. B1, B4.

26. Robert E. Wilkes and Debra A. Laverie, "Purchasing Decisions in Non-Traditional Households: The Case of Lesbian Couples," *Journal of Consumer Behavior* 6, no. 1, 2007, pp. 60–73.

27. Harry L. Davis, "Dimensions of Marital Roles in Consumer Decision Making," *Journal of Marketing Research*, May 1970, pp. 168–177; and Conway Lackman and John M. Lanasa, "Family Decision Making Theory: An Overview and Assessment," *Psychology and Marketing*, March–April 1993, pp. 81–93.

28. P. Doyle and P. Hutchinson, "Individual Differences in Family Decision Making," *Journal of the Market Research Society*, October 1973, pp. 193–206; Jagdish N. Sheth, "A Theory of Family Buying Decisions," in ed. J. N. Sheth, *Models of Buyer Behavior* (New York: Harper & Row, 1974), pp. 17–33; and Daniel Seymour and Greg Lessne, "Spousal Conflict Arousal: Scale Development," *Journal of Consumer Research*, December 1984, pp. 810–821.

29. Alice Gronhoj, "Communication About Consumption: A Family Process Perspective on 'Green' Consumer Practices," *Journal of Consumer Behavior* 5, no. 6, 2006, pp. 491–503.

30. Sheth, "A Theory of Family Buying Decisions"; and Michael A. Belch, George E. Belch, and Donald Sciglimpaglia, "Conflict in Family Decision Making: An Exploratory Investigation," in ed. Jerry C. Olson, *Advances in Consumer Research*, vol. 7 (Chicago: Association for Consumer Research, 1980), pp. 475–479.

31. W. Christian Buss and Charles M. Schaninger, "The Influence of Family Decision Processes and Outcomes," in eds. Richard P. Bagozzi and Alice M. Tybout, *Advances in Consumer Research*, vol. 10 (Ann Arbor, Mich.: Association for Consumer Research, 1983), pp. 439–444.

32. Terry L. Childers and Akshay R. Rao, "The Influence of Familial and Peer-Based Reference Groups on Consumer Decisions," *Journal of Consumer Research*, September 1992, pp. 198–211.

33. Harry L. Davis and Benny P. Rigaux, "Perception of Marital Roles in Decision Processes," *Journal of Consumer Research*, June 1974, pp. 5–14; and Mandy Putnam and William R. Davidson, *Family Purchasing Behavior: 11 Family Roles by Product Category* (Columbus, Ohio: Management Horizons, Inc., a Division of Price Water-house, 1987).

34. Rosann Spiro, "Persuasion in Family Decision Making," *Journal of Consumer Research*, March 1983, pp. 393–402; and Alvin Burns and Donald Granbois, "Factors Moderating the Resolution of Preference Conflict," *Journal of Marketing Research*, February 1977, pp. 68–77.

35. Pierre Filiarault and J. R. Brent Ritchie, "Joint Purchasing Decisions: A Comparison of Influence Structure in Family and Couple Decision Making Units," *Journal of Consumer Research*, September 1980, pp. 131–140; Dennis Rosen and Donald Granbois, "Determinants of Role Structure in Financial Management," *Journal of Consumer Research*, September 1983, pp. 253–258; Spiro, "Persuasion in Family Decision Making"; and Kim P. Corfman and Donald R. Lehmann, "Models of Cooperative Group Decision-Making and Relative Influence: An Experimental Investigation of Family Purchase Decisions," *Journal of Consumer Research*, June 1987, pp. 1–13.

36. William J. Qualls, "Household Decision Behavior: The Impact of Husbands' and Wives' Sex Role Orientation," *Journal of Consumer Research*, September 1987, pp. 264–279; and Giovanna Imperia, Thomas O'Guinn, and Elizabeth MacAdams, "Family Decision Making Role Perceptions Among Mexican-American and Anglo Wives: A Cross-Cultural Comparison," in eds. Elizabeth C. Hirschman and Morris B. Holbrook, *Advances in*

Consumer Research, vol. 12 (Provo, Utah: Association for Consumer Research, 1985), pp. 71–74.

37. Michael Flagg, "Asian Marketing," *Asian Wall Street Journal*, March 19, 2001, p. A12.

38. Jack Neff, "The Consumer Is Not a Moron, He Is Your Child's Father," *Advertising Age*, October 17, 2011, www.adage.com.

39. Robert T. Green, Jean-Paul Leonardi, Jean-Louis Chandon, Isabella C. M. Cunningham, Bronis Verhage, and Alain Strazzieri, "Societal Development and Family Purchasing Roles: A Cross-National Study," *Journal of Consumer Research*, March 1983, pp. 436–442; Leonidas C. Leonidou, "Understanding the Russian Consumer," *Marketing and Research Today*, March 1992, pp. 75–83; and Sak Onkvisit and John J. Shaw, *International Marketing: Analysis and Strategy* (Columbus, Ohio: Merrill, 1989).

40. Michael B. Menasco and David J. Curry, "Utility and Choice: An Empirical Study of Wife/Husband Decision Making," *Journal of Consumer Research*, June 1989, pp. 87–97; and Qualls, "Household Decision Behavior: The Impact of Husbands' and Wives' Sex Role Orientation."

41. C. Whan Park, "Joint Decisions in Home Purchasing: A Muddling-Through Process," *Journal of Consumer Research*, September 1982, pp. 151–162; Harry L. Davis, Stephen J. Hoch, and E. K. Easton Ragsdale, "An Anchoring and Adjustment Model of Spousal Predictions," *Journal of Consumer Research*, June 1986, pp. 25–37; Gary M. Munsinger, Jean E. Weber, and Richard W. Hansen, "Joint Home Purchasing by Husbands and Wives," *Journal of Consumer Research*, March 1975, pp. 60–66; Lakshman Krisnamurthi, "The Salience of Relevant Others and Its Effect on Individual and Joint Preferences: An Experimental Investigation," *Journal of Consumer Research*, June 1983, pp. 62–72; and Robert F. Krampf, David J. Burns, and Dale M. Rayman, "Consumer Decision Making and the Nature of the Product: A Comparison of Husband and Wife Adoption Process Location," *Psychology and Marketing*, March–April 1993, pp. 95–109.

42. Benjamin Scheibehenne, Jutta Mata, and Peter M. Todd, "Older but Not Wiser," *Journal of Consumer Psychology*, 2011, vol. 21, pp. 184–191; Davy Lerouge and Luk Warlop, "Why It Is So Hard to Predict Our Partner's Product Preferences," *Journal of Consumer Research* 33, no. 3, 2006, pp. 393–402; and Chenting Su, Edward F. Fern, and Keying Ye, "A Temporal Dynamic Model of Spousal Family Purchase-Decision Behavior," *Journal of Marketing Research*, August 2003, pp. 268–281.

43. Scott I. Rick, Deborah A. Small, and Eli J. Finkel, "Fatal (Fiscal) Attraction," *Journal of Marketing Research*, April 2011, pp. 228–237.

44. Tamara F. Mangleburg, "Children's Influence in Purchase Decisions: A Review and Critique," in eds. Marvin E. Goldberg, Gerald Gorn, and Richard W. Pollay, *Advances in Consumer Research*, vol. 17 (Provo, Utah: Association for Consumer Research, 1990), pp. 813–825; Ellen R. Foxman, Patriya S. Tansuhaj, and Karin M. Ekstrom, "Family Members' Perceptions of Adolescents' Influence in Family Decision Making," *Journal of Consumer Research*, March 1989, pp. 481–490; George Belch, Michael A. Belch, and Gayle Ceresino, "Parental and Teenage Influences in Family Decision Making," *Journal of Business Research*, April 1985, pp. 163–176; and Lackman and Lanasa, "Family Decision Making Theory: An Overview and Assessment."

45. Mary Lou Roberts, Lawrence H. Wortzel, and Robert L. Berkeley, "Mothers' Attitudes and Perceptions of Children's Influence and Their Effect on Family Consumption," in ed. Jerry C. Olson, *Advances in Consumer Research*, vol. 8 (Ann Arbor, Mich.: Association for Consumer Research, 1981), pp. 730–735; and Ellen Foxman and Patriya Tansuhaj, "Adolescents' and Mothers' Perceptions of Relative Influence in Family Purchase Decisions: Patterns of Agreement and Disagreement," in ed. Michael J.

Houston, *Advances in Consumer Research*, vol. 15 (Provo, Utah: Association for Consumer Research, 1988), pp. 449–453.

46. Sharon E. Beatty and Salil Talpade, "Adolescent Influence in Family Decision Making: A Replication with Extension," *Journal of Consumer Research*, September 1994, pp. 332–341; Christopher Power, "Getting 'Em While They're Young," *BusinessWeek*, September 9, 1991, pp. 94–95; and Scott Ward and Daniel B. Wackman, "Children's Purchase Influence Attempts and Parental Yielding," *Journal of Marketing Research*, November 1972, pp. 316–319.

47. William K. Darley and Jeen-Su Lim, "Family Decision Making in Leisure Time Activities: An Exploratory Analysis of the Impact of Locus of Control, Child Age Influence Factor and Parental Type on Perceived Child Influence," in ed. Richard J. Lutz, *Advances in Consumer Research*, vol. 13 (Ann Arbor, Mich.: Association for Consumer Research, 1986), pp. 370–374; George P. Moschis and Linda G. Mitchell, "Television Advertising and Interpersonal Influences on Teenagers' Participation in Family Consumer Decisions," in ed. Lutz, *Advances in Consumer Research*, vol. 13, pp. 181–186; and Beatty and Talpade, "Adolescent Influence in Family Decision Making: A Replication with Extension."

48. June Cotte and Stacy L. Wood, "Families and Innovative Consumer Behavior: A Triadic Analysis of Sibling and Parental Influence," *Journal of Consumer Research*, June 2004, pp. 78–86.

49. Anirban Mukhopadhyay and Catherine W. M. Yeung, "Building Character: Effects of Lay Theories of Self-Control on the Selection of Products for Children," *Journal of Marketing Research*, April 2010, pp. 240–250.

50. Kay M. Palan and Robert E. Wilkes, "Adolescent–Parent Interaction in Family Decision Making," *Journal of Consumer Research*, September 1997, pp. 159–169.

51. Les Carlson and Sanford Grossbart, "Parental Style and Consumer Socialization of Children," *Journal of Consumer Research*, June 1988, pp. 77–94.

52. Belch, Belch, and Ceresino, "Parental and Teenage Influences in Family Decision Making."

53. Andrea Gordon, "Big Brands Are Lining up to Harness the Clout of Online Moms," *The Star (Toronto)*, October 13, 2011, www.thestar.com.

54. John Paul Rathbone, "The Last Word: Advertiser-Funded Theme Parks That Make the World of Work Child's Play," *Financial Times*, June 24, 2011, p. 12; and Miho Inada, "Playing at Professions," *Wall Street Journal*, February 9, 2007, p. B1.

55. Amanda C. Kooser, "Virtual Playground," *U.S. News & World Report*, April 1, 2008, www.usnews.com.

56. Dave Lee, "Look Out, There Are Monsters About," *BBC News*, September 24, 2011, www.bbc.co.uk.news.

57. Les Carolson, Russell N. Laczniak, and Chad Wertley, "Parental Style," *Journal of Advertising Research*, June 2011, pp. 427–435.

58. Pierre Bourdieu, *Language and Symbolic Power* (Cambridge, Mass.: Harvard University Press, 1991).

59. Richard P. Coleman, "The Continuing Significance of Social Class to Marketing," *Journal of Consumer Research*, December 1983, pp. 265–280; and Wendell Blanchard, *Thailand, Its People, Its Society, Its Culture* (New Haven, Conn.: HRAF Press, 1990), cited in Sak Onkvisit and John J. Shaw, *International Marketing: Analysis and Strategy* (Columbus, Ohio: Merrill, 1989), p. 293.

60. Edward W. Cundiff and Marye T. Hilger, *Marketing in the International Environment* (Englewood Cliffs, N.J.: Prentice-Hall, 1988), as cited in Mariele K. DeMooij and Warren Keegan, *Advertising Worldwide* (Englewood Cliffs, N.J.: Prentice-Hall, 1991), p. 96.

61. Onkvisit and Shaw, *International Marketing: Analysis and Strategy*.

62. Ernst Dichter, "The World Consumer," *Harvard Business Review*, July–August 1962, pp. 113–123, as cited in Cundiff and Hilger, *Marketing in the International Environment*, p. 135.

63. Richard P. Coleman, "The Significance of Social Stratification in Selling," in ed. Martin L. Bell, *Marketing: A Maturing Discipline* (Chicago: American Marketing Association, 1960), pp. 171–184.

64. Douglas E. Allen and Paul F. Anderson, "Consumption and Social Stratification: Bourdieu's Distinction," in eds. Chris T. Allan and Deborah Roedder John, *Advances in Consumer Research*, vol. 21 (Provo, Utah: Association for Consumer Research, 1994), pp. 70–73.

65. Pierre Bourdieu, *Distinction: A Social Critique of the Judgment of Taste* (Cambridge, Mass.: Harvard University Press, 1984).

66. Coleman, "The Continuing Significance of Social Class to Marketing."

67. See Joan M. Ostrove and Elizabeth R. Cole, "Privileging Class: Toward a Critical Psychology of Social Class in the Context of Education," *Journal of Social Issues*, Winter 2003, pp. 677–692; and Charles M. Schaninger, "Social Class Versus Income Revisited: An Empirical Investigation," *Journal of Marketing Research*, May 1981, pp. 192–208.

68. "Pleased to Be Bourgeois," *Economist*, May 14, 2011, p. 58.

69. Diane Crispell, "The Real Middle Americans," *American Demographics*, October 1994, pp. 28–35; and Michael Hout, "More Universalism, Less Structural Mobility: The American Occupational Structure in the 1980s," *American Journal of Sociology*, May 1988, pp. 1358–1400.

70. Tiffany Julian and Robert Kominski, "Education and Synthetic Work-Life Earnings Estimates," *U.S. Census Bureau American Community Survey Reports*, September 2011, p. 2.

71. Peter Francese, "The College–Cash Connection," *American Demographics*, March 2002, http://adage.com/article/american-demographics; and Patricia Cohen, "Forget Lonely. Life Is Healthy at the Top," *New York Times*, May 15, 2004, p. B9.

72. William L. Wilkie, *Consumer Behavior*, 2nd ed. (New York: Wiley, 1990).

73. See Mary Ellen Slayter, "Succeeding with an Upbringing That's Not Upper Crust," *Washington Post*, May 2, 2004, p. K1; and Aaron Bernstein, "Waking Up from the American Dream," *BusinessWeek*, December 1, 2003, p. 54.

74. Allen and Anderson, "Consumption and Social Stratification: Bourdieu's Distinction."

75. Jake Ryan and Charles Sackrey, *Strangers in Paradise: Academics from the Working Class* (Boston: South End Press, 1984).

76. Andrew D. Gershoff and Katherine A. Burson, "Knowing Where They Stand," *Journal of Consumer Research*, October 2011, pp. 407–419.

77. Ariel Zirulnick, "US Losing Its Competitive Edge Due to Higher Costs of Higher Education: OECD," *Christian Science Monitor*, September 13, 2011, www.csmonitor.com; Amelia Hill, "Upward Mobility Less Likely for Women and Low Earners, Says Study," *Guardian (UK)*, September 23, 2011, www.guardian.co.uk; Mary Janigan, Ruth Atherley, Michelle Harries, Brenda Branswell, and John Demont, "The Wealth Gap," *Maclean's*, August 28, 2000, pp. 42; and Bernstein, "Waking Up from the American Dream."

78. M. R. Haque, "Marketing Opportunities in the Middle East," in ed. V. H. Manek Kirpalani, *International Business Handbook* (New York: Haworth Press, 1990), pp. 375–416.

79. Katherine S. Newman, *Falling from Grace: The Experience of Downward Mobility in the American Middle Class* (New York: Free Press, 1988); and Benita Eisler, *Class Act: America's Last Dirty Secret* (New York: Franklin Watts, 1983).

80. Scott D. Roberts, "Consumer Responses to Involuntary Job Loss," in eds. Rebecca H. Holman and Michael R. Solomon, *Advances in Consumer Research*, vol. 18 (Provo, Utah: Association for Consumer Research, 1988), pp. 40–42.

81. Kenneth Labich, "Class in America," *Fortune*, February 7, 1994, pp. 114–126.

82. Ibid.

83. John Brooks, *Showing Off in America: From Conspicuous Consumption to Parody Display* (Boston: Little, Brown, 1981).

84. Aron O'Cass and Hmily McEwen, "Exploring Consumer Status and Conspicuous Consumption," *Journal of Consumer Behavior* 4, no. 1, 2004, pp. 25–39.

85. Wilfred Amaldoss and Sanjay Jain, "Pricing of Conspicuous Goods: A Competitive Analysis of Social Effects," *Journal of Marketing Research*, February 2005, pp. 30–42.

86. Nailya Ordabayeva and Pierre Chandon, "Getting Ahead of the Joneses," *Journal of Consumer Research*, June 2011, pp. 27–41.

87. Jamie Arndt, Sheldon Solomon, Tim Kasser, and Kennon M. Sheldon, "The Urge to Splurge: A Terror Management Account of Materialism and Consumer Behavior," *Journal of Consumer Psychology* 14, no. 3, 2004, pp. 198–212.

88. Janeen Arnold Costa and Russell W. Belk, "Nouveaux Riches as Quintessential Americans: Case Studies of Consumption in the Extended Family," in ed. Russell W. Belk, *Advances in Nonprofit Marketing*, vol. 3 (Greenwich, Conn.: JAI Press, 1990), pp. 83–140.

89. "You Choose," *Economist*, December 18, 2010, pp. 123–125; and Mustapha Harzallah Ibtissem, "Application of Value Beliefs Norms Theory to the Energy Conservation Behaviour," *Journal of Sustainable Development*, June 2010, pp. 129ff.

90. Rebecca H. Holman, "Product Use as Communication: A Fresh Appraisal of a Venerable Topic," in eds. Ben M. Enis and Kenneth J. Roering, *Review of Marketing* (Chicago: American Marketing Association, 1981), pp. 106–119.

91. Jonah Berger and Morgan Ward, "Subtle Signals of Inconspicuous Consumption," *Journal of Consumer Research*, December 2010, pp. 555–569; and Ben Steverman, "Conspicuous Consumption Is Back," *Businessweek*, January 27, 2011, www.businessweek.com.

92. Naomi Mandel, Petia K. Petrova, and Robert B. Cialdini, "Images of Success and the Preference for Luxury Brands," *Journal of Consumer Psychology* 16, no. 1, 2006, pp. 57–69.

93. Tamara Abraham, "As Sales Soar 54 Percent in a Year, How Nail Polish Replaced Lipstick as Women's Favourite Recession-Proof Luxury," *Daily Mail (UK)*, September 30, 2011, www.dailymail.co.uk; and Rebecca Gardyn, "Oh, the Good Life," *American Demographics*, November 2002, pp. 30–35.

94. Brooks, *Showing Off in America: From Conspicuous Consumption to Parody Display*.

95. Stephen Buckley, "Brazil Rediscovers Its Culture; Poor Man's Cocktail, Martial Art Hip Among Middle Class," *Washington Post*, April 15, 2001, p. A16.

96. Teri Agins, "Now, Subliminal Logos," *Wall Street Journal*, July 20, 2001, p. B1.

97 Derek D. Rucker and Adam D. Galinsky, "Desire to Acquire: Powerlessness and Compensatory Consumption," *Journal of Consumer Research*, August 2008, pp. 257–267.

98. Russell W. Belk and Melanie Wallendorf, "The Sacred Meanings of Money," *Journal of Economic Psychology*, March 1990, pp. 35–67.

99. Abraham McLaughlin, "Africans' New Motto: 'Charge It,'" *Christian Science Monitor*, February 14, 2005, p. 6.

100. Adrian Furnham and Alan Lewis, *The Economic Mind: The Social Psychology of Economic Behavior* (Brighton, Sussex: Harvester Press, 1986); and Belk and Wallendorf, "The Sacred Meanings of Money."

101. Rebecca Gardyn, "Generosity and Income," *American Demographics*, December 2002–January 2003, pp. 46–47.

102 Jennifer L. Aaker, Melanie Rudd, and Cassie Mogilner, "If Money Does Not Make You Happy, Consider Time," *Journal of Consumer Psychology* 21, 2011, pp. 126–130.

103. Elizabeth W. Dunn, Daniel T. Gilbert, and Timothy D. Wilson, "If Money Doesn't Make You Happy, Then You Probably Aren't Spending It Right," *Journal of Consumer Psychology* 12, 2011, pp. 115–125.

104. Christopher K. Hsee, Yang Yang, Naihe Li, and Luxi Shen, "Wealth, Warmth, and Well-Being: Whether Happiness Is Relative or Absolute Depends on Whether It Is About Money, Acquisition, or Consumption," *Journal of Marketing Research*, June 2009, pp. 396–409.

105. Leonardo Nicolao, Julie R. Irwin, and Joseph K. Goodman," *Journal of Consumer Research*, August 2009, pp. 188–198.

106. C. Rubenstein, "Your Money or Your Life," *Psychology Today* 12, 1980, pp. 47–58.

107. See Joseph Chancellor and Sonja Lyubomirsky, "Happiness and Thrift: When (Spending) Less Is (Hedonically) More," *Journal of Consumer Psychology* 21, 2011, pp. 131–138.

108. Marshall Heyman, "At New York Parties, Visions of Grandeur," *Wall Street Journal*, October 6, 2011, www.wsj.com.

109. Bert Archer, "Still Upwardly Mobile," *Toronto Life*, November 2007, p. 95.

110. E.J. Schultz, "Packages Shrink to Fit Spending-Power Decline," *Advertising Age*, October 17, 2011, www.adage.com.

111. "How Marketers Sell to the Long-Term Jobless," *Advertising Age*, October 16, 2011, www.adage.com.

112. Shen Jingting, "HTC, Unionpay Target Mobile Wallets," *China Daily*, August 10, 2011, www.chinadaily.com.cn.

113. Shayndi Raice, "Zynga Devices a New Plan to Break Its Facebook Habit," *Wall Street Journal*, October 12, 2011, www.wsj.com.

114. Mercedes M. Cardona, "Affluent Shoppers Like Their Luxe Goods Cheap," *Advertising Age*, December 1, 2003, p. 6.

115. See "Old Money," *American Demographics*, June 2003, pp. 34–37.

116. "India's Luxury Market," *India Knowledge@Wharton*, September 1, 2011, http://knowledge.wharton.upenn.edu; and Shobhana Chandra and Anthony Feld, "Rich Americans Raise Consumer Spending with Little Help from Middle Class," *Bloomberg News*, January 18, 2011, www.bloomberg.com.

117. Elizabeth Ody, "U.S. Millionaires' Ranks Increase 8%, Remain Below '07 High of 9.2 Million," *Bloomberg News*, March 16, 2011, www.bloomberg.com.

118. Kathryn Kranhold, "Marketing to the New Millionaire," *Wall Street Journal*, October 11, 2000, pp. B1, B6.

119. Carole Ann King, "The New Wealthy: Younger, Richer, More Proactive," *National Underwriter Life & Health–Financial Services Edition*, February 12, 2001, p. 4.

120. "U.S. Affluent Classes Dwarf China and India," *Reuters*, October 7, 2011, www.reuters.com.

121. Brad Tuttle, "The Sad, Sorry State of the Middle Class," *Time*, September 8, 2011, http://moneyland.time.com.

122. Elisabeth Malkin, "Mexico's Working Poor Become Homeowners," *New York Times*, December 17, 2004, p. W1.

123. Patrick McGroarty, "Africa's Middle Class to Boom," *Wall Street Journal*, October 13, 2011, www.wsj.com.

124. Coleman, "The Continuing Significance of Social Class to Marketing."

125. Paul C. Henry, "Social Class, Market Situation, and Consumers' Metaphors of (Dis)Empowerment," *Journal of Consumer Research* 31, no. 4, 2005, pp. 766–778.

126. Prasad, "Socioeconomic Product Risk and Patronage Preferences of Retail Shoppers"; Stuart Rich and Subhish Jain, "Social Class and Life Cycle as Predictors of Shopping Behavior," *Journal of Marketing Research*, June–July 1987, pp. 51–59.

127. John Fetto, "Watering Holes," *American Demographics*, June 2003, p. 8.

128. Ronald Paul Hill and Mark Stamey, "The Homeless in America: An Examination of Possessions and Consumption Behaviors," *Journal of Consumer Research*, December 1990, pp. 303–321; and Frank Caro, *Estimating the Numbers of Homeless Families* (New York: Community Service Society of New York, 1981).

129. "Hunger and Homelessness Remain Most Pressing Issues for U.S. Cities," *U.S. Conference of Mayors*, January 1, 2011, www.citymayors.com; "Federal Report Takes Snapshot of Country's Homeless Population," *The Nation's Health*, May 2007, p. 10; and National Coalition for the Homeless, "How Many People Experience Homelessness?" February 1999, http://nch.ari.net/numbers.html.

130. Richard B. Freeman and Brian Hall, "Permanent Homelessness in America?" *Population Research and Policy Review* 6, 1987, pp. 3–27.

131. Ronald Paul Hill, "Homeless Women, Special Possessions, and the Meaning of 'Home': An Ethnographic Case Study," *Journal of Consumer Research*, December 1991, pp. 298–310.

132. Marla Dickerson, "Mexican Retailer, Partner to Build Cars," *Los Angeles Times*, November 23, 2007, p. C1; and Peter Katel, "Petro Padillo Longoria: A Retailer Focused on Working-Class Needs," *Time International*, October 15, 2001, p. 49.

133. Prior and Nagel, "P&G's McDonald Out to Cover Globe."

134. Alessandro Di Fiore, "A Different Premium Brand Strategy," *Harvard Business Review*, October 10, 2011, www.hbr.org.

135. Sally Shin, "Target Partners with Designer Jason Wu," *CNBC*, October 7, 2011, www.cnbc.com.

136. Sonya A. Grier and Rohit Deshpandé, "Social Dimensions of Consumer Distinctiveness: The Influence of Social Status on Group Identity and Advertising Persuasion," *Journal of Marketing Research* 38, May 2001, pp. 216–224.

137. "Increased Sales of Tablet Computers Drive Shopping in Advertising Breaks," *Deloitte News Release*, August 22, 2011, www.deloitte.com.

138. Rich and Jain, "Social Class and Life Cycle as Predictors of Shopping Behavior."

139. Diana ben-Aaron and Matthew Campbell, "Diamond-Crusted Vertu Phone Defies Slump," *Bloomberg News*, September 29, 2011, www.bloomberg.com.

140. Christine Page, "A History of Conspicuous Consumption," in eds. Floyd Rudmin and Marsha Richins, *Meaning, Measure, and Morality of Materialism* (Provo, Utah: Association for Consumer Research, 1993), pp. 82–87.

141. "Grocery Shoppers Leave Walmart for Dollar Stores," *NPR*, August 19, 2011, www.npr.org.

142. Francine Kopun, "IKEA Sets up Playpen for Men," *Star (Toronto, Canada)*, September 23, 2011, www.thestar.com; Kwanchai Rungfapaisarn, "IKEA Launches 2012 Catalogue Ahead of First Store," *The Nation*, October 1, 2011, www.nationmultimedia.com; "IKEA Sales Up as Shoppers' Time in Store Doubles," *Express and Star (UK)*, October 16, 2011, www.expressandstar.com; "The Swedish Revolution," *Bangkok Post*, September 19, 2011, www.bangkokpost.com; "IKEA Has Launched the First Ever Personalised 3D Showroom on YouTube," *Social Media Today*, August 25, 2011, www.socialmediatoday.com; Natalie Zmuda, "With Home Sales Down, Focus Turns to Upkeep," *Advertising Age*, July 25, 2011, p.11; Nick Pisa, "'We Are Open to All Families,'" *Daily Mail (UK)*, March 18, 2011, www.dailymail.co.uk; and "The Secret of IKEA's Success," *Economist*, February 26, 2011, p. 68.

PSYCHOGRAPHICS: VALUES, PERSONALITY, AND LIFESTYLES

After studying this chapter, you will be able to

1. Define values and the value system and show how they can be described.

2. Identify some values that characterize Western cultures, outline the main factors that influence values, and describe how values can be measured.

3. Discuss the personality characteristics most closely related to consumer behavior, and show why these are important from a marketing perspective.

4. Explain how lifestyles are represented by activities, interests, and opinions.

5. Describe how psychographic applications in marketing combine values, personality, and lifestyle variables.

© AP Images/PRNewsFoto/Zazzle

INTRODUCTION

The Dazzle of Customizing via Zazzle

Founded in 2005, Zazzle's vision is "To re-define commerce, powered by the world's imagination." Anyone with a computer and Internet access can express his or her individuality by creating designs for any of Zazzle's 3,000 basic products, from sneakers and speakers to postage stamps and pet shirts. The customer's tastes and interests dictate what the final product looks like—bold or baroque, sedate or sassy, but always unique. "When you give consumers the tools to do whatever they want, they go wild," explains Jeff Beaver, Zazzle's chief product officer. For example, he says buyers really enjoy designing the minute details of their Keds athletic shoes, right down to the colors of the stitching and the shoelace eyelets.

Zazzle has found that preferences for customized products vary from country to country. For instance, custom-designed skateboards are particularly popular in Germany, while custom-designed sneakers are particularly popular in Japan. To accommodate differences in both product preferences and shopping behavior, Zazzle has set up 17 country-specific websites (with content translated for local buyers), and it will ship across borders to more than 70 nations. On any given day, Zazzle mails tens of thousands of customized products to consumer designers eager to show off who they are and what they have made.[1]

The trend toward customization illustrates the influence of values, personality, and lifestyles on consumer behavior, all topics discussed in this chapter. Values determine whether consumers care more about individualism or put more emphasis on social groups, for instance. A consumer whose personality leans toward creativity will be more likely to try Zazzle than someone who is more reserved. Also, customizing a skateboard fits the lifestyles of consumers interested in that activity.

Together, values, personality, and lifestyles constitute the basic components of **psychographics,** the description of consumers based on their psychological and behavioral characteristics (see Exhibit 14.1). Traditionally, psychographics measured consumer lifestyles, but more modern applications also include the consumers' psychological makeup, values, personality, and behavior with respect to specific products (usage patterns, attitudes, and emotions). Marketers use psychographics to gain a more detailed understanding of consumer behavior than they can get from demographic variables like ethnicity, social class, age, gender, and religion.

Psychographics
A description of consumers based on their psychological and behavioral characteristics.

VALUES

Values Abstract, enduring beliefs about what is right/ wrong, important, or good/bad.

Values are enduring beliefs that a given behavior or outcome is good or bad.[2] For example, you may believe that it is good to be healthy, keep your family safe, have self-respect, and be free. As enduring beliefs, your values serve as standards that guide your behavior across situations and over time. Thus, how much you value the environment generally determines the extent to which you litter, recycle, or buy products made from recycled materials. Values are so ingrained that people are usually not conscious of them and have difficulty describing them.

Value system Our total set of values and their relative importance.

Our total set of values and their relative importance to us constitute our **value system**. The way that we behave in a given situation is often influenced by how important one value is to us relative to others.[3] For instance, deciding whether to spend Saturday afternoon relaxing with your family or exercising will be determined by the relative importance that you place on family versus health. You feel *value conflict* when you do something that is consistent with one value but inconsistent with another equally important value. This dynamic can be illustrated with the example of parents who place equal value on convenience and concern for the environment. They may experience value conflict if they buy disposable diapers for their babies. Consumers facing such decisions consider not only the product's immediate consumption outcomes but also the product's general effect on society, including how the manufacturer behaves (e.g., toward the environment).[4]

Because values are among the first things that children learn, value systems are often in place by age 10. As discussed in Chapter 11, people learn values through the process of socialization, which results from exposure to reference groups and other sources of influence.[5] You may therefore value education because your parents went to college and because they and your teachers encouraged

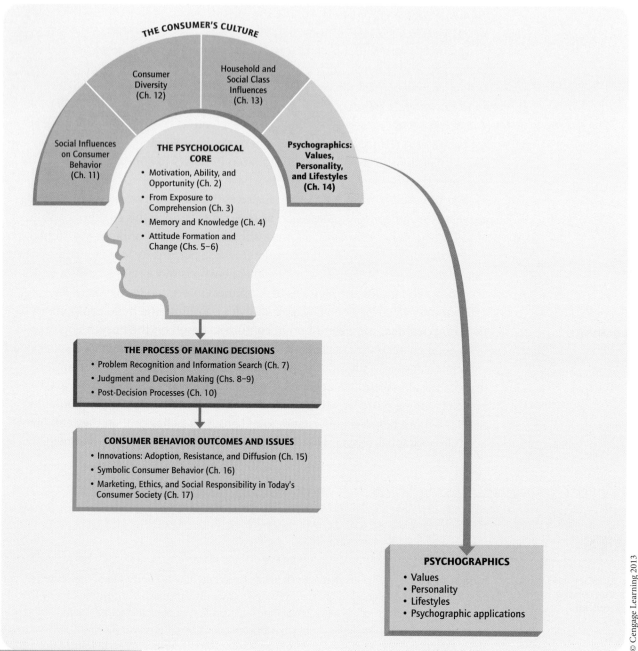

Exhibit 14.1

Chapter Overview: Psychographics: Values, Personality, and Lifestyles

Previous chapters demonstrated how membership in certain cultural groups (regional, ethnic, social class, and so on) can affect group behaviors. This chapter examines the effect of these cultural influences on an individual level—namely, on values (deeply held beliefs), personality (consumer traits), and lifestyles (behavioral patterns that are manifestations of values and personality). Each of these factors is useful in understanding consumer behavior; in addition, marketers often combine them to obtain an overall psychographic profile of consumers.

this value. Because individuals learn values through exposure to others in institutions and cultures, people within the same group often hold similar values.

Acculturation is the process by which individuals learn the values and behaviors of a new culture (see Chapter 12). For example, immigrants arriving in the United States must learn new values to acculturate to American life. Consumers are more likely to adopt the values of a new culture if they view that culture as attractive and as having values similar to their own. Acculturation also happens faster when people in the new culture are cohesive, give a lot of verbal and nonverbal signals about what their values are, and express pride in the values that they hold.[6]

How Values Can Be Described

Global values A person's most enduring, strongly held, and abstract values that hold in many situations.

Terminal values Highly desired end states such as social recognition and pleasure.

Instrumental values The values needed to achieve the desired end states such as ambition and cheerfulness.

Values can vary in terms of their specificity. At the broadest level are **global values**, which represent the core of an individual's value system. These highly enduring, strongly held, and abstract values apply in many situations. For example, because much of U.S. political philosophy is based on the idea of freedom, that value permeates many domains of our lives. We believe in the freedom to speak, to go where we want, to dress as we please, and to live where we want.

One of the many ways of characterizing global values is depicted in Exhibit 14.2. This scheme divides global values into seven categories: maturity, security, prosocial behavior (doing nice things for others), restrictive conformity, enjoyment, achievement, and self-direction. Note that similar categories are placed close together. Thus, achievement and self-direction reflect a similar orientation toward the individual as a person, whereas prosocial behavior and restrictive conformity reflect values that relate to how an individual should deal with others.

Within the seven domains there are two types of global values: terminal and instrumental. **Terminal values** (shown with an asterisk) are highly desired end states, and **instrumental values**

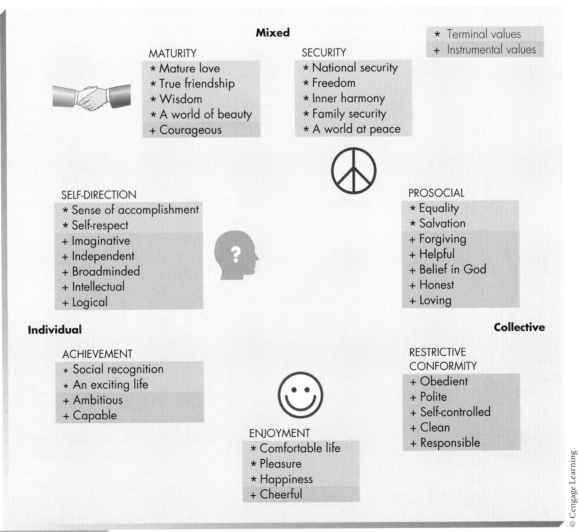

© Cengage Learning

Exhibit 14.2

Global Values and Value Categories

One scheme for classifying global values identifies seven major categories. Some values are individual oriented (e.g., self-direction, achievement); others are more collective or group oriented (e.g., prosocial, restrictive conformity). Note that categories close to each other are similar; those farther apart are less so. Terminal values (or highly desired end states) are marked with an asterisk (∗); instrumental values have a plus sign (+).

(shown with a plus sign) are those needed to achieve these desired end states. For example, the two terminal values in the prosocial category are equality and salvation. The instrumental values of loving, forgiving, helpfulness, honesty, and belief in God help one achieve these terminal values.[7] Also notice in Exhibit 14.2 that values tend to be polarized: Consumers who place a high value on one set of terminal values place less value on the set on the opposite side of the figure. This situation means that individuals who value security, maturity, and a prosocial orientation might place less value on enjoyment (on the opposite side). Those who emphasize self-direction and achievement would value prosocial behaviors and restrictive conformity less.

Domain-specific values Values that may only apply to a particular area of activities.

Global values are different from **domain-specific values**, which are relevant only to particular areas of activity, such as religion, family, or consumption. Materialism is a domain-specific value because it relates to the way that we view the acquisition of material goods. Although they differ, global and domain-specific values can be related in that achievement of domain-specific values (such as health) can be instrumental to the achievement of one or more global values (such as inner harmony or self-respect).

The Values That Characterize Western Cultures

Materialism Placing importance on money and material goods.

Given that values are an important influence on behavior, marketers need to understand some of the values that characterize consumption in Western societies. These include materialism, the home, work and play, individualism, family and children, health, hedonism, youth, authenticity, the environment, and technology.

Materialism

One value that has become increasingly prevalent in Western cultures is **materialism**.[8] In a materialistic society, people gauge satisfaction in terms of what they have or have not acquired in life and in terms of desired possessions. Materialistic individuals tend to value items like cars, jewelry, and boats (see Exhibit 14.3). In contrast, symbolic items such as a mother's wedding gown, family mementos, and photos are more important to those low in materialism.[9]

Materialistic consumers might believe that they would be happy if they had a bigger house, a nicer car, or more expensive clothes—beliefs that can lead to stress if family or life changes disrupt their financial situation.[10] Yet research actually indicates a weak connection between material possessions and happiness. During the recent recession, financially strapped consumers who previously placed a high value on materialism began shifting away from this value. They have been seeking to spend their time wisely and gain hedonic value from positive experiences, smaller purchases, and other alternatives to materialism.[11] Refocusing on experiences makes sense because the happiness associated with acquired possessions fades quickly, while the positive feelings associated with experiences lingers longer.[12] Another explanation for the movement away from materialism is that the value conflict between the individual orientation of materialism and the group orientation of family-oriented values is associated with a reduced sense of well-being.[13]

Materialism may relate to several of the terminal values noted in Exhibit 14.2. For example, possessions may be instrumental in achieving the higher-order value of social recognition. Or materialism may reflect a high value on accomplishment if people

Image Courtesy of The Advertising Archives

Exhibit 14.3

Materialism

Ads for expensive items, like Coach, Prada, and Gucci, target consumers who focus on materialism as a gauge of satisfaction.

judge self-worth by what they have acquired or by their achievement of a comfortable life. According to *terror management theory* (see Chapter 13), materialism is rooted, in part, in consumers' drive to relieve anxiety over the inevitability of death by deriving self-esteem and status from acquiring and possessing things.[14] On the other hand, members of communes and certain religious orders have chosen a lifestyle that rejects material possessions.[15]

Nevertheless, U.S. consumers generally have a materialistic bent, as do consumers in Japan, China, and many other nations.[16] In a materialistic society, consumers will be receptive to marketing tactics that facilitate the acquisition of goods, such as phone-in or online orders, special pricing, convenient distribution, and communications that associate acquisition with achievement and status, like ads for a Rolex watch. Consumers also want to protect their possessions, creating opportunities for services such as insurance and security companies that protect consumers against loss, theft, or damage.

Home

Many consumers place a high value on the home and believe in making it as attractive and as comfortable as possible (see Exhibit 14.4). Currently, 69 percent of U.S. citizens own their own home, and they spend more time there than they did in the past. Because the outside world is becoming more complex, exhausting, and dangerous, consumers often consider their home a haven, but they also look for opportunities to connect with others.[17] The home is "command central"—a place to coordinate activities and pool resources before family members enter the outside world. For example, more than 70 million Americans use online banking to control family finances from their home computers.[18] IKEA even ran an emotional global ad campaign reflecting how strongly people feel about their homes. "It marks commitment to putting the heart back into the home and serves as our manifesto for the future," says an IKEA marketing manager.[19]

Work and Play

Not everyone in every culture shares the same values of work and play. In the United States, consumers are working harder and longer than ever before, partly due to corporate downsizing and an emphasis on productivity. In fact, when career-minded consumers go on vacation, nearly half regularly communicate with work colleagues through cell phone, e-mail, and fax.[20] However, consumers increasingly value work for its instrumental function in achieving other values such as a comfortable lifestyle, family security, and accomplishing their life goals. Thus, the idea of valuing work itself and delaying gratification to the exclusion of leisure and pleasure is less characteristic of U.S. consumers than it was a century ago.

When people work longer hours, they value leisure time as much as they value money, and they will pay for services so that they can spend more nonwork time on leisure activities. For

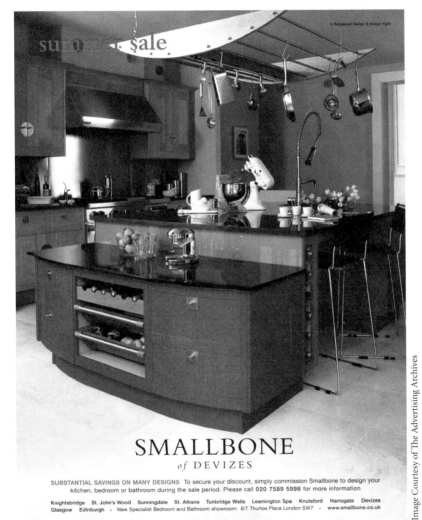

Image Courtesy of The Advertising Archives

SMALLBONE *of* DEVIZES

SUBSTANTIAL SAVINGS ON MANY DESIGNS To secure your discount, simply commission Smallbone to design your kitchen, bedroom or bathroom during the sale period. Please call **020 7589 5998** for more information

Knightsbridge St. John's Wood Sunningdale St. Albans Tunbridge Wells Leamington Spa Knutsford Harrogate Devizes
Glasgow Edinburgh · New Specialist Bedroom and Bathroom showroom: 6/7 Thurloe Place London SW7 · **www.smallbone.co.uk**

Exhibit 14.4

Placing a High Value on the Home

As consumers are placing a greater value on the home and are spending more time there, companies are advertising more to appeal to that value.

instance, the online grocery retailer Peapod, owned by the Dutch supermarket company Royal Ahold, has built a multimillion-dollar business catering to U.S. consumers who have better things to do than go to the supermarket to pick out tomatoes and tissues.[21] Many consumers make leisure-time choices with the express purpose of getting completely away from work, a goal that has made remote vacation spots and spas more popular in recent years.[22]

Individualism

Western cultures generally place a high value on individualism. The traditional "rugged individualist" consumer values independence and self-reliance, tending to see the individual's needs and rights as a higher priority than the group's needs and rights.[23] Marketers who target men for products such as hunting gear often use advertising imagery and words to make explicit the connection between owning and using these products and expressing rugged individualism. Despite the frontier roots of individualism in America, some consumers worry about violence and other possible negative consequences of unbridled individualism.

Even in a generally individualistic society, there are *allocentric* consumers who prefer interdependence and social relationships. In contrast, *idiocentric* consumers tend to put more emphasis on individual freedom and assertiveness. The behavior of these two types of consumers reflects such differences. Idiocentric consumers in the United States exhibit more interest in sports and adventure, financial satisfaction, gambling, and brand consciousness. Allocentric consumers exhibit more interest in health consciousness, group socializing, reading, and food preparation.[24]

Family and Children

Cultures also differ in the values that they place on their families and children. Parents in Europe and Asia, for example, tend to value education more than U.S. parents do. Among Asian middle-class families, educating children is second in priority only to providing food. Nevertheless, American consumers still place a high value on children. Rather than move their families when they change jobs or get promoted, some parents commute to work in another city or state and use e-mail and other technologies to stay in touch with the other parent and their children during the week.[25]

U.S. parents are generally quite receptive to child-related products, as are families in many cultures (see Exhibit 14.5). LEGO, a Danish company, now enjoys a 6 percent share of the global toy market because so many families are buying its plastic interlocking blocks for children who want to build structures straight out of the Harry Potter books and Star Wars movies.[26] Photo-related goods and service are in high demand as indulgent parents capture images of their children to save and view in the future. Snapfish, a photo service owned by Hewlett-Packard, has 90 million members in 22 countries who have stored 2 billion photos on the site for printing and putting into photo books. Marketers are targeting children with an endless range of cereals, juices, desserts, soft drinks, and other snack products, not to mention games and other playthings.

Image Courtesy of The Advertising Archives

Exhibit 14.5

Valuing Family and Children
Advertisers target children and family, by focusing on the value of spending quality time together with games or hobbies.

Exhibit 14.6

Annual Sales of Organic
Food and Nonfood Products
From 2006 to 2010, sales of
organic foods and organic
nonfood products rose year
after year.

Type of Organic Product	Sales (in billions)				
	2006	2007	2008	2009	2010
Organic foods	$ 17.2	$ 20.4	$ 23.6	$24.8	$26.7
Organic nonfoods	$ 0.94	$ 1.2	$ 1.6	$1.8	$2

Source: Organic Trade Association, *2011 Organic Industry Survey*, www.ota.com/organic/mt.html.

Health

Many U.S. consumers place a high value on health due to reasons of self-esteem (the way the body looks) and concerns about longevity and survival. The value of health is reflected in the popularity of foods low in fat, calories, carbohydrates, salt, sugar, or cholesterol, as well as foods with special nutritional benefits. Grocery chains such as Dave's Supermarkets in Cleveland now use green "Go! Food" stickers to show shoppers which fruits, vegetables, side dishes, and entrees are low in fat and sodium.[27] Responding to trends in health consciousness, the Wendy's fast-food chain has introduced a gluten-free menu and notifies consumers of all potential allergens in its foods.[28]

Growing concern about pesticides, additives, food-related illnesses, and contaminants has enhanced U.S. demand for organic foods year after year. As Exhibit 14.6 shows, sales of organic nonfood products have also increased, doubling in only five years as U.S. consumers seek out natural products in all categories.[29] Moreover, consumers who value health tend to be less price sensitive than consumers who do not hold that value—an important consideration because organic foods sometimes cost more than nonorganic foods.[30]

The emphasis on health has also paved the way for walk-in medical clinics located inside popular stores such as CVS and Walmart, as the case at the end of this chapter explains.[31] Antismoking campaigns, bans on smoking in public places, and tobacco and alcohol warning labels in many Western nations are consistent with health values.

Values and behavior can differ, however. Although many Americans talk about a healthy diet, more than 30 percent of U.S. adults are obese, and obesity is also on the increase in Europe and other regions.[32] Some marketers have been criticized for offering excessively large food portions or packages, whereas others have come under fire for the ingredients they put into (or do not take out of) food products (see Chapter 17 for more on this issue). These concerns have resulted in fast-food restaurants posting nutritional information on their websites and on their menus, as well as prompting them to add healthier menu items. McDonald's has downsized the packet of fries that comes with Happy Meals and also includes apple slices with each order to encourage children to eat healthier.[33]

Hedonism

Hedonism The principle of pleasure seeking.

Consumers are increasingly operating on the principle of **hedonism**, or pleasure seeking, searching for goods, services, and experiences that simply make them feel good, such as luxury cars, home entertainment centers, and exciting vacations. Grilled cheese restaurants such as the The American Grilled Cheese Kitchen in San Francisco and gourmet cupcake bakeries like the Michigan chain Just Baked illustrate the hedonistic search for food that tastes good and makes people happy.[34] Hedonism has led to some interesting eating patterns that contradict health values, witnessed by the successes of Häagen-Dazs (the first superpremium ice cream) on the one hand and Healthy Choice low-fat foods (a $700 million brand) on the other.[35] Furthermore, despite their concerns about health, consumers will not switch to low-fat, low-calorie varieties unless they taste good. In fact, one study found that consumers possess an implicit intuition that healthy foods taste bad.[36,37]

Youth

Compared with other cultures, the United States has long placed a high value on youth, as evidenced by the wide range of offerings for combating or reducing signs of aging (think of wrinkle creams, hair coloring, and hair transplants). Cosmetic surgery is one of the fastest-growing medical specialties for both men and women. Beauty products are riding the wave of this emphasis on youth: For instance, L'Oréal, a global cosmetic brand based in France, is seeing profitable results from marketing campaigns targeting women in the United States, China, and India who buy hair coloring, makeup, and nail polish.[38] Marketing communications also indicate the value placed on youth and products that help consumers feel youthful.

Authenticity

People generally value authentic things, either the original article (such as the actual furniture that George Washington owned, which is displayed in his Mount Vernon home) or a faithful reproduction (such as furniture made to look like that of George Washington and shown in a museum or available for purchase).[39] Cheap knockoffs or counterfeits tend to be valued much less. Consumers may feel a close attachment to brands they perceive to be "authentic"—and may drop or even disparage brands that cease to seem authentic.[40] For example, U.S. craft beer brands, brewed locally or in small batches, are often viewed as more authentic than mass-produced beer brands.[41] A service or experience may also be valued for its authenticity. For example, some consumers may perceive the experience of sipping espresso in a small, locally owned coffee shop as a more authentic experience than going to Starbucks, which has a global presence and a consistent in-store brand identity. Sports teams such as the Toronto Maple Leafs hockey team sometimes make small changes to their logos, but they rarely change team colors or emblems because fans value the authenticity of these traditional elements.[42]

The Environment

Environmental protection has become an important value among U.S. and European consumers, who are interested in conserving natural resources, preventing pollution, and supporting environmentally friendly goods, services, and activities. Businesses can profit from many aspects of environmental values. Procter & Gamble, for example, is demonstrating its green side by replacing petroleum-based packaging and products with sustainable materials, which appeals to consumers who want to buy and use eco-friendly goods.[43] The Nissan LEAF and the Toyota Prius are two car models attracting a growing number of buyers because they run more cleanly and deliver more fuel efficiency (see Exhibit 14.7). H&M and other retailers are involved with a Natural Resources Defense Council initiative to increase efficiency, which can make any business's bottom line look greener.[44]

Technology

Consumers in many cultures are fascinated by technological advances. More than ever before, consumers in the United States, Japan, and other nations believe that computers, smart phones, digital cameras, and the Internet improve the quality of their lives. Nevertheless, technological changes can be so rapid that we have trouble keeping up, resulting in a renewed emphasis on simplicity or at least on managing complexity. Still, products with features that work automatically are popular because they make it easier for consumers to use the products properly. Thus, consumers appear to value technology for what it can do to make their lives easier rather than for its own sake, making technology an instrumental rather than a terminal value. Intel, which makes computer chips for computers and smartphones, is fine-tuning its marketing strategy in line with that insight. "A brand that helps people achieve and offers opportunity has a phenomenal brand attribute," says Intel's director of marketing research.[45]

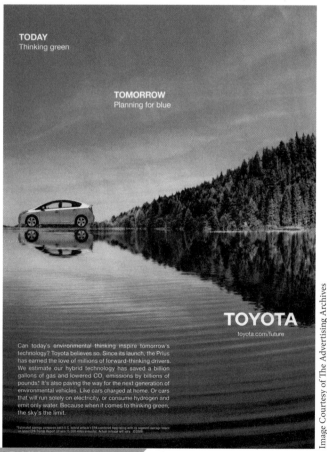

Image Courtesy of The Advertising Archives

Exhibit 14.7

Valuing the Environment
Environmental concerns are an increasingly important value trend, for consumers and businesses alike.

Why Values Change

Because societies and their institutions are constantly evolving, value systems are also changing. In addition to the key trends already discussed, U.S. values are moving toward casualness in living, greater sophistication in behavior, a change in sex roles, and the desire to be modern.[46] Although the United States was different from Western Europe 100 years ago, both cultures (and to a certain extent Japan as well) are now becoming more similar in values, even though differences still exist. This increase in value consistency is driven in part by the increase in global communication. For example, Western Europeans regard some U.S. consumption patterns as attractive. Affluent Japanese consumers are starting to place greater value on personal preferences, a balanced life, and experiences and less value on traditional expectations, work, and possessions.[47]

Influences on Values

How do values differ across groups of consumers? This section explores the ways that culture, ethnicity, social class, and age can influence our values.

Culture and Values

People in different countries are exposed to different cultural experiences, a situation that leads to cross-cultural differences in values. One study found that the three most important values among Brazilians are true friendship, mature love, and happiness, whereas U.S. consumers named family security, world peace, and freedom.[48] Consumers in China place the most importance on values such as preserving the best that one has attained, being sympathetic to others, having self-control, and integrating enjoyment, action, and contemplation. A study of women in Germany, France, and the United Kingdom found that the value of "having a familiar routine" is most important for German women, but only tenth in importance for the British and twenty-third for the French.[49] On the other hand, some values cross national boundaries. Research spanning 28 countries found that an emphasis on materialism is associated with positive attitudes toward global and local products, for example.[50]

In a classic study, Geert Hofstede found that cultures can vary along four main value dimensions:[51]

▶ *Individualism versus collectivism.* The degree to which a culture focuses on the individuals rather than the group.

▶ *Uncertainty avoidance.* The extent to which a culture prefers structured to unstructured situations.

▶ *Masculinity versus femininity.* The extent to which a culture stresses masculine values (as defined by Hofstede) such as assertiveness, success, and competition over feminine values such as quality of life, warm personal relationships, and caring.

▶ *Power distance.* The degree to which a society's members are equal in terms of status.

All cultures can be classified according to these fo[...]
culture falls may provide insight into cross-cultural di[...]
tipping in restaurants is less likely to occur in coun[...]
avoidance are low, feminine values are strong, and indi[...]
humorous ad themes are more likely to focus on grou[...]
South Korea and more likely to focus on unequal statu[...]
distance like the United States and Germany.[53] Finally[...]
consumption to support their view of themselves as [...]
masculinity.[54]

Ethnic Identification and Values

Ethnic groups within a larger culture can have some[...]
nic subcultures. As noted in Chapter 12, Hispanic Am[...]
similarly, African American and Asian American con[...]

family.[55] Consumers in different countries may have different ethnic values. For example, consumers in China tend to hold the traditional Confucian value of respect for older family members. Knowing this, Nestlé advertises milk-based meal supplements to adults by appealing to their respect and responsibility for aging parents.[56]

Social Class and Values

Different social classes hold specific values, as discussed in Chapter 13, which in turn affect their acquisition and consumption patterns. As countries in Eastern Europe and Latin American are now embracing market economies, the size of the global middle class is increasing dramatically, along with middle-class values of materialism and a desire for less government control over their lives and greater access to information. Upper–upper-class consumers value giving back to society, a characteristic that explains why they become active in social, cultural, and civic causes. These consumers also prize self-expression as reflected in their homes, clothing, cars, and other forms of consumption.[57]

Age and Values

Members of a generation often share similar values that differ from those of other generations. For example, your grandparents may value security over hedonism, not because they are older but because they grew up during the Great Depression and suffered economic hardship as children. Many of that generation therefore view hedonic activities as frivolous and unacceptable. Baby boomers who grew up in the 1960s—a time of political upheaval, self-indulgence, and rebellion—often value hedonism, morality, self-direction, and achievement.[58] Note that it is sometimes very difficult to distinguish values we acquire with age from those we learn from our era. Nevertheless, differences by virtue of age or cohort do exist, and they influence the way that we behave as consumers.

Marketing Implications

Marketers need to understand how consumer values affect consumption patterns, market segmentation, new product development, ad development strategy, and ethics.

Consumption Patterns

Consumers usually buy, use, and dispose of products in a manner consistent with their values.[59] Thus, marketers can know more about what consumers like if they understand their values. For example, those who value warm relationships with others are more likely to buy gifts and send cards than those who place less value on relationships.[60] When the U.K. supermarket chain Tesco studied its customers' values, it found such strong environmental concerns that it launched a program to label the carbon footprint of every product it sells. It has also undertaken a program of sustainable retail development in China, where the chain is expanding amid strong competition.[61] However, marketers sometimes adopt an ethnocentric perspective, assuming that consumers in other cultures hold values similar to their own.

Market Segmentation

value segmentation The grouping of consumers by common values.

Marketers can identify groups of consumers who have a common set of values that differ from those of other groups, a process called **value segmentation**. Even the market for something as basic as pencils can be segmented in this way. Faber-Castell, for example, which sells two billion pencils every year, offers products for different value segments, including consumers who value quality, creativity, the environment, status, and style.[62] Marketers also can use values to understand the attributes that consumers in a particular segment may find important in a product and that may motivate them to choose one brand over another. When buying clothes, individuals who value status might look for attributes like price and luxury, those who value fitting in with the crowd might look for clothing that is trendy, and those who value uniqueness might look for new or nonmainstream styles. For example, uniqueness is a key segmentation variable for Of a Kind, an online retailer that offers limited-edition fashion clothing by up-and-coming designers.[63]

New Product Ideas

Values can also influence consumers' reactions to new and different products. The more a new product is consistent with important consumer values, the greater the likelihood of its success. For example, good-tasting, microwaveable, low-fat, and low-calorie frozen entrees have succeeded in part because these items are consistent with multiple values like hedonism, time, convenience, health, and technology. Yet sometimes balancing conflicting values can be a challenge for marketers with new product ideas. This was the case for the Campbell Soup Company, which tried to balance hedonism and health values. When the firm noticed that sales of its all-natural Select Harvest soups had plateaued, the company increased the amount of salt because consumers "didn't come back," according to a spokesperson. "The reality is, if it doesn't taste good, people are not going to buy it."[64]

Ad Development Strategy

Examining the target segment's value profile can help marketers design more appealing ads.[65] Value-laden ads can instigate value-consistent behavior (such as buying a product related to that value), especially when consumers have a positive attitude toward the advertising.[66] The more compatible the ad copy is with consumers' values, the more likely consumers are to become involved in the message and find it relevant. Clearly, marketers must connect product attributes and benefits to consumer values because these represent the end state consumers desire to achieve—the driving force behind their consumption of the product. To stay in tune with its customers, Harley-Davidson, for example, is using crowdsourcing via Facebook to generate advertising ideas and, in the process, learn more about the target audience. A Harley-Davidson official says: "The added benefit is we get insights into what people are thinking about the brand."[67] Marketers must also avoid communications that conflict with cultural values within one nation or when reaching audiences in multiple nations.

Ethical Considerations

Consumers use values to gauge the appropriateness of others' behaviors—including the behavior of marketers. For example, those who value morality might disapprove of products such as cigarettes and X-rated videos, consumption practices like prostitution and gambling, and sexually explicit ads. In Valencia, Spain, a bus company removed transport ads promoting escort bars and erotic phone services after receiving many complaints about the nature of the ads.[68] Consumers also evaluate marketers' behavior for fairness, ethics, and appropriateness.[69] As Chapter 17 explains, marketers should be aware that consumers may boycott, protest, or complain about practices that seem inconsistent with their values of fairness. ⎯⎯⎯⎯⎯⎯⎯⎯⎯⎯⎯⎯⎯

How Values Can Be Measured

To segment the market by values, marketers need some means of identifying consumers' values, gauging their importance, and analyzing changes or trends in values. Unfortunately, values are often hard to measure. One reason is that people do not often think about their values and may therefore have a hard time articulating what is really important to them. Another reason is that people may sometimes feel social pressure to respond to a values questionnaire in a certain way to make themselves look better in the eyes of the researcher. Therefore, marketers usually use less obtrusive or more indirect ways of assessing values.

Inferring Values from the Cultural Milieu

The least obtrusive way to measure values is to make inferences based on a culture's milieu. Advertising has often been used as an indicator of values.[70] Research examining the values portrayed in U.S. print ads between 1900 and 1980 revealed that practicality, the family, modernity, frugality, wisdom, and uniqueness were among the values that appeared most frequently. Researchers can also use ads to uncover cross-cultural differences and track trends in values. One study found that because the People's Republic of China, Taiwan, and Hong Kong are at different levels of economic development and have different political ideologies, different values were reflected in each country's ads.[71] At the time, ads from China focused on utilitarian themes and promised a better life, Hong Kong ads stressed hedonism and an easier life, and Taiwan ads fell between the other two. Now, with the economic changes occurring in China, the trend in local advertising is away from utilitarian themes and toward variety in products and product assurances.

Marketers can infer values just by looking at product names. Product names reflecting values of materialism (Grand Hyatt hotels), hedonism (Obsession perfume), time (Ronzoni Quick Cook Pasta), technology (Microsoft), and convenience (Reddi-wip topping) are common in the United States. Values are also reflected in magazine titles (such as *Money*), book and movie titles, TV programs, the types of people regarded as heroes or heroines, and popular songs. In China, foreign brands are more valued than local brands, so companies like Cadillac and Hilton simply translate their brand names phonetically to emphasize their U.S. origins.[72]

One criticism of cultural milieu as an indicator of values is that researchers never know whether culture reflects values or creates them. In light of this problem, researchers have introduced other methods to measure values.

Means-End Chain Analysis

> **Means-end chain analysis** A technique that can help to explain how values link to attributes in products and services.

Marketers can use the **means-end chain analysis** to gain insight into consumers' values by better understanding which attributes they find important in products. Armed with this information, researchers can work backward to uncover the values that drive consumer decisions.[73] One way to do this is through *value laddering*, determining the root values related to product attributes that are important to consumers.[74] Suppose a consumer likes light beer because it has fewer calories than regular beer. If a researcher asks why it is important to have a beer with fewer calories, the respondent might say, "Because I don't want to gain weight." If the researcher asks why not, the consumer might respond by saying, "I want to be healthy." If asked why again, the consumer might say, "Because I want to feel good about myself." This example is illustrated in the top line of Exhibit 14.8.

Note that this means-end chain has several potential levels. First, the consumer mentioned an important attribute followed by a concrete benefit that the attribute provides. Then the consumer indicated that this benefit was important because it served some instrumental value. This entire process is called a *means-end chain* because the attribute provides the means to a desired end state or terminal value (in this case, self-esteem).

Looking at Exhibit 14.8, you can also see that a particular attribute can be associated with very different values. For example, first, rather than valuing light beer for its health benefits, some consumers may like light beer because they drink it in a social context that leads to a greater sense of belonging. Second, the same value may be associated with very different products and attributes. Thus, attributes associated with both light beer and rice may appeal equally to the value of belonging. Third, a given attribute may be linked with multiple benefits and/or values, meaning that a consumer might like light beer because it makes her feel healthier and because it facilitates belonging.

> **Exhibit 14.8**
>
> **An Example of Means-End Chains**
>
> According to the means-end chain analysis, product and service attributes (e.g., fewer calories) lead to benefits (e.g., I won't gain weight) that reflect instrumental values (e.g., helps make me healthy) and terminal values (e.g., I feel good about myself). This analysis helps marketers identify important values and the attributes associated with them. Can you develop a means-end chain for toothpaste or deodorant?

Product	Attribute	Benefit	Instrumental Value (driving force)	Terminal Value
Light beer (I)	Fewer calories	I won't gain weight.	Helps make me healthy	I feel good about myself (self-esteem).
Light beer (II)	Fewer calories Great taste Light taste	Less filling Enjoyable/relaxing Refreshing	Good times/fun Friendship	Belonging
Rice	Comes in boiling bag	Convenient No messy pan to clean up	Saves time	I can enjoy more time with my family (belonging).

Source: Adapted from Jonathan Gutman, "A Means-End Chain Model Based on Consumer Categorization Processes," *Journal of Marketing*, Spring 1982, pp. 60–72; and Thomas J. Reynolds and John P. Rochan, "Means-End Based Advertising Research: Copy Testing Is Not Strategy Assessment," *Journal of Business Research*, March 1991, pp. 131–142.

Image Courtesy of The Advertising Archives

Exhibit 14.9

Products' Benefits and Values
Marketers are finding new ways to appeal to both a Products' benefits (such as 0% fat) and its valuable attributes (100% pleasure).

Rokeach Value Survey (RVS) A survey that measures instrumental and terminal values.

List of Values (LOV) A survey that measures nine principal values in consumer behavior.

Marketers can use means-end chain analysis to identify product attributes that will be consistent with certain values.[75] At one time, consumers generally considered sports cars to be expensive and uncomfortable, and ownership of them took on an aspect of "arrogance and irresponsibility." Then, to be more in line with current values, manufacturers began offering comfortable cars positioned for "people who have friends."[76] The means-end chain model is also useful for developing advertising strategy. By knowing which attributes consumers find important and which values they associate with those attributes, advertisers can design ads that appeal to these values and emphasize related attributes. Note that the ad need not explicitly link a given attribute with a motive, but it can allow consumers to implicitly make the linkage.

Finally, marketers can use the means-end chain to segment global markets and appeal to consumers on the basis of specific benefits and related values.[77] To market yogurt, for instance, a company could identify one segment that values health and reach this segment by focusing on product attributes such as low fat and could identify a second segment that values enjoyment and reach this segment through attributes such as fruit ingredients (see Exhibit 14.9).

Value Questionnaires

Marketers can directly assess values by using questionnaires. Some types of questionnaires, such as the material values scale, focus only on specific aspects of consumer behavior.[78] Others cover a range of values. One of the best known of these is the **Rokeach Value Survey (RVS)**. This questionnaire asks consumers about the importance that they attach to the 19 instrumental values and 18 terminal values identified in Exhibit 14.2. This questionnaire is standardized, and everyone responds to the same set of items, a procedure that helps researchers identify the specific values that are most important to a given group of consumers, determine whether values are changing over time, and learn whether values differ for various groups of consumers. One drawback is that some values measured by the RVS are less relevant to consumer behavior (such as salvation, forgiving, and being obedient). Some researchers have therefore recommended using a shortened form of the RVS containing only the values most relevant to a consumer context.[79]

Others have advocated the use of the **List of Values (LOV)**. Consumers are presented with nine primary values and asked either to identify the two most important or to rank all nine values by importance. The nine values are (1) self-respect, (2) warm relationships with others, (3) sense of accomplishment, (4) self-fulfillment, (5) fun and enjoyment in life, (6) excitement, (7) sense of belonging, (8) being well respected, and (9) security.[80] The first six are internal values because they derive from the individual; the others are external values. The values can also be described in terms of whether they are fulfilled through interpersonal relationships (warm relationships with others, sense of belonging), personal factors (self-respect, being well respected, self-fulfillment), or nonpersonal things (sense of accomplishment, fun, security, and excitement).

In one study, the LOV predicted consumers' responses to statements that describe their self-reported consumption characteristics (e.g., "I am a spender, not a saver"), their actual consumption behaviors (the frequency with which they watch movies or the news, read certain magazines, and engage in activities like playing tennis), and their marketplace beliefs ("I believe the consumer movement has caused prices to increase"). Compared with the RVS, the LOV is a better predictor of consumer behavior, is shorter, and is easier to administer. Finally, the LOV is useful for identifying segments of consumers with similar value systems.[81]

PERSONALITY

Personality An internal characteristic that determines how individuals behave in various situations.

Although individuals with comparable backgrounds tend to hold similar values, it is important to remember that people do not always act the same way even when they hold the same values. In listening to a sales pitch, one consumer may state demurely that she finds the product interesting but is not ready to make up her mind right now. Another might act more assertively, interrupting the salesperson midway through his pitch to indicate that she has no interest whatsoever in the product. Therefore, consumers vary in terms of their personality or the way in which they respond to a particular situation.

Personality consists of the distinctive patterns of behaviors, tendencies, qualities, or personal dispositions that make one individual different from another and lead to a consistent response to environmental stimuli. These patterns are internal characteristics that we are born with or that result from the way we have been raised. The concept of personality helps us understand why people behave differently in different situations.

Research Approaches to Personality

The social sciences provide various approaches to studying personality. This section reviews five approaches that consumer researchers apply: psychoanalytic approaches, trait theories, phenomenological approaches, social-psychological theories, and behavioral approaches.

Psychoanalytic Approaches

According to psychoanalytic theories, personality arises from a set of dynamic, unconscious internal struggles within the mind.[82] The famous psychoanalyst Sigmund Freud proposed that we pass through several developmental stages in forming our personalities. In the first stage, the oral stage, the infant is entirely dependent on others for need satisfaction and receives oral gratification from sucking, eating, and biting. At the anal stage, the child is confronted with the problem of toilet training. Then in the phallic stage, the youth becomes aware of his or her genitals and must deal with desires for the opposite-sex parent.

Freud believed that the failure to resolve the conflicts from each stage could influence one's personality. For example, the individual who received insufficient oral stimulation as an infant may reveal this crisis in adulthood through oral-stimulation activities like gum chewing, smoking, and overeating or by distrusting others' motives (including those of marketers). At the anal stage, an individual whose toilet training was too restrictive may become obsessed with control and be overly orderly, stubborn, or stingy, resulting in neatly organized closets and records, list making, and excessive saving or collecting. These individuals may also engage in extensive information search and deliberation when making decisions. On the other hand, those whose training was overly lenient may become messy, disorganized adults.

Although some of Freud's theories were later questioned by many researchers, the key point is that the subconscious can influence behavior. Consequently, some advertising agencies conduct research to delve deep into consumers' psyches and uncover subconscious reasons why they buy a particular product.[83] This type of research led to the discovery of a deep-seated desire for milk that the dairy industry used in its "Got Milk?" campaign.

Trait Theories

Trait theorists propose that personality is composed of characteristics that describe and differentiate individuals.[84] For example, people might be described as aggressive, easygoing, quiet, moody, shy, or rigid. Psychologist Carl Jung developed one of the most basic trait theory schemes, suggesting that individuals could be categorized according to their levels of introversion and extroversion.[85] Introverts are shy, prefer to be alone, and are anxious in the presence of others. They tend to avoid social channels and may not find out about new products from others. They are also less motivated by social pressure and more likely to do things that please themselves. In contrast, extroverts are outgoing, sociable, and typically conventional.

Research in social psychology has found that five major personality traits tend to account for the most variance in personality (the "Big 5"): agreeableness, conscientiousness, emotional

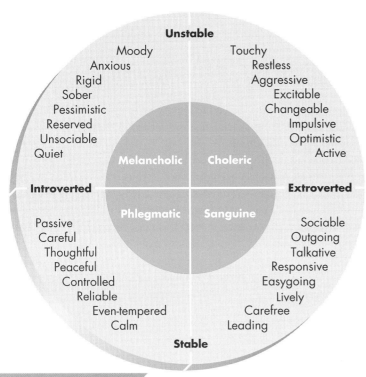

Unstable

Moody
Anxious
Rigid
Sober
Pessimistic
Reserved
Unsociable
Quiet

Touchy
Restless
Aggressive
Excitable
Changeable
Impulsive
Optimistic
Active

Melancholic   **Choleric**

Introverted   **Extroverted**

Phlegmatic   **Sanguine**

Passive
Careful
Thoughtful
Peaceful
Controlled
Reliable
Even-tempered
Calm

Sociable
Outgoing
Talkative
Responsive
Easygoing
Lively
Carefree
Leading

Stable

Exhibit 14.10

A Trait Conception of Personality Types
Consumers can be classified according to whether they have introverted or extroverted personality traits. These traits can lead to the identification of various personality types (e.g., moody, peaceful, lively, and aggressive). Interestingly, these traits can be collected into four major groups that correspond to the basic temperaments identified by the ancient Greek physician Hippocrates many centuries ago. How would you classify your personality according to this scheme?

Source: Adapted from Hans Eysenck and S. Rachman, *The Causes and Cures of Neurosis: An Introduction to Modern Behavior Therapy Based on Learning Theory and Principles of Conditioning* (San Diego, Calif.: Knapp, 1965–, p. 16.) Reprinted by permission from EdITS.

Locus of control How people interpret why things happen (internal versus external).

stability, openness, and extraversion.[86] Recent work has also found that the trait of stability, or consistency in behavior, when combined with the introversion/extroversion dimension, can be used as a basis to represent various personality types (see Exhibit 14.10). For example, a person who is reliable tends to be high on both introversion and stability. In contrast, a passive person is introverted but neither highly stable nor highly unstable. One interesting feature about this scheme is that the personality types identified by these two dimensions match the four temperaments identified by the Greek physician Hippocrates centuries ago—for example, a phlegmatic person is introverted and stable; a melancholic person is introverted and unstable.

Phenomenological Approaches

Phenomenological approaches propose that personality is largely shaped by an individual's interpretations of life events.[87] For example, according to this approach, depression is caused by the way that someone interprets key events and the nature of that interpretation rather than by internal conflicts or traits.

A key concept of the phenomenological approaches is **locus of control**, or people's interpretations of why specific things happen.[88] Individuals with an internal locus of control attribute more responsibility to themselves for good or bad outcomes, so they might blame themselves or see themselves as having been careless when a product fails. Externally controlled individuals place responsibility on other people, events, or places rather than on themselves. Thus, they might attribute product failure to faulty manufacturing or poor packaging.

Locus of control can heavily influence consumers' perceptions of satisfaction in a consumption experience and determine how the consumer feels. To illustrate, consumers who blame themselves for product failure might feel shame, whereas those who blame product failure on an external source might feel anger and irritation. In addition, someone's life theme or goals (concerns that we address in our everyday lives) can greatly influence the meanings that he or she derives from ads.[89] As a result, a person who is more concerned with family might interpret an ad differently than someone who is more concerned with his or her private self.

Social-Psychological Theories

Another group of theories focuses on social rather than biological explanations of personality, proposing that individuals act in social situations to meet their needs. The researcher Karen Horney, for instance, believed that behavior can be characterized by three major orientations.[90] *Compliant* individuals are dependent on others and are humble, trusting, and tied to a group. *Aggressive* individuals need power, move away from others, and are outgoing, assertive, self-confident, and tough-minded. *Detached* individuals are independent and self-sufficient but suspicious and introverted. These three orientations are measured by the CAD scale.[91] One study found that assertiveness and aggressiveness were significantly related to styles of interaction with marketing institutions.[92] In particular, highly assertive and aggressive people were likely to perceive complaining as acceptable and to enjoy doing it.

In social-psychological theory, researchers distinguish between state-oriented consumers, who are more likely to rely on subjective norms to guide their behavior, and action-oriented consumers, whose behavior is based more on their own attitudes.[93] Consumers also vary in terms of their attention to information that helps them compare themselves with others (social comparison information). Individuals high on this factor are more sensitive to normative pressure than are those low on this factor.

Behavioral Approaches

In contrast to other explanations of personality, behavioral approaches propose that differences in personality are a function of how individuals have been rewarded or punished in the past. According to behavioral approaches, individuals are more likely to have traits or engage in behaviors for which they have received positive reinforcement. They are less likely to maintain characteristics and behaviors for which they have been punished.[94] Thus, an individual might be extroverted because parents, caretakers, and other individuals rewarded outgoing behaviors and punished introverted behaviors. Likewise, a consumer might prefer colorful clothing if he or she previously received positive reinforcement for wearing it. Note that these behavioral approaches to personality involve the principles of operant conditioning discussed in Chapter 9.

Determining Whether Personality Characteristics Affect Consumer Behavior

Much of the consumer-related personality research has followed the trait approach and focused on identifying specific personality traits that explain differences in consumers' purchase, use, and disposition behavior. Although studies have attempted to find a relationship between personality and consumer behavior, personality is not always a good predictor of consumer behavior.[95] One major problem is that researchers developed many of the trait measurement instruments for identifying personality disorders in clinical settings, so these instruments may not be applicable for identifying traits related to consumption behaviors.

Although some studies have been problematic, other researchers believe that more reliable measures of traits, developed in a consumer context, would reveal a relationship.[96] For instance, researchers created a consumer self-confidence scale to examine how this trait affects the choice of higher-price alternatives.[97] Also, the association between personality and consumer behavior may be stronger for some types of consumer behavior than for others. For example, although personality may not be very useful in understanding brand choice, it may help marketers understand why some people are more susceptible to persuasion, particularly like a certain ad, or engage in more information processing.

Marketers may also find personality more useful for targeting some product and service categories than others. In particular, our choice of offerings that involve subjective or hedonic features such as looks, style, and aesthetics may be somewhat related to personality. A good example is the selection of a greeting card, which represents a personal message and therefore is an extension of the sender's personality. Finally, certain types of personality traits may be more related to consumer behavior than others. As described below, these include optimal stimulation level, dogmatism, need for uniqueness, creativity, need for cognition, susceptibility to influence, frugality, self-monitoring behavior, national character, and competitiveness.

Optimal Stimulation Level

Some activities have the potential to provide some sort of physiological arousal. For example, you might feel more aroused when you speed on the highway, ride a roller coaster, see a scary movie, or go to new and unfamiliar surroundings. Things that are physically stimulating, emotionally energizing, or novel have arousal-inducing potential. However, highly stimulating activities are not always desirable. According to the theory of optimal stimulation level (OSL), people prefer things that are moderately arousing to things that are either too arousing or not arousing at all.[98] For example, you might prefer eating at a restaurant that offers moderately imaginative food to eating at one that offers boring food or one that offers unusual food.

Even though people generally prefer moderate levels of stimulation, individuals differ in the level of arousal they regard as moderate and optimal. Individuals with a low optimal stimulation level tend to prefer less arousing activities because they want to avoid going over the edge.

In contrast, individuals with a high optimal stimulation level are more likely to seek activities that are very exciting, novel, complex, and different. Consumers with a high need for stimulation might enjoy activities like skydiving, gambling, and river rafting.[99] They are also more likely to be innovative and creative.

Individuals with high and low needs for stimulation also differ in the way in which they approach the marketplace. Those with high stimulation needs tend to be the first to buy new products, to seek information about them, and to engage in variety seeking (buying something different).[100] They are more curious about the ads they see but may also be easily bored by them. These consumers are more likely to buy products associated with greater risk, enjoy shopping in malls with many stores and products, and prefer offerings that deviate from established consumption practices.

Dogmatism

Dogmatism A tendency to be resistant to change or new ideas.

Consumers can vary in terms of being open- or closed-minded. **Dogmatism** refers to an individual's tendency to be resistant to change and new ideas. Dogmatic, or closed-minded, consumers are relatively resistant to new products, new promotions, and new ads. In support, one study found that Nigerian consumers' acceptance of new products depended on how dogmatic the consumers were. The study also found that Muslims were more dogmatic than Christians.[10]

Need for Uniqueness

Need for uniqueness (NFU) The desire for novelty through the purchase, use, and disposition of products and services.

Consumers who pursue novelty through the purchase, use, and disposition of goods and services display a **need for uniqueness (NFU)**.[102] A need for uniqueness covers three behavioral dimensions: creative choice counterconformity (the consumer's choice reflects social distinctiveness yet is one that others will approve of), unpopular choice counterconformity (choosing products and brands that do not conform to establish distinctiveness despite possible social disapproval), and avoidance of similarity (losing interest in possessions that become commonplace to avoid the norm and hence reestablish distinctiveness). In one study, consumers with a high need for uniqueness who were asked to explain their decisions made unconventional choices, showing that they were aware that their choices and reasoning were outside the norm.[103] Thus, consumers with a high need for uniqueness may avoid well-known global brands in favor of small, local brands.[104] They may also dispose of clothing that has become too popular in favor of emerging fashion trends, seek out handcrafted or personalized items, and customize products to their own specifications, as described in this chapter's opening example.

Creativity

In terms of consumer behavior, *creativity* means "a departure from conventional consumption practice in a novel and functional way."[105] For instance, if confronted with an everyday problem such as lacking the right ingredients to make dinner, a consumer high in creativity would locate substitutes. This solution would enable the consumer to complete the activity in a novel yet practical way. Such creativity enhances the consumer's mood as well.[106] To illustrate, the Pillsbury website and Facebook pages encourage creativity with videos demonstrating cooking techniques, recipes organized by ingredient and occasion, and forums for consumers to exchange ideas about menus, entertaining, and more.[107]

Need for Cognition

Need for cognition (NFC) A trait that describes how much people like to think.

Consumers who enjoy thinking extensively about things like products, attributes, and benefits are high in the **need for cognition (NFC)**.[108] Those with a low need for cognition do not like to think and prefer to take shortcuts or to rely on their feelings. Consumers with different needs for cognition differ in terms of their product interests, information search, and reaction to different ad campaigns. Specifically, those with a high need for cognition enjoy products and experiences that carry a serious learning and mastery component such as chess, educational games, and TV shows like *Jeopardy*. They derive satisfaction from searching for and discovering new product features and react positively to long, technically sophisticated ads with details about products or services. They might also scrutinize messages more carefully than other consumers do, considering the credibility or merits of the message.[109] Consumers with a low need for cognition, on the other hand, react more positively to short messages using attractive models, humor, or other cues. These individuals tend to make decisions that involve little thinking.

CUT YOUR HEATING AND COOLING COSTS UP TO 80%.

Cut your energy bills. ClimateMaster geothermal systems tap the constant temperature of the earth to provide heating, cooling, and hot water. Your home stays comfortable year-round while trimming your energy use by up to 80%. And now with new federal tax credits, you will save an additional 30% on the total installation. Best of all, ClimateMaster systems are not only a good investment, they are a cleaner choice for the environment. To learn more about how the geothermal technology leader can help you cut your energy bills, visit climatemaster.com or call 877-436-6263 today.

CLIMATEMASTER®
Geothermal Heat Pump Systems
An LSB Industries, Inc. Company (NYSE: LXU)

Courtesy of ClimateMaster Inc.

Exhibit 14.11

Appealing to Frugality
Some consumers posses the value of frugality, especially in tough economic times, so some ads stress these saving money values.

National character The personality of a country.

Susceptibility to Influence

Consumers also vary in their susceptibility to persuasion attempts, especially those who are interpersonal or face to face. Some consumers have a greater desire to enhance their image as observed by others and are therefore willing to be influenced or guided by them.[110] Consumers with lower social and information processing confidence tend to be more influenced by ads than are those with higher self-confidence.

Frugality

Frugality is the degree to which consumers take a disciplined approach to short-term acquisitions and are resourceful in using products and services to achieve longer-term goals. Consumers who are high on frugality will, for example, pack leftovers for lunch at work (rather than buy take-out food or eat in a restaurant). Such consumers are less materialistic, less susceptible to the influence of others, and more conscious of price and value.[111] Sometimes governments or firms will actively encourage frugality to conserve scarce resources such as electric power.[112] During the recent recession, with unemployment high and economic uncertainty an ongoing concern, many consumers embraced a deeper sense of frugality, dramatically changing their saving and spending habits.[113] These consumers switched to lower-priced, private-label brands; postponed nonessential purchases; limited their use of credit; and actively comparison shopped to stretch their budgets (see Exhibit 14.11). However, it is unclear yet whether this embrace of frugality will endure as a long-term trait once the economy has recovered.

Self-Monitoring Behavior

Individuals differ in the degree to which they look to others for cues on how to behave. High self-monitors are typically sensitive to the desires and influences of others as guides to behavior, and low self-monitors are guided more by their own preferences and desires and are less influenced by normative expectations.[114] High and low self-monitors also differ in their responsiveness to advertising appeals. High self-monitors are more responsive to image-oriented ads and more willing to try and pay more for products advertised with an image consistent with high self-monitoring. In contrast, low self-monitors are generally more responsive to ads that make a quality claim and are more willing to try these products and pay extra for them. Marketers can prime awareness of self-monitoring through techniques such as calling the consumer by name. In turn, this higher awareness can encourage the consumer to make decisions that better fit their personal preferences and therefore improve satisfaction.[115] These consumers are also less likely to accept compromise options (see Chapter 8) and variety in their choice set. Yet studies also show that consumers do not always accept information they learn about themselves—which means they may not apply their knowledge of themselves to make more informed decisions.[116]

National Character

Personality traits can sometimes be used to stereotype people of a particular country as having a **national character**. These characterizations represent only very broad generalizations about a particular country; obviously, individuals vary a great deal. To illustrate, French people and

Italian people are often characterized as emotional and romantic; the British as more reserved; and German, French, and Americans have been characterized as more assertive than their British, Russian, or Italian counterparts. German, British, and Russian consumers can be viewed as "tighter" compared with the "looser" French, Italian, and U.S. consumers.[117]

U.S. consumers are considered more impulsive, risk-oriented, and self-confident than Canadians, who are stereotyped as more cautious, restrained, and reserved. Researchers have characterized how countries differ in their needs for achievement, levels of introversion and extroversion, perceptions of human nature, and flexibility.[118] Marketers must consider how differences in national character may influence reactions to advertising and other communications. For example, when German retailer Media Markt ran ads in Turkey depicting human bodies with animal heads—intended to suggest that only animals would be foolish enough to overpay for certain products—outraged consumers forced the removal of the ads.[119]

Competitiveness

The personality trait of competitiveness has been associated with the desire to outdo others through conspicuous consumption of material items such as electronic gadgets. It also plays a role in consumers' wanting to do better than others in a direct way (e.g., through a sport or by gambling) or an indirect way (such as when watching a sporting event).[120] Marketers who want to appeal to competitive consumers often use messages emphasizing the opportunity to be among the first to try or buy a new product or service. Some marketers appeal to competitiveness by downplaying explicit branding on products in favor of subtle status cues that can be recognized by consumers who are "in the know."[121] Note that when lower-status consumers focus on conspicuous consumption and are aware of their potential for gains relative to higher-status consumers, this creates a competitive mindset and stimulates them to increase consumption.[122]

Marketing Implications

Because some personality traits may be related to consumption behavior, marketers can develop offerings and communications that appeal to various personality types. For example, ads targeting compliant or extremely self-monitoring consumers should focus on the approval of others, whereas ads and promotions appealing to high optimal stimulation-level consumers or those with a strong need for uniqueness might focus on trying something new and different.

Targeting consumers who enjoy stimulation, Ben & Jerry's ice cream recently launched a Facebook app in Europe that combines a "personality test" based on ice cream preferences with an invitation to vote for new ice cream flavors.[123] Appealing to consumers who are competitive, the Los Angeles Kings hockey team added a game to its website so that visitors get points for activities such as posting messages about the Kings to social media sites. As they earn points, winners unlock exclusive rewards such as personalized messages from team members.[124]

LIFESTYLES

Lifestyles People's patterns of behavior.

Activities, interests, and opinions (AIOs) The three components of lifestyles.

Lifestyles relate closely to consumers' values and personality. Whereas values and personality represent internal states or characteristics, **lifestyles** are manifestations or actual patterns of behavior. In particular, they are represented by a consumer's **activities, interests, and opinions (AIOs)**, as illustrated in Exhibit 14.12.

Lifestyle and Behavior Patterns

What people do in their spare time is often a good indicator of their lifestyle. One consumer might like outdoor activities such as skiing, whereas another might prefer to surf the Web. Political opinions, ideology, and involvement also can affect acquisition, consumption, and disposition decisions.[125] Consumers who engage in different activities and have differing opinions and interests may in fact represent distinct lifestyle segments for marketers. For instance, one lifestyle segment

Activities	Interests	Opinions	Demographics
Work	Family	Themselves	Age
Hobbies	Home	Social issues	Education
Social events	Job	Politics	Income
Vacations	Community	Business	Occupation
Entertainment	Recreation	Education	Family size
Club membership	Fashion	Economics	Dwelling
Community	Food	Products	Geography
Shopping	Media	Culture	City size
Sports	Achievements	Future	Life cycle stage

Source: Joseph T. Plummer, "The Concept and Application of Life Style Segmentation," *Journal of Marketing*, January 1974, pp. 33–37. Reprinted with permission.

consists of people with an affinity for *nostalgia*, or the desire for old things.[126] This segment clearly represents a key market for old movies, books, and antiques. As another example, consumers who participate in extreme sports such as snowmobiling are a key market for companies that sell related equipment.[127]

Lifestyle research can help marketers understand how a product fits into consumers' general behavior patterns. For example, the Slow Food movement, which began in Italy, has spread around the world and now influences the lifestyle of many consumers, including how they buy foods and beverages and their attitudes toward cooking and eating with others. Slow Food enthusiasts favor locally grown ingredients, enjoy the process of cooking, and welcome the social experience of sharing a meal with friends and family.[128]

Importantly, consumers in different countries may have characteristic lifestyles. For instance, compared with U.S. women, Japanese women are more home focused, less price sensitive, and less likely to drive.[129] Given these preferences, Japanese women would probably spend more time than U.S. women would preparing meals at home and would therefore pay more for products that enhance meal quality. Popular lifestyle activities among Russian consumers include going to the movies and theater and participating in sports like soccer, ice hockey, and figure skating.[130]

Voluntary Simplicity

As defined in the previous chapter, *voluntary simplicity* means consciously limiting acquisition and consumption for a less materialistic, more eco-friendly lifestyle. Voluntary simplicity is not the same as frugality. Whereas frugality is a personality trait reflecting disciplined spending and consumption of goods and services, voluntary simplicity is a lifestyle choice for consumers who do not want the accumulation of possessions to be the focus of their lives. Instead, those who follow this lifestyle will borrow items when needed, buy used or share products with family and friends, pay in cash to avoid debt, and reuse items (such as coffee mugs) rather than buying disposable products.[131]

Marketing Implications

Consumer lifestyles can have important implications for market segmentation, communication, and new product ideas.

Segmentation and Targeting

Marketers can use lifestyles to identify consumer segments for specific offerings. Services such as day-care centers and housecleaning services save time and provide convenience, two benefits that particularly appeal to dual-career couples, working women, and other consumers with busy lifestyles.[132] For example, a group of Dutch

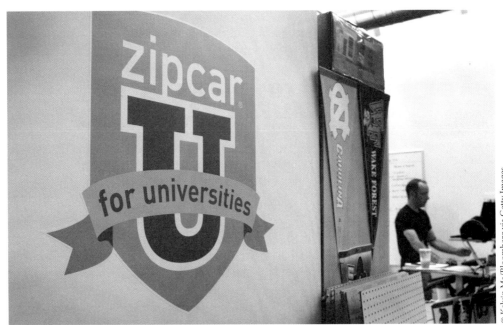

firms that export flowering bulbs to U.S. garden centers is targeting busy gardening hobbyists with a campaign that explains how easy it is to plant and grow blooms from bulbs.[133]

As another example, Ford is using lifestyles to target busy, eco-minded college students who are the new car buyers of tomorrow (see Exhibit 14.13). Ford is supplying Zipcar—the by-the-hour rental firm—with 1,000 Ford Focus and Escape vehicles for rent on college campuses, and subsidizing students' rental fees. "This program enables today's new drivers to experience our latest fuel-efficient vehicles, while helping them reduce their cost of living and help relieve [traffic] congestion on campus," explains Bill Ford Jr., the company's executive chairman.[134]

Marketers also monitor lifestyle changes to identify new opportunities.[135] For instance, time-pressured consumers all over the world are now seeking services at all hours. That's why a Singapore branch of Standard Chartered Bank located in a popular shopping center stays open until late evening. The branch has been so successful, in fact, that Standard Chartered is planning to open several 24-hour branches in South Korea.[136]

Communications

Marketers can design ad messages and promotions to appeal to certain lifestyles, featuring products in the context of desired lifestyles.[137] For instance, One Kings Lane, an online furniture retailer, does this by photographing furniture groupings arranged with accessories, just as they would appear in an upscale home environment, to accompany its item listings. Each grouping receives a lifestyle name, such as "Little Bit of Luxe."[138] Using the Internet, social media, and mobile marketing can be very targeted ways to communicate with a variety of lifestyle segments. This is why sites like mycoke. com and others regularly post new features such as music and games on the Web, on Facebook pages, on YouTube, and via Twitter links to keep younger visitors returning again and again. For example, Flip-Pal, a small, portable scanning device, advertises on genealogy blogs to reach consumers who are interested in researching their family trees and need a easy way to digitize photos and documents.

New Product Ideas

Often marketers can develop new product and service ideas by uncovering unfulfilled needs of certain lifestyle segments. For example, Japan's NTT DOCOMO recognized that many of its customers are avid travelers who like to try different foods when out of the country. In response to this need, the company developed a smartphone app that can instantly translate any restaurant menu written in Chinese or English to

Japanese.[139] In another example, Canadian company lululemon has built its retail business on yoga-inspired clothing for active, fitness-oriented consumers who want to feel comfortable while they work out in style.[140]

PSYCHOGRAPHICS: COMBINING VALUES, PERSONALITY, AND LIFESTYLES

This chapter opened by observing that psychographic research today combines values, personality, and lifestyle variables. To illustrate this key point, this last section provides a brief description of several psychographic applications in marketing.

VALS™

One of the most widely known psychographic tools is *VALS*, formerly known as *Values and Lifestyles*, and is owned by Strategic Business Insights. VALS analyzes the behavior of U.S. consumers to create segments based on two factors. The first is resources, including income, education, self-confidence, health, eagerness to buy, intelligence, and energy level. The second is primary motivation. Consumers motivated by ideals are guided by intellectual aspects rather than by feelings or other people's opinions. Those who are motivated by achievement base their views on the actions and opinions of others and strive to win their approval. And those who are motivated by self-expression desire social or physical action, variety, activity, and personal challenge.[141]

Combining the resource and motivation variables, VALS has identified eight consumer segments (see Exhibit 14.14). At the low end of the resource hierarchy are the survivors, who have the lowest incomes. Their focus is on meeting basic day-to-day needs; they are not active consumers, so they are not described by a primary motivation. Believers are conservative and motivated by ideals; they have somewhat modest resources and, because they do not change easily, tend to prefer familiar, established products and brands. The other group motivated by ideals is the thinkers, who are mature and well educated and who actively conduct information searches when planning purchases. Thinkers have more resources than believers and are value oriented in their consumption practices, valuing durability over style.

The two achievement-oriented segments are the strivers (who have limited discretionary income yet strive to emulate more successful people) and achievers (who have higher resources, are focused on work and families, and prefer status-symbol products). In the self-expression segment, makers value self-sufficiency, buy basic products, and are focused on family, work, and constructive activities. Experiencers have more resources overall though often less household income than makers, stay active, seek stimulation and novelty, and spend money on socializing and entertainment. Innovators have the greatest resource base, with plenty of self-confidence, high incomes, and education, so they can indulge in all three primary motivations to some extent. These consumers will accept new products and technologies, and they choose upscale offerings reflective of their personal style.

Other Applied Psychographic Research

Although VALS is well-known and widely used, there are other ongoing psychographic surveys. One is the Futures Company's MindBase, a psychographic segmentation system with eight broad segments.[142] Based on attitudes, life-stage data, gender, age, and other inputs, MindBase determines how consumers in each segment behave and why, and then interprets this information for marketing purposes. Consumers in MindBase's "I am at capacity" segment, for instance, have as their motto "Time is of the essence" because they are extremely busy; therefore, this segment values convenience, control, and simplification. Those in the "I am expressive" believe in "carpe diem." They live in the moment and express their personality freely, meaning they value creative and hedonic offerings.

Some researchers question whether psychographic techniques fully capture all the variation in consumers' lifestyles. Rather than relying on the traits measured in the preceding research, one

Exhibit 14.14

VALS American Segments
VALS classifies consumers into eight major segments based on two dimensions: resources (education, income, intelligence, and so on) and primary motivation (ideals, achievement, self-expression), as described in this exhibit. Into which group would you fall? Go to www .strategicbusinessinsights .com/vals and take the VALS survey to find out.

Source: Reprinted with permission from VALS™ Program. SRI Consulting Business Intelligence (SRIC-BI); www.sric-bi.com/VALS.

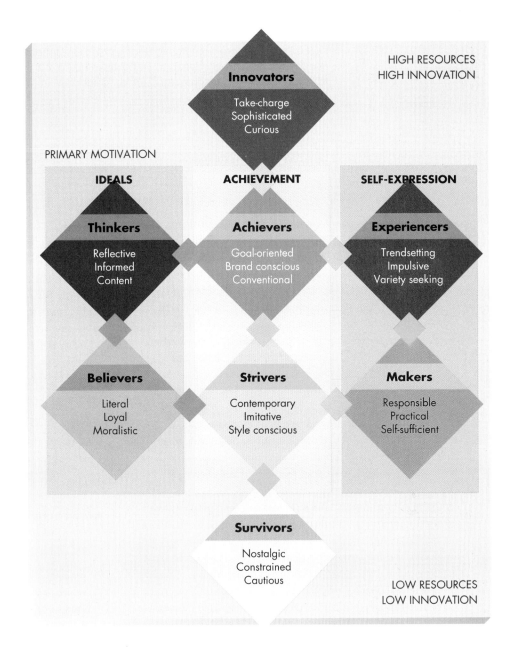

researcher identifies some consumption patterns that do not fit into the VALS framework. These include canonical aesthetics (which relates to traditional Western thought and artistic tastes), nurturing mother (in which consumption centers on the home and child-care), and Jeffersonian America (related to the styles and traditions of a pastoral United States).[143] Another researcher warns that segments can shift with societal changes, economic changes, technological changes, and competitive changes.[144]

Marketing Implications

Marketers use tools such as VALS and other psychographic applications for market segmentation, new product and promotion ideas, and ad development. One area being pursued is methodology for analyzing social media interactions for more precise targeting, message development, and media selection according to individuals' interests and lifestyle activities.[145]

Often, marketers will use psychographic applications in combination with demographic analyses to understand and reach their target markets. This is what Hilton Garden Inn does when it plans its communications and promotional targeting. A recent "Life's Ultimate To-Do List" contest, promoted on the hotel chain's Facebook page, appealed to a target market of experienced, knowledgeable, active travelers in the 30- to 54-year-old age group with a $75,000 household income and a drive to succeed in life. Such promotions support Hilton Garden Inn's advertising slogan, "We Speak Success."[146] _____

SUMMARY

Consumers learn values—enduring beliefs about things that are important—through the processes of socialization and acculturation. Our values exist in an organized value system, in which some are viewed as more important than others. Terminal values are desired end states that guide behavior in many situations, whereas instrumental values help people achieve those desired end states. Domain-specific values are relevant within a given sphere of activity. Marketers use value-based segmentation to identify groups within the larger market that share a common set of values that differ from those of other groups. Three methods for identifying value-based segments are inferring values based on the cultural milieu of the group, using the means-end chain analysis, and using questionnaires.

Personality consists of the patterns of behaviors, tendencies, and personal dispositions that make people different from one another. Approaches to the study of personality include (1) the psychoanalytic approach, which sees personality as the result of unconscious struggles to complete key stages of development; (2) trait theories, which attempt to identify a set of personality characteristics that describe and differentiate individuals; (3) phenomenological approaches, which propose that personality is shaped by an individual's interpretation of life events; (4) social-psychological theories, which focus on the ways that individuals act in social situations; and (5) behavioral approaches, which view personality in terms of behavioral responses to past rewards and punishments.

Marketers are also interested in examining lifestyles, which are patterns of behavior or activities, interests, and opinions, for additional insight into consumer behavior. Finally, some marketing researchers use psychographic techniques involving values, personality, and lifestyles to predict consumer behavior.

Questions for Review and Discussion

1. Explain the differences among global values, terminal values, instrumental values, and domain-specific values.

2. What are the four main value dimensions along which national cultures can vary?

3. How do marketers use means-end chain analysis, the Rokeach Value Survey, and the List of Values?

4. What are three personality traits which affect consumer behavior?

5. How does the locus of control affect personality?

6. What are the three components of a consumer's lifestyle?

7. Define *psychographics*, and discuss its use and potential limitations.

CONSUMER BEHAVIOR CASE

Earache Treatment, Aisle 3: The Rise of Retail Walk-In Clinics

Thousands of retailers across America will soon feature walk-in clinics to accommodate people who need to shop and want to get a flu shot or have an achy ear inspected on the same shopping trip. Nights, weekends, holidays, or almost any time, consumers with minor medical complaints are already stopping into local store's walk-in clinics for quick, convenient, affordable care,

filling an important gap between getting urgent care at the hospital emergency room and a scheduled visit to the doctor for in-depth consultation. Many of these stores also have on-site pharmacies, an added convenience for clinic patients who must fill a prescription right away.

Some consumers choose the walk-in clinics because their lives are so hectic that they can't see a doctor during regular office hours. "It works for parents with that little one with an ear infection the day before Christmas," says a nurse practitioner who works in a MinuteClinic located inside a New England CVS Pharmacy. Others have no regular doctor or prefer to visit a walk-in clinic rather than waiting in a crowded doctor's office or going to the emergency room to have a sore throat checked. "Access to health care is key," explains an official at Take Care Health Systems, which runs 350 walk-in clinics located in Walgreens drug stores. "Over 40 percent of our patients tell us that if it weren't for our clinics, they would go to the emergency room, urgent care clinic, or wouldn't seek treatment."

Today, about 1,500 clinics are located inside U.S. stores of all kinds; within five years, as many as 4,000 may be operating inside stores, taking advantage of the built-in customer base and good retail locations. Two companies—MinuteClinics that serve CVS stores and Take Care Health System clinics that serve Walgreens stores—account for three-quarters of the U.S. walk-in medical market. CVS plans to open 500 additional clinics during the next few years, even as Walmart moves to aggressively expand its network of walk-in, quick-service clinics, all operated by outside health-care providers.

Grocery retailers are also offering walk-in clinics as an extra convenience for their shoppers. For example, at the Giant Eagle supermarket in Lyndhurst, Ohio, the FastCare Clinic operated by University Hospitals is open seven days a week to treat routine illnesses and administer vaccines. Appointments are available, but if consumers walk in and find a line, they can take a vibrating pager and continue shopping until the clinic signals that it's their turn for medical treatment. If the patient usually sees a doctor affiliated with University Hospitals, clinic personnel update the electronic medical records and send them to the doctor immediately after the visit.

One big reason for the growing popularity of walk-in clinics is the lower cost: Consumers pay significantly less than they would pay at the doctor's office or the emergency room. Walk-in clinics treat only a limited range of ailments and refer more serious cases to a doctor or hospital. Although some clinics are staffed by doctors, most are staffed by nurse practitioners or physician's assistants. Other trends affecting demand for walk-in clinic treatment are a looming shortage of primary-care doctors and ongoing legislative changes that affect the nation's health-care system. All of this means that soon an even higher number of consumers could find themselves shopping for earrings in aisle 2 and then choose to have an earache or bug bite checked in aisle 3 at the in-store clinic.[147]

CASE QUESTIONS

1. How are retailers using in-store clinics in their marketing to consumers on the basis of lifestyle?
2. What consumer values are represented by the growth in demand for in-store medical clinics during recent years?
3. Develop a means-end chain for an in-store medical clinic. What attributes are associated with the values you have identified?
4. How might personality characteristics such as dogmatism and frugality apply to consumers' interest in and use of in-store medical clinics?

ENDNOTES

1. Jason W. Lloren, "Website Lets Customers Do the Designing," *San Francisco Chronicle*, February 21, 2011, p. D1; Ryan Underwood, "Clicks from Round the World," *Inc.*, December 2010, p. 146; and Jill Duffy, "Zazzle," *PC Magazine*, November 10, 2011, www.pcmag.com.
2. Milton Rokeach, *The Nature of Human Values* (New York: Free Press, 1973), p. 5.
3. Wagner A. Kamakura and Jose Alfonso Mazzon, "Value Segmentation," *Journal of Consumer Research*, September 1991, pp. 208–218; see also Milton Rokeach and Sandra J. Ball-Rokeach, "Stability and Change in American Value Priorities, 1968–1981," *American Psychologist*, May 1989, pp. 775–784; Milton Rokeach, *Understanding Human Values* (New York: Free Press, 1979); and Shalom H. Schwartz and Wolfgang Bilsky, "Toward a Universal Psychological Structure of Human Values," *Journal of Personality and Social Psychology*, September 1987, pp. 550–562.
4. Kim A. Nelson, "Consumer Decision Making and Image Theory," *Journal of Consumer Psychology* 14, no. 1/2, 2004, pp. 28–40.
5. Francesco M. Nicosia and Robert N. Mayer, "Toward a Sociology of Consumption," *Journal of Consumer Research*, September 1976, pp. 65–75; and Hugh E. Kramer, "The Value of Higher Education and Its Impact on Value Formation," in eds. Robert E. Pitts and Arch G. Woodside, *Personal Values and Consumer Psychology* (Lexington, Mass.: Lexington Books, 1984), pp. 239–251.
6. Mary Gilly and Lisa Penaloza, "Barriers and Incentives in Consumer Acculturation," in eds. W. Fred van Raaij and Gary J. Bamossy, *European Advances in Consumer Research*, vol. 1 (Provo, Utah: Association for Consumer Research, 1993), pp. 278–286.

7. Rokeach, *The Nature of Human Values*; and Schwartz and Bilsky, "Toward a Universal Psychological Structure of Human Values."

8. Russell W. Belk, "Materialism: Trait Aspects of Living in the Material World," *Journal of Consumer Research*, December 1985, pp. 265–280; and Russell W. Belk, "Three Scales to Measure Constructs Related to Materialism," in ed. Thomas P. Kinnear, *Advances in Consumer Research*, vol. 11 (Provo, Utah: Association for Consumer Research, 1984), pp. 291–297.

9. Marsha L. Richins, "Special Possessions and the Expression of Material Values," *Journal of Consumer Research*, December 1994, pp. 522–533.

10. James A. Roberts, John F. Tanner Jr., and Chris Manolis, "Materialism and the Family Structure–Stress Relation," *Journal of Consumer Psychology* 15, no. 2, 2005, pp. 183–190.

11. Elizabeth W. Dunn, Daniel T. Gilbert, and Timothy D. Wilson, "If Money Doesn't Make You Happy, Then You Probably Aren't Spending It Right," *Journal of Consumer Psychology* 21, 2011, pp. 115–125; Jennifer L. Aaker, Melanie Rudd, and Cassie Mogilner, "If Money Does Not Make You Happy, Consider Time," *Journal of Consumer Psychology* 21, 2011, pp. 126–130; and Joseph Chancellor and Sonja Lyubomirsky, "Happiness and Thrift: When (Spending) Less Is (Hedonically) More," *Journal of Consumer Psychology* 21, 2011, pp. 131–138.

12. Leonardo Nicolao, Julie R. Irwin, and Joseph K. Goodman, "Happiness for Sale: Do Experiential Purchases Make Consumers Happier than Material Purchases?" *Journal of Consumer Research*, August 2009, pp. 188–198.

13. James E. Burroughs and Aric Rindfleisch, "Materialism and Well-Being," *Journal of Consumer Research*, December 2002, pp. 348–370.

14. Jamie Arndt, Sheldon Solomon, Tim Kasser, and Kennon M. Sheldon, "The Urge to Splurge: A Terror Management Account of Materialism and Consumer Behavior," *Journal of Consumer Psychology* 14, no. 3, 2004, pp. 198–212; Jamie Arndt, Sheldon Solomon, Tim Kasser, and Kennon M. Sheldon, "The Urge to Splurge Revisited," *Journal of Consumer Psychology* 14, no. 3, 2004, pp. 225–229; Durairaj Maheswaran and Nidhi Agrawal, "Motivational and Cultural Variations in Mortality Salience Effects," *Journal of Consumer Psychology* 14, no. 3, 2004, pp. 213–218; and Aric Rindfleisch and James E. Burroughs, "Terrifying Thoughts, Terrible Materialism? Contemplations on a Terror Management Account of Materialism and Consumer Behavior," *Journal of Consumer Psychology* 14, no. 3, 2004, pp. 219–224.

15. Marsha L. Richins and Scott Dawson, "A Consumer Values Orientation for Materialism and Its Measurement," *Journal of Consumer Research*, December 1992, pp. 303–316.

16. Mary Yoko Brannen, "Cross Cultural Materialism: Commodifying Culture in Japan," in eds. Floyd Rudmin and Marsha Richins, *Meaning, Measure, and Morality of Materialism* (Provo, Utah: The Association for Consumer Research, 1992), pp. 167–180; and Dorothy E. Jones, Dorinda Elliott, Edith Terry, Carla A. Robbins, Charles Gaffney, and Bruce Nussbaum, "Capitalism in China," *BusinessWeek*, January 1985, pp. 53–59; see also David K. Tse, Russell W. Belk, and Nan Zhou, "Becoming a Consumer Society: A Longitudinal and Cross-Cultural Content Analysis of Print Ads from Hong Kong, the People's Republic of China, and Taiwan," *Journal of Consumer Research*, March 1989, pp. 457–472.

17. Meg Dupont, "Cocooning Morphs into Hiving," *Hartford Courant*, October 29, 2004, p. H2.

18. "One Third of Americans Regularly Bank Online," *Information Week*, February 19, 2008, www.informationweek.com.

19. "Ikea Ads Home in on Soul Objective," *Marketing Week*, September 20, 2007, p. 12; and Suzanne Vranica, "Ikea to Tug at Heartstrings," *Wall Street Journal*, September 18, 2007, p. B6.

20. John Fetto, "Nowhere to Hide," *American Demographics*, July–August 2002, pp. 12.

21. Robin van Daalen, "Ahold Cuts Costs, Ups Dividend with New Strategy," *Wall Street Journal*, November 21, 2011, www.wsj.com.

22. Michelle Higgins, "To Plug in or Unplug for the Pedicure," *New York Times*, September 16, 2007, sec. 5, p. 6.

23. Elizabeth C. Hirschman, "Men, Dogs, Guns, and Cars," *Journal of Advertising*, Spring 2003, pp. 9–22.

24. Mohan J. Dutta-Bergman and William D. Wells, "The Values and Lifestyles of Idiocentrics and Allocentrics in an Individualist Culture," *Journal of Consumer Psychology*, 12 (3), 2002, pp. 232–242.

25. Sue Shellenbarger, "Technology Is Helping 'Commuter Families' to Stay in Touch," *Wall Street Journal*, February 14, 2001, p. B1.

26. Simon Goodley, "Lego Profits Boosted by Harry Potter Magic," *Guardian (UK)*, March 3, 2011, www.guardian.co.uk.

27. Evelyn Theiss, "Dave's Supermarkets Joins Cleveland Clinic's Healthy Food Program," *Cleveland Plain Dealer*, November 18, 2011, www.cleveland.com.

28. Tiffany Hsu, "Diners to Get More Details to Digest," *Los Angeles Times*, October 26, 2011, www.latimes.com.

29. "U.S. Organic Industry Overview," *Organic Trade Association's Organic Industry Survey*, 2011, www.ota.com.

30. Ashutosh Prasad, Andrei Strijnev, and Qin Zhang, "What Can Grocery Basket Data Tell Us About Health Consciousness?" *International Journal of Research in Marketing* 25, 2008, pp. 301–309.

31. Robert Vosburgh, "Whole Health: Remaking Walk-in Clinics," *Supermarket News*, September 12, 2011, www.supermarketnews.com; and Milt Freudenheim, "Wal-Mart Will Expand In-Store Medical Clinics," *New York Times*, February 7, 2008, p. C4.

32. Tanya Albert Henry, "U.S. Obesity Rate Projected to Reach 50% by 2030," *American Medical News*, September 12, 2011, www.ama-assn.org.amednews.

33. Donna Goodison, "How 'Bout Them Apples?" *Boston Herald*, October 26, 2011, www.bostonherald.com.

34. Jill Wendholt Silva, "The Classic Grilled Cheese Is Trendy Again," *Times Leader (Wilkes-Barre, Pa.)*, October 26, 2011, www.timesleader.com; and Nathan Skid, "Cupcakes Rising," *Crain's Detroit Business*, November 20, 2011, www.crainsdetroit.com.

35. "Häagen Dazs: Coming In from the Cold," *Marketing Week*, April 3, 2008, p. 29; and "Low-Fat Chance," *Advertising Age*, February 19, 2007, p. 14.

36. Raj Raghunathan, Rebecca Walker Naylor, and Wayne D. Hoyer, "The 'Unhealthy = Tasty Intuition' and Its Effects on Taste Inferences, Enjoyment, and Choice of Food Products," *Journal of Marketing* 70, no. 4, 2006, pp. 170–184.

37. Renee Schettler, "America's Artificial Sweetheart," *Washington Post*, February 23, 2005, p. F1.

38. Jack Neff, "Zigging Where Others Zagged, L'Oréal Focuses on U.S., to Beautiful Effect," *Advertising Age*, November 7, 2011, www.adage.com.

39. Kent Grayson and Radan Martinec, "Consumer Perceptions of Iconicity and Indexicality and Their Influence on Assessments of Authentic Market Offerings," *Journal of Consumer Research* 31, no. 2, 2004, pp. 296–312.

40. Craig J. Thompson, Aric Rindfleisch, and Zrsel Zeynep, "Emotional Branding and the Strategic Value of the Doppelganger Brand Image," *Journal of Marketing*, January 2006, pp. 50–64.

41. Gerry Khermouch, "Secret Origins of Authentic Brands," *BEV-NET*, November 14, 2011, www.bevnet.com.

42. Peter Goddard, "Design's in Play in World of Sports," *Toronto Star*, November 6, 2011, www.thestar.com.

43. Mara Lemos Stein, "Talking About Waste with P&G," *Wall Street Journal*, September 12, 2011, www.wsj.com.

44. Paul Keegan, "The Trouble with Green Product Ratings," *Fortune*, July 25, 2011, pp. 130-134.

45. Adam L. Penenberg, "NeuroFocus Uses Neuromarketing to Hack Your Brain," *Fast Company*, August 8, 2011, www.fastcompany.com.

46. Sak Onkvisit and John J. Shaw, *International Marketing: Analysis and Strategy* (Columbus, Ohio: Merrill, 1989), p. 243.

47. Robert Wilk, "INFOPLAN: The New Rich: A Psychographic Approach to Marketing to the Wealthy Japanese Consumer," ESOMAR Conference, Venice, Italy, June 1990, reported in de Mooij and Keegan, *Advertising Worldwide*, pp. 122–129.

48. K. S. Yang, "Expressed Values of Chinese College Students," in eds. K. S. Yang and Y. Y. Li, *Symposium on the Character of the Chinese* (Taipei, Taiwan: Institute of Ethnology Academic Sinica, 1972), pp. 257–312; see also Oliver H. M. Yau, *Consumer Behavior in China: Customer Satisfaction and Cultural Values* (New York: Rutledge, 1994).

49. Alfred S. Boote, cited in Rebecca Piirto, *Beyond Mind Games* (Ithaca, N.Y.: American Demographic Books, 1991).

50. Jan-Benedict E. M. Steenkamp and Martijn G. de Jong, "A Global Investigation into the Constellation of Consumer Attitudes Toward Global and Local Products," *Journal of Marketing*, November 2010, pp. 18–40.

51. Geert Hofstede, "National Cultures in Four Dimensions," *International Studies of Management and Organization*, Spring–Summer 1983, pp. 46–74.

52. Michael Lynn, George M. Zinkhan, and Judy Harris, "Consumer Tipping: A Cross-Country Study," *Journal of Consumer Research*, December 1993, pp. 478–488.

53. Dana L. Alden, Wayne D. Hoyer, and Chol Lee, "Identifying Global and Culture-Specific Dimensions of Humor in Advertising," *Journal of Marketing*, April 1993, pp. 64–75.

54. Douglas B. Holt and Craig J. Thompson, "Man-of-Action Heroes: The Pursuit of Heroic Masculinity in Everyday Consumption," *Journal of Consumer Research* 31, no. 2, 2004, pp. 425–440.

55. Van R. Wood and Roy Howell, "A Note on Hispanic Values and Subcultural Research: An Alternative View," *Journal of the Academy of Marketing Science*, Winter 1991, pp. 61–67; see also Humberto Valencia, "Hispanic Values and Subcultural Research," *Journal of the Academy of Marketing Science*, Winter 1989, pp. 23–28; and Thomas E. Ness and Melvin T. Smith, "Middle-Class Values in Blacks and Whites," in eds. Pitts and Woodside, *Personal Values and Consumer Psychology*, pp. 231–237.

56. "China's Golden Oldies," *Economist*, February 26, 2005, p. 65.

57. Richard P. Coleman, "The Continuing Significance of Social Class to Marketing," *Journal of Consumer Research*, December 1983, pp. 265–280.

58. William Strauss and Neil Howe, "The Cycle of Generations," *American Demographics*, April 1991, pp. 25–33, 52; see also William Strauss and Neil Howe, *Generations: The History of America's Future, 1584 to 2069* (New York: William Morrow, 1992).

59. Sharon Beatty, Lynn R. Kahle, Pamela Homer, and Shekhar Misra, "Alternative Measurement Approaches to Consumer Values: The List of Values and the Rokeach Value Survey," *Psychology and Marketing*, Fall 1985, pp. 181–200.

60. Lynn R. Kahle, *Social Values and Social Change: Adaptation to Life in America* (New York: Praeger, 1983).

61. "Mofcom Inks Deal with Tesco for Sustainable Retail Development," *China Retail News*, May 4, 2011, www.chinaretailnews.com; and Heather Green and Kerry Capell, "Carbon Confusions," *BusinessWeek*, March 17, 2008, pp. 52–55.

62. "Face Value: At the Sharp End," *Economist*, March 3, 2007, p. 73.

63. Raquel Laneri, "Of a Kind," *Forbes*, October 7, 2011, www.forbes.com.

64. Katie Moisse, "Campbell's Panned for Adding Salt to Soups," *ABC News*, July 14, 2011, http://abcnews.go.com.

65. Patricia F. Kennedy, Roger J. Best, and Lynn R. Kahle, "An Alternative Method for Measuring Value-Based Segmentation and Advertisement Positioning," in eds. James H. Leigh and Claude R. Martin Jr., *Current Issues and Research in Advertising*, vol. 11 (Ann Arbor, Mich.: Division of Research, School of Business Administration, University of Michigan, 1988), pp. 139–156; and Daniel L. Sherrell, Joseph F. Hair Jr., and Robert P. Bush, "The Influence of Personal Values on Measures of Advertising Effectiveness," in eds. Pitts and Woodside, *Personal Values and Consumer Psychology*, pp. 169–185.

66. Christine Defever, Mario Pandelaere, and Keith Roe, "Inducing Value-Congruent Behavior Through Advertising and the Moderating Role of Attitudes Toward Advertising," *Journal of Advertising*, Summer 2011, pp. 25–37.

67. Rick Barrett, "Harley Draws on Fan Base for Ad Ideas," *Journal Sentinel (Milwaukee)*, November 9, 2011, www.jsonline.com.

68. Jennifer Leighfield, "Valencia Bus Company Removes 'Explicit' Ads," *Euro Weekly News*, November 2, 2011, www.euroeweeklynews.com.

69. Robert E. Pitts, John K. Wong, and D. Joel Whalen, "Consumers' Evaluative Structures in Two Ethical Situations," *Journal of Business Research*, March 1991, pp. 119–130.

70. Russell W. Belk and Richard W. Pollay, "Materialism and Status Appeals in Japanese and U.S. Print Advertising," *International Marketing Review*, Winter 1985, pp. 38–47; see also Russell W. Belk, Wendy J. Bryce, and Richard W. Pollay, "Advertising Themes and Cultural Values: A Comparison of U.S. and Japanese Advertising," in eds. K. C. Mun and T. S. Chan, *Proceedings of the Inaugural Meeting of the Southeast Asia Region Academy of International Business* (Hong Kong, China: The Chinese University of Hong Kong, 1985), pp. 11–20.

71. Tse, Belk, and Zhou, "Becoming a Consumer Society: A Longitudinal and Cross-Cultural Content Analysis of Print Ads from Hong Kong, the People's Republic of China, and Taiwan."

72. Michael Wines, "Picking Brand Names in China Is a Business Itself," *New York Times*, November 12, 2011, www.nytimes.com.

73. For more on means-end chain analysis, see Beth A. Walker and Jerry C. Olson, "Means-End Chains: Connecting Products with Self," *Journal of Business Research*, March 1991, pp. 111–118; Thomas J. Reynolds and John P. Richon, "Means-End Based Advertising Research: Copy Testing Is Not Strategy Assessment," *Journal of Business Research*, March 1991, pp. 131–142; Jonathan Gutman, "Exploring the Nature of Linkages Between Consequences and Values," *Journal of Business Research*, March 1991, pp. 143–148; Thomas J. Reynolds and Jonathan Gutman, "Laddering Theory, Method, Analysis and Interpretation," *Journal of Advertising Research*, February/March 1988, pp. 11–31; and Thomas J. Reynolds and Jonathan Gutman, "Laddering: Extending the Repertory Grid Methodology to Construct Attribute–Consequence–Value Hierarchies," in eds. Pitts and Woodside, *Personal Values and Consumer Psychology*, pp. 155–167.

74. Dawn R. Deeter-Schmelz and Jane L. Sojka, "Wrestling with American Values," *Journal of Consumer Behavior* 4, no. 2, 2004, pp. 132–143.

75. Thomas J. Reynolds and J. P. Jolly, "Measuring Personal Values," *Journal of Marketing Research*, November 1980, pp. 531–536; Reynolds and Gutman, "Laddering"; and Jonathan Gutman, "A Means-End Model Based on Consumer Categorization Processes," *Journal of Marketing*, Spring 1982, pp. 60–72.

76. T. L. Stanley, "Death of the Sports Car?" *Brandweek*, January 2, 1995, p. 38.

77. Frenkel Ter Hofstede, Jan-Benedict E. M. Steenkamp, and Michel Wedel, "International Market Segmentation Based on Consumer–Product Relations," *Journal of Marketing Research* 36, February 1999, pp. 1–17.

78. Marsha L. Richins, "The Material Values Scale," *Journal of Consumer Research*, June 2004, pp. 209–219.

79. J. Michael Munson and Edward F. McQuarrie, "Shortening the Rokeach Value Survey for Use in Consumer Research," in ed. Michael J. Houston, *Advances in Consumer Research*, vol. 15 (Provo, Utah: Association for Consumer Research, 1988), pp. 381–386.

80. Lynn R. Kahle, Sharon Beatty, and Pamela Homer, "Alternative Measurement Approaches to Consumer Values: The List of Values (LOV) and Values and Life Style (VALS)," *Journal of Consumer Research*, December 1986, pp. 405–409; and Kahle, *Social Values and Social Change: Adaptation to Life in America*.

81. Wagner Kamakura and Thomas P. Novak, "Value-System Segmentation," *Journal of Consumer Research*, June 1992, pp. 119–132.

82. Sigmund Freud, *Collected Papers*, vols. I–V (New York: Basic Books, 1959); Erik Erickson, *Childhood and Society* (New York: Norton, 1963); and Erik Erickson, *Identity: Youth and Crisis* (New York: Norton, 1968).

83. Yumiko Ono, "Marketers Seek the 'Naked' Truth," *Wall Street Journal*, May 30, 1997, pp. B1, B13.

84. Gordon Allport, *Personality: A Psychological Interpretation* (New York: Holt, Rinehart, & Winston, 1937); and Raymond B. Cattell, *The Scientific Analysis of Personality* (Baltimore: Penguin, 1965).

85. Carl G. Jung, *Man and His Symbols* (Garden City, N.Y.: Doubleday, 1964); see also Hans J. Eysenck, "Personality, Stress and Disease," *Psychological Inquiry*, vol. 2, 1991, pp. 221–232.

86. For example, see Lara K. Kammrath, Daniel R. Ames, and Abigail R. Scholer, "Keeping Up with Impressions: Inferential Rules for Impression Change Across the Big Five," *Journal of Experimental Social Psychology* 43, 2007, pp. 450–457; and William Fleeson, "Situation-Based Contingencies Underlying Trait-Content Manifestation in Behavior," *Journal of Personality* 75, no. 4, 2007, pp. 825–862.

87. Carl R. Rogers, "Some Observations on the Organization of Personality," *American Psychologist*, September 1947, pp. 358–368; and George A. Kelly, *The Psychology of Personal Constructs*, vols. 1 and 2 (New York: Norton, 1955).

88. Bernard Weiner, "Attribution in Personality Psychology," in ed. Lawrence A. Pervin, *Handbook of Personality: Theory and Research* (New York: Guilford, 1990), pp. 465–484; and Harold H. Kelly, "The Processes of Causal Attribution," *American Psychologist*, February 1973, pp. 107–128.

89. David Glen Mick and Claus Buhl, "A Meaning-Based Model of Advertising Experiences," *Journal of Consumer Research*, December 1992, pp. 317–338.

90. Karen B. Horney, *Our Inner Conflicts* (New York: Norton, 1945).

91. Joel B. Cohen, "An Interpersonal Orientation to the Study of Consumer Behavior," *Journal of Marketing Research*, August 1967, pp. 270–277; and Jon P. Noerager, "An Assessment of CAD," *Journal of Marketing Research*, February 1979, pp. 53–59.

92. Marsha L. Richins, "An Analysis of Consumer Interaction Styles in the Marketplace," *Journal of Consumer Research*, June 1983, pp. 73–82.

93. Richard P. Bagozzi, Hans Baumgartner, and Youjae Yi, "State Versus Action Orientation and the Theory of Reasoned Action," *Journal of Consumer Research*, March 1992, pp. 505–518; William O. Bearden and Randall L. Rose, "Attention to Social Comparison Information," *Journal of Consumer Research*, March 1990, pp. 461–471; and Bobby J. Calder and Robert E. Burnkrant, "Interpersonal Influence on Consumer Behavior," *Journal of Consumer Research*, December 1979, pp. 29–38.

94. B. F. Skinner, *About Behaviorism* (New York: Knopf, 1974); and B. F. Skinner, *Beyond Freedom and Dignity* (New York: Knopf, 1971).

95. Jacob Jacoby, "Multiple Indicant Approaches for Studying New Product Adopters," *Journal of Applied Psychology*, August 1971, pp. 384–388; and Harold H. Kassarjian, "Personality and Consumer Behavior: A Review," *Journal of Marketing Research*, November 1971, pp. 409–418; see also Harold H. Kassarjian, "Personality: The Longest Fad," in ed. William L. Wilkie, *Advances in Consumer Research*, vol. 6 (Ann Arbor, Mich.: Association for Consumer Research, 1979), pp. 122–124.

96. John L. Lastovicka and Erich A. Joachimsthaler, "Improving the Detection of Personality–Behavior Relationships in Consumer Research," *Journal of Consumer Research*, March 1988, pp. 583–587; and Kathryn E. A. Villani and Yoram Wind, "On the Usage of 'Modified' Personality Trait Measures in Consumer Research," *Journal of Consumer Research*, December 1975, pp. 223–228.

97. William O. Bearden, David M. Hardesty, and Randall L. Rose, "Consumer Self-Confidence," *Journal of Consumer Research* 28, June 2001, pp. 121–134.

98. D. E. Berlyne, *Conflict, Arousal and Curiosity* (New York: McGraw-Hill, 1960); and D. E. Berlyne, "Novelty, Complexity, and Hedonic Value," *Perception and Psychophysics*, November 1970, pp. 279–286.

99. Marvin Zuckerman, *Sensation Seeking: Beyond the Optimal Level of Arousal* (Hillsdale, N.J.: Lawrence Erlbaum, 1979); and Elizabeth C. Hirschman, "Innovativeness, Novelty Seeking, and Consumer Creativity," *Journal of Consumer Research*, December 1980, pp. 283–295.

100. R. A. Mittelstadt, S. L. Grossbart, W. W. Curtis, and S. P. DeVere, "Optimal Stimulation Level and the Adoption Decision Process," *Journal of Consumer Research*, September 1976, pp. 84–94; P. S. Raju, "Optimum Stimulation Level," *Journal of Consumer Research*, December 1980, pp. 272–282; Jan-Benedict E. M. Steenkamp and Hans Baumgartner, "The Role of Optimum Stimulation Level in Exploratory Consumer Behavior," *Journal of Consumer Research*, December 1992, pp. 434–448; and Erich A. Joachimsthaler and John Lastovicka, "Optimal Stimulation Level—Exploratory Behavior Models," *Journal of Consumer Research*, December 1984, pp. 830–835.

101. Leon G. Schiffman, William R. Dillon, and Festus E. Ngumah, "The Influence of Subcultural and Personality Factors on Consumer Acculturation," *Journal of International Business Studies*, Fall 1981, pp. 137–143.

102. Kelly Tepper Tian, William O. Bearden, and Gary L. Hunter, "Consumers' Need for Uniqueness," *Journal of Consumer Research* 28, June 2001, pp. 50–66

103. Itamar Simonson and Stephen M. Nowlis, "The Role of Explanations and Need for Uniqueness in Consumer Decision Making," *Journal of Consumer Research* 27, June 2000, pp. 49–68.

104. Craig J. Thompson and Zeynep Arsel, "The Starbucks Brandscape and Consumers' (Anticorporate) Experiences of Globalization," *Journal of Consumer Research* 31, no. 3, 2004, pp. 631–642.

105. James E. Burroughs and David Glen Mick, "Exploring Antecedents and Consequences of Consumer Creativity in a Problem-Solving Context," *Journal of Consumer Research*, September 2004, pp. 402–411.

106. Ibid.; and Alice M. Isen, "Positive Effect," in eds. Tim Dageleisch and Mick Power, *Handbook of Cognition and Emotion* (New York: Wiley, 1999), pp. 521–539.

107. Stuart Elliott, "A Push to Promote Familiar Brands Online," *New York Times*, November 17, 2011, www.nytimes.com.

108. John T. Cacioppo, Richard E. Petty, and Chuan F. Kao, "The Efficient Assessment of Need for Cognition," *Journal of Personality Assessment*, June 1984, pp. 306–307; Curtis R. Haugtvedt, Richard E. Petty, and John T. Cacioppo, "Need for Cognition and Advertising: Understanding the Role of Personality Variables in Consumer Behavior," *Journal of Consumer Psychology* 1, no. 3, 1992, pp. 239–260; Rajeev Batra and Douglas M. Stayman, "The Role of Mood in Advertising Effectiveness," *Journal of Consumer Research*, September 1990, pp. 203–214; and John T. Cacioppo, Richard E. Petty, and K. Morris, "Effects of Need for Cognition on Message Evaluation, Recall and Persuasion," *Journal of Personality and Social Psychology*, October 1983, pp. 805–818.

109. Susan Powell Mantel and Frank R. Kardes, "The Role of Direction of Comparison, Attribute-Based Processing, and Attitude-Based Processing in Consumer Preference," *Journal of Consumer Research* 25, March 1999, pp. 335–352.

110. William O. Bearden, Richard G. Netemeyer, and Jesse H. Teel, "Measurement of Consumer Susceptibility to Interpersonal Influence," *Journal of Consumer Research*, March 1989, pp. 472–480; and Peter Wright, "Factors Affecting Cognitive Resistance to Ads," *Journal of Marketing Research*, June 1975, pp. 1–9.

111. John L. Lastovicka, Lance A. Bettencourt, Renée Shaw Hughner, and Ronald J. Kuntze, "Lifestyle of the Tight and Frugal," *Journal of Consumer Research* 26, June 1999, pp. 85–98.

112. Terrence H. Witkowski, "World War II Poster Campaigns," *Journal of Advertising*, Spring 2003, pp. 69–82.

113. Matthew Egol, Andrew Clyde, and Kasturi Rangan, "The New Consumer Frugality," *Strategy + Business*, March 15, 2010, www.strategy-business.com.

114. Richard C. Becherer and Lawrence C. Richard, "Self-Monitoring as a Moderating Variable in Consumer Behavior," *Journal of Consumer Research*, December 1978, pp. 159–162; and Mark Snyder and Kenneth G. DeBono, "Appeals to Image and Claims about Quality," *Journal of Personality and Social Psychology*, September 1985, pp. 586–597.

115. Caroline Goukens, Siegried Dewitte, and Luk Warlop, "Me, Myself, and My Choices: The Influence of Private Self-Awareness on Choice," *Journal of Marketing Research*, October 2009, pp. 682–692.

116. Eugenia C. Wu, Keisha M. Cutright, and Gavan J. Fitzsimons, "How Asking 'Who Am I?' Affects What Consumers Buy: The Influence of Self-Discovery on Consumption," *Journal of Marketing Research*, April 2011, pp. 296–307.

117. Dean Peabody, *National Characteristics* (Cambridge, England: Cambridge University Press, 1985); and Allan B. Yates, "Americans, Canadians Similar but Vive La Difference," *Direct Marketing*, October 1985, p. 152.

118. Terry Clark, "International Marketing and National Character: A Review and Proposal for an Integrative Theory," *Journal of Marketing*, October 1990, pp. 66–79.

119. Adam Wooten, "Marketers Beware of Using Animals in International Campaigns," *Deseret News (Salt Lake City)*, September 23, 2011, www.deseretnews.com.

120. John C. Mowen, "Exploring the Trait of Competitiveness and its Consumer Behavior Consequences," *Journal of Consumer Psychology* 14, no. 1/2, 2004, pp. 52–63.

121. Jonah Berger and Morgan Ward, "Subtle Signals of Inconspicuous Consumption, *Journal of Consumer Research*, December 2010, pp. 555–569.

122. Nailya Ordabayeva and Pierre Chandon, "Getting Ahead of the Joneses: When Equality Increases Conspicuous Consumption Among Bottom-Tier Consumers," *Journal of Consumer Research*, June 2011, pp. 27–41.

123. "Social Media: PepsiCo and Unilever Aim to Connect with Consumers," *Just-Food*, June 30, 2011, www.just-food.com.

124. Zachary Sniderman, "L.A. Kings Are First Pro Sports Team to Get Gamified," *Mashable*, October 20, 2011, www.mashable.com.

125. David Crockett, "The Role of Normative Political Ideology in Consumer Behavior," *Journal of Consumer Research* 31, no. 3, 2004, pp. 511–528.

126. Morris B. Holbrook, "Nostalgia and Consumption Preferences," *Journal of Consumer Research*, September 1993, pp. 245–256.

127. Sandra Yin, "Going to Extremes," *American Demographics*, June 1, 2001, p. 26.

128. Egle Juozenaite, "A Rushed World Reconsiders Its Food," *Baltic Times*, November 3, 2011, www.baltictimes.com.

129. Onkvisit and Shaw, *International Marketing: Analysis and Strategy*, p. 283.

130. Leonidas C. Leonidou, "Understanding the Russian Consumer," *Marketing and Research Today*, March 1992, pp. 75–83.

131. Wendy Koch, "Why Are We Obsessed with Stuff and More Stuff?" *USA Today*, March 24, 2010, www.usatoday.com; and Wendy Koch, "Getting to the Heart of 'Simple Living,'" *USA Today*, June 2, 2010, www.usatoday.com.

132. See Leonard L. Berry, Kathleen Seiders, and Dhruv Grewal, "Understanding Service Convenience," *Journal of Marketing Research*, July 2002, pp. 1–17.

133. Sara Tambascio, "Refreshing the Bulb Market with Dig, Drop, Done," *Today's Garden Center*, July 2011, www.todaysgardencenter.com.

134. Joann Muller, "Ford's Zipcar Deal Is a Clever Marketing Move," *Forbes*, August 31, 2011, www.forbes.com.

135. Jerri Stroud, "'Bankers' Hours' Now Include Evenings and Sundays," *St. Louis Post-Dispatch*, September 4, 2007, n.p.

136. "SC First Bank Mulls 24-Hour Service Branches," *Korea Herald*, November 4, 2011, www.koreaherald.com.

137. Basil G. Englis and Michael R. Solomon, "To Be and Not to Be: Life Style Imagery, Reference Groups, and the Clustering of America," *Journal of Advertising*, Spring 1995, pp. 13–28.

138. Katherine Rosman, "Buy This Lifestyle, Furniture Included," *Wall Street Journal*, November 23, 2011, www.wsj.com.

139. "'Smart' Apps Becoming Lifestyle Game-Changer," *Japan Times*, November 25, 2011, www.japantimes.co.jp.

140. Timothy Taylor, "CEO of the Year: Christine Day of Lululemon," *Globe and Mail (Canada)*, November 24, 2011, www .theglobeandmail.com.

141. Strategic Business Insights, www.strategicbusinessinsights.com/vals.

142. "Who Will Buy and Why? MindBase," The Futures Company, 2010, www.thefuturescompany.com/page/MindBase.

143. Douglas B. Holt, "Poststructuralist Lifestyle Analysis," *Journal of Consumer Research*, March 1997, pp. 326–350.

144. Marvin Shoenwald, "Psychographic Segmentation: Used or Abused?" *Brandweek*, January 22, 2001, p. 34.

145. See, for example, Michael Learmonth, "Penry Price: Why Social Is the Next Frontier of Ad Targeting," *Advertising Age*, June 23, 2011, www.adage.com.

146. Tanya Irwin, "Hilton Garden Inn Launches 'To-Do List' Contest," *Mediapost*, August 9, 2011, www.mediapost.com.

147. Laura Landro, "Informed Patient: Hospital Systems Move into the Walk-In Market," *Wall Street Journal*, November 22, 2011, www.wsj.com; Laura Landro, "At the Mall: New Clinics Let Patients Skip the ER," *Wall Street Journal*, November 22, 2011, www.wsj.com; Julie Appleby and Sarah Varney, "Wal-Mart Plans Ambitious Expansion into Medical Care," *National Public Radio*, November 9, 2011, www.npr.org; Priyanka Dayal; "Walk-in Non-emergency Clinics on the Rise," *Worcester Telegram & Gazette (MA)*, October 30, 2011, www .telegram.com; Janet Cho, "Giant Eagle Adds Walk-In Clinics Staffed by University Hospital Nurse Practitioners," *Cleveland Plain Dealer*, May 6, 2010, www.cleveland.com; and "Buy Health Care at the Store?" *MSN Money*, March 18, 2011, http://money.msn.com.

Consumer Behavior Outcomes and Issues

PART 5

15 Innovations: Adoption, Resistance, and Diffusion   414

16 Symbolic Consumer Behavior   442

17 Marketing, Ethics, and Social Responsibility in Today's Consumer Society   472

PART FIVE EXAMINES key issues related to the influences, processes, and outcomes that were examined in Parts Two, Three, and Four. Chapter 15 builds on the topics of decision making and group processes by exploring how consumers adopt innovative offerings and how their adoption decisions affect the spread (diffusion) of a new offering through a market. This chapter also looks at factors that make a difference in consumers' resistance to an innovation, an adoption of an innovation, and the diffusion of an offering through a marketplace.

Chapter 16 discusses the fascinating topic of symbolic consumer behavior. Both goods and services can have deeply felt and significant meanings for consumers. These meanings may be affected by rituals related to acquisition, ownership, use, and disposal. Moreover, the meaning of an offering can be transferred through gift giving.

Chapter 17 examines the role of ethics and social responsibility in marketing. It also looks at positive and negative aspects of consumer behavior and marketing, including problematic behaviors such as compulsive buying and productive behaviors such as consumer-led marketing efforts to benefit charities.

THE CONSUMER'S CULTURE

Consumer Diversity (Ch. 12)

Household and Social Class Influences (Ch. 13)

Social Influences on Consumer Behavior (Ch. 11)

THE PSYCHOLOGICAL CORE
- **Motivation, Ability, and Opportunity (Ch. 2)**
- **From Exposure to Comprehension (Ch. 3)**
- **Memory and Knowledge (Ch. 4)**
- **Attitude Formation and Change (Chs. 5–6)**

Psychographics: Values, Personality, and Lifestyles (Ch. 14)

THE PROCESS OF MAKING DECISIONS
- Problem Recognition and Information Search (Ch. 7)
- Judgment and Decision Making (Chs. 8–9)
- Post-Decision Processes (Ch. 10)

CONSUMER BEHAVIOR OUTCOMES AND ISSUES
- Innovations: Adoption, Resistance, and Diffusion (Ch. 15)
- Symbolic Consumer Behavior (Ch. 16)
- Marketing, Ethics, and Social Responsibility in Today's Consumer Society (Ch. 17)

© Cengage Learning 2013

413

INNOVATIONS: ADOPTION, RESISTANCE, AND DIFFUSION

After studying this chapter, you will be able to

1. Describe how innovations can be classified in terms of their type, the benefits they offer, and their breadth.

2. Explain how consumers adopt an innovation, why they might resist adoption, and why marketers must understand the timing of adoption decisions.

3. Define diffusion and discuss how diffusion curves relate to the product life cycle.

4. Outline the main factors that affect adoption, resistance, and diffusion, and show how marketers can use their knowledge of these factors to market more effectively.

© Dai Sugano/MCT/Newscom

INTRODUCTION

Will Consumers Pay with Their Phones?

Visa, Google, Verizon, and PayPal—among many other firms—are all competing to provide "mobile wallet" technology that allows consumers to quickly and conveniently pay for purchases via smartphone. But why pay by phone? "People's phones are closer to their hands than their wallets most of the time," explains a Visa executive. This mobile wallet concept is still so novel that each company utilizes different concepts and no one technology has yet won out over the others. For example, Google Wallet stores the consumer's credit card number on the phone and transmits it when the phone is tapped against a wireless reader at the point of purchase. On the other hand, PayPal's system, which runs through an app, offers consumers the unique ability to choose from multiple payment options (credit, debit, PayPal account, store gift card) even *after* the purchase.

Mobile-banking or *m-banking* is expected to grow enormously across the world. It includes all kind of banking services conducted via smartphones, such as mobile billing and Web payments. It can provide consumers with immediate feedback about their credit status and provide SMS information, such as promotional offers or any fraudulent activity with the account. In Japan, millions of consumers already use NTT DOCOMO's mobile wallet system, and a group of telecommunications is operating a mobile wallet program in Germany. U.S. consumers, however, have generally been slow to embrace this payment innovation. One reason is that some mobile wallet systems require a special phone chip. Another reason is that not every store and restaurant is equipped to accept mobile wallet payments. Security is also a concern, which is why Google Wallet requires users to enter a PIN code for every purchase. And consumers have an ever-increasing number of mobile payment options from which to choose. Starbucks, for instance, has a proprietary app for consumers who want to pay via mobile at its U.S. and U.K. cafes. But how many consumers will choose to pay with their phones, and how soon?[1]

The question of whether and when consumers will use mobile wallets illustrates some of the factors that influence consumers' decisions about innovative offerings, the subject of this chapter (see Exhibit 15.1). First, the chapter describes types of innovations, which can vary in both novelty and benefits, the way PayPal's mobile wallet system differs from that of Google Wallet. Next, we examine what affects whether consumers will resist a new product or adopt it. (Why have Japanese consumers enthusiastically embraced mobile wallets, while U.S. consumers have been more hesitant?) The final section examines the factors affecting how quickly a new product spreads, or diffuses, through a market.

INNOVATIONS

The ability to develop successful new products is critical to a company's sales, future growth, and long-term survival potential. Selling nearly one million iPad2 tablet computers during the product's launch weekend not only boosted Apple's profits but also riveted media attention on the company's innovations and reinforced the brand's market dominance.[2] Innovation is so important to the future of the food company Nestlé that the top management team receives monthly reports on the 10 most promising products in development.[3] Given the role that new products play in a company's sales and profitability, it is vital for marketers to understand new products and what drives their success in the market.

Defining an Innovation

Innovation An offering that is perceived as new by consumers within a market segment and that has an effect on existing consumption patterns.

A new product, or an **innovation**, is an offering that is new to the marketplace. More formally, an innovation is any product, service, attribute, or idea that consumers within a market segment perceive as new and that has an effect on existing consumption patterns.[4] Services such as movie downloads and identity fraud insurance can be innovations, as can ideas. For example, social marketers have been active in persuading consumers to adopt such ideas as practicing safe sex and preventing bullying.

Products, services, attributes, packages, and ideas are innovations if they are *perceived* as being new by consumers, whether or not they actually are new. On the other hand, although products can be marketed as new offerings, they can fail if consumers do not view them as providing any unique benefits.[5] Marketers also define an *innovation* with respect to a market segment. Consumers in developing countries may regard certain appliances and electronic gadgets as entirely new, even though Americans and consumers in other Western countries regard these items as near necessities. On the other hand, U.S. and European consumers may consider something to be new which has been available to consumers in developing countries for some time, such as the ability to complete cash transactions via cell phones, already available in many African countries, India, and other developing countries.[6]

THE CONSUMER'S CULTURE

Consumer Diversity (Ch. 12)

Household and Social Class Influences (Ch. 13)

Social Influences on Consumer Behavior (Ch. 11)

Psychographics: Values, Personality, and Lifestyles (Ch. 14)

THE PSYCHOLOGICAL CORE
- Motivation, Ability, and Opportunity (Ch. 2)
- From Exposure to Comprehension (Ch. 3)
- Memory and Knowledge (Ch. 4)
- Attitude Formation and Change (Chs. 5–6)

THE PROCESS OF MAKING DECISIONS
- Problem Recognition and Information Search (Ch. 7)
- Judgment and Decision Making (Chs. 8–9)
- Post-Decision Processes (Ch. 10)

CONSUMER BEHAVIOR OUTCOMES AND ISSUES
- **Innovations: Adoption, Resistance, and Diffusion (Ch. 15)**
- Symbolic Consumer Behavior (Ch. 16)
- Marketing, Ethics, and Social Responsibility in Today's Consumer Society (Ch. 17)

| INNOVATIONS | ADOPTION OR RESISTANCE | DIFFUSION |

FACTORS AFFECTING ADOPTION, RESISTANCE, AND DIFFUSION
- Perceived value
- Uncertainty
- Consumer learning requirements
- Social relevance
- Legitimacy and adaptability
- Social factors

© Cengage Learning 2013

Exhibit 15.1

Chapter Overview: Innovations: Adoption, Resistance, and Diffusion

Consumers may decide to adopt (e.g., purchase) or resist adopting a new offering (an innovation). Diffusion reflects how fast an innovation spreads through a market. Adoption, resistance, and diffusion can be influenced by the type of innovation, its breadth, its characteristics, and the social system into which it is introduced.

Innovations can bring about changes in acquisition, consumption, and disposition patterns. Microwave ovens have changed the way we cook; e-mail and text messaging have changed the way we communicate; digital cameras and camera phones have changed the way we take photographs and share them with others. Increased attention to recycling has brought about innovations such as recyclable and reusable packaging. Finally, online sites such as eBay, craigslist, and Freecycle provide innovative ways for consumers to dispose of unwanted items.

Marketers classify innovations in three main ways: in terms of (1) the innovation's type (2) the type of benefits it offers, and (3) its breadth. In addition, consumers are increasingly involved in the innovation process, via cocreation.

Innovations Characterized by Degree of Novelty

One way to characterize innovations is to describe the degree of change that they create in our consumption patterns.[7]

Continuous innovation
An innovation that has a limited effect on existing consumption patterns.

▶   **Continuous innovations** have a limited effect on existing consumption patterns; the innovation is used in much the same way as the products that came before it. Not surprisingly, most new products are continuous innovations.

Dynamically continuous innovation An innovation that has a pronounced effect on consumption practices and often involves a new technology.

▶   **Dynamically continuous innovations** have a pronounced effect on consumption practices. Often these innovations incorporate a new technology. Pocket-size video cameras such as the Flip were dynamically continuous innovations when first introduced because they changed the way that consumers took, stored, and shared videos. Having revolutionized the camcorder business, the Flip was discontinued only a few years later, due to the widespread availability of smartphones and digital cameras that double as handy video cameras.[8]

Discontinuous innovation An offering that is so new that we have never known anything like it before.

▶   **Discontinuous innovations** are so new that we have never known anything like it before.[9] Airplanes and Internet service were once discontinuous innovations that radically changed consumer behavior. Like dynamically continuous innovations, discontinuous innovations often spawn a host of peripheral products and associated innovations. For example, after microwave ovens were introduced, marketers began offering new pans, temperature probes, food products, and cookbooks tailored specifically for microwave cooking. Campbell's microwavable Soup at Hand, for example, allows people to enjoy soup while away from home, which changes how, when, and where soup is eaten.

Based on these three broad innovation types—continuous, dynamically continuous, and discontinuous—innovations can be characterized more specifically according to their degree of novelty on a continuum of newness (see Exhibit 15.2).

High	Moderate	Low

Behavioral Change Required

Discontinuous	Dynamically Continuous	Continuous
Computer	• Personal computer • Laptop computer • Notebook computer • Tablet computer	• Tablet with e-book reader • Tablet with in-cloud data storage • Tablet with front/rear digital and video cameras

© Cengage Learning 2013

Exhibit 15.2

The Innovation Continuum

Innovations vary in how much behavioral change they require on the part of consumers. Discontinuous innovations (products that are radically new when they are first introduced) require considerable change in consumption patterns, whereas continuous innovations (often extensions of existing products) require very little change.

Innovations Characterized by Benefits Offered

In addition to their degree of novelty, innovations can be characterized by the type of benefits that they offer.

Functional innovation A new product, service, attribute, or idea that has utilitarian benefits that are different from or better than those of alternatives.

Hedonic or aesthetic innovation An innovation that appeals to our aesthetic, pleasure-seeking, and/or sensory needs.

Symbolic innovation A product, service, attribute, or idea that has new social meaning.

▶ **Functional innovations** offer functional performance benefits that are better than those provided by existing alternatives. For example, hybrid vehicles are more fuel-efficient than traditional gasoline-powered vehicles, a functional performance benefit that saves consumers money on fuel costs and reduces pollution at the same time. Functional innovations often rely on new technology that makes the product better than existing alternatives.

▶ **Hedonic or aesthetic innovations** appeal to our aesthetic, pleasure-seeking, and/or sensory needs.[10] New forms of dance or exercise, new types of music, new clothing styles, and new types of food all qualify as hedonic or aesthetic innovations. Hedonic innovations are a point of differentiation and also affect consumers' processing of feature performance. Interestingly, consumers may sometimes exhibit a bias in favor of aesthetically less appealing products because they are stimulated to elaborate on the contrast between the look of the product and information about its performance.[11]

▶ **Symbolic innovations** have new social meanings carried by their use and ownership. In some cases, a symbolic innovation is a new offering that is used exclusively by a particular group of consumers. Using the innovation, therefore, conveys meaning about a consumer's group membership. New styles of clothing that convey membership in a particular ethnic, age, or gender group may be regarded as symbolic innovations. In some cases, it is the meaning of the product and not the product itself that is new. For example, although condoms have been around for a long time, their meaning is now couched in terms of preventing the spread of AIDS or STDs as opposed to controlling conception. Earrings, once worn by women, are now fashionable for men as well. Finally, tattoos, once a symbol of machismo, have gained wide appeal and have different meanings among various consumer groups.

Many new products represent blends of innovation types. Nutrition bars are designed to offer the functional benefits of protein and vitamins, with the hedonic benefit of good taste, and the social meanings of being health conscious.

Innovations Characterized by Breadth

Innovations can also be characterized in terms of their *breadth*, or the range of new and different uses for a particular product. (see Exhibit 15.3) Baking soda, for example, has enjoyed a long life in part because it has innovation breadth; it has been used as a baking ingredient, a tooth polisher, a carpet deodorizer, and a refrigerator deodorizer. Teflon, originally developed to keep food from sticking to cookware, is now used in oven mitts, men's clothing (to help repel stains caused by spills), snow shovels (so snow will slide off the shovel), and many other products. The cell phone became the personal organizer, camera, global positioning system, and central device for socializing.

Innovations and Cocreation

Traditionally, companies have controlled the innovation process, developing new offerings based on detailed knowledge of their customers' needs and purchasing patterns, specific customer requests, new technology, and similar market inputs.[12] Today, however, many companies are pursuing innovations via

Exhibit 15.3

Innovations and Cocreation
Nivea used cocreation to create a new product in their line—deodarant.

Image Courtesy of The Advertising Archives

Cocreation Actively involving consumers in creating value through participation in new product development, among other marketing activities.

cocreation, actively involving consumers in creating value through participation in new product development, among other marketing activities. Consumers who get involved enjoy the cocreation experience and get satisfaction from seeing some of these ideas transformed into innovative products.[13] From the company's perspective, it is particularly useful to involve consumers who are capable of imagining how a product concept might be developed for the mainstream marketplace.[14]

The Internet and social media have accelerated the cocreation trend by providing convenient, accessible forums for interaction between marketers and consumers. One way consumers may become involved is by submitting new product ideas and voting on other consumers' ideas. Dell set up the site ideastorm.com just for this purpose; its most active consumer participants have suggested more than 200 ideas each and voted on thousands of other ideas.

Potential benefits of cocreation include:[15]

▶ Innovations that spring from cocreation are likely to better fit consumer needs.

▶ Gathering ideas from consumers via social media or a website is relatively fast and inexpensive.

▶ Involving consumers in cocreation strengthens the relationship with the company.

▶ Consumers who are involved in selecting the products to be marketed exhibit higher demand for them, because they feel a sense of psychological ownership.[16]

Marketing Implications

Cocreation is increasingly popular and is now used in a wide variety of industries. Nivea, for example, recently used cocreation to develop a new deodorant product, and it is involving consumers in other innovation projects, as well.[17] Dell, best known for its computers, has refined the site ideastorm.com since its launch in 2007, enhancing the transparency of the process so that consumers know what is happening to every idea, from company review and posting for votes to acceptance and implementation in the form of a new or improved product. Consumer votes help Dell determine which ideas are the most popular, although the company's business criteria must be met before any ideas are implemented.

Despite the benefits, marketers that employ cocreation must deal with concerns such as the secrecy of new product ideas and the challenges of developing an idea into a commercially feasible innovation. They also must attract, retain, and motivate a community of consumers to participate in cocreation.[18]

RESISTANCE VERSUS ADOPTION

Adoption A purchase of an innovation by an individual consumer or household.

Because the success of their new offerings is so important to companies, marketers need to understand how a consumer or household chooses to buy or adopt an innovation. Initially, marketers are interested in learning whether consumers would even consider the **adoption** of an innovation or whether they would choose to resist buying it. Marketers also want to know how consumers adopt products and how they decide whether to buy an innovation. Finally, marketers are interested in learning when a consumer would buy an innovation in relation to when other consumers would purchase it.

Whether Consumers Adopt an Innovation

Resistance A desire not to buy the innovation, even in the face of pressure to do so.

Adoption will take place only if consumers do not resist the innovation. Consumers who resist an innovation choose not to buy it, even in the face of pressure to do so.[19] Consumers sometimes resist adopting an innovation because it is simpler or seems preferable for them to continue using a more familiar product or service. **Resistance** may also be high if consumers think that using the new product would involve some risk. Lengthy battles between incompatible technology standards, for instance, affected adoption of products such as DVD players.[20]

Exhibit 15.4

Eight Central Paradoxes of Technological Products
Consumers sometimes have mixed reactions to technologies because they create some of the paradoxes noted here. When the negative sides of these paradoxes are salient, consumers will likely resist an innovation.

Source: From David Glen Mick and Susan Fournier, "Paradoxes of Technology: Consumer Cognizance, Emotions, and Coping Strategies," *Journal of Consumer Research* 25, September 1998, p. 126. Reprinted with permission of The University of Chicago Press.

Paradox	Description
Control/chaos	Technology can facilitate regulation or order, and technology can lead to upheaval or disorder.
Freedom/enslavement	Technology can facilitate independence or fewer restrictions, and technology can lead to dependence or more restrictions.
New/obsolete	New technologies provide the user with the most recently developed benefits of scientific knowledge, and new technologies are already or soon to be outmoded as they reach the marketplace.
Competence/incompetence	Technology can facilitate feelings of intelligence or efficacy, and technology can lead to feelings of ignorance or ineptitude.
Efficiency/inefficiency	Technology can facilitate less effort or time spent in certain activities, and technology can lead to more effort or time spent in certain activities.
Fulfills/creates needs	Technology can facilitate the fulfillment of needs or desires, and technology can lead to the development or awareness of needs or desires previously unrealized.
Assimilation/isolation	Technology can facilitate human togetherness, and technology can lead to human separation.
Engaging/disengaging	Technology can facilitate involvement, flow, or activity, and technology can lead to disconnection, disruption, or passivity.

Exhibit 15.4 shows that consumers often resist new technologies until they perceive that the negative effects from having to deal with something new are outweighed by the positive effects the new product might bring.[21] Research also indicates that consumers with low needs for change and cognition are most likely to resist innovations, whereas consumers with high needs for change and cognition are least likely to resist them.[22] Moreover, when consumers identify with a brand, they will resist switching to a new innovation marketed under a different brand.[23]

Note that resistance and adoption are separate concepts. An individual can resist purchasing an innovation without ever progressing to the point of adoption. If an individual does adopt a product, he or she has presumably overcome any resistance to purchasing that might have existed initially. Marketers have to understand whether, why, and when consumers resist innovations—because the product will fail if resistance is too high. Typically, marketers can use a number of tactics to reduce consumers' resistance to an innovation. As discussed later in this chapter, the characteristics of the innovation, the social system in which the consumers operate, and marketing tactics all influence consumers' resistance to innovations.

How Consumers Adopt an Innovation

Whether consumers choose to adopt or resist an innovation depends, in part, on whether they are prevention- or promotion-focused. Prevention-focused consumers, whose priority is safety and protection, are more likely to resist new offerings because of the perceived risk and uncertainty that new offerings entail.[24] Promotion-focused consumers, whose priority is advancement and growth, are more likely to adopt new offerings, at least when the risks are not salient.[25]

The way in which consumers adopt innovations can vary, depending on whether the adoption decision is a high- or low-effort one. The **high-effort hierarchy of effects**, illustrated in the top half of Exhibit 15.5, corresponds to the high-effort information search, attitude formation, judgment, and choice processes described in earlier chapters. Here, the consumer becomes aware of an innovation, thinks about it, gathers information about it, and forms an attitude based on this information. If his or her attitude is favorable, the consumer may try the product. If the trial experience is favorable, the consumer may decide to adopt the new product.

High-effort hierarchy of effects A purchase of an innovation based on considerable decision-making effort.

The High-Effort Hierarchy of Effects

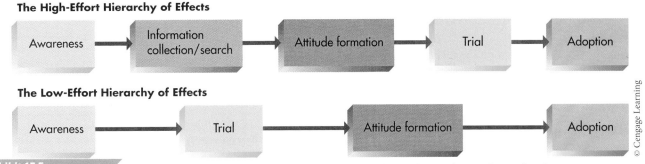

The Low-Effort Hierarchy of Effects

© Cengage Learning

Exhibit 15.5

Adoption Decision Process

The amount of effort we engage in before we decide to adopt an innovation varies. In some cases, we engage in considerable effort (e.g., extensive information search and evaluation of an offering). In other cases, the adoption process involves limited effort. In such cases, we first adopt the innovation and then decide whether we like it.

Consumers' motivation, ability, and opportunity (MAO) determine whether a high-effort adoption process occurs. A high-effort adoption process often takes place when consumers see that the innovation not only has benefits but also incurs psychological, social, economic, financial, or safety risks. For example, the consumer may think that wearing a new style of clothing is socially risky and will wait for others to buy it first. At one time, consumers carefully considered the benefits of buying a DVD player because of the high cost of replacing an entire collection of videotapes with DVDs. These days, DVD sales are decreasing as consumers adopt Internet-capable gadgets they can use to stream movies and TV shows from online sources such as Netflix.[26] A consumer may consider buying an e-book reader but may worry about having to get rid of all the regular printed books.

Consumers are more likely to follow a high-effort decision-making process when the innovation is discontinuous (as opposed to continuous) because they know less about the innovation and must learn about it. Novice consumers need more information before they can understand and appreciate the benefits of a discontinuous innovation.[27] Also, a high-effort adoption process may be used when many people are involved in the decision, as in a family or an organization.[28]

When the new product involves less risk (as might be the case with a continuous innovation) and when fewer people are involved in the buying process, decision making may follow the low-effort hierarchy of effects illustrated in the bottom half of Exhibit 15.5. Here, consumers devote less decision-making effort to considering and researching the product before they try it, and then they form attitudes based on the trial. If their attitudes are positive, they may adopt the innovation. With a low-effort hierarchy of effects, the time between awareness of the innovation and its trial or adoption may be brief.

Marketing Implications

Understanding whether consumers' adoption decisions are based on a high- or low-effort adoption process has important implications for marketers. For example, if the adoption involves low effort, marketers need to do all they can to encourage trial. Because the time between trial and purchase is low, trial may be very effective at encouraging consumers to adopt and buy the product. This is true for free offerings, as well. To illustrate, Google's Wave service, which combined the communication capabilities of e-mail with the immediacy of instant messaging, was launched with much fanfare in 2009. Although Google tried various methods to induce trial, Wave never attracted the many thousands of consumers it was created to serve. The company dropped Wave after two years, saying it "has not seen the user adoption we would have liked."[29]

If the adoption process is a high-effort one, marketers need to do all they can to reduce the perceived risk of adopting the innovation. For example, consumers have largely resisted adopting the Segway, a self-balancing scooter with a top speed of about 13 miles per hour and a maneuverability well suited to paved streets and park paths. Some of this resistance may be due to the high price and some due to concerns about learning to ride safely. Despite high awareness of the product after intense media coverage of its introduction in 2001, relatively few consumers have actually seen or tried riding a Segway. Now, years after its launch, the Segway is most often purchased by travel businesses for use by tour groups and by municipalities for use by police officers on patrol.[30] An initial trial experience of the Segway as part of a tour group may convince consumers to buy one for their own use.

When Consumers Adopt Innovations

Consumers differ in when they adopt an innovation. One framework identifies five adopter groups based on the timing of their adoption decisions, as shown in Exhibit 15.6.[31] The first 2.5 percent of the market to adopt the innovation are described as *innovators*. The next 13.5 percent are called *early adopters*. The next 34 percent are called the *early majority*. The *late majority* represent the next 34 percent of adopters, and the last 16 percent to purchase the product are called *laggards*.

Characteristics of Adopter Groups

The adopter groups tend to exhibit different characteristics, as shown in the exhibit. Research indicates, for example, that innovators who are enthusiastic about technology want to be the first to get a new high-tech product, even if there are a few bugs or inefficiencies.[32] For example, devotees of Apple iPhones and iPads have been known to endure hours of waiting in front of local Apple stores just to be among the first buyers of each new version. Some electronic games inspire similar enthusiasm.

Early adopters are visionaries in the product category. They admire a technologically new product not so much for its features as for its abilities to create a revolutionary breakthrough in how things are done. One research company has suggested that approximately 16 percent of U.S. households are technologically advanced families—early adopters. These families want faster, newer, and more advanced products that help make home and work life more efficient and fun. Although they know that additional products that will follow the new product's introduction will likely be cheaper, faster, and easier to use than the innovation on the market right now, they do not want to wait for the future products. Technologically advanced families tend to be younger and better educated and to have more children than the average U.S. family.[33]

Exhibit 15.6

Profile of Adopter Groups
Researchers have identified five groups of consumers that differ in when they adopt an innovation relative to when others do. Innovators are the first in a market to adopt an innovation, and laggards are the last. Certain characteristics are associated with each adopter group.

Source: Based on *Diffusion of Innovations*, 3rd Edition by Everett M. Rogers. Copyright © 1962, 1971, 1983 by The Free Press. All rights reserved.

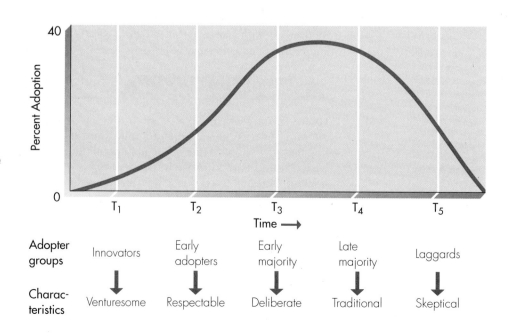

The early majority are pragmatists, seeking innovations that offer incremental, predictable improvements on an existing technology. Because they do not like risk, they care deeply about who is making the innovation and the reputation of the company. They are interested in how well the innovation will fit with their current lifestyle and the products they own now, and they are concerned about the innovation's reliability. They are price sensitive, and they are happy when competitors enter the market because they can then compare features and be more assured about the product's ultimate feasibility.

Late-majority consumers are more conservative, wary of progress, and rely on tradition. They often fear high-tech products, and their goal in buying them is to not get stung. They like to buy preassembled products that include everything in a single, easy-to-use package. Laggards, the slowest group to adopt, are skeptics. Although laggards may resist innovations, marketers can gain insights from understanding why this group is skeptical of an innovation. Why, for example, do some people shun electronic book readers in favor of other methods of acquiring, reading, and storing book and magazine content? Do they fear they will never learn to use the product properly? Are they worried about product reliability or rapid obsolescence? Knowing the answers to these questions can help firms such as Amazon and Barnes & Noble market more effectively to this group. The answers can also help companies develop add-ons to the innovation that would resolve consumers' fears.

Application of Adopter Group Categories

An important implication of adopter groups is that if an innovation is to spread through the market, it must appeal to every group. Unfortunately, many potentially useful innovations have never gained mass-market appeal because the marketing efforts for them did not acknowledge the characteristics of the adopter groups. This result was the case with short-lived products such as the Apple Newton MessagePad and the Flooz system of online buying credits.[34]

The five-category scheme of adopter groups is a useful but somewhat idealized way of looking at who adopts innovations when. That is, there may be more or fewer adopter groups, depending on the innovation.[35] For example, when Vespa scooters became a fashion item in Europe, some early adopters in America imported their own before the product was introduced to the U.S. market. Such consumers could be called "preinnovators," because they adopt the innovation before it is even officially introduced.

Also, the shape of adoption curves may differ from the regular bell-shape, such as the positively skewed shape of fashion adoption curves (steep growth, sometimes with steep declines) or the negatively skewed shape of certain health-related innovations (slow growth, slow decline). Thus, instead of attracting the percentages of adopters that form the bell-shaped curve in Exhibit 15.6, certain products may attract the first 1 percent of adopters as innovators, the next 60 percent as early adopters, the next 30 percent as the early majority, the following 5 percent as the late majority, and the last 4 percent as laggards. It is important that marketers use the idea of adoption groups and adoption curves flexibly, and examine how many groups, of which size, and at what times consumers adopt new products in the specific markets where the company operates. We return to this issue later in the chapter when describing the diffusion of innovations.

Marketing research suggests that it can be useful to examine the rate of use and variety of use to understand how an innovation diffuses through the market.[36] As an example, the use-diffusion model in Exhibit 15.7 identifies specific types of users of home technology such as PCs: intense users (who have many uses for an innovation and show a high rate of use), specialized users (high rate of use but low variety of uses), nonspecialized users (high variety of uses but low rate of use), and limited users (low variety of uses and low rate of use).

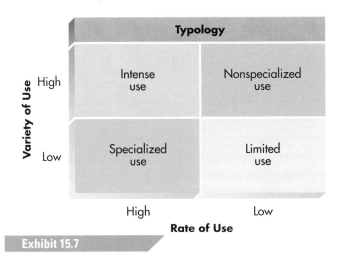

Exhibit 15.7

Use-Diffusion Patterns for Home Technology Innovations
Studying the difference in diffusion and usage patterns of consumers can help marketers to understand the diffusion of innovations.

Source: From R. James H. McAlexander, John W. Schouten, and Harold F. Koenig, "Building Brand Community" *Journal of Marketing* 66, no. 1, January 2004, pp. 38–54. Reprinted with permission of American Marketing Association.

Marketing Implications

Whether or not marketers accept the five-category adopter scheme, they recognize that consumers who are the first to buy a new product are important for several reasons. First, because innovators adopt new products independently of the opinions of other people, they are more likely to be receptive to information about new products, including information provided by marketers. Second, by virtue of their experience with the innovation, they may also communicate information to others and thus exact normative and informational influence through the adoption decisions of others (see Chapter 11). Given these issues, many researchers want to better understand who innovators are and how they can be reached through marketing communications and appropriate media.

Demographics

Several of the demographic variables described in Chapters 12 and 13 have been linked with innovators.[37] For example, innovators tend to be younger, more affluent, and better educated than other consumers; laggards are typically older, have less income and education, and have lower occupational status. Yet, even here, marketers need to be aware that unexpected opportunities may emerge. For example, when the new cholesterol-free Becel margarine targeted to younger consumers was introduced in Europe, older consumers in particular were ready to adopt it early on. Religion is sometimes linked with innovation adoption. Amish consumers, for example, avoid many innovations, including cars, electricity, and telephones.

The general links between these demographic variables and innovativeness make sense. First, highly educated people tend to be heavier users of media and therefore tend to learn about new products earlier than less educated people do. Second, high-income consumers can afford to buy innovations, and they may perceive less financial risk in adopting something new. Demographic variables such as culture of origin have also been linked with innovativeness. Consumers in Japan, for example, are regarded as innovators for new technology. This market was among the first to adopt high-tech offerings such as paying for purchases via smartphone, even as the "mobile wallet" has been slow to catch on elsewhere.[38]

Social Influence

Innovators have been linked with the social influence factors discussed in Chapter 11.[39] They tend to have a great deal of social influence beyond their immediate groups, and they tend to be opinion leaders. Although this finding has not been observed in all research, it makes sense that innovators have influence because their opinions are shared with and respected by nonadopters. Importantly, consumers who participate in a brand community are more likely to adopt a new product marketed by that brand—and to resist adoption of new products from competing brands.[40]

Personality

Several personality characteristics have also been linked with the adoption of innovations.[41] For example, innovators are high in their need for stimulation, are inner directed, and are less dogmatic than other consumers. Still, the relationships between personality traits and innovativeness are not very strong.[42] Innovators also do less planning and deliberate less than other consumers do when making buying decisions.[43]

Therefore, it is better to use a mixed approach to understanding innovativeness. That is, in addition to measuring "innate innovativeness" (as a personality trait that some consumers are high on, across all consumption domains) it is useful to examine consumers' willingness to be innovative in a specific consumption domain. For example, an innovator of alternative music might respond positively to statements like "In general, I am among the first in my circle of friends to download a new alternative-rock song" or "I know the names of new alternative-rock acts before other people do." Innovators in the area of fashion, however, might not respond similarly to these statements.[44] Consumers may be innovators or early adopters in one domain but laggards in another, and some consumers may more generally be ready to adopt innovations.

Cultural Values

Adoption of innovations has been linked with culture of origin and the values tied to the culture. One study of 11 European countries found that innovativeness was associated with cultures that value individualism over collectivism, those that value assertiveness over nurturing, and those that value openness to change over conservatism.[45]

Media Involvement

Innovators have been shown to be heavy media users and to rely extensively on external information.[46] They tend to think of themselves as active seekers and disseminators of information.[47] This finding makes sense because to affect others' adoption decisions, innovators must not only get their information somewhere but also be willing to transmit it.

Usage

Finally, innovators may be heavy users within the product category.[48] Consumers who frequently drink soft drinks may be innovators of new beverages because they are in the market often and hence are likely to notice these new products. In addition, innovators are usually experts in the product category, perhaps because of their heavy media involvement and product usage. ⎯⎯⎯⎯⎯⎯⎯⎯⎯⎯⎯⎯⎯⎯⎯⎯⎯⎯⎯⎯⎯⎯⎯⎯

DIFFUSION

Diffusion The percentage of the population that has adopted an innovation at a specific point in time.

As increasing numbers of consumers in a market adopt an innovation, the innovation spreads or diffuses through the market. While adoption reflects the behavior of an individual, **diffusion** reflects the behavior of the marketplace of consumers as a group. More specifically, diffusion reflects the percentage of the population that has adopted an innovation at a specific point in time. To illustrate, cell phones are used by more than three-quarters of the population in the United States, Argentina, Chile, South Africa, and many European countries.[49]

Because marketers are interested in successfully spreading their offering through a market, they want to understand two important diffusion issues: how an offering diffuses through the market and how quickly it does so.

How Offerings Diffuse Through a Market

One way to examine how offerings spread through a market is to look at the pattern of adoption over time. From the marketers' perspective, life would be easy if everyone adopted the new offering just as soon as it was introduced into the market (assuming sufficient production capacity to meet the demand). However, this occurrence is rarely the case; in fact, several diffusion patterns have been identified.

The S-Shaped Diffusion Curve

S-shaped diffusion curve A diffusion curve characterized by slow initial growth followed by a rapid increase in diffusion.

Some innovations exhibit an **S-shaped diffusion curve**, as shown in Exhibit 15.8(a).[50] Following this pattern, adoption of the products begins relatively slowly; as the exhibit shows, a relatively small percentage of the total market has adopted the product between times 1 and 2 in the exhibit. After a certain period, however, the rate of adoption increases dramatically, with many consumers adopting the product within a relatively short period of time. Between times 2 and 3, a dramatic increase occurs in the number of consumers adopting the product. Then adoptions grow at a decreasing rate, and the curve flattens out.

As an example, the diffusion of electronic book readers was initially very slow. Then it began to increase as more consumers became aware of and knowledgeable about the technology and as a larger number of companies entered the market. As a wider variety of downloadable content (books, magazines, newspapers) became available, and more popularly priced devices were introduced by Amazon, Barnes & Noble, and other firms, millions of consumers decided to buy their first e-book reader. Hybrid gadgets such as the Kindle Fire—a combination e-reader/tablet computer—have been fueling even more rapid diffusion. Now Amazon says it sells more electronic books than printed books, another sign that consumers are continuing to adopt e-book readers at a rapid rate.[51]

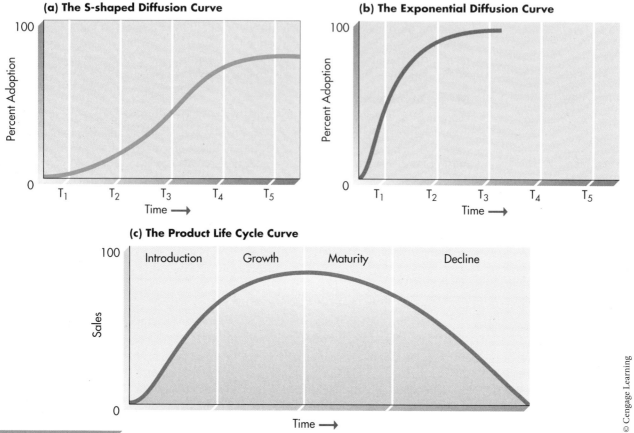

© Cengage Learning

Exhibit 15.8

Diffusion and Product Life Cycle Curves

Several diffusion patterns have been identified: (a) with an S-shaped diffusion curve, diffusion starts out slowly, increases rapidly, and then flattens out again; (b) with an exponential diffusion curve, many people adopt the innovation quickly; and (c) the product life cycle curve depicts sales (not cumulative diffusion) of an offering over time.

Exponential diffusion curve A diffusion curve characterized by rapid initial growth.

The Exponential Diffusion Curve

Another type of adoption curve is the **exponential diffusion curve**, illustrated in Exhibit 15.8(b).[52] In contrast to the S-shaped curve, the exponential diffusion curve starts out much more quickly, with a large percentage of the market adopting the product as soon as it is available. However, with each additional time period, the adoption rate increases at a slower pace.

Factors Affecting the Shape of the Diffusion Curve

Many factors influence the ultimate shape of the diffusion curve. In general, marketers might expect an S-shaped diffusion curve when the innovation is associated with some social, psychological, economic, performance, or physical risk. In such situations, consumers might wait to see how other people use and react to the innovation before adopting it. Diffusion may also be slow initially if consumers are not sure whether the product will be on the market for long or whether its use carries high switching costs. The diffusion of computers and CD players followed this S-shaped curve. An S-shaped diffusion pattern might also occur when consumers are physically far apart, do not discuss the innovation with others, or do not share the same beliefs.

In contrast, when the innovation involves little risk, when switching costs are low, when consumers are similar in their beliefs and values, and/or when people talk often about the product and quickly disseminate knowledge throughout the social system, the product may have a rapid takeoff period that follows the exponential curve for diffusion. Note that these curves reflect only the rate at which consumers in the market adopt a product, not the time period under analysis. In other words, an S-shaped or an exponential curve could reflect diffusion that has occurred over a 1-year or a 30-year period. Furthermore, the curves could reflect the diffusion of either a functional, symbolic, or hedonic innovation.

How Diffusion Relates to the Product Life Cycle

Product life cycle A concept that suggests that products go through an initial introductory period followed by periods of sales growth, maturity, and decline.

The **product life cycle** concept, illustrated in Exhibit 15.8(c), proposes that products initially go through a period of introduction, followed by relatively rapid growth as more competitors enter the market and more consumers adopt the product. With greater competition, weaker competitors drop out, and product sales plateau. At some point, however, consumer acceptance wanes, and product sales decline.

Product diffusion and the product life cycle are related but different concepts. Diffusion focuses on the *percentage of the market* that has adopted the product; diffusion is complete when 100 percent of the market has purchased the product. The product life cycle, on the other hand, deals with *sales of the product* over time. Moreover, diffusion curves are generally cumulative—that is, they continue to increase or at least level off over time. However, the product life cycle curve may decline as consumers decide not to purchase the product in the future. For instance, after an innovation such as the cell phone diffused through an entire market, it was replaced by another innovation, the multifunction smart phone, and sales of the old product eventually declined as the new innovation took hold.

Marketing Implications

Marketers who understand a product's life cycle can try to prevent that product's decline—perhaps by finding new uses for it. For example, nylon has enjoyed a long life cycle given the myriad uses to which it has been put since its introduction in the 1940s—as an ingredient in clothing, rope, fishing lines, and so on. To the extent that marketers develop new uses for a product or encourage use innovativeness, they can lengthen their product's life cycle.

Fad A successful innovation that has a very short product life cycle.

Marketers can also try to diagnose the likely life cycle pattern of their offering. Just as diffusion curves differ, so too are there different product life cycle curves. A **fad** is a successful innovation that has a very short product life cycle. Teenage Mutant Ninja Turtles, scooters, and certain diets are examples of fads. Some fads experience a revival years after their first appearance. Hula hoops, for example, came back, more than 40 years after the original fad, as a product to use to stay fit.[53] As another example, yo-yos have been through multiple fashions and fads in usage since the 1930s.

Fashion A successful innovation that has a moderately long and potentially cyclical product life cycle.

A **fashion** or trend is a successful innovation with a lengthier and potentially cyclical life. For example, certain aesthetic styles like art deco run in fashion cycles, as do styles of clothing and shoes. Colors of laptops, coffeemakers, washing machines, and other electrical items run in fashion cycles, as well. For example, a few years ago, when Dirt Devil wanted its handheld vacuums included in Target's back-to-school displays, the retailer insisted that the vacuums be made in teal and in pink, two colors then in fashion for appliances.[54] In contrast, a **classic** is a successful innovation that has a lengthy product life cycle. For example, Jeans are an American classic, as are rock 'n' roll music and hamburgers.

Classic A successful innovation that has a lengthy product life cycle.

Although the terms *fad, fashion*, and *classic* have most often been applied to aesthetic or hedonic innovations, they can also describe functional and symbolic innovations because the life cycle of these innovations similarly can be variable.

INFLUENCES ON ADOPTION, RESISTANCE, AND DIFFUSION

Knowing that innovations may diffuse quickly or slowly through a market and that the success of a new product depends on how many people within the market adopt it, marketing managers need to understand the factors affecting resistance, adoption, and diffusion. A number of factors, including characteristics of the innovation and of the social system into which it is introduced, are described below.

Characteristics of the Innovation

Characteristics of the innovation that can affect resistance, adoption, and diffusion include perceived value, benefits, and costs.

Sometimes your hands could use a hand.

TOUCH₂O® TECHNOLOGY. TOUCH IT ON, TOUCH IT OFF.

Touch anywhere on the spout or handle with your wrist or forearm to start and stop the flow of water. Another way that Delta® is more than just a faucet. For a demo, visit www.deltafaucet.com/touch

△ **DELTA**
see what Delta can do

Courtesy of Delta Faucets Company

Exhibit 15.9

Relative Advantage

Innovations that have a clear relative advantage tend to be adopted more quickly.

Relative advantage Benefits in an innovation superior to those found in existing products.

Use innovativeness Finding use for a product that differs from the product's original intended usage.

Perceived Value

Consumers perceive that an innovation has value if it offers greater perceived benefits or lower perceived costs than existing alternatives do. Products with high perceived value may be more readily adopted than those with low perceived value. Portable digital music players, for instance, were adopted quickly because consumers perceived the value in a small, handheld device, like an iPod, that could store and play thousands of songs. This was a big improvement over portable CD players, which were larger than the digital devices and required a collection of CDs.

Perceived Benefits

An innovation's value to consumers is affected by its perceived **relative advantage**, the extent to which it offers benefits superior to those of existing products. Something new offers a relative advantage if it can help consumers avoid risks, fulfill their needs, solve problems, or achieve their goals—criteria that affect consumers' adoption decisions. In fact, research indicates that product advantage is one of the most important predictors of new-product success (see Exhibit 15.9).[55] Note that a relative advantage is something the product does for the consumer—not something that exists in the product. Thus, the relative advantage of hybrid cars such as the Toyota Prius lies not in their features but rather in the owners' ability to save money on gasoline and help save the environment.

However, if consumers do not perceive a new product's advantage over the benefits of existing alternatives or think the advantage is unimportant, the innovation will face resistance. This happened to Microsoft's Windows Vista operating system. Vista was supposed to be more secure and have expanded functionality compared to its predecessor, Windows XP. However, after publicity about conflicts between Vista and other software, consumers began to resist the new operating system. Some PC buyers even insisted on having the older XP software loaded on the new computer instead of Vista.[56]

Consumers often have difficulty concretely imagining the circumstances of buying and using a radically new product.[57] Yet consumers who are able to visualize the value of the novel new benefits will have higher evaluations of a dramatically different innovation.[58] Consumers are likely to perceive a product's benefits as being more valuable when they can adapt it for use in different contexts. **Use innovativeness** means using products in a new or creative way, as in the way that a consumer might use baking soda to solve problems like deodorizing a kitty litter box.[59]

Perceived Costs

Another aspect of the value of a product is its perceived costs, meaning all types of costs, including the money, time and effort required to adopt the product. The higher the purchase cost, the greater the resistance, and hence the slower the diffusion. Consider hybrid gas-electric cars like the Prius, which tend to have a higher initial cost than comparable conventional cars. Although the higher perceived cost slowed its adoption at first, the car's relative advantage became apparent after the pump price of gasoline skyrocketed, resulting in higher demand for fuel-efficient cars. In contrast, digital music players have experienced much more rapid diffusion as competition and manufacturing efficiencies have brought prices down. *Switching costs*—the costs of changing from the current product to a new one—are part of the total costs. For example, consumers who upgrade computer operating systems may have to replace a peripheral device such as a printer because of incompatibility with the new system.

> ## Marketing Implications

If consumers do not perceive that an innovation has a relative advantage, marketers may need to add one by physically redesigning or reengineering the innovation.

Communicate and Demonstrate the Relative Advantage

The company must educate consumers who do not understand a product or its relative advantages. For instance, when Amazon.com introduced its Kindle wireless reading device, the company posted video demonstrations on its website showing how the product works. Now Amazon sells more than 15 million Kindles every year, and this diffusion has also driven sales of digital books higher than sales of printed books.[60] Another way to communicate an innovation's advantage is through highly credible and visible opinion leaders. Amazon did this by sending Kindle samples to influential reviewers at the *New York Times* and other leading media outlets.

Use Price Promotions to Reduce Perceived Costs

If consumers perceive that a product is too costly, the company can use special price-oriented sales promotions such as price-offs, rebates, or refunds to reduce the perceived cost. Marketers can also provide guarantees or warranties that make the product seem less expensive. Alternatively, the marketer may find a cheaper way to manufacture the product and pass on the savings in the form of lower prices for consumers, a strategy that marketers of digital watches used.

Provide Incentives for Switching

If innovations are not adopted because consumers think switching costs are high, marketers might provide incentives for switching. This situation explains why razor companies often give away free razor handles to get consumers to switch to new-generation blades. Companies might also use advertising to inform consumers about the costs associated with *not* switching. Finally, marketers might be able to force their innovation to become the industry standard, for instance, by having such high quality, ease of use, or low price that they become the dominant alternative. ⎯⎯⎯⎯⎯⎯⎯⎯⎯⎯⎯⎯

Uncertainty

In addition to the characteristics of the innovation, uncertainty surrounding the innovation can affect its adoption, resistance, and diffusion. Several aspects of uncertainty are particularly important. One is doubt about what will become the industry standard. For example, when Sony first introduced its PlayStation 3 game console with Blu-ray DVD, a battle raged over whether Blu-ray would become the new DVD standard. Sales of the PlayStation 3 lagged until Blu-ray became the industry standard. Now consumers are rapidly adopting streaming of movies and TV shows through PlayStation and other game consoles.[61]

Another aspect is uncertainty about the relative advantage of a product that requires the consumer to make significant behavioral changes.[62] Consumers are often more uncertain about the usefulness of a discontinuous (vs. a continuous).[63] Surprisingly, giving consumers more information about a high-tech product that combines a new interface with new functionality actually makes consumers more uncertain about the product's advantages. This phenomenon may happen because consumers pay more attention to the new interface and, in processing the information, reason through the possible negative outcomes of product adoption.[64]

A third aspect of uncertainty is the length of the product life cycle. Consumers are more likely to resist buying a fad than a fashion or a classic. For example, you may forgo spending $100 on spike-heeled shoes if you think they will soon be out of style, or you may wait to buy a tablet computer because you think the next generation will have longer battery life. This type of uncertainty is a legitimate concern in clothing and high-tech markets, where products are frequently changed or improved.

Finally, consumers' specific uncertainty concerns differ according to the length of time before adoption. For example, people are more concerned about the downside of uncertainties such as switching costs when they plan to adopt an innovation in the near future, compared to when adoption is in the distant future.[65]

Marketing Implications

When consumers resist innovations because they are worried about an offering's short life cycle, marketers might show how adaptable the product is and hence how likely it is to have a long life cycle. For example, marketers of digital book readers can address consumers' fears of the product's rapid obsolescence by demonstrating how their products may be upgraded, connected to advanced systems, or used in other ways that extend the life cycle by continuing to deliver perceived value.

Consumer Learning Requirements

A third characteristic affecting resistance, adoption, and diffusion is consumer learning requirements—or what consumers need to do to use the innovation effectively. These learning requirements involve compatibility, trialability, and complexity.

Compatibility

Compatibility The extent to which an innovation is consistent with one's needs, values, norms, or behaviors.

Consumers often resist innovations because they see them as incompatible with their needs, values, norms, or behaviors.[66] The more **compatible** the innovation is with consumers' values, norms, and behaviors, the less their resistance and the greater the product diffusion. For example, when Patagonia introduced the first jacket made of Polartec polyester fleece, it was an immediate hit because it was warm yet lightweight, durable, and washable. Today, Polartec is made from recycled material, adding to the eco-friendly appeal.[67] On the other hand, Bernard Matthews Farms, a large U.K. turkey grower, withdrew a line of gourmet-branded turkey steaks in crust and turkey roasts with stuffing after only six months on the market. Why? Turkey is not as mature a product category in the United Kingdom as it is in the United States, and U.K. consumers are accustomed to cooking whole turkeys rather than buying ready-to-cook specialty turkey entrees positioned on the basis of convenience.[68]

Some potentially serious consequences can arise when an innovation is incompatible with consumers' values, goals, and behaviors. One case in particular is marketers' attempts to encourage bottle-feeding by mothers in Latin American, African, and Asian markets. Manufacturers' ads showed pictures of mothers with beautiful, fat, healthy babies. The ad copy read, "Give your baby love and Lactogen" (Lactogen is an infant formula). The modern look of the ad attracted upper-income, well-educated consumers as well as peasant families who aspired to be like the well-educated. Unfortunately, most peasant families could not afford the expensive formula, so they diluted it with water, leaving their babies malnourished. Furthermore, they were unfamiliar with practices like sterilizing nipples and bottles; as a result, bacteria in these items made the babies sick. The lack of compatibility between the innovation and the consumers' behavior therefore caused unanticipated problems.[69]

Trialability

Trialability The extent to which an innovation can be tried on a limited basis before it is adopted.

A second aspect of consumer learning requirements is the **trialability** of the innovation, the extent to which the product can be tried on a limited basis before it is adopted. Products like microwaveable meals can be tested and tasted in just a few minutes (see Exhibit 15.10). Similarly, many software firms offer limited-use trials so consumers can experience the features and benefits before they buy. However, trialability is virtually impossible with innovations like laser eye surgery. Because a trial allows a consumer to assess the product's relative advantages and potential risks, products that are easy to try tend to diffuse through the market more quickly than those that do not.

Trialability is often important to innovators and early adopters because they have little else on which to base the value of the innovation. Trialability can be less important for later adopters, who are likely to know people who have already adopted the innovation and who can therefore speak to its efficacy.[70]

Exhibit 15.10

Trialability
Consumers' learning experience benefits from a products' trialability, such as trying samples of food, before they purchase.

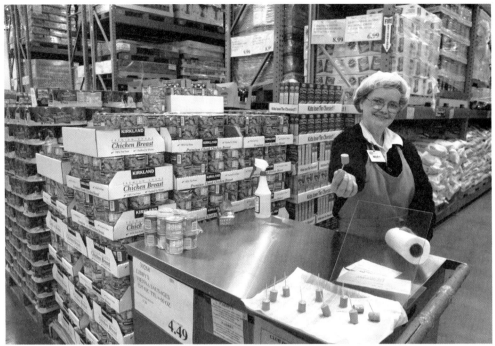

Complexity

Complexity The extent to which an innovation is complicated and difficult to understand or use.

Complexity is a final learning requirement related to adoption and diffusion. Diffusion is likely to be slow when consumers perceive they will have difficulty understanding or using a new product. Then, the mental or thinking costs are high. Products that are loaded with many features may appear useful, yet the fact that they have so many features leads them to be perceived as being overly complex.[71] In fact, consumers may form a lower evaluation of a complex product with novel attributes because they worry about the time needed to understand the new features.[72] This perception is a challenge for marketers because consumers tend to underestimate how well they can manage complexity.[73] Digital photography initially diffused at a relatively slow rate because consumers perceived that it would be complex to transfer digital images from the camera to the computer, figuring out the software for enhancing images, and printing high-quality photos.[74]

Marketing Implications

Marketers can use several tactics to reduce consumers' resistance to innovations.

Enhance Compatibility or Reduce Complexity

Marketers may be able to reposition an innovation so that it is viewed as more consistent with consumers' needs and values. For example, after experiencing lower sales, Campbell Soup Company recently implemented a marketing campaign to reposition its soup products as both healthy and convenient—two benefits highly valued by consumers, as research shows.[75] Sometimes, however, companies must redesign an offering to overcome incompatibility and reduce complexity. Apple's iPod was not the first digital music player, but it became a runaway success because it was the simplest and easiest to operate, compared with competing players. Many brands followed Apple's lead in reducing complexity, and soon sales in the entire category soared.

Educate About Compatibility

Companies can use promotions to show how their innovations actually are compatible with consumers' needs, values, norms, or behaviors. For example, connecting with friends via texting and using touch screen electronics are common behaviors for many millennial generation consumers, the target market for PepsiCo's innovative "Be Social" soft-drink vending machines. To promote this innovation, PepsiCo created a how-to video for YouTube, showing the steps that users can take to send a code for a free PepsiCo beverage via text through the new machines, along with a brief personalized video message.[76] Advertising can also show how a new offering is easier to use or has more benefits than current alternatives do, even if it requires adopting new behaviors.

Use Change Agents

Another way to enhance perceived compatibility is to use change agents such as opinion leaders. Marketers in diverse industries have aimed new products at influential and highly respected people who can be convinced of a new product's merits and who will then spread positive word of mouth to others. For example, companies are eager to have their products included in the gift bags distributed to movie stars at the annual Academy Awards event because product adoption by these celebrities (or a few words of praise) will encourage trial among fans. Cadillac, eager to be associated with the glamour of the Oscars, recently put into the bag a certificate good for a free two-week test-drive of one of its luxury vehicles.[77] The tour operators using Segways to guide tourists though cities, as described earlier, may be helpful in getting consumers to try the product and experience its benefits.

Fit with a System of Products

Some marketers address incompatibility by designing the innovation to fit with a system of existing products. Procter & Gamble's Mr. Clean AutoDry car cleaning sprayer was designed to be hooked up to any garden hose, making the product simple and easy for consumers to use. The rate of diffusion was "beyond our wildest dreams," a P&G spokesperson comments. And once consumers adopt the product, the hope is that many will also buy P&G's complementary products, such as Mr. Clean car-wash soap.[78]

Force the Innovation to Be the Industry Standard

Marketers can sometimes work with regulators to require adoption of the innovation. For example, smoke detectors, seat belts, and lead-free gasoline are all innovations that have been forced into usage by government mandate. Manufacturers are introducing more hybrid cars because states' clean-air requirements are mandating zero-emission vehicles.[79]

Use Promotions to Enhance Trialability

Companies can stimulate trial through various promotions. Free samples, for example, encourage trial by people who might otherwise resist using the product. Many supermarkets encourage trial by distributing samples of new food products, and Costco is known for the number and variety of sampling opportunities that shoppers encounter as they browse its cavernous stores.

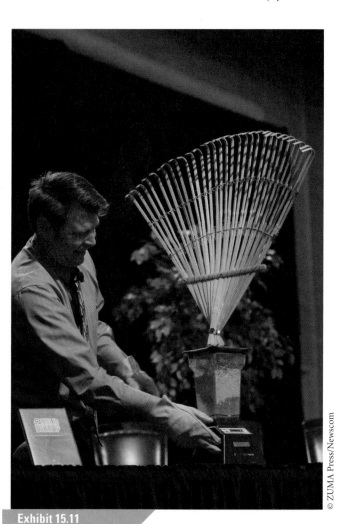

© ZUMA Press/Newscom

Exhibit 15.11

Compatibility and Simplicity
Consumers respond to innovations that are shown to be simple and compatible with their values, like the live demonstrations of the Blendtec's blenders.

Demonstrate Compatibility and Simplicity

Live demonstrations (at trade shows or conducted by salespeople) and demonstrations in ads and online videos can show a product's ease of use and its compatibility with consumers' needs, values, and behaviors. Sales of Blendtec's blenders increased by 500 percent after the firm posted videos on YouTube to demonstrate how rugged the blenders are and how quickly and easily they work (see Exhibit 15.11). The company continues to film and post at least one new "Will It Blend?" video each month, showing products such as iPhones being pulverized in moments. In all, Blendtec's YouTube videos have been viewed more than 12 million times.[80]

Simulate Trial

At times, a company may need to *simulate* trial rather than have consumers actually try the product. Tea, for example, an online children's clothing retailer, offers a free iPad app that allows parents to mix and match children's outfits on the screen, see how outfits look in a "virtual dressing room," and share views of the outfits on social media sites before buying.[81] On Benjamin Moore's website, consumers can use a "personal color viewer" to preview how different paint colors would look on the walls of different rooms. _____

Social Relevance

Social relevance The extent to which an innovation can be observed or the extent to which having others observe it has social cachet.

A fourth major factor that affects resistance, adoption, and diffusion is the innovation's **social relevance**, particularly its observability and social value. *Observability* is the extent to which consumers can see others using the innovation. In general, the more consumers can observe others using the innovation, the more likely they are to adopt it.[82] For example, a new shoulder strap designed to distribute the weight of a golf bag gained acceptance among caddies after they saw others using the product.[83] On the other hand, a new scale that announces your body weight is unlikely to be very observable because few people want to weigh themselves in public (or want others to hear their weight!).[84] Thus, diffusion is also affected by the public or private nature of the product's consumption, as described in Chapter 11.

Social value reflects the extent to which the product has social cachet, which means that it is seen as socially desirable and/or appropriate and therefore generates imitation, speeding diffusion. One study found that farmers adopted certain farming innovations because the innovations were expensive and thus had social prestige value. These studies also found that the earlier someone adopted the innovation, the more prestige was associated with it.[85] Consumers sometimes adopt aesthetic innovations like new fashions, hairstyles, and cars based on the social prestige they confer on the user.

Although social value may enhance diffusion, the diffusion of a product based on a prestige image may actually shorten its life cycle because once a product is adopted by the masses, it is no longer prestigious. For example, designer jeans, once associated with prestige and exclusivity, lost prestige when everyone in the market started to wear them.[86]

Marketing Implications

Observability can be enhanced by the use of distinctive packaging, styling, and color or unique promotions,[87] using the attention and perception enhancement techniques described in Chapter 3. Also, associating the product with a well-known person or creating ads to suggest that the consumer will be socially rewarded for using the product may enhance observability. An innovation's social relevance can be heightened through advertising—particularly advertising that ties product use with potential social approval. Finally, marketers can enhance social value by associating the product with some social entity, cause, or value. For example, China-based Yingli Green Energy, which makes solar panels, is a sponsor of the Fifa World Cup because it wants a high-profile way to associate its brand with the world's most popular sport—especially now that the company is targeting final consumers, not just business customers.[88] _____

Legitimacy and Adaptability

Legitimacy The extent to which the innovation follows established guidelines for what seems appropriate in the category.

Legitimacy and adaptability also influence resistance, adoption, and diffusion, particularly for symbolic and aesthetic innovations.[89] **Legitimacy** refers to the extent to which the innovation follows established guidelines for what seems appropriate in the category. An innovation that is too radical or that does not derive from a legitimate precursor lacks legitimacy.

Exhibit 15.12

Legitimacy
Innovations must be based on a legitimate precursor, or push the boundaries to prove their legitimacy, like Blue Bottle Coffee.

When Starbucks, for example, introduced the coffee culture to U.S. consumers, it also had to educate consumers to the benefits of waiting a few extra minutes for made-to-order espressos or lattes. Once Starbucks paved the way, other coffee chains that brewed to order were not perceived as too radical. Blue Bottle Coffee, a small but fast-growing chain of cafes, is now expanding the boundaries of that legitimacy. Customers have to wait about five minutes while an employee grinds fresh-roasted beans and brews each cup individually, using a special filtering system. "There's a chance that people are going to be enraged by us and hate us," admits Blue Bottle's founder. With annual revenue of $20 million, however, the company has found that once customers taste its top-quality coffee, most are willing to wait (see Exhibit 15.12).[90]

Adaptability The extent to which the innovation can foster new styles.

Adaptability, the innovation's potential to fit with existing products or styles, is another factor affecting adoption and diffusion.[91] For example, certain fashion or furniture is highly adaptable because it can fit with a variety of other fashion or furniture trends. Some functional products, such as cell phones, have high adaptability because they can perform a variety of functions.

Marketing Implications

Marketers may enhance legitimacy by demonstrating how the innovation came into being or marketing it in a way that is consistent with consumers' perceptions of what is appropriate for the category. Frito-Lay did this when it tried marketing Latin-flavored Doritos and Lay's chips to Hispanic Americans. Adoption was slow because the targeted consumers "were looking for authentic flavors but didn't expect to see them on those brands," says Frito-Lay's chief marketing officer. Instead, the firm started importing its Sabritones Chile & Lime wheat snacks from Mexico, initially stocking them only in stores serving Mexican American communities. Adoption was so enthusiastic that the product was soon made available in other outlets.[92]

Conversely, if consumers believe the product lacks adaptability, marketers can show that it has uses beyond its original function. For example, the makers of cranberry sauce ask consumers to consider other uses for their product besides serving it as a condiment at Thanksgiving dinner.[93]

Characteristics of the Social System

Innovations diffuse rapidly or slowly in part because of product characteristics and in part because of the characteristics of the social system into which they are introduced. Both the kinds of people in the target market and the nature of the relationships among the people in the social system will affect the innovation's acceptance.

Modernity The extent to which consumers in the social system have positive attitudes toward change.

▶ *Modernity.* Resistance, adoption, and diffusion are affected by the social system's **modernity**, the extent to which the system's consumers have a positive attitude toward change. Consumers in modern systems value science, technology, and education and are technologically oriented in terms of the goods produced and the skill of the labor force.[94] The more modern the social system, the more receptive its consumers are to novel products.

▶ *Physical distance.* Diffusion tends to be faster when members of the social system are physically close. Some marketers in Japan have found that high school girls excel at setting trends. No doubt this ability is due to the physical and emotional proximity of girls and their tendency to talk about new products they have seen and used.[95] Likewise, an innovation may experience slower diffusion when consumers are physically separated.[96]

▶ *Homophily.* Diffusion tends to be faster when consumers in the market are similar in education, values, needs, income, and other dimensions.[97] This type of similarity, called homophily, is another type of closeness. Why does similarity increase diffusion rate? First, the more similar people's backgrounds are, the more likely they are to have similar needs, values, and preferences. Second, similar people are more likely to interact with one another and transmit information. Third, similar people tend to model each other. Also, normative influence is likely to be higher as homophily grows, increasing the pressure for adopting the innovation and speeding adoption and diffusion.

▶ *Opinion leadership.* As noted in Chapter 11, people with credibility, such as experts or opinion leaders, can have considerable influence on product adoption and diffusion because they may spread positive or negative product information to others.[98] Interestingly, opinion leaders both influence others and are influenced by information from others when they are central to their social network—meaning they have many ties within the network and serve to connect individuals within the network.[99]

Marketing Implications

Marketing efforts can influence resistance, adoption, and diffusion by affecting the social system. For example, if members of the target market are very different from one another, companies may need to use targeted communications that show the product's relevance to consumers' unique needs, values, or norms and may need to place the messages in specialized (target market–specific) media to reach these consumers.

Companies might also identify consumers who have not adopted the innovation yet. There are three types of nonadopters: (1) passive consumers who have tried the product but are unlikely to provide much information to others about it; (2) active rejectors who have tried the product and are likely to provide unfavorable word of mouth to others; and (3) potential adopters who have not yet tried the product but who may be influenced by active rejectors, active acceptors, or marketers. Different marketing strategies may be appropriate for different adopter and nonadopter groups.[100] If potential adopters are unaware of the innovation, for instance, advertising can help build awareness and encourage adoption. Product improvements may, however, be necessary to attract active rejectors.

Because marketing activities can influence diffusion by affecting both the innovation and the social system, it is not surprising that the more intensive the marketing effort, the faster the innovation spreads through a market.[101] Media coverage of an innovation generally has more credibility than the company's communications do. Targeting opinion leaders and targeting the network, rather than the consumer, can also stimulate positive word of mouth, as can new product demonstrations at trade shows and in online videos. And marketers can take a number of steps to track word of mouth, generate positive word of mouth, and counteract negative word of mouth.

THE CONSEQUENCES OF INNOVATIONS

Although innovations often offer relative advantages that may not have previously existed, they need not always be good for society at large. One study examined the diffusion of the steel ax among a tribe of aborigines who lived in the Australian bush.[102] Before the innovation was introduced, the stone ax had served as the tribe's principal tool. It was used only by men and was awarded to them as a gift and as payment for work performed. It was generally regarded as a symbol of masculinity and respect. However, missionaries came into the social system with the steel ax and distributed it to men, women, and children. This distribution scheme disrupted the sex and age roles among tribal members and thus affected the social system.

Innovations may also have negative socioeconomic consequences. For example, a study examining the diffusion of the CAT scanner through the medical community identified two important sociological consequences. First, the innovation tended to diffuse to markets that were generally wealthy, leaving the technology unavailable to families who lived in poorer rural areas. Second, the innovation was expensive and was viewed as driving up health-care costs.[103] As another example, the diffusion of electronic payment systems may lead to increased borrowing and debts, without the proper socialization of consumers. Marketers, policy makers, and we as consumers should be aware of the potential unanticipated social and economic consequences of the adoption and diffusion of innovations, and try to prevent or minimize the negatives.

SUMMARY

Innovations are products, services, ideas, or attributes that consumers in a market segment perceive to be new. Innovations can be characterized as functional, symbolic, or hedonic and may vary in the degree of behavioral change their adoption requires. Companies are increasingly using cocreation to develop innovative new products. Product innovativeness ranges along a continuum from continuous to discontinuous. Innovations may represent fads, fashions, or classics and hence may exhibit a short, moderate, or long life cycle. Marketers can extend a product's life cycle by enhancing the breadth of the innovation and encouraging consumers to find innovative uses for familiar products.

Strategies for marketers of innovations include reducing consumers' resistance to innovations, facilitating consumers' adoption of the innovation, and affecting the diffusion of the innovation through the marketplace. A high-effort as opposed to low-effort hierarchy-of-effects adoption process occurs when the innovation is seen as risky. Some individuals, called *innovators*, are among the first to adopt new products independently of the decisions of other people. Companies may target innovators because their adoption of products influences other consumers' adoption decisions through word of mouth or social modeling.

Resistance, adoption, and diffusion are affected by the characteristics of the innovation and the social system into which it is introduced. Overcoming resistance is easiest when the innovation is perceived to provide value to consumers such as a relative advantage, low price, or low switching costs. Resistance will be lower when the innovation requires minimal learning and is highly compatible with consumers' existing needs, values, and behaviors; easy to try; easy to use; and low risk. Innovations viewed as high in social relevance, legitimacy, and adaptability encounter less resistance than those regarded as low in such factors. The characteristics of the social system in which the innovation operates also affect resistance, adoption, and diffusion. However, it is possible that the diffusion of an innovation may entail some negative social and economic consequences.

Questions for Review and Discussion

1. How can innovations be described in terms of degree of novelty and types of benefits? How does the degree of novelty affect consumers' behavioral change?

2. What is cocreation and what are its potential benefits?

3. What is the difference between adoption and diffusion? How does the concept of *resistance* relate to adoption?

4. Under what circumstances might a consumer follow the high-effort hierarchy of effects in adopting an innovation?

5. How can consumers be categorized in terms of their timing of adoption relative to that of other consumers?

6. What is the product life cycle, and how does it differ from product diffusion?

7. How do consumer learning requirements and social relevance affect resistance, adoption, and diffusion?

8. What characteristics of the social system affect an innovation's acceptance within a market?

29. Michael Arrington, "Wave Goodbye to Google Wave," *TechCrunch*, August 4, 2010, www.techcrunch.com; and "Google Kills Off Seven More Products, Including Wave," *BBC News*, November 23, 2011, www.bbc.co.uk.

30. "Segway Tours: Two Wheels Good, Two Legs Bad," *Economist*, November 7, 2011, www.economist.com; and "The Segway, Billed as the Next Big Thing, Is Still Finding Its Place After Hype," *Canadian Press*, February 27, 2008, n.p.

31. Rogers, *The Diffusion of Innovations*.

32. Geoffrey A. Moore, *Crossing the Chasm* (New York: HarperBusiness, 1991).

33. Cristina Lourosa, "Understanding the User: Who Are the First Ones Out There Buying the Latest Gadgets?" *Wall Street Journal*, June 15, 1998, p. R17a.

34. Bill Machrone, "The Most Memorable Tech Flops," *PC Magazine*, January 2008, pp. 88–89.

35. Robert A. Peterson, "A Note on Optimal Adopter Category Determination," *Journal of Marketing Research*, August 1973, pp. 325–329; see also William R. Darden and Fred D. Reynolds, "Backward Profiling of Male Innovators," *Journal of Marketing Research*, February 1974, pp. 79–85; and Steven A. Baumgarten, "The Innovative Communicator in the Diffusion Process," *Journal of Marketing Research*, February 1975, pp. 12–17a. Schemes based on consumers' involvement in the new-product development process, for example, might be utilized by managers (see Jerry Wind and Vijay Mahajan, "Issues and Opportunities in New Product Development: An Introduction to the Special Issue," *Journal of Marketing Research*, February 1997, pp. 1–12).

36. Chuan-Fong Shih and Alladi Venkatesh, "Beyond Adoption: Development and Application of a Use-Diffusion Model," *Journal of Marketing*, January 2004, pp. 59–72.

37. See review in Thomas S. Robertson, Joan Zielinski, and Scott Ward, *Consumer Behavior* (Glenview, Ill.: Scott, Foresman, 1984); see also Dickerson M. D. and J. W. Gentry, "Characteristics of Adopters and Non Adopters of Home Computers," *Journal of Consumer Research* 10, no. 2, pp. 225–235; Duncan G. Labay and Thomas C. Kinnear, "Exploring the Consumer Decision Process in the Adoption of Solar Energy Systems," *Journal of Consumer Research*, December 1981, pp. 271–277; Kenneth Uhl, Roman Andrus, and Lance Poulsen, "How Are Laggards Different? An Empirical Inquiry," *Journal of Marketing Research*, February 1970, pp. 51–54; and Rogers, *The Diffusion of Innovations*, pp. 383–384.

38. Richard Mader, "Year of the Mobile Payment," *Stores*, August 2011, www.stores.org.

39. Rogers, *The Diffusion of Innovations*; see also Mark S. Granovetter, "The Strength of Weak Ties," *American Journal of Sociology*, May 1973, pp. 1360–1380; and John A. Czepiel, "Word-of-Mouth Processes in the Diffusion of a Major Technological Innovation," *Journal of Marketing Research*, May 1974, pp. 172–181.

40. Scott A. Thompson and Rajiv K. Sinha, "Brand Communities and New Product Adoption: The Influence and Limits of Oppositional Loyalty," *Journal of Marketing*, November 2008, pp. 65–80.

41. Manning, Bearden, and Madden, "Consumer Innovativeness and the Adoption Process"; Jan-Benedict E. M. Steenkamp and Hans Baumgartner, "The Role of Optimum Stimulation Level in Exploratory Consumer Behavior," *Journal of Consumer Research*, December 1992, pp. 434–448; and P. S. Raju, "Optimum Stimulation Level: Its Relationship to Personality, Demographics, and Exploratory Behavior," *Journal of Consumer Research*, December 1980, pp. 272–282.

42. Thomas S. Robertson and James H. Myers, "Personality Correlates of Opinion Leadership and Innovative Buying Behavior," *Journal of Marketing Research*, May 1969, pp. 164–167.

43. Gordon R. Foxall and Christopher G. Haskins, "Cognitive Style and Consumer Innovativeness," *Marketing Intelligence and Planning*, January 1986, pp. 26–46; and Gordon R. Foxall, "Consumer Innovativeness: Novelty Seeking, Creativity and Cognitive Style," in eds. Elizabeth C. Hirschman and Jagdish N. Sheth, *Research in Consumer Behavior*, vol. 3 (Greenwich, Conn.: JAI Press, 1988), pp. 79–114.

44. Ronald E. Goldsmith and Charles F. Hofacker, "Measuring Consumer Innovativeness," *Journal of the Academy of Marketing Science*, Summer 1991, pp. 209–221.

45. Jan-Benedict E. M. Steenkamp, Frenkel ter Hofstede, and Michael Wedel, "A Cross-National Investigation into the Individual and National Cultural Antecedents of Consumer Innovativeness," *Journal of Marketing*, April 1999, pp. 55–69.

46. Hubert Gatignon and Thomas S. Robertson, "A Propositional Inventory for New Diffusion Research," *Journal of Consumer Research*, March 1985, pp. 849–867; see also John O. Summers, "Media Exposure Patterns of Consumer Innovators," *Journal of Marketing*, January 1972, pp. 43–49.

47. James J. Engel, Robert J. Kegerreis, and Roger D. Blackwell, "Word-of-Mouth Communication by the Innovator," *Journal of Marketing*, July 1969, pp. 15–19.

48. Dickerson and Gentry, "Characteristics of Adopters and Non Adopters of Home Computers"; Robertson, *Innovative Behavior and Communication*; and James W. Taylor, "A Striking Characteristic of Innovators," *Journal of Marketing Research*, February 1977, pp. 104–107; see also Gatignon and Robertson, "A Propositional Inventory for New Diffusion Research"; Elizabeth C. Hirschman, "Innovativeness, Novelty Seeking and Consumer Creativity," *Journal of Consumer Research*, December 1980, pp. 283–295; and Engel, Kegerreis, and Blackwell, "Word-of-Mouth Communication by the Innovator."

49. Aaron Smith, "Smartphone Adoption and Usage," *Pew Internet*, July 11, 2011, www.pewinternet.org; and Zweli Mokgata, "Vodacom Ready to Ring the Changes," *The Times (South Africa)*, February 26, 2008, n.p.

50. Frank M. Bass, "New Product Growth Models for Consumer Durables," *Management Science*, September 1969, pp. 215–227; Wellesley Dodds, "An Application of the Bass Model in Long-Term New Product Forecasting," *Journal of Marketing Research*, August 1973, pp. 308–311; Roger M. Heeler and Thomas P. Hustad, "Problems in Predicting New Product Growth for Consumer Durables," *Management Science*, October 1980, pp. 1007–1020; and Douglas Tigart and Behrooz Farivar, "The Bass New Product Growth Model: A Sensitivity Analysis for a High Technology Product," *Journal of Marketing*, Fall 1981, pp. 81–90.

51. Ian Sherr, "Kindle Catches Fire," *Wall Street Journal*, November 29, 2011, www.wsj.com; Suzanne Choney, "E-Book Sales, Devices Soar," *MSNBC*, August 18, 2011, www.msnbc.com; and "Amazon Sells More EBooks than Print Books," *International Business Times*, May 19, 2011, www.ibtimes.com.

52. William E. Cox Jr., "Product Life Cycles as Marketing Models," *Journal of Business*, October 1967, pp. 375–384; Rolando Polli and Victor Cook, "Validity of the Product Life Cycle," *Journal of Business*, October 1969, pp. 385–400; D. R. Rink and J. E. Swan, "Product Life Cycle Research: A Literature Review," *Journal of Business Research*, September 1979, pp. 219–242; and Robertson, *Innovative Behavior and Communication*.

53. Rayna McInturf, "Crash Course: Fitness Goals Lagging a Bit?" *Los Angeles Times*, February 17, 2005, p. E23.

54. Sarah Nassauer, "A Season (or 13) for Shopping," *Wall Street Journal*, August 17, 2011, www.wsj.com.

55. David H. Henard and David M. Szymanski, "Why Some New Products Are More Successful Than Others," *Journal of Marketing Research*, August 2001, pp. 362–375.

56. Don Reisinger, "10 Epic Tech Failures of All Time," *CIO Insight*, November 8, 2011, www.cioinsight.com.

57. David L. Alexander, John G. Lynch Jr., and Qing Wang, "As Time Goes by: Do Cold Feet Follow Warm Intentions for Really New Versus Incrementally New Products?" *Journal of Marketing Research*, June 2008, pp. 307–319.

58. Min Zhao, Steve Hoeffler, and Darren W. Dahl, "The Role of Imagination-Focused Visualization on New Product Evaluation," *Journal of Marketing Research*, February 2009, pp. 46–55.

59. James E. Burroughs and David Glen Mick, "Exploring Antecedents and Consequences of Consumer Creativity in a Problem-Solving Context," *Journal of Consumer Research* 31, no. 2, 2004, pp. 402–411.

60. Erick Schonfeld, "Citi Analyst: Kindle Will Be 10 Percent of Amazon Sales in 2012," *TechCrunch*, June 7, 2011, www.techcrunch.com; and Randall Stross, "Freed from the Page, but a Book Nonetheless," *New York Times*, January 27, 2008, p. BU3.

61. Chloe Albanesius, "Half of Netflix Users Connect Via Game Consoles," *PC Magazine*, July 27, 2011, www.pcmag.com; and Se Young Lee and Jay Alabaster, "Sony's PS3 Gets Boost From Its Blu-ray Drive," *Wall Street Journal*, March 12, 2008, p. D7.

62. Jan-Benedict E. M. Steenkamp and Katrijn Gielens, "Consumer and Market Drivers of the Trial Probability of New Consumer Packaged Goods," *Journal of Consumer Research*, December 2003, pp. 368–384.

63. Steve Hoeffler, "Measuring Preferences for Really New Products," *Journal of Marketing Research*, November 2003, pp. 406–420.

64. Paschalina Ziamou and S. Ratneshwar, "Promoting Consumer Adoption of High-Technology Products: Is More Information Always Better?" *Journal of Consumer Psychology* 12, no. 4, 2002, pp. 341–351.

65. Raquel Castano, Mita Sujan, Manish Kacker, and Harish Sujan, "Managing Consumer Uncertainty in the Adoption of New Products," *Journal of Marketing Research*, June 2008, pp. 320–336.

66. Gatignon and Robertson, "A Propositional Inventory for New Diffusion Research"; and Vijay Mahajan, Eitan Muller, and Frank M. Bass, "New Product Diffusion Models in Marketing: A Review and Directions for Research," *Journal of Marketing*, April 1990, pp. 1–27.

67. Hilary Greenbaum and Dana Rubinstein, "Who Made That? Fleece," *New York Times Magazine*, November 27, 2011, p. 28.

68. Julia Glotz, "Marco's Range Dropped as Bernard Changes Tack," *Grocer*, August 20, 2011, p. 31; and "Marco Pierre White's Bernard Matthews Turkey Meals Are Chopped After Just Six Months," *Daily Mail (UK)*, August 21, 2011, www.dailymail.co.uk.

69. Rogers, *The Diffusion of Innovations*.

70. Ibid.

71. Debora Viana Thompson, Rebecca W. Hamilton, and Roland T. Rust, "Feature Fatigue: When Product Capabilities Become Too Much of a Good Thing," *Journal of Marketing Research*, November 2005, pp. 431–442.

72. Ashesh Mukherjee and Wayne D. Hoyer, "The Effect of Novel Attributes on Product Evaluation," *Journal of Consumer Research*, December 2001, pp. 462–472.

73. Katherine A. Burson, "Consumer–Product Skill Matching: The Effects of Difficulty on Relative Self-Assessment and Choice," *Journal of Consumer Research* 34, no. 1, 2007, pp. 104–110.

74. Al Doyle, "Getting the Perfect Picture," *Technology & Learning*, January 2002, pp. 9–11.

75. "Campbell Planning $100 Million Repositioning Effort," *Radio Business Report*, July 13, 2010, www.rbr.com.

76. Tim Hornyak, "Pepsi Vending Machines Like Your Social Network," *CNet*, April 29, 2011, http://news.cnet.com.

77. "Inside the Academy Awards Gift Bags," *Boston Globe*, n.d., www.boston.com/business/gallery/award_show_gift_bags/bostonglobe.com.

78. "Car Wash Tech," *DSN Retailing Today*, July 19, 2004, p. 15.

79. Kathryn Kranhold, "Toyota Makes a Bet on New Hybrid Prius," *Wall Street Journal*, July 20, 2000, p. B18.

80. David Gianatasio," Will Siri Blend? Blendtec Takes on the iPhone 4S," *AdWeek*, October 17, 2011, www.adweek.com; and Raymund Flandez, "Lights! Camera! Sales!" *Wall Street Journal*, November 29, 2007, ww.wsj.com.

81. Claire Cain Miller, "Retailers Enliven Catalog Offerings Through Apps," *New York Times*, November 20, 2011, www.nytimes.com.

82. Robert J. Fisher and Linda L. Price, "An Investigation into the Social Context of Early Adoption Behavior," *Journal of Consumer Research*, December 1992, pp. 477–486.

83. Sandra D. Atchison, "Lifting the Golf Bag Burden," *BusinessWeek*, July 25, 1994, p. 84.

84. June Fletcher, "New Machines Measure That Holiday Flab at Home," *Wall Street Journal*, December 26, 1997, p. B8.

85. Rogers, *The Diffusion of Innovations*, p. 99.

86. C. Whan Park, Bernard J. Jaworski, and Deborah J. MacInnis, "Strategic Brand Concept–Image Management," *Journal of Marketing*, October 1986, pp. 135–145.

87. Fisher and Price, "An Investigation into the Social Context of Early Adoption Behavior."

88. Bill Wilson, "Bright Start for Fifa's Chinese World Cup Sponsor," *BBC News*, November 23, 2011, www.bbc.co.uk.

89. Petrosky, "Extending Innovation Characteristic Perception to Diffusion Channel Intermediaries and Aesthetic Products."

90. Michael V. Copeland, "The Best Coffee You May Ever Drink," *Fortune*, September 26, 2011, pp. 38–44.

91. Alfred Petrosky labels this factor *genrefication* and discusses it in the context of aesthetic innovations in "Extending Innovation Characteristic Perception to Diffusion Channel Intermediaries and Aesthetic Products."

92. Diane Brady, "A Thousand and One Noshes," *BusinessWeek*, June 14, 2004, pp. 54–56.

93. Jagdish N. Sheth and S. Ram, *Bringing Innovation to Market* (NewYork: Wiley, 1987).

94. Everett M. Rogers and F. Floyd. Shoemaker, *Communication of Innovations* (New York: Free Press, 1971); and Elizabeth C. Hirschman, "Consumer Modernity, Cognitive Complexity, Creativity and Innovativeness," in ed. Richard P. Bagozzi, *Marketing in the 80s: Changes and Challenges* (Chicago: American Marketing Association, 1980), pp. 152–161.

95. Seth Stevenson, "I'd Like to Buy the World a Shelf-Stable Children's Lactic Drink," *New York Times Magazine*, March 10, 2002, p. 38; John C. Jay, "The Valley of the New," *American Demographics*, March 2000, pp. 58–59; and Norihiko Shirouzu, "Japan's High-School Girls Excel in Art of Setting Trends," *Wall Street Journal*, April 24, 1998, pp. B1, B7.

96. Gatignon and Robertson, "A Propositional Inventory for New Diffusion Research"; and Lawrence A. Brown, Edward J. Malecki, and Aron N. Spector, "Adopter Categories in a Spatial Context," *Rural Sociology*, Spring 1976, pp. 99–117a.

97. Jaishankar Ganesh, V. Kumar, and Velavan Subramaniam, "Learning Effect in Multinational Diffusion of Consumer Durables," *Journal of the Academy of Marketing Science* 25, Summer 1997, pp. 214–228; and Gatignon and Robertson, "A Propositional Inventory for New Diffusion Research."

98. Dorothy Leonard-Barton, "Experts as Negative Opinion Leaders in the Diffusion of a Technological Innovation," *Journal of Consumer Research*, March 1985, pp. 914–926.

99. Seung Hwan (Mark) Lee, June Cotte, and Theodore J. Noseworthy, "The Role of Network Centrality in the Flow of Consumer Influence," *Journal of Consumer Psychology* 20, 2010, pp. 66–77.

100. Everett M. Rogers and D. Lawrence Kincaid, *Communication Networks: Toward a New Paradigm for Research* (New York: Free Press, 1981).

101. Frank M. Bass, "The Relationship Between Diffusion Curves, Experience Curves, and Demand Elasticities for Consumer Durable Technological Innovations," *Journal of Business*, July 1980, pp. s51–s57; Dan Horskey and Leonard S. Simon, "Advertising and the Diffusion of New Products," *Marketing Science*, Winter 1983, pp. 1–17; Vijay Mahajan and Eitan Muller, "Innovation Diffusion and New Product Growth Models in Marketing," *Journal of Marketing*, Fall 1979, pp. 55–68; and Mahajan, Muller, and Bass, "New Product Diffusion Models in Marketing: A Review and Directions for Research."

102. Lauriston Sharp, "Steel Axes for Stone Age Australians," in ed. Edward H. Spicer, *Human Problems in Technological Change* (New York: Russell Sage Foundation, 1952).

103. H. David Banta, "The Diffusion of the Computer Tomography (CT) Scanner in the United States," *International Journal of Health Services* 10, 1980, pp. 251–269, as reported in Rogers, *The Diffusion of Innovations*, pp. 231–237.

104. Marina Strauss, "Starbucks Tries to Build a Bridge from Cafes to Grocery-Stores Shelves," *Globe & Mail (Toronto)*, April 14, 2011, p. B1; Joshua Levine, "Pod of Gold," *Time*, March 7, 2011, www.time.com; Harry Wallop, "Espresso Cups Outsell Mugs," *Telegraph (UK)*, November 11, 2011, www.telegraph.co.uk; and Leslie Patton, "Green Mountain's Expiring K-Cup Patents Attract Coffee Rivals," *Bloomberg*, November 18, 2011, www.bloomberg.com.

SYMBOLIC CONSUMER BEHAVIOR

After studying this chapter, you will be able to

1. Discuss how products, special possessions, and consumption activities gain symbolic meaning and how this meaning is conveyed from one consumer to another.

2. Identify how marketers can influence or make use of the symbolic meaning that consumption may have for consumers.

3. Distinguish between sacred and profane entities, and show why this distinction is important for marketing strategy.

4. Understand the process of gift giving and describe how marketers can use knowledge of this process to market more effectively.

© Frances Roberts/Alamy

INTRODUCTION

Spin It Again: The Vinyl LP Is Back

The vinyl long-playing (LP) record album is back after decades of dormancy. By the start of the 21st century, LPs were all but extinct as consumers enthusiastically embraced the convenience of CDs and, later, rushed to download digital music. Now vinyl has emerged as a favorite of collectors, audiophiles, and younger fans who care about the album artwork, the liner notes, the superior sound reproduction, and the "hip" factor, not just the music. By one estimate, as many as half of all LPs sold these days never make it onto a turntable. Instead, the owners preserve the vinyl and use a code received with the purchase to download and listen to the music electronically.

Vinyl sales have been rising in many global markets, with U.S. sales up by 41 percent and U.K. sales up by 55 percent. Turntable sales are also going up, and independent record stores are popping up to serve this new generation of vinyl fans. Why? "Today's music has been stripped away of all packaging," explains a record store owner in Illinois, "and I think that has people reflecting on vinyl. Plus, there's something to be said about people standing around in a store and talking about music." Performers such as Adele, Arcade Fire, Radiohead, and Arctic Monkeys are releasing new albums on vinyl, even as vintage LPs draw new interest in stores and online auction sites. Oldies record labels are issuing collectible LPs on colored vinyl or with special artwork, targeting collectors who want a second chance to own the rock music they loved as teens—in that same format.[1]

Vinyl LPs can have symbolic meaning, the focus of this chapter. The first section examines how symbolic meaning develops in products or consumption experiences, the functions symbolic consumption serve, and how symbolic consumption can affect our self-concept. The next section explains why some products (such as colored-vinyl LPs) are more meaningful than others. Some are special—even sacred—and require consumption practices to keep them so, the way LP buyers may download music instead of playing their vinyl records. The final section discusses how meaning is transferred from person to person through gift giving (see Exhibit 16.1). Knowing how symbolic meaning affects consumer behavior can help marketers develop and identify target markets, create needs-satisfying offerings, and plan appropriate communications.

SOURCES AND FUNCTIONS OF SYMBOLIC MEANING

To understand why some consumers believe vinyl LPs are special, consider where the meaning associated with these products comes from and what functions these offerings and practices fulfill. As shown in Exhibit 16.2, this meaning can stem from either our culture or ourselves as individuals.

Meaning Derived from Culture

Cultural categories The natural grouping of objects that reflect our culture.

Part of the meaning associated with products comes from our culture (see Exhibit 16.3).[2] Anthropologists show that we have **cultural categories** for such things as time (as in work time and leisure time), space (such as home, office, and safe or unsafe places), and occasions (such as festive versus somber events). We also have cultural categories that reflect characteristics of people, such as categories of gender, age, social class, and ethnicity.

Cultural principles Ideas or values that specify how aspects of our culture are organized and/or how they should be perceived or evaluated.

Implicit in cultural categories are **cultural principles**—ideas or values that specify how aspects of our culture are thought about and evaluated. For example, the cultural principles associated with "work time" dictate time that is structured, organized, and precise, and that we should feel tired afterward. The principles associated with "leisure time" are quite different. Cultural principles give meaning to products. This explains why the clothing we associate with work time is also more structured and organized than the clothing we associate with leisure time. In addition, we have categories for occasions, including festive (vibrant, active, and energetic) and somber (dark, quiet, and inactive) occasions. The clothing that we consider appropriate for those occasions mirrors these qualities.

We also have cultural principles linked with social status, gender, age, and ethnicity. For example, the category "women" has historically been associated with concepts like delicate, whimsical, expressive, and changeable. In contrast, the category "men" has historically been associated with concepts like disciplined, stable, and serious. Marketers make products and consumers use them in ways that are consistent with these principles. Thus, women's clothing in many cultures has traditionally been more delicate, whimsical, expressive, and changeable than men's clothing. Exhibit 16.3 indicates that by matching product characteristics with cultural principles and categories, we transfer the meaning associated with the cultural principles to the product. For example, we might classify certain clothing as "feminine" or as "suitable for work" because we associate it with the corresponding cultural principles and categories.

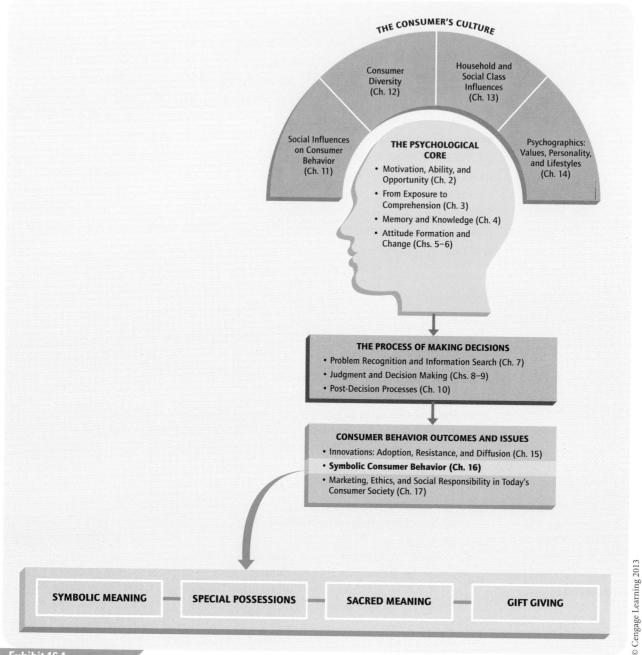

THE CONSUMER'S CULTURE

Consumer Diversity (Ch. 12)

Household and Social Class Influences (Ch. 13)

Social Influences on Consumer Behavior (Ch. 11)

THE PSYCHOLOGICAL CORE
• Motivation, Ability, and Opportunity (Ch. 2)
• From Exposure to Comprehension (Ch. 3)
• Memory and Knowledge (Ch. 4)
• Attitude Formation and Change (Chs. 5–6)

Psychographics: Values, Personality, and Lifestyles (Ch. 14)

THE PROCESS OF MAKING DECISIONS
• Problem Recognition and Information Search (Ch. 7)
• Judgment and Decision Making (Chs. 8–9)
• Post-Decision Processes (Ch. 10)

CONSUMER BEHAVIOR OUTCOMES AND ISSUES
• Innovations: Adoption, Resistance, and Diffusion (Ch. 15)
• **Symbolic Consumer Behavior (Ch. 16)**
• Marketing, Ethics, and Social Responsibility in Today's Consumer Society (Ch. 17)

SYMBOLIC MEANING   **SPECIAL POSSESSIONS**   **SACRED MEANING**   **GIFT GIVING**

© Cengage Learning 2013

Exhibit 16.1

Chapter Overview: Symbolic Consumer Behavior

Products and consumption activities can symbolize something about ourselves and our relationships with others. In this chapter, we consider how products and consumption activities take on and communicate meaning. We also show how some possessions and consumption activities take on special or even sacred meaning. Finally, we discuss how gift giving can symbolize how we feel toward a gift recipient.

Exhibit 16.3 also shows that many agents can play a role in this association and matching process. First, product designers and manufacturers introduce new products with characteristics that reflect cultural principles. For example, the Harley-Davidson motorcycle has characteristics that make it "macho." This fit between cultural principles and offerings explains why U.S. consumers perceive a rodeo as more authentic if it reflects freedom, independence, and competition, qualities closely associated with the American West.[3] Marketers may also confer meaning by associating their offerings with certain cultural categories or myths. Therefore, Harley-Davidson develops clothing, accessories, and information that communicate what it means to be a "biker."[4]

Exhibit 16.2

The Sources and Functions of Consumption Symbols
Consumers use products with various meanings to achieve a set of functions. Combined, these functions help define the consumer's self-concept.

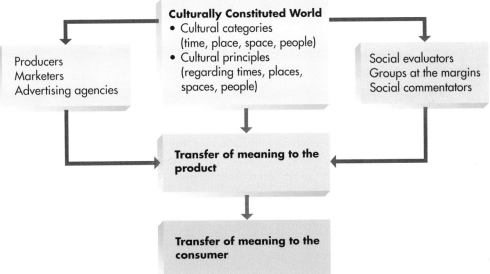

Exhibit 16.3

Transfer of Meaning from the Culture to the Product and to the Consumer
Meaning that exists at the level of the culture (e.g., youthfulness) can become associated with a product (e.g., Burton snowboards). Both marketers and nonmarketers (e.g., opinion leaders, the media) can play a powerful role in this association process. The meaning associated with the product can in turn be transferred to the consumer who uses it.

Source: Adapted from Grant McCracken, "Culture and Consumption: A Theoretical Account of the Structure and Movement of the Cultural Meaning of Consumer Goods," *Journal of Consumer Research*, 1986, pp. 71–84. Reprinted with permission of The University of Chicago Press.

Meaning comes from nonmarketing sources, as well. Specific people may serve as opinion leaders who shape, refine, or reshape cultural principles and the products and attributes they are linked to (see Chapter 11). For example, musical artists can serve as opinion leaders for fans who see LPs as desirable because their favorite performers prefer the sound quality of vinyl. Sometimes groups on the margins of society can be agents of change, as when brash, distinctive street-smart clothing worn by inner-city teens influences what mainstream designers produce.[5]

Journalists also shape cultural principles and the products associated with them. For example, restaurant reviewers may determine whether a restaurant is associated with principles like status, and style editors may determine whether clothes are associated with young and hip categories. Magazines like *Runner's World* communicate meanings associated with the runner category, such as what runners wear and eat, and what they like to do. Websites like www.bicycling.com communicate the meanings of extreme biking trips and the shoes, gloves, helmets, and energy bars that go with such activities. Celebrities like Lady Gaga can also create meaning in products by how they use them. Through all of these sources, the meaning inherent in the product is transferred to the consumer.

Meaning Derived from the Consumer

In addition to the way that products derive symbolic meaning from the surrounding culture, consumers can develop their own individual meanings associated with products, such as when a product was a gift from a friend or relative. Whether meaning stems from the culture or the consumer, however, consumption symbols can be used to say something about the consumer as a member of a group or as a unique individual. Combining these two dimensions produces the emblematic, role acquisition, connectedness, and expressiveness functions of symbols described in the next section.

The Emblematic Function

Emblematic function
The use of products to symbolize membership in social groups.

Meaning derived from culture allows us to use products to symbolize our membership in various social groups—what we call an **emblematic function**. Dresses are associated with women, and robes are associated with judges and school graduation. The music we listen to may symbolize our age, and the car we drive may symbolize our social status. Consciously or unconsciously, we use brands and products to symbolize the groups to which we belong (or want to belong[6]). At the same time, people who observe us using these products may consciously or unconsciously categorize and make inferences about us and the groups to which we belong. Just by looking at someone and his or her possessions, we might be able to tell whether that person is a member of the "surfer," "fraternity type," or "rich kid" social categories.[7] In particular, offerings can serve as geographic, ethnic, or social class emblems.

Geographic Emblems

Products can symbolize geographic identification. For example, brightly colored, loose-fitting clothing symbolizes identification with sunnier regions of the United States, such as California, Arizona, and Hawaii. Products may also symbolize geographic identification with a region even if they are used by people who live elsewhere.

Ethnic Emblems

Products and consumption activities can symbolize identification with a specific culture or subculture. African Americans sometimes wear African garb to symbolize identification with that culture. In India, Sikh men wear five Ks as symbols of their ethnic and religious affiliation: *kesh* (hair), *kada* (bangle), *kangha* (comb), *kacha* (underpants), and *kirpan* (dagger). Some consumers use ethnic emblems of other cultures or subcultures to differentiate themselves.

Consumers also use food to express ethnic identity. For example, grilled chicken, chicken mole, and steamed yellowfish reflect U.S., Mexican, and Chinese identities, respectively. U.S. consumers put ketchup on their fries, but Dutch consumers use mayonnaise. Cornmeal serves as an ethnic emblem for Haitians immigrating to the United States.[8] In addition, we can express ethnic identification by how and when we eat. Cultures differ in whether all elements of the meal are served at once or one item at a time.[9] U.S. families typically eat dinner before 7:00 P.M., but dinnertime is much later in Spain and Italy.

Social Class Emblems

Products can also symbolize social class. For example, in China, emblems of status include large luxury yachts (for the very wealthy), high-end imported cars, imported whisky, and fine imported wine (for younger consumers).[10] Rolls-Royce is a particularly prized status symbol among car buyers worldwide (see Exhibit 16.4). Overall, the brand's sales have tripled during the past three years, despite difficult economic conditions in many nations. Its top three markets are the United States, China, and Great Britain; in India, Rolls-Royce sales are up by 400 percent per year.[11]

Different social classes use different symbols in consumption rituals. For example, higher and lower social classes in the United States differ greatly in the types of clothing they wear at holiday time, the importance they place on etiquette, the types of serving dishes they use at formal family dinners, and even the way that they serve certain foods. Upper-class consumers may express their values, status, and group membership via subtle clues that set them apart from the mainstream while identifying them to others of their class.[12] Countering this type of social-class emblematic function, a growing number of U.S. schools (both public and private) require students to wear uniforms, as is common in many other countries. The purpose of this policy is to help curb gang activity, remove social class emblems, reduce students' anxiety about keeping up with peers, and encourage identification with the school community.[13]

Gender Emblems

Food, clothing, jewelry, and alcoholic beverages are only some of the product categories associated with membership in the male and female gender categories. One study of consumers in France revealed that meat and certain other foods are viewed as "man" foods, whereas celery and other foods are viewed as "woman" foods. The way that a food is eaten also reflects its gender

Social Class Emblems
Products can indicate consumer's social class, for example, Rolls-Royce is considered a highly prized status symbol worldwide.

© Liu Dawei/Xinhua/Photoshot/Newscom

appropriateness: Steak and meats that may be cut roughly and chewed intensively are viewed in some cultures as more consistent with male characteristics.[14] Other researchers have found gender differences in food preferences, with boys preferring chunky peanut butter, for instance, and girls preferring the smooth variety. These preferences may be related to culturally derived associations with boys (rough) and girls (not rough).[15]

Large, rugged, powerful vehicles such as pickup trucks are often associated with male characteristics and, not surprisingly, are marketed primarily to men. For example, most commercials and Facebook promotions for Ford's F-150 and F-250 trucks feature images of guys driving heavily laden pickups across rough terrain. Ford's tagline, "Built Tough," sums up the masculine feeling of the trucks and the ads. Yet Ford also sees an opportunity to target women who want to drive a pickup. Without changing the exterior of its pickups, Ford now adds small touches that appeal to women buyers, such as pedals for shorter drivers and back-seat DVD players for children's use.[16]

Reference Group Emblems

Harley-Davidson merchandise is a good example of how products can serve as emblems of membership in a reference group. One reason why Harley-Davidson consumers adopt "outlaw" symbols is that they like being members of a reference group with a counterculture ideology and independence. In general, consumers like a reference group emblem (like a T-shirt with the Harley-Davidson logo) more when an identity-consistent aspect of their self-concept (such as their image of themselves as fiercely independent) has been activated.[17] Varsity jackets, special hats, particular colors, or gang-designated jewelry may also symbolize reference group membership. Conversely, consumers may shun certain products to avoid being seen as members of a reference group—which, in turn, symbolizes membership in another reference group.

In addition to products, rituals are sometimes important indicators and affirmations of group membership. For example, rituals like attending graduation may reinforce our membership in the "college graduate" group. Other rituals serve as public confirmation that we have become members of a group or that we have made a life transition via a rite of passage. Among families of Hispanic heritage, the *Quinceañera* is a ritual that marks the transition of 15-year-old girls from childhood into adulthood. Another ritual is the debutante ball, which formally introduces upper-class 16-year-old girls into the group of women eligible for dating.[18]

Marketing Implications

Marketers can play three roles in establishing the emblematic function of products.

Symbol Development

Marketing can link a product and its attributes to a specific cultural category and its principles. For example, when Toyota wanted to develop the symbolic associations of its re-designed Tundra pickup truck, it targeted opinion leaders it calls "true truckers," men who work in rugged situations like construction or ranching, because "they're the taste makers, the influentials," a Toyota executive explained.[19] Sometimes marketers need to ensure that product attributes are appropriately linked with cultural principles. Miller, for example, positioned the *lite* in Miller Lite as meaning "less filling and has fewer carbohydrates"—an appropriate attribute for men—rather than *diet*, which would have made the beer seem more feminine.[20]

Symbol development can be a challenge, as India's Tata Motors learned with its Nano car. Designed as the world's cheapest car, it was advertised with stripped-down features and high fuel efficiency. Its actual price, though, wound up slightly above original estimates, which put it out of reach of the upwardly mobile, first-time car buyers who were the original target market. Consumers with a little more income could afford the Nano but did not want to be associated with its low-price symbolism. Instead, they aspired to better-than-basic cars that were less obviously low-end. As a result, the Nano has not sold as well as Tata expected.[21]

Symbol Communication

A company can use advertising to imbue a product with meaning through the setting for the ad (whether fantasy or naturalistic, interior or exterior, or rural or urban) and through other details such as the time of day and the types of people in the ad—their gender, age, ethnicity, occupation, clothing, body postures, and so on.[22] Each ad element, including the headline and words, reinforces the meaning associated with the product. For example, Disney—known for its Disney Princess products—ran ads featuring DisneyWorld as a festive destination for *quinceanera* celebrations, showing dinner-dance packages fit for a 15-year-old princess, such as *La Bella del Baile* (Belle of the Ball) and *Bailandu con una Estrella* (Dancing with a Star).

Symbol Reinforcement

Firms can design other elements of the marketing mix to reinforce the symbolic image.[23] For instance, a company can use various pricing, distribution, and product strategies to maintain a product's status image. It may give the product a premium price, distribute it through outlets with an upscale image, and incorporate certain features that are appropriate only for the targeted segment. For example, Diageo reinforces Johnnie Walker whisky's status-symbol image in Africa by emphasizing the significance of the label color (e.g., Red Label is lower priced than Black Label or Blue Label), promoting the unique taste and drinking experience, associating the brand with opinion leaders such as runner Haile Gebrselassie, and offering apps to educate consumers about whisky's finer points. This strategy is working: Although general whisky purchases are increasing in Africa, Johnnie Walker's sales are growing even more quickly.[24] A product's symbolic image may be damaged if the elements of the marketing mix clash with each other.

Symbol Removal

Some marketers have made a business of helping consumers erase symbols associated with groups with which they no longer identify. For example, the tattoo removal market is growing. Consumers often want tattoos removed because they are emblematic of an earlier time of life or an abandoned reference group and therefore impede the development of new personal identities.[25] There may even be a market in erasing symbols left behind on social media sites and Web pages.

Role acquisition function The use of products as symbols to help us feel more comfortable in a new role.

The Role Acquisition Function

In addition to serving as emblems of group membership, offerings can help us feel more comfortable in new roles. This function is called the **role acquisition function** (look back at Exhibit 16.2).

Role Acquisition Phases

Consumers fill many roles in their lives, and these roles constantly change. You may currently occupy the role of student, son or daughter, brother or sister, and worker. At some point in your life (perhaps even now), you may occupy the role of husband or wife, uncle or aunt, parent, divorcee, grandparent, retiree, widow or widower, and so on. People typically move from one role to another in three phases.[26] The first phase is *separation* from the old role. This often means disposing of products associated with the role we are leaving, the way that children give up security blankets in their transition from baby to child. Consumers who are breaking up a relationship may symbolize the relationship's end by giving away, throwing away, or destroying products that remind them of their former partners.[27] The second phase is the *transition* from one role to another, which may be accompanied by experimentation with new identities. During this transition, consumers may be willing to accept new possessions or styles that they otherwise would have rejected. Consumers may also construct a new identity through plastic surgery, dieting, new hairstyles, branding, body piercing, and tattooing. The final phase is *incorporation*, in which the consumer takes on the new role and the identity associated with it.

Use of Symbols and Rituals in Role Transitions

Exhibit 16.5 illustrates how and why we use symbols and rituals when we acquire a new role. We often feel uncomfortable with a new role because we are inexperienced in occupying it and have little knowledge about how to fulfill it. A common reaction is to use products stereotypically associated with that role. For example, MBAs who are insecure about their job prospects are more likely than other MBAs to use symbols generally associated with the role of a businessperson.[28] We often use a group of products to symbolize adoption of a new role. Having the right combination of products is important because without it we may not elicit the appropriate response from others. Imagine the reaction you would get at work if you wore white socks or sneakers with a dark business suit.

Rituals (sometimes called *rites of passage*) are an important part of role transitions. In the United States, a number of rituals mark the transition from single to married status—engagement party, wedding shower, bachelor party, rehearsal dinner, wedding, reception, and honeymoon—each with relevant enabling products.[29] In the social media era, one ritual is changing your Facebook relationship status as part of a role transition.[30] Funeral rituals in different cultures involve symbolic

Exhibit 16.5

Model of Role Acquisition

When we first enter a new role (e.g., parenthood), we may lack some role confidence. As a result, we engage in activities (e.g., have baby showers) and buy groups of products (e.g., strollers) typically associated with that role. These activities and products, along with the way that others react to our behaviors, enhance our role confidence.

Source: Adapted from Michael Solomon, "The Role of Products as Social Stimuli: A Symbolic Interactionism Perspective," *Journal of Consumer Research*, December 1983, pp. 319–329. Reprinted with permission of The University of Chicago Press.

consumption activities such as presenting or consuming special foods, buying flowers and cards, and displaying pictures or valuables that reflect on the deceased and the bereaved.[31]

Rituals often involve others whose participation helps validate the role transition. As Exhibit 16.5 shows, we use symbols and engage in rituals to get feedback from participants about whether we are fulfilling the role correctly. This feedback, called **reflexive evaluation**, helps us feel more confident in our role and thus validates our new status. Newly minted MBAs, for example, feel more confident in their role when experienced businesspeople acknowledge them as fellow businesspeople. The next section focuses on marital role transitions and products as symbols of this transition process.

Reflexive evaluation
Feedback from others that tells us whether we are fulfilling the role correctly.

Marital Transitions

Products are often an important component in the transition from single to married status. As part of separating from the old phase, the couple must decide which of their possessions to dispose of and which to move to their new household. Often presents from old boyfriends or girlfriends are discarded, as are products symbolizing one's former single status. As part of the incorporation phase, the couple acquires new products that are culturally appropriate for the married role and that help them create a mutual history. Clearly, different cultures have different marital rituals. For example, the mother-in-law often gives the keys to the house to a Hindu bride following the wedding, symbolically handing over the charge of running the house.

A similar process operates in the transition from married to divorced status. Here, each person takes back what was his or hers, and they divide their joint possessions. People may deliberately dispose of possessions that remind them of the other person. As one set of researchers notes, "Jettisoning symbols of the ex-spouse … may be psychologically necessary in the process of ending the relationship.[32]" Some people destroy possessions, an action that perhaps serves several functions—symbolically representing the destruction of the marriage, punishing the ex-spouse, and eliminating possessions that symbolize the marriage.

People may have difficulty fulfilling other symbolic functions as a result of ending a marriage. For example, one spouse may no longer have the conspicuous consumption items that once communicated social status. Thus, someone who loses a house (an important symbol of social prestige) may feel a loss of identity. On the other hand, people may acquire products symbolic of their new single status during this role transition, as some people do by purchasing a sports car or road bike at this time.

Cultural Transitions

Consumers also may change roles when they move to a new culture, often abandoning or disposing of old customs and symbols and adopting new ones in the process. Research suggests that Mexican immigrants faced different and sometimes difficult experiences in moving to the United States.[33] Among these were living in densely grouped housing, shopping in stores with a sometimes overwhelming number of choices, and dealing with unfamiliar currency. Another study shows that Indians moving to the United States needed to acquire status symbols they did not need in India, where caste and family designate class membership.[34]

Expatriates often face frustrating and formidable barriers to inclusion in a new culture. To reduce these barriers, they may participate in local events and rituals, adapt consumption to local customs, and become brand conscious, even though they may hold on to certain aspects of their home culture, like food, language, videos, photos, and jewelry.[35] Whether someone abandons or retains possessions that symbolize the old role may depend on how long the role is expected to last. The study of expatriates from India showed that consumers held onto possessions reminiscent of their culture of origin because they still considered the possibility of someday returning to India.

Social Status Transitions

Newly wealthy individuals, the "nouveaux riches," use possessions—usually ostentatious ones—to demonstrate their acquired status and validate their role. This behavior is consistent with the model of symbols and role transitions in Exhibit 16.5, which shows the importance of reflexive evaluation from others to indicate successful role performance. As one author notes, "Consumer satisfaction is derived from audience reactions to the wealth displayed by the purchaser in securing the product or service rather than to the positive attributes of the item in question."[36] In other words, "new money" consumers wear brand labels on the outside of their clothes to communicate, whereas "old money" consumers leave labels on the inside.

Marketing Implications

Marketers can apply their knowledge of consumers' role transitions in several ways.

Role Transitions and Target Consumers

Consumers in transition represent an important target market for many firms. As Procter & Gamble's global marketing officer says, "Newlyweds are in some ways the ultimate consumer."[37] Many companies target engaged couples who will soon buy offerings related to the wedding, honeymoon, and new housing. For example, a campaign from De Beers, a diamond trading company, targets women with messages reinforcing how wearing jewelry on different hands can symbolize marriage or self-expression. The tag line is "Your left hand says 'we.' Your right hand says 'me.'"[38]

Role Transitions as a Means for Developing Inventory

Because product disposition can be an important aspect of role separation, marketers of secondhand products can acquire inventory by marketing to people engaged in role transitions. For example, secondhand stores might target college students before graduation, knowing that in their role transitions many may wish to dispose of student-related paraphernalia such as furniture and clothing. Similarly, online auction sites such as www.ebay.com profit when consumers decide to dispose of items made obsolete or irrelevant by role transitions.

Role Transitions and Product Promotions

Marketers may find it useful to promote their products as instrumental in incorporating a new role. For example, marketers tout everything from shower fixtures to stock shares as acceptable wedding gifts. Bloomingdale's is one of many retailers targeting partners planning same-sex marriages, and wedding registries are showing up in places as diverse as Ace Hardware and the Metropolitan Museum of Art stores.[39] Baby gift registries have become a $240 million business, helping new parents acquire products that are important to their new role.[40]

Selling Product Constellations

Marketers can stress the importance of groups of products to consumers in the process of role acquisition.[41] Businesses featuring product constellations include websites such as www.theknot.com and www.weddingchannel.com, which offer access to one-stop shopping for wedding apparel, photographers, florists, limousines, catering companies, and related offerings. Company advertising can suggest that consumers will earn positive reflexive evaluation from others if they use an appropriate constellation of products associated with a given role.

Managing Rituals

Marketers can also be instrumental in developing services that help in planning and implementing rituals surrounding transitions, as funeral homes do by performing services in the death ritual. Rituals such as sending a greeting card on the occasion of a life transition have helped Hallmark build annual revenue beyond $4 billion. The company offers paper and electronic cards for consumers to send for such diverse occasions as being newly single and losing a job. Despite the rise of e-mail and social media, greeting cards remain an important part of the rituals that mark new roles during these transitions. "Electronic communication is great for sharing information," says a Hallmark spokesperson. "Cards are better for sharing emotions."[42] ⸻

Connectedness function
The use of products as symbols of our personal connections to significant people, events, or experiences.

The Connectedness Function

Although the meaning of offerings that serve emblematic or role acquisition functions comes from the culture, product meaning can also come from the groups consumers belong to (review Exhibit 16.2).[43] Products and consumption activities that serve the **connectedness function** express our membership in a group and symbolize our personal connections to significant people, events, or experiences in our lives. For example, you may particularly like a painting or a hat because it was a gift from a close friend. Heirlooms and genealogy studies connect people with their ancestors; family photos connect them to their descendants. People may also value concert programs, ticket stubs, and other souvenirs as reminders of special people, events, and places.[44]

Other products and acts can also symbolize connectedness. For instance, Chinese consumers use large round tables in restaurants to symbolize wholeness and the group's connectedness; Chinese New Year celebrations emphasize family ties. During Muslim feasts, everyone shares food from a community plate; those who ask for a separate plate are considered rude. Rituals such as the U.S. celebration of Thanksgiving may also symbolize connectedness. Often family members show their commitment by attending the Thanksgiving gathering—even if they have to travel long distances. Moreover, cultures like those of the United States and England emphasize family connectedness during the Christmas ritual. In other cultures, such as those of some Inuit villages in Alaska, the Christmas ritual has more of a community focus.[45]

Each family maintains its own traditions that foster connectedness. Members often strongly resist deviating from these traditions (such as trying a new stuffing recipe). Many families foster connectedness by looking at old family photographs or videos and telling family stories. Other families pass certain cherished objects from one generation to the next as symbols of the family's connectedness, with each owner acting as guardian of the special possessions.[46] This sense of connectedness may not only reaffirm social ties but may also make us nostalgic about past times.

The Expressiveness Function

Expressiveness function
The use of products as symbols to demonstrate our uniqueness—how we stand out as different from others.

As a symbol, a product has the potential to say something about our uniqueness.[47] This **expressiveness function** reflects how unique we are, not how we relate to other people. According to research, Eastern European youths like Western products because these offerings are used to create a distinct appearance that sets them apart from others.[48] We express our unique personalities through offerings like clothing, home decoration, art, leisure activities, and food consumption. We might find certain product categories, such as hairstyles or music, particularly appropriate for indicating who we are as individuals.[49] Some consumers use body piercing, branding, and tattooing to symbolize their individuality and expressiveness.[50]

Marketing Implications

The connectedness and expressive functions lead to several marketing implications. For example, marketers may wish to invoke feelings of nostalgia by connecting their product with people, places, or events. Marketers of toys and games, movies, and music have successfully encouraged consumers to connect these products with special times in their lives.[51] Colorforms, owned by University Games, recently celebrated its 60th anniversary with ads promoting the rerelease of its colorful geometric set and its Michael Jackson Dress-Up Set. The target: Parents who remember playing with a Colorforms set when they were young. "Everything you loved about it as a child will be appealing to your children," says the head of University Games.[52]

In addition, marketers can suggest that their products enhance uniqueness.[53] The British fashion house Burberry invites consumers to express themselves by custom-designing a trench coat to suit their own taste. "Luxury consumers are very interested in self-expression," says a Forrester Research analyst. "If they can put a little twist on a product that makes it individualized, it suddenly sounds like a very good value proposition."[54] See the chapter-ending bicycle case for more about this aspect of symbolic consumer behavior. _____

Multiple Functions

A given product may serve several of the functions we just described. Crystal wine goblets received as a wedding present from the bride's grandparents could serve an emblematic function because their high price tag communicates social status. They may also serve a role acquisition function, helping the newlyweds to internalize their new marital roles. In addition, as a present from grandparents, the goblets may serve a connectedness function, symbolizing the newlyweds' special relationship with their family. Finally, if the goblets are personally appealing to the couple, they may symbolize the newlyweds' individual aesthetic tastes, thus also serving an expressiveness function. We are not always aware of a product's symbolic function. We may expect certain types of gifts when we go through role transitions like graduation and marriage, but we are probably not conscious of the fact that these products are helping us adjust to our new roles. Finally, we may really like an item that we received as a gift without realizing that we are reacting in this way because it serves as a reminder of the gift giver.

Symbols and Self-Concept

The symbolic functions of products and consumption rituals are important because together they help to define and maintain our self-concept, our mental conception of who we are.[55] Social identity theory proposes that we evaluate brands in terms of their consistency with our individual identities.[56] According to the theory, our self-concept can be decomposed into many separate identities called **actual identity schemas**, including student, worker, daughter, and so on. These identities may be driven, at least in part, by the roles that we fulfill. Some identities may be especially salient or central to our self-concept. Our actual identity may be shaped by an **ideal identity schema**—a set of ideas about how the identity that we seek would be realized in its ideal form.

Our actual and ideal identity schemas influence which products we use and which consumption practices we engage in, even among consumers who object to the overcommercialization of contemporary culture.[57] Our actual identity might affect which symbols of ourselves (such as family photos or personal mugs) we bring to our workplace or put up in dorm rooms to reflect who we are.[58] Identity can also influence the amount donated to nonprofit groups. In one study, consumers contributed more when informed that another contributor who shares their identity has donated a significant amount of money.[59]

The fact that possessions help to shape our identity may explain why people who lose their possessions in natural disasters or war and people who are in institutions like the military, nursing homes, or prisons sometimes feel a loss of identity.[60] Indeed, loss of cherished possessions can induce a state of grief that resembles the death of a loved one. Some institutions, such as the military and prisons, deliberately strip individuals of their possessions to erase old identities.[61] School and work uniforms also do this, on a more subtle level. On the other hand, millions of consumers have personal websites, blogs, and other Internet places where they use words, images, audio, links, and other elements to construct and project identities digitally, shaping and sharing their self-concept online with friends.[62]

Actual identity schema A set of multiple, salient identities that reflects our self-concept.

Ideal identity schema A set of ideas about how the identity would be indicated in its ideal form.

Marketing Implications

Marketers need to consider several implications stemming from the preceding concepts.

Marketing and the Development of Consumer Self-Concepts

Marketers can play a role in both producing and maintaining an individual's self-concept. Although products may help define who we are, we also maintain our self-concept by selecting products with images that are consistent with it. For example, Converse, the athletic shoe company, allows consumers shopping in its stores or on its website to personalize their sneakers in many different ways, in line with their own self-concept. Its stores, in major cities worldwide, are equipped with special fabric printers so buyers can design and then wear their newly designed shoes on the same day. These sneakers are a good fit with self-concept because, explains a Converse executive, "the Converse customer is very creative."[63]

Exhibit 16.6

Fit with Self-Concepts
Products are most successful when brand images fit with consumers' self-concepts, such as the Japanese girl singing group, AKB48.

Product and Brand Fit with Self-Concepts

Marketers seek to create a close fit between the image of their brand and the actual or ideal identity of the consumer. The more similar a product's image is to a consumer's self-image, the more the consumer likes the product.[64] For example, in Japan, the wildly successful 60-member AKB48 all-girl singing group appeals to teen girls who see the members as *kawaii* (Japanese for "cute") and very much like themselves (see Exhibit 16.6). AKB48 has released one chart-topping song after another, and its branded merchandise is sold in the group's official stores in Japan, Hong Kong, and Taiwan.[65] A close fit between the brand and the consumer's self-concept can enhance brand loyalty and reduce the possibility of brand-switching.[66]

Product Fit with Multiple Self-Concepts

Because self-images are multifaceted, marketers must also determine whether products consistent with one aspect of the target customers' identity may be inconsistent with another aspect. For example, a new father may react negatively to disposable diapers because even though the product is consistent with his new parent identity, it is inconsistent with his environmentally conscious identity.

Advertising Fit with Self-Concepts

Finally, ads should appeal to the identity concept appropriate for the targeted segment's gender and culture.[67] Thus, some ads that target women might emphasize mutual reliance, whereas some ads that target men might emphasize autonomy. Similarly, ads geared toward consumers in China might stress culturally appropriate themes of group goals and achievement, whereas ads for U.S. consumers might stress culturally appropriate themes of personal goals and achievement.

Frame switching
Stimulated by language cues, a consumer who identifies with more than one culture will activate the aspects of his or her self-concept that relates to that language's cultural background.

Increasingly, consumers are involved in two cultures and fluent in two languages due to immigration or because they leave their home country to work. When these consumers are exposed to an ad in one of the languages they know, they experience **frame switching**, activating the aspects of their self-concepts that relate to that language's cultural background. In other words, they adopt the cultural frame of the language contained in the ad—but only if they are both bicultural and bilingual.[68] A U.S.-born consumer who lives and works in Japan will switch to an American cultural frame when exposed to an English-language billboard, for instance. As a result, marketers must consider how frame switching will affect consumers' emotional and cognitive processing of the arguments and images in their communications. ———

SPECIAL POSSESSIONS AND BRANDS

We may feel emotionally attached to certain possessions and certain brands because we see them as part of ourselves.[69] However, some products come to hold a special, valued position in our minds, whether or not they are relevant to our self-concepts.[70] For example, one consumer may regard his lawn mower as a special possession because it is very functional, whereas another may view her skis as special because they provide such enjoyment, yet neither consumer may view these items as relevant to their self-concept.[71] This section looks at what makes a brand or product special to a consumer.

Special Brands

A brand becomes special to consumers when they feel emotionally attached to it in some way. As this emotional connection strengthens, consumers become more likely to buy the special brand over and over again. Ultimately, a special brand may be able to command a price premium and will retain loyal customers even after a crisis such as a product recall or less-than-stellar product reviews.[72] For example, the influential magazine *Consumer Reports*, which reviews all kinds of products, waited a year to recommend Apple's iPhone 4, until "a flaw with its reception" was fixed.[73] Yet, the iPhone was a runaway hit because Apple is a special brand that has earned unusual brand loyalty. Brands such as Apple and Coca-Cola have carefully nurtured their brand connections over the years.

Types of Special Possessions

Although almost any possession can be special, researchers have found that special possessions typically fall into one of several categories: pets, memory-laden objects, achievement symbols, and collections.[74]

Pets

U.S. consumers tend to regard their pets as very special and spend an estimated $55 billion every year on pet products.[75] More than 60 percent of U.S. households have a pet. Whether the economy is booming or struggling, retailers such as Petco see higher demand for gourmet pet food and other premium products because, says Petco's CEO, "we are in a pretty emotional category."[76] Not every culture treats pets as special possessions. For example, cats and dogs are not treasured as pets in the Middle East, and dog owners in Korea typically feed their pets leftovers rather than dog food.

Memory-Laden Objects

Some products acquire special meaning because they evoke memories or emotions of special people, places, or experiences.[77] Examples include heirlooms, antiques, souvenirs, and gifts from special people. You may value a ticket stub—otherwise just a piece of paper—because it evokes memories of going to see your favorite band in concert. Such possessions can be therapeutic for elderly people because they evoke links to other people and happy times. Several researchers report the case of an individual who had to sell a favorite automobile because of a divorce but saved the license plates as a memento of this special possession. Many consumers consider photographs special because they are reminders of special people, and they create "shrines" by displaying photos on bureaus, mantles, and pianos.[78] Particular memory-laden objects can become *fetish objects*, viewed as extraordinarily magical objects. Even replicas or copies of a particularly valued item may become fetish objects. For example, a guitar reputed to have been played by George Harrison of the Beatles can be a fetish object for some consumers, even without evidence that it was actually Harrison's guitar.[79]

Achievement Symbols

People also regard possessions that symbolize achievement as special. One researcher who studied the Mormon migration to Utah in the 1800s found that people often moved possessions that demonstrated competence. For example, men brought tools, and women brought sewing machines and

Collections

Products can be collectible items for consumers, viewing the products as an extension of themselves.

© Gary Coronado/ZUMA Press/Newscom

other objects that had a practical function but also symbolized domestic achievement.[80] Modern-day symbols of achievement might include college diplomas, sports trophies, recognition plaques, or even conspicuously consumed items like Rolex watches or Porsches.

Collections

Collections are special possessions for many people. Common collectible items include model cars, sports memorabilia, seashells, minerals, coins, and childhood objects like baseball cards and dolls (see Exhibit 16.7).[81] Uncommon collectibles include spark plugs and drain tiles. Firms like the Bradford Exchange, the Franklin Mint, GovMint.com, and the Danbury Mint produce collectible items for consumers, but rarity makes some items particularly special. For instance, a collector paid nearly $700,000 for a Richard Mille wristwatch worn by tennis superstar Rafael Nadal during his highly successful 2010 season.[82]

Collectors often view their collections as extensions of themselves—sometimes symbolizing an aspect of their occupation, family heritage, or appearance. Collectors have the urge to "complete" the collection, such as finding the last Babe Ruth baseball card or all Beatles bootleg records, as a form of "symbolic self-completion." Researchers have studied a grocery store owner who collected antique product packages, an engineer who collected pocket watches, a woman named Bunny who collected rabbit replicas, and wealthy women who collected monogrammed silver spoons.[83] For some, collections represent a fantasy image of the self. For example, men who collect baseball cards may be keeping alive the fantasy of themselves as ball players. As is often the case with people who have special possessions, collectors tend to believe that they take better care of their collections than anyone else would.[84]

The Characteristics That Describe Special Possessions

Special possessions have several distinct characteristics.[85] First, special possessions (like our family dog or the cherished silver pencil sharpener) have *few or no substitutes* according to their owners. Insurance may pay to replace furniture that was damaged in a fire, but new furniture cannot compensate for heirloom pieces that were passed down through generations. In fact, consumers see special possessions as irreplaceable because of their associations with certain events and people in their lives.[86]

Second, because of this sentimentality, consumers will not sell special possessions at market value, if at all, and often buy special possessions with little regard for their price. Economists say that special possessions have unusually low *price elasticity*, because increasing their price has very little effect on reducing demand for them. We could never, for example, sell at any price our family pet or an afghan made by our grandmother. Collectors may pay exorbitant prices to acquire particularly sought-after objects like rare coins and one-of-a-kind wristwatches.

Third, people experience a *reluctance to discard* special possessions, even when they lose their functional value. Children often have a hard time parting with security blankets and stuffed animals and will keep these favorite objects until they are mere threads of fabric. Others have a hard time tossing out their favorite jeans. Do your parents still keep your old report cards and pictures that you drew for them? Do you still have the special gifts you got?

Some special possessions, however, are not always used for their original purpose. Some people who buy Altoids "Curiously Strong" mints retain the tin container to keep small special possessions safe.[87] Some consumers believe that a prized possession will lose valued properties if it is used to fulfill its original function, which is why some consumers preserve their new vinyl LPs and download the songs instead.

Finally, consumers frequently personify special possessions. Some name individual items in a collection, name their houses, or use a feminine or masculine pronoun when referring to their cars or boats. Perhaps even more significant, we may treat these possessions as though they were our partners, feeling such commitment and attachment that we would be devastated by their loss.[88]

Why Some Products Are Special

Possessions take on special meaning for several reasons, including their symbolic value, mood-altering properties, and instrumental importance. Exhibit 16.8 shows more specific reasons that underlie these three general categories.

▶ *Symbolic value.* Possessions may be special, in part, because they fulfill the emblematic, role adoption, connectedness, and expressiveness functions noted earlier in the chapter. For example, we may value art, heirlooms, and jewelry because they express our style or because they were gifts and tie us to special people.[89] Thus, consumers are very reluctant to part with a possession (such as a Christmas ornament or a piece of jewelry) that has symbolic meaning because it was acquired from a much-loved family member or close friend.[90]

▶ *Mood-altering properties.* Possessions may be special because they have mood-altering properties. For example, trophies, plaques, collections, and diplomas can evoke feelings of pride, happiness, and joy.[91] Pets can evoke feelings of comfort. A consumer in one study described her refrigerator as a special possession because making snacks always cheered her up. Others cited music players and music as favorite possessions because these put consumers in a good mood.[92]

▶ *Instrumental importance.* Possessions may also be special because they are extremely useful. A consumer who describes her cell phone or computer as special because she uses it constantly to get things done throughout the day is referring to this possession's instrumental value.

Consumer Characteristics Affect What Is Special

Social class, gender, and age are among the background characteristics that affect the types of things that become special to each of us.

▶ *Social class.* One study examined the meanings that people of different social classes in England gave to their possessions. People in the business class were concerned about possessions that symbolized their personal history and self-development. Unemployed people were concerned about possessions that had utilitarian value.[93] In addition, consumers who aspire to a higher social class may use particular possessions to associate themselves with that social class, even misrepresenting those products to support the self-image of belonging to the higher class.[94]

Take a possession that you regard as special, and answer the following questions using a 7-point scale (1 = not true of me; 7 = very true of me).

This possession is important to me because it ...

Symbolic Value	Symbolizes personal history	Reminds me of particular events or places Is a record of my personal history Required a lot of effort to acquire or maintain
	Represents achievement	Required a lot of effort to acquire or maintain Reminds me of my skills, achievements, or goals Reminds me of my relationship with a particular person Reminds me of my family or a group of people that I belong to Represents my family heritage or history
	Facilitates interpersonal ties	Allows me to spend time or share activities with other people
	Demonstrates status	Has social prestige value Gives me social status Makes others think well of me
	Is self-expressive	Allows me to express myself Expresses what is unique about me, different from others
Mood-Altering Properties	Provides enjoyment	Provides enjoyment, entertainment, or relaxation Improves my mood Provides comfort or emotional security
	Is spiritual	Provides a spiritual link to divine or higher forces
	Is appearance related	Is beautiful or attractive in appearance Improves my appearance or the way I look
Utilitarian Value	Is utilitarian	Allows me to be efficient in my daily life or work Has a lot of practical usefulness Provides me freedom or independence
	Has financial aspects	Is valuable in terms of money

Exhibit 16.8

Reasons Why Possessions Are Special

Take a possession that you regard as special. Most likely it is special to you because it has symbolic value, mood-altering properties, and/or utilitarian value.

Source: Adapted from Marsha Richens, "Valuing Things: The Public and Private Meanings of Possessions," *Journal of Consumer Research* 21, December 1994, pp. 504–521.

▶ *Gender.* For men, products are special when they symbolize activity and physical achievement and when they have instrumental and functional features. On the other hand, women often value symbols of identity and products that symbolize their attachment to other people.[95] A study of consumers in Niger and the United States found that women's special possessions were those that symbolized their children's accomplishments or connected consumers to others. For the U.S. women, these possessions included heirlooms and pictures; for the Niger women, they included tapestries, jewelry, and other items passed on through generations. Men chose objects that showed material comfort and possessions that indicated mastery over the environment.[96] Men are more likely to collect cars, books, and sports-related objects, and women are more likely to collect jewelry, dishes, and silverware.[97]

▶ *Age.* Although individuals have special possessions at all ages, what they regard as special changes with age. For example, stuffed animals are very important for children, music and motor vehicles are highly prized among teenagers, and photographs take on increasing importance as consumers enter adulthood and old age.

Rituals Used with Special Possessions

We often engage in rituals designed to create, energize, or enhance the meaning of special possessions. These rituals can occur at the acquisition, usage, or disposition stage of consumption.

Possession ritual Ritual we engage in when we first acquire a product that helps to make it "ours."

At the acquisition stage, **possession rituals** enable the consumer to claim personal possession of new goods.[98] When you buy new jeans, for example, you may change the length, cut them at the knees, or add embellishments. You may adorn a new car with personal markers like seat covers or pillows. When you move to a new house or apartment, you hang pictures, buy curtains, and position the furniture.

Possession rituals for previously owned goods include wiping away traces of the former owner.[99] For example, when you buy a new home, you thoroughly clean it, tear down old wallpaper, and take down personal markers like the name on the mailbox. However, it is not always possible to wipe away meaning. In China, for example, consumers often build new houses because of a sense that older structures are "contaminated" by the former occupants. This is the reverse of the "magic" that consumers feel when acquiring possessions that were once owned or touched by a famous person (or that person's relative), such as George Harrison's guitar or a baseball autographed by a Major League team. Some studies show that the feeling of disgust that consumers feel for certain products (such as raw meat) can carry over to products that are in physical contact with those "disgusting" products. With this in mind, grocery stores often provide plastic bags so shoppers can keep meat packages from touching other products in their shopping carts.[100]

Grooming ritual Ritual we engage in to bring out or maintain the best in special products.

At the consumption stage, consumers may engage in **grooming rituals** to bring out or maintain the best in special products.[101] Some consumers spend hours washing and waxing their cars or cleaning house before visitors arrive. Sometimes the grooming ritual extends to you personally, as when you spend a lot of time making yourself look good for a special event.

Divestment ritual Ritual enacted at the disposition stage that is designed to wipe away all traces of our personal meaning in a product.

Finally, when the offering loses its symbolic meaning, consumers engage in **divestment rituals**—wiping away all traces of personal meaning.[102] For example, many people remove the address labels before giving away magazines that they subscribe to or delete personal files before selling or donating a computer. We might even get rid of a possession in stages, moving it from the living room to the attic before finally selling it or throwing it away.

Disposing of Special Possessions

People dispose of special possessions for different reasons and in different ways. Consumers dispose of special possessions during life transitions, such as when moving to a university, to one's first home, getting married, and so on. Older consumers make disposition decisions when experiencing periods of crisis, when moving to an institution, when approaching death, and when marking rites of passage and progression—although some transfer special possessions only after death through a will. Sometimes the consumer hopes that giving the object to a relative will invoke memories, express love, or lead to a symbolic immortality; at other times the consumer seeks to control disposition decisions and timing. An older consumer generally considers which recipient will best appreciate the special object's meaning, continue to use or care for it, or uphold family traditions, or he or she may simply give it to the person who asks for it first.[103]

SACRED MEANING

Sacred entities People, things, and places that are set apart, revered, worshiped, and treated with great respect.

Profane things Things that are ordinary and hence have no special power.

Although many possessions are considered special, some are so special that they are viewed as sacred. **Sacred entities** are people, things, and places that are set apart, revered, worshiped, and treated with great respect. We may find such entities deeply moving, and we may feel anger and revulsion when they are not respected. In contrast, **profane things** are ordinary, without special power. Profane objects are often distinguished from sacred ones by the fact that they are used for more mundane purposes.[104]

Movie stars, popular singers, historic figures like John F. Kennedy and Martin Luther King Jr., and religious leaders such as the pope and Buddha are regarded by many people as sacred. The sacred status of famous people is exemplified by the crowds visiting the graves of celebrities like Princess Diana and the homes of living or dead celebrities, such as Elvis's Graceland.

One reason why heirlooms and photographs of ancestors take on sacred status is that we may view our ancestors as heroes. A similar phenomenon explains why we treat items associated with

HAMILTON
THE AMERICAN BRAND SINCE 1892

Automatic movement
Sapphire crystal
Swiss made
www.hamiltonwatch.com
VENTURA XXL
ELVIS® ANNIVERSARY COLLECTION

© EPE, Reg. U. S. Pat & TM Off

Image Courtesy of The Advertising Archives

Exhibit 16.9

Sacred Entities

Some famous objects, places, or people—like Elvis—are so special that they attain a sacred status and elicit emotions in consumers. That is why some ads, like this watch ad, may be successful if they combine products with an emotional response.

famous statesmen such as George Washington and Winston Churchill as sacred. Although not part of our actual past, these heroes were instrumental in formulating national identities. Consumers demonstrate their reverence by visiting the places that mark these historic figures.[105]

Many consumers also regard as sacred such objects as national flags, patriotic songs, art, collections, family recipes, and the Bible and such places as museums, the Alamo, the Taj Mahal, and the Great Wall of China. These sacred objects and places evoke powerful feelings, sometimes causing people to weep or feel emotional when viewing them. In addition to sacred people, objects, and places, we may identify certain times and events, religious holidays, weddings, births, deaths, and grace before meals as sacred. Sacred entities involve some mystery or myth that raises them above the ordinary.[106] The pope, for example, is viewed as being almost godlike. And legendary figures such as Elvis Presley, Marilyn Monroe, and John F. Kennedy are associated with mystery (see Exhibit 16.9). Sacred entities have qualities that transcend time, place, or space. When you enter the Alamo, for instance, you may feel as if you are back in the period when the historic fighting took place.

Sacred objects also possess strong approach/avoidance characteristics and create an overwhelming feeling of power and fascination. For example, you may simultaneously desire to be close to but also watch from a distance people you view as heroes and heroines. Encountering sacred entities may evoke certain feelings, such as ecstasy or the sense of being smaller and humbler than the sacred entity. For instance, some people may feel that they have accomplished little in life in comparison with the achievements of heroes like Martin Luther King Jr. Some people feel humbled by the mass of humanity represented by the Vietnam Memorial. Moreover, sacred objects can create strong feelings of attachment, such as the need to take care of and nurture the sacred entity. Often sacred objects involve rituals that dictate how we should behave in the object's presence, such as the right and wrong way to treat the American flag.

Sacredness may be maintained by scarcity and exclusivity.[107] For example, the sacred status of special works of art derives from their uniqueness and the fact that their high price maintains their exclusivity. Entities that were once sacred can be made profane if they are not treated with due respect or if their sacred status is eliminated through commercialization. We can feel anger and disgust at the profaning of a sacred person or sacred object. In one study, some *Star Trek* fans said they were "barely" able to "stand watching the show" because of the way that the series was being commercially exploited.[108]

Marketing Implications

Marketers need to be aware of the sacred meanings that people, objects, places, and events can have to consumers.

Creating and Maintaining Sacredness

Sometimes marketers create sacredness in objects or people. For example, the promoters of a famous movie star might heighten his sacred status by creating or enhancing his mystery and myth, making him exclusive, and promoting the powerful emotional effect he has on people. Marketers may also help maintain sacredness—for example, by keeping the price of sacred objects like collections, fine art, and rare jewelry very high. Before Charles Leski Auctions accepts autographed Beatles memorabilia for auction in Australia, its experts authenticate the signatures so buyers will know they are getting what they pay for. Because some items were signed by the group's road manager rather than one of the Fab Four, "we end up breaking a lot of hearts," says an auction official. And as the 50th anniversary of the Beatles' first Australian concert approached, auction prices for the group's memorabilia—considered sacred by fans—continued to rise.[109]

Avoiding the Profaning of Sacred Objects and Entities

Marketers sometimes unintentionally profane sacred objects through commercialization. Some consumers believe that Elvis Presley has been profaned by commercial Elvis paraphernalia. Selling religious trinkets outside the sacred properties of certain religious sites may profane these places as well. Benetton, the Italian apparel firm, touched off a worldwide controversy when its ad agency digitally manipulated photos of religious and political leaders to show them kissing each other. The company said this "Unhate" campaign was intended to "combat the culture of hatred in all its forms." One ad depicted a digitally created kiss between Pope Benedict XVI, the head of the Roman Catholic Church, and Ahmed Mohamed el-Tayeb, the leader of Cairo's al-Azhar mosque. Public outrage and official protests from the Vatican prompted Benetton to end the campaign within hours of its introduction.[110]

Product Involvement in Sacred Activities and Rituals

In some cases, marketers sell products regarded as instrumental to the continuation or conduct of sacred occasions and rituals. Marketers like Hallmark profitably capitalize on sacred rituals such as Christmas celebrations by selling products (tree ornaments, ribbons, wrapping paper, cards) regarded as important parts of these events. _____

THE TRANSFER OF SYMBOLIC MEANING THROUGH GIFT GIVING

This chapter has shown how consumers invest products, times, activities, places, and people with symbolic meaning. Some meanings enhance the special and/or sacred status of the product, and some are instrumental in developing or maintaining the consumer's self-concept. Another important aspect of symbolic consumption involves transferring meaning from one individual to another through gifts of physical goods (such as clothing) or experiences (such as a gift card for a restaurant).[111]

The Timing of Gifts

Some gift-giving occasions are culturally determined and timed. In the United States, these include Valentine's Day, Mother's Day, and Father's Day. Koreans celebrate the 100th day of a baby's life, and families in China celebrate when a baby is one month old. Koreans also give gifts to elders and family members on New Year's Day. Consumers in cultures around the world also celebrate various gift-giving holidays such as Valentine's Day, Hanukkah, and Kwanzaa.[112]

Some gift-giving occasions are culturally prescribed but occur at a time that is specific to each individual.[113] These are often the transitions discussed earlier: anniversaries, graduations, birthdays, weddings, bridal and baby showers, retirement parties, and religious transitions such as baptism, first communion, or bar mitzvah. Still other gift-giving occasions are ad hoc, as when we give gifts as part of a reconciliation attempt, to celebrate the birth of a child, to cheer up someone who is ill, or to thank someone for helping us.

Three Stages of Gift Giving

Gift giving consists of three stages, as shown in Exhibit 16.10. In the **gestation stage**, we consider what to give the recipient. The **presentation stage** occurs with the actual giving of the gift. Finally, in the **reformulation stage**, we reevaluate the relationship based on the gift-giving experience.

The Gestation Stage

The gestation stage before a gift is given involves the motives for and emotions surrounding giving, the nature and meaning of the gift, the value of the gift, and the amount of time spent searching for the gift.

Gestation stage The first stage of gift giving, when we consider what to give someone.

Presentation stage The second stage of gift giving, when we actually give the gift.

Reformulation stage The final stage of gift giving, when we reevaluate the relationship based on the gift-giving experience.

Exhibit 16.10

A Model of the Gift-Giving Process

The process of gift giving can be described in terms of three stages: (1) the *gestation stage*, at which we think about and buy the gift; (2) the *presentation stage*, at which we actually give the gift; and (3) the *reformulation stage*, at which we reevaluate our relationship based on the nature of the gift-giving experience. At each stage we can identify several issues that affect the gift-giving process.

Gestation Stage
- Motives
- Nature of the gift
- Value of the gift
- Search time

Presentation Stage
- Ceremony
- Timing and surprise elements
- Attention to the recipient
- Recipient's reaction

Reformulation Stage
- Relationship bonding
- Reciprocation

Motives for and Emotions Surrounding Giving

During the gestation stage we develop motives for gift giving.[114] On the one hand, people may give for altruistic reasons—to help or show love for the recipient. For example, a relative may give a large cash gift to help a young couple start their married life. We may also give for agnostic reasons because we derive positive emotional pleasure from the act of giving. Or we may give a gift for instrumental reasons, expecting the recipient to give something in return, as when a student gives a teacher a small gift in hopes of a higher grade. Consumers may also give for purely obligatory reasons because they feel the situation or the relationship demands it. Indeed, sometimes we do not react positively to gifts given by others because we now feel the obligation to reciprocate.

Sometimes we give gifts because we want to reduce guilt or alleviate hard feelings. In divorce, for example, the spouse who feels responsible for the breakup tends to give the partner more than a fair share in what is called *compensatory giving*.[115] Sometimes people have antagonistic motives for gift giving. For example, if you are invited to the wedding of someone you do not like, you might give the couple something you think is not very beautiful. Sometimes givers feel anxiety about giving a gift.[116] They may feel that the gift has to be absolutely perfect or worry if they lack the time or money to find a suitable gift.

The Appropriateness and Meaning of the Gift The appropriateness of the gift depends on the situation and the relationship between the gift giver and the recipient. For example, a worker would not give a boss a gift of lingerie because such items are too personal. Likewise, you would not give good friends a token wedding gift because the relationship dictates something more substantial. Although token gifts may not be appropriate on a clearly defined gift-giving occasion, they can be highly significant when no gift is expected. Spontaneously giving a gift, even something small, can signify love and caring.[117]

Thus, you may feel quite touched when your significant other buys you "a little something." Token gifts are quite important for recipients with whom we do not have strong ties. It is appropriate and desirable to send holiday and birthday cards to people we see infrequently.[118]

The gift may also symbolize a particular meaning to the receiver.[119] For example, gifts can represent values we regard as appropriate for the recipient, such as domesticity for new brides and grooms or a new set of expectations. An engagement ring symbolizes expectations regarding commitment and future fidelity, just as giving golf clubs at retirement symbolizes expectations regarding future leisure. Gifts can also be symbolic of the self, as when giving a piece of art or something that the giver has created.

The Value of the Gift The value of the gift is an important element of the gift-selection process. You might splurge on a Mother's Day gift to show your mother how much you love her. The consumer's culture can influence decisions about the value of a gift. In Japan, for example, people lose face if the gift they receive exceeds the value of the gift they have given.[120] Interestingly, consumers perceive that gifts they buy for others are more valuable, in economic terms, than gifts received from others. When giver and receiver had close connections, however, the receiver perceived higher economic value in the gift.[121] A giver may also use the value of a gift to repay a favor done by the receiver. Here, the giver's motive is to avoid feeling indebted to the receiver for the favor. The value of the purchased gift helps change what was a social exchange into an economic exchange.[122]

The Amount of Time Spent Searching   The amount of time spent searching for a gift symbolizes the nature and intensity of the giver's relationship with the recipient. Men and women differ in how much time and effort they invest in the search for a gift. Women are reportedly more involved in holiday gift shopping than are men.[123] Women also appear to spend more time searching for the perfect gift, whereas men are more likely to settle for something that "will do."[124]

The Presentation Stage

The presentation stage describes the actual exchange of the gift. Here, the ritual or ceremonial aspects of the giving process become very important.[125]

Ceremony   During the presentation stage, the giver decides whether to wrap the gift and, if so, how. Wrapping the present nicely in appropriate paper helps to de-commodify, or make more personal, a mass-produced product.[126] However, the importance of the gift packaging depends on the formality and spontaneity of the occasion. For example, unanticipated gifts, such as a boss's surprise gift to an assistant or a wife's surprise gift to her husband, may be less formally wrapped and may even be appropriate if left unwrapped.

Timing and Surprise   Both the timing and the possibility of surprise may be important in gift giving. For example, although we know that gift giving is part of the Christmas ritual and that the wrapped gifts are even prominently displayed under the tree—sometimes for days before the actual exchange—being surprised by what they contain is often a key element. The excitement of unwrapping an item is heightened by having the recipient guess what the package contains. Although surprise is a valued part of the ritual, it is not always achieved. One study found that right before Christmas, some husbands purchase items that have been chosen in advance by their wives. Here, the gift giving is an orchestrated event with the husband playing the role of "purchasing agent."[127]

Attention to the Recipient   Paying attention to the recipient can be a critical dimension in the presentation stage. For example, attendees at wedding showers are expected to watch closely as the bride-to-be opens her gifts. Another factor to be considered is the congruence between the gift, the recipient's self-concept, and the giver's self-concept. Specifically, giving a gift that conflicts with the giver's self-concept can have a negative effect on the giver. As an example, if you give your best friend a T-shirt with an image he likes, but you find it offensive because it conflicts with your self-concept, you will not feel good about your choice.[128]

Recipient's Reaction   Another aspect is the reaction that the giver hopes to elicit from the recipient, the recipient's actual reaction, and the giver's response to the recipient's reaction. If you spent a lot of time and effort looking for the perfect gift and then the recipient opens the package quickly and goes on to the next gift without a word, you will probably feel hurt. As noted earlier, you may also feel anxious at the presentation stage if you are not sure about whether the recipient will like your gift.[129]

The Reformulation Stage

The reformulation stage marks the third and final stage of the gift-giving process. At this stage, the giver and the recipient reevaluate their relationship based on the gift-giving process.

Relationship Bonding   A gift may affect the relationship between giver and recipient in different ways, as shown in Exhibit 16.11. A gift can either maintain, strengthen, or weaken the relationship between the giver and receiver. One study found that gifts could strengthen a relationship by communicating feelings of connection, bonding, and commitment. Gifts can also affirm the relationship, validating existing feelings of commitment. Research suggests that a romantic relationship is likely to last longer when one member gives the other a gift to publicly announce their relationship. On the negative side, inappropriate gifts or those showing limited search effort or interest in the recipient's desires can weaken a relationship, creating the perception that the relationship lacks bonding and connection.[130] In many cultures, it is inappropriate to give money as a gift, in particular

Exhibit 16.11

Possible Effect of Gift Giving on the Relationship

Gifts can have many different effects on a relationship— effects that range from strengthening to severing the relationship.

Relational Effect	Description	Experiential Themes
Strengthening	Gift receipt improves the quality of the relationship between giver and recipient. Feelings of connection, bonding, commitment, and/or shared meaning are intensified.	Epiphany
Affirmation	Gift receipt validates the positive quality of the relationship between giver and recipient. Existing feelings of connection and/or shared meaning are validated.	Empathy Adherence Affirming farewell Recognition
Negligible effect	The gift-receipt experience has a minimal effect on perceptions of relationship quality.	Superfluity "Error" Charity Overkill
Negative confirmation	Gift receipt validates an existing negative quality of the relationship between giver and recipient. A lack of feelings of connection, bonding, and/or shared meaning is validated.	Absentee Control
Weakening	Gift receipt harms the quality of the relationship between giver and recipient. There is a newly evident or intensified perception that the relationship lacks connection, bonding, and/or shared meaning, but the relationship remains.	Burden Insult
Severing	Gift receipt so harms the quality of the relationship between giver and recipient that the relationship is dissolved.	Threat Nonaffirming farewell

Source: Julie A. Ruth, Cele C. Otnes, and Frédéric F. Brunel, "Gift Receipt and the Reformulation of Interpersonal Relationships," *Journal of Consumer Research* 25, March 1999, p. 389. Reprinted by permission of The University of Chicago Press.

between friends and loved ones. Rituals such as wrapping the money or converting it into a gift card aim to transform money into a personal symbol.[131]

Reciprocation The reformulation stage also has implications for how and whether the recipient will reciprocate on the next gift-giving occasion. If you gave someone a nice gift on one occasion, you would generally expect the recipient to reciprocate on the next occasion. If, on the other hand, you gave a gift that weakened the tie between you and the recipient, the latter may not give you a very nice gift or may give no gift at all on the next gift-giving occasion.

Some kinds of gift-giving situations or recipients are exempt from reciprocation.[132] For example, if you give someone a gift because she is ill or has experienced some tragedy (say, her house burned down), you will not expect her to reciprocate. However, if someone unexpectedly gives you a Christmas gift, you will usually feel guilty and want to rush out and buy him a gift, too. People of limited financial means (children, students) or lower status (a clerk, as opposed to a boss) may be regarded as exempt from giving to higher status people. Thus, it is appropriate for parents to give their children gifts and expect nothing in return. Women have also been reported to feel less obligated to reciprocate in date-related gift giving, perhaps because of culturally prescribed notions regarding men's generally higher economic power.[133]

Expectations of reciprocation depend on the culture and the relationship between the giver and the recipient. In China and Hong Kong, for instance, where gifts are commonly exchanged during certain festivals and other important occasions, reciprocity is discouraged among family members and close friends because there is no need to build ties through gift giving.[134]

Marketing Implications

Firms can build on several aspects of gift giving to market more effectively to consumers.

Promoting Products and Services as Gifts

Many marketers promote their products for gift-giving occasions, and often gift-giving occasions are the primary focus of their business. Consider the greeting card industry, which gets its biggest U.S. sales boost from the Christmas/Hanukkah/Kwanzaa season, when roughly 1.5 billion commercially produced greeting cards are bought and mailed. This figure doesn't even include homemade cards created by scrapbooking enthusiasts or the hundreds of millions of electronic cards that consumers send.[135] In some cases, uncommon gifts are promoted as appropriate for various gift-giving occasions. For example, engaged couples can now register for gift-givers to contribute toward a honeymoon trip, a home down payment, or a charitable donation in honor of the bride and groom.[136]

Technology and Gift Shopping

Technology has created major changes in the gift-giving process. Online shopping is faster and more convenient than ever, and many retail sites invite consumers to post "wish lists" showing the gifts that they would like to receive for holidays, weddings, and other occasions. Another major change affecting consumers and retailers is the growing use of gift cards, which have become a $100 billion business.[137] Knowing that consumers who receive gift cards for Christmas often go shopping right after the holiday, retailers are boosting profit margins by displaying new, full-priced products as well as discounting seasonal merchandise for postholiday shoppers. In fact, the day after Christmas is now the third-busiest shopping day for stores because of the widespread use of gift cards—and because recipients tend to spend more freely when they have a gift card.[138]

Alternatives to Traditional Gifts

Knowing that consumers are tiring of the commercialism, hassle, and materialism surrounding gift-giving occasions like Christmas, some charities ask consumers to instead give gifts to people in need. For example, the nonprofit organization Heifer International publishes a holiday catalog inviting consumers to purchase "gift" animals such as geese or bees to help families around the world become self-sufficient. As another example, giving to the United Nations refugee agency helps provide shelter and food to families displaced by famine in East Africa. Why give a donation instead of a traditional gift? "These gifts are more fun, more inspiring, and more meaningful than most gifts," according to Melissa Winkler of International Rescue Committee, a nonprofit organization.[139]

SUMMARY

Some offerings have symbolic meaning. Consumers use some products as conscious or unconscious badges that designate the various social categories to which they belong. Products and rituals hold symbolic significance when people undergo role transitions; serve as symbols of connection to meaningful people, places, and times; and are symbols of individuality and uniqueness. The symbolic uses of products and rituals affect the consumer's self-concept.

Consumers regard some possessions and brands as very special, nonsubstitutable, and irreplaceable. These items may be purchased with little regard for price and are rarely discarded, even if their functional value is gone; they may not even be used for their original purpose. In part, possessions are special

because they serve as emblems, facilitate role transitions, connect us to others, or express our unique styles. They are special because they indicate personal mastery and achievements or are mood enhancing. Background characteristics such as social class, gender, and age all influence the type of object someone regards as special.

Some entities (possessions, people, places, objects, times, and events) are so special that they are regarded as sacred. Consumers care for and nurture these possessions and often devise special rituals to handle them. However, sacred objects can be profaned or made ordinary by commercialization, inappropriate usage, or divestment patterns. Gift giving is a process of transferring meaning in products from one person to another in three phases: gestation, presentation, and reformulation. Such occasions are often culturally prescribed but may vary in the timing. The manner in which the first two phases of gift giving are enacted can affect the long-term viability of the relationship between giver and recipient.

Questions for Review and Discussion

1. Contrast the emblematic function of a product with the role acquisition function; also contrast the connectedness function of a product with the expressive function.

2. What is reflexive evaluation, and how does it affect role acquisition?

3. How does the ideal identity schema relate to a person's actual identity schema?

4. What is frame switching, and why do marketers have to consider it when targeting bilingual, bicultural consumers?

5. What are the three main reasons why possessions take on special meaning?

6. Why do consumers engage in possession, grooming, and divestment rituals?

7. What are sacred entities, and how are they profaned?

8. Identify the three stages of gift giving, and explain how gift giving can affect relations between the giver and the recipient.

CONSUMER BEHAVIOR CASE

Bicycles: More than Pedal Power

Not so long ago, a bicycle was, well, just a pedal-powered way to get around. Today, the bicycle is not just two-wheeled transportation—it has become a major industry worldwide. A growing number of consumers are buying bikes for commuting, for fun, for status, for personal style, and for environmental reasons.

Especially in developing nations, where incomes are rising and middle-class consumers are looking for more than basic transportation, demand for better bicycles is rising year after year as the product category takes on new significance as a sign of wealth and of interest in a healthy leisure-time activity. "As people become more affluent, they tend to go to global brands," says the director of international sales for Wisconsin-based Trek Bicycles, "and that's where global brands have advantages." Trek's high-quality bikes are now marketed in two dozen nations, with even wider distribution on the way.

Some top automotive firms are putting their brands on upscale bicycles. Porsche, for example, offers high-end bicycles with precision-made bodies and brakes so riders can glide smoothly on paved paths and navigate off-road trails. Each carries the red, black, and gold brand badge positioned below the handle bars, signaling that the rider is pedaling a Porsche.

Luxury designer brands are also involved in the burgeoning bicycle business. Gucci's creative designer has developed a lightweight, high-performance bicycle and accessories (such as a helmet and riding gloves)

for Bianchi, decorated with the red and green stripes that are Gucci's brand symbol. Missoni's colorful bicycle, marketed by cheap chic retailer Target at a more affordable price, is for city-dwellers or suburbanites who want to pedal along in style.

Folding bicycles are increasingly popular, everywhere from Kentucky to Kuala Lumpur. On a recent World Car-Free Day, cyclists rode folding bicycles along Kuala Lumpur roads to nearby mass-transit stations, folded their bikes, and took them on board. They were not just demonstrating a greener alternative to gas-powered vehicles—they were also showing the convenience and ease of taking folding bikes on commuter trains. Another use of bicycles is for tourist transportation. In Santiago, Chile, cyclists have ridden through the streets to promote environmentally friendly bicycle tourism and encourage the construction of bicycle paths throughout Patagonia.

From the great outdoors to the inner city, bicycles are often used to show off the rider's personal style. In particular, youngsters who aren't yet old enough to drive four-wheeled vehicles like to cruise the streets in home-decorated two wheelers. One urban trend in bicycle bling is the "scraper bike," a small-framed bike with special touches such as dashes of color, duct tape detailing, aluminum foil wrapped around the wheel spokes, and flashy, outsized accessories. A scraper bike song by the California hip-hop group Trunk Boiz has attracted more than 3 million YouTube views and spread the look's popularity far beyond the West Coast. "It just makes you feel like a star," says one teen of the scraper bike he spray painted and outfitted with foiled-wrapped spokes. A gallery in Berkeley, California, even exhibited scraper bikes as objects of art.

Consumers who are serious about their bicycling look carefully at specifications and notice which brands the top athletes endorse. Cannondale, for example, is endorsed by women's triathlete champion Chrissie Wellington. Many enthusiasts attend bicycle shows, watch bicycle races, test-ride new models, and compare every technical detail before deciding what to buy. One purchase leads to another as enthusiasts acquire all the gear they need—bike racks, locks, seats, tools, and anything else they must have to keep their

bikes looking good and working properly. No wonder the two-wheeler business is gaining speed.[140]

CASE QUESTIONS

1. What emblematic functions can a bicycle serve? Be specific.
2. How can a bicycle be part of a social status transition?
3. Do scraper bikes derive their product meaning from the culture or the individual? Explain your answer.
4. What sacred meaning(s) might a bicycle hold for a consumer? What are the implications for marketers?

ENDNOTES

1. Christopher Morris, "Pros Hope Oldies Can Still Spin Gold," *Variety*, November 19, 2011, www.variety.com; Lainie Steelman, "Vinyl Records Making a Comeback," *McDough Voice (Macomb, IL)*, December 6, 2011, www.mcdonoughvoice.com; "The Revival of Vinyl: Back to Black," *Economist*, August 20, 2011, p. 56; Michael Christopher, "Rock Music Menu: Making the Case for Vinyl," *Delaware County Daily Times (Penn.)*, September 9, 2011, www.delcotimes.com; Yusuf Omar, "Vinyl Destination," *Independent Online (South Africa)*, December 1, 2011, www.iol.co.za; and Ben James, "Re-Vinylised," *Impact (University of Nottingham, England)*, December 6, 2011, n.p.

2. Grant McCracken, "Culture and Consumption," *Journal of Consumer Research*, June 1986, pp. 71–84; and Grant McCracken, *Culture and Consumption* (Indianapolis, Ind.: Indiana University Press, 1990).

3. Lisa Peñaloza, "Consuming the American West: Animating Cultural Meaning and Memory at a Stock Show and Rodeo," *Journal of Consumer Research*, December 2001, pp. 369–398.

4. See Craig J. Thompson, "Marketplace Mythology and Discourses of Power," *Journal of Consumer Research*, June 2004, pp. 162–175; Elizabeth C. Hirschman, Linda Scott, and William B. Wells, "A Model of Product Discourse," *Journal of Advertising*, Spring 1998, pp. 33–50; Barbara A. Phillips, "Thinking into It: Consumer Interpretation of Complex Advertising Images," *Journal of Advertising*, Summer 1997, pp. 77–86; Cele Otnes and Linda Scott, "Something Old, Something New: Exploring the Interaction Between Ritual and Advertising," *Journal of Advertising*, Spring 1996, pp. 33–50; and Jonna Holland and James W. Gentry, "The Impact of Cultural Symbols on Advertising Effectiveness: A Theory of Intercultural Accommodation," in eds. Merrie Brucks and Debbie MacInnis, *Advances in Consumer Research*, vol. 24 (Provo, Utah: Association for Consumer Research, 1997), pp. 483–489.

5. Ruth La Ferla, "Young Shoppers Chase Up-from-the-Asphalt Niche Designers," *New York Times*, December 21, 2007, pp. G1, G10.

6. Jennifer Edson Escalas and James R. Bettman, "You Are What They Eat: The Influence of Reference Groups on Consumers' Connections to Brands," *Journal of Consumer Psychology* 13, no. 3, 2003, pp. 339–348.

7. For a discussion of how consumers use fashion to characterize their identity and infer aspects of others' identities, see Craig J. Thompson and Diana L. Haytko, "Speaking of Fashion," *Journal of Consumer Research*, June 1997, pp. 15–42.

8. Laura R. Oswald, "Culture Swapping: Consumption and the Ethnogenesis of Middle-Class Haitian Immigrants," *Journal of Consumer Research*, March 1999, pp. 303–318.

9. Elisabeth Furst, "The Cultural Significance of Food," in ed. Per Otnes, *The Sociology of Consumption: An Anthology* (Oslo, Norway: Solum Forlag, 1988), pp. 89–100.

10. Frederick Balfour, "China's Next Port of Call: Luxury Yachts," *Business Week*, May 9–15, 2011, pp. 20–21; and "Breaching the Grape Wall of China," *Business Week*, February 10, 2005, www.businessweek.com.

11. Andrew Cave, "Rolls-Royce Seeks Slice of South American Luxury Car Market," *Telegraph (UK)*, October 23, 2011, www.telegraph.co.uk; and "The New High Rollers," *Economist*, January 15, 2011, p. 61.

12. Jonah Berger and Morgan Ward, "Subtle Signs of Inconspicuous Consumption," *Journal of Consumer Research*, December 2010, pp. 555–569.

13. Tina A. Brown, "Kids Uniformly Love the Clothes, Parents Love the Prices," *Hartford Courant*, August 9, 2007, p. B2.

14. Pierre Bourdieu, *Distinction: A Social Critique of the Judgment of Taste* (Cambridge, Mass.: Harvard University Press, 1984); for other research on gender associations with food, see Deborah Heisley, "Gender Symbolism in Food," doctoral dissertation, Northwestern University, 1991.

15. Sidney Levy, "Interpreting Consumer Mythology," *Journal of Marketing* 45, no. 3, 1982, pp. 49–62.

16. Dean Reynolds, "Ford Marketing Trucks to Women," *ABC News*, January 7, 2011, http://abcnews.go.com.

17. Americus Reed II, "Activating the Self-Importance of Consumer Selves," *Journal of Consumer Research* 31, no. 2, 2004, pp. 286–295.

18. Jennifer Edison Escalas, "The Consumption of Insignificant Rituals: A Look at Debutante Balls," in eds. Leigh McAlister and Michael L. Rothschild, *Advances in Consumer Research*, vol. 20 (Provo, Utah: Association for Consumer Research, 1993), pp. 709–716.

19. Jon Gertner, "From 0 to 60 to World Domination," *New York Times Magazine*, February 18, 2007, pp. 34+.

20. James B. Arndorfer, "Miller Lite: Bob Mikulay," *Advertising Age*, November 1, 2004, p. S12; and "Miller Lite," *Beverage Dynamics*, January–February 2002, p. 40.

21. Jyoti Thottam, "The Little Car That Couldn't," *Time*, October 24, 2011, pp. B1–B4; and "Tata's Nano: Stuck in Low Gear," *Economist*, August 20, 2011, pp. 60–61.

22. Michael R. Solomon, "Building Up and Breaking Down: The Impact of Cultural Sorting on Symbolic Consumption," in eds. Elizabeth C. Hirschman and Jagdish N. Sheth, *Research in Consumer Behavior* (Greenwich, Conn.: JAI Press, 1988), pp. 325–351.

23. Solomon, "Building Up and Breaking Down: The Impact of Cultural Sorting on Symbolic Consumption"; and James H. Leigh and Terrace G. Gabel, "Symbolic Interactionism," *Journal of Consumer Marketing*, Winter 1992, pp. 27–39.

24. "Persuading Africans to Switch from Beer to Scotch," *Economist*, October 1, 2011, www.economist.com.

25. Emily Wax, "Rethinking the Ink: Laser Tattoo Removal Gains Popularity," *Washington Post*, December 11, 2011, www.washingtonpost.com; and Myrna L. Armstrong and Donata C. Gabriel, "Motivation for Tattoo Removal," *Archives of Dermatology*, April 1996, pp. 412–416.

26. John W. Schouten, "Personal Rites of Passage and the Reconstruction of Self," in eds. Rebecca H. Holman and Michael R. Solomon, *Advances in Consumer Research*, vol. 18 (Provo, Utah: Association for Consumer Research, 1991), pp. 49–51.

27. Melissa Martin Young, "Dispositions of Possessions During Role Transitions," in eds. Rebecca H. Holman and Michael R. Solomon, *Advances in Consumer Research*, vol. 18 (Provo, Utah: Association for Consumer Research, 1991), pp. 33–39.

28. Robert A. Wicklund and Peter M. Gollwitzer, *Symbolic Self-Completion* (Hillsdale, N.J.: Lawrence Erlbaum, 1982).

29. Diane Ackerman, *A Natural History of Love* (New York: Random House, 1994).

30. Angela Woodall, "When Is It Time to Change Your Facebook Relationship Status?" *Oakland Tribune*, December 2, 2011, www.mercurynews.com.

31. See, for example, Samuel K. Bonsu and Russell W. Belk, "Do Not Go Cheaply into That Good Night: Death-Ritual Consumption in Asante, Ghana," *Journal of Consumer Research*, June 2003, pp. 41–55.

32. James H. McAlexander, John W. Schouten, and Scott D. Roberts, "Consumer Behavior and Divorce," in eds. Janeen Arnold Costa and Russell W. Belk, *Research in Consumer Behavior*, vol. 6 (Greenwich, Conn.: JAI Press, 1993), pp. 162; see also Rita Fullerman and Kathleen Debevec, "Till Death Do We Part: Family Dissolution, Transition, and Consumer Behavior," in eds. John F. Sherry and Brian Sternthal, *Advances in ConsumerResearch*, vol. 19 (Provo, Utah: Association for Consumer Research, 1992), pp. 514–521.

33. Melanie Wallendorf and Michael D. Reilly, "Ethnic Migration, Assimilation, and Consumption," *Journal of Consumer Research*, December 1983, pp. 292–302; Rohit Deshpande, Wayne Hoyer, and Naveen Donthu, "The Intensity of Ethnic Affiliation: A Study of the Sociology of Hispanic Consumption," *Journal of Consumer Research*, September 1986, pp. 214–220; for a discussion of acculturation of Chinese Americans, see Wei-Na Lee, "Acculturation and Advertising Communication Strategies: A Cross-Cultural Study of Chinese Americans," *Psychology and Marketing*, September–October 1993, pp. 381–397; for a study of the immigration of Haitian consumers, see Laura R. Oswald, "Culture Swapping: Consumption and the Ethnogenesis of Middle-Class Haitian Immigrants."

34. Annamma Joy and Ruby Roy Dholakia, "Remembrances of Things Past: The Meaning of Home and Possessions of Indian Professionals in Canada," in ed. Floyd W. Rudmin, *To Have Possessions: A Handbook of Ownership and Property*, Special Issue, *Journal of Social Behavior and Personality* 6, no. 6, 1991, pp. 385–402; see also Raj Mehta and Russell W. Belk, "Artifacts, Identity, and Transition," *Journal of Consumer Research*, March 1991, pp. 398–411.

35. Craig J. Thompson and Siok Kuan Tambyah, "Trying to Be Cosmopolitan," *Journal of Consumer Research* 26, December 1999, pp. 214–241.

36. Priscilla A. LaBarbera, "The Nouveaux Riches," in eds. Elizabeth C. Hirschman and Jagdish N. Sheth, *Research in Consumer Behavior* (Greenwich, Conn.: JAI Press, 1988), pp. 181–182.

37. Sarah Ellison and Carlos Tejada, "Mr., Mrs., Meet Mr. Clean," *Wall Street Journal*, January 30, 2003, pp. B1, B3.

38. Blythe Yee, "Ads Remind Women They Have Two Hands," *Wall Street Journal*, August 14, 2003, pp. B1, B5; for more about life transitions and related products, see Paula Mergenhagen, *Targeting Transitions* (Ithaca, N.Y.: American Demographics Books, 1995).

39. Ian Mount, "Alternative Gift Registries," *Wall Street Journal*, March 2, 2004, p. D1; and Julie Flaherty, "Freedom to Marry, and to Spend on It," *New York Times*, May 16, 2004, sec. 9, p. 2.

40. Pamela Paul, "What to Expect When Expecting? A Whole Lot of Loot," *New York Times*, June 24, 2007, p. BU5.

41. Otnes and Scott, "Something Old, Something New: Exploring the Interaction Between Ritual and Advertising."

42. Angela Hill, "Has Facebook Killed the Holiday Card?" *Oakland Tribune*, November 26, 2011, www.mercurynews.com.

43. In line with our notion that the meaning of the symbol may derive from the culture instead of from the individual and that symbols may have public or private meaning, see Marsha L. Richins, "Valuing Things: The Public and Private Meaning of Possessions," *Journal of Consumer Research*, December 1994, pp. 504–521.

44. N. Laura Kamptner, "Personal Possessions and Their Meanings," *Journal of Social Behavior and Personality* 6, no. 6, 1991, pp. 209–228.

45. Adam Kuper, "The English Christmas and the Family," in ed. Daniel Miller, *Unwrapping Christmas* (Oxford, England: Oxford University Press, 1993), pp. 157–175; and Barbara Bodenhorn, "Christmas Present: Christmas Public," in ed. Daniel Miller, *Unwrapping Christmas* (New. York: Oxford University Press, 1993), pp. 193–216.

46. Carolyn Folkman Curasi, Linda L. Price, and Eric J. Arnould, "How Individuals' Cherished Possessions Become Families'

Inalienable Wealth," *Journal of Consumer Research*, December 2004, pp. 609–622.

47. Kelly Tepper Tian, William O. Bearden, and Gary L. Hunter, "Consumers' Need for Uniqueness," *Journal of Consumer Research* 28, June 2001, pp. 50–66; Howard L. Fromkin and C. R. Snyder, "The Search for Uniqueness and Valuation of Scarcity," in eds. Kenneth Gergen, Martin S. Greenberg, and Richard H. Willis, *Social Exchanges: Advances in Theory and Research* (New York: Plenum, 1980), pp. 57–75; and Mihaly Csikszentmihalyi and Eugene Rochberg-Halton, *The Meaning of Things* (Cambridge, England: Cambridge University Press, 1981).

48. Gabriel Bar-Haim, "The Meaning of Western Commercial Artifacts for Eastern European Youth," *Journal of Contemporary Ethnography*, July 1987, pp. 205–226.

49. Jonah Berger and Chip Heath, "Where Consumers Diverge from Others: Identity Signaling and Product Domains," *Journal of Consumer Research*, August 2007, pp. 121–134.

50. Robert P. Libbon, "Datadog," *American Demographics*, September 2000, p. 26.

51. Stacy Baker and Patricia Kennedy, "Death by Nostalgia," in *Advances in Consumer Research*, vol. 21 (Provo, Utah: Association for Consumer Research, 1994), pp.169–174; and Morris B. Holbrook and Robert Schindler, "Echoes of the Dear Departed Past," in *Advances in Consumer Research*, vol. 18 (Provo, Utah: Association for Consumer Research, 1991), pp. 330–333.

52. Gregory Schmidt, "Toy Companies Turn to Nostalgia to Celebrate Anniversaries," *New York Times*, July 11, 2011, www.nytimes.com.

53. Stuart Elliott, "A Two-Wheeled Ride Down Memory Lane," *New York Times*, May 4, 2004, www.nytimes.com.

54. Roya Wolverson, "Styling for the Subcontinent," *Time*, December 11, 2011, p. B4; and William Lee Adams, "In the Trenches: Will Burberry Customers Pay Big for a DIY Coat?" *Time*, December 5, 2011, p. 82.

55. Vanitha Swaminathan, Karen L. Page, and Zeynep Gürhan-Canli, "'My' Brand or 'Our' Brand: The Effects of Brand Relationship Dimensions and Self-Construal on Brand Evaluations," *Journal of Consumer Research*, August 2007, pp. 248–259; Matthew Thomson, Deborah J. MacInnis, and C. Whan Park, "The Ties That Bind: Measuring the Strength of Consumers' Emotional Attachments to Brands," *Journal of Consumer Psychology* 15, no. 1, 2005, pp. 77–91; Jennifer Edson Escalas, "Narrative Processing," *Journal of Consumer Psychology* 14, no. 1/2, 2004, pp. 168–180; Jennifer Edson Escalas and James R. Bettman, "Self-Construal, Reference Groups, and Brand Meaning," *Journal of Consumer Research* 32, no. 3, 2005, pp. 378–389; Russell W. Belk, "Possessions and the Extended Self," *Journal of Consumer Research*, September 1988, pp. 139–168; A. Dwayne Ball and Lori H. Tasaki, "The Role and Measurement of Attachment in Consumer Behavior," *Journal of Consumer Psychology* 1, no. 2, 1992, pp. 155–172; and Robert E. Kleine, Susan Schultz Kleine, and Jerome B. Kernan, "Mundane Consumption and the Self," *Journal of Consumer Psychology* 2, no. 3, 1993, pp. 209–235.

56. Kleine, Kleine, and Kernan, "Mundane Consumption and the Self"; see also M. Joseph Sirgy, "Self-Concept and Consumer Behavior," *Journal of Consumer Research*, December 1982, pp. 287ff; and George M. Zinkhan and J. W. Hong, "Self-Concept and Advertising Effectiveness," in eds. Rebecca Holman and Michael Solomon, *Advances in Consumer Research*, vol. 18 (Provo, Utah: Association for Consumer Research, 1991), pp. 348–354.

57. For example, see Robert V. Kozinets, "Utopian Enterprise: Articulating the Meanings of *Star Trek*'s Culture of Consumption," *Journal of Consumer Research*, June 2001, pp. 67–88; and Douglas B. Holt, "Why Do Brands Cause Trouble? A Dialectical Theory of Consumer Culture and Branding," *Journal of Consumer Research*, June 2002, pp. 70–90.

58. Kelly Tian and Russell W. Belk, "Extended Self and Possessions in the Workplace," *Journal of Consumer Research* 32, no. 2, 2005, pp. 297–310.

59. Jen Shang, Americus Reed II, and Rachel Croson, "Identity Congruency Effects on Donations," *Journal of Marketing Research*, June 2008, pp. 351–361.

60. Kleine, Kleine, and Kernan, "Mundane Consumption and the Self."

61. C. R. Snyder and Howard L. Fromkin, *Uniqueness: Human Pursuit of Difference* (New York: Plenum, 1981).

62. Hope Jensen Schau and Mary C. Gilly, "We Are What We Post? Self-Presentation in Personal Web Space," *Journal of Consumer Research*, December 2003, pp. 385–404.

63. Amanda Gaines, "Breaking the Retail Code," *Retail Merchandiser,* July–August 2011, p. 1; and Emilia Terzon, "Australian First for Converse," *Inside Retail*, December 13, 2011, www.insideretailing.com.au.

64. Sirgy, "Self-Concept and Consumer Behavior."

65. "AKB48 Takes Equal Parts Choir, Slumber Party and Beauty Pageant, Mixes Well," *Advertising Age*, December 4, 2011, www.adage.com.

66. Ashutosh Dixit, William Lundstron, and Glenna Pendleton, "Social Meanings and Brands in Marketing," *Journal of the Academy of Business and Economics* 10, no. 4, 2010, pp. 108–117.

67. Cheng Lu Wang, Terry Bristol, John C. Mowen, and Goutam Chakraborty, "Alternative Modes of Self-Construal," *Journal of Consumer Psychology* 9, no. 2, 2000, pp. 107–115.

68. David Luna, Torsten Ringberg, and Laura A. Peracchio, "One Individual, Two Identities: Frame Switching Among Biculturals," *Journal of Consumer Research*, August 2008, pp. 279–293.

69. Thomson, MacInnis, and Park, "The Ties That Bind: Measuring the Strength of Consumers' Emotional Attachments to Brands"; Jennifer Edson Escalas, "Narrative Processing," *Journal of Consumer Psychology* 14, no. 1/2, 2004, pp. 168–180; and Jennifer Edson Escalas and James R. Bettman, "Self-Construal, Reference Groups, and Brand Meaning," *Journal of Consumer Research* 32, no. 3, 2005, pp. 378–389.

70. Richins, "Valuing Things: The Public and Private Meaning of Possessions"; and Marsha L. Richins, "Special Possessions and the Expression of Material Values," *Journal of Consumer Research*, December 1994, pp. 522–533.

71. Richins, "Valuing Things: The Public and Private Meaning of Possessions."

72. Thomson, MacInnis, and Park, "The Ties That Bind: Measuring the Strength of Consumers' Emotional Attachments to Brands"; C. W. Park and Deborah J. MacInnis, "What's In and What's Out: Questions on the Boundaries of the Attitude Construct," *Journal of Consumer Research* 33, no. 1, 2006, pp. 16–18; Rohini Ahluwalia, Robert Burnkrant, and H. Rao Unnava, "Consumer Response to Negative Publicity: The Moderating Role of Commitment," *Journal of Marketing Research* 37, no. 2, May 2000, pp. 203–214; Michael D. Johnson, Andreas Herrmann, and Frank Huber, "The Evolution of Loyalty Intentions," *Journal of Marketing* 70, April 2006, 122–132; and Matthew Thomson, "Human Brands: Investigating Antecedents to Consumers' Strong

Attachments to Celebrities," *Journal of Marketing* 70, no. 3, July 2006, pp. 104–119.

73. "At Last, a New IPhone We Can Recommend," *Consumer Reports*, January 2012, p. 29.

74. Richins, "Valuing Things: The Public and Private Meaning of Possessions."

75. Andrew Martin, "'For the Dogs' Has a Whole New Meaning," *New York Times*, June 5, 2011, pp. BU–1, BU–7.

76. Diane Brady and Christopher Palmeri, "The Pet Economy," *Business Week*, August 6, 2007, pp. 44–54; Richard C. Morais, "Dog Days," *Forbes Global*, June 21, 2004, p. 30; and Martin, "'For the Dogs' Has a Whole New Meaning."

77. Russell W. Belk, "Possessions and the Sense of Past," in ed. Russell W. Belk, *Highways and Buyways* (Provo, Utah: Association for Consumer Research, 1991) pp. 114–130; Susan Schultz Kleine, Robert E. Kleine III, and Chris T. Allen, "How Is a Possession 'Me' or 'Not Me'? Characterizing Types and an Antecedent of Material Possession Attachment," *Journal of Consumer Research*, December 1995, pp. 327–343; McAlexander, Schouten, and Roberts, "Consumer Behavior and Divorce"; and Lisa L. Love and Peter S. Sheldon, "Souvenirs: Messengers of Meaning," in eds. Joseph W. Alba and Wesley Hutchinson, *Advances in Consumer Research*, vol. 25 (Provo, Utah: Association for Consumer Research, 1998), pp. 170–175.

78. Belk, "Possessions and the Sense of Past."

79. Karen V. Fernandez and John L. Lastovicka, "Making Magic: Fetishes in Contemporary Consumption," *Journal of Consumer Research,* August 2011, pp. 278–299.

80. Russell W. Belk, "Moving Possessions: An Analysis Based on Personal Documents from the 1847–1869 Mormon Migration," *Journal of Consumer Research*, December 1992, pp. 339–361.

81. Russell W. Belk, Melanie Wallendorf, John F. Sherry Jr., and Morris B. Holbrook, "Collecting in a Consumer Culture," in ed. Russell W. Belk, *Highways and Buyways* (Provo, Utah: Association for Consumer Research, 1991), pp. 178–215.

82. Michael Clerizo, "Weird, Wild Watches," *Wall Street Journal*, August 13, 2011, www.wsj.com.

83. Russell W. Belk, Melanie Wallendorf, John F. Sherry Jr., Morris Holbrook, and Scott Roberts, "Collectors and Collecting," in ed. Michael J. Houston, *Advances in Consumer Research*, vol. 15 (Provo, Utah: Association for Consumer Research, 1988), pp. 548–553.

84. Belk, Wallendorf, Sherry, Holbrook, and Roberts, "Collectors and Collecting."

85. Russell W. Belk, "The Incluctable Mysteries of Possessions," in ed. Floyd W. Rudmin, *To Have Possessions: A Handbook on Ownership and Property*, Special Issue, *Journal of Social Behavior and Personality* 6, no. 6, 1991, pp. 17–55.

86. Kent Grayson and David Shulman, "Indexicality and the Verification Function of Irreplaceable Possessions: A Semiotic Analysis," *Journal of Consumer Research* 27, June 2000, pp. 17–30.

87. Daniel Terdiman, "Curiously High-Tech Hacks for a Classic Tin," *New York Times*, February 3, 2005, www.nytimes.com.

88. Susan Fournier, "The Development of Intense Consumer–Product Relationships," *Winter AMA Educator's Conference*, St. Petersburg, FL (February 1994).

89. Mihalyi Csikszentmihalyi and Eugene Rochberg-Halton, *The Meaning of Things*; M. Wallendorf, and E. J. Arnould, "My Favorite Things: A Cross-Cultural Inquiry into Object Attachment, Possessiveness, and Social Linkage," *Journal of Consumer Research*, March 1988, pp. 531–547; and Belk, "Moving Possessions: An Analysis Based on Personal Documents from the 1847–1869 Mormon Migration."

90. A. Peter McGraw, Philip E. Tetlock, and Orie V. Kristel, "The Limits of Fungibility," *Journal of Consumer Research*, September 2003, pp. 219–228.

91. Csikszentmihalyi and Rochberg-Halton, *The Meaning of Things*.

92. Ibid.

93. Helga Dittmar, "Meaning of Material Possessions as Reflections of Identity," in ed. Rudmin, *To Have Possessions*, pp. 165–186; see also Helga Dittmar, *The Social Psychology of Material Possessions* (New York: St. Martin's, 1992).

94. Jaideep Sengupta, Darren W. Dahl, and Gerald J. Gorn, "Misrepresentation in the Consumer Context," *Journal of Consumer Psychology* 12, no. 2, 2002, pp. 69–79.

95. Dittmar, "Meaning of Material Possessions as Reflections of Identity"; and Kamptner, "Personal Possessions and Their Meanings."

96. Wallendorf and Arnould, "My Favorite Things: A Cross-Cultural Inquiry into Object Attachment, Possessiveness, and Social Linkage."

97. Russell W. Belk and Melanie Wallendorf, "Of Mice and Men: Gender Identity in Collecting," in eds. K. Ames and K. Martinez, *The Gender of Material Culture* (Ann Arbor, Mich.: University of Michigan Press), reprinted in ed. Susan M. Pearce, *Objects and Collections* (London: Routledge, 1994), pp. 240–253; and Belk, Wallendorf, Sherry, Holbrook, and Roberts, "Collectors and Collecting."

98. McCracken, "Culture and Consumption"; and McCracken, *Culture and Consumption*.

99. Ibid.

100. Andrea C. Morales and Gavan J. Fitzsimons, "Product Contagion: Changing Consumer Evaluations through Physical Contact with 'Disgusting' Products," *Journal of Marketing Research*, March 2007, pp. 272–283.

101. McCracken, "Culture and Consumption"; and McCracken, *Culture and Consumption*.

102. John L. Lastovicka and Karen V. Fernandez, "Three Paths to Disposition: The Movement of Meaningful Possessions to Strangers," *Journal of Consumer Research* 31, no. 4, 2005, pp. 813–823.

103. Linda L. Price, Eric J. Arnold, and Carolyn Folkman Curasi, "Older Consumers' Disposition of Special Possessions," *Journal of Consumer Research* 27, September 2000, pp. 179–201.

104. Russell W. Belk, Melanie Wallendorf, and John F. Sherry Jr., "The Sacred and the Profane in Consumer Behavior," *Journal of Consumer Research*, June 1989, pp. 1–38.

105. Belk, "Possessions and the Sense of Past."

106. Belk, Wallendorf, and Sherry, "The Sacred and the Profane in Consumer Behavior."

107. Amitai Etzioni, "The Socio-Economics of Property," in ed. Rudmin, *To Have Possessions: A Handbook on Ownership and Property*, Special Issue, *Journal of Social Behavior and Personality* 6, no. 6, 1991, pp. 465–468.

108. Robert V. Kozinets, "Utopian Enterprise: Articulating the Meanings of *Star Trek*'s Culture of Consumption," *Journal of Consumer Research* 28, June 2001, pp. 67–88.

109. James Cockington, "Beatles Fans Can't Let It Be," *Sydney Morning Herald*, December 7, 2011, www.smh.com.au.

110. Rupal Parekh, "Netanyahu, Abbas Smooch in Benetton Ad," *Advertising Age*, November 16, 2011, www.adage.com.

111. Jackie Clarke, "Different to 'Dust Collectors'? The Giving and Receiving of Experience Gifts," *Journal of Consumer Behavior* 5, no. 6, 2006, pp. 533–549.

112. For historical and sociological accounts of Christmas, see Daniel Miller, "A Theory of Christmas," in ed. Daniel Miller, *Unwrapping Christmas*, pp. 3–37; Claude Levi-Strauss, "Father Christmas Executed," in ed. Miller, *Unwrapping Christmas*, pp. 38–54; Belk, "Materialism and the Making of the Modern American Christmas"; Barbara Bodenhorn, "Christmas Present: Christmas Public," in ed. Miller, *Unwrapping Christmas*, pp. 193–216, Oxford, UK: Oxford University Press; William B. Waits, *The Modern Christmas in America* (New York: New York University Press, 1993); and Stephen Nissenbaum, *The Battle for Christmas* (New York: Vantage Books, 1997).

113. John F. Sherry Jr., "Gift Giving in Anthropological Perspective," *Journal of Consumer Research*, September 1983, pp. 157–168.

114. For a discussion of these motives, see Sherry, "Gift Giving in Anthropological Perspective"; for research on gender differences in motives, see Mary Ann McGrath, "Gender Differences in Gift Exchanges: New Directions from Projections," *Psychology and Marketing*, August 1995, pp. 229–234; Cele Otnes, Kyle Zolner, and Tina M. Lowry, "In-Laws and Outlaws: The Impact of Divorce and Remarriage upon Christmas Gift Exchange," in eds. Chris Allen and Debbie Roedder-John, *Advances in Consumer Research*, vol. 21 (Provo, UT: Association for Consumer Research, 1994), pp. 25–29; and Russell W. Belk, "The Perfect Gift," in eds. Cele Otnes and Richard Beltrami, *Gift Giving Behavior: An Interdisciplinary Anthology* (Bowling Green, OH: Bowling Green University Popular Press, 1996); for a discussion of the roles played by gift, see Cele Otnes, Tina M. Lowrey, and Young Chan Kim, "Gift Selection for Easy and Difficult Recipients," *Journal of Consumer Research*, September 1993, pp. 229–244; and Kleine, Kleine, and Allen, "How Is a Possession 'Me' or 'Not Me'?"

115. McAlexander, Schouten, and Roberts, "Consumer Behavior and Divorce."

116. David B. Wooten, "Qualitative Steps Toward an Expanded Model of Anxiety in Gift-Giving," *Journal of Consumer Research* 27, June 2000, pp. 84–95.

117. Russell W. Belk and Gregory S. Coon, "Gift Giving as Agapic Love," *Journal of Consumer Research*, December 1993, pp. 393–417.

118. Sherry, "Gift Giving in Anthropological Perspective"; and Mary Searle-Chatterjee, "Christmas Cards and the Construction of Social Relations in Britain Today," in ed. Miller, *Unwrapping Christmas* (New York: Oxford University Press, 1993), pp. 176–192.

119. Belk and Coon, "Gift Giving as Agapic Love"; see also Sherry, "Gift Giving in Anthropological Perspective."

120. Sak Onkvisit and John J. Shaw, *International Marketing: Analysis and Strategy* (Columbus, Ohio: Merrill, 1989), pp. 241–242.

121. "The Efficiency of Gift Giving: Is It Really Better to Give than to Receive?" *Marketing: Knowledge at Wharton*, December 15, 2004, http://knowledge.wharton.upenn.edu.

122. Jean-Sebastian Marcoux, "Escaping the Gift Economy," *Journal of Consumer Research,* December 2009, pp. 671–685.

123. Sandra Yin, "Give and Take," *American Demographics*, November 2003, pp. 12–13; and Eileen Fischer and Stephen J. Arnold, "More Than a Labor of Love: Gender Roles and Christmas Shopping," *Journal of Consumer Research*, December 1990, pp. 333–345.

124. John F. Sherry Jr. and Mary Ann McGrath, "Unpacking the Holiday Presence: A Comparative Ethnography of Two Gift Stores," in ed. Elizabeth C. Hirschman, *Interpretive Consumer Research* (Provo, Utah: Association for Consumer Research, 1989), pp. 148–167.

125. See, for example, Theodore Caplow, "Rule Enforcement Without Visible Means: Christmas Gift Giving in Middle-town," *American Journal of Sociology*, March 1984, pp. 1306–1323.

126. James G. Carrier, "The Rituals of Christmas Giving," in ed. Daniel Miller, *Unwrapping Christmas* (New York: Oxford University Press, 1993), pp. 55–74.

127. Mary Ann McGrath, "An Ethnography of a Gift Store: Trappings, Wrappings, and Rapture," *Journal of Retailing*, Winter 1989, p. 434.

128. Morgan K. Ward and Susan M. Broniarczyk, "It's Not Me, It's You: How Gift Giving Creates Gift Identity Threat as a Function of Social Closeness," *Journal of Consumer Research*, June 2011, pp. 164–181.

129. Wooten, "Qualitative Steps Toward an Expanded Model of Anxiety in Gift-Giving."

130. Julie A. Ruth, Cele C. Otnes, and Frederic F. Brunel, "Gift Receipt and the Reformulation of Interpersonal Relationships," *Journal of Consumer Research*, March 1999, pp. 385–402; and Ming-Hui Huang and Shihti Yu, "Gifts in a Romantic Relationship: A Survival Analysis," *Journal of Consumer Psychology* 9, no. 3, 2000, pp. 179–188.

131. See P. Webley, S. E. G. Lea, and R. Portalska, "The Unacceptability of Money as a Gift," *Journal of Economic Psychology*, vol. 4, 1983, pp. 223–238.

132. Belk, "Gift Giving Behavior"; see also Sherry, "Gift Giving in Anthropological Perspective."

133. Belk and Coon, "Gift Giving as Agapic Love."

134. Annamma Joy, "Gift Giving in Hong Kong and the Continuum of Social Ties," *Journal of Consumer Research*, September 2001, pp. 239–256.

135. Peg Quann, "Christmas: It's in the Cards," *Burlington County Times (PA)*, December 12, 2001, www.phillyburbs.com.

136. Meena Hartenstein, "Getting Registered: Unusual Wedding Registry Options," *New York Daily News*, March 27, 2011, www.nydailynews.com.

137. Mitch Lipka, "When Shopping for Gift Card Deals, Think High-End," *Reuters*, December 9, 2011, www.reuters.com.

138. Tim Feran, "Day After Christmas Will Be Busy for Stores," *Columbus Dispatch*, November 23, 2011, www.dispatch.com; and Louise Lee, "What's Roiling the Selling Season," *BusinessWeek*, January 10, 2005, p. 38.

139. Betsy Anderson, "Why Goats and Chickens Make Great Holiday Gifts," *CNN*, December 14, 2011, www.cnn.com.

140. Tony C. Dreibus and Danielle Rossingh, "British Women's Triathlon Domination Boosts Sport's Image, Equipment Sales," *Bloomberg News*, December 19, 2011, www.bloomberg.com; Robert E. Kleine III, Susan Schultz-Kleine, and Jerone B. Kernan, "Mundane Everyday Consumption and the Self: A Conceptual Orientation and Prospects for Consumer Research," *Advances in Consumer Research*, eds John F. Sherry Jr. and Brian Sternthal (Provo, Utah: Association for Consumer Research, 1992), pp. 411–415; Simon Usborne, "Wheels, Etc.: Porsche Bike RS," *The Independent (UK)*, December 8, 2011, www.independent.co.uk; Noel Achariam, "Folding Bikes Welcome on LRT," *New Straits Times (Malaysia)*, December 19, 2011, www.nst.com; Susan Monroe, "Cycling Activists Peddle Through Patagonia," *Santiago Times (Chile)*, December 12, 2011, www.santiagotimes.cl; Sam McManis, "15-year-old Hopes 'Scraper Bikes' Hold Key to His Creative Future," *Sacramento Bee*, December 18, 2011, www.sacbee.com; and Nicole Formosa, "Red Tape Slows Entry into Latin America," *Bicycle Retailer*, December 2, 2011, www.bicycleretailer.com.

CHAPTER 17

MARKETING, ETHICS, AND SOCIAL RESPONSIBILITY IN TODAY'S CONSUMER SOCIETY

LEARNING OBJECTIVES

After studying this chapter, you will be able to

1. Distinguish between social and temporal dilemmas, and explain the search for balance in decisions that involve such dilemmas.

2. Define marketing ethics and consumer ethics, and identify some of the issues that arise from unethical or deviant acquisition, consumption, and disposition behaviors.

3. Discuss some of the ways in which consumers and organizations use marketing for socially responsible purposes.

4. Describe what consumers can do to resist unwanted marketing practices.

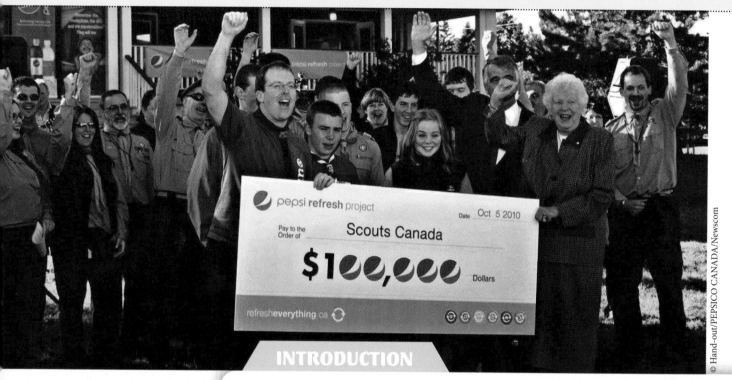

© Hand-out/PEPSICO CANADA/Newscom

INTRODUCTION

Pepsi Refresh Pours On the Community Grants

In 2010, PepsiCo decided not to air commercials for its soft drinks during the Super Bowl. Instead, it spent the money on a community grant initiative called Pepsi Refresh, seeking "refreshing ideas that change the world." Pepsi invited individuals and organizations to submit applications for projects that would do something worthwhile for local communities, such as building playgrounds and starting arts programs. Then Pepsi posted the ideas online and asked consumers to vote for their favorites.

Even Pepsi was surprised at what happened next. Thousands of volunteers got involved with the proposed programs, and local media coverage spread the word and praised the brand. Many applicants created special Facebook pages to generate excitement and encourage voting. In all, 76 million votes were counted, and Pepsi awarded a total of $20 million in grants. Pepsi Refresh attracted such positive response in the first year that it was expanded beyond North America during the second year. And what have the community grants done for Pepsi? In the words of

CEO Indra Nooyi: "It's a matter of 'What does this brand stand for in terms of doing something positive in the world.'"[1]

The Pepsi Refresh campaign supercharged the fundraising and volunteer efforts of community groups working on socially responsible projects that benefit many thousands of people. This example illustrates how, in today's consumer society, marketers and consumers have the power to achieve constructive outcomes—the "bright side" of marketing. In particular, the rise of social media has empowered individuals and consumer groups to make a real difference to the planet and to the lives of others.

On the other hand, ethical issues such as whether advertising contributes to obesity and whether marketing invades consumer privacy are part of the discussion about the "dark side" of marketing. Consumer behavior can have a "dark side," as well, including illegal acts (such as theft) and the compulsion to buy unneeded goods and services. Despite these extremes, marketers and consumers both seek balance when making decisions that involve dilemmas, such as between self-interest and the interests of others, and between immediate interests and long-term interests. Also, consumers can, individually and in groups, resist marketing efforts or pressure marketers to take certain steps, as this chapter explains. Exhibit 17.1 summarizes key points in marketing ethics and social responsibility.

IN SEARCH OF BALANCE

Social dilemma Deciding whether to put self-interest or the interests of others first.

Temporal dilemma Deciding whether to put immediate interests or long-term interests first.

When marketers and consumers make decisions, they often face potentially conflicting priorities and outcomes. Attempts to resolve these conflicts can raise ethical issues. For example, the question of who takes priority represents a **social dilemma**: Whose interests are the priority, our own or those of others? As another example, when time is the issue, consumers face a **temporal dilemma**: Which is the priority, immediate interests or long-term interests? Exhibit 17.2 shows the dimensions of these two dilemmas.

As you learned in previous chapters, focusing on our own immediate self-interest may actually increase our happiness. At the same time, focusing on the future interests of others may increase our sense of satisfaction or be congruent with our self-concept as someone who is altruistic or charitable. But what about the extreme case of focusing on ourselves at the expense of others who might be harmed (such as exposing someone else to secondhand smoke when we light up a cigarette)? Or making an impatient choice (eating an unhealthy snack now) that may result in a negative long-term outcome (becoming overweight)?

Self-interest Versus the Interests of Others

If we focus concretely on people close to us (such as family members or friends), our decision may be framed as concerning *me versus we*. If our focus is more abstract, such as on strangers or society at large, the decision may be framed as *me versus them*. When marketers make decisions, they may focus on *me*, meaning their own professional or personal goals. Focusing on the interests of others may frame the decision as *me or we* (the brand, product, company, or coworkers) or *me or them* (competitors or others outside the organization).

Choosing to focus on *me, we*, or *them* is not intrinsically bad. One example of *helpful other-focus* is the sharing of ideas, such as answering the questions of friends or strangers posted on social media such as Twitter or Facebook, or posting product reviews that will help others make good purchase decisions.[2]

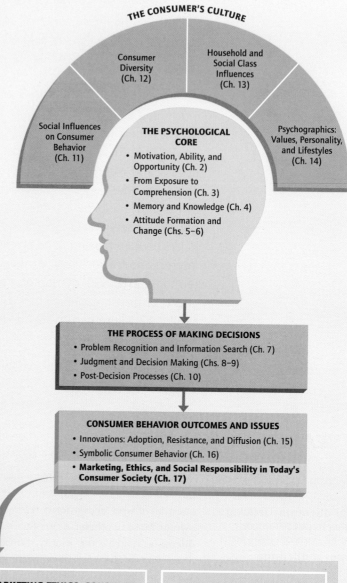

Exhibit 17.1

Chapter Overview: Marketing, Ethics, and Social Responsibility in a Consumer Society

When making decisions, marketers and consumers must balance their self-interests with the interests of others and immediate interests with long-term interests. Certain decisions about acquisition, consumption, and disposition raise "dark side" issues of marketing ethics and consumer ethics. The "bright side" of marketing and consumer behavior is reflected in social responsibility activities geared toward constructive outcomes.

Social Dilemma	Temporal Dilemma
Whose interests take priority?	*What timing takes priority?*
• Me (as an individual) **OR**	• Short-term interests **OR**
• We (my family, friends, colleagues, my employer, human beings) **OR**	• Long-term interests
• Them (others, such as competitors, people in other nations, or society at large)	

Exhibit 17.2

Social and Temporal Dilemmas

Social dilemmas focus on "who," whereas temporal dilemmas focus on "when."

An example of *harmful self-focus* is shoplifting. The shoplifter may perceive no or little harm to others or society because "it is only a single book, DVD, or steak." In reality, however, this illegal and unethical behavior costs the store money, which in turn causes it to raise prices—in effect, penalizing other shoppers while the shoplifter benefits. Every day, U.K. retailers lose merchandise worth an estimated $3 million to shoplifters, which means the financial impact on U.K. shoppers, in the form of higher prices, is quite significant.[3] Here again is the balancing act: If U.K. retailers install antitheft devices that make honest shoppers feel spied upon, or if they raise prices too high to make up for losses, shoppers may avoid their stores, which will hurt sales and profits.

Immediate Versus Long-Term Interests

In the case of a temporal dilemma, the central issue is: How will the decision affect my interests, our interests, or their interests *immediately*, compared with the *future*? In the Pepsi Refresh example, the company was focusing on long-term brand results. It did not require any purchases to qualify for funding, nor did it expect an immediate financial gain. Instead, its marketers relied on the positive word of mouth from the campaign to encourage future purchases and reinforce long-term brand loyalty. The same kind of reasoning can be applied to consumers who focus on the future. When parents save money for a child's college education, or when adults put money into a retirement fund, they are making an "investment" with the expectation of a positive future outcome.

Decisions that emphasize short-term interests may have positive or negative implications for the future. If you have an opportunity to buy a used car at a bargain price, you might decide to make the purchase right away, because you will come out ahead. If you overspend on a car, however, you may feel good about your purchase initially but discover later that you have jeopardized your financial situation. Of course, decisions that emphasize future interests may also have positive or negative implications. For instance, by focusing on the future, you might neglect or downplay pleasurable experiences in the present (forgetting to "stop and smell the roses"). This is why it's so important to balance the interests of today with the interests of tomorrow when making decisions.

"Dark Side" Versus "Bright Side" Outcomes

Conflicts that arise from dilemmas in marketing sometimes lead to "dark side" outcomes, which can potentially harm consumers or marketers. For example, as discussed in the next section, should marketers advertise to children, with the goal of making sales today and encouraging loyalty tomorrow? Should consumers be able to download or share digital entertainment that they have not officially purchased or registered to receive (benefiting "me" or "we"), even if that deprives the marketers and creators ("them") of revenue?

On a larger scale, when managers in public corporations get ready to report financial results, their decisions entail both a social and a temporal dilemma. In rare and extreme cases, individuals who feel pressure to improve profits may focus too narrowly on "me" or "we" (themselves, their colleagues, company stockholders) and "now" (making today's financial performance look better). They may take unethical actions, such as inflating financial results, and when their actions are exposed, the "dark side" outcome is bankruptcy (e.g., Enron), which can hurt stockholders and put thousands of people out of work.

Of course, such extreme and far-reaching decisions are not commonplace. Most companies seek a better balance, aiming for long-term profitability *and* broadening their focus on "we" to achieve constructive, sustainable outcomes for people and the planet—the "bright side" outcome. Initially, such programs are usually funded from the firm's profits, which would seem to go against the drive for profitability. Over time, however, these programs can shape positive brand attitudes, reinforce brand loyalty, reduce costs, and ultimately lead to higher sales and profits from new products, new markets, and new customers. Moreover, such programs toward sustainable business fit the morality of the firms and its owners. These are some "bright side" outcomes not only for the marketer but for the consumer as well. Consumers can benefit directly from new products that meet their needs and indirectly from programs that help their communities or society at large.

MARKETING ETHICS, CONSUMER ETHICS, AND DEVIANT CONSUMER BEHAVIOR

Marketing ethics Rules of acceptable conduct that guide individuals and organizations in making honest, fair, and respectful decisions about marketing activities.

Marketing ethics are rules or standards of acceptable conduct that guide individuals and organizations in making honest, fair, and respectful decisions about marketing activities, internal and external. Marketing ethics apply not just only to relationships with customers but also to relationships with employees, managers, suppliers, and other stakeholders. These standards, often formalized in ethical codes of conduct adopted by companies, professional associations, and industry groups, cover everything from targeting and communications to promotions and pricing (see Exhibit 17.3).

It is important to remember that unethical marketing behavior may not be illegal; it is unethical if it violates generally accepted rules of conduct or a formal ethical code observed by the marketer. Further, not all ethical standards are static. For instance, the growing movements toward the ethical sourcing of coffee, cocoa, lumber, and other materials as well as concerns about the ethical treatment of employees who work for overseas suppliers are relatively recent developments.

Consumer ethics Rules of acceptable conduct (such as honesty, fairness, and respect) that apply to the range of consumer behaviors.

Consumer ethics are rules of acceptable conduct (such as honesty, fairness, and respect) that apply to the range of consumer behaviors. When consumers act unethically, they may not be breaking the law, but their behavior is in some way dishonest, unfair, or disrespectful to individuals or to

Exhibit 17.3

Marketing and Consumer Ethics

Brands like the Body Shop actively promote their marketing ethics in their ads.

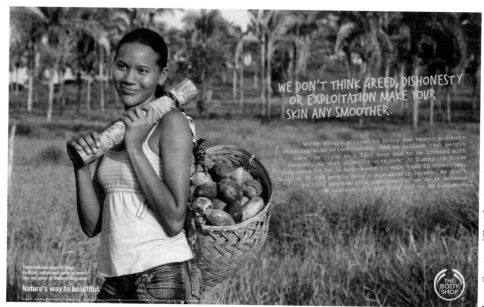

organizations. In contrast, *deviant consumer behavior* is behavior regarded as deviant if it is either unexpected or not sanctioned by members of the society (whether or not the behavior is illegal or unethical). Unethical behavior—perceived or actual, intentional or not—on the part of marketers and consumers, as well as deviant consumer behavior, can create controversies in the context of acquisition, consumption, and disposition situations.

Acquisition Controversies

Five key controversies related to questions of ethics in marketing and consumer behavior in terms of acquisition are: (1) materialistic behavior, (2) addictive and compulsive behavior, (3) consumer theft, (4) black markets, and (5) targeting vulnerable segments.

Materialistic Behavior

Materialism is a value in many cultures (as noted in Chapter 14), not just in the West but increasingly in Asia, as well. In part, the rise in materialism among consumers in China can be attributed to wider exposure to media and marketing and to increases in income.[4] Purchases of luxury brands are increasing in Japan, Singapore, Hong Kong, and China, even during economic downturns—another sign of materialistic behavior.[5] Although materialism is a neutral value and neither unethical nor deviant, some are critical of this focus on acquiring possessions, such as consumers buying items they do not always need, sometimes do not even want, and at times, cannot afford.

Family influences can be quite strong: The children of materialistic parents tend to be more materialistic than other children.[6] Materialistic adolescents shop more, save less, and are more responsive to marketing efforts.[7] And with more marketing and media emphasis on brands, it is not surprising that children are aware of more than 200 brands by the time they reach first grade.[8] Social comparison theory would predict that if advertising and the media show individuals with many material possessions, consumers might use advertising as a means of judging their own personal accomplishments.

Consumers who perceive that they are less well off than the comparison population may be less satisfied with their lives. Some evidence supports this idea. Consumers exposed to a lot of advertising tend to overestimate how well off the average consumer is.[9] This misperception sets up a potentially false frame of reference regarding how much the average consumer owns. Furthermore, materialistic consumers may pay undue attention to the possessions of others and make inferences about these people based on the possessions that they own.[10]

Addictive and Compulsive Behavior

Addiction Excessive behavior typically brought on by a chemical dependency.

Addiction reflects continued, excessive behaviors despite adverse consequences, which is typically brought on by a chemical dependency. Addicted consumers feel a great attachment to and dependence on a product or activity and believe that they must use it to function.[11] Individuals can become addicted to many goods and services, including cigarettes, drugs, alcohol, Internet use, and video games. In many cases, an addiction involves repeated acquisition and/or use of a product, even if consumption is dangerous. Although addicted individuals may want to stop, they believe doing so is beyond their control ("I can't help myself"). Often individuals feel shame and guilt about their addiction and try to hide it. Some addicted consumers find strength in programs like Alcoholics Anonymous and SmokeEnders.

Addictive behaviors can be harmful to people involved and to those around them. For example, cigarette smoking is a preventable cause of death, and a leading cause of cancer, cardiovascular disease, and chronic obstructive lung disease. According to the World Health Organization, tobacco use contributes to more than five million deaths worldwide each year, killing smokers and those around them who are exposed to secondhand smoke.[12]

Compulsive behavior An irresistible urge to perform an irrational act.

Compulsive behavior is an irresistible urge to perform an irrational act. Unlike addictive behavior, which involves a physiological dependency, compulsive behavior occurs because the consumer cannot stop doing something. For example, some individuals buy compulsively, purchasing many items that they do not need and sometimes cannot afford; they gain satisfaction from *buying*, not from *owning* (see Exhibit 17.4).

Quotes from Compulsive Buyers

Compulsive buying can be an emotionally involving experience. Consumers may engage in compulsive buying to feel a thrill, gain attention, or feel that they are pleasing someone else. But this emotional high may be followed by serious financial and negative emotional consequences.

Emotional Aspects of Compulsive Buying

a. "I couldn't tell you what I bought or where I bought it. It was like I was on automatic."
"I really think it's the spending. It's not that I want it, because sometimes I'll just buy it and I'll think, Ugh, another sweatshirt."

b. "But it was like, it was almost like my heart was palpitating. I couldn't wait to get in to see what was there. It was such a sensation. In the store, the lights, the people; they were playing Christmas music. I was hyperventilating and my hands were starting to sweat, and all of a sudden I was touching sweaters and the whole feel of it was just beckoning to me. And if they had a SALE sign up, forget it; I was gone. You never know when you're going to need it. I bought ten shirts one time for $10.00 each."

"It's almost like you're drunk. You're so intoxicated; ... I got this great high. It was like you couldn't have given me more of a rush."

Factors Influencing Compulsive Buying

c. "The attention I got there was incredible. She waited on me very nicely, making sure it would fit and if it didn't, they would do this and that. And I guess I enjoyed being on the other end of that. I had no idea how I was going to pay for it. I never do."

"I never bought one of anything. I always buy at least two. I still do. I can never even go into the Jewel and buy one quart of milk. I've always got to buy two ... It's an act of pleasing. I had been brought up to please everybody and everyone around me because that was the way you got anything was to please. So I thought I was pleasing the store."

Financial and Emotional Consequences of Compulsive Buying

d. "I would always have to borrow between paychecks. I could not make it between paychecks. Payday comes and I'd pay all my bills, but then I'd piss the rest away, and I'd need to borrow money to eat, and I would cry and cry and cry, and everyone would say, 'Well just make a budget.' Get serious. That's like telling an alcoholic not to go to the liquor store. It's not that simple."

e. "My husband said he couldn't deal with this, and he said, 'I'm leaving you. We'll get a divorce. That's it. It's your problem. You did it. You fix it up.'"

"I didn't have one person in the world I could talk to. I don't drink. I don't smoke. I don't do dope. But I can't stop. I can't control it. I said I can't go on like this ... My husband hates me. My kids hate me. I've destroyed everything. I was ashamed and just wanted to die."

Source: Thomas O'Guinn and Ronald Faber, "Compulsive Buying: A Phenomenological Perspective," *Journal of Consumer Research*, September 1989, pp. 147–157. © 1989 University of Chicago. All rights reserved.

Compulsive buying has a strong emotional component, and the emotions run the gamut from the most negative to the most positive.[13] Compulsive buyers feel anxious on days when they do not buy; thus, compulsive buying may be a response to tension or anxiety. While in the store, compulsive buyers may feel great emotional arousal at the stimulation evoked by the store's atmosphere. Buying brings an immediate emotional high and a feeling of loss of control. This reaction is followed by feelings of remorse, guilt, shame, and depression.

Why do people buy compulsively? For one thing, compulsive buyers tend to have low self-esteem. In fact, the emotional high consumers experience from compulsive buying comes in part from the attention and social approval they get when they buy. The salesperson can provide considerable satisfaction—being a doting helper, telling consumers how attractive they look in a particular outfit. Consumers can also feel that they are pleasing the salesperson and the company by making purchases. This attention and the feeling of pleasing others may temporarily raise compulsive buyers' self-esteem and reinforce buying behavior (see part c of Exhibit 17.4).

The financial, emotional, and interpersonal consequences of compulsive buying can be devastating. These consumers rely extensively on credit cards, have high credit card debt, and tend to pay only the minimum monthly balance. They are also more likely to write checks for purchases, even though they know they cannot afford them. And compulsive buyers are more likely to borrow money from others to make it from paycheck to paycheck.[14] Finally, children, spouses, and friends can all be hurt by the spending habits of compulsive buyers.

Consumer Theft

Whereas compulsive buying reflects an uncontrollable desire to *purchase* things, consumer theft reflects a desire to *steal* things, which is both unethical and illegal. For U.S. retailers, shoplifting is pervasive and significant, with yearly merchandise losses topping $37 billion; worldwide, yearly shoplifting losses are estimated at $107 billion.[15] Consumer theft is a problem for nonretailers as well as for retailers. Automobile insurance fraud; credit card fraud; theft of cable TV services; piracy of music, movies, and software; fraudulent returns; and switching or altering price tags are just some of the forms of consumer theft with which companies must contend.[16] During the recent recession, consumers seeking multiple copies of store coupons began stealing newspapers from stores and driveways.[17]

As shown in Exhibit 17.5, two psychological factors seem to explain theft: (1) the temptation to steal and (2) the ability to rationalize theft behavior. These factors are, in turn, affected by aspects of the product, the purchase environment, and the consumer.

Temptation to Steal

The *temptation* to steal arises when consumers want products that they cannot legitimately buy, either to satisfy real needs or due to greed. Some researchers suggest that marketers are involved by perpetuating materialistic tendencies and creating insatiable desires for new goods and services.[18] Consumers may also be tempted to steal items that they are too embarrassed to buy through conventional channels (e.g., condoms) or that they cannot legally buy (e.g., an underage consumer stealing alcohol).[19]

Temptation is greater when consumers think that they can get away with stealing and that it is worth doing. Thus, consumers may assess the perceived risks associated with stealing and getting caught and may consider the benefits of having a product or using a service that they did not pay for.[20] Many factors in the environment affect the perceived risks of shoplifting.[21] Stores may be noisy or crowded, have little or no security, have lax return policies, have few salespeople, contain hidden

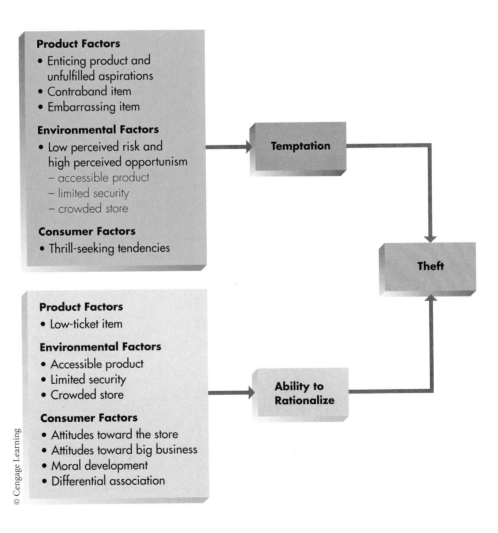

Exhibit 17.5

Motivations for Consumer Theft

Consumers may engage in theft because they (1) feel the temptation to steal and (2) can somehow rationalize their behavior. Various factors associated with the product, the environment, and the consumer can influence temptation and the ability to rationalize.

Product Factors
- Enticing product and unfulfilled aspirations
- Contraband item
- Embarrassing item

Environmental Factors
- Low perceived risk and high perceived opportunism
  - accessible product
  - limited security
  - crowded store

Consumer Factors
- Thrill-seeking tendencies

Temptation

Product Factors
- Low-ticket item

Environmental Factors
- Accessible product
- Limited security
- Crowded store

Consumer Factors
- Attitudes toward the store
- Attitudes toward big business
- Moral development
- Differential association

Ability to Rationalize

Theft

© Cengage Learning

nooks and crannies, or use price tags that are easily switched—leading consumers to believe their theft will be unnoticed. Also, a tendency toward thrill-seeking has been associated with many forms of consumer theft, including price tag switching and shoplifting.[22]

Rationalizations for Stealing

Consumers also steal because they can somehow *rationalize* their behavior as being either justified or driven by forces outside themselves. For example, consumers may justify stealing a low-ticket item such as a grape from a bunch at the grocery store because the item's cost seems so negligible that the word *stealing* hardly seems to apply. Some consumers may reason that a marketer "asked for it" by keeping merchandise displays open, having no security guards, or using price tags that can be readily switched.

"Everybody does it" is another rationalization, in which people feel they are "licensed to steal." After they act in a virtuous way, consumers may feel "licensed" to act less virtuously later on.[23] In one study, 11 percent of the respondents agreed that it was wrong to download online music without paying and to copy software without paying—but if they believe that "everybody else does it," they may still follow suit.[24] Interestingly, consumers who behave a little dishonestly want the expected benefits, yet try to remain honest enough to preserve their positive self-concept.[25]

Black Markets

Black market An illegal market in which consumers pay often exorbitant amounts for items not readily available.

Whereas theft represents acquisition situations in which consumers refuse to pay for available items, **black markets** represent situations in which consumers *pay* (often exorbitant amounts) for items *not* readily available. These are called "black" markets because the sellers are unauthorized, which means that the buying-selling process is usually illegal. Black markets for goods like sugar, salt, blankets, matches, and batteries fulfill functional needs; black markets for drugs, entertainment, and sexual services fulfill experiential needs; and black markets for watches and jewelry may fulfill symbolic needs.

Some items sold on the black market are legal but in short supply. For example, some consumers buy blocks of tickets to popular sporting events and concerts and resell them at much higher prices.

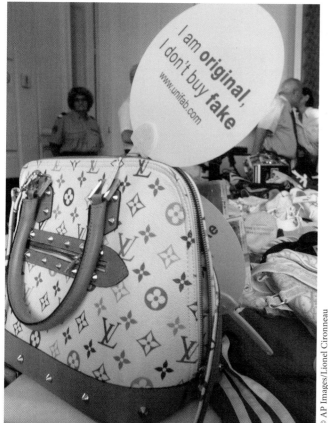

Princeton University and other universities are cracking down on black-market sales of graduation tickets.[26] Some goods and services that *cannot legally be sold* to consumers, such as components to build bombs, are sold on black markets. For example, after the Iranian government banned the sale of Barbie dolls and toys based on the TV show *The Simpsons*, consumers began to acquire such products on the black market.[27]

Another problem is that some goods offered on black markets are fake (see Exhibit 17.6). Counterfeits of luxury products have long been a black-market problem, fueled in part by purchases by consumers who knowingly acquire counterfeit branded items to gain the approval of others.[28] Online sales are now a problem for marketers of products in all price ranges, costing marketers up to $135 billion in lost revenue worldwide.[29] In such cases, consumers do not always know that the products they buy are fake—they only know that the prices are lower than usual.

Targeting Vulnerable Segments

Certain consumer segments are vulnerable to questionable marketing practices because of their age or because they are unprepared or unable to rationally evaluate marketing stimuli. Seniors, for instance, tend to have more difficulty processing and interpreting marketing information as they age. As another example, consumers in developing nations who have not been exposed to marketing in the past are more likely to believe a marketer's false claims or fall prey to other unethical marketing actions.

© AP Images/Lionel Cironneau

Advertising to children, in particular, has been the subject of considerable controversy focusing on the effects these ads may have on young, impressionable consumers. Research shows that by the age of two, 90 percent of U.S. children are watching videos or TV on a regular basis.[30] Youngsters, particularly those under seven years, are not able to distinguish between the ad and the TV program.[31] Even at an age at which children can recognize this difference, they may not understand that the purpose of the ad is to sell them something.[32] Thus, young children do not possess the same critical reflection as adults do and are more likely to believe what they see in ads. Nonetheless, children are better at understanding the informational intent ("ads tell you about things") than the persuasive intent.[33]

Also, ad messages may prey on children's strong needs for sensual satisfaction, play, and affiliation, influencing them to choose material objects over socially oriented options.[34] Critics argue that ads teach children to become materialistic and expect immediate gratification. Unfortunately, many parents do not watch television with their children and do not educate them about advertising. As a result, children may be subject to having their attitudes and behaviors influenced by ads. Exposure to ads often prompts children to step up requests to parents about buying products, leading to family conflict and disappointed children. Children are also exposed to ads for products that shape, often negatively, their impressions of what it means to be an adult.[35] Another controversy centers on the types of products advertised, whether toys or unhealthy foods or another product.

Concerns have also been raised about the fact that many websites targeting children feature some form of advertising.[36] Although parents can use software to block access to some sites, children may not understand the need to avoid giving out personal data and e-mail addresses. Internet access therefore raises concerns about family privacy as well as about children's ability to differentiate between advertising and nonadvertising material on the Web.

Marketing Implications

Acquisition controversies raise a number of important questions that affect marketers and their relationships with consumers and other stakeholders.

Does Marketing Perpetuate Materialism?

Clearly, many marketing activities are designed to influence consumers by making acquisition both attractive and convenient, with a wide variety of options. Despite this marketing influence, consumers in many cultures did slow their spending during the recent recession. Some entirely changed their buying habits, shopping in discount stores rather than the mid- or higher-priced stores they once preferred. Even as the economy improved, a number of these consumers continued their new, more frugal buying patterns (see Chapter 14 for more on frugality). The 99p Stores retail chain in England, for example, has retained many bargain-loving customers who were originally attracted by the availability of brand-name products priced at 99 pence.[37] To reduce the influence of materialism on their lives, some consumers are choosing voluntary simplicity, as you saw in Chapter 13, often with an eye toward sustainability.

Does Marketing Encourage Addictive and Compulsive Acquisition Behaviors?

Some might argue that marketing activities encourage such behaviors. For example, cigarettes are heavily promoted in the United States—despite regulations that outlaw ads in broadcast media—and the nicotine in cigarettes is addictive (which is why it is now regulated by the Food and Drug Administration).[38] Public policy makers clearly view marketers as perpetuating this form of addictive consumption. Some countries have banned cigarette ads, and more than three dozen countries require graphic warning labels on cigarette packages because the images are presumably more effective in conveying smoking dangers than words alone.[39]

In another example, in Australia, where tobacco advertising has been forbidden since 1992, fewer than 3 percent of teenagers smoke, far fewer than in nations where ads are permitted.[40] In Canada, where graphic, full-color warnings on cigarette packs have been required for years, studies indicate that the warnings increase smokers' motivation to quit.[41] Many government and nonprofit marketers go further, running multimedia antismoking campaigns to change perceptions of and attitudes toward smoking, with the ultimate goal of discouraging consumers from buying tobacco products in the first place. Research continues on advertising appeals that can effectively discourage young consumers from smoking.[42]

However, in response to these bans on mass media advertising and strict regulations on tobacco packaging warnings, the tobacco industry has increased its emphasis on sponsorship marketing. Marlboro was co-sponsor of the Ferrari Formula One car racing team until 2010. Tobacco companies are now also leveraging the power of social media to communicate with their target segments.

How Can Marketers Deal with Consumer Theft?

Businesses spend billions of dollars every year trying to prevent or reduce theft through the use of antitheft devices and improved security systems. Some companies combine closed-circuit TVs with sophisticated computer software to track suspicious behavior. With the rise of social media and some incidents of "flash mobs" in which consumers converge on a store and shoplift in a group, retailers are now monitoring social media and Internet sites for early warning signs so they can be prepared.[43]

Although security systems and procedures may reduce theft, they also may interfere with retailers' abilities to service customers. For example, retailers may have to keep merchandise in glass display cases, locked cabinets, and so on. This added security increases consumers' search costs, making it more difficult and more time-consuming for consumers to examine products and for salespeople to service customers. The added security systems may also feel intimidating to consumers.

How Can Marketers Deal with Black Markets?

Marketers are taking a variety of actions to thwart black markets, especially buying and selling online. In many cases, products sold though black market channels are fake. A lawyer at World Wrestling Entertainment (WWE), for example, scours the Internet for auctions that offer fake WWE DVDs and clothing and then takes legal action against the sellers.[44] U.K.-based Barbour, an upscale apparel firm, fights back against counterfeiters' online marketing by buying search engine ads that appear when consumers use keywords such as "fake Barbour." One of Barbour's ads warns consumers: "Don't get caught buying fakes, see which fake websites to avoid."[45] Fake merchandise may be hazardous, such as some counterfeit food or medicines.

Should Marketers Target Children?

In light of concerns about marketers targeting children, both the Federal Trade Commission (FTC) and the Federal Communications Commission (FCC) have recommended that television stations use a separator between the program and the ad whenever the program is directed toward younger children. They recommend including a message prior to and directly after the ads—such as "We will return after these messages" before the commercial break, followed by "We now return to [name of the program]" at the end of the break—to help children to distinguish between ads and programming.[46]

The advertising industry has developed guidelines for children's advertising that are enforced by the Children's Advertising Review Unit (CARU), a wing of the Council of Better Business Bureaus. The guidelines encourage truthful and accurate advertising that recognizes children's cognitive limitations and avoids promoting unrealistic expectations about what products can do. Other countries also have agencies that regulate children's advertising and take action when necessary. For example, the U.K. Advertising Standards Authority investigates complaints about ads that target children inappropriately. It recently ruled that a commercial for the Morrisons, a supermarket chain, promoting collectible trading cards and the chance to win a trip to Disneyland Paris, could no longer air because it encouraged children to pester parents into making purchases.[47]

Consumption Controversies

Consumption situations can also give rise to ethical controversies. Here we discuss concerns about (1) underage drinking and smoking, (2) idealized self-images, (3) compulsive gambling, (4) overeating and obesity, and (5) privacy.

Underage Drinking and Smoking

As mentioned earlier, addictions to alcohol and tobacco represent one form of deviant consumer behavior. *Illegal use* of these products by minors is another deviant consumer behavior. Nearly one-third of high school students and nearly 45 percent of college students have engaged in "binge drinking" (drinking more than five drinks in one sitting).[48] One million young consumers begin smoking every year, and 90 percent of new smokers are teenagers.[49] These figures are even higher in countries where there are few bans on cigarette advertising. Underage drinking and smoking have consequences for the individual and for society.[50] Overuse of alcohol has been implicated in campus violence, campus property damage, academic failures, teen highway fatalities, youth suicides, and campus hazing deaths.

Idealized Self-Images

Some critics say that advertising contributes to an idealized self-image (see Exhibit 17.7). Most male models shown in advertisements are trim with well-developed muscles and handsome features. The female models are mostly young, very thin, and beautiful. Because these ads represent society's conception of the ideal man or woman, they exemplify traits that many men and women will never actually achieve. A particularly salient issue for both men and women is how their bodies compare with those of thin models. Indeed, one study found that 11 percent of men said that they would trade more than five years of their lives to achieve personal weight goals—statistics that closely track women's responses.[51]

Particularly in Westernized countries, thinness is viewed as a characteristic of attractive men and women. Unfortunately, this value can be carried to extremes and can lead to eating disorders such as anorexia and bulimia, disorders that affect approximately 10 million U.S. women and 1 million U.S. men. These disorders are also increasing dramatically among young women in Japan.[52] On the other hand, binge eating is a problem for an estimated 25 million Americans.[53] But do ads with thin models serve as an impetus to consumers with predispositions to eating disorders? Does identification with very thin models create dissatisfaction with one's own body and appearance?[54] Some evidence suggests the answer to these questions is yes.

Featuring the Women's Hazel Wedge in Violet

UGG australia

Image Courtesy of The Advertising Archives

Social comparison theory A theory that proposes that individuals have a drive to compare themselves with other people.

Social comparison theory proposes that individuals have a drive to compare themselves with other people.[55] Consistent with this theory, research shows that young women do compare themselves with models in ads and that such self-comparisons can affect self-esteem.[56] As a result, consumers feel inadequate if they do not measure up to the comparison person. Consumers who feel threatened by such comparisons will lie about their behavior to protect their self-esteem.[57] Interestingly, some research has also found that consumers who view ads with beautiful models reduce their attractiveness ratings of average-looking women. A potential conclusion, based on the research, is that advertising can have an unintended but negative impact on how satisfied men and women are with their appearance.[58] Note that consumers do not feel bad about the comparison if the models in ads are extremely thin.[59]

Compulsive Gambling

Compulsive gambling, a problematic consumption behavior, affects an estimated six to nine million Americans. In one study, 85 percent of the participants aged 18 to 24 said that they had gambled, and 5 percent admitted having gambling problems.[60] Scientists have established systematic links between compulsive gambling and consumption of alcohol, tobacco, and illicit drugs.[61] Typically, compulsive gambling behavior evolves over a series of stages. Sometimes, but not always, the consumer first experiences the pleasure of a "big win."[62] Next, gambling becomes more reckless, losses pile up, and gambling becomes a central force in the individual's life. The compulsive gambler promises to stop gambling, but cannot. The final stage occurs when the gambler realizes that he or she has hit rock bottom.

Industry and marketing practices may also perpetuate behaviors like compulsive gambling.[63] Gambling is a profitable industry; although attendance at horse races is decreasing, casino gambling is on the rise, with nearly 1,000 casinos now located in 41 states in the United States—many with high-tech video slot machines.[64] Seeing the potential for higher revenue, some states spend millions of dollars advertising their lottery programs. New York, for example, takes in more than $6.5 billion in lottery revenue and spends $43 million annually to advertise its lottery and scratch-off tickets.[65] Online gambling has grown into a $12 billion industry, even though U.S. citizens cannot legally bet in online casinos.[66]

Overeating and Obesity

Scientists say that the rapid rise of obesity worldwide constitutes an "epidemic."[67] Overeating remains a serious problem in the United States, where one-third of all adults and 17 percent of children and teens are obese.[68] Researchers are investigating a variety of issues that may contribute to overeating and, over time, to obesity. For example, do consumers feel less guilty about eating "low fat" snack foods and therefore overeat? Marketers can help combat this tendency by making serving size information more salient.[69]

Also, consumers tend to underestimate the calorie content of foods they consume, a situation that explains the regulatory move to have restaurants post nutrition information about menu items.[70] Another issue is that consumers tend to perceive unhealthy foods as being tastier and more enjoyable than healthy foods. To address this perception, food marketers can reformulate foods to make foods healthier as well as better tasting—and revamp marketing to promote healthy foods.[71]

Privacy Controversies

Privacy controversies have received more attention in recent years because a great deal of detailed information is being collected about consumers as they click around the Internet and use social media.[72] When consumers post a photo on Facebook or a message on Twitter, click on an advertising link, or watch an online video, their activities are being tracked—sometimes by more than one company. The marketing purpose is to show relevant ads to consumers, based on their online behavior and browsing history.[73] This is useful because consumers can thus learn about products and brands that they are or might be interested in, rather than being bombarded by irrelevant ads. However, the amount and type of data collected, and what marketers might do with the data, has some consumers and privacy advocates worried.[74]

Many consumers believe that businesses collect too much personal information and are concerned about threats to their personal privacy.[75] In another study, 61 percent of the participants decided not to use a financial website because of concerns about how their personal data would be handled.[76] They also worry about identity theft, especially in the wake of incidents involving theft of personal data such as credit card numbers.[77]

The extent of consumer concern and the willingness to give personal information varies according to the type of information that marketers want to collect.[78] However, although consumers often complain about privacy concerns, many still willingly provide information that could compromise their privacy.[79] Most websites post privacy policies to explain what consumer data they gather, what they do with it, how consumers can review it, and how it is protected—although often these statements do not offer complete explanations.[80] Companies can help consumers make informed decisions by describing what data they collect and how they use data to improve the consumers' online experience (such as customized offers that better fit the consumers' interests).[81]

Marketing Implications

The consumption issues just discussed are both complex and challenging. Yet marketers must understand the questions raised by such controversies as they plan their strategy and activities. They concern balancing the interests of consumers and their own interests, in both the short and long run.

Does Marketing Encourage Underage or Excessive Drinking and Smoking?

Youngsters are exposed to a large amount of alcohol advertising as well as to non–TV-based tobacco advertising,[82] a situation that has led to calls for companies to limit kids' exposure to such advertising.[83] Although the tobacco industry avoids deliberately marketing to children, some brands continue to be advertised in adult publications that teens also read. Evidence suggests that the more young consumers view alcohol ads, the more they know about these products, and the more likely they are to use them.[84]

Similarly, most youthful smokers choose the most heavily advertised brands—which shows that advertising works and also implicates it as a cause of smoking behavior. Adolescents who have the greatest exposure to cigarette advertising in general tend to be the heaviest smokers, and the brands that do the most advertising tend to attract a greater proportion of teenagers than of adults. In particular, tobacco and alcohol ads featuring human actors or models have been found to directly produce more positive attitudes toward the ad, the brand, and the product category.[85] Children are also exposed to images of cigarette consumption in nonadvertising contexts. In fact, research indicates that up to one-third of the children who see smoking in movies rated G, PG, and PG-13 will start to smoke.[86]

However, others argue that advertising for these products has little effect on children; more critical determinants are said to include peer influence, parental smoking, and self-esteem. The alcohol industry stresses that it does not target young consumers and notes that it has invested heavily to promote responsible drinking among adult consumers (see Exhibit 17.8). Recently, Heineken, which markets beer brands worldwide, introduced a global campaign to encourage responsible alcohol consumption. "You can't build a long term sustainable business on excessive consumption," explains the senior director of the Heineken brand.[87] Even when alcohol marketers present messages such as "Don't drink and drive," consumers may not react positively because the source is a corporate sponsor.[88]

Does Advertising Affect Self-Image?

Some companies are becoming more sensitive to the potentially negative effects of promotional messages on self-image. In the fashion industry, demand for plus-size models is up—perhaps in response to consumers' demands for different types of women in fashion products and ads.[89] Also, online retailers give consumers the option of buying and trying on clothing at home.[90] Although some women may be unhappy about how they compare with models in ads, others are comfortable with themselves and are hostile toward advertisers that perpetuate unrealistic images of women.[91] However, because some women

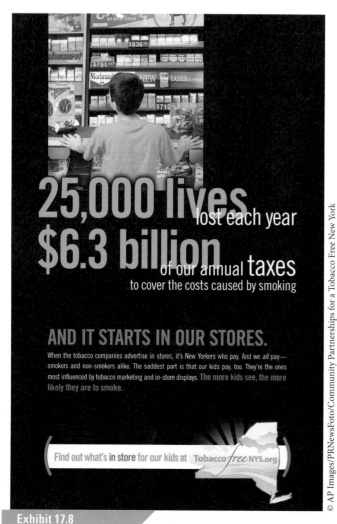

25,000 lives lost each year
$6.3 billion of our annual taxes to cover the costs caused by smoking

AND IT STARTS IN OUR STORES.

When the tobacco companies advertise in stores, it's New Yorkers who pay. And we *all* pay—smokers and non-smokers alike. The saddest part is that our kids pay, too. They're the ones most influenced by tobacco marketing and in-store displays. The more kids see, the more likely they are to smoke.

Find out what's **in store** for our kids at TobaccofreeNYS.org

© AP Images/PRNewsFoto/Community Partnerships for a Tobacco Free New York

Exhibit 17.8

Publicizing Health Concerns
To combat the advertising of tobacco and alcohol to children, federal and state agencies, interest groups, and companies publicize the adverse effects of these substances on children's health.

will still be willing to use products that entail some risk to achieve an idealized body image, marketers must disclose risks (e.g., of pharmaceutical products or dietary supplements) so that consumers can evaluate any potential negative outcomes.

Does Marketing Affect Compulsive Gambling Behavior?

The expansion of legalized gambling operations—and the marketing of such facilities—may be a problem for consumers with a tendency toward or a history of compulsive gambling. Most government-run lotteries and many casino companies set aside some funding for consumer education and treatment of compulsive gambling. Australian Leisure and Hospitality Group, for example, runs an award-winning program to combat problem gambling at hundreds of its facilities where consumers can play electronic poker.[92] Online gambling is generally illegal in the United States but legal in many countries. However, because multiple jurisdictions regulate online gambling that occurs across national borders, no one approach has been put in place to help consumers who compulsively gamble online. Finally, some research suggests that a slot machine's physical appearance—specifically, whether consumers see a hint of human resemblance—can affect consumers' perceptions of risk, a finding that may help in developing effective anti-gambling messages.[93]

Does Marketing Contribute to Overeating and Obesity?

The World Health Organization believes that evidence connecting junk food advertising and childhood obesity is convincing enough that governments should discourage marketing activities that promote unhealthy eating among youngsters.[94] In some countries, advocacy groups are campaigning for stronger restrictions on marketing of high-sugar or high-fat foods to children, whether through traditional promotions, online, or in social media. The Children's Food Campaign, for example, has complained to U.K. authorities that marketers' use of brand characters, animation, and other tools make junk foods more appealing to children who surf the Web.[95] Availability is another concern: In many cases, children can buy unhealthy snacks from vending machines at school—a distribution practice under scrutiny by states and federal regulators.[96]

On the other hand, more companies and media are using marketing to encourage healthier behaviors. For example, Sesame Street's Cookie Monster now tells kids that cookies are a "sometimes food."[97] Food manufacturers are also emphasizing the good taste of healthy foods and providing nutrition information. PepsiCo, known for its cola drinks and salty snacks, has introduced dozens of healthy snacks, from yogurt drinks to oatmeal bars, to broaden its appeal.[98] As another example, Bolthouse Farms, one of the largest U.S. growers of baby carrots promotes consumption of its products with catchy ads carrying the slogan: "Eat 'em like junk food" (see this chapter's ending case for more detail).[99] Pick n Pay, a South African grocery retailer, discounts healthy foods by up to 25 percent to encourage healthier eating.[100] Fast-food restaurants not only post nutrition data, some are making healthy foods a default menu choice for children. The McDonald's Happy Meals now come with apples and small fries, for instance.[101] The SUBWAY chain of restaurants has long emphasized healthy food options.

Do Marketers Invade Consumers' Privacy?

Online privacy is a headline issue, even though other aspects of privacy do affect consumers (such as names on mailing lists and credit card numbers retained in company databases). Giants such as Google and Facebook have become embroiled in controversy after controversy as they seek to use the volume of data they collect to better target consumers with personalized ads. Concerns about privacy are only intensifying as billions of consumers worldwide go online for information, entertainment, shopping, and more. Although privacy policies are almost universally available, privacy advocates say consumers rarely read them or understand the sophisticated tracking and data collection procedures used by marketers.

Some regulators are taking action. For example, the European Union has some of the strictest online privacy rules on the planet, covering disclosure of what data is being gathered and requiring consumers to consent to being tracked by cookies.[102] Even tighter rules are on the way, giving European consumers more say over how their information may be used.[103] U.S. regulators are considering a "Do Not Track" list to protect children's privacy online, similar to the "Do Not Call" list that allows millions of Americans to opt out of telemarketing calls.

Meanwhile, many marketers are doing more to explain their privacy policies and reassure consumers that personal data are being safeguarded. Major Internet browsing programs have features that enable users to reject or delete cookies and avoid being tracked as individuals. Advertisers who are members of the Digital Advertising Alliance—including American Express and Walmart—voluntarily invite consumers to opt out of seeing online and mobile ads by clicking on a special icon.[104] At the same time, concerns about privacy open up the potential for marketers to develop new offerings designed to protect consumer privacy, such as software that allows anonymous browsing.[105] _____

Disposition Controversies

As discussed in Chapter 10, consumers have many options for voluntarily disposing of possessions. Some of these disposition outcomes can be controversial, especially now that more consumers and marketers are embracing sustainability and trying to protect the environment, now and into the future. This section will discuss two specific concerns: (1) disposing of products that still function and (2) disposing of products that are no longer functional.

Disposing of Products That Still Function

When products can be used, consumers who want to dispose of them can give them away to another consumer, trade for useful items, sell or auction them, donate them, or recycle them. Research about recycling demonstrates that specific beliefs about its importance and attitudes toward recycling in general can directly affect whether consumers engage in recycling behaviors and whether they perceive that recycling is inconvenient.[106]

On occasion, useful products are thrown away, a disposition behavior that can be controversial, not just because it may be perceived as wasteful. When consumers upgrade their electronics products, for example, they don't always have or take advantage of proper recycling or disposal services for their old products (in workable condition), through stores or recycling centers. As a result, many old but functional cell phones, televisions, computer monitors, and other electronics wind up in landfills, posing an environmental hazard because of materials contained in the products. In fact, this is why the European Union and individual countries have enacted strict laws regarding the safe disposal of electronic and electrical goods, whether in working order or not.[107]

Disposing of Products That Do Not Function

When consumers seek to dispose of products that no longer function, they can throw them away in a socially acceptable way (in the proper trash bin or recycle center) or abandon them in a socially unacceptable way (e.g., littering), which is controversial. Some nonfunctioning products retain a value and can be sold to consumers or businesses that want the parts or the materials. In some countries, controversy surrounds the practice of dismantling and selling old, uninhabitable buildings and other artifacts that are nonfunctional in the traditional sense, but have important historic value.

Marketing Implications

What role can or should marketers play in the disposition of functioning and non-functioning products, especially in controversial situations? Businesses and nonprofit organizations such as eBay, Freecycle Network, Goodwill Industries International, Oxfam, and others facilitate the disposition of functional products, as do marketing policies that encourage trade-ins toward the purchase of new goods. IKEA and others invite customers to recycle used batteries for free through bins in their stores, a responsible way to deal with products that otherwise would pile up in landfills. Marketers working for businesses, nonprofit groups, and government agencies are doing more to encourage consumers to recycle products. And nonprofit groups like the National Trust for Historic Preservation are raising money (often in partnership with businesses) to help buy and restore historic sites like crumbling buildings, so they will not be lost forever.

In addition, many companies are being pushed by both consumers and retailers to use less product packaging or more environmentally friendly product packaging.[108] Product designers are now building in features and components that allow products to be easily disassembled for recycling or disposal. Even when products are thrown away, they can serve as raw material for companies like TerraCycle, which transforms trash into new products, marketed to green-minded consumers.[109] Such efforts may become part of the lifestyle for larger segments of consumers or perhaps entire nations or regions. Germany, for example, strictly limits the amount of waste sent to landfills, and therefore consumers have developed the habit of recycling everything that can be recycled.[110]

SOCIAL RESPONSIBILITY ISSUES IN MARKETING

Economist Milton Friedman famously stated that "the social responsibility of business is to increase its profits."[111] Now, decades after his statement, most businesses do not take an "either-or" approach. Rather than framing the decision as "higher profits *or* social responsibility," they are pursuing both higher profits *and* social responsibility through marketing.

Businesses are, for the most part, thinking long-term and seeing their stakeholders as "we," making social responsibility an integral part of their overall strategy. And marketers—not just giants like Walmart, but smaller firms as well—are starting to use their influence over suppliers to encourage more socially responsible, sustainable behavior throughout the supply chain, even across national borders.[112] Although marketers sometimes take the lead in addressing an issue, consumers now have the power and the voice to take the initiative; at other times, marketers and consumers collaborate to address important issues.

The following sections offer a brief overview of three social responsibility issues receiving particular marketing attention: (1) environmentally conscious behavior, (2) charitable behavior, and (3) community involvement.

Environmentally Conscious Behavior

Marketers are directly and indirectly involved in efforts to foster environmentally conscious behavior and to address concerns about global warming. Car companies, their suppliers, and gasoline companies all must comply with government requirements such as the use of unleaded gasoline and adherence to stricter emission controls to reduce environmental damage. These efforts sometimes increase marketing costs but may also open new profit opportunities. The trend toward the use of environmentally friendly products is growing, paving the way for companies like Seventh Generation, which markets eco-friendly household cleaning products.[113]

Conservation behavior
Limiting the use of scarce natural resources for the purposes of environmental preservation.

An important aspect of behavior related to the environment is **conservation behavior**, actions taken to limit the use of scarce natural resources. Consumers are most likely to conserve when they accept personal responsibility for the pollution problem.[114] For example, consumers who perceive that there is an energy shortage because of consumption by all consumers (including themselves) are more likely to do something about it. However, consumers often do not feel accountable for many environmental problems and are not motivated to act. Thus, for conservation programs to succeed, messages must make the problem personally relevant, such as educating consumers about how much energy and money they will save by cutting electrical usage. Environmentally conscious behaviors are, in fact, most likely to occur when consumers perceive that their actions will make a difference—called *perceived consumer effectiveness*.[115]

A study in the Netherlands points out the importance of using social norms to influence consumers' environmental behaviors. This study found that consumers generally perceive that they are more motivated to engage in proenvironmental behavior than other households are but that they have less ability to do so.[116] Furthermore, they believe that ability is the greatest determinant and that their own behavior is influenced by others. In another study of social norms, researchers examining the behavior of hotel guests concluded that normative appeals (such as "the majority of guests in this room reuse their towels") are more effective than environmental-protection appeals in encouraging conservation behavior.[117]

Many organizations and agencies are trying to motivate consumers to be environmentally friendly. Ads sometimes encourage consumers to use products or packages that conserve resources or to engage in conservation behaviors. Providing consumers with detailed information about how to be environmentally friendly can be helpful, as well. For example, the U.S. Environmental Protection Agency and the U.S. Department of Energy's joint program ENERGY STAR, promoted through on-package labeling and manufacturers' advertising, helps consumers choose energy-efficient appliances and computers (see Exhibit 17.9). Moreover, marketers can encourage consumers to include eco-friendly products in their consideration set by proposing a list of prescreened alternatives (such as products that have earned green certification).[118]

Another promising approach is to provide consumers with incentives to conserve. Providing consumers with a free shower-water flow device, for instance, significantly increased participation in an energy conservation program. Consumers prefer incentives such as tax credits to coercive tactics such as higher taxes. In addition, setting goals and providing feedback can help consumers curtail their energy use.

Exhibit 17.9

Publicizing Health Concerns
The Environmental Protection Agency's Energy Star program labels energy-efficient appliances and computers, promoting consumer energy conservation.

© Justin Sullivan/Getty Images

Greenwashing The misleading use of environmental claims for marketing purposes.

Public interest in and support for environmentally conscious behavior has resulted in a backlash against **greenwashing**, the misleading use of environmental claims for marketing purposes. When marketers promote nonexistent or minimally beneficial eco-friendly claims, they risk being perceived negatively because they seem to be exploiting consumers' interest in green goods or services. To avoid confusion and deception, government regulators in many nations have established specific guidelines for how marketers can use phrases like "environmentally friendly." In addition, to reassure consumers that their eco-claims are legitimate, some marketers seek certification from groups like the Marine Stewardship Council (to show that fish come from sustainable sources).

Charitable Behavior

The influence of marketing on charitable behavior has been the focus of considerable research. For example, consumers' cognitive resources can become depleted after being exposed to a charity's foot-in-the-door techniques. In turn, it reduces their self-control and increases their tendency to respond positively to donation requests, a finding that can help charities plan more effective appeals.[119] Other research shows that asking consumers about their intentions to volunteer *time* for a charity cause activates an emotional reaction that makes more salient the idea of "giving leads to happiness." This positive mindset, in turn, increases *money* contribution. Yet, as Exhibit 17.10 shows, asking about intentions to donate money prompts consideration of monetary value, and ultimately results in a lower charitable contribution.[120]

It is important to recognize that charitable behavior can vary by culture. According to one global survey, U.S. consumers are the most generous in volunteering their time, donating money, and helping strangers. In terms of financial contributions, Thailand ranks first, with 85 percent of consumers saying they donate to charity monthly, followed by the United Kingdom, and a tie between Ireland and the Netherlands.[121]

Thanks to social and online media, marketing to encourage charitable behavior can extend its reach and multiply its impact. Consider Comic Relief, a U.K.-based charity that holds two star-studded events—Red Nose Day and Sport Relief—to raise money for fighting poverty and helping at-risk youth. Among the marketing tools it uses are the Web, Twitter, Facebook, iPhone apps, YouTube, public relations, celebrity spokespeople, and sales promotion. Comic Relief also encourages consumers and businesses to further get involved by holding local fundraisers, all of which helps the charity raise tens of millions of dollars and help thousands of people every year.[122]

Exhibit 17.10

How Requests for Time and Money Affect Charitable Contributions
Source: Wendy Liu and Jennifer Aaker, "The Happiness of Giving: The Time-Ask Effect," *Journal of Consumer Research,* October 2008, figure 1, p. 546.

Community Involvement

As the opening example shows, companies can use marketing as a catalyst for community-based social responsibility. By inviting groups to compete for grants—and giving consumers a say in which groups should receive money—Pepsi encouraged active involvement in the groups and among community members.

Marketers, large companies in particular, often have policies that encourage employees to get involved in the communities where they do business.[123] While this involvement usually generates goodwill and positive word of mouth, it can also benefit the company in other ways (e.g., by

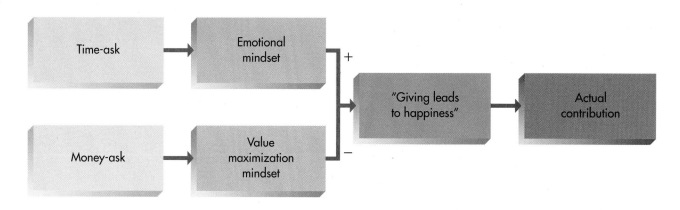

increasing employee satisfaction).[124] Many employees of Target, for example, volunteer as "reading buddies," reading to patients in local hospitals and to youngsters in local schools. General Electric has a Volunteers Foundation that coordinates employee volunteer efforts in 41 nations.

HOW CAN CONSUMERS RESIST MARKETING PRACTICES?

Any marketing, even "bright side" marketing in support of socially responsible outcomes, may irritate some consumers. Whether these consumers believe that they are being barraged with messages or for any other reason, consumers who are upset about certain marketing practices can resist them and try to bring about change individually, through advocacy groups, and through boycotts.[125] Consumers who are dissatisfied or unhappy with marketing practices can choose *not* to patronize the offending marketer in the future, complain to the marketer, and spread negative word of mouth. These individual consumer resistance strategies can be very effective, especially when social media are leveraged to repeat the message.

Group strategies are potentially even more powerful than unorganized consumer efforts. Some formally organized advocacy groups engage in resistance by informing the public about business practices that they regard as socially inappropriate.[126] The Center for the Study of Commercialism, for example, distributes information and uses lobbying to stop marketing practices such as advertising in schools. *Adbusters*, a magazine published by Canada's Media Foundation, informs consumers about commercial excess.[127]

Boycott An organized activity in which consumers avoid purchasing products or services from a company whose policies or practices are seen as unfair or unjust.

A **boycott** is an organized activity in which consumers avoid purchasing products or services from a company whose policies or practices are seen as unfair or unjust. Boycotting is a way for consumers to hold companies accountable for perceived objectionable actions. Thus, many consumers are motivated by the opportunity and likelihood of making a difference. Also, consumers who are particularly susceptible to the normative influences of the reference group conducting the boycott will be more likely to participate than those who are less susceptible. Finally, consumers may seek to feel less guilty and hope to boost or sustain their self-esteem by joining a particular boycott.[128]

Organized boycotts are able to gain publicity and are likely to have more impact than the same number of consumers acting on their own.[129] Sometimes boycotts are directed against a company's activities rather than against a product. The primary indicators that a boycott has been successful are not that it has caused financial effects but rather that it (1) has changed the offending policies, (2) has made businesses more responsible in their plans for future activities, and (3) has forced changes in the behavior of nontargeted businesses that engage in similar practices.

SUMMARY

Marketing and consumer behavior can have a "bright side," leading to constructive outcomes, and a "dark side," leading to negative outcomes. Decision-makers often face ethical issues when they try to balance social dilemmas (whose interests will take priority) and temporal dilemmas (if immediate or long-term interests take priority). Marketing ethics are rules or standards of acceptable conduct that guide marketing decisions. Consumer ethics are rules of acceptable conduct that apply to the full range of consumer behaviors. Deviant consumer behavior is either unexpected or not sanctioned by society.

Five areas of controversy related to acquisition situations are materialistic behavior, addictive and compulsive behavior,

consumer theft, black markets, and targeting vulnerable segments. In the context of consumption situations, controversies include underage drinking and smoking, idealized self-images, compulsive gambling, overeating and obesity, and privacy.

Disposition controversies include disposing of functional and nonfunctional products. Social responsibility issues receiving special marketing attention are environmentally conscious behavior, charitable behavior, and community involvement. Consumers can resist unwanted, disreputable, objectionable, and/or unethical marketing through individual actions, support of advocacy groups, and boycotts.

Questions for Review and Discussion

1. Why is balance needed in decisions that involve social dilemmas and temporal dilemmas?

2. What is deviant consumer behavior, and is it always unethical?

3. How does addictive behavior differ from compulsive behavior?

4. How do temptation and rationalization affect consumer theft?

5. What is social comparison theory, and how does it apply to advertising?

6. What influences conservation behavior and charitable behavior?

7. What can consumers do to resist unwanted marketing practices?

CONSUMER BEHAVIOR CASE

Marketing Baby Carrots Like Junk Food

Can marketing encourage people to snack on baby carrots as if they were junk food? That's what California-based Bolthouse Farms has set out to do, with the help of Colorado advertising agency Crispin Porter + Bogusky. Bolthouse CEO Jeff Dunn, a former Coca-Cola marketing executive, remembers thinking that his firm's baby carrots are "a perfect snack"—low-calorie, inexpensive, good tasting, and nutritious. "But people aren't eating as much of them as we'd like. So what do we do?"

Crispin's advertising experts told Dunn that baby carrots have a lot in common with junk food. "They're neon orange, they're crunchy, they're dippable, they're kind of addictive," said Omid Farhang, the agency's creative director. Baby carrots may be healthy, but Dunn wanted to avoid messages that discuss nutrition, which he calls "the rational approach." Instead, the agency aimed to reposition baby carrots by emphasizing their eat-anywhere, bite-size snackability and associating them with skateboarding and other popular, contemporary activities. "It's about getting baby carrots into a different category," says Crispin's CEO.

What baby carrots needed was the right positioning, messages, packaging, and distribution. A new campaign was born. Crispin created a catchy slogan: "Baby carrots: Eat 'em like junk food." Next, they designed a flashy new bag, much like the packaging that chips come in, with a window so buyers can see that they're buying fresh vegetables. It set up a Twitter account and YouTube channel to reach out to social media-savvy consumers, tested three TV commercials, and printed store displays promoting baby carrots as "the original orange doodle." Also, the agency developed colorful baby carrot vending machines that resemble the machines used to sell chips and other snacks. Finally, it posted engaging online content, marketing baby carrots with fun games and apps.

During test-marketing, Bolthouse found that its sales in the test cities were as much as 12 percent higher than its sales in non–test-markets. The vending machines sold as many as 90 snack packs each week, and a number of schools called about putting the machines in cafeteria areas. In short, baby carrot snacks were beginning to catch on.

To keep the campaign fresh, Crispin added new online content and designed additional packaging alternatives to catch the eye of shoppers. Meanwhile, Bolthouse experiments with new flavored baby carrots, following the lead of snack marketers that add flavors to their basic chips or pretzels. This variety gives novelty-seekers more options and may even win over snackers who prefer flavored carrots to plain ones. Other vegetable and fruit marketers are paying close attention because the marketing that makes baby carrots appealing as junk food could very well work for apples and other foods.

Baby carrots aren't going to replace every other snack food on the shelf, but sales are growing little by little as more consumers get the message. For example, U.S. consumers buy millions of bags of chips, order millions of pizza slices, and stock up on fizzy soft drinks for Super Bowl Sunday. Lately, however, baby carrots are starting to score: Bolthouse Farms now ships 28 percent more baby carrots during the week leading up to the Super Bowl than in an ordinary week.[130]

CASE QUESTIONS

1. Which is likely to be more effective—marketing baby carrots to young consumers or to parents of young consumers? Why?

2. Does the marketing of baby carrots raise any social or temporal dilemmas?

3. Is there a potential "dark side" to marketing baby carrots as junk food?

4. Do you agree with this strategy of marketing baby carrots as junk food instead of as a healthy snack? Explain your answer.

ENDNOTES

1. Duane D. Stanford, "PepsiCo May Boost Marketing Budget to Take on Coca-Cola," *Bloomberg*, January 17, 2012, www.bloomberg.com; Valerie Bauerlein, "Pepsi Hits 'Refresh' on Donor Project," *Wall Street Journal*, January 30, 2011, www.wsj.com; and Todd Wasserman, "Pepsi Refresh Project Netted 61 Million Votes," *Mashable*, December 15, 2010, www.mashable.com.

2. For more about sharing, see Russell Belk, "Sharing," *Journal of Consumer Research*, February 2010, pp. 715–734.

3. Stephen Hayward, "Britain's Shoplifting Bill Hits 840 Million Pounds a Year," *Sunday Mirror (UK)*, January 15, 2012, www.mirror.co.uk.

4. Flora F. Gu and Kineta Hung, "Materialism Among Adolescents in China: A Historical Generation Perspective," *Journal of Asia Business Studies* 3, no. 2, 2009, pp. 56–64. For another perspective, see: Harold Ogden and Shen Cheng, "Cultural Dimensions and Materialism: Comparing Canada and China," *Asia Pacific Journal of Marketing and Logistics* 23, no. 4, 2011, pp. 431–447.

5. Karl Wilson, "In Love with Luxury amid Global Gloom," *China Daily*, January 16, 2012, www.chinadaily.com.cn.

6. Aaron C. Ahuvia and Nancy Y. Wong, "Personality and Values Based Materialism: Their Relationship and Origins," *Journal of Consumer Psychology* 12, no. 4, 2002, pp. 389–402; and Marvin E. Goldberg, Gerald J. Gorn, Laura A. Peracchio, and Gary Bamossy, "Understanding Materialism Among Youth," *Journal of Consumer Psychology* 13, no. 3, 2003, pp. 278–288.

7. Goldberg, Gorn, Peracchio, and Bamossy, "Understanding Materialism Among Youth."

8. Noel C. Paul, "Branded for Life?" *Christian Science Monitor*, April 1, 2002, www.csmonitor.com.

9. Marsha L. Richins, "Media, Materialism, and Human Happiness," *Advances in Consumer Research* 14, 1987, pp. 352–356.

10. See, for example, James M. Hunt, Jerome B. Kernan, and Deborah J. Mitchell, "Materialism as Social Cognition: People, Possessions, and Perception," *Journal of Consumer Psychology* 5, no. 1, 1996, pp. 65–83.

11. Elizabeth C. Hirschman, "The Consciousness of Addiction," *Journal of Consumer Research*, September 1992, pp. 155–179.

12. "Tobacco Fact Sheet," World Health Organization, July 2011, www.who.int.

13. Ronald Faber, Gary Christenson, Martina DeZwaan, and James Mitchell, "Two Forms of Compulsive Consumption: Comorbidity of Compulsive Buying and Binge Eating," *Journal of Consumer Research*, December 1995, pp. 296–304; Thomas C. O'Guinn and Ronald J. Faber, "Compulsive Buying," *Journal of Consumer Research*, September 1989, pp. 147–157; Ronald J. Faber and Thomas C. O'Guinn, "Compulsive Consumption and Credit Abuse," *Journal of Consumer Policy*, March 1988, pp. 97–109; Gilles Valence, Alain D'Astous, and Louis Fortier, "Compulsive Buying: Concept and Measurement," *Journal of Consumer Policy*, December 1988, pp. 419–433; Rajan Nataraajan and Brent G. Goff, "Compulsive Buying," in ed. Floyd W. Rudman, *To Have Possessions: A Handbook on Ownership and Property* (Corte Madera, Calif.: Select Press, 1991), pp. 307–328; and Wayne S. DeSarbo and Elizabeth A. Edwards, "Typologies of Compulsive Buying Behavior," *Journal of Consumer Psychology* 5, no. 3, 1996, pp. 231–262.

14. Faber and O'Guinn, "Compulsive Consumption and Credit Abuse"; Ronald J. Faber and Thomas C. O'Guinn, "A Clinical Screener for Compulsive Buying," *Journal of Consumer Research*, December 1992, pp. 459–469; O'Guinn and Faber, "Compulsive Buying"; and James A. Roberts, "Compulsive Buying Among College Students," *Journal of Consumer Affairs*, Winter 1998, pp. 295–319.

15. "Shrinkage on the Rise," *National Retail Federation news release*, June 14, 2011, www.nrf.com; and "Shoplifting: Five-Fingered Discounts," *Economist*, October 23, 2010, p. 81.

16. Joseph C. Nunes, Christopher K. Hsee, and Elke U. Weber, "Why Are People So Prone to Steal Software?" *Journal of Public Policy and Marketing* 23, Spring 2004, pp. 43–53.

17. Rick Jervis, "Discount-Seeking Consumers Swipe Newspapers to Pad Savings," *USA Today*, August 17, 2011, www.usatoday.com.

18. Ronald A. Fullerton and Girish Punj, "The Unintended Consequences of the Culture of Consumption," *Consumption, Markets, and Culture* 1, no. 4, 1998, pp. 393–423.

19. Dena Cox, Anthony P. Cox, and George P. Moschis, "When Consumer Behavior Goes Bad," *Journal of Consumer Marketing*, September 1990, pp. 149–159.

20. Paul Bernstein, "Cheating—The New National Pastime?" *Business*, October–December 1985, pp. 24–33; and Ronald A. Fullerton and Girish Punj, "The Unintended Consequences of the Culture of Consumption: A Historical-Theoretical Analysis of Consumer Misbehavior," *Consumption, Markets and Culture* 1, no. 4, 1998, pp. 393–423.

21. Ronald A. Fullerton and Girish Punj, "Choosing to Misbehave," in eds, Leigh McAlister and Michael Rothschild, *Advances in Consumer Research*, vol. 20 (Provo, Utah: Association for Consumer Research, 1993), pp. 570–574; and Donald R. Katz, *The Big Store* (New York: Penguin, 1988).

22. Cox, Cox, and Moschis, "When Consumer Behavior Goes Bad"; George P. Moschis, Dena S. Cox, and James J. Kellaris, "An Exploratory Study of Adolescent Shoplifting Behavior," in eds. Melanie Wallendorf and Paul Anderson, *Advances in Consumer Research*, vol. 14 (Provo, Utah: Association for Consumer Research, 1987), pp. 526–530; and Fullerton and Punj, "The Unintended Consequences of the Culture of Consumption."

23. Uzma Khan and Ravi Dhar, "Licensing Effect in Consumer Choice," *Journal of Marketing Research*, May 2006, pp. 259–266.

24. John Fetto, "Penny for Your Thoughts," *American Demographics*, September 2000, pp. 8–9.

25. Nina Mazar, On Amir, and Dan Ariely, "The Dishonesty of Honest People: A Theory of Self-Concept Maintenance," *Journal of Marketing Research*, December 2008, pp. 633–644.

26. Diana Ransom, "The Black Market in College-Graduation Tickets," *Wall Street Journal*, May 8, 2007, p. D1.

27. Samantha Grossman, "Simpsons Dolls Join Barbie on Iran's Banned-Toy List," *Time*, February 7, 2012, www.time.com.

28. Keith Wilcox, Hyeong Min Kim, and Sankar Sen, "Why Do Consumers Buy Counterfeit Luxury Brands?" *Journal of Marketing Research*, April 2009, pp. 247–259.

29. Shan Li, "Counterfeiters Go Downscale," *Sacramento Bee*, February 8, 2012, www.sacbee.com; and MaryLou Costa, "The New Copycats," *MarketingWeek*, September 27, 2011, www.marketingweek.co.uk.

30. F. J. Zimmerman, D. A. Christakis, and A. N. Meltzoff, "Television and DVD/Video Viewing in Children Younger Than 2 Years," *Archives of Pediatric and Adolescent Medicine* 161, no. 5, 2007, pp. 473–479.

31. Andreas I. Andronikidis and Maria Lambrianidou, "Children's Understanding of Television Advertising: A Grounded Theory Approach," *Psychology & Marketing*, April 2010, pp. 299–322; Scott Ward, "Consumer Socialization," *Journal of Consumer Research*, September 1974, pp. 1–13; Laurene Krasney Meringoff and Gerald S. Lesser, "Children's Ability to Distinguish Television Commercials from Program Material," in ed. R. P. Adler, *The Effect of Television Advertising on Children* (Lexington, Mass.: Lexington Books, 1980), pp. 29–42; and S. Levin, T. Petros, and F. Petrella, "Preschoolers' Awareness of Television Advertising," *Child Development*, August 1982, pp. 933–937.

32. M. Carole Macklin, "Preschoolers' Understanding of the Informational Function of Advertising," *Journal of Consumer Research*, September 1987, pp. 229–239; and Merrie Brucks, Gary M. Armstrong, and Marvin E. Goldberg, "Children's Use of Cognitive Defenses Against Television Advertising," *Journal of Consumer Research*, March 1988, pp. 471–482.

33. Mary C. Martin, "Children's Understanding of the Intent of Advertising: A Meta-Analysis," *Journal of Public Policy and Marketing*, Fall 1997, pp. 205–216.

34. Jon Berry, "The New Generation of Kids and Ads," *Adweek's Marketing Week*, April 15, 1991, pp. 25–28; Marvin E. Goldberg and Gerald J. Gorn, "Some Unintended Consequences of TV Advertising to Children," *Journal of Consumer Research*, June 1978, pp. 22–29; and Gary M. Armstrong and Merrie Brucks, "Dealing with Children's Advertising," *Journal of Public Policy and Marketing* 7, 1988, pp. 98–113.

35. Gerald J. Gorn and Renee Florsheim, "The Effects of Commercials for Adult Products on Children," *Journal of Consumer Research*, March 1985, pp. 962–967.

36. "For Kids on the Web, It's an Ad, Ad, Ad, Ad World," *Business-Week*, August 13, 2001, p. 108.

37. Erin Maclaughlin, "How '99p' Stores Made African Businessman Millions," *CNN*, February 10, 2012, www.cnn.com.

38. Michael Felberbaum, "Q&A: Former FDA Commissioner Talks about Tobacco," *Associated Press*, August 5, 2011, http://abcnews.go.com.

39. Gary Strauss, "Graphic Cigarette Labels: Will They Work?" *USA Today*, June 22, 2011, www.usatoday.com.

40. Denis Campbell, "'Plain Packs Will Make Smoking History,'" *Guardian (UK)*, January 24, 2012, www.guardian.co.uk.

41. Scott Hensley, "Be Warned: FDA Unveils Graphic Cigarette Labels," *NPR*, June 21, 2011, www.npr.org.

42. See, for example, Kathleen Kelly, Maria Leonora G. Comello, Linda R. Stanley, and Gabriel R. Gonzalez, "The Power of Theme and Language in Multi-Cultural Communities," *Journal of Advertising Research*, September 2010, pp. 265–278.

43. Whit Richardson, "NRF Issues Guidelines, But Finds Flash Mobs Less Serious than Assumed," *Security Director News*, August 9, 2011, www.securitydirectornews.com.

44. Maija Palmer, "Cyberspace Fakes Make Brands Truly Worried," *Financial Times*, April 11, 2007, p. 10.

45. Loulla-Mae Eleftheriou-Smith, "Barbour Shells Out on Search Ads to Fight Fakes," *Marketing*, February 3, 2012, www.marketingmagazine.co.uk.

46. Meringoff and Lesser, "Children's Ability to Distinguish Television Commercials from Program Material."

47. Mark Sweney, "Morrisons Ad Banned for Targeting Kids," *Guardian (UK)*, October 26, 2011, www.guardian.co.uk.

48. "Underage Drinking in the United States: A Status Report, 2004," Georgetown University Center on Alcohol Marketing and Youth, February 2005, p. 2; and Mindy Sink, "Drinking Deaths Draw Attention to Old Campus Problem," *New York Times*, November 9, 2004, p. A16.

49. "Tobacco Use, Access, and Exposure to Tobacco in Media Among Middle and High School Students, United States, 2004," *Morbidity and Mortality Weekly Report, Centers for Disease Control and Prevention*, April 1, 2005, www.cdc.gov/mmwr.

50. Charles S. Clark, "Underage Drinking," *The CQ Researcher* 2, no. 10, 1992, pp. 219–244; and Courtney Leatherman, "College Officials Are Split on Alcohol Policies," *Chronicle of Higher Education*, January 31, 1990, pp. A33–A35.

51. Catherine Fitzpatrick, "How Buff Is Enough? Reality Check Is in the Male," *Milwaukee Journal Sentinel*, June 24, 2001, p. 1–L.

52. Isabel Reynolds, "Japan: Feature—Eating Disorders Plague Young Japanese," *Reuters*, June 20, 2001, www.reuters.com.

53. Laura Landro, "The Informed Patient: Amid Focus on Obesity and Diet, Anorexia, Bulimia Are on the Rise," *Wall Street Journal*, March 30, 2004, p. D1.

54. See also Debra Lynn Stephens, Ronald P. Hill, and Cynthia Hanson, "The Beauty Myth and Female Consumers: The Controversial Role of Advertising," *Journal of Consumer Affairs*, Summer 1994, pp. 137–154.

55. Leon Festinger, "A Theory of Social Comparison Processes," *Human Relations*, May 1954, pp. 117–140.

56. Michael Häfner, "How Dissimilar Others May Still Resemble the Self," *Journal of Consumer Psychology* 14, no. 2, 2004, pp. 187–196; Mary C. Martin and James W. Gentry, "Stuck in the Model Trap: The Effects of Beautiful Models in Ads on Female Pre-Adolescents and Adolescents," *Journal of Advertising*, Summer 1997, pp. 19–33; Marsha L. Richins, "Social Comparison and the Idealized Images of Advertising," *Journal of Consumer Research*, June 1991, pp. 71–83; and Richard W. Pollay, "The Distorted Mirror: Reflections on the Unintended

Consequences of Advertising," *Journal of Marketing*, April 1986, pp. 18–36.

57. Jennifer J. Argo, Katherine White, and Darren W. Dahl, "Social Comparison Theory and Deception in the Interpersonal Exchange of Consumption Information," *Journal of Consumer Research* 33, no. 1, 2006, pp. 99–108.

58. Charles S. Gulas and Kim McKeage, "Extending Social Comparison: An Examination of the Unintended Consequences of Idealized Advertising Imagery," *Journal of Advertising* 29, no. 2, Summer 2000, pp. 17–28.

59. Dirk Smeesters and Naomi Mandel, "Positive and Negative Media Image Effects on the Self," *Journal of Consumer Research* 32, no. 4, 2006, pp. 576–582.

60. Hannah Karp, "The Senior Trip to the Strip," *Wall Street Journal*, April 8, 2005, p. W4.

61. Laurence Arnold, "Link to Other Addictions Raises New Questions About Gambling," *Associated Press*, June 12, 2001.

62. Jeffrey N. Weatherly, John M. Sauter, and Brent M. King, "The 'Big Win' and Resistance to Extinction When Gambling," *Journal of Psychology*, November 2004, pp. 495–504.

63. Kevin Heubusch, "Taking Chances on Casinos," *American Demographics*, May 1997, pp. 35–40; Rebecca Quick, "For Sports Fans, The Internet Is a Whole New Ball Game," *Wall Street Journal*, September 3, 1998, p. B9; and Stephen Braun, "Lives Lost in a River of Debt," *Los Angeles Times*, June 22, 1997, pp. A1, A14–A15.

64. Paul Davies, "New York's Bad Bet," *New York Times*, January 22, 2012, www.nytimes.com; "Report Outlines Grim Future for Racing Industry," *Associated Press*, August 14, 2011, www.wsj.com; and "Slot Machines: The Big Gamble," *CBS News*, June 23, 2011, www.cbsnews.com.

65. Stuart Elliott, "It Only Takes an Instant, Lottery Ads Declare," *New York Times*, May 9, 2011, www.nytimes.com.

66. Matthew Garrahan, "Call for Change to US Gambling Laws," *Financial Times*, August 14, 2011, www.ft.com; and Matt Viser, "Internet Gambling Is a Target of Patrick Bill: Casino Initiative Makes It Illegal," *Boston Globe*, November 10, 2007, p. A1.

67. Ron Winslow and Peter Landers, "Obesity: A WorldWide Woe," *Wall Street Journal*, July 1, 2002, pp. B1, B4.

68. Shari Roan, "Obesity Rates in U.S. Appear to Be Finally Leveling Off," *Los Angeles Times*, January 17, 2012, www.latimes.com.

69. Brian Wansink and Pierre Chandon, "Can 'Low-Fat' Nutrition Labels Lead to Obesity?" *Journal of Marketing Research*, November 2006, pp. 605–617.

70. Pierre Chandon and Brian Wansink, "Is Obesity Caused by Calorie Underestimation?" *Journal of Marketing Research*, February 2007, pp. 84–99.

71. Rajagopal Raghunathan, Rebecca Walker Naylor, and Wayne D. Hoyer, "The Unhealthy = Tasty Intuition and Its Effects on Taste Inferences, Enjoyment, and Choice of Food Products," *Journal of Marketing*, October 2006, pp. 170–184.

72. Eve M. Caudill and Patrick E. Murphy, "Consumer Online Privacy: Legal and Ethical Issues," *Journal of Public Policy and Marketing* 19, no. 1, Spring 2000, pp. 7–19.

73. Julia Angwin, "Latest in Web Tracking: Stealthy 'Supercookies,'" *Wall Street Journal*, August 18, 2011, www.wsj.com.

74. Ellen Foxman and Paula Kilcoyne, "Information Technology, Marketing Practice, and Consumer Privacy," *Journal of Public Policy and Marketing*, Spring 1993, p. 106; and Kim Bartel Sheehan and Mariea Grubbs Hoy, "Dimensions of Privacy Concern Among Online Consumers," *Journal of Public Policy and Marketing* 19, no. 1, Spring 2000, pp. 62–73.

75. Carol Krol, "Consumers Reach the Boiling Point Over Privacy Issues," *Advertising Age*, March 29, 1999, p. 22; and "Survey Results Show Consumers Want Privacy," *Direct Marketing*, March 1999, p. 10.

76. Michael Moss, "A Web CEO's Elusive Goal: Privacy," *Wall Street Journal*, February 7, 2000, pp. B1, B6.

77. Bob Tedeschi, "Poll Says Identity Theft Concerns Rose After High-Profile Breaches," *New York Times*, March 10, 2005, p. G5.

78. Pamela Paul, "Mixed Signals," *American Demographics*, July 2001, pp. 45–49; and Joseph Phelps, Glen Nowak, and Elizabeth Ferrell, "Privacy Concerns and Consumer Willingness to Provide Personal Information," *Journal of Public Policy and Marketing* 19, no. 1, Spring 2000, pp. 27–41.

79. Patricia A. Norberg and Daniel R. Horne, "Privacy Attitudes and Privacy-Related Behavior," *Psychology and Marketing* 24, no. 10, 2007, pp. 829–847.

80. Mary J. Culnan, "Protecting Privacy Online: Is Self-Regulation Working?" *Journal of Public Policy and Marketing* 19, no. 1, Spring 2000, pp. 20–26; and Anthony D. Miyazaki and Ana Fernandez, "Internet Privacy and Security," *Journal of Public Policy and Marketing* 19, no. 1, Spring 2000, pp. 54–61.

81. George R. Milne, "Privacy and Ethical Issues in Database/Interactive Marketing and Public Policy," *Journal of Public Policy and Marketing* 19, no. 1, Spring 2000, pp. 1–6.

82. Joan Ryan, "Steroids? Alcohol Is the Real Problem," *San Francisco Chronicle*, March 17, 2005, www.sfgate.com; Vanessa O'Connell and Christopher Lawton, "Alcohol TV Ads Ignite Bid to Curb," *Wall Street Journal*, December 18, 2002, p. B2; "Study: Kids Remember Beer Ads," *ClariNet Electronic News Service*, February 11, 1994; Fara Warner, "Cheers! It's Happy Hour in Cyberspace," *Wall Street Journal*, March 15, 1995, pp. B1, B4; and Kirk Davidson, "Looking for Abundance of Opposition to TV Liquor Ads," *Marketing News*, January 6, 1997, pp. 4, 30.

83. Nicholas Bakalar, "Ad Limits Seen as Way to Curb Youth Smoking and Drinking," *New York Times*, May 22, 2007, p. F5.

84. Alyssa Bindman, "Children Exposed to Alcohol Ads More Likely to Drink," *The Nation's Health* 37, no. 6, 2007, p. 24; Elizabeth M. Botvin, Gilbert J. Botvin, John L. Michela, Eli Baker, and Anne D. Filazolla, "Adolescent Smoking Behavior and the Recognition of Cigarette Advertisements," *Journal of Applied Social Psychology*, November 1991, pp. 919–932; and Richard W. Pollay, S. Siddarth, Michael Siegel, Anne Hadix, Robert K. Merritt, Gary A. Giovino, and Michael P. Eriksen, "The Last Straw? Cigarette Advertising and Realized Market Shares Among Youths and Adults, 1979–1993," *Journal of Marketing*, April 1996, pp. 1–16.

85. Kathleen J. Kelly, Michael D. Slater, and David Karan, "Image Advertisements' Influence on Adolescents' Perceptions of the Desirability of Beer and Cigarettes," *Journal of Public Policy and Marketing*, Fall 2002, pp. 295–304.

86. "Smoking in Movies Linked to Kids Lighting Up," *Health Day*, January 8, 2008, www.nlm.nih.gov/medlineplus.

87. Russell Parsons, "Heineken Bids to Make Responsible Drinking 'Aspirational,'" *MarketingWeek*, December 12, 2011, www.marketingweek.co.uk.

88. Lisa R. Szykman, Paul N. Bloom, and Jennifer Blazing, "Does Corporate Sponsorship of a Socially Oriented Message Make a Difference?" *Journal of Consumer Psychology* 14, no. 1/2, 2004, pp. 13–20.

89. Calmetta Y. Coleman, "Can't Be Too Thin, but Plus-Size Models Get More Work Now," *Wall Street Journal*, May 3, 1999, pp. A1, A10.

90. José Antonio Rosa, Ellen C. Garbarino, and Alan J. Malter, "Keeping the Body in Mind: The Influence of Body Esteem and Body Boundary Aberration on Consumer Beliefs and Purchase Intentions," *Journal of Consumer Psychology* 16, no. 1, 2006, pp. 79–91.

91. Sally Goll Beatty, "Women's Views of Their Lives Aren't Reflected by Advertisers," *Wall Street Journal*, December 19, 1995, p. B2.

92. Michelle Ainsworth, "David Schwarz's Responsible Gambling Program Named Best in the World," *Herald Sun (Australia)*, January 25, 2012, www.heraldsun.com.au.

93. Sara Kim and Ann L. McGill, "Gaming with Mr. Slot or Gaming the Slot Machine? Power, Anthropomorphism, and Risk Perception," *Journal of Consumer Research*, June 2011, pp. 94–107.

94. Betsy McKay, "The Children's Menu: Do Ads Make Kids Fat?" *Wall Street Journal*, January 27, 2005, pp. B1, B7.

95. Gemma Charles, "Junk Food 'Super Complaint,'" *Marketing*, February 9, 2012, www.marketingmagazine.co.uk.

96. Steven Reinberg, "Many U.S. Kids Still Buy Unhealthy Snacks at School," *U.S. News & World Report*, February 6, 2012, http://health.usnews.com.

97. Claudia Kalb and Karen Springen, "Pump Up the Family," *Newsweek*, April 25, 2005, pp. 62+.

98. Duane Stanford, "Indra Nooyi Rediscovers the Joy of Pepsi," *Businessweek*, February 2, 2012, www.businessweek.com.

99. David Wright, "Baby Carrots: The Next Snack Food?" *ABC News*, February 7, 2012, http://abcnews.go.com.

100. "Getting on the Treadmill," *Economist*, October 8, 2011, p. 80.

101. Lisa Jennings, "Kids' Ads Under Fire," *Nation's Restaurant News*, August 8, 2011, p. 1.

102. John Naughton, "EU Cookie Laws Could Cause Unwary Firms to Get Their Fingers Burnt," *Guardian (UK)*, December 17, 2011, www.guardian.co.uk.

103. Teri Schultz, "EU Outlines Online Privacy Recommendations," *NPR*, January 27, 2012, www.npr.org.

104. Tim Peterson, "DAA Debuts Consumer Education Campaign for Online Behavioral Advertising," *Direct Marketing News*, January 20, 2012, www.dmnews.com.

105. Roland T. Rust, P. K. Kannan, and Peng Na, "The Customer Economics of Internet Privacy," *Journal of the Academy of Marketing Science* 30, Fall 2002, pp. 455–464.

106. John A. McCarty and L. J. Shrum, "The Influence of Individualism, Collectivism, and Locus of Control on Environmental Beliefs and Behavior," *Journal of Public Policy and Marketing* 20, no. 1, Spring 2001, pp. 93–104.

107. "Europe Expands Electronic Waste Collection, Recycling Law," *Environment News Service*, January 20, 2012, www.ens-newswire.com.

108. Jack Neff, "Eco-Wal-Mart Costs Marketers Green," *Advertising Age*, October 1, 2007, pp. 3, 42.

109. Tom Szaky, "The Myth of Biodegradability," *New York Times*, February 9, 2012, www.nytimes.com.

110. See "Leaders Say Europe's Waste-recovery Goal Is Achievable," *European Plastics News*, February 7, 2012, www.plasticsnews.com.

111. See Steve Lohr, "First, Make Money. Also, Do Good," *New York Times*, August 13, 2011, www.nytimes.com.

112. Wong Lai Cheng and Jamilah Ahmad, "Incorporating Stakeholder Approach in Corporate Social Responsibility," *Social Responsibility Journal*, 6, no. 4, 2005, pp. 593–610.

113. Jack Neff, "Seventh Generation," *Advertising Age*, November 12, 2007, p. S13.

114. Russell Belk, John Painter, and Richard Semenik, "Preferred Solutions to the Energy Crisis as a Function of Causal Attributions," *Journal of Consumer Research*, December 1981, pp. 306–312.

115. Pam Scholder Ellen, Joshua Lyle Wiener, and Cathy Cobb-Walgren, "The Role of Perceived Consumer Effectiveness in Motivating Environmentally Conscious Behaviors," *Journal of Public Policy and Marketing*, Fall 1991, pp. 102–117; and Thomas C. Kinnear, James R. Taylor, and Sadrudin A. Ahmed, "Ecologically Concerned Consumers: Who Are They?" *Journal of Marketing*, April 1972, pp. 46–57.

116. Rik Peters, Tammo Bijmo, H. Fred van Raaij, and Mark de Kruijk, "Consumers' Attributions of Proenvironmental Behavior, Motivation, and Ability to Self and Others," *Journal of Public Policy and Marketing*, Fall 1998, pp. 215–225.

117. Noah J. Goldstein, Robert B. Cialdini, and Vladas Griskevicius, "A Room with a Viewpoint: Using Social Norms to Motivate Environmental Conservation in Hotels," *Journal of Consumer Research*, October 2008, pp. 472–482.

118. Julie R. Irwin and Rebecca Walker Naylor, "Ethical Decisions and Response Mode Compatibility: Weighting of Ethical Attributes in Consideration Sets Formed by Excluding versus Including Product Alternatives," *Journal of Marketing Research*, April 2009, pp. 234–246.

119. Bob M. Fennis, Loes Janssen, and Kathleen D. Vohs, "Acts of Benevolence: A Limited-Resource Account of Compliance with Charitable Requests," *Journal of Consumer Research*, April 2009, pp. 906–924.

120. Wendy Liu and Jennifer Aaker, "The Happiness of Giving: The Time-Ask Effect," *Journal of Consumer Research*, October 2008, pp. 543–557.

121. David Mills, "World Giving Index 2011," *Guardian (UK)*, December 20, 2011, www.guardian.co.uk.

122. "Helen Skelton Reaches the South Pole," *Telegraph (UK)*, January 22, 2012, www.telegraph.co.uk.

123. Debra Basil, Mary Runte, Michael Basil, and John Usher, "Company Support for Employee Volunteerism," *Journal of Business Research*, January 2011, pp. 61–66.

124. David A. Jones, "Does Serving the Community Also Serve the Company?" *Journal of Occupational and Organizational Psychology*, December 2010, pp. 857–878.

125. N. Craig Smith and Elizabeth Cooper-Martin, "Ethics and Target Marketing," *Journal of Marketing*, July 1997, pp. 1–20; Robert O. Hermann, "The Tactics of Consumer Resistance: Group Action and Marketplace Exit," in eds. Leigh McAlister and Michael Rothschild, *Advances in Consumer Research*, vol. 20 (Provo, Utah: Association for Consumer Research, 1993), pp. 130–134; and Lisa Penaloza and Linda L. Price, "Consumer Resistance: A Conceptual Overview," in eds. Leigh McAlister and Michael L. Rothschild, *Advances in Consumer Research*, vol. 20 (Provo, Utah: Association for Consumer Research, 1993), pp. 123–128.

126. Robert V. Kozinets and Jay M. Handelman, "Adversaries of Consumption: Consumer Movements, Activism, and Ideology," *Journal of Consumer Research* 31, no. 3, 2004, pp. 691–704.

127. Richard W. Pollay, "Media Resistance to Consumer Resistance," in eds. Leigh McAlister and Michael Rothschild, *Advances in Consumer Research*, vol. 20 (Provo, Utah: Association for Consumer Research, 1993), p. 129.

128. Jill Gabrielle Klein, N. Craig Smith, and Andrew John, "Why We Boycott: Consumer Motivations for Boycott Participation," *Journal of Marketing Research*, July 2004, pp. 92–109; and Sakar Sen, Zeynep Gürhan-Canli, and Vicki Morwitz, "Withholding Consumption: A Social Dilemma Perspective on Consumer Boycotts," *Journal of Consumer Research*, December 2001, pp. 399–417.

129. Jonathan Baron, "Consumer Attitudes About Personal and Political Action," *Journal of Consumer Psychology* 8, no. 3, 1999, pp. 261–275.

130. Valerie Bauerlein, "Carrots Vie for a Spot on Game Day," *Wall Street Journal*, February 2, 2012, www.wsj.com; David Wright and Mary Marsh, "Baby Carrots: The Next Snack Food?" *ABC News*, February 7, 2012, http://abcnews.go.com; and Douglas McGray, "How Carrots Became the New Junk Food," *Fast Company*, April 1, 2011, www.fastcompany.com.

Glossary

A

Ability The extent to which consumers have the resources needed to make an outcome happen.

Absolute threshold The minimal level of stimulus intensity needed to detect a stimulus.

Accommodation theory The more effort one puts forth in trying to communicate with an ethnic group, the more positive the reaction.

Acculturation Learning how to adapt to a new culture.

Acquisition The process by which a consumer comes to own an offering.

Activities, interests, and opinions (AIOs) The three components of lifestyles.

Actual identity schema A set of multiple, salient identities that reflects our self-concept.

Actual state The way things actually are.

Adaptability The extent to which the innovation can foster new styles.

Addiction Excessive behavior typically brought on by a chemical dependency.

Additive difference model Compensatory model in which brands are compared by attribute, two brands at a time.

Adoption A purchase of an innovation by an individual consumer or household.

Affect Low-level feelings.

Affect referral A simple type of affective tactic whereby we simply remember our feelings for the product or service.

Affect-related tactics Tactics based on feelings.

Affective decision-making model The process by which consumers base their decision on feelings and emotions.

Affective forecasting A prediction of how you will feel in the future.

Affective function How attitudes influence our feelings.

Affective involvement Interest in expending emotional energy and evoking deep feelings about an offering, activity, or decision.

Affective response When consumers generate feelings and images in response to a message.

Agentic goal Goal that stresses mastery, self-assertiveness, self-efficacy, strength, and no emotion.

Alternative-based strategy Making a noncomparable choice based on an overall evaluation.

Ambiguity of information When there is not enough information to confirm or disprove hypotheses.

Ambivalence When our evaluations regarding a brand are mixed (both positive and negative).

Anchoring and adjustment process Starting with an initial evaluation and adjusting it with additional information.

Appraisal theory A theory of emotion that proposes that emotions are based on an individual's assessment of a situation or an outcome and its relevance to his or her goals.

Approach-approach conflict An inner struggle about which offering to acquire when each can satisfy an important but different need.

Approach-avoidance conflict An inner struggle about acquiring or consuming an offering that fulfills one need but fails to fulfill another.

Aspirational reference group A group that we admire and desire to be like.

Associative reference group A group to which we currently belong.

Attention How much mental activity a consumer devotes to a stimulus.

Attitude A relatively global and enduring evaluation of an object, issue, person, or action.

Attitude accessibility How easily an attitude can be remembered.

Attitude confidence How strongly we hold an attitude.

Attitude persistence How long our attitude lasts.

Attitude resistance How difficult it is to change an attitude.

Attitude toward the act (Aact) How we feel about doing something.

Attitude toward the ad (Aad) Whether the consumer likes or dislikes an ad.

Attraction effect When the addition of an inferior brand to a consideration set increases the attractiveness of the dominant brand.

Attractiveness A source characteristic that evokes favorable attitudes if a source is physically attractive, likable, familiar, or similar to ourselves.

Attribute balancing Picking a brand because it scores equally well on certain attributes rather than faring unequally on these attributes.

Attribute-based strategy Making a noncomparable choice by making abstract representations of comparable attributes.

Attribute determinance Attribute that is both salient and diagnostic.

Attribute processing Comparing brands, one attribute at a time.

Attribution theory A theory of how individuals find explanations for events.

Autonomic decision Decision equally likely to be made by the husband or wife, but not by both.

Availability heuristic Basing judgments on events that are easier to recall.

Avoidance-avoidance conflict An inner struggle about which offering to acquire when neither can satisfy an important but different need.

B

Baby boomers Individuals born between 1946 and 1964.

Base-rate information How often an event really occurs on average.

Behavioral intention (BI) What we intend to do.

Behavior (B) What we do.

Belief discrepancy When a message is different from what consumers believe.

Bias for the whole The tendency to perceive more value in a whole than in the combined parts that make up a whole.

Black market An illegal market in which consumers pay often exorbitant amounts for items not readily available.

Boycott An organized activity in which consumers avoid purchasing products or services from a company whose policies or practices are seen as unfair or unjust.

Brand-choice congruence The purchase of the same brand as members of a group.

Brand community A specialized group of consumers with a structured set of relationships involving a particular brand, fellow customers of that brand, and the product in use.

Brand extension Using the brand name of a product with a well-developed image on a product in a different category.

Brand familiarity Easy recognition of a well-known brand.

Brand image Specific type of schema that captures what a brand stands for and how favorably it is viewed.

Brand loyalty Buying the same brand repeatedly because of a strong preference for it.

Brand personality The set of associations included in a schema that reflect a brand's personification.

Brand processing Evaluating one brand at a time.

C

Central-route processing The attitude formation and change process when effort is high.

Choice tactics Simple rules of thumb used to make low-effort decisions.

Class average Families with an average income in a particular class.

Classic A successful innovation that has a lengthy product life cycle.

Classical conditioning Producing a response to a stimulus by repeatedly pairing it with another stimulus that automatically produces this response.

Closure The principle that individuals have a need to organize perceptions so that they form a meaningful whole.

Clustering The grouping of consumers according to common characteristics using statistical techniques.

Co-branding An arrangement by which the two brands form a partnership to benefit from the power of both.

Cocreation Actively involving consumers in creating value through participation in new product development, among other marketing activities.

Coercive power The extent to which the group has the capacity to deliver rewards and sanctions.

Cognitive decision-making model The process by which consumers combine items of information about attributes to reach a decision.

Cognitive function How attitudes influence our thoughts.

Cognitive involvement Interest in thinking about and learning information pertinent to an offering, activity, or decisions.

Cognitive response Thought we have in response to a communication.

Communal goal Goal that stresses affiliation and fostering harmonious relations with others, submissiveness, emotionality, and home orientation.

Comparative message A message that makes direct comparisons with competitors.

Compatibility The extent to which an innovation is consistent with one's needs, values, norms, or behaviors.

Compensatory consumption The consumer behavior of buying products or services to offset frustrations or difficulties in life.

Compensatory model A mental cost-benefit analysis model in which negative features can be compensated for by positive ones.

Complexity The extent to which an innovation is complicated and difficult to understand or use.

Compliance Doing what the group or social influencer asks.

Comprehension The process of extracting higher-order meaning from what we have perceived in the context of what we already know.

Compromise effect When a brand gains share because it is an intermediate rather than an extreme option.

Compulsive behavior An irresistible urge to perform an irrational act.

Concreteness The extent to which a stimulus is capable of being imagined.

Confirmation bias Tendency to recall information that reinforces or confirms our over all beliefs rather than contradicting them, thereby making our judgment or decision more positive than it should be.

Conformity The tendency to behave in an expected way.

Conjoint analysis A research technique to determine the relative importance and appeal of different levels of an offering's attributes.

Conjunctive model A noncompensatory model that sets minimum cutoffs to reject "bad" options.

Connative function How attitudes influence our behavior.

Connectedness function The use of products as symbols of our personal connections to significant people, events, or experiences.

Conservation behavior Limiting the use of scarce natural resources for the purposes of environmental preservation.

Consideration (or evoked set) The subset of top-of-mind brands evaluated when making a choice.

Conspicuous consumption The acquisition and display of goods and services to show off one's status.

Conspicuous waste Visibly buying products and services that one never uses.

Construal level theory Theory describing the different levels of abstractness in the associations that a consumer has about concepts (people, products, brands, and activities) and how the consumer's psychological distance from these concepts influences his or her behavior.

Consumer behavior The totality of consumers' decisions with respect to the acquisition, consumption, and disposition of goods, services, time, and ideas by human decision-making units (over time).

Consumer ethics Rules of acceptable conduct (such as honesty, fairness, and respect) that apply to the range of consumer behaviors.

Consumer memory The persistence of learning over time, via the storage and retrieval of information, either consciously or unconsciously.

Consumer socialization The process by which we learn to become consumers.

Continuous innovation An innovation that has a limited effect on existing consumption patterns.

Counterargument (CA) Thought that disagrees with the message.

Credibility Extent to which the source is trustworthy, expert, or has status.

Cultural categories The natural grouping of objects that reflect our culture.

Cultural principles Ideas or values that specify how aspects of our culture are organized and/or how they should be perceived or evaluated.

Culture The typical or expected behaviors, norms, and ideas that characterize a group of people.

Customer retention The practice of keeping customers by building long-term relationships.

Cutoff level For each attribute, the point at which a brand is rejected with a noncompensatory model.

D

Data mining Searching for patterns in a company database that offer clues to customer needs, preferences, and behaviors.

Deal-prone consumer A consumer who is more likely to be influenced by price.

Decay The weakening of memory strength over time.

Decision framing The initial reference point or anchor in the decision process.

Decision making Making a selection among options or courses of action.

Diagnostic information That which helps us discriminate among objects.

Differential threshold/just noticeable difference (j.n.d.) The intensity difference needed between two stimuli before they are perceived to be different.

Diffusion The percentage of the population that has adopted an innovation at a specific point in time.

Disconfirmation The existence of a discrepancy between expectations and performance.

Discontinuous innovation An offering that is so new that we have never known anything like it before.

Disjunctive model A noncompensatory model that sets acceptable cutoffs to find options that are "good."

Disposition The process by which a consumer discards an offering.

Dissatisfaction The feeling that results when consumers make a negative evaluation or are unhappy with a decision.

Dissociative reference group A group we do not want to emulate.

Divestment ritual Ritual enacted at the disposition stage that is designed to wipe away all traces of our personal meaning in a product.

Dogmatism A tendency to be resistant to change or new ideas.

Domain-specific values Values that may only apply to a particular area of activities.

Door-in-the-face technique A technique designed to induce compliance by first asking an individual to comply with a very large and possibly outrageous request, followed by a smaller and more reasonable request.

Downward mobility Losing one's social standing.

Dramas Ads with characters, a plot, and a story.

Dual-mediation hypothesis Explains how attitudes toward the ad influence brand attitudes.

Dynamically continuous innovation An innovation that has a pronounced effect on consumption practices and often involves a new technology.

E

Earned status Status acquired later in life through achievements.

Ego depletion Outcome of decision-making effort that results in mental resources being exhausted.

Elaboration Transferring information into long-term memory by processing it at deeper levels.

Elimination-by-aspects model Similar to the lexicographic model but adds the notion of acceptable cutoffs.

Embedded market Market in which the social relationships among buyers and sellers change the way the market operates.

Emblematic function The use of products to symbolize membership in social groups.

Embodiment Connection between mind and body that influences consumer self-control and behavior.

Emotional accounting The intensity of positive or negative feelings associated with each mental "account" for saving or spending.

Emotional appeal A message designed to elicit an emotional response.

Emotional contagion A message designed to induce consumers to vicariously experience a depicted emotion.

Emotional detachment Emotionally disposing of a possession.

Encoding of evidence Processing the information one experiences.

Endowment effect When ownership increases the value of an item.

Enduring involvement Long-term interest in an offering, activity, or decision.

Episodic (autobiographical) memory Knowledge we have about ourselves and our personal, past experiences.

Equity theory A theory that focuses on the fairness of exchanges between individuals, which helps in understanding consumer satisfaction and dissatisfaction.

Estimation of likelihood Judging how likely it is that something will occur.

Ethnic group Subculture with a similar heritage and values.

Ethnographic research In-depth qualitative research using observations and interviews (often overrepeated occasions) of consumers in real-world surroundings. Often used to study the meaning that consumers ascribe to a product or consumption phenomenon.

Evaluative conditioning A special case of classical conditioning, producing an affective response by repeatedly pairing a neutral conditioned stimulus with an emotionally-charged unconditioned stimulus.

Even-a-penny-will-help technique A technique designed to induce compliance by asking individuals to do a very small favor—one that is so small that it almost does not qualify as a favor.

Expectancy-value model A widely used model that explains how attitudes form and change.

Expectation Belief about how a product/service will perform.

Explicit memory When consumers are consciously aware that they remember something.

Exponential diffusion curve A diffusion curve characterized by rapid initial growth.

Exposure The process by which the consumer comes in physical contact with a stimulus.

Exposure to evidence Actually experiencing the product or service.

Expressiveness function The use of products as symbols to demonstrate our uniqueness—how we stand out as different from others.

Expressive roles Roles that involve an indication of family norms.

Extended family The nuclear family plus relatives such as grandparents, aunts, uncles, and cousins.

External search The process of collecting information from outside sources, for example, magazines, dealers, ads.

Extremeness aversion Options that are extreme on some attributes are less attractive than those with a moderate level of those attributes.

F

Fad A successful innovation that has a very short product life cycle.

Fairness in the exchange The perception that people's inputs are equal to their outputs in an exchange.

Family life cycle Different stages of family life, depending on the age of the parents and how many children are living at home.

Fashion A successful innovation that has a moderately long and potentially cyclical product life cycle.

Favorability The degree to which we like or dislike something.

Fear appeal A message that stresses negative consequences.

Felt involvement Self-reported arousal or interest in an offering, activity, or decision.

Figure and ground The principle that people interpret stimuli in the context of a background.

Financial risk The extent to which buying, using, or disposing of an offering is perceived to have the potential to create financial harm.

Focus group A form of interview involving 8 to 12 people; a moderator leads the group and asks participants to discuss a product, concept, or other marketing stimulus.

Foot-in-the-door technique A technique designed to induce compliance by getting an individual to agree first to a small favor, then to a larger one, and then to an even larger one.

Frame switching Stimulated by language cues, a consumer who identifies with more than one culture will activate the aspects of his or her self-concept that relates to that language's cultural background.

Fraudulent symbol Symbol that becomes so widely adopted that it loses its status.

Frequency heuristic Belief based simply on the number of supporting arguments or amount of repetition.

Functional innovation A new product, service, attribute, or idea that has utilitarian benefits that are different from or better than those of alternatives.

Functional need Need that motivates the search for offerings that solve consumption-related problems.

G

Gatekeeper A source that controls the flow of information.

Gender Biological state of being male or female.

Generation X Individuals born between 1965 and 1979.

Gestation stage The first stage of gift giving, when we consider what to give someone.

Global values A person's most enduring, strongly held, and abstract values that hold in many situations.

Goal Outcome that we would like to achieve.

Goal-derived category Things viewed as belonging in the same category because they serve the same goals.

Gray market Individuals over 65 years old.

Greenwashing The misleading use of environmental claims for marketing purposes.

Grooming ritual Ritual we engage in to bring out or maintain the best in special products.

Grouping The tendency to group stimuli to form a unified picture or impression.

H

Habit Doing the same thing time after time.

Habituation The process by which a stimulus loses its attention-getting abilities by virtue of its familiarity.

Hedonic dimension When an ad creates positive or negative feelings.

Hedonic need Need that relates to sensory pleasure.

Hedonic or aesthetic innovation An innovation that appeals to our aesthetic, pleasure-seeking, and/or sensory needs.

Hedonism The principle of pleasure seeking.

Heuristics Simple rules of thumb that are used to make judgments.

High-effort hierarchy of effects A purchase of an innovation based on considerable decision-making effort.

Homophily The overall similarity among members in the social system.

Household A single person living alone or a group of individuals who live together in a common dwelling, regardless of whether they are related.

Household decision roles Roles that different members play in a household decision.

Husband-dominant decision Decision made primarily by the male head-of-household.

Hypothesis generation Forming expectations about the product or service.

Hypothesis testing Testing out expectations through experience.

I

Ideal identity schema A set of ideas about how the identity would be indicated in its ideal form.

Ideal state The way we want things to be.

Imagery Imagining an event in order to make a judgment.

Implicit memory Memory without any conscious attempt at remembering something.

Impulse purchase An unexpected purchase based on a strong feeling.

Incidental learning Learning that occurs from repetition rather than from conscious processing.

Independent variable The "treatment" or the entity that researchers vary in a research project.

Inept set Options that are unacceptable when making a decision.

Inert set Options toward which consumers are indifferent.

Informational influence The extent to which sources influence consumers simply by providing information.

Inherited status Status that derives from parents at birth.

Inhibition The recall of one attribute inhibiting the recall of another.

Innovation An offering that is perceived as new by consumers within a market segment and that has an effect on existing consumption patterns.

Instrumental roles Roles that relate to tasks affecting the buying decision.

Instrumental values The values needed to achieve the desired end states such as ambition and cheerfulness.

Integration of evidence Combining new information with stored knowledge.

Intensity of ethnic identification How strongly people identify with their ethnic group.

Interference When the strength of a memory deteriorates over time because of competing memories.

Internal search The process of recalling stored information from memory.

J

Judgment Evaluation of an object or estimate of likelihood of an outcome or event.

Judgment of goodness/badness Evaluating the desirability of something.

L

Law of small numbers The expectation that information obtained from a small number of people represents the larger population.

Legitimacy The extent to which the innovation follows established guidelines for what seems appropriate in the category.

Lexicographic model A noncompensatory model that compares brands by attributes, one at a time in order of importance.

Lifestyles People's patterns of behavior.

List of Values (LOV) A survey that measures nine principal values in consumer behavior.

Locus of control How people interpret why things happen (internal versus external).

Low-effort hierarchy of effects Sequence of thinking-behaving-feeling.

M

Market maven A consumer on whom others rely for information about the marketplace in general.

Market test A study in which the effectiveness of one or more elements of the marketing mix is examined by evaluating sales of the product in an actual market, e.g., a specific city.

Marketing The activity, set of institutions, and processes for creating, communicating, delivering, and exchanging offerings with value for individuals, groups, and society.

Marketing ethics Rules of acceptable conduct that guide individuals and organizations in making honest, fair, and respectful decisions about marketing activities.

Marketing source Influence delivered from a marketing agent, for example, advertising, personal selling.

Marketing stimuli Information about offerings communicated either by the marketer (such as ads) or by nonmarketing sources (such as word of mouth).

Match-up hypothesis Idea that the source must be appropriate for the product/service.

Materialism Placing importance on money and material goods.

Means-end chain analysis A technique that can help to explain how values link to attributes in products and services.

Mental accounting Categorizing spending and saving decisions into "accounts" mentally designated for specific consumption transactions, goals, or situations.

Mere exposure effect When familiarity leads to a consumer's liking an object.

Metacognitive experiences How the information is processed beyond the content of the decision.

Millennial Individuals born between 1980 and 1994; also known as Generation Y.

Modernity The extent to which consumers in the social system have positive attitudes toward change.

Motivated reasoning Processing information in a way that allows consumers to reach the conclusion that they want to reach.

Motivation An inner state of arousal that provides energy needed to achieve a goal.

Multiattribute expectancy-value model A type of brand-based compensatory model.

Multibrand loyalty Buying two or more brands repeatedly because of a strong preference for them.

Multicultural marketing Strategies used to appeal to a variety of cultures at the same time.

Mystery ad An ad in which the brand is not identified until the end of the message.

N

National character The personality of a country.

Need An internal state of tension caused by disequilibrium from an ideal/desired physical or psychological state.

Need for cognition (NFC) A trait that describes how much people like to think.

Need for uniqueness (NFU) The desire for novelty through the purchase, use, and disposition of products and services.

Negative word-of-mouth communication The act of consumers saying negative things about a product or service to other consumers.

Netnography Observing and analyzing the online behavior and comments of consumers.

Noncomparable decision The process of making a decision about products or services from different categories.

Noncompensatory model A simple decision model in which negative information leads to rejection of the option.

Nonmarketing source Influence delivered from an entity outside a marketing organization, for example, friends, family, the media.

Norm Collective decision about what constitutes appropriate behavior.

Normative choice tactics Low-elaboration decision making that is based on others' opinions.

Normative influence How other people influence our behavior through social pressure.

Nuclear family Father, mother, and children.

O

Objective comprehension The extent to which consumers accurately understand the message a sender intended to communicate.

Offering A product, service, activity, experience, or idea offered by a marketing organization to consumers.

One-sided message A marketing message that presents only positive information.

Ongoing search A search that occurs regularly, regardless of whether the consumer is making a choice.

Online processing When a consumer is actively evaluating a brand as he/she views an ad for it.

Operant conditioning The view that behavior is a function of reinforcements and punishments received in the past.

Opinion leader An individual who acts as an information broker between the mass media and the opinions and behaviors of an individual or group.

Optimal stimulation level (OSL) The level of arousal that is most comfortable for an individual.

Overprivileged Families with an income higher than the average in their social class.

P

Parody display Status symbols that start in the lower-social classes and move upward.

Perceived risk The extent to which the consumer is uncertain about the consequences of an action, for example, buying, using, or disposing of an offering.

Perception The process of determining the properties of stimuli using vision, hearing, taste, smell, and touch.

Perceptual fluency The ease with which information is processed.

Perceptual organization The process by which stimuli are organized into meaningful units.

Performance The measurement of whether the product/service actually fulfills consumers' needs.

Performance-related tactics Tactics based on benefits, features, or evaluations of the brand.

Performance risk The possibility that the offering will perform less than expected.

Peripheral cues Easily processed aspects of a message, such as music, an attractive source, picture, or humor.

Peripheral-route processing The attitude formation and change process when effort is low.

Peripheral route to persuasion Aspects other than key message arguments that are used to influence attitudes.

Personal relevance Something that has a direct bearing on the self and has potentially significant consequences or implications for our lives.

Personality An internal characteristic that determines how individuals behave in various situations.

Physical detachment Physically disposing of an item.

Physical (or safety) risk The extent to which buying, using, or disposing of an offering is perceived to have the potential to create physical harm or harm one's safety.

Possession ritual Ritual we engage in when we first acquire a product that helps to make it "ours."

Post-decision dissonance A feeling of anxiety over whether the correct decision was made.

Post-decision feeling Positive or negative emotion experienced while using the products or services.

Post-decision regret A feeling that one should have purchased another option.

Preattentive processing The nonconscious processing of stimuli in peripheral vision.

Prepurchase search A search for information that aids a specific acquisition decision.

Presentation stage The second stage of gift giving, when we actually give the gift.

Price-related tactics Simplifying decision heuristics that are based on price.

Primacy and recency effect The tendency to show greater memory for information that comes first or last in a sequence.

Primary data Data originating from a researcher and collected to provide information relevant to a specific research project.

Primary reference group Group with whom we have physical face-to-face interaction.

Priming The increased sensitivity to certain concepts and associations due to prior experience based on implicit memory.

Problem recognition The perceived difference between an actual and an ideal state.

Product life cycle A concept that suggests that products go through an initial introductory period followed by periods of sales growth, maturity, and decline.

Profane things Things that are ordinary and hence have no special power.

Prominence The intensity of stimuli that causes them to stand out relative to the environment.

Prototype The best example of a cognitive (mental) category.

Protoypicality When an object is representative of its category.

Psychographics A description of consumers based on their psychological and behavioral characteristics.

Psychological risk The extent to which buying, using, or disposing of an offering is perceived to have the potential to harm one's sense of self and thus create negative emotions.

R

Reactance Doing the opposite of what the individual or group wants us to do.

Recall The ability to retrieve information from memory without being reexposed to it.

Recognition The process of identifying whether we have previously encountered a stimulus when reexposed to it.

Reference group A group of people consumers compare themselves with for information regarding behavior, attitudes, or values.

Reflexive evaluation Feedback from others that tells us whether we are fulfilling the role correctly.

Reformulation stage The final stage of gift giving, when we reevaluate the relationship based on the gift-giving experience.

Relative advantage Benefits in an innovation superior to those found in existing products.

Representativeness heuristic Making a judgment by simply comparing a stimulus with the category prototype or exemplar.

Research foundation A nonprofit organization that sponsors research on topics relevant to the foundation's goals.

Resistance A desire not to buy the innovation, even in the face of pressure to do so.

Response involvement Interest in certain decisions and behaviors.

Retrieval The process of remembering or accessing what was previously stored in memory.

Retrieval cue A stimulus that facilitates the activation of memory.

Rokeach Value Survey (RVS) A survey that measures instrumental and terminal values.

Role acquisition function The use of products as symbols to help us feel more comfortable in a new role.

S

Sacred entities People, things, and places that are set apart, revered, worshiped, and treated with great respect.

Salient attribute Attribute that is "top of mind" or more important.

Satisfaction The feeling that results when consumers make a positive evaluation or feel happy with their decision.

Satisfice Finding a brand that satisfies a need even though the brand may not be the best brand.

Schema The set of associations linked to a concept.

Script A special type of schema that represents knowledge of a sequence of actions involved in performing an activity.

Secondary data Data collected for some other purpose that is subsequently used in a research project.

Secondary reference group Group with whom we do not have direct contact.

Self-concept Our mental view of who we are.

Self-control Process consumers use to regulate feelings, thoughts, and behavior in line with long-term goals.

Self-referencing Relating a message to one's own experience or self-image.

Semantic memory General knowledge about an entity, detached from specific episodes.

Sensation seeker A consumer who actively looks for variety.

Sensory memory Input from the five senses stored temporarily in memory.

Sexual orientation A person's preference toward certain behaviors.

Shaping Leading consumers through a series of steps to create a desired response.

Simple inferences Beliefs based on peripheral cues.

Situational (temporary) involvement Temporary interest in an offering, activity, or decision, often caused by situational circumstances.

Sleeper effect Consumers forget the source of a message more quickly than they forget the message.

Social class fragmentation The disappearance of class distinctions.

Social class hierarchy The grouping of members of society according to status high to low.

Social comparison theory A theory that proposes that individuals have a drive to compare themselves with other people.

Social dilemma Deciding whether to put self-interest or the interests of others first.

Social influence Information by and implicit or explicit pressures from individuals, groups, and the mass media that affects how a person behaves.

Social relevance The extent to which an innovation can be observed or the extent to which having others observe it has social cachet.

Social risk The extent to which buying, using, or disposing of an offering is perceived to have the potential to do harm to one's social standing.

Source derogation (SD) Thought that discounts or attacks the source of the message.

Source identification The process of determining what the perceived stimulus actually is.

Spreading of activation The process by which retrieving a concept or association spreads to the retrieval of a related concept or association.

S-shaped diffusion curve A diffusion curve characterized by slow initial growth followed by a rapid increase in diffusion.

Status crystallization When consumers are consistent across indicators of social class income, education, occupation, etc.

Status float Trends that start in the lower and middle classes and move upward.

Status symbol Product or service that tells others about someone's social class standing.

Storytelling A research method by which consumers are asked to tell stories about product acquisition, usage, or disposition experiences. These stories help marketers gain insights into consumer needs and identify the product attributes that meet these needs.

Strong argument A presentation that features the best or central merits of an offering in a convincing manner.

Subjective comprehension What the consumer understands from the message, regardless of whether this understanding is accurate.

Subjective norm (SN) How others feel about our doing something.

Subliminal perception The activation of sensory receptors by stimuli presented below the perceptual threshold.

Support argument (SA) Thought that agrees with the message.

Survey A method of collecting information from a sample of consumers, predominantly by asking questions.

Symbolic innovation A product, service, attribute, or idea that has new social meaning.

Symbolic need Need that relates to how we perceive ourselves, how we are perceived by others, how we relate to others, and the esteem in which we are held by others.

Symbols External signs that consumers use to express their identity.

Syncratic decision Decision made jointly by the husband and wife.

T

Taxonomic category How consumers classify a group of objects in memory in an orderly, often hierarchical way, based on their similarity to one another.

Temporal dilemma Deciding whether to put immediate interests or long-term interests first.

Terminal values Highly desired end states such as social recognition and pleasure.

Terror management theory (TMT) A theory which deals with how we cope with the threat of death by defending our world view of values and beliefs.

Theory of planned behavior An extension of the TORA model that predicts behaviors over which consumers perceive they have control.

Theory of reasoned action (TORA) A model that provides an explanation of how, when, and why attitudes predict behavior.

Thin-slice judgments Evaluations made after very brief observations.

Tie-strength The extent to which a close, intimate relationship connects people.

Time risk The extent to which buying, using, or disposing of the offering is perceived to have the potential to lead to loss of time.

Top dog A market leader or brand that has a large market share.

Trade group A professional organization made up of marketers in the same industry.

Traditional hierarchy of effects Sequential steps used in decision making involving thinking, then feeling, then behavior.

Transformational advertising Ads that try to increase emotional involvement with the product or service.

Trialability The extent to which an innovation can be tried on a limited basis before it is adopted.

Trickle-down effect Trends that start in the upper classes and then are copied by lower classes.

Truth effect When consumers believe a statement simply because it has been repeated a number of times.

Two-sided message A marketing message that presents both positive and negative information.

U

Underdog A lower-share brand.

Underprivileged Families below the average income in their class.

Unity When all the visual parts of a design fit together.

Upward mobility Raising one's status level.

Usage The process by which a consumer uses an offering.

Use innovativeness Finding use for a product that differs from the product's original intended usage.

Utilitarian (or functional) dimension When an ad provides information.

V

Valence Whether information about something is good (positive valence) or bad (negative valence).

Value segmentation The grouping of consumers by common values.

Value system Our total set of values and their relative importance.

Values Abstract, enduring beliefs about what is right/wrong, important, or good/bad.

Variety seeking Trying something different.

Vicarious exploration Seeking information simply for stimulation.

Viral marketing Rapid spread of brand/product information among a population of people stimulated by brands.

Voluntary simplicity Limiting acquisition and consumption to live a less material life.

W

Wearout Becoming bored with a stimulus.

Weber's law The stronger the initial stimulus, the greater the additional intensity needed for the second stimulus to be perceived as different.

Wife-dominant decision Decision made primarily by the female head-of-household.

Word of mouth Influence delivered verbally from one person to another person or group of people.

Working memory (WM) The portion of memory where incoming information is encoded or interpreted in the context of existing knowledge, and kept available for more processing.

Z

Zapping Use of a remote control to switch channels during commercial breaks.

Zipping Fast-forwarding through commercials on a program recorded earlier.

Zone of acceptance The acceptable range of prices for any purchase decision.

Name/Author Index

A

Aaker, David A., N123n51, N180n87, N180n89
Aaker, Jennifer L., N67n16, 109, N123n42, N125n65, N153n114, N154n122, N154n141, N178n32, N291n16, N352n104, N352n106, N353n150, N381n102, N408n11, N412n38, 490, N496n120
Abdul-Muhmim, Alhassan G., N211n127
Abe, Shuzo, N151n29
Abelson, Jenn, N178n33
Abelson, Robert P., N123n46
Abendroth, Lisa J., N25n49, N291n4
Abraham, Tamara, N180n106, N380n93
Achenreiner, Gwen Bachmann, N325n62
Ackerman, Diane, N468n29
Acohido, Byron, N26n65
Adams, William Lee, N469n54
Adaval, Rashmi, N180n86, N237n57, N239n130, N264n87
Adele, 442–443
Aditham, Kiran, N94n13
Adkins, Natalie Ross, N25n60
Adler, R. P., N494n31
Adomowicz, Wiktor, N239n128
Aggarwal, Pankaj, N326n84
Agins, Teri, N380n96
Agrawal, Nidhi, N67n6, N69n71, N153n95, N153n96, N154n140, N408n14
Ahearne, Michael, N438n23
Ahluwalia, Rohini, N123n60, N150n4, N155n182, N178n37, N178n48, N236n18, N469n72
Ahmad, Jamilah, N496n112
Ahn, Sun Joo, N180n105
Ahuvia, Aaron C., N25n53, N493n6
Ainslie, Andrew, N263n54
Ainsworth, Michelle, N496n92
Ajzen, Icek, N150n6, N151n31, N155n179
Akerman, Iain, N95n38
Akhter, Syed H., N67n17
Aksoy, Lerzan, N292n42, N292n45
Al, Lee, N324n32
Alabaster, Jay, N440n61
Alba, Joseph W., N70n96, N70n97, N96n88, N98n125, N98n131, N98n142, N122n33, N123n51, 124n76, N124n91, N125n93, N125n102, N125n107, N125n117, N126n127, N177n22, N178n42, N208n4, N208n11, N208n15, N209–210n48, N211n108, N211n116, N236n21, N264n84, N292n19, N327n107, N438n11, N470n77
Albanesius, Chloe, N440n61
Albert, Terri C., N353n125, N353n148
Alden, Dana L., N70n81, N95n41, N98n138, N182n137, N263n38, N264n89, N292n49, N293n50, N409n53
Alexander, David L., N440n57
Alexander, James H., N296n159, N378n14
Algesheimer, Rene, N326n89

Allen, Chris T., N125n98, N153n111, N179n67, N179n68, N380n64, N470n77, N471n114
Allen, Douglas E., N380n64, N380n74
Allenspach, Kevin, N24n34
Alleyne, Sonia, N353n152
Allison, Ralph I., N265n114
Allport, Gordon, N410n84
Alpert, Frank H., N125n109
Alpert, Judy I., N180n120, N181n122
Alpert, Mark I., N180n120, N181n122, N209n35
Alpha, Wolfram, 208
Alsop, Ronald, N352n91, N378n24, N378n25
Altsech, Moses B., N181n130
Alwit, Linda F., N97n117
Amaldoss, Wilfred, N380n85
Ambady, Nalini, N177n7, N262n18
Ames, Daniel R., N410n86
Ames, K., N470n97
Amir, On, N71n121
Amschewitz, Dennis, N153n102
Anand, Punam, N151n25
Anckaert, Pascal, N178n46
Anderson, Beverlee B., N210n94
Anderson, Eugene W., N292n34, N293n52
Anderson, Mae, N42n14, N95n42, N324n30
Anderson, Paul, N239n129, N380n64, N380n74, N494n22
Anderson, Roy C., N42n15
Andrade, Eduardo B., N25n52, N25n54, N69n63, N240n134
Andreasen, Alan R., N294n103, N378n6
Andrews, J. Craig, N67n17, N178n77, N327n111
Andriuli, Frank J., N122n38
Andronikidis, Andreas I., N494n31
Andrus, Roman, N439n37
Ang, Swee Hoon, N208n13
Angwin, Julia, N495n73
Ansari, Asim, N26n92, N211n100, N327n132
Anthony, Marc, 249
Anthony, Scott, N352n80
Antil, John H., N182n167
Aparicio, Manuel, IV, N210n73
Appleby, Julie, N412n147
Appleton, Sara L., N122n26
Arar, Yardeena, N94n15
Archer, Bert, N381n109
Areni, Charles S., N152n67, N154n125, N180n93, N351n61
Argo, Jennifer J., N25n51, N96n80, N326n95, N326n103, N495n57
Aribarg, Anocha, N26n90
Ariely, Dan, N27n105, N24n12, N71n124, N210n73, 233, N237n46, N293n62
Armstrong, Gary M., N494n32, N494n34
Armstrong, Myrna L., N468n25
Arndorfer, James B., N468n20
Arndt, Jamie, N380n87, N408n14

Arndt, Johan, N327n134
Arndt, Jonathan, N24n14
Arnett, Dennis B., N294n100
Arnold, Eric J., N470n103
Arnold, Laurence, N495n61
Arnold, Stephen J., N471n123
Arnould, Eric J., N25n40, N25n59, N27n115, N67n20, N468–469n46, N470n89, N470n96
Arrington, Michael, N439n29
Arsel, Zeynep, N411n104
Asch, Solomon E., N326n85
Ashmore, Richard D., 305
Ashworth, Laurence, N27n98, N293n61
Askegaard, Søren, N68n34, N239n112, N350n6
Assael, Henry, N152n79, N327n122
Atchison, Sandra D., N440n83
Atherley, Ruth, N380n77
Au, Kevin, N70n102
Austin, Erica Weintraub, N153n85
Avila, Ramon, N327n113
Avnet, Tamar, N153n114, N154n121
Aydinoglu, Nilufer Z., N212n142

B

Baack, Daniel W., N353n127
Baack, Donald, N353n127
Baar, Aaron, N296n165
Backer, Stacy, N469n51
Bae, Soonyong, N352n78
Bagchi, Rajesh, N68n45
Bagnall, Andy, N378n25
Bagozzi, Richard P., N25n46, 54, N68n43, N69n50, N69n52, N123n46, N151n29, N154n123, N293n66, N293n67, N296n167, N323n6, N324n38, N326n87, N378n31, N410n93, N440n94, N42n29
Bailenson, Jeremy N., N180n105
Bailey, Sarah, N153n102
Bakalar, Nicholas, N495n83
Bakamitsos, Georgios A., N25n52, N178n26
Baker, Eli, N495n84
Baker, Julie, N178n39, N264n82
Baker, Rosie, N264n69, N352n81
Baker, William E., N126n120, N178n51, N263n35
Bakir, Aysen, N351n69
Balasubramanian, Siva K., N351n44, N351n47
Baldinger, Allan L., N178n78
Balfour, Frederick, N467n10
Ball, A. Dwayne, N469n55
Ball, Deborah, N438n3
Ball-Rokeach, Sandra J., N407n3
Baluja, Tamara, N351n66
Bamossy, Gary J., N123n51, N407n6, N493n6, N493n7
Banta, H. David, N441n103
Barbaro, Michael, N208n3
Barbera, Priscilla L., N354n166
Barg, Nitika G., N25n54

Bargh, John A., N25n62
Bar-Haim, Gabriel, N469n48
Barnes, James, N153n86
Baron, Jonathan, 497n129
Baron, Robert S., N182n149
Barone, Michael J., N123n55, N153n88, N153n92, N180n84
Baroniarczyk, Susan M., N123n51
Barrett, Rick, N409n67
Barsalou, Lawrence W., N122n31, N124n70, N124n71, N124n81
Bartl, Michael, N438n17
Basil, Debra, N496n123
Basil, Michael, N496n123
Basnjak, Michael, N24n27
Bass, Frank M., N24n14, N439n50, N440n66, N441n101
Bastin, Mike, N154n134
Basu, Kunal, N181n136, N240n133
Basuroy, Suman, N328n138
Batra, Rajeev, N71n122, N98n138, N122n37, N122n39, N151n27, N154n116, N154n145, N155n163, N180n87, N180n88, N411n108
Battle, John, N94n3
Bauer, Raymond A., N69n79, N210n98
Bauerlein, Valerie, N493n1, 497n130
Baumeister, Roy F., N68n30, N69n57, N71n121, N266n143
Baumgarten, Steven A., N439n35
Baumgartner, Hans, N68n37, N122n13, N154n118, N180n85, N209n43, N294n86, N410n93, N410n100, N439n41
Bazdarich, Colleen, N96n84
Bearden, William O., N68n31, N293n66, 314, N294n105, N325n47, N326n85, N326n93, N326n96, N326n106, N327n123, N327n124, N410n93, N410n97, N411n102, N411n110, N439n41, N469n47
Beattie, Ann, N97n117
Beatty, Sally Goll, N155n165, N182n168, N350n13, N496n91
Beatty, Sharon E., N97n101, N379n46, N379n47, N409n59, N410n80
Beaver, Jeff, 382
Becherer, Richard C., N411n114
Bechwati, Nada Nasr, N295n110
Becker-Olsen, Karen L., N27n95, N152n63
Beckham, David, 136
Beem, Dan, N265n120
Beene, Ryan, N151n34
Belch, George E., N122n25, N155n167, N178n55, N178n79, N181n126, N378n30, N379n44, N379n52
Belch, Michael A., N181n126, N378n30, N379n44, N379n52
Belk, Russell W., N24n10, N24n22, N24n29, N68n34, N239n112, N266n152, N296n154, N296n160, N326n91, N378n14, N380n88, N380n98, N380n100, N408n8, N408n16, N409n70, N409n71, N468n31, N468n32, N468n34, N469n55, N469n58, N470n77, N470n78, N470n80, N470n81, N470n83, N470n84, N470n85, N470n89, N470n97, N470n104, N470n105, N470n106, N471n112, N471n114, N471n117, N471n119, N493n2, N496n114
Bell, David R., N266n158

Bell, Martin L., N380n63
Bell, Reginald L., N350n9
Bellenger, Danny N., N263n44, N266n152
Bellizzi, Joseph A., N27n112, N180n91
Bellman, Steven, N94n9
Beltrami, Richard, N471n114
Beltrone, Gabriel, 84, N156n188
Ben-Aaron, Diana, N381n139
Bendapudi, Neeli, N293n75
Benedict XVI, Pope, 461
Bennett, Peter, N211n118
Benwick, Bonnie S., N293n69
Bergadaa, Michelle M., N240n139
Bergami, Massimo, N151n29
Berger, Ida E., N150n3, N155n173, N155n176, N178n44, N291n14
Berger, Jonah, N26n93, N265n134, N380n91, N467n12, N469n49
Berger, Paul D., N352n90
Berk, Christina Cheddar, N182n160
Berkeley, Robert L., N379n45
Berkowitz, Leonard, N155n171
Berkowitz, Nancy, N154n137
Berlyne, D. E., N410n98
Berning, Carol A., N24n15, N24n32, N212n147, N296n149, N296n151
Berns, Dave, N352n93
Bernstein, Aaron, N380n73, N380n77
Bernstein, Elizabeth, N354n169, N493n20
Bernthal, Matthew J., N24n28
Berry, Jon, N494n34
Berry, Leonard L., N293n53
Berscheid, Ellen, N294n79
Berthon, Pierre R., N323n9
Best, Arthur, N294n103
Best, Roger J., N409n65
Bettencourt, Lance A., N411n111
Bettman, James R., N25n45, N26n69, N69n80, N122n13, N122n31, N209n43, N211n116, N212n144, N212n152, N236n28, N237n60, N238n65, N238n66, N238n76, N239n102, N239n127, N240n136, N265n107, N324n34, N467n6, N469n55, N469n69
Beverland, Michael B., 196, N151n14
Bhadury, Roop K., N181n132
Bhat, Subodh, 196
Bhatla, Sunil, N155n164, N181n114
Bhattacharya, C. B., N294n100
Bickart, Barbara A., N98n149
Biehal, Gabriel, N208n22, N208n23, N209n41
Biel, Stefan, N438n17
Bierley, Calvin, N179n67, N179n68
Biggart, Nicole Woolsey, N325n56
Bijmolt, Tammo H. A., N125n98, N125n104, N125n108, N352n77, N496n116
Bilgin, Baler, N24n7
Bilgram, Volker, N438n17
Bilsky, Wolfgang, N407n3, N408n7
Bilton, Nick, N180n92
Bindman, Alyssa, N495n84
Biocca, Frank, N210n79
Bird, Laura, N151n43
Biswas, Abhijit, N296n164
Biswas, Dipayan, N125n103
Bither, Stewart W., N238n70
Bitner, Mary Jo, N293n73, N295n126

Bittar, Christine, N42n13
Bizer, George Y., N69n71
Bjork, Robert A., N122n26
Blackmore, Judith E. O., N325n69
Blackwell, Roger D., N439n47, N439n48
Blair, Adam, N71n120
Blair, Ireen V., N237n61
Blair, Margaret Henderson, N179n56
Blanchard, Wendell, N379n59
Blattberg, Robert, N264n94
Blazing, Jennifer, N495n88
Bless, Herbert, N98n128, N123n53
Blevins, Jason, N151n17
Bloch, Peter B., N67n11, N67n20, 202, N210n97, N292n35
Block, Lauren G., N67n6, N209n38, N236n17, N237n31, N293n63, N293n64
Blodgett, Jeffrey, N328n155
Bloom, Paul N., N67n7, N495n88
Blumberg, Stephen J., N294n96
Boatwright, Peter, N27n107, N264n84
Boccaccio, Katherine Field, N212n132
Bodapati, Anand, N325n54
Bodenhorn, Barbara, N471n112
Bodur, H. Onur, N153n106
Bohner, Gerd, N152n77, N208n24
Boland, Michael, N212n158
Boller, Gregory W., N178n35
Bolt, Usain, 72
Bolton, Lisa E., N67n7, N264n84, N326n86, N327n107
Bolton, Ruth N., N293n52, N294n82, N295n125
Bone, F. P., N150n11
Bonfrer, Andre, N152n80
Boninger, David S., N177n4, N180n107
Bonsu, Samuel K., N468n31
Boone, Lisa, N70n107
Boote, Alfred S., N409n49
Booth, David, N26n72
Booth, Hannah, N95n61
Boothby, Rita, N325n69, N325n71
Bordenhorn, Barbara, N468n45
Bornemann, Torsten, N212n140
Bornmann, Torsten, N212n140
Bosmans, Anick, N96n71, N180n85
Botti, Simona, N293n57
Bottomley, Paul A., N95n56
Botvin, Elizabeth M., N495n84
Bourdieu, Pierre, N379n58, N380n65, N467n14
Bourgeois, Jacques C., N354n162
Bousch, David M., N123n51, N123n53, N265n111
Boutilier, Robert, 361
Boutlon, Clint, N212n158
Bower, Gordon H., N126n123
Bowman, Douglas, N26n67, N212n151, N292n46
Brady, Diane, N440n92, N470n76
Brady, Shirley, N354n171
Brady, Tom, 93
Brakus, J. Joško, N292n33, N438n25
Brandal, Hege, N94n18
Brandau, Mark, N265n124
Brannen, Mary Yoko, N408n16
Branswell, Brenda, N380n77
Brasel, S. Adam, N67n16, N94n8, N124n65, N291n16
Brashear, Thomas G., N150n7
Braun, Kathryn A., N122n20

Braun, Stephen, N495n63
Braun-LaTour, Kathryn A., N122n14, N122n19
Braus, Patricia, N378n9
Bray, Hiawatha, N178n41
Brayton, N328n159
Brendl, C. Miguel, N68n27
Brenner, Lyle, N238n67, N239n100
Bridges, Sheri, N123n51
Briggs, Rex, N125n112
Briley, Donnel A., N326n105, N352n105, N353n151
Brinberg, David, N153n106, N211n115
Briñol, Pablo, N152n52
Bristol, Terry, N325n72, N469n67
Bristor, Julia, N210n81
Britton, Julie Edell, N154n148, N263n32
Brock, Timothy C., N94n24, N178n29
Broniarczyk, Susan M., N98n131, N210n71, N211n105
Bronnenberg, Bart J., N27n99
Brooks, Charles, N24n27
Brooks, John, N380n83, N380n94
Brown, Abram, N350n28
Brown, B. Bradford, 305
Brown, Christiana L., N239n126
Brown, Jacqueline J., N324n47, N325n51, N325n55, N326n79, N327n125, N328n140
Brown, James, 121
Brown, Lawrence A., N441n96
Brown, Mark R., N181n132, N182n142
Brown, Stephen, N23n3
Brown, Steven P., N179n75, N178n79, N178n81, N265n115
Brown, Tina A., N467n13
Brown, Tom J., N125n98
Browne, Beverly A., N325n68
Browning, Frank, N42n40
Bruce, Grady D., N324n45, N326n94
Brucks, Merrie, N70n97, N122n31, N124n91, N208n28, N211n113, N211n116, N292n18, N467n4, N494n32, N494n34
Brumbaugh, Anne M., N178n3, N352n110, N353n131, N353n150
Brunel, Frédéric F., N352n105, 464
Bruner, Gordon C., N181n120
Brunner, Thomas A., N239n119
Bruno, Ken, N152n59
Bryant, Chris, N156n188
Bryce, Wendy J., N409n70
Buchanan, Lauranne, N98n149
Bucholz, Laura M., N67n17
Buckley, M.R.F., N209n36
Buckley, Stephen, N380n95
Bucklin, Randolph E., N42n22, N210n74, N211n126, N325n54
Buda, Richard, N263n33
Buesing, Thomas, N264n94
Buhl, Claus, N410n89
Bulbul, Cenk, N182n158
Bulik, Beth Snyder, N124n90, N350n33
Buncombe, Andrew, N179n73
Burda, Benedicta, N70n113
Burette, John J., N155n161
Burgarino, Paul, N350n11
Burke, Marian, N179n61
Burke, Marian Chapman, N180n82, N180n87
Burke, Raymond, N125n98, N125n104

Burnett, John J., N351n55
Burnkrant, Robert, N71n115, N95n33, N122n25, N151n25, N155n182, N178n29, N178n35, N178n37, N178n43, N236n18, N325n74, N326n85, N326n96, N410n93, N469n72
Burns, Alvin, N378n34
Burns, David J., N379n41
Burns, Mary Jane, N294n95
Burroughs, James E., N408n13, N408n14, N411n105, N440n59
Burroughs, Jeffrey, N95n34
Burroughs, W. Jeffrey, N126n123
Burson, Katherine A., N324n35, N380n76, N440n73
Burton, Jonathan, N354n155, N354n161
Burton, Scott, N98n145, N264n95, N327n111
Bush, Alan J., N180n108, N353n142, N353n146
Bush, R. F., N262n2
Bush, Robert P., N409n65
Bush, Victoria D., N180n108
Buskin, John, N210n81
Busler, Michael, N154n133
Buss, Dale, N26n72, N27n111, N124n63, N208n1
Buss, W. Christian, N354n162, N378n31
Byrnes, Nanette, N212n132
Byron, Ellen, N42n16, N353n120, N353n122, N353n128

C

Caalan, J., N327n113
Caballero, Marjorie J., N180n98, N180n99
Cacioppo, John T., N66n4, N68n22, N68n36, N150n9, N155n169, N156n186, N177n3, N180n96, N411n108
Cadotte, Ernest R., N293n51
Cafferata, Pat, N126n123, N126n125, N182n161
Cain, W. S., N96n67, N96n68
Calder, Bobby J., N326n85, N326n96, N327n114, N410n93
Camerer, Colin F., N42n31
Cameron, David, 298
Cameron, Glen T., N94n10
Campbell, Colin, N323n9
Campbell, Dennis, N494n40
Campbell, Leland, N181n125, N181n128
Campbell, Margaret C., N71n123, N179n58, N264n93, N323n4
Campbell, Matthew, N381n139
Campoy, Ana, N353n124
Caniglia, John, N350n24
Cao, Huan, N26n81
Capell, Kerry, N350n13, N409n61
Capon, Noel, N71n118, N211n117
Cardona, Mercedes M., N381n114
Carey, Bridget, N210n80
Carey, Elizabeth, N265n138
Carey, Susan, N208n7
Carlson, Kurt A., N67n6, N212n138
Carlson, Les, N152n54, N325n59, N325n66, N379n51, N379n57
Carmon, Ziv, N23n4, N24n12, N27n105, N291n10, N293n62
Carpenter, Gregory S., N98n136, N124n71
Carrillat, Francois A., N124n79
Carroll, John, N236n10
Carter, Bill, N94n19
Casey, Susan L., N352n83

Castano, Raquel, N440n65
Cattell, Raymond B., N410n84
Caudill, Eve M., N495n72
Cave, Andrew, N467n10
Celsi, Richard L., N67n10, N67n11, N67n20, N67n22, N95n31, N97n112
Censky, Annalyn, N42n42
Ceresino, Gayle, N379n44, N379n52
Chaiken, Shelly, N70n113, N71n114, N177n20, N178n24, N180n99
Chakraborty, Goutam, N469n67
Chakravarti, Amitav, N126n128, N151n36, N212n150, N237n36, N438n20
Chakravarti, Dipankar, N26n68, N208n22, N208n23, N209n41
Chan, Elaine, N154n142, N292n36
Chan, Hamilton, 203
Chan, Kimmy Wa, N294n88
Chan, T. S., N409n70
Chanasawatkit, Suchart, N25n57
Chancellor, Joseph, N381n107, N408n11
Chandler, Jesse, N123n43
Chandon, Jean-Louis, N379n39
Chandon, Pierre, N25n43, N25n50, N95n55, N155n175, N380n86, N495n69, N495n70
Chandra, Shobhana, N381n116
Chandran, Sucharita, N27n99, N237n54
Chandrashekaran, Murali, N125n109
Chandy, Rajesh, N24n18, N69n76, N154n146, N438n15
Chang, Andrew, N27n109
Chaplin, Lan Nguyen, N123n49
Chapman, Mary M., N94n14
Chappell, Lindsay, N295n118
Charles, Gemma, N496n95
Chartrand, Tanya L., N97n99, N262n16
Chatterjee, Rabikar, N264n85
Chatterjee, Subimal, N237n41, N328n138
Chattopadhyay, Amitava, N94n10, N95n60, N125n102, N153n101, N180n82, N181n136, N209–210n48, N239n115, N328n153
Cheema, Amar, N24n12, N68n44, N68n45, N328n151
Chen, Haipeng (Allan), N352n102
Chen, Qimei, N178n40
Chen, Yubo, N328n149
Chen, Zinlei (Jack), N296n157
Cheng, Shen, N493n4
Cheng, Wong Lai, N496n112
Cherian, Joseph, N353n119
Chernev, Alexander, N26n84, N69n60, N69n77, N98n136, N237n40, N237n45, N238n74, N240n140, N240n142, N438n24
Chestnut, Robert W., N67n20, N97n113, N210n94, N212n133, N263n62
Chiang, Kuan-Pin, N24–N25n38
Childers, Terry L., N96n75, N122n28, N124n70, N126n121, N209n47, N324n21, N378n32
Chillingworth, Mark, N325n52, N325n73
Chintagunta, Pradeep K., N210n69, N263n54
Cho, Janet, N412n147
Choi, Candice, N124n63
Choi, Jinhee, N69n53
Choi, Yung Kyun, N153n83
Chow, Jason, N294n85
Christakis, D. A., N494n30
Christensen, Glenn L., N295n124

Christensen, Jen, N378n22
Christenson, Gary, N493n13
Christiansen, Ann, N327n111
Christopher, Michael, N467n1
Churchill, Gilbert A., N182n166, N293n66, N438n28
Churchill, Winston, 459–460
Cialdini, Robert B., N151n30, N151n40, N327n113, N380n92, N496n117
Clark, Charles S., N494n50
Clark, Gary, L., N328n155
Clark, Jackie, N470n111
Clark, Margaret, N126n123
Clark, Margaret S., N265n107
Clark, Ronald A., N324n26
Clarke, Charlotte, N26n91
Clarkson, Joshua J., N155n178
Claus, Jasper, N97n97
Claxton, John O., N210n96
Clee, Mona A., N326n88
Clemons, D. Scott, N294n95
Clerizo, Michael, N470n82
Clifford, Stephanie, N352n79
Clift, Vicki, N324n14
Cline, Thomas W., N181n129, N181n130
Clooney, George, 143
Close, Angeline G., N210n90
Clyde, Andrew, N411n113
Cobb, Cathy J., N262n29, N266n150
Cobb-Walgren, Cathy J., N263n46, N496n115
Cocanougher, A. Benton, N324n45
Cockington, James, N470n109
Cohen, Joel B., N25n54, N67n7, N68n41, N150n3, N150n11, N150n11, N151n13, N151n32, N154n125, N236n6, N240n134, N410n91
Cohen, Noam, N94n11
Cohen, Patricia, N380n71
Cohn, D'Vera, N377n2
Cokely, Kevin, N353n124
Cole, Catherine A., N70n106, N97n111, N122n30, 126n122, N212n154, N240n135, N351n44, N351n47, N351n57
Cole, Elizabeth R., N380n67
Cole, John, N97n111
Coleman, Calmetta Y., N211n101, N496n89
Coleman, Richard P., 365, N379n59, N380n63, N380n66, N381n124, N409n57
Colliander, Jonas, N324n13
Collins, Sarah, N70n109
Colvin, Geoff, N42n20
Comello, Leonora G., N494n42
Commuri, Suraj, N378n20
Coney, Suzanne, N439n51
Cooil, Bruce, N292n42
Cook, Victor, N439n52
Cooke, Alan D. J., N210n72
Coon, Gregory S., N471n117, N471n119
Cooper, M. Bixby, N293n70, N295n121
Cooper-Martin, Elizabeth, N496n125
Copeland, Michael V., N440n90
Corfman, Kim P., N210n81, N210n82, N239n122, N263n51, N326n80, N378n35
Corneille, Olivier, N179n71
Cornwell, T. Bettina, N125n111
Corsten, Daniel, N266n158
Coskun, A., N328n155

Costa, Janeen, N378n14
Costa, Janeen Arnold, N98n129, N351n61, N351n73, N380n88, N468n32
Costa, MaryLou, N494n29
Costley, Carolyn, N153n86, N208n28
Cotte, June, N23n5, N24n33, N379n48, N441n99
Coulter, Keith S., N27n104, N42n12, N152n72
Coulter, Robin A., N27n104, N42n12, N180n95
Coupey, Eloïse, N153n106, N236n3
Courtney, Alice E., N181n135
Cousineau, Alain, N325n74
Cowley, Elizabeth, N124–125n92, N209n45, N237n41
Cox, Anthony D., N95n35, N179n67, N493n19, N494n22
Cox, Dena, N95n35, N493n19, N494n22
Cox, William E., Jr., N439n52
Craig, Adam W., N26n87
Craig, Samuel, N95n37, N181n128
Craik, Fergus I. M., N122n23, N126n122, N351n46
Credeur, Mary Jane, N291n1
Crispell, Diane, N380n69
Crocker, Kenneth E., N180n97
Crocket, Susan, N123n53
Crockett, David, N24n28
Cronley, Maria L., N98n144, N98n147, N124n87, N237n37
Croson, Rachel, N469n59
Crossen, Cynthia, N70n108
Crowley, Ayn E., N27n112, N180n90, N180n91
Crutchfield, Dean, N121n1
Cruz, Julie, N94n13
Csikszentmihalyi, Mihaly, N469n47, N470n89, N470n91
Culnan, Mary J., N495n80
Cummings, William H., N291n2
Cundiff, Edward W., 366, N379n60, N380n62
Cunningham, Isabella C. M., N379n39
Cunningham, R. M., N263n67
Curasi, Carolyn Folkman, N25n40, N25n59, N468–469n46, N470n103
Currim, Imran, N211n100
Curry, David J., N379n40
Curtis, W. W., N410n100
Cutright, Keisha M., N411n116
Czellar, Sandor, N68n25, N154n143
Czepiel, John A., N439n39

D

Dabholkar, Pratibha, N296n167
Dacin, Peter A., N70n96, N124n91, N182n164
Dade, Corey, N353n113
Dageleisch, Tim, N411n106
Dahl, Darren W., N25n50, N25n51, N70n112, N95n60, N96n80, N154n128, N154n150, N182n143, N239n115, N294n80, N324n40, N326n92, N326n95, N438n11, N440n58, N470n94, N495n57
Dahlen, Micael, N324n13
Dalakas, Vassilis, N325n63
Danaher, Peter J., N152n80
Danckert, Sarah, N94n1
Daniels, Chris, N353n134
Danko, William D., N378n3
Danziger, Shai, N208n25
Darby, D. L., N327n113

Darden, William R., N439n35
Darke, Peter, N27n98, N293n61, N294n80
Darley, William K., N351n70, N379n47
Das, Enny H. H., N151n26
Dasgupta, Srabana, N296n157
D'Astous, Alain, N493n13
Daugherty, Terry, N210n79
Daughtridge, Christopher, N296n164
Davenport, J. William, Jr., N95n32
Davidson, Kirk, N495n82
Davidson, William R., N378n33
Davies, Paul, N495n64
Davis, B. P., N151n26
Davis, Harry, L., N325n51, N325n56, N325n57, N378n27, N378n33, N379n41
Davis, Joyce E., N42n9
Davis, Meryle, 47
Davis, Rece, 191
Davis, Roger, N71n118, N211n117
Dawar, Niraj, N124n64
Dawson, Scott A., N67n20, N408n15
Day, Ellen, N180n111
Day, George S., N263n62, N264n68
Day, Ralph L., N294n102, N294n103, N294n107
Dayal, Priyanka, N412n147
de Angels, Matteo, N295n115
Dearden, Chris, N96n63
DeBerry-Spence, Benét, N27n115
Debevec, Kathleen, N178n29, N180n99, N468n32
DeBono, Kenneth G., N411n114
DeCarlo, Thomas E., N27n101
Deen, Paula, 304
Deeter-Schmelz, Dawn R., N410n74, N23n3
Defever, Christine, N409n66
DeGeneres, Ellen, 176
Deighton, John, N182n161, 270, 271, N291n9, N292n26, N292n28
de Jong, Martijn G., N41n4, N409n50
de Kruijk, Mark, N496n116
Dellande, Stephanie, N27n100, N293n55, N327n118
Delo, Cotton, N26n94, N323n8
DeLosier, M. Wayne, N327n121
DeLucia, Lenore A., N325n69
DelVecchio, Devon, N27n104
DeMello, Gustavo, N25n47, N67n9
Demont, John, N380n77
De Moss, M., N68n40
Dempsey, Melanie A., N179n74, N262n17
Deng, Xiaoyan, N95n57
De Pelsmacker, Partrick, N178n46
Derbaix, Christian M., N179n75
de Ruyter, Ko, N210n68
Desai, Kalpesh Kaushik, N123n54, N208n9
DeSarbo, Wayne S., N293n65, N493n13
Deshpande, Rohit, N210n98, N262n2, N263n36, N325n48, N353n117, N353n129, N381n136, N468n33
Deutsch, Ronald, N25n45, N265n140, N325n74, N327n119
Deveny, Kathleen, N263n59, N264n100
DeVere, S. P., N410n100
Dewitte, Siegried, N69n58, N182n144, N411n115
DeZwaan, Martina, 493

Dhar, Ravi, N68n46, N69n49, N69n59, N69n64, N69n73, N71n121, N237n32, N237n33, N240n138, N240n141, N494n23, N294n92, N294n97

Dhar, Sanjay, N152n80

Dholakia, Ruby Roy, N24–N25n38, N151–153n45, N468n34

Dholakia, Utpal M., 54, N68n43, N69n50, N69n52, N152n60, N323n6, N324n38, N326n87, N326n89

Diallo, Mariamo, N296n177

Diaz, Andrea Narholz, N211n108

Diaz, Ann-Christine, N27n118

Dibb, Sally, N67n15

Dichter, Ernest, N68n40, N380n62

Dickerson, M. D., N439n37, N439n48

Dickinson, Tom, 136

Dickson, Peter D., N264n78

Dickson, Peter R., N181n114, N211n99, N262n7

Didow, Nicholas M., N295n122

Diehl, Kristin, N25n49, N210n77, N211n102, N211n115, N212n135, N291n4, N293n59

Diener, E., N294n96

Dietworst, Thomas F., N24n15, N24n32, N296n149, N296n151

DiFiore, Alessandro, N381n134

Dijksterhuis, Ap, N26n62, N177n5, N262n14, N262n23

Di Justo, Patrick, N152n76

Dillon, William R., N410n101

DiMeo, Joan, N354n153

Dimofte, Claudia V., N26n83, N353n130

Dittmar, Helga, N470n93, N470n96

Dixit, Ashutosh, N469n66

Djokovic, Novak, 170

Dobel, Linda, N295n130

Dodd, G. H., N96n69

Dodds, Wellesley, N439n50

Dogg, Snoop, 89

Donkers, Bas, N179n57

Donkin, Richard, N150n1

Donnelly, Tim, 203

Donthu, Naveen, N325n48, N353n117, N353n119, N468n33

Doong, Her-Sen, N263n65

Dornoff, Ronald, N125n109

Dorotic, Matilda, N24n18, N69n76, N438n15

Douglas, Susan P., N98n137

Dover, Philip A., N151n19

Dowd, Casey, N350n41

Dowling, Grahame R., N69n79

Downey, Robert, Jr., 170

Doyle, Al, N440n74

Doyle, John R., N95n56

Doyle, P., N378n28

Dreier, Hannah, N350n11

Drew, James H., N293n52

Drèze, Xavier, N68n47, N69n48, N122n15

Droge, Cornelia, N293n70, N295n121

Drolet, Aimee, N238n66, N238n77, N351n56

D'Sousa, Giles, N71n122

Du, Rex Y., 359, N377n3

Dubé, Jean-Pierre, N210n69

Dubé, Laurette, N98n129, N351n72, N352n82

Dubitsky, Tony M., N125n118

Duff, Brittany R. L., N94n4

Duffy, Jill, N407n1

Dugan, Lauren, N97n124, N24n24

Duhachek, Adam, N25n56, N27n115, N154n140, 279, N294n91

Duhan, Dale, N323n12

Duhigg, Charles, N96n90

Dunai, Marton, N26n71

Duncan, Calvin P., N181n126, N181n128, N211n106, N211n107, N236n16

Duncan, Robert, N438n28

Dunn, Elizabeth W., N381n103, N408n11

Dunn, Jeff, 492

duPlessis, Erik, N94n7

Dupont, Meg, N408n17

Durante, Kristina M., N351n63

Durvasula, Srinivas, N67n17, N178n77

Dutta-Bergman, Mohan J., N408n24

Duty, Jason, N209n46

Dwyer, Paula, N350n17

Dwyer, Sean, N27n100

E

Eagly, Alice, N70n113, N71n114

East, Robert, N94n12, N328n152

Eaton, John, N124n62

Eberhardt, Tim, N26n64

Edell, Julie A., N66n4, N97n117, N155n166, N179n61, N180n82, N180n87, N237n59, N238n75

Edwards, Elizabeth A., N493n13

Edwards, Steven M., N94n11

Efrati, Amir, N438n1

Egol, Matthew, N411n113

Ehrich, Kristine R., N24n26

Ehrlich, Kristine R., N24n26

Einwiller, Sabine, N152n77

Eisenberg-Berg, Nancy, N325n69, N325n71

Eisend, Martin, N152n78, N181n126, N351n67

Eisenstein, Eric M., N291n12

Eisingerich, Andreas B., N155n181

Eisler, Benita, N380n79

Ekstrom, Karin M., N379n44

Elam, Stephanie, N328n159

Eleftheriou-Smith, Loulla-Mae, N494n45

Ellen Pam Scholder, N496n115

Ellen, S. P., N150n11

Elliot, Richard, N351n73

Elliott, Dorinda, N408n16

Elliott, Michael, N94n5

Elliott, Stuart, N68n38, N154n151, N156n188, N177n1, N180n109, N239n116, N328n165, N411n107, N469n53, N495n65

Ellis, Andrew W., N97n120, N350n16

Ellis, Elwood A., N327n120

Ellison, Sarah, N182n157, N468n37

Elmer-DeWitt, Philip, N438n2

Elmore-Yalch, Rebecca, N71n117

Elpers, Josephine L. C. M. Woltman, N95n39, N95n41, N181n131

Emshwiller, John R., N351n59

Engel, Cole J., N350n9

Engel, James J., N439n47, N439n48

Engen, Trygg, N96n66

Engle, Randall W., N179n68

Englis, Basil G., N324n43

Enis, Ben M., N377n3, N380n90

Enright, Allison, N262n1

Ensor, Benjamin, N438n1

Eppright, David R., N155n153

Epstein, Seymour, N238n68, N239n99

Erb, Hans-Peter, N152n77

Erdem, Tülin, N152n64, N212n131, N264n79

Erffmeyer, Robert C., N351n54

Erickson, Erik, N410n82

Eriksen, Michael P., N495n84

Erlichman, Howard, N96n70

Ernst, Holger, N438n12

Escalas, Jennifer Edson, N69n70, N121n10, N152n70, N154n148, N177n16, N178n28, N182n162, N239n114, N324n3, N467n6, N468n18, N469n55, N469n69

Essegaier, Skander, N327n132

Etzel, Michael J., N326n93, N42n41

Etzioni, Amitai, N470n107

Eugene, Thomas L., N325n70

Eysenck, Hans, 397, N410n85

F

Faber, Ronald, N25n45, N68n40, N94n4, N266n144, 478, N493n13, N493n14

Fan, Xiucheng, N70n102

Fang, Xiang, N178n48

Farivar, Behrooz, N439n50

Farley, John U., N326n85

Farrelly, Francis J., N151n14

Fastenburg, Dan, N378n19

Faulds, David J., N26n89

Faullant, Rita, N26n75

Fay, Brad, N328n143

Faycon, Benoit, N236n25

Fazekas, Dave, N210n89

Fazio, Russell H., N155n171, N155n173, N178n38, N292n23

Fedorikhin, Alexander, N240n135, N265n109

Feick, Lawrence, N124n91, N324n19, N324n21, N324n25, N324n26, N324n46, N327n120

Fein, Greta, N325n69, N325n71

Feinberg, Fred M., N42n29, N42n31

Feinberg, Richard A., N95n34, N97n101

Feitelberg, Rosemary, N98n151, N177n19

Felberbaum, Michael, N494n38

Feld, Anthony, N381n116

Feng, Yang, N354n161

Fennis, Bob M., N151n26, N496n119

Fera, Rae Ann, N263n51

Ferber, Robert, N68n40

Ferguson, Joey, N350n15

Fern, Edward F., N153n86, N327n113, N379n42

Fernandez, Ana, N495n80

Fernandez, Karen V., N265n122, N470n79, N470n102

Fernandez, Sofia, N26n86

Ferraro, Rosellina, N25n45, N266n147

Ferrell, Elizabeth, N495n78

Fessel, Florian, N291n8

Festinger, Leon, N494n55

Fetto, John, N182n153, N352n91, N354n156, N378n12, N381n127, N408n20, N494n24

Fickenscher, Lisa, N352n93

Fiedler, Klaus, N124n83

Filazolla, Anne D., N495n84

File, Karen Maru, N328n155

Filiarault, Pierre, N378n35

Finkel, Eli J., N379n43

Finn, Adam, N94n2

Finott, John, N350n39

Fischer, Eileen, N210n81, N351n61, N471n123
Fishbach, Ayelet, N68n46, N69n49, N69n53, N177n6
Fishbein, Martin, N150n6, N151n31, N155n179
Fisher, Robert J., N266n153, N325n75, N326n101, N352n82, N440n82, N440n87
Fisher, William A., N210n94, N212n133
Fiske, Susan T., N265n107, N265n111, N265n112
Fitzgerald, Kate, N96n64
Fitzgerald, Matthew, N96n96
Fitzpatrick, Catherine, N494n51
Fitzsimons, Gavan J., N97n99, N155n172, N155n175, N237n39, N293n63, N411n116, N470n100
Fitzsimons, Grainne, M., N97n99
Flagg, Michael, N379n37
Flaherty, Julie, N468n39
Flandez, Raymund, N440n80
Fleeson, William, N410n86
Fleming, Monique A., N155n177
Fletcher, June, N70n109, N440n84
Fling, Sheila, N325n71
Florsheim, Renee, N494n35
Folger, Jean, N177n19
Folkes, Valerie, N24n30, N95n54, N124n68, N154n152, N177n18, N262n5, N293n72, N293n74, N295n109, N328n160
Ford, Bill, Jr., 403
Ford, Gary T., N98n132
Ford, Jeffrey D., N327n120
Ford, John B., N352n83
Ford, Peter, N181n112
Forehand, Mark R., N180n104, N353n130
Fornell, Claes, N292n34, N293n52, N295n122, N295n123
Förster, Jens, N69n52, N177n10, N262n20
Fortier, Louis, N493n13
Fost, Dan, N295n113
Foster, Brian, N326n79
Fournier, Susan, N67n16, N124n65, N291n16, N293n56, 420, N438n21, N470n88
Fowler, Geoffrey, A., N352n84
Fox, Jean-Paul, N41n4
Foxall, Gordon R., N263n65, N265n129, N439n43
Foxman, Ellen R., N379n44, N379n45, N495n74
Francese, Peter, N24n20, N380n71
Frank, Ronald E., N263n66
Franses, Philip Hans, N179n57
Fraser, S., N327n112
Freeman, J. L., N327n112
Freeman, Mike, N352n101
Freeman, Richard B., N381n130
French, John R., N326n102, N327n123
Frenzen, Jonathan K., N325n51, N325n55, N325n56, N325n57
Freud, Sigmund, 396, N410n82
Freudenheim, Milt, N408n31
Frey, Dieter, N291n2
Friedman, Milton, 488
Friedman, Ronald S., N177n10, N262n20
Friend, David, 145
Friestad, Marian, N151n20, N182n159
Fritz, Ben, N263n57
Frohlich, Cheryl J., N328n155
Fromkin, Howard L., N469n47, N469n61
Fry, Joseph N., N210n96
Fuchs, Christoph, N438n16

Füller, Johann, N26n75
Fullerman, Rita, N468n32
Fullerton, Ronald A., N493n18, N493n20, N493n21, N494n22
Furnham, Adrian, N380n100
Furse, David H., N95n35, N125n108, N181n125, N211n100, N211n129
Furst, Andreas, N295n114
Furst, Elisabeth, N467n9

G
Gabel, Terrance G., N468n23
Gable, Myron, N97n101
Gabriel, Donata C., N468n25
Gaeth, Gary J., N70n106, N97n111, N351n44, N351n47
Gaffney, Charles, N408n16
Gaidis, William C., N263n39, N263n55
Gainer, Brenda, N210n81
Gaines, Amanda, N469n63
Gal, David, N69n60, N69n68
Galica, Matthias, 203
Galinsky, Adam D., N380n97
Gallo, Carmine, N239n116
Gamble, Molly, N239n116
Ganesh, Jaishankar, N441n97
Ganzach, Yoav, N237n58
Garbarino, Ellen, N66n4, N238n75, N496n90
Gardial, Sarah Fisher, N294n95
Gardner, Meryl Paula, N25n41, N180n120, N208n26, N209n34, N236n19, N239n102
Gardyn, Rebecca, N354n156, N380n93, N381n101
Garfield, Bob, N124n75, N156n188
Garland, Susan B., N324n17
Garlic, Rick, N350n5
Garner, Randy, N41n3
Garrahan, Matthew, N495n66
Garretson Judith A., N152n55, N180n110
Gaski, John F., N42n41
Gasparro, Annie, N23n1
Gates, Fliece R., N97n109
Gatignon, Hubert, N438n4, N439n46, N439n48, N440n66, N441n96, N441n97
Gauri, Dinesh K., N212n139
Gebrselassie, Haile, 448
Geistfeld, Loren V., N351n59
Gelato, Paola, N153n102
Gelb, Betsy D., N181n126, N182n152
Gelfand, Elizabeth, N236n20
Gengler, Charles, N178n31, N264n105
Gentry, J. W., N439n37, N439n48
Gentry, James W., N211n119, N378n20, N467n4, N494n56
Genturk, Esra, N123n53
Ger, Güliz, N68n34, N239n112
Gerard, Harold B., N325n74, N327n119
Gergen, Kenneth, N469n47
Germain, Richard, N153n113
German, Steve D., N294n100
Gershoff, Andrew D., N210n71, N262n31, N324n35, N380n76
Gerstner, Etian, N98n145
Gertner, Jon, N468n19
Geuens, Maggie, N178n46
Geyskens, Kelly, N69n58
Gianatasio, David, N440n80

Gibson, Richard, N96n94
Gielens, Katrijn, N440n62
Gies, Erica, N328n162
Giesler, Markus, N24n26
Gilbert, Daniel T., N294n96, N381n103, N408n11
Gillespie, Kate, N328n139
Gilligan, Stephen, N126n123
Gilly, Mary C., N27n100, N293n55, N324n46, N327n118, N328n140, N351n48, N377n3, N407n6, N469n62
Giner, Brenda, N351n61
Giopalakrishna, Srinath, N351n68
Giovino, Gary A., N495n84
Gips, James, N94n8
Gittelsohn, John, N26n74
Glazer, Emily, N25n39
Glotz, Julia, N440n68
Gneezy, Ayelet, N24n9
Goddard, Peter, N409n42
Godek, John, N153n89, N155n177
Goerne, Carrie, N353n115
Goff, Brent G., N493n13
Goh, Charlene, N352n107
Goh, Khim Yong, N210n69
Goi, Fedele J., N122n38
Goldberg, Marvin E., N70n88, N152n62, N182n164, N208–209n31, N240n133, N379n44, N493n6, N493n7, N494n32, N494n34
Golden, Linda L., N293n72
Goldenberg, Jacob, N328n153
Goldhaben, Gerald M., N24n31
Goldman, Kevin, N152n57
Goldschmidt, Bridget, N353n123
Goldsmith, Elizabeth, N324n26
Goldsmith, Ronald E., N151n45, N324n26, N439n44
Goldstein, David, N177n23
Goldstein, Noah J., N151n30, N496n117
Gollwitzer, Peter M., N468n28
Gonzalez, Gabriel R., N494n42
Gonzalez, Silvia, N328n139
Goodale, Gloria, N181n112
Goode, Miranda R., N154n128
Goodison, Donna, N181n134, N408n33
Goodley, Simon, N408n26
Goodman, Joseph K., N381n105, N408n12
Goodman, Phil, N351n43
Goodstein, Ronald C., N66n4, N97n100, N177n4, N177n17, N180n107
Goodwin, Cathy, N294n106
Gopinath, Mahesh, N25n46, N69n52
Gordon, Andrea, N379n53
Gorn, Gerald J., N96n87, N125n119, N154n150, N179n65, N181n120, N182n164, N208–209n31, N239n115, N240n133, N379n44, N470n94, N493n6, N493n7, N494n34, N494n35
Gotlieb, Jerry B., N153n90, N153n97
Goukens, Caroline, N411n115
Gourville, John T., N27n106, N237n56, N327n114
Graham, John L., N27n100, N293n55, N293n74, N324n46, N327n118
Granbois, Donald H., N262n30, N328n155, N378n34, N378n35
Granhoj, Alice, N378n29

Granitz, Neil A., N210n82
Granovetter, Mark S., N325n51, N439n39
Grayson, Kent, N408n39, N470n86
Greatorex, Michael, N70n82
Green, Corliss L., N353n143, N353n147
Green, Donald P., N237n61
Green, Heather, N409n61
Green, Penelope, N24n17, N296n176
Green, Robert T., N70n81, N379n39
Greenbaum, Hilary, N440n67
Greenberg, Barnett A., N263n44
Greenberg, Martin S., N469n47
Greenfeld, Karl Taro, N378n11
Greenleaf, Eric A., N25n49, N67n20, N95n47, N239n109, N239n117
Greenwald, Anthony G., N97n101, N66n4, N67n22, N327n116
Gregan-Paxton, Jennifer, N70n100, N70n105, N97n121, N150n12
Gregory, Sean, N154n129, N264n104
Greifender, Rainer, N123n53, N210n78, N239n118
Grether, David, N238n78
Grewal, Dhruv, N125n103, N153n86, N153n97, N211n113, N212n136, N264n82, N264n91, N292n41, N293n53
Grey, Brian, N350n30
Grier, Sonya A., N352n110, N353n150, N381n136
Griffin, David A., N178n40
Griffin, Jill G., N211n105
Griffith, Chris, N94n16
Grillo, Thomas, N181n134
Griskevicius, Vladas, N151n30, N351n63, N496n117
Grobart, Sam, N438n8
Grohmann, Bianca, N122n40, N150n8, N327n117
Gronhaug, Kjell, N295n111
Gross, Grant, N26n65
Grossbart, S. L., N410n100
Grossbart, Sanford, N325n59, N379n51
Grossman, Randi Priluck, N179n69
Grossman, Samantha, N494n27
Groth, Markus, N25n5, N294n90
Grove, Stephen J., N126n123
Gruenwedel, Erik, N263n57
Grunert, Suzanne, N352n74
Gu, Flora F., N493n4
Guetzkow, H., N326n85
Gulas, Charles S., N326n98, N495n58
Gunasti, Kunter, N98n127
Gupta, Kamal, N24n30
Gürhan-Canli, Zeynep, N98n140, N122n32, N122n37, N209n42, N469n55, 497n128
Guskey-Federouch, Audrey, N324n23
Gustafsson, Anders, N292n38, N292n40
Gutchess, Angela H., N42n31
Gutman, Jonathan, 394, N409n73, N410n75
Gwinner, Kevin P., N124n62

H
Ha, Young-Won, N292n21
Haber, R. N., N121n3
Haddock, Rafael, N27n103
Hadix, Anne, N495n84
Häfner, Michael, N494n56
Hagerty, James R., N296n177
Hagerty, Michael R., N180n87

Hagtvedt, Henrik, N181n116
Hair, Joseph F., Jr., N409n65
Haley, Russell I., N178n78
Hall, Brian, N381n130
Hall, Edward T., N97n115
Halpern, Jack N., N96n70
Halstead, Diane, N293n70, N295n121, N354n170
Hamilton, Jon, N42n20
Hamilton, Rebecca W., N153n99, N237n43, N440n71
Hamilton, Ryan, N237n40
Hammond, Kathy, N94n12, N211n108, N328n152
Hampp, Andrew, N94n19, N352n112
Han, Jin K., N121n4
Han, Seunghee, N69n56, N239n103, N239n104
Hancock, Robert S., N69n79, N210n98
Handelman, Jay M., N496n126
Hannah, Darlene B., N152n61
Hansen, Eric N., N42n15
Hansen, Richard W., N379n41
Hanson, Cynthia, N494n54
Haq, Amber, N42n33
Hardesty, David M., N154n144, N410n97
Harley, Bryan, N123n50
Harrell, James, N296n150, N323–324n12
Harries, Michelle, N380n77
Harris, Eric G., N124n79
Harris, Judy, N68n31, N409n52
Harris, Lynn, N97n101
Harris, Rachel Lee, N354n168
Harrison, George, 459
Hartwick, Jon, N151n31, N152n62, N238n73
Hasher, Lynn, N94n21, N177n23
Haskinsl Christopher G., N439n43
Hastak, Manoj, N125n102, N209n41
Hastie, Reid, N209n40, N292n24
Hasty, Ronald W., N27n112, N180n91
Hatchman, Mark, N264n96
Häubl, Gerald, N263n63
Haugtvedt, Curtis P., N179n61, N180n96, N411n108
Hauser, John R., N208n5, N211n125
Hausknecht, Douglas, N70n113
Hawkins, Del I., N97n101
Hawkins, Scott A., N71n122, N126n122, N177n23, N351n46
Hayden, Noel, N122n22
Hayes, Paula J., N354n170
Hays, Constance L., N42n20
Haytko, Diana L., N467n7
Hayward, Stephen, N493n3
Healey, Spencer, N152n50
Healy, Melissa, N26n66
Heath, Chip, N469n49
Heath, Robert, N94n29
Heath, Timothy B., N97n111, N152n74, N237n41
Heckler, Susan E., N23n5, N94n28, N122n28, N208n14, N209n47, N296n170, N296n174
Heckman, Robert L., N324n23
Heeler, Roger M., N439n50
Heilman, Carrie M., N26n67, N70n87, N212n151
Heine, Christopher, N327n109
Heisley, Deborah, N125n114, N42n11, N467n14
Helft, Miguel, N41n1
Heline, Holly, N263n40, N264n70
Hemetsberger, Andrea, N24n18

Henard, David H., N292n38, N440n55
Hennig-Thurau, Thorsten, N25n55, N264n75, N294n90
Henry, Paul C., N381n125
Henry, Tanya Albert, N408n32
Hensley, Scott, N494n41
Herman, C. P., N177n20
Hermann, Robert O., N496n125
Herr, Paul M., N151n45, N178n38, N180n102, N208n29, N209n37, N236n24, N237n62, N292n23, N323n11, N328n144
Herrmann, Andreas, N155–156n182, N177n8, N262n19, N326n89, N469n72
Herzenstein, Michael, N438n25
Hetzner, Christiaan, N26n71
Heubusch, Kevin, N495n63
Heussner, Ki Mae, N353n149
Heyman, Marshall, N350n23, N381n108
Higgins, E. Tory, N69n52, N153n114, N265n111
Higgins, Michelle, N408n22
Higie, Robin M., N324n21, N324n25, N324n46
Hilger, Marye T., 366, N379n60, N380n62
Hill, Amelia, N380n77
Hill, Angela, N468n42
Hill, Ronald Paul, N381n128, N381n131, N494n54
Hill, Sarah E., N351n63
Hillyer, Clayton L., N123n47
Hippocrates, 397
Hirsch, Jerry, N26n79
Hirschman, Elizabeth C., N67n20, N68n40, N121n7, N208n10, N239n101, N266n149, N353n117, N354n166, N378n10, N378–379n36, N408n23, N410n99, N439n43, N439n48, N440n94, N467n4, N468n22, N468n36, N471n124, N493n11
Ho, Edward A., N237n38
Ho, Prudence, N294n85
Hoch, Stephen J., N24n6, N69n61, N177n23, N239n126, 270, 271, N291n9, N292n21, N292n28, N379n41
Hockman, Dennis, N121n12
Hoefer, Hans, N354n164
Hoeffler, Steve, N440n58, N440n63
Hoegg, JoAndrea, N96n88, N438n1, N126n128
Hof, Robert, N181n117, N328n165
Hofcker, Charles F., N439n44
Hoffman, Donna L., N438n14
Hofstede, Frenkel Ter, N410n77, N439n45
Hofstede, Geert, 391, N409n51
Hogan, Daniel, N177n7, N262n18
Holbek, Jonny, N438n28
Holbrook, Morris B., N24n10, N25n41, N42n12, N67n20, N95n46, N121n7, N122n17, N155n163, N180n87, N208n10, N239n101, N239n102, N353n117, N378n10, N378–379n36, N469n51, N470n81, N470n83, N470n84, N470n97
Holden, Reed K., N98n146
Holland, Jonna, N467n4
Hollis, Nigel, N125n112
Holm, Cynthia K., N42n43
Holman, Rebecca H., N122n17, N296n158, N296n159, N380n80, N380n90, N438n10, N468n26, N468n27, N469n56
Holmes, Elizabeth, N266n160, N324n44

Holmes, Jake, N328n163
Holmes, Selina J., N97n120, N350n16
Holt, Douglas B., N351n62, N409n54, N412n143, N469n57
Holzwarth, Martin, N210n67
Homans, R., N237n35
Homburg, Christian, N68n25, N154n143, N212n140, N292n37, N292n39, N292n44, N294n94, N295n114
Homer, Pamela M., N122n39, N125n108, N155n167, N178n79, N180n97, N180n99, N180n102, N409n59, N410n80
Honea, Heather, N25n50, N126n120, N154n150
Honeycutt, Earl D. Jr., N352n83
Hong, J. W., N469n56
Hong, Jiewen, N125n94, N237n40
Hong, Sung-Tai, N98n137, N98n141, N236n26
Horn, Jennifer, N177n1
Horne, Daniel R., N495n79
Horney, Karen B., 397, N410n90
Horng, Der-Juinn, N152n48
Hornik, Jacob, N96n78
Hornyak, Tim, N440n76
Horovitz, Bruce, N124n63, N177n12
Horskey, Dan, N441n101
Horwitt, Elisabeth, N42n28
Houghton, David C., N237n37
Houpt, Simon, N354n163
Houston, Michael J., N67n12, N67n20, N71n115, N97n111, N122n30, N123n46, 124n73, N126n122, N152n67, N180n96, N209n47, N236n2, N262n5, N263n44, N293n58, N324n22, N379n45, N410n79, N470n83
Hout, Michael, N380n69
Hoverstad, Ronald, N209n40
Howard, Daniel J., N27n105, N95n33, N178n31, N178n35, N264n105
Howard, Theresa, N182n160
Howe, Neil, N409n58
Howell, Roy D., N294n107
Howell, Roy, N409n55
Howenstein, E., N296n168
Hoy, Mariea Grubbs, N495n74
Hoyer, Wayne D., N24n1, N67n5, N68n25, N69n76, N70n81, N95n39, N95n41, N97n109, N97n117, N98n133, N123n45, N151n39, N154n143, N156n183, N181n131, N182n137, N208n9, N210n98, N262n2, N262n12, N262n28, N262n29, N263n36, N263n37, N263n38, N263n45, N265n115, N265n130, N266n150, N292n37, N294n94, N324n21, N325n48, N353n117, N408n36, N409n53, N438n12, N438n15, N440n72, N468n33, N495n71
Hsee, Christopher, N381n104, N493n16
Hsu, Tiffany, N408n28
Hu, Ye, N438n23
Huang, Liang, N182n139
Huang, Peng, N210n95
Huber, Frank, N155–156n182, N469n72
Huber, Joel, N178n29, N212n149, N236n4, N236n12, N237n41, N240n145
Hudson, Kris, N353n124
Huffman, Cynthia, N212n143
Hughes, G. David, N122n25, N150n11, N236n6
Hughner, Reneé Shaw, N411n111
Hui, Michael K., N70n102, N293n54

Humphreys, Michael S., N125n111
Hung, Iris W., N69n62, N121n11, N177n11
Hung, Kineta, N493n4
Hunt, David M., N25n48, N155n157
Hunt, H. Keith, N264n94, N294n107
Hunt, James B., N155n153, N493n10
Hunt, S. D., N262n2
Hunt, Shelby D., N294n100
Hunter, Gary L., N68n31, N411n102, N469n47
Hustad, Thomas P., N439n50
Hutchings, Emma, N42n35
Hutchinson, J. Wesley, N70n96, N70n97, N98n125, N122n33, 124n91, N125n93, N125n107, N125n117, N126n127, N178n42, N208n4, N208n10, N208n11, N208n12, N208n15, N208n18, N211n108, N211n116, N265n123, N291n12, N292n19, N470n77
Hutchinson, P., N378n28
Hutter, Katja, N26n75
Hwang, Suein, N124n75
Hymowitz, Carol, N350n13

I

Iacobucci, Dawn, N25n56, N155n181, N294n91
Ibtissem, Mustapha Harzallah, N380n89
Idson, Lorraine Chen, N69n52
Imperia, Giovanna, N378n36
Inada, Miho, N379n54
Inman, J. Jeffrey, N25n54, N263n52, N264n90, N265n130, N265n131, N266n147, N266n148, N266n149, N266n156, N291n6, N291n7, N294n83, N326n103
Innis, Daniel E., N181n115
Invik, Lauren, N291n1
Irmak, Caglar, N293n63
Irwin, Julie R., N24n26, N236n3, N381n105, N408n12, N496n118
Irwin, Tanya, N126n129, N412n146
Isen, Alice M., N126n123, N126n124, N126n125, N411n106
Ives, Nat, N262n11
Iyengar, Sheena S., N265n133
Iyer, Easwar S., N24n16, N123n46, N211n124, N240n137

J

Jaccard, James T., N211n100
Jack, Louise, N27n118
Jackson, Michael, 349
Jacobs, Emma, N350n22
Jacobs, Randy D., N353n125, N353n148
Jacoby, Jacob N., N23n2, N24n15, N24n32, N27n103, N70n84, N97n109, N97n113, N97n117, N209n32, N210n94, N211n100, N212n133, N212n146, N212n148, N212n152, N212n155, N236n7, N240n146, N263n52, N263n62, N263n64, N296n149, N296n151, N324n21, N410n95
Jaffe, Lynn J., N352n90
Jain, Ambuj, N178n31
Jain, Dipak, N212n154
Jain, Sanjay, N380n85
Jain, Shailendra Pratap, N67n6, N69n51, N70n94, N123n54, N153n94, N153n95, N153n96
Jain, Subhish, N381n126, N381n138
James, Ben, N467n1
Janigan, Mary, N380n77

Janiszewski, Chris, N94n25, N94n26, N94n27, N95n49, N98n135, N122n25, N122n35, N123n51, N123n58, N151n36, N178n43, N178n52, N179n64, N179n68, N179n70, N210n67, N211n121, N212n150, N237n36, N262n22, N264n80
Janssen, Loes, 496
Jantsch, John, N26n76
Janus, Eunika, N209n45
Jass, Jeffrey, N126n121
Jaworski, Bernard J., N66n2, N66n4, N68n29, N70n95, N123n51, N153n112, N154n119, N155n162, N440n86
Jay, John C., N440n95
Jedidi, Kamel, N236n7
Jeffries, Scott, N262n2, N263n36
Jenkins, Roger L., N293n51
Jennings, Brandon, 317
Jennings, Lisa, N350n14, N496n101
Jensen, Thomas, D., N152n54
Jervis, Rick, N493n17
Jewell, Robert D., N26n73, N125n100, N154n126
Jiang, Lan, N262n21
Jim, Sung Youl, N123n51
Jingting, Shen, N381n112
Joachimsthaler, Erich A., N265n135, N410n96, N410n100
Johansson, Johny K., N98n137
Johar, Gita Venkataramani, N25n45, N69n65, N123n42, 125n113, N150n5, N155n170, N177n15, N236n7, N262n31, N326n90
John, A., 497n128
John, Deborah Roedder, N70n100, N70n105, N97n121, N122n30, N123n44, N123n48, N123n49, N123n54, N123n57, N124n91, N150n12, N212n144, N325n60, N325n62, N325n65, N351n44, N351n57, N380n64
Johnson, Allison R., N25n46, 56, N69n54
Johnson, David, N325n69
Johnson, Eric J., N70n97, N211n116, N211n128, N212n153, N236n5, N238n65, N238n66, N239n127, N262n5, N292n20
Johnson, Michael D., N155–156n182, N236n2, N239n121, N240n136, N292n34, N292n38, N293n52, N469n72
Johnson, Richard D., N98n125
Johnson, Scott, N323–324n12
Joiner, Christopher, N123n57, N124n80
Jolie, Angelina, 170
Jolly, J. P., N410n75
Jones, David A., N496n123
Jones, Dorothy, N408n16
Jones, Hadley, N327n115
Jones, Marilyn Y., N182n152
Jones, Sandra M., N98n143
Joseph, Sebastian, N182n169
Joy, Annamma, N468n34
Judd, Ben B., N328n155
Julian, Tiffany, N380n70
Jun, Sung Youl, N263n34
Jung, Carl, 396, N410n85
Jurkowitsch, Andreas, N208n24

K

Kacen, Jacqueline, N266n141
Kacker, Manish, N440n65

Kadet, Anne, N98n148

Kaelin, Lee, N212n158

Kahle, Lynn R., N180n97, N180n99, N180n102, N409n59, N409n60, N409n65, N410n80

Kahn, Barbara E., N95n57, N98n134, N265n127, N265n128, N265n132, N265n139, N326n90

Kahneman, Daniel, N124n74, N236n7, N237n50, N262n2, N262n3, N262n9, N265n127, N294n96

Kaikati, Andrew M., N328n151

Kakkar, P., N212n153

Kalb, Claudia, N496n97

Kalra, Ajay, N97n100

Kaltcheva, Velitchka D., N27n113

Kalyanaram, Gurumurthy, N125n109

Kalyanaraman, Sriram, N95n46

Kamakura, Wagner A., N292n35, 359, N377n3, N407n3, N410n81

Kamins, Michael A., N125n109, N152n79, N180n98, N328n160

Kaminski, Peter F., N328n155

Kammrath, Lara K., N410n86

Kamptner, N. Laura, N468n44, N470n95

Kane, Yukari Iwatani, N294n101

Kang, Dong Kyoon, N98n141

Kang, Yong-Soon, N151n45, N180n102

Kannan, P. K., N496n105

Kao, Chuan Fang, N156n186, N411n108

Kapferer, Jean-Noel, N67n12, N67n14, N67n22

Kaplan, Leon, N70n84

Kapoor, Kareena, 167

Karan, David, N495n85

Kardes, Frank R., N68n36, N98n125, N98n144, N98n147, N124n87, N125n109, N177n9, N208n29, N209n37, N237n37, N237n39, N292n22, N323n11, N328n137, N328n144, N411n109

Karp, Hannah, N378n5, N495n60

Karp, Lynn, N126n123

Karremans, Johan C., N97n97

Kary, Tiffany, N295n116

Kashyap, Rajiv K., N24n16

Kassarjian, Harold, N68n40, N68n41, N125n107, N150n2, N154n136, N154–155n152, N178n42, N179n72, N180n102, N208n4, N264n80, N325n59, N410n95, N438n4

Kasser, Tim, N380n87, N408n14

Kates, Steven, N352n92, N352n107

Kats, Rimma, N150n1

Katz, Donald R., N493n21

Katz, Elihu, N328n145

Kaufman, Betsy, 58

Kaufmann, Patrick J., N24n27

Kavanoor, Sukumar, N153n86

Keegan, Paul, N409n44

Keegan, Warren, N238n69, 366, 369, N379n60, N409n47

Keenan, Greg, N354n163

Kegerreis, Robert J., N439n47, N439n48

Keh, Hean Tat, N327n107

Keinan, Anat, N25n49, N291n5

Keiningham, Timothy L., N292n42, N292n45

Kellaris, James J., N23n5, N95n35, N95n40, N98n144, N98n147, N179n67, N181n129, N181n130, N494n22

Keller, Ed, N328n143

Keller, Kevin Lane, N71n123, N122n34, N123n47, N123n51, N123n51, 125n98, N179n58

Keller, Punam Anand, N150n11, N151n40, N209n38, N237n47, N237n51, N239n111, N240n147

Kelly, George A., N410n87

Kelly, Harold H., N410n88

Kelly, J. Patrick, N263n58

Kelly, J. Steven, N97n101

Kelly, Kathleen, N494n42, N495n85

Keltner, Dacher, N69n56, N239n103, N239n104

Kempf, Deanna S., N263n42, N291n13

Kennedy, Ellen, N123n53

Kennedy, John F., 459, 460

Kennedy, Patricia F., N409n65, N469n51

Kenning, Peter, N26n64

Kent, Ray, N94n18

Kent, Robert J., N95n35, N125n98

Keras, Michelle, N66n1

Kerber, Ross, N210n76

Kerin, Michelle R., N182n156

Kerin, Roger A., N27n105

Kermond, Clare, N27n96

Kernan, Jerome B., N154n135, N180n99, N293n72, N325n54, N328164, N469n55, N469n56, N469n60, N493n10

Key, W. B., N96n96

Khan, Shah Rukh, 127

Khan, Uzma, N69n59, N494n23

Khandelwal, Payal, N68n35

Khang, Hyoungkoo, N26n88

Khare, Adwait, N263n52

Khermouch, Gerry, N409n41

Ki, Eyun-Jung, N26n88

Kidwell, Blair, N154n144, N211n115

Kiecker, Pamela, N351n61

Kiesler, Tina, N154n152

Kilcoyne, Paula, N495n74

Kim, David, N180n93

Kim, Hyeong Min, N124n72, N494n28

Kim, John, N124n87, N208n29, N209n37, N323n11, N328n137, N328n144

Kim, Jooyoung, N154n117

Kim, JungKeun, N237n41

Kim, Kyeongheui, N123n48

Kim, Sara, N496n93

Kim, Susanna, N182n148

Kim, Tae-Hyung, N327n108

Kim, Young Chan, N471n114

Kincaid, D. Lawrence, N441n100

King, Brent M., N495n62

King, Carol Ann, N381n119

King, Martin Luther, Jr., 459, 460

King, Ronald H., N237n55

Kinnear, Thomas, C., N181n126, N265n130, N294n102, N327n120, N408n8, N496n115

Kinnear, Tim, N68n22, N180n99

Kintsch, Walter, N208n31

Kirby, Patrick N., N27n102

Kirk-Smith, M. S., N96n69

Kirmani, Amna, N152n51, N177n21, N323n4

Kirpalani, V. H. Manek, N380n78

Kirsner, Scott, N155n158

Kiselius, Jolita, N209n37

Kivetz, Ran, N25n49, N66n3, N237n49, N240n141, N240n148, N263n43, N264n73, N264n74, N291n5

Kjeldgaard, Dannie, N350n6

Klara, Robert, N156n188

Klein, Jill Gabrielle, 497n128

Klein, Noreen, N238n70

Kleine, Robert E., N469n55, N469n56, N469n60, N470n77, N471n114

Kleine, Susan Schultz, N153n111, N469n55, N469n56, N469n60, N470n77, N471n114

Klopp, Charlotte, N292n48

K'naan, 349

Knowles, E. S., N151n26

Knowles, Patricia, A., N126n123

Knox, George, N266n158

Kochhar, Rakesh, N377n2

Koenig, Frederick, N323n11

Koenig, Harold, N324n36, N324n37, 423

Kohler, Clemens F., N210n68

Kohli, Rajeev, N327n132

Koletsky, Susan, N293n74

Kominski, Robert, N380n70

Koo, Minjung, N177n6

Kooser, Amanda C., N379n55

Kopalle, Praveen K., N293n51

Koperski, Scott, N41n5

Kopun, Francine, N381n142

Korgaonkar, P. K., N266n152

Kornish, Laura J., N212n135

Koschate, Nicole, N292n37, N294n94, N295n114

Koslow, Scott, N353n133

Kosslyn, Stephen M., N121n6

Kosson, Nancy, N325n69

Kowitt, Beth, N122n36

Kozinets, Robert V., N42n21, 16, N27n115, N469n57, N470n108, N496n126

Krabbenhoft, Mary Ann, N177n7, N262n18

Krafft, Manfred, N24n18, N69n76, N438n12, N438n15

Kramer, Hugh E., N407n5

Kramer, Patricia, N352n83

Kramer, Thomas, N293n64

Krampf, Robert F., N379n41

Kranhold, Kathryn, N381n118, N440n79

Krieger, Katrin, N438n12

Krishna, Aradhna, N95n47, N96n81, N212n142, N264n87

Krishnamurthy, Parthasarathy, N152n69

Krishnan, H. Shanker, N27n104, N122n29, N123n53, N125n110, N125n116

Krishnan, S., N294n108

Krishnan, Shanker H., N125n99, N155n180, N156n185

Krisnamurthi, Lakshman, N379n41

Kristel, Orie V., N470n90

Krober-Riel, Werner, N95n46

Krohmer, Harley, N123n45, N156n183

Krol, Carol, N495n75

Kroll, Karen M., 203

Kropp, Fredric, N325n63

Kruglanski, Arie W., N97n105

Krugman, Dean M., N94n10

Krugman, Herbert E., N70n113, N178n54, N262n25

Kukar-Kinney, Monika, N210n90

Kuman, Anand, N125n99

Kumar, V., N441n97

Kunda, Ziva, N67n6

Kuntze, Ronald J., N411n111

Kuper, Adam, N468n45
Kurschmann, Thorston, N123n53
Kurt, Didem, N326n103
Kurzbard, Gary, N182n145
Kuss, Alfred, N209n32, N211n100
Kwak, Hyokjin, N327n129
Kyner, David B., N263n52, N263n62

L

LaBarbera, Priscilla, N70n113, N468n36
Labich, Kenneth, N380n81
Labroo, Aparna A., N69n62, N97n119, N122n21, N124n88, N153n114, N177n11, N179n75
Lach, Jennifer, N42n19
Lackman, Conway, N325n67, N378n27, N379n44
Laczniak, Russell N., N67n17, N325n66, N379n57
Laden, Rich, N26n85
Lady Gaga, 72, 445
Lafferty, Barbara A., N124n79, N151n45
La Ferla, Ruth, N467n5
Lakshmi-Ratan, R. A., N123n46
Lalwani, Ashok K., N352n104
Lam, Kevin, N327n108
Lam, Son K., N438n23
Lambert, Zarrel V., N264n86
Lambert-Pandraud, Raphaelle, N351n50
Lamberton, Cait Poynor, N210n85
Lambrianidou, Maria, N494n31
Lan, Huang, N26n81
Lanasa, John M., N325n67, N378n27, N379n44
Landers, Peter, N495n67
Landro, Laura, N412n147, N494n53
Landwehr, Jan R., N177n8, N262n19
Laneri, Raquel, N409n63
Lang, Bodo, N152n71
Langley, Kyle, N350n5
Lapersonne, N351n50
Laroche, Michel, N182n139, N323n7
LaRue, Asenath A., N325n69
Lascu, Dana-Nicoleta, N326n106, N327n123
Lastovicka, John L., N182n165, N265n135, N410n96, N410n100, N411n111, N470n79, N470n102
LaTour, Kathryn A., N123n61
LaTour, Michael S., N122n14, N122n19, N123n61, N182n150
LaTour, Stephen A., N293n51, N327n131
Lau-Gesk, Loraine, N121n2
Laufer, Daniel, N328n139
Laurent, Gilles, N67n12, N67n14, N67n22, N122n15, N351n50
Laverie, Debra A., N378n26
Law, Sharmistha, N71n122, N122n27, N126n122, N351n46
Lawrence, Dallas, N328n156
Lawson, Robert, N68n42, N123n54
Lawton, Christopher, N495n82
Lazarfeld, Paul F., N328n145
Learmonth, Michael, N412n145
Leatherman, Courtney, N494n50
Leavitt, Clark, N66n4, N67n22, N151–152n45, N152n60
LeBoeuf, Robyn A., N24n7, N24n11
Leclerc, France, N98n129, N212n145
Lee, Angela Y., N69n52, N97n119, N122n21, N125n97, 126n126, N153n114
Lee, Cheng-Wen, N26n82

Lee, Chol, N182n137, N409n53
Lee, Christina Kwai-Choi, N354n161
Lee, Dave, N266n161
Lee, David, N379n56
Lee, Euehun, N378n23
Lee, Jinkook, N351n59
Lee, Joo-Hyun, N94n11
Lee, Julie Anne, N266n141
Lee, Leonard, N237n46
Lee, Myung-Soo, N212n130
Lee, Seung Hwan (Mark), N441n99
Lee, Sheng-Hsien, N152n48
Lee, Taesik, N352n78
Lee, Wei Na, N468n33
Lee, Wendy, N328n165
Lee, Yih Hwai, N95n40, N125n115, N153n110, N154n120, N182n140, N264n106
Leek, Sheena, N25n57
Lehman, Donald L., N211n124
Lehmann, Donald R., N95n46, N97n114, N239n117, N293n51, N378n35, N438n9, N438n27
Leigh, James H., N155n159, N181n124, N181n135, N409n65, N468n23
Leigh, Thomas W., N67n20, N123n46
Leighfield, Jennifer, N409n68
Lemon, Katherine N., N123n47, N294n82
Leonard-Barton, Dorothy, N324n27, N441n98
Leonardi, Jean-Paul, N379n39
Leone, Robert P., N293n75
Leong, Siew Meng, N208n13, N263n38, N263n47, N265n116
Leonidou, Leonidas C., N379n39
Lepkowska-White, Lizbieta, N150n7
Lerman, Dawn, N353n137
Lerner, Jennifer S., N69n56, N239n103, N239n104
Lerouge, Davy, N379n42
Lesser, Gerald, S., N494n31, N494n46
Lessig, Parker, N326n100
Le Turck, Mark A., N24n31
Lev, Michael, N96n96
Levav, Jonathan, 233, N236n14
Levere, Jane L., N327n129
Levey, Richard H., N328n165
Levick, Richard S., N324n18
Levin, Irwin P., N98n125, N237n53
Levin, S., N494n31
Levine, Joshua, N182n146, N441n104
Levi-Strauss, Claude, N471n112
Levy, Piet, N354n167
Levy, Sidney J., N42n11, N68n40, N125n114, N296n152, N467n15
Lewis, Alan, N380n100
Lewis, S. K., N327n113
Lewisn, Jeffrey E., N323n10
Li, Hairong, N94n11, N210n79
Li, Jet, 72
Li, Jin, N328n148
Li, Naihe, N381n104
Li, Norman P., N351n63
Li, Shan, N94n13, N494n29
Li, Shibo, N24n27
Li, Wai-kwan, N98n137
Liao, Chi-Shun, N26n82
Libbon, Robert P., N469n50
Liberman, Nira, N124n82, N124n8
Licata, Jane W., N296n164

Lichtenstein, Donald, N24n27, N98n145, N264n80, N264n95
Lichtenstein, Meryl, N292n24
Lieb, Daniel, N212n138
Lieber, Ronald B., N42n9
Lim, Elison Ai Ching, N153n110, N154n120, N182n140
Lim, Jeen-Su, N379n47
Lin, Chien-Huang, N67n8
Lin, Chin-Lung, N152n48
Lin, Ying Ching, N67n8
Lindauer, Martin S., N121n9
Lindsay, Peter H., N95n59
Lindsey, Charles D., N125n116, N153n96
Lindstrom, Martin, N262n13
Lipkus, Isaac M., N237n51
Little, Morgan, N26n65
Liu, Wendy, N69n68, N265n134, 490, N496n120
Liu, Yong, N328n141
Liver, Jamie, 304
Lloren, Jason W., N407n1
Lloyd, B., N124n66
Locander, William B., N266n140
Lockhart, R. S., N122n23
Lodahl, Thomas L., N263n66
Loewenstein, George F., N42n31, N69n61
Loftus, Elizabeth F., N122n19, N125n105
Loftus, Tom, N42n23
Lohr, Steve, N42n8, N42n20, N496n111
Loken, Barbara, N123n48, N123n53, N123n57, N124n71, N124n80 N208n12, N209n40, N265n111
Lomax, Wendy, N94n12, N328n152
Lombardi, Candace, N152n65, N208n1
Lonial, Subhaus C., N211n116
Lonner, W., N124n89
Lopez, Jennifer, 249
Lorange, Frederic, N123n51
Lord, Kenneth R., N71n115, N151n25, N181n114, N296n173
Louie, Therese A., N181n113
Loureiro, Yuliya Komarova, N26n87
Lourosa, Cristina, N439n33
Love, Lisa, N470n77
Lowenstein, George, N294n96
Lowrey, Tina M., N68n42, N125n118, N296n163, N296n169, N326n81
Lowry, Tina M., N471n114
Luca, Michael, N328n147
Lucas, Louise, N154n138
Luce, Mary Frances, N152n70, N154n124, N177n16, N238n66, N238n75, N238n76, N238n77
Lukovitz, Karlene, N69n74, N153n100
Luminet, Olivier, N179n71
Luna, David, N97n118, N125n101, N353n137, N469n68
Lundstrom, William, N469n66
Luo, Xueming, N25n45, N266n154, N292n39, N292n44
Lurie, Nicholas H., N210n95, N212n156, N327n126
Lurie, Nicole H., N71n119, N210n75, N210n84
Lussier, Denis A., N238n66
Lutz, Richard J., N67n17, N124n71, N152n67, N155n167, N178n79, N208n12, N209n32, N263n35, N263n45, N264n78, N324n25, N325n61, N379n47

Lynch, John G., N25n61, N155n174, N178n42, N208n4, N208n11, N208n15, N208n27, N210n81, N210n82, N237n48
Lynch, John G., Jr., N125n92, N125n107, N210n73, N212n135, N262n8, N291n14, N440n57
Lynn, Michael, N68n31, N409n51
Lysonski, Steven, N178n77
Lyubomirsky, Sonja, N381n107, N408n11

M
MacAdams, Elizabeth, N378n36
Macarthur, Kate, N153n100
Machleit, Karen A., N153n111
Machrone, Bill, N439n34
MacInnis, Deborah J., N25n47, N26n63, N66n2, N66n4, N67n9, N67n16, N68n29, N70n95, N71n114, N94n27, N94n28, N95n35, N96n87, N121n5, N121n6, N122n34, N123n51, N151n27, N153n109, N153n111, N153n112, N154n119, N154n146, N155n162, N155n181, N155n182, N179n59, N208n14, N210n84, N236n11, N239n108, N239n111, N240n131, N263n34, N266n146, N294n96, N327n126, N440n86, N467n4, N469n69, N469n72
Mack, Chantal, N26n66
MacKenzie, Scott B., N66n4, N67n17, N94n24, N95n48, N155n167, N178n79, N208n26, N209n34
Macklin, M. Carole, N265n117, N494n32
Maclaran, Pauline, N23n3
Maclaughlin, Erin, N494n37
Mac-Laughlin, James, N70n113
Macleod, Ishbel, N179n62
Madden, Mary, N351n52
Madden, Thomas, N95n37, N179n67, N181n125, N181n133, N180n135, N439n41
Mader, Richard, N24n28, N439n38
Madrigal, Robert, N325n49
Magliore, Grey, N124n69
Maguire, Angela M., N125n111
Mahajan, Vijay, N24n14, N439n35, N440n66, N441n101
Maheswaran, Durairaj, N67n6, N69n51, N69n71, N70n94, N70n99, N98n139, N98n140, N153n95, N153n96, N292n25, N351n70, N408n14
Mahoney, Sarah, N210n83
Maimaran, Michal, N262n16
Main, Kelley, N293n61
Maio, Gregory, N151n16
Malar, Lucia, N123n45, N156n183
Malaviya, Prashant, N178n26, N178n45, N179n63
Malhortra, Naresh K., N42n29, N25n46, N69n54
Malkin, Elizabeth, N381n122
Mallozzi, Vincent M., N26n77
Malter, Alan J., N496n90
Malviya, Sagar, N352n7
Manchanda, Puneet, N210n69
Manchanda, Rajesh V., N25n50, N25n51, N326n95, N352n105
Mandel, Naomi, N24n36, N211n128, N237n29, N294n98, N380n92, N495n59
Mandese, Joe, N42n39

Mangleburg, Tamara, N325n72, N379n44
Mangold, W. Glyn, N211n116, N26n89
Mani, Gayathri, N122n34, N123n51
Manning, Kenneth C., N153n88, N153n92, N325n47, N439n41
Mano, Haim, N292n31, N292n32, N294n86
Manoj, Thomas, N27n102
Manolis, Chris, N408n10
Manosevitz, Main, N325n71
Manrai, Ajay, N327n131
Mantel, S. P., N23n5
Mantel, Susan Powell, N411n109
Mao, Huifang, N123n53, N123n54
Marcel, A. J., N97n98
Marcoux, Jean-Sebastian, N471n122
Markman, Arthur B., N68n27, N97n114, N438n9, N438n27
Marks, Lawrence J., N71n122, N178n50
Markus, Hazel B., N262n27
Marmorstein, Howard, N177n22, N208n27, N212n136, N264n91
Marsh, Mary, N497n130
Martin, Andrew, N26n85, N470n75
Martin, Brett A. S., N152n71, N354n161
Martin, Claude R., N155n159, N181n124, N181n135, N409n65
Martin, Craig A., N180n108, N353n142, N353n146
Martin, Hugo, N94n1
Martin, Ingrid W., N24n30, N68n42, N123n54
Martin, Mary, N494n33, N494n56
Martin, Michael, N350n9
Martinec, Radan, N408n39
Martinez, K., N470n97
Masanauskas, John, N350n12
Maslow, Abraham H., 49, 50, N68n28
Mason, Charlotte H., N71n119, N94n30
Mason, Marlys J., N25n58
Massy, William F., N263n66
Mata, Jutta, N379n42
Mathur, Anil, N378n23
Mathur, Pragya, N69n51
Mathwick, Charla, N67n19, N210n66
Matson, Tom, N325n69, N325n71
Matta, Shashi, N95n54, N124n68
Maxhamm, James G., III, N294n84, N295n119
May, F., N237n35
Mayer, Robert N., N407n5
Mayhew, Glenn, N264n79
Mazar, Nina, N494n25
Mazumdar, Tridib, N27n105
Mazursky, David, N209n32
Mazzon, Jose Alfonso, N407n3
McAlexander, James H., N324n36, N324n37, 423, N468n32, N470n77, N471n115
McAlister, Leigh, N265n126, N468n18, N493n21, N496n125, N496n127
McBride, Brad, N328n139
McCabe, Deborah Brown, N24n36, N96n77
McCarthy, Michael S., N26n86, N152n74, N179n72
McCarty, John A., N296n163, N296n169, N496n106
McClellan, Steve, N94n7
McClintock, Pamela, N66n1

McCracken, Grant, N95n34, 445, N467n2, N470n98, N470n101
McCrea, Bridget, N152n73
McFerran, Brent, N154n150
McGill, Ann L., N150n11, N151n40, N177n8, N239n111, N262n19, N293n57, N496n93
McGlone, Matthew S., N240n144
McGrath, Mary Ann, N68n40, N296n152, N471n114, N471n124
McGraw, A. Peter, N236n14, N326n90, N470n90
McGray, Douglas, N497n130
McGregor, Jena, N71n127, N154n127
McGroarty, Patrick, N381n123
McHugh, Kenna, N354n171
McInturf, Rayna, N440n53
McKay, Betsy, N496n94
McKeage, Kim, N326n98, N495n58
McKean, Michael, N327n129
McKee, Daryl, N296n164
McKinnon Gary F., N263n58
McLaughlin, Abraham, N380n99
McManamon, Mary K., N352n85
McNair, James, N295n129
McNatt, Robert, N26n80
McQuarrie, Edward F., N67n11, N95n43, N410n79
McQueen, Josh, N182n161
McSweeny, Frances K., N179n67, N179n68
McWilliam, Gil, N211n108
McWilliams, Jeremiah, N26n70
Mead, Kate, N70n92
Mead, Nicole L., N68n30
Medvec, Husted, N212n147
Mehraian, Albert, N265n136
Mehta, Raj, N468n34
Mehta, Ravi, N126n128
Meier, Robert J., N350n9
Meirick, Patric, N153n84
Mela, Carl F., N26n92, N264n89
Mellor, William, N350n1
Melnyk, Valentyna, N352n77
Meloy, Margaret G., N67n6, N180n83, N212n138, N212n147, N236n20
Meltzoff, A. N., N494n30
Menasco, Michael B., N379n40
Menon, Geeta, N25n45, N67n6, N70n93, N96n62, N182n158, N208n26, N208n28, N236n17, N237n30, N237n31, N237n54, N262n6, N266n142
Menon, Satya, N95n40, N265n132
Meredith, Geoffrey, N350n2
Mergenhagen, Paula, N468n38
Meringoff, Laurene Krasney, N494n31, N494n46
Merritt, Robert K., N495n84
Messer, M., N180n101
Messner, Claude, N68n27
Metcalf, Barbara L., N211n120
Metz, Rachel, N296n161
Meulenbert, T. G., N98n137
Meyer, Robert J., N238n66
Meyer, Tracy, N98n147
Meyers-Levy, Joan, N70n94, N94n25, N95n40, N125n117, N178n29, N181n121, N211n111, N236n8, N262n21, N351n60, N351n70, N351n71, N352n104
Meyvis, Tom, N98n135, N123n51, N123n58, N178n43, N178n52, N239n106, N24n8

Michaelidou, Nina, N67n15
Michaels, Daniel, N324n28
Michela, John L., N495n84
Mick, David Glen, N23n5, N24n33, N68n40,
    N95n43, N97n108, N208n31, N293n56,
    N410n89, N411n105, 420, N438n21,
    N440n59
Mickelson, Phil, 127
Micu, Camelia C., N180n95
Milberg, Sandra, N123n54
Milkman, Katherine L., N26n93
Miller, Claire Cain, N440n80
Miller, Cyndee, N182n146
Miller, Daniel, N468n45, N471n112, N471n118
Miller, Elizabeth G., N98n134
Miller, John A., N293n68
Miller, Lisa, N354n169
Miller, Ronald, N353n143
Miller, Steve, N123n50
Millet, Kobe, N211n123
Milliman, Ronald E., N27n112, N96n83,
    N96n85, N351n54
Mills, David, N496n121
Milmo, Cahal, N97n104
Milne, George R., N495n81
Min, Kyeong Sam, N178n29
Minahan, Dan, N155n168
Miniard, Paul W., N153n88, N153n92, N155n164,
    N180n84, N181n114, N181n115
Minis, Wevonneda, N352n75
Minshall, Bettie, N123n53
Miracle, Gordon E., N153n83, N327n127
Mirren, Helen, 72
Mishra, Arul, N97n106, N236n15, N266n155
Mishra, Himanshu, N27n108, N97n106,
    N266n155
Mishra, Sanjay, N237n41
Misra, Shekhar, N409n59
Misurell, Dennis, N123n53
Mita, Sujan, N25n48
Mitchell, Andrew A., N68n22, N70n96, N97n117,
    N122n31, N124n91, N124–125n92, N150n3,
    N155n173, N178n44, N179n74, N179n75,
    N179n76, N181n114, N182n149, N262n17,
    N291n14, N377–378n3
Mitchell, Deborah J., N493n10
Mitchell, James, N493n13
Mitchell, Linda G., N379n47
Mitchell, Robert L., N71n127
Mitchell, Susan, N352n96, N352n100
Mitchell, Vincent W., N70n82
Mithas, Sunhil, N292n45
Mitra, Anusre, N125n102
Mitra, Sabyasachi, N210n95
Mittal, Banwari, N66n2, N68n23
Mittal, Vikas, N67n21, N266n141, N291n3,
    N292n35, N293n76
Mittelstadt, R. A., N410n100
Mitts, Heather, 93
Miyazaki, Anthony D., N495n80
Mizerski, Richard W., N293n72, N328n137
Moberg, D. Paul, N327n111
Moe, Wendy W., N212n150, N327n130
Mogilner, Cassie, N265n133, N381n102, N408n11
Moisio, Risto, N27n115
Moisse, Katie, N409n64
Mokgata, Zweli, N439n49

Moldovan, Sarit, N328n153
Monga, Alokparna Basu, N123n48, N123n54
Monga, Ashwani, N237n52, N293n58
Monroe, Kent B., N27n103, N70n111, N98n145,
    N122n31, N212n133, N237n57, N264n80,
    N264n88, N295n111, N324n21, N327n113
Monroe, Marilyn, 460
Montiero, Kenneth, N126n123
Monty, Lynn, N209n39
Mooij, Mariele K., N238n69, 366, 369, N379n60,
    N409n47
Mookerji, Nivedita, N210n93
Mooradian, Todd A., N292n39
Moore, Danny L., N70n113
Moore, David J., N154n123, N353n151
Moore, Demi, 176
Moore, Elizabeth, N178n79, N325n61
Moore, Geoffrey, A., N439n32
Moore, Malcolm, N324n33
Moore, Marian Chapman, N154n148
Moore, Timothy E., N97n103
Moore, William L., N211n124
Moorman, Christine, N66n2, N211n115,
    N211n121
Moorman, Marjolein, N178n47
Moorthy, Sridhar, N211n104
Morago, Greg, N95n58
Morais, Richard C., N470n76
Morales, Andrea C., N96n80, N293n77,
    N470n100
Moran, Simone, N208n25
Moreau, C. Page, N70n112, N97n114, N154n128,
    N294n94, N438n9, N438n27
Morello, Carol, N378n21
Morgan, Carol M., N351n43
Morgan, Michael S., N351n72
Morgeson, Forrest V., III, N292n45
Morrin, Maureen, N96n73, N123n56, N295n110
Morris, Christopher, N467n1
Morris, Jon D., N154n117
Morris, K., N411n108
Morris, Katherine, N68n36
Morrison, Maureen, N236n27, N264n81
Morrison, Michelle, N327n129
Morrow, Geoff, N209n44
Morwitz, Vicki G., N27n99, N27n102, N155n175,
    N236n23, 497n128
Moschis, George, N324n46, N325n59, N325n67,
    N352n109, N378n23, N379n47, N493n19,
    N494n22
Moskin, Julia, N324n31
Moss, Michael, N351n49, N495n76
Mothersbaugh, David L., N124n91, N152n74
Mount, Ian, N468n39
Mourali, Mehdi, N323n7
Mowen, John C., N326n97, N469n67
Mowen, Robert, N327n113
Moyer, John, N154n137
Moylan, Martin, N351n42
Muehling, Darrel D., N67n17, N122n17,
    N178n30
Mueller, Barbara, N67n18, N151n44, N153n103
Mukherjee, Ashesh, N95n39, N95n41, N151n39,
    N181n131, N440n72
Mukhopadhyay, Anirban, N25n45, N69n65,
    N292n36, N325n64, N379n49
Muller, Eitan, N24n14, N440n66, N441n101

Mulvihill, Amanda, N350n10
Mun, K. C., N409n70
Munch, James M., N178n35, N182n167
Muniz, Albert M., Jr., N324n36, N324n39
Munsinger, Gary M., N379n41
Munson, J. Michael, N410n79
Murphy, David, N151n41, N350n8
Murphy, Patrick E., N495n72
Murray, H., N68n40
Murray, John P., N182n165
Murray, John P., Jr., N182n164
Murray, Keith B., N211n99
Murray, Kyle B., N69n66, N263n63
Murray, Noel M., N181n123
Murray, Sandra B., N181n123
Murtha, Brian R., N154n144
Mussen, Paul, N23n2
Mustafa, Isaiah, 176
Muthukrishnan, A. V., N27n99, N153n93,
    N153n101, N292n22
Myers, James H., N439n42

N

Na, Li, 143
Na, Peng, N496n105
Nadal, Rafael, 456
Nagel, Andrea, N377n1, N381n133
Nagle, Thomas T., N98n146
Nair, Manoj, N42n36
Nakamoto, Kent, N122n34, N123n51, N124n71,
    N325n51, N325n55
Nakamoto, Michiyo, N212n141
Narayandas, Das, N292n46
Nassauer, Sarah, N27n114, N95n58, N263n50,
    N266n157, N440n54
Nataraajan, Rajan, N69n52, N493n13
Naughton, John, N496n102
Nayakankuppam, Dhananjay, N27n108,
    N97n106, N155n177, N236n15
Nayankuppum, D. J., N153n89
Naylor, Rebecca Walker, N98n133, N210n85,
    N265n110, N408n36, N495n71, N496n118
Nedungadi, Prakash, N180n82, N208n10,
    N208n12, N208n18
Needleman, Sarah E., N291n1
Neff, Jack, N122n18, N182n169, N208n6,
    N264n71, N379n38, N408n38, N496n108,
    N496n113
Neijens, Peter C., N178n47
Nelson, Andy, N69n69
Nelson, James E., N181n126
Nelson, Kim A., N407n4
Nelson, Leif D., N239n106, N24n8
Nelson, Michelle R., N151n16, N352n105
Nepomuceno, Vinhal, N182n139
Ness, Thomas E., N409n55
Netemeyer, Richard G., N42n38, N178n77,
    N264n95, N294n84, N295n119, 314,
    N326n96, N327n111, N327n124, N411n110
Netzer, Oded, N66n3, N240n141
Neumann, Marcus M., N210n67
Newell, Alan, N262n2
Newell, Stephen J., N151n45
Newman, Joseph W., N211n118
Newman, Katherine S., N380n79
Newtown, Cam, 93
Ng, Irene C. L., N236n13

Ng, Sharon, N123n59, N124n73, N352n102
Ngumah, Festus E., N410n101
Nicholls, Charles, N210n91
Nicholls, Walter, N95n50
Nicolao, Leonardo, N381n105, N408n12
Nicosia, Francesco M., N407n5
Nieburg, Oliver, N323n1
Niedrich, Ronald W., N124n78, N152n55, N180n110
Nielsen, Jesper H., N94n30
Nissenbaum, Stephen, N471n112
Noel, Hayden, N122n26
Noerager, Jon P., N410n91
Nolan, Catherine A., N211n120
Nonaka, Ikujiro, N98n137
Nooyi, Indra, 472–473
Norberg, Patricia A., N495n79
Nord, Walter A., N263n39
Nordhielm, Christie L., N179n60
Norman, A. T., N23n5
Norman, Donald A., N95n59
Norton, David A., N210n85
Noseworthy, Theodore J., N441n99
Notani, Arti Sahni, N151n33
Novak, Thomas P., N410n81
Novemsky, Nathan, N69n64, N294n92, N294n97
Nowak, Glen, N495n78
Nowlis, Stephen M., N24n36, N71n116, N96n77, N151n37, N237n33, N240n138, N294n98, N411n103
Nudd, Tim, N154n151, N180n103
Nunes, Joseph C., N27n107, N25n44, N68n47, N69n48, N264n84, N493n16
Nussbaum, Bruce, N408n16
Nuttavuthisit, Kristtinee, N27n115
Nyer, P. U., N25n46
Nyffenegger, Bettina, N123n45, N156n183

O
Obermeier, Dirk, N24n27
Obermiller, Carl, N71n122, N178n49, N181n113
O'Connell, Vanessa, N495n82
O'Curry, Sue, N237n41
Odekerken-Schröder, Gaby, N295n124
Ody, Elizabeth, N381n117
Ofir, Chezy, N262n8, N293n60
Ogden, Harold, N493n4
O'Guinn, Thomas C., N324n36, N378n36, 476, N493n13, N493n14
Ohno, Apolo, 176
Okada, Erica Mina, N24n6, N24n37, N239n101, N296n156
Oliva, Terrence A., N67n20
Oliveira, Michael, N266n161
Oliver, James M., N292n39
Oliver, Richard L., N155n161, N292n31, N292n32, N292n49, N293n65, N293n66, N294n79, N294n81, N294n86, N294n89, N294n93
Olney, Thomas J., N155n163
Olsen, Anton, N150n12
Olshavsky, Richard W., N211n106, N211n107, N236n16, N238n66, N262n30, N293n68, N327n119
Olson, Clark D., N378n10
Olson, Elizabeth, N122n24
Olson, James M., N151n16, N177n20

Olson, Jerry C., N27n103, N67n10, N67n11, N67n22, N95n31, N97n112, N151n19, N178n29, N179n75, N179n76, N181n114, N293n51, N378n30, N379n45, N409n73
Omar, Yusuf, N467n1
O'Neal, Charles R., N438n28
Onkvisit, Sak, N96n79, N97n115, N97n116, N182n157, N326n85, N354n162, N379n39, N379n61, N409n46, N471n120
Ono, Yumiko, N410n83
Oosterhouse, Carter, 306
Ordabayeva, Nailya, N95n55, N380n86
O'Reilly, Kelly, N152n66
O'Reilly, Lara, N208n21
Orsingher, Chiara, N295n115
Ostrom, Thomas, N94n24
Ostrove, Joan M., N380n67
Ostrow, Joanne, N126n129
Oswald, Laura R., N467n8, N468n33
Otnes, Cele C., N326n81, 464, N467n4, N467n9, N468n40, N471n114
Ott, Bryant, N350n3
Ottman, Jacquelyn, N124n67
Ouellet, Jean-Francois, N352n111
Oyserman, Daphna, N352n103
Ozanne, Julie L., N25n60, N211n113
Ozersky, Josh, N238n64
Özil, Mesut, 303

P
Pace, Gina, N69n72, N293n71
Padgett, Dan, N154n118
Padgett, Marty, N26n71
Padgett, Sonya, N96n82
Paek, Hye-Jin, N182n156
Page, Christian M., N237n62, N381n140
Page, Karen L., N122n32, N469n55
Painter, John, N496n114
Painton, Scott, N211n119
Paivio, Allan, N121n6
Palan, Kay M., N351n69, N379n50
Palmer, Kaija, N494n43
Palmeri, Christopher, N470n76
Pan, Yigang, N237n41
Pandelaere, Mario, N211n123
Pandelaere, Mario, N409n66
Papatla, Purushottam, N27n105
Parasuraman, A., N264n82, N293n53
Parekh, Rupal, N97n110, N470n110
Parent, Michael, N323n9
Park, Bernadette, N209n40
Park, C. Whan, N26n63, N66n2, N67n13, N67n16, N68n29, N71n114, N95n35, N96n87, N123n46, 123n51, N123n54, N124n91, N151n27, N153n109, N154n115, N155n181, N155n182, N180n120, N211n116, N211n124, N239n108, N239n123, N239n127, N240n131, N240n137, N263n34, N294n96, N326n100, N379n41, N438n5, N440n86, N469n55, N469n69, N469n72
Park, Daniel, N239n123
Park, Ji Kyung, N123n44
Park, Jong-Won, N153–154n114, N209n41, N237n41
Park, Kiwan, N150n5, N153n89
Park, Se-Bum, N178n26

Paronen, Lars, N328n162
Parsons, Amy L., N181n127
Parsons, Russell, N495n87
Pascal, Vincent J., N122n17, N178n30
Passyn, Kirsten, N25n48, N155n156
Patrick, Vanessa M., N26n63, N124n88, N181n116, N239n108, N266n146, N294n96
Patterson, Paul G., N293n66
Patton, Leslie, N441n104
Patton, W. E., N237n55
Paul, Michael, N25n55, N294n90
Paul, Noel C., N493n8
Paul, Pamela, N350n34, N378n12, N378n16, N468n40, N495n78
Pavelchak, Mark A., N182n167, N265n111
Pavia, Teresa, N25n58, N98n129
Pavio, Allan, N291n11
Pavlika, Holly, N350n38
Pavlov, Ivan, 165
Payne, John, N212n149, N236n4
Payne, John W., N236n3, N237n41, N237n59, N238n65, N238n66, N238n76, N240n136, N263n32
Peacock, Peter, N264n94
Peak, Krystal, N178n36
Pearce, Susan M., N470n97
Pearce, Tralee, N350n26
Pearo, Lisa Klein, N323n6, N326n87
Peat, Nancy C., N293n51
Pechmann, Cornelia, N70n88, N98n145, N152n81, N152–153n81, N153n87, N153n91, N153n98
Peck, Joann, N96n75, N96n76, N124n80
Penaloza, Lisa, N352n109, N353n116, N407n6, N467n3, N496n125
Pendleton, Glenna, N469n66
Penenberg, Adam L., N42n32, N42n34, N409n45
Penn, David, N97n102
Pennington, Sylvia, N150n1
Peracchio, Laura A., N125n101, N152n75, N178n29, N211n110, N353n137, N469n68, N493n6, N493n7
Percy, Larry, N125n95
Pereira, Arun, N353n127
Perilloux, Carin, N351n63
Perkins, Andrew, N180n104
Perner, Lars, N328n160
Perrault, William D., N237n35
Perry, Katy, 75
Pervin, Lawrence A., N410n88
Pessemier, Edgar A., N151n28, N238n73
Pessin, Jaime Levy, N69n78
Peter, Anil C., N264n90
Peter, J. Paul, N69n79, N70n84, N263n39
Peters, Cara Okleshen, N327n129
Peters, Rik, N496n116
Peterson, Laurie, N264n77
Peterson, Robert A., N182n155, N439n35
Peterson, Robin T., N351n55
Peterson, Tim, N496n104
Petrecca, Laura, N182n151
Petrella, F., N494n31
Petros, T., N494n31
Petroshius, Susan M., N98n145, N180n97, N264n80

Petrosky, Alfred, N438n10, N440n89, N440n91
Petrova, Petia K., N151n40, N380n92
Petty, Richard E., N66n4, N68n22, N68n36, N69n71, N94n24, N150n2, N150n5, N150n9, N151n22, N151n24, N152n52, N152n67, N154n131, N155n169, N156n186, N177n3, N180n96, N180n102, N411n108
Pham, Michel Tuan, N125n113, N150n11, N151n40, N153n108, N154, 121, N236n6, N239n101
Phelps, Joseph, N495n78
Phillips, Barbara A., N467n4
Phillips, Diane M., N294n86
Pick, A. D., N124n89
Pickett, Charles M., N181n126
Pickrell, Jacqueline E., N122n19
Pierleoni, Allen N328n146
Pieters, Rik, N24n9, N25n49, N26n87, N26n90, N41n4, N42n30, N69n55, N94n22, N94n23, N95n44, N95n51, N95n52, N97n107, N125n98, N125n104, N125n108, N239n107, N291n7, N296n166, N296n171, N327n133
Pietz, John, N264n97
Piirto, Rebecca, N409n49
Pillutla, Madan M., N124n64
Pinel, Elizabeth C., N294n96
Pinkleton, Bruce E., N153n85
Pitt, David, N264n101
Pitt, Leyland F., N323n9
Pitts, Robert E., N182n150, N237n41, N409n55, N409n65, N409n69, N409n73
Plank, Kevin, 93
Plassmann, Hilke, N42n29
Pleyers, Gordy, N179n71
Plummer, Joseph T., N122n38, 402
Pocheptsova, Anastasiya, N71n121
Pofeldt, Elaine, N263n61
Pogue, 302
Pokhrel, Pallav, 305
Polk, Thad A., N42n31
Pollay, Richard W., N208–209n31, N379n44, N409n70, N494–495n56, N495n84, N496n127
Polli, Rolando, N439n52
Pollio, Howard R., N266n140
Polman, Paul, 23
Pons, Frank, N323n7
Pope, Nigel K. Li, N181n132, N182n142
Portis, Bernard, N210n96
Posavac, Steven S., N98n144, N98n147, N153n94, N237n38, N237n39, N438n25
Poulsen, Lance, N439n37
Poulter, Sean, N182n141
Powell, Martha C., N155n173, N178n38
Power, Christopher, N379n46
Power, Mick, N411n106
Poynor, Cait, N293n59
Pracejus, John W., N150n11, N236n6
Prandelli, Emanuela, N438n16
Prasad, Ashutosh, N381n126, N408n30
Pratkanis, Anthony R., N97n101
Prelec, Drazen, N42n31
Presley, Elvis, 459, 460, 461
Price, Linda L., N25n40, N25n59, N67n20, N121n5, N121n6, N180n95, N236n11, N239n111, N265n137, N324n21, N324n25, N324n26, N324n46, N327n120, N440n82,

N440n87, N468–469n46, N470n103, N496n125
Pride, William M., N180n99
Priester, Joseph R., N150n5, N152n46, N153n89, N155n177, N155n182
Prince, Russ A, N328n155
Principe, Victor, N71n115
Prior, Molly, N377n1, N381n133
Pritchard, Jennifer, N262n1
Pruyn, Th. H., N151n26
Puccinelli, Nancy M., N180n94
Pullig, Chris, N42n38, N296n164
Pullins, Ellen Bolman, N264n72
Punj, Girish, N123n47, N152n72, N211n114, N211n100, N211n106, N211n129, N239n125, N493n18, N493n20, N493n21, N494n22
Puri, Radhika, N266n153
Putnam, Mandy, N378n33
Puto, Christopher, P., N236n2, N237n41, N237n55, N262n5

Q

Qualls, William J., N353n151, N378n36, N379n40
Qui, Cheng, N264n106
Quick, Rebecca, N495n63
Quinton, Brian, N177n1
Quittner, Jeremy, N71n127

R

Rachman, S., 397
Radiohead, 442–443
Rafaely, Vered, N208n25
Raghubir, Priya, N24n21, N27n99, N67n8, N69n67, N70n93, N95n47, N208n26, N208n28, N237n30, N262n6, N263n51, N264n90, N264n92
Raghunathan, Rajagopal, N98n133, N265n110, N326n80, N408n36, N495n71
Ragsdale, E. K. Easton, N379n41
Raj, S. P., N27n105
Raju, P. S., N68n37, N211n116, N266n152, N410n100, N439n41
Raju, Sekar, N156n184
Ram, S., N438n19, N440n93
Ramanathan, Suresh, N25n45, N67n6, N179n75, N236n17, N237n31, N265n110, N266n142
Ramaswami, S., N153n93
Ramaswamy, Venkatram, N98n138
Ramesh, M., N291n1
Rampl, Linn Viktoria, N26n64
Rangan, Kasturi, N411n113
Ransom, Diana, N494n26
Rao, Akshay R., N98n145, N352n102, N378n32
Rao, Ambar, N179n59
Rao, Ram C., N71n122
Rappaport, Stephen D., N153n107
Ratchford, Brian T., N211n100, N211n104, N212n130
Rathbone, John Paul, N379n54
Ratner, Rebecca K., N265n127, N265n128
Ratneshwar, S., N23n5, N24n33, N96n73, N98n145, N153n91, N153n105, N178n24, N208n16, N208n31, N237n41, N440n64
Raucem Shayndi, N381n113
Raven, Bertram, N326n102, N327n123
Ravid, S. Abraham, N328n138

Rawn, Catherine D., N68n30
Ray, Michael, N71n122, N122n25, N154n116, N155n154, N180n88, N262n26
Rayman, Dale M., N379n41
Raymond, Joan, N378n13
Reardon, Marguerite, N296n177
Reckard, E. Scott, N354n159
Reed, Americus, II, N68n24, N15n3, N150n11, N151n13, N151n16, N151n32, N325n50, N326n86, N326n99, N327n123, N468n17, N469n59
Reeves, Bradley, N24n19
Reibling, Ellen Thomas, N70n88
Reilly, Michael D., N293n67, N296n162, N468n33
Reily, Stephen, N350n35
Rein, Shaun, N266n159
Reinartz, Werner J., N155n175
Reinberg, Steven, N496n96
Reingen, Peter, N154n135, N180n99, N324n46, N325n51, N325n55, N326n79, N327n125, N328n104, N328n140, N328n164
Reingold, Jennifer, N377n1
Reinhard, M., N180n101
Reisinger, Don, N440n55
Reiss, Craig, N182n169
Reitinger, Gail, N208n31
Reitz, Stephanie, N295n120
Rethans, Arno, N71n122, N123n46, N178n50
Rever, Rolf, N240n144
Reynolds, Dean, N468n16
Reynolds, Fred D., N439n35
Reynolds, Isabel, N494n52
Reynolds, Jonathan, N42n21
Reynolds, Mike, N353n126
Reynolds, Thomas J., 394, N409n73, N410n75
Rice, Ronald, N95n40
Rich, Stuart, N381n126, N381n138
Richard, Lawrence C., N411n114
Richard, Marie-Odile, N182n139
Richard, Orlando, N27n100
Richardson, Alan, N121n7
Richardson, Whit, N494n43
Richins, Marsha L., N67n11, N292n35, N294n102, N295n127, N324n22, N327n135, N408n9, N408n15, N408n16, N410n78, N410n92, 458, N468n43, N469n70, N469n71, N470n74, N493n9, N494n56
Richon, John P., N409n73
Rick, Scott I., N379n43
Rickey, Carrie, N66n1
Ridgway, Nancy M., N67n20, 202, N210n97, N265n130, N265n137
Rigaux, Benny P., N378n33
Rigdon, Edward, N67n19, N210n66
Rigdon, Joan E., N211n109
Riggs, Larry, N328n165
Rimer, Barbara K., N237n51
Rindfleisch, Aric, N408n13, N408n14, N408n40
Ringberg, Torsten, N295n124, N469n68
Rink, David R., N328n155
Ritchie, J. B., N95n60
Roan, Shari, N495n68
Robbins, Carla A., N408n16
Roberts, Daniel, N26n81
Roberts, James A., N408n10, N493n14
Roberts, Kristal, N325n58
Roberts, Mary Lou, N379n45

Roberts, Scott D., N380n80, N468n32, N470n77, N470n83, N470n84, N470n97, N471n115
Robertson, D. H., N266n149
Robertson, Thomas S., N125n107, N150n2, N154n136, N154–155n152, N178n42, N179n72, N180n102, N208n4, N264n80, N265n126, N325n59, N438n4, N438n7, N439n37, N439n42, N439n46, N439n48, N439n52, N440n66, N441n96, N441n97
Robinson, E. Doyle, N263n58
Robinson-Jacobs, Karen, N66n1
Rochan, John P., 394
Rochberg-Halton, Eugene, N469n47, N470n89, N470n91
Rochford, Linda, N123n53
Rockoff, Jonathan D., N152n46
Rodder-John, Debbie, N471n114
Rodriguez, Regina, N156n186
Roe, Keith, N409n66
Roedder, Deborah, N97n111
Roehm, Harper A., N25n52, N264n72
Roehm, Michelle L., N25n52, N70n101, N264n72, N328n161
Roering, Kenneth J., N380n90
Roese, Neal J., N291n8
Rogers, Carl R., N410n87
Rogers, Everett M., 422, N438n4, N439n31, N439n37, N439n39, N440n69, N440n70, N440n85, N440n94, N441n100, N441n103
Rogers, Martha, N96n96
Rogers, Stuart, N96n95
Roggeveen, Anne L., N125n103, N153n97, N177n15
Rohn, Andrew J., N210n68
Rokeach, Milton, N407n2, N408n7
Romeo, Jean B., N178n29, N180n84
Romer, Daniel, N182n161
Rook, Dennis W., N68n40, N265–266n140, N265n151, N266n153, N325n75
Rooney, Jennifer, N151n38
Roos, Inger, N292n38
Root-Shafer, Teri, N324n22
Rosa, José Antonio, N496n90
Rosbergen, Edward, N94n22, N95n52
Rosch, Eleanor, N124n66, N124n70, N124n88
Rosch, Marita, N291n2
Rose, Derrick, 75
Rose, Gregory M., N325n63
Rose, Kevin, 176
Rose, Randall L., N24n28, N67n20, N68n26, N153n88, N153n92, N155n164, N325n47, N326n85, N326n96, N326n106, N327n123, N410n93, N410n97
Roselius, Ted, N263n53
Rosen, Dennis L., N97n101, N265n122, N327n119, N378n35
Rosenbloom, Stephanie, N263n56
Rosenzweig, Mark, N23n2
Ross, Ivan, N294n106
Ross, William T., Jr., N98n127, N293n76
Rossiter, John R., N125n95, N237n41
Rossman, Marlene, N353n115
Rotfeld, Herbert J., N155n159
Roth, Bryan, N208n30, N238n79
Roth, Robert, N68n39
Rothbart, Myron, N292n24

Rothschild, Michael L., N67n12, N67n20, N68n22, N125n98, N263n39, N263n44, N263n55, N468n18, N493n21, N496n125, N496n127
Rottenstreich, Yuval, N238n67, N239n100
Rouner, Donna, N325n70
Roux, Elyette, N123n51
Rozin, Paul, N326n76
Rubenstein, C., N381n106
Rubinstein, Dana, N440n67
Rucker, Derek D., N155n178, N380n97
Rudd, Melanie, N381n102, N408n11
Rudmin, Floyd, N408n16, N468n34, N470n85, N470n93, N470n107
Rudnick, Tamar, N265n133
Rudolph, Thomas, N264n75
Ruggless, Ron, N23n1, N350n1
Rui, Juliet, N181n121
Rumpel, Joan H., N350n9
Rungfapaisarn, Kwanchai, N381n142
Runte, Mary, N496n123
Runyon, Kenneth E., N68n41
Rusli, Evelyn M., N438n8
Russell, C. A., N23n5
Russell, Cheryl, N350n32
Russell, Cristel Antonia, N126n120
Russell, Gary J., N211n120
Russell, James, N265n136
Russo, J. Edward, N67n6, N70n97, N211n120, N212n145, N212n147, N212n153, N236n5, N236n20, N239n125, N239n127, N292n20
Rust, Roland T., N123n47, N440n71, N496n105
Ruth, Julie A., N123n51, N326n81, 464
Ruvio, Ayalla A., N42n29
Ryan, Jake, N380n75
Ryan, Joan, N495n82
Ryan, John C., N210n87
Ryu, Gangseog, N324n19

S
Sackrey, Charles, N380n75
Saegert, Joel, N97n101
Said, Carolyn, N94n20
Salas, Randy A., N438n26
Saliba, Clare, N210n86
Salter, Michael D., N495n85
Salvail, Andre, N353n121
Sampson, Hannah, N262n24
Samu, Sridar, N125n110
Sanbonmatsu, David M., N237n37, N237n38, N237n39
Sanburn, Josh, N96n72
Sapong, Emma, N351n58
Sarel, Dan, N122n25, N153n90
Sarno, David, N94n13
Sass, Erik, N350n19
Sattler, Henrik, N123n53
Sauer, Abe, N97n123, N121n1
Sauter, John M., N495n62
Sawyer, Alan G., N122n25, N122n26, N264n78
Sayid, Ruki, N212n157
Sazky, Tom, N496n109
Scalf, Abby, N151n15
Scgneider, W., N94n21
Schab, Frank P., N96n70
Schaffer, David R., N152n53

Schaller, Mark, N27n98
Schaninger, Charles M., N211n118, N354n162, N378n3, N378n31, N380n67
Schau, Hope Jensen, N324n39, N351n48, N469n62
Scheibehenne, Benjamin, N210n78, N239n118, N379n42
Schemper, T., N96n67
Schettler, Renee, N408n37
Schewe, Charles D., N350n2
Schiffman, Leon G., N410n101
Schillewaert, Niels, N438n23
Schindler, Robert M., N27n102, N122n17, N469n51
Schkade, David A., N294n96
Schlossberg, Howard, N353n141
Schlosser, Ann E., N67n19, N125n106, N239n113, N326n82, N327n136
Schmidt, Gregory, N469n52
Schmitt, Bernd H., N98n129, N124n89, N155n182, N292n33
Schmitt, Philipp, N324n20, N327n110
Schmitz, Laura, N262n1
Schneider, Kenneth C., N42n43
Schneier, Wendy L., N179n61
Scholer, Abigail, N410n86
Schonfeld, Erick, N440n60
Schouten, John W., N324n36, N324n37, 423, N468n26, N468n32, N470n77, N471n115
Schreier, Martin, N438n16
Schreiner, Bruce, N265n120
Schrift, Rom Y., N66n3
Schul, Yaacov, N237n58
Schultz, E. J., N178n80, N208n17, N381n110
Schultz, Teri, N496n103
Schumann, David W., N155n169, N177n3, N179n61, N294n95
Schutte, Reinhard, N26n64
Schwartz, Evan I., N182n151
Schwartz, John, N124n77
Schwartz, Shalom H., N407n3, N408n7
Schwarz, Norbert, N98n128, N122n16, N123n43, N177n2, N208n28, N240n143, N240n144, N240n145, N294n96
Schweda, Anika, N94n9
Schweitzer, George, N328n150
Sciglimpaglia, Donald, N211n118, N378n30
Scott, Carol A., N212n144
Scott, Linda, N467n4, N468n41
Seader, Stuart, N122n38
Searle-Chatterjee, Mary, N471n118
Sebastian, Simone, N296n175
Seetharaman, P. B., N26n67, N263n54
Seiders, Kathleen, N292n41
Seiler, Christine A., N96n96
Sela, Aner, N265n134
Semansky, Matt, N156n188
Semenik, Richard, N496n114
Sen, Sankar, N237n41, N294n100, N494n28, 497n128
Sen, Subrata K., N264n94
Sengupta, Jaideep, N123n42, N124n85, 125n119, N125n118, N154n142, N155n170, N155n172, N177n4, N180n107, N182n143, N212n137, N470n94
Sengupta, Sanjit, 196
Sentis, Keith, N178n29

Seth, Dilasha, N210n93
Sethi, Rajesh, N438n5
Sethuraman, Raj, N212n154
Severman, Ben, N380n91
Severson, Kim, N98n150
Sewall, Murphy S., N122n25
Sewell, Dan, N377n1
Seymour, Daniel, N378n28
Shahin, Kimary N., N95n60
Shaich, Ron, 2
Shalker, Thomas, N126n123
Shambora, Jessica, N70n90
Shamdasani, Prem N., N353n133
Shang, Jen, N469n59
Shank, Roger C., N123n46
Shapiro, Stewart A., N25–26n62, N94n27,
    N94n28, N94n30, N208n14, N209n33,
    N240n131
Sharapova, Maria, 161
Sharma, Arun, N264n91
Sharma, Shailaja, N208n8
Sharma, Subhash, N124n78
Sharp, Lauriston, N441n102
Shavitt, Sharon, N68n42, N151n16, N178n29,
    N326n82, N352n104
Shaw, Hillian, N352n89
Shaw, Hollie, N182n169
Shaw, John J., N96n79, N97n115, N97n116,
    N182n157, N326n85, N354n162, N379n39,
    N379n59, N379n61, N409n46, N471n120
Shayon, Sheila, N266n161, N350n18
Sheehan, Kim Bartel, N495n74
Shehryar, Omar, N25n48, N155n157
Sheikh, Aness, N121n7, N121n9
Sheldon, Kennon M., N380n87, N408n14
Sheldon, Peter S., N470n77
Shellenbarger, Sue, N408n25
Sheluga, David A., N97n109
Shen, Luxi, N381n104
Sheng, Shibin, N154n144
Shepherd, C. David, N27n100
Sheppard, Blair H., N151n31, N238n73
Sherman, Elaine, N239n129
Sherman, Steven J., N292n23
Sherr, Ian, N294n101, N439n51
Sherrell, Daniel, N67n20, 202, N210n97,
    N409n65
Sherry, John B., N296n152
Sherry, John F., N27n115, N68n40, N94n27,
    N122n34, N296n160, N468n32, N470n81,
    N470n83, N470n84, N470n97, N470n104,
    N470n106, N471n113, N471n118, N471n124
Sheth, Jagdish, N42n29, N211n118, N324n25,
    N354n166, N378n28, N378n30, N438n19,
    N439n43, N440n93, N468n22, N468n36
Shiffrin, R. M., N94n21
Shih, Chuan-Fong, N439n36
Shimp, Terence A., N154n139, N179n68,
    N179n72, N179n75, N264n89
Shin, Jiwoong, N264n83
Shin, Sally, N381n135
Ship, Shannon, N123n53
Shirouzu, Norihiko, N440n95
Shiv, Baba, N24n12, N25n45, N42n29, N71n116,
    N152n51, N236n12, N237n59, N239n103,
    N263n32, N265n109, N293n62
Shlachter, Barry, N96n86

Shocker, Allan D., N123n51, N208n16, N237n41
Shoemaker, F. Floyd, N440n94
Shoenwald, Marvin, N412n144
Shrum, L. J., N125n118, N296n163, N296n169,
    N353n151, N496n106
Shu, Suzanne B., N24n9
Shulman, David, N470n86
Siddarth, S., N94n10, N495n84
Siebler, Frank, N152n77
Siegel, Michael, N495n84
Silberman, William, N97n113, N210n94
Silva, Jill Wendholt, N408n34
Silverstein, Barry, N178n25
Simhan, T. E. Rana, N291n1
Simison, Robert L., N323n5
Simmons, Carolyn J., N27n95, N42n38, N98n149
Simon, Herbert A., N154n137, N262n2
Simon, Leonard S., N441n101
Simonin, Bernard, N123n51
Simons, Marlise, N42n40
Simonsohn, Uri, N152n49
Simonson, Itamar, N69n73, N151n37, N177n13,
    N212n149, N236n4, N237n32, N237n40,
    N237n42, N237n49, N238n65, N238n71,
    N239n110, N240n148, N264n73, N264n74,
    N293n60, N411n103
Sindhav, Birud, N438n13
Singer, Jed, N177n1
Singer, Natasha, N262n1
Singh, Jagdip, N294n107, N295n112
Singh, Leher, N326n76
Singh, Nitish, N353n127
Singh, S. N., N182n166
Singh, Siddharth S., N24n18, N69n76, N438n15
Singh, Surendra N., N97n101, N178n48,
    N182n165
Sinha, Indrajit, N27n105
Sinha, Rajiv K., N439n40
Sink, Mindy, N494n48
Sirdeshmukh, Deepak, N125n98, N181n115
Sirgy, M. Joseph, N68n23, N469n56, N469n63
Sismeiro, Caterina, N42n22, N210n74, N211n126
Sivararman, Anuradha, N152n69
Skelton, Helen, N496n122
Skid, Nathan, N408n34
Skiera, Bernd, N324n20, N327n110
Skinner, B. F., N410n94
Slattery, Laura, N126n129
Slayter, Mary Ellen, N380n73
Slotegraaf, Rebecca J., N294n83
Slutsky, Irina, N24n25, N353n139
Small, Deborah A., N154n149, N379n43
Smeesters, Dirk, N495n59
Smit, Edith G., N178n47
Smith, Aaron, N439n49
Smith, Amy K., N295n125
Smith, Daniel C., N27n104, N123n46, N211n124,
    N240n137, N438n5
Smith, Daniel P., N98n150
Smith, Ellis, N293n78
Smith, Jamie, 304
Smith, Karen H., N292n49, N293n50
Smith, Kirk H., N96n96
Smith, Melvin T., N409n55
Smith, N. Craig, N496n125, 497n128
Smith, Pamela K., N26n62, N177n5, N262n14,
    N262n23

Smith, Paul M., N351n68
Smith, Rachel, N353n142, N353n146
Smith, Ray, N26n85
Smith, Robert E., N67n17, N125n110, N155n171,
    N155n174, N155n180, N156n185, N263n41,
    N263n42, N263n49, N291n13, N351n70
Smith, Ronn J., N327n117
Smith, Ruth Ann, N98n132, N123n46
Smith, Ruth Belk, N239n129
Smith, Timothy M., N351n68
Snook-Luther, David C., N182n150
Snyder, Beth, N350n4
Snyder, C. R., N469n47, N469n61
Snyder, Mark, N156n187, N411n114
Snyder, Rita, N153n82
So, Sherman, N323n1
Sojka, Jane L., N23n3, N410n74
Soldow, Gary, N71n115
Soley, Lawrence, N182n145
Solomon, Michael R., N122n17, N296n158,
    N296n159, N324n43, N380n80, N438n10,
    449, N468n22, N468n23, N468n26,
    N468n27, N469n56
Solomon, Paul J., N180n98
Solomon, Sheldon, N380n87, N408n14
Solon, Olivia, N27n110
Soman, Dilip, N24n13, N24n35, N27n106,
    N68n44, N95n40
Song, Sangyoung, N236n22
Sood, Alex, N352n86
Sood, Sanjay, N123n51, N238n67, N239n100
Sorenson, Chris, N98n151
Sorrentino, R. M., N265n111
Spangengerg, Eric R., N68n25, N96n85, N150n8,
    N154n143, N327n116, N327n117
Spanier, Gideon, N323n1
Spannenberg, Eric, N27n112
Spaulding, George, N350n18
Spears, Nancy, N153n113, N178n27
Speck, Paul Surgi, N94n5, N181n124
Spector, Aron N., N441n96
Spence, Mark T., N209n33
Spencer, Steven J., N96n97
Spira, Joan Scattone, N180n100
Spiro, Rosann, N378n34
Sporer, S. Ludwig, N180n101
Spotts, Harlan E., N181n124, N181n127,
    N181n133, N182n138
Spreng, Richard A., N66n4
Springen, Karen, N496n97
Springer, John, N208n20
Sprott, David, N68n25, N122n17, N154n143,
    N327n116, N327n117
Srinivasan, Kannan, N24n27
Srinivasan, Narasimhan, N211n100
Srinivasan, V., N240n141
Srivastava, Ishan, N295n117
Srivastava, Joydeep, N24n21, N69n67, N212n156,
    N264n92
Srivastava, Mehul, N208n7
Srivastava, Rajendra K., N97n117
Srull, Thomas K., N125n98, N125n104,
    N126n124, N180n120, N263n38, N292n24
Staelin, Richard, N97n117, N155n166, N211n106,
    N211n114, N211n120, N240n147
Stafford, James E., N326n83
Stafford, Marla Royne, N24n27, N180n111

Stafford, Thomas F., N180n111
Stambor, Zak, N27n117, N178n53, N210n92, N266n161
Stamey, Mark, N381n128
Stanaland, Andrea J. S., N182n152
Stanford, Duane D., N493n1, N496n98
Stanley, Linda R., N494n42
Stanley, T. L., N324n41, N410n76
Stayman, Douglas M., N68n36, N70n81, N151n27, N153n111, N154n145, N179n75, N178n79, N178n81, N180n87, N180n89, N292n49, N293n50, N325n48, N353n129, N411n108
Steel, Emily, N42n18
Steele, Chandra, N121n1
Steelman, Lainie, N467n1
Steenkamp, Jan-Benedict E. M., N68n37, N98n137, N98n138, N409n50, N410n77, N410n100, N439n41, N439n45, N440n62
Steidley, T., N180n96
Stein, Mara Lemos, N409n43
Stephens, Debra Lynn, N494n54
Sterlickhi, John, N292n48
Stern, Barbara B., N24n27, N182n161, N182n162, N351n70
Stern, Donald E., N237n41
Stern, Stefan, N438n18
Sternthal, Brian, N70n99, N70n101, N94n27, N95n36, N122n34, N125n94, N126n126, N151n25, N151–152n45, N152n60, N152n61, N178n26, N178n45, N181n128, N209n37, N327n114, N468n32
Stevens, J. C., N96n67
Stevenson, Seth, N440n95
Stewart, David W., N25n46, N25n47, 56, N67n9, N68n41, N68n42, N69n54, N95n35, N123n54, N125n108, N152n81, N152–153n81, N153n87, N153n91, N181n125, N211n100, N211n129, N237n41, N239n125
Stilley, Karen M., N266n148
Stillman, Tyler F., N68n30
Stipp, Horst, N350n29
Stoltman, Jeffrey J., N67n17
Stork, Linda, N325n69
Storm, Diana, N27n115
Stout, Patricia, N70n113, N181n122
Strack, Fritz, N25n45, N265n140
Strahan, Erin J., N96n97
Strathman, Alan J., N150n2, N150n9, N151n24, N152n67, N154n131, N180n102
Strauch, Jesse, N324n42
Strauss, Gary, N494n39
Strauss, Marina, N441n104
Strauss, William, N409n58
Strazzieri, Alain, N379n39
Strebel, Judi, N212n131
Strijnev, Andrei, N408n30
Strobel, John, N123n53
Stroebe, Wolfgang, N97n97
Stross, Randall, N291n1, N294n104, N440n60
Strutton, David, N323n10
Stuart, Elnora W., N154n139, N179n68
Sturdevant, Matthew, N126n129, N350n31
Su, Chenting, N379n42
Subramaniam, Velavan, N441n97
Subramanian, Anusha, N150n1
Suciu, Peter, N438n1

Sudhir, K., N212n139
Sujan, Harish, N210n72, N265n107, N440n65
Sujan, Mita, N122n13, N124n91, N154n118, N155n156, N209n43, N210n72, N236n28, N237n60, N265n107, N265n112, N440n65
Sullivan, Mary, N98n129
Summers, John O., N439n46
Summerville, Amy, N291n8
Sun, Baohung, N264n79
Sundar, S. Shyam, N95n46
Sundaram, Karthikeyan, N208n7
Sung, Baohong, N24n27
Sung, Yongjun, N122n341
Supphellen, Magne, N352n105
Supranant, Carol, N293n66
Suri, Rajneesh, N70n111
Suris, Oscar, N70n98
Sussman, Steve, 305
Swait, Joffre, N152n64, N212n131, N239n128, N438n22
Swaminathan, Vanitha, N70n86, N122n32, N469n55
Swan, John E., N294n79, N294n81, N439n52
Swan, Suzanne, N68n42
Swan, William B., N156n187
Swazy, John L., N71n122, N178n35, N178n50
Sweldens, Steven, N179n64, N179n70
Sweney, Mark, N494n47
Swinyard, William R., N155n171, N155n174, N263n41, N291n13
Szabo, Liz, N70n103, N378n18
Szaky, Tom, N24n17
Szykman, Lisa R., N495n88
Szymanski, David M., N292n38, N440n55

T

Tai, Christopher, N327n108
Talbot, David, N42n27
Talbot, Margaret, N326n78
Talpade, Salil, N379n46, N379n47
Talukdar, Debabrata, N211n104, N212n130, N212n139
Tambyah, Siok Kuan, N468n35
Tan, Chin Tiong, N326n85
Tanner, John F., N155n153, N408n10
Tansuhaj, Patriya S., N379n44, N379n45
Tarpey, Lawrence X., N69n79, N70n84
Tasaki, Lori H., N469n55
Tavassoli, Nader T., N121n4, N125n115
el-Tayeb, Ahmed Mohamed, 461
Taylor, Charles R., N327n127
Taylor, David G., N323n10
Taylor, James R., N496n115
Taylor, James W., N439n48
Taylor, Timothy, N412n140
Taylor, Valerie A., N354n170
Tedeschi, Bob, N292n17, N495n77
Teel, Jesse E., N294n105, 314, N326n85, N326n96, N327n124, N411n110
Tejada, Carlos, N468n37
Tellegen, Cassandra L., N125n111
Tellis, Gerard J., N154n146
Tepper, Kelly, N68n31
Terdiman, Daniel, N42n17, N470n87
Terry, Edith, N408n16
Terzon, Emilia, N469n63

Tetlock, Philip E., N326n90, N470n90
Texeira, Thales, N26n87, N42n30
Thaivanich, Pattana, N154n146
Tham, Lai Leng, N208n13
Thamodaran, Kanchana, N70n113
Theiss, Evelyn, N408n27
Thomas, Greg Metz, N323n2
Thomas, Monoj, N236n23
Thompson, Craig J., N70n89, N266n140, N351n62, N408n40, N409n54, N411n104, N467n4, N467n7, N468n35
Thompson, Debora Viana, N153n99, N440n71
Thompson, Linda, N378n12
Thompson, Scott A., N439n40
Thompson, Steven R., N42n14
Thomson, Matthew, N67n16, N155n182, N156n182, N469n55, N469n69, N469–470n72
Thorelli, Hans B., N438n28
Thornton, Corliss G., N352n110
Thorson, Esther, N182n159
Thottam, Jyoti, N468n21
Tian, Kelly, N469n58
Tian Kelly-Tepper, N68n31, N411n102, N469n47
Tierney, Jim, N295n131
Tigart, Douglas, N439n50
Till, Brian D., N154n133, N179n69
Timmons, Heather, N208n7
Tinkham, Spencer F., N122n41
Tkacik, Maureen, N350n20
Todd, Peter M., N210n78, N239n118, N379n42
Tofighbakhsh, Jessica, N240n144
Toppino, Thomas, N177n23
Torelli, Carlos J., N352n104
Tormala, Zakary L., N151n22, N152n52, N155n178
Totty, Michael, 196
Touchstone, Ellen E., N353n13e
Toy, Daniel R., N151n19, N151n23
Triandis, Harry C., N124n89, N154n132
Trijp, Hans C. M., N265n130
Tripp, Carolyn, N152n54
Trope, Yaacov, N124n82, N124n84
Troutman, Tracy, N209n32, N211n100
Trudel, Remi, N69n66
Trusov, Michael, N325n54, N327n130
Tsao, Amy, N352n79
Tse, David K., N293n65, N294n88, N408n16, N409n71
Tsiros, Michael, N70n87, N291n3, N293n76
Tsui, Bonnie, N125n96
Tsui, Enid, N98n139
Tsurulnik, Giselle, N208n1, N323n3, N353n145
Tuggle, Kathryn, N96n65
Tuten, Tracy L., N24n27
Tuttle, Brad, N381n121
Tversky, Amos, N124n74, N236n7, N237n40, N237n50, N262n2, N262n3, N262n9
Tybout, Alice, N70n94, N95n40, N123n46, N126n123, N126n125, N178n26, N182n161, N211n110, N211n111, N236n8, N293n66, N293n67, N327n114, N328n161, N378n31
Tylee, John, N153n102

U

Uhl, Kenneth P., N265n114, N439n37
Ulkumen, Gulden, N212n150

Um, Nam-Hyun, N153n85
Umesh, U., N., N237n41
Underwood, Ryan, N407n1
Unnava, H. Rao, N26n73, N122n25, N125n98,
   N125n100, N150n2, N150n9, N151n24,
   N152n67, N154n126, N154n131, N155n182,
   N156n184, N178n29, N178n43, N180n102,
   N181n114, N236n18, N469n72
Urban, Glen L., N211n125, N438n28
Urbany, Joel E., N211n99, N264n89
Urminsky, Oleg, N263n43
Ursic, Anthony C., N351n55
Ursic, Michael L., N351n55
Ursic, Virginia L., N351n55
Usher, John, N496n123
Utterback, James M., N438n28

V

Valence, Gilles, N493n13
Valencia, Humberto, N353n117, N353n132,
   N409n55
Valentini, Sara, N295n115
Valle, S. A., N294n108
Van Allen Peter, N354n160
Van Baaren, Rick B., N26n62, N177n5, N262n14
Van Daalen, Robin, N408n21
Van den Bergh, Bram, N68n33, N182n144,
   N211n123
Van den Bulte, Christophe, N324n20, N327n110
van der Voo, Lee, N42n37
van de Ven, Niels, N69n55, N239n107
Van Diepen, Merel, N179n57
Van Dyk, Tuen A., N208n31
Van Herpen, Erica, N327n133
Vanhuele, Marc, N122n15
Vannieuwkerk, Renee, N179n67, N179n68
van Olst, Janna, N153n102
van Osselaer, Stijn M. J., N122n35, N179n64,
   N179n70, N236n21, N262n22, N352n77
van Raaij, W. Fred, N407n6, N496n116
Vanscoy, Holly, N210n86
Van Toller, C., N96n69
Varab, Duane, N94n9
Varney, Sarah, N412n147
Vasquez, Ignacio, N352n95
Vavra, Terry, N292n47
Vaynerchuk, Gary, N182n169
Vázquez-Carrasco, Rosario, N265n129
Vendemia, Jennifer M. C., N26n87
Venkatesan, M., N265n126, N291n2
Venkatesh, Alladi, N351n64, N439n36
Venkatesh, R., N264n85
Venter, Irma, N151n34
Veremis, Lindsay, N151n42
Verhage, Bronis, N379n39
Verhage, Bronislaw J., N70n81
Verlegh, Peeter W. J., N98n137
Verrochi, Nicole M., N154n149
Veryzer, Robert W., N265n123
Vijayraghavan, Kala, N352n76
Villani, Kathryn E A., N410n96
Vincent, J. E., N327n113
Virzi, Anna Maria, N27n118
Viser, Matt, N495n66
Vissm S., N96n67
Viswanathan, Madhubalan, N124n70
Vlahos, James, N262n15

Vlessing, Etan, N42n25
Voegele, Erin, N151n35
Voges, Kevin E., N182n142
Vohs, Kathleen D., N25n45, N68n30,
   N69n57, N182n143, N266n144, N266n145,
   N496n119
Voight, Joan, N152n59
Volkmann, Kelsey, N208n1
Volkner, Franziska, N123n53
Vonn, Lindsey, 317
von Raiij, Fred, N123n51
Vosburgh, Robert, N408n31
Vosgerau, Joachim, N23n4
Voss, Glenn B., N264n82, N292n41, N293n53
Voss, Kevin E., N150n8
Vranica, Suzanne, N97n110, N182n147, N408n19
Vruyneel, Sabrina, N69n58

W

Wachter, Jason, N378n7
Wackman, Daniel B., N379n46
Waddell, Ray, N325n53
Wade, Matt, N351n65
Waenke, Michaela, N208n24
Wagner, Janet, N295n125
Wagner, Judy A., N178n39
Wagner, Mary, N264n87
Wagner, Tillmann, N264n75
Waits, William B., N471n112
Wakefield, Kirk, N178n39, N266n148, N326n101
Wakslak, Cheryl, N124n82
Walker, Alexis, N378n12
Walker, Andrea K., N98n151, N327n128
Walker, Beth A., N409n73
Walker, Bruce, N265n137
Walker, Chip, N328n142
Wallace, Amy, N69n75
Wallendorf, Melanie, N239n129, 285, N296n153,
   N296n155, N296n160, N296n162,
   N327n125, N380n98, N380n100, N468n33,
   N470n81, N470n83, N470n84, N470n89,
   N470n96, N470n97 N470n104, N470n106,
   N494n22
Wallop, Harry, N441n104
Walsh, Ann, N325n66
Walsh, Mark, N354n171
Walster, Elaine G., N294n79
Walster, G. William, N294n79
Walter, Ekaterina, N27n118, N328n158
Wan, Echo Wen, N155n178
Wan, Lisa C., N293n55
Wand, Qing, N440n57
Wang, Cheng Lu, N469n67
Wang, Hui-Chih, N263n65
Wang, Jim, N237n44
Wang, Jing, N69n52, N294n92, N294n97
Wang, Liz C., N178n39
Wang, Qu, N328n149
Wang, Tuo, N264n85
Wänke Michaela, N68n42, N98n128, N239n119
Wansink, Brian, N25n43, N25n50, N25n54,
   N265n139, N495n69, N495n70
Ward, James, N124n71, N208n12
Ward, James C., N210n82
Ward, Morgan, N380n91, N467n12
Ward, Scott, N154n136, N265n126, N325n59,
   N379n46, N439n37, N494n31

Warlop, Luk, N98n142, N124n76, N182n144,
   N264n84, N379n42, N411n115
Warner, Fara, N495n82
Warren, N., N124n89
Warren, Susan, N296n172
Warren,Wendy L., N179n61
Warshaw, Paul R., N151n31, N238n73
Washington, George, 459–460
Wasserman, Lisa, N325n69
Wasserman, Todd, N156n188, N294n99, N493n1
Waters, Florence, N126n129
Waterson, James, N181n112
Wathieu, Luc, N27n99
Watson, Bruce, N96n89
Wax, Emily, N468n25
Weatherly, Jeffrey, N., N495n62
Webb, Amy L., N94n6
Weber, Elke U., N493n16
Weber, Ernst, 85
Weber, Jean E., N379n41
Webster, Cynthia, N353n118, N352n119
Webster, Donna M., N97n105
Webster, Frederick E., N154n136
Wechasara, Guntalee, N182n137, N263n38
Wedel, Michel, N42n30, N26n87, N26n90,
   N94n22, N94n23, N95n44, N95n51,
   N95n52, N97n107, N410n77, N439n45
Wedell, Douglas H., N124n78
Weeks, Clinto S., N125n111
Weentraug, Pamela, N96n70
Weigl, Karl, N210n94
Weigold, Michael F., N208n27
Weinberg, Bruce D., N211n125
Weinberger, Marc G., N95n37, N150n7,
   N181n124, N181n124, N181n125,
   N181n127, N181n128, N181n133,
   N181n135, N182n138
Weiner, Bernard, N292n27, N293n72, N410n88
Weiss, Allen M., N179n59, N210n84, N327n126
Weiss, Michael, N352n97
Weitz, Barton A., N27n113, N210n72
Wellington, Chrissie, 467
Wells, Ryan, N70n104
Wells, William D., N71n122, N122n38,
   N182n161, N265n108, N408n24, N467n4
Wentz, Laurel, N353n135, N353n136
Wernerfelt, Birger, N208n5, N295n122
Wertenbroch, Klaus, N23n4, N291n10
Werth, Lioba, N25n45, N265n140
Wertley, Chad, N379n57
West, Patricia M., N178n29, N210n71, N239n126,
   N291n15
Westaway, Luke, N438n1
Westbrook, Robert A., N293n67, N294n86,
   N294n87, N294n89, N295n123
Wetzels, Martiin, N210n68
Whalen, D. Joel, N409n69
Whalen, Jeanne, N96n89, N152n76
Wheatley, John J., N155n160
Wheatley, Thalia P., N294n96
Wheeler, Carolynne, N350n1
Wheeler, D., N327n113
Wheeler, S. Christian, N69n71, N262n16
Whipple, Thomas, N181n135, N352n85
White, Candace McKearney, N94n10
White, Charlie, 47
White, Joseph B., N323n5

White, Katherine, N324n40, N326n92, N495n57
White, Shaun, 132
White, Tiffany Barnett, N238n77
Whitney, John C., Jr., N122n30, N124n91
Whittler, Tommy E., N180n100, N354n153, N354n154
Wickens, Thomas D., N122n26
Wicklund, Robert A., N326n88, N468n28
Wiener, Joshua Lyle, N293n70, N496n115
Wieseke, Jan, N68n25, N154n143, N292n44
Wigboldus, Daniel H. J., N26n62, N177n5, N262n14
Wiggins, Jennifer, N96n76
Wilcox, James, N323–324n12
Wilcox, Keith, N236n22, N494n28
Wilde, Louis, N238n78
Wilk, Robert, N409n47
Wilkens, Henry T., N97n101
Wilkes, Robert E., N353n132, N378n4, N378n26, N379n50
Wilkie, Maxine, N96n91
Wilkie, William L., N68n22, N151n28, N155n154, N211n99, N238n73, N294n108, N325n61, N380n72, N410n95
Williams, Carol J., N155n173
Williams, Derrick, 93, 167
Williams, Patti, N154n122, N154n141, N351n56
Willis, Richard, H., N469n47
Wilson, Bill, N440n88
Wilson, Eric, 149
Wilson, Karl, N493n5
Wilson, Peter C., N293n65
Wilson, R. Dale, N327n127
Wilson, Timothy, N294n96, N381n103, N408n11
Wind, Jerry, N439n35
Wind, Yoram, N410n96
Winer, Russell S., N264n86, N266n147, N266n149, N266n156
Wines, Michael, N409n72
Winkler, Melissa, 465
Winkler, Rolfe, N266n161
Winslow, Ron, N495n67
Winterich, Karen Page, N266n141
Witkowski, Terrence H., N411n112
Witt, Kathy, N350n37
Witt, Robert, E., N326n94
Wolfinbarger, Mary, N324n46, N351n48
Wolverson, Roya, N469n54
Wong, Elaine, N182n163
Wong, John K., N409n69
Wong, Nancy, N151n29
Wong, Stephanie, N152n71
Wood, Stacy L., N26n87, N68n26, N125n92, N210n88, N239n102, N294n94, N379n48, N438n22
Wood, Van R., N409n55
Woodell, Angela, N468n30

Woodifield, Peter, N265n118
Woodruff, Robert B., N293n51, N294n95
Woods, Tiger, 137
Woodside, Arch G., N95n32, N211n118, N327n121, N409n55, N409n65, N409n73
Woodward, Kevin, N27n117
Woodyard, Chris, N181n118
Wooten, David B., N326n77, N326n99, N327n123, N471n116
Worth, Marc, N262n10
Worthington, Don, N264n76
Wortzel, Lawrence H., N379n45
Woyke, Elizabeth, N438n1
Wright, Alice A., N291n14
Wright, David, N496n99, 497n130
Wright, Gordon P., N212n151
Wright, Peter L., N70n110, N151n18, N151n20, N155n160, N265n108, N238n70, N411n110
Wright, Richard L., N97n120, N350n16
Wu, Chenghuan, N152n53
Wu, Eugenia C., N411n116
Wu, Jason, 374
Wyer, Robert S., Jr., N98n137, N121n11, N123n52, N126n124, N236n26, N237n44, N240n132, N293n54, N326n105, N353n151

X

Xie, Jinhong, N328n149, N438n20
Xu, Jing, N122n16
Xun, Jiyao, N42n21

Y

Yalch, Richard, N26n83, N27n112, N71n117, N96n85
Yale, Laura, N324n46, N328n140
Yan, Dengfeng, N124n85, N212n137
Yang, Eric, N265n119
Yang, K. S., N409n48
Yang, Yang, N381n104
Yap, Jamie, N212n158
Yates, J. Frank, N239n103
Yau, Oliver H. M., N409n48
Yavas, Ugur, N70n81
Ye, Keying, N379n42
Ye, Lan, N26n88
Yee, Blythe, N468n38
Yee, Chen May, N351n64
Yeo, Junsang, N153–154n114
Yeung, Catherine W. M., N123n52, N240n132, N264n106, N325n64, N379n49
Yi, Youjae, N292n30, N292n49, N293n50, N295n128, N410n93
Yim, Chi Kin (Bennett), N294n88
Yin, Sandra, N42n10, N350n36, N352n94, N378n24, N471n123
Yin, Sara, N266n161
Yingling, Cathy, N152n58

Yip, Nick K. T., N236n13
Yoon, Carolyn, N42n29, N42n31, N264n87, N351n45
Yorkston, Eric, N96n62
Young, Melissa Martin, 285, N296n153, N296n155, N296n158, N468n27
Young, S. Mark, N67n13, N71n114, N96n87, N154n115, N181n120
Yurcan, Bryan, N24n28
Yzerbyt, Vincent, N179n71

Z

Zacks, R. T., N94n21
Zaichkowsky, Judith Lynne, N26n78, N67n14, N67–68n22, N126n121
Zajonc, Robert B., N262n27
Zaltman, Gerald R., N42n12, N295n111, N327n125, N438n28
Zanna, Mark P., N96n97, N155n171, N177n20
Zarantonello, Lia, N292n33
Zauberman, Gal, N25n61, N210n77, N211n102, N211n103, N237n48
Zeelenberg, Marcel, N24n9, N25n49, N69n55, N239n107, N291n6, N291n7, N291n10, N327n133
Zeithaml, Valerie A., N123n47, N293n53
Zemborain, Martin R., N150n5
Zeynep, Zrsel, N408n40
Zhan, Lingjing, N328n148
Zhang, Jie, N95n51
Zhang, Jing, N352n104
Zhang, Mod-Yong, N181n136
Zhang, Qin, N408n30
Zhang, Shi, N124n89
Zhang, Ying, N69n49
Zhang, Yinlong, N67n21, N266n141
Zhang, Yong, N263n33
Zhao, Guangzhi, N70n88
Zhao, Min, N440n58
Zhao, Xiande, N70n102
Zheng, Yuhuang, N263n43
Zhou, Nan, N408n16, N409n71
Zhou, Rongrong, N24n35
Zhu, Rui (Juliet), N69n52, N237n52, N262n21, N296n157
Ziamou, Paschalina (Lilia), N153n105, N440n64
Zielinski, Joan, N439n37
Zimmerman, F. J., N494n30
Zinkhan, George M., N122n14, N181n126, N327n129, N409n52, N469n56
Ziobro, Paul, N95n53
Zirulnick, Ariel, N380n77
Zmuda, Natalie, N182n160, N211n112, N328n154, N354n171, N381n142
Zolner, Kyle, N471n114
Zuckerman, Marvin, N410n99

Product Index

A

Abercrombie & Fitch, 306
Ace Hardware, 451
Adidas
    endorsements, 136–137
    NEO stores, 75
Aflac (American Family Life Assurance
        Company), 88
AKB48, 454
Alcohol, 483, 485, 486
Altoid mints, 457
Amazon
    cell phone recycling, 290
    customer service, 276
    prototypical brand, 112
    saving items, 64
AMC Entertainments, 44
American Airlines, 345
American Cancer Society, 309
American Greetings cards, 345
American Grilled Cheese Kitchen, 389
Anchor Spreadable ad, 273
Angry Birds, 298, 319
Angry Birds Mooncake Festival, 298
Apple
    anchor products, 217
    comparative advertising, 195
    customer service, 280
    distinctive design, 21
    logo, 99–100
Apple iPad, 112, 191, 192
    repositioning product, 431
Apple iPad2, 415
Apple iPhone
    brand loyalty, 455
    prototypical brand, 112
Apple Newton MessagePad, 423
Ariel laundry detergent, 356
AT&T
    animated commercial, 76
    cell phone recycling, 290–291
    endorsements, 137
Audi
    hedonic message, 146
    nostalgic commercials, 121
    QR code, 185
AXA Equitable Life Insurance, 335
Axe, 22, 176
Aybrey-Organics, 49

B

Baby Orajel, 140
Baidu, 208
Bailandu con una Estrella, 448
Baking soda, 418
Banana Flame, 135
Barbie dolls, 480

Barbour, 482
Barilla
    cross-cultural affect, 258
    value-driven attitude, 132
Baskin-Robbins, 87
BBC America, 76
Becel margarine, 424
Ben & Jerry's
    consumer goals, 53
    "personality test," 401
Benetton, 461
Benjamin Moore, 433
Berlitz language schools, 78
Bernard Matthews Farm, 430
Bertolli, 22
Best Buy, 303
Bicycles, 466–467
Big Y supermarket, 282
Bike by Me, 217
Blendtec, 136, 432–433
Blockbuster, 250–251
Bloomingdale, 451
Blue Bottle Coffee, 434
BMW, 90
Bobbi Brown cosmetics, 250
Body Shop, 476
Bollé goggles, 14
Bolt Barbers, 320
Bolthouse Farms, 486, 492
Boston Consulting Group, 370
Botox Cosmetic, 232
Bradford Exchange, 456
Brand Match, 206–207
Bridgestone, 79
Brown Bear Car Wash, 284
Buckley's Cough Mixture, 83–84,
        138–139
Budwiser Budvar, 273
Bulgari sunglasses, 372
Burberry
    body fragrance, 197
    custom-design, 452
Burton snowboards, 445
Busch Gardens, 11

C

Cadbury
    nostalgic ads, 121
    seasonal advertising, 19
    snack foods, 157, 158
Cadillac, 432
Campbell Soup Company
    microwave soups, 417
    new products, 393
    prototypical brand, 112
    quick-serve meals, 334
    repositioning products, 431

    senior market, 336
    soup pouches, 80
Cannondale, 467
Carbonite, 58, 145
Cartoon Network, 334
Cathay Pacific Airways, 137
CDW, 188
Cesar, 141
Charles Leski Auctions, 460
Charming Shoppes
    baby boomers, 336
    social media, 35
Cheetos, 36
Chevrolet, 78, 192
Chevy Volt, 192, 221,
        223, 321
Chico's, 336
Chow Tai Fook, 279
Christian Deals, 348
Christian Louboutin shoes, 51
Chrysler, 76
Cialis, 132
Cigarette advertising, 15, 481–482, 483,
        485, 486
Cisco, 137
Cleveland Public Library, 334
ClimateMaster, 400
Club Penguin site, 363
CM Photographics, 165
Coach, 386
Coca-Cola
    distinctive script, 81
    downward mobility, 372
    Freestyle vending machine, 253
    iconic bottle, 191
    marketing communication, 142
    online purchase panel, 34
    pleasant smell, 84
    product placement, 89
    slogan, 273
    transformational advertising, 174
    teen market, 349
Cold Stone Creamy, 257
Cole Hardware, 284
Colgate, 90
College Hunks Hauling Junk, 267
Colorforms, 452
Comic Relief, 308, 310, 490
Converse shoes, 453
Costco
    bargains, 205
    cell phone recycling, 290
    retail atmospherics, 91
    sampling opportunities, 432
Crème Egss, 157
Crutchfield, 267
CVS, 389, 407

D

Daimler, 16
Daiso Japan, 255
Danbury Mint, 456
Dannon, 61
Darn Tough Vermont, 60
Dave's Supermarkets, 389
De Beers, role transition, 451
Debenhams, 64, 170
Deep River Snacks, 251
Dell
    cocreation, 419
    INTERBRAND ranking, 137
    "listening post," 194
    social media, 321
Del Monte Foods
    advertising jingle, 120–121
    online purchase panel, 34
Delta Air Lines, 267, 268
Delta faucets, 428
Denny's, 337
Dentastix, 172
Diet Pepsi, 201
Dirt Devil, 81, 427
DISH Network, 250, 251
Disney, 112
Disney Princess products, 448
Dollar General, 255
Dollar tree, 375
Domino's Pizza
    artisan Pizzas, 249
    digital billboards, 339
    promotions, 249
Dongsuh Foods, 84
Dove
    brand extensions, 109–110
    customer connection, 22
Dr. Pepper Snapple, 33
Duane Reade drug store, 91
Duke University, 223
Dunkin' Donuts, 193
Earthbound Organic, 249

E

eBay, 488
Ebtune dashboard, 213
Eggies, 58
Elektra retail chain, 374
Energizer batteries, 252
ENERGY STAR, 489
EPIC hotel, 245
Erlanger Health System, 228
ESPN Deportes, 344

F

Faber-Castell, 392
Facebook
    privacy issues, 486–487
    prototypical brand, 112
FarmVille game, 157
FastCare Clinic, 407
Febreze, 84
Ferrero, 157
First Tennessee Bank, 278
Flipkart, payment plan, 199
Flip-Pal, 403

Flip video camera, 417
Flooz system, 423
Flying Bison Brewing Company, 259
Ford
    car gizmos/gadgets, 213
    truck marketing, 447
    video ads, 19
    and Zipcar, 403
Ford Focus, 6
Forty Putney Road Beer and
        Breakfast, 193
Franklin Mint, 456
Freecycle Network, 9, 488
Frito-Lay
    neuroscientific information, 36, 37
    new flavors, 259
    product legitimacy, 434
    regional marketing, 341
    snack foods, 157–158, 167
Frosted Flakes, 191

G

Gatorade
    endorsements, 137
    social media monitoring, 320
GEICO
    brand image, 109
    elaboration, 105
    Gecko spokesman, 136
General Mills
    and baby boomers, 336
    and mothers, 363
General Motors
    African American market, 346
    Buicks in China, 342
    car gizmos/gadgets, 213
    categories, 111
    crisis management, 321
Gillette razors, 133
Girl Scouts, 309
Glad bags, 162, 163
GO Daddy, 173
Goodwill Industries International, 488
Google
    netnography, 35
    privacy issues, 486–487
    search competition, 208
    Wave service, 421
Google Offers, 261
Google Wallet, 414, 415
GovMint.com, 456
Graff, 372
Green Mountain Coffee Roasters, 437
Gucci
    high-end bikes, 466
    materialism, 386

H

H&M
    chunking, 105
    nostalgic ads, 121
    eco-friendly products, 390
    UNICEF support, 137
Häagen-Daz
    content reduction, 85
    hedonism, 389

Haier appliances, 244
Hallmark cards
    African American market, 345
    and blended families, 360
    card-sending rituals, 451
    job loss, 372
    prototypical brand, 112
    representative heuristics, 242
    and sacred rituals, 461
Harley-Davidson
    ad strategy, 393
    customer satisfaction, 280
    HOGs group, 16, 235
    in India, 235
    "macho" characteristics, 444
    "outlaw" symbols, 447
    prototypical brand, 112
    self-concept, 49
    social media, 335
    sonic identity, 81
    women customers, 338
Harley Owners Group (HOG), 235
Healthy Choice, 389
Heineken, 485
Heinz
    "Dip & Squeeze" packets, 255
    downward mobility, 372
    prototypical brand, 112
    recycling efforts, 289
Hermès, 188
Hertz, 60, 112
Hewlett-Packard
    INTERBRAND ranking, 137
    photo service, 388
Hilton Garden Inn, 405–406
Hindustan Unilever, 338
Home Plus, 20
Honda, 137
Hornby trains, 388
Huggies, 33
Hyundai, 135

I

IKEA
    assembly instructions, 62
    advertising campaigns, 37
    customer experience, 376–377
    home ad campaign, 387
    product disposal, 488
    referrals, 315
    service representative, 197
In-N-Out hamburger chain, 83
IRN-BRU, 257
ITALIKA motorbike, 223
ITC hotels, 348

J

JC Penney
    African American market, 345
    fund raising campaign, 131
    "haul videos," 334
    social media complaints, 283
Johnnie Walker whiskey, 448
Johnson & Johnson
    African American market, 346
    INTERBRAND ranking, 137

K

KB Toys, 39
Kellogg's
    prototypical brand, 112
    share love, 191
Kenny Rogers Roasters, 217–218
Keurig, 437
KFC
    chunking, 105
    cross-cultural affect, 258
    regional preferences, 329–330
Kia Motors, 171
Kid Nation, 306
KidZania, 363
Kimberly-Clark, 33
Kindle devices, 219, 429
Kindle e-book, 193
Kindle Fire, 425
Kit Kat bars, 115, 121
Kitzbühel, 13, 14
Kleenex tissues, 260
Kohl's
    clothing lines, 249
    senior discounts, 337
Kraft
    concentrated flavors, 162
    emotional marketing, 145
Kyochon Chicken, 225

L

L. L. Bean
    guarantees, 277
    product review monitoring, 320
    reputation, 142
La Bella del Baile, 448
Lactogen formula, 430
Lakme cosmetics, 167
LEAF electric car
    new features, 226
    sales promotion, 229
    sound symbolism, 81
LEGO
    global toy market, 388
    opinion leaders, 304
    virtual blocks, 163
LEGO Games, 221
Lenovo computers
    product placement, 89
    representative heuristics, 244
Liberty Mutual, 270
Lipton, 22
Living Social, 261
Lone Star Steakhouse, 252–253
LoroPiana clothing, 374
Los Angeles Kings, 401
Louis Vuitton Company, 170
Lululemon, 404
Lux, 22

M

M&M World, 82
Macy's
    Bobbi Brown cosmetics, 250
    Independence Day fireworks, 194

marketing sources, 299
    Thanksgiving day parade, 194
    WiFi service, 204
Madame Tussauds, 72–73
Magic Eraser, 189
Magnum Ecuador, 51
Mall of America, 322
Marlboro, 482
Mary Kay cosmetics, 315
Mazda
    interactivity, 161
    QR code, 185
McDonald's
    brand familiarity, 191
    emotional cognition, 144
    hamburger size, 85
    Happy Meals, 486
    lobster rolls, 287
    marketing sources, 299
    multicultural sector, 343
    pricing strategy, 254
    prototypical brand, 112
    sonic identity, 81
Media Market, 401
Megabus services, 224
Melt restaurants, 221
Meow Mix cat food, 120–121
Mercedes Benz
    electric car, 113
    endorsements, 143
    millennial consumers, 333
    status symbol, 370
Merlin Entertainments Group, 72
Metropolitan Museum of Art stores, 451
MGM Grand hotels, 83
Michael Jackson Dress-Up Set, 452
Milk ads, 13
Miller Lite, 448
MinuteClinics, 407
Minute Maid, 16
Mocavo, 208
Moon Dough, 304
Morrisons supermarket, 482
Morton Salt, 119
Moshi Monsters site, 363
Mountain Dew, 5
Movie Tavern, 44–45
Mr. Clean Auto Dry, 432
Mustang car, 19
MyFord Touch, 213

N

National Geographic cruise, 13
National Rifle Association, 133
National Trust for Historic Preservation, 488
NBC
    musical tags, 171
    sonic identity, 81
NBC Sports Network, 18
NEO stores, 75
Nespresso
    endorsements, 143
    single-serve coffeemakers, 437

Nestlé
    adult supplements, 392
    innovation developments, 415
    positioning, 115
    single-serve coffee makers, 437
    yogurt marketing, 395
NetCost supermarket, 82
Netflix
    ratings, 198–199
    rental fees, 250
New Balance, 163
Newegg, 198
Nielsen, 38
Nike
    endorsements, 143, 161
    gender marketing, 339
    logos, 93
99p Store, 481
Nissan
    brand image management, 17
    car gizmos/gadgets, 213–214
    customer complaints, 282
    eco-friendly products, 390
    sales promotion, 229
    sound symbolism, 81
Nivea
    competition, 176
    emotional messaging, 144
    invisible deodorant, 418, 419
Nokia, 375
Nordstrom, 91
North Face parka, 14
Northstar Ski Resort, 132
Novo Nordisk, 304
NPD Group, 32
NTT DOCOMO, 403–404, 414–415
Nutella, 157

O

Ocado groceries, 284
Of a King, 392
Old Spice, 176
Oleadas, 343
Omo, 22
One Kings Lane, 403
OnStar system, 213
Oogavé sodas, 82
Oregon Institute of Technology, 198
Oscar Mayer, 112
Oxfam, 488

P

Palladium Mall, 51
Panasonic, 137
Pandora jewelry, 227
Panera Bread, 2
Panera Cares restaurants, 2–3
Panerai, watches, 127
Pantene, 355
Patagonia, 31
Patek Philippe, 127
PayPal, 414, 415
Peapod, 387–388

PepsiCo
    community grants, 472–473, 490
    healthy snacks, 486
    multiple media, 64
    new can designs, 259
    product disposal, 5
    recycling efforts, 289
    teen market, 349
    vending machines, 431–432
Petco, 455
Pew Research Center, 29
Philips
    consume knowledge, 115
    Senseo coffeemaker
Pizza Hut
    endorsements, 137
    regional preferences, 329, 330
Playstation 3, uncertainty, 429
Polartec, 430
Porsche, 466
Prada, 386
Pretzel Crisps, 19
Procter & Gamble
    advertising to mothers, 339
    African American market, 346
    car cleaning sprayer, 432
    class-differentiated products, 374
    eco-friendly products, 390
    Febreze, 84
    Magic Eraser, 189
    multicultural sector, 343, 344
    newlywed consumption, 451
    Old Spice, 176
    online purchase panel, 34
    Pampers ads, 342
    product positioning, 18
    social media, 35
    Swiffer products, 226
    $2 dollar consumers, 355–356, 368
Provo Craft, 103
Publix supermarkets, 343

R
RadioShack, 290
Radisson Hotels, 224
Ragú, 22–23
Raymond, 38
ReCellular, 290
Red Bull, 334
Red Sox Nation, 306
RedLaser, 197
Regal, 44
Restaurant of the Future, 39
Richard Mille wristwatch, 456
Right Guard, 176
Ritz-Carlton hotels
    scents, 245
    training system, 228
Rock and Roll Fantasy Camp, 335
Rolex
    endorsements, 143
    prestige watches, 127, 128
    materialism, 387

Rolls-Royce, 446, 447
Rovio, 298
Royal Ahold, 387–388
Royal Enfield engine, 235
Royal Ocean Racing Club, 127
Runner's World, 445

S
Sabritones Chile & Lime snacks, 434
Sainsbury, 206–207
Saks Fifth Avenue, 189
Sanibel Recreation Center, 64
Santander Bank, 284
Segway, 421–422
Senseo, 437
Sharan car system, 213
ShopSmart, 302
Siemens, 137
Sierra Club, 13
Smallbone of Devizes, 387
Snack Factory, 19
Snapfish, 388
Snausage Breakfast Bites, 34
Social Tattoo Project, 6
Soup at Hand, 417
South Bend Silver Hawks, 194
Southern Comfort Fiery Pepper, 257
Spacer Camp, 13
Speck, 34
Sport Relief, 308, 490
Standard Chartered Bank
    customer service, 267
    late hours, 403
Star beer, 191
Starbucks
    analogies, 131
    brewed coffee, 434
State Farm Insurance, 344
Strategic Business Insights, 404
Subaru
    customer service, 270
    marketing communication, 142
    subculture marketing, 347
SUBWAY
    comparative message, 140
    foot-long sandwich, 255
    fresh fit line, 58
    healthy food options, 486
Sunbeam Toasters, 81
Sunsilk, 22
Super Mercado, 343
Surf, 22
SurveyMonkey, 29
Sveltesse yogurt, 395
Swarovski, 17
Swiffer products, 226
Swiss Army knife, 131
Syracuse University, 198

T
Taco Bell, 330
Tag Heuer, 127
Take Care Health Systems, 407

Target
    bull's eye symbol, 191, 192
    cell phone recycling, 290
    dorm-room shopping, 241–242
Tastefully Simple, 303
Tata Nano, 448
TCBY, 58
Teenage Mutant Ninja Turtles, 427
Teflon, 418
Telstra, 336
TerraCycle, 289, 488
Tesco
    eco-friendly products, 392
    grocery chain, 76
    recycling incentives, 289
    virtual store, 20
Threadless, 17
3M, 137
Ticketmaster, 309
Tide
    prototypical brand, 112
    representative heuristics, 242
Tide Dry Cleaners, 18
Timberland shoes, 5
Tobacco, 481–482, 483, 485, 486
Toll Brothers, 16
Toronto Maple Leafs, 390
Toyota
    car gizmos/gadgets, 213
    INTERBRAND ranking, 137
Toyota Prius, 112, 390
Toyota Tundra, 448
Trader Joe's, 360
Trek Bicycles, 466
Trunk Boiz, 466–467

U
U.S. Postal Service, 17
Ueshima coffee shops, 336
Under Armour
    brand exposure, 93
    endorsements, 167
    rehearsal, 105
UNICEF, 170
Unilever
    brand connection, 22–23
    cosmetic endorsements, 167
    shampoo products, 257
UNIQLO, 205
United States Automobile Association
    (USAA), 65–66
University Games, 452
University of Central Florida, 241
University of Utah, 241
USAA Federal Savings Bank, 284

V
Velcro, 112
Verizon
    Coupe cell phones, 335
    payment by phone, 414
Verizon Video, 90
Versus sports channel, 18

Vertu cell phones, 375
Vespa scooters, 423
Vicks, 342
VideoSurf, 208
Vintage Tub & Bath, 199
Vinyl LPs, 442–443
Virgin Atlantic Airways, 267
Visa, 414
Vista operating system, 428
Volkswagen
    car gizmos/gadgets, 213
    nostalgic ads, 121
Volkswagen Group, 59, 137, 149–150

W
Walmart
    database marketing, 34
    Hispanic market, 343

lower middle class
    customers, 375
    medical clinics, 389
Walt Disney Company, 216
WeCar, 223
Weight Watchers, 57, 315
Wendy's, 389
Whirlpool, 267
Whole Foods Market
    customer information, 277
    recharging stations, 225
Wilkinson Sword razor blades, 252
Window of the World theme
    park, 17
Woodward Dream Cruise, 76
Woolworth, 76
World of Wrestling Entertainment
    (WWE), 482

Y
Yandex, 208
Yellow Pages, 257
Yingli Green Energy, 433
Your Shape, 205
Yum! Brands, 329, 330

Z
Zane's Cycles, 274, 277
Zazzle, 382–383
Zipcar, 403

Subject Index

('e' indicates an exhibit)

A

Ability, 11, 45, 60. *See also* Consumer ability, MAO (motivation, ability and opportunity)
   influences, 46e
   recycling, 288
Absolute threshold, 84, 85
Abstract goal, 55
Abstractness, and attention, 80e
Academics
   consumer behavior research, 39
   high school reference group, 305e
Acceptable cutoff, 225
Accessibility/availability, brand name recall, 191
Accommodation theory, 344
Acculturation, 342, 384
Achievement symbols, 455–456
Acquisition
   consumer behavior, 4
   controversies, 477–482, 491
   and gender, 338
   methods, 7e
Active coping, 279e
Activists, complainer, 281
Activities, interests, and opinions (AIOs), 401, 402e
Actual identity schema, 453
Actual state, 187
Adaptability, innovation, 433
Addiction, 477
   and marketing, 481–482
Additive difference model, 225
Adopter groups, 422–423
   application, 423
Adoption
   innovation, 419
   innovation influences, 427–436
Advertising
   boomers, 336–337
   and consumer behavior, 18–19
   fit and self-concepts, 454
   generation X, 334
   Hispanic Americans, 344
   position and exposure, 73
   and self-image, 485–486
   teens, 333–334
   values influence, 393
Advertising agencies, 37
Advertorial, 88
Aesthetic innovations, 418
Affect, definition, 256
Affective (emotional) function
   attitudes, 128
   decision-making, 222, 226–229
   high effort, 141–143
   high effort influences, 143–146
   low-effort attitudes, 164–165

low-effort attitude influences, 169–175
Affective forecasting, 227–228, 280
Affective involvement, 47, 141
Affective responses (ARs), 142
African American consumers, 345–346
Age
   and consumer ability, 62
   and consumer behavior, 330–337, 348
   and special possessions, 458
   United States consumer spending, 6e
   and values, 392
Agentic goal, 337
Aggressive personality, 397
Alcohol, minor's illegal use, 483
Allocentric consumers, 388
Alternative-based strategy, 229
Ambiguity of information, 272
Ambivalence, definition, 128
American Consumer Satisfaction Index (ACSI), 274e
Amount of information, and consumer opportunity, 63
Analogy, attitude reasoning, 131
Analysis of reason, attitude/behavior prediction, 147
Anchoring and adjustment process, judgment, 216
Appraisal theory, 55, 56e, 227
Approach-approach conflict, 52
Approach-avoidance conflict, 52
Appropriateness, gift, 462
Argument quality, message, 138
Asian Americans consumers, 346–347
Aspirational reference group, 305, 306
Associative networks, 106–108, 106e, 107e
Associative reference group, 305, 306
Athletes, high school reference group, 305e
Attention
   characteristics, 76–77, 77e
   and consumer behavior, 11
Attitude, definition, 76, 92, 128
Attitude accessibility, 128
   and behavior prediction, 147
Attitude-behavior relationship
   factors affecting, 146–147
   over time, 147
Attitude confidence, 128, 147
Attitude persistence, 128
Attitude resistance, 128
Attitude toward the act (A_{act}), TORA, 133, 134e
Attitude toward the ad (A_{ad}), high-effort, 146
Attitude toward the ad (A_{ad}), low-effort, 167
Attitudes
   affective (emotional) foundations, 141–146
   analytical processes, 132–135
   behavior prediction, 146–148
   change strategies, 135
   characteristics, 128–129

cognitive foundations, 131–140
   in consumer behavior, 11
   external search, 200
   forming and changing, 129
   foundations, 129, 130e, 131, 132–135
   low-effort situations, 158
   and motivation, 60
   research, 146
   specificity and behavior prediction, 147
   unconscious influences, 160–161
Attraction effect, 219
Attractive sources, 78, 169–170
Attractiveness, 143
   reference groups, 307
Attribute balancing, high-effort decisions, 231
Attribute determination, 192
Attribute information, external search, 204, 205
Attribute processing, 224–225
Attribution theory, 277, 278
Attributes, and decision-making, 223, 224–225
Authenticity, 389
Autobiographical (episodic) memory, 103
Autonomic decision, 362
Availability heuristic, 242, 244
Avoidance, consumption coping, 279e
Avoidance-avoidance conflict, 52

B

Baby carrots marketing, 492
Back-to-school shopping events, 241–242
Bargain-a-day websites, 261
Base-rate information, 244
Basic level, hierarchical structure, 112
Behavior (B), TORA, 133, 134e
Behavior intention (BI), TORA, 133, 134e
Behavior prediction, from attitudes, 146–148
Behavioral approaches, personality, 398
Behavioral change, and innovations, 417e
Belief discrepancy, 133
Beliefs, change strategies, 135
Bias for the whole, 87
Biases, 216–217, 272–273
Bicycles, 466–467
Black Friday, 322–323
Black markets, 480
   prevention, 482
Blocking exposure to evidence, 273
Body feedback, 160
Boomerangers, 332
Boomers, 335
Boomtown Singles, 341
Bottom-up processing, 229
Boycott, 491
Brand-choice congruence, 311–312
Brand community, 305, 306
Brand extensions, 109–110
Brand familiarity, 190, 257

Brand image, 108
  creation, 109
  maintenance, change and protection, 110
Brand loyalty, 251
  development, 252
  teens, 333
Brand names
  consumer inferences, 90
  external search, 203
  liking and pre-attentive processing, 77
Brand personality, 108, 109e
  creation, 109
  maintenance, change and protection, 110
Brand preference, 190
Brand processing, and decision-making, 223
"Bright side" outcomes, 475–476, 491
Buyer, family role, 361, 361e
Buying, and smell, 82

C

Categories, knowledge structure, 110–113
Category, attitude reasoning, 131
Category-consistent information, 162
Causality and blame, 277–278
Celebrity sources, 170
Cell phones, disposition, 290–291
Central-route processing, 131
  high-effort, 129e
Ceremony, gift-giving, 463
Change agents, and innovation, 432
Channel selection, social class influence, 375
Charitable behavior, 490, 490e
Children
  and household decision influence, 363
  targeting, 482
Choice, and affective forecasting, 227–228
Choice tactics learning, 247–248
Chunking, memory, 105
Class average families, 365
Classic, innovation, 427
Classical conditioning, 165, 166e
Closure, 87
Clustering, 340, 348
Co-branding, 257
Co-creation
  definition, 419
  and innovations, 418–419, 436
  process, 58
Coercive power, 313
Cognition needs, 51
Cognitive abilities, external search, 201
Cognitive decision-making model, 222
  choice models, 222e
Cognitive function
  attitudes, 128, 129
  high-effort attitudes, 131–135
  high-effort attitude influences, 135–140
  low-effort attitudes, 161, 162
  low-effort attitude influences, 162–164
Cognitive involvement, 47
Cognitive resources, and consumer ability, 61
Cognitive responses, 132
Cognitive style, consumers, 61
Collections, special possessions, 456
Color, and perception, 81
Communal goal, 337

Communication source, influence of, 170.
  See also Sources
Communications, cognitive responses to,
  132–133
Community grants, 472–473
Community involvement, 490–491
Company reputation, 137
Comparative messages, 139–140
Compatibility, innovation, 430
Compensatory consumption, 370–371
Compensatory method, decision-making, 222
Competing stimuli, and attention, 79
Competitive brand marketing, 253
Competiveness, and consumer behavior, 401
Complaint-resolution, 281–282
Complaints, 281, 289
Complexity, innovation, 431
Complexity of information, and consumer
  opportunity, 63
Compliance, techniques, 315
Compliant personality, 397
Comprehension
  in consumer behavior, 11
  and culture, 89
  definition, 87, 92
  and MAO, 88–89
  message identification, 88
  source identification, 87–88
Compromise effect, high-effort decisions, 231
Compulsive behavior, 477–478, 478e
  and marketing, 481–482
Computerized Status Index (CSI), 367
Concrete goal, 55
Concreteness, and attention, 79, 80e
Conditioned response (CR), 165
Conditioned stimulus (CS), 165
Confirmation bias, 194, 216
Conformity, definition, 311
Conformity pressure creation, 315
Conjoint analysis, consumer behavior research, 33
Conjunctive model, decision-making, 223
Connative function, attitudes, 128
Connectedness function, symbols, 451–452
Conscious low-effort decision-making, 245–246
Conservation behavior, 489
Consideration (evoked set), 189
Consideration set, 219, 229
  external search, 199
Consistency with self-concept, 48–49
Conspicuous consumption, 369
Conspicuous waste, 369
Construal level theory, 114, 220
Consumer
  ability, 60–62
  diversity, 331e, 348
  inferences, 90–92
  and meaning, 445
  memory, 100, 120
  invasion, 41
  resistance to commercial excess, 491
  socialization, 309–310
Consumer access, and information, 64
Consumer behavior
  and age, 330–337
  attention, 76–80
  comprehension, 22, 87–92

  decisions, 6–9
  definition, 3
  dimensions, 4–5, 4e
  emotions and coping, 9
  ethnic influences, 342–347
  exposure, 73–76
  gender, 337–340
  household influences, 356, 357e, 376
  income versus social class, 366–367
  influences, 10–14
  and innovation, 417
  and normative influence, 311–312
  outcomes and issues, 13
  perception, 80–87
  and personality, 398–401, 406
  processes, 5, 10e, 11–13
  regional influences, 340–342
  religious influences, 347–348
  sexual orientation, 339
  social class influences, 364, 376
  social influences, 300e, 322
  study benefits, 14–15, 22
Consumer behavior cases
  baby carrots marketing, 492
  bargain-a-day websites, 261
  bicycles, 466–467
  Black Friday, 322–323
  cell phones, 290–291
  Cyber Monday, 323
  Harley-Davidson, 235–236
  IKEA's household appeal, 376–377
  Old Spice, 176–177
  research and marketing, 22–23
  retail walk-in clinics, 406–407
  search engines, 207
  single-serve coffeemakers, 437
  teens and music, 349
  Under Armour, 93
  USAA (United States Automobile Association),
    65–66
  Volkswagen Group, 149–150
Consumer behavior research
  ethical issues, 39–41
  methods, 28–36
  negative aspects, 40–41
  positive aspects, 40
  researchers, 36–39
  tools, 28e–29e
Consumer characteristics
  high-effort decisions, 230–231
  informational influence, 316–317
  memory retrieval, 119
  normative influence, 313
Consumer ethics, 476–477
Consumer experience, learning from, 270–271, 271e
Consumer knowledge, external search, 200–201
Consumer learning, and innovation, 430–431
Consumer opportunity, 62–64
Consumer organizations, consumer behavior
  research, 39
Consumer protection, definition, 39
Consumer theft, 479–480
  motivations, 479e
  prevention, 482
Consumption behaviors, and gender, 338
Consumption controversies, 483–484, 491

Consumption experiences, and episodic memory, 103
Consumption patterns, 405
    values impact, 391
Consumption symbols, 445e
Context
    group decision-making, 233–234
    and informational influence, 317
    message, 164, 175
Continuous innovation, 417
Contrast, and attention, 80
Control of information, and consumer opportunity, 64
Controllability, cause and effect, 277
Coping
    and consumer behavior, 9
    consumption problems, 279–280
Correlated associations, 113
Counterargument (CA), 132
Country of origin, and consumer inferences, 91
Creativity, and consumer behavior, 399
Credibility
    definition, 136
    marketing influence, 302
Cross-cultural needs, 52
Cross-cultural values, 391
Cultural categories, 443
Cultural milieu, and advertising, 393–394
Cultural principles, 443
Cultural resources, and consumer ability, 62
Cultural transitions, symbols, 450
Culture
    definition, 12
    class structure, 366e
    and comprehension, 89
    consumer behavior influences, 341–342
    context and needs, 52
    and decision-making, 222
    external consumption processes, 12–13
    and external search, 196
    and humor in ads, 173, 174e
    and innovation, 425
    and knowledge content and structure, 115
    resources and consumer ability, 62
    and meaning, 443–445
    and values, 391
Curiosity, and ad response, 146
Customer-company relationship, complaint-resolution, 281
Customer loyalty, and satisfaction, 283–284
Customer-oriented marketing, 16
Customer psychographics, complaint-resolution, 282
Customer segments, 16
    and attention, 80
Customized products, 382–383
Cutoff levels
    acceptable, 225
    decision-making, 222
Cutting-edge cars, 213–214
Cyber Monday, 323

D
"Dark side" outcomes, 475–476, 491
Database marketing, consumer behavior research, 34

Data mining, definition, 34
"Deal fatigue," 261
Deal sites, 261
Deal-prone consume, 254
Deals, 255
Decay, memory, 116
Deceptive research practices, 41
Decider, family role, 361
Decision characteristics, high-effort decisions, 231–234
Decision delay, 229–230
Decision framing, definition, 220
Decision-making
    affective, 226–229
    in consumer behavior, 12
    criteria, 220–226
    definition, 214
    and high-effort, 218–222, 230–234
    low-effort processes, 245–247, 260
    and personal relevance, 48
    post-decision, 268–270, 269e
    process, 186e, 215e
    thought-based, 222
    and variety, 258–259
Decision roles, family, 361e
Decisions, in consumer behavior, 5–9
Degree of contact, reference groups, 307
Degree of identification, reference groups, 307
Delayed marriage and cohabitation, 358–359
Demographics
    external search, 201
    and innovation, 424
Demonstration, innovation compatibility and simplicity, 432–433
Denial, consumption coping, 279e
Density, reference groups, 307
Desire, and goals, 56
Detached personality, 397
Development and communication, symbols, 448
Deviants, high school reference group, 305e
Diagnostic information, definition, 191
Diagnosticity, brand name recall, 191
Diaries, consumer behavior research, 31–32
Differential thresholds, 84
    marketing implications, 85
Diffusion
    definition, 425
    factors, 426
    influences, 427–436
    product life cycle, 426e, 427
Direct comparative advertising, 139
Direct experience, attitudes, 131
Disconfirmation, definition, 275
Disconfirmation paradigm, 275e
Discontinuous innovation, 417
Disjunctive model, decision-making, 223
Displays, and consumer inferences, 91
Disposition
    consumer behavior, 4–5
    controversies, 487–488, 491
    products, 285–287, 289
    options, 285e
Dissatisfaction
    coping with, 279
    definition, 274
    feelings-based, 279–280

responses to, 281–283
    thought-based, 275–279
Dissociative reference group, 305, 306
Distraction, and consumer opportunity, 63
Distribution
    and consumer behavior, 20–22
    and consumer inferences, 91
    definition, 4
Diversity influences, 13
Divestment ritual, 459
Divorce, 360
Dogmatism, and consumer behavior, 399
Domain-specific values, 386
Door-in-the-face technique, 315
Downward mobility, 368
Dramas, ad message as, 174
Dual-career families, 359
Dual coding, memory retrieval, 119
Dual-mediation hypothesis, 167
Dynamically continuous innovation, 417

E
Early adopters, 422e
Early majority, 422e
Earned status, 367
Easily processed stimuli, and attention, 79
Echoic memory, 100
Education
    and consumer ability, 62
    and social class, 367
Effort. See also High-effort, Low-effort
    in attitude formation and change, 129, 131
    and goals, 54–55
    and persuasion, 158
Ego depletion, 55
Egoistic needs, 50e
Elaboration
    attitude/behavior prediction, 146–147
    and attitudes, 129
    memory, 104, 105
Elites, high school reference group, 305e
Embedded market, 309
Emblematic function, symbol, 446–448
Embodiment, 57
Emotional accounting, 216
Emotional appeals, 142, 144, 174
Emotional attachment, attitude/behavior prediction, 147–148
Emotional contagion, 144
Emotional detachment, disposition, 286
Emotional expression, and music, 171e
Emotional resources, and consumer ability, 61
Emotions
    and attitudes, 129
    and consumer behavior, 9
    gift-giving, 462
Empathy, and episodic memory, 103
Encoding of evidence, 271
Encouragement, specific behaviors, 58
Enduring involvement, 47
Energy Star, EPA program, 489
Engagement, 141
Enhancement, motivation, 57
Environment, Western value, 390
Environmentally conscious behavior, 488–490
Episodic (autobiographical) memory, 103

Equity theory, 278
Estimation of likelihood, 214
Ethic groups
    global, 347
    United States, 343–347
Ethnic emblems, 446
Ethnic group, definition, 342
Ethnic identification, and values, 391–392
Ethnic influences, on consumer behavior,
    342–347
Ethnographic research
    definition, 34
    consumer behavior research, 33–34
Evaluations, change strategies, 135
Evaluative conditioning, 165, 166e
Even-a-penny-will-help technique, 315
Evoked set, 189
Expectancy-value models, 133
Expectation, definition, 275
Expectations and performance, 275–276
Experience, attitude/behavior prediction, 147
Experience goods, 198
Experienced emotions, and coping, 279–280
Experiential search, 196
Experiments, consumer behavior research, 32–33
Expertise, high-effort decisions, 230
Experts
    and informational influence, 317
    knowledge content and structure, 115–116
Explaining the experience, 273
Explicit memory, 103
Exponential diffusion curve, 426, 426e
Exposure
    and consumer behavior, 11
    definition, 73, 92
    influences, 73, 74e
Exposure to evidence, 271
Expressive roles, 361
Expressive support seeking, consumption coping,
    279e
Expressiveness function, symbols, 452
Extended family, 356
External consumption processes, 12–13
External marketing research firms, 37
External search, 194–206
    accuracy, 204
    definition, 194, 206
    extent of, 198–202
    information acquired, 203–204
    sources, 195–198
    steps, 204–205
    types, 195e
Extremeness aversion, high-effort decisions, 231

F
Fad, definition, 427
Fairness and equity, 278
Fairness in the exchange, 278
False memories, 117
Family and children, Western value, 388
Family life cycle, 358
Fashion, definition, 427
Fast food restaurants, 2–3
Favorability
    associations, 108
    attitudes, 128
Favorable word of mouth, engineering, 320

Fear appeals, 145
Feeling-based decisions
    high-effort, 143–146
    low-effort, 256–257
Feeling-based satisfaction/dissatisfaction,
    279–280, 289
Feelings
    simplifying strategy, 256–257
    source of information, 141
Felt involvement, 46e, 47–48
Field experiments, consumer behavior research,
    33
Figure and ground, 86, 87e
Financial resources, and consumer
    ability, 60–61
Financial risk, 59
Focal attention, 77
Focus, cause and effect, 277
Focus group
    definition, 30
    consumer behavior research, 30
Foot-in-the-door technique, 315
Formality, reference groups, 307, 308
Frame switching, 454
Framing, and decision-making, 220–221
Fraudulent symbol, 370
Frequency heuristic, 161, 162
Frugality, and consumer behavior, 400
Functional (utilitarian) dimension of ad, 146
Functional innovations, 418
Functional needs, 50–51
Future-oriented customers, 231

G
Gains and losses, decision-making, 225–226
Gambling, compulsive, 484
Gatekeeper
    family role, 361
    marketing influence, 304
Gender
    and consumer behavior, 337–340, 348
    and special possessions, 458
Gender emblems, 446–447
Generation X, 332, 334
Generation Y, 332
Geographic function, symbol, 446
Gestation stage, gift-giving, 461–463
Gift-giving
    process, 462e
    reciprocation, 464
    relationship impact, 464e
    stages, 462e, 463–464
    timing, 461–463
Global values, 385, 385e
Goal-derived categories, 114, 115
Goals
    brand name recall, 190, 192
    consumer decision-making, 233e
    and decision-making, 220
    and effort, 54–55
    and emotions, 55, 56e
    and knowledge content and structure, 115
    to regulate action, 57
    to regulate feeling, 57
    setting and pursuit, 53–54, 54e
    types, 55
Good and evil, money as, 371

Government agencies, consumer behavior
    research, 39
Graded structure, and prototypicality,
    111–112
Gray market, 336
Green brands, global top 10, 137e
Greenwashing, 490
Grooming ritual, 459
Group characteristics
    informational influence, 317
    normative influence, 313–314
Group context, decision-making, 233–234
Grouping, 87
Guarantees, 277

H
Habit, definition, 249
Habitual purchases, other brand marketing, 250,
    251
Habituation, 80
Happiness, money as, 371–372
Harmful self-focus, 475
Health, Western value, 389
Hearing
    and perception, 81
    sensory marketing, 83
Hedonic dimension of ad, 146
Hedonic experience, interruption, 227
Hedonic innovations, 418
Hedonic needs, 51
Hedonism, 389
Helpful other-focus, 473
Hemispheric lateralization, 77
Heuristics, 161
    in consumer evaluation, 61
Hierarchical structure, 112
High-context cultures, message comprehension,
    89
High-effort attitudes
    affective function, 141–143
    cognitive function, 131–135
    formation and change, 130e
    influences, 135–140, 143–145
High-effort behavior, 45, 46e
High-effort decision-making, 12, 215e, 218–222
    influences, 230–234
High-effort hierarchy of effects, innovation, 420,
    421e
High-effort information processing and
    decision-making, 45, 46e
High-effort judgments, 215e, 218–222
High-involvement, and satisfaction, 274
High school reference groups, 305e
High self-monitors, 148
Hispanic American consumers, 343–345
Home, Western value, 387
Homeless, consumption patterns, 373–374
Homophily
    group membership, 307, 308
    social system and innovation, 435
Horizontal versus vertical orientation, 341
Household
    changes, 338e, 358–360
    consumer behavior influences, 13, 356,
        357e, 376
    definition, 356
    life cycles, 359e

roles, 361–363
types, 356, 358
Humor
and attention, 78
low-involvement offerings, 172
Husband-dominant decision, 362
Hypothesis generation, 271
Hypothesis testing, 271

I
Iconic memory, 100
Ideal identity schema, 453
Ideal state, 185, 187
Idealized self-image, 483
Identification, and episodic memory, 103
Idiocentric consumers, 388
Image location, and perception, 81
Imagery
emotional decision-making, 228
judgment, 216
memory impact, 102
Imagined experience
attitude change, 135
attitudes, 131
Immediate versus long-term interests, 475
Implicit memory, 103–104
Impulse purchase, 259
Incidental learning, 164
Income, and social class, 366–367
Inconsistency, and attitudes, 60
Incorporation, new role, 449
Independent search, 196
Independent variable, definition, 32
Indirect comparative advertising, 139
Individual-alone goals, 233
Individual-group goals, 233
Individualism, Western value, 388
Individualism versus collectivism, 341, 391
Industry standards, and innovation, 432
Inept set, 219
Inert set, 219
Inferences, definition, 90
Influence
sources of, 299–305
types of, 311e
Influencer, family role, 361
Infomercials, 88, 138
Information
dimensions, 318
sources of, 316–322
Information availability
external search, 201
high-effort decision, 232
Information discrepancy, external
search, 200
Information format
external search, 201
high-effort decision, 232
Information gathering, group decision-making,
233
Information overload, external search, 197
Information processing
ability, 200–201
motivation factors, 199–200
opportunity, 201–202
Information transmission, reference groups,
308–309

Informational influence, marketing source, 311e,
316–322
Informative ads, 146
Inherited status, 367
Inhibition, and internal search, 194
In-house marketing research departments, 36–37
Innovation, definition, 415, 436
Innovations, 416e
adoption or resistance, 419–425
characteristics, 417–419, 427–429
consequences, 436
consumer learning requirements, 430–433
diffusion, 425–427
influences, 427–435
legitimacy and adaptability, 433–434
social relevance, 433
and social system, 435
uncertainty influence, 429–430
Innovators, 422e
Instrumental importance, special possessions, 457
Instrumental roles, 361
Instrumental values, 385
Integration of evidence, 271
Interference, memory, 116–117
Internal consumption processes, 11
Internal search
accuracy, 193–194
definition, 188, 206
and recall, 188–193
Internet
external search sources, 196–197
searcher types, 200
Interviews
definition, 30
consumer behavior research, 30–31
Involvement
affective, 141
attitude/behavior prediction, 146–147
external search, 199
objects of, 47–48
and risk, 59
types, 47
Involvement with a brand, 48
Involvement with a medium, 48
Irates, complainer, 281

J
Joint household decisions, 362
Judgment
biases, 216–217
definition, 214, 234
goodness/badness estimation, 214, 216
low-effort processes, 242
process, 215e
satisfaction, dissatisfaction, 273–280
Just noticeable difference (j.n.d.), 84

K
Kids & Cul-de-sac consumers, 340
Knowledge
attitude/behavior prediction, 147
and consumer behavior, 11
Knowledge content, 105, 106, 109, 120
Knowledge flexibility, 113–114
Knowledge structure, 105–106, 110
associative networks, 106
categories, 111–113
schemas, 106

L
Laggards, 422e
Late majority, 422e
Law of small numbers, 244
Learning
and choice, 247–248, 248e
consumer experience, 270–271, 271e
factors, 272
Legitimacy, innovation, 433
Lettering, and perception, 81
Lexicographic model, 225
Lifestyles
and behavior patterns, 401–402
consumer influence, 13
definition, 401, 406
Likable sources, 170
Liking
and color, 81
and smell, 82
List of Values (LOV), 395
Locus of control, 397
Long-term memory (LTM), 102–103, 120
Low-context cultures, message
comprehension, 89
Low-effort attitudes
affective function, 164–165
cognitive function, 161
formation and change, 159e
influences, 162–164, 169–175
Low-effort decision-making, processes, 245–247,
260
Low-effort hierarchy of effects, 246, 421, 421e
Low-effort situation, 158
Low-elaboration decisions, 246
and choice tactics, 247
Lower Americans, 365e
Low-level construals, 220
Low self-monitors, 148
Luxury watches, 127–128

M
MAO (motivation, ability and opportunity), 46e
and complaining, 281
and comprehension, 88–89
and direct comparative messages, 140
and effort, 129, 131, 148, 158, 175, 218
and emotion-based attitudes, 143
and high-effort adoption process, 421
and internal search, 188
in low-effort decisions, 246
and post-decision dissonance, 268
Marital transitions, and products, 450
Market
segments, 16
segmentation values impact, 391
as socializing agent, 310
Market maven, 304
Market test, 33
Marketing
and consumer behavior, 4e
and consumers' privacy, 486–487
consumers' resistance, 491
and consumption controversies, 485–486
definition, 14
ethics, 14–15, 393, 476
and materialism, 481
social responsibility issues, 488–491

Marketing communications. *See also* Messages
 and consumer ability, 62
 and enhanced motivation, 57
 memorability, 116
 opinion leaders, 304
 and perceived risk, 58
 and repetition, 64
Marketing implications
 acquisition controversies, 481–482
 affective decision-making, 228
 African Americans, 345–346
 age, 332–337
 alternatives comparison, 229–230
 Asian Americans, 346–347
 attention, 78–80
 attitude affective/emotional foundations,
  142–143
 attitude cognitive foundations, 133
 attitude-toward-the-brand theory, 146, 168
 attribution theory, 278
 brand loyalty, 252–253
 classical/evaluative conditioning, 166–167
 comprehension, 89–90
 connectedness and expressiveness, 452
 consumer ability, 62
 consumer behavior, 15–22
 consumer characteristics, 234
 consumer dissatisfaction, 280, 282
 consumer opportunity, 64
 consumer satisfaction, 274–275, 276–277
 consumption controversies, 485–487
 cultural influences, 341–342
 customer retention, 284
 decision delay, 229
 decision-making, 221, 223, 224
 disposition controversies, 488
 disposition decisions, 286–287
 emblematic function of products, 448, 453–454
 emotional arousal, 145
 episodic memory, 103
 exposure, 75–76
 external search, 198, 202–203, 205–206
 fairness and equity, 278–279
 fear appeals, 145
 feelings, 257–258, 259
 gender, 338
 gift-giving, 465
 hedonic enhancement, 146
 Hispanic Americans, 343
 household changes, 360
 household roles, 363–364
 humor and low-involvement offerings, 172
 impulse purchases, 260
 informational influences, 317
 innovation, 419, 421–422, 427, 429,
  430, 433, 434
 innovation adoption, 424–425, 431–433, 436
 internal search, 193, 194
 judgment process, 217–218
 knowledge content, 109–110
 knowledge flexibility, 115
 knowledge structure, 113–114
 lifestyles, 402–404
 low-effort attitudes, 160–161, 163, 164–165
 low-effort decision-making, 249
 low-effort judgments, 244, 245
 memory, 105

message quality, 138–141
 mood, 169
 motivation, 57–58
 negative word-of-mouth communication, 283
 normative influences, 314–316
 perceived risk, 60
 perception, 83–84
 personality traits, 401
 post-decision dissonance, 270
 pricing techniques, 255
 problem recognition, 187–188
 processing biases, 273
 psychographic applications, 405–406
 recycling, 289
 reference groups, 306, 308–309
 role transitions, 451
 service recovery, 283
 sex, 173–174
 sexual orientation, 339–340
 social class, 372, 374
 source attractiveness, 143
 source credibility, 136–137
 sources, 303
 Theory of Reasoned Action (TORA), 134–135
 values, 392
 word of mouth, 319–322
 working memory, 102
Marketing sources, 299–305, 301e
 credibility, 302
 informational influence, 316–322
 mix, 303
 normative influence, 310
 reference groups, 305–310
Marketing stimuli, 73
Masculinity versus femininity, 391
 cultures, 341
Maslow's Hierarchy of Needs, 49–50, 50e
Mass media
 marketing influence, 299
 reach, 301
Match-up hypothesis, 143
Materialism, 386–387, 477
 and marketing, 481
Me versus them, 473
Meaning
 and consumer, 445
 and culture, 443–445
 emblematic function, 446
 gift-giving, 461–466
 sacred, 459–460
 and special possessions, 457
 symbolic, 444e, 446–454
 transfer from culture to product, 445e
Means-end chain analysis, 394e, 394–395
Media
 African American marketing, 345–346
 Asian American marketing, 347
 Hispanic American marketing, 343–344
 and innovation, 425
 social class influence, 374–375
 as socializing agent, 310
Media planning firms, 37
Media search, 196
Medium, memory retrieval stimulus, 118
Memory
 and consumer behavior, 11
 enhancement, 104

explicit and implicit, 103–104
 long-term, 102–103
 and retrieval, 116–117
 sensory, 100
 working, 102
Memory-laden objects, 455
Mental accounting, 216
Mental calculation difficulties, and
  judgment, 217
Mere exposure effect, 164, 175
Message
 boomers, 336–337
 cognitive-based high-effort attitudes, 138–140
 cognitive-based low-effort attitudes, 162–164
 comprehension, 88
 context and repetition, 164, 175
 emotion-based high-effort attitudes, 143–146
 emotion-based low-effort attitudes, 171–175
 generation X, 334
 lifestyles, 403
 social class influence, 374
 teens, 333–334
Metacognitive experiences, 231
Middle Americans, 365e
Middle class, consumption patterns, 373
Millennials, consumer behavior, 332
MindBase, psychograhic segmentation
  system, 404
Mind-body connection
 behavior influence, 58
 and self-control, 56
Miscomprehension, 88
Mispredictions, emotions, 280
Mobile wallets, 414–415
Mobility Blues, 341
Modality, informational information, 318
Modernity, social system and innovation, 435
Money, meanings of, 371
Mood-altering properties, special possessions,
  457, 458e
Mood-congruent direction, attitudes, 168
Moods
 and bias, 217
 and color, 81, 169
 high-effort decisions, 230–231
 and internal search, 194
 and lighting, 169
 and smell, 82
Morals, influence, 311
Motivated reasoning, 47
Motivation, 11. *See also* MAO (motivation, ability
  and opportunity)
 and attitudes, 60
 consumer theft, 479e
 definition, 45, 65
 and emotions, 55
 gift-giving, 462
 and goals, 53–55
 and learning, 272
 influences, 46e
 marketing implications, 57–58
 and needs, 49–52
 personal relevance, 48–49
 recycling, 287
 and self-control, 55–57
 values, 49
Movie and meal combinations, 44–45

Multiattribute expectancy-value models, and decision-making, 223
Multibrand loyalty, 251
Multicultural marketing, 343, 348
Multiple items, external search, 201
Music
    and attention, 78
    and emotional expression, 171e
    sensory marketing, 83, 171
    teens marketing, 349
Mystery ad, 163

N
National character, 400–401
Need, definition, 49
Need for cognition (NFC), 399
Need for uniqueness (NFU), 399
Needs
    categorizations, 50e
    characteristics, 51–52
    identification, 52
    and personal relevance, 49–50
Negative word-of-mouth-communication, 275, 283
    preventing and responding, 320
Negativity bias, 217
Netnography
    definition, 34
    consumer behavior research, 34–35
Network targeting, 308
Neuroscience, consumer behavior research, 35–36
Noncomparable decision, 229
Noncompensatory model, decision-making, 222
Nonfocal attention, 77
Nonmarketing sources, 299, 301e
    credibility, 302
Nonsocial needs, 50
Norm(s)
    definition, 311
    creation, 315
Normative beliefs, targeting, 135
Normative influences, 134, 256
    attitude/behavior prediction, 148
    marketing source, 311e, 310–312
    strength impact, 312–314, 322
Nostalgia marketing, 120–121
Novelty, innovations, 417
Nuclear family, 356
Nutrition labels, information format, 201e

O
Obesity "epidemic," 484
Objective comprehension, 88
Objective knowledge, external search, 200
Observability, 433
Observations, consumer behavior research, 33–34
Occupation, and social class, 367
Offering
    acquisition, use and disposal decisions, 6–9
    definition, 3
Olfactory memory, 100
One brand at a time evaluation, 224
One-sided messages, 138–139
Ongoing search, 195
Online community, 197–198
Online processing, consumer evaluation, 192
Online word of mouth, 318–319

Operant conditioning, 247
    episodic memory, 103
Opinion leaders, 303–304
    referral to, 305
    social system and innovation, 435
    targeting, 304
Opportunity, 11, 45. See also Consumer opportunity, Motivation, MAO (motivation, ability and opportunity)
    influences, 46e
    recycling, 288
Optimal stimulation level (OSL), 258, 398–399
Optimizing, best possible, 246
Organic food and nonfood products, annual sales, 389e
Overeating and obesity, 484
Overprivileged families, 365

P
Packaging, consumer inferences, 91
Parody display, 370
Passives, complainer, 281
Perceived benefits, innovation, 428
Perceived consumer effectiveness, 489
Perceived costs
    external search, 199
    innovation, 428
Perceived risk
    definition, 58
    external search, 199
    marketing implications, 60
    types, 59
Perceived value, innovation, 428
Perception
    and consumer behavior, 11
    definition, 80
    hearing, 81
    and smell, 82
    stimuli thresholds, 84–85, 92
    taste, 82
    and touch, 82–83
    visual, 81
Perception of problem, complaint-resolution, 281
Perceptual fluency, 89
Perceptual organization, 86
Performance risk, 59
Performance-related tactics, 249
Peripheral cues, 158
Peripheral-route processing, 131
    low-effort, 129e
    persuasion, 158
Personal characteristics, complaint-resolution, 282
Personal marketing delivery, 299, 300
    two-way communication, 302
Personal relevance, and motivation, 48–49
Personality
    attitude/behavior prediction, 148
    and consumer behavior, 13, 398–401, 406
    definition, 396, 406
    and innovation, 424
    research approaches, 396–398
Personally relevant stimuli, 78
Persuasion, and effort, 158
Pervasive and persuasive, word of mouth, 318
Pets, 455
Phenomenological approaches, personality, 397

Photography and pictures, consumer behavior research, 31
Physical (safety) risk, 59
Physical detachment, disposition, 286
Physical distance, social system and innovation, 435
Physical resources, and consumer ability, 61–62
Physiological needs, 50e
Physiological response
    color, 81
    smell, 82
Pleasant stimuli, and attention, 78
Positioning
    and consumer behavior, 17–18
    for teens, 333
Possession ritual, 459
Post-decision evaluations, 12
Post-decision feeling, definition, 279
Post-decision levels of happiness, forecasting, 228
Post-decision processes
    dissonance, 268, 289
    regret, 268–270, 289
Power distance, 391
Pre-attentive processing, 77
Preference dispersion, 189
Pre-purchase search, 195
Presentation stage, gift-giving, 463
Present-oriented customers, 231
Prevention-focused goals, 55, 141
Price
    consciousness variability, 255
    and consumer behavior, 19–20
    consumer inferences, 91
    external search, 203–204
    simplifying strategy, 253
Price perception, 254
Primacy and recency effects, 117
Primary reference group, 307
Priming, associations, 107
Prior brand evaluations, and judgment, 217
Prior experience
    and judgment, 217
    and knowledge content and structure, 115–116
    and learning, 272
Privacy controversies, 484–485
Problem recognition
    definition, 185
    and information search, 186e
Processing biases, 272–273
Product(s)
    African American marketing, 345
    Asian American marketing, 346
    and choice tactics, 248
    disposition, 285–287, 289, 487
    distribution and shelf placement, and exposure, 73
    features and consumer inferences, 90–91
    fit and self-concepts, 454
    fit with system, 432
    Hispanic American marketing, 343
    informational influence, 316
    large market share (top dog), 273
    lifestyles influence, 403–404
    lower-share brand (underdog), 273
    and motivation, 57–58
    normative influence, 312–313
    positioning for teens, 333

Product(s) (*Continued*)
quality and brand loyalty, 252
sacred and ritual involvement, 461
social class influence, 374
and symbols, 446–448
technological paradoxes, 419e
values influence, 393
Product development, and consumer behavior, 16–17
Product life cycle, 426e, 427
Product placement, 88
and comprehension, 89
Product trial, and smells, 81
Profane things, 459
Prominence, and attention, 79
Promotion-focused goals, 55, 141
Promotions, and innovation trialability, 432
Prototype, definition, 112, 120
Prototypical brands, 112e
Prototypicality
brand name recall, 189–190, 190e
definition, 112
memory retrieval stimulus, 118
Psychoanalytic theories, personality, 396
Psychographics, 383, 384e
applications, 404–406
lifestyles, 401–404
personality, 396–401
values, 383–395
Psychological core
attitude formation and change, 130e, 159e
exposure to comprehension, 74e
internal consumer processes, 11
memory and knowledge, 101e
motivation, ability and opportunity (MAO), 46e
Psychological risk, 59
Psychophysiological reactions, consumer behavior research, 35–36
Punishment, 247–248, 248e
Purchase panels, consumer behavior research, 34
Puzzles, and attention, 79

Q
QR (quick response) codes, 184–185, 299
dos and don'ts, 202e
Quality and price inference, 91

R
Reach, mass media, 301
Reactance, definition, 311
Recall, memory, 104
Recall of attributes, 190–192
Recall of brands, 189–190
Recall of evaluations, 192
Recall of experiences, 192–193
Recirculation, memory, 105
Recognition, memory, 104
Recycling, 287–289
selected materials, 288e
Reducing time needed to buy, use and learn product or service, 64
Reducing time pressure, 64
Redundant cues, memory retrieval stimulus, 118
Reference group(s)
characteristics, 306–308
and consumer socialization, 309–310

definition, 12
emblems, 447
product influence, 313e
types, 305–306, 322
Referrals, and normative influence, 315
Reflexive evaluation, definition, 450
Reformulation stage, gift-giving, 463–464
Regional influences, on consumer behavior, 340–342, 348
Regret minimizing, group decision-making, 233
Regulatory fit, attitudes, 141
Rehearsal, memory, 105
Reinforcement, 247, 248e
Reinforcement and removal, symbols, 448
Relationship bonding, gift-giving, 463–464
Relationship impact, gift-giving, 464e
Relative advantage, 428
Relative brand uncertainty, external search, 199–200
Religion, and consumer behavior, 347–348
Repeat purchase, 248
development, 250
Repeating marketing communications, 64
Repetition
and brand awareness, 164
and consumer opportunity, 63–64
and top-of-mind, 219
Representativeness heuristic, 242
Reputation restoration, 320e
Research, and marketing, 22–23
Research foundation, 38
Resistance, innovation, 419
innovation influences, 427–436
to commercial excess, 491
Response involvement, 48
Retail atmospherics, consumer inferences, 91, 92e
Retail walk-in clinics, 406–407
Retailer search, 196
Retailers, consumer research, 38
Retrieval
and consumer characteristics, 119
cues, 118, 190, 191e
definition, 100, 120
enhancing, 117
errors, 117
failures, 116
stimulus, 118–119
Rewards and sanctions, product use, 314
Risk
and involvement, 59
perceived, 58–59
Rites of passage, 449
Rituals, role transitions, 449
Rituals, special possessions, 458–459
Rokeach Value Survey (RVS), 395
Role acquisition function, symbol, 448–450
Role acquisition
model, 449e
phases, 449
Rumors, handling, 321

S
Sacred entities, 459, 465
Sacred objects, 460
Sacredness
avoiding profaning, 461
creating and maintaining, 460

Safety
need, 50e
risk, 59
Sales promotions, and brand loyalty, 252–253
Salience
associations, 108
memory retrieval stimulus, 118
Salient attributes, 191–192
Same-sex couples, 360
Satisfaction
definition, 273
feelings-based, 279–280
service recovery, 283–284
thought-based, 275–279
Satisfice, good enough, 246
Scandals, handling, 321
Schema
brand image and personality, 108
definition, 106
Schema-consistent information, 162
Script, definition, 108
Search engines, 207
Search goods, 199
Searching by attribute, 205
Searching by brand, 205
Secondary reference group, 307
Segmentation, lifestyles, 402–403
Selective exposure, 73–75
Self-actualization, 50e
Self-concept, 48
and symbols, 453
Self-control, 55
and goal conflict, 55–57
Self-image, idealized, 483
Self-interest versus interests of others, 473–475
Self-monitoring behavior, 400
Self-positivity bias, 217
Self-presentation, group decision-making, 233
Self-referencing message, 163
Semantic memory, 103
Seniors, 336
Sensory marketing, 83
Sensory memory, 100, 120
Separation, old role, 449
Service provider similarity, 315
Service recovery, 282–283
Service, social class influence, 374
Sex, as communication technique, 173
Sex roles, 337–338
Sexual orientation, and consumer behavior, 339
Shaping, 250
Shopping, and needs, 52
Signal-to-noise ratio, and attention, 80
Simple inferences, 161
Simplifying strategies, 249
brand loyalty, 251–253
feelings, 256–257
habit, 249–250
normative influences, 256
price, 253–255
Simulations, external search, 197
Single-serve coffeemakers, 437
Situational factors, attitude/behavior prediction, 148
Situational involvement, 47
Size and shape, and perception, 81
Sleeper effect, 137
Smaller families, 360

Smell
  and perception, 82
  sensory marketing, 84
Snack foods, and social media, 157–158
Social class
  changes over time, 367–369
  consumer behavior influences, 13, 364, 376
  and consumption, 369–372
  consumption patterns, 372–375
  determination, 366–367
  emblems, 446
  fragmentation, 368
  hierarchy, 364
  indexes, 367
  segmentation variability, 375
  and special possessions, 457
  structures, 365–366, 366e
  system types, 364–365
  and values, 392
Social comparison information, and susceptibility, 314e
Social comparison theory, 484
Social dilemma, 473, 475e
Social identity-based attitudes, 132
Social influences, 298–299, 300e, 301e
  and innovation, 424
  and tie-strength, 308e
Social media
  and customer service, 267–268
  generation X, 335
  marketing influence, 301
  teens, 334
  word of mouth, 319
Social needs, 50
Social norms, and environmental behaviors, 489
Social-psychological theories, personality, 397–398
Social-relational theory, 212
Social relevance, definition, 433
Social resources, and consumer ability, 62
Social responsibility, 488
Social risk, 59
Social status transitions, symbols, 450–451
Social system, and innovative products, 435–436
Source credibility, 136
Source derogation (SD), 132
Source identification, 87–88
Source of confusion, retrieval error, 117
Sources
  cognitive-based high-effort attitudes, 136–138, 162
  cognitive-based low-effort attitudes, 162
  emotion-based high-effort attitudes, 143
  emotion-based low-effort attitudes, 169–171
  of influence, 299–305, 311e
  of information, 316–322
Spanish/English messages, Hispanic American marketing, 344
Special brands, 455
Special events, teens, 334
Special possessions, 455–456, 465
  characteristics, 456–457, 458e
  consumers, 457–458
  disposal, 459
Special pricing, 255
Speedy response, complaint-resolution, 282
Spouses, decision roles, 362
Spreading of activation, associative networks, 107

S-shaped diffusion curve, 425, 426e
Stability, cause and effect, 277
Status crystallization, 367
Status float, 366
Status panic, 368
Status symbol, 370
Stealing
  rationalizations, 480
  temptation to, 479
Stimulation needs, 51
Stimuli thresholds, perception, 84–85
Stimulus, memory retrieval, 118
Strong argument, definition, 138
Strong effect, subliminal advertising, 86
Storytelling, consumer behavior research, 31
Subjective comprehension, 88, 89
Subjective knowledge, external search, 200
Subjective norm (SN), TORA, 133, 134e
Subliminal perception, 85–86
Subordinate level, hierarchical structure, 112
Superordinate level, hierarchical structure, 112
Support argument (SA), 132
Surprise, gift-giving, 463
Surprising stimuli, and attention, 79
Survey, definition, 29
Surveys, consumer behavior research, 29–30
Susceptibility
  to influence, 400
  interpersonal influence, 314e
Symbolic innovations, 418
Symbolic meaning, 444e, 465
  consumption symbols, 445e
Symbolic needs, 51
Symbolic value, special possessions, 457, 458e
Symbols
  definition, 14
  connectedness function, 451–452
  consumer inferences, 90
  emblematic function, 446–448
  expressiveness function, 452
  role acquisition function, 448–451
  role transitions, 449
  and self-concept, 453–454
Syncratic decision, 362
Syndicated data services, consumer research, 38

T
Target market selection, 16
Targeting
  children, 482
  lifestyles, 402–403
  vulnerable segments, 480–481
Taste
  and perception, 82
  sensory marketing, 83–84
Taxonomic category, 111, 111e
Technological products, paradoxes of, 419e
Technology, Western value, 390
Teens, consumer behavior, 330–332
Temporal dilemma, 473, 475e
Temporary (situational) involvement, 47
Temptation to steal, 479
Terminal values, 385
Terror Management Theory (TMT), 145
Theory of planned behavior, 131, 134, 148
Theory of Reasoned Action (TORA), 131, 133–134, 134e, 148

behavior prediction, 146
decision-making, 223
Thinking-behaving-feeling sequence
  low-effort, 246
  traditional, 245
Thin-slice judgments, 160
Thought-based decisions
  high-effort, 222, 234
  low-effort, 249
Thought-based satisfaction/dissatisfaction, 275–279, 289
Tie-strength, and social influence, 308e, 309
Time
  and consumer opportunity, 63
  and decision-making, 220
  risk, 59
Time available, external search, 201
Time pressure, high-effort decisions, 231
Tobacco, minor's illegal use, 483
Top-dog strategies, product, 273
Top-down processing, 229
Top-of-mind accessibility, 147
Top-of-mind and repetition, 219
Top-of-mind brands, 189
Touch
  and perception, 82–83
  sensory marketing, 84
Trade group, definition, 38
Traditional hierarchy of effects, 245
Traditional media
  generation X, 335
  seniors, 337
  teens, 334
Trait theories, personality, 396–397, 397e
Transformational advertising, 174
Transition, roles, 449
Trial simulation, innovation, 433
Trialability, innovation, 430
Trickle-down effect, 365
Trivial attributes, high-effort decision, 233
Truth effect, repetition, 161
Two brands at a time evaluation, 225
"$2 a Day" consumers, 355–356
Two-sided messages, 138–139
Two-way communication, personally delivered sources, 203, 302

U
Uncertainty, innovation, 429–430
Uncertainty avoidance, 391
Unconditioned response (UCR), 165
Unconditioned stimulus (UCS), 165
Unconscious influences, on attitudes, 160–161
Unconscious low-effort decision-making, 245
Underage drinking and smoking, 483
Underdog strategies, product, 273
Underprivileged families, 365
Unexpectedness, and attention, 79
Uniqueness, associations, 108
United States
  ethnic groups, 343–347
  household life cycles, 359e
  population age, 330, 332e
  regions, 340
  social class, 365e, 366e
  spending by age, 6e
Unity, design, 257

Upper Americans, 365e
Upper class, consumption patterns, 372–373
Upward mobility, 368
Usage
    brand name recall, 190
    consumer behavior, 4
    and innovation, 425
    methods, 7
Use-diffusion patterns, home technology
        innovations, 423e
Use innovativeness, 428
User, family role, 361, 361e
Utilitarian (functional) dimension of ad, 146
Utilitarian value, special possessions, 458e

V
Vacation choices, 13e
Valence, informational information, 318
VALS™ (Values and Lifestyles), 404, 405e
Value(s)
    changes, 391
    definition, 383, 406
    gift, 462
    importance of, 255

influences, 13, 391–393
    and innovation, 425
    measurement, 393–395
    and personal relevance, 49
    types, 385–386, 406
    Western cultures, 386–391
Value conflict, 383
Value laddering, 394
Value questionnaires, 395
Value segmentation, 391
Value system, definition, 383
Values-driven attitudes, 132
Variety seeking, definition, 258
Variety seeking needs, 258–259
Vinyl long-playing (LP) record albums,
        442–443
Viral marketing, 319
Vision, and perception, 81
Vision, sensory marketing, 83, 171
Vividness, brand name recall, 192
Voicers, complainer, 281
Voluntary disposition, 285e
Voluntary simplicity, 369, 402
Vulnerable segments, targeting, 480–481, 482

W
Weak effect, subliminal advertising, 86
Weak ties, and word-of-mouth, 309
Wearout, 165
Weber's law, 85
Wife-dominant decision, 362
Will-power, and goals, 56
Word-of-mouth communication
        influence, 300, 318–319
        negative experience, 275, 283, 318, 322
        tracking, 321
        weak ties, 309
Work and play, Western value, 387–388
Working class, consumption patterns, 373
Working memory (WM), 102, 120
Working memory, stimulus processing, 119

Y
Young digiterati, 340
Youth, Western value, 389–390

Z
Zapping, 75
Zipping, 75